Beyond
the
Down
Low

Sex, Lies, and Denial in Black America

KEITH BOYKIN

Foreword by E. Lynn Harris

CARROLL & GRAF PUBLISHERS

NEW YORK

BEYOND THE DOWN LOW
Sex, Lies, and Denial in Black America

Carroll & Graf Publishers
An Imprint of Avalon Publishing Group Inc.
245 West 17th Street
11th Floor
New York, NY 10011

AVALON
publishing group incorporated

Library of Congress Cataloging-in-Publication Data is available.

ISBN-10: 0-7867-1704-1
ISBN-13: 978-0-78671-704-0

10 9 8 7 6 5 4 3 2 1

Book design by Maria E. Torres
Printed in the United States of America
Distributed by Publishers Group West

Contents

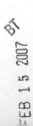

Foreword

When I self-published my first novel, *Invisible Life,* in 1991, the subject of bisexuality in the black community was rarely discussed in the mainstream media. Eight bestselling novels later, it is now clear that many of us were starving for these stories all along. Not only black women, but men and women of all races have begun to pay attention. Then a few years ago, I started getting phone calls from reporters asking about men on the down low who were in relationships with women but secretly having sex with men. Some of these men were becoming infected with HIV and passing the virus to their wives and girlfriends. Ever since then, the down low story has made front-page headlines in the *New York Times* and other newspapers across the country.

I first met Keith Boykin more than ten years ago when he was working in the White House for President Clinton. Since that time, I have seen him become an author, then an activist, and even a reality TV star. Now I'm pleased to see him writing a new book about an important topic once again.

As the AIDS epidemic grows in the black community, *Beyond the Down Low: Sex, Lies, and Denial in Black America* is timely and necessary. Over the years, I have met far too many black women and men whose lives have been dramatically affected by HIV, and I have seen how the down low discussion has drawn some of them apart. Indeed, the most visible public discussions about the down low lately have been more about finger-pointing and dividing the community than about establishing honest and open dialogue. Rather than blaming black men or black women, Keith offers a smart, thoughtful approach that suggests we try to move beyond fear to find ways to love ourselves and love one another.

Perhaps just as importantly, Keith reminds us that the down low is not a new phenomenon. In fact, his is the first book to identify the long history of the DL. He takes us back to the Harlem Renaissance and walks us through the popular culture and music of the twentieth century. From there, we continue on the journey through contemporary America. He takes us into the modern world of big-time professional sports, backstage in the hip-hop music industry, and behind the pulpit in the powerful black church.

Keith's purpose is to challenge us to think beyond the down low and to get us to re-think what we *think* we know. I have no doubt that this provocative book will spark controversy in some quarters, but it is time for us to have a healthy and informed discussion about these issues. Fortunately, Keith is not content to critique the problems without solutions, and he provides specific answers to what we can do. In fact, he gives us lists of concrete steps that any of us can take. All told, *Beyond the Down Low* is healing medicine for all of us.

E. Lynn Harris
November 2004

Introduction

In February 2005, I arrived at the CNN headquarters in New York to appear on *Anderson Cooper 360*. I was there to discuss my new book, *Beyond the Down Low*. However, I had been struggling for days to figure out a simple way to communicate the ideas in my book to the press. How do you condense a 300-page book that challenges virtually all we've been told about the down low into a 30-second soundbite? I stumbled on a golden nugget during the interview that night.

"Of the 7,000 black female AIDS cases in 2003, only 118 reported sex with a bisexual male as the method of exposure," I reported. At first that seemed like the perfect statistic to quote. It was a simple message that put the whole down low story in perspective. Only 1.6 percent of black women diagnosed with AIDS reported sex with a bisexual male, but nearly 100 percent of the public discussion about AIDS in the black community focused on the down low. Unfortunately, those numbers did little to quiet the storm.

The following week, I taped an interview for Voice of America radio, which gave me a chance to clear up some more misconceptions about African Americans and AIDS. I explained that black women did not make up 68 percent of all new AIDS cases, as was widely reported. Instead, they made up only 18 percent of all new AIDS cases, a dramatic difference, and yet many reporters continued to get the story completely wrong.

I soon realized that what began as a book tour had grown into something much larger. Somewhere along the tour, my purpose had changed. At first it was primarily an opportunity to communicate an important message. As it developed, however, the book tour became much more than that. It became a mission, a cause, a campaign. When I read a national news headline one day that said "U.S. HIV Cases Soaring Among Black Women," I knew something was wrong. The headline was grossly inaccurate. The rates had not soared; they had fallen.

The black female AIDS rate had actually *declined* 6 percent in the previous four years, according to the Centers for Disease Control. But newspapers kept printing the same old story about African American women facing skyrocketing AIDS rates without checking the facts. Meanwhile, they neglected to print sympathetic stories about black men. There were almost twice as many black men diagnosed with AIDS as black women. Black men have the highest AIDS rates of any segment of the population, but the media rarely discussed black men with AIDS unless they were black men who infected black women.

To be fair, I must admit that a lot has changed over the past year. R&B singer Luther Vandross passed away. Author Terry McMillan divorced Jonathan Plummer, her recently discovered gay husband. And Minister Louis Farrakhan, the leader of the Nation of Islam, began a groundbreaking dialogue with black gays and lesbians. But in many ways, a lot has not changed and misinformation is still widespread.

It was always easier to believe the stereotypes than to challenge them. That's because this story was always much bigger than the down low. It was about lies that demonized black men, stigmatized black women, and perpetuated the assumption of black pathology. If nothing else, I hope this book helps to fight those dangerous lies.

CHAPTER 1

A Thousand Different Meanings

I STARTED WORKING at Sears in the fall semester of my last year in high school. It was the best job I had ever had. That was not a great achievement because my other jobs had been pretty lousy. Well, actually, they were great jobs for a teenager. My first job was stuffing bags as a courtesy clerk at a local grocery store called Family Mart. I did that for six months and then moved up to fast food. In my next job, I cooked Big Macs and Quarter Pounders at McDonald's. Then I got my first big break.

I had just gotten back from a weeklong junior congressional internship in Washington, D.C., when my father offered me a job working for him in the summer before my senior year of high school. It was a desk job as a clerk/typist for my dad's beauty supply store in Clearwater, Florida. Working for family can be stressful, but it can be even more complicated when your boss doesn't pay you on time. My father felt I needed to have a more professional job if I was soon going to college, but I quickly realized that my father's business was not nearly as successful as McDonald's. By the beginning of the fall, I was still broke and eager to find a new job that could pay me consistently and where I didn't have to flip burgers. I found my salvation at Sears.

I started selling shoes at Sears in November of my last year in high school. I knew nothing about shoes or sales, but I knew how to count, and that was really the most important qualification I needed for the job. I could count the money that came into the register, and I could count the code numbers on the bottom of the shoes to match them with the code numbers in the stockroom. It was an easy job and a great way to meet people. It paid the bills and kept gas in the motorcycle that I drove to work. I did not ask for much more because I was too busy to know what I wanted. By the time I was seventeen, I was on the school's varsity track team and the debate team, president of the student government, writing a monthly column for the local newspaper, and serving a term on the city's parks and recreation board. In many ways, I was a model citizen and a model employee.

I loved working at Sears. It gave me a sense of pride to know they trusted me, and I stayed there for seven months, the longest period I had ever worked for anyone at that time. My career at Sears started to draw to a close after I graduated from high school. I had just been accepted at Dartmouth College, and I was spending the summer preparing myself for my first year away from home. A few weeks after graduation, I came into work one evening and was told to report to the manager's office before I punched in on the clock. I took the escalator upstairs to the manager's office, where I found my supervisor and the manager waiting for me in an office. "Sit down," they told me, "We have some questions we'd like to ask you." I sat down apprehensively. The tone of their voices was solemn, and immediately my mind started thinking about what I might have done wrong. Had I shown up late? No. I was still on time. Did I forget to put the shoes back on the rack the last time I closed? No.

It wasn't that. Was I dressed inappropriately? No again. I was wearing slacks, a dress shirt, and a tie. What had I done wrong? I could not think of what it might be.

My supervisor did most of the talking during the conversation, while the manager looked on from behind his desk. The supervisor told me that my drawer came up short the last time I worked. I did not remember any discrepancy the night I closed, but I knew I was not the only one who worked that night. "Do you know what happened to the money?" my supervisor asked. "No," I replied honestly. "I didn't know there was any money missing." My answer did little to convince either of them. Apparently, they had already decided what had happened to the money and they had already decided what to do about it. "Keith, we're gonna have to let you go," the manager told me. I listened to what he said, but I was so young and unaccustomed to the language of the work world that I did not understand what it meant to "let you go." I sat and stared for a moment until my supervisor told me himself. "You're being fired," he said. "I'm sorry we have to do it, but we won't report it to the police." And with those ignoble words, my career at Sears came to an abrupt and involuntary end.

The news left me in a daze. I slowly walked out of the office, down the escalator, past the shoe department, and out to my motorcycle. As I fastened the helmet, I could feel the fresh moisture of sorrow on my cheek. I would have to face my family and tell them what happened. I had just been fired from my job for stealing. But the worst part was even harder to accept and understand. The worst part was that I was not guilty.

There is nothing worse than being blamed for something you did not do. I know. The more I thought about being fired, the more frustrated I became. I had been accused, tried, and convicted without any real chance to explain my side of the story. In fact, I was never even told how much money was missing. I guess that was not important. For seven months, I had been a loyal and honest employee without a blemish on my record, and then suddenly I was dismissed for an incident I knew nothing about. In the end, I realized that I was guilty after all. I was guilty of an offense that I had forgotten was a crime. My crime was simple. I was a young black man in America.

I discovered early in life that black men make easy targets to blame for many of the problems in America. I had never thought of myself as a problem before, but from that day forward I realized that I was. Over the following years, I would be blamed for many more crimes that I had not committed. I made white women nervous and white men anxious. They created an image of me that even black people started to believe. I was responsible for murder, rape, drugs, guns, poverty, homelessness, welfare, illiteracy, teen pregnancy, and AIDS. And all because I am a black man.

As I said, there is nothing worse than being blamed for something you have not done. And that is exactly why the public discussion about black men on the down low is so dangerously wrong. Almost every time I hear talk about the down low, I remember the feeling of being blamed for something I did not do. Facts are not important in this environment. Perception is reality. I live in a world that has already been trained to fear and despise me. It is not because of what I have done. I have never murdered anyone. I have never smoked crack. I have never been in prison. And I have never passed a deadly disease to anyone. But none of that matters. I am still guilty, and I will be held accountable for the rest of my life.

Perhaps I should have learned my lesson in high school. I should have realized that perception is more important than truth. I should have known that I would be judged by the preconceived perception of me instead of the truth about me. But somehow I never learned that lesson. For some reason, I held fast to the belief that truth would always prevail eventually. Against all evidence to the contrary, I remained convinced that no lie, no matter how widely repeated, could stand forever. Maybe I was wrong, but deep in my heart I still believe the truth will always emerge.

In the meantime, I am forced to face the lies.

This is a story about lies. Actually, these days, anytime you read anything about the down low, you probably know it is about lies. But this is a different story. It's not just about the lies that men on the down low tell. It is a story about the lies that men *and women* tell themselves about their relationships. It is a story about the lies that we tell the media, which the media in turn tell back to us about who we are. Yes, it is a story about lies in black America, but it is also a story about lies in white America. It is a story about men lying, but it is also a story about women lying. It is a story about the way in which lies become mistaken for truth when repeated often enough, and how we use those lies to deny our personal responsibility to find the truth.

America's recent obsession with the down low is not about the truth. It is about avoiding the truth. The truth is, more than a generation after the so-called sexual revolution and decades after the beginning of the AIDS epidemic, we are still a nation in deep denial about sex, race, and relationships. In black America, with the all-too-willing assistance of white America, we are still afraid to hear, understand, and process the truth. And as a nation, we would rather talk about the down low than talk candidly about racism, homophobia, and AIDS, and about our collective responsibility to find solutions for these problems. Of course, it is easier to believe the hype than to engage in a sensible dialogue based on real information, but we cannot find solutions in a sensationalistic conversation based on fear and blame. The solutions lie in a conversation about love and personal responsibility. So it's time to get past the fear and the blame. It's time to go beyond the down low.

We begin in February 2001. George W. Bush has just been inaugurated as president after a controversial election in which he lost the popular vote yet won a disputed contest for the electoral ballot in Florida. Former President Bill Clinton has moved to New York with his wife, who has just been elected a U.S. senator from that state. Clinton has been hounded by a "vast right-wing conspiracy" throughout his tenure in office and impeached by a Republican Congress because he lied about a sexual relationship with an intern. I feel the president's pain. After eight years of living in Washington, I am ready to leave. I had moved to Washington to work in the Clinton White House as a special assistant to the president, and the city suddenly feels unwelcoming to an exiled Democrat. Then one day in 2001, I'm invited to dinner with three friends who were in town for an AIDS conference, and that's where I first heard about "the down low," a term I vaguely understood to mean men who have sex with men but do not identify as gay. As a black gay man, I had known about such men for a decade. Since I came out in 1991, I had been working on issues of race and sexuality during most of that time, and I had met or interviewed dozens of men who would qualify as down low. What could possibly be new about such an old occurrence, I wondered. Was it just a new word for an old behavior?

Over the years, I had heard a number of terms to describe these men and their behavior. Some were dismissed as "closeted." Many called themselves "bisexual." Some said they were only "messin' around" while others accused them of "creeping." Most of the supposedly straight men I had met had always seemed resistant to labels. Their interest in me was usually physical, not intellectual, so they were seldom willing to answer probing questions about their lives. Nevertheless, I had interacted with these men for years. There was the police officer I met in Los Angeles, the postal worker in Chicago, the corporate executive in Maryland, the Web designer in North Carolina, and the government official in Washington, D.C. All of them were black, several of them were married, and a few of them had young children. Then, there were dozens of men I had met at an infamous gym on L Street in Washington. Many of these guys seemed to be making hookups on a regular basis. It didn't seem very underground to me, but that was because I saw it happen so often. A few of the guys would talk to me on the sly, while others— who had seen me talking about gay issues on television or in the newspaper—would walk a country mile to steer clear of me. In fact, I could almost identify who was in the closet based on how much effort they put into avoiding me.

By 2001, the down low was old news to me, but for the mass media it was the beginning of a profitable period of exploitation of black grief. To some in the media, the down low seemed the missing link to explain the AIDS epidemic in the black community. HIV seemed to be spreading more rapidly among black women than in almost any other demographic group, and if these women were unknowingly having sex with black men on the down low, then that could explain the problem. The overwhelming majority of black women with HIV contracted the virus from heterosexual sex, and some black men who call themselves heterosexual also had sex with men. So these black men could have been responsible for spreading the virus to unsuspecting women. It all seemed to make sense.

Others were a bit more skeptical. There was no research to prove the down low was responsible for the spread of AIDS in the black community, and no one knew how to study a population that was unwilling to be identified. These skeptics feared that focusing on the down low would distract public attention and public resources from what they perceived were the real needs of the community. Focusing on the down low would mislead people into thinking that AIDS was spread by men on the DL rather than by HIV. And instead of encouraging individuals to focus on their own safe sex behavior, we would encourage them to focus on the behavior of their partners. Even worse, public policy decisions would have to rely on anecdotal evidence from those men who had once been on the down low, a group that was admittedly notorious for its untruthfulness. In other words, we would have to trust the liars to tell the truth about their lies.

Despite the uncertainty about the issue, just mention the words "down low" to someone in the media, and you're likely to hear remarkable tales of sex, lies, and deception—all supposedly brought on by a small, dangerous and influential fraternity of black men leading double lives.

Ever since the down low story broke, many journalists have been convinced that men on the down low are responsible for the spread of AIDS in the black community. Books have been published that claim to teach women "the signs" to tell if a man is on the down low. Black women have been deputized as down low detectives and told to watch to see if their male partners stare too long at other men. The media and the public have developed a whole new fascination with all things down low.

But is all this hype really necessary? Is the information even true?

We should start with a basic question that needs to be asked at the beginning of any serious discussion about this issue: What is the down low? Before you answer, here are a few examples to help us understand the question. Try to figure out which of these people are on the down low.

Raheem is a twenty-four-year-old black man in northeast Washington, D.C. He looks just like any other young man on the street on a hot summer afternoon. He is wearing an XXXL-size plain white T-shirt, oversized baseball cap, droopy jeans, and sneakers. But Raheem is different. Raheem says he's "on the DL." He only "messes with" brothas, and he has a computer at home that he uses to find them in chat rooms and Web sites on the Internet. Although he has not been involved with a woman since he graduated from high school, six years ago, he still dreams that one day he will settle down with the right woman and get married. Is Raheem on the down low?

David is a thirty-six-year-old black man in Stone Mountain, Georgia. He lives with his wife and two kids in a two-story, three-bedroom house and commutes to work in midtown Atlanta. He wears a business suit to the office but brings his gym clothes to work out at the gym near his job. A few years ago, he started meeting men at the gym and taking them to hotels to have sex with them. Eventually, he worked up the nerve to go home with the men he met. He enjoys his sexual encounters with men, but he has no plans to leave his wife and kids, and they do not know about his homosexual experiences. David has recently heard of the term "down low," but he does not identify with it. He calls himself "straight." David is HIV negative. He doesn't want to run the risk of getting caught, so he always uses a condom with his male sex partners, and he only plays the role of a "top." Is David on the down low?

Jabbar is a twenty-nine-year-old black man in Dayton, Ohio. He's a shoe salesman for a high-end department store, and he prides himself on the way he dresses. He's fashionably conservative and considers himself very masculine. Jabbar's deep bass voice and tall good looks help make him an effective salesman, but Jabbar has a not-so-secret life away from the department store. Once or twice a month, Jabbar drives his BMW to the gay clubs in Cincinnati. He's very popular with the black men there, who see him as a good catch, but he's never allowed himself to be caught. He has sex with men but has never been in a relationship with one. Jabbar loves being single, he loves the attention he gets from men and women, and he loves being so "unclockable" that no one can tell his sexuality. Is Jabbar on the down low?

Joyce is a thirty-eight-year-old black woman in Little Rock, Arkansas. She's the HR director for a major local hospital and has been involved in three long-term relationships in her life: two with men and one with a woman. Joyce's feminine good looks make her very desirable to women and men, but she won't commit to either. She's dating a man right now, but she's also seeing a woman on the side. Her man thinks she's straight. Her woman thinks she's on the DL. Is Joyce on the down low?

Shawn is a twenty-two-year-old white man in Brooklyn. He wants to be an electrical engineer, and he's got a part-time job to help him pay his way through community college. He has a white girlfriend he met at school and a black boyfriend he met in a club one night. Shawn grew up around blacks and Latinos in a racially mixed neighborhood in the Bronx, so he has always been comfortable developing friendships and relationships with people who are different from him. He knows he can never tell his girlfriend about his boyfriend, but he has told his boyfriend about his girlfriend. Shawn considers himself "on the down low." Is Shawn on the down low?

Jerry is a forty-six-year-old black man in Los Angeles. He's a semisuccessful visual artist who made a name for himself fifteen years ago and has continued to grow in popularity in local arts circles. Jerry lives with his wife and their twelve-year-old daughter, but Jerry also has a long-term male lover. Years ago, Jerry told his wife that he was bisexual, and after a heartfelt discussion she allowed him to date men outside of their marriage as long as he was safe. Jerry and his wife have made peace with their living situation, but they haven't told anyone else about it. When their daughter found out about the situation recently, she had a name for their relationship. She told her parents that they were a "down low couple." Is Jerry on the down low?

Luis is a nineteen-year-old mixed-race Hispanic man in Chicago. He planned to join the military until he realized the armed forces did not allow gays to serve openly. Almost everyone seems to know or assume that Luis is gay. He says he's very proud of his sexuality, and most of his good friends are gay or transgendered. But his friends don't know the whole truth. Luis has a girlfriend he's been hiding from them. Is Luis on the down low?

Those are the seven people. Now here's the question again. Which of the people mentioned above are on the down low? The question is not as easy as it seems. To answer the question, we have to start with an acceptable definition of what it means to be on the down low in the first place. And that's the problem. In the years since the media began to hype the down low, no one has ever really defined it. You start to realize the problem when you try to pick which of the seven people are on the down low.

Let's start with Raheem. Raheem raises the difficult issue of self-identification. He doesn't fit neatly into a gay stereotype. He doesn't look gay and he doesn't call himself gay. He self-identifies as "down low," but he has not had sex with a woman since he was a teenager. So here's the question. Can you be on the down low merely by self-identifying as being on the down low? Most of the recent media definitions of the down low seem to assume that you have to be unfaithful to a woman in order to be on the down low. Raheem, however, doesn't even date women, but he does considers himself on the down low. For Raheem, being on the down low simply means being a man who doesn't look gay and isn't public about being gay.

David raises the other side of self-identification. By most accounts, David fits the classic definition of a man on the down low.

He's black, he's married to a woman, and he secretly sleeps with men. But unlike Raheem, David doesn't consider himself to be on the down low. In fact, he's barely even familiar with the term, and he calls himself straight. If self-identification determines whether you're on the down low, then David is not down low, even though most observers would say he is.

David's story raises another issue as well. Since David is HIV negative and always practices safe sex, David's life challenges the assumption that down low men are spreading HIV to black women. In fact, David's wife is actually safer having sex with him than with an HIV positive man who is exclusively heterosexual.

Next there's Jabbar. On the surface, Jabbar seems to be another candidate for the down low, but beneath the surface he raises troubling questions about looks and behavior. Some would say that you can't be on the down low if you go out to gay bars and night clubs. For Jabbar, however, being down low simply means being what he considers masculine and discreet. Most people think he looks like he's straight, and since he never hangs out with gay guys in his hometown, he thinks that makes him down low. Is he right?

Then there's Joyce. Joyce's story complicates the simplicity of the down low formula by introducing the issue of gender. Like the men on the down low, she's cheating on her partner with someone of the same sex. What makes her different is that Joyce is a woman, and her partner is a man. Most of the public discussion about the down low seems to assume that women don't engage in the same unfaithful behavior that men do. Women are portrayed as the victims, not the perpetrators. Joyce's story forces us to reexamine our simplistic stereotypes about female fidelity and male deceit.

Shawn's situation complicates matters even more. If we define a down low man as someone who cheats on his wife or girlfriend with a man, then Shawn perfectly fits the bill. The only issue is that

Shawn is white. If white men can be on the down low, why all the fuss over black men on the down low? Is the down low specific to race? There's no evidence to prove that black men are more likely to be on the down low than white men. Perhaps the focus on black men can be explained because white men on the down low are not spreading the HIV virus to their female partners at the same rate as black men. If so, why not? Is it because white men engage in safer sex, and if so, shouldn't our prevention efforts focus on how to get black men on the down low to take the same precautions?

What can we say about Jerry and his wife? If you knew them as a couple and then discovered that Jerry was sleeping with another man, you might think that Jerry was on the down low. He's black, he's married to a woman, and he's secretly sleeping with a man. What else does it take to be on the down low? Well, in this case, Jerry's secret is not a secret from his wife. His wife already knows. The rest of the world doesn't. Does that make Jerry on the down low? Jerry's life raises the issue of disclosure. Once you tell your wife, does it matter that you keep the secret from everyone else?

Finally, let's look at Luis. Luis is a proud Hispanic gay man. He goes to gay bars, he has gay friends, and he calls himself gay. Doesn't sound very down low. But Luis has a secret. He recently started dating a woman, and he doesn't know how to break the news to his gay friends. If being on the down low means lying to the world about your sexuality, then Luis may very well be a member of the group. But if being on the down low only means lying to your opposite-sex partner about your same-sex partner, we've created a very narrow field of concern.

At the end of this exercise, we still don't have a common definition of what it means to be on the down low. So how is the down low defined in the media? To position this story as a cautionary tale about AIDS, the media seem to have accepted a popular definition of the down low that suggests five basic traits for those on the DL. According to the media, those on the down low are:

(1) black,
(2) male,
(3) HIV positive,
(4) in relationships with women, and
(5) secretly having sex with men.

We've considered seven examples of people who could be on the down low, but each of them challenges the popular definition. Raheem is not in a relationship with a woman. David is not HIV positive. Jabbar is a closeted gay man. Joyce is a woman. Shawn is white. Jerry is out to his wife. And Luis is gay.

Is it possible than none of the seven people mentioned above are on the down low? To resolve this dilemma, I asked several of the most visible black figures who have talked publicly about the down low to answer a simple question: What is the down low?

I began with J. L. King, the author of a book called *On the Down Low: A Journey into the Lives of "Straight" Black Men Who Sleep with Men*. I could not find a clear definition of the down low in his book, so I decided to ask him myself. He responded to each of my four e-mails but never answered the question, so I went back to his book and tried to piece together a definition from his own words. The subtitle of the book presents one possible definition: "'straight' black men who sleep with men." But that definition doesn't require the men to be involved in relationships with women. The dedication for the book seems to explain more. King dedicates the book, in part, to "all the women whose health has been jeopardized and emotional state compromised by men living on the DL," a dedication that suggests men on the down low are responsible for the spread of AIDS to black women. Should we also be concerned about down low men who are HIV negative and always practice safe sex? King uses other terms such as "double lifestyle" and "duplicitous behavior" to give us more understanding of what the down low means to him. The closest definition he provides, however, is in response to a question from an Ohio health official who asks about the secret lives of bisexual men. "The secret," he writes, "is that men who look like me, talk like me, and think like me are having sex with men but still love and want to be with their women. And they do not believe they're gay." King's definition seems to exclude men who date women just to conceal their homosexuality. In other words, men on the down low would be inherently bisexual. But if they are bisexual and not just in denial about their homosexual desires, then why should we vilify these man who are acting out on their natural desires?

I put the same question to Phill Wilson, the director of the Black AIDS Institute in Los Angeles. "Like many slang terms, 'DL' means different things to different people," he said. "Some DL men identify as straight and have wives or girlfriends but secretly have sex with other men. Others are younger men who are still questioning or exploring their sexuality. Some are closeted gay men. And then there are African-American brothers who openly have relationships with other men but reject the label 'gay' or 'bisexual' because they equate those terms with white men."

Many of those black men who do not consider themselves gay would still feel perfectly comfortable cavorting in a predominantly black gay bar. By rejecting the homosexual label, they are not necessarily rejecting the sexual behavior associated with it. Black men often reject the term "gay" to repudiate white social constructs of homosexuality but not to reject their own homosexual sexual behavior. Some black men who openly acknowledge that they have sex with other men have simply found other words to describe themselves, including the term "same-gender-loving." They reject the term "gay" not because of internalized homophobia or because they are on the down low. Instead, they simply want to create their own identities outside of what they perceive to be a racially insensitive white gay world.

The journalist Kai Wright in New York shares Wilson's sense of complexity about the definition. Wright has written extensively about the down low, and he finds the act of defining the term problematic. "It's whatever the person using the phrase wants it to be," he explains.

For black gay men, labeling themselves on the down low is a way to validate their masculinity. Wright mentions an example of a black gay bar in Brooklyn that advertised in a local gay magazine as "Brooklyn's down low choice," despite the fact that "there couldn't be a less down low place," he says. "It's one of the oldest black gay bars in the city, first off, and it's packed with gay-identified men watching a male strip show!"

For white gay men, "the down low has become the latest way to fetishize the scary, roughneck black men of their porns," says Wright. He fears that "this racist fantasy bleeds into the AIDS activism" of some white gay men as well.

For black women, the down low provides an easy way to deal with difficult issues, he says. By focusing on the behavior of men on the DL, black women are not required to reconsider their own behavior and may be left disempowered to protect themselves.

"That's just the problem with this issue," according to Wright. "It's the perfect boogeyman: a group of shady, dangerous men who are, by definition, hidden and unidentifiable." Kai Wright raises an excellent point. How do you define someone who doesn't want to be defined? How do you identify someone who doesn't want to be identified? And once you get the person to be identified, that person is, by definition, no longer on the down low.

Dr. Darrell Wheeler of New York's Hunter College defines the term more broadly than most. The down low is "a term used by some men to describe behaviors that they do not want others to know about," he says. Dr. Wheeler's definition seems to open the door to those who are white, gay, HIV negative, and not in relationships. The down low is also a term used to describe men "or women" who are homosexually active but do not identity themselves as lesbian, gay or bisexual, he adds. In other words, almost everyone who hides his or her behaviors from others can be on the down low.

The Arkansas-based columnist Alicia Banks, who writes an online column called *Eloquent Fury*, says she resents the media characterization of the down low as "an exclusively ethnic moniker to trivialize and exploit a universal issue." Banks also identifies a link between racism and homophobia in the common definition of the down low. All humans cheat, she said, and men of all races creep with women and men. Cheating and lying are both "fatal infections," according to Banks, "whether your partner is creeping with a woman or a man." Her comment implies that the public might not be as concerned about infidelity when practiced in a traditional male-female relationship. But for Banks, the down low is nothing to be proud of. The DL, she says, is both a "damned lie" and a "deceitful life."

Dr. David Malebranche, assistant professor of medicine at Emory University in Atlanta, provides historical perspective in his definition of the DL. "The 'down low' is a phrase that has been part of the black community for ages, and historically meant something that is 'secretive' or 'covert.'" he says. Dr. Malebranche cites several examples where the down low simply means to keep something—a loan, a love affair—a secret. "Only within the past couple of decades has the term become a more specific catch phrase to describe black men who have wives or girlfriends, but also mess around with other men on the side."

Dr. Ron Simmons, a former assistant professor of communications at Howard University in Washington, D.C., also associates the term "down low" with its history, describing it as "a hip-hop expression meaning something secret or undercover." Today, however, he says the term "is commonly used to refer to men who have sex with men but self-identify as heterosexual." Simmons runs Us Helping Us, a Washington-based AIDS organization for black gay and bisexual men that provides a down low telephone help line, Internet outreach, and barbershop intervention. "Part of the problem," he finds with the definition of the term "is that self-identified gay men also refer to themselves as being on the down low." The situation can be confusing to outsiders, and Dr. Simmons recalls an incident when a reporter called him to find men on the down low. "I told her that down low men do not have a physical place or area where they can be found," he said. "She remarked that she had heard that there was a down low party during D.C. Black Gay Pride. I had to explain to her that this was a party of gay men who were using the term but not the kind of 'down low' men as she was investigating."

The reporter who called Dr. Simmons is not alone. Since the down low story hit the media in 2001, every major newspaper in the country has scrambled to find down low men in their community. Black magazines like *Essence* and gay publications like *The Advocate* have covered the down low story, while many of their reporters have struggled to find men on the down low and others have stretched to define the community they were covering. An August 2004 article in *The Advocate* starts with a visit to a popular black gay bar called The Study, but for black gay men in Los

Angeles, the location—situated on a major street in Hollywood—is hardly a secret. Do "real" down low men go to gay bars? The story quotes a young man named Ezel, who declined to give his last name but is described as a volunteer for the Minority AIDS Project and who is distributing condoms at a table in the bar. He's married, bisexual, and in the closet. But is he on the down low? It is hard to imagine that a man on the down low would volunteer for a gay-identified AIDS organization that hands out condoms at gay bars. It's even harder to imagine that such a man would give out his first name to a reporter. It wouldn't take a lot for a curious reader to piece together the details of his life and blow his cover. If someone like Ezel is on the down low, then just about anyone can be on the down low. And that's exactly the problem. Without a uniform definition of the down low, we are left with no clear boundaries in defining this mysterious group of men.

Dr. Greg Millett, a behavioral scientist in the epidemiology branch of the U.S. Centers for Disease Control and Prevention (CDC), has studied the down low issue for the federal government. To generate a sense of clarity about the meaning of the term, Millett developed his own definition of the down low as a "man who is heterosexually identified and has sex with other men without the knowledge of their primary female partner."

Millett acknowledges "there are many other definitions that people have for the down low that you see in the media. Some people are considering down low [to be] men who are not out about their sexuality. Some people consider down low men just men who are bisexually active. Some people consider down low men many other things—men who are having sex with other men, have female partners and having unprotected sex with their male and female partners," he said.

While Millett's definition may not be universally accepted in the public, his objective was to "define it and operationalize it for the scientific community" so that future researchers could work with the same basic understanding of the population to be studied. That may help settle any scientific disputes, but it does not settle the raging debate in the public.

The down low has become so pervasive in the public discourse that the term has even crept its way into Internet encyclopedias, but the definitions employed by these reference materials often simply repeat popular perceptions. One online encyclopedia explains, "Among some sectors of African-American homosexual sub-culture . . . same-sex sexual behavior is sometimes viewed as solely for physical pleasure. Men on the 'down-low' may engage in regular (though often covert) sex acts with other men while continuing sexual and romantic relationships with unsuspecting women." Another source defines the down low as "men who discreetly have sex with other men while in sexual relationships with women." These are fairly common definitions, but they exclude a large segment of the population who self-identify as "down low" but do not have relationships with women. In addition, the first definition seems to exclude whites and others who are not black, while the second definition excludes women on the down low.

So once again, what is the down low? The answer may challenge everything we think we know about the subject. The only point on which the experts seem to agree is that the down low is about secrecy in our sexual behavior. You don't have to be black, you don't have to be male, you don't have to be HIV positive, and you don't even have to be in a relationship to be on the down low. The down low is everything and nothing. In fact, the down low seems a bit like water. It has no shape, no form, and no color of its own. Like water, it is flexible enough to adapt to the shape and color of any container. It can mean whatever the user wants it to mean.

For closeted black gay and bisexual men, the down low is a way to validate their masculinity. For straight black women, the down low is a way to avoid the difficult issues of personal responsibility. For white America, the down low is a way to pathologize black lives. And for the media, the down low is a story that can be easily hyped.

For a phrase that is subject to multiple interpretations with no uniform definition, the "down low" is a term that is widely used and even more widely misunderstood.

Chapter 2

Since the Beginning of Time

I REMEMBER MY first experience with the down low. The summer before I started law school, I worked out at a Bally's gym in St. Louis and developed an acquaintance with a tall, muscular black man named Mike. I was young and naïve and totally clueless about the culture of the down low. Mike knew the culture well. When I would speak to him at the gym, he would stare into my eyes with a penetrating look that seemed to indicate that he knew more about me than I knew about myself. "We should hang out," he told me shortly after we met. I politely agreed but never followed up with him. There was something about Mike that I found both intriguing and terrifying. He turned me on and turned me off at the same time. Every time I looked into his eyes, I knew at some level that I was looking into my own, and the experience scared me to death.

I did not know why Mike decided to introduce himself to me the day we met, but I'm sure he knew that I was willing to talk. Maybe he caught me studying the curve of his biceps or peeking beneath his tank top to see his chest. There must have been something about me that told him I was safe for conversation. I had never been involved with a man, and I had no intention of ever doing so. I was in deep denial about my sexual orientation, and he knew it before I did.

Mike was also a master at smooth talk. He made me feel safe and comfortable when we spoke, but there was something enticingly mischievous about him. He would wink his eye to say good-bye. He would glance me over from head to toe as though he were contemplating a meal. And then there was his handshake. It was a normal handshake at first, but soon it became more intimate. I noticed it one day when he held my hand for an extra second as his middle finger ever so casually brushed across my palm. I did not respond, a reaction that I thought was appropriately neutral. But instead of sending him a red light signal I had actually given him a green light, or at least a yellow light to proceed with caution. Mike was a master at nonverbal communication. If I had flinched at his gesture, he could have easily dismissed it as unintentional contact. But since I did not flinch, he assumed it was okay with me. The next time we shook hands, he tried it again, this time clearly stroking my palm as he watched for a response. "We should hang out and get together some time," he suggested. I agreed, but we made no plans.

As the summer ended, I paid my last visit to the gym one night and found Mike on the bench press. As we had done before, we worked out together. He spotted me when I did my sets, and I spotted him on his. At the end of the workout, I reminded him that I was leaving town and moving to Boston to go to school. Sensing an opportunity would be lost, he suggested that we get together when we left the gym that evening.

"We've been talking about getting together for the longest time," he said. "What are you doing tonight?"

"Nothing," I said.

"Why don't we hang out?"

"Sure, what do you want to do?"

"We can just hang out. Come on over to my place for a while," he said.

I agreed, and when we left the gym I followed him in my car to his house. We walked through the family room, where he yelled to someone in the kitchen that he was home. He led me to his bedroom, and I asked if the person who answered was his roommate. "No, that's my wife," he told me. I felt strangely comforted by this knowledge, feeling safe that his wife was in the house. But then he locked the door in his bedroom, turned on the television, and sat on the edge of the bed next to a chair where I was seated. His seductive stare made me nervous and confused. I turned my attention to the television, but his eyes remained fixed on me. A few minutes into an awkward conversation, he reached out and touched my hand, caressing my palm with his middle finger once again. I felt guilty and excited all at once. What was I doing in this man's house? And what would his wife think about all this if she saw us together? How do you bring home another man while your wife is at home, lock him in the bedroom, and not tell her about it? I knew he was a smooth talker, but this was hard to understand.

I did not have much time to think about what was happening, and Mike did not have time to waste. He continued touching me, stroking my palm and caressing both sides of my hand. He never said a word. There was no need. He gestured for me to sit next to him on the bed, and I got up and moved closer. He moved his hands up my arm and found a position between my shoulders and back. Then his hands moved under my T-shirt and across my chest, and I felt a guilty pleasure in his touch. The feel of another man's body so close to mine was a new and exciting experience for me, but Mike was not satisfied with a simple touch. He lifted my shirt and threw it on the floor, forcing me back on the bed as he lay on top of me. That was the moment that scared me the most. I could not focus on what he was doing because I could not stop thinking about what I was doing there and how I had allowed myself to get into such an awkward situation. I stopped suddenly and pushed him off of me, clearing my head as I fumbled for my T-shirt.

"What's the matter?" he asked.

"I have to go."

"Why? You just got here."

"No, you don't understand. This is, this is not for me," I said. "I have never done this before, and I'm not about to start right now. I can't do this. I have to go home, right now." He tried to talk me into staying but I was determined to leave. Finally, he relented, but he must have realized the turmoil going on inside of me. No matter how awkward I felt, I had enjoyed the experience at some level, and he knew it. Mike must have known that this would not be my last encounter with a man, and he predicted the future with his final words as I left. "You'll be back," he snapped.

"I don't think so," I objected, and walked out the door.

I met Mike in 1989 when I was a completely different person from who I am now. I had not started law school, had never worked in the White House and had never written a book. I had been involved with a girlfriend and had no intention of ever being with a man. Most important, I did not consider myself to be gay. I had a profound and deep-seated physical attraction to men that I did not understand and did not acknowledge. I never acted on the feelings inside of me, and I did everything I could to repress them. I was so far in denial that I was in the closet even to myself. Had I continued along my path of self-deception, I would have ended up on the down low. I would have been married with children only to wake up one day and realize I was living a lie.

The lie in which I was involved began long before the current down low sensation. In fact, it began long before 1989, when I had my first experience with a man. To tell the truth, the lie began before I was even born. The lie to which I refer is the lie we tell ourselves about who we are as a people. And that lie is what makes the recent obsession with the down low so painfully problematic. Given what we already know or should know, it is hard to believe that anybody with an ounce of real-world experience would think the down low is new. Let's be honest. Men have been secretly sleeping with other men since the beginning of time.

As I said before, this is a book about lies, and one of the biggest lies we have told ourselves about the down low is that this story is new. Sometimes, we passingly acknowledge that the down low has been around for a while, but then we continue on with the discussion as though we are engaged in a bold new conversation. It's not. However you define it, the down low has been going on since the beginning of recorded history. In the Bible's first chapter of the second book of Samuel, a supposedly straight David says to Jonathan, "Thy love to me was wonderful, passing the love of women." Yes, David is speaking to another man. At one point in the story, Jonathan goes to a secret hiding place where he and David "kissed one another, and wept one with another, until David exceeded." That story took place more than two thousand years ago. The down low has been around for a long time.

Just how far back does it go? The writer Cary Alan Johnson has uncovered evidence of homosexuality in pre-colonial Africa. Professor Charles Nero at Bates College has exposed a centuries-old slave narrative that reveals the existence of homosexuality among black slaves. And scores of scholars have documented the influence of black lesbian, gay, bisexual, and transgendered writers, artists, musicians and entertainers in the Harlem Renaissance of the 1920s and 1930s.

Homosexuality and bisexuality have always been somewhat difficult for many of us to understand, but the notion of a married man sleeping with another man seems to be irresistibly scandalous. It seems every generation produces artists who "expose" this drama. Ma Rainey's 1926 song "Sissy Blues" provides an example. Rainey sings:

> *I dreamed last night that I was far from harm*
> *Woke up and found my man in a sissy's arms.*

Two years later, the bisexual Rainey had moved from victim to culprit in her song "Prove It on Me Blues." Exposing the down low culture of the times, Rainey plays the role of the cagey defendant who secretly acknowledges her activity but demands that her accuser "prove it" to the world because "ain't nobody caught me." In that song, she sings:

> *Went out last night with a crowd of my friends,*
> *They must have been women, 'cause I don't like no men.*

Of course, women weren't the only ones who sang about the experience. In 1926, Pinewood Tom (Josh White) seemed to have given up on the hope of finding a "good woman" when he sang:

> *If you can't bring me a woman*
> *Bring me a sissy man.*

And no chronology of the down low is complete without acknowledging what may be the first popular song in history to connect the words "down low" with closeted homosexuality. In the 1930 song "Boy in the Boat," George Hanna exposes a culture among lesbian women who socialize at dimly lit venues designed to protect their identities:

If you see two women walking hand in hand
Just look 'em over and try to understand
They'll go to these parties, have their lights down low
Only those parties where women can go.

There was a name for these women living in the shadows. Bessie Jackson (Lucille Bogan) called them "B.D. women" in her song "B.D. Woman's Blues." The B.D. stood for "bulldagger." Reinforcing socially constructed gender norms, Bessie Smith referred to a "mannish-acting woman" and a "womanish-acting man." Some of the men were simply called "sissies."

The Depression at home and the war in Europe brought an end to the sexual candor of the twenties and thirties, but homosexuality and bisexuality persisted nonetheless. In the 1940s, *Ebony* magazine reported on a Harlem nightclub called Lucky's Rendezvous at 148th Street and St. Nicholas Avenue where "male couples are so commonplace . . . that no one looks twice at them." In 1953, the civil rights activist Bayard Rustin was arrested in Pasadena, California, and convicted of a morals charge for having sex with two men. Three years later, James Baldwin wrote a gay love story in his novel *Giovanni's Room.* And the following year, the young playwright Lorraine Hansberry wrote a letter to *The Ladder,* an early lesbian publication, where she condemned "homosexual persecution and condemnation" as "social ignorance." By the 1960s, Hansberry, Baldwin, and Rustin had become genuine black celebrities. Hansberry had won critical acclaim for her play *A Raisin in the Sun,* Baldwin's books were selling in the millions, and Rustin had won fame as the architect of the famous 1963 March on Washington.

History provides plenty of evidence of black homosexuality and bisexuality, but we don't have to go back in time to find examples of men sleeping with men. We can find them in our own circles. They have always been there, but we did not always talk about them. We saw them leading the church choir. We spotted them on the street. We recognized them at our family reunions, funerals, and weddings, and they were obviously gay. They were the easy ones to understand because they fit neatly into a box that allowed us to reduce and define them into a simple stereotype. They made us feel good about ourselves because they could make us laugh, but, just as important, we felt good because we were not them. We were married with children and trying our best to live the prototypical American dream of happiness while they were perpetually lonesome and single, we thought, and yet they were somehow fun-loving and excited about life.

We liked them, in part, because they knew their place. They knew the role they were supposed to play in our lives, and they performed it on cue. We liked them because they did not threaten us by forcing us to challenge our preconceived notions of homosexuality. And that was the great paradox. By being so different, they actually made us feel at ease. If they had looked and spoken and acted just like us, we might not have been as comfortable. How would we pick them out and identify them if they were just like us? But they were identifiable, or so we thought, and so we could relax because we knew who *they* were. They were not us.

What we did not know, or did not want to know, is that there was never an "us" or "them." We were always the same. They were not just the "flamboyant" florists and the "sensitive" male friends. They were the "masculine" construction workers and the "married" men with children. All of them had been there all along, but we continued to live intoxicated by the narcotic power of a collective lie. Like the characters in the film *The Matrix,* we had swallowed the blue pill that made life simple and easy to understand instead of the red pill that made life complicated and truthful. Unfortunately for us, life is not always simple and easy. But the truth did not matter because our virtual reality had already told us what was true. It was a perfect matrix. Straight women could identify straight men, and straight men could identify straight women, and both of them could identify gay men, who could in turn identify one another. But there was actually a fundamental flaw in the system, and it produced an anomaly. In order for the system to work, everyone had to believe it.

The matrix worked well when most homosexuals were confined to the closet. In that world, a few out gay men were free to be themselves while the vast majority of gay men lived their lives in hiding. Closeted gay men who did not want to risk the disclosure of their sexual orientation would carefully adapt their public lives to society's expectations. Homosexuality was not to be discussed. It was, after all, "the love that dare not speak its name." So as long as we remained hooked up to the matrix, we kept ourselves oblivious to the secret lives and torment in which many gays and lesbians lived.

The matrix functioned most smoothly in a world where oppression was common and expressions of difference were forced underground. While the world tolerated injustice for blacks and women and others, few people had any need to worry about the concerns of homosexuals. But with the rise of the civil rights and women's rights movements, ordinary people began to question the premise of their own oppression and to challenge the notion that one group of people had a right to rule over others. Alice Paul led thousands of women through the streets of Washington, D.C., in March 1913 in a demonstration for women's right to vote. A black seamstress in Montgomery, Alabama, named Rosa Parks sparked a boycott in December 1955 when she was arrested after refusing to give up her seat to a white man on a bus. Martin Luther King, Jr., led a quarter of a million people at an August 1963 civil rights march on Washington. And a quarter of a million people marched through the nation's capital in November 1969 to protest the Vietnam War.

By the end of the 1960s, the vocal defenders of oppression more often quietly slipped into the closet while the oppressed spoke out loudly. A string of assassins' bullets had silenced the most audible voices of the decade and threatened to wake us from the stupor of the matrix. Although some could overlook the murder of four little girls in Birmingham, they could not ignore the deaths of John Kennedy and Malcolm X and Martin Luther King and Bobby Kennedy. Nor could they ignore the thousands of American soldiers who were being killed in the war in Southeast Asia.

America in 1969 was a much different country from America in 1960. Our heroes were dead, Richard Nixon was president, and NASA was making plans to send the first man to the moon. It was in that environment that a group of drag queens and gay men would stage an unlikely revolt at a popular bar in New York's Greenwich Village. On Friday, June 27, 1969, eight New York City police officers raided the Stonewall Inn and ordered the patrons to leave. Many of them had seen police raids before, and they knew the drill all too well. But this time was different. As they congregated outside the bar, some of the patrons began to resist. Some taunted the police. Others threw bricks and bottles. The crowd did not disperse. We have conflicting reports about how the night ended, but the event became legendary in gay history.

A riot at a gay bar may seem like an odd event to mark the beginning of a revolution, but word spread quickly, and protests continued at the bar for several days afterward. It is impossible to know how many gays and lesbians outside of New York even heard about the Stonewall incident during the summer of 1969, but by the 1970s, cities across the country were celebrating something called gay pride on the anniversary of Stonewall.

Suddenly, Americans started seeing large numbers of lesbian, gay, bisexual, and transgendered (LGBT) people who were willing to be visible in public. Thousands of them marched in annual pride parades through the streets of major cities like New York and San Francisco. America slowly warmed up to a campy 1970s version of gayness that had been constructed by cultural icons like Elton John and Peter Allen, while black gays found representation in disco divas like Sylvester and the Village People. Once again, Hollywood was available to help us understand another complicated social issue. The comedian Redd Foxx and the singer Pearl Bailey depicted a black couple coming to terms with their son's homosexuality in the comic 1976 film *Norman, Is That You?* Then there was the actor John Ritter, who deployed every gay stereotype he could summon in his role as Jack Tripper, a straight man pretending to be gay in order to live with two female roommates in the 1970s sitcom *Three's Company.* The gay stereotypes worked quite well for most Americans by providing us a comfortable way to process homosexuality through the lens of comedy, but by the time the AIDS epidemic surfaced in the early 1980s, a problem developed. The matrix was beginning to unravel at its seams.

The matrix had always depended on our faith in a collective lie that gay men were readily identifiable. We believed they could be picked out by their behavior, their dress, their walk, their sense of style. The AIDS epidemic, however, began to challenge our assumptions about homosexuality by presenting us with real-life images of gay men who were not the stereotypes we imagined them to be. As thousands of gay men became sick and died, we realized that many of them were our brothers, our cousins, our uncles, our fathers, and sometimes even our husbands. We realized it, but many of us still denied it. Many of us acted as though the truth was not the truth, and we continued to generate and perpetuate outdated but reassuring images of homosexuality.

As gays became more vocal and visible as the victims of AIDS and the fighters against it, the backlash against them became more strident. Increased gay visibility provided fertile ground for televangelists like Jerry Falwell and Pat Robertson and others to exploit America's discomfort with homosexuality. The televangelists misled Americans to believe that liberal political and cultural changes had produced legions of new homosexuals. Although it seemed that gays and lesbians were suddenly coming out of nowhere, in reality they had always been there. The gay movement did not make them gay; it simply gave them the courage to tell the world that they were gay. Before the movement, they had been invisible and silent. After the movement, they were visible and vocal.

Meanwhile, by the 1980s, gay men had learned to morph themselves from a homosexual stereotype into a heterosexual one. A community that was being destroyed by a deadly new disease now exalted men who fit into a stereotypical image of masculine fitness and health. An extensive gym culture developed, and a new gay icon emerged. The new gay model was not just the guy next door. He was a better version of the guy next door. And that was one of the secrets that had been exposed by the unraveling of the matrix. While the matrix told us that gay men looked a certain way, gay men themselves knew that the matrix was wrong. They could see it in their social circles, and they could see it in the mirror. What's more shocking, however, is that some of the antigay conservatives knew the same thing. While they continued to profit from their perpetuation of a gay stereotype, some of them knew all along that the stereotype was wrong. They knew because they helped to design the system. As lawmakers, ministers, corporate executives, and beneficiaries of the status quo, they were the architects of the matrix.

Ironically, the architects of the matrix maintained the system with the complicity of the very people it oppressed. By creating a utopian vision of heterosexuality, the architects produced a social norm that helped to push gay men into false and unnatural relationships with women. The men in these sham relationships knew better than anyone that the matrix was a fraud, but they could never reveal the fraud without revealing their homosexuality. Their ability to operate without suspicion in society depended on their silence. So they persisted in the lie that gay men were simply stereotypes, and as long as they avoided the stereotypes they also avoided detection. That is, until the AIDS epidemic.

With their lives in jeopardy, white gay men quickly mobilized to respond to AIDS in the 1980s. They raised money, created new organizations, educated the community, provided services to people with AIDS, lobbied for public policy, and funded research efforts to produce a cure. The new activism generated concrete results, but it also exposed deep-seated racial fault lines in the gay community. In the 1990s, the AIDS infection rates were declining more significantly among white gay men than among homosexual and bisexual men of color. In spite of all the AIDS education efforts, large numbers of black men who have sex with men (MSM) were still not being reached. While white gay men were coming out of the closet, many black gay men were battening down the hatches.

The AIDS outbreak had also mobilized a cadre of trailblazing black gay poets, writers, artists, and film makers in the 1980s. Many of these men had already told us about a culture that predated the down low. Presumably straight black men had been having sex with one another on the down low for decades. Essex Hemphill's 1991 book *Brother to Brother* included a poem called "The Tomb of Sorrow" about black men secretly having sex in Washington's Malcolm X Park. But by 1995, nearly all the top black gay figures—Joe Beam, Steven Corbin, Melvin Dixon, Craig Harris, Essex Hemphill, Marlon Riggs and Assotto Saint—had died of AIDS-related complications. The memory of their work disappeared from the collective consciousness of the black community as the brightest stars in the black gay constellation slowly faded away into obscurity. An old era had ended, and a new one was beginning as a fresh breed of writers stepped forward to represent the changing times.

In the new era, black gay writers were able to break out of the gay label and reach mainstream black audiences with new images of black gay and bisexual men. E. Lynn Harris opened the doors with his immensely popular groundbreaking debut novel, *Invisible Life.* For many African Americans, Raymond Winston Tyler, Jr., became the embodiment of black bisexuality, and suddenly the secret was out. Harris had introduced the nation to black gay men who did not fit the common stereotypes and to black bisexual men who liked sports, held professional jobs, dated women, and looked just like other black men. At the same time, the writer James Earl Hardy rounded out the new image with his depiction of a young black male couple in his first novel *B-Boy Blues,* in which a streetwise Raheim "Pooquie" Rivers negotiated his relationship with a young journalist named Mitchell "Little Bit" Crawford. Black America was slowly waking up from a long slumber of denial about homosexuality and bisexuality. The blue pill was gradually wearing off.

Our history is not difficult to find in our popular culture, so it is hard to understand how we missed the truth all these years. It is hard to understand how we could believe the down low did not exist until now. Unless, of course, we were not awake. And that is exactly what happened. For a long time, we had been hypnotized by the rhetoric of our own alternative reality. We did not acknowledge what we had seen or what we should have known all along. We had been living in a matrix, but the down low was always there.

Whether through popular culture or real life, we have always known that there were men (and women) on the down low. Like the invisible man in Ralph Ellison's famous novel, they have always been there. Often, they have hidden from us, but sometimes there was no need to hide. As long as we believed that our collective lie was the truth, we were unable to see anything but what we believed to be true. For years, we lived in denial. And for years, we ignored the truth that they, like us, possess the free will to see the truth. "I am invisible," Ellison wrote, "simply because people refuse to see me."

CHAPTER 3
Everybody's Doing It

WHEN I WAS a child, I had an uncle on the down low. People in the family never really talked about Uncle Michael, but we knew he was gay. He was a well-known organist at a popular church in St. Louis, and he had a fraternity of male friends whose association with him raised a few eyebrows in the community. Nevertheless, as far as I can recall, Uncle Michael was very well liked and respected. That is, until he was murdered one night in his own apartment. We never found out who killed him, and no one was ever convicted of the crime. But Michael was not the one on the down low. Uncle Larry was. Uncle Larry lived in a beautiful ranch house in the suburbs of St. Louis County. He was married with children and had a successful job as an up-and-coming businessman. From the outside, it appeared that Uncle Larry had the perfect life. From the inside, we knew it was a lie. Uncle Larry was living a double life. He was on the down low.

Before you make any assumptions about Uncle Larry, you should know this. Uncle Larry considered himself to be straight. He did not sleep with men or have sex with them. If anything, he considered himself a ladies' man. And that, actually, was the problem. Uncle Larry was married, but he also had a long-time girlfriend on the side. You see, Uncle Larry not only *considered* himself to be heterosexual; he *was* heterosexual. Uncle Larry was straight in his sexual orientation and in his behavior, and yet he was on the down low. He was on the down low because he cheated on his wife. When his wife found out, she confronted him, challenged him, and ultimately left him. She refused to be married to a man on the down low.

Quiet as it's kept, there is a dirty little secret about the down low that most of the media have not discussed. Here's the secret. The down low is not only about closeted gay men and bisexuals. Straight men and women are on the down low too. In fact, if gay men and bisexuals have now popularized the down low, then heterosexuals might actually have perfected it. Long before the current down low scare, heterosexuals were cheating in their marriages and in their relationships, just like everyone else. History is filled with heterosexual examples of men cheating with women and women cheating with men. From the ancient Greek tragedies to the Christian Bible to Shakespeare, few themes are more constant than infidelity. We have been writing about it, singing about it, and creating art about it for centuries. The only thing that has changed is what we call it.

I learned that lesson when I was driving my car down U Street in Washington, D.C., one day when a new song came on 95.5/WPGC. The infectious beat quickly had me bobbing my head in the car, and I recognized the artist's voice as soon as I heard the words:

> *My body wants you so*
> *For what I miss at home*
> *Nobody has to know*
> *Keep it on the down low.*

The year was 1995, the artist was Brian McKnight, the song was "On the Down Low," and Maxine became one of the first modern poster girls for the DL. Back then, the down low was simply an expression of secret intimacy outside a relationship, and because Maxine yearned for satisfaction that her man could not provide, she was portrayed as a sympathetic figure, the forlorn woman abandoned by her unsympathetic partner. Poor Maxine. Her man "doesn't take her anywhere," McKnight explains. He used to "say sweet things" but now he "acts like he doesn't even care." Who could be upset at a woman rebelling against the heartbreak of a loveless relationship? She was a woman who simply "needed someone to hold" and whose lonely nights were "oh so cold." Brian McKnight, the handsome young man with a smooth voice and sensitive looks, became the perfect paramour for the lonesome woman, able to sweep her off her feet with a song and rescue her from her tragic relationship. When McKnight's song was released, there was little public concern about the decline of moral values or the problem of infidelity in the black community. At the time, the down low was seen as a heterosexual thing, acknowledging the reality that both men and women often go unfulfilled in their relationships and seek comfort elsewhere.

Brian McKnight may have been the first artist to mention the down low in a *title* of a popular song, but he was not the first popular recording artist to sing about the heterosexual down low. The female R&B trio TLC had already introduced us to the down low in their 1994 song "Creep." As in McKnight's story, the lonely woman in "Creep" decides to cheat on her man because she needs "some affection." She suspects her man is unfaithful to her, but rather than confront him, she takes a different approach—she cheats as well. Behind a flaring trumpet interlude and a jazzy sexual overtone, the TLC trio sings the now-famous chorus:

So I creep, yeah
Just keep it on the down low
Said nobody is supposed to know.

The song that played on the radio presented a morally neutral view of the woman's actions, but TLC also released a socially conscious remix of the song that seemed to question the values of the down low. The remix added a new verse that sounds more like a public health warning than a typical R&B song. The added lyrics warned that creepin' could lead to passionate crime, unwanted pregnancy, incest, family breakup, AIDS, and death, and the remixed song explicitly warned that "HIV is often sleepin' in a creepin' cradle."

In the 1990s, "creeping" became a widely used slang term to describe unfaithful behavior. Meanwhile, the down low that TLC sang about was an intangible place or space where secrets were kept, but it was not a description commonly used to identify someone. People were not *on* the down low, but people would *do things* on the down low. The down low was not a description of who they were, it described something that they did. Our early understanding of the heterosexual down low operated in much the same way as our understanding of sexual orientation in the late nineteenth and early twentieth century. In prewar America, homosexuals and bisexuals did not identify themselves based on their sexual orientation. What they did in bed described their behavior, not their identity. But times change, and similarly some words and ideas change their meaning over time. The word "gay," for example, once meant "happy" and "cheerful" but now means "homosexual" as well. The word "black" was once avoided by African Americans but was later embraced by the black nationalists of the 1960s. When Luther Vandross sang about "creepin'" in his 1989 song of the same name, the word had a somewhat positive connotation as Vandross sang to a lover who creeps into his dreams. It was the ultimate expression of loyalty that a man would fantasize about his partner at night. Five years later, TLC had changed the perception of the term by associating it with the disloyalty of the down low.

Even as TLC tried to cover its tracks with its warning about the risks of the down low, the music that they and others created still seemed to romanticize heterosexual infidelity. Brian McKnight's 1995 *I Remember You* CD led with his "On the Down Low" song as the first track. McKnight was pictured on the cover of the CD in a sexy pose with his shirt open and chest exposed, but inside the liner notes he was shown in another photo that portrayed him embracing his two young sons, B. J. and Niko, who actually introduced the down low song. Thus began the contradiction associated with the down low. Here was Brian McKnight, a family man still married to his college sweetheart, but he was singing a song that rationalized cheating. The crooner known for his melodic love ballads was striking a chord as a bad boy. In a CD filled with endearing songs about "crazy love," the down low tune seemed strangely out of place, but the song helped to reposition McKnight in line with the emerging anything goes hip hop mentality of the early 1990s.

In the 1990s, top hip hop performers were becoming the new kings and queens of the music world. The rap group Naughty by Nature glamorized both male and female cheating in their 1991 crossover hit "O.P.P.," an abbreviation loosely interpreted to mean "other people's property." Long before "the down low" term became popular, people were asking each other another question: "Are you down with O.P.P.?" In the words of that song:

> *Have you ever known a brother who had another like a girl or wife*
> *And you just had to stop and look cuz he look just that nice.*

Never mind the girl or wife. The man was going to be "yours anyway," the song claims. In the bold new world of hip hop, men and women could openly celebrate their disrespect for marital vows. Despite a woman's repeated claim that "I Got a Man" in a 1993 song of the same name, the rap artist Positive K nonetheless repeatedly asks: "What's your man got to do with me?"

Hip hop opened up new opportunities and new challenges for women as well. With its provocative female MCs and its sexual depiction of women in rap videos, hip hop had ushered in a controversial new sexual revolution for black women. Perhaps that explains why many of the first songs about the down low were songs *about women* on the down low. One major exception was a song recorded *by women,* as the female group Salt-N-Pepa rapped about a man on the down low. Back in 1993, before Brian McKnight's "On the Down Low" or TLC's "Creep," Salt-N-Pepa released a song called "Whatta Man," recorded with the female group En Vogue, that repeatedly boasts about the virtue of a particularly good man. But rather than praise his faithfulness, the artists appreciate his discretion, while tacitly acknowledging his cheating:

> *Although most men are hos*
> *He flows on the down low*
> *Cuz I never heard about him with another girl.*

The reference to "another girl" makes it very clear that Salt-N-Pepa are thinking about heterosexual infidelity. But more importantly, the lyrics indicate that some women, almost a decade before the most recent down low sensation, were publicly excusing their men for their down low behavior.

In 1993, the down low was, arguably, acceptable, or at least expected, behavior for some men in relationships. Long before J. L.

King was writing about the down low, black women were acknowledging and living with the reality that men cheat. Although Salt-N-Pepa acknowledge "that ain't nobody perfect," the man they applaud in their song seems pretty damn close. When it comes to monogamy, however, he's given a pass. Here's a man who is described in the song as funny, smooth, masculine, muscular, handsome, intelligent, caring, well-dressed, good in bed, patient, dependable, polite, and respectful of his elders. But there's one tiny little glitch: he's a ho. And what's the woman's response? "I don't sweat it because it's just pathetic to let it get me involved in that 'he said/she said' crowd." That's an odd statement, suggesting that monogamy is too much to expect or even discuss with an otherwise good man. But if the man is really as caring and sensitive as he's described, it's hard to understand why their relationship would be hurt by a little candor.

Salt-N-Pepa were not one-dimensional. The group also tried to balance their overtly sexual messages with public education about the dangers of AIDS. The artists even allowed a Boston youth group to record a three-minute public service announcement called "I've Got AIDS" that was included on their *Very Necessary* CD. The PSA, presented as a skit between a young man and a young woman, is introduced by Salt in her speaking voice. "Well, for a long time, me, Pep, and Spin have been involved in the fight against AIDS, and we always say the best cure is not to get it and not to spread it. You should be responsible if you're gonna have sex." Although seemingly at odds with the implicit message of much of their music, the PSA was actually consistent with the idea behind their 1992 hit "Let's Talk About Sex," a song that encouraged America to "talk about all the good things and the bad things that may be." The PSA also communicated the need for safe sex, not for abstinence. "All we had to do was just use protection," says the young woman who learns she's HIV positive in the skit. "I mean, the condoms were right there." It was a valuable public service message, but it underscored a paradox in American sexual behavior. In 1990s America, it was still easier to talk about sex than it was to talk about safe sex. Condom ads were banned from the same airwaves that made TV shows more sexually explicit than ever before. Music videos and cable television programming promoted graphic sexual depictions, and yet Surgeon General Joycelyn Elders was fired from her job because she talked about masturbation as a method of safe sex. In that climate, Salt-N-Pepa would be best known for such hit songs as "Push It," "Let's Talk About Sex," "None of Your Business," and "Shoop," and not for their efforts to promote safe sex and HIV awareness through their PSA.

On the surface, Salt-N-Pepa's most popular music seemed to send a different message from the PSA on their CD, but the predominant message of empowering women remained the same in the PSA as in their music. In "None of Your Business," for example, the rappers present an image of women empowered to make their own sexual decisions without regard to the opinions of others. That sentiment was hardly new in black music and culture. The song was reminiscent of Billie Holiday's legendary recording of "Ain't Nobody's Business If I Do." In the old song, Holiday sang:

> *If I go to church on Sunday*
> *Then cabaret all day Monday*
> *Ain't nobody's business if I do.*

In the new song, Salt-N-Pepa sing:

> *If I wanna take a guy home with me tonight*
> *It's none of your business.*

Hidden behind the lyrics of the two songs was a deeper meaning. At first blush, the songs represented the right of women to make their own decisions about their sexuality. Upon closer inspection, the songs revealed a long held but seldom discussed truth about relationships. Many of us knowingly remain in complex, even problematic relationships. Even when we know our partners are lying, cheating, and abusing us, we find it difficult to admit the truth. And when we do admit the truth, we still find it difficult to make a change. In "Ain't Nobody's Business," written by Porter Grainger and Everett Robbins, Holiday claims that she would rather her man "would hit me" than to "jump up and quit me." Sometimes, stability is more important than peace, but Holiday takes it to a new level when she promises not to call the police even if her man should beat her up. Similarly, although less dramatically, Salt-N-Pepa seem to indicate they won't be filing divorce papers if an otherwise good man cheats on one of them. In reality, we all make different choices about what we will and will not tolerate in a relationship, and many of us compromise our convictions out of love.

Salt-N-Pepa's 1993 song opened the door to the truth about men on the down low, but the next major musical references to the down low focused on women on the DL instead of men. There was TLC in 1994, followed by Brian McKnight in 1995, and then the R&B singer R. Kelly joined the crowd with his popular 1996 slow jam called "Down Low (Nobody Has To Know)." In R. Kelly's song, the featured character is once again a woman in an unhappy relationship. The woman approaches the man and whispers to him to keep it on the down low, and then like every other song of the genre she adds the familiar refrain: "nobody has to know." It's the exact same phrase used by Maxine in Brian McKnight's song ("nobody has to know") and strikingly similar to the phrase used in TLC's song ("nobody is supposed 2 know"). In the highly derivative world of contemporary music, it is not uncommon for artists to sample each other's music or lyrics or even their ideas, but the 1990s down low craze seemed to represent a new extreme as one artist after another jumped into the mix with his or her own version of the down low.

Not content with one song about the subject, R. Kelly decided to milk the down low concept again. In the 1998 song "Down Low Double Life," he plays the role of a down low man cheating on his wife until he's busted by his caller ID. But even before he gets caught, his wife seems to suspect his double life, which becomes clear when she tries to stop him from leaving the house one day. R. Kelly sings:

> *You pulled me to the side and you begged for me to stay*
> *But I was caught up in a life that forced me to walk away.*

In the end, he confesses to his "creepin'" only when he's thrown out of his house and forced to live with his momma, and even then his own mother scolds him and tells him he's pathetic. His response: "Must be because of what my old man did to her." Yes, the down low has been around for a long time.

In some form or another, the down low story has been told for generations. Long before there was a name attached to it, men and women were cheating on each other and singing about it in their music. In a popular 1955 song, Chuck Berry asks his sweetheart: "Oh Maybellene, why can't you be true?" In 1968, Marvin Gaye "heard it through the grapevine" that his woman was cheating on him. In 1972, Bill Withers asked the question, "Who is he and what is he to you?" And in 1985, Stevie Wonder sang about "part-time lovers."

We can learn a lot about the way we see ourselves as a people by taking a look at our popular culture. To the extent that popular music reflects our real-life concerns, we learn about the down low by looking back at the music of various periods in our history. In many ways, music has provided a virtual soundtrack for our lives, where art imitates reality imitating art. Music survives when the public consumes it, and the public consumes what they think is real, which is based, in part, on perceptions that are reinforced by what they hear from their music. Music helps us to realize that the down low is not just about supposedly straight men sleeping with other men. Instead, as we see through our music, the down low is also about men and women cheating on each other. It's about finding outlets to satisfy our needs when our partners cannot or will not do that for us. It's about men sleeping with women, women sleeping with men, men sleeping with men, and women sleeping with women. It's about infidelity and trust, victimhood and blame, and the difference between life as we would like it to be and life as it really is.

Despite the recent narrative of the down low that assumes a male perpetrator and a female victim, the musical history of infidelity—like its real life counterpart—cannot be reduced to simple equations where male equals bad and female equals good. In fact, the complex discography of the down low is filled with examples of men as both victims and participants in illicit affairs. A lonesome Hank Williams warned his ex-lover "your cheating heart will tell on you" in a 1952 song. The Eagles cautioned a young girl, "You can't hide your lyin' eyes" in 1975. Prince asked his woman "What's it gonna be? Is it him or is it me?" in his 1984 song "The Beautiful Ones." In each song, the man is portrayed as the victim of the woman's cheating.

Men, of course, have played the perpetrator role as well. The Doors' lead singer Jim Morrison bragged that he was the "Back Door Man" in a 1967 song of the same name. The back door man was the guy who had sex with another man's wife while the husband was away. Twenty years later, Bobby Womack sang "I Wish He Didn't Trust Me So Much," a song about a man who wants to sleep with his best friend's wife. And in 2000, the reggae recording artist Shaggy counsels a cheating friend "never to admit to a word that she say" in his song "It Wasn't Me." Even when his friend's girlfriend catches him naked with another woman, Shaggy tells him to deny it.

It's not always easy to determine who to blame. Like men, women have also played dual roles in the discourse of the down low. In some examples, women were not only active participants but actually initiated the affairs they had. Bessie Smith, for example, plays the role of a moneygrubbing, love-hungry woman who threatens her man in the 1923 song "If You Don't, I Know Who Will." Portraying herself as both victim and perpetrator, she warns her man that her "other papa" will take care of her if her needs are not met. The country singer Loretta Lynn plays the same dual role as victim and perpetrator in her 1971 song "Another Man Loved Me Last Night." Although Lynn expresses some remorse for her betrayal, she seems to justify her actions because "not being loved" was more than she could take. In contrast, Meshell Ndegeocello unapologetically flaunts her success in stealing somebody else's man in her 1992 breakthrough song "If That's Your Boyfriend (He Wasn't Last Night)." In a schoolyard-style chant, Ndegeocello sings, "Boyfriend, boyfriend, yes I had your boyfriend" and boasts that she's "the kind of woman [to] do almost anything to get what I want."

Women are often portrayed somewhat sympathetically in songs about cheating, but Bessie Smith, Loretta Lynn, and Meshell Ndegeocello provide a different and more complicated image of the woman as an empowered figure making her own choices about fidelity. Perhaps it's significant that a white country music singer and two black bisexual women could present such an image, while many other black women recording artists seem to shy away from such depictions.

One of the lies we tell ourselves about the down low is that women are only the innocent victims of men on the down low. Even when women are the coconspirators in a man's infidelity, we sometimes think of them with sympathy. In many of the popular R&B songs where women sing about their participation in an affair, the women portray themselves as lonely mistresses waiting for their men to come back to them. Gladys Knight plays the role of mistress in the 1970 song "If I Were Your Woman," where she justifies her affair with a married man because the man's wife does not treat him well. Like so many other deluded mistresses, she imagines that the man's cheating would somehow stop if she were his woman. "If I were your woman and you were my man, you'd have no other woman," she sings.

"A few stolen moments" is all that Whitney Houston shares with her fictional man in the 1985 song "Saving All My Love For You." True to the traditional story line, she complains that "it's not very easy living all alone," and she remembers the days when her man told her they'd run away together. Houston's song positions her in the classic victim-as-participant role, a common template through which our society understands women in extramarital affairs. It's no accident, for example, that the guilty female murderers in the musical "Chicago" reflexively revert to the victim-as-participant position in their "Cell Block Tango." When one of their soon-to-be victims comes home and accuses his wife of "screwing the milkman," rather than address his accusation, the wife responds by stabbing him nine times. Nevertheless, she claims "he had it coming," that he deserved his fate, and through the lens of politically correct preconceived notions about gender, the calculated appeal to victimhood may have been perfectly timed. After all, the woman is often seen as a victim, whether it's from domestic abuse, infidelity, or even from previously latent effects of child abuse. It may be true that all criminals can be seen as victims of their environment, but men are rarely afforded the same presumption of victimhood that is sometimes conferred upon women. There is no need to explore the male inner psyche when we have already concluded that "men are dogs."

The truth is that being involved in an extramarital affair can be emotionally stressful for both men and women on both sides of the relationship. Sometimes, the pressure of being "the other woman" can be too much to bear, as Stephanie Mills discovers in her 1987 song "Secret Lady." After struggling in a role behind the scenes, she finally breaks down and announces, "I just can't go on being your secret lady, mystery baby," a chorus that is repeated until the end, as Mills becomes more and more defiant. In contrast, one of the most amusing examples of the victim role comes from Candi Staton's 1978 disco tune appropriately called "Victim," where the woman who counsels other women not to fall in love finds herself in a relationship with a cheating man. As Staton explains, "I'm a victim of the very song I sing."

One of the problems with the caricature of women solely in the victim role is that such roles ignore the obvious inconsistency of typecasting both the wife and the mistress as victims. If the wife is a victim, shouldn't the mistress be a perpetrator or at least a coconspirator with the husband? Instead, the mistress is usually viewed as a coconspirator if the story is told from the wife's perspective, but even then it's not always a critical depiction of the other woman. In "Clean Up Woman," for example, the R&B singer Betty Wright realizes that her own indifference to her man may have "made it easy" for another woman to get him. Still, it's more of a warning to married women than a criticism of the other woman. Similarly, in "All The Way

Lover," the raunchy recording artist Millie Jackson chides married women for their general inattentiveness to their men and warns them that some other woman might come and "steal your man." But even in that song, the other woman is portrayed more as an opportunist than as a predator. Perhaps no song depicts the rival mistress as more sympathetic and complex than Nina Simone's "The Other Woman." Although "the other woman" has time to manicure her nails and do her hair, she's still lonesome most of the time, crying herself to sleep because she "will never have his love to keep" and "will spend her life alone." In other words, she is to be pitied, not condemned.

The image of the sympathetic female culprit is not universal in contemporary pop culture. Compare those earlier songs with Shirley Brown's 1975 single "Woman to Woman." Brown picks up the phone and calls the other woman, Barbara, and tells her, "The man you're in love with, he's mine." In a calm, respectful tone, she appeals to Barbara's sense of dignity as a woman. "If you were in my shoes," Brown asks, "wouldn't you have done the same thing too?" More recent music has taken the woman-to-woman concept and applied it to dramatic face-to-face scenes in music videos such as "Gettin' In The Way," where Jill Scott marches over to the other woman's house, rolls her neck and pulls off the woman's wig. Confrontation is also a major element in musical duets such as Brandy and Monica's 1998 hit song "The Boy Is Mine" or Whitney Houston's duo with Deborah Cox, "Same Script, Different Cast." By presenting both the wife figure (or girlfriend) and the mistress, those songs break new ground by acknowledging the conflict between the two, and yet at some level the listener is left conflicted because the women are arguing over an apparently unfaithful man.

Only a few moments in life compare to the drama involved when a woman confronts her man about his infidelity. It happens every day in real life, and it's often reflected in our popular culture.

Whitney Houston tells her man "My Name Is Not Susan" when she hears him call out the other woman's name in his sleep in her 1990 song. Toni Braxton struggles with what to do in a similar situation when she catches her husband mentioning the other woman in her 1996 song "Talking In His Sleep." Meanwhile, the members of the female musical group Destiny's Child develop a creative way to find out if a man is lying when he's on the phone. "Say My Name," they say in their 1999 song. "If no one is around you, say baby I love you, if you ain't running game."

Some of the most striking scenes about cheating are viewed not from the perspective of the victim but from the viewpoint of the cheaters themselves. In the 1972 song, "Me and Mrs. Jones," Billy Paul seems almost tearful as he sings of his "thing going on" with his married mistress. Back then, artists sang euphemistically about their other "obligations" as an indication that they were already involved in other relationships. The same "obligations" language comes up in The Manhattans' 1976 classic "Kiss and Say Goodbye," where a man meets with his lover at their usual rendezvous to break off their down low relationship. Knowing that the two can never meet again, the man calls it "the saddest day of my life." The same sense of sorrow hangs over Shirley Murdock's 1985 song "As We Lay," as she and a married man wake up to the consequences of a one-night stand.

While some of us were busy making amends for our infidelity and moving forward, Luther Ingram took issue with that view of morality in his 1972 classic "(If Loving You Is Wrong) I Don't Wanna Be Right." Even with a wife and two kids at home, Ingram sings about holding on to his lover, whom he calls "the best thing I ever had." But one of the most memorable examples of cheaters singing about their relationship comes from the tune "Secret Lovers," recorded by Atlantic Starr in 1986. As in earlier songs, the cheating man and the cheating woman are both married to other people, but in this song the cheaters come together to sing to each other. In one verse, the man acknowledges the difficulty of "living two lives" after he sings:

> *How could something so wrong be so right*
> *I wish we didn't have to keep our love out of sight.*

Unlike so many other songs about cheating, the "secret lover" songs acknowledge the reality that it takes two people to cheat. The man and the woman are both involved.

We know that many women find it embarrassing when a man is cheating on them. Imagine the response, then, when men discover that a woman is cheating on them. The reaction to being cheated on (or played) begins to change with the increased machismo of modern times, as men feel the need to assert their dominance against newly liberated women. The passive response of Hank Williams, Chuck Berry, and Marvin Gaye started to be replaced by a more vengeful retaliation in the 1980s. Early hip hop music provides an example. At first, hip hop seemed to follow the pattern of its musical predecessors. "If your woman steps out with another man," said Kurtis Blow, "and she runs off with him to Japan," all you were expected to do is "clap your hands" and go dancing because, hey, "these are the breaks." By 1986, however, Oran "Juice" Jones catches his woman "walking in the rain" and "holding hands" with another man and waits till she gets back home to confront her. In the modern male reinterpretation of responding to female infidelity, the cuckold has been taught to respond strategically but forcefully. If he responds with violence, he could end up in jail for abuse, but if he does nothing, he risks looking weak. In this song, Jones's character says he chose not to be violent because he did not want to mess up his $3,700 lynx coat, so instead he goes to the bank, closes her account, cancels her credit cards, and packs her belongings in the guest room, all in an effort to teach her "a valuable lesson." Similarly, in Justin Timberlake's 2002 song "Cry Me a River," Timberlake cuts off his relationship with his cheating girlfriend and plots his revenge against her. "The damage is done so I guess I'll be leaving," the background vocalist sings.

Vengeance works for women too, as we see in Blu Cantrell's 2001 song, "Hit 'Em Up Style (Oops!)," where the woman exacts her revenge by taking her man's credit card on an expensive shopping spree at Neiman Marcus. Angela Bassett follows a more destructive path in the 1995 film *Waiting To Exhale,* based on the novel by Terry McMillan, when she burns her husband's expensive suits in his BMW after she discovers his infidelity. In the accompanying song from the soundtrack, Mary J. Blige promises she's "Not Gon' Cry." Today, it's not unusual to find women who are defiant to unfaithful men. Whitney Houston sang "It's not right, but it's okay" in 1998 as she told her man to pack his bags and leave. In the 2002 hit "Heard It All Before," Sunshine Anderson explained, "Your lies ain't working now" and told her man, "I had to shut you down."

In Carl Thomas's 2000 song "I Wish," one of the most memorable songs about the down low, he tells the story of a deceptive woman. Thomas sings about meeting her, falling in love and spending long days and nights together until one day she tells him that she's married with children. She goes back to her life, while he is left alone and devastated. She's just another woman on the down low.

With all the popular musical references to heterosexuals on the down low, there are considerably fewer songs about homosexuals and bisexuals on the down low. Nevertheless, those references exist too. In 1984, long before the current down low sensation, Barbara Mason released the song "Another Man (Is Beating My Time)," which was a follow-up to a seemingly endless stream of spin-off songs from an earlier tune called "She's Got Papers On Me." But unlike most songs from the perspective of women as victims of cheating, this song actually challenged the man's masculinity. "There was a little too much sugar and you were a little too sweet," Mason sings. Mason also sings of her suspicion that her man borrowed her new dress, she says she saw him "switching" his hips on the steps, and she caught him holding hands with another man. Like many other women who are challenged by homosexuality, Mason describes her man as "a waste," presumably because she believes he cannot fulfill her needs. She thought she had a real man, she says, but instead she had "a facsimile thereof," whose sexual orientation she sees as a "defect" or as evidence that "something went wrong" after he was created.

The scandalous gay song of the nineties was a simple blues tune called "Bill" by Peggy Scott-Adams, where she catches her husband in the arms of another man named Bill and sees them "breathing hard and french-kissing." Describing the pain involved, she sings:

> *I was ready for Mary*
> *Susan, Helen and Jane*
> *When all the time it was Bill*
> *That was sleeping with my man.*

Her sense of betrayal is directed not only at her husband, but at Bill, who she said was a friend and a god uncle to her son. Then in a particularly demeaning reference to her former friend, she says, "Now it looks like Uncle Billy wants to be his step mom." Her song, like Barbara Mason's before it, is filled with outdated stereotypes about flamboyant homosexuals, but she does raise one very provocative question that vexes other women in her position. In broken English, she asks, "How do a woman compete with a man for another man?" She seems genuinely interested in learning more about bisexuality, but her curiosity is clouded by her prejudice. When she asks her husband why he did not tell her that he was gay, he explains his hope that being with a woman "would change me." Fortunately, she says she does not feel ashamed and does not take the blame, but she does place blame on her man, whom she describes as "just a queen . . . that thought he was a king."

It seems the absence of visible black openly gay recording artists has left a one-dimensional image in the black community's musical depiction of male homosexuality. Since Sylvester kicked down the music industry's closet door with his 1978 hit "You Make Me Feel (Mighty Real)," most black gay recording artists—like their white gay counterparts—have labored in obscurity or hidden in the closet. The black gay performer Carl Bean, who later founded the Unity Fellowship Church, created what some called a "gay national anthem" with his 1985 recording of "I Was Born This Way." In the 1980s, the once and future Prince was confusing everybody with questions about his sexuality. Before Prince, the rock 'n' roll legend Little Richard had generated speculation for years about his sexual orientation. It was always easier to dodge the issue than to confront it directly. Those who have been openly gay have rarely met with the same public success as those who have dwelled in the closet. When the R&B recording artist Tevin Campbell was arrested in 1999 for soliciting a male prostitute, his career was ruined. On the other hand, recent "homo hop" artists like Tori Fixx, Tim'M West, Rainbow Flava, and DeepDickCollective have become legendary in the underground scene but have not been introduced to the public at large. The drag queen RuPaul seemed to open up new possibilities with her early 1990s anthem "Supermodel (You Better Work)," but her visibility, without other balancing images, merely confirmed popular beliefs that gay men wanted to be women.

Among today's major figures in the industry, Meshell Ndegeocello stands alone as an openly bisexual black recording artist, and much of her music explores the complexity of sexual identity. When Ndegeocello remade Bill Withers's classic "Who Is He (And What Is He to You)," she complicated the formula of the song without changing a word. When Withers had asked the question in the title of the song, it seemed clear he was asking his woman about a man they had just passed on the street. But when Ndegeocello sang the exact same verse, it automatically introduced a homosexual relationship into the picture. If she was asking the question to her man in the traditional heterosexual equation, then the man must have been involved with the other man who was walking down the street. In order to make that illicit relationship into a heterosexual affair, Ndegeocello's partner would have to be a woman, meaning that Ndegeocello was in a homosexual relationship. Either way, whether it's two men or two women, somebody was sleeping with someone else of the same gender.

Ndegeocello introduced another form of sexual nuance in her 2002 song "Berry Farms." In front of a slow go-go beat, she raps about an ex-girlfriend who "liked to flirt with me, and act like she didn't know me when her friends came around." After people begin to wonder about their relationship, the girl stops talking to her and starts dating a man. Then one day the ex-girlfriend spots Ndegeocello, approaches her and confesses that she misses her. Oh really, Ndegeocello asks, "What do you miss?" The ex-girlfriend replies in a whisper: "Can't nobody eat my pussy the way that you do."

Meshell Ndegeocello is not impressed by the obvious attempt at flattery, and she knows exactly what is going on—her ex-girlfriend is on the down low. As Meshell explains in the chorus to the song:

She couldn't love me without shame
She only wanted me for one thing
But you can teach your boy to do that.

Ndegeocello's music tells us that men are not the only ones who have been having secret same-gender relationships without telling their opposite-sex partners. Just as there have been men who have sex with men but do not identify as gay, there have also been women who have sex with women but do not identify as lesbian. These women rarely get talked about in the recent media hype about the down low, but they have been discussed from time to time in music. In Michael Coleman's 1987 blues song "Woman Loves a Woman," he confesses that he's in love with a woman, and then he drops the catch line: "She's in love with a woman too." Listeners to the blues have always known the real deal. Even as far back as the 1930s, "the blues reflected a culture that accepted sexuality, including homosexual behavior and identities, as a natural part of life," according to the historian Eric Garber in an essay called *A Spectacle in Color: The Lesbian and Gay Subculture of Jazz Age Harlem.* While the mainstream media were documenting an official company line about America, the blues became the real paper of record that told us who we were, not just who we wanted to be. Thank goodness for the blues.

In the end, the down low in popular culture is almost as complicated as the down low in real life. There are women on the down low as well as men. They are black and white, straight, gay, and bisexual. Film makers, authors, song writers, and recording artists have romanticized, scandalized, and fantasized about it. And whether they called it cheating, creeping, O.P.P. or something else, it's the same old song that's been playing for generations. As we see from our culture, we've heard it all before. We just weren't listening.

CHAPTER 4

It's Not Just a Black Thing

I MET YVONNE in my first year of law school. She was almost everything I thought I wanted in a woman: attractive, intelligent, articulate, spiritual, and physically fit. She didn't drink too much. And she didn't smoke cigarettes. She was a modern woman. She would have made a perfect wife. A perfect wife for someone else, that is. When Yvonne and I started dating, we were at a difficult point in our lives, trying to sort our way through the maze of the first year of law school. Harvard was a whole new world for both of us, and we were each looking for ways to bring stability to the otherwise chaotic experience.

Before I started Harvard, everyone had told me not to worry about dating. Those who had been through law school warned that I would have little time to do anything but study. Law school, they told me, was not at all like college. In most college courses, professors give you midterms, final exams, and papers to write. In law school, however, your entire course grade is based on a single exam you take at the end of the semester. If you're not prepared or if you have a bad day, three months of course work can go down the drain in a three-hour exam. In order to do well, you have to keep up with the reading, attend classes, and form study groups. Several people advised me to do *nothing* but study. I listened carefully to what they said, but I could not follow their advice. I knew I would go crazy if I spent three years of my life in the library. That has never been my style.

I thought I would function well in school if I followed the same strategies that had worked for me in college. That meant trying to maintain balance in my life, which I found by going to the gym, hanging out with friends, joining organizations, and dating Yvonne. Yvonne and I had a wholesome relationship. We went out to dinner, spent time at each other's apartments, and went to church from time to time. One Sunday after church, however, I made an important and dramatic discovery about our relationship. I realized I was not in love with Yvonne.

The streets were bustling with activity as Yvonne and I walked down Massachusetts Avenue from St. Paul's A.M.E. Church to the subway stop at Central Square. Yvonne reached out to grab my hand while we walked. I recoiled for a split second and then returned my hand back to hers. I had hoped she had not noticed my reaction but the gesture was far too obvious for her to miss. She waited a few seconds as we walked and then turned to me with a smile and called me on it. "You don't like holding my hand, do you?" I smiled back, trying to think of what to say, so I asked a dumb question in response. "Why do you say that?" Yvonne knew I was stalling. "You just pulled your hand away from mine," she said. Seconds had passed, and I still hadn't thought of what to say. To be honest, I did not know what to say. I did not know why I had pulled my hand away from hers. I knew I liked her, and I was not the least bit ashamed to be seen with her. But I guess, deep down, something told me not to hold her hand at that moment. Something about the intimacy felt fake.

"I'm not a very touchy-feely person," I told her. That was true. My family was never physically expressive, and I guess I had picked up their behavior. I had dated a couple of girls in high school and one woman in college, and I don't recall ever really holding hands with any of them. Yvonne seemed to accept that explanation, but I knew she suspected there was more to it than I was telling her. She was very perceptive, and she was right. Yvonne could see things about me that I was unwilling to see, and shortly after that day our relationship began to fizzle out. We stopped talking as much, then we stopped hanging out, and soon we just stopped dating.

A few months after Yvonne and I broke up, I started to feel burned out from school and life. I felt as though I had been on a treadmill from grade school to junior high to high school to college to law school, and I was exhausted. Like the unnamed protagonist in Ellison's *Invisible Man,* I had been running all my life from one task to the next, and suddenly it had all caught up to me. I was tired of going to school, tired of being involved in extracurriculars, and tired of living my life in confusion about my identity.

In the spring of my second year of law school, I decided to resign from my position as an editor of the *Civil Rights–Civil Liberties Law Review,* and I withdrew from my role as a spokesman for the campus Coalition for Civil Rights. For the first time in my life, I was pulling back from the activities that had defined my existence. I realized suddenly that my whole identity had been wrapped up in my work and not in my relationships. My work had become my life, and my life had become my work. Then one day, I decided to step off the treadmill and live, and that was the day I realized I had been living a lie. I had never lied to my girlfriends. I had never lied to my friends or my family. I had not lied to the rest of the world. Instead, most tragically, I had lied to myself.

In April of 1991, I finally stopped lying to myself and acknowledged the sexual orientation I had tried to repress my entire life. I called my mom and came out to her, and the next day I told a friend on campus. Coming out to my family and friends was liberating and frightening at the same time. It felt good to finally speak the words, "I'm gay," but it was difficult to repeat the monologue over and over again with each person I told.

That's why I decided not to tell everyone. I realized it would be easier to *be* out than to come out, and I quickly discovered one of the first rules of coming out. That is, if you tell the right people, you don't have to tell everyone else. It worked. Within days of coming out to a few friends at school, it seemed as if everyone on campus knew I was gay. One of my professors even asked me about it. "I heard you came out recently," he said. "Yes," I replied, "but how did you hear about it?" His response shocked me. "One of the other professors told me," he said. It was an unusual admission of academic gossip. For a long time, I had labored under the delusion that professors at Harvard Law School had more important things to do with their time than to speculate on the sexual orientation of their students, but apparently I was wrong. It was fitting irony, especially since many of my classmates had spent our time speculating on the sexual orientation of our professors.

Except for a few close friends I spoke to directly, everyone on campus found out through the grapevine that I was gay. Everyone, including Yvonne. She and I had almost stopped talking by that time. We would see each other in passing and speak to each other briefly, but we had not hung out since the day we broke up months earlier. I heard from a friend that Yvonne felt betrayed when she found out I was gay. I never spoke to her about it, and she never asked me, but I imagine she felt a sense of awkwardness in being the last person to date me before I came out of the closet.

It took me thirteen years to understand exactly what Yvonne

must have felt. That was the day when I realized the real meaning of the down low. I was visiting my family in Chicago one day when my friend Maurice called on the cell phone. "Are you watching TV?" he said. It was the middle of the day, so I had no reason to be watching television. But the urgency of the question suggested that something was happening that was important enough to be broadcast live on several different networks. Immediately, my mind sped back to September 11, and I remembered the call I got early that morning. "Are you watching television?" a friend had asked that day as well. What could it be this time? Another terrorist attack in Manhattan? Had the White House been attacked? Could it be another hijacking? A thousand different thoughts raced through my head before I could answer the question. I fumbled for the remote and clicked on the television as I asked what happened. I could see the image slowly brighten on the screen as Maurice spoke. "Governor McGreevey is holding a press conference," he said. "I think he's going to announce that he's gay."

It was hard to believe at first, but here was the governor of New Jersey holding a press conference that was being televised on MSNBC. I switched to CNN and to other networks, and there he was again on almost every channel. "He hasn't said it yet, but I can just feel it," Maurice told me. "He said something about grappling with his identity since he was a child. And he talked about having some 'feelings' that made him different from the other kids. I really think he's gonna come out," Maurice said. I was still doubtful—no governor of any state had ever come out before—but I could not deny the obvious code language in the words Maurice had quoted to me. Separated by thousands of miles, Maurice and I watched the television together in stunned silence as McGreevey finally reached the climax of his speech. "At a point in every person's life, one has to look deeply into the mirror of one's soul and decide one's unique truth in the world, not as we may want to see it or hope to see it, but as it is. And so my truth is that I am a gay American."

I was shocked. I had never seen or heard anything like this before. It all seemed surreal. Flanked by his parents and his wife, the governor of the ninth-largest state in America had just told the world that he had been living a lie. He had been married once before to a woman named Kari. They had a daughter together and then, as McGreevey delicately put it, Kari "chose to return to British Columbia." After their divorce, McGreevey married Dina Matos, and the new couple had a daughter as well. It was a perfect rebound. From the outside looking in, they were an ideal family. On the inside, known perhaps to no one but James McGreevey himself, there was a secret that could ruin everything.

Like many observers of the scene, I tried to stare into the soul of Dina McGreevey as her husband made his announcement. I wondered if her eyes would betray her disappointment, or if she would reveal an inner peace that suggested she had known all along. Was this an arranged marriage, a marriage of convenience, a marriage of love, or perhaps some combination of all of the above? I could not tell. In the end, it was not important for me to know. It was a matter between the two of them, and Dina McGreevey appropriately kept it that way. Nevertheless, I wondered what it must have felt like to stand there while her husband told the media that their marriage was not what it appeared.

Then I remembered Yvonne. It was not the same thing, of course. Yvonne and I had never gotten even close to marriage. But the public nature of my own decision to come out made me realize how hurtful it might have been to Yvonne. Fortunately, I did not come out in the middle of a scandal, but I did come out in a very public setting. I had been a leader in the movement for faculty diversity at Harvard, and I had been quoted frequently in the newspapers. I took part in student sit-ins, vigils, and other protests to register our support for women and minorities to be hired as professors. We had occupied the dean's office, taken over the administration building, marched to the president's office, and demonstrated outside faculty meetings. But my claim to fame was as one of several students who filed a lawsuit against Harvard for discriminating in the hiring of its faculty. We lost the lawsuit but won the war to bring national attention to the issue. I was quoted in newspapers around the country talking about the issue, and my picture showed up more than once in the *Boston Globe*. A few weeks after I came out, I gave a speech on campus at an outdoor rally where I announced that I was speaking as a "black gay student." Anyone on campus who had not known by that time surely knew then. Some of those watching the speech might have thought I was still dating Yvonne, and that, I'm sure, only made matters worse.

For a long time, I felt guilty about coming out so publicly, but slowly I realized that I had to be true to myself. Truth was the common element here. Yvonne had to be true to herself as well. No doubt, dating someone who turns out to be gay, lesbian, or bisexual can produce feelings of self-doubt and guilt. "Did I do this? Did I cause this person to be gay? Was there something I could have done?" Those are the questions that are sometimes expressed but more often simply held inside. Women who have been involved in relationships with men who are gay or bisexual must negotiate their way through a complex series of issues that often reach the core of their own sense of identity. SaraKay Smullens, a family therapist, explained more about the challenges involved in a column in the *Philadelphia Daily News* shortly after McGreevey came out. Smullens, who has worked with a number of women who have been married to gay men, said the names used to describe these women ("cover girls" or "beards," for example) are "cruel and humiliating." Women who are attracted to gay men are described as having "the curse of the pink wand" and those who have gay male friends are often called "fag hags," she explained. Smullens tells us that women in these situations go through a range of emotions in deciding whether to continue in their relationships, and all of us could be a little more understanding.

Governor McGreevey's wife must have been going through a full range of emotions the day she stood next to her husband at his press conference. The governor's disclosure of his sexual orientation was not the end of the issue. McGreevey also admitted to "an adult consensual affair with another man," which he said "violates my bonds of matrimony." That was the real bombshell McGreevey dropped that day. Many of us were already surprised to hear him announce that he was gay, but we were more shocked to learn that he had carried on an affair. Yes, the governor of New Jersey was on the down low.

By announcing his affair with another man, Governor McGreevey immediately provided a clear example of the reach of the down low. He was young, attractive, masculine, successful, powerful, and married with children. And he was white. With one stunning example, McGreevey proved that the down low is not just a black thing.

In hindsight, we should not have been surprised. Surely, we must have known that white men lived on the down low as well. We should have known that black men were not the only ones who cheated on their wives. Or had we bought into the myth of black male identity that constructs black manhood solely as pathology? Did we really believe that black men were the only ones?

James McGreevey provides an ideal example of the white down low, but he is only an example. He is not the only white man on the down low. He is not even the only white politician on the down low. He is just one who got caught, in public. We perpetuate a lie to ourselves if we believe that McGreevey is simply a rare exception. White men on the down low are everywhere. They are professional athletes, famous entertainers, powerful businessmen, and influential elected officials. More important, they are our coworkers, neighbors, and friends. Perhaps what makes the McGreevey case stand out is that it seems so new and different. When was the last time a prominent married politician came out and announced that he was not heterosexual? Well, actually, it was just a few years before.

With degrees from Stanford and Harvard and a career as vice-chairman of his family-owned energy business, Michael Huffington seemed to be on the rise when he decided to run for Congress as a conservative Republican in the early 1990s. He had a prominent wife, Arianna, and he had already accumulated impressive experience in federal government when he served as a deputy assistant secretary of defense in the Reagan administration. After spending $5 million on his campaign, it was not a surprise when Huffington was elected to Congress from California's Twenty-second District in November 1992. But Huffington was not finished. He had not even completed his first term in the House of Representatives when he agreed to run for the U.S. Senate, a race in which he spent $28 million of his personal wealth to try to beat Dianne Feinstein. In what was then the most expensive nonpresidential election in American history, Huffington lost by less than 1.6 percent of the vote. Afterward, his career in politics survived, but he could not shake the personal demons that haunted him about his sexuality. Finally, in 1998, Huffington came out of the closet. In an interview with David Brock in *Esquire* magazine, Huffington explained that he once had homosexual feelings years earlier but had renounced them after watching a critical discussion about homosexuality on Pat Robertson's *700 Club* television show. So the path he decided to follow at the time was one of self-deception. "I am straight. I will get married. I will have children. I will never sleep with another man again," Huffington told himself.

But no matter how hard he tried over the years, he could not deny the truth inside of him. Huffington had been living on the down low.

And then there is the case of Edward Schrock, an investment broker, retired Navy officer, Vietnam veteran, and loyal family man who was married with one son. Schrock was born and raised in Middletown, Ohio, and married a school teacher from Long Beach, California. The couple settled in Virginia Beach and became active members of the Atlantic Shores Baptist Church. After a few years in Virginia politics, Schrock decided to run for Congress. Elected in 2000, he was chosen to be the chairman of the Republican Freshman Class and quickly became one of the most conservative members in the U.S. House of Representatives. He cosponsored the Federal Marriage Amendment, which would have amended the U.S. Constitution to prohibit same-sex marriage, and he sought to block gays and lesbians from entering the military. From all outward appearances, he was a classic social conservative. But others had doubts about his personal life. When a Web site called Blogactive.com released an audio recording of what it said was Schrock calling into a gay telephone sex line, the congressman never admitted his behavior. Instead, Schrock announced he was leaving the Congress and would not seek reelection.

It happens outside the world of politics too. The entertainment industry is filled with stories of white men and women on the down low. One of the most famous relationships of the 1970s involved a pop recording star and a music mogul on the down low. It was September 1973, and Neil Young was headlining at the opening night of the Roxy nightclub, a new Los Angeles spot on Sunset Boulevard. David Geffen, the owner of the new club, had made a name for himself by working with some of the top talent in the music industry and had recently sold his new music company, Asylum Records. On the opening night at the Roxy, Geffen met Cher. They seemed to like each other, and the two soon started dating. While

Cher waited for her divorce from her husband and business partner, Sonny Bono, she and Geffen became a Hollywood item and reportedly planned to get married. But Cher abruptly called it off in early 1974 and decided against the marriage. Geffen, meanwhile, kept his reputation as a ladies' man, dating Marlo Thomas and other women over the years. By the early 1990s, however, Geffen's homosexuality had become an open secret, and Geffen had been a very generous contributor to numerous ostensibly gay-related AIDS causes over the years. In 1990, he sold his company, Geffen Records, to MCA and became a billionaire. Then in November 1992, Geffen said the words that shocked the industry. He publicly came out of the closet in a speech at AIDS Project Los Angeles. David Geffen had been on the down low.

Like Geffen, many of Hollywood's leading men were also on the down low. None was more famous than Roy Harold Scherer, Jr., of Winnetka, Illinois. Scherer moved to Hollywood to become an actor, and his agent, Henry Willson, promptly renamed him. It was to be one of many contrivances to advance his career. When rumors circulated that Scherer was homosexual, Willson quickly arranged for Scherer to marry Phyllis Gates, Willson's secretary. The marriage lasted three years, but it may have salvaged Scherer's career. Scherer, known publicly as Rock Hudson, became even more successful the following year when he played opposite Doris Day in the film *Pillow Talk.* For decades, Rock Hudson (Roy Scherer) became the veritable embodiment of heterosexual masculinity. Men wanted to be him, and women wanted to be with him. But like so many other Hollywood celebrities, his life was a lie. While he played the role of the heterosexual playboy on screen, he was a closeted homosexual off screen. When Hudson died of AIDS-related complications in October 1985, his lover, Marc Christian, successfully sued his estate because Hudson had not informed him of his HIV status. Hudson had been married to a woman and maintained his heterosexuality, but he slept with men, and he was HIV positive. Even by today's definitions, Rock Hudson might be a poster boy for the down low. Except for one inconvenient fact. Rock Hudson was white.

When black men become involved in fake relationships, we process the issue by ascribing negative characteristics to an entire group of people, and we tend to think in global terms concerning the breakdown of the black family and other such nonsense. When white men become involved in fake relationships, we simply call it what it is and move on. We don't make sweeping generalizations about all white men, and we don't try to study the pathology of their behavior.

When Peter Allen married Liza Minnelli in 1967 or Elton John married Renate Blauel in 1984, there was no public outcry about celebrity men on the down low. But when ordinary black men marry ordinary black women under similar circumstances, suddenly we are told we have a crisis in the black community. Black men are dishonest, irresponsible liars, cheaters, pimps, and thugs—if you believe the rhetoric. But similarly situated white men are just white men, and they are relieved of the unrealistic burden of bearing the responsibility for an entire race.

We should have known decades ago that white men were doing the same things that black men were doing. It never made sense to assume otherwise. Remember the story in the 1982 film *Making Love*? The relationship between a happily married heterosexual couple (Kate Jackson and Michael Ontkean) begins to unravel when the husband comes to terms with his homosexuality and falls in love with another man (Harry Hamlin). That was a warning sign that white men were also on the down low.

In fact, we knew the truth all along. For years, both black and white America convinced each other that homosexuality was merely a "white thing." When the gay rights movement grew in the 1970s, we pretended that it only concerned the rights of white gays and lesbians, and we continued to deny the existence of lesbian, gay, bisexual, and transgendered people of color. Then, as white gays and lesbians emerged as public figures, we assumed that black openly gay and bisexual public figures would never emerge because homophobia was too widespread among blacks, as if homophobia did not exist in the rest of America.

The truth is, we created this lie, and now we have to find our way out of it. Homosexuality, like homophobia, is widespread in the black community and in the white community. White men do not live in a parallel universe where homosexuality is widely accepted. They live in the same country as everyone else—a country where no federal law prohibits workplace discrimination against gays and lesbians and where a president of the United States has tried to write antigay discrimination into the U.S. Constitution. White men make many of the same compromises and false choices that black men do, and because they tend to have access to power and opportunity that elude most blacks, they may have more to lose by coming out. White men are on the down low just like black men, and since we live in a country with far more white men than black men, it stands to reason that there are far more white men on the down low than black men. They, too, are secretly sleeping with men while they plan their lives with their wives. Some of them may even bring home sexually transmitted diseases to their unsuspecting partners. But if more white men are doing it than black men, where is the outcry about white men on the down low? And why aren't more white women being infected with HIV from these white men on the down low? How do we reconcile the black infection rates with the white infection rates? Those questions never even get asked. Instead, we find it much easier to continue using a racial typecast that confirms our preconceived beliefs about black male guilt.

I know what it feels like to live with the burden of proof always resting on your shoulders. Ever since the day I was fired at Sears, I have carried that burden. I do not claim to be perfect, and I am not always innocent. But I do believe that those who make scurrilous accusations against black men bear the burden to prove their assertions with facts. Instead, what we usually get is the same old tired circumstantial case built on the same old racial stereotypes.

We know this much. The down low is not just a black thing. We have packaged it as such because it provides a simple and convenient mechanism to understand a complex issue. But for every black man on the down low, there is a Jim McGreevey, a Michael Huffington, a David Geffen, a Rock Hudson, or a no-name white man who is also on the down low. So we are left with this possibility to consider. If the white down low is not leading to a new outbreak of AIDS in the white community, then maybe, just maybe, the black down low is not responsible for the spread of AIDS in the black community either.

CHAPTER 5

When a Disease Becomes an Excuse

BY CHANCE OR fate, I found myself in the thick of the down low story when it first broke in the media in 2001. I had little interest in exploring the story at the time, but the universe had other plans for me. I had known, or come to know, all the major players involved in the story—the reporters, the advocates, and the critics. I knew Linda Villarosa, the reporter for the *New York Times* who wrote about the down low in the most influential paper in America. I knew Phill Wilson, the founder of the Black AIDS Institute who introduced the down low at a mainstream black AIDS conference. And that was the year I met J. L. King, the chief advocate and poster boy for the down low. It was not my intention to be involved in this story, but it happened. On the day when the story first developed, I was there.

Linda Villarosa's presence was striking. A thin, fair-skinned woman with long curly hair, she radiated energy and charisma. I met her at a writers' conference in Boston in March 1995. She was executive editor of *Essence* magazine and had recently published a book about black women's health, but her real claim to fame was from an *Essence* article she had written in May 1991. In that article, Linda, with her mother Clara by her side, told the world that she was a lesbian. It was the first time that any prominent black woman had come out so publicly, and it happened on the cover of the nation's leading black women's magazine. Linda quickly became a lightning rod for attention, provoking hate mail and angry phone calls from detractors and enormous praise and encouragement from supporters. Personally, I was impressed that *Essence* would even publish an article about a black woman coming out, and more impressed that the subject of the article was an editor at *Essence* as well.

Essence was also breaking down barriers about black women and AIDS. A few months before I met Linda, and years before the current down low hype, *Essence* had published a dramatic cover story of a heterosexual black woman with AIDS. Her name was Rae Lewis-Thornton, and she was a well-educated, drug-free, thirty-two-year-old self-described "Buppie." Lewis-Thornton said she had "never been promiscuous" and "never had a one-night stand," but she was "dying of AIDS." Like so many other women, she had contracted the virus from unprotected sex.

Many of us in the black community had enormous respect for *Essence* and especially for Linda for pushing the envelope on issues that were difficult for black people to understand and accept. The gay community was also eager to embrace Linda. As the keynote speaker at a gay and lesbian writers conference in 1995, Linda drew attention from nearly everyone as she entered the main room in the Park Plaza Hotel. I was excited to see her as well, but the hall was packed, and I had no special privileges, so I took a seat far away and squinted my eyes from the balcony. I was writing my first book and wanted to interview Linda, but I was not sure I would ever get a chance to speak to her one-on-one, so I tape recorded her speech from the audience.

Linda had a fast-pitched conversational speaking style that was part educational, part inspirational, and part comical. It was almost like listening to someone talk in a living room after dinner. But despite her disarming appearance, her speech was hard-hitting, especially when she challenged the way majority cultures typecast minorities to justify their oppression. "Black men and women were told that we were hypersexual in order to justify slavery," she said. To prove her point, she read from the journal of a seventeenth-century slave trader who once wrote that "negro nature is so craven and sensuous in every fiber of its being, so deeply rooted in [the] immorality part on negro people, that they turn in aversion from any sexual relation which does not invite sensuous embraces."

I thought I might have missed a word in the transcription from the tape recorder, so I went back and did some research on Linda's point, but I could not find the quote. I did find, however, a strikingly similar statement made by a different person at a different time. In the book, *The American Negro,* William Hannibal Thomas wrote that "Negro nature is so craven and sensuous in every fiber of its being that a Negro manhood with decent respect for chaste womanhood does not exist."

The words were almost identical, but there were two significant differences between Thomas's statement and the statement from the slave trader. Thomas wrote his words in 1901, not in the seventeenth century. And unlike the slave trader of centuries past, Thomas was black. Not surprisingly, Thomas was roundly criticized by the black community for his comments, but the fact that he made them at all, and that they were widely published, demonstrates three important points.

First, black people have been trained to internalize and repeat the very prejudices used against us. Second, a few opportunistic blacks are all too willing to tell white America exactly what they want to hear about us. And third, white America is all too willing to publicize and promote controversial black figures who are severely ill-informed.

Those thoughts came to mind when I met with Linda at a trendy Washington restaurant called Jaleo in February 2001. As I mentioned before, this was the dinner when I first heard about the down low. Linda was in Washington for an African-American AIDS conference she was covering for the *New York Times*. Two of our mutual friends, Phill Wilson and Maurice Franklin, were also in town for the conference, and the three of them invited me to join them for dinner. I had interviewed Linda in 1995 after I met her at the Boston writers' conference, but I had never had the chance to sit down with her for a meal. Phill, on the other hand, I knew very well. We had met at a White House meeting in March 1993, in the early months of the Clinton administration. In an effort to involve the gay and lesbian community in the administration, the White House Office of Public Liaison set up a series of meetings between LGBT leaders and administration officials. As an openly gay staff member, I was eager to participate in the discussion when I walked into the ornate board room in the Old Executive Office Building. I sat down at the long wooden table just as the meeting began. A few minutes later, Phill walked in.

He was a handsome, well-dressed black man in a room filled with white gay men, so my eyes immediately focused on him. I learned during the meeting that Phill was the public policy director of AIDS Project Los Angeles and the founder of the National Black Lesbian and Gay Leadership Forum. After the meeting, we spoke and agreed to stay in touch. Our friendship developed quickly when Phill invited me to dinner a few days later. When I returned the favor and invited him to the White House Mess for lunch, Phill surprised me with a kiss in the entrance foyer to the West Wing. I suppose most of the staff already knew I was gay, but the Secret Service agents who stood guard at the door did not, until then.

The following month, Phill returned to the White House with a group of seven gay and lesbian leaders, including Nadine Smith, a black lesbian activist from Florida, for a meeting with the president. The gay community was preparing to hold a massive march in Washington in April 1993, and they wanted President Clinton to speak at the event. Clinton had been elected as a friend of the gay community, and they expected he would speak at their rally, but I knew that would never happen. Hundreds of groups hold marches and rallies in Washington every year, and presidents rarely, if ever, attend these functions. At the most, the president might send a statement to be read at the event, but the White House had no interest in seeing the president too closely identified with the gay community.

As I sat across from Phill during the meeting in the Oval Office, I could not help thinking about the significance of that moment. Although the White House tried to downplay the meeting by scheduling it on a Friday afternoon when the media were winding down for the weekend, everyone in the room knew it was the first time *any* president had ever met with leaders of the gay and lesbian community in the Oval Office. That made it historic. But there was another thought on my mind that day. It was also historic for African-American involvement. Alexis Herman, the straight black woman who ran the White House Office of Public Liaison, and I, a black gay man who served as special assistant to the president, sat in the room on behalf of the staff. Along with the other two African Americans in the room, it had to be the first time in history when two black openly gay men, an open black lesbian and a straight black woman all met with the president of the United States, in the Oval Office of the White House, on any civil rights issue.

Some people merely watch history while others make it. Phill and Maurice, who were on the front lines of the battle to educate America about AIDS and sexuality, seemed to be making history and had been at the center of several historic events, from the thirtieth anniversary of the March on Washington to the Million Man March. But neither of them knew that the discussion at dinner that night with Linda would also mark a historic turning point in the black community. That may have been the night when the down low media story was born.

George W. Bush had just been sworn into office, and there was a bitter sense of acrimony in the capital. At the dinner table, I griped about the changing political scene with the Republicans in town. After eight years of living in D.C., I was ready to go somewhere else. I had decided to leave politics and move to New York, and I was eager to learn about my new city from Linda, who was then a reporter for the *New York Times*.

The four of us had ordered *tapas* and were comparing notes about New York, Washington, and Los Angeles when the conversation turned to the down low. I had heard the term before, but I had never heard it connected to AIDS policy, so I was a little confused. "What is the down low?" I asked.

"It's about these black men who sleep with men but don't identify as gay," Maurice replied.

"Oh, you mean MSM," I said, using a term I knew for "men who have sex with men."

"Well, these men on the down low are MSM, but not all MSM are on the down low," he explained. It took me a second to register what he meant. Researchers had long ago replaced the term "gay" with "MSM." Under pressure from minority activists who felt the word "gay" was too limiting for men of color, the CDC started using "MSM" in its 1991 *HIV/AIDS Surveillance Report*. Although it sounded clinical, "men who have sex with men" more accurately identified the range of men who engaged in same-sex behavior. It also shifted the focus of AIDS prevention away from "identity" and toward "behavior." A large number of these MSM, even those who were open about their sexuality, had never identified with the more white-oriented and political term "gay."

I asked another question. "So are you talking about men who have sex with men but who are in the closet?"

"They wouldn't necessarily consider themselves in the closet," Maurice said.

"So you mean they're in denial?"

Maurice paused. "I guess you could say that," he said with a smile. I wasn't sure if he agreed with me, or if I had just worn him down with my persistent questions, but I had more to say.

"So what else is new? That's been going on since the beginning of time," I said. Maurice seemed to agree, but there was one aspect of the story that did seem to be new. Black women were being infected with HIV at alarming rates, and no one had a good explanation for why it was happening. No one except for James L. King.

Linda had her reporter's cap on that night. She wanted to write a story about the conference, and the down low angle provided the most promising opportunity. Earlier in the day, a lively exchange had taken place at the conference when Phill, Maurice, and a former down low man named James L. King (later known as J. L. King) took part in a luncheon. Phill, who was then the director of the Los Angeles-based Black AIDS Institute, moderated the panel, while Maurice and James were the two panelists. Maurice let us know at dinner that he felt King was an "ill-informed black gay man masquerading on the down low." That was a strong indictment, but I had no reason to distrust Maurice. King seemed to have little real experience in AIDS policy, while Maurice had been involved in the trenches for years.

When I met Maurice back in 1993, he was a young civil rights activist who had worked for Dr. Joseph Lowery at the Southern Christian Leadership Conference. A veteran of the Navy, he had come to Washington as a lobbyist for the newly formed Campaign for Military Service, an organization that was fighting to lift the ban on gays in the military. But with his attractive chocolate face, muscular body, and medium-length dreadlocks, Maurice stood out like a sore thumb among the bland legion of gray-suited lobbyists in Washington. After the campaign ended, he became intensely involved in AIDS policy work and had recently become a director at New York's Gay Men of African Descent (GMAD).

Based on what Maurice and Phill said that night, I was a little wary of Linda's plan to write a story about the down low. I knew that other reporters would cover the down low angle even if Linda did not write about it, but I felt that a prominent *New York Times* article might give the story credibility it did not deserve. The *Times* had already mentioned the down low once in an article a few weeks before, but there was a big difference between writing an article that mentioned the down low and writing an article *about* the down low. It also made a difference that the new article would be written by Linda Villarosa, who was one of the most respected black women in journalism. But Linda seemed to be genuinely intrigued by the story. She knew that black women all over America were clamoring for information, and this story could help them sort through the confusing issues involved with the epidemic. It seemed like a perfect story. It combined the public health issue of AIDS with a new angle that could get people to wake up and pay attention. In addition, the down low seemed to provide an obvious answer to lingering questions about the alarming HIV infection rates among black women.

There was one big question that black women wanted answered in 2001. Could the down low be a bridge that brings the virus from closeted black gay and bisexual men to straight black women? The idea seemed reasonable. If men on the down low were secretly sleeping with other men and then bringing HIV back to their female partners, that could explain the infection rates among black women. But there was not much evidence to support the theory, and I was concerned that focusing attention on the issue would divert our energy from the factors we already knew were responsible for the problem, including unprotected heterosexual intercourse and intravenous drug use with infected needles.

Maurice and I were also concerned that the down low story might have the potential to divide the black community into a battle of the sexes, to demonize black gay and bisexual men, and to distract the public's attention from the personal responsibility to protect themselves instead of expecting someone else to protect them. Little did we realize that our conversation would serve as a harbinger of the public dialogue to follow.

Part of what concerned me was that the connection between the down low and black women seemed a bit illogical. There were two ways to look at it. Either the down low was new or the down low was old, but either way it did not make sense. If the down low was new in 2001, it could not have been responsible for an epidemic that was twenty years old. On the other hand, if the down low was old in 2001, then we should have been alarmed about high HIV infection rates among black women ten to fifteen years earlier when the epidemic was raging out of control.

AIDS had not just arrived in black America in 2001. We had been affected by it since the early days of the epidemic, but we did not always pay attention. For a long time, the African-American community responded to AIDS as if it were somebody else's disease. In the first few months of the epidemic, the virus was thought to be limited to a notorious group known as the four Hs: homosexuals, hemophiliacs,

Haitians, and heroin users. But in June 1982, just a year after the beginning of the epidemic, the U.S. Centers for Disease Control (CDC) reported that 23 percent of initial AIDS cases were among African Americans. We were just 12 percent of the population, but we accounted for nearly a quarter of the first AIDS cases.

Just two years later, the CDC reported that African Americans accounted for 50 percent of all new AIDS cases among children. And two years after that in 1986, CDC reported that black women accounted for half of all AIDS cases among women. Right from the beginning, in the first five years of the outbreak, African Americans were put on notice about the reach of the epidemic, but instead of reacting with action, we continued to pretend that it was a white gay disease.

In December 1988, it became harder to deny the truth when ABC's Max Robinson, the first black man to anchor a network news broadcast, died of AIDS-related complications. A year after Robinson passed away, the dancer and choreographer Alvin Ailey died of AIDS as well. Then in February 1991, the gospel recording artist James Cleveland died of AIDS-related complications. By the time the basketball superstar Magic Johnson announced that he was HIV positive in November 1991, we had no reason to be surprised anymore. But then, five months after Johnson's stunning announcement, the tennis legend Arthur Ashe announced that he too had AIDS.

At the dawn of the nineties, black America knew that the epidemic had crossed over to the black community. Some experts suspected the problem was related to drug users transferring HIV to one another by sharing dirty needles. Others felt that convicted felons were a major source of transmission after being infected in prison and bringing home the virus to their unsuspecting partners upon their release. While black America struggled to explain the heterosexual AIDS cases, far fewer people seemed concerned about the thousands of black gay and bisexual men who were already dying in cities all across the country. At the end of 1991, the CDC reported that more than 30,000 black men had died from AIDS, and only a tiny percentage of them reported that they had acquired the virus solely from heterosexual contact. That posed a challenge in getting straight black men to pay attention to an epidemic that did not appear to affect them.

The Marketing of An Epidemic

The AIDS community of funders, researchers, activists, and sympathetic government officials had a problem. In the early 1990s, some AIDS activists knew that Americans would not pay attention to the growing epidemic if they thought the disease primarily affected black drug users and black gay men. That's when some activists apparently decided to market the epidemic for middle America. As a result, in their well-intentioned desire to motivate the country to do something about AIDS, the activists provided the media with a more palatable story line that was technically accurate but misrepresented the greatest impact of the disease. Phill Wilson confirms this strategic decision. "There definitely was a concerted effort to make AIDS more compelling to the black community," he recalled, "and that process entailed a de-gaying of the epidemic." Perhaps as a result, we saw stories about children with AIDS and women with AIDS and other "innocent" victims of the disease. In fact, African Americans might have gotten the impression that women and children were the primary black victims of AIDS. But they were not. At the end of 1993, 52,259 black men, 12,875 black women and 1,517 black children had died from AIDS. In the black community, AIDS was still a disease of black gay men and black drug users.

While the media presented a cleaned-up version of the black AIDS epidemic, there was a dramatic shift in the demographics of the international AIDS problem. AIDS became a black disease in the 1990s. Not a black American's disease. Not a black gay disease. Not a black drug user's disease. Not even a black ex-convict's disease. AIDS became a black disease, period. Early in the decade, the World Health Organization estimated that two-thirds of the 15 million people who were infected with HIV were sub-Saharan African. That meant that AIDS was killing black people all over the world.

Meanwhile, in this country, AIDS had become the leading cause of death for black men between the ages of twenty-five and forty-four and the second leading cause of death for black women in the same age group. The primary difference between the AIDS epidemic in Africa and in black America was the method of exposure. In Africa, AIDS was primarily a heterosexual disease. In black America, it was not. But there was one other sobering fact that should have caused alarm. In 1995, the CDC reported that the AIDS incidence rate for blacks had surpassed the rate for whites. For the first time, there were more new black AIDS cases than white AIDS cases. Twelve percent of the population was driving the entire nationwide AIDS epidemic. We knew that in the nineties.

Despite the trends in the epidemic, much of the mainstream media continued to ignore the issue of AIDS in the black community. Thus, the decision to focus on media-friendly AIDS stories may seem understandable when you consider the lack of coverage given to minorities and AIDS.

Cathy J. Cohen, a political science professor at Yale, researched the media's coverage of AIDS in her 1999 book, *The Boundaries of Blackness: AIDS and the Breakdown of Black Politics.* She looked closely at the coverage in the *New York Times,* widely considered the American "newspaper of record" for its extensive coverage of national and international news. In her analysis of all *Times* articles written about AIDS from the beginning of the epidemic in 1981 to the first year of the Clinton administration in 1993, Cohen discovered that the *Times* published just 231 articles focused on African Americans. That may seem like a high number until you consider the fact that the *Times* published a total of 4,671 articles on AIDS during this time period. In other words, only 5 percent of all *Times* articles about AIDS focused on African Americans.

Even more disturbing, Cohen found that 62 percent of the articles about blacks focused on just two celebrities, Magic Johnson and Arthur Ashe. That meant that only 1.9 percent of all *New York Times* stories about AIDS focused on ordinary black people, even though blacks made up 32 percent of all AIDS cases during that period, according to Cohen.

Stories about gays were almost as rare. In the thirteen years of her study, Cohen found only 369 stories that focused on gay men. That amounts to 7.9 percent of all *New York Times* stories on AIDS, even though the CDC reported that men who had sex with men made up 60 percent of all AIDS cases during that period. If ordinary blacks made up 1.8 percent of the AIDS news coverage and gay men made up only 7.9 percent of the news coverage, we can expect that even less coverage was devoted to those double minorities who were both black and gay. Never mind the fact that 80 percent of all AIDS cases in America at that time involved either blacks or men who had sex with men, and in many cases the two categories overlapped.

Unfortunately, the racial disparity between the epidemic and the media coverage has not been limited to the *New York Times*. Kai Wright has done more to separate fact from fiction about AIDS than almost any reporter on the beat. He's traveled the world and written about AIDS in Africa and in black America. In the spring of 2004, Wright wrote an article in the *Columbia Journalism Review* that analyzed a media survey conducted by the Kaiser Family Foundation. The results were shocking.

The Kaiser study looked at twenty-two years of media coverage on AIDS from 1981 through 2002. They examined more than 9,000 new stories from four major national newspapers (*New York Times, Wall Street Journal, Washington Post,* and *USA Today*), three major regional papers (*San Francisco Chronicle, Miami Herald,* and *Los Angeles Times*), and three major network news programs (*ABC World News Tonight, CBS Evening News,* and *NBC Nightly News*). Amazingly, they found only 3 percent of news stories in the major media outlets focused on U.S. minorities. Just 3 percent.

Why was the number so low? The study offered an explanation. The media tend to operate with a pack mentality that focuses primarily on specific and dramatic episodes in the AIDS epidemic instead of the ongoing challenges. "In the early years," Wright explained, "it was the effect on the blood supply and debate over San Francisco bathhouses being shut down. Next came the public infections of Rock Hudson and Magic Johnson, followed by a pair of very large events, the discovery of the drugs that have staved off death for so many people, and, finally, by the AIDS devastation in Africa." In other words, the media were covering episodes, but they were not really covering the epidemic.

Ironically, the new HIV drug treatments and the proliferation of AIDS in Africa may have actually hindered the possibility of generating sustained media attention for AIDS in black America. Just when black America started paying attention to AIDS in the mid 1990s, the powerful new drugs that were released in 1996 began to extend the lives of people living with AIDS. As a result, the media stopped covering the old story about people dying and started reporting the new story about people living. In November 1996, for example, the *New York Times Magazine* published a cover story by Andrew Sullivan, a prominent white gay conservative, who suggested the AIDS epidemic had been won.

In his article, "When Plagues End," Sullivan told the world "this ordeal as a whole may be over." Yet even Sullivan knew that prediction did not apply to everyone. In a single paragraph at the beginning, he passingly acknowledged the enormous socioeconomic disparities that separated him from most others. "The vast majority of H.I.V.-positive people in the world, and a significant minority in America, will not have access to the expensive and effective new drug treatments now available," he wrote. "And many Americans—especially blacks and Latinos—will still die." Despite that caveat, the tone and title of his piece was unmistakably optimistic. A few weeks later, *Newsweek* magazine followed suit and declared "The End of AIDS" on its cover. That was in 1996.

Given the media hype about the end of AIDS, it's no wonder that America, including black America, stopped paying attention. Most African Americans get their information about AIDS from the media, so many of us in the black community allowed our attention to drift elsewhere—or return our focus to other urgent matters in the black community —as the news coverage declined. In 1995, 56 percent of African Americans considered AIDS to be the nation's most urgent health problem, according to a Kaiser study. By 2000, that number had dropped to 41 percent.

Black America, like the rest of America, simply let down our guard. We still knew that AIDS was affecting significant numbers of black people, but the black people who were affected did not engender our concern. For the first time in the history of the epidemic, people with means could buy their way out of much of their suffering, so those who were left were the ones who could not afford the expensive drugs to save their lives. They were gay, bisexual, drug users, sex workers, and low-income people. Middle-class black America was not as directly affected in the same way that marginalized blacks were.

But blacks were still bearing a disproportionate burden of the epidemic in the late 1990s, and black activists and journalists were rightly concerned that America was not paying attention. The easiest way to get the story back in the headlines and generate community sympathy and action was to create an image of law-abiding, middle-class, heterosexual black people facing AIDS.

The "Bisexual Bridge"

In January 2000, the CDC issued a press release noting that HIV infection had "increased significantly in women of color over the last decade." Researchers at CDC suggested a possible answer. They suspected that men who had sex with men might be bringing the virus from the gay community to heterosexual women. Since black men who have sex with men often do not identify as gay, CDC speculated that "these men may not accept their own risk for HIV, and therefore, may unintentionally put their female partners at risk." Notice the language used by the CDC. The word "unintentionally" suggests that the men involved were not necessarily guilty of doing anything purposefully harmful. The language from CDC was typically nonjudgmental, but the language used in the black community would be a different story.

By July 2000, Linda Valleroy (not to be confused with the *Essence* magazine editor Linda Villarosa), a researcher at the CDC, coined a name for the theory that black men were bringing AIDS to black women. Valleroy called it a "bisexual bridge for HIV." The idea was that black men who have sex with men were also having sex with women and therefore might be acting as a bridge for the virus to cross over into the black heterosexual community. The bridge theory coincided with new information about the AIDS epidemic among black gay and bisexual men. Earlier that year, the CDC reported for the first time that gay and bisexual men of color made up more AIDS cases than white gay and bisexual men. Even more alarming, 24 percent of HIV-positive black men who had sex with men identified as "heterosexual" in a separate CDC study. For some observers, that was all the proof they needed. Black men who had sex with men were becoming infected, and since a quarter of them considered themselves heterosexual, they were *probably* taking the virus back to black women. That seemed logical, but it did not tell us everything we needed to know.

The problem with most of the media analyses about the down low is that they were based on circumstantial evidence. A more thorough analysis might have approached the story from the perspective of a homicide detective. Think about it this way. Imagine finding a suspicious weapon in the course of a murder investigation. What looks like a smoking gun from a distance may appear more innocent upon closer investigation. If the gun is actually smoking, does that mean it was used to kill anybody? Even if the gun was used to kill, does that prove that it killed the victim in the investigation? And if it did kill that victim, does it tell us who pulled the trigger? Those are the questions you need to ask in a criminal case. Who? What? When? Where? Why? How? And the same basic level of analysis used in a homicide investigation should be used in examining the down low theory. Yes, there is definitely a bridge between men on the down low and black women. That has never been in dispute. The real question is how large is that bridge, and that we do not know. To show that the bridge is wide, as most of the media stories assume it is, you would have to prove several different assumptions from various studies.

First, you would have to prove that the black women in question were becoming infected by heterosexual sex and not from injection drug use. Given the legal ramifications and social stigma attached to drug use, some women may not want to admit, or may not know, that they were infected by drug use.

Second, you would have to prove that the women who did become infected by heterosexual sex were not having sex with drug users. Just because a woman contracts the virus from male-female sex does not mean the man was initially infected by another man.

Third, you would have to prove that the same women were becoming infected by black men, not men of other races. This seems likely given the racial segregation in American dating, but you would still have to prove it.

Fourth, you would have to prove that the MSM who identified as heterosexual were actually having sex with women. Social stigma against same-sex behavior might discourage many of these men from admitting that they only had male partners. Just because they claim they are heterosexual on a survey does not mean they really are in practice.

Fifth, you would have to prove that the men involved were HIV positive. Obviously, HIV cannot be transmitted across the down low bridge unless the person has HIV.

Sixth, you would have to prove that the same men were having sex with the same women who were becoming infected. It may seem a reasonable assumption, but you still have to prove it.

And then seventh, you would have to prove that the men were having *unprotected* or *unsafe* sex with the same women. Even if a bisexual man is HIV positive, it is very difficult to spread the virus to anyone unless he engages in unprotected sex.

That was the logical challenge. All seven elements had to be proven. But no CDC study had ever been able to answer all those questions at once. No study had ever told us what percentage of black men who had sex with men were HIV positive. Nor had the CDC told us what percentage of black bisexual men were HIV positive. Those had always been complicated questions. But in early

2001, there was a deceptively simple answer waiting across the horizon.

One Out of Three Black Gay Men

In February 2001, CDC's Linda Valleroy announced the preliminary results of a major new study. Speaking at a conference in Chicago, Valleroy announced that one out of three young black gay men were HIV positive. Well, that's not exactly what she said, but that's how the media reported it. What she said, of course, was more nuanced. But here's how it happened.

From 1998 to 2000, the CDC conducted a survey of young men who have sex with men (MSM) in six cities (Baltimore, Dallas, Los Angeles, Miami, New York, and Seattle). The CDC recruited the men at gay bars, nightclubs, bookstores, shopping areas and other locations that gay men visited in those cities. They found 2,401 MSM between the ages of 23 and 29. They tested the men for HIV and 293 (12 percent) of them tested positive. The more troubling number was that 30 percent of the African-American men in the group tested positive. That was the number that sent headline writers into a frenzy.

Newspapers across the country printed the story the next day. *USA Today*'s headline said, "1 in 3 young gay black men are HIV-positive." The *Milwaukee Journal* headline read, "HIV hits 30% of gay black males." The *Boston Herald* simply said, "Gay black men hit hard by AIDS virus." The *Washington Post, Los Angeles Times, Chicago Sun-Times,* and *Atlanta Journal* all ran stories, as did several radio and television news programs. It seemed to be a breakthrough moment—the first time the major media seriously addressed the issue of black gay men and AIDS. But the breakthrough was not what it appeared, and it was very short-lived.

Despite the flurry of news stories, many of them were not exactly accurate. Take the *USA Today* article, for example. That paper claimed that "1 in 3 young gay black men are HIV-positive." But the CDC never really said that. Instead, what they said was that 30 percent of the black gay men in the survey *of those six cities* were HIV positive. It was important to understand the distinction between those six cities and the rest of the nation. Five of the six cities in the study were among the hardest hit by the epidemic, and the sixth city (Seattle) did not have a large enough African-American population to provide many black participants. That meant most of the blacks surveyed came from Baltimore, Dallas, Los Angeles, Miami, and New York, the same cities where the AIDS epidemic was at its worst.

We know that 73 percent of blacks living with AIDS are located in just ten states. Since the survey relied heavily on those states, that meant that the places chosen for the survey were not necessarily representative of the rest of America. The black AIDS epidemic in New York and Los Angeles, for example, was always much worse than it was in smaller cities. That was the problem with the *USA Today* headline. The CDC never said that 1 in 3 of *all* young gay black men were HIV positive. It was only about the people in the survey from those six cities.

Of course, surveys routinely use small sample sizes to determine a larger picture of the country. Public opinion polls do that every week. A thousand people are interviewed by telephone and then an anchorman on the network news tells us that 60 percent of Americans feel this way or that way about something. We're used to that, but most of those surveys that purport to represent American public opinion do so by sampling a wide cross-section of people from various backgrounds. The CDC survey, however, was never designed to give us a complete national picture. It was only a snapshot of the places hardest hit.

The headline in the *Milwaukee Journal* was also problematic, but for different reasons. The *Journal* claimed that 30 percent of black gay males were HIV positive, but once again, the CDC never said that either. Remember, the CDC only surveyed people who were between twenty-three and twenty-nine years old, one of the age groups hardest hit by the epidemic. The results would have been dramatically different had the CDC taken a survey of black gay men who were fifty-three to fifty-nine, a group with a much smaller AIDS incidence rate. The point is that we cannot draw conclusions about all black gay men based on a survey of twenty-three- to twenty-nine-year-olds. What the *Journal* did was like going to Harlem to get a sample of New York City and then drawing the conclusion that 90 percent of New York is black. Certainly, 90 percent of Harlem might be black, but that's not the case in the rest of New York City. That's why any time you draw broad conclusions from a survey, the survey has to be wide enough to include the diversity in the community.

The *Boston Herald*, in comparison to the other two papers, played it safe with its headline: "Gay black men hit hard by AIDS virus." That was a lot more accurate. But there was one tiny little problem. The men in the study were not necessarily "gay." The term that CDC used was MSM, which in this case meant "men who have *ever* had sex with men." As used here, MSM is a broad term that could include gay men, bisexual men, men on the down low, or men who had only one sexual experience with another man. In other words, the men in the study were not all gay.

There appeared to be one other flaw in the reporting about this study as well. It was very basic. Most of the news stories did not tell us how many people in the survey were black. We knew there were 2,401 men in the study. We knew they were drawn from public venues in six cities. We knew that 293 of the men tested HIV positive. And we knew that only 85 of the 293 men knew they were infected before the testing. That's a lot of numbers to digest. But the numbers that were curiously missing were the number of black people in the study and the number of blacks who tested positive. That was critical. Say, for example, there were only three blacks in the study. In that case, a shift of just one person would cause a dramatic difference of 33 percent in the statistics. It is much harder to make accurate generalizations from small numbers than from larger numbers, which is why we needed to know how many blacks were in the study before we could draw any broad conclusions.

Despite the absence of this critical piece of information, the *USA Today* article on February 6 never mentioned the number of blacks in the study. Neither did the *Milwaukee Journal* article on February 6 or the articles in the *Los Angeles Times* or *Washington Post* on February 7. That information was even missing from the *New York Times* article on February 11. Did the reporters simply forget to mention the numbers? No, the real story is actually more complex than that. The media did not report the numbers because the CDC did not tell them. It's not that the CDC purposefully hid the information, but they certainly did not make it easy to find.

Journalists often develop their stories based on news releases provided to them by reputable government agencies such as the CDC. (The CDC, for example, was very helpful to me in the writing of this book.) The communications department of the government agency usually helps the reporters by giving them press releases with the basic information they need for their stories. These press releases are extremely valuable to guide reporters who cover conferences where there are many different events going on in a short period of time. That's exactly where the story about young black men was released, during a CDC conference in Chicago on February 5, 2001. Unfortunately, the CDC press release never mentioned the number of black men in the study. The release did mention the number of total study participants (2,400) and the number of HIV-positive men (293) in the study, but it failed to mention the number of black men who were in the study or the number of black men who tested positive. That was crucial information that could have helped provide context for the headlines that screamed across the nation's newspapers the next day.

Day-to-day reporters seldom have time to dig deeply into the numerous issues that come across their desk, but beat reporters who cover a specific topic or beat often have more time to develop their stories. Many of these beat reporters wanted to know the story behind the story. Why were so many young black gay and bisexual men becoming infected? Eager to find explanations for the statistics, reporters called on the usual suspects to interpret the study. Here's what they said.

Cornelius Baker, the director of Washington's Whitman-Walker Clinic, said the study's findings were "no surprise." Other AIDS activists blamed the high infection rates on the "stigma" of being black and gay. Doug Nelson, the executive director of the AIDS Resource Center of Wisconsin said the study confirms "how vital it is to repeat and reinforce the AIDS prevention message." The director of Boston's AIDS Action group said the problem is that many black gay men are afraid to "come out."

The problem with those answers is that the experts were saying the same thing that they had been saying all along, and reporters wanted something new to explain the new infections. Cleo Manago, the head of the AMASSI Center in Inglewood, California, offered one perspective that seemed to be fresh and different from what the rest of the experts were saying. "The CDC and the public health departments need to reevaluate who they're funding and why they're funding people to do this work, because clearly it's not working," he told the *Los Angeles Times*. But even Manago's provocative comments were not necessarily new. Many members of the community in Los Angeles had heard him deliver that same message several times before. Reporters were still stumped. No one—at least not one of the usual suspects—could provide a new or definitive explanation for the infection rates.

Then came the down low.

A Star Is Born

Just two days after the CDC study was released about black gay men, there seemed to be an answer ready to be served. That was the day the down low first appeared in the mainstream media. The first major media reference to the down low took place on February 7, 2001, in the *Los Angeles Times*. The *Times* article—the same article that quoted Cleo Manago—came up with a possible new answer to the infection rates. The article featured a twenty-eight-year-old black man named Charles. Described by the reporter as "young and attractive," Charles said he had a steady girlfriend but occasionally slept with men. Five years earlier, Charles had made a fateful decision that changed his life when he had decided not to use condoms while having sex with someone who he later discovered was HIV positive. But despite his pattern of sleeping with men and women, Charles did not consider himself to be gay or bisexual. Charles was on the down low.

Jocelyn Y. Stewart and Sharon Bernstein had introduced America to a new lifestyle and a new term: "the down low." The two reporters had also introduced other phrases that were rarely seen in newspapers at the time. They described terms like "homo thug" and "same-gender-loving" and used these words synonymously with "down low." As discussed previously, in the early days of the DL, the term "down low" had a much broader meaning than it often does today. By today's standards, homothugs (gay men who dress and act like hip hop thugs) would not be down low. Likewise, men who call themselves "same-gender-loving," a politically conscious term associated widely with Cleo Manago, would not be considered down low either. But back then, any man who had sex with men who did not look gay or talk gay or call himself gay might have been labeled on the down low. That was also the impression given by a *New York Times* article four days after the Los Angeles article appeared. The *New York Times* piece quoted two mysterious men (Walter and Jay) who were supposed to be on the down low, but without last names and photographs we were left to our imagination to visualize them.

A good reporter can smell a story before it develops. Linda Villarosa was one of the best health reporters, and I think she knew something that Maurice and Phill and I did not realize the night we had dinner. She knew the down low story had to be told. Somebody was going to tell the story, so she might as well tell it in a candid, nonsensationalized way. So on April 3, 2001, Linda's article finally appeared in the *New York Times* under the headline "AIDS Education Is Aimed 'Down Low'." Not surprisingly, hers was one of the most thorough stories about the down low, and it teased out the complexity of the term itself. In Linda's story, James L. King had described the down low as "men who have sex with men but do not identify themselves as gay or bisexual," according to Villarosa. That was a definition that did not require the men to be involved in relationships with women. But Linda also interviewed our mutual friend Maurice Franklin, who said that half of the men in the focus groups conducted by his organization, Gay Men of African Descent, described themselves as being on the DL. Men who were willing to identify themselves at a focus group run by a gay organization were calling themselves down low. That posed a major challenge for the down low story from the beginning. Nobody had a clear, universally accepted definition of what it meant.

There was also a problem with the timing of the down low story in the news. "It has long been known that men of all races have sex with men but prefer not to be labeled gay or even bisexual," Linda wrote in her article. Maurice echoed that sentiment in his quote: "There has always been a secret society of men who were undetectably gay and continued to live in the black community," he told Linda. That begged an obvious question. If the down low had "long been known" and these men had "always" been there, why was this suddenly becoming an issue in the spring of 2001?

Perhaps it was because of the CDC study that showed that one fourth of the HIV-positive black men who had sex with men identified themselves as heterosexual. Linda mentioned the study in her article, but that information had been released more than a year earlier. Then, maybe it was because 54 percent of women newly reported with AIDS had acquired the virus from heterosexual relations. Linda mentioned that study as well, but the information came from 1998. In fact, the only major new information that had been released about AIDS in the black community was the CDC study that showed 30 percent of young black gay and bisexual men were HIV positive. But that study had nothing to do with the down low. It was a study of men in six cities who were found at gay-identified venues and other locations where gay men tend to go. "There were very few down low guys in this sample," the study's author Linda Valleroy told *Gay City News*. "Down low guys don't tend to appear at the more obvious type places [where men who have sex with men go]," she said.

The study may have raised more questions than answers. Nobody could explain the high prevalence of HIV among young black gay and bisexual men. The CDC researchers could not explain it. The AIDS activists could not explain it. And the reporters could not explain it. The only thing we did know is that they were *not* becoming infected because of the down low. After all, the men in the study were self-acknowledged "men who had sex with men" who had been recruited at public venues. By King's own definition, they were not on the down low.

So if there was no new information about the down low, how did the media leap from black gay and bisexual men to men on the down low?

At least four factors may have played a role in the shift to the down low. First, the twentieth anniversary of the AIDS epidemic was coming up in June 2001, and many reporters were looking for ways to understand the past two decades and predict the challenges ahead. Second, the statistics about black gay and bisexual men were staggering, but they were not entirely surprising, and since no one had a clue what caused the numbers, those statistics could still be used as a springboard to talk about other black AIDS issues that were easier to discuss. Third, HIV seemed to be increasing among black women, and a story line that incorporated black women was more likely to generate public concern than a new batch of stories solely about black gay and bisexual men. Fourth, although the down low may have been around forever, no one had any personal investment in pushing the story until James L. King came along at the conference in February 2001.

A Story with No Proof
After the February conference, dozens of stories about the down low appeared, and many of them quoted King. What the stories did not provide, however, was any proof that the down low was responsible for the black AIDS epidemic. I did a Nexis search of all the articles I could find about the down low from 2001. I found articles in the *New York Times, Los Angeles Times, USA Today, Chicago Sun-Times, Atlanta Journal, San Francisco Chronicle, St. Louis Post-Dispatch, San Diego Union-Tribune, Columbus Dispatch, Village*

Voice, VIBE, Essence, and *JET.* All the stories referenced the down low, but not a single article mentioned a black woman who had been recently infected with HIV by a man on the down low. Not one case. Here's what I found.

February 7: The *Los Angeles Times* runs the first article that mentions the down low, but the story never cites any women who had been infected by a man on the DL.

February 11: The *New York Times* runs a story that mentions the down low. It quotes five men, but not a single woman is mentioned.

March 15: *USA Today* runs an article about "the danger of living 'down low'" with a subtitle about how these men "can put women at risk." The story quotes six men and one woman but provides not one case in which a man transmitted HIV to his female partner.

March 19: An extensive article about the down low runs in the *Columbus Dispatch* in Ohio. The article quotes seven men and four women, and mentions several others. Two of the men had passed HIV to their female partners, but they were not necessarily on the down low. The first man had "experimented" with homosexual sex before his marriage but never did so while he was married. The second was an African exchange student who had infected his female partner in 1993, but the article never said that he engaged in any homosexual or bisexual behavior.

April 1: An article in the *St. Louis Post-Dispatch* quotes a man named Tyrone who had been married for ten years and had two daughters before he divorced his wife and came to terms with his sexuality. Tyrone, however, was not HIV positive.

April 3: A *New York Times* article quotes five men and two women. All of the people quoted were experts, and not a single person mentioned in the article had given HIV to his partner.

April 22: The *Chicago Sun-Times* runs an article about a new film called *Kevin's Room*. The film includes a "church brother who's having sex with men on the down low" and the article concludes that "secrets are endangering our lives." However, not a single person in the article had passed HIV to a partner.

June 3: A columnist in the *Atlanta Journal* explains that men on the down low "stubbornly resist the safe-sex messages that have helped to curb the epidemic among whites." Nevertheless, the article never mentions a single example in which a man on the down low passed HIV to his partner.

June 4: An article in the *San Francisco Chronicle* quotes six men and one woman. The woman is HIV positive, but "she believes she contracted the virus through unprotected sex with someone she met through a singles telephone line." Once again, there is no evidence of the down low.

June 6: A *Village Voice* article titled "The Great Down-Low Debate" profiles a twenty-five-year-old down low man named Tevin who has a relationship with a man and a woman. However, there is no evidence that Tevin is HIV positive or that he has passed any viruses to his female partners. In fact, Tevin says "he always uses condoms."

July: *VIBE* magazine runs an article called "A Question of Identity" about homothugs and men on the down low. The article never mentions any women who were infected by men on the down low.

July 3: A lengthy *New York Times* article about the toll of the AIDS epidemic on black women never mentions anyone on the down low. Instead, it quotes a doctor who specializes in AIDS and identifies other problems for women such as the absence of fathers, the lack of insurance, alcohol, drugs and a history of sexually transmitted disease.

September 8: An article in *JET* magazine explains "why AIDS is rising among black women." It is the first article I can find that actually mentions a woman (identified as Hannah) who was given

HIV by a man on the down low. But there's one catch. The story took place in 1991, ten years before the down low hype began.

October: An article in *Essence* magazine quotes six men and two women to prove that "brothers on the down low pose a serious AIDS risk to black women." Despite that claim, not one black woman mentioned in the article was even HIV positive. The closest case was Julie Posey, a San Francisco fashion merchandiser who discovered that her ex-husband was living with HIV and on the down low. Two paragraphs later, we learn that Posey herself was HIV negative.

December 2: A story in the *San Diego Union-Tribune* mentions a man on the down low who passed HIV to his female partner. Ava Gardner, a minister's wife in Sacramento, learned just before her second wedding anniversary that her husband had AIDS and had infected her. On his deathbed, her husband told her: "Ava, I did what I did to you purposefully because I didn't want to die by myself." It's definitely a story about the down low, but when we look closer at the article we see the story took place in 1996, five years before the 2001 down low craze.

December 7: A *Los Angeles Times* article profiles Tony Wafford, a community activist who has set up an innovative HIV testing facility in a local beauty salon. The article mentions men on the down low but never mentions a case in which a man on the down low passed the virus to his partner.

At the end of the year, out of all the articles I could locate, not one of them mentioned a woman who had been recently infected with HIV by a man on the down low. Most of the articles did not even come close. The only two articles that were close involved stories that were five to ten years old.

The argument for the down low has always rested on a very shaky circumstantial case. Without statistical evidence to back up the claim that the down low was spreading AIDS in the black community, the media had to rely on anecdotal evidence. It found plenty of stories about black men on the down low and black women who had been infected, but almost none of the stories ever connected the men on the down low with the women who were being infected. In most cases, there was a missing link. In some examples, the man was on the down low, but he was not HIV positive. In other examples, he was HIV positive, but he always practiced safe sex. In a few examples, the woman was HIV positive, but she was not infected by a man on the down low. Or if her man was on the down low, he had not infected her. If the down low argument had been introduced in a court of law, any good lawyer would have found plenty of reasonable doubt, and a judge might have dismissed the case before it even got to the jury.

After a year of media hype in 2001, the media could not produce a single example of a man on the down low who had recently given HIV to his female partner. That is not to say that it didn't happen. Of course, there were men on the down low spreading HIV in 2001. But how many? The media never told us. Perhaps the full story was too complex to explain or not as dramatic as the down low sensation, but the public had a right to know the truth.

The real issues around AIDS are very complex, sometimes boring, and not easy to follow. I know. In the months I spent researching AIDS issues for this book, I had to talk to scientists and researchers and translate their techno-speak into plain English. I had to pore over dozens of dry research documents with titles about "prevalence, predictors and presumptions" and "noncordant HIV serostatus." And then I had to study the CDC's own HIV surveillance data for every year from 1982 to 2002. Twelve years of primary and secondary school, four years of college, and three years of law school were all more interesting than reading through the CDC's raw data and statistics. But it had to be done. There was no other way to make sense of the down low story and AIDS.

One of the first statistics I read led me to question the whole principle behind the down low. Here it is. In 1991, 51 percent of AIDS cases among black men (24,118) reported homosexual contact as a method of exposure. In 2001, the figure had dropped to 33 percent (4,605). In other words, the number and percentage of black men exposed to AIDS because of homosexual contact had declined sharply over that decade. Why is that important? Because those men were the primary potential source of the down low infection "bridge," and if there were fewer of them around in 2001 than in 1991, there should have been fewer black women becoming infected as well. In other words, the "bridge" should have been much wider back in 1991 when there were five times as many black MSM AIDS cases than in 2001.

What could explain the discrepancy? The answer was remarkably simple but rarely revealed. The number of black female AIDS cases from heterosexual contact *did not* rise from 1991 to 2001. It actually fell. In 1991, there were 3,784 adult and adolescent black female AIDS cases from heterosexual contact. In 2001, the number had fallen to 2,606, a reduction of 1178 cases per year. So despite the media frenzy that gave us the impression of skyrocketing numbers, the number had actually decreased.

Much of that drop was due to the life-sustaining AIDS drugs introduced in 1996 that enabled people with HIV to live longer, healthier lives. But even when we look at the *percentage* of black women exposed by heterosexual contact, the change is not dramatic. In 1991, the CDC reported that 34 percent of black women with AIDS were exposed by heterosexual contact, and in 2001 the figure had increased to 37 percent. A year's worth of media hype had been based on an increase of 3 percent over 10 years, and there was almost no evidence that the increase was connected to men on the down low. In fact, out of the 7,023 total black female adult and adolescent

AIDS cases reported in 2001, only 111 (1.6 percent) reported sex with a bisexual male as the method of exposure. No wonder it was so hard for reporters to find people to interview for their news stories.

Anatomy of a Media Frenzy

Facts are rarely as important as impressions when we talk about black men, and the down low story would not be stopped because of lack of statistics. This was a story with several ups and downs over the years, beginning with its dramatic launch in February 2001. The story died for a few months following the September 11 terrorist attacks but picked up again in 2002 when the television show *E.R.* unveiled a plot involving a rapper on the down low who was diagnosed with HIV. Then the story died again.

Like a cat with nine lives, the story resurrected itself in August 2003 when the *New York Times Magazine* ran a controversial cover article called "Double Lives On the Down Low." That story also took me by surprise. I had been reading the *New York Times Magazine* since college, during the height of the AIDS epidemic, but in the years since that time I had never seen a cover story about black men who have sex with men. It seemed the first time the *New York Times Magazine* took any interest in the lives of black gay and bisexual men was in the context of a scandalous story about the down low, and that story was written by a white reporter, Benoit Denizet-Lewis, who did not seem to have all the facts. Early in the story, Denizet-Lewis made an incredible and completely unfounded claim that caught my attention. "There have always been men— black and white—who have had secret sexual lives with men," he wrote. "But the creation of an organized subculture largely made up of black men who otherwise live straight lives is a phenomenon of the last decade." The last decade? Was he joking? Black men have been on the down low for as long as black men have been getting married to women. I knew black men in my family who had been on the down low in the 1970s. But the reporter offered not one shred of evidence to back up his outrageous claim.

I continued reading with skepticism. The article begins at a bathhouse in Cleveland, where the reporter acknowledges that he is one of the few white people in the facility. That, too, raises a troubling question. Given the racial dynamics in America, it seems plausible that black men on the down low might be reluctant to open up to a white reporter trying to expose them. The story goes on to reveal one of the many contradictions about who is and is not on the down low. "Most DL men identify themselves not as gay or bisexual but first and foremost as black," writes Denizet-Lewis. That may be true, but how does the reporter know this? No studies have ever been conducted about men on the down low, so we cannot really say how most of them identify. If, on the other hand, you claim that a *real* down low man would not identify as gay or bisexual, then you have constructed a circular argument. It goes like this. How do we know men on the down low do not identify as gay? Because only men who do not identify as gay are on the down low. That is the circularity.

In fact, the story itself, like much of the down low hype, is one big contradiction. Some, like King, claim that men on the down low do not go to identifiably gay places, but throughout the *New York Times Magazine* story Denizet-Lewis reports finding men on the down low at gay places, including bathhouses and gay nightclubs. In Atlanta, Denizet-Lewis goes to a nightclub for "young guys on the DL." In one scene, two men on the DL are driving around Atlanta with a third man who is openly gay.

In another scene, the reporter visits the office of a Cleveland Web site that produces live video of down low men having simulated sex "for anyone who cares to log on." No one points out the obvious contradiction as to how a man on the down low can have sex in front of a camera for public consumption. Writing in New York's *Gay City News,* Duncan Osborne said the reporting in the *Times Magazine* article was "sloppy." Osborne directly challenged Denizet-Lewis on his assumptions. "He never tells us why he chose to believe [the men who said they were on the DL] when they claim to have sex with women while he also asserts that these men were lying to those women. These men may be lying when they say they have girlfriends," writes Osborne.

Although the *Times Magazine* story is fascinating and extensive, it does not even attempt to prove that men on the down low are spreading HIV to their female partners. It was one of the longest articles ever written about the down low, and yet it never mentions even one woman who was infected with HIV by a man on the down low. Ostensibly, that was the whole rationale for the down low story in the first place. Or was it?

The public obsession with the down low from 2001 to 2003 was fueled, in part, by a well-intentioned but completely irrational media frenzy. The same energy that had been spent on uncovering a story that wasn't there could have been spent on breaking down stereotypes by showing black gay and bisexual men who were in healthy relationships, or exposing the problem in the assumption that all blacks are straight and all gays are white, or educating the public about how to prevent the spread of HIV/AIDS. Apparently those stories were not as exciting.

Black gay and bisexual men have been living with HIV and dying of AIDS for a quarter of a century now. The HIV infection rates for this group are among the highest in the country. But the media and the black community have never treated this crisis with the same energy now devoted to the down low. Ironically, a story that began because of alarming statistics about black gay and bisexual men had somehow evolved into a completely different story about straight black women. And after all the media attention, we still could not explain the cause of the high infection rates among young black gay and bisexual men. The media did not stick around long enough to answer those questions. Instead, they moved onto sexier topics—straight black women and the implicitly guilty black men who infect them.

If we seriously care about the spread of HIV, we cannot isolate our concern and efforts on one segment of the community and ignore another. We have to create a climate of love instead of fear, where black men who have sex with men are not stigmatized by the church, the media, their families, and their friends. In fact, the whole DL mythology at some level acknowledges the struggle of the black man on the down low. The legend tells us he does not identify with the white gay community, and he is not accepted by the black community, so he goes underground and creates a secret fraternity of sex partners.

But if that is true, then our solutions are way off base. If we accept the premise that black homosexuality is that difficult, then why not break down those barriers? Why not use the media to portray the black gay and bisexual men who are out of the closet, living openly in their relationships, and who have reconciled their careers, their families, and their faith with their sexuality. If it is really that hard to be black and gay and out, then those who are black and gay and out are the true heroes who deserve recognition. The *New York Times Magazine* should profile that group of people. Black media should tell their stories.

Instead, the down low story sailed on and picked up more steam after the *Times Magazine* piece. The subject had fascinated reporters in 2001, provided story lines for television shows in 2002, and then provided a major magazine cover story for 2003. Then, like clockwork, it rose again in 2004.

In the spring of 2004, the down low reemerged. The *New York Times* reporter Linda Villarosa wrote another story about the down low in the *Times*. The comedian Mo'Nique was featured on the front page of a special edition of *POZ* magazine talking about the down low. Even the television show *Law and Order: SVU* aired an episode about the down low during this time. Then, the story made the biggest splash yet. It made it to *Oprah*. The story was about to become big news.

The down low had legs, as reporters would say to describe a story that could go on for a while. For that reason, it could not continue on disembodied. Stories with legs need a voice, a look, a visual. They also need to have a face. To sell the down low to the public, it needed someone who was willing to be the image. It needed a real-life human being who could speak on the record and on camera about this underground movement. It needed a book to generate new media hype and to validate the old media hype. But most important, it needed a poster boy.

CHAPTER 6

Down Low Detectives

THE PHONE RANG, and I sat down at my desk to see the caller ID. I value my privacy, so I rarely answer the phone without knowing who is on the other end. There was no phone number on the screen, so I waited. The phone rang again before the message finally appeared on the caller ID box. "OUT OF AREA," it said. I was not expecting anyone to call, but I answered the phone anyway. "Hello," I said cautiously. Then I heard the voice on the other line.

"Keith Boykin?"

No one ever called me by my full name except for telemarketers and bill collectors. Nevertheless, after a brief moment of suspicion, I responded.

"Who's calling?" I said. I wanted to get the other person's name before I would confirm my own identity.

"This is J. L. King," the voice replied. I was surprised to get the phone call. I had heard of J. L. King before, and he surely must have known that I knew him. In fact, I knew a lot more about him than I could say in the phone call. I knew people in Ohio who knew him, and I knew people in Chicago who knew him. I knew men who had dated him, and I knew men he had tried to date. I had never seen him in person, and I had no idea what he looked like. All I had was his voice on the other end of the telephone.

King introduced himself and told me about a new project of his. I listened intently, but I was not quite sure why he was sharing this information. He told me he was writing a book about the down low, and he wanted to reach out to me. He had heard positive things about me, he said, and he respected the work I had done. I was honestly flattered by the praise, but I still did not know why he had called me. I was not on the down low, and I did not have much to say about it. I was openly gay, and I had been quoted in a *Village Voice* article that Kai Wright had written about the down low. "It doesn't mean that we have to go out carrying rainbow flags," I was quoted as saying. "But we do have to acknowledge sexual orientation." That message contradicted everything I thought I knew about the down low. So why me?

What King told me next floored me. He had signed, or was about to sign, a huge new book deal to write about the down low. He had another deal with ABC News that was going to generate major publicity and exposure for him and the book. He was getting offers to speak at conventions and conferences and schools all across the country. He had so much going on with these new career developments that he had to be selective about what he chose to do.

I was impressed by his accomplishments, but, I have to admit, I was also shocked. To listen to him on the telephone, I did not get the impression that he was the most articulate communicator, but I had to question myself for thinking that. Perhaps I was imposing my own biases on his experience. Maybe I needed to be more open-minded, I thought. But that led me to the central question of the conversation. Why would he contact me?

That's the part that floored me. He had not called simply to chat about his achievements. He had called with a purpose and a proposal. Then he told me the purpose. He wanted me to help him write his book. I must have expressed some noticeable reluctance to accept his offer because he immediately started selling the idea to me as if I needed to be persuaded, and at the same time he backtracked a bit from the offer. He mentioned one or two other names of writers he thought might be suitable to help him with the book, which I took as a convenient exit sign for both of us to think about different options. I threw out a few names of writers for him to think about, and he seemed to take them seriously. But I needed to know more about what he wanted the writer to do.

"Do you need a ghost writer or a co-author?" I asked. Ghost writing (writing without any credit) is much less interesting than co-authoring. Many authors would be reluctant to devote the time and energy it takes to write a book without some hope of recognition for their work. There was, however, one advantage to ghost writing, especially since I expected that King and I would have different perspectives on the down low. If I were to ghost write the book for him, no one would ever know that I had anything to do with it. But, of course, I would know the truth, and if I did not like the final product, I would feel partly responsible. With that in mind, I told him I was reluctant to accept his offer.

King was not finished. He had another card to play, which he had mentioned several times already in the conversation. That may have been his ace in the hole. He had money. He let me know repeatedly and in no uncertain terms that he would be making a lot of money off the deal. That part I understood. But there was more. Not only had he signed a deal that would make money for him, he had also expected that the co-author or ghost writer of the book would make plenty of money as well. He never said exactly how much money was at stake, but he repeatedly let me know that I would be well paid for helping with his book. In fact, as the conversation ended, it seemed to me that money was the primary, if not the sole, motivation behind the book, the media appearances, and the lucrative speaking engagements he was doing. It was as if money was everything to him.

I can't lie about it. I felt a mix of emotions after I hung up the phone. At first, the conversation felt sort of slimy. I had no desire to become a literary mercenary to be sold off to the highest bidder. The conversation felt even worse when I thought about the message that King was communicating about the down low. It was not my message at all. I did not want to trivialize and sensationalize the lives of black men, no matter how they identified (or chose not to identify) their sexuality.

A part of me remained deeply suspicious about the whole transaction with King. I wondered if he had really gotten a deal with a publisher and a television network. He had mentioned ABC's *20/20*, but I could hardly imagine Barbara Walters wanting to do an interview with him. But maybe I was wrong. After all, J. L. King was providing a perfect iconic image for white America to understand. It was the stereotypical image of black men as pathological liars, surreptitiously satisfying their primitive sexual cravings by cheating on their wives. That would have been an easier image for white news anchors to swallow than the image of black men who accept their sexuality and are comfortable with it. To promote positive images of black gay and bisexual men might actually help some black men to deal with their sexual orientation. And soon there would be no scandal to cover.

But another part of me wondered if I should give some serious thought to King's proposal anyway. It was 2001, and I had just moved to New York. I had not written a book in two years. I was self-employed, and the cost of living in Manhattan was much higher than it had been in Washington, D.C. I was $60,000 in debt from college and law school and paying $1,000 a month for a one-bedroom apartment in Harlem that had no air conditioner, dishwasher, or washer and dryer. And I lived on a block with half a dozen abandoned buildings.

Part of me felt it was time to give in to reality and give up the pipe dream of working for myself. My last nine-to-five job was in the White House, and since that time I had struggled to support myself, first while working for a fledgling nonprofit organization and then teaching at a local college. I had once heard "if you do what you love, the money will follow," but fourteen years out of college the money had still not found me. It was all my fault, of course. Over the years, I had turned down several high-paying jobs so I could spend my life in public service. My first job out of college paid me just $250 a week, before taxes, but I was working for Mike Dukakis's presidential campaign, and I loved it. When Dukakis lost, I moved in with my father in Stone Mountain, Georgia, so that I could save money while I taught at a nearby high school. Then, a few months after I graduated from law school, I quit a lucrative position working for a San Francisco law firm, and moved to Little Rock, Arkansas, to work on Bill Clinton's first presidential campaign. And rather than stay in the comfortable White House job I landed, I eventually left the Clinton administration and signed up with a black gay organization that had no money to pay me.

Yes, it was my own fault. I was happy with my life experiences, but I had plenty of reasons to question the economic wisdom of my decisions. My grandmother was particularly persistent in questioning me. How could anyone turn down six-figure job opportunities, she wanted to know. And how could someone with an Ivy League college degree and a Harvard law degree leave a prestigious job in the White House to go work for the black gay community?

She suggested that I move to St. Louis, where I could live like a king if I practiced law. Or if I insisted on writing books, I should write something more interesting. "Why don't you write one of those books like E. Lynn Harris?" she asked. "It's not that easy," I told her, but something about her message stuck with me. Maybe she was right about one thing. Maybe it was time for me to make some money instead of trying to save the world.

I finally hit rock bottom one day when I drove almost an hour in traffic out to Jacob Riis Park, a beach in Brooklyn, and realized I did not have enough money to pay the toll to get across the bridge. There was no money in my wallet. No money in my checking account. No money in my savings. And my credit cards were maxed out. I drove back to the nearest gas station, searched through my car for stray quarters and then worked up the courage to ask someone at the gas station to lend me the last dime I needed. Once I got over the bridge, I realized I needed more money to park the car and to cross the bridge back to the mainland. Again, I had to find a gas station where I could "borrow" some money. When I got back to my apartment that evening, I knew it was time to change my life, and working on King's book seemed to offer an easy way out.

The drive back to the house had given me plenty of time to think about the book, but I still wanted to know more about J. L. King. I remembered that King had encouraged women to be down low detectives, so I decided to do a little detective work of my own to find about him. Was he credible? Did he know what he was talking about? What did other people think about him? My friend Maurice would surely have something to say. I remembered the strong words Maurice expressed about King when we were at the restaurant in Washington, so I called him on the phone to get his opinion. "What do you know about J. L. King?" I asked. Maurice told me that he and King had both been on a recent television segment on *The News*

Hour with Jim Lehrer. I looked it up on the Internet and found the transcript. King's comments on that show concerned me. They played right into the media hype about the down low and set him up as the sole person who could speak on the topic.

"Most down low brothers look at themselves at being nothing but a heterosexual man—with a twist, every now and then wanting to have sex with another man," King told the reporter on the show. "To a down low brother, [sex is] more gratification and not orientation. It's all about, let's get together do the sexual thing, then I'm outta here. Don't ask me any questions whatsoever. That's what makes it so dangerous."

That was an incredible statement filled with generalizations and unprovable assertions. *Most* down low brothers? How did King know what *most* down low brothers wanted to do? Had he met all the men on the down low? Had he done a survey or a poll? How could he possibly know what *most* of these men thought, especially if they prided themselves on maintaining their secrecy and privacy. It was a ridiculous claim, but no one challenged him on it. He was the only one who was actually speaking from the perspective of the down low, so reporters listened uncritically to what he said. But how did one individual's personal experience become the basis for a cultural obsession?

"When I look at gay men, when I look at what they call their culture, how they have their own churches, and they have their own clubs, and bars, and they do their own thing—I don't relate to that," King said. "You will not find a down low brother in a gay bar—a real, true down, bona fide low brother," he said. That statement indicated that King himself knew very little about black gay and bisexual men. Many black men who have sex with men do not identify with the "gay community" either, but they do not necessarily consider themselves down low. A 2002 study conducted by the

National Gay and Lesbian Task Force found a significant percent of black men surveyed at black gay and lesbian pride events did not identify as gay. Some said that they were "same-gender-loving," "in the life," "open to love," "questioning," and "curious," while other respondents simply wrote in "I like what I like." It's also true that some bona fide men on the down low do go to black gay clubs and bars. I have met some of these men myself. They may not go out in the same town where they live, but they will go out in other places. I have also met a number of men on the down low—men with wives and families—who have socialized among black gay men. What I would not do, however, is generalize from my own experiences and then declare that most men on the down low are exactly like the down low men I have met.

J. L. King has also criticized traditional AIDS prevention messages. "The message so far has been to the gay community," he said. "They have not sent those messages out to where 'down low,' or men who don't relate to or are labeled," he said. Wait a minute. That statement made no sense either. By his own testimony, down low men did not go to any special place to meet each other, so how could you target a message for a particular place if they were not going to be there? King talked about the absence of "safe sex messages" at barber shops, shopping malls, and gyms, but once again, he was off base. Was he saying that men on the down low do actually go to certain places? If so, then those places would not be very down low. And the places he mentioned were the exact same places where all men, including gay and bisexual men, could be found.

The story gets more convoluted if you listen closely to the contradictions in the message. If we take King's suggestion and target barber shops and gyms, would that reach men on the down low? Not if you follow King's other logic. Maurice reminded me about the exchange that he and King had at the African-American AIDS conference earlier that year. When asked how to change the behavior of men on the down low, King told the audience, "You can't." I found the transcribed notes from the conference on the Internet, and they confirmed Maurice's description of King's response. But King's defeatist attitude seemed to contradict his message about going to barber shops and gyms. What would be the point of doing outreach to men on the down low if, as King suggested, these men could never be reached? For that matter, what was the point of raising the issue of the down low in the first place if there was nothing that could be done about it?

My next call was to Phill Wilson. I told him about King's offer and asked him if he thought I should accept it. Phill was characteristically evenhanded in his response. On the one hand, working on the book might give me the opportunity to help shape and influence King's message in a positive direction, Phill said. On the other hand, working on the book might prove to be a frustrating experience if the book did not turn out well. Phill's response was so impartial that I wondered if he felt responsible for creating the whole down low monster in the beginning. It was Phill who had given J. L. King his first national platform when he invited him to speak at the African-American AIDS Conference back in February, and Phill moderated the panel where King launched his down low profile. During the panel, King had described the typical attitude of men on the down low when he said, "I don't go to gay clubs and I don't talk to gay people. I go to straight clubs. The pickings are better there." That statement made little sense either. Obviously, some men on the down low had to talk to gay men. They may not have done so openly, but they still talked to them. How else could these men meet their sexual partners, unless King was suggesting that men on the down low only slept with other men on the down low. But that could not be the case either. If they were only sleeping with each other, then it undermined the whole argument that they were bringing back HIV from the gay community into the straight community. How could they bring a virus from the gay community if they had no contact with that community?

The statement was also confusing because King said the "pickings are better" in straight clubs than in gay clubs. That begs an obvious question. How do you know the pickings are better if you have never been to the gay clubs? It didn't add up. In fact, almost nothing he said made sense. It reminded me of the words Phill had spoken at the beginning of the down low panel where J. L. King was first introduced. Likening the situation to Lewis Carroll's *Alice in Wonderland,* Phill described the scene in which Alice finds herself in a place where "What is, is not, and what is not, is." That seemed a fitting description of J. L. King as well. The more I learned about him, the more questions I had.

I had not been following the public down low discussion since I had dinner with Linda, Phill, and Maurice months earlier. I had been finishing my last semester teaching at American University and spending every weekend of the spring driving up to New York to find an affordable place to live. While I was making a transition in my life, J. L. King was making one of his own. Following the African-American AIDS Conference, King had been deluged by reporters who wanted to know more about the mysterious world of the down low. He gave several interviews, and a string of articles appeared in major newspapers across the country.

USA Today's article on March 15, 2001, was the first to focus exclusively on the down low. But that article shifted the focus away from the high infection rates facing black gay and bisexual men and instead focused on black women who were victims of certain deceitful black men. I realized that something was missing, and I quickly figured out what it was. Black men were victims too. They were being infected at an alarming rate, and the overwhelming majority of black AIDS cases were among black men, not black women. But black men in crisis was an old story, and the idea of black men as victims did not fit into our preconceived image of black men as perpetrators. Every few months, somebody was releasing a disturbing new study about black men who were supposedly unemployed, in prison, abandoning their children, or dropping out of school. America knew that story line well. The down low, however, provided a sexy new vehicle to drive home a more predictable message about AIDS in the black community. With hints of closeted sexuality and talk of double lives, it played right into our stereotypical image of black men, and it conjured up the secrecy of a mysterious underground lifestyle. King called it "a culture that represents probably millions of men . . . from the pulpit to the police force." And that made the story exciting.

The *USA Today* article helped to initiate the dramatic change in public concern from black men to black women. The headline read: "The danger of living 'down low': Black men who hide their bisexuality can put women at risk." And with that message, a story that began from a study about black gay men had been transformed into a story about the risk to straight black women. The soon-to-be repeated statistics about HIV among black men became a mere mechanism to show why black women should be concerned. Twenty years after the epidemic began, we were finally starting to engage in the fight against AIDS, but even as we approached the battlefield, we seemed reluctant to fight the full war.

The *USA Today* story began with an imaginary black "Prince Charming" figure who was "well-paid, well-educated, nicely dressed, active in church and devoted to family." But despite his other virtues, we were told, he was "secretly having sex with men" and "might bring home an unwelcome guest—HIV, the AIDS virus."

Unfortunately, that story was a scare tactic for black America. The image of the well-paid, nicely dressed, churchgoing black man on the down low played right into the fears of middle-class black women all across America. But the image was not supported by any evidence in the scientific research. To bolster the claim in the article, the story cited a CDC study that showed that 25 percent of young gay and bisexual men surveyed had unprotected sex with both men and women. True, but that study was conducted with men from fifteen to twenty-two, they were not all black, they came from just seven urban settings, and they were recruited at "venues frequented by young MSM." In other words, they were not the middle-class black men in stable relationships. Most of the men in the study were adolescents who were way too young to be well-paid, well-educated, nicely dressed family men. And since many of them were recruited at gay bars and other places where down low men supposedly fear to tread, they hardly fit J. L. King's description of the DL. All the men in the study were comfortable enough with their identity that they were willing to tell a total stranger that they had sex with men. That was not the down low.

Even for middle-class black men who were on the down low, there was no evidence that they were HIV positive. Often, we make the assumption that all, or most, down low men are HIV infected, but that assumption has never been proven and seems highly unlikely. Nor has it been shown that large numbers of middle-class men on the down low were having unprotected sex with their male partners. In fact, it seemed illogical that they would, given their need to protect their secrecy. Middle-class down low men might be more inclined than others to use condoms. If you don't want your wife to know that you're sleeping around, then you would probably want to use a condom with your outside sex partners so you don't bring home any diseases and end up getting caught.

The stories of the two bisexual men quoted in the *USA Today* article actually undermined the connection between men on the down low and HIV infections among women. The article quoted King, who described himself as "a life member" of the down low but never said anything about being HIV positive. The other bisexual man quoted in the story was Raenard Brown, a forty-nine-year-old man who had a four-year relationship with a woman when he was HIV negative. It seems that neither of the bisexual men quoted in the article ever passed HIV to his female partner. That is an important point to make because the premise of the down low obsession is that DL men are spreading the virus to black women. Nobody would doubt that there are men on the down low who pass HIV to black women, but, again, not one of the men *in the article* had done so. There was not one iota of evidence in the *USA Today* article to prove that large numbers of down low men were infecting black women with HIV. It was all speculation.

The *USA Today* story was the first major newspaper article that mentioned J. L. King, and I was still trying to withhold judgment on him when I read it. The article was already troubling, but there was one part that finally helped me decide what to do about his book proposal. The article said the title of King's new book would be *Secrets: The Official Handbook of the Lifestyles of African-American Men Who Have Sex with Men.* That sensationalistic title was not a good sign, but I would not judge his book by the cover. After all, book titles often change, and King might be willing to change the title and focus of his book. Next, I read King's description of the personality types for men on the DL. There was the "Rough Neck Player," a thuglike figure who King said was the most popular down low type. Then there was the "Brooks Brothers Brother," a professional man who refuses to deal with men below his level. And finally there was the "Bi-Curious Brother," the ex-convict who, out of curiosity, lets men perform sex acts on him.

I chuckled at the descriptions. I had certainly met all three types of men in my life experiences, and I suppose the descriptions were amusing. But I soon realized that the personality types were amusing because they were simply broad, meaningless generalizations. His whole argument was internally contradictory. On the one hand, he claimed that down low men were so secretive that they could not be picked out in a crowd. But on the other hand, he was writing a book to tell black women how to pick them out in a crowd. That was more than I could take.

I spoke to King on the phone and told him that I could not do the book, and I gave him the names of two other writers who might be interested instead. He seemed prepared for my decision but did not give up entirely. He had some other writers in mind anyway, he said, and he thought it might be better to have a female writer since the book would be marketed toward black women. As the conversation ended, however, I got the impression that the door of opportunity was still open as he tried to sweeten the pot. "We're gonna make a lot of money off this," he said, almost enticingly. At first, I was skeptical of that claim. You can't fool all the people all the time, and King's plan seemed so transparently venal that I expected his publishers would see right through him. If not his publishers, then the public would surely challenge him, and King might self-destruct from the weight of his own contradictions. But deep in my heart, I knew he was probably right about the money. After all, no one ever went broke exploiting the fears of the American public. I knew King would do well by exploiting our fears, and although I could have used the money he was offering, I could not be a part of his book. We said our good-byes, I hung up the phone, and I hoped that would be the end of it. But, of course, the down low story did not end with that phone call.

Instead, the down low became increasingly ridiculous. Bloggers on the Internet started writing about it. Women on Internet message boards and listservs started trading secrets on how to spot a man on the down low. Some even started spying on their own men. A few weeks after the *New York Times Magazine* story appeared in the summer of 2003, I heard about a book called *How to Tell If Your Man Is Gay or Bisexual.* The author, Shahrazad Ali, was once the queen of controversy with her book *The Black Man's Guide to Understanding the Blackwoman* (1989). In that book, she provided ridiculous advice on how to deal with a black woman. "Soundly slap her in her mouth," she told black men. Her follow-up book, *The Black Woman's Guide to Understanding the Blackman* (1992) was just as dumb. There, she claimed that her research showed that black gay men became homosexual because of unsuccessful relationships with females, that 95 percent of them grew up in homes with either no father or a weak father, that "they feel no special connection or responsibility to other Blacks" and that they "can cook, sew and bake and are determined to be a better woman than all the women they know." If all those stereotypes were true, then Ali would have a hard time explaining the "unclockable" black men on the down low. Many of them were in relationships with females, grew up in homes with strong fathers, were very connected to the black community, and couldn't or wouldn't cook to save their lives. Given everything I knew about Ali, I could not allow myself to buy her new book without doing some basic research online. There I found one reviewer had retitled it *How to Tell If This Book Is Flammable* and urged readers to light it on fire. With that said, I decided to save my money.

A few months before J. L. King's book was published, an article about him in the *Chicago Sun-Times* raised even more concern. Early in the piece, the article claimed that "the Centers for Disease Control and Prevention connected black men on the down low with the rise of HIV infection rates among black women." In reality, that never happened. By its own admission, the CDC had never made any connection between men on the down low and HIV infections among black women.

As I read through the article, something else concerned me. It seemed as though King had not changed much over the years. I recognized the same J. L. King I had met on the telephone years earlier. He talked about his $4,000 lecture fee, his publicist in New York, and his lecture agent. He also mentioned a media consultant and said, "She's working with me to help me refine my whole image." Even the sympathetic reporter noted that King had "plenty of handlers." To read the story, it seemed as if King was more interested in making money off the down low hype than helping the community with honest information. He told the *Sun-Times* reporter that he was using his speaking opportunities to push a new brand of condoms and was actively looking for paid endorsement deals. And his comments suggested that the book might not actually help black men and women learn to trust each other. Instead, King promised his book was "probably going to set back black male-female relationships."

Black women "finally got somebody who looks like them or their husband, and doesn't act like a sissy," King said of himself. But he never really explained his own identity. "I no longer want to be promoted as this DL person," he acknowledged. "I look at myself as going through a transformation of acceptance." That may be true, but what exactly did he accept? A few months after the article, his identity was much less clear when he appeared on *Oprah*. He was not gay, he was not bisexual, he was not on the down low. He simply refused to be labeled. A few months after that, when *A&U* magazine featured him on a cover story, his story changed again. "All my life I was a bisexual man who was living on the DL," he said.

Perhaps it is difficult for reporters to challenge King, because it is was difficult to understand where he stood. In a May 2004 interview with *The Advocate,* for example, King complained that "the media needs to show two strong black men in a committed relationship, living together and being positive in their community. Instead, you see sissies, faggots, and clownlike characters." But when asked about his own sexual orientation, King replied, "If I could settle down today, it would be with a woman. My life will be easier if I have a woman in my life, living the American dream. I don't see myself with a man, growing older, being with him for the rest of my life. No way. It's easier to be heterosexual in our culture." Apparently, King did not even see the contradiction in his own words. How did he expect the media to show black men in "committed relationships" when he disparaged those relationships in the very next sentence out of his mouth? And when he did talk about black gay men, he talked about sissies, faggots, and clowns.

What is, is not, and what is not, is.

After a life spent deceiving everyone around him, King may now feel the need to make amends for the lies of his past, but that has not stopped him from sensationalizing serious issues into dramatic parody. When a reporter from *The Advocate* asked King about a story line on the television show *Law & Order: SVU* involving a black man on the down low who murders his white male sex partner, King had a ready answer. "I know a brother right now who's fucking a white guy, and if [the white guy] ever outed him, he'd kill him," said King. If nothing else, reporters can always count on J. L. King for a good quote.

So how does a story based entirely on anecdotal and circumstantial evidence become a mainstream media sensation big enough to generate headlines in the *New York Times* and *Washington Post* and to be discussed on the nation's most respected daytime television talk show?

First, it helps if you have a major publicity budget from Random House. The media feed off the other media. If the *Wall Street Journal* runs a story, then the *New York Times* is more likely to run a story, and if the *Times* runs a story, then the *Washington Post* may run a story, and the cycle continues on and on. By the time the down low subject got to *Oprah,* it had been vetted and filtered through every respected newspaper in the country, giving it the pedigree of a serious story. If the nation's most respected journalists were writing about it, then there was no reason why Oprah Winfrey shouldn't talk about it as well. But Oprah was not the problem. The problem was that the mainstream media had never really challenged the logic behind the down low in the first place.

Second, if you want to start a media frenzy, it also doesn't hurt to have a provocative spokesman who is willing to make controversial remarks about a taboo topic. "The reason why this makes *Oprah* is because of the homosexual story line," according to Phill Wilson of the Black AIDS Institute. He may be right, and yet the fascination with homosexuality and bisexuality can blind us to other realities, including the possibility that men who are not on the down low can also spread HIV to their partners.

The worst part of the down low story is that it is being promoted by a black man who is using America's fear of black men to advance his own agenda. Few black figures are more compelling to white America than the black man who is willing to criticize his own people. Remember the example of William Hannibal Thomas who wrote the 1901 book, *The American Negro.* Thomas, you may recall, said that "Negro nature is so craven and sensuous in every fiber of its being that a Negro manhood with decent respect for chaste womanhood does not exist." In Thomas's case, the Macmillan Company was willing to publish multiple printings of his incendiary book despite the fact that Thomas lived "a life shrouded in ambiguity, controversy and secrecy," as he was described by his biographer John David Smith in *Black Judas*. But controversy sells books. If you add ambiguity and secrecy to the mix, you could easily have a best-seller.

It's even easier when you are demonizing black men. Perception is more important than reality when it comes to black men. In 1901, it was easy for Thomas to portray black men as indecent sexual creatures because people in society already saw us that way. Since that time, it has been easy for others throughout history to portray black men as sexual predators because many people in society still see us that way.

When nine black boys were wrongly convicted of gang raping two white women on an Alabama train in 1931, the "Scottsboro Boys" were portrayed as sexual predators. When fourteen-year-old Emmett Till was lynched in Mississippi in August 1955, the white men who murdered him imagined him as a sexual predator because he had whistled at a white woman. And when black men are discussed today in the context of the down low, we too are portrayed as sexual predators.

"The thing that makes this down low story a major media issue is that fact that these men are sleeping with other men," says Phill Wilson. "That's why it's so easy to totally exclude from the conversation the fact that black women might be at risk because their male partners might be sleeping with HIV positive women," he adds. That message is more difficult for us to hear. It may be easier for us to understand the image of the closeted black gay man as the evildoer who is coming into our lives to break up our happy homes. A commentator named "Blackbrit" on the *New York Times Magazine* Web forum put it this way: "Too often the DL brother is constructed as the vessel of contagion." He blamed this perspective on a "hetero-sexist assumption that AIDS is born and bred in gay communities then venomously spread to pure, sterile black communities." In reality, he reminded us, "straight black people are HIV-positive and spreading the disease among themselves without any help from 'evil' black gay men."

The down low story also appealed to us because J. L. King offered answers that no one else would. AIDS rates were relatively high in black America, and King, at least, offered an explanation. Men on the down low, he said, were responsible for the spread of the AIDS epidemic to black women. No one else in America seemed willing to say that. The CDC wouldn't say that. The leading researchers wouldn't say that. The AIDS advocates in the field wouldn't say that either. Of course, no one denied that there were men on the down low. Everyone in the AIDS field already knew that. But they did not know who they were, how many they were, how many were in relationships, how many were HIV positive, or how many were using protection. The down low story only made sense if we could answer those questions, but it would have been very difficult to do so. The only way to verify any information about this group was to ask the people who were on the down low, which was already complicated. First, you would have to find them, and how do you find people who are trying not to be found? Next, you would have to trust them. The same people who would admit that they were habitual liars would have to be trusted to tell the truth about their lies. It was very convoluted, but it was a perfect oppor-tunity for a smooth-talking "expert" who had admittedly spent his adult life deceiving people.

J. L. King had an answer that no one could challenge. As the only one who was talking publicly about this secret lifestyle, anything he said was taken as fact because no one could repudiate it. He had constructed quite a clever ploy. If he said certain people were on the down low, how could anyone prove that they were *not* on the down low? The "suspects" could never admit it because that would blow their cover. If, however, they denied it, King could still argue that they were on the down low. Thus, without any other evidence to back up his claims, King skillfully turned his individual life stories into a public, and soon to be profitable, truth.

It's not clear whether all those handlers paid off. On the *Oprah* show, King "misquoted HIV statistics" and provided "sensationalistic rhetoric," according to Dr. David Malebranche, a doctor, HIV specialist, and assistant professor at Emory University in Atlanta. When Oprah asked King how he could tell who is on the down low, he told her, "we do it by the eyes" and said "I could make a connection in this room." That may be true, but that is not specific to the down low. In fact, gay men have been doing the same thing for centuries. Some call it "gaydar." In a culture that represses open expression of homosexuality, men with same-sex attraction often find other men simply by looking at them and seeing if they look back. It's not complicated, it's not rocket science, and it's not a mystery. It's the same technique that many heterosexuals use to gauge interest from those they find attractive. But King's comments on the *Oprah* show made me more concerned about his book.

The book was not yet in the stores when King appeared on *Oprah,* so I went to his Web site to try to find out more. There, I found his list of the "top questions" asked about the down low, and the first question listed was an indication of what to expect: "How can I tell if my man is on the DL?" I was not surprised by the response. "The answers to these questions and much more will be in the book. Please make sure you get your copy on May 10, 2004."

A few weeks after the *Oprah* appearance, I finally picked up

King's book, *On The Down Low,* and read it on a flight to Seattle. In some ways, the book was better than I expected it to be. The writing, in particular, was much better than I expected and seemed clearly different from King's own voice. He had obviously found an excellent ghost writer. Some big-time celebrities do not write their own books. Many don't have the time, some don't have the knowledge, and others simply don't know how to write. Celebrity ghost writers can be valuable for artists, athletes, and entertainers who want to tell their stories in print, but they can also useful for non-celebrities if they have the money. J. L. King was not yet a celebrity, but he was not an author either. However, he was smart enough to pick one of the best celebrity biographers in the business—Karen Hunter.

Karen Hunter had written celebrity biographies and autobiographies for several of the leading figures in black America. She co-authored LL Cool J's bestselling book *I Make My Own Rules* in 1997. She co-wrote Queen Latifah's bestselling book *Ladies First* in 1999. And when the rapper Mase published his book *Revelations* in 2001, he too chose Karen Hunter to help him out. Even the Reverend Al Sharpton's book, *Al on America,* was co-authored by Karen Hunter.

One of Hunter's most valuable connections was with New York's popular radio personality Wendy Williams. Williams had often spoken on the radio about homothugs, gay rappers, and closeted performers in the entertainment industry, and she had a reputation for dealing with hot topics. With access to A-list celebrities and a huge media market, Wendy Williams could help to make or break a new artist, entertainer, or author. The guests on the highly rated *Wendy Williams Show* were some of the same entertainers who had come to Karen Hunter to write their books, so it was no surprise that Williams chose Hunter to co-write her own books, *Wendy's Got the Heat* in 2003 and *The Wendy Williams Experience* in 2004. And perhaps it should come as no surprise that J. L. King chose Karen Hunter to write his book as well.

Parts of King's book were informative and entertaining, other parts seemed unrealistic, and much of the book was, quite frankly, contradictory. In many ways, the book, like the author, was the proverbial riddle wrapped in a mystery inside an enigma. Every answer seemed to raise at least two questions, which never got answered. The more you peeled away, the more confused you became. Even in the introduction to the book, King claims that his success was "ordained by God" and describes how speaking engagements and media appearances found their way to him "seemingly out of nowhere." As King said, "I had no connections to help me get invited to speak. Nor did I have a public relations professional promoting my message to the media." Yet in the first chapter of his book, he tells a different story. There, he explains that he resigned from his job in 2001 and had a friend put together a brochure called "Secrets of the African-American Bisexual Man." That wasn't all. "I had been in marketing for my entire professional career," King wrote, "so I knew how to do this part of it." King then acknowledges that he sent his brochure to fifty-two health departments throughout the country. Given that extensive marketing campaign, it's hard to understand his claim that the speaking engagements came "out of nowhere."

In another apparent contradiction, King admits his lack of knowledge about AIDS issues when he first started talking about the down low in 2001. "I wasn't a health expert," he wrote. "I didn't know much about HIV and AIDS or the statistics." But on the back jacket of his book, he identifies himself as "an HIV/STD prevention activist, educator and author" whose "expertise" has been cited in various national publications. That's fine. If he is now an expert, then he should be expected to know the basic research to support his argument.

But in the very first chapter of his book, King completely misquotes important CDC statistics that any expert should know. For example, on page 10 of his book he claims that "sixty-eight percent of all new AIDS cases are black women." That's just plain wrong, and anyone who calls himself an AIDS expert should know better. Based on the latest statistics available when King published his book, black women made up just 18 percent of all new AIDS cases, not 68 percent, as King claimed. That's a huge difference, but King did not appear concerned about facts and statistics when asked a question by a reporter for *Southern Voice* newspaper in August 2004. "King brushed off criticism from public health experts about his lack of data, saying he has done more for introducing blacks to safe-sex education in the past year than anyone else in the past two decades," the reporter wrote. That is an insulting statement that shows just how little King really knows about the work of HIV/AIDS activists who have been fighting the epidemic for decades without the publicity of a major book tour.

King is unashamed of his newfound fame and talks about it frequently. A woman would "have to be from another planet by now not to have heard of me," King told the *Houston Chronicle*. "I travel with bodyguards because there are so many people who want to silence the messenger," he added. And he is not afraid to take credit for saving the black community. "I'm making the everyday common folks hear about this epidemic," he told the *Southern Voice*. "Now there's more of a demand for everyday people to learn about it, and that wasn't happening before me." Finally, in an interview with *Salon.com*, King confessed his real agenda. "I want people to say thank you, J. L., for forcing us to take a look at sexuality and sexual orientation. Hopefully when the [HIV/AIDS] numbers start decreasing, people will say it's because of this guy who stepped forward and put a face on this behavior—that it's because of his vision that we're seeing a decrease." In other words, it's all about J. L. King. One man spreading misinformation wants to get credit for saving the entire black community. Apparently, it does not matter to him that the conversation that is now taking place—the conversation that he says he started—is based on fear instead of facts.

King may have been right about one thing. His book may actually set back black male-female relationships, just as he predicted months before its publication. As the author Darryl James observed in an article about the down low, "This issue has not provided any intrinsic awareness, and has not served to create more open discussions about sex, sexuality or sexually transmitted diseases. What it has done is to drive a wedge between the already divided pools of single Black men and women." And there are consequences. A black woman in Tampa told the *St. Petersburg Times* that the book frightened her to the point that she looks at the men in church differently. "It made me not want to date," she confessed. Stephanie Edgecombe in Washington, D.C., expressed similar feelings in an interview with *Salon.com.* "When I first heard about the DL, fear immediately set in . . . Now you have to be an FBI agent? This is what is so frightening to me."

It's hard to believe that those are just some of the minor problems and contradictions in King's book. The other contradictions call into question the seriousness of his "research" and the purpose of his message. For example, in Chapter 2 of his book, King says that down low men are in "denial" about "being a homosexual." Then he adds, "If they tell the truth and say they're gay or bisexual, they will be called a 'fag.'" In essence, King is admitting that down low men are gay or bisexual. But in several other places in the book, he claims that DL men are *not* gay or bisexual. He never clarifies the contradiction.

On one page King says "the DL man is indistinguishable from every other man in the crowd. And that's the way he likes it." Four pages later, he says a DL man is "the first one to stand up in church and shout, 'Get the homosexuals out of here!'" It's hard to figure out how standing up and shouting against gays in a church would make someone "indistinguishable" in the crowd, but that's the kind of inconsistency we see throughout King's book and his message.

The third chapter of King's book is even more perplexing. In that chapter, King reveals a salacious homosexual affair that supposedly ended his seven-year marriage to his wife, Brenda. When she found out about the affair, she locked him out of his own house and cut him off, he says. In describing that affair, King makes a big deal about not using a condom with his male sex partner. "We never even talked about safe or safer sex," King wrote. "We never used protection. Never." Seems like a clear problem until you get to the very end of the chapter. That's when King tells us that the story took place when he was twenty-seven years old. And when was King twenty-seven years old? He does not tell us. It is difficult to be exactly sure of King's age because a number of newspaper articles about him curiously skip over that fact, but there is some reliable information out there. *USA Today* reported that King was forty-four years old in March 2001. In August 2004, an article on King in *Salon.com* reported that he was forty-nine years old. I don't understand how someone jumps from forty-four to forty-nine in just three years, but let's assume the more recent article is correct.

If King was forty-nine in 2004, then he would have been twenty-seven in 1982. His marriage would have taken place from approximately 1975 to 1982. In other words, the melodramatic unsafe sex story that King details in his book actually took place long before *anyone* knew about HIV. The first cases of AIDS were reported in June 1981, and the government did not even create a name for it until 1982. At that time, there were no safe sex messages about using condoms. Nobody was using condoms to stop HIV because nobody knew how it was spread back then. Most men were only using condoms to prevent pregnancy, not to stop a virus that they had never heard about. King's failure to disclose the year in which his affair took place seems purposefully designed to mislead the reader not only about his own safe sex practices, but also about the safe sex practices of other men on the down low. A story about a man not using condoms from 1975 to 1982 is completely irrelevant to the down low today.

The 1982 story raises questions about King's credibility, but it also raises questions about the credibility of the down low story itself. For example, if black men were on the down low twenty years ago, why are we just now talking about it now, especially since King's own marriage provides a clear example that the down low has been around for decades. And here's another question. If black men on the down low have been sleeping around for twenty years, why are black women only now becoming infected by these men? King never answers those questions in his book.

Of the many troubling questions and contradictions in King's book, the most disturbing are the questions about what he calls "DL behavior types" and about "the signs" to tell if a man is on the DL. King claims to have conducted extensive "research" involving "DL focus groups" and has used that research to develop five DL behavior types. King never explains the methodology used to conduct the focus groups or to select the participants, nor does he explain what exactly constitutes a "DL focus group." By his own definition, men on the down low would have nothing to do with anything—especially a focus group—that identified them as being on the down low. Maybe King recruited some of his own down low friends from his secret society. That's a plausible explanation, but it seems unlikely that one person's network of contacts could be broad enough to draw conclusions about what he claims are "millions of men." It seems even less plausible when the men are consciously trying not to be detected. Of course, he might have met some of the men because they wanted to hook up with him, but that would not necessarily create a diverse pool for a focus group unless we assume that men of all ages, lifestyles, and backgrounds wanted to hook up with him. But at forty-nine years old, King was probably not as connected to men in the younger age range who are most affected by the epidemic. The participants in the CDC studies of young black men, for example, were fifteen to twenty-nine years old, not the group of people who typically hang out with forty-nine-year-olds.

The five personality types in King's book were similar to the three types I had read about years before. In addition to the "thug brother" and the "curious brother," King also included the "mature brother" and the "I have a wife/girlfriend brother." He also renamed the "Brooks Brothers Brother" the "professional brother." At the beginning of the chapter, however, King zeroes in on the major flaw in his own research. The behavior types are so broad that they describe "every man in our communities." King says that's the point because "DL men don't stand out." But if that's the case, then why go through the whole exercise of writing a chapter about the five behavior types? He never answers that question. Instead, he provides a litany of stereotypes under the guise of research. The mature brother, for example, "knows how to get what he wants and keep what he has." He's older than the other types, but don't expect much more analysis from King. This character type gets just four paragraphs of text in the book.

The "thug brother," on the other hand, gets several pages. King calls him a "homo-thug," a term most often used to describe black gay and bisexual men who dress in "thuggish" urban gear. But homo-thugs often go out to gay clubs, as Malcolm Venable explained in his groundbreaking July 2001 *VIBE* magazine article "A Question of Identity." In a gross generalization about a whole group of people, King says the thug brother "has little knowledge" about HIV because "he doesn't read." And just to make it easier to spot the thug from a distance, King says the thug brother "might have braids or dreads or sport a baldie." That narrows the field to about half of all black men.

King's "professional brother" is described as a metrosexual who is "always dressed very GQ." But this brother "will tend to have safer sex and may take an HIV test every time he has sex with a man," King says. Safer sex? HIV tests? Those words contradict almost everything the public has been told about the down low. Furthermore, that message actually acknowledges that the stereotypical middle-class professional black man at the very core of the whole down low frenzy is more likely than others to practice safe sex. If that is true, then it calls into question the hysterical media frenzy about middle-class black women becoming infected by their down low partners, and it undermines the whole point of J. L. King's book—that all women are at great risk from the down low.

King dispenses with the "'I have a wife/girlfriend' brother" in just three short paragraphs and then moves onto the personality type that gets most of his attention—the curious brother. Men in this group are described by King as "the only one of the five types of DL brothers I've met who will go to a local gay bar, party, or event." That is a perfectly fair statement because King limits his assertion to the extent of his own knowledge, but in so doing he demonstrates the very limits of his knowledge. Malcolm Venable's article in *VIBE* found homo-thugs in a black gay nightclub in the Bronx, and King himself admitted in Chapter 12 of his book that some other types of DL men may go out to gay bars. In the end,

King's five behavior types do more harm than good by alarming black women with little or no basis in evidence.

As a result, he has helped to create a culture in which women are learning to be "down low detectives." They are trading tips on how to spot men on the down low and posting messages on Web sites to find the tricks of the trade. "I am new to figuring this out," writes one woman on a Yahoo group for women "betrayed" by men on the down low. "But I think there are hand gestures involved such as scratching a part of the face." Another poster encourages women to slip a finger or two up their man's ass. "If he accepts two fingers up his butt then he surely is DL." On a different message forum on Bravenet, women are also upset but they are fighting back by posting photographs of men who they say are on the down low.

It's happening in the mainstream media as well. A counselor quoted in a September 2004 article in the *Detroit News* tells women to look for "low sexual appetite," gay friends, or homophobia. It seems a bit of a circular argument. If the man is homophobic, then he is probably gay, but if he is not homophobic and has gay friends, then he is still probably gay.

In his chapter on the signs, King reprints a letter to the editor written to *USA Today* in which a woman asks a gay friend to make a pass at her husband to see if he responds. The scheme worked for the woman, and based on her experience she offered a suggestion. "My advice to women is get you a gay man and have him come on to your man," she wrote. And if a woman has no gay friends, King has some simple advice to help them as well. Watch the eyes, he says. Men communicate with their eyes, he warns. But of course they also communicate with their mouths, so if your man says the word "S'up," that should cause some suspicion as well, King suggests. "The signs are very subtle," he insists. It could be a "hug that is just a second too long" or if your man wants to have anal sex in your heterosexual relationship. In fact, King's signs are so broadly constructed that just about anything a man does might raise a red flag.

This is where King's message gets muddled in its own contradictions again. To his credit, King says "a woman should not automatically label her man 'on the DL' when his actions change." He also admits that "not every black man is on the DL" and "not every black man in your life is on the DL." That is an accurate and important message to deliver. But at the same time he counsels caution, he tacitly encourages the very behavior he supposedly discourages. He does tell women not to "overdo" it, but he never tells them not to do it—not to spy on their partners. Instead, in two consecutive pages of his book, King seems to deliver repeatedly conflicting advice. First, on page 129, King says that women might hire a private investigator or find a "masculine-looking gay man" to try to seduce their man. But then on page 130 he says couples "should strive to have a relationship where they can talk freely about sex, where they can have the power of choice through open, honest discussion." Later on the same page, he changes his message again and says a woman "can't just approach her man and ask, 'Baby, are you fooling around with another man?'" Instead, he says women should follow "their intuition" and "start playing detective" to find out if their man is on the DL.

How does a couple create an open and honest relationship in this climate of distrust? According to King, just pretend that you're doing good things while you're discreetly checking up on your man. Get to know your man's schedule, King says, and change your own schedule while you're at it. "Drop in on him at work and take him to lunch one day out of the blue. Come home early from work one day; surprise him." King says it's more difficult for men to get away with DL activity if their women keep surprising them. No doubt that's true, but it's also horrible advice for managing a relationship. If your man really wants to be with another man, it's just a matter of time before it happens. It probably doesn't matter how many times you come home early from work to interrupt him. If he's going to do it, he's going to do it somewhere, somehow, away from you.

Men and women in relationships cannot form healthy bonds if they create patterns of distrust. Instead of becoming down low detectives, we need to get to know our partners before we enter relationships with them. Once in those relationships, we have to learn to trust one another and communicate to each other. If you need to snoop around to check on your partner's e-mails and cell phone messages, then maybe you shouldn't be involved in a relationship with him in the first place. Maybe you need to find someone you can trust.

Of course, many women are legitimately concerned about dishonesty from their men, but the way to change the culture of untruthfulness is to practice honesty in your own behavior. Deputizing yourself as a down low detective will not make your man heterosexual if he is not, and it will not save your relationship if it is built on mutual mistrust. You can spend the rest of your life going to down low seminars and reading the latest magazine articles on how to tell if your man is gay, but the truth is there is no way to tell. There are no real "signs" to spot a man on the down low, and there are no real "behavior types" of these men. Despite the contradictory messages in his book, King himself admits that men on the down low do not look a certain way or act a certain way.

If you want to protect yourself, you cannot make assumptions based on appearances, sexual orientation, performance in bed, marital status, or old test results. If you don't want to be infected with HIV, then you have the responsibility to protect yourself. Nobody else can do that for you. The best way to know the truth is not to spy on your partner but to create an environment where sexuality can be discussed openly.

The truth is, you cannot tell if a man is on the down low, and you should never trust anyone who says you can.

CHAPTER 7
Victims and Villains

AS I WALKED off the plane, I could not remember the last time I had been to Atlanta. The city had changed a lot since I had lived there. My father and sister relocated to Atlanta in the 1980s and had moved between Stone Mountain, Marietta, and Smyrna. Between semesters at school and in between jobs, I bounced back and forth to the Atlanta area as a place of refuge. In one of my early jobs during a semester away from college, I sold jeans and things at the Gap at Cumberland Mall. Although they called it the New South, I still felt a bit of the old when some of the elderly white customers would come in shopping. With their strong southern accents and years of wrinkles, I could not help wondering which side they had chosen during the civil rights struggles of the past. Were these the same people who had screamed racial obscenities at my parents and grandparents, and if so, how did they reconcile the passionate beliefs of their past with the racial realities of integration?

That racial history was inescapable in Atlanta. It left its imprint on nearly every institution, and it forced future generations to decide whether to forgive or forget. From Auburn

Avenue to Stone Mountain, I felt connected to the past almost everywhere I traveled. But after my years of absence, the city had been reduced to a kaleidoscopic blur of images in my mind. I remembered working on a political campaign, teaching eighth grade social studies, and hiking to the top of Stone Mountain. And I could never forget the time when I marched with Mrs. King as an honorary grand marshal in the annual King Day Parade. But the most profound image in my mind was the sight of a small band of KKK leaders marching through the streets of downtown Atlanta in 1989 under the protection of black police officers who kept them separated from hundreds of counter demonstrators. That was the paradox of Atlanta. Surrounded by some of the most conservative places in the south, the Atlanta metropolitan area was an oasis of culture and diversity where you could forgive but you could never forget.

I had come to Atlanta to make a presentation about the down low at a CDC HIV Prevention Conference. I was a little nervous about speaking to a group of experts about a topic they all knew well, so I decided to talk about what I knew. I talked about victims and villains, wherein I questioned the need to assign blame to men on the down low. Instead, I suggested that we create a culture that destigmatizes homosexuality and bisexuality so men will not feel the pressure to enter into duplicitous relationships.

I thought I had offered a fairly innocuous recommendation, but after I spoke I was peppered with questions from the audience. Most of the questions were fairly straightforward, but one question shot right through me. A black woman stood at the microphone and looked me directly in the face as she spoke. "It figures they would get a gay man to come up here and speak," she said. "All I hear from you is blame," she continued. "You make it seem like black women are the perpetrators. Until you've been in a relationship with a man for fourteen years and had three kids and had him leave you for another man, then you don't understand," she said.

It seemed as if the room stood still when she finished speaking. Maybe we were all stunned. With one single question, the entire tone in the room had changed. She was definitely right about one thing. I could hardly imagine the pain involved in learning that my partner had lied to me for fourteen years. But, unfortunately, that was not the issue. The subject of the panel was not about infidelity and relationships. It was about HIV and AIDS. The two issues were connected, but they needed to be understood in context. No one would dispute the importance of honesty in relationships, but dishonesty does not spread AIDS. An honest man with HIV can still spread the virus to his partner, but a dishonest man without HIV cannot.

I think the woman who asked the question came to the panel to hear from someone who could affirm her pain rather than question her rage, and my presentation must have been a big disappointment to her. I was unable to provide the comfort she needed. Even as I tried to respond diplomatically, I may have made things worse with my reply.

"Thank you for your comment," I said. "I have three thoughts I'd like to share. First, I did not select the panel, so I cannot take responsibility for who is or is not on the stage. Second, I do hear your frustration, but I am not going to apologize for being a gay man. Third, the purpose of my remarks is not to blame black women. But I am also not here to blame black men. My whole point," I said, "is that we need to get beyond the blame game."

I had hoped that my answer would help resolve the question, but I sensed that it had encouraged more frustration among a few members of the audience. After the session ended, another black woman confronted me and told me that my comments were "insensitive" and "disrespectful." With a half-completed evaluation sheet in her hand, she listened carefully as I tried to explain my position. I got the sense that my comments might dictate her evaluation, but I could not hold back what I felt. "The down low is not responsible for the AIDS epidemic," I said. "It's time we recognize that HIV is spread by behavior, not identity. And it's time to stop pitting female victims against male villains in this discussion. We're all in this together, and we can't afford to have a battle of the sexes in the middle of an epidemic."

On the plane ride home, I thought about what I had said and how I could have handled the situation better. Some of my friends have accused me of responding to life rationally instead of emotionally, and I realized that was the disconnect in my message. I was providing facts and figures and information, but some of the people affected by the down low wanted emotion instead. I was explaining why blame was a counterproductive emotion that would not change reality, but that explanation missed the point for some listeners. Their reality was that they needed someone to blame. They had been lied to and cheated on, and they needed someone to be responsible. They needed a villain.

The man on the down low was the perfect boogeyman. If the subject was AIDS, somebody had to be responsible for transmitting the virus, and if the subject was relationships, the one who cheated was the obvious wrongdoer. It made me think of a conversation I had with J. L. King in 2001. I called to interview him for a story I was writing about AIDS in the black community. I asked him how to reach men on the down low, and what he thought about the trend toward demonizing those men. "As far as DL brothers being demonized, yeah, I think that's what it's going to take in order for women to know that they are sleeping with the enemy," said King. "A lot of guys who are on the DL who are doing this, they have no shame," he said.

Dr. David Malebranche, assistant professor of medicine at Emory University, has a theory about all this. In an essay called "Black Dick as a Weapon of Mass Destruction," Malebranche compares the demonization of men on the down low to the vilification of Arab enemies in the war on terror, and he even provides a formula for how it works. "You identify a group of people in the midst of tough emotional and economic times (the American people or heterosexual black women), and you give them a face or profile of someone they can blame (any Middle Eastern Muslim man or the "Down Low" brutha). 'He is the reason for your problems. He is the cause of your sickness. He is the one we are fighting against.' And *voilà!* Instant fear, instant outrage, instant division, instant war, instant excuses."

The down low fit perfectly into larger cultural dynamics because it confirmed stereotypical values that many of us already believed. For some whites, it confirmed their hypersexualized perception of black people, and for some blacks it confirmed their hypersexualized perception of gay men. Given society's stereotypical view of black men combined with societal beliefs about homosexuality, the story became more believable because it vilified a group of people we did not understand and many of us did not want to know. And for those of us who had been victimized by black men, it gave us a way to express our grief and our rage.

In her controversial book *On Death and Dying,* Dr. Elisabeth Kübler-Ross defined five common stages of grief—denial, anger, bargaining, depression, and acceptance. The stages apply to other forms of grief besides dying, and they operate fluidly to allow us to move back and forth as we try to cope. Similarly, the Straight Spouse Network in San Francisco identifies five steps for heterosexuals to cope with the news that a partner is gay—shock, face reality, let go, heal, and reconfigure. But I realized on the plane trip home that many of those most affected by the down low are still struggling with Kübler-Ross's first two stages. Denial and anger are normal human responses to tragedy, and we should definitely be understanding to those women and men in those stages, but we cannot allow emotion alone to dictate our public policy.

When friends of mine are angry and call me for advice on how to confront a friend or a partner, I usually ask them a question and give them two choices. The question is this: What outcome do you hope to achieve by your behavior? If you want to vent and release your frustration, then an angry confrontational approach makes perfect sense. However, if you want to change someone's behavior, you have to be more strategic about how you approach them. That advice applies to the down low as well as to friendships and relationships. If we simply want to vent, then by all means we should get it off our chest with as much anger as necessary. If, however, we want to encourage people to change their behavior, we need to think about the best way to reach them.

Demonizing men on the down low will not change their behavior. It may make us feel better about ourselves, but it will not make those men straight. Nor will it make them come clean. Instead, the anger involved in the demonization process may cloud our judgment as we try to think of rational solutions. Despite that reality, the tone of the down low story has become considerably angrier since the media frenzy began in 2001. The first stories talked about men who were unknowingly spreading HIV to their female partners, but by 2004 the women in the stories were portrayed as being much more upset about it. For example, a September 2004 article in *POZ* magazine begins with the line "Patricia Nalls is mad as hell." Nalls is the founder of a Washington, D.C., AIDS agency for black women called The Women's Collective, and she is HIV positive. According to *POZ,* she was infected in 1984 by her late husband, an IV drug user.

Although Nalls was not infected by a man on the down low, she has seen women who were. "I can't tell you how many married women we've served, some of whom were infected by husbands sleeping with the best man from their wedding or the baby's god-father. I can't believe these men are being so selfish," she said. It is important to understand what she is and is not saying. Her agency has served a number of married women, but not all of them were infected by their husbands, and of those who were, not all of their husbands were on the down low. Some were likely to have been drug users like her own husband. And some may have contracted the virus in prison or from women.

The article quotes another woman who was infected with HIV, but she "isn't sure whether the man who gave her HIV got it from sex with another woman or with another man or from sharing nee-dles." As a heavy drinker, a crack user, an injection drug user, and an incarcerated felon, her former boyfriend fit into numerous risk groups that have nothing to do with the down low.

The story that looked like a condemnation of men on the down low actually turned out to be a broader analysis of complex social phenomena in the black community. Perhaps there is a lesson in that experience. If we allow our anger about the down low to guide us into obsession—however righteous and well intended the anger may be—we may miss the numerous other factors that determine behavioral risk that have nothing to do with the down low. When we approach the issue from the assumption that the down low is the problem, we tend not to see the other problems out there, or we may misunderstand how those problems really affect our behavior.

An August 2004 article in *Essence* magazine provides an example. The article is titled "Deadly Deception" and the pull-out quote on the first two page sets the tone: "Men on the down low view dis-honesty as survival. Problem is, their lies are killing us." Writer Taigi

Smith acknowledges the burdens faced by men who have sexual desires for other men but argues that "shame and social stigma don't make it okay for men on the DL to cheat on their female partners, especially when those liaisons are infecting black women with HIV." Of course she's right. Few people would dispute the argument that cheating or infecting someone with a disease is inappropriate behavior in a relationship, but Smith never cites any evidence to prove how commonly this occurs. Instead, she develops an analysis that seems to be influenced by her anger.

> Why now does it seem that so many more Black men are secretly choosing to have sex with other men? Part of the answer has to do with the oversexualization of American culture in general. Today any child old enough to reach for the remote can be bombarded with sexual images of video girls shaking their booties, showing their boobs or otherwise displaying sex set to music. . . . By the time a boy reaches 18, he is already desensitized to both the sexual act and the feelings of women. It's no wonder that as our men become sexually desensitized, it takes more to stimulate them physically. They start to crave sex that is a bit more risky and a lot more lewd as the ante is upped on what will satisfy them.

Smith's critique is based entirely on the assumption that more black men are having sex with men now than ever before. Of course, there is no way to measure that claim, and Smith does not even attempt to do so. The truth is that black men have been secretly having sex with men since the beginning of time. If it seems that more of them are doing it now than ever before, you can thank the media for creating that impression. There may be more black men talking about it now, but there is no evidence that more black men are actually doing it. Besides, how do you measure a secret? Smith argues that more black men are "secretly choosing to have sex with other men," but if they are really doing it secretly, how do we know how many are doing it? And how do we know how many were doing it before? The evidence we do have seems to contradict Smith. As I mentioned before, 52 percent of African-American male AIDS cases resulted from homosexual contact in 1991 but in 2001 the percentage had dropped to 33 percent, suggesting that homosexuality is less prevalent among black men in this decade than it was in the early 1990s.

Statistics are easy to overlook, so it is not a surprise that reporters would think that the reach of black male homosexuality is a relatively new phenomenon. Smith's other argument, however, is dangerously misinformed. Her claim that black men *choose* homosexuality over heterosexuality because music videos have desensitized them to women is ridiculous and insulting. That statement feeds into the misapprehension that homosexuality is simply a convenient lifestyle choice, like which peanut butter to buy, instead of a fundamental reality for some humans. Moreover, it seems patently illogical that straight men would no longer want to have sex with women after watching music videos with sexy women in them. If anything, we should expect the videos would stimulate their heterosexual desires, but Smith assumes that straight videos actually turn straight men gay.

Unfortunately, Smith's article illustrates the danger in allowing emotion instead of reason to dictate our thinking on the down low. Smith confesses that she is "terrified" after reading an article about the DL in the *New York Times* and she admits: "I no longer make eye contact with attractive men because I'm afraid that perhaps they're living life on the down low." And despite the evidence to the contrary, she is "incensed by the dramatic numbers of African-

American women becoming infected with HIV, mainly from men who sleep around with other men."

Lynn Norment makes a much more reasonable argument in the August 2004 issue of *Ebony*. "Come out of the closet, out of the basement," she tells down low brothers. "Face up to who you are, and let us live." An April 2004 comment from a visitor on Oprah.com conveys a similar sentiment. "We can sit and talk about this for years to come but we should constantly pray that these people can get deliverance from this lifestyle. This epidemic is out of control and souls have to be saved. Be true to the ones you so call love and be true to yourself. Be honest!"

Those are powerful statements that convey the real-life concerns of black women. Black women have a right to be outraged by the deception of the men in their lives who lie to them about their sexual behavior. Outrage is a perfectly understandable emotion, but unfortunately it seems unlikely to change the behavior of the men who lie. In fact, men on the down low may become more resistant to being honest in an environment where they feel hostility and anger directed at them.

Black male-female relationships have already become a casualty in the war on the down low. We have created a new black version of the battle of the sexes in which black men and women fight about who is to blame for the AIDS epidemic. The problem with this battle is that it misleads us about the identity of the enemy. The real enemy is not black men. Nor is it black women. The real enemy is AIDS, and we cannot afford to allow this disease to defeat us with a divide-and-conquer strategy that pits black men against black women.

Unfortunately, we are headed in the wrong direction. On a message board on BET.com, one writer blames men on the down low for spreading AIDS. Another responds angrily: "That's not the reason why black women are infected with HIV." Then the conversation continues with a different post: "We all need to shut up and take responsibility for ourselves." Then: "sad how U dont care what black men do to U." Then another writer: "So many black females with aids n U still say its not black males." Followed by another: "you a fool with a capital F, the reason black people is getting aids is cause women like you who will sleep with my best friend & his best friend & his best friend the whole neigborhood."

For many of those who are angry, the down low is not just about men who cheat. It's about men being cheaters. It fuels a discussion that some believe to be anti-male, not just anti–down low male. Part of that results from the nature of the cheating. When a man and a woman are involved in an affair outside a relationship, it is harder to make negative generalizations by gender than when *two men* are involved in an affair. With a male-female liaison, both a man and a woman are engaged in inappropriate conduct, but with two men it is just two men, and suddenly it is easier to frame the issue through the lens of a gender war, where all the men involved are seen as perpetrators and the women left behind are viewed as victims.

Our obsession with the down low unnecessarily pits black men against black women and reinforces existing negative public perceptions of black men. Black men are constantly portrayed by society as the perpetrators of pathology. We are repeatedly studied and examined for what we are said to do wrong, but these analyses rarely attempt to understand the root causes of our behavior. That is not to say that black men are blameless. In fact, some of us seem to have no shame in the lies we tell or the deception we practice. Women have every right to blame us when we do wrong by them. But blame alone will not solve the problems in our community.

That's why the effort to vilify men on the down low is a mistake. Vilifying men on the down low will not solve the problem with the down low. Pointing fingers will only make the problem worse. I know that some women and some down low educators are heavily invested in demonizing these men, but our resources would be better spent on creating an environment where black women and men can talk candidly and openly about sexual expression. Even if you accept the premise that men on the down low are chiefly responsible for the spread of HIV among black women, it's hard to understand how pushing these men further into denial about their sexuality will help solve the problem. Instead, it's likely to exacerbate the problem as men on the down low become so vilified that they avoid testing, counseling, treatment, and any serious effort to address their HIV status, not to mention their sexuality.

One of the problems in looking at the down low in terms of villains and victims is that the characterization of victims may actually discourage women from taking personal responsibility. Webster's defines a victim as "one that is acted on and usually adversely affected by a force or agent." There is no doubt that some women are real-life victims of men on the down low, but when you think of all black women as victims or potential victims you run the risk of disempowering them as well. If we label women as being "acted on" by outside forces, we assume incorrectly that women are not strong enough to stand up on their own to these deceptive men. Those labels create an unflattering image of women as helpless victims instead of powerful agents of change.

Blame is usually reactive, not proactive. To blame someone for infecting us with HIV means we are already infected. All we can do is react. On the other hand, to stop someone from infecting us with HIV requires us to be proactive, not reactive. The most important lesson that all people need to learn about AIDS is that the disease is entirely preventable. It is our behavior, not our identity, that creates the conditions for the spread of HIV. But the DL phenomenon may discourage women from exercising personal autonomy. To the extent that we can point our fingers at someone else, we implicitly excuse ourselves from responsibility.

The *New York Times Magazine* article may help us to understand the dilemma. The introduction to the piece set the tone for the article to follow. "To their wives, they're straight. To the men they have sex with, they're forging an exuberant new identity. To the gay world, they're kidding themselves. To health officials, they're spreading AIDS throughout the black community."

Is it possible that they're all wrong? Maybe some of the wives just don't want to deal with the reality of their husbands' sexuality. Maybe men on the down low don't think they're "forging an exuberant new identity." Maybe some gay men should not be so upset about the down low when they're busy seeking "masculine" or "straight-acting" men. And maybe men on the down low are not primarily responsible for spreading AIDS in the black community.

We cannot allow the media hysteria about the down low to drive our public policy, and we especially cannot allow that hysteria to misdirect public resources in responding to the larger public health crisis in America. The down low story encourages us to focus our attention on a tiny subpopulation of the black community that is not responsible for the vast majority of black AIDS cases. For the black community to do so would mark a tragic abdication of our responsibility to help all those in need, not just the most sympathetic victims.

One of our biggest obstacles to overcome is our unwillingness to talk candidly about sex. When it comes to sex, we've created a culture of lies. Men on the down low lie about having sex with men. Men who are infected sometimes lie about their HIV status. Some gay and bisexual men lie about their sexual interests. And some women lie to themselves when they know or suspect their men are cheating. What makes us think people are going to suddenly start telling the truth when we start calling them dirty names?

The truth is, we can't deal with the down low until we learn to deal with our hang-ups about sex. Unfortunately, that's not going to happen right away. That's why we have to accept personal responsibility for our behavior. We all know the drill by now. If you have unprotected sexual intercourse without knowing your partner's HIV status, you're putting yourself at risk. Period.

It doesn't matter that your man is "fine." It doesn't matter that he's good in bed. It doesn't matter that he looks like a "real man." Unprotected sex is still risky behavior. If we want to fight the spread of AIDS, we need to understand what we can do to stop it. Men blaming women and women blaming men will not stop the AIDS epidemic. Changing the way we conduct our relationships, on the other hand, can stop the spread of AIDS.

That also means we have to move beyond some of the conspiracy theories. Some of us have speculated that HIV is a biological warfare agent developed in secret laboratories in the 1950s. Others have suggested that AIDS was introduced as a population control measure in the developing world. A few have argued that HIV was specifically designed to wipe out blacks and gays. Those theories may be appropriate for researchers and activists to explore, but they do not change the reality of the AIDS epidemic today. As the activist Tony Wafford told the *Los Angeles Times,* "Too many people are still talking about 'AIDS comes from the white man, AIDS is a gay disease,'" he says. But "the white man ain't in the room with you telling you not to put the condom on," he adds.

Therein lies the challenge. For some reason, we in the black community just can't seem to stay focused about AIDS. First, we denied it affected us. Then, we ignored it because we thought it only affected a few of us. Next, we preached morality because we thought it only affected the ones we didn't like. Then, we tried to figure out which secret laboratory developed it. And, finally, we dramatized it by creating a self-destructive story line about victims and villains. At what point do we just deal with it? That point is now.

No matter how good it makes us feel to lash out at the men on the down low, that is not the answer. Demonizing men on the down low as "villains" will not make them straight, and stereotyping women as "victims" will not keep them safe. AIDS is a huge problem in our community. It doesn't matter how we got here. We're here. It doesn't matter how anyone got it. They have it. It doesn't matter who's to blame. It matters how we respond to it. The biggest lie of the down low is not just the lie that men tell their women. The biggest lie is the lie we tell ourselves about AIDS—that it's somebody else's responsibility.

CHAPTER 8
Seven Deadly Lies and Other Myths

THE FORMER SURGEON General Joycelyn Elders once said that 90 percent of American men report that they masturbate on a regular basis, and 70 percent of American women report that they masturbate regularly. The rest, she said, lie.

Elders was joking, of course, but the truth about sex is no joke. People lie about sex every day. We lie about who we have it with, who we want to have it with, and how often we have it. Some of us lie to our spouses, our lovers, our friends, and even our doctors about sex. Lying about sex is to be expected in a culture where many of us have been conditioned to believe that sex is dirty and wrong. But lying about sex can still have harmful consequences, and believing the lies can be just as dangerous.

When it comes to lies, the down low is second to none in the number it generates. First, there is the lie that men and women on the down low tell themselves about who they are. Then, there is the lie they tell their partners about who they are. But that is not where the lying ends. There is also the lie we use to convince ourselves that we are not at risk. There is the lie that enables us to deny our own complicity in our risk. And there is the lie that precludes us from accepting personal responsibility for our behavior. The down low is filled with lies, myths, and contradictions, but it is not just the usual suspects who do the lying. Yes, the men and women on the down low are lying, but many of the rest of us are lying as well.

With that in mind, I have put together a list of the seven deadly lies about the down low and thirteen myths that follow. The research is still fluid and not always conclusive, but it does allow us to dispel some of the common myths and lies we've been told about the down low.

Seven Deadly Lies

1. *We all agree on what the down low means.* Not true. The down low means different things to different people. Since its debut in 2001, it has never been universally defined. Some say it refers to men who have sex with men but do not identify as gay, while others say the men must be bisexual and involved with women. On the other hand, some self-acknowledged gay men call themselves "down low" because they perceive it as a stamp of masculinity.

2. *The down low is new.* No. The down low is definitely not new. It's been around since the beginning of time. The only thing that's new is the name we call it. We can find examples in the Bible, in literature, and in popular culture to show that men have been secretly having sex with men for centuries.

3. *The down low is about bisexual men.* Wrong. The down low is about cheating. It doesn't matter if you're straight, gay, bisexual, male, or female. People of all races, genders, and backgrounds cheat. That's what the down low is really about. Bisexual men have become the recent focus of the down low, but the actual term in black popular culture

seems to have originated in the 1990s in reference to black men and women cheating on each other in heterosexual relationships.

4. *The down low is primarily black.* Not by a long shot. When New Jersey's Governor Jim McGreevey came out in August 2004, he laid to rest the lie that black men are the only ones on the down low. White, Hispanic, Latino, Asian-American, Native American, and other men and women have all dabbled on the down low.

5. *The concern about the down low is because of AIDS.* Not exactly. The down low was around long before AIDS and will continue on long after it. Contrary to popular belief, AIDS is not spread by the down low. AIDS is caused by a virus, and those without it can't spread it. Some men on the down low do have AIDS, but so do some heterosexual men who have never been on the down low. Those who are concerned about HIV should be concerned about their own behavior, and not about their partner's identity. Despite the widespread media hype, the down low is not responsible for the AIDS epidemic in the black community.

6. *You can tell if someone is on the down low.* Wrong again. This one seems obvious. If you could tell that someone was on the down low, they wouldn't be very down low. But many of us have invested considerable time and energy in this type of amateur sleuthing. Don't waste your time. There are no signs to tell if someone is on the down low, and don't believe anyone who tells you there are.

7. *Demonizing men on the down low will help solve the problem.* That's not likely. Those who have been lied to by men on the down low have the right to be upset. But demonizing men on the down low as "villains" will not make them

straight, and stereotyping women as "victims" will not make them safe. Vilifying men as demons may actually push them further into denial, and stereotyping women as victims may discourage them from exercising personal responsibility to protect themselves.

Those are the seven big lies about the down low, but there is a lot more to be said. Here are the other little lies that also need to be challenged.

8. *Blacks don't know as much about AIDS as whites do.* Not true. A study conducted by the Kaiser Family Foundation and reported in August 2004 found that blacks may actually know more than whites about HIV prevention. For example, 93 percent of blacks and only 91 percent of whites knew that HIV could be transmitted from unprotected oral sex. Blacks were also more likely than whites to know that a pregnant woman with HIV can take drugs to reduce the risk of her baby becoming infected (48 percent to 42 percent), that one in three people with HIV don't know they're infected (89 percent to 83 percent), and that having another sexually transmitted disease increases a person's risk of getting HIV (54 percent to 36 percent). In addition, almost all black adults (99 percent) knew that HIV could be transmitted by unprotected intercourse or from sharing an IV needle. These statistics contradict the widespread assumption that black HIV infection rates result from lack of education about AIDS.

9. *Blacks are less likely to be tested for HIV.* Not so. Blacks are much more likely than whites to report that they have been tested, according to the August 2004 Kaiser Family

Foundation study. Two-thirds of blacks (67 percent) reported that they had been tested for HIV but less than half of whites (44 percent) reported the same. In fact, blacks were twice as likely as whites to report that they had been tested recently. Only 15 percent of whites reported that they had been tested in the previous 12 months, but 36 percent of blacks reported that they had been tested during the same time period.

10. *More black women are getting AIDS than ever before.* We have to be very careful with this one. In 1991, the CDC reported 11,156 black female AIDS cases. In 2001, the CDC reported just 7,023 such cases. While the percentage of women with AIDS who are black has increased steadily, the percentage of blacks with AIDS who are women has not increased as dramatically. Because of HIV education and the introduction of powerful new drugs in 1996, overall AIDS incidence has decreased significantly since the late 1990s. The problem is that the rates decreased much less significantly for blacks than for whites. Thus, black women make up an increasing share of overall female AIDS cases because the number of white females with AIDS has dropped sharply.

11. *Black women make up two-thirds of all new AIDS cases.* Not true. This figure has gotten a lot of play since the publication of J. L. King's book, *On The Down Low.* Fortunately for black women, it's not true. Black women actually make up 18 percent of all new AIDS cases, not 68 percent. The confusion comes when people misinterpret CDC data. Black women are grossly overrepresented among *female* AIDS cases, but they have never been even close to a majority of *all* AIDS cases. Nor are black women the

majority of *black* AIDS cases. In 2001, for example, there were almost twice as many black men diagnosed with AIDS as black women.

12. *Black women are the fastest growing group for HIV.* Not according to the CDC. Commentators often claim that black women are the fastest growing risk group for HIV, but the CDC has never made that claim. In fact, the information available during the down low media crazy seemed to contradict that claim. In November 2003, the CDC reported that "the number of new HIV diagnoses did not change significantly during 1999–2002 among females." Nor did it change among African Americans. "No significant changes were observed for non-Hispanic blacks" during this time period, the CDC reported. That was exactly the time period involved in the down low media hype, but there was no significant change in HIV infections for blacks or for women.

13. *Black women who become infected tend to be in mongamous relationships.* Not necessarily. A February 2001 study of 441 blacks in North Carolina found high levels of "concurrent sexual partnerships" among blacks, and especially among those who were HIV positive. The term "concurrent sexual partnership" refers to sexual activity outside of a relationship. Involvement in concurrent partnerships was "particularly high among those with recently reported heterosexually transmitted HIV." In addition, a December 2003 study of 5,156 HIV-positive MSM found only 12 percent of bisexuals in the group reported having one female partner and multiple male partners. More than half of bisexuals with multiple male partners also had multiple female partners. According to the researchers, "This

finding contradicts the common belief that bisexual men often are in a committed relationship with a woman and have many male sex partners that she doesn't know about."

14. *Most women don't know their men are cheating on them.* This may be true, but it requires some background information. A 2002 study published by *Psychology Press* looked at sex differences in response to partners' infidelity and found that women sometimes stay with their men even when they know or suspect the men are cheating. One of the dirty little secrets about the down low is not just that men don't tell their female partners about their clandestine affairs. Another secret is that some of the female partners already know *or suspect* the affairs in the first place. In a culture where so-called good men are considered hard to find and keep, some women have been conditioned to take whatever they can get, leaving some men with little incentive to change.

15. *Black men on the down low are more likely to be HIV positive.* Actually, we don't know for sure, but some of the evidence from the CDC seems to contradict this assumption. The reason we don't know for sure is because no research has been published about men on the down low. The closest we have is research about bisexual men or bisexual men who do not disclose their sexual orientation. A 2003 study of 5,589 MSM found that black MSM who do not disclose their sexual orientation were actually more likely to be safe in some of their sexual practices and more likely to be HIV negative than other black MSM. For example, 72 percent of black disclosers reported five or more lifetime partners but only 56 percent of black nondisclosers

reported the same number of sexual partners. Similarly, 41 percent of black disclosers reported unprotected anal intercourse while only 32 percent of black nondisclosers reported the same. But once again, we have to be careful not to draw conclusions either way about men on the DL because the men in the study were not necessarily on the down low.

16. *Black men with AIDS are usually on the down low.* That is definitely not the case. At the end of 2002, the CDC reported that 48 percent of the 111,000 black men living with AIDS were infected by injection drug use or heterosexual contact. Fifty percent of black men with AIDS reported male-to-male sexual contact, and 8 percent of them were also drug users. In the end, only 42 percent of black men with AIDS were exposed solely by male-to-male sexual contact. But even that figure does not tell us the whole story. No doubt, some of those men openly identify their sexual orientation. Others are not involved with women. And of those who are involved with women, given the disproportionate incarceration rates of black men, we can expect that some of them contracted the virus in prison, not on the down low. The truth is that most black men with AIDS are probably not on the down low.

17. *Bisexuals are more likely to engage in unsafe behavior than gay men.* Not necessarily. A 2000 study of 3,492 men who have sex with men (MSM) conducted by Dr. Linda Valleroy of the CDC found that bisexual men were actually less likely than their gay counterparts to have unprotected receptive anal sex. Another study of 2,500 bisexual men conducted by the San Francisco Department of

Health also found that bisexual men may have fewer risk behaviors than exclusively homosexual men. In other words, bisexuals may be less likely to engage in unsafe behavior.

18. *Black bisexuals are more likely than white bisexuals to lie about their bisexuality.* Yes and no. A December 2003 study published in *AIDS CARE* looked at 5,156 men and found that black bisexuals were actually more likely than their white or Hispanic counterparts to identify themselves to researchers as bisexual. However, they did tend to be less honest than others in dealing with their intimate partners.

19. *Black gay and bisexual men don't practice safe sex.* Not true. Despite the widespread belief that black gay and bisexual men are not using condoms, a December 2001 study by Dr. John Peterson indicated that black MSM were actually less likely than other minority MSM to engage in unprotected anal intercourse. Another study in February 2003 confirmed this report and found that black MSM in Los Angeles engaged in less risky behavior than white MSM. That raises a difficult question. If black men are actually safer than their counterparts, why are they more likely to be HIV infected?

The answer may lie in the social networks of black MSM, suggests Dr. John Peterson. Imagine two groups of men and two swimming pools. Now imagine that a certain percentage of men in both groups use an antibacterial agent to prevent them from becoming infected from pool germs. Even if a greater percentage of black men use the protection, black men as a group could be more likely to become infected if the black pool is not as clean from the beginning. Since black MSM tend to socialize with one another in a fairly closed population, this could allow HIV to be spread efficiently within that network. Another possible factor is that young black MSM tend to socialize with older partners, according to the Los Angeles study, and older partners may be more likely to have HIV.

20. *Men on the down low are responsible for the black AIDS epidemic.* We see this claim everywhere. "The Centers for Disease Control and Prevention connected black men on the down low with the rise of HIV infection rates among black women," the *Chicago Sun-Times* reported. But there's one problem. It's not true. The CDC has never made any connection about men on the down low and HIV infections among black women because no research has ever been reported about men on the down low. Once again, it is hard to figure out how to define the men in this group, and it is even harder to find them. Even the widely quoted Young Men's Survey (YMS) did not blame men on the DL for the black AIDS epidemic. That was the study that first launched the down low media frenzy back in February 2001. Three years later, the lead researcher for that study, Dr. Linda Valleroy, told the Fifteenth International AIDS Conference in Bangkok that the YMS study was not about men on the down low. As Dr. David Malebranche has said, "The majority of public health and behavioral research doesn't support the theory of 'Down Low' black men as the 'bridge' of HIV to the general black community."

Those are the facts. They don't answer all the questions but they do raise new questions about what we've been told before. So much of the information we've been told about the AIDS epidemic in the black community is just not accurate. And so much of our hysteria about the down low has been rooted in this misinformation. Now that we know the truth behind the facts and the statistics, it's time to think about the issues that led us here in the first place. It's time to think about sexism, racism, homophobia, and classism. It's time to think about the role of the government, the media, the church, and the family in shaping our values. It's time to deconstruct our perception of morality, masculinity, sex, and relationships.

It's time to move beyond the down low.

CHAPTER 9

Never Underestimate the Power
of a Woman

A FEW YEARS ago, I was invited to speak at the University of California at Santa Cruz. The crowd seemed stiff the night of my speech so I started with a joke. A man goes to a doctor and discovers that he is ill but the doctor cannot figure out the problem, so he recommends a specialist. A few days later, the man and his wife go to the specialist's office. The specialist notices their interaction in the waiting room and summons the couple to talk to him. "I know exactly what the problem is," he announces. "Let me speak to your wife for a minute and I'll be right back," he tells the man. In his office, the doctor tells the wife the secret. "Your husband has a rare case of Affection Deficit Disorder. To save him, you have to attend to his every need for the next year, or he will die. Do you understand what you have to do?" The shocked woman nods, and then returns to the waiting room. The anxious husband runs up to her: "What did the doctor say?" he asks. The woman looks at her husband straight in his eye and says, "You're gonna die."

A few members of the audience laughed at the joke while one or two others chuckled or smiled. But most of the audience reacted with stony silence. I tried to explain the point of the joke. It's always a bad sign if you have to explain the point of your joke. Anyway, I told the audience, "The point is this. Knowing the right thing to do is not the same as doing it. In this case, even knowing the right thing to do, the wife was unable to help her husband. And similarly," I said, "knowing the right thing to do is not the same as doing it when we talk about public policy."

I thought the joke was a lighthearted but clever segue to discuss more serious issues, but I completely misread the audience. Before I could even finish my speech, a woman's hand shot up from the crowd. "Are you saying that a woman's job is just to attend to her husband's needs?" she asked. "No, not at all. I was just trying to tell a joke to get the crowd warmed up." Silence.

I continued cautiously. "Regardless of whether it's the husband or the wife, if you assume that a spouse's role is to take care of a partner in sickness or health, then knowing that and doing that are two different things," I said. More silence. I thought about how to dig my way out of the hole but decided to give up instead. Knowing the right thing to do is not the same as doing it.

Despite the criticism that day, I considered telling the joke again a few months later at another speech. This time, it was World AIDS Day, and the stakes were higher. World AIDS Day takes place every year on December 1 to remind us of the millions of lives lost to the disease and to encourage us to continue the struggle. I did not want to minimize the real-life disease that is AIDS with the fictitious "disorder" I had created for my joke, so I knew to tread carefully. An offensive speech would have alienated the audience on what was supposed to be a special day, but a dry speech about statistics would have bored the audience and motivated no one. There had to be a balance, but it was going to be a difficult decision. A high school teacher once told me, "When in doubt, do without." That seemed like a wise strategy for the occasion, but another teacher once told me that "nothing worthwhile is accomplished without risk." I weighed the options. If it worked, the speech would be a hit, and the audience would be energized. If it failed, I would never be asked to speak there again.

The host started the program by introducing two speakers who were living with AIDS and one speaker who had lost a family member to AIDS. Then, it was my turn to deliver the keynote address. With the familiar red AIDS ribbon fastened to the lapel of my suit jacket, I walked confidently to the podium and thanked the host for inviting me. I was still not sure if I should tell the joke, so I spent a few moments praising the institution for holding the event. With no more time to stall, I finally started the speech. "A man goes to a doctor," I said. And from there, it was too late to stop. The audience looked perplexed. Was this a serious story or a warm-up joke for the speech? A few eyeballs darted back and forth to gauge the reaction from the other audience members, and then a smile broke out in the middle of the story. By the time I reached the scene with the husband and the wife, the audience members were eagerly waiting for the funny part. I plunged forward with the punchline. "You're gonna die," I said. And almost everyone in the crowd seemed to get it.

It was an unusual joke to tell in the middle of an epidemic, but there seemed to be a collective sense of relief and enjoyment in the audience. Some of them might have experienced survivors' guilt after burying their loved ones. Others certainly knew the physical, emotional, and mental challenge involved in taking care of someone who had once been independent. And a few may have wondered how they would have responded if posed with the challenge of a year's worth of intense commitment to a partner. But almost everyone seemed to get the point of the story before I could even explain it. "Knowing the right thing to do is not the same as doing it," I said.

The health professionals in the audience knew the statistics better than I did. They knew that blacks were 12 percent of the U.S. population but made up more than half of all new AIDS cases. They knew that two-thirds of the international AIDS cases were in sub-Saharan Africa. And they knew that many of us had stopped paying attention to AIDS when the new drug treatments were introduced in the late 1990s. Many of the AIDS activists in the room also believed that we needed to develop more "culturally relevant" prevention messages specifically targeted to the communities at greatest risk. But there was another, more controversial question I wanted to raise that day. Were we fighting the wrong battle?

I knew it was politically and statistically incorrect to suggest that the battle against AIDS was over, and that was not my point at all. The fight against AIDS was actually a war, not a battle, I said, and the AIDS community had achieved two major victories in the first twenty years. The first was the development of the highly active antiretroviral therapy (HAART) in 1996. Those powerful new drugs cut the mortality rate in half. In 1995, there were more than 52,000 U.S. deaths related to AIDS, but two years later the number dropped to 22,000 and continued to drop for several years afterward.

The second victory was in the battle for education. By 2001, almost everyone in America knew the basics about HIV and AIDS. Blacks were no exception to this rule. A Kaiser Foundation study released that year showed that 99 percent of African-American adults knew that a person could become infected with HIV by having unprotected intercourse or sharing an IV needle. Ninety-nine percent! The public was already educated. But if everyone knew how to prevent the spread of HIV, why were 40,000 new infections occurring every year? That brings me back to the joke I told at the beginning. The answer to the question was in that joke. *Knowing the right thing to do is not the same as doing it.*

Almost everybody already knew the right thing to do. What they did not know was how to do it. It was not enough to teach people to use condoms. They already knew that. We had to teach people how to talk about condoms. And it was not enough to teach people about clean needles. They knew that too. Instead, we would have to provide those needles and then change our policy to encourage treatment instead of incarceration for drug users. That would require a dramatic shift in thinking, but there was no other choice. We could not moralize our way out of the epidemic. We had to take a radically different approach to the problem.

Like it or not, we have reached a turning point in the battle against AIDS. We can continue along the current path with mostly stable levels of HIV infection that are increasingly concentrated in people of color. Or we can take a different route and expand our approach to the war on AIDS. Either way, we cannot win the war with the equipment that has been provided to us. We need new resources for new challenges. We cannot limit our concern to the surface issues that lead to HIV infection. We—the government, the church, the community, the family—have to deal with the deeper socioeconomic conditions that lead people to engage in risky behavior in the first place. We will not stop the AIDS epidemic by AIDS education alone. Instead, we have to deal with jobs, health care, education, homelessness, poverty, drugs, and the disproportionate incarceration of minorities. We have to deal with racism, sexism, classism, misogyny, homophobia, heterosexism, and cultural imperialism.

We have a new battle to fight. The purpose of this battle is to empower people who have been disenfranchised so that they can begin to protect themselves. Who has time to think about AIDS when you don't have a roof over your head, or food on your table, or diapers for your baby? It's hard to make the right decisions when you don't know where your next check is coming from or don't know how you're going to pay your light bill. Before we can expect people to make healthy decisions, they have to have jobs, health care, education, and homes. They have to be invested in their own future. They have to be convinced that their lives are worth saving. Men who have sex with men need to be empowered to protect themselves in a world that seems to despise them. Poor people need to be empowered in a society that neglects them. Drug users need to be empowered in a culture that criminalizes them. And women need to be empowered in a climate that reduces and objectifies them.

That is the real challenge. It is one thing to know to use a condom, but it is quite another to negotiate the use of a condom in the passion of intimacy. What do you say to your partner? When do you bring it up? Will it ruin the moment? Could it turn off your partner? Those are some of the real questions that women want to know. The Kaiser study that found nearly universal knowledge about the way HIV is spread also found widespread hunger for other information. More than half of African Americans said they needed more information on how to talk to children about AIDS, nearly four in ten wanted to know how to talk to their partner about AIDS and 34 percent wanted more information on how to talk to a doctor about AIDS. Learning to talk about AIDS without fear or embarrassment is the next challenge.

We cannot simply tell women to make sure their male sexual partners wear a condom. We also have to understand women's relationships with their men. Women who are economically dependent on men might make different choices from women who are financially independent. Women in abusive relationships might feel pressured to engage in unprotected intercourse while other women might have more leverage to be able to influence their partners. And women involved with drug users or ex-convicts might make entirely different decisions from the others.

There's another reality that we sometimes gloss over in our discussion about black woman with HIV. Many of the women becoming infected with HIV are poor, and unfortunately, many of them are not practicing safe sex. A study by Professor Ellen Yancey at the Morehouse School of Medicine found that nearly half of low-income African-American women surveyed in Atlanta did not use a condom during any sexual encounter in the previous two months and 60 percent did not know their partner's HIV status. Those are troubling numbers that should lead us to face the larger reality. For many poor black women, HIV is far from their minds. In an interview with the *New York Times,* Hamza Brimah, a physician in Mississippi who specializes in HIV, explained the challenge. "There are issues of looking after children, trying to get insurance, the lack of a father in the home, alcohol [and] drugs. They have so much going on," he said. Many of his patients already knew that HIV could be spread from unprotected heterosexual sex, but many of them placed themselves at risk nonetheless, Dr. Brimah told the *Times.* That seems consistent with the research from the Kaiser Foundation showing that almost all African Americans know how HIV is spread. *But knowing the right thing to do is not the same as doing it.* We cannot fight the AIDS epidemic among black women if we do not deal with the attendant issues of poverty, homelessness, substance abuse, unemployment, access to health care, and lack of education.

A small study published in 2004 by Lisa Bowleg, a psychology professor at the University of Rhode Island, found that young black women expressed a range of different reasons for using and not using condoms. The results, published in the *Psychology of Women Quarterly,* found that issues other than HIV prevention affected women's decisions about using condoms. Infidelity was one such issue. At least one woman said she used condoms as punishment, mostly on days when she thought her man was with another woman. Some women simply did not like the feeling of condoms during sex. Even some of the women at high risk for HIV did not like to use condoms. Some stopped using condoms after they got tested for HIV, while some wanted to use condoms at the beginning of the relationship but not throughout. The results of the study seem to contradict the assumption that all women want to use condoms until their men persuade them not to do so. Yes, that often happens, but it's not always the case, and our approach to HIV prevention has to go beyond the stereotype that men alone reject condoms and understand that many women do not like condoms either.

The study also noted that African-American women often deal with something other researchers called "psychological androgyny." According to Merriam Webster's Collegiate Dictionary, things that are androgynous are "neither specifically feminine nor masculine," and that definition may also apply to the psychological condition of many African-American women. Long before white women started to enter the work force in droves in the 1970s and 1980s, black women were already working outside their homes to support their families. But black women were also expected to maintain traditional gender roles at home, and this division of labor created added stress in black relationships. In addition, because society limits the options available to black men, African-American women often compensate for racism by building up the men in their community and in their relationships.

I had never heard the term "psychological androgyny" before, but it seemed to make sense to me. I remember thinking about a similar idea during the Clarence Thomas confirmation hearings in October 1991. I was upset that President George H. W. Bush had nominated a conservative black opponent of affirmative action to replace Thurgood Marshall on the U.S. Supreme Court. I was also disappointed with some of the black leaders in the country who chose to remain silent instead of criticizing another African American. As I watched the hearings with my friends from law school, I thought it was obvious that Thomas was lying through his teeth. In my judgment, he had already perjured himself once in his official hearings a month earlier when he denied that he had ever thought about the famous 1973 abortion case *Roe v. Wade* while he was in law school. Here was a man who wanted to sit on the highest court in America, and he had no opinion on the most controversial Supreme Court decision to come down since *Brown v. Board of Education* outlawed racial segregation in schools in 1954. Thomas was at Yale Law School when *Roe* was decided, and he expected us to believe that none of his friends or professors even mentioned what some consider the most divisive case ever to be decided by the U.S. Supreme Court. That had to be a lie, and I felt that if he lied about what he did in law school, he was just as likely to lie about everything else.

When Anita Hill, a law professor and former colleague of Thomas's, came forward to testify in the hearings a month later, she was immediately attacked by the right-wing propaganda machine. They impugned her character, questioned her sexuality, and argued that she had a political axe to grind. And it was not just the Republicans. Mississippi's Democratic Senator Howell Heflin turned to Professor Hill with his thickest southern drawl and asked, "Are you a scorned woman?" Even the question, however innocently intended, was offensive. The attack on Hill seemed patently unfair. Why would she lie about Clarence Thomas? She had little to gain from her testimony and much to lose by speaking out against an influential judge who was likely to become a member of the

Supreme Court. And her testimony was so vivid and detailed that it was hard to imagine how or why she would have fabricated such a startling tale about Thomas. The pubic hair, the Coke can, the porn videos, and all the other elements of sexual harassment she detailed seemed quite real, and Hill seemed extremely credible and almost reluctant to raise the issues. She had not sought the limelight; it was brought to her.

The anti-Hill forces did their best to portray Professor Hill as the perpetrator and Thomas as the victim. In denying Professor Hill's allegations, Thomas even called the hearings "a high-tech lynching for uppity blacks who in any way deign to think for themselves." The same man who said we should move beyond race was suddenly willing to play the race card when it suited his personal interests. It sickened me, and I thought it was an obvious ploy, even though it would probably work to pacify guilty whites who were too afraid to challenge a black Republican on his own racial hypocrisy. But in black America, I thought Thomas's ploy would backfire. Apparently, I thought wrong.

A few days after Anita Hill testified, I took a trip to St. Louis to visit my grandmother. Exhausted from class, I sat in the den and watched television for much of the time I was in her house. My grandmother walked in one afternoon just as I flipped to a news channel that was covering the Thomas hearings. She glanced at the screen, shook her head at the image of Anita Hill, and then shocked me with her statement. "I wish that woman would stop lying on that man," she said.

Before I could even register what she had said, she walked off to another room. I followed her to continue the conversation. My grandmother had never been old-fashioned. She was active in Democratic Party politics and had run for local office once herself. She was a strong woman who spent her life working for the federal government and always had a job, even after she retired. Outside of politics, she kept herself busy as an member of the local and national Daughters of Isis and Delta Sigma Theta sorority and was an active member of her church. My grandmother had always been outspoken and independent, so I was shocked to hear her comments about Anita Hill. But as I listened to her explain, I definitely understood the dual role that strong black women play in black families all the time. The black woman, especially in my grandmother's generation, was expected to be a co-provider, but she was always taught that the black man is the cornerstone of the family and the community. When a strong black man gets a good job, a black woman was not supposed to tear him down. She was supposed to support him. That was my grandmother's way of thinking, and it made perfect sense for her and her generation.

But it did not stop with my grandmother's generation. It continues even today. My mother is another strong, outspoken black woman, and she too spent her life working for the federal government. A talented singer and gifted pianist, she was told that a woman's role is to find a husband, not to nurture her own interests. Like many of the women in my family, she was taught to balance a work role outside the house with a traditional gender role at home. But that experience seems common today. Women of all colors develop their careers and simultaneously help run their families. The feminist movement and the women's liberation movement opened up opportunities for millions of women to join the workforce. Naturally, then, white women and other women should experience the same conflict of emotions.

What's different about black women is that their husbands (usually black men) have been disempowered by the racial prejudice in society, while white women have husbands (usually white men) who have been the greatest beneficiaries of America's prejudice. Thus, black women often feel the need to build up their black men who have already been beaten down by the world. In a culture that attempts to emasculate black men in so many ways, the black woman can provide a sanctuary where the male figure can be the man of the house. Professor Bowleg speculates that some black women may "allow men to control some aspects of relationships as a way to compensate" for other things the men may not be able to bring to the table.

Of course, not all black women think this way, but we still have to understand the connection between our cultural norms and our sexual choices. Our understanding of what is romantic may complicate the problem. Traditional images of male-female romance envision a passive woman, and a strong man who sweeps her off her feet. But according to some researchers, this Prince Charming idea of romance may actually discourage women from playing an active role in generating a dialogue about safe sex. If you believe that the man should be the one to initiate sex, you may also believe that the man should be the one to initiate *safe sex*, making it less likely that the woman will raise the issue of condoms. When you add the concerns of many black women about the lack of suitable black male partners, you can understand why some women may be reluctant to give up on a good man. One woman in the Bowleg study put it this way: "If I want a serious relationship and he is a professional and I would like to be with a professional . . . well there are certain things that I'm going to have to actually be a little more lenient about." Another woman described her man as "completely crazy," but at the same time she admitted "no matter what he did I found a way to deal with it and put it into perspective."

The most troubling aspect of the Bowleg research was that many women described infidelity as the norm in male-female relationships. Several women in the study were willing to tolerate infidelity, and some seemed to think that cheating was to be expected by both partners in a relationship. More than half of the women in the focus group suspected their partners had other sexual partners. But the women were not just victims sitting at home waiting for their men. More than half of the women themselves also reported having other sexual partners.

Yes it's true. Sometimes women cheat on their partners too. We spend a lot of time analyzing male infidelity but we often neglect the fact that women sometimes do the same thing. In fact, a survey of 8,000 women in the October 2004 issue of *Ebony* magazine found that 48 percent of women were "very concerned" about "brothers on the down low," but almost the same percentage of women (44 percent) admitted they too had cheated on their partners. And those are just the ones who admitted it. It seems that both male and female infidelity are far more common in our relationships than we like to acknowledge.

Perhaps that explains why women sometimes continue in relationships where they suspect or know their partner is cheating. It is difficult to question someone else's behavior when you are doing the same thing. Professor Bowleg reported that not one of the women in her focus group said she had ended a relationship with a cheating partner. That observation seems consistent with other research that shows women of all races often stay with men who they know are cheating on them. For example, in a study published in 2002 called "Forgiveness or breakup," Professor Todd Shackelford of Florida Atlantic University and two other researchers found that women tend to be more upset about "emotional infidelity" than about "sexual infidelity." Similarly, women were much less likely than men to end a relationship because of "sexual infidelity."

Remember the Salt-N-Pepa song "Whatta Man" from 1993? The female rap artist seems ready to apologize for her man's infidelity in that familiar verse about the down low: "Although most men are hos / He flows on the down low / Cuz I never heard about him with another girl." Truth be told, many of us—male and female, regardless of sexual orientation—have a "don't ask, don't tell" policy about dating and relationships. What we don't know can't hurt us, many of us think, but that assumption is not necessarily true. A woman in the Bowleg study provides an example of the risk. She said she suspected her partner of eight years was having unprotected sex with men and women, but she was willing to tolerate it "as long as he just don't flaunt it in my face [and] . . . don't give me no sexual diseases or anything." That's a dangerous perspective to take. If you wait until your man brings home a sexually transmitted disease before you question his infidelity, you may be putting your health at risk.

With all the recent hype about the down low, some black women may even be thrilled to find a man who cheats with a woman instead of a man. That's a big mistake. HIV is not spread by identity, it's spread by behavior. A completely straight man can give you HIV, but a down low man who has sex with men may not. It all depends on which one has HIV, not on the man's identity.

There's another reason for concern. If your man cheats on you with women, he may also cheat on you with men. We have this perception that men on the down low tend to have one steady female partner and multiple male sex partners. There's no evidence to support that perception, and some evidence actually contradicts it. For example, a December 2003 study in Michigan by the researcher J. P. Montgomery looked at 3,000 women and more than 5,000 men who have sex with men. The study found more than half of bisexual men with multiple male partners also had multiple female partners. Only 12 percent of bisexual men reported having one female partner and multiple male partners. What does this mean? To put it more bluntly, the men who cheat with other men may also be cheating with other women. A cheater is a cheater, and a ladies' man may also be a man's man. While many women have been taught not to confront a man or end a relationship because of a man's infidelity with another woman, that lesson may be a big problem. If you don't pay attention when your man is cheating with women, don't be surprised to find your man is cheating with men. And even if your man is only cheating with women, don't be surprised if he brings home HIV or some other STD from other women.

Let's be honest. Some women enter into relationships where they know their partner is sleeping with other women. That is a choice for women to make, but if you make that choice and also choose to have unprotected sex with your partner, you are putting yourself in danger. You cannot blame your partner for a risk you knowingly accept. And you cannot and should not assume that it is safe to have unprotected sex with your man just because you know, or think you know, that he is heterosexual. Women need to be educated, empowered, and encouraged to stand up for themselves. Pointing fingers at men on the down low is an easy way to take the finger of responsibility away from ourselves, but it does not change that fact that we are individually responsible for our own health and safety.

Unfortunately, a lot of the dialogue we have heard about the down low is based on misinformation and fear. That path will not lead toward a solution. Our solutions have to be based on real facts and information, even if that information challenges our stereotypical assumptions about gender.

Fortunately, there are some constructive steps we can take to move beyond the sensationalism of the down low and deal with the real issues. Our solutions to the AIDS epidemic among black women have to be understood in a comprehensive context, says Professor Bowleg. "Comprehensive interventions that address a variety of aspects of African American women's lives (e.g., employment, relationships, education, etc.) may prove more effective than those that focus solely on HIV, particularly when other life realities supersede concerns about HIV," she writes. That means we have to change the way we sometimes structure our relationships. We have to encourage black women to exercise personal responsibility to protect themselves. We need to communicate a new message. It is okay to trust your partner, but your partner should also trust you. If you want to use protection or want to be tested, a good man, a "real" good man will want you to do so, too.

We also have to change the culture of finding partners. Many black women have been conditioned to settle for a halfway decent man instead of waiting for a good man. Many are simply tired of waiting. AIDS organizations, women's groups, sororities, churches, and other organizations need to provide safe sex counseling, support groups, and role-playing models to teach women how to have these difficult conversations.

One of the most important things we need to do is to destigmatize homosexuality in our families and our communities. I've heard scores of black women complain about the no-good, low-down, two-timing knucklehead "bisexual" men who can't make up their minds and end up ruining the lives of black women. That's a fair complaint, but let's understand how to address the matter. Many of these men have been pressured into heterosexual relationships that they know are not sincere. Where does that pressure come from? From us. They get pressure from their parents, their aunts, their uncles, their godparents, their siblings, their friends, and their peers. They get this same message from their churches, their schools, the movies they see and the television shows they watch. Even the comedians on BET's *Comic View* have an impact. We all know the comedians who tell the funny little fag jokes that we laugh about. But while we're laughing, the man in the third row who is struggling with his sexuality decides that he cannot be accepted even among his own people, the same people he expected to be there for him in a world full of racial hatred.

We may wonder where these men get off by endangering the lives of women, but we should also stop to think about the ways in which we contribute to our own oppression by participating in a culture that drives these men underground. If we do not want so many men to be on the down low, then we need to stop helping to push them there in the first place. We need to challenge the homophobia in our own lives, in our families, in our churches, and in our social settings. If we participate in this homophobia or fail to challenge it, we are part of the very problem we supposedly seek to end.

At least some comedians seem to understand this problem. Interviewed by *POZ* magazine, an AIDS-themed publication, the comedian Mo'Nique was wise enough to explain why down low men exist in the first place. "They're on the down low because nobody's talking to them," she said. "We can't deal with the honesty. We want to be lied to."

Destigmatizing homosexuality and changing cultural norms about relationships will not happen overnight, but fortunately there are little things that women can do that can protect their lives and make a huge difference about AIDS and the down low. But we also have to understand that AIDS is a disease of opportunity. HIV is a virus that is spread by behavior, not by lifestyle. The most common and dangerous behavior for the spread of HIV is unprotected intercourse. So here are five things you can begin to do right now.

First, talk to your partner about safe sex. Let your partner know that protection is important to you. This is usually easier to do at the beginning of a relationship than after a pattern of unprotected intimacy has already been established. But even after the relationship has begun, you still have power. Don't give it away if you don't want to, and don't be manipulated by a partner who tries to use your suggestion against you.

Second, go to the drugstore and buy condoms. Many AIDS organizations and community groups supply condoms for free, so you don't even have to spend the money if you don't have it. Once you have condoms, carry a couple with you at all times. Put them in a secure part of your purse if you need to, but always keep them on you. One of the main reasons men and women don't use condoms is because they don't have them at the point of intimacy. You can eliminate that excuse by carrying your own.

Third, use the condoms. Don't use them only when you think a man might be HIV positive or might be on the down low. You have no way of knowing that, and your life is too important to risk on a gamble. One rule of thumb is to assume that everyone you sleep with is HIV positive and act accordingly. It might seem overly cautious, but the rule actually does make some sense. If you ask your partner about his HIV status, how many men do you think are really going to tell you that they are HIV positive? Some may, while others won't. But why should you have to ask? If they're willing to have unprotected sex with you without volunteering that information, that's a bad sign.

There is also another reason to use this rule of thumb. Many men simply don't know their HIV status. A 2001 study of young men who have sex with men found that only 29 percent of those who were HIV positive knew they were infected. If you rely on your partner's word, you're taking a risk. Your partner may tell you what he thinks is the truth, but your partner may not know the real truth. That doesn't mean your partner lied to you. It means he just did not know. But which is most threatening—an honest partner who infects you without knowing it or a dishonest partner who does not infect you because you use protection?

Every time you have sex with someone without a condom and you don't know his HIV status, you put your life at risk. Every time! It doesn't matter what your partner looks like, how healthy he appears, or what his sexual orientation may be. Your man may be straight as an arrow, but he could still carry HIV, or your man may be on the down low and he may not have HIV. We have to let go of the down low thing. It is not the answer.

Phill Wilson of the Black AIDS Institute gives us a simple reminder. It takes two people to spread HIV, he says, but it only takes one person to stop it.

Fourth, get tested with your partner before you have unprotected intercourse. Using a condom is an effective strategy for single women who do not want to become pregnant, but married women often face a different set of challenges. Once you get to the point where you are ready to have unprotected sex, then both of you should go get tested together. If you both test negative, you can feel some sense of safety before you begin unprotected intercourse, but you should know that HIV tests do not always detect recent infections, so you may want to wait awhile and get tested again to be sure that nothing has changed.

Fifth, get tested regularly. Remember, it takes less than a minute to become HIV infected. Although you may begin your relationship with both partners testing negative, one partner could easily acquire HIV later in the relationship. An HIV test only measures one point in time. It does not give you or your partner lifetime immunity against future infection. So get tested again. Make an annual event out of HIV testing. You might even pick a date and get tested every year on that date with your partner. Regular testing is important to detect the virus before it progresses to an advanced stage. HIV is more likely to be treatable if it is detected early. It is also important to be tested if you become pregnant. Even if you and your partner test positive, you can still take drugs that can significantly reduce the risk of infecting your baby.

Fortunately, many black women are already taking a stand. They are moving beyond the fear and moving toward positive solutions in their own lives. Many of them have found good men by refusing to accept the behavior of the men who do not meet their standards. In Professor Bowleg's research, all the women who refused to tolerate infidelity in their relationships were also involved in relationships with "emotionally invested partners." That can make a big difference.

All women have a right to expect the men in their lives to treat them with respect, and women have the responsibility to make sure that they set the standards for their relationships. One woman in Professor Bowleg's study told her partner that she would leave him if she caught him cheating. Both partners knew the expectations of the relationship. Another woman told herself what she would do in that situation. "I know that I'm a strong person and I love myself," she said. "So I know that if anything came up that would compromise the relationship as far as breaking up, I don't mind being alone because I've been alone."

That message reminds me of the lyrics from an old Whitney Houston song. "I'd rather be alone than unhappy," Houston sang, but most of us would rather we didn't have to make that choice. That is why we search to find a way to balance our desire for love and intimacy with our need to maintain respect for ourselves and our integrity. Writing in *Ebony* magazine in April 1996, Nicole Walker, then a junior at Northwestern University, warned black women not to lock themselves in what she called "emotional prisons." In a commentary on the 1995 film *Waiting to Exhale,* Walker encouraged women to reject the "Prince Charming fallacy" and instead find true peace and happiness inside themselves. "We are ready to stop giving men the burden of making our lives complete," she wrote. "We are ready to be the authors of our own joy and serenity. We are ready to live our lives for ourselves. We are ready to exhale."

CHAPTER 10

Black Men: Married, in Jail, or Gay?

THEY SAY A good black man is hard to find. "All the black men are either married, in jail, or gay," I've been told. Many of us who are black men have heard this complaint over and over. We've heard it so many times that we have begun to believe it and repeat it. But is it true?

From a casual observer's perspective, it certainly looks like the odds are not good for black women hoping to find a black male partner. It seems a new report is issued every month that confirms the plight of the black man. We've all heard the bad news.

From the criminal justice system, a study by the Justice Policy Institute showed there were more black men incarcerated than in college. A different study from the American Sociological Association found more young black men have done time than have served in the military or earned a college degree. And a Justice Department study found more than 12 percent of black men in their twenties and early thirties were in prison or jail in 2002.

In terms of the economy, nearly half of all black men in New York City between the ages of sixteen and sixty-four were not working in 2002, according to an organization called the Community Service Society. Another study found that one of every four black men in the United States was idle all year long in 2002, twice the rate for white and Hispanic males.

On the health care front, AIDS is the leading cause of death for black men between the ages of 25 and 44. Black men born in 1999 have a life expectancy of just 67.8 years, while black women and white men born the same year can expect to live about 75 years.

The statistics around education are no brighter. More black women than black men have earned a bachelor's degree, according to the Census Bureau. The college graduation rate of black men is lower than that of any other group. Only 35 percent of black men who entered college in 1996 graduated within six years, compared with 59 percent of white men and 45 percent of black women. Even in college enrollment, only 37 percent of eligible black men are enrolled, compared with 42 percent of black women.

To hear the barrage of statistics, it seems as though we've created a culture that robs black women of equal partners for relationships just at the time when more black women are going to college and becoming professionals. And for those without a college background, the disparity seems even worse. The employment rate for young black men with a high school education or less has dropped from 62 percent in 1982 to 52 percent in 2002, according to a study from the Georgetown Public Policy Institute. In contrast, the employment rate for young black women with the same background rose from 37 to 53 percent in the 1990s.

Is the situation really that grim for black men? It certainly seems that way to the media, and also to some black women.

You can read about it on the Internet. A woman on SistaPower.com writes: "I find it very hard to find a good black man who is a professional, down to earth, loving and kind, exciting, who secretly gets my engines going. I am an attractive black woman in my 40's and I am smart, [I have a] good job, my own car and place, nice shape and lovely personality. But when I do meet a professional black man he just wants to have fun and kick it. (Sex) No type of meaningful relationship, and I am not having it. I am tired of games, and drama. The other men are drug addicts, jailbirds, or down low brothers. Now I know there has to be the other good ones out there, right? I am not giving up on men."

We see a similar story in the newspapers, on the radio, and on television. In addition to all the negative statistics, we also hear a few names over and over. O. J. Simpson, Michael Jackson, R. Kelly, Kobe Bryant, John Lee Malvo, John Allen Muhammad, and Jayson Blair have practically moved into our living rooms for the evening news. It seems like the only time black men make the news these days is when we're accused of violence or deception.

So let's look at the question. Are most black men really married, in jail, or gay?

Let's start with marriage. The percentage of black men age fifteen and older who are married dropped from 64 percent in 1950 to 42.8 percent in 2000, according to the Joint Center for Political and Economic Studies. That is a dramatic reduction in the number of married black men, but that is exactly the point. For better or worse, the rumor that the "good black men" are already taken may not be true. If less than half of black men are married, that means more than half of black men are still available. The Census Bureau confirms this conclusion. In 2001, 5.1 million black men over 18 were married, leaving 5.7 million black men who were still available.

Are black men in jail? In 2002, there were 819,000 black men in jail or prison, and 73 percent of them were in their twenties and thirties, the prime age for dating and marriage. That's an extraordinarily high number. Twelve percent of black males in their twenties or early thirties were in jail. But as shocking as that number is, we have to remember that 88 percent of young black men were not in jail. So when we subtract the 819,000 incarcerated black men from the 5.7 million left after marriage, we still have about 4.9 million black men available.

Well, are they gay? There's no way to answer this question for sure, but it does seem unlikely that most of the black men who are not married or in jail would be gay. The U.S. Census Bureau does not measure the number of black gay men. Nor does the CDC. Even if they tried, it's unlikely that they could identify and record the thousands of black gay and bisexual men who may not want to identify their sexual orientation to the U.S. government. We do know there were 10.8 million adult black men listed in the the 2002 U.S. Census data. If we use the widely quoted (but just as widely discredited) assumption that 10 percent of the male population is homosexual, that would give us a little more than 1 million black gay and bisexual men. And when we subtract the 1 million black gay and bisexual men from the number left after incarceration, we still have more than 3.8 million straight black men who are available.

Perhaps those straight men are involved with white women. After all, the number of black men with white wives more than doubled from 1980 to 2002. In 1980, there were 122,000 such couples, but by 2002 there were 279,000. That is a huge increase, but it only accounts for 2.6 percent of the 11 million adult black men in the United States. And since the men who are married to white women are already included in the overall number of black men who are married, there's nothing left to subtract here. That means there were 3.8 million single, potentially eligible African-American men in 2002.

But here's the problem. There were 13.5 million African-American women over the age of 18 in 2002. That's a huge disparity with the 10.8 million black men in that age range. Before we consider who is married, incarcerated, or gay, we have to remember that there were 2.7 million more black women in the population than black men. That is a big part of the problem. Even if every black man in America was single, straight, and not in jail, there would still not be enough for all the black women in the population.

Of the 13.5 million adult black women in America, 5.2 million were married in 2002. Another 3.1 million were widowed or divorced. That leaves more than 5 million black women who have never been married. Some of these women may not want to be married, some may be interested in men of other races, and some may even be homosexual or bisexual. But if you assume that most of these women want to marry black men, then the odds are not good. But again here's the point. The problem is not that black men are married, in jail, or gay. The problem is that there are not enough black men to go around in the first place. The incarceration rates exacerbate the problem more than any other factor, but they are not the cause of the problem itself. Nor should we place the blame on those who are married or gay. If the objective is to encourage black men to be married, we should be grateful for the 5 million black men who are married. And if the objective is to encourage black marriages to endure, we should not try to pressure the black men who might be gay or bisexual into a heterosexual marriage that may not last.

If there are not enough black men for the black women in America, are the available black men really as bad as America seems to think they are? The truth about black men is much more complicated than the statistics we hear all the time on the news. In many ways, black men are in crisis today, but it is precisely because of that crisis that we should recognize the black men who are surviving and succeeding in a world that seems out to get them.

Let's not forget about the black men who have run major companies such as American Express, Fannie Mae, Merrill Lynch, and

AOL Time Warner. And don't neglect to mention the ordinary black men who work hard and stay out of trouble. Everyday, millions of black men go to work, support their families, and obey the law, but don't expect to see that on the news anytime soon. That's why we may need a new standard to measure the performance of black men. Considering all that black men have to overcome, it's actually amazing that we're doing as well as we are.

Black men still have to deal with racism. More than half of all black men report that they have been the victims of racial profiling by police, according to a study conducted in 2001. Given that profiling, it's no wonder that the Justice Department estimates that 30 percent of young black men will end up in jail at some point in their lives. And we're still the most likely *victims* of crime, not just the perpetrators. Young black men ages twelve to nineteen were 25 percent more likely to be victims of crime than whites of the same age group, according to a 1992 study. Considering all that black men go through, maybe we're not doing so badly after all. But when researchers look at our condition, they tend not to look at the unique situation of black men in America. Instead, they often compare black men to black women. That is a fair comparison, but it needs some context. First, as I mentioned earlier, there are far more black women than black men. Second, men and women are different in all races. The vast majority of the people in prison, for example, are men. Even among whites, the white male prison population dwarfs the white female prison population. Men of all races, including whites, have a lower life expectancy than women of the same race. And the population of women of all races outnumbers men of all races. White women also face a shortage of men. In 2002, there were 78 million adult white women and only 73 million adult white men.

But there is another reason for caution with the comparison

between black men and black women. It seems part of the assumption behind the comparison is that black men are falling behind and unable to be the leaders of their families and their communities that they are expected to be. That seems to be a reasonable argument, but it also appears to be based on the paternalistic assumption that men should be better off than women because women cannot take care of themselves. If that assumption is the foundation of our comparison, then we are simply replicating antiquated notions of patriarchy from the majority community and imposing those ideas on the African-American community. To change that pattern, we should not expect black men to do better than black women. Nor should we expect them to do worse. Instead, we should expect both black men and black women to do well.

In some ways, black men are doing relatively well as compared to black women. For example, there seems to be an assumption in the dialogue that black men are not making as much money as our female counterparts. But the truth is that black men still make considerably more money than black women, according to the National Committee on Pay Equity. That is not good news for black women, but it does challenge the notion that black men are falling behind economically. In fact, there has been no dramatic change in the black male-female wage gap in thirty years. But even if black men earn more, they might not have as many job opportunities as black women, so we might expect the unemployment rate to be higher. But the numbers do not support that argument either. From 1980 to 2003, unemployment for black men was not dramatically different from unemployment for black women, according to the U.S. Labor Department. In August 2003, for example, the unemployment rate for black men was 10 percent and the unemployment rate for black women was 10.1 percent.

Black men are doing okay in education too. Black male college enrollment has increased steadily in recent decades. In 1980, less than 8 percent of black men over 25 had completed college, but by 2000 the figure had doubled to more than 16 percent. This is about the same increase for black women (from 8.1 percent to 16.8 percent). And black men have actually done better than black women in high school graduation. In 1980, a slightly larger percentage of black women (51.5) than black men (51.2) graduated from high school, but by 2000 the roles had reversed, as 79.1 percent of black men graduated from high school compared to 78.7 percent of black women.

Even in the criminal justice system, the overwhelming majority of black men will never see the inside of a jail or prison. Remember the study mentioned earlier that said there were more black men in prison than in college? Well, that was very misleading. The reason that imbalance exists is because the authors of the study looked at the black male prison population of all ages instead of the college-aged prison population. In other words, there were more black men in prison because there were more black men in the sampled population, but if you just look at black men between the ages of eighteen and twenty-four, there are actually twice as many black men in college than there are in prison and jail. In 2002, there were 195,500 black men ages 18–24 in prison or jail. However, there were 469,000 black men in this age group who were enrolled in college in 2000.

But for every statistic showing that black men are doing well, someone else can produce another statistic that appears to show the opposite. And some African Americans fear that positive statistics about blacks may be used against us by giving white America an excuse to ignore the continuing racial imbalances in society. That is not my intention. However we choose to measure the success or failure of black men, we have to consider the unique circumstances of being a black man in America. It's the same sentiment reflected in Lorraine Hansberry's classic play *A Raisin in the Sun* when the family matriarch, Lena Younger, admonishes her daughter for criticizing her brother. "When you starts measuring somebody," she says, "measure him right, child, measure him right. Make sure you done taken into account what hills and valleys he come through before he got to wherever he is."

So how do you measure a good black man? Despite some of the imagery in popular culture, black manhood is more than just muscles, guns, sex, sports, and rap. Being a black man has nothing to do with being on the down low, but the down low story is so popular because it confirms our one-dimensional image of black men. The truth, of course, is more complicated. No doubt, we have plenty of issues to deal with as black men. The news media portray us as criminals and thugs, and then our own culture reinforces that image as a legitimate expression of black masculinity. But even if we are not in the dire predicament the media say we are, we are also not where we should be or could be. We still have much more work to do as black men. So here are some constructive steps that we can take to move beyond the down low.

First, we should examine our outdated concepts of masculinity and rethink what is masculine. The down low promoter J. L. King helps us understand the problem. "Some little, dainty-looking guy who is five feet five, weighing a buck twenty-five, can be packing a nine-inch penis. That's power," says King. No it's not. With all due respect to King, our power is not in the size of our dicks, or how well we use them, or how many kids we've made with them. If we see our penis as the sole source of our power, then we should not be surprised by society's attempts to reduce us to one-dimensional hypersexual creatures.

Nor should we judge our masculinity by our physical stature.

King's notion that a man who is five-five and 125 pounds is not masculine without a big dick is itself problematic. The brain, not the dick, is the most powerful organ in our bodies, and we as black men must emphasize mental strength as much as we highlight physical prowess. Perhaps in a premodern era before computers and technology, physical strength was an important measurement of masculinity. And in many neighborhoods today, a boy's physical ability is still the symbol of his maturity. But black men will not succeed in the modern business-oriented world on the basis of our physical power alone.

In fact, popular culture, in quiet complicity with African Americans, has been very successful at perpetuating an idea of physically dominant black men, and that image has traveled all across the globe. I experienced the effect of the stereotype when I visited a souvenir shop in St. Thomas in the Virgin Islands. While my partner Nathan and I were looking for magnets to take back home, we overheard an older white customer in a very loud and long conversation with an Indian store employee. I thought to myself, that poor sales clerk probably wants to do his job but the old guy won't stop talking. But I was wrong.

When we finally picked out our magnets, we took them to the counter to purchase, and the old guy finally stopped talking and walked away. Then the sales clerk asked us if we were basketball players. No, we told him. "Well, you look like ball players," he said. But we're not, we said again.

We had already gotten the basketball player look a few times on the trip. I'm six feet tall, and Nathan is six feet three inches. We were two black guys traveling together in the Caribbean, so we had to be basketball players or brothers. Never mind the fact that we don't look alike and we're not as tall as most professional basketball players. In the eyes of many in the Caribbean, we were athletes.

"Why is it that black American men are so athletic?" the store clerk asked.

I guess he thought he was praising our race, but I had my doubts. I know the secret code that black men are not supposed to challenge the racial stereotypes that confirm our physical superiority and sexual prowess, but I just could not see how that code would help us in this situation.

"Not all black men are athletic," I corrected him, thinking that would do the trick. But again I was wrong.

"Did you see the man who just left?" he asked. Nathan and I nodded. "He used to play basketball with Oscar Robertson, and he said that black men have something in their legs that makes them stronger, faster, and jump higher."

"That's not true," we said.

"But he said it is. He said he's played with several blacks, and that's why you're such good athletes."

"But I'm telling you it's not true," I told him.

"Why would he say that if it's not true? He seems to know what he's talking about."

"But he's wrong," we said. "Are you going to believe him or us? We're black. We know. Jimmy the Greek said the same thing a few years ago and got in trouble for making that remark."

"Then why are so many black athletes dominating sports? Whites can't compete. Indians can't compete. You guys are built differently."

"No, we're not built any differently," I said. "I've studied the issue of race for years, and most scientific evidence shows there are more differences within a race than between the races."

"But he . . ."

"He doesn't know what he's talking about."

"Then why are there so many black kids who go into sports?"

"Many of these kids come from backgrounds where sports are seen as the only way out of the community," Nathan said.

"It's a stereotype," I added. "It's just like the stereotypes about Indians, whatever that is."

"That we're all computer programmers," he said.

"Right, and you're not a computer programmer are you?"

"I am," he said.

I guess you don't have to be a logical thinker to program a computer, I thought to myself. He seemed incapable or unwilling to hear what we were saying.

"We all own businesses," he said. "In fact, most of the businesses on this strip are owned by Indians."

"And that's partly because of economic opportunity," I said. "Many African Americans don't necessarily have the same access to resources that people in your community may have."

"Sports is really a way out for many of the kids in the black community," Nathan said. "That's why they excel at it, because they're driven."

"It's very interesting," he said. "I hadn't thought about that before. Now I have something to think about." He finished the conversation and rang up our orders. "Enjoy St. Thomas," he said as we left the store. But somehow we knew the dialogue was not over. My guess is that the store clerk was not likely to believe us until our words were confirmed to him by an "objective" white source. In his estimation, we were just a couple of black athletes. What did we know?

The widespread perception of black physical and sexual prowess may make us proud as black men, but it does very little to advance a more realistic image of who we are. Now it's time for us to redefine what manhood is all about.

When I was in college, I won an award at the end of my freshman year as the outstanding freshman man in the class. The award was called the William S. Churchill Prize, and I actually thought it was a mistake when I first heard about it. I had done reasonably well my first year but a dismal grade in spring semester Spanish ruined my GPA. I figured the school would take back the award once the Spanish professor reported the final grade, but they never took it back. Instead, I got a cash prize to buy whatever books I wanted through the library. Every book was inscribed with a plaque that defined the purpose of the award. It read very simply. *"Honesty with oneself, fairness toward others, sensitivity to duty and courage in its performance: these qualities make manhood, and on manhood rests the structure of society."*

I was eighteen years old when I first read that inscription, and ever since that time I have used those words to define manhood. The definition applies to men of all races, but black men would do well to adopt that philosophy as our own. If each of us could just apply the four principles in the definition, we would eliminate the down low right away. If we could be honest with ourselves, fair toward others, sensitive to our duties, and courageous in performing those duties, we would have no reason to be on the down low in the first place. We can respond to the down low by creating an environment of honesty among ourselves as black men.

But far beyond the down low, we should remember that honesty, fairness, duty, and courage are important principles for men in any situation. That is what manhood is all about. It's not about how many women we've fucked or how much money we've earned. It's not about how much weight we can bench press or how many free throws we can sink. Manhood is much simpler than that, and much more difficult. It is honesty with ourselves, fairness toward others, sensitivity to duty, and courage in its performance.

Second, we have to practice safe sex. Many of the same rules that apply to women apply to men as well. Talk to your partner about safe sex, get condoms, use them, and get tested regularly. But as men, we have a greater responsibility not to mislead our partners about our sexual orientation or about our HIV status. In male-female relationships, women often look to us to set the tone of the relationship, and men often have more power to determine the nature of the relationship. What will our relationship be like? Will we talk about safe sex or not? Will we use condoms or not? Many women will go along with us if we integrate safe sex as a part of our sexual practice. The study by Professor Lisa Bowleg confirms that "when men initiated condom use at first sex, women readily accepted the use of condoms." One participant in the study described at as "just a thing he does." Even after first sex, "men also controlled current condom use in terms of initiating or refusing condoms, regardless of whether women wanted to use condoms," according to the study.

Every time you have sex with someone without a condom and you don't know their HIV status, you put your life at risk. It doesn't matter if you're having sex with a man or a woman or if you're a top or a bottom, and it doesn't matter what your own HIV status may be. A negative HIV test is not a license to practice unsafe sex. As men, we have great power to make a positive influence on our relationships. But with great power comes great responsibility.

Third, we have to deal with our hangups around homosexuality. In his book *Who's Gonna Take The Weight,* Kevin Powell talks to black men about homophobia. But Powell, a straight black man, explains how he overcame his own biases when he rented an apartment from a landlord who was a middle-aged black gay man. The experience taught him that his homophobia was a misplaced expression of his own weakness as a man. "And this man," Powell writes, "this gay Black man, taught me more lessons about manhood than one would think possible: that one could be a man, be responsible, be kind, be loving, show love, give love, without compromising one's self-worth and dignity."

That's what being a man is all about. It's about responsibility, kindness, love, principle, and dignity. We don't dignify ourselves when we demean others because of their sexual orientation. Those who are comfortable with their own sexuality have no reason to make light of anyone else's sexuality. But those who are uncomfortable with their own sexuality are sometimes the most vocal critics of homosexuality and bisexuality.

The burden to challenge homophobia falls on the shoulders of all black men, regardless of their sexual orientation. Unfortunately, black gay and bisexual men and black men on the down low can be just as homophobic as their heterosexual counterparts. Many of us have sat quietly through homophobic sermons, antigay comedy routines, vicious music lyrics, and offensive conversations with our friends. Many of us are concerned about being typecast as gay if we simply speak in defense of the rights of those who are. Those fears are understandable, but they must be overcome. Being a man is about standing up for what is right, even when you are sometimes afraid to do so. It will not get any easier to stand up until we simply stand up. Society will not change on its own until we begin to change it.

I have been through the experience of overcoming my own fears many times, and I know how difficult it can be, but I also know how empowering it can be. One of those experiences took place in the fall of 1995 when I had just started a job as the executive director of a national black gay organization based in Los Angeles. I asked the men in the office where to get a haircut and they recommended two places in the 'hood. The first, they told me, was closer to the office. The barbers were older and pleasant, but they were not as skilled as the younger barbers at other shops. The second location was a barbershop in South Central that was much more popular but also homophobic, they told me. In the interest of vanity, I decided on the second shop. A good haircut was more important than a good conversation.

I walked into the barbershop and waited patiently while thumbing through some old magazines and watching television. When my turn came about an hour later, I finally sat in the barber's chair. Most of the conversation in the shop that day was about sports, and none of it was homophobic. Except for the long wait at the beginning, the experience at the barbershop was fine, and the haircut was great. The guys must have been mistaken, I thought to myself. To show my appreciation for the barber and to keep me from waiting on my next visit, I gave him a big tip, and he told me to look for him when I returned.

More than a month later, I returned to the same barbershop and sat in the same barber's chair. The barber asked me where I had been, and I told him that I was out of town. I explained that I worked in Los Angeles but I actually lived in Washington, D.C. He seemed interested in my bicoastal living arrangements so he kept talking. "Where do you work?" he asked. For some reason, I wasn't expecting that question. When most people get that question, they can usually answer without telling too much about themselves. For me, it was a little different. My job was a part of my identity, and I was still learning how to talk about that in awkward situations like this one. I decided to simply tell him the truth.

"I work for the National Black Gay and Lesbian Leadership Forum," I said. The barber paused and pulled back his clippers for a moment. I could almost feel the wheels processing in his brain as he prepared his next question. "The National Black what?" he asked. I told him once more. "The National Black Gay and Lesbian Leadership Forum." He turned off the clippers and continued with the questions. "So how did you get that job?" he asked. I took a second to question my decision to return to the same barbershop with the reputation for homophobia, but I mustered up the courage to keep speaking. "I applied for the job, and I got selected," I said, but clearly he was not satisfied with my response. He wanted to know more. He knew that I knew what he wanted, and I knew that he knew that I knew what he wanted. We both danced around the issue for a few moments, and then he finally blurted it out. "So are you gay?"

I know the TV was still on, and the conversations around me were still taking place, but for a brief moment when he asked that question and I prepared to respond, it felt as if the entire barbershop was staring at me and waiting for my reply. Why did I come here? The guys at the office already warned me about this place, and now the barber is standing behind me waiting for my answer. I took a quick breath, and I told him. "Yes, I am."

The barber stopped for a split second, then turned the clippers back on. "That's cool," he said. And he continued cutting my hair. There was no big incident. No drama. No angry confrontation. No preaching. Just a barber and his client having a conversation about the client's job. When he finished the hair cut, I gave him another tip and promised I would come back on my next visit a month later. And I returned as promised. For two years, I continued to patronize the same barber at the same barbershop that everyone had warned me to avoid. And for two years I never heard a homophobic word out of anyone in the shop.

I learned from that experience the importance of standing up for who we are and what we believe. It doesn't matter what your sexual orientation may be. It doesn't matter what people think about you. It matters what you think about yourself. If we expect people to treat us badly, they will. If we expect our communities to forsake us, they will. If we walk around in shame with a chip on our shoulders, someone will try to knock it off. But when we have the courage to be open and honest about who we are, people in our community not only accept us, they respect us more.

One of the main reasons men are on the down low is because many of them do not believe that they can be who they are in a culture where homophobia and heterosexism are widespread. Homophobia exists not just in black America, it's in all of America, but the feeling of hurt can be much more profound when it comes from your own people. Most black men grow up in a world where we are feared, despised, and distrusted. We respond to that environment by creating a safe space of our own, but for those men who are not heterosexual, their sexual orientation can become an obstacle to their full acceptance in their own community. Since they already face prejudice as black men, they are reluctant to acknowledge their sexual orientation and take on even more prejudice because of whom they love.

If we truly hope to break the cycle of the down low, we have to create an environment where men can be free to be who they are, and not just who we expect them to be. Being a black man has nothing to do with your sexual orientation. It has everything to do with your sense of honesty, fairness, duty, and courage. And many of the greatest black men who personify that courage were gay or bisexual themselves.

Civil rights activists, like Bayard Rustin, who organized Dr. King's historic 1963 march on Washington, have helped to motivate us. Soldiers, like Perry Watkins, have defended us. Authors like James Baldwin, Countee Cullen, Alain Locke, Samuel R. Delany, Essex Hemphill, E. Lynn Harris, and James Earl Hardy, have educated and enlightened us. Performers, like Johnny Mathis, Billy Strayhorn, and Alvin Ailey, have inspired and entertained us. Filmmakers, like Paris Barclay, Isaac Julien, and Lee Daniels, have told our stories. Playwrights, like George C. Wolfe, have drama-tized us. Athletes, like the baseball player Glenn Burke, the body-builder Chris Dickerson, and the soccer player Justin Fashanu, have excited us. Politicians, like Ron Oden and Ken Reeves, have led our cities. And ministers, like the Reverend James Cleveland and the Reverend Peter Gomes, have led our congregations.

Black men come in all different shapes, sizes, colors, and back-grounds. We are straight, gay, bisexual, same-gender-loving, ques-tioning, and on the down low. All of us have something to contribute, and we cannot expect to advance as black men if we create a culture that deprives us of the talents, skills, and contribu-tions of some of our very own.

Fourth, let's take control of our image. The playwright and director George C. Wolfe once said, "Anytime anyone comes up with a def-inition of who you are, it has absolutely nothing to do with who you are. It has to do with how they can process in a way that they can feel in command of whatever impact you're having."

So let's tell the truth about who we really are as black men. Most black men are not in jail and not on the down low. Millions of black men are hard-working, law-abiding, tax-paying citizens. We are not all saints, but we are certainly not all criminals either. The mass media have constructed an image of us that reduces black manhood to a cultural commodity to be bought and sold in the marketplace. But we are more than XXXL T-shirts, oversized jeans, and basket-ball jerseys. That is a part of who we are, but it is not all of who we are. And we are more than just rappers and ballplayers too. That is also a part of who we are, but it is not all of who we are.

The problem with many discussions about our image is that we often end up trading one stereotype for another. Some of those who reject the image of black men as pimps and thugs would like to replace it with a sanitized image of black men as lawyers and doctors.

But we don't need censorship to make our point. We need reality. Some black men are doing very well, but too many of us are not. Too many of us are in jail or prison or out of work, but we have to figure out a balanced way to say that without feeding into the stereotype that *all* black men are in jail or prison or out of work.

To do all that will require a delicate balancing act. We cannot ignore the suffering in our community, but we cannot be defined by it either. We must find a way to challenge America's persistent racial barriers without allowing those barriers to paralyze us into inaction. We have to fight against our one-dimensional media identity without fighting against the black men who embrace that identity. We have to create a culture that discourages the dishonesty of the down low without shaming men on the down low into more denial.

It will not be easy work, but we have faced many difficult challenges before. Ten years before I wrote this book, I took part in a defining event that helped to shape the collective sense of possibility for black men. It was the Million Man March. Many of us worried about the exclusionary message in producing an all-male event, and many of us also worried about the exclusion of gay and bisexual men from the podium. But on October 16, 1995, more than a million black men took a leap of faith and came together. We stood on the mall in the nation's capital in all of our beautiful diversity. We were young and old, rich and poor, straight and gay, standing side by side. Men with college degrees marched alongside men without high school diplomas. Black men from the south joined hands with black men from the north, east, and west. It was a day that began with a chilly morning and ended with a balmy afternoon. The police and the media expected violence, but there was none. A million black men came to the nation's capital peacefully to show our unity as a people and to commit ourselves to heal and rebuild and grow. No one had ever seen anything like it, and almost all of us left with a sense of awe and wonder in the possibilities for the future. If we could get a million black men to come together in Washington, we thought, we could do almost anything. We could empty the jails, educate our children, eliminate diseases, inspire our families, rebuild our communities, lead our churches, change our diets, write our own books, produce our own films, create our own music, buy our own homes, and start our own businesses. The opportunities were endless.

Those of us who were there that day promised to go back to our communities and our families and be better men. Some of us did not survive, while others made great strides toward that goal. But all of us knew the challenge would last throughout our lifetimes. As black men, we have always known that we have much more work to do. And we know that we must do it.

That is what being a man is all about.

Chapter 11
Homothugs, Helmets & Hip Hop

LIKE MANY YOUNG men, I was pushed to play sports at a very early age. From the time I entered grade school to the time I graduated from college, I was almost always on a team. In grade school, it was Little League baseball. In high school, it was football, wrestling, cross country, and track. In college, it was track once again. From my experience, I can think of no place in America that is as homophobic and as homoerotic as the sports team locker room.

The sport I know best is track and field. Track has always seemed a very homoerotic sport. Men prance around the track with hip-hugging tights and tiny tank tops that tuck into their tiny shorts. Even as a teenage runner, it seemed to me there were quite a few gay men in the track world, and one of them was on my high school team. If Steve was in any way trying to hide his sexual orientation, I could not tell. It was an open secret on the track team that he was gay. But he had one quality that made him acceptable even to his most homophobic teammates: He was fast. He could outrun anyone on the team, and he helped us win track meets when no one else could. But a few years after high school, a classmate called me with bad news. Steve had passed away. He died of AIDS.

Over the years, I had almost forgotten about Steve and forgotten about the idea of gay athletes. When I ran track in college, there were no openly gay members of our team. A year after I graduated, however, I got a call from a friend that one of our teammates who was still on the team had come out of the closet. That was a bold move. Gay men were not exactly welcome in the locker room of most sports teams at the time. And that was in the late 1980s. Then things started to change. Pushed forward by the impact of the AIDS epidemic, gay men began to play a much more visible role in society in the 1990s. Instead of ignoring the existence of homosexuality, America found itself speculating about gays in the miltary, gay marriage, gays in sports, and gays in hip hop.

By the end of the twentieth century, homosexual and bisexual men seemed to be visible almost everywhere, and yet there were still a few bastions of masculinity that were reluctant to acknowledge the presence of gay men in their midst. Professional sports was one of those places. In a 1998 speech to the Wisconsin legislature, the Green Bay Packers defensive end Reggie White said gay men were "malicious and backstabbing," equated them with "liars" and "cheaters," and blamed homosexuality for the decline of Western civilization. So when the track star Derrick Peterson appeared in the pages of a gay magazine in the summer of 2002, it seemed a breakthrough for gay and bisexual athletes. Peterson, an American champion 800-meter runner, was hailed as the first active black professional athlete to come out of the locker room closet.

Genre magazine, the gay publication that interviewed Peterson, said that his willingness to announce his sexuality would "make an enormous impact on the issue of gays in sports." Outsports.com, a gay Web site, called Peterson a "rare" and "courageous" individual.

The *Daily Pennsylvanian* newspaper described Peterson's "revolutionary" actions as a "lesson in heroism."

When the Peterson story broke, only a handful of black college or professional athletes had come out to the public, and almost all of them suffered through tragedy or controversy. Glenn Burke, the first black professional athlete to come out, was eventually run out of the Los Angeles Dodgers team in 1979. A dozen years later, he was reported to be living on the streets and drug addicted until he died of AIDS in 1995. The British soccer star Justin Fashanu was described as "erratic" after he came out of the closet. He claimed and then retracted a statement that he had had sex with two British cabinet ministers. Accused of sexually assaulting a teenager in Maryland, Fashanu took his own life in 1998. The former New York Giants guard Roy Simmons came out on the *Phil Donahue Show* in 1992 but then disappeared from the public, and had not been heard until he appeared on an ESPN show in 2004. The Stanford football player Dwight Slater came out to his coach and teammates after hearing homophobic conversations that left him feeling depressed. Slater soon quit the team altogether.

Until Peterson's announcement, Chris Dickerson and Kisha Snow provided the only positive examples of coming out experiences for black athletes. But Dickerson, the first black bodybuilder to win the title "Mr. America," came out years after his career had ended, and Snow, the top-ranked female heavyweight boxing contender, later announced that she was engaged to be married to a man.

The negative experiences of black gay and bisexual athletes who did come out made Peterson's disclosure all the more significant. But the story was not the breakthrough it appeared to be. Even in the *Genre* interview, Peterson was very careful about what he said. "One thing I will say for sure [is that] I'm definitely not heterosexual," the magazine quoted him. But Peterson never said he was homosexual or bisexual either. Was Peterson on the down low? It's hard to be on the down low when you're interviewed in a national gay magazine.

When I interviewed Peterson for a magazine article, he denied that he was gay or bisexual and declined to define his sexual orientation. "I don't want to be called something or labeled something that I am not," he said. His comments echoed earlier remarks reported in *Genre,* in which he said, "I hate labels. I don't really care what people think of my sexual orientation. I like men and women."

Irritated by the press, Peterson reserved much of his outrage for the media coverage of his sexuality. Although a friend of Peterson's wrote the *Genre* article, Peterson said he was "very very appalled and upset at being labeled as a gay person in the article." When asked if he was upset at the writer, he acknowledged, "I wasn't so much upset with him, with what he did, I think I was more upset with what people were saying or doing on websites." But Peterson also seemed a bit naïve about the media. "I honestly thought it was just going to be another story . . . that had nothing to do with my sexuality," he said, adding that he expected the story to focus on his "athletic prowess." But why announce your sexual orientation in a story about athletics? "I like to see everyone represented equally," he replied, describing himself as an activist concerned about the underrepresentation of African Americans in the gay media. The comments about his sexuality, he said, were "fabricated by myself."

Derrick Peterson's coming out reversal is complicated and unusual, but in some ways it mirrors the larger problem for black gay and bisexual athletes. Many of these athletes are "following the script that was given to them," according to the author Randy Boyd. "You're black, you're an athlete, you're a Man with a capital M, and this is what you do," he said, describing the script.

Sports plays a unique role in the black community. It provides a social ladder that motivates thousands of young black men, undaunted by the slim odds of professional success, to pick up basketballs and footballs with dreams of future glory. It is a counterweight to racism and white supremacy that instills a sense of pride in many African Americans, as when Jesse Owens won four gold medals at the 1936 Olympics in Hitler's Germany, or when Jackie Robinson passed through baseball's color barrier in 1947, or when Tommie Smith and John Carlos gave the defiant black power salute at the 1968 Mexico City Olympics. In a world where black men are beaten down every day, sports enables black men to establish masculinity. When the all-black men's 4 x 100 meter relay team stripped off their shirts and posed with flexed muscles after winning at the 2000 Olympics, or when the legendary basketball player Wilt Chamberlain boasted that he had slept with 20,000 women in his career, they were demonstrating not their athletic prowess but their perception of their masculinity. In few other public arenas are black men afforded the luxury of creativity and individuality or excused for the excesses of bravado. We see this freedom in the colorful pranks of the Harlem Globetrotters, the artful dancing of the boxer Muhammad Ali, or the fancy footwork of the football player "Neon" Deion Sanders.

Although a few white athletes have revealed their sexual orientation to the public, very few black athletes have taken the same step, leaving many to speculate that it is more difficult for black athletes to come out than it is for whites. If so, black hypermasculinity and homophobia may be to blame. The openly gay track coach Eric Anderson cites the "cool pose," adopted by African-American men as an indication of a "hypermasculine" image that may be "partially based on homophobia" or "hyperheterosexuality."

Despite social changes in recent decades, coming out of the closet is difficult for athletes of all colors. If the issue affected only black athletes, then more white athletes would be out of the closet too. But only a handful of major white athletes have come out, and their stories are not all positive. Greg Louganis only came out after winning the Olympic gold medal in diving. But the openly gay football player Dave Kopay and the baseball player Billy Bean both emphasized how difficult it is for any gay or bisexual athlete to come out in their footsteps. And the tennis players Billie Jean King and Martina Navratilova both lost some support and endorsements after they came out.

But coming out may not be necessary for African-American sports figures. Black athletes have long brought a flamboyant presence to their game. With a name, a style, or a flair, they teased audiences and moved athletics to the edge of acceptable sexual expression. In the 1960s, the pro wrestler Sweet Daddy Siki dyed his hair blond, wore dark sunglasses, and carried a mirror with him into the ring. Georgia Tech's offensive guard Roy Simmons won the nickname "Sugar Bear" a dozen years before he came out of the closet. The Olympic gold medalist Carl Lewis teased his fans in a pair of red stilettos in a famous picture for the photographer Annie Leibovitz in a Pirelli tire ad. "Power is nothing without control," the ad said. The basketball player Dennis Rodman once showed up in a wedding dress as a publicity stunt. And the NFL running back Ricky Williams posed on the cover of a popular sports magazine in a wedding gown as well.

Athletes can get away with some things that other black men, perhaps, cannot do. Magic Johnson of the Los Angeles Lakers and Isaiah Thomas of the Detroit Pistons made history in 1988 when they began kissing each other before their basketball games. When Mark Aguirre was traded from the Dallas Mavericks to the Pistons, he too joined in the kissing game, but virtually no one suggested that any of the three black athletes might be same-gender-loving. On the other hand, Dennis Rodman of the Chicago Bulls acknowledged "many homosexual aspects of sports" in his 1996 memoir, *Bad as I Wanna Be.* "Watch any football game. What's the first thing guys do when they win a big game? They hug each other. What does a baseball manager do when he takes his pitcher out? He takes the ball and pats him on the ass . . . Man hugs man. Man pats man on ass. Man whispers in man's ear and kisses him on the cheek. This is classic homosexual or bisexual behavior," Rodman says.

Rodman became the first active black professional athlete to acknowledge a same-sex attraction in a 1995 *Sports Illustrated* article, where he said he "fantasized" about being with another man. Although he parties at gay clubs, paints his fingernails, colors his hair, and sometimes wears women's clothes, Rodman says he is not homosexual. "I'm not gay," he said in his book. "I would tell you if I was. If I go to a gay bar, that doesn't mean that I want another man to put his tongue down my throat—no. It means I want to be a whole individual." Rodman added, "Mentally, I probably am bisexual."

Even when athletes do engage in homosexual behavior, it does not necessarily mean that they are homosexual. Homosexuality and homoeroticism have played a secret role in sports for decades, but is it not always labeled gay. Phil Petrie was a college athlete at Tennessee State University in the 1950s, and he recalls that "it was common for athletes to, in effect, sell themselves . . . to have sex for men." Petrie, who is married with children, remembered football players who talked about receiving oral sex or "packing shit," but the athletes at the time did not consider their actions to be homosexual. Instead, it was a business transaction between cash-strapped players and men who wanted to have them. "If you have a group of people who are considered desirable, and you live in a capitalistic society, can you get them with money?" Petrie asked. "And the answer is you can get some." It took a kind of cognitive dissonance for some of the straight athletes to engage in homosexual sex without acknowledging what they were actually doing. But it was not uncommon.

In some ways, the pro sports world has been more receptive toward out black athletes than what society expects. Blacks are actually well represented among the relatively few out gay athletes in the top sports. As of 2004, a third of the pro football players (one out of three), half of the pro baseball players (one out of two), and the only pro basketball player to acknowledge a same-sex attraction (Dennis Rodman) were all black. But for every out black athlete, there are two or three examples of athletes who have denied that they are homosexual or bisexual. When the boxer Hasim Rahman accused Lennox Lewis of "gay moves," Lewis, who was thirty-six and still single at the time, responded firmly to London's *Daily Telegraph:* "I am definitely, definitely not gay and never have been." He said, "I love women."

When rumors spread about the Pittsburgh Steelers quarterback Kordell Stewart in 1999, Stewart confronted the rumors in a private locker room session with his teammates. Using graphic descriptions of heterosexual acts he said he enjoyed, Stewart told his teammates, "You'd better not leave your girlfriends around me, because I'm out to prove a point." Three years later, when asked to comment on a rumor about another player, Stewart replied: "I'm a man . . . 110 percent man. . . . My daddy did a wonderful job of raising a man, period, hands down, no more, no less."

When Magic Johnson made his stunning announcement about his HIV status in 1991, a few eyebrows were raised about his sexual behavior as well. To stop the speculation, Johnson quickly arranged an appearance on the *Arsenio Hall Show* the next day and told Hall and the audience exactly what they wanted to hear. "I'm far from being homosexual," he said. "But that's the whole thing. [People] think it can only happen to gay people, and that's so wrong. Even I was naïve to think, 'well it can't happen to me.' Well that's wrong. [For] heterosexuals it's coming fast and we all have to practice safe sex."

Johnson was right about one thing. We all do have to practice safe sex, but at the time there was little evidence that the HIV epidemic was "coming fast" in the heterosexual community, at least not for straight black men. In fact, in the year that Johnson tested positive, only 7 percent of all black male AIDS cases resulted from heterosexual contact. When you exclude sex with injection drug users and with members of other risk groups, the percentage shrinks to less than one-tenth of one percent. Only 383 of the 47,000 black men diagnosed with AIDS in 1991 contracted the virus exclusively from heterosexual sex with no other risk factors. When you consider the likelihood that some of these 383 men lied in reporting their behavior, it makes you realize that AIDS was not a disease that seriously threatened drug-free straight black men in 1991. But Johnson dutifully stayed on message.

Johnson's confirmation of his sexual orientation reminded me of the energy some people spent in proving that the ABC News anchor Max Robinson was straight after he died from AIDS in 1988. After Robinson's death, the author Haki Madhubuti made it clear that Robinson was not gay. "It was [Max's] wish to let people know he died of AIDS and that he did not contract it through the *assumed avenues* of drug use or homosexual activity," Madhubuti wrote. "Max was a woman's man to the bone," he explained. Of course that explanation was possible but highly unlikely. Of the nearly 18,000 black male AIDS cases the CDC reported in 1988, only 40 of them (not 40 percent, but 40) resulted from heterosexual sex with a woman who was not a drug user or a member of some other obvious risk group. Yes, that is not a misprint. Only 40 out of 18,000 cases. That is just two-tenths of 1 percent of all black male

AIDS cases. And again that number is probably inflated because some of the 40 men may have lied about how they contracted the virus. In other words, Max Robinson would have been *extremely* unlucky to have been infected from heterosexual sex with a woman who was not a drug user. It's not impossible, just highly unlikely. But AIDS was still a dirty word in the 1980s and 1990s, and the black community was heavily invested in protecting the reputation of its heroes like Robinson and Johnson. The last thing we needed was another reason to "beat down" a good black man.

If Magic Johnson were gay, it would be his own business. And the sports reporters who know the truth would never reveal his secret, according to some observers who see a conspiracy of silence among reporters, athletes, and teammates. Although the public does not realize that many professional athletes are gay or bisexual, some of those closest to the athletes do know. As with the military, the policy seems to be "don't ask, don't tell." For example, at the 2002 National Basketball Association draft, when Charles Barkley was asked by a television crew if there were any gay players in the NBA, he replied: "I don't kiss and tell."

The truth is that many high-level athletes live in glass closets visible to those around them. The sports columnist Wallace Matthews wrote in *Newsweek* that "it is a common practice among ballplayers who suspect a teammate is gay to confide to friendly reporters, 'He's a little funny,' with a roll of the eyes." Some black professional athletes even take their boyfriends to sporting events, according to the author Randy Boyd. "There are reporters who know this and they don't report about it," he said, in part because they "don't want to breach trust and be thrown out of the inner circle." Boyd likens the situation to the media's relationship with the 1960s Kennedy White House, where some reporters knew of the president's alleged extramarital affairs but never reported on them.

Another sports author told me a "sad story" of a black college basketball player whose boyfriend would sit and watch the games in the stands but could never be recognized. "Everybody knew who the girlfriends were, but nobody knew about the boyfriend," he said. When the games were over, the player would join his teammates and their girlfriends to celebrate, while his own boyfriend would be left to himself. "Teams can deal when a guy has a drug problem or an alcohol problem," says Dennis Rodman, "but not when they find out someone's doing something they don't like in the privacy of their own bedroom. It doesn't make sense."

The same double standards apply to the hypermasculine world of hip hop. Privately, everyone in the industry knows there are gay and bisexual men in the hip hop world, but publicly the industry seems unwilling to admit the presence of homosexuality, except in stereo-typical expressions. Several of the most powerful men in hip hop are gay or bisexual. Some have arranged marriages. Some date women and sleep with men. Some have never really tried to hide. And some just don't talk about it. Almost everybody on the inside knows the deal, but they don't talk about it on the outside.

They don't talk about it because they know the public has its own double standard about homosexuality. If a rapper gets arrested, goes to jail, or spends time in prison, we not only forgive him, we anoint him with praise and street credibility. If he's a drug addict, an alco-holic or a womanizer, the public will barely bat an eyebrow. But if there's even a hint of a rumor that someone is gay, then the public is up in arms. That is a classic double standard. The rap artist 50 Cent becomes a legend for being shot nine times as a drug dealer. The rapper Shyne goes to prison on gun charges and ends up with a record deal behind bars. And R. Kelly's album sales soar after he is busted for allegedly videotaping himself having sex with a minor. We can forgive all that, but we can't forgive an artist for being gay?

But don't think the public isn't interested. No, the public is fascinated by the idea of homosexuality in hip hop. Just ask New York's most popular urban radio and television personality, Wendy Williams. Her audience was once riveted by tales of a gay rapper on the down low. Many of us pretend we don't want to know, but deep down we do. I've seen the interest at events I've attended all across the country.

A few years ago, I walked into a crowded room on the campus of the University of Pennsylvania for a panel discussion. The audience members had taken all the chairs and occupied all the wall space, so my fellow panelists and I stood near the doorway as the organizers rushed in new chairs to accommodate the overflow. I had no idea the audience would be so large, but the topic was hot—"Hip Hop and Homosexuality."

I began by speaking about hip hop artists who have recorded homophobic music. My list included Brand Nubian, Canibus, Common, Cypress Hill, DMX, Eazy E, Eminem, Goodie Mob, Allen Iverson, Ice Cube, Ja Rule, Jay Z, Mase, Mobb Deep, Public Enemy, Snoop Dogg, T.O.K., and 50 Cent.

Then I moved to hip hop artists who have challenged homophobia, and here the list was much shorter. I cited Queen Pen, Queen Latifah, Common (who reformed after dating Erykah Badu), Meshell Ndegeocello, and Will Smith (who played a gay man in the film *Six Degrees of Separation*). The moderator also reminded me of the Disposable Heroes of Hiphoprisy, a hip hop group who recorded an underground CD back in 1992 but hadn't surfaced since.

I was also intrigued by P. Diddy and LL Cool J, both of whom are popular hip hop artists who have rarely, if ever, used antigay lyrics in their music. And I mentioned some openly gay hip hop artists, including Caushun, DeepDickCollective, Dutchboy, Tori Fixx, and Rainbow Flava.

But before you can understand hip hop's role in homophobia, you have to understand hip hop's role in black culture. I am left to wonder if hip hop is still as revolutionary as it once was. The answer depends on how you define hip hop. Hip hop is not all about music, and it is not all about rap music, and even then, not all rap music is homophobic. Gay activists tend to focus on the most offensive artists who record music with homophobic lyrics and neglect to mention the scores of other hip hop artists without homophobic lyrics. Some hip hop is still on the cutting edge, while other hip hop music has become so commercialized that it seems to have lost its soul. It seems that a lot of the radio-friendly hip hop has become more evolutionary than revolutionary as it has evolved deeper and deeper into mainstream culture. Rather than communicate progressive messages that challenge the status quo, too much of mainstream hip hop seems willing to generate materialistic videos, overproduced music, and watered-down messages. How can performers complain about rundown projects in the ghettoes when they're driving their Hummers and their Bentleys and drinking expensive bottles of Cristal?

With jobs disappearing and the country at war, the political side of hip hop re-emerged in 2004. The entertainment mogul Russell Simmons and Dr. Benjamin Chavis at the Hip Hop Summit Action Network have persuaded hip hop artists to encourage young people to vote, and P. Diddy's Citizen Change organization sparked a revolution of politics through fashion with his "Vote or Die" campaign. But I imagine the artists can only go so far. In today's consumer-driven hip hop music culture, it seems the public may not want to hear the most controversial messages, and the most successful artists may not be the right messengers. Meanwhile, a few popular artists record increasingly political music, like Public Enemy's "Son of a Bush," Wyclef Jean's "President," and Eminem's "Mosh."

Maybe we should expect nothing at all from hip hop artists. After all, hip hop music is a business. It's a business that often uses black talent to generate hundreds of millions of dollars for nonblack record companies. And many of the hip hop artists are themselves businesspeople. No matter what they say, you cannot be a practicing gangsta and a successful hip hop artist at the same time.

So who am I to expect more from hip hop than I expect from the rest of the community? It's just entertainment, after all. Snoop Dogg once said he can't knock nobody's hustle, and he was right. It is, after all, a hustle. But it's a hustle that has extremely important consequences on the larger society and on the black community.

Hip hop creates and reinforces exaggerated images of black masculinity and then uses its market power to regulate and restrict our perceptions of black authenticity. Thus, hip hop enables the commercialization and commodification of black culture for nonblack business interests. Those who don't fit the newly popular pimp and thug image can be easily discredited by their own communities, creating a vicious cultural cycle that values style over substance, money over mission, and ignorance over education.

But maybe I was wrong. During the discussion at the University of Pennsylvania, a gay rapper named Caushun said that he did not feel the hip hop music industry is particularly homophobic. He cited his own positive experiences with various industry leaders as an indication that the business may not be what it appears to be from the outside. I don't have the direct experience he does as an artist, but I do think it's important to distinguish between an artist's personal relationships and an executive's institutional obligation. Personally, the music executives may be very friendly, but I think we should demand more than a polite smile and a pat on the back to get new music and new talent released.

Given the trends in our culture, perhaps it is not surprising to find gay artists, producers, musicians, stylists, and song writers in hip hop. But few of these people are out publicly, and many sit by silently while their artists seemingly promote intolerance of gays and lesbians. Although Caushun said that he was not offended by homophobic music lyrics, I was not so sanguine about it. Caushun suggested that we give too much power to words sometimes, and perhaps he was right. Words can only hurt us if we allow them to do so, but that philosophy works best for well-adjusted adults who are secure in their identity. I am not convinced that young people struggling with their identity have the same capacity to dismiss the significance of homophobic lyrics from the mouths of the artists they and their peers most admire. The thirteen-year-old boy or the fifteen-year-old girl who internalizes the animus in the words "fag" or "dyke" may not react as positively as adults do.

Strangely enough, many black adults who are gay or bisexual seem to have made peace with homophobic music. Only a few minutes after watching the drag queen Harmonica Sunbeam host her popular Sunday night variety show at Escuelita's nightclub in New York, black and Latino men were dancing with each other to the familiar melody of Tok's "Chi Chi Man," a reggae song that appears to encourage the burning and killing of gay ("chi chi") men.

From dem a par inna chi chi man car
Blaze di fire mek we bun dem!!!! (Bun dem!!!!)

At a party in Washington a few year ago, black gay men were tapping their feet to the beat of Jay-Z's *Blueprint* CD, in which the artist uses some variation of the word "fag" three times on different songs. And in the same year, black gay men across the country were buying DMX's new *Great Depression* CD, which criticizes "faggots" in the song "Bloodline Anthem."

233

What once seemed unimaginable has now become reality. Mainstream black gay male identity now embraces a popular music and culture that often seems inconsistent with homosexuality. Many of these men have constructed themselves as homothugs, every bit the image of the hard-edged thugs in the rap music videos, indistinguishable from the Tims-wearing men in the 'hood. In fact, many of them have been living the thug life for as long as they have being dealing with men. The two images are perfectly consistent, particularly if you do not identify with the term "gay" or with the popular representation of gayness.

The marriage of hip hop and homosexuality has created a divide in the black community with surprising new fault lines. The new divide is not so much between black homosexuals and heterosexuals as it is among black homosexuals themselves, split along generational, political, and social boundaries. The divide appears more clearly in the music. In the 1980s and early 1990s, house music reigned supreme in black gay nightlife, but by the year 2000 it seemed an ancient religion, practiced primarily by "oldheads" in tight-fitting spandex muscle shirts. Aided by the hypermasculinity of hip hop culture, black homosexual identity in the nineties evolved away from house music and other gay-identified representations of self and instead created the homothug and the down low. Some would argue that black gay and bisexual men were adopting this new thug drag even before their straight counterparts had embraced it.

As a result of the changing norms, many black men have been left to reconcile their sexuality with their newly exaggerated sense of masculinity. At a town meeting of black same-gender-loving men in Washington, one man explained that the homophobic lyrics in some rap songs did not refer to him. Another explained that the lyrics did not offend him. No matter what the explanation, increasing numbers of black same-gender-loving men are making peace with a music and culture that sometimes appears to be anti-homosexual and antibisexual.

Older black gay men sometimes do not understand the younger hip hoppers who adopt the new culture, and yet the embrace of hip hop among black gay youth seems strikingly similar to the embrace of black church culture among many older black gay men who socialize in gay settings on Saturdays and then attend homophobic churches on Sundays. In different times, we find different ways to identify with our communities.

For years, I have struggled to understand how and why same-gender-loving men and women can embrace homophobia in their midst, but I have come to realize the difficulty in separating one's self from the dominant cultural paradigm. Hip hop is the dominant popular culture for millions of Americans. Most of society has embraced hip hop at some level. Everything from soda pop to pop music is being promoted by and influenced by hip hop, and young people from the suburbs to Serbia shake their booties to hip hop beats. If music is truly the universal language, then hip hop is the hot new slang.

I realized just how much the world had changed one day while I was looking for a pair of shorts to wear to the gym. I walked into an Urban Outfitters store where they were playing "Rapper's Delight" on the sound system. Afterward, I walked a few blocks to an Old Navy, where the speakers were blaring the sounds of "Five Minutes of Funk." The white people strolling through the store seemed just as comfortable as I did singing the lyrics of the songs. The cutting-edge music of the 1980s and 1990s had become the commercially marketable sounds of the new generation.

But even the newer, harder music is becoming more widely accepted. I remember, for example, an experience on the campus of Oberlin College in Ohio. I was visiting for a speech and staying at the Oberlin Inn, a quaint little place in a liberal-arts-college town. When I walked down to Main Street for a bite to eat, I heard the familiar thumping of a bass line pumping out hard rap music into the street. It was a sound I had heard many times walking in Harlem and Brooklyn, but I had never expected it in a rural white college town. Still, Oberlin had a small but active black community, so I was not entirely surprised. I heard the word "nigga" punctuated throughout the music from the car speakers, but even that was old news to me by then. It was only when the car drove by and I looked inside that I really understood what was going on. Much to my surprise, the three young men in the car were all white.

That took place years ago, and since that time almost everyone has heard that young white men are the primary consumers of rap music. The bold black masculinity of the early rap artists is no longer as threatening to white America as it was in the 1980s and early 1990s. Even black rage has become a commodity to be bought and sold, played on the latest CD, or worn with the latest urban designer wear. Young white men in the suburbs seem to identify with the culture of rebellion as much as, if not more than, the black and Latino youth in the inner city. No longer subjected to the legacy of derision left by Vanilla Ice, white rap artists like Eminem have become more widely accepted. And so black men have won. The cultural dominance of black manhood has been acknowledged and commercialized. But what exactly have we won?

With whiteness comes privilege in America, and young white men are still afforded the luxury of experimentation rarely granted to African-American youth. The white kid arrested for selling marijuana to his suburban classmates calls his parents, who hire a lawyer to negotiate a deal that spares a conviction, while the black kid could go to prison simply for smoking weed. The young white guy who tries and fails to succeed as an athlete falls back on other opportunities made available to him, while the young black guy falls back onto the streets. And the white youth who spend their college days listening to the hardest of the hard rap artists can still graduate and assimilate into the white elite network, while the young black fans of rap may not find those opportunities.

The problem here is not with hip hop, helmets, or homothugs. The problem is the lack of options available to too many young black men. Black youth in the cities deserve the same opportunities made available to white youth in the suburbs. They deserve the right to make minor mistakes as juveniles that do not jeopardize their future as adults. They deserve the right to receive a quality education that gives them the opportunity to make choices about academics and athletics. They deserve the right to listen to the music of their choice and still find good jobs to support themselves. And they deserve the right to express their manhood and their sexuality with all the diversity of options available to other men in society.

It is unfair to complain about the choices that many young black men make without understanding the limited options that we make available to them. We need to communicate positive messages to them to make healthy choices, but they need to be encouraged to make their own choices, not just the choices that we would make. Even if they never listen to hip hop, pick up a ball, or sleep with a woman, they can still be strong black men. And if they do love hip hop, love to play ball, and love to make love to women, that's not a problem either. Black males do not have to be stereotypes, caricatures, or clones. They do not have to dress a certain way, talk a certain way, or act a certain way. It doesn't matter if they are straight, gay, bisexual, questioning, or something else. We need all kinds of black men in our community—football players as well as construction workers, rappers as well as businessmen, doctors as well as actors. We need them all.

CHAPTER 12

Let's Talk About Sex

LET'S TALK ABOUT sex. Ever since Salt-N-Pepa released their 1992 hit single with that name, people have been using the song title to underscore the need to talk about sex. But for many of us, it's easier to talk about the need to talk about sex than to actually talk about sex. That's why I like to acknowledge and applaud the courageous people who do get us to talk about sex. One of those people is Dr. Joycelyn Elders.

Hers was one of the first names I learned to spell when I worked in the White House. She started her job some time after I started mine, but I knew who she was from the beginning. Her name was pronounced "Jocelyn" but for some reason it was spelled "Joycelyn," and it took me awhile to remember to add the extra "y" in the first syllable. She was the Arkansas state health director that President Clinton had appointed to be the United States Surgeon General, and she was one of a few powerful black women in the Clinton Administration.

To be honest, I had little or no reason to deal with Dr. Elders in my position as White House director of specialty media. I was working with the press, while she was dealing with health policy. But I respected her outspokenness and candor, and I wanted to know more about her. There were only a few African Americans who ran things in the U.S. government. There was Alexis Herman, the White House director of public liaison who later became secretary of labor. There was Rodney Slater, the secretary of transportation, and Mike Espy, the secretary of agriculture. And of course there was Ron Brown, the influential secretary of commerce who was killed in a plane accident. In the first year of the Clinton administration, there was also Colin Powell, a Bush appointee who remained on to serve as the chairman of the Joint Chiefs of Staff.

I had met all of them before, and I had worked closely with Alexis Herman in the White House. They were all dedicated public servants who had risen to the top of their fields. But Dr. Elders was different. She was not just a public servant. She was a lightning rod for attention. Unlike so many people in government, she spoke her mind publicly, and that pissed off a lot of people in both parties. She talked about sex education, AIDS, teen pregnancy, condoms in schools, and other issues that health care professionals should be able to discuss openly and candidly.

In one speech in which she compared high school drivers' education with sex education, Dr. Elders said that we have taught teenagers what to do in the front seat of cars, so now we have to teach them what to do in the back seat. In other remarks, she said that girls who go to the high school prom should carry condoms in their purses. That was honest advice, but as a reward for her candor, the right wing labeled her a "condom queen" and vowed to stop her at all costs. Even then, she refused to back down. "If I could get every teenager engaged in sex to use a condom, I'd gladly wear a crown of condoms on my head," she wrote in her memoir.

Confirmed after a divisive Senate debate in the summer of 1993,

Joycelyn Elders refused to hold her tongue, even after she was appointed. That made her a star in my book, and I tried to think of any excuse I could to meet her. You meet a lot of famous people when you work in the White House. Almost everybody who is well known comes through the West Wing at some point. World leaders, senators, governors, cabinet secretaries, business executives, five-star generals, movie stars, musicians, professional athletes, and television news anchors have all walked through the hallways of the Executive Mansion. I had seen everyone from Nelson Mandela to Yasser Arafat, but there were few people I wanted to meet more than Joycelyn Elders.

After the first few months of working in the White House, I was starting to get a little restless. Then I made an important discovery. I realized that working in the White House was just like working in any other job. There were good moments and bad moments. The good moments were unlike any experience you could have at any other job. But the bad moments were much worse than anything at any other job. And there were times when it seemed that everything was falling apart and that the administration was unraveling at the seams. There was also office politics and personality conflicts and all the other work-related drama you would find in any other office in America. After a few months, going to work was just like going to work.

I was unhappy with my job, so I quickly involved myself in a number of other issues that went well beyond my job description. Although I was paid to work in media affairs, I made time to work on civil rights issues, gay and lesbian issues, and AIDS issues as well. It was in that capacity that I finally arranged to meet with Dr. Elders. I joined a White House colleague on a trip to her office, and we sat down with Dr. Elders for a wide-ranging discussion about administration policy. Her office was surprisingly unimpressive. There were no big flags and formality and such. It looked just like any other government office. Dr. Elders explained that she spent a lot of time on the road, so I assumed there was no reason to get attached to an office. My impression was that the office fit her personality. She was down-to-earth and honest, and I was impressed that she was willing to sit and spend a few minutes in her busy day talking to us.

Meanwhile, back at the White House, the Clinton administration started to change dramatically in 1994. Reporters were writing stories that the staff was too young and undisciplined and the president needed to do something about it, so he did. The president appointed Leon Panetta as his chief of staff, and he was given the task of imposing order. I resisted some of the discipline that came from above. The new deputy chief of staff made a number of changes in the way our department operated, and I resented the sense of micromanagement that was being imposed. We were told to take shorter lunch breaks and to return reporters' phone calls within the same news cycle, and we were given other basic instructions that I thought were insulting. From my vantage point, we were all professionals and should be treated as such, and I did not want someone in the West Wing telling me when to use the bathroom.

At the same time, I was frustrated by the conservative shift in White House policy. We were still recovering from the defeat of the president's policy on gays in the military, and no one wanted the president's health care plan to be defeated as well. Health care was supposed to be the defining legacy of the Clinton administration, while the issue of gays in the military was merely a diversion for the White House. I had worked on the military issue from the beginning, and I knew what a distraction it was for the president. Still, I expected he would keep his promise and lift the ban, but I was wrong.

A few weeks before the president announced his final decision, I got a call from my boss, George Stephanopoulos, on Air Force One. It was almost six o'clock in the morning, and I was still in bed. George asked me to write a memo to the president listing the public statements Bill Clinton had made about the issue of gays in the military. I quickly prepared a memo that I thought might influence the president's thinking, but I was wrong again. Two weeks later, the president finally announced his policy. It was called "don't ask, don't tell, don't pursue." Instead of banning gays from the military, the government would simply stop asking recruits about their sexual orientation as long as gays and lesbians in the services stopped talking about it. It was a horrible policy, and it seemed to undermine the sense of duty, honor, and integrity expected from members of the armed forces. How could the military expect to uphold a sense of honesty if soldiers were essentially encouraged to be dishonest? With the wave of a magical presidential wand, the military would begin to implement a policy of winks and nods.

It was supposed to be a compromise, but instead it was a disaster. The liberals were upset because the president did not lift the ban, and the conservatives were upset because he tried to change the ban. Nobody was happy about the outcome. As a result of the debacle, the White House staff became gun-shy about all things gay. "Don't ask, don't tell" became the unofficial policy of the Clinton administration in acknowledging its own positions. When Deval Patrick, the assistant attorney general for civil rights, wanted to testify at the congressional hearings on the Employment Non-Discrimination Act (ENDA), the White House told him not to do it. The bill would have outlawed workplace discrimination based on sexual orientation. In most states in the country, it was still legal to fire gay and lesbian employees because of their sexuality. President Clinton wanted to change that. He had endorsed ENDA long before he was elected. But that was before the gays in the military failure.

In the long conference table in the Roosevelt Room of the West Wing, Deval Patrick and I argued the issue for more than an hour. There was no federal law that prohibited sexual orientation discrimination in the workplace. Most states did not prohibit this discrimination. The president had already endorsed the legislation. What could be the issue? The issue was the president's ability to govern. Influential senior staff members felt that the White House had already taken a big hit with the gays in the military debacle, and they did not want to risk expending any political capital when the president needed all his energy to push for health care reform. That made sense, but this was not a controversial position. This was not the military. Most Americans agreed that job discrimination was wrong, and I felt the public would respect the president more if he stood up for his beliefs. And to be honest, most Americans were not going to pay attention to the testimony of an assistant attorney general. I argued more passionately that day than I had argued with anyone about anything in the White House. But at the end of the discussion, we lost that debate almost unanimously. Even the top liberals in the White House disagreed with us. In the end, we worked out a compromise for Deval Patrick to send written testimony instead of appearing in person.

After that experience, I began to question what I was accomplishing by working in the White House, and I started thinking about an exit strategy. There was one good option I had dismissed earlier, but maybe it was time to reconsider. I had received a phone call from a writer named E. Lynn Harris who had self-published a novel called *Invisible Life*. Lynn had since signed with Doubleday, and his editor told him about an essay I wrote for a book that was never published. When we talked on the phone, I felt a breath of fresh air just thinking about other opportunities outside of politics. Lynn was the one who suggested that I develop my essay into a book. That was a new direction for me. I had never seriously thought about writing a book, but with Lynn's encouragement, I contacted an agent and created a book proposal. The agent sent the proposal directly to Doubleday, and I waited for a response.

I had almost forgotten about the book proposal when an intern came into my office on a Friday afternoon in December and told me that Joycelyn Elders had just resigned from her job. "No way," I said. I knew there had been controversy swirling around her, but I had no idea it had escalated to this. I called around to some of the other White House staff members until I found someone who could tell me what happened. Apparently, Dr. Elders had been forced to resign because of some controversial comments she made during a World AIDS Day appearance at the United Nations. One of the people in the audience at the event asked Dr. Elders a question about a sensitive but important topic. "What do you think are the prospects for a discussion and promotion of masturbation?" Dr. Elders's only mistake that day was her honesty. She did not try to sugarcoat her answer or develop a politically correct response. She simply told the truth.

"In regard to masturbation, I think that is part of human sexuality, and perhaps it should be taught," Dr. Elders responded. That was it. No one in the room was alarmed. None of the reporters even asked a followup question about it. All she said was that masturbation should be discussed in the context of sex education. She had not advocated that schools should teach kids *how* to masturbate, but that was how her comments would be reported later. Eight days after the speech, the transcript of that exchange made its way to Donna Shalala, the secretary of health and human services (HHS). Although the surgeon general is appointed by the president, she works under the HHS secretary. Shalala was apparently concerned about the remarks and spoke to White House Chief of Staff Leon Panetta. Panetta then called Elders and asked for her resignation. Dr. Elders said she refused to resign unless the president personally asked her to do so. That was a bold move, but it did not work. By the time I left the office that night for the weekend, Elders was already history. She was another casualty of the policy of "don't ask, don't tell."

I returned to work dispirited the following Monday. Dr. Elders had been forced to resign, the Republicans had just won control of the Congress for the first time since Franklin Roosevelt was elected president, and I was no longer happy working in the White House. Then came an important phone call. Later that day, I received good news from my agent in New York. Doubleday had agreed to publish my book. To accept the offer would require me to give up my job working in the White House and spend six months writing the book. It took me less than a minute to decide what to do. After I hung up the phone, I walked into my boss's office and announced that I was resigning from my job. It was the easiest decision I ever made, and I never looked back.

Two years after I left the White House, I met with Dr. Elders once again. This time I introduced her at a conference where she was speaking in Long Beach, California. When she recounted the experience of being fired, she simply explained that she was a doctor, not a politician. I understood exactly what she meant. Politicians are afraid to talk about sex. They are not afraid to have it, of course, but they are afraid to talk about it approvingly. The rest of us, on the other hand, would be wise not to follow the example of politicians in how we conduct our sex lives.

That means it's time to talk about sex. We need to talk about it openly, honestly, candidly, even passionately. We need to talk about it with our partners. We need to talk about it with our families. We need to talk about it with our friends. And we definitely need to talk about it with our children.

Far too often, we avoid discussions about sex because we are uncomfortable with the dialogue. We are ashamed to talk to our friends and family about our sexual behavior, or we are afraid that the conversations may turn off our partners. But we have to have those discussions in order to save our lives. There are at least five different conversations we need to have about sex.

First, parents should talk to their children about sex, sexual orientation, pregnancy, and sexually transmitted diseases before they become sexually active. My parents never talked to me about sex when I was growing up. Maybe they were afraid. Maybe they didn't think I was having sex. Maybe they thought I would learn on my own. I don't know. But I grew up with lots of misinformation and misconceptions about sex and sexuality. My life would have been a lot easier if my parents had talked to me about sexuality, homosexuality, and bisexuality when I was younger. I might not have deceived myself for ten years about my own sexual orientation. I might have come to terms with my identity when I was in high school or college instead of when I was twenty-five years old. I'm just fortunate that I didn't do anything that jeopardized my life when I was young and dumb and impressionable. In any case, I would not want my children to grow up with the same misinformation I had.

Second, middle schools and high schools should provide regular sex education sessions with accurate information. I went to middle school in St. Louis and high school in Clearwater, Florida. Aside from a passing reference in a health education course, I don't recall a single instance when a teacher, a nurse, a counselor, or a school official even acknowledged the fact that we were sexual beings as adolescents. The policy there was "don't ask, don't tell," and the assumption seemed to be that students would not have sex if the schools just didn't talk about it. That assumption was way off base. Almost everyone I knew was having sex in high school, and many of us were getting our information about sex from the same unreliable sources—each other. I know that some parents do not want their kids to learn about sex from a school teacher, but too many parents just don't talk about sex with their children, and the schools have a responsibility to teach. If the parents don't like what the schools teach, they should teach their kids in their own way, but they should not deprive the overwhelming majority of students of the vital information they need to protect themselves against pregnancy, HIV, and other sexually transmitted diseases.

Third, families, friends, and community institutions need to talk about sex. Too many people are isolated in their sexual lives, and developing a healthy dialogue about sex can help to break the isolation. Let's talk about masturbation. How often do we really do it? Let's talk about intercourse. How many different ways do we explore it? And let's talk about safe sex. How do we get our partners to try it, and how do we make it exciting?

Over the years, I've been conducting an unofficial and unscientific experiment with friends, acquaintances, and strangers. From time to time at parties and dinner tables, I'll wait for the right moment and then strike up a spicy conversation that has something to do with sex. "Have you ever cheated on a partner? How many times a month do you have sex? When was the last time you masturbated?" Those are the types of questions I like to ask. And you would be surprised how receptive most people are to answering those questions. Even the ones I don't expect to participate in the discussion will often become very engaged. Although I cannot draw any scientific conclusions from my experiments, I do think they confirm my belief that we are nation in denial about our sexual desires. I think people respond to these conversations because they have pent-up sexual energy and they don't have as many outlets as they would like to have where they can talk about sex. At some level, they want their own sex lives to be validated by the experiences of others, even strangers, and they want to know that it's okay to be who they are and to do what they do.

The fourth conversation we need to have is even more public. That's the conversation the media needs to initiate with us. Media outlets should develop story lines that show couples negotiating safe sex issues in the context of intimacy. It's not a big stretch. You can hardly turn on the television these days without seeing a couple in bed, making out on a sofa, or simulating intimacy. But for all the sexuality in the media, images of safe sex are not nearly as frequent. Sitcoms and drama series went through a stage in the 1990s when they started talking about safe sex more often, but that conversation needs to continue on today. Most adults already know about safe sex. They already know to use condoms to protect themselves from pregnancy and HIV. But they don't know how to talk to their partners about it. The media can show us how to do it by providing useful examples of couples who talk about safe sex in the heat of the moment. Almost everyone acknowledges the difficulty of initiating those conversations, so why not use our popular television shows and movies to give us some ideas on how to do it?

That leads us to the fifth and final conversation. Sexual partners need to be able to talk to one another without shame or judgment. Of course, that is much easier said than done, but we still have to find a way to talk to our sexual partners about our deepest fears and desires. That level of dialogue seems pretty basic in a relationship, but the research suggests that a lot of couples are just not having those conversations. So we should not be surprised to see more HIV infections and more STDs until we begin to talk about safe sex to our partners. As one AIDS activist told me, if you can't have a conversation with your partner about safe sex, should you really be having sex with that person in the first place?

But once we do start talking, what should we talk about? Should those who are HIV positive reveal their status? Should men on the down low admit their preferences? Should women who practice infidelity disclose their behavior patterns? The simple and politically correct answer is yes to all these questions. But the truth is not always simple and politically correct. The truth is that people lie. For various reasons, some more noble than others, a lot of people tend to lie about their sex lives. If that's the case, how do we know whom to trust? The answer may disappoint you. We don't. Instead, we make judgments that are sometimes irrational about the level of risk involved in having sex with various people. Yes, we know he just got out of prison, but he looks so hard that we can't believe he would let a man inside of him. Yes, we know he said he's bisexual, but he will surely give up on men once he falls in love with the right woman. Yes, we know he's a drug user, but he looks clean to me. Or even worse, no, we don't know anything about him, but what we don't know can't hurt us. Ignorance is bliss, we tell ourselves. But ignorance is no excuse for blindness.

Over the years, I've dated several men who told me they were HIV positive. I respected them for their honesty, and we always practiced safe sex. But I did not assume that everyone else was HIV negative because they didn't tell me otherwise. Instead, in all my years of dating, I have never asked anyone, male or female, about his or her HIV status. I have told my partners that I am HIV negative, but I have never insisted that they tell me about their own status. It's not because I'm afraid to ask. Instead, it is because I want to be safe with everyone. So I assume that everyone I have sex with is HIV positive, and I act accordingly.

I believe the recent trend toward demonizing those who are HIV positive for failure to disclose their HIV status sends the wrong signal. It stems from our need to blame other people for our own failures, and it is based in an unhelpful concept of victim-based morality that takes away our personal responsibility and assigns all the blame and puts all the responsibility on those who are HIV positive. Blaming someone else for our own actions will not change our actions, nor will it change the past. By the time you get to the point of blame, you have already passed the point of responsibility.

Some people lie about their HIV status. That doesn't mean we have to become distrustful cynics, but it does mean we are on notice. The best way to protect yourself is to protect yourself, not to let someone else do it for you. Another truth is that many people do not know their HIV status. Far too many people have never been tested, and many others have only been tested once or twice. Those who think they are negative may actually be positive. We can't blame them for their ignorance and then fail to take precautions on our own. The only way to be sure is to be tested, and even that is not the end of the process. When a person is infected with HIV, the body's immune system produces antibodies to fight off the virus. HIV tests measure the presence of these antibodies, but it often takes up to two months before the antibodies are detected, and in some rare cases it can take considerably more time to detect the antibodies. Therefore, some people may get negative test results after the body has been exposed to the virus but before the antibodies are detectable. That's why health officials encourage follow-up tests and regular testing for those who engage in risky behavior. And that's why using protection is much safer than trusting your partner's word.

One of the biggest mistakes we can make in dealing with our sexual partners is falling into the trap that using protection means we don't trust them or we don't love them. Nothing could be further from the truth. In fact, using protection is the ultimate form of love because it reflects a desire to protect both partners from harm.

Once we start having an open dialogue about sex, we can finally dismiss some of the misinformation that's already out there. For example, no matter what you may have heard to the contrary, AIDS is not a curse on homosexuals. In fact, most of the people in the world with AIDS are not gay. Moralistic misinformation in the 1980s and early 1990s led to collective neglect of the AIDS pandemic because too many of us thought it was somebody else's problem until we woke up one day and realized it was our own.

In addition, AIDS is not a curse on the promiscuous. Promiscuity does not cause AIDS. HIV does. Many people wrongly believe they are not at risk for HIV because they are monogamous or because they practice serial monogamy. But AIDS doesn't care if you are the biggest slut on the street or a virgin on a first date. It only takes one time to be infected. You can sleep with a different person every night of the year and never get infected, or you can sleep with only one person one time in your life and be infected the same day.

The truth is that AIDS is entirely preventable. From this day forward, there's no reason why anyone in the world has to be infected with HIV. We may not have a cure, but we do know how to stop it. HIV is spread by behavior and ignorance, so let's talk honestly about changing our behavior and ending our ignorance.

The most effective way to prevent the spread of HIV is by abstinence. HIV cannot be spread by casual contact such as kissing or sharing water glasses, so as long as you refrain from sexual activity, then you're not likely to be exposed to the virus. Of course, HIV can also be spread by infected blood, but unless you're a health care worker or an injection drug user, you're not likely to come in contact with such blood on a regular basis.

Human beings are sexual creatures, so the idea of abstinence is not practicable for most adults. Therefore, we have to come up with other mechanisms to protect ourselves from the virus. Maybe Joycelyn Elders was right about masturbation. You cannot get HIV by having sex with yourself. But the morality police are so hell-bent on controlling our sexuality that they want us to hate ourselves for it. There's nothing wrong with masturbation, and those who want the enjoyment of sexual pleasure without the risk of sexual intercourse should be encouraged to do it.

If abstinence and masturbation aren't enough, then safe sex is the best option to prevent the spread of HIV. That means using a new condom every time with every partner, not just for the partners who you think might be HIV positive. Some argue that we should limit the number of our sexual partners. That may or may not be a good idea, but it will not necessarily limit our risk of getting HIV. That argument has more to do with morality than reality. HIV is not spread by sex, and it does not matter how frequently you have it. HIV is spread by sex with someone who is infected. That is the only way to get the virus from sexual contact.

Sexual intercourse without a condom is inherently risky. There is no way around it. Even married heterosexual couples should seriously consider the risks of condomless sex. The best way to protect yourself in this situation is for both partners to get tested before unprotected intercourse and to continue doing so on a regular basis. By exercising simple caution and using basic common sense, you can protect yourself even in this situation.

Unfortunately, all the talk about sexually transmitted diseases has convinced some of us that sex is something to fear instead of something to embrace. But we need not fear these discussions. Knowledge is power, and knowledge about sex can give us the power to save our lives and enjoy our sexual experiences. Sex is a wonderfully healthy form of human expression, and we would be wise to learn to talk about it. We would be wiser still to protect ourselves.

CHAPTER 13
Can I Get a Witness?

IN MY TWO and a half years as executive director of the National Black Lesbian and Gay Leadership Forum, I had three distinctly memorable experiences. The first was in 1995 when I joined more than two hundred black gay and bisexual men in a controversial contingent in the Million Man March. The second was in the summer of 1997 when I traveled to Zimbabwe on a presidential delegation with Coretta Scott King and the Reverend Jesse Jackson. The third was in October 1997 when I appeared with Angie and Debbie Winans on *BET Tonight* hosted by Tavis Smiley.

In some ways, the Million Man March and the trip to Zimbabwe prepared me for the BET appearance. Some of us had expected condemnation from the Nation of Islam for joining in the Million Man March, but there was hardly a whisper of criticism as we marched along that day. The crowd of men on the mall split like the parting of the Red Sea as we marched and chanted, and most of those who had any reaction at all simply clapped. Similarly, I was not sure what to expect from the homophobic leadership of the government of Zimbabwe when I arrived in Harare. President Robert Mugabe had announced a crackdown to arrest gays and lesbians and had made incredibly offensive remarks about homosexuality. But when I got to Zimbabwe, I met with the president and with members of his cabinet, and I traveled on my own to meet with the leaders of the national gay and lesbian organization. The experience was empowering and productive with no drama or confrontation.

Perhaps those experiences softened me. If I could participate as an openly gay man in the Million Man March and travel as an openly gay man to Zimbabwe, then I had no reason to be concerned about appearing on BET. I had been on BET several times before. I had appeared on the *Bev Smith Show* years earlier, and I had appeared on Tavis Smiley's show to promote my first book, *One More River to Cross*. Those experiences were mostly enjoyable, but the issue of religion always managed to surface whenever I appeared.

I had no plans to make any new appearances on BET until I received a couple of phone calls on Friday, October 24. The first was from a friend who told me that two gospel recording artists, Angie and Debbie Winans, had recorded a new song called "Not Natural." The song was a direct attack on homosexuality, and more specifically on the comedian Ellen DeGeneres, who had recently come out of the closet. We quickly put out an alert to our e-mail network and asked our members to call the record company about the song. The second call was from BET. They wanted me to appear on a show with Angie and Debbie Winans the following Tuesday. I accepted the invitation without thinking of the possible controversy surrounding my appearance.

The day before the appearance, I got a second phone call from BET. This time, the news was not good. I had been disinvited. Angie and Debbie Winans would not appear on the show if I was also a guest. I could not believe it. I tried to persuade the producers to change their opinion, but they would not budge. In all my years working with the media, I had never been so outraged. A few hours later, we issued the strongest press release we had ever put out. Not only did we take on Angie and Debbie Winans, we also took on BET "for providing a biased, one-sided forum for the Winans to promote their homophobia." That was just the beginning.

"BET has stooped to a new low of cowardice by caving in to the homophobic demands of two anti-gay performers," I wrote. "To allow controversial guests to dictate the content of a news show reflects a complete and total lack of journalistic integrity by BET-TV," I added. Mindful that we had less than a day to turn things around, we threatened a boycott and a protest. "When we go to BET headquarters Tuesday afternoon, we're going to show BET and the Winans once and for all that we will not be the whipping boy for the black church," the press release said. "The black church and the gospel music industry are filled with black gays and lesbians, and it's time to open the closet doors and show the world who's who," it said.

Within a few hours of issuing the press release, we were getting inundated with phone calls from people who had called BET to protest their decision and from reporters who wanted to know what was going on. We were even more outraged when we learned that Angie and Debbie Winans were also scheduled to appear on another BET show, *Teen Summit,* which was directed at African-American youth. But that was not the big shocker. The big surprise was when I heard that the publicist for Angie and Debbie Winans who had started the controversy was a black gay man. When I found out, I publicly accused him of "serving as a mercenary in the Winans' battle to denigrate his very own community." That may have been a low blow, but I was fed up with the hypocrisy of self-hating homosexuals who were profiting from religious homophobia.

Although they came from a prominent family in gospel music—

the Detroit-based family had been recording albums since 1981—nobody had ever heard of Angie and Debbie Winans before that controversy, and some of my colleagues felt the whole incident had been manufactured by the publicist to sell records. Cathy Renna, a spokesperson for the Gay and Lesbian Alliance Against Defamation (GLAAD) told the *Washington Post* that the first time her organization heard of the controversy was from a press release issued by the publicist, which seemed to be promoting a controversy that did not yet exist.

His press release launched a back-and-forth media war about the Bible and homosexuality. Quoted in the *Washington Times,* Angie and Debbie Winans said, "What we're saying is not what we think but what Jesus thinks." Our organization quickly put out a press release to remind the public that Jesus never mentions homosexuality in the Bible. "Not only is their music mediocre, but so is their knowledge of the Bible," the press release said. "For that matter, the Bible says that women should 'adorn themselves with modest apparel' and 'not with gold or costly array' (I Timothy 2:9), but that doesn't stop the Winans sisters from sporting gold necklaces and diamond earrings in their promotional photos. If they really believe in every word of the Bible, then they can't have it both ways."

We were harsh, quick, and effective. I had learned the lesson from my experience in the 1992 Clinton campaign when we ousted the incumbent, George H. W. Bush, from office, and the strategy worked. Under pressure, BET finally backed down and re-invited me. Tavis called me himself to apologize for the controversy and told me he was not responsible for disinviting me. I have always respected Tavis so I had hoped he would come through for us.

When the show finally appeared, I sat in the BET studio in Washington with Bishop Noel Jones of Los Angeles, while Angie and Debbie Winans joined us via satellite. The Reverend James

Forbes from Riverside Church in Harlem also joined us by satellite. And for one hour, we had a wide-ranging debate about the Bible and homosexuality. Bishop Jones and the Winans sisters were against homosexuality, while the Reverend Forbes and I argued on behalf of love and equality. I have never been convinced that these biblical debates are as useful as we like to think they are. Most of the observers tend to have preformed opinions about the issue, so it is difficult to really change anybody's thinking. One side quotes a biblical passage to make its case, and then the other side quotes its own. At the end of the debate, it all comes down to which side you agreed with in the beginning. In addition, these debates rarely delve into the related issues about the role of religion in society. For example, in the unlikely event that we could develop a consensus about what the Bible says, should we use the Bible to dictate our public policy? How do we reconcile the use of biblical beliefs to guide our laws with the separation of church and state?

Despite my misgivings about these types of debates, I thought it was important to be on the show. If the discussion helped to save the life of one kid who was struggling with his sexuality, then it would be worth all the effort. And even if the discussion failed to change a single mind, it would at least present a debate instead of a one-sided diatribe against homosexuality. The viewers would at least get to see the split in opinion about what the Bible really does and does not say. That had to be better than an unfiltered hour of Angie and Debbie condemning homosexuality.

The dialogue was heated and passionate but mostly respectful. The Winans sisters explained why they recorded the song. I explained my concerns that the song would adversely influence young people. And the two ministers debated the biblical implications. We each had our role on the show, but when Angie and Debbie ventured away from their role and started talking about

Jesus, I interjected. Jesus says nothing about homosexuality any-where in the Bible, I said. "I beg to differ," Angie said, shaking her head in disagreement. "I have a stack of Bibles at home that say otherwise." Bishop Jones also joined in on the attack, accusing me of distorting the Bible. But to this day, years after that appearance, no one has ever produced a single scripture where Jesus mentions homosexuality. They haven't produced such a scripture because none exist. Jesus never mentions homosexuality anywhere in the Bible.

Maybe I was misunderstood. Maybe they thought I was saying that homosexuality is never discussed by anyone in the Bible. But that was not my point and not what I said. I was talking specifically about Jesus. Based on the previous comments that the Winans sisters made in the media, I think they honestly thought that Jesus had discussed the issue. But they were wrong.

For some reason, a lot of Christians who use religion to justify their dislike of homosexuality seem to think that no one else has read the Bible, or that everyone else who has read it has reached the same conclusions that they have. Religious scholars who have studied the Bible in its original languages have reached different conclusions about what it says, and doesn't say, about homosexuality. Instead of taking my word for it, I usually try to direct critics to a few other books that discuss the issue. The first, *What the Bible Really Says About Homosexuality,* was written by the Reverend Daniel Helminiak, and it goes through each one of the biblical passages that has any connection to homosexuality. The second text, *The Good Book: Reading the Bible with Heart and Mind,* was written by the Reverend Peter Gomes, and it provides understanding of how the Bible has been used and misused by various groups over time.

Over the years, I have found a lot of misinformation and mis-representation about the Bible and homosexuality. I used to argue with people toe to toe when they questioned my sexual orientation, but I realized that many of them had never really studied the biblical passages related to homosexuality. Many of them were too busy quoting bumper stickers to quote the Bible itself. "God made Adam and Eve, not Adam and Steve," they would say. If I had a nickel for every time I heard that, I would be a rich man. The argument is based on an overly simplistic reading of the creation story in the book of Genesis of the Bible. Since the creation story mentions Adam and Eve, a few people would like to interpret that to mean that God did not also create Steve. But the creation story fails to mention a lot of things in the world that we now believe to exist. Chief among these is race. The story never mentions blacks or whites, but no one would argue that the absence of race from the story means that God did not create black people.

Religion has been misused by many well-intentioned believers to justify their dislike for others. The Bible was used for centuries to justify the slavery and oppression of blacks ("slaves be obedient to your masters," Ephesians 6:5–9), and we, of all people, should know not to use the Bible to justify the oppression of others. But instead we practice the same prejudice practiced against us, and with the same hypocrisy used by our oppressors in selecting which parts of the Bible to accept and reject. Religious critics of homosexuality often quote the passage from Leviticus 18 that man should not lie with man, but they conveniently overlook the passages in Leviticus 19 that prohibit haircuts, tattoos, and shaving a beard. Leviticus 19 even prohibits wearing mingled fabrics such as wool and linen together, but we rarely condemn people to Hell for wearing polyester-cotton blends. Other passages outlaw the eating of pork and seafood (Leviticus 11), but we seldom follow those rules either. That's because the prohibitions in Leviticus were developed to separate the Jews from the Gentiles of the time and bear little relevance to modern-day life. Leviticus cannot be taken seriously as a guide to twenty-first-century living. But when it comes to homosexuality and bisexuality, many of us do not operate out of logic. We operate out of fear and bias. That is true for people of all races, but the religious hypocrisy is particularly disappointing among African Americans.

I was out on tour for my first book when I sat down for an interview at a black radio station in Chicago. I never discussed religion on my own, but almost every caller wanted to debate with me about the Bible. When one self-described Christian caller told me that Jesus condemned homosexuality, I corrected him. "Actually, Jesus never discussed the issue," I said. He questioned my information, so I challenged him to find a passage where Jesus mentions it. He thought about it for a moment, admitted he could not think of a passage, and then decided to take another route. "What Jesus says is irrelevant," he told me. I did not even bother to point out the inconsistency in using Jesus to justify an argument and then denying the importance of Jesus once the argument failed.

After a speech to a conference of college student leaders meeting on diversity in Seattle, two students stood up and argued with me about the Bible. When I responded with my own knowledge of the Bible, they retreated. But they ended the confrontation with a promise to pray for me. Anyone who had a different opinion from the one they had been taught was wrong. Then, shortly after the Massachusetts Supreme Court struck down the state's discriminatory marriage law in 2004, a black minister in Chicago was so outraged that he told the *New York Times* that he would march with the Ku Klux Klan against gays and lesbians. On a television show in Washington, another minister told me that God doesn't like my "lifestyle." And in an interview for my first book, a different minister told me that homosexuality is the worst possible sin. That's a lot of criticism for anyone to take.

Given all the religion-based venom spewed out against homosexuality and bisexuality, it is no wonder that so many same-gender-loving men have difficulty accepting their sexual orientation. Who would want to acknowledge their real identity in a world that teaches them they are immoral just for being who they are? We cannot expect most men on the down low to come to terms with their sexuality when the rest of society has not yet come to terms with it either. And when the people who claim to be following the teachings of Jesus communicate hatred and fear instead, we are only fooling ourselves if we think we have created a climate for openness. In fact, if you want one explanation as to why men are on the down low, look no further than our local churches.

The church is the arbiter of moral decency in the black community. Whether or not we attend church, we learn most of our values and our sense of right and wrong from what the church teaches us. Even as we breach the rules expected of us, many of us have a sense that the rules laid down are right. And the church, for the most part, has told us that homosexuality is wrong. In fact, many of our churches have invented special ministries and campaigns simply to convert the homosexual men in their midst. They are not interested in talking about it or learning about it. They are more interested in preaching against it. And that attitude is exactly the cause of the problem.

I am not on the down low and have never been on the down low, but I have met enough men who are to understand why they exist. We create them. Yes, you and I create them. We create them with our condemnation of homosexuality. We create them with our insulting stereotypes. And we certainly create them with the offensive words we use in our families, our communities, and our churches. And every single time we complain about men on the down low without acknowledging the ways in which we create the conditions that make them exist, we become the hypocrites.

Over the past few years, I have heard dozens of women who want to know why men on the down low just don't "come out" and stop living a lie. That is a valid concern—in fact, many in the gay community have asked the same question—but it is often not a very deep one. If we want the men on the down low to be honest with us, then we first have to be honest with ourselves. The problem is not just that the men are on the down low. The problem is that they feel *the need* to be on the down low. And that is where we as a community come in.

Unfortunately, too many black churches have become active co-conspirators in the silencing of black men on the down low. More than almost any other institution in our community, our churches have perfected the policy and practice of "don't ask, don't tell." As a result, the black church has developed a paradoxical reputation as the most homophobic institution in the black community and also the most homo-tolerant. When ministers deliver the company line fire-and-brimstone sermon, the church is at its most homophobic. But when you look behind the minister at the members of the choir, the choir director, the music director, the organist, and the deacons, the church is often homotolerant. In few other places in the community do black gay and bisexual men play such a visible leadership role. Anyone who has been to black churches knows that our churches are filled with gay and bisexual men, and yet many of these churches rarely acknowledge the odd reality that these men support and fund the very institutions that beat them down. Many of our churches are still in denial about homosexuality in their own congregations.

Fortunately, there are some ministers and churches that are beginning to change that pattern. The Reverend Jeremiah Wright of Trinity United Church of Christ in Chicago, the Reverend Cecil Murray of First AME Church in Los Angeles, the Reverend James Forbes at Riverside Church in Harlem, and the Reverend Cecil

Williams at Glide Memorial Church in San Francisco have led the way to develop open and welcoming congregations. These churches are coming to grips with sexuality and opening up a dialogue with heterosexuals, homosexuals, and bisexuals in the pews. Other churches have begun to re-examine biblical texts with new eyes. And a few new churches have opened with affirming ministries. Some churches actually started to deal with sexuality back in the 1980s and 1990s at the height of the AIDS epidemic when many of them learned that many of those who died were homosexual or bisexual. They also have help from organizations like Balm In Gilead, a New York–based nonprofit that helps churches across the nation to develop their own AIDS ministries.

Then there are churches that cater to the needs of the black LGBT community. The biggest of these is the Unity Fellowship Church, which has opened up churches in cities across America. But there is also the Breath of Life Fellowship Community Church, which welcomes black gays and lesbians in Tampa, and the Church of the Open Door, which has been serving the black LGBT community in Chicago for years.

If the bad news is that we have much more work to do in our churches, the good news is that many churches are already setting an example of what can be done. There will be plenty of resistance to change, but it needs to happen. What exactly can churches do? In an ideal world, we would get our churches to initiate a long-overdue dialogue about sexuality and to stop preaching against homosexuality. In reality, that will take time. In the meantime, we still have an epidemic to fight, and there are things that churches can do to save lives without compromising on their own positions.

Most important, churches should develop active AIDS ministries. The church leadership should help set a positive tone for the ministry, but members of the congregation—male, female, straight,

gay, and bisexual—should be encouraged to become active participants. There are several major components that could be included
in these ministries.

First, provide safe sex education to the members. This information
can be in the form of a pamphlet inserted in the program or flyers
given out at the end of the service. Just make sure the information
is accurate and up to date. Consult with an established AIDS organization to develop the literature or to prepare your own.

Second, provide free HIV testing in the church. It could happen
once or twice a year, or once a month, depending on the needs and
size of the church. Again, churches can work with local agencies to
administer the program, and with the development of new oral
fluids rapid testing, this can be conducted without drawing blood
or other invasive procedures. The oral tests simply swipe a sample
from inside the mouth and test that sample for the HIV antibodies.

Third, provide free condoms to church members. We know that one
of the factors that contributes to unprotected sex is the absence of a
condom. If women and men can pick up these condoms at church
instead of buying them at a drug store, we may be able to increase
the number of sexually active people who use protection. In addition, when churches provide condoms, they can also provide
instruction booklets to teach people how to use them, and they can
provide educational materials to advise members how to prevent
pregnancy, HIV, and sexually transmitted diseases. They can even
use the condom distribution materials to encourage abstinence.

Fourth, develop peer support groups. Too many people living with
HIV feel isolated and alone. To avoid prejudice and judgment, some
of them may not want to identify themselves to members of the
church. Support groups made up of other members of the church
may provide a mechanism to deal with the isolation. Churches
might even develop two different types of support groups—one for

anyone who is concerned about HIV and AIDS, and another, confidential group exclusively for those who are living with HIV.

Fifth, offer financial assistance to low-income members with HIV needs. Drug therapy for HIV can be very expensive, and many African Americans with HIV cannot afford the treatment. Some government programs, such as the AIDS Drug Assistance Program (ADAP), help to fund access to prescription drugs for those with HIV. Churches can help members prepare the paperwork for the ADAP application and for other government assistance programs. Churches can also incorporate people with HIV and AIDS into their sick and shut-in programs. In addition to prayer, church members can provide free meals, temporary housing, grocery shopping assistance, and other necessities to low-income members with HIV or AIDS who may need these services.

Sixth, provide nonjudgmental counseling. Far too often, our approach to sexuality and AIDS is shaped by our prejudice. Many of us have been taught to "love the sinner but hate the sin." That's a clever little bumper sticker, but like the "Adam and Steve" refrain, it's not in the Bible. If we approach people with AIDS as sinners instead of children of God, we communicate a message of condemnation. That is not our role. Let God decide on judgment. Our role is to comfort those in need. If we truly want to encourage people with HIV or AIDS to come forward in the church, the best way to do that may be to open our arms and welcome them, listen to them, and help them where they need help. Not everyone with HIV or AIDS wants or needs counseling, and they certainly don't all need the same counseling. Our counseling approach should fit the individual, not the stereotype, and the only way to determine people's individual needs is to listen to their concerns in an environment that encourages them to be open and honest.

Religion plays an important role in the lives of many African

Americans. Whether we go to church or not, we are influenced by the church. Whether we are Christian or not, we have been exposed to Christian teachings. In our darkest hours, many of us turn to faith for hope and salvation. Religion has long been used for good in our community, to fight against slavery and segregation, to challenge society, and to comfort those in need. That is the proud tradition of the African-American church. We know that religion should be used as a tool for love, not as a weapon of hate.

CHAPTER 14

Sick and Tired of Being
Sick and Tired

NIKKO BRITERAMOS STARTED college in South Dakota in the fall of 2001. Even as a freshman, he was tall, attractive, muscular, and athletic. He had a 3.6 grade point average, was one of the leading scorers on the school's basketball team, and he never had a problem with the law. As an African-American city kid from Chicago in an overwhelmingly white rural community, he stood out, both literally and figuratively.

From the outside, Briteramos was a great kid with a world of opportunity before him, but on the inside he was having a rough first year in school. In the spring of 2002, the eighteen-year-old Briteramos tried to do his part to help out the local community by donating blood. Not long afterward, the health officials who screened the blood discovered that it was infected with HIV. They could not accept the donation, and they told Briteramos that he was HIV positive. It is not clear whether Briteramos fully understood the consequences of his HIV status or if he was still in denial about it, but a few weeks after he learned of the test results, he was arrested in his dorm room for having intimate relations with his girlfriend.

Although his girlfriend was not infected with the virus, he was charged with violating the state's tough new HIV transmission law, which prohibits any persons with HIV from having unprotected sex without disclosing their status to their partners.

In a matter of days, Briteramos went from star college athlete to public enemy number one. Before the trial even began, the governor of South Dakota—the one public official with the power to grant clemency—publicly accused Briteramos of attempted murder. Not surprisingly, Briteramos was later tried, convicted, and imprisoned for his crime.

South Dakota passed its HIV transmission law after another AIDS scare involving another African American in a different state. In 1996 and 1997, NuShawn Williams, a twenty-year-old black man, was accused of spreading HIV to at least ten women in upstate New York, which is mostly white. Without an HIV transmission law to use, the state of New York had to prosecute Williams on a related charge of statutory rape since one of his sexual partners was under age. Following the uproar, dozens of states rushed to pass their own legislation to criminalize HIV transmission, and South Dakota passed its law in 2000. Until Nikko Briteramos was arrested in 2002, no one in the state of South Dakota had ever been charged under the law.

To many observers, the HIV transmission laws appear to be reasonable measures to discourage those with sexually transmitted diseases from passing them on to unsuspecting partners. But these new laws will not reduce the spread of HIV. Instead, they will make it worse. The best way to stop the spread of HIV is to encourage testing and protection, but the HIV transmission laws accomplish neither goal. By punishing those who fail to disclose their HIV status, the laws actually discourage those in need from being tested. If a man thinks he may be HIV positive but knows he will have to reveal his HIV status to all of his partners if he is, the requirement to disclose his status may stop him from being tested. Why find out the truth if you can't be blamed for your ignorance? If you penalize someone with HIV for *knowingly* having unprotected sex, then you simply discourage people from knowing, because as long as you don't get tested you can never go to jail.

The laws could also discourage us from self-protection by providing us with a false sense of security as long as we believe our partners will not behave inappropriately because of the legal consequences of their deception. The problem with these legal approaches is that they fail to recognize our own ability to protect ourselves, and in so doing they actually discourage us from doing so. The governor, the mayor, and the sheriff cannot protect us from HIV. Only we can do that for ourselves.

We all want to reduce the spread of HIV and encourage those with the virus to be open and honest in their sexual relations, but the HIV transmission laws fail to achieve those goals and instead add to one of the biggest problems in our community—the disproportionate incarceration of black men. With staggering HIV rates among African Americans and two black men as the poster boys for bad behavior, the new HIV transmission laws create another opportunity to send more black men to prison. Although I firmly believe that sexual partners should honestly disclose their HIV status to one another, I do not believe the police should put people in jail who fail to do so. The punitive approach fails to solve the problem and instead adds tragedy on top of tragedy.

Sexual activity is a joint responsibility that requires joint accountability. More than two decades after the AIDS epidemic, almost every adult in America knows that HIV can be spread by unprotected sex. That's why both partners should bear the burden of protecting themselves. It is not a good thing that people lie about their HIV status, but it should not be a criminal thing either.

Instead of putting people with HIV in jail, let's provide them with access to valuable services that can save their lives and the lives of others. What Nikko Briteramos needed was counseling and treatment, not incarceration. With our prisons already swelling with minority inmates locked up during the war on drugs, the last thing we need is more black men in jail for a crime that shouldn't be a crime in the first place. Should we lock up men like Mor Rondo Roberts, a thirty-one-year-old black gay man who was convicted in Ohio for failing to tell a sex partner that he was HIV positive? Although Roberts had no criminal record, was active in the gay community, and his female sex partner tested negative for HIV, he was sentenced to four years in prison. "Putting him in prison will kill him," said his attorney, Tom Adgate, who claimed the jail staff would not treat Roberts's HIV infection effectively, leading to the onset of AIDS.

Roberts and Briteramos knew their HIV status, but one of the reasons some people refuse to get tested is because they have no resources to help themselves if they test positive. HIV testing seems pointless without HIV treatment and access to expensive, life-saving medication. Forty-five million Americans lack health insurance, and many of them are young and poor, the groups most vulnerable to HIV. Even if they knew they were HIV positive, some of these people may wonder what they could possibly do about it when they have no health insurance and the drug treatments can cost up to $15,000 a year.

Perhaps the biggest problem with the passage of HIV transmission laws is that they lead our attention down the wrong path. As with the down low, we find ourselves fighting against the people who engage in irresponsible behavior rather than fighting against the socioeconomic conditions that encourage the behavior. The men and women with HIV in America are not the enemy. They are caught up in a larger struggle that we must not ignore. Our society, our nation, and our community are ailing, and we need to remember how we got in this situation.

I remember Fannie Lou Hamer. Born poor and black as the last of her parents' twenty children in segregation-era Mississippi, Hamer suffered from polio in her youth and was left with a lifelong disability. But despite her physical limitations, the defiant sharecropper became legendary for her efforts to register blacks to vote in the 1960s. After being arrested, intimidated, and beaten repeatedly, she continued to fight. "I'm sick and tired of being sick and tired," she said. Rather than allow her circumstances to paralyze her into inaction, she turned her outrage into activism, and we would be wise to follow in her footsteps.

Personal Steps To Take

Those of us who are sick and tired of the down low and concerned about the spread of HIV in our communities need to turn our outrage into activism. We do not have to become statistics in the latest CDC casualty count. Here's what we can do.

First, get tested regularly. If you are sexually active, you owe it to yourself to get tested. Then go back and get tested again. Make it an annual event, and be sure to keep the promise to yourself.

Second, encourage your friends and partners to be tested. One of the best ways to show our love for one another is to express our concern for our mutual health. Tell your friends that you want them to be around to share the memories of the experiences you've had together. And tell your partner too. Encourage your partner to be tested with you. A loving partner should want to protect both of you.

Third, use protection in your sexual encounters. Don't fall into the trap of assuming that you are safe or your partner is safe. Find out for sure by being tested, and until you do, be sure to use a condom.

Fourth, talk about HIV. Let's erase the stigma that closes off conversation about AIDS. Talk about HIV to your children. Tell them how it's spread and how to avoid it. And talk about it to your friends, your family, and your sexual partners.

Fifth, disclose your HIV status to your sexual partners. People with HIV do continue to lead healthy sex lives, and if you have HIV you can do the same. But give your partners a choice to decide whether and how to be intimate with you. When one partner is positive and the other is not, researchers call this "noncordant HIV serostatus." It happens more often than we may think, but it works best when both parties make informed decisions.

Sixth, share your techniques to talk about safe sex. Many of us are dying to know how to bring up the issue of condoms without ruining an intimate moment. Do we just produce the condoms and use them without discussion? Should we raise the issue before we go to bed? Is there a certain way to say it? If you have helpful ideas, please share them with your friends, family, and others who may need some advice.

Seventh, join HIV vaccine clinical trials. Vaccine clinical trials are used to test the efficacy of HIV preventive treatments, but we need people of all races to participate in the trials to determine how potential vaccines work with different populations. In one example in February 2003, a company called Vaxgen released data from a clinical trial for a vaccine called AIDSVAX that seemed to show some distant promise of protecting African-American participants from infection with HIV. Unfortunately, the number of black participants in this trial was too small to draw any conclusions.

In light of the infamous Tuskegee experiments where blacks were knowingly injected with syphilis, many African Americans express understandable skepticism about participating in new testing trials. But this dilemma poses a catch-22. Some of us fear becoming racial guinea pigs if we participate in the studies, but if we don't participate in the studies, many of us will complain about the absence of blacks. Somehow, we have to find a way to break down the stigmas and myths regarding clinical trial participation and continue to educate ourselves about HIV vaccine research efforts. To do so, we have to work with activists, community leaders, health care workers, scientists, and physicians to build mutual trust.

Eighth, join local HIV community planning boards. Many of the decisions about the use of federal and state funds are determined by local planning boards made up of community citizens, activists, experts, and government officials. If you are concerned about the way money is spent in your community, you can make a difference by participating in the local planning board that makes the decisions.

Ninth, support community-based organizations. Many local AIDS service organizations are struggling to serve the community and stay afloat financially. Many need your help. You can make a difference by calling a local AIDS organization and volunteering your time. If you don't have a lot of time to volunteer in an office, you can make a financial contribution, donate a computer, or offer your professional services. You can even host an event in your home to raise funds for a worthy organization.

Public Policy Action to Support

In many ways, the individual steps we can take are much easier than implementing the policy steps, but changing our government policies offers the best hope for developing long-term solutions. After years of conservative political restrictions that limit the most creative and potentially effective HIV prevention tools, AIDS activists are well aware of the challenges involved in developing new public policy. Over the past ten years, I have spent a lot of time asking experts what should be done about the AIDS crisis in the black community. The answers vary widely depending on the individual. Many observers believe that more money needs to be dedicated to the domestic AIDS problem, but they also agree that money alone is not enough. An AIDS activist in Chicago said we needed a "multi-faceted approach" that involves "saturation of the message." A community leader in Los Angeles suggested an approach that understands and considers "black history, culture and circumstances." Another Los Angeles activist argued for a "big emphasis on black masculinity." An activist in Ohio pushed for changing the way safe sex messages are marketed. And a New York activist said "we need to demand that those organizations that are funded are accountable." These are all reasonable ideas, but we cannot afford an "either-or" approach to saving our lives. We have to adopt many different approaches for the many different elements in our communities.

Despite all the work that needs to be done, many of our elected officials and political leaders are still not prepared to respond to the epidemic in our community. When Gwen Ifill of PBS moderated the 2004 U.S. Vice Presidential Debate between Dick Cheney and John Edwards, she asked one question that caught both candidates off guard. "I want to talk to you about AIDS," she said. "And not about AIDS in China or Africa, but AIDS right here in this country where black women between the ages of 25 and 44 are 13 times more likely to die of the disease than their counterparts. What should the government's role be in helping to end the growth of this epidemic?"

Vice President Cheney pleaded ignorance. "I had not heard those numbers with respect to African-American women," he said. "I was not aware that it was that severe an epidemic there." Senator Edwards talked about the international AIDS crisis and the lack of universal health care coverage in America. Those were important issues too, but they missed the point of the question. Government can play an important role in preventing the spread of AIDS in the black community. Government cannot do it alone, but it can provide the valuable resources we need to fight the epidemic. Here's what the candidates could have said.

First, we need free, universally accessible, easily administered HIV testing. If we really want to encourage people to be tested, we have to make it easy for them. Many local AIDS organizations and city health clinics already provide free HIV testing. We need to expand the number of facilities that offer these services so that everyone in America has access to free testing.

Testing should also be anonymous or confidential. There has been a big debate for years about anonymous testing versus confidential testing. Anonymous testing allows patients to find out their HIV status without revealing their name or identity. Confidential testing collects their personal information but keeps it away from unauthorized outsiders. Each form of testing has its advantages. Anonymous testing is likely to encourage more people to be tested because they don't have to worry about divulging their identity, but confidential testing enables government researchers to track reliable information about the spread of the epidemic.

In addition, we should also encourage and support noninvasive HIV testing with rapid results. Recently developed oral fluids tests can provide almost immediate HIV results without drawing blood from the patient. This solves two problems, getting patients to come back to the doctor's office to get their results and getting over their fears about needles and blood.

Second, we need to abolish HIV transmission laws. In November 2004, 32-year-old Anthony Whitfield was convicted of exposing 17 women to HIV by having unprotected sex with them in Washington state. Five of the women tested positive and Whitfield faced a minimum sentence of 137 years in prison. Whitfield is black and his victims were white. It's the same scenario with Briteramos and Williams and likely for future high-profile cases of HIV transmission. These laws appear to be innocent and well-meaning in their intent, but in their enforcement they serve as a tool to regulate black sexuality and penalize black male sexual activity with white women. In Washington state, for example, hundreds of homes were leafleted after Whitfield was arrested. Some were given fliers that read "Don't Have Sex With Blacks; Avoid AIDS!"

As I mentioned earlier, these laws discourage testing and self-protection. People with HIV need treatment and counseling, not incarceration. Let's invest our resources in positive and constructive tools to get people into treatment.

Third, we need publicly financed needle exchange programs for drug users. Injection drug use was listed as an exposure category for 40 percent of black men and 36 percent of black women living with AIDS in 2002. In the year 2000, more than half of all AIDS deaths of African Americans aged 25 to 44 were caused by contaminated needles, according to a 2002 report by Dr. Dawn Day. Some lawmakers fear that needle exchange programs will encourage the use of illegal drugs, but studies have shown that such programs do not encourage new drug use and do prevent the spread of HIV. Needle exchanges target people who already inject drugs. Many of them are poor and do not have access to clean needles, but the simple act of providing them with clean needles in exchange for their dirty needles can significantly reduce the spread of HIV in our communities.

Fourth, we need free condom distribution in prisons. Whether or not we like to admit it, men have sex with other men in prison. The confirmed AIDS rate in state and federal prisons was more than three times higher than in the total U.S. population, according to a study of HIV in prisons in 2001. Given the disproportionate incarceration of black men in the U.S. penal system, black men bear an even greater risk than white men of being exposed to HIV while incarcerated and then bringing the virus back to their community upon release. In the federal prison system, 97 percent of inmates will eventually be released back into society. But condoms are banned or unavailable in more than 95 percent of U.S. prisons, according to the *New York Times*. We cannot think of the prison crisis as unrelated to the larger AIDS epidemic. If we want to protect the non-incarcerated population, we must also protect the incarcerated.

Fifth, we need targeted prevention funding to fight AIDS in the hardest hit communities. Almost everyone agrees we need more money to fight AIDS, but everyone also agrees that money alone will not solve the problem. How we spend the money is just as important as how much money we spend. That's why we need to use our resources wisely. Those communities hardest hit by AIDS need the bulk of the funding, and the funding needs to be administered in a way that not only targets the communities but empowers them by building up an infrastructure. We need more community-based organizations that understand both the scientific research and the community needs. We have too few of these organizations in our communities, and some other groups lack the capacity to administer major grant awards from the government. We cannot develop long-term solutions to the problems that contribute to HIV without also developing and supporting community institutions that can address the problems that go beyond the AIDS epidemic.

Sixth, we need to fund resources for low-income people living with AIDS. What we once mistakenly believed to be a disease of well-heeled gay men has now clearly become a disease that affects people of all income levels. One in four blacks lives in poverty, according to the U.S. Census Bureau, and studies have found a link between higher AIDS incidence and lower income. Low-income people with HIV and AIDS are at great risk for developing deadly symptoms, particularly if they do not have adequate housing, meals, medicine, and counseling. Federal, state, and local government programs help provide assistance to people with AIDS, and these programs need our support.

The Housing Opportunities for Persons with HIV/AIDS (HOPWA) program, run by the U.S. Department of Housing and Urban Development, makes grants to local communities, states, and nonprofit organizations for projects that benefit low-income people with HIV/AIDS and their families. The AIDS Drug Assistance Program (ADAP), run by the U.S. Department of Health and Human Services, provides medications for the treatment of HIV and enables eligible clients to purchase health insurance. Many communities and nonprofit organizations have also developed meals on wheels programs that help provide food to those in need.

Seventh, we need more research on AIDS in the black community. In addition to AIDS vaccine trials with black participants, we also need more behavioral research in the black community. We need to understand what factors encourage men and women to engage in risky behavior and determine what interventions are most effective in discouraging unhealthy behavior. We also need to understand that interventions may vary from group to group, age to age, or region to region, even within very narrowly defined subpopulations of the black community. What works for eighteen- and nineteen-year-old black gay and bisexual men hanging out in New York's Greenwich Village may not work for eighteen- and nineteen-year-old black gay and bisexual college students in North Carolina. What works for college-educated professional women in Chicago may not work for low-income women in Atlanta. And what works for self-identified men on the down low may not work for those men who do not even realize that they are on the down low.

In the early days of HIV prevention, "we were employing various strategies from card parties to rap groups, in bars, parks and bathhouses, from Long Island to Long Beach to discuss risk and behaviors," according to George Bellinger, Jr., a leading activist in the AIDS community. He continues, "If you are more concerned about the men's political affiliations than their activities then you may never get to them change their behaviors. And we all know that knowledge alone does not mean behavior change."

Despite the apparent connection between black gay men and white gay men, prevention methods that have largely worked for white gay men do not appear to be as effective among black gay men. And for that matter, we should not expect that prevention models for black people, at large, will be as specifically effective with every subpopulation of the African-American community.

We need to consider unconventional approaches to reach those African-American subpopulations that are most difficult to access. Many of our AIDS service organizations are already targeting churches, social functions, bars, nightclubs, bath houses, fraternal organizations, barbershops, beauty salons, and the Internet. But many of those in the target groups will not be accessible even in these locales. Those who do not self-identify or acknowledge their identity by their sexual behavior may have to be approached in completely different settings.

Although government resources are limited, multifaceted, multipronged black prevention research can prove cost effective if it leads to practical prevention methods that will reduce HIV infection rates, reduce the strain on our public health system, and reduce the costs to our government and our economy.

Eighth, we need to develop creative treatment and discipline options instead of incarceration for nonviolent drug users. According to the U.S. Bureau of Prisons, 54 percent of inmates in federal prisons in 2004 were being held for drug offenses. Back in 1980, before the Reagan Administration initiated the war on drugs, only 25 percent of federal inmates were incarcerated for drug-related crimes. Most of these inmates will eventually return to our communities, and many will be left without employable skills that can keep them productively engaged, away from drugs and out of trouble. Incarcerating nonviolent young people for drug offenses provides a quick fix to the drug problem, but it misses an opportunity to reach those youth and make a significant positive impact in their lives. Creative solutions that provide job training, child care, education, and basic discipline can help those in need and help the communities at the same time.

Ninth, we need realistic safe-sex education in public schools. An abstinence-only approach to secondary-level sex education is optimistic, but not realistic. Abstinence is an admirable objective that we should strongly encourage among youth, but we should not let our political and moral boundaries blind us to the reality that teenagers do have sex. Most young people begin having sex in their mid-to-late teens, according to the Alan Guttmacher Institute, and more than half of seventeen-year-olds have had sexual intercourse.

Tenth, we need health care coverage for the 45 million Americans who are uninsured. More than 19 percent of blacks had no health insurance in 2003, and a 1996 study found that blacks with HIV/AIDS were more likely to be publicly insured or uninsured than their white counterparts. According to the study, 59 percent of blacks with HIV/AIDS relied on Medicaid (medical support for the indigent) compared to 32 percent among whites. Only 14 percent of blacks with HIV/AIDS were privately insured, compared to 44 percent of whites. Given those statistics, it is no wonder that blacks with HIV/AIDS were less likely to receive adequate treatment and more likely to die.

Of all the public policy action items listed here, the only subject the vice-presidential candidates discussed was the issue of health care coverage. But the candidates need to know about all these issues, and we need to put these items on their agenda and demand action. As long as we allow the media to divert our attention from the serious issues to the sensationalized ones, we give the politicians an excuse to neglect our public policy agenda and ignore our concerns.

Much needs to be done, and we need holistic approaches that address the complex issues of race, gender, class, and culture. Rather than approach the litany of work as a cause for confusion, we should consider it an opportunity for discovery, where careful investment of resources can reap enormous dividends for the populations that have previously appeared to be most immune to intervention efforts. In virtually every area, from the prison system to the health care system, we need to do more. We need more clinical, epidemiological, and behavioral research. We need to support successful prevention efforts and reexamine failing strategies. And we need to direct our resources where they can provide the most benefit.

Since the beginning of the epidemic in the early 1980s, we have taken many positive steps forward to reduce the spread of AIDS. Now, it is time to take bold new action. We cannot micromanage the disease into nonexistence. More Americans have died from AIDS than from battle during all the wars of the twentieth century combined, and so we must respond to the epidemic with the same level of seriousness we give to terrorism, war, and the other important issues facing our country. There is much we can do in our personal lives to prevent the spread of HIV, but our government must provide strong and visionary leadership. Many of us are waiting for our country to take these issues seriously. Like Fannie Lou Hamer, we are sick and tired of being sick and tired, but we soldier on another day.

CHAPTER 15
Love and Fear

IN THE FALL of 1995, I received a very disturbing phone call from an angry colleague. I had just become executive director of the National Black Lesbian and Gay Leadership Forum, and this colleague had heard that the Forum was planning to apply for a federal HIV/AIDS contract. He called to express his concern.

"I want you to know that if you move forward with this," he said, "I will do everything in my power to prevent you from being funded."

I was stunned that a black man leading a major AIDS organization could be so threatened by another black organization that wanted to help fight AIDS. He feared that the Forum would ultimately compete with his organization for the limited federal AIDS dollars targeted at the black community. "What would you do if you were in my shoes?" he asked. I gave him an answer that he did not believe. "I would be relieved to have an ally because I know that no one organization can do it all," I replied.

My colleague was not impressed, and he refused to back down from his threat. Although my competitive instincts told me to fight back, after discussing the issue with some of my associates in the Leadership Forum, I decided to back off rather than fight. We never applied for the grant, and a few years later, his organization and mine both closed down.

In some ways, I guess we were both victims of the politics of fear. Fear paralyzes our productivity by turning our constructive energy into panic and defensiveness. With fear, rather than see the opportunities for growth and learning, we focus attention on the obstacles that could lead to failure. The battle for limited government AIDS dollars is based on fear and scarcity. We do have the resources to fight AIDS in America, but first we have to change our way of thinking.

A number of writers have published books and articles about the personal choice between fear and love. They suggest that fear is a negative emotion and love is a positive emotion. "The spiritual journey is the relinquishment—or unlearning—of fear and the acceptance of love back into our hearts," writes Marianne Williamson. I believe that fear teaches us to think in terms of scarcity, while love encourages us to think in terms of abundance. With scarcity, we imagine the world has limited resources and, therefore, we must be constantly engaged in battle with one another to acquire and protect our own. With abundance, however, we see the world with plentiful resources at our disposal to be used and managed responsibly.

With trillions of dollars in debt, if our government can find the resources to fight a war on terror and a war on drugs, we ought to be able to find the resources to fight and win the war on AIDS. We can find the resources if we work together. We have to stop falling into the trap of pitting organization against organization, men against women, gays against straights, and bisexuals against everybody else. We have to stop blaming one another for the crisis and start focusing on the answers. We have to stop obsessing about the down low and start focusing on the larger issues that contribute to the down low.

After years of watching African Americans fight among ourselves for a small portion of the federal pie, I am encouraged when I see community leaders moving proactively to set the agenda and engage with the government we elect to represent us. I am encouraged when I see organizations working together instead of against one another. And I am encouraged when I see positive solutions that offer constructive ideas instead of sensationalized stereotypes.

The fundamental choice we face comes down to one simple question: Will we live in love or fear? Every challenge, every obstacle, every difficulty comes down to this choice. And the answer is love.

But fear is not easily conquered. I know women who live in fear of men on the down low and men on the down low who live in fear that they will be discovered. Some gay and bisexual men fear that they will be vilified by the down low, while some straight men fear that they will be unfairly blamed by the actions of men on the down low. Too many of us are operating out of fear, and we cannot build healthy relationships with one another, or with ourselves, in a climate of fear.

As with most things in life, overcoming fear is easier said than done. Perhaps that explains why Audre Lorde, the poet and author, teaches us to use fear to our advantage. Lorde explains: "When I dare to be powerful—to use my strength in the service of my vision—then it becomes less and less important whether I am afraid."

What I like about her statement is that she never says she is not afraid. She simply refuses to allow her fear to paralyze her. Some of our Hollywood action heroes seem to define courage as the absence of fear. They walk into a scene with a swagger and a joke, but we see little of their inner emotional turmoil. I define courage differently.

To me, courage is not the absence of fear, but the willingness to act in spite of fear.

Every time we act in defiance of our fears, we diminish the power they have over us. When we allow fear to disable us, we cannot overcome it. But every time we overcome our fear, we implicitly give permission for others to do the same. When ordinary people do extraordinary things, it inspires other ordinary people to believe that they can do it too. I have seen this happen many times in my own life.

When my partner Nathan and I agreed to take part in a reality television series on Showtime in the summer of 2004, we were both a little concerned about putting our lives and our relationship on display to the public. We weighed the advantages and disadvantages, and ultimately we decided to participate in spite of the fear. In the end, we were glad we did, and we received hundreds of e-mails, letters, and phone calls of support. Many of those who contacted us had never seen two black men involved in a relationship. Without even knowing it, we were able to make a positive impact on the lives of those we had never met.

The same is true for Karamo, a young black gay man who appeared on the MTV series *The Real World* in the fall of 2004. I spoke to Karamo a few weeks after the series began, and he seemed excited about the show, but I doubt he had any idea what an impact his presence would have in the black community and beyond. After fourteen seasons of the longest running reality show in America, he would become the first openly gay African-American cast member on the show. A few weeks into the series, when he met and dated another young man named Dorian, America got a chance to see two young black men holding hands and kissing each other on national television. With his do rag and hip hop clothing, Karamo helped to challenge the monolithic image of black homosexuality, while his friend Dorian—a muscle-bound trainer at a Philadelphia gym—also helped to shatter the stereotypes.

The media images did not end there. There were more images of black gay and bisexual men on television and film in 2004 than in any other time I can remember in my life. ABC's 2004 reality series, *The Benefactor,* featured a black gay man named Kevin, and Bravo's 2004 series *Manhunt: the Search for America's Most Gorgeous Male Model,* included a black gay man named Ron. On scripted television, the HBO series *The Wire* and *Six Feet Under* both featured black gay characters. Meanwhile, four new films and TV shows about black gay and bisexual men—*Noah's Arc, The Ski Trip, Brother to Brother,* and *The Closet*—were released in the summer of 2004.

The notion that black men choose to be on the down low because they do not see healthy images of themselves in the media is slowly starting to change. New images are being developed and created in the media, and more and more real-life black men and women are talking about issues of sexuality in their own lives with their family, friends, and partners. They are acting out of love instead of fear.

There is a story in the Bible that illustrates the choice between fear and love. In Matthew 22:37, Jesus is approached by the Pharisees, who ask him which is the greatest commandment in the law. Jesus responds, "Thou shalt love the lord thy God with all thy heart, and with all thy soul, and with all thy mind. This is the first and great commandment. And the second is like unto it, Thou shalt love thy neighbor as thyself. On these two commandments hang all the laws and the prophets."

I love that passage for its simplicity and its instructional value. It seems to me, the principle of love applies to all of us, regardless of our faith. Jesus tells us in that story that we cannot love our neighbors if we do not love ourselves first. Many of us are upset about our failed relationships, broken marriages, and poisoned friendships. We are quick to hold others responsible for making our lives miserable, but we also need to take responsibility for making our own lives better. As long as we focus our energy primarily on what someone else has done to us, we limit the energy we have left to do for ourselves. If we turn our attention outside, we lose sight of all that we can do inside. Most important, we have to love ourselves before we can love anyone else. We have to love ourselves enough to forgive ourselves for our mistakes and to learn from them. We have to love ourselves enough to overcome our fears. We have to love ourselves enough to be honest about who we are and to protect ourselves from harm.

As Marianne Williamson has written, "Our deepest fear is not that we are inadequate. Our deepest fear is that we are powerful beyond measure. It is our light, not our darkness, that most frightens us. . . . And as we let our own light shine, we unconsciously give other people permission to do the same. As we're liberated from our own fear, our presence automatically liberates others."

I discovered early in life not to live in fear. When I was wrongly fired from my job at Sears as a teenager, I learned that fear can stop us from taking action. Fear can discourage us from telling the truth. And fear can prevent us from standing up for what we believe.

I believe that facts are important in the world. Perception is not reality. And despite all that has happened, I still hold fast to the belief that truth will prevail eventually. I remain convinced that no lie, no matter how widely repeated, can stand forever. Maybe I am naïve, but deep in my heart I still believe the truth will always emerge.

Acknowledgments

It took six years from the publication of my last book to find the time, courage, and energy to write this book. Over the years, I have written several book proposals and partial manuscripts that I never finished, and I would never have finished this book if it were not for the love, encouragement, and support of my partner, Nathan Williams. More than just a partner and a lover, he has also been my lawyer, campaign manager, motivator, stylist, makeup artist, travel agent, travel companion, soulmate, and best friend. Thank you, Nathan, for believing in me.

I also need to thank my family, and especially my mom, Shirley Parker, for encouraging me to be myself, and supporting me along the way. I also want to thank Bill, Krystal, Doris, Delores, Michael, Rochelle, Cheryl, Jardin, and Cameron.

I get a lot of e-mails from people who want to know how to get published. Part of it is luck, part of it is talent, and part of it is hard work. I have been very lucky to have three wonderful advisers in my corner. First, I can't say enough about my agent, Mondella Jones, who immediately "got it" with this book. Thanks, Mondella, for saving me. Next, I have to thank my editor, Don Weise, who has been extremely patient, supportive and easy to work with. Every author should have an editor as helpful as Don. Finally I must thank E. Lynn Harris, who got me started as a writer years ago when I was still working in politics.

Someone once told me, when you find good friends, you should hold on to them. I have many wonderful friends who have supported me over the years, but some of them went far above and beyond the call of friendship for this book. Maurice Franklin of Bristol-Myers Squibb was there from the beginning to help me remember the events of the past and discuss solutions for the future. Phill Wilson of the Black AIDS Institute answered dozens of my spontaneous phone calls when I just wanted to find one little piece of information that I knew he would have. Justin Smith of Rutgers University was an invaluable research assistant. And John Peterson at Georgia State University kept me on the phone for hours talking about AIDS research in the black community. I also want to thank Frank Roberts and Brian Keith Jackson for inspiring me. Then there were friends like Mike Ramsey and Gordon Chambers, who helped me locate the music I used in the chapter on pop culture.

Much of the information I used in the book I owe to the professionals who provided it to me. Thanks to Greg Millett and Karlie Stanton at the Centers for Disease Control, David Malebranche at Emory University and Lisa Bowleg at the University of Rhode Island. I also thank the wonderful reporters who have set the standard in their coverage of the down low—Linda Villarosa at *Essence* magazine, freelance journalist Kai Wright and Duncan Osborne of *Gay City News*. I also thank the readers of my Web site, keith-boykin.com, who provided great ideas and resources when I announced I was writing this book.

Finally, no writer can launch a book without the help of great bookstores. Independent bookstores and big chains have both supported me, and I particularly want to thank a few. In New York: Hue-Man Books in Harlem and Barnes & Noble in Chelsea. In Washington, D.C.: Lambda Rising, SisterSpace, Vertigo, and Books-A-Million. In Atlanta: Outwrite Books and Shrine of the Black Madonna. In my hometown, St. Louis: Left Bank Books and Afrocentric Expressions. In Los Angeles: Eso Wan and Different Light. And I can't forget Giovanni's Room in Philadelphia, Crossroads in Texas, Marcus Books in Oakland, California, and Open Book in Columbus, Ohio. Thank you all for spreading the word.

Index

Contents

DISCOVER
Oregon

Truly epic in its breadth, Oregon's landscape is diverse and dramatic. A broad deep-green swath, lush with farmland and studded with old-growth Douglas firs, runs between the rugged Pacific coast and the volcanic peaks of the Cascades. Farther east, you'll find high desert, alpine mountains, and deep river canyons—spectacular country that's largely unexplored by visitors.

But Oregon is much more than a scenic abstraction. In few places has human civilization meshed so agreeably with the natural environment. What helps make Oregon unique is the attitude of its citizens, who are fiercely proud of their state, its culture, and its open spaces. Equal to the great outdoors, the arts are cherished and draw crowds by multitudes. The state also celebrates its historical heritage, ethnic makeup, and straightforward high spirits with a thousand festivals. And the food? Much of Oregon is a huge garden where vegetables, fruit, wine grapes, and farm and ranch products reach perfection. Mighty rivers and 360 miles of Pacific coast provide shellfish, salmon, tuna, and halibut.

Clockwise from top left: salmon fisherman sculpture; Multnomah Falls; Coquille River Lighthouse; Cottonwood Canyon State Park; water fountain in Portland; Oregon coastline.

Whether it's "three days and four plays" at the Oregon Shakespeare Festival in Ashland, shopping for wild morel mushrooms at the Sisters farmers market, dueling pinot noir tastings in Carlton, or kiteboarding near Hood River, you'll find that Oregonians engage with everyday life with a verve that's at once intensely local yet tied to a larger, more universal perspective. In Portland, where "organic" and "local" are assumptions, not exceptions, life is rich with the culture and cuisine options of a cosmopolitan center, yet as comfortable and cozy as in a small town.

Oregonians tell a fable about a crossroads on the old Oregon Trail. Pointing south toward the California goldfields was a sign with a drawing of a bag of gold. Pointing north was another sign with the words "To Oregon." The punch line? Only those pioneers who could read continued to Oregon.

Of course, the Oregon Trail is history now, but that doesn't mean that the movement to Oregon is over. The same vaguely agrarian and utopian ideals that drew the pioneers still work magic on a new crop of immigrants eagerly moving to the Beaver State to seek the good life.

Clockwise from top left: Portland's iconic sign; fly fishing, Deschutes River; trail at Cape Perpetua; pears growing in the Hood River Valley.

Planning Your Trip

Where to Go

Portland

Graced by the presence of the Columbia and Willamette Rivers and nearby Mount Hood, Portland is the state's green urban core. Just north of downtown, find the vibrant **Pearl District.** To the west, **Washington Park** is home to rose gardens; trails here connect to **Forest Park,** the nation's largest urban forested park. Cross the Willamette River to the east side to explore thriving neighborhoods.

Columbia River Gorge and Mount Hood

This is the Pacific Northwest's primal landscape: towering waterfalls, moss-draped rainforests, snowcapped volcanoes—all in a chasm 5 miles wide, 80 miles long, and 3,000 feet deep. The **Historic Columbia River Highway** ushers travelers to hiking trails. Hood River has a lovely setting at the foot of **Mount Hood;** drive up the mountain to the landmark **Timberline Lodge** to more hiking trails and nearly year-round skiing.

The Willamette Valley

The historic end of the Oregon Trail, the Willamette Valley is still agriculturally rich, with the emphasis now on **wine grapes.** Nearly the entire west side of the valley is a wine lover's pilgrimage route. **Cycling** the wine country adds an active dimension to such a tour. Hike past some of the state's prettiest waterfalls at **Silver Falls State Park.**

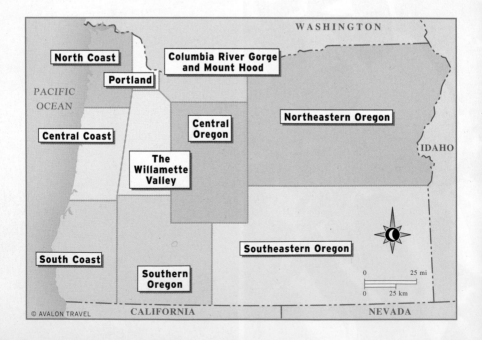

vineyards in the Willamette Valley

North Coast

Sandy beaches along the northern coastline are separated by headlands, most traced by a hiking trail. Lots of beach towns, ranging from quirky spots that are lost in time to sophisticated resort communities, mean that everyone can find a place to adopt as their own. Vibrant **Astoria** has a rich history; **Cannon Beach** is a favorite Portlanders' getaway; and the **Three Capes Scenic Loop** west of Tillamook provides access to spectacular beaches, including the one at **Cape Kiwanda.**

Central Coast

The central coast is anchored at its northern end by sprawling **Lincoln City** and exemplified by **Newport,** with charming neighborhoods, an active fishing port, and the **Oregon Coast Aquarium.** At the southern end of the region, **Florence** and **Reedsport** are great bases for visits to the **Oregon Dunes,** which form an otherworldly sandscape dotted with lakes and bisected by broad estuaries.

South Coast

The south coast feels far from everything, a landscape of mountains, dense forest, wild rivers, and beaches punctuated with dramatic rock formations. West of **Coos Bay** are wild and beautiful natural areas. **Bandon** is cozy and full of tourists, many there for the world-class golf courses at **Bandon Dunes.** The southernmost part of Oregon's coastline may be its most scenic, especially the stretch between **Gold Beach** and **Brookings.**

If You Have . . .

- **A LONG WEEKEND:** Visit Portland with day trips to the Willamette Valley wine country and the Columbia River Gorge.

- **ONE WEEK:** Add a trip down the coast from Astoria to Newport, then head east to Bend and central Oregon's alpine lakes and volcanoes. Return to Portland via Mount Hood.

- **TWO WEEKS:** Add eastern Oregon (catch the Wallowa Mountains in late summer), Crater Lake, and Ashland's Shakespeare Festival.

Southern Oregon

Southern Oregon is a land of opposites, ranging from the arts town of **Ashland,** known for its **Shakespeare Festival,** to some of the state's most secluded backcountry. The valleys of the **North Umpqua and Rogue Rivers** are both attractive to hikers and anglers; the Rogue is a top-notch white-water river. **Crater Lake** is a mesmerizing highlight in Southern Oregon.

Central Oregon

The high desert of central Oregon is cut through by the **Deschutes and Crooked Rivers** and dotted with volcanic peaks. In **Bend,** visitors can find good food and a comfortable place to spend the night as well as skiing at nearby **Mount Bachelor** and easy access to hiking and mountain biking. Raft trips vary from tame floats to the rip-roaring rapids outside **Maupin.** Visit the **Warm Springs Indian Reservation** to get a sense of Native American history and culture.

Northeastern Oregon

You'll hear echoes of the Old West in northeastern Oregon, whether you're touring Chief Joseph's homeland, tracing the steps of Oregon Trail pioneers, or cheering rodeo athletes at the **Pendleton Round-Up.** Go even further into the past at the **John Day Fossil Beds,** or explore the

John Day Fossil Beds and the Painted Hills

geology of Hells Canyon with a boat ride down the **Snake River.**

Southeastern Oregon

This high-desert region boasts deep blue skies, geologic marvels, and plenty of elbow room. Soak in natural hot springs, view migrating birds at the vast **Malheur National Wildlife Refuge,** and get to know your fellow travelers at the **Frenchglen Hotel.** A visit to this corner of Oregon will reconnect you with nature and give you time and space for reflection.

When to Go

Although **summer** weather is usually beautiful, June can be cloudy and cool in the Willamette Valley. When the Willamette Valley heats up, the coast usually remains cool, with morning fog. Trails in the Cascades are often snowy until mid-July—find early summer hikes in the Columbia Gorge or along the Rogue River Trail.

Spring is ideal for touring southeastern Oregon, unless you want to make it all the way to the top of Steens Mountain, which is usually closed by snow until early July.

Autumn's first rains appear in September, but October's weather often starts off clear and beautiful. Even after the rains start, remember that cloudy days with scattered rain are the norm, and that "sun breaks" are common.

Although the mountainous parts of the state accumulate huge amounts of snow during the **winter,** snowfall is rare on the coast and in the western valleys. Wintertime temperatures are usually above freezing, though the dampness can make it seem colder.

sea lions in Astoria's harbor

The Best of Oregon

It's almost impossible to cover all of Oregon in a week, so we've crafted a 10-day tour that hits most of the highlights. Although we think it would be a great trip, don't take this itinerary too seriously—and don't hesitate to stay longer at one site or discover your own favorite places along this route. With a mere 10 days to explore the entire state in this itinerary, we couldn't quite get you into the heart of eastern Oregon, but that doesn't mean we don't highly recommend this part of the state. In fact, we like it so much we've devoted an entirely different itinerary to it.

Day 1
PORTLAND
Fly into **Portland International Airport** and either pick up a rental car or take the MAX light rail train into town and arrange to get a rental car in downtown Portland. Spend the afternoon strolling around downtown, visiting Powell's Books and the **Pearl District.** Spend the night at the Heathman Hotel and dine nearby at old

fave Higgins Restaurant & Bar or, a slightly longer walk away, at Tasty n Alder.

Day 2
NORTH COAST
Head northwest out of Portland on U.S. 30 to **Astoria.** Explore this historic town at the mouth of the Columbia River, including a visit to the replica of Fort Clatsop, which served as Lewis and Clark's winter home in 1805-1806. Then continue south and spend the night in **Cannon Beach** at the Stephanie Inn.

Day 3
NORTH COAST TO CENTRAL COAST
Head south out of town on U.S. 101 and stop for a walk at **Oswald West State Park,** where you can follow a short trail through an old-growth forest to Short Sands Beach to watch the surfers. Then drive down the coast as far as **Yachats** and spend the night at Overleaf Lodge. Eat dinner and catch some live music at the Drift Inn Pub.

Mount Hood

Day 4
CENTRAL COAST TO THE WILLAMETTE VALLEY

Spend the morning exploring the tidepools and old-growth forest around **Cape Perpetua**. Take a tour of **Sea Lion Caves** (or just peer down from the road with your binoculars). From the seaside town of Florence, cut east on Route 126 to **Eugene,** with a detour south to Lorane for a visit to the King Estate Winery tasting room. Spend the night near Eugene's riverside trails at the elegant Inn at the 5th.

Days 5-6
ASHLAND AND SOUTHERN OREGON

Drive south along I-5 to **Ashland** to attend a world-class play. Dine at New Sammy's Cowboy Diner (reserve well in advance) or Amuse, and spend the night at the Ashland Springs Hotel.

From Medford, just north of Ashland, drive up the Rogue River on Route 62 through the tiny towns of Prospect and Union Creek to **Crater Lake National Park,** where you'll spend the night at the Crater Lake Lodge.

Day 7
BEND AND CENTRAL OREGON

Head north on U.S. 97 to **Bend,** visiting the **Lava Lands Visitor Center** and **High Desert Museum** on the way. Stay downtown at the Oxford Hotel or a few miles out of town along the Deschutes River at the Mount Bachelor Resort.

Day 8
CENTRAL OREGON TO MOUNT HOOD

Continue north to **Maupin** to meet your raft guide for a daylong float down the Deschutes. At the end of the day, drive up **Mount Hood** and spend the night at Timberline Lodge.

Day 9
COLUMBIA RIVER GORGE AND MOUNT HOOD

Hike along the **Timberline Trail** (or spend the morning skiing—even in August) and then drive to Hood River. Take a hike to **Upper Horsetail Falls** and then continue west to **Troutdale,** where you'll spend your final night at **McMenamins Edgefield.**

Day 10
RETURN TO PORTLAND

It doesn't take long—about 20 minutes—to get from Edgefield to the Portland airport. If you have a late flight, spend the day in **Portland,** visiting Washington and Forest Parks.

Best Bike Rides

PORTLAND AREA
Waterfront Park and the Eastbank Esplanade
3-5 miles, easy

In downtown Portland, **Waterfront Park and the Eastbank Esplanade** run along either bank of the Willamette River. Cross the Steel Bridge's pedestrian and bike bridge (it's beneath the bridge's main span) at the northern end of the loop, and ride the Hawthorne Bridge's sidewalk at the loop's south end. It's a car-free three-mile loop, so it's good for the whole family. If you want to ride a couple of miles farther, continue south on the east side past the Oregon Museum of Science and Industry to the **Tillikum Bridge,** which has separate lanes for bikes, pedestrians, buses, MAX trains, and the streetcar. Bike lanes on the west side of the bridge usher you back north to Waterfront Park.

More ambitious cyclists should stay on the east side and continue south; the trail will jog a couple of blocks east and become the **Springwater Corridor,** which runs 21 miles to the town of Boring.

Banks-Vernonia Trail
42 miles roundtrip, moderate

The **Banks-Vernonia State Trail** runs along the route of an old logging train and includes 80-foot-high railroad trestles, one of which is safety-improved for cyclists. Catch the trail west of Portland; Banks is on Route 47 just south of Route 26. The trail passes through sprawling Stub Stewart State Park, which has a campground and great mountain biking. If you want to cut a few miles off your ride, turn around at Stub Stewart.

COLUMBIA GORGE
Mosier Twin Tunnels
7 miles roundtrip, easy

Another family-friendly ride is along the five-mile **Mosier Twin Tunnels** stretch of the Historic Columbia River Highway between Hood River and Mosier. This is a restored portion of the old road, now open only to bike and foot traffic. Park at the Mark O. Hatfield Trailhead at the east end of Hood River, near exit 64 from I-84 ($3 parking fee) or ride up from town (it's a steep approach).

WILLAMETTE VALLEY
Aufderheide National Scenic Byway
60 miles one way, challenging

Oakridge is known for its network of mountain bike trails, but a wonderful road ride starts here, too, and goes north along the **Aufderheide National Scenic Byway** to Rainbow, a site on the McKenzie River Highway (Route 126). Near the northern end of the ride, you'll pass Terwilliger Hot Springs. Believe us when we tell you that you'll be too tired to turn around and ride back the way you came, so a car drop is recommended.

SOUTHERN OREGON
Crater Lake Loop
33 miles, challenging

Don't plan to ride the loop around **Crater Lake's rim** too early in the summer, or you'll run into snow. And don't count on riding it too fast, either; most of the ride is above 7,000 feet, and you'll be stopping not only to suck air but also to admire the great views of the lake. There's a window, usually in late June, when most of the snow has melted but the road is not yet entirely open to cars. A car-free weekend is also held during the third weekend of September.

OREGON COAST
Oregon Coast Bike Route
342 miles one way, challenging

The Oregon Coast Bike Route, a hilly 342-mile ride along busy U.S. 101, is popular for its spectacular ocean views and ample opportunities for eating and sleeping, whether in a hotel bed or in a sleeping bag at a campground.

STATEWIDE
Cycle Oregon
Mileage varies, usually about 400 miles, challenging

Cycle Oregon has mapped out some great routes over the years for its weeklong mid-September tours. One of these makes a 365-mile loop through northeastern Oregon, starting in Baker City, heading east to Halfway, north along Forest Road 39 to Joseph, northwest through Enterprise and Lostine to Elgin, then south along back roads through Cove and Union back to the starting point. Train well for this ride: It's wild, rugged, and beautiful country, and the stretch from Halfway to Joseph climbs over 7,000 feet in 61 miles.

RIDE OREGON
Find a ride anywhere in the state at www.rideoregonride.com. Here you can find notices of upcoming bicycling events as well as rides along scenic bikeways, mountain trails, and roads. Each ride includes detailed directions and cue sheets, elevation profiles, and maps. Try the 38-mile Covered Bridges Scenic Bikeway out of Cottage Grove, a challenging 79-mile mountain bike ride along the North Umpqua Trail, or a 135-mile figure-eight tour of northeastern Oregon's back roads, starting and ending in La Grande.

One of the things residents love most about Portland is how easy it is to get out of town. The following places are within a couple of hours of downtown Portland:

- **Columbia River Gorge:** It only takes 45 minutes to drive to the Gorge. If all you want to do is see Multnomah Falls, go early in the day (the parking lot fills up on nice days) and you'll be back in town by lunchtime. Extend your trip by hiking to the top of the falls, catching the Larch Mountain trail to the Wahkeena Falls trail (trail 420), and hiking down via Wahkeena Falls. The final half-mile of this five-mile loop is on the road.

- **Oregon Coast:** Head west on U.S. 26, and within two hours you'll be gazing at tidepools at the base of Haystack Rock. Grab lunch in Cannon Beach, then head south to Oswald West State Park for hiking or surfing (rent surf gear in Cannon Beach). Finish with a visit to Manzanita for a burrito or some pizza; hang around long enough to miss the evening rush hour into Portland.

- **Mount Hood:** In the winter, a ski trip is a no-brainer. Mount Hood Meadows is our favorite place for downhill, but a day on the slopes at Timberline Ski Area is enhanced by an après-ski

hot cocoa (or beer, if you're not driving) in the lodge. Cross-country and snowshoe trails abound; stop at Otto's in the town of Sandy for rental gear and maps.

- **Pacific Crest Trail:** In summer, hike the Pacific Crest Trail in the area around Timberline Lodge.

- **Willamette Valley wine country:** A loop that includes Dundee, McMinnville, and Carlton makes a good day trip in the wine country. Don't be tempted to stop at every tasting room you see on the way, and remember that all three of these towns have excellent places to eat. Consider taking back roads on your return to Portland (you'll need a map!).

- **Silverton:** East of Salem, the area around Silverton has a number of lovely places to visit. Hike the trails at Silver Falls State Park—they're especially attractive in the winter—or visit the Oregon Gardens, with cultivated gardens and a house designed by Frank Lloyd Wright. Before heading home, stop at the Mount Angel Abbey for a visit to the library there (designed by Finnish architect Alvar Aalto). The views and the peaceful atmosphere will chill you out for the drive back to Portland.

Silver Falls State Park

Oregon's vineyards feature many different varietals.

The Wine Route

There are over 400 wineries in the state, producing more than 1.7 million cases per year. Wine grape production takes place across the state, even in the dry rangelands of eastern Oregon. Planning a trip through Oregon's many wine regions is a good way to explore the state and track down little-known vintages that don't make it across state lines.

Southern Oregon

DAY 1

Start your wine odyssey in Ashland, where Shakespeare and fine restaurants make good companions for wine exploration. Near town are **Ashland Vineyards,** famous for the white wine Shakespeare's Love, and **Weisinger's Vineyard,** which produces fine viognier and cabernet sauvignon. The area's best wines, and the greatest concentration of wineries, are over the ridge in the Applegate Valley. High summer heat here enables the production of red wines such as cabernet and syrah as well as some California-style chardonnays; check out the wines at **Valley View Winery** or **Troon Vineyard.**

Spend the night at the Ashland Creek Inn, a luxury inn right on the water, and dine at Peerless Restaurant, known for its wine cellar and dedication to regional foods.

DAY 2

Travel north toward Roseburg, central for the wines of the Umpqua Valley. **Abacela** is noted for the many varieties of wine grapes it grows, offering unusual-for-Oregon varietals such as tempranillo, dolcetto, and sangiovese. **Henry Estate Winery** is one of the state's oldest, and has lovely gardens that make an excellent picnic destination. The wines range from full-bodied pinot noir and merlot to refreshing Riesling. **Girardet** produces a range of wines, such as chardonnay, cabernet sauvignon, and pinot noir, and also makes wine from more unusual grapes such as baco noir.

The historic, riverside **Steamboat Inn,** 38 miles up the North Umpqua River, is the region's best dining and lodging choice.

The Willamette Valley

The Willamette Valley is Oregon's primary wine-growing region. Here the weather is cooler in than the Umpqua and Applegate Valleys, favoring the production of pinot noir and chardonnay, the

Touring the Taps

If you're serious about craft brews, plan your trip around the Oregon Brewers Festival, held in Portland during the last full weekend of July.

PORTLAND

- **Cascade Brewing Barrel House:** Try the gose—a lemony, herbal beer that may have a slightly salty finish. It's a good summer beer, and it's also relatively low in alcohol.

- **Hair of the Dog:** HOTD, known for bold, rich flavors and alcohol contents of about 10 percent, also brews some lower-alcohol beers that leave you able to bike home. It's right near the Eastbank Esplanade, making it a good biking destination.

- **Loyal Legion:** If you can't travel to every brewery in the state, just come here. The 99 taps represent only Oregon beers.

COLUMBIA RIVER GORGE

Hood River has two great brewpubs, and the Hood River Hotel is an easy walk from both of these spots.

- **Double Mountain Brewery:** Stop here for pizza and a Double Mountain Hop Lava.

- **Full Sail Brewery:** Brewery tours, good beer, and a spectacular river view from the deck make this a great place to spend the afternoon.

THE WILLAMETTE VALLEY

- **Ninkasi Brewing Company:** Ninkasi was the ancient Sumerian goddess of fermentation, and she's easy to worship with a glass of Believer Double Red Ale in your hand.

- **Rogue Farms Hopyard:** If you've never seen hops growing, head to this Willamette River-side farm in Independence, where, if you visit around the fall harvest time, you'll be able to drink fresh-hopped brew.

- **Brewers Union Local 180** in Oakridge is a favorite with the mountain bikers who come to ride the local trails.

NORTH COAST

- **Fort George Brewery and Public House** in downtown Astoria brews some of the state's best beers. Even if you can't make it to the pub, pick up a can of Belgian-style Quick Wit at a grocery store.

- **Pelican Pub and Brewery** in Pacific City has a spectacular oceanside setting at the foot of Cape Kiwanda and a popular cream ale, in addition to the requisite IPAs.

SOUTHERN OREGON

- **Caldera Tap House:** Tucked away near Ashland Creek, Caldera is just a couple of blocks from the Oregon Shakespeare Festival's theaters.

- **Wild River Brewing** has locations in Grants Pass, Cave Junction, and Brookings Harbor. The pizza at their family-friendly pubs is a local favorite.

CENTRAL OREGON

- **Deschutes Brewery and Public House:** The Mirror Pond pale ale is an Oregonian staple.

- **10 Barrel:** You'll want the award-winning S1NIST0R black ale.

- **Boneyard Brewing:** Only a tasting room, but look for Boneyard on tap around town.

- **GoodLife Brewing:** Bring your dog, sit outside, and get to know the locals over a pint of Descender IPA.

NORTHEASTERN OREGON

Some would say northeastern Oregon is itself off the beaten path, but plenty of brewpubs await to quench your thirst.

- **Prodigal Son Brewery and Pub:** Cowboy up at this lively and pleasant pub on the edge of downtown Pendleton.

- **Terminal Gravity Brewing:** Enjoy a mighty IPA in a creekside setting in Enterprise.

- **Mutiny Brewing:** Avoid Joseph's more touristy choices with this friendly and authentic pub.

- **Barley Brown's Brew Pub:** Make a pilgrimage to Baker City for a pint of Barley Brown ales—if you see a BB brew on tap elsewhere around the state, order it!

Oregon has great bird-watching destinations. Pack your binoculars and go birding at these scenic sanctuaries.

- **Cape Meares Rocks:** This Pacific coast fastness combines rocky headlands (for nesting seabirds such as cormorants, common murres, tufted puffins, and pigeon quillemots) and coastal old-growth forest (home to northern spotted owls, bald eagles, and marbled murrelets).

- **Sauvie Island:** This large, lake-filled island in the Columbia River is a good spot for fall and winter birding, when you might see snow geese and sandhill cranes, plus massive flocks of migrating waterfowl. Bald eagles and peregrine falcons are the primary raptors.

- **Malheur National Wildlife Refuge:** Over 320 bird species have been observed at Malheur Lake; during spring migration it's a top viewing area for sandhill cranes, tundra swans, northern pintails, many types of geese, white pelicans, double-crested cormorants, western grebes, long-billed curlews, and American avocets. Sage grouse are also prevalent.

- **Upper Klamath National Wildlife Refuge:** Large, marshy Upper Klamath Lake is most noted as the winter home of hundreds of bald eagles. In spring breeding season, you may see white pelicans, great egrets, and black-crowned night herons, and, if you're lucky, western and Clark's grebes doing their mating dance on the water.

Make dinner reservations at **Marché** restaurant and spend the night a few steps away at the **Inn at the 5th.**

DAY 2

Between Rickreall and Carlton is the greatest concentration of wineries in the state. Here are the pinot noir vineyards that have put Oregon on the world wine map. With over 200 wineries in a relatively compact area, there's no single route to recommend, so pick up a copy of the widely available Willamette Valley Winery Association's winery map, and follow your instincts.

That said, here are a few tips: Not to be missed is **Sokol Blosser Winery,** with a stunning tasting room perched on a hill just above Dundee. **Domaine Drouhin,** also near Dundee, is the Oregon outpost of France's famed Drouhin family and makes excellent pinot noirs in the Burgundy style. **Anne Amie Vineyards** makes fine pinot noirs and has a beautiful facility with one of the most panoramic views in the valley. The **Rex Hill Vineyards** is just east of Newberg, and it is one of the closest vineyards to Portland, with premium pinot noir and a lovely garden setting.

DAY 3

If it seems like there are just too many wineries to choose from, consider a stop at **Carlton Winemakers Studio,** a cooperative where small winemakers share a winemaking facility and tasting room.

Stay at the **Allison Inn** near Newberg and plan to dine at **Thistle,** in nearby McMinnville.

Columbia River Gorge

Microclimates in the Columbia River Gorge create niches where cool-climate grapes like pinot noir thrive, while just up the road vineyards of syrah and merlot, which require intense summer heat to ripen, may be planted.

DAY 1

There are wineries on both the Oregon and Washington sides of the gorge, so don't hesitate to cross bridges to taste wine. Across the Columbia

grapes of France's Burgundy valley, and pinot gris from northern Italy and the French Alsace region.

DAY 1

Near Eugene, be sure to stop at **King Estate Winery,** with a hilltop tasting and winemaking facility near Lorane that is literally palatial. **Territorial Vineyards & Wine Company** has vineyards near the Coast Range, but a winemaking facility and tasting room in downtown Eugene. From its estate-grown pinot noir grapes, Territorial makes a series of regular pinot noir bottlings and a fantastic rosé.

Top Tents and Trails

COLUMBIA RIVER GORGE

Eagle Creek Campground: The tent campground here is the Forest Service's oldest. The classic gorge trail starts down the hill from the campground and follows Eagle Creek past waterfalls and springtime wildflowers. Your face will be misted with spray, and in places you'll need to grab hold of cables bolted into the basalt cliffs as the trail narrows.

THE WILLAMETTE VALLEY

Silver Falls State Park: Ten waterfalls cascade off canyon walls in a forest of Douglas firs, ferns, and bigleaf and vine maple. Come during fall foliage season when there are few visitors. The campground here offers easy access to hiking and biking trails.

Paradise Campground: This campground provides access to the 26.5-mile McKenzie River National Recreation Trail and the nearby Belknap Lodge and Hot Springs.

NORTH COAST

Fort Stevens State Park: The campground here is large and family-oriented, with lots of yurts. The trails are best for biking around the sprawling park. Hiking is mostly along the beach.

CENTRAL COAST

Carl G. Washburne State Park: Pile your gear into a wheelbarrow (provided) and trundle it to one of the great walk-in campsites. After pitching your tent, take a hike along the Hobbit Trail.

SOUTH COAST

Humbug Mountain State Park: The campground here is pretty close to the road, but traffic quiets down at night. Stay here, and in the morning you'll beat the crowds on the hike up Humbug Mountain, an excellent trail along which to acquaint yourself with native plants.

CENTRAL OREGON

Devils Lake: These prime lakeside campsites, along the Cascade Lakes Highway, are set away from the parking area, so you'll have to schlep your gear. Across the highway is the climber's trail for South Sister.

Metolius River Campgrounds: The many campgrounds here, especially those downstream from Camp Sherman, offer a chance to linger by central Oregon's most magical river. Take a short walk to the headwaters of the Metolius or a longer hike along the river.

Smith Rock State Park: The campground here is a rough-and-ready climber's bivouac, but anyone who's willing to leave their car in the parking area--and return to the parking area to cook dinner (no fires allowed in tent area)--is welcome. Majestic spires tower above the Crooked River at this state park. Seven miles of well-marked trails follow the Crooked River and wend up the canyon walls.

NORTHEASTERN OREGON

Strawberry Campground: This campground offers a quick 1.25-mile hike to Strawberry Lake. Make sure your car has a bit of clearance and good tires before heading up here.

Grande Ronde Lake Campground: Small Grande Ronde Lake lies in a meadow of tiny streams that is the headwaters of the Grande Ronde River. Hiking trails into the Elkhorn Mountains start nearby.

SOUTHEASTERN OREGON

Hart Mountain National Antelope Refuge: This hot springs campground is four miles south of the refuge headquarters. Soak in the hot springs, then explore the area on foot or by mountain bike.

Page Springs: This campground is just a few miles from Frenchglen, at the base of Steens Mountain. Get up early to check out the birds on a hike along the Donner und Blitzen River.

are such notable producers as **Syncline Wine Cellars** and **Domaine Pouillon.**

Stay at the grand and historic **Columbia Gorge Hotel** in Hood River, and dine at **Celilo Restaurant and Bar** for sophisticated fine dining and a wine list rich in local vintages.

Northeastern Oregon

DAY 1

Route 11 runs north from Pendleton up toward Walla Walla, Washington. About a third of the official Walla Walla wine-growing area is in Oregon, and several tasting rooms in Walla Walla call for serious attention from lovers of cabernet and merlot. On the Oregon side, stop in Pendleton at **Great Pacific Wine and Coffee Co.,** where wines from Walla Walla and the Columbia Valley are featured.

Book a room at **Pendleton House Bed and Breakfast** for the night.

The High Desert

Day 1

If you're starting from Portland, drive east on U.S. 26 over the hump of Mount Hood and spend your first afternoon at **Smith Rock State Park.** Hike the trails and watch climbers scale the rocks, then drive down to Bend and settle into your room at **McMenamins Old St. Francis School.**

Day 2

Begin the day with an ocean roll (and a sandwich to go) at **Sparrow Bakery** and a stroll or bike ride along the Deschutes River Trail in town.

Then head about seven miles up the Cascade Lakes Highway and turn off onto Forest Road 41 to hike a more outlying section of the Deschutes trail to Lava Island Falls, Dillon Falls, and Benham Falls. Head back to town for one more night at the St. Francis.

Days 3-4

Now get serious about heading up the Cascade Lakes Highway to hike, fish, or just hang out on a lakeshore. Camp at a hike-in site at **Todd Lake,** or find a more convenient car-camping

Todd Lake

site at one of the other lakes along the road. (If you're not camping, several lakeside resorts rent rustic cabins.) Consider spending more than one night here; once you've found the perfect camping spot, it seems a shame to leave it, and there are plenty of trails to hike, including the tough but rewarding hike from Devils Lake to the top of **South Sister.**

Day 5

Drive down to Sunriver on Route 42 (catch it just past Crane Prairie Reservoir), then south a few miles on U.S. 97 to the turnoff for **Newberry Volcano.** Head up to the caldera, where you can hike the trail through the **Big Obsidian Flow,** and then find your new campground at either **Paulina** or **East Lake** (or a cabin at one of the rustic lakeside resorts).

Day 6

After you break camp, head back down the volcano and north on U.S. 97. Stop to explore the **Lava River Cave.** Continue north and spend the afternoon at the **High Desert Museum** (don't worry, they have a café), then spend the night in either Bend or Sisters.

Day 7

Finish your week with a river trip. Get up early

on the Deschutes River

and drive north of Madras to Maupin, where you'll meet your river guide for a day trip on the **Deschutes River.** Wear sunscreen and quick-dry shorts, and take a swim down the Elevator Rapids.

The Oregon Outback

Jettison your notions of Oregon as a cloud-enshrouded spot and get set for expansive views, lots of wildlife, and a dose of the West in this tour of an area sometimes referred to as "Oregon's outback."

If you're flying in for this trip, consider using the Boise, Idaho airport. It's much closer to Baker City, where this itinerary begins and ends, than the Portland airport.

Day 1

Start your tour of eastern Oregon in **Baker City,**

but don't linger in town for too long; head west to the near-ghost town of **Sumpter** (30 miles) and then up a ways into the Elkhorns for more gold-era history and mining ghost towns. North of Sumpter, follow the **Elkhorn Drive National Scenic Byway** to the near-ghost town of **Granite.** If you're enjoying the drive, continue north and east to Anthony Lakes; from there, continue east back to I-84 and Baker City.

Day 2

Visit the **National Historic Oregon Trail**

Interpretive Center near Baker City, then head about 70 miles east on Route 86 to **Hells Canyon** at Oxbow, where you can take a look at the Snake River's gorge by car, jet boat, or on foot. Backtrack and stay the night in **Halfway,** just beneath the southern edge of the **Wallowa Mountains.**

Day 3

From Halfway, head about 15 miles east on Route 86, then turn north on Forest Road 39. This 54-mile summer-only road will take you up the eastern edge of the Wallowas—and past the area's most accessible viewpoint onto **Hells Canyon**—to lodgings in the artsy town of **Joseph** or at nearby **Wallowa Lake.**

Day 4

Take the **Wallowa Lake Tramway** from Wallowa Lake. The tram lets you off at the top of Mount Howard, where there is a network of hiking trails. Then head west to I-84 at La Grande and follow the interstate to Pendleton. Tour the

Pendleton Underground and spend the night in town.

Day 5

Hop back on I-84 and take it west to Arlington. From Arlington, drive south on Route 19 to the **John Day Fossil Beds.** Just south of the Thomas Condon Paleontology Center, turn west onto U.S. 26 and take it to your night's lodging in John Day.

Day 6

It's a pretty drive south from John Day on U.S. 395 through Burns to the **Malheur National Wildlife Refuge.** Visit the refuge headquarters a few miles east of Route 205, then continue south on Route 205 to lodgings in **Frenchglen.**

Day 7

If the snows have melted, drive the **Steens Mountain Byway.** Spend another night in Frenchglen, or head north to Burns before driving back to Boise to fly home.

Wallowa Lake

Although we can't direct you to the Northwest Passage, we can suggest great river trips in every corner of the state.

- **Portland:** Paddle the Willamette with a sea kayak or stand-up paddleboard from **Portland Kayak Company** (6600 SW Macadam Ave., 503/459-4050, www.portlandkayak.com) on the west side of the Willamette River or **Alder Creek Kayak** (1515 SE Water St., 503/285-1819, www.aldercreek.com) just off the Eastbank Esplanade immediately south of the Hawthorne Bridge. An easy afternoon tour circumnavigates Ross Island and offers a chance to see bald eagles nesting just a couple of miles from downtown.

- **The Willamette Valley:** In mid-August join the Willamette Riverkeepers' **Paddle Oregon** event (www.paddleoregon.org) to run 107 miles of the Willamette in a canoe or sea kayak. It's also easy to do this trip, or a shorter one, on your own.

- **Columbia Gorge and Mount Hood:** Catch some wind on the mighty Columbia. **Big Winds** (207 Front St., Hood River, 541/386-6086, www.bigwinds.com) offers board and full rig rentals, lessons, and all the necessary windsurfing equipment. Or give kiteboarding a try.

- **North Coast:** Rent a surfboard and wetsuit at **Cleanline Surf** (171 Sunset Blvd., 503/436-9726) in Cannon Beach, drive a few miles south, and hike down to Short Sands Beach at Oswald West State Park.

- **Central Coast:** Explore a quiet coastal stream and wetland and its abundant wildlife at **Beaver Creek,** south of Newport. Make reservations in advance for a **guided tour** (Brian Booth State Park, 541563-6412).

- **South Coast:** Board a jet boat and travel upstream from the mouth of the Rogue River through a Wild and Scenic stretch that's loaded with wildlife and lush vegetation. **Jerry's Rogue Jets** (29985 Harbor Way, Gold Beach, 541/247-4571 or 800/451-3645, www.roguejets.com) has been running these trips for many years, and the boat pilots are known for their excellent commentary.

- **Southern Oregon:** Take a multiday raft trip on the Rogue River starting seven miles west of Grants Pass. This stretch not only has some of the best white water in the United States, but also backcountry riverside lodges. The Rogue is also ideal for half- and full-day rafting trips, with most outfitters putting in near the town of Merlin and continuing downstream as far as Foster Bar. **Morrison's Rogue River Lodge** (8500 Galice Rd., Merlin, 541/476-3825 or 800/826-1963, www.rogueriverraft.com) leads a variety of trips.

- **Central Oregon:** Spend a day rafting the Deschutes River surrounded by sage-covered grasslands and wild rocky canyons, where you might see bald eagles, pronghorn, and other wildlife. The town of Maupin is home base for many outfitters, including **All Star Rafting and Kayaking** (405 Deschutes Ave., 541/395-2201 or 800/909-7238, www.asrk.com).

- **Northeastern Oregon:** The undammed John Day River winds through unpopulated rangeland and scenic rock formations; plan to spend a few days away from everything. It's easy enough for almost everybody to paddle on their own; **Service Creek Stage Stop** (38686 Hwy. 19, Fossil, 541/468-3331, www.servicecreek.com) rents rafts and can set you up with a car shuttle. Farther east, an early-summer raft trip on the **Wallowa and Grande Ronde Rivers** starts in Minam and heads into a rugged, remote canyon. Find rentals, shuttles, and a guide at **Minam Raft Rentals** (541/437-1111, www.minamrafterentals.com).

- **Southeastern Oregon:** The Owyhee River is a prime springtime destination for white-water enthusiasts. The 53 miles from Rome to the Owyhee Reservoir have two sections of exceptionally heavy rapids, but the many pools of short, intense white water alternating with easy drifts make for a well-paced trip. **Ouzel Outfitters** (541/385-5947 or 800/788-7238, www.oregonrafting.com) is one of several companies with guided Owyhee trips.

Portland

Look for ★ to find recommended
sights, activities, dining, and lodging.

Highlights

★ **Portland Art Museum:** Portland's green and shady South Park Blocks are home to this excellent collection of art and artifacts (page 37).

★ **Tom McCall Waterfront Park:** This riverside park is home to lots of summer festivals, great people-watching, a fountain, and over a mile of seawall to stroll (page 38).

★ **International Rose Test Garden:** The most spectacular sights in Washington Park are these famed gardens containing 10,000 rose plants (page 39).

★ **Portland Japanese Garden:** Five gardens in one, this is one of the most authentic Japanese gardens in the United States (page 40).

★ **Lan Su Chinese Garden:** A magical enclave in historic Chinatown, this replica of a Ming Dynasty garden was built by craftspeople from Suzhou, China (page 43).

★ **Pearl District:** This upscale shopping and dining district is Oregon's most densely populated neighborhood, home to many of the city's top galleries and restaurants (page 44).

★ **Hawthorne District:** This neighborhood, with its kick-back hippie vibe, is a good place to sip coffee and people watch (page 50).

★ **Forest Park:** In the nation's largest forested urban park, you can mountain bike or walk on Leif Erikson Drive or explore part of the 30-plus-mile-long Wildwood Trail (page 52).

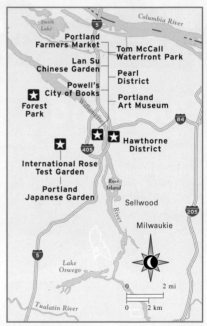

★ **Portland Farmers Market:** On Saturdays, the South Park Blocks explode with the fresh bounty of the Willamette Valley (page 67).

★ **Powell's City of Books:** As the Pearl District has flourished, so has this huge bookstore, known for its mix of new and used titles (page 69).

Perhaps the headline in the *San Francisco Chronicle* said it best—"Newsflash: When we weren't looking, Portland got hip."

At some point in the past decade, Portland's place in the popular culture firmament has vaulted from that of a friendly, flannel-clad, rain-scrubbed city solidly lodged in the nation's second tier to being a major trendsetter in cuisine, wine, arts, design, and up-to-the-second lifestyles.

Oregon's largest city, Portland is cosmopolitan and has a metro area population of 2.34 million, although the city's easygoing and quirky spirit makes it feel like a much smaller town. It's extremely easy to feel at home here—many's the tale of visitors coming to stay for a few days and finding a few pleasant years later that they forgot to leave.

Newcomers are drawn here to live out their dream of launching a startup, opening a coffee shop, founding a clothing design firm, or establishing a microdistillery. It's Portland's combination of youthful idealism and entrepreneurial zeal that really sets the city apart, and it is currently one of the top West Coast destinations for "young creatives"—that is, college-educated 25- to 34-year-olds.

And then there's the politics. Portland is famously liberal and irreverent. In fact, even as the city grows, its reputation as a center of unconventional lifestyles and alternative and populist politics increases. But there's more to Portland than tribal tattoos and indolent coffee shops. Amid lush greenery rare in an urban environment, high-tech business ventures, top-notch cultural institutions (including a first-rate symphony, opera company, and art museum), and distinctive architecture lend an air of worldly sophistication. A latticework of bridges spanning the Willamette River adds a distinctive profile, while parks, plazas, and other public spaces give Portland a heart and a soul.

The result is a small city with lots of personality; an urban area equally suffused with green space and creative energy. A recent *New York Times* article declared Portland to be the most European city in the United States, but most Portlanders were too busy biking, drinking handcrafted ale, and buying local cheese at the farmers market to have noticed.

Previous: International Rose Test Garden in Washington Park; Portland's skyline. **Above:** view of downtown Portland from the Eastbank Esplanade.

Greater Portland Area

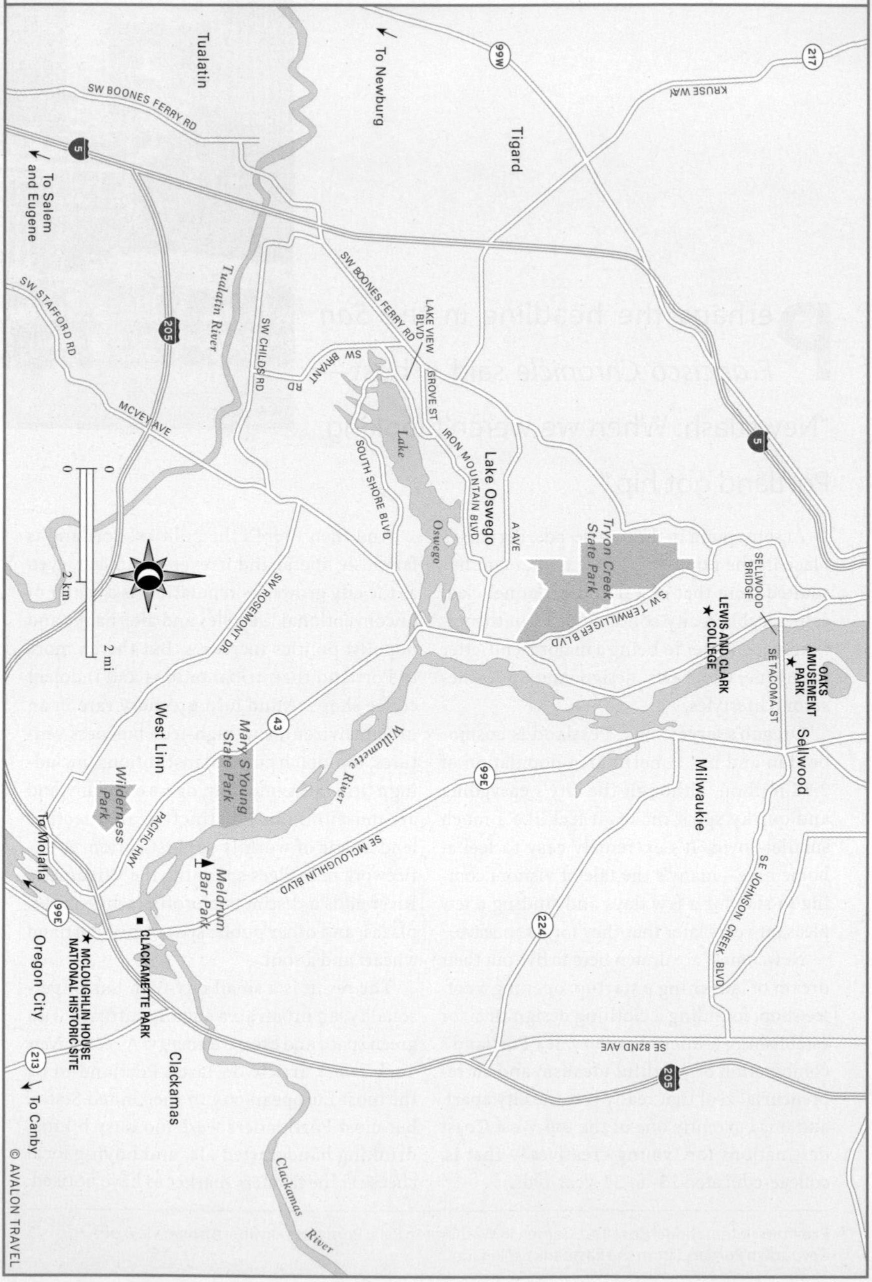

To Newburg

Tualatin

SW BOONES FERRY RD

99W

Tigard

217

KRUSE WAY

5

To Salem
and Eugene

205

SW STAFFORD RD

Tualatin River

MCVEY AVE

SW BOONES FERRY RD

SW CHILDS RD

SW BRYANT RD

LAKE VIEW BLVD

GROVE ST

IRON MOUNTAIN BLVD

Lake

Oswego

SOUTH SHORE BLVD

Lake Oswego

A AVE

SW TERWILLIGER BLVD

Tryon Creek
State Park

5

SELLWOOD
BRIDGE

★ LEWIS AND CLARK
COLLEGE

SE TACOMA ST

OAKS
AMUSEMENT
★ PARK

Sellwood

0

0

2 km

2 mi

SW HOMESMONT DR

West Linn

Mary S Young
State Park

43

Wilderness
Park

PACIFIC HWY

Willamette River

Meldrum
Bar Park

SE MCLOUGHLIN BLVD

99E

Milwaukie

SE JOHNSON CREEK BLVD

224

SE 82ND AVE

205

To Molalla

99E

Oregon City

213

To Canby

★ MCLOUGHLIN HOUSE
NATIONAL HISTORIC SITE

■ CLACKAMETTE PARK

Clackamas

Clackamas River

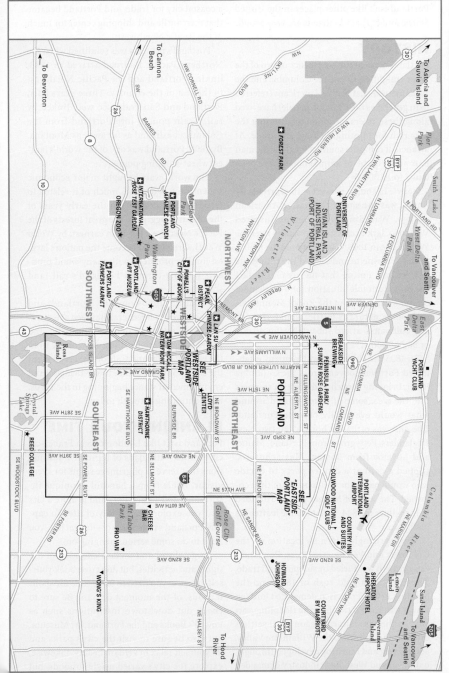

Portland isn't like other places in the United States, and of that its citizens are very proud.

HISTORY

Portland sits near the confluence of two of the West's mightiest rivers, the Columbia and the Willamette. Local Native Americans (referred to in general as the Chinook people) have lived along these rivers for millennia, finding the area rich for hunting, fishing, and trade. At an ancient campsite south of Portland, human hair and a cache of animal bones have been dated to 10,000 BC.

Sauvie Island, northwest of the current city limits, was the site of the Native American village, Wal-lamt, whose name inspired William Clark to christen the nearby river the Willamette in 1805. Clark explored the mouth of the Willamette and viewed the future site of Portland, noting that the area "is in fact the only desirable situation for a settlement on the western side of the Rocky Mountains, and, being naturally fertile, would, if properly cultivated, afford subsistence for 40,000 or 50,000 souls."

In 1825 the Hudson's Bay Company established Fort Vancouver across the Columbia River, bringing French and Scottish trappers into the area, some of whom retired around what would eventually become Portland. The city was officially born when two New Englanders, Pettygrove from Portland, Maine, and Lovejoy from Boston, Massachusetts, flipped a coin at a dinner party to decide who would name the 640-acre claim they co-owned. The state-of-Mainer won and decided in the winter of 1844-1845 to name it after his birthplace.

Unsurprisingly, given its location on the Columbia and Willamette rivers, Portland's early growth was fueled by shipping and trade. The California gold rush of 1849 and the building of San Francisco demanded lumber, which was routed through the fledgling port city. At the same time, Oregon Trail settlers brought agriculture to the Willamette Valley, and mining and ranching developed throughout the inland West. Each industry demanded a coastal city for trade, and Portland became that mercantile and shipping center for much of the Pacific Northwest.

Portland's primacy was solidified when the Northern Pacific Railroad arrived in 1883, linking Portland and the Pacific Northwest to the rest of the country. Three years later, Portland and San Francisco were linked by rail. Grain poured into Portland from the Columbia basin and as far away as Montana. By 1890, Portland was one of the world's largest wheat-shipping points.

The world wars brought major economic expansion to Portland, much of it related to resource exploitation. In the early years of the century, logging of the great forests of the Pacific Northwest began in earnest; by World War II, Oregon had become the nation's largest lumber producer, with many wood products passing through Portland's rail- and shipyards.

From the 1960s onward, Portland, and western Oregon in general, has seen a new migration of settlers. Educated, idealistic, and politically progressive, these newcomers from the eastern states and California served to tilt the city's political balance toward a liberal and environmental stance beginning in the 1970s, and continuing through today.

PLANNING YOUR TIME

Portland isn't like London or San Francisco, cities filled with loads of top-notch destinations that serve as pilgrimage sights for every visitor. Aside from a handful of unique institutions and sights, Portland is more a city that you explore for its way of life. To capture Portland's potent allure—to "get it"—you need to do some serious hanging out.

So go ahead and make a checklist of top sights and activities, but don't overbook yourself, because you need to leave time for spontaneous, of-the-moment detours. Be sure to check out downtown institutions such as Powell's Books and the Portland Art Museum, but also be sure to visit the city's parks and let yourself relax in verdant beauty. Likewise, explore the city's varied neighborhoods, but take time to chat with new best friends in a brewpub or coffee shop. The point is that the Portland experience is more a lifestyle than a set of destinations.

ORIENTATION

Familiarizing yourself with directional reference points will help you smoothly navigate the city. The line of demarcation between north and south in addresses is Burnside Street; between east and west it's the Willamette River. These give reference points for the address prefixes southwest, southeast, north, northwest, and northeast. Avenues run north-south and streets run east-west.

Sights

Portland offers the visitor a wealth of attractions and experiences, from cultural and historic to hands-on and avant-garde. Alongside the built environment are Portland's myriad beloved parks, which range from meticulously tended to sprawling and untamed. Portland has all the amenities you expect from a city, but with a healthy dose of the great outdoors.

Before you arrive, check out **Travel Portland** (1000 SW Broadway, Ste. 2300, Portland, OR, 97205, 503/275-9750 or 800/962-3700, www.travelportland.com) for free maps and their informative magazine-like publication *Travel Portland*.

For a fun overview of Portland's top sights, join Big Pink Sightseeing's **Hop-On Hop-Off Trolley Tour** (503/241-7373, www.graylineofportland.net, $32). A daylong ticket lets you jump off and on an open-air, covered bus anywhere along its 12-stop route.

DOWNTOWN

Portland's modern downtown core is located on a broad ledge of land between the north-flowing Willamette River and a steep volcanic ridge just to the west called the West Hills. These "hills" are more accurately called the Tualatin Mountains, and they form a backdrop that towers over 1,000 feet above downtown. The forested West Hills are home to one of Portland's oldest and most beautiful residential neighborhoods and to Washington Park, the city's grandest.

Portland's city center is a pleasant area with lots of green spaces and tree-lined streets. Cafés and bars spill onto the pavement, and a handsome blend of modern office towers, turn-of-the-20th-century storefronts, and office buildings lends architectural interest.

What Portland doesn't have is massive skyscrapers. Building heights are restricted to no more than 400 feet to maintain the city's "human scale." In addition, city blocks in downtown Portland are only 200 by 200 feet, which makes the city seem more accessible, pedestrian-friendly, and fun and easy to explore.

The best introduction to downtown Portland is a walking tour that also takes advantage of the city's excellent mass transit. Ask for a free *Walking Tour Map* of Portland published by Powell's Books, available from the bookstore, from Travel Portland's visitor center in Pioneer Courthouse Square, or by download at www.powells.com/portland_walking_map.pdf.

Pioneer Courthouse Square

The nominal center of downtown Portland is **Pioneer Courthouse Square** (SW 6th Ave. and Broadway at Morrison St.), a block-square redbrick plaza at the intersection of the city's shopping, transportation, business, and cultural districts. In addition to serving as an urban park and entertainment venue, the square houses a ticket and information office for **TriMet** (701 SW 6th Ave., 503/238-7433, www.trimet.org, 8:30am-5:30pm Mon.-Fri.), which operates the city's public transportation, and Travel Portland's **Visitor**

Portland

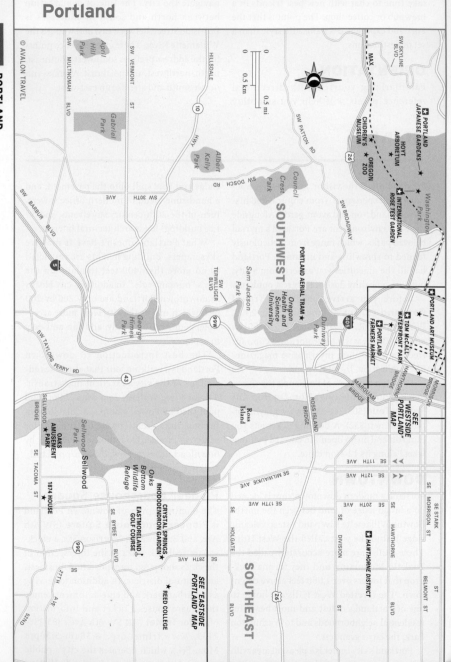

© AVALON TRAVEL

SW SKYLINE BLVD

MAX

April Hill Park

SW MULTNOMAH BLVD

SW VERMONT ST

Gabriel Park

HILLSDALE

Albert Kelly Park

Council Crest Park

SW DOSCH RD

SW 30TH AVE

SW PATTON RD

Hwy 10

26

SW BROADWAY

✚ PORTLAND JAPANESE GARDENS

CHIDREN'S MUSEUM

HOYT ARBORETUM

★ OREGON ZOO

✚ INTERNATIONAL ROSE TEST GARDEN

Washington Park

SOUTHWEST

PORTLAND AERIAL TRAM ★

Sam Jackson Park

Oregon Health and Science University

SW TERWILLIGER BLVD

Dunway Park

✚ PORTLAND ART MUSEUM

★ TOM McCALL WATERFRONT PARK

✚ PORTLAND FARMERS MARKET

SW BARBUR BLVD

5

99W

405

SW TAYLORS FERRY RD

George Himes Park

43

MARQUAM BRIDGE

SEE "WESTSIDE PORTLAND" MAP

HAWTHORNE BRIDGE

MORRISON BRIDGE

SELLWOOD BRIDGE

Sellwood Park

★ OAKS AMUSEMENT PARK

SE TACOMA ST

Sellwood

Ross Island

ROSS ISLAND BRIDGE

SE 11TH AVE

SE 12TH AVE

SE MORRISON ST

SE STARK ST

Oaks Bottom Wildlife Refuge

★ 1874 HOUSE

SE BYBEE BLVD

CRYSTAL SPRINGS RHODODENDRON GARDEN ★

EASTMORELAND GOLF COURSE

SE 17TH AVE

SE MILWAUKIE AVE

SE 20TH AVE

SE HOLGATE BLVD

DIVISION ST

✚ HAWTHORNE DISTRICT

HAWTHORNE BLVD

BELMONT ST

99E

SE 27TH AVE

★ RED COLLEGE

SE 28TH AVE

SE 52ND

SOUTHEAST

SEE "EASTSIDE PORTLAND" MAP

0 ——— 0.5 mi
0 ——— 0.5 km

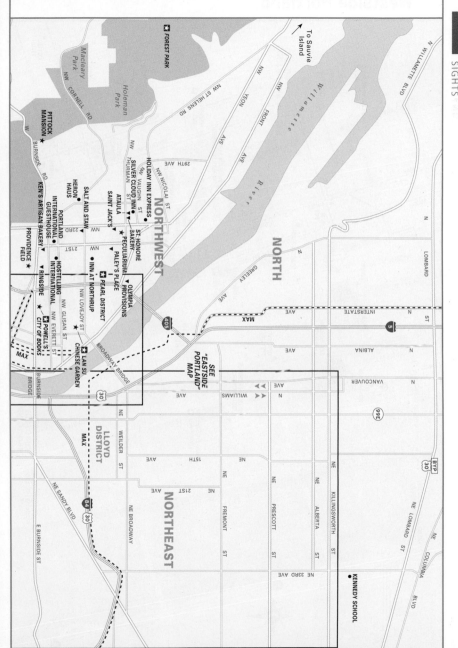

To Sauvie Island

✚ FOREST PARK

Macleary Park

Holeman Park

NW CORNELL RD

PITTOCK MANSION ★

W BURNSIDE RD

KEN'S ARTISAN BAKERY ▼

PROVIDENCE FIELD ★

HERON HAUS ●
SALT AND STRAW ▼
PORTLAND INTERNATIONAL GUESTHOUSE ●
HOSTELLING INTERNATIONAL ✚
RINGSIDE ▼
POWELL'S CITY OF BOOKS ✚ ★

SILVER CLOUD INN ▼
HOLIDAY INN EXPRESS
ATAULA ▼
SAINT JACK'S ▼
ST HONORÉ BAKERY ★
PECULIARIUM ★
PALEY'S PLACE ▼
INN AT NORTHRUP ●
PEARL DISTRICT ✚
OLYMPIA PROVISIONS ▼

NW VAUGHN ST
NW THURMAN ST
NW NICOLAI ST
NW 29TH AVE
NW ST HELENS RD

NW YEON AVE
NW FRONT AVE

Willamette River

NW 23RD
NW 21ST

NW NORTHRUP
NW LOVEJOY ST
NW GLISAN ST
NW EVERETT ST

LAN SU CHINESE GARDEN ✚ ★

BROADWAY BRIDGE
405
MAX
BURNSIDE BRIDGE
30

NORTHWEST

N GREELEY AVE
N INTERSTATE AVE
N ALBINA AVE
N VANCOUVER AVE
N WILLIAMS AVE

NORTH

5
MAX

"SEE EASTSIDE PORTLAND" MAP

99E

BYP 30

LLOYD DISTRICT

NE WEIDLER ST
NE BROADWAY
NE 16TH AVE
NE 21ST AVE

NORTHEAST

MAX
84
30
NE SANDY BLVD
E BURNSIDE ST

NE FREMONT ST
NE PRESCOTT ST
NE ALBERTA ST
NE KILLINGSWORTH ST
NE LOMBARD ST
NE COLUMBIA BLVD

N WILLAMETTE BLVD
N LOMBARD ST

NE 33RD AVE

KENNEDY SCHOOL ●

Westside Portland

SW 13TH AVE
SW 12TH AVE
SW 11TH AVE
SW 10TH AVE
SW 9TH AVE

SW MORRISON ST
SW YAMHILL ST
SW MAIN ST
SW SALMON ST
SW TAYLOR ST

SOUTH PARK BLOCKS CULTURAL DISTRICT

PORTLAND FARMERS MARKET

SOUTH PARK BLOCKS

PORTLAND STATE UNIVERSITY

SOUTH PARK BLOCKS

PORTLAND ART MUSEUM

STREET CAR

STREET CAR

CENTRAL LIBRARY

HOTEL DELUXE

RED/BLUE

GRUNER

SW ALDER ST

SW WASHINGTON ST

GOVERNOR HOTEL

HABIBI

PARK AVE

OREGON HISTORICAL SOCIETY MUSEUM

HEATHMAN HOTEL AND RESTAURANT

ANTOINE HATFIELD HALL

SOUTHPARK

PIONEER COURTHOUSE SQUARE/ TRAVEL PORTLAND

HOTEL VINTAGE PLAZA

PORTLAND WESTIN

SW HALL ST
SW MONTGOMERY ST
SW MILL ST

MAX

BROADWAY AVE

PARK AVE

SW COLUMBIA ST

SW JEFFERSON ST

SW MADISON ST

HIGGINS

ARLENE SCHNITZER HALL

PORTLAND HILTON

THE NINES/ URBAN FARMER

HOTEL LUCIA/ TYPHOON

MAX

SW 6TH AVE

STREET CAR

SW 5TH AVE

AAA

GREEN/YELLOW

HOTEL MONACO

SW 4TH AVE

HOTEL MODERO

IRA'S FOUNTAIN

GREEN/YELLOW

TRANSIT MALL

SW HARRISON ST

SW 3RD AVE

CARAFE

SW 2ND AVE

PORTLANDIA

PORTLAND BUILDING

PIONEER PLACE

SW 1ST AVE

KELLER AUDITORIUM

SW FRONT AVE (SW NAITO PKWY)

MARRIOTT WATERFRONT

VERITABLE QUANDARY

SW CLAY ST

SW MARKET ST

SW ALDER ST

YAMHILL HISTORIC DISTRICT

SW STARK ST

SW OAK ST

SKIDMORE HISTORIC DISTRICT

To Marquam Bridge

RIVERPLACE HOTEL

Riverplace

SALMON STREET SPRINGS FOUNTAIN

TOM McCALL WATERFRONT PARK

NW FRONT AVE

RED/BLUE

OREGON MARITIME CENTER AND MUSEUM

W i l l a m e t t e

R i v e r

HAWTHORNE BRIDGE

MORRISON BRIDGE

OREGON MUSEUM OF SCIENCE AND INDUSTRY

Eastbank Esplanade

SE MADISON ST

SE HAWTHORNE BLVD

200 yds
200 m

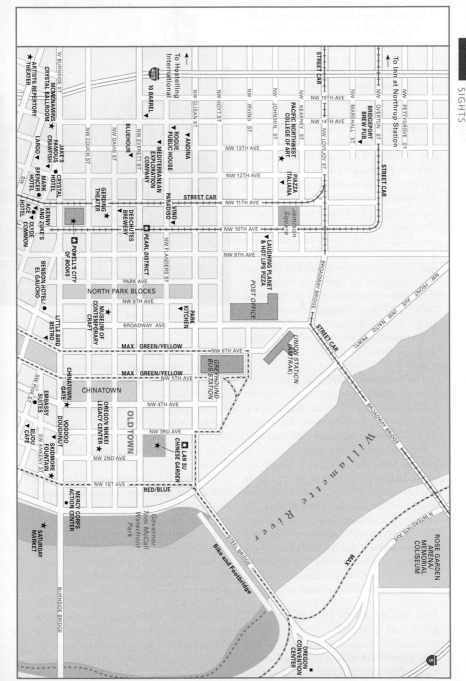

Information and Services Center (701 SW 6th Ave., 503/275-8355 or 877/678-5263, www. travelportland.com, 8:30am-5:30pm Mon.-Fri., 10am-4pm Sat., and 10am-2pm Sun. May-Oct.; 8:30am-5:30pm Mon.-Fri., 10am-4pm Sat. Nov.-Apr.).

Always busy, in good weather the square is filled with brown-bag lunchers, Hacky Sack-kickers, chess players, political activists, and dozens of free spirits that defy characterization. The square is ringed by fanciful columns supporting nothing in particular, and a portion of the plaza is a hillside of steps that serve as seating or stairways, depending on your needs. A few food carts line the south edge of the square, and many more are within a few blocks, making this a good destination for an open-air lunch. In summer, free midday concerts add to the zest; for information on square events, contact the **Pioneer Courthouse Square office** (503/223-1613). A waterfall fountain (not always working) flanks the doors to the TriMet and Travel Portland offices; through the same doors you'll find access to public toilets.

The "courthouse" alluded to in the square's name is just east across 6th Avenue. **Pioneer Courthouse** (555 SW Yamhill St., no public facilities) is the oldest public building in the state, constructed between 1869 and 1873.

Pioneer Courthouse Square is also at ground zero for downtown shopping. Immediately west, across Broadway, is Nordstrom; across the corner at Morrison Street and 6th Avenue is Macy's; and one block east along Morrison or Yamhill Streets is Pioneer Place, a two-section upscale shopping development that is linked by a skywalk to fashion bargains at H&M. The lower level of Pioneer Place features a food court with a wide array of fast-food concessions.

The South Park Blocks Cultural District

Southwest of the square, paralleling Broadway, is the **South Park Blocks Cultural District.** Many of the city's cultural institutions open

Pioneer Courthouse Square

onto the South Park Blocks, a delightful thread of tree- and statuary-filled greenways established in the 1850s and now running through the midst of downtown. The stands of American elms found here (and in the Pearl District's North Park Blocks) are among the largest remaining in North America, most of the rest having succumbed to Dutch elm disease.

Strolling the lanes through the South Park Blocks, which are flanked by many of Portland's most important museums, civic buildings, and early landmark churches, evokes memories of European parks. What makes this very civilized scene notable is that Portland's founders established this park in 1852, when wilderness stretched in every direction for thousands of miles.

Twice weekly from spring to fall—on Saturday and Wednesday—the **Portland Farmers Market** fills the South Park Blocks with the agricultural bounty of the Willamette Valley. The farmers market is also a great option for a casual bite to eat—many

the South Park Blocks Cultural District

by a confetti-like glass dome. The Schnitzer Concert Hall isn't usually open for casual visits, so you'll need a concert ticket to see its glittering interior, but the Antoinette Hatfield Hall is open all day and during the evening when performances are scheduled; the lobby bar makes a nice spot for a drink.

OREGON HISTORICAL SOCIETY MUSEUM

The **Oregon Historical Society Museum** (1230 SW Park Ave., 503/222-1741, www.ohs. org, 10am-5pm Mon.-Sat., noon-5pm Sun., $11 adults, $9 seniors and students, $5 children ages 6-18), holds the collection of the Oregon Historical Society. The museum tells the rich story of the state's Native American and settlement heritage; the combined gift shop and bookstore is a good place to pick up quality gifts.

★ Portland Art Museum

The **Portland Art Museum** (1219 SW Park Ave., 503/226-2811, www.portlandartmuseum.org, 10am-5pm Tues.-Wed. and Sat.-Sun., 10am-8pm Thurs.-Fri., $15 adults, $12 seniors 55 and older and students ages 18 and older, free children ages 17 and under) encompasses two grand structures along the South Park Blocks, the original Pietro Belluschi-designed building from 1932 and the adjacent and imposing Portland Masonic Temple, which together offer 112,000 square feet of galleries housing a collection of 42,000 objects. It's the oldest art museum on the West Coast (from 1892) and houses Oregon's most significant art collection, including a small but engaging collection of European Old Masters and Impressionists and a noteworthy Asian art collection. In 2001, the museum acquired the private collection of renowned New York art critic Clement Greenberg, which is on permanent display in the Center for Modern and Contemporary Art. The Pacific Northwest Native Art collection is also excellent. At least one major traveling exhibition is presented most of the time (usually with separate admission).

food vendors purvey freshly prepared food in addition to selling fruits, vegetables, cheese, and meats. Also opening onto the park is the multibuilding Portland Art Museum. The southern edges of the parks dissolve into Portland State University, an urban campus that boasts the state's largest higher-education enrollment.

PORTLAND CENTER FOR THE PERFORMING ARTS

Backing up to the South Park Blocks are two units of the **Portland Center for the Performing Arts** (503/248-4335, www.pcpa. com), including the ornate **Arlene Schnitzer Concert Hall** (1037 SW Broadway), home to the Oregon Symphony. This jewel-box concert venue was once a 1920s vaudeville hall, but you'd never know it after a 1980s makeover turned the neglected theater into the city's premier concert space. Directly across Main Street is the **Antoinette Hatfield Hall** (SW Broadway at Main), which houses the Newmark Theater and a soaring lobby topped

Portland Architecture

Portland has many notable buildings, both old and new. From its beginnings in the 1840s to the 1870s, Portland was built mostly of wood. However, after a series of fires in the 1870s, which together burned much of the original downtown, Portland was rebuilt in brick and stone. By this time the merchant kings of Portland felt like displaying their affluence, and a brand-new and very glamorous city went up between 1880 and 1915.

From Pioneer Courthouse Square you can see a number of notable buildings. On SW Morrison Street between 6th Avenue and Broadway is the **American Bank Building,** built in 1913 from a design by famed architect A. W. Doyle. Doyle is also responsible for the design of the building just to the east, the block-square **Meier & Frank Building** (now Macy's and the Nines Hotel), built in 1909. Both these buildings (and the **Jackson Tower/Oregon Journal Building,** across the Square at Broadway and SW Yamhill Street, 1912) are faced in white-glazed terra-cotta tile.

Immediately east of the Square is the **Pioneer Courthouse** itself. Begun in 1869, it's the oldest public building in Oregon and the second-oldest west of the Mississippi. Kitty-corner to the square to the southwest is one of Portland's most pleasing modern buildings, the 27-story **Fox Tower,** built in 2000 with a curving facade that looks like a cruise ship.

North on Broadway are two other very handsome historic structures. At SW Washington Street and Broadway is the **Vintage Plaza Hotel,** a marvelous example of late Victorian (1894) Romanesque, built of local basalt and red brick. The **U.S. National Bank Building** (1917), at SW Broadway and Stark Street (main entrance on SW 6th Ave.), is a grand neoclassical structure faced with 54-foot Corinthian columns. Just around the corner, at SW 6th Avenue and Burnside Street, is **U.S. Bankcorp Tower,** at 43 stories the city's second-tallest building. Commonly called "Big Pink" for its pink granite and rose glass facade, it's one of Portland's most distinctive buildings.

The **Dekum Building** (SW 3rd Ave. and Washington St.), with its massive basalt columns, arches, and gargoyles, is a prime example of Richardson Romanesque from 1891. The striking **Haseltine Building** (1893) at 133 SW 2nd Avenue was once a hansom cab stable, its arches open for the to-ing and fro-ing of carriages.

Central Library

Portland is a city of readers, with the busiest library system in the United States. A landmark for bibliophiles, Multnomah County Library system's **Central Library** (801 SW 10th Ave., 503/988-5123, www.multcolib.org, 10am-8pm Mon., noon-8 Tues.-Wed., 10am-6pm Thurs.-Sat., 10am-5pm Sun.) is an architecturally stunning renovation of a 1913 building designed by Alfred Doyle (architect of the Benson Hotel and the U.S. Bank downtown). Climb the sweeping staircases to the top floor to get a sense of the scale of this building—three stories have never seemed so monumental.

Portland Building

Raymond Kaskey's *Portlandia,* a statue that is said to symbolize the city, ranks right behind the Statue of Liberty as the world's largest hammered copper sculpture. Located outside Michael Graves's postmodern **Portland Building** on SW 5th Avenue between Main Street and Madison Street, the crouching female figure holding a trident recreates the Lady of Commerce on the city seal. Inside the Portland Building on the second floor is the **Portland Public Art Gallery** (8am-5:30pm Mon.-Fri.), operated by the **Regional Arts and Culture Council, or RACC** (503/823-5111, www.racc.org), where you can also pick up a walking tour map of the city's murals, fountains, sculptures, statues, and other public art pieces.

★ Tom McCall Waterfront Park

Tom McCall Waterfront Park is named for the governor credited with helping to reclaim

Oregon's rivers. In the early 1970s the park's grassy shore replaced Harbor Drive, a freeway that impeded access to the Willamette River. Today, the park is frequently the scene of summer festivals, while the wide, paved riverside esplanade is a favorite for joggers, cyclists, and strolling families.

Begin your introduction to mile-long Tom McCall Waterfront Park at **RiverPlace,** an attractive string of restaurants, specialty shops, and boating facilities overlooking the Willamette River in the shadow of the Marquam Bridge. Follow the paved riverside walkway north to the **Salmon Street Springs Fountain** at the base of Salmon Street. The fountain water's ebb and flow are meant to evoke the rhythms of the city and provide a refreshing shower on a hot day.

North along the seawall is the sternwheeler USS *Portland,* which houses the **Oregon Maritime Center and Museum** (at the foot of SW Pine, 503/224-7724, www.oregonmaritimemuseum.org, 11am-4pm Wed. and Fri.-Sat., $7 adults, $5 seniors, $4 students ages 13-18, $3 children ages 6-12). The museum offers a window into the fascinating maritime heritage of Portland and the Columbia and Willamette River systems, and it features ship models, historic diving equipment, and other ship artifacts.

Farther north in the shadow of the Burnside Bridge is the home of the **Portland Saturday Market** and the **Battleship Oregon Memorial,** which commemorates a famed 1893 fighting ship named after the state; the ship's block juts out of the grass.

Old Town and the Skidmore Fountain Historic District

From the 1870s through the 1920s, **Old Town** was the heart of Victorian-era Portland. After a disastrous fire in 1873 burned Portland's original wood-built commercial district, the city was rebuilt with multistory brick buildings, many faced with cast-iron facades. Iron could be cast in myriad forms, and the most popular in this period were Italianate columns and what look like elaborately carved plinths

and capitals. Portland has the second-largest inventory of cast-iron-fronted buildings in the country.

Portland's original harbor area fell on hard times after commercial shipping traffic moved to docks farther downriver and passenger trains replaced boats.

Today, even though there's still a scruffy edge to Old Town, many of the city's hottest nightclubs and bars are here. At the heart of Old Town is **Skidmore Fountain** (SW 1st Ave. and SW Ankeny St.). Built at great expense with a bequest from an early Portland dentist, it was intended as a source of water for "horses, men, and dogs."

Just north of the Skidmore Fountain is the **Mercy Corps Action Center** (28 SW 1st Ave., 503/896-5002, www.actioncenter.org, 11am-5pm Mon.-Fri., 11am-4pm Sat.), where you can learn about many of the projects sponsored by Mercy Corps, a Portland-based aid organization.

WASHINGTON PARK

The crown jewel of Portland's magnificent park system is **Washington Park,** which encompasses 130 acres of forest, formal gardens, and such civic institutions as the Oregon Zoo, International Rose Test Garden, Portland Japanese Garden, and the Portland Children's Museum. Adjacent to the park is the Hoyt Arboretum.

The park had its beginnings in 1871, and in its early years was modeled on European parks, with winding drives, shady walkways, fountains, noble statuary, formal plantings, lawns, and ornamental flower displays. To reach the park from downtown, take TriMet bus 63, with weekday service. If you're driving, biking, or walking, take Park Place west from SW 23rd Avenue and wind up the hill. The road passes a number of fountains and statues as it loops upward.

★ International Rose Test Garden

Encompassing 4.5 acres of roses, manicured lawns, other formal gardens, and an outdoor concert venue, the **International Rose Test Garden** is wedged onto the steep slopes of the West Hills in Washington Park. In addition to intoxicating scents and incredible floral displays, the garden also offers the classic view of Portland—Mount Hood rising above the downtown office towers. Bring a camera.

Today, the rose garden features over 6,800 rose bushes representing 557 varieties, both old and new. A charming annex to the rose garden is the **Shakespearean Garden,** which includes only herbs, trees, and flowers mentioned in Shakespeare's plays.

From June through the third Saturday in September, free tours of the rose garden are led by trained volunteers at 11:30am and 1pm Tuesday and 1pm Thursday, Saturday, and Sunday. Meet at the sign outside the Rose Garden Store. Donations are gladly accepted for the tour.

Just above the rose gardens are a set of tennis courts, beautifully situated beneath towering firs, and up a flight of steps is the terminus for the 30-inch narrow-gauge Washington Park and Zoo Railway, which links these two popular family destinations with a trip through Washington Park's dense forests; note that riders who take the train from the

rose gardens must pay zoo admission in addition to train fare.

Just beyond the rose gardens is the **Rose Garden Children's Park,** a large and elaborate play area with quite fantastic play structures.

★ Portland Japanese Garden

The beautiful **Portland Japanese Garden** (611 SW Kingston Ave., 503/223-1321, www.japanesegarden.com, noon-7pm Mon., 10am-7pm Tues.-Sun. Mid-Mar.-Sept., noon-4pm Mon., 10am-4pm Tues.-Sun., Oct.-mid Mar., $9.50 adults, $7.75 seniors and college students with ID, $6.75 children ages 6-17) is just up the slope from the rose gardens. The Portland Japanese Garden is a magical five-acre Eden with tumbling water, pools of koi, bonsai, elaborately manicured shrubs and trees, and five separate gardens linked by winding paths.

From the rose gardens, you can walk up the short but relatively steep trail that leads to the Japanese Garden, or hop on the free open-air shuttle that climbs up the hill every 10 minutes or so.

Oregon Zoo

The **Oregon Zoo** (4001 SW Canyon Rd., 503/226-1561, www.oregonzoo.org, 9am-6pm

the International Rose Test Garden

daily Memorial Day-Labor Day, 9am-4pm daily Mar.-late May and early Sept.-Dec., 10am-4pm daily Jan.-Feb., $11.50 visitors ages 12-64, $10 seniors, $8.50 children ages 3-11) has exhibits representing various geographic areas of the world. A series of major expansions through 2019 will see new elephant, rhino, primate, and polar bear habitats; nearly half the zoo grounds will get an upgrade. The zoo collection contains nearly 2,000 individual animals representing 232 species of birds, mammals, reptiles, amphibians, and invertebrates. The zoo is especially noted for its elephant program, which has one of the most successful breeding programs in the world. The zoo features two year-round eating establishments, a series of educational events for children, and summertime concerts. The zoo is easily reached from the Blue and Red MAX light rail lines or, on weekdays, via the number 63 bus from downtown.

If you're planning on visiting both the zoo and the International Rose Test Garden, consider linking these two family-favorite sites along the 30-inch narrow-gauge **Washington Park and Zoo Railway** (503/226-1561, 10:30am-5:30pm daily Memorial Day-Labor Day weather permitting, $5, children under

age 3 free), a two-mile rail service through Washington Park's dense forests. Since the train's upper station is within the zoo precincts, riders who board the train at the rose gardens must also purchase admission to the zoo.

The train also runs during the holiday ZooLights season, from the Friday after Thanksgiving through the Sunday after New Year's Day. During this time, you can visit the zoo with the added enhancement of a holiday light display with over one million LED lights. ZooLights trains run 5pm-8pm Sunday-Thursday and 5pm-8:30pm Friday and Saturday. You can also visit the zoo via public transportation or private car during the same hours.

Portland Children's Museum

Adjacent to the zoo is the **Portland Children's Museum** (4015 SW Canyon Rd., 503/223-6500, www.portlandcm.org, 9am-5pm Fri.-Wed., 9am-8pm Thurs. Mar. 1-Labor Day, 9am-5pm Tues.-Sun. Labor Day-Feb., $10.75 adults and children, $9.75 military and seniors age 55 and older), featuring events and activities for kids aged six months to 10 years old.

the Portland Japanese Garden

Hoyt Arboretum

Along the crest of the West Hills above Washington Park is **Hoyt Arboretum** (4000 SW Fairview Blvd., 503/865-8733, www.hoytarboretum.org, 6am-10pm daily, free), with 12 miles of trails winding through an expansive 187-acre tree garden boasting the world's largest collection of conifers. The arboretum's collection is made up of over 8,000 individual trees and plants that represent over 1,000 species from all corners of the globe. Most of the collection is linked by trails and labeled with botanical names. The trees throughout are presented in taxonomically organized groups, surrounded by other members of the same order, family, and genus; in other words, oaks are with oaks, and maples are with other maples. Visitors should stop by the visitors center and pick up a trail map before setting out. A one-mile trail is paved and suitable for wheelchairs.

NORTHWEST

Northwest Portland is in reality an entire quadrant of the city, but when most Portlanders talk about the Northwest, they are talking about a rather compact set of neighborhoods just to the north of downtown.

Old Town/Chinatown

From the 1870s through the 1910s, the entire Willamette River waterfront was the city's harbor, an extended area now called **Old Town.** By the 1870s the more northerly neighborhoods of Old Town, roughly bounded by NW 2nd and 4th Avenues and Burnside and Everett Streets, became known as **Chinatown,** an enclave of historic red-brick buildings that was home to Chinese and Japanese immigrants who came to Oregon seeking work and then made their homes here.

At its peak, around 1890, Portland's Chinatown had a population of around 5,000, second in size only to San Francisco's. As the Chinese in Chinatown grew old or moved on, they were replaced by Japanese people, and Chinatown became **Japantown;** by 1940, Portland's Japantown had over 100 Japanese-owned businesses and a population of some 3,500 Japanese and Japanese American residents.

Portland's thriving Japanese community came to a sudden end in 1942 when President Franklin D. Roosevelt issued Executive Order 9066, leading to the evacuation and internment of thousands of Japanese American citizens. Almost overnight, Japantown became a ghost town. With all the Japanese gone,

Chinatown Gate

Chinese businesses moved back in, and the area once again became known as Chinatown; but in many ways, this neighborhood has never recovered. (Today's Asian community in Portland can now be found along SE 82nd Avenue.)

Wandering the streets of Old Town/Chinatown alone late at night is probably not a good idea, but traveling safely to and from the restaurants and clubs is easy. Taxis are usually easily found in this entertainment hotbed, MAX light rail trains run along 1st, 5th, and 6th Avenues, and buses pass along 5th and 6th Avenues and on Everett Street.

OREGON NIKKEI LEGACY CENTER

For insights into Portland's immigrant Japanese community and the internment, visit the **Oregon Nikkei Legacy Center** (121 NW 2nd Ave., 503/224-1458, www.oregonnikkei.org, 11am-3pm Tues.-Sat., noon-3pm Sun., $5 adults, $3 seniors), in the heart of old Japantown; it is one of the most fascinating small museums in Portland.

CHINATOWN GATE

Presented as a gesture of goodwill from the Chinese community to the city of Portland, the colorful **Chinatown Gate** (W. Burnside St. and SW 4th Ave.) is the largest of its kind in the United States and marks the entrance to historic Chinatown. Dedicated in 1986, the Chinatown Gate comprises five roofs, 64 dragons, and two huge lions.

★ LAN SU CHINESE GARDEN

Colorful in a different way, the **Lan Su Chinese Garden** (239 NW Everett St., 503/228-8131, www.lansugarden.org, 10am-6pm daily Apr.-Oct., 10am-5pm daily Nov.-Mar., $9.50 adults, $8.50 seniors, $7 students ages 6-18 and college students with ID) is a formal Chinese garden built in the style of the Ming Dynasty. The block-square green space is the result of a joint effort between two famed gardening centers, Portland and its Chinese sister city, Suzhou. Over 60 landscape designers and craftspeople from Suzhou lived and worked in Portland for a year to complete the gardens, which are the largest traditional Chinese gardens in the United States. Nearly all the materials and tools used were also brought from China, including roof and floor tiles, all of the hand-carved woodwork, the latticed windows, and over 500 tons of swiss cheese-like Taihu granite boulders. A tea shop keeps the same hours as the gardens and is a delightful spot for a light lunch.

The Lan Su Chinese Garden is a quiet spot in the middle of busy Old Town.

UNION STATION

To the north, Old Town/Chinatown ends at Union Station (800 NW 6th Ave.), the glorious Italianate rail station that still serves as Portland's Amtrak depot. The station has been in continuous use since it was built in 1896 and is the second-oldest still-operating train station in the country. With its terra-cotta tile roof and 150-foot campanile with a four-sided Seth Thomas clock, this is one of Portland's most beloved landmarks.

North Park Blocks

Established in the 1860s as an extension of the South Park Blocks, the leafy confines of the North Park Blocks (bounded by NW Park Ave., 8th Ave., W. Burnside St., and NW Glisan St.) now serve as the front yard and a dog-walk destination for Pearl District dwellers. As with the South Park Blocks, the stand of American elms includes some of the largest remaining in the nation. The park also contains an elaborate children's playground, basketball and bocce ball courts, and lots of benches for contemplation and people watching.

Museum of Contemporary Craft

In the streets surrounding the North Park Blocks is the city's greatest concentration of commercial art galleries. A stroll along NW 9th Avenue reveals nearly a dozen galleries, and adjacent to the North Park Blocks at NW Davis Street and NW 8th Avenue is the DeSoto Building, once an automobile showroom. Today, it has been converted into a hub for art galleries, including three of Portland's top retail galleries, and the Museum of Contemporary Craft (724 NW Davis St., 503/223-2654, www.museumofcontemporarycraft.org, 11am-6pm Tues.-Sat., 11am-8pm first Thurs. of month, $4 adults, $3 seniors and students ages 13 and older), a showcase for local crafts.

★ Pearl District

A former warehouse district, the Pearl District is lined with upscale condos, home decor boutiques, fine restaurants, and art galleries.

A good place to begin your exploration is along NW 10th and 11th Avenues. At the corner of West Burnside Street and 10th Avenue is the mother ship of Powell's Books, one of the nation's largest bookstores and a classic place for Portlanders to spend rainy weekday afternoons. Continuing north on 11th Avenue, you pass the castellated Gerding Theater, a former armory and home to Portland Center Stage. If you're looking to decorate your home, the myriad furniture and decor stores along NW Glisan Street between 10th and 14th Avenues ought to provide inspiration.

If you're wondering why Portland has so many art galleries, perhaps a stop at Pacific Northwest College of Art (1241 NW Johnson St., 503/226-4391, www.pnca.edu) will explain. Since 1909 this art school, originally housed by the art museum, has provided a hands-on education for multiple generations of artists, many of whom remain in Portland to pursue their careers. The lobby of this converted warehouse contains two art galleries, and student art is usually on display in the central atrium.

Farther north, bounded by NW 10th and 11th Avenues and Johnson and Kearney Streets, is Jamison Square, a public park with a fountain that's a favorite destination for the neighborhood's children to get wet and cool down.

From downtown, the Pearl District is easily reached on the Portland Streetcar, which travels along NW 10th and 11th Avenues.

NW 21st and 23rd Avenues

Sometimes referred to as Nob Hill, the lovely Victorian neighborhoods around NW 21st and 23rd Avenues represent an island of upscale dining and shopping. Victorian homes have been remodeled into boutiques to join stylish clothing shops, restaurants, bars, and theaters. Generally speaking, NW 21st Avenue has the greater number of restaurants while NW 23rd Avenue has more shops—a mix of upper-end, locally owned boutiques and national chains such as Pottery Barn, Lush Handmade Cosmetics, and Kiehl's.

This area makes a good destination if you have an afternoon to while away. Coffee shops and unique little stores are abundant, and on a nice day, the streets are absolutely thronged with intriguing-looking people. Street parking is often difficult to find in Northwest Portland; if you're coming in from downtown or the Pearl District, consider taking the Portland Streetcar, which crosses both NW 21st and 23rd Avenues along Marshall and Lovejoy Streets.

Peculiarium

From the bloody Frankenstein dummy dozing in a wheelchair outside the entrance to the creepy fake-alien dolls, Bigfoot exhibit, and gross-out ice cream sundaes ("Crime Scene Massacre," anybody?) and gag gifts sold to keep the place in business, the **Peculiarium** (2234 NW Thurman St., 503/227-3164, www.peculiarium.com, 11am-7pm Thurs.-Sun., plus 11am-5pm Wed in Dec., free) does its bit to keep Portland weird. Even weirder, it's right around the corner from toney 23rd Avenue, though at the somewhat less vaunted north end of the neighborhood.

Pittock Mansion

Occupying a 1,000-foot promontory on 46 acres in the West Hills is **Pittock Mansion** (3229 NW Pittock Dr., 503/823-3623, http://pittockmansion.org, 11am-4pm daily Feb.-June and Sept.-Dec., 10am-5pm daily July-Aug., closed Jan., $8.50 adults, $7.50 seniors, $5.50 children ages 6-18), a grand 1914 home built by the then-editor of the *Oregonian* newspaper. The 22-room mansion was designed to contemporary tastes, and is a showcase of early-20th-century style and design. Guided tours of the mansion are available, but it's also worth the trip up to this pinnacle vantage point simply for the fabulous views of Portland and the Cascade peaks rising to the east (bring a picnic).

NORTHEAST

North and Northeast Portland cover an enormous area, all the way from East Burnside Street north to the Columbia River, and from the Willamette River east to beyond Portland International Airport. However, for visitors, the quadrant's main draws are the inner Northeast neighborhoods directly across from downtown as well as a handful of districts that represent the outposts of Portland's DIY nation.

Lloyd District

Just east of Old Town, across the Willamette River, is the **Lloyd District.** Named for Lloyd Center—Portland's (and the nation's) first shopping mall, which lies at its center –Lloyd District is basically an extension of downtown, with towering office buildings, major public buildings, sports stadiums (such as the Rose Garden Arena and the Memorial Coliseum), convention facilities, and a number of midrange hotels. The monumental **Oregon Convention Center** (777 NE M. L. King Jr. Blvd., 503/235-7575, www.oregoncc.org) is easy to spot with its twin glass steeples. Encompassing nearly 20 square blocks, this massive structure is the largest convention facility in the Pacific Northwest.

All of these destinations are easily reached by the Red and Blue MAX light rail lines and the eastside Portland Streetcar. On the north edge of Lloyd District is NE Broadway, a major arterial linking the northeast residential neighborhoods with downtown Portland via the Broadway Bridge (take TriMet bus #17 from downtown).

North Mississippi Avenue

If you had to choose a single poster child to represent Portland's do-it-yourself spirit, it could easily be the recently gentrified stretch of North Mississippi Avenue between North Fremont and North Skidmore Streets (take bus #44 from downtown).

Even in 2000, this neighborhood was a collection of mostly vacant turn-of-the-20th-century storefronts that had

Portland Bridges

Of all the metro areas in the United States, Portland is arguably *the* City of Bridges. With 13 bridges on the Willamette and two on the Columbia, the spans are both numerous and diverse. The three oldest were built prior to World War I (the Broadway, Steel, and Hawthorne). Bridge-ophiles can also revel in the broad array of types on view; all were designed by the preeminent engineers of their day. Many of the Willamette River crossings are illuminated at night by strategically placed floodlights, adding yet another pleasing visual dimension. The two spans of the **Steel Bridge** (1912) can be raised and lowered independently. The lovely **St. John's Bridge** (1931) is the only steel suspension bridge in Portland and one of only three major suspension bridges in Oregon.

From the newest bridge, the **Tillicum Crossing** (2015), to the oldest, the **Hawthorne Bridge** (1910), downtown bridges are located a third of a mile from each other and are, for the most part, safe and accessible for bicyclists and pedestrians (only the I-5 Marquam and I-405 Fremont Bridges are off-limits to nonmotorized vehicles and pedestrians).

the Tillicum Crossing

---

fallen into disrepair and dereliction. Then Portland's influx of "young creatives" discovered this historic community hub and found it an inexpensive place to start restaurants, art galleries, bars, brewpubs, coffeehouses, bakeries, and other one-of-a-kind enterprises. Fast-forward to today, and Mississippi Avenue is a testament to progressive politics and entrepreneurial instincts, with six blocks of Portland's renowned neighborhood-oriented lifestyle and enough nightlife and restaurant choices for travelers staying downtown to justify a trip across the river.

Any trip to North Mississippi Avenue should include a stop at **The Rebuilding Center** (3625 N. Mississippi Ave., 503/331-1877, http://rebuildingcenter.org, 9am-6pm Mon.-Sat., 10am-5pm Sun.), the largest nonprofit resource for used building materials in North America. Building salvage of all sorts finds its way to this 64,000-square-foot warehouse and lumberyard. If you're a homeowner and looking for a cheap sink, a period match for picture molding, or used-once two-by-fours, this labyrinth of old house stuff is fascinating.

NE Alberta Street

Once a thriving commercial strip, by the late 1980s Alberta Street had become a symbol of neglect, redlining, drug dealing, and gang activity. A decade later, the surrounding neighborhood was among the most rapidly gentrifying in the country, with all the change that entails. Nowadays Alberta Street, between NE Martin Luther King Jr. Boulevard and NE 33rd Avenue, is known to a new generation as a trendy arts district and a center for drinking and fine dining, perhaps the closest thing you'll find in Portland to a Latin Quarter of bohemian artists, cafés, bars, and bonhomie.

Part of the charm of Alberta Street is that it hasn't been razed and remade; there are still barbershops and body shops, storefront churches and comfortably seedy bars amid all the new construction and renovation. Alberta Street is also home to several art galleries, which play host along with studios and

the Rebuilding Center's whimsical entranceway

SE Hawthorne Boulevard, these Victorian residential neighborhoods are still home to Portland's Youth Culture, even though some of these folks are reaching retirement age. To the graying hippies, add in a thick overlay of goth kids, gays and lesbians, and street musicians, and you've got a people watching nexus. The Southeast quadrant stretches east across leafy neighborhoods filled with antique mansions to busy SE 82nd Avenue, the hub of today's immigrant Asian community. Two of Portland's greatest parks are in Southeast Portland—one designed by the famed Olmsted firm a century ago, the other situated on the only extinct volcano in a U.S. city—along with some of the city's most critically acclaimed independent restaurants.

Oregon Museum of Science and Industry

The **Oregon Museum of Science and Industry** (OMSI, 1945 SE Water Ave., 503/797-4000, www.omsi.edu, 9:30am-7pm daily late June-Labor Day, 9:30am-5:30pm Tues.-Sun. Labor Day-late June, $13.50 adults, $9.75 seniors and children ages 3-13, $2 parking) is a family-oriented hands-on interactive museum encompassing 219,000 square feet with five exhibit halls and eight science labs, making it one of the largest science and natural history museums in North America. The museum's 18.5-acre riverfront campus also features an OmniMax Theater with a five-story-high domed screen, the Pacific Northwest's largest planetarium, and the **USS** *Blueback* (503/797-4624, www.omsi. edu/submarine, tour $6.75), the last fast-attack diesel-powered submarine built by the U.S. Navy, now moored just west of OMSI in the Willamette River. OMSI also offers a variety of kids' camps and classes during the summer. During the school year, OMSI is open 9:30am-5:30pm on Mondays that are school holidays. The Portland Streetcar's CL line has a stop at OMSI, and it's at the east end of the car-free Tillicum Crossing bridge.

Oregon Rail Heritage Center (2250 SE Water St., 503/233-1156, www.orhf.org,

street vendors to thousands of revelers the last Thursday evening of every month for the Art Walk, otherwise known as Last Thursday.

The best way to get to Alberta Street by public transport is by TriMet bus #6, which crosses Alberta Street on NE Martin Luther King Jr. Boulevard, or bus #8, which crosses Alberta Street on NE 15th Avenue. Once on Alberta Street, take bus #72, which travels on Alberta between NE Martin Luther King Jr. Boulevard and NE 30th Avenue.

SOUTHEAST

When you think of Portland, do you conjure images of a slightly stoned hippie utopia? Or do you envision mobs of twenty-something hipsters flashing tattoos and piercings in a slacker coffeehouse? Rest assured that both stereotypes are alive and well—in fact thriving—in Southeast Portland.

The inner Southeast is a gentrifying warehouse district flanked to the east by Portland's most alternative neighborhoods. Centered on

Eastside Portland

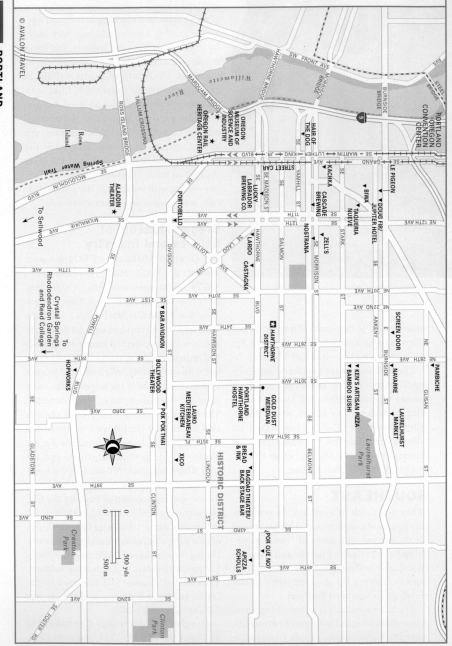

© AVALON TRAVEL

Willamette River

Ross Island

To Sellwood

To Rhododendron Garden
and Reed College

Crystal Springs

Creston Park

Clinton Park

Laurelhurst Park

HISTORIC DISTRICT

PORTLAND
OREGON
CONVENTION
CENTER

Bridges / Landmarks: ROSS ISLAND BRIDGE, MARQUAM BRIDGE, HAWTHORNE BRIDGE, MORRISON BRIDGE, BURNSIDE BRIDGE, STEEL BRIDGE, TALLUM CROSSING, Spring Water Trail

OREGON RAIL HERITAGE CENTER
OREGON MUSEUM OF SCIENCE AND INDUSTRY
HAIR OF THE DOG
LE PIGEON
KACHKA
BIWA
CASCADE BREWING
DOUG FIR/ JUPITER HOTEL
TAQUERIA NUEVE
ZELL'S
NOSTRANA
LUCKY LABRADOR BREWING CO.
PORTOBELLO
ALADDIN THEATER
LARDO
CASTAGNA
SCREEN DOOR
NAVARRE
PAMBICHE
LAURELHURST MARKET
KEN'S ARTISAN PIZZA
BAMBOO SUSHI
BAR AVIGNON
HOPWORKS
BOLLYWOOD THEATER
POK POK THAI
LAURO MEDITERANEAN KITCHEN
PORTLAND HAWTHORNE HOSTEL
GOLD DUST MERIDIAN
XICO
BREAD & INK
BAGDAD THEATER/ BACK STAGE BAR
¿POR QUE NO?
ARIZA SCHOLLS
HAWTHORNE DISTRICT
STREET CAR

0   500 yds
0   500 m

SW FRONT AVE
SE MARTIN LUTHER KING JR. BLVD
SE GRAND AVE
SE 11TH
SE 12TH
SE MADISON ST
SE HAWTHORNE BLVD
SE LADD AVE
SE DIVISION
SE ELLIOT AVE
SE 20TH
SE 21ST AVE
SE 24TH
HARRISON ST
SE 26TH AVE
SE 28TH AVE
SE 30TH AVE
SE 33RD AVE
SE 35TH AVE
SE 35TH PL
LINCOLN ST
CLINTON ST
SE 39TH
SE 42ND AVE
SE 43RD ST
SE 49TH AVE
SE 50TH AVE
SE 52ND
SE FOSTER RD
GLADSTONE AVE
POWELL BLVD
MILWAUKIE AVE
MCLOUGHLIN BLVD
YAMHILL
SALMON ST
MORRISON ST
STARK
ANKENY
BURNSIDE ST
GLISAN ST
BELMONT ST
NE 12TH AVE
NE 20TH AVE
NE 22ND AVE
NE 28TH AVE

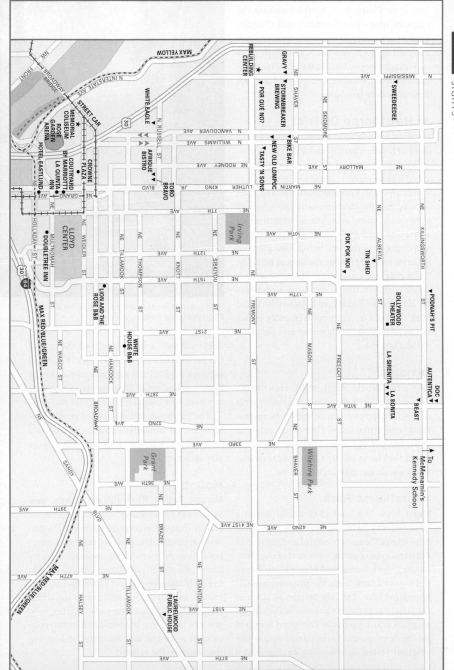

1pm-5pm Thurs.-Sun., free) focuses on the railroad history of Portland and Oregon. This new facility displays vintage engines and rolling stock, and offers 45 minute rides on vintage Oregon Pacific Railroad trains to Oaks Bottom Wildlife Refuge and back ($5, Saturdays only Jan.-Nov.).

★ Hawthorne District

Portland has a longtime reputation as an enclave of hippie lifestyles and a hotbed of progressive politics, and if that's the Portland you'd like to explore, come to the neighborhoods along SE Hawthorne Boulevard. Rest assured that the idealistic early 1970s haven't aged much around here. Stores purveying fine coffees, secondhand clothing, imported arts and crafts, antiques, and books join cafés and galleries recalling the hip enclaves of Berkeley, California, and Cambridge, Massachusetts. A dense concentration of these establishments on Hawthorne Boulevard between 30th and 50th Avenues is catnip for a friendly population of idealists both young and old; take TriMet bus #14.

Division

Just a few blocks south of SE Hawthorne Boulevard is SE Division Street, another strip of hipster enterprises thick with bars, restaurants, and coffee shops. One major hub is at **D Street Village** at SE 30th Avenue, where you'll find some of city's best casual dining and a few shops; take TriMet bus #4.

Laurelhurst Park

Until 1909, the land that would become **Laurelhurst Park** (SE 39th Ave. and Stark St.)—one of the most beautiful and beloved of Portland's many parks—was part of the then-mayor's stock farms, and blue-ribbon Jersey milk cows drank from the property's small spring-fed lake. The city bought 30 acres of the farmland to create Laurelhurst Park based on plans drawn up by the Olmstead Brothers for the development of Portland's parks. The original watering hole was enlarged and

Spring is the time to visit the Crystal Springs Rhododendron Garden.

deepened into a small lake, and the rest of the park was divided into a series of distinct sections. In 2001 the park was named to the National Register of Historic Places, the first city park ever listed on the national register.

The south side of the park has tennis, volleyball, and basketball courts; nearby is a large playground for children, with a large play structure.

Mount Tabor Park

Mount Tabor Park (SE 60th Ave. and Salmon St.) rises above Southeast Portland, and its distinctive cone shape reveals its primary attribute: The park contains the country's only extinct volcano within the city limits of a major population center. Roping in nearly 200 acres, Mount Tabor Park is large enough to offer several miles of hiking trails, and a large off-leash dog park. During July, you can catch free Wednesday-evening concerts at a natural amphitheater. A looping road leads to the summit.

Crystal Springs Rhododendron Garden

Ten-acre **Crystal Springs Rhododendron Garden** (SE 28th Ave. and Woodstock Blvd.) is a colorful place mid-April-June when some 600 varieties of rhododendrons and azaleas, represented by about 2,500 individual specimens, are in bloom. The floral display peaks in mid-May; strolling the woodland trails on Mother's Day is a Portland tradition. A $4 admission fee is charged 10am-6pm Wednesday-Sunday March-Labor Day.

Sports and Recreation

PARKS

Portland is famous for more park acreage per capita than any other major U.S. city—more than 37,000 acres are preserved as parkland, with 8 percent of the city's area devoted to public recreational venues. Within these holdings, the city has more urban wilderness than any other municipality in the country.

Portland Parks and Recreation (503/823-7529, www.portlandonline.com/parks) is the bureau that operates the city's 250 parks.

Waterfront Park and the Eastbank Esplanade

This 2.8-mile loop trail rings the Willamette River in the very heart of Portland, linking two bridges and Waterfront Park with a floating walkway on the river's eastern bank. The trail can be walked in either direction and accessed at many points; to follow the loop clockwise from downtown, walk the riverfront embankment trail north through Waterfront Park to the Steel Bridge. Cross the lower span of the bridge, a pedestrian- and cyclists-only crossing called the Steel Bridge RiverWalk.

On the east side of the Willamette, the trail heads south, dropping onto the Eastbank Esplanade, about half of which is a floating walkway (at 1,200 feet, the longest in the country) and the rest a paved path along the riverbank. At the Hawthorne Bridge, climb up the stairs and cross the bridge to downtown, completing the loop. Or add a couple more miles to your walk by continuing south

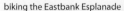
biking the Eastbank Esplanade

and crossing on the new Tillicum Crossing bridge.

★ Forest Park

The largest urban wilderness in the United States, with over 5,100 acres and 70 miles of trails, **Forest Park** stretches along the crest of Portland's West Hills. It is 8.5 miles long and 1.5 miles wide. As much a statement of Portland's priorities and values as a leafy refuge for hikers, joggers, and cyclists, Forest Park is home to an abundance of wildlife (more than 112 bird and 62 mammal species, including bears, elk, deer, and cougars), all found just minutes from the urban center.

For hikers, the park's centerpiece is 30-mile **Wildwood Trail,** which links various parklands in the West Hills with Forest Park. The southern end of the trail starts just past the Vietnam Veterans of Oregon Memorial near the Oregon Zoo. From here it runs through Washington Park and Hoyt Arboretum and past Pittock Mansion. At Cornell Road, the trail crosses the edge of the **Audubon Sanctuary** (5151 NW Cornell Rd., 503/292-6855, www.audubonportland.org, dawn-dusk daily), where the Audubon Society of Portland administers a 148-acre free-to-the-public nature preserve that is a showcase for native flora and fauna. The sanctuary has over four miles of forested hiking trails in the verdant West Hills.

From the Audubon Sanctuary, the Wildwood Trail enters Forest Park and runs north for another 22 miles. The trail can be accessed at any of the points described above or at several more northerly trailheads. One convenient access point is the western end of NW Upshur Street at Macleay Park; another is the end of NW Thurman Street (the number 15 Thurman Street bus from downtown stops about 0.25 mile downhill from this entrance to the park).

Tryon Creek State Park

The only Oregon state park within the Portland metro area, 645-acre **Tryon Creek State Park** (11321 SW Terwilliger Blvd.,

The Wildwood Trail runs for 30 miles through Forest Park.

503/636-9886 or 800/551-6949, http://oregonstateparks.org) offers eight miles of nature trails in a vernal woodland setting. Cyclists bike along the paved trail on the park's eastern edge. The park's many events include summer day camps for kids, guided nature walks, and special activities; for a list of events, go to www.tryonfriends.org. Streamside wildlife includes beavers and songbirds. In late March there are wondrous displays of trilliums, a wild marsh lily. To reach the park, take I-5 Exit 297 south of Portland, follow SW Terwilliger Boulevard for 2.5 miles past Lewis and Clark College, and watch for signs for the park.

BICYCLING

Portland has twice been selected by *Bicycling* magazine as the most bike-friendly city in the nation, and indeed the city has a comprehensive infrastructure devoted to cycling. Unless you're from Amsterdam, you'll be amazed at the number of people who get around Portland on bikes.

The website of the **City of Portland's Office of Transportation** (www.portland-oregon.gov/transportation/34772) lists up-to-date information for cyclists. Keep up on local cycling issues at bikeportland.org, an excellent bike blog; find fun rides and details on **Pedalpalooza** events (held throughout June) at shift2bikes.org. An indispensable map called *Bike There!* published by the government agency Metro, is sold at bike shops and bookstores across town, and is available online at www.oregonmetro.org/tools-living/getting-around/bike-there.

Cyclists should know that Portland is a city of bridges, but that not all bridges are recommended for cyclists. A river-level foot-and-bike bridge forms the lower level of the Steel Bridge and connects Waterfront Park and downtown to the Eastbank Esplanade; otherwise, the Hawthorne, Broadway, and Burnside Bridges are best, although bikes must share sidewalks with pedestrians. The new Tillicum Crossing bridge is dedicated to cyclists, pedestrians, and public transport. Bikes are allowed on TriMet buses (bike racks are mounted on the front of every bus), the MAX, and the Portland Streetcar.

For a recreational ride that's almost entirely on bike paths, check out the 16.8-mile **Springwater Corridor,** a bike thoroughfare built on a reclaimed rail line from the east base of the Tillicum Crossing bridge through Gresham to Boring. Views of Mount Hood abound along much of the route. Along the way, easy access to Leach Botanical Gardens, Powell Butte, and other worthy detours are available.

An easy choice for mountain bikers is **Leif Erikson Road** in Forest Park. From the park gate at the end of NW Thurman Street, the dirt road is closed to motor vehicles; it's a steady but gentle six-mile climb through mature forest to the junction at Salzman Road, and another six miles to the trail's end at Germantown Road. Bikes are not allowed on the park's hiking trails, but they can go on selected (steep) fire lanes as marked by signs.

North of Portland at the confluence of the Columbia and Willamette Rivers is **Sauvie Island** (http://sauvieisland.org), a perfectly flat island where farms and truck gardens share space with wildlife refuges. The island's 12-mile loop road is a scenic delight reminiscent of rural France. Sauvie Island is 10 miles north of Portland off U.S. 30.

Bike Rentals

As you might expect in bicycle-mad Portland,

Escape to Sauvie Island

Ten miles northwest of Portland at the confluence of the Willamette and Columbia Rivers is the rural enclave of **Sauvie Island** (http://sauvieisland.org), a scant 20 minutes from downtown. On clear days here, views of the snowcapped Cascades Range backdrop oceangoing freighters and cruise ships. Visitors enjoy horseback riding, swimming, and U-pick farms. A favorite spot for bird-watching, the island sees eagles, great blue herons, geese, and sandhill cranes among the 250 species that pass through on the Pacific Flyway. Wildlife aficionados may glimpse red foxes and black-tailed deer on the island's northern half. In addition, anglers come to Sauvie's lakes and sloughs for panfish and bass, and to the Columbia side for sturgeon, salmon, and steelhead. Bikers come for the 12-mile "hill-less" biking loop. Nearby is **Collins Beach** (4am-10pm daily), which is clothing optional.

Be aware that if you park at one of Sauvie Island's public beaches or wildlife viewing areas, you'll need a parking certificate, available for $7 per vehicle at the Cracker Barrel Convenience Store on Sauvie Island Road; turn left after coming off the bridge. Also remember to gas up and hit the ATM before heading to the island; neither are here.

To reach Sauvie Island, take U.S. 30 northwest to Sauvie Island.

it's no problem to rent a bike; average rates run $25-60 for a 24-hour rental, depending on the model. Convenient to Waterfront Park and with a large rental fleet is **Waterfront Bikes** (10 SW Ash St., 503/227-1719, www.waterfrontbikes.com, 10am-6pm Mon.-Fri., 9am-6pm Sat.-Sun.). On the way to Forest Park trails is **Fat Tire Farm** (2714 NW Thurman St., 503/222-3276, www.fattirefarm.com, 11am-7pm Mon.-Fri., 10am-6pm Sat., noon-5pm Sun.). Just east of the Hawthorne Bridge, **Clever Cycles** (900 SE Hawthorne Blvd., 503/334-1560, http://clevercycles.com, 11am-6pm Mon.-Fri., 11am-5pm Sat.-Sun.) rents Dutch city bikes, Brompton folding bikes, and Bakfiets cargo bikes. At **Pedal Bike Tours** (133 SW 2nd Ave., 503/243-2453, www.pedalbiketours.com, 9am-6pm daily), you can rent a bike or join a tour around town or out to the Columbia Gorge or Willamette Valley. One of their most fun trips is the self-guided Forest Park ride; cyclists and bikes are transported to a trailhead and ride, generally downhill, through the park back to town. Hardened cyclists looking for organized 30- to 100-mile rides at a touring pace should hook up with the **Portland Wheelmen Touring Club** (503/257-7982, www.pwtc.com).

BIRD-WATCHING

To the far south of the Southeast district, the Sellwood neighborhood offers access to wetlands along the Willamette River. **Oaks Bottom Wildlife Refuge** (SE 7th Ave. and Sellwood Blvd., www.portlandonline.com, 5am-midnight daily) is a 163-acre area of woods, open fields, and wetlands. This is a popular spot for birders, since it attracts some 125 species of birds, including blue herons, red-tailed hawks, and eight species of warblers. To explore the bottoms, hike down the bluff from the parking lot at the north end of Sellwood Park.

CLIMBING

The top inner-city destination for climbers is **Portland Rock Gym** (21 NE 12th Ave., 503/232-8310, http://portlandrockgym.com,11am-11pm Mon., Wed., and Fri., 7am-11pm Tues. and Thurs., 9am-9pm Sat., 9am-6pm Sun.), with a 12,000-square-foot climbing area, 40-foot top-rope and lead walls, and a large bouldering area. A day pass ($15 adults, $7.50 seniors,$10 children ages 13 and under) includes unlimited access to the gym for one day, including climbing areas, fitness facilities, and drop-in yoga classes.

GOLF

For golfers, Portland has more publicly owned golf courses per capita than any other U.S. city. Two of these, Heron Lakes and Eastmoreland, are ranked by *Golf Digest* as among the top 75 public courses in the country; both are operated by Portland Parks and Recreation. Portland public course fees average around $32-43 for 18 holes.

Heron Lakes (3500 N. Victory Blvd., 503/289-1818, http://heronlakesgolf.com) is the premier public golf facility in Portland, with 36 holes (the Greenback and Great Blue courses), a grass driving range, and good short-game practice areas. The two courses offer varying challenges for different greens fees. The easier and shorter Greenback is good for beginners and moderate players, though it doesn't drain as well. The more challenging—and costlier—Great Blue, designed by Robert Trent Jones Jr., is better manicured and drains better in wet weather.

Eastmoreland Golf Course (2425 SE Bybee Blvd., 503/775-2900, www.eastmorelandgolfcourse.com) is Oregon's second-oldest course and one of the most beautiful. Located near Reed College in Southeast Portland, the mature and lengthy (6,529 yards) 18-hole course is lined with statuesque trees and gardens. Eastmoreland features a two-tier driving range, a pro shop, and full bar and restaurant facilities. The course was designed by former U.S. Amateur champion H. Chandler Egan, who later helped redesign Pebble Beach Golf Links in the early 1900s.

PADDLING

If you're tempted to get out onto the Willamette River, take a tour or rent a sea kayak from **Portland Kayak Company** (6600 SW Macadam Ave., 503/459-4050, www.portlandkayak.com) on the west side of the Willamette River near Willamette Park. They also maintain a fleet of boats at RiverPlace Marina, which is used as a base for three-hour beginner-friendly tours around Ross Island (offered at 10am and 2pm daily, $45); on these tours, paddlers have a chance to see great blue herons and, oftentimes, ospreys and eagles.

On the east side of the river, **Alder Creek Kayak** (1515 SE Water St., 503/285-1819, www.aldercreek.com) has a boathouse near the Eastside Esplanade immediately south of the Hawthorne Bridge, near the junction of SE Water Avenue and Clay Street. A three-hour tour of Ross Island is $39. Rent a canoe, kayak, or stand-up paddleboard ($30-40 for four hours) here; from the boathouse it's easy to launch into the Willamette River.

RUNNING

Thanks to its relatively mild climate, wealth of trails (especially in Forest Park), and the influence of Nike and Adidas, which are headquartered here, Portland is widely regarded as a great running town and host to many running and walking events, including the early-October **Portland Marathon** (503/226-1111, www.portlandmarathon.org). To find out about these and other events, contact the **Oregon Road Runners Club** (message phone 503/646-7867, www.orrc.net); they'll be glad to recommend the best places to run.

SWIMMING

The indoor Portland Parks pool at **Dishman Community Center** (77 NE Knott St., 503/823-3673) is open year-round and convenient to downtown. A little less convenient, but quite nice, is the **Southwest Community Center and Pool** (6820 SW 45th Ave., 503/823-2840). In summer the outdoor pool at **U. S. Grant Park** (503/823-3674),

near the corner of NE 33rd Avenue and U. S. Grant Place, is a great place for hot kids.

Public beaches and swimming along the Willamette and Columbia Rivers are popular in summer. **Sellwood Riverfront Park,** at the east end of the Sellwood Bridge, is a good place for a picnic and a wade in the Willamette River; there's also an outdoor pool in **Sellwood Park** (7951 SE 7th Ave., 503/823-3679). Ten miles north of Portland, the beaches along the east side of **Sauvie Island** are popular; they are reached from U.S. 30. Once on the island, nude sunbathing becomes more the norm the farther north you go along its beaches. If you're headed up the Columbia River Gorge, **Rooster Rock State Park** (I-84 Exit 25) has three miles of sandy beaches on the Columbia River, with the easternmost beaches being clothing-optional.

TENNIS

A number of Portland parks offer free tennis courts. Most convenient to visitors staying downtown are the courts near the Rose Gardens in **Washington Park** (SW Park Place, www.portlandonline.com). On the east side of the Willamette River there are outdoor courts at **Laurelhurst Park** (SE 39th Ave. and Stark St.).

SPECTATOR SPORTS

Portland is more a town for athletes than for devotees of spectator sports. Nonetheless, a couple of professional sports teams have many ardent fans.

Directly across the Willamette River from downtown in Northeast Portland, the Rose Quarter area is home to two of Portland's sports stadia. The larger (20,339 seats) and newer is the **Rose Garden Arena** (at the east end of the Steel Bridge, 503/235-8771, www.rosequarter.com), which is home to the National Basketball Association's Portland Trailblazers. While most seats are reserved for season ticket holders, some are available at Ticketmaster outlets or through the Rose Garden Arena box office (503/797-9619). Of course, there are always the offerings of ticket brokers on Craigslist (www.craigslist.org) and the scalpers who may be found beyond a four-block radius of the Rose Garden. You can also buy tickets directly from the **Blazer website** (www.nba.com/blazers). Regular season play is October-April.

Adjacent to the Rose Garden Arena is the 12,000-seat **Memorial Coliseum** (1401 N. Wheeler Ave., 503/235-8771), which hosts sporting events, concerts, and other local teams, including the **Winter Hawks** (503/238-6366, www.winterhawks.com), a minor league team in the Western Hockey League. Both are easily reached on the Red, Green, Yellow, and Blue MAX trains (take the train to Rose Quarter Transit Center).

Across the river, **Providence Park** (1844 SW Morrison St., 503/553-5400, www.timbers.com) is home to Major League Soccer's **Portland Timbers.** The stadium's nearly 20,000 seats are usually filled, with a substantial number occupied by the Timbers Army, an enthusiastic legion of green-scarfed fans. The **Portland Thorns** (www.timbers.com/thornsfc), owned by the same franchise as the Timbers, is Portland's National Women's Soccer League team and also plays at Providence Park stadium.

Tickets for all of these teams' games are available through **Ticketmaster** (800/277-1700, www.ticketmaster.com).

Entertainment and Events

As Portland has grown in recent years, its arts scene has become more diverse and sophisticated. The traditional institutions of symphony, opera, and classical ballet are strong, and contemporary dance and theater are represented by an eclectic bunch of adventurous companies. In addition to the more formal music and theater listings that follow, there's a very active summer festival itinerary that ranges from the superb Chamber Music Northwest series, Portland Opera's summer performances, to blues and jazz festivals.

In Portland, bars are allowed to stay open until 2:30am, though few do so on weekdays. During the week, most places close at midnight or 1am, though may stay open later if there's entertainment. Cover charges usually kick in at 9pm when there's live music.

NIGHTLIFE

Portland has a very full-bodied live music and club scene: On any given night, some 300 clubs offer live music, and with typical Portland character, what you'll find in these venues is often a bit different than you might expect. In addition to live music and dancing, you'll also find lots of theme nights, often accompanied

by a combination of cabaret, performance art, magic, and burlesque—think *Cabaret's* Kit Kat Klub. These unscripted evenings can often provide very diverting entertainment.

Much of the nightlife is concentrated in a few easily reached neighborhoods, most with safe and dependable public transport to and fro. Be sure to pick up a copy or check the websites of *Willamette Week* or the *Portland Mercury,* two free weeklies that follow the music and nightlife scene closely. Most music events in bars are restricted to ages 21 and older. Cover charges, which range $3-10 in most nightclubs, are frequently levied, though there's often no cover charge for live music early in the week or even early in the evening. Also note that smoking is not permitted in Oregon bars, though nudity is: Because of Oregon's liberal laws regarding nudity, Portland is home to many strip clubs.

Bars

Portland is a nightlife kind of city, with bars everywhere. You won't find it difficult to find places to drink, but here's a primer on some of the city's best bars.

The most sought-after bar stools in

Portland are at the **Multnomah Whisk{e}y Library** (1124 SW Alder, 503/954-1381, www. mwlpdx.com, 4pm-midnight Mon.-Thurs., 4pm-1am Fri.-Sat.), an ornate, membership-driven bar with an extensive collection of liquors: This library has some 1,500 bottles on its shelves, almost 1,000 of them whiskies. The bar room is very attractive and clubby, and the service top-notch. Nonmembers can have a drink at the street-level bar or ask if there's room in the library up the stairs; at night, the lines can be long.

In the hip Ace Hotel, **Clyde Common** (1014 SW Stark St., 503-228-3333, 11:30am-midnight Mon.-Sat., 10am-11pm Sun.) is where young downtown execs enjoy hand-crafted cocktails and nicely curated local ales in a bright, bustling bar. There's quite a different vibe in the Ace's other bar, **Pepe Le Moko** (407 SW 10th, 503/546-8537, 4pm-2am daily), a tiny, subterranean speak-easy-type joint with classic cocktails, oysters on the half shell, and the sense of traveling back in time to the 1920s.

One of Northeast Portland's top cocktail bars is **Expatriate** (5424 NE 30th, 503/867-5309, 5pm-midnight daily), a moody, candle-lit lounge with a romantic travel theme. Drinks are excellent, and the Asian fusion snacks are from recipes of Naomi Pomeroy, the award-winning chef whose Beast restaurant is just across the street.

Along a humdrum stretch of NE Broadway is Portland's top tiki bar, **Hale Pele** (2733 NE Broadway, 503/662-8454, 4pm-midnight Sun.-Thurs., 4pm-1am Fri.-Sat.), a hole-in-the-wall decorated with shrunken heads, pufferfish lights, and a smoking volcano. The tropical-themed drinks are delicious, and the collection of rums here is formidable.

There's a cluster of bars in inner Southeast Portland (near the east end of the Morrison Bridge, just across the river from downtown) where you can stumble from bar to excellent bar and have a completely different experience in each. Here are some favorites. **Bit House Saloon** (727 SE Grand, 503/954-3913, 3pm-2:30am daily) is a large and rollicking redbrick bar with a nice patio. The specialties here are barrel-stored spirits poured through a tap system and high falutin' cocktails both fresh squeezed and draft-style. Across the street is **Kachka** (720 SE Grand, 503/235-0059, http://kachkapdx.com, 4pm-midnight daily) with vodka flights and delicious Russian snacks. One block further east is **Trifecta Tavern** (726 SE 6th Ave., 503/841-6675, http://trifectapdx.com, 5pm-9pm Mon., 5pm-10pm

Bit House Saloon

Tues.-Thurs., 4pm-11pm Fri.-Sat., 4pm-9pm Sun.) an excellent bakery and restaurant with a bar up front. The cocktails are updated classics, accompanied by fresh oysters, thin-sliced American hams, and wonderful breads.

Of the dozens of McMenamin locations in Portland, the **Back Stage Bar** (3702 SE Hawthorne Blvd., 503-236-9234, 4pm-1:30am Mon.-Thurs., 4pm-2:30am Fri., noon-2:30am Sat., noon-1:30am Sun.) is the most amazing. At the front of the building is the **Bagdad Theater,** a former vaudeville hall converted to a pub-slash-movie theater. In the old days, when the painted scrims and backdrops that set the scene for its live song-and-dance routines weren't in use, they were hung in the Back Stage, a seven-story curtain storehouse directly behind the theater. Today's Back Stage Bar makes the most of this narrow towering space. On the ground floor is the handsome bar and pool tables, but catwalks and staircases lead to secluded spots tucked into the walls. And there's nothing like a bar with a seven-story-high ceiling to start a conversation.

The **Crow Bar** (3954 N. Mississippi Ave., 503/280-7099, http://crowbarpdx.com, 3pm-2am daily) feels comfortable and slightly old-fashioned, a narrow space with exposed red brick, high ceilings, and a long wooden bar. However, the crowds are anything but old-fashioned—this is a favorite watering hole for the many 20- and 30-somethings who have refashioned the adjoining North Portland neighborhoods in their image.

Gold Dust Meridian (3267 SE Hawthorne Blvd., 503/239-1143, http://golddustmeridian.com, 2pm-2:30am daily) started out as a 1960s-era accountant's office, which it remained until it was transformed into a swank temple of drink. This is a lively spot, with a pool table, good cocktails, and a high-energy vibe. The young, attractive crowd, chatting above blaring techno-pop, is easy on the eyes as well.

The side-by-side **Mint** and **820** (816 N. Russell St., 503/284-5518, www.mintand820.com, 4pm-11pm Tues.-Thurs., 4pm-midnight Fri.-Sat.) are owned by Lucy Brennan, a renowned mixologist whose cocktail creativity has won her accolades from *Food and Wine* and *Bon Appetit.* Inventive cocktails that incorporate fresh (and sometimes unusual) fruit and juices are the hallmark of Brennan's creations. Mint is nominally the restaurant side of things, with Caribbean-infused cooking, while 820 is the lounge (with outdoor seating), but these popular and richly decorated nightspots, located under the soaring Fremont Bridge, are easily thought of as a two-for-one destination. The **Teardrop Lounge** (1015 NW Everett St., 503/445-8109, http://teardroplounge.com, 4pm-12:30am Sun.-Thurs., 4pm-2am Fri.-Sat.) is a small and stylish see-and-be-seen bar in the midst of the Pearl District where highly creative drinks are crafted from handmade elixirs, hard-to-find Oregon liquors, and tinctures of a very local variety. While the bar celebrates the classic drinks of the cocktail age, it also makes sure that everything is sourced locally.

Gay and Lesbian

Portland's gay bar scene used to be concentrated along SW Stark Street downtown, but the scene has dispersed, both into new neighborhoods (there are now as many gay bars on the East Side as downtown) and to regular bars. Gay people are welcome pretty much anywhere in Portland, and you certainly don't need to seek out a gay bar just to have drinks with gay friends.

SW Stark Street is the traditional hub of Portland's gay bar scene, and **Scandals** (1038 SW Stark St., 503/227-5887, www.scandalspdx.com, noon-2:30am daily) has been a fixture here since the 1970s. The bar is bright and airy, and in summer the floor-to-ceiling windows slide open and the scene spills onto the sidewalk. While there are pool tables and DJs spinning tunes, this is an easygoing, cruisy bar where (mostly) men come to hang out and meet friends.

The longtime favorite **CC Slaughters** (200 NW 3rd Ave., 503/248-9135, http://cc-slaughterspdx.com, 3pm-2:30am daily) has

The *Real* Portland Spirit

Portland is famed as a center for brewing, with more breweries than any city in the world, and it's a short drive from world-class wineries in the northern Willamette Valley and the Columbia Gorge. What you may not know, but shouldn't surprise you, is that Portland is also a major center for artisanal **micro-distilleries.** There are over a dozen small distilleries in Portland, producing specialty vodka, gin, whiskey, rum and eau-de-vie. Several offer tasting rooms where you can sample the Portland spirit.

In addition to the following distilleries, also check out the small-batch liquors at brewpubs **Edgefield** (2126 SW Halsey St., Troutdale, 503/669-8610 or 800/669-8610, www.mcmenamins. com) for Hogshead whiskey, Penney's gin, and various brandies; and **Rogue Distillery & Public House** (1339 NW Flanders St., 503/241-3780, www.rogue.com) for three kinds of rum, a Scotch-style whiskey, and spruce (not juniper-based) gin.

- **Clear Creek Distillery** (2389 NW Wilson St., 503/248-9470, www.clearcreekdistillery.com, noon-6pm Mon.-Fri., 10am-6pm Sat.): Famous for pear brandy and other fruit-based eaux-de vie; check out the Oregon Single Malt Whiskey, if the year's tiny production isn't already sold out.

- **House Spirits Distillery** (2505 SE 11th Ave., 503/235-3174, www.housespirits.com, noon-6pm daily): Most noted for its Aviation Gin, but also try the Medoyeff vodka and aquavit.

- **Eastside Distilling** (1512 SE 7th Ave., 503/926-7060, www.eastsidedistilling.com, noon-8pm daily): Check out the very popular Burnside Bourbon and potato vodka, and investigate three types of rum.

- **New Deal Distillery** (900 SE Salmon St., 503/234-2513, http://newdealdistillery.com, noon-6pm Wed.-Sun.): This operation specializes in vodka and gin.

- **Stone Barn Brandy Works** (3315 SE 19th Ave., 503/775-6747, www.stonebarnbrandy-works.com, noon-6pm Mon. and Fri.-Sun.): Unsurprisingly, there's brandy, but so much more, such as grappa, ouzo, rye whiskey, oat whiskey, and strawberry, apricot, cranberry, and coffee liqueur.

undergone a lot of changes in the past few years. Up front, the Rainbow Room is a frosty-cool cocktail lounge, a place to sip cocktails and play pool in high-style surroundings; food is available as well. The nightclub is entered along NW Davis Street and contains a large bar and dance floor where DJs keep the rhythms pounding. The crowd is mostly male and of all ages, but all are welcome.

Crush (1400 SE Morrison St., 503/235-8150, www.crushbar.com, noon-2am Mon.-Sat., noon-1am Sun.) is a bar that defies easy categorization. There are three separate bar areas, each with its own ambience, including the lounge with its old-fashioned curved bar and the Blue Room for dancing and live music; other evenings may feature theme nights, burlesque, or Tarot readers. Crush is a fun, high-energy place to hang.

Darcelle XV Showplace (208 NW 3rd Ave., 503/222-5338, www.darcellexv.com, shows at 8pm Wed.-Thurs., 8pm and 10:30pm Fri.-Sat.) is one of those Portland institutions, like biking and brewing, that may not make sense until you get here. Darcelle is a female impersonator extraordinaire who has, over the years, cozied up to all of the political leaders in Oregon and whose outsize personality has made her an entertainment legend for over 40 years. The stage show ($20), a combination of lip-synching and comedy by a bevy of lovely queens, is very funny and rather raunchy, just as it should be. Reservations are recommended, especially on weekends. If it's midnight on Friday or Saturday, bring on the male strippers!

In super-tolerant Portland, it's easy to ask why gay bars still even exist. Well, places like

Embers (110 NW Broadway, 503/222-3082, 11:30am-2:30pm daily) hang on because they are so much damn fun. Part drag showcase (up front), part disco inferno (the back room), Embers is a Portland institution from the days when dancing all night beneath a mirrored ball to "I Will Survive" seemed like an act of defiant liberation. This is still Portland's premier gay dance club, though the crowds here are very inclusive of gays and straights and everyone in between.

In the heart of Old Town, **Hobo's** (120 NW 3rd Ave., 503/224-3285, www.hobospdx.com, 4am-close) combines the classic red-brick good looks of an authentic 1890s bar with the courtly rhythms of a contemporary piano lounge. Wednesday-Sunday evenings starting at 8pm, pianists tickle the ivories (jazz, show tunes, occasional classical numbers) while the well-dressed clientele—a friendly mix of gays, lesbians, and their straight friends—enjoy cocktails. Hobos is a classy spot for an after-dinner drink.

Darcelle XV Showplace is Portland's top drag bar.

Live Music

One of the pioneers along gentrifying North Mississippi Avenue is a tiny, acoustically rich recording studio called **Mississippi Studios** (3939 N. Mississippi Ave., 503/288-3895, www.mississippistudios.com, hours vary), where local and regional bands go to record music and perform in the studio's intimate space. Check the website to find out what concerts may be offered during your visit; this is a great spot to catch rising stars.

The **Alberta Rose Theatre** (3000 NE Alberta St., 503/719-6055, www.albertarosetheatre.com, hours vary) hosts a selection of folk, world music, cabaret and circus music, comedy, and whatever else is slightly alternative and cool.

If you're looking for the punk edge of the Portland live music scene, one good place to start is **The Know** (2026 NE Alberta St., 503/473-8729, 3pm-2am daily), often referred to as Portland's CBGB.

Speaking of the cool kids, you'll find them on NE Russell Street, in the wood-paneled

Victorian-era bar at the **Secret Society** (116 NE Russell St., 503/493-3600, thesecretsocietylounge.com, 5pm-midnight Sun.-Thurs., 5pm-1am Fri.-Sat.) or smoking outside the **Wonder Ballroom** (128 NE Russell St., 503/284-8686, wonderballroom.com, hours vary). The upstairs ballroom at the Secret Society hosts shows ranging from choro to bluegrass to jazz; the ground-level Wonder's shows tend to be rock or acoustic, including some pretty big names on the indie circuit (this is where you may have caught locals Blitzen Trapper or Colin Meloy a couple of years ago).

At **Holocene** (1001 SE Morrison St., 503/239-7639, www.holocene.org, hours vary), the nightly entertainment can be live music, DJs, performance art, or regularly scheduled evening events. Many events hover at the intersection of music, performance, and technology, and the crowds are fun and varied.

Before you hit town, check out the performers scheduled at the **Aladdin Theater** (3017 SE Milwaukie Ave., 503/233-1994, www.

aladdin-theater.com, hours vary). This 1920s burlesque house has been gussied up to host an eclectic array of touring performers including Steve Earle, the Buena Vista Social Club, and Rufus Wainwright. Many folk, world beat, and indie rock bands play here, and it's a wonderful small theater for taking in a concert.

Kell's Irish Restaurant and Pub (112 SW 2nd Ave., 503/227-4057, www.kellsportland.com, 11am-2am Sun.-Thurs., 11am-2pm Fri.-Sat.) is a landmark not just because of its Victorian good looks, but also thanks to live Celtic music. The musicians are usually local—Portland has a large Celtic music community—although touring bands are also featured.

JAZZ AND BLUES

The hottest jazz club in Portland is **Jimmy Mak's** (221 NW 10th Ave., 503/295-6542, www.jimmymaks.com, 5pm-midnight Mon.-Thurs., 5pm-1am Fri.-Sat.). There's live music every night except Sunday, frequently featuring local drummer Mel Brown and his band. National touring jazz groups also often appear. The lounge at the back of the popular steakhouse **Clyde's** (5474 NE Sandy Blvd., 503/281-9200) usually has live music on Friday and Saturday evenings at 9pm; especially popular are the Sunday evening jazz jam sessions (beginning at 8:30pm) led by local drummer extraordinaire Ron Steen. The atmosphere is friendly and inclusive.

The exquisite and formal **Tea Court** (1009 SW Broadway, 503/790-7752, www.heathmanhotel.com) at the Heathman Hotel, paneled in eucalyptus and illuminated by crystal chandeliers, is a delightful counterpoint to live jazz music, performed Wednesday-Saturday nights with no cover charge. This is the spot to dress up a bit, sip cocktails, and slip into a reverie about the golden age of jazz. Located in historic Union Station, **Wilf's** (800 NW 6th Ave., 503/223-0070, www.wilfsrestaurant.com) is an atmospheric spot to take in live jazz. The large, high-ceilinged, redbrick space was created as the formal dining room for rail travelers during the golden age of the railroad. Jazz is normally offered starting at 7pm Wednesday-Saturday evenings. Many of Portland's top local performers cycle through.

Over in Southeast, **Duff's Garage** (1635 SE 7th Ave., 503/234-2337, www.duffsgarage.com) hosts blues, roots, and rockabilly bands. In addition to regular 9pm shows, Duff's has 6pm-8pm Tuesday-Friday happy hour music and a popular Wednesday night blues jam. With live jazz and blues seven nights a week, newcomer **Blue Diamond** (2016 NE Sandy Blvd., 503/230-9590, www.bluediamondpdx.net, 10:30am-1am Mon.-Fri., Sat., 5pm-1am, 5pm-10pm Sun.) is a laid-back, insider's place to enjoy top local bands.

ROCK

Just west of the Burnside Bridge is **Dante's** (SW 3rd Ave. and Burnside St., 503/226-6630, www.danteslive.com, 11am-2:30am daily), where, in addition to live alternative bands, you'll find often outrageous cabaret and burlesque shows.

One stronghold of the concert scene is the **Crystal Ballroom** (1332 W. Burnside St., 503/225-0047, www.mcmenamins.com, hours vary), where a mix of rock, indie, and world beat artists play in a large ballroom. There, you can "dance on air" thanks to the floating dance floor—perhaps the only one in the United States.

Portland's East Side has a lively music scene. A major destination in any tour of Portland's music hotbeds would include **Doug Fir** (830 E. Burnside St., 503/231-9663, www.dougfirlounge.com, 7am-2:30pm daily), which attracts some of Portland's most interesting acts and is part of a hip development that includes a vintage motor court motel and late-night restaurant.

If you came to Portland to find the remnant of its hippie Grateful Dead roots, then the **Laurelthirst Public House** (2958 NE Glisan St., 503/232-1504, 4pm-midnight Mon., 10:30am-midnight Tues.-Wed., 10:30am-1am Thurs., 10:30am-2am Fri.-Sat., 10:30am-midnight Sun.) is where you need to be. This venerable and funky tavern has excellent local folk and country swing bands along with a feel-good vibe that takes you back to the Summer of Love.

Comedy

Portland's veteran comedy club, **Harvey's** (436 NW 6th Ave., 503/241-0338, www.harveyscomedyclub.com, hours vary), might suffer from poor acoustics and a lack of intimacy if you sit in the back, but it's got the classic comedy club vibe and the talent is usually good. A reasonably priced menu and a full bar are available. For rollicking comedy improv, go to **ComedySportz** (1963 NW Kearney St., 503/236-8888, www.portlandcomedy.com, 8pm Fri.-Sat., $12), where two teams compete for laughs using suggestions from the audience. If you're into standup, check out **Curious Comedy Theater** (5225 NE M. L. King Jr. Blvd., 503/477-9477, www.curiouscomedy.org, $5-12), a nonprofit theater that offers a variety of shows, including "comedy showdowns," audience-participation "random acts of cruelty," lesbian stand-up, improv classes and more.

Newest on the scene is the ultra-hip **Helium Comedy Club** (1510 SE 9th Ave., 888/643-8669, www.heliumcomedy.com/portland, $15-30) which caters to the edgier side of Comedy Central humor. This venue has quickly become a hub of "alt comedy" in Portland; each weekend, stars perform to a packed house of Portland's hip, bespectacled locals.

THE ARTS
Performing Arts

The **Oregon Symphony** (503/228-1353, www.orsymphony.org) is the oldest orchestra west of the Mississippi, and it performs in a historic jewel-box of an auditorium, the **Arlene Schnitzer Concert Hall** (1037 SW Broadway). **Portland Opera** (503/241-1802, www.portlandopera.org) has moved to a summer festival format with four operas presented May through July. The opera also hosts traveling Broadway shows. Other classical music organizations include the **Portland**

The Oregon Symphony performs at Arlene Schnitzer Concert Hall.

Baroque Orchestra (503/222-6000, www.pbo.org), led by Monica Huggett and presenting 18th-century music on period instruments; **Portland Piano International** (503/228-1388, www.portlandpiano.org), which presents world-renowned pianists in recital; and the **Third Angle New Music Ensemble** (503/331-0301, www.thirdangle.org), presenting contemporary classical music.

Oregon Ballet Theatre (503/222-5538, www.obt.org) is the city's classical dance troupe, usually performing at Keller Auditorium. **White Bird Dance** (503/245-1600, www.whitebird.org) brings an impressive number of world-class modern dance troupes to Portland. White Bird sponsors two different series each year, one at Arlene Schnitzer Concert Hall that features established troupes such as Paul Taylor or Mark Morris, the other featuring edgier and more intimate dance pieces held at various venues in Portland. Portland's homegrown modern dance troupe, **BodyVox** (1201 NW 17 Ave.,

503/229-0627, bodyvox.com), is known for its energy and wit.

Theater

More than a dozen theatrical troupes make up a significant presence on Portland's cultural scene. **Imago Theatre** (17 SE 8th Ave., 503/231-9581, www.imagotheatre.com) is an internationally acclaimed troupe that employs multimedia visuals, masks, puppets, dance, and animation to achieve dramatic resonance. Imago performs in an old Masonic hall that is at once intimate and spacious enough for the ambitious visual effects and movement of this cutting-edge troupe. Like Imago, **Do Jump Extremely Physical Theater** (Echo Theater, 1515 SE 37th Ave., 503/231-1232, www. dojump.org) wows its audiences with innovative productions that meld trapeze and other circus arts with whimsical choreography.

For more traditional theater, **Portland Center Stage** (503/445-3700, www.pcs. org) operates out of the renovated **Portland Armory Building** (128 NW 11th Ave.) in the Pearl District. PCS productions encompass classical, contemporary, and premiere works in addition to an annual summer playwrights' festival. Portland's other major theater group, **Artists Repertory Theater** (1515

SW Morrison St., 503/241-1278, www.artistsrep.org), produces intimate, often edgier productions from its "black box" theater just west of downtown.

Art Galleries

Portland has a dynamic fine art scene. Many of the top galleries are in the Pearl District and other neighborhoods in Northwest Portland. To preview some of Portland's leading galleries, go to the **Portland Art Dealers Association** website (www.padaoregon.org), which has details of monthly shows at a dozen of the city's top galleries.

One of the best times to explore Portland's galleries is on the first Thursday of every month during the **First Thursday Gallery Walk.** More than 30 gallery owners coordinate show openings the first Thursday of every month, and many offer complimentary refreshments. Visit the agglomeration of galleries in the Pearl District, where the biggest crowds gather. In this neighborhood, **Elizabeth Leach Gallery** (417 NW 9th Ave., 503/224-0521, www.elizabethleach.com) is one of Portland's most successful and long-established galleries, presenting challenging and inventive art pieces from top regional and national artists. Also check out the nearby

Portland Center Stage mounts its productions at the Portland Armory Building.

DeSoto Building (724 NW Davis St.), which houses three of Portland's top galleries and the Museum of Contemporary Craft.

For something completely different, plan to attend **Last Thursday,** an event at month's end that highlights the dynamic district of galleries and independent designers on Northeast Alberta Street. A mix of street fair, performance art, and gallery tour, Last Thursday is much more raucous than First Thursday, with live bands, fire-eaters, and other high jinks adding an almost circuslike atmosphere to the Alberta Street art scene.

Portland Institute for Contemporary Art, or PICA (224 NW 13th Ave., 503/242-1419, www.pica.org), is Portland's leader in cutting-edge performance, experimental theater, new music, and dance. Throughout the year PICA offers lectures, performances, and exhibitions at many venues throughout the city, but the organization's top event, September's **Time-Based Art Festival** (TBA), is a contemporary art festival of regional, national, and international artists presenting theater, dance, music, film, visual exhibitions, and installations.

Art in the Pearl (503/722-9017, www.artinthepearl.com) is an outdoor arts and crafts fair held over Labor Day weekend in the North Park Blocks, bounded by NW Park and 8th Avenues and Burnside and Glisan Streets along the eastern edge of the Pearl District. This street fair showcases the creations of the local artistic community and also features food and music.

CINEMA

Portland has plenty of multiscreen movie theaters that show the latest Hollywood releases. Thankfully, it also has a rich selection of alternative and repertory cinemas that feature independent, foreign, and vintage movies as well. Almost 85 percent of the city's first-run movie theaters are controlled by the **Regal Cinemas** chain (www.regalcinemas.com), including the following cinemas convenient to central Portland: **Fox Tower**

Stadium 10 (846 SW Park Ave., 503/221-3280), the **Broadway Metroplex 4** (1000 SW Broadway, 503/243-1404), **Pioneer Square Stadium 6** (340 SW Morrison St., 503/295-0909), the **Lloyd Mall 8 Cinema** (2320 Lloyd Center Mall, 503/335-3760), and the **Lloyd Center 10 Cinema** (1510 NE Multnomah St., 503/287-0338).

Portland offers an array of genre movie houses, such as **Cinema 21** (616 NW 21st Ave., 503/223-4515, www.cinema21.com), which is the city's principal independent art-house movie theater. Another independent theater that shows offbeat, foreign, and cult movies is **Hollywood Theatre** (NE 41st Ave. and Sandy Blvd., 503/281-4215, www.hollywoodtheatre.org), housed in a vintage movie palace. The **Clinton Street Theater** (2522 SE Clinton St., 503/238-8899, www.clintonsttheater.com) is an art-house cinema featuring films that generally would not have a market in most other theaters. This might mean *The Rocky Horror Picture Show* every Saturday night, vintage concert films, or dated propaganda films from the Cold War.

Courtesy of brewpub-meisters the brothers McMenamin, Portland also features several restored vintage theaters, among other screening facilities, featuring just-past-first-run flicks ($3) along with pub grub and beer. The most convenient to central Portland neighborhoods are the **Mission Theater** (1624 NW Glisan St., 503/223-4527) and the neo-Moorish **Bagdad Theater & Pub** (3710 SE Hawthorne Blvd., 503/236-9234). For info on what's playing at McMenamins establishments, check out www.mcmenamins.com.

It's not a McMenamins operation, but the budget-priced **Laurelhurst Theater** (NE 28th Ave. and Burnside St., 503/232-5511, www.laurelhursttheater.com) offers beer and pizza to accompany vintage and slightly dated first-run films.

Another twist in the drinks-with-movies trend is **Living Room Theaters** (341 SW 10th Ave., 971/222-2010, www.livingroomtheaters.com), which blends the offerings of a six-theater cinema with a high-end cocktail bar. The films tend toward a mix of art-house flicks, foreign films, and revivals of classics.

Part of the Portland Art Museum, the **Northwest Film Center** (934 SW Salmon St., 503/221-1156, ext. 10, www.nwfilm.org) is the Pacific Northwest's foremost school of filmmaking and media production. As part of its curriculum and community outreach, it offers an ongoing series of foreign, classic, experimental, and independent films that showcase an extremely broad array of cinema and video art forms. Included are thematic series (for example, contemporary films of Egypt), special retrospectives (Fassbinder, Milos Forman, Derek Jarman), and visiting artist programs. Most films are screened at the Whitsell Theater at the Portland Art Museum.

FESTIVALS AND EVENTS

The February **Portland International Film Festival** (503/221-1156, www.nwfilm.org/festivals/piff) is a two-week-plus showcase of foreign and art films that are screened in various theaters across the city.

The **Cinco de Mayo Fiesta** (www.cincodemayo.org) celebrates Latino heritage at Tom McCall Waterfront Park the first weekend

Portland Rose Festival

the Rose Queen and her court

The **Portland Rose Festival** (503/227-2681, www.rosefestival.org) has been the city's major summer event for over a century. The Rose Queen and her court (chosen from among local high school entrants), Navy sailors, and floats from several parades clog Portland's traffic arteries during this 18-day citywide celebration each June. Check out the website for a schedule of what is essentially a small-town festival done with big-town flair.

Two of the more colorful events of the June fete are the **Grand Floral Parade** and the **Festival of Flowers** at Pioneer Courthouse Square. In the latter, all manner of colorful blossoms fill the square to overflowing during the first week of the festival. The Grand Floral Parade usually begins the Saturday following the opening of the festival. You can reserve seats in the Coliseum ahead of time, but save your money and station yourself on an upper floor along the parade route or visit the floats at Oregon Square between Lloyd Center and the Convention Center during the week following the parade. Any lofty perch is sufficient for taking in all the hoopla, drill teams, the Rose Queen, and equestrian demonstrations. This procession is the second-largest all-floral parade in the United States.

(Thurs.-Sun.) in May. This has become one of the largest celebrations of its kind in the country. Mariachis, folk dance exhibitions, a large selection of Mexican food, and fireworks displays are included in the festivities. Admission is $8 adults, $4 children ages 6-12.

Portland is a bicycle town that loves a festival, but it questions authority. Put this all together and you get **Pedalpalooza** (www.shift2bikes.org/pedalpalooza), a decentralized, even anarchic celebration of Portland's bike culture. The festival is extremely free-form and is held in multiple locations with only a few organized annual events. The **Waterfront Blues Festival** (503/282-0555, www.waterfrontbluesfest.com) is the largest festival of its kind on the West Coast. It takes place the first weekend in July at Tom McCall Waterfront Park and features some of the biggest names in the blues. The $10 admission and donations (two canned-good items) go to the Oregon Food Bank.

From the end of June through July, **Chamber Music Northwest** (503/294-6400, www.cmnw.org) presents five weeks of classical music concerts in two locations: Reed College in Southeast Portland and the Catlin Gabel School in Northwest Portland. Ticket prices begin at $25.

No longer Gay Pride, not even Gay and Lesbian Pride, it's now just the **Pride Festival** (503/295-9788, www.pridenw.org): Portland's largest gay festival celebrates Stonewall and affirms the city's LGBTQ

community, held on Father's Day weekend in June. The Waterfront Park main stage has entertainment all weekend, but Sunday is the big day, when some 50,000 people attend the Pride Parade.

Taking place the last full weekend in July in Portland's Tom McCall Waterfront Park, the **Oregon Brewers Festival** (www.oregonbrewfest.com) is North America's largest gathering of independent brewers. The four-day event showcases the wares of more than 100 breweries and attracts more than 90,000 beer lovers. Admission is free, but you'll need to spend $11 for a souvenir mug and four drink tokens. Live musical entertainment accompanies the beer.

An August festival, **The Bite of Oregon** (Tom McCall Waterfront Park, 503/248-0600, www.biteoforegon.com), offers samples of local culinary specialties, and proceeds go to the Special Olympics. Live music is also a highlight.

Portland is confident enough to compare its live music scene to Austin, Texas, and the citywide **Music Fest Northwest** (www.musicfestnw.com) is Portland's answer to Austin's SXSW festival. Over the course of three days and nights in early September, over 200 bands gather in Portland to play their music for large and enthusiastic audiences at Waterfront Park. To attend the concerts, you'll need to buy a wristband ($45-60 per day, or $140 for a 3-day pass), which gets you into the concert grounds.

Shopping

Oregon has no sales tax, so you'll find Portland shopping especially satisfying.

DOWNTOWN AND SOUTHWEST
Shopping Centers and Malls

In the heart of the downtown shopping district, **Pioneer Place** (SW 5th Ave. and Morrison St., 503/228-5800, www.

pioneerplace.com) is an upscale shopping development that features a number of national merchandisers, including Eddie Bauer, Ann Taylor, J. Crew, Coach, and more. The lower level features a vast food court amidst pleasant fountains.

H&M (340 SW Morrison St.), the Swedish clothier, offers stylish but inexpensive clothing and accessories. It's linked to Pioneer

Place via skywalks. Based in the Pacific Northwest, **Nordstrom** (701 SW Broadway) offers downtown shoppers quality clothing and shoes from its location just west of Pioneer Courthouse Square; **Macy's** (621 SW 5th Ave.) is a couple of blocks east.

Niketown (920 SW 6th Ave., 503/221-6453, www.nike.com/NikePortland, 10am-8pm Mon.-Sat., 11am-6pm Sun.) is the flagship store of Oregon's largest sportswear manufacturer, and you'll find a large selection of elite shoes and sports gear in a whiz-bang retail environment. If you're looking for Nike quality and logoed goods at a lower price, head to the **Nike Outlet Store** (2650 NE Martin Luther King Jr. Blvd., 503/281-5901) in inner Northeast Portland.

Farmers Markets
★ **PORTLAND FARMERS MARKET**
One of the institutions that characterize Portland, the **Portland Farmers Market** (South Park Blocks, www.portlandfarmersmarket.org, 8:30am-2pm Sat. Mar.-Nov., 9am-2pm Sat. Nov.-Feb.) attracts throngs of people, and not just for food shopping. Every Saturday, upwards of 15,000 people come to the market to gaze at locally produced food and socialize with friends. This teeming

market features breads and baked goods, locally grown fruits and vegetables, artisan cheeses, wild mushrooms, organic meat and poultry, freshly caught fish and seafood, and nursery stock. For entertainment, there's always live music, and local chefs give cooking demonstrations. In addition, this is a great place to come for breakfast or lunch, as a number of food carts offer freshly made food. People watching is of the highest caliber here. On Wednesday from 10am-2pm, there's a smaller version of this farmers market a few blocks to the north, at the end of the South Park Blocks near SW Salmon and Park. Pets are not allowed at either market.

There are other farmers markets in Portland neighborhoods throughout the week. In fact, during summer and fall, Monday is the only day without a market somewhere. For a complete list of farmers markets in Portland, follow the links at www.oregonfarmersmarkets.org.

Clothing and Accessories
You don't have to be in Oregon very long before plaid woolen shirts begin to look sensible and stylish. Pendleton Woolen Mills is an Oregon company, and at downtown's **Pendleton Store** (900 SW 5th Ave.,

shopping at the Portland Farmers Market

503/242-0037,9:30am-5:30pm Mon.-Fri., 10am-5pm Sat., noon-5pm Sun.) you can pick up distinctive wool shirts, skirts, and blankets that will last for years.

Portland's most upscale menswear store is **Mario's** (833 SW Broadway, 503/227-3477, http://marios.com, 10am-6pm Mon.-Sat., noon-5pm Sun.), with the best of casual and formal wear from the world's top designers. **Parallel** (1016 SW Washington St., 503/274-8882, www.parallelportland.com, 11am-6pm Mon.-Sat., noon-5 Sun.) is a fun spot for women's designer clothing and accessories from small, specialty fashion houses, many based in Portland or the Pacific Northwest.

Looking for women's fashion? A Portland fashion leader for over 40 years, **The Mercantile** (729 SW Alder St., 503/223-6649, www.mercantileportland.com, 10am-6pm Mon.-Sat., noon-5 Sun.) is a top choice for sophisticated clothing, both hip and professional. The Mercantile carries many New York and LA clothing lines, and has exclusive representation of several Portland-based designers.

Crafts

Real Mother Goose (901 SW Yamhill St., 503/223-9510 or 800/968-1070, www.therealmothergoose.com, 10am-5:30pm, Mon.-Thurs., 10am-6pm Fri.-Sat.) is a quality crafts gallery that presents jewelry, pottery, woodcrafts, and other design goods from hundreds of Pacific Northwest artists and craftspeople. It's an excellent place to buy one-of-a-kind gifts.

In operation since 1974, **Portland Saturday Market** (just south of the Burnside Bridge in Waterfront Park, www.portlandsaturdaymarket.com, 10am-5pm Sat., 11am-4:30pm Sun. Mar.-Dec. 24,) is the largest outdoor arts and crafts fair in the United States, attracting an estimated 750,000 visitors each year. The handicrafts range from exquisite woodwork (at reasonable prices), pottery, paintings, and jewelry to more uniquely Portland items like tie-die baby clothes and handmade juggling equipment. The high

quality that's been maintained here for decades is astonishing.

Outdoor Clothing and Gear

Based in the Portland metro area, **Columbia Sportswear** (911 SW Broadway, 503/226-6800, 9:30am-7pm Mon.-Sat., 11am-6pm Sun.) has its flagship store downtown on SW Broadway. This is the place to go for fashionable, hardworking outerwear for recreation and heavy weather. For discounts on the same quality clothing and gear, go to the **Columbia Sportswear Outlet** (1323 SE Tacoma St., 503/238-0118, 9am-7pm Mon.-7pm Mon.-Sat., 11am-6pm Sun.) in Sellwood.

NORTHWEST
Clothing and Accessories

If all Portland hipsters had money, they'd be shopping at **Lizard Lounge** (1323 NW Irving St., 503/416-7176, www.lizardlounge-pdx.com, 10am-7pm Mon.-Sat., 11am-7pm Sun.), where you can pick up functional, ecofriendly, stylish duds from local company Nau and others.

Popina Swimwear Boutique (318 NW 11th Ave., 503/243-7946, www.popinaswimwear.com, 11am-6pm Mon.-Wed., 11am-7pm Thurs.-Sat., noon-5pm Sun.) is a fabulous shop for women's bathing suits and swim accessories, with 25 international brands and Popina's own line of updated, retro-chic swimwear.

Founded in Portland in 1983, **Hanna Andersson** (327 NW 10th Ave., 503/321-5275, www.hannaandersson.com, 10am-6pm Mon.-Fri., 10am-5pm Sat., 11am-5pm Sun.) sells clothing for kids in bright, simple Swedish-inspired designs and soft, durable cotton. It's decidedly upscale children's wear, but it's high quality and well-wearing, destined to be handed down.

One of Portland's best sources for refined, upscale women's fashion is **Physical Element** (416 NW 12th Ave., 503/224-5425, www.physicalelement.com, 11am-5pm Mon., Tues.-Fri. 11am-6pm, 11am-5pm Sat., noon-5pm Sun.). While the styles here tend to be classic, sprinkled throughout are more sassy fashions from local designers.

Up on NW 23rd is another hot spot for small, locally owned boutiques. For fun children's clothes, go to **Duck Duck Goose** (525 NW 23rd Ave., 503/916-0636, http://shopduckduckgoose.com, 10am-6pm Mon.-Sat., 11am-5pm Sun.) and, for a wide selection of high-end shoes from mostly European designers, to **Zelda's Shoe Bar** (633 NW 23rd Ave., 503/226-0363, www.zeldaspdx.com, 10am-6pm Mon.-Sat., 11am-5pm Sun.).

Books
★ **POWELL'S CITY OF BOOKS**
For many visitors, **Powell's City of Books** (1005 W. Burnside St., 503/228-0540 or 800/878-7323, www.powells.com, 9am-11pm daily) is one of Portland's primary attractions. A block square and three stories tall, Powell's combines new, used, and out-of-print books and is usually absolutely thronged with bibliophiles. In addition to miles of bookshelves, Powell's offers a coffee shop as well as free author events and book signings.

Outdoor Clothing and Gear
The Northwest Portland outpost of **REI** (1405 NW Johnson St., 503/221-1938, 10am-9pm

Mon.-Fri., 10am-9pm Sat., 10am-7pm Sun.) is where to head if you forgot your bike helmet or crampons, or if you are shopping for functional, all-weather clothing for active lifestyles.

Synonymous with earth-friendly and socially responsible manufacturing, **Patagonia** (907 NW Irving St., 503/525-2552, 11am-7pm Mon.-Fri., 10am-6pm Sat., 11am-6pm Sun.) shares a large and strikingly handsome historical storefront with the Ecotrust Foundation in the Pearl District. Patagonia offers gear and clothing for those serious about the outdoors.

NORTHEAST
Built in 1960, **Lloyd Center** (NE 15th Ave. and Weidler St., 503/282-2511, www.lloydcenter.com) was the first shopping center in North America and is still one of Portland's major shopping destinations. Centered around an Olympic-size indoor ice-skating rink (Tonya Harding once trained here), Lloyd Center boasts more than 200 retail outlets (including Sears and Macy's), a food court, and two multiplex cinemas.

One of Northeast Portland's top destinations for strolling, window shopping, and shopping at independent shops is North Mississippi Avenue between Fremont and

Prepare to spend some time browsing at Powell's City of Books.

Skidmore Streets. Here you'll find dozens of locally own boutiques; fun bars, restaurants, and food carts; and excellent people watching. Favorite shops include **Gypsy Chic** (3966 N. Mississippi Ave., 503/234-9779, http://shop. gypsy-chic.com, 11am-8pm Mon.-Fri., 10am-8pm Sat., 10am-7pm Sun.) for casual but elegant women's clothing and **Manifesto** (3806 N. Mississippi Ave., 503/546-0910, www. manifestoshoes.com, 11am-6pm Mon.-Sat., 11am-5pm Sun.) for men and women's shoes. You'll need to stop in at **Meadow** (3731 N. Mississippi Ave., 503/288-4633, www.at-themeadow.com, 10am-7pm daily). What's not to like in a shop that sells dozens of different finishing salts, wine, flowers, artisan chocolate, and the largest selection of bitters imaginable?

A few blocks east on Williams Avenue is another hotbed of hipster-focused shops, pubs, and restaurants. If you wonder where Portland's "put a bird on it" aesthetic hails from, look no further than **Queen Bee Creations** (3961 N. Williams Ave., 503/232-1755, www.queenbee-creations.com, 10am-7pm Mon.-Sat., 11am-5pm Sun.) where you'll find handmade bags, wallets, bike packs, and other fun leather cases, many in fact with whimsical birds on them.

SOUTHEAST
Housewares and Home Decor

Acres of upholstery fabric from around the world make the **Whole Nine Yards** (1820 E. Burnside St., 503/223-2880, http://w9yards. com, 10am-6pm Mon-Fri., 10am-5pm Sun.) a must-stop for home decorators.

A Portland original, **Hippo Hardware** (1040 E. Burnside St., 503/231-1444, www. hippohardware.com, 10am-5pm Mon.-Thurs., 10am-5pm Fri.-Sat., noon-5pm Sun.) has been collecting period lighting, plumbing, hardware, and architectural components since 1976, when, as they say, the "notion of selling things that many people threw away was considered strange at best." The great thing about Hippo Hardware is that it hasn't gone upscale or hipster like Portland's other salvage

and house part businesses—it's still the very funky operation it's always been. Equal parts secondhand shop, antiques store, and house salvage emporium, it's a vast and fascinating place to explore.

The showroom for **Pratt & Larson Tile** (1201 SE 3rd Ave. 503/231-9464, www.prat-tandlarson.com, 9am-5pm Mon.-Fri., 10am-2pm Sat.,), a local ceramic tile manufacturer and retailer, offers an amazing display of the tiling arts. Pratt & Larson creates its own distinctive tiles in dozens of colors and hundreds of shapes, sizes, and textures, and also displays hand-painted and handcrafted tiles from dozens of other tile makers from around the country. If that weren't dizzying enough for anyone contemplating a house remodel or tilework upgrade, much of the showroom is made up of beautifully tiled tableaus of kitchens and bathrooms.

If you're into "upcycling"—finding new uses for old house parts and industrial salvage—then check out **Grand Marketplace**'s (1005 SE Grand, 503/208-2580, http://grand-marketplacepdx.com, 10am-6pm daily), 18,000 feet of vintage, salvaged, and industrial furniture and collectibles.

Music

A quintessential Portland business, **Music Millennium** (3158 E. Burnside St., 503/248-0163, www.musicmillennium.com, 10am-10pm Mon.-Sat., 11am-9pm Sun.) is a vast and funky CD, record, and music store of the sort that typified the 1970s. You'll find almost every kind of music—old, new, rare, foreign—you name it, it's probably here. Next door is Classical Millennium, which offers the same expansive selection for opera and classical music fans.

Anyone who plays an acoustic stringed instrument, or who appreciates folk music, should stop by **Artichoke Music** (3130 SE Hawthorne Blvd., 503/232-8845, http://artichokemusic.org, 11am-5pm daily), Portland's premier acoustic instrument emporium. Artichoke offers a rich selection of folk instruments made by North American craftspeople, as well as a growing selection of vintage instruments.

Plants

Portland is famed for its parks and gardens, and no wonder—the climate here is so mild and nurturing that gardeners can grow almost anything. To prove the point, there's **Portland Nursery** (5050 SE Stark St., 503/231-5050, www.portlandnursery.com, 9am-7pm daily). If you've got a green thumb or just enjoy plant life, consider a trip to this block-square nursery, the city's largest and most comprehensive.

SELLWOOD

Sellwood, about five miles south of downtown Portland on the east banks of the Willamette River, is synonymous with antique stores. Walk along Southeast 13th Avenue between Marion and Malden Streets and check out its many shops, starting at **1874 House** (8070 SE 13th Ave., 503/233-1874). Take bus #70 from the Rose Quarter.

Accommodations

Portland has a broad range of lodging choices—but few are particularly cheap. The good news is that many of the best lodging options are in the central city, close to the arts, restaurants, and nightlife. In general, downtown presents the most lodging options, while Northeast Portland, near Lloyd Center and the Convention Center, offers another wide selection at somewhat lower prices, with convenient links to downtown by MAX light rail.

The rates quoted are for double occupancy summer high-season rooms. Winter off-season rates are usually about 25 percent lower. Shopping for rooms on Internet discount lodging sites such as www.hotels.com can yield unexpected deals, even in high season.

DOWNTOWN

Unless otherwise noted, you'll pay to park at downtown hotels. Parking fees range $15-30 per night, so be sure to ask when booking a room, as these fees add up fast (and you'll be charged lodging tax on them, which is currently 14.5 percent assessed in lodgings with more than 50 rooms).

$100-150

Downtown Portland's newest hotel, ★ **McMenamins Crystal Hotel** (303 SW 12th Ave., 503/972-2670 or 855/205-3930, www.mcmenamins.com/CrystalHotel,

$145-180, parking $25), is also one of its least expensive. The McMenamins crew has rehabilitated this once-decrepit building with the company's trademark whimsy and Oregonian informality (guests in the less-expensive rooms will find bathrooms down the hall). The ground floor is dominated by the Zeus Café; down in the basement, you'll find Al's Den, with live music nightly and a huge soaking pool, in memory of when this building housed downtown's liveliest gay baths.

$150-200

The renovation of the 1912 ★ **Ace Hotel Portland** (1022 SW Stark St., 503/228-2277, www.acehotel.com/portland, $199-395, parking $37) has turned a historic but down-at-heel property in an unbeatable downtown location into a distinctive, quintessentially Portland hotel. Spare but stylish guest rooms reflect the city's recycling ethic with a mix of salvaged fir, vintage fixtures, and army surplus, while custom-made Pendleton blankets and eclectic murals by local artists enhance the unique sense of place. The less expensive rooms share a bathroom, while the top-floor suites offer understated luxury.

The large **Portland Waterfront Marriott Downtown** (1401 SW Naito Pkwy., 503/226-7600, www.portlandmarriott.com, $199-309, parking $35) is a convention hotel that faces

Waterfront Park, with half the views over the Willamette River toward Mount Hood. It's an excellent location if you're visiting Portland for a waterfront festival; when it's not booked with conventioneers, it's also one of the most affordable of the downtown hotels. Facilities include an indoor saline pool, a large fitness area, a restaurant, a large sports bar, a coffee shop, and free wireless Internet.

The **Benson Hotel** (309 SW Broadway, 503/228-2000 or 800/663-1144, www.benson hotel.com, $170-329, valet parking $35) was built in 1913 as the city's most luxurious hotel, and thankfully this grande dame retains nearly all of its spectacular early-20th-century fittings, particularly the grand lobby with its walnut paneling, Belgian chandeliers, Italian marble floors, and massive oriental carpets. If you're feeling important, go for the Presidential Suite: Every U.S. president since Taft has stayed here. Facilities include a restaurant and a cozy lobby bar.

With nearly 800 rooms, the **Portland Hilton** (921 SW 6th Ave., 503/226-1611, www.portland.hilton.com, $199-329, parking $30-37) is Oregon's largest hotel. And while there's no denying that the Hilton is largely a business and convention hotel, the hotel is absolutely in the center of the city, close to shopping, the arts, and public transport. Online specials mean that standard guest rooms frequently represent the best value in the city center, and the 12,000-square-foot athletic club with indoor pool is the best hotel facility in downtown. The **Rivers Edge Hotel & Spa** (0455 SW Hamilton Ct., 503/802-5800, www.riversedgehotel.com, $137-279, parking $25), although a couple of miles south of downtown, is worth noting for its quiet setting along the Willamette River, stylish rooms, excellent fitness center and spa (no swimming pool), and lovely adjacent restaurant with riverside dining. Spend the extra $30 or so for a riverside room.

$200-250

Mark Spencer Hotel (409 SW 11th Ave., 503/224-3293 or 800/548-3934, www.mark spencer.com, $219-339, parking $20), is a former residential hotel that's now a comfortable

McMenamins Crystal Hotel

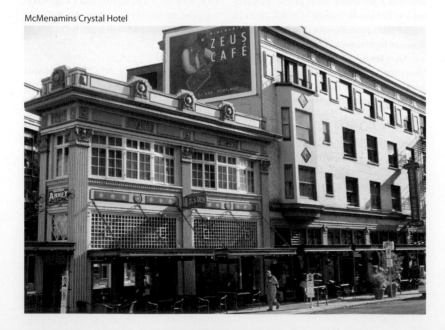

The Ace Hotel is a hip place to stay downtown.

lodging just a few blocks from shopping and dining in the Pearl District. The rooms once rented as apartments, so even the standard guest rooms are spacious and have complete kitchens. Rates include continental breakfast.

At the vintage but beautifully updated ★ **Hotel deLuxe** (729 SW 15th Ave., 503/219-2094 or 866/895-2094, www.hoteldeluxeportland.com, $229-299, parking $31) a Hollywood theme prevails throughout, with hundreds of movie stills and other photos celebrating the golden age of film in guest rooms, hallways, and on a screen that dominates the lobby. The least expensive rooms are rather small, but well appointed, and service is strong on details. The hotel is just west of downtown.

Chic and conveniently located, **Hotel Lucia** (400 SW Broadway, 503/225-1717 or 866/986-8086, www.hotellucia.com, $249-339, valet parking $40) is a top choice for travelers looking for high-design comfort and a frisson of cool urban style. Edgy art fills the lobby along with modern leather furniture

that bespeaks cool elegance. Standard guest rooms aren't vast but are very comfortable and beautifully furnished; consider stepping up to a Superior or Deluxe room if you need space.

Sleek and stylish, **Hotel Modera** (515 SW Clay St., 503/484-1084 or 877/484-1084, www.hotelmodera.com, $239-399, valet parking $32) showcases an updated, mid-century aesthetic. The large art-draped lobby, lined with marble and dark woods, opens onto a very spacious courtyard with lots of outdoor seating, three fire pits, and a "living wall" of greenery. Guest rooms carry on the Euro-chic look, with a streamlined aesthetic that's both bold and whimsical. Hotel Modera is at the center of downtown and right on the MAX line. Guests can use the nearby 24-Hour Fitness.

A historic hotel with a stunning Romanesque facade, ★ **Hotel Vintage** (422 SW Broadway, 503/228-1212 or 800/263-2305, www.hotelvintage-portland.com, $243-356, valet parking $43) is a temple of discreet luxury, perfect for a romantic weekend or a highly civilized business stay. Standard rooms are sumptuous, but if you're here for a special occasion, the hotel's many unique suites (there are 57 different guest-room floor plans) make this a top choice—check out the two-story townhouse suites and the Garden Spa rooms, with a flower-decked rooftop patio and outdoor hot tub. Amenities include the Pazzo Ristorante and bar, a manager's wine reception, an honor bar, fitness and business centers, and free wireless Internet. Pets are welcome.

Don't let the corporate moniker mislead you. ★ **Embassy Suites Portland** (319 SW Pine St., 503/279-9000, www.embassyportland.com, $249-309, valet parking $30, self-parking $30) is in fact the palatial Multnomah Hotel, built in 1912 as the largest and grandest hotel in the Pacific Northwest. When Embassy Suites remodeled this aging beauty, the company reduced the number of guest rooms from 700 to just 276 suites. These are the largest standard rooms in downtown Portland. Amenities include a free breakfast, and an indoor pool and fitness center that resemble a Roman bath.

Over $250

A true Portland landmark, ★ **The Sentinel** (614 SW 11th Ave., 503/224-3400 or 800/554-3456, www.sentinelhotel.com, $288-413, parking $39) has two wings: the original 1909 hotel with an imposing white tile facade (look for the Transformer-like figures along the roofline) and the adjoining Portland Elks Lodge, a very ornate structure built in 1932 to resemble the Farnese Palace in Rome. This is one of Portland's most regal hotels. The standard Superior level guest rooms are large and nicely furnished, but the suites are really outstanding. Amenities include Jake's Grill restaurant, a Starbucks coffee shop, and a large and airy fitness center.

The interior of the historic and luxurious ★ **Heathman Hotel** (1009 SW Broadway, 800/551-0011, www.heathmanhotel.com, $250-379, parking $39), built in 1927, offers a tantalizing balance between old and new, between its old-fashioned opulence and the refreshing brio of the hotel's vast collection of modern art. The entry-level Deluxe rooms aren't huge but offer every luxury and very refined furnishings. For more room, book an Executive King or a Symphony Suite. Facilities include the **Heathman Restaurant,** one of Portland's finest; a wonderful two-story wood-paneled tearoom with daily high tea and live jazz music Wednesday-Saturday; the see-and-be-seen Marble Bar; and a hot chocolate-coffee lounge.

The conveniently located **Hotel Monaco** (506 SW Washington St., 503/222-0001 or 888/207-2201, www.monaco-portland.com, $256-373, valet parking $41) is a showcase of vivid color, oversize art, and unconventional furnishings. The zippy decor continues into the large stylish guest rooms, which are designed with a sense of humor, using color and fabric to create a mood of relaxed whimsy. Amenities include a day spa, fitness and business centers, and the very good **Red Star Tavern** restaurant.

The Nines (525 SW Morrison St., 877/229-9995, www.thenines.com, $348-578, valet parking $43) occupies the top nine floors of the downtown Macy's store, a magnificent glazed terra-cotta landmark from 1908. A dramatic nine-story interior atrium is flanked by large stylish guest rooms. Guest rooms feature original art from students at the Pacific Northwest College of Art. Facilities include fitness and business centers, the organic steak house Urban Farmer, and the rooftop Departures, which has cocktails and lighter Asian-influenced fare.

One of the few hotels right on the Willamette River, **RiverPlace Hotel** (1510 SW Harbor Way, 503/228-3233 or 800/227-1333, www.riverplacehotel.com, $311-518, valet parking $33) sits above a marina at the edge of Waterfront Park, yet it's just moments from downtown shopping and activities. A warm and pleasing Arts and Crafts aesthetic pervades the lobby and bar, and guest rooms are large and comfortable. RiverPlace also offers eight one-bedroom and two two-bedroom condos for either nightly or extended rental. With the notable position right on the river, the bar and restaurant, both with large outdoor decks, are very popular.

NORTHWEST
Under $100

Hostelling International—Portland, Northwest (425 NW 18th Ave., 503/241-2783 or 888/777-0067, www.nwportlandhostel.com, bunks $29 for HI members, $32 nonmembers, private rooms $71-99, parking permit $2/day) has a great location at the heart of Northwest Portland's most exciting neighborhoods. The main hostel is in a restored turn-of-the-20th-century building and features dorms with as few as two and up to eight beds per room, private rooms, a fully equipped kitchen, and a coffee bar. Some of the private guest rooms are in nearby buildings.

Another simple place to stay in Northwest Portland is the **Portland International Guesthouse, Northwest** (2185 NW Flanders St., 503/224-0500 or 877/228-0500, www.pdxguesthouse.com, $70-80), a historic home with six rooms sharing three bathrooms, a sitting room, and a kitchen.

$150-200

A couple of quite decent but rather generic hotels on the industrial edge of Northwest Portland are very convenient to the neighborhood, the streetcar, the freeway, and good restaurants: the **Silver Cloud Inn** (2426 NW Vaughn St., 503/484-2400, www.silvercloud.com, $189-239) and **Holiday Inn Express** (2333 NW Vaughn St., 503/248-4055, www.hiexpress.com, $208-229). Both have free parking.

One of Portland's most engaging lodging choices, the ★ **Inn at Northrup Station** (2025 NW Northrup St., 503/224-0543 or 800/224-1180, www.northrupstation.com, $259-309, free parking) is an older motel in Northwest Portland that has been totally renovated into a retro-hip showcase with a wild color palette. Each room has a kitchen and boldly designed furniture, and there's a rooftop garden. The inn is right on the Portland Streetcar line, so you can get to the Pearl District or downtown in minutes without having to worry about parking.

The top B&B in Northwest Portland is **Heron Haus Bed & Breakfast Inn** (2545 NW Westover Rd., 503/248-4055, www.heronhaus.com, $185-250). Built in 1904 and perched in a prime West Hills location, this ivy-covered 10,000-square-foot English Tudor home is one of the city's most impressive lodging options. It offers six guest rooms on the second and third floors, all with fireplaces, modern private baths, cable TV, and terrific views of the city and the Cascades.

NORTHEAST

Between downtown Portland and the Lloyd Center are the Portland Oregon Convention Center and the Rose Garden sports arena, along with a number of good-value chain hotels. There are often deep discounts on these hotels at Internet reservation sites. Most of the hotels are no more than five minutes'

walk from the MAX line. The downside is that many of these close-in hotels sit in a busy urban neighborhood with lots of traffic whizzing by, but that's the price you pay for convenience.

The historic Irvington neighborhood north of Broadway, studded with lovely vintage homes, offers a couple of fine bed-and-breakfast options.

$50-100

A historic saloon and hotel near the foot of the Fremont Bridge in a gentrifying industrial neighborhood, **McMenamins White Eagle** (836 N. Russell St., 503/335-8900 or 866/271-3377, www.mcmenamins.com, $60, free on-street parking) is one of the best lodging deals in town. The 11 sparsely furnished but comfortable rooms share two toilets and two showers, European style. The saloon features live music nightly—here's the rub if you're only here for the accommodation: It's loud until at least midnight. Earplugs are available for free.

$100-150

★ **Kennedy School** (5736 NE 33rd Ave., 503/249-3983 or 888/249-3983, www.kennedyschool.com, $185-215, free parking) is a quirky McMenamins hotel in the Concordia neighborhood, about six miles northeast of downtown. The hotel is set in an old elementary school that has been transformed into a brewpub, movie theater, restaurant, several school-themed bars (including the Detention Lounge), and a concert venue. You have a choice of rooms: whimsically decorated former classrooms that have become guest rooms, complete with chalkboards and private bathrooms, and king bedrooms in the "English Wing," a newly built addition in a lush courtyard behind the school.

The historic Irvington neighborhood north of the Lloyd Center has several fine B&Bs. The opulent ★ **White House Bed and Breakfast** (1914 NE 22nd Ave., 503/287-7131 or 800/272-7131, www.portlandswhitehouse.com, $145-250) gives you the presidential treatment. Located just off Broadway near an avenue of shops and restaurants and only 5-10 minutes from the Lloyd Center and downtown, this lovingly restored 1912 lumber baron's mansion is one of the city's top B&Bs. It really does look like its namesake in D.C.

$150-200

Across from the Lloyd Center shopping mall, right on the MAX line and a short walk from the convention center is the large and nicely renovated ★ **DoubleTree by Hilton** (1000 NE Multnomah St., 503/281-6111 or 800/996-0510, www.doubletreeportland.com, $159-259 parking $10). The Doubletree is a full-service hotel with two restaurants, a lounge, fitness room and indoor pool, room service, and convention facilities.

The landmark **Lion and the Rose Victorian Bed and Breakfast Inn** (1810 NE 15th Ave., 503/287-9245 or 800/955-1647, www.lionrose.com, $185-235) is a 1906 Queen Anne mansion listed on the National Register of Historic Places. The seven guest rooms and apartment, all with private baths, are each unique, and although they are charming in an authentically Victorian way, they're also up-to-date, with air-conditioning, telephones, and cable TV. The B&B is within walking distance of good restaurants and shopping on Northeast Broadway.

$200-250

Just across the street from the Oregon Convention Center and immediately on the MAX line, **Hotel Eastlund** (1021 NE Grand Ave., 503/235-2100 or 800/343-1822, http://hoteleastlund.com, $229-279, parking $25) offers recently updated rooms in a very convenient location. The rooftop Altabira City Tavern offers fantastic views over Portland.

The **Crowne Plaza Hotel Portland** (1441 NE 2nd Ave., 503/233-2401 or 877/277-6963, $208-235, parking $19) offers upscale rooms in addition to its excellent location near (but not on) the MAX line, the Portland Streetcar, and other major Northeast Portland arterials.

In a quiet corner of this busy neighborhood, the nine-story Crowne Plaza also has good views from the upper floors. Facilities include a beautiful indoor pool and fitness center, plus a restaurant and bar.

SOUTHEAST
Under $50

No other lodgings capture the ecofriendly vibe of Portland—and especially the woolly Hawthorne neighborhood—quite like **Portland Hawthorne Hostel** (3031 SE Hawthorne Blvd., 503/236-3380 or 866/447-3031, www.portlandhostel.org, bunks $29 for HI members, $32 nonmembers). Among its most prominent features is an "eco-roof" over the front porch, a runoff filtering system planted in sedum and yarrow and cisterns to capture rainwater for landscaping and toilet flushing. The 1909 house offers men's, women's, and coed dorm rooms, plus two private rooms ($64 members, $67 nonmembers). Amenities include a fully equipped kitchen (make your own pancakes for a buck!), lockers, and bike rentals.

$100-150

On SE Clinton Street, near the restaurant hotbed along SE Division Avenue, the ★ **Clinton Street Guesthouse** (4220 SE Clinton St., 503/234-8752, www.clintonstreetguesthouse.com, $110-155) offers four nicely furnished, but not overly fussy, guest rooms in one of Portland's most coveted neighborhoods. Two of the rooms have private baths, while the other two rooms share two bathrooms (not en suite), and everything is tip-top, including breakfast. If you're traveling with a small group, inquire about the small two-bedroom bungalow and cottage (breakfast not included; three-night minimum).

$150-200

On the east side of the Burnside Bridge, as Burnside Street mounts the hill, are a number of older motor court motels, some of dubious quality. However, one of these older properties has an interesting tale to tell. The **Jupiter Hotel** (800 E. Burnside St., 503/230-9200 or 877/800-0004, www.jupiterhotel.com, $189-550, parking $10) is what you might call a boutique motel, an older motel that has been totally updated with a chic modern look and such stylish accoutrements as fine linens, eye-grabbing art, and high-end toiletries. Best of all, the Jupiter Hotel is also home to the Doug Fir Restaurant and Lounge, one of Portland's top music clubs with a popular dining room open till 4am daily. Weekends can get pretty noisy, so bring earplugs or just dance till dawn.

On the edge of beautiful Laurelhurst Park, the opulent **Portland Mayor's Mansion** (3360 SE Ankeny St., 503/232-3588, http://pdxmayorsmansion.com, $150-275) is indeed the home of a former Portland mayor. Built in 1912 of red brick in colonial revival style, the mansion is filled with intriguing period detail and offers four lodging options (all with private bathrooms), including a three-room executive suite. This mansion is at the heart of one of early Portland's most exclusive neighborhoods, and a walk in any direction will reveal dozens of beautiful architectural specimens.

AIRPORT

There are a lot of hotels at I-205 Exit 23, the exit for PDX airport. Except on holiday weekends, you probably won't need reservations, but here are a few options from all price categories if you want to call ahead. All of the following offer free shuttle service to and from the airport.

- **Ramada Portland Airport:** 6221 NE 82nd Ave., 503/255-6511, www.ramada.com, $82-109

- **Country Inn and Suites:** 7025 NE Alderwood Rd., 503/255-2700 or 888/987-2700, www.countryinns.com, $126-179

- **Aloft Portland Airport Hotel:** 99920 NE Cascades Pkwy., 503/200-5678, www.aloft-portlandairport.com, $159-249

- **Sheraton Portland Airport Hotel:** 8253 NE Airport Way, 503/281-2500 or 800/325-3535, www.sheratonportlandairport.com, $149-239

CAMPING

Portland isn't particularly convenient for campers. South of Portland, with easy access off I-5, is **Champoeg State Heritage Area** (503/678-1251, www.oregonstate-parks.org, $19-28), a lovely park along the Willamette River. Campsites are in shaded groves alongside the river, and bike and hiking paths and museums make this park a worthy recreational destination. In addition to year-round tent ($19) and RV ($26-28) sites, there are also yurts ($40) and rustic cabins ($40-50). Champoeg is about 30 miles south of downtown Portland, off I-5 Exit 278. Reserve campsites at 800/452-5687 or www.reserveamerica.com.

For those who enjoy rural serenity within commuting distance of downtown, there's camping in **Milo McIver State Park** (503/630-7150 or 800/551-6949, www.oregonstateparks.org, mid-Mar.-Oct., $18 tent, $24 RV). This retreat, set on the banks of the Collowash River five miles northwest of Estacada, is 25 miles (but about 45 minutes) from downtown Portland. To get to the park, take I-84 east to I-205 south and follow it to the exit for Route 224/Estacada. The road forks right at the town of Carver to go 10 miles (look for Springwater Road) to the campground. East of Portland, a few miles north of I-84 on the Sandy River, is **Oxbow Park** (503/797-1850, $22 with additional $5 vehicle entrance fee), operated by Metro, the Portland regional government agency. Oxbow Park is right on a bend in the river in a quiet woodsy setting and offers flush toilets, but no showers. There's a strict no-dog policy. To reach Oxbow Park, take I-84 Exit 17, follow 257th Avenue to Division Street, turn east (right), and follow signs to the park.

Food

Portland is known for its restaurants, especially those focusing on locally sourced ingredients, and increasingly people structure their trips here around eating. Even if you're not a foodie, be sure to bring your appetite.

In this neighborhood-oriented city, restaurants have strong associations with their locale. The restaurant scene—and dining experience—will be very different in the Pearl District than in the Mississippi Avenue neighborhood, for instance, though both offer top quality and selection. You may find it as tempting to choose a neighborhood in which to dine as to choose a specific restaurant or type of cuisine, because many of the dining neighborhoods have a strong and appealing character of their own.

Brewpubs

Portland, also known as Beervana, is the epicenter of the craft brewing revival in North America, boasting more breweries than any other city in the world—91 were in operation in the metro area at press time.

All brewpubs are required to serve food, and many double as restaurants. This means that in almost all cases, families are welcome in brewpubs within dining hours and sometimes in designated nonbar areas. Portland brewpubs come in all shapes and sizes, from garden tents to converted warehouses to funeral chapels. Locally brewed beer is one of the pillars of Portland life—cheers!

The McMenamins Brewpub Empire

Whether or not you're a beer drinker, you're likely to run into a McMenamins brewpub during a trip to Portland. This highly successful local enterprise now has over 50 pubs and related businesses in Washington and Oregon, and whenever a historic venue goes on sale, there's at least a large minority of Pacific Northwesterners who hope that it will become a McMenamins brewpub. The McMenamins are in fact brothers Brian and Mike, who are equally devoted to brewing beer, designing fun spaces to drink it in, and preserving distinctive buildings.

The **Crystal Ballroom** (1332 W. Burnside St., 503/225-0047), a former dance hall, is a singular place to catch a concert or have a beer. Constructed in 1914, the top-story ballroom has a mechanical "floating on air" dance floor (there's a layer of ball bearings and springy rubber beneath the hardwood flooring). One block away is another extension of this massive entertainment citadel: the **Crystal Hotel** (303 SW 12th Ave., 503/972-2670), a hotel set in a former gay bathhouse, with an appropriately labyrinthine set of basement bars culminating in the just-right **Ringler's Annex,** a tiny subterranean bar in a Flatiron Building-like structure for in-the-know hipsters.

The **Kennedy School** (5736 NE 33rd Ave., 503/249-3983 or 888/249-3983) is an unusual enterprise—a block-square 1915 grade school that's been converted into a brewpub, restaurant, and hotel, plus a movie theater (think couches in the auditorium). In the suburbs of Portland is one of the grandest extensions of the McMenamins dream. On the way to the Columbia Gorge, **Edgefield** (2126 SW Halsey St., Troutdale, 503/669-8610 or 800/669-8610) began its existence as the Multnomah County Poor Farm and now contains multiple restaurants and drinking establishments, plus a delightful period hotel, movie theater, winery, and "pub golf" course.

Lest we forget, the McMenamins pioneered the notion of cinema brewpubs, where you can buy a microbrew, chow down on a burger, and watch a recent movie. The **Bagdad Theater & Pub** (3702 SE Hawthorne Blvd., 503/236-9234) is in the thick of the Hawthorne neighborhood.

For more info on locations and music and movie offerings within the McMenamins empire, visit www.mcmenamins.com or call 503/249-3983.

Food Carts

If you're on a budget or looking for inexpensive al fresco dining, join the bus commuters, cyclists, and pedestrians on the go who eat at street food carts. **Food carts** are scattered all over the city, purveying all sorts of street food (burritos, bento, stir-fry, barbecue, Indian, Korean, Lebanese, and so on). The selection is staggering; an estimated 800 food carts operate around Portland. Downtown, find a hub, or "pod," of carts at SW Alder Street at 9th and 10th Avenues (with a total of 60 carts) or on the bus mall around SW 5th Avenue and Stark Street. Other major pods include **Cartopia** at 12th and SE Hawthorne, where half a dozen carts remain open until late at night, and the **Mississippi Marketplace** on N. Mississippi and N. Skidmore. Head to SE 28th and Division to check out the food carts at the **Tidbit** pod, which include a couple of the city's best. If you're serious about exploring Portland cart culture, be sure to visit www.foodcartsportland.com, where you'll find maps, reviews, and apps for your smartphone.

DOWNTOWN AND SOUTHWEST
American

A longtime favorite for a hearty morning meal, the **Bijou Café** (132 SW 3rd Ave., 503/222-3187, bijouxcafepdx.com, 7am-2pm Mon.-Thurs., 7am-2pm and 6pm-10pm Fri., 8am-2pm Sat.-Sun., breakfast $8-16) is a friendly, light-filled little diner that has staked its reputation on perfecting breakfast classics. While fried cinnamon bread, red snapper, or roast beef hash are morning mainstays in this cheery café, ordinary breakfast foods are done perfectly with the freshest local ingredients.

The famous **Voodoo Doughnut** (22 SW 3rd Ave., 503/241-4704, www.voodoodoughnut.com, 24 hours daily) is in the thick of the Old Town bar zone and offers all-night doughnuts to club kids and anyone else who stumbles by. But by now, Portlanders tend to roll their eyes when they see folks at the airport flying home with Voodoo's pink to-go boxes; locals line up at **Blue Star Donuts** (1237 SW Washington St., 503/265-8410, www.bluestardonuts.com, 8am-7pm daily), where the donuts are made with brioche dough; try the matcha donut for a nice blend of bitter and sweet.

Next door to the Ace Hotel, **Kenny and Zuke's Delicatessen** (1038 SW Stark St., 503/222-3354, www.kennyandzukes,com, 7am-8pm Mon.-Thurs., 7am-9pm Fri., 8am-9pm Sat., 8am-8pm Sun., $7-16) turns out

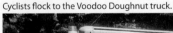
Cyclists flock to the Voodoo Doughnut truck.

hearty breakfasts and sandwiches in the style of a New York Jewish deli. The thick-sliced pastrami has a strong following, and the selection of soda pop is unsurpassed in this town.

Meaty sandwiches, including the tasty pork meatball banh mi, are specialties at **Lardo** (1205 SW Washington St., 503/241-2490, and 1212 SE Hawthorne Blvd., 503/234-7786, htpp://lardosandwiches.com, 11am-10pm daily, $8-12), a casual sandwich shop with a good beer list. Vegetarians should come in for the broccoli rabe sandwich and the absolutely delicious kale Caesar salad.

French

Portland chef Gabriel Rucker, who has gained national attention for his cooking at Le Pigeon on East Burnside, now has a downtown outpost, ★ **Little Bird** (219 SW 6th Ave., 503/688-5952, http://littlebirdbistro.com, 11:30am-midnight Mon.-Fri., 5pm-midnight Sat.-Sun., $14-29), where French bistro favorites such as steak tartare and duck confit are served up in a dining room that looks like a Parisian bistro staffed by hip, friendly Pacific Northwesterners. Don't skip the not-quite-French "Le Pigeon" burger, a favorite both here and at the eastside restaurant.

Swedish

Maurice (921 SW Oak St., 503/224-9921, 10am-7pm Mon.-Sat.), a cute downtown "pastry luncheonette" that's named for a rabbit and celebrates "fika," or an extra-leisurely coffee break, is the place to head for a chocolate brioche roll, black pepper cheesecake, or a lunchtime salad.

Mediterranean

The large, comfortably informal dining room at **SouthPark** (901 SW Salmon St., 503/326-1300, http://southparkseafood.com, 11:30am-3pm daily and 5pm-10pm Sun.-Thurs., 5pm-11pm Fri.-Sat., $20-32) is, as its name suggests, just a block from the South Park Blocks and the busy cultural venues at the Portland Center for the Performing

Arts. The focus is on the sunny foods of the Mediterranean, with an especially strong selection of fresh fish. The adjacent wine bar is a favorite for a pre- and post-symphony quaff.

Pacific Northwest

A pioneer of Portland's seasonal, regional, locavore food movement, **Higgins** (1239 SW Broadway, 503/222-9070, http://higginsportland.com, 11:30am-midnight Mon.-Fri., 4pm-midnight Sat.-Sun., $20-39) is the best exemplar of Pacific Northwest cuisine in downtown Portland. Although Higgins cures its own hams and specializes in charcuterie, this is also a good spot for vegetarians, as there's usually a broad selection of meat-free dishes. Budget tip: the classy wood-paneled bar is a great spot for a light meal from the bistro menu ($8-20) and a beer from the one of the carefully curated taps.

One of Portland's most elegant dining venues, the **Heathman Restaurant** (1001 SW Broadway, 503/790-7752, www.heathmanrestaurantandbar.com, 6:30am-3pm and 5:30pm-10pm Mon.-Fri., 9am-3pm and 5:30pm-11pm Sat.-Sun., $26-49) is synonymous with fine dining. This is very sophisticated, artful food. The dining room is formal and the service is attentive, but the ambience is anything but stuffy.

A longtime insider favorite, the ★ **Veritable Quandary** (1220 SW 1st Ave., 503/227-7342, www.veritablequandary.com, 11:30am-3pm Mon.-Fri., 9:30am-3pm Sat.-Sun. and 5pm-10pm daily, $25-34) is a shoebox-size bar and restaurant at the foot of the Hawthorne Bridge. Up front is a wood-paneled bar usually propped up with attorneys and city hall types. The dining room is serves well-prepared hearty Pacific Northwest cuisine without fussy pretensions. In summer, the VQ has one of the city's best outdoor dining areas.

Housed on the ground floor of the hip Ace Hotel, **Clyde Common** (1014 SW Stark St., 503/228-3333, www.clydecommon.com, 11:30am-3pm Mon.-Fri. and 6pm-midnight Mon.-Fri., 10am-3pm and 6pm-midnight Sat.,

10am-3pm and 6pm-11pm Sun., $12-17) is an airy space with long communal tables and a focus on boldly flavored small plates. The convivial bar is one of the city's great late-night spots.

Steak and Seafood

Although the dinner menu at ★ **Tasty n Alder** (580 SW 12th Ave., 503/621-9251, www. tastynalder.com, 9am-10pm Sun.-Thurs., 9am-11pm Fri.-Sat., $11-19) tends toward steaks, there's plenty for everyone to enjoy (and share, since the emphasis is on small plates) at this downtown corner spot where big windows draw in the downtown scene. Brunch is popular, but our favorite time to visit is in the mid-afternoon, when there's rarely a wait and a good bar menu.

Jake's Famous Crawfish (401 SW 12th St., www.mccormickandschmicks.com, 503/226-1419, 11:30am-10pm Sun.-Thurs., 11:30am-midnight Fri.-Sat., $17-41) has been one of Portland's most popular restaurants since 1892. An old-fashioned fish and steak house, Jake's is emblematic of traditional Pacific Northwest cooking at its best—dozens of fresh fish choices, hefty cuts of beef, and oysters on the half shell from the region's most pristine bays are all well prepared and served up by a knowledgeable white-jacketed staff. The dining room is full of character, and the adjacent bar is simply full of characters.

NORTHWEST

Northwest Portland begins just north of downtown across Burnside Street. Three of the city's most vibrant dining districts are here, within minutes of downtown hotels. **Old Town** also encapsulates historic Chinatown and is a hotbed of music clubs and late-night bars. The Portland Streetcar travels through the **Pearl District,** with its wealth of restaurants, linking it with downtown. Another restaurant destination along the streetcar line is **NW 21st and 23rd Avenues,** two pedestrian-friendly streets that are at the heart of an attractive 19th-century neighborhood.

Bakeries and Cafés

With Portland's profusion of excellent bakeries, it's easy to get into a squabble by asking people to identify their favorite. One thing's for certain: **Ken's Artisan Bakery** (338 NW 21st Ave., 503/248-2202, www.kensartisan. com, 7am-9:30pm Mon., 7am-6pm Tues.-Sat., 8am-5pm Sun.) is always among the top choices for wonderful French-style breads and pastries; the croissants—light, flaky, and

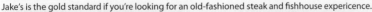

Jake's is the gold standard if you're looking for an old-fashioned steak and fishhouse expericence.

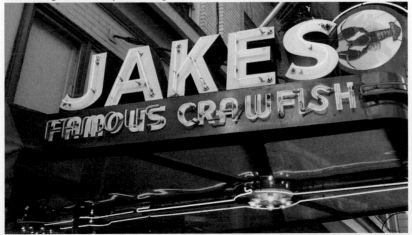

crunchy at once—are masterful. At this busy NW 21st Avenue fixture, you can also pick up a lunchtime sandwich (11am-3pm, $7-8). Monday evenings only, Ken's stays open late and serves delectable pizza ($11-15).

A traditional French *boulangerie* and café for light meals, **St. Honoré Bakery** (2335 NW Thurman St., 503/445-4342, www.sthonorebakery.com, 6:30am-8pm daily, $5-14) is a neighborhood institution in Northwest Portland. Of course, there's a broad selection of pastries, and the bakery is a good spot for

lunch or an early, informal dinner; sandwiches, soups, excellent salads, and savory tarts are available.

Chinese

While Portland's longtime Chinatown is in the Old Town district, the business and culinary center for today's Chinese immigrants long ago shifted to the area around SE 82nd Avenue and Division Street. In the Pearl District, **Seres** (1105 NW Lovejoy St., 971/222-7327, seresrestaurant.com,

Local Chains

If you're out exploring and need a decent bite to eat without too much fuss or expense, chances are you'll find one of these local chains around. You can feed yourself for $5-10 at any of these cafés.

A simple pleasure of summer is sitting on the deck outside the Pearl District's Ecotrust Building with a slice of **Hotlips Pizza** (NW 10th Ave. and Irving St., 503/595-2342, 11am-9pm Sun.-Thurs., 11am-10pm Fri.-Sat.) and a beer or a bottle of Hotlips's homemade fruit soda. Other convenient Hotlips outlets are near PSU (1909 SW 6th Ave., 503/224-0311), at Southeast Hawthorne Street and 22nd Avenue (503/234-9999), and across from Providence Field (SW 18th Ave. and Morrison St., 503/517-9354).

The other café housed in the Ecotrust Building, **Laughing Planet** (NW 10th Ave. and Irving St., 503/505-5020, 11am-9pm daily), serves healthy, mostly vegetarian variations on rice and bean bowls, burritos, soups, and salads. Other Laughing Planet locations include 3320 SE Belmont Street (503/235-6472), 922 NW 21st Avenue (503/445-1319), and 3765 N. Mississippi Avenue (503/467-4146), as well as outposts in Bend, Corvallis, and Eugene.

Some Portland bakeries and sandwich shops are dining destinations. **Grand Central Bakery** is the place for a reliably good (actually, rather addictive) midmorning scone or a sandwich served up without hipster foodie attitude. Find Grand Central bakeries at 2230 SE Hawthorne Boulevard (503/445-1600), in Sellwood (7987 SE 13th Ave., 503/546-3036), or just off N. Mississippi (714 NE Fremont Ave., 503/546-5311).

If you're near the convention center, there's no need to fear the fast food at **Burgerville** (1135 NE M. L. King Jr. Blvd., 503/235-6858, 6:30am-11pm daily). Even here you can dine on the seasonal (celebrate spring with batter-fried asparagus and a strawberry shake) and the local (beef from an Eastern Oregon ranchers' cooperative and smoked salmon from Astoria). In Portland, stop by for Walla Walla onion rings (in season) at 1122 SE Hawthorne Boulevard (503/230-0479) or at SE 25th Avenue and Powell Boulevard (503/239-5942).

If you need a simple, relatively quick, and inexpensive place to eat downtown, **Pastini Pastaria** (911 SW Taylor St., 503/863-5188, 11am-9pm Mon.-Thurs., 11am-10pm Fri.-Sat., 3pm-9pm Sun.) fits the bill. The pasta dishes are pretty tasty, and they're served with excellent Pearl Bakery ciabatta bread. Pastini also has restaurants at 1506 NW 23rd Avenue (503/595-1205) and 1426 NE Broadway (503/288-4300).

Although it's not a restaurant, **New Seasons Market** (2170 NW Raleigh St., 503/224-7522, 8am-10pm daily) is a great place to grab deli food to go. Many of the seven stores are in the suburbs, but Portland visitors may find themselves near the Sellwood (1214 SE Tacoma St., 503/230-4949), Seven Corners (1954 SE Division St., 503/445-2888), Hawthorne (4034 SE Hawthorne Blvd., 503/236-4800), or inner NE store (3445 N. Williams Ave.).

11am-10pm Mon.-Sat., 4pm-10pm Sat., $13-24) extends the fresh, organic, and sustainable ethos of Portland restaurants to Chinese cooking. While the menu offers tastes and textures from multiple regions of China, many dishes reflect the spicy, hearty cooking of Szechuan province. The dining room is stylishly modern; this is the best Chinese cooking in the central Portland area.

French

Reserve a table at ★ **Saint Jack's** (1610 NW 23rd Ave., 503/360-1281, stjackpdx.com, 9am-9:30pm Sun.-Thurs., 9am-10:30pm Fri.-Sat., $25-40) for dinner or, as is our preference, drop by for a light meal ($11-27) or late evening drink and snack at the bar. Either way, you'll feel like you've landed in a Paris bistro, with food inspired by the meaty cuisine of Lyons such as pan-roasted sweetbreads with figs, arugula and onion. No surprise that it's also a good place for a glass of wine.

Italian

Café Mingo (807 NW 21st Ave., 503/226-4646, caffemingonw.com, 5pm-10pm Mon.-Sat., 4:30pm-9:30pm Sun., $17-29) is an always-bustling trattoria along a busy section of NW 21st Avenue. The dining room is intimate yet casual, with the kitchen opening out to diners. The menu is a bit idiosyncratic; don't expect to dine in traditional *antipasti, primi,* and *secondi* courses. The dishes are well-prepared, however, and the service is gracious. Next door, **Bar Mingo** (811 NW 21st Ave., 503/445-4646, http://barmingonw.com, 4pm-11pm Sun.-Thurs., 4pm-midnight Fri.-Sat., $8-24) has different, but equally good, food in a casual atmosphere. The handmade pasta here is excellent, and many dishes are small plates.

Italian cooking "like Mama used to make" conjures up associations of red-checkered tablecloths and a rosy-cheeked maternal presence in the kitchen. **Piazza Italiana** (1129 NW Johnson St., 503/478-0619, www.piazza-portland.com, 11:30am-3pm and 5pm-10pm daily, $11-16) isn't like that. This is a hearty trattoria with European league soccer on the TV, effusive Italian conversation bouncing off the walls, and a persistent bustle that verges on rowdiness. Everyone comes for the pasta, particularly *bucatini all'Amatriciana* (bucatini pasta with pancetta, onion, and pecorino in a red wine and tomato reduction sauce).

Middle Eastern

Be sure to visit ★ **Mediterranean Exploration Company** (133 NW 13th Ave., 503/222-0906, www.mediterranean-explorationcompany.com, 5pm-10pm Sun.-Thurs., 5pm-11pm Fri.-Sat., small plates $8-19), where the warm freekah salad with pistachio oil, the grilled octopus salad, and the chreime, or Tripolitany Jewish fish stew, go far beyond Middle Eastern standards such as humus or falafels (also available here, with tasty twists that make them special). This is one of our favorite Pearl District restaurants.

Latin American

At **Andina** (1314 NW Glisan St., 503/228-9535, www.andinarestaurant.com, 11:30am-2:30pm

The Mediterranean Exploration Company features modern Israeli cooking in the Pearl District.

and 5pm-9:30pm Sun.-Thurs., 11:30am-2:30pm and 5pm-10:30pm Fri.-Sat., bar open later, $17-35), the take on South American cooking is unexpectedly delicious. The many small plates are rich in vegetarian choices—like quinoa-stuffed piquillo peppers—and can make a meal. Alternately, go for traditional Peruvian such as lamb shanks braised in black beer, or a new cuisine hybrid like quinoa-crusted diver scallops with wilted spinach and potato-parsnip puree.

Spanish

Find the city's best Spanish food on a side street at the far north end of Northwest Portland, where ★ **Ataula** (1818 NW 23rd Pl., 503/894-8904, ataulapdx.com, 4:30pm-10pm Tues.-Sat.) serves beautifully presented and exquisitely flavored tapas ($6-16) and cocktails (special sangria!) in a relaxed gastropub atmosphere. If you can resist ordering more and more tapas, it's good to know that the paella ($32-38, serves two) is also excellent.

Pacific Northwest

It's in a lovely spot, directly across from the shady North Park Blocks where the locals toss balls in a game of bocce, but **Park Kitchen** (422 NW 8th Ave., 503/223-7275, www.parkkitchen.com, 5pm-9pm daily, $28-36) has a lot more going for it than its location. Seasonal and regional ingredients ensure the height of freshness and flavor, but an eclectic touch of genius makes even ordinary ingredients shimmer. The small plates ($7-15) make a meal here a bit less pricey. The dining room and tiny bar seem simultaneously very urban, and as friendly as a well-loved neighborhood joint.

Bluehour (250 NW 13th Ave., 503/226-3394, www.bluehouronline.com, 11:30am-2:30pm and 5:30pm-10pm Mon.-Thurs., 11:30am-2:30pm and 5:30pm-10:30pm Fri., 5:30pm-10:30pm Sat., $17-39) is one of Portland's few really swanky restaurants. The cooking is nominally Italian, though the kitchen is fluent in many cuisines, resulting in very sophisticated dishes that are flavor-focused, revelatory, and fun all at the same

time. If you don't feel like getting dressed up for the dining room, the bar has its own menu and a more relaxed vibe.

There's no better place to taste the *terroir* of Oregon than ★ **Paley's Place** (1204 NW 21st Ave., 503/243-2403, www.paleysplace. net, 5:30pm-10pm Mon.-Thurs., 5pm-11pm Fri.-Sat., 5pm-10pm Sun., $26-42), an intimate bastion of fine dining. Chef Paley has a firm grasp of traditional French techniques and uses the best local ingredients in dishes such as king salmon cooked on a wood plank with tomato-tinted béarnaise sauce. The wine list features many hard-to-find Oregon pinot noirs. This is one of Portland's best special-occasion restaurants; for an affordable treat, eat in the bar (less romantic) or order the half-portions offered on the dining room menu.

Tucked beneath the Fremont Bridge, you'll find one of two locations of **Olympia Provisions** (1632 NW Thurman St., 503/894-8136, 107 SE Washington St., 503/954-3663, www.olympiaprovisions.com, 11am-10pm Mon.-Fri., 10am-10pm Sat.-Sun., $20-27), known for excellent sausages and charcuterie but also serving up some wickedly good fish dishes, such as pan-roasted halibut with forest mushrooms and cabbage. The southeast location has a different, but similar, menu; the NW Thurman location is also a butcher shop, with most of the building taken up by production of chorizo, saucisson, and the like.

Steak

Portland has a full contingent of upscale expense-account steak houses, but if you're hungry for beef, go to one of the city's originals, the **Ringside** (2165 W. Burnside St., 503/223-1513, www.ringsidesteakhouse. com, 5pm-11:30pm Mon.-Wed., 5pm-midnight Thurs.-Sat., 4pm-11:30pm Sun., $29-69, reservations recommended). Family owned for nearly 70 years, the Ringside retains its 1960s look of red Naugahyde and dark lighting even after a remodel. The steaks, prime rib, and seafood are excellent, and James Beard once proclaimed the onion rings "the best I ever had." Come before 6pm for a special three-course dinner menu for $39.

Ice Cream

Come on a cold day and maybe there won't be a line at **Salt & Straw** (838 NW 23rd Ave., 971/271-8168, and 5829 SE Milwaukie Ave., 503/232-9440, saltandstraw.com, 10am-11pm daily), but don't count on it. The flavors here can be weird and intense, but servers offer up plenty of tastes, so if olive oil doesn't do it for you (we love it!), move on to pear and blue cheese. Salt & Straw also has locations at 3345 SE Division St. (503/208-2054, 11am-11pm daily) and 2035 NE Alberta St. (503/208-3867, 11am-11pm daily).

Brewpubs

Portland's first microbrewery, the **BridgePort Brewpub** (1313 NW Marshall St., 503/241-3612, www.bridgeportbrew.com, 11:30am-1pm Tues.-Thurs., 11:30am-midnight Fri.-Sat., 11:30am-10pm Sun., $9-14), started out in an old rope factory in the then-derelict Pearl District. Depending on the time of year, try a pint of the Ebenezer or a fresh-hopped IPA.

Oregonians shrieked when **10 Barrel** (1411 NW Flanders St., 503/224-1700, www.10barrel.com, 11am-11pm Sun.-Thurs., 11am-midnight Fri.-Sat.) was sold to InBev Anheuser-Busch, but almost immediately thereafter a Pearl District branch of this Bend brewery opened, and there's rarely been an open seat since. Come by for an Apocalypse IPA or, on a hot summer day, a glass of Swill, a radler with a lemon twist. A smoked trout salad ($13) goes with beer just as well as the pizza and burgers also offered.

Right across the street is **Rogue Distillery & Public House** (1339 NW Flanders St., 503/222-5910, www.rogue.com, 11am-12:30am Mon.-Thurs., 11am-1:30am Fri.-Sat., 11am-10:30pm Sun., $8-16), a Portland outlet of Rogue Brewing in Newport. This is some of Oregon's best beer: Most of the elixirs here are wonderful, but check out the Maibock-style Dead Guy Ale and St. Rogue Red.

Although its headquarters are in Bend, **Deschutes Brewery's Portland Public House** (210 NW 11th Ave., 503/296-4906, www.deschutesbrewery.com, 11am-11pm Sun.-Thurs., 11am-midnight Fri.-Sat., $12-29), in the midst of the Pearl District, is large and well located. While much of the space is dedicated to restaurant service, there's also a large bar area for worship of these local brewing gods, creators of the classic Mirror Pond Pale Ale and Black Butte Porter. This is a great place to come before or after a play at neighboring Portland Center Stage.

Wine Bars

Very stylish and even glamorous, the Pearl District wine bar **Coppia** (417 NW 10th Ave., 503/295-9536, www.coppiaportland. com, 4pm-10pm Tues.-Sat., $11-29) will make you feel young and good-looking (or is that the wine talking?). The food and wine selections focus on Italy's Piedmont region—with a flight of nebbiolo, savor fresh porcini mushroom agnolotti pasta or grilled salmon with hazelnuts and capers.

NORTH AND NORTHEAST

Linked to downtown by MAX light rail trains and near the Lloyd Center hotels, the area along **NE Broadway** (between NE 8th and NE 28th Avenues) is the hub of close-in Northeast Portland. Other Northeast Portland destinations for diners looking for casual yet cutting-edge food are **North Mississippi Avenue** and **Northeast Alberta Street.** Out past the Hollywood neighborhood along **Sandy Boulevard** is the heart of today's Vietnamese community, where you'll find inexpensive and delicious *pho* and other Southeast Asian specialties.

American

Portland's breakfast hot spot is right on the southern edge of Northeast, where you can spot the ★ **Screen Door** (2337 E Burnside St., 503/541-0880, www.screendoorrestaurant. com, 8am-2pm and 5:30pm-10pm Mon.-Fri.,

9am-2pm and 5:30pm-10pm Sat.-Sun., $10-15) by the line outside. Southern food such as delicious fried chicken and the homey atmosphere draw the crowds. Weekend brunch is the real deal.

Alberta Street is especially blessed with friendly and informal places for breakfast and lunch. The **Tin Shed** (1438 NE Alberta St., 503/288-6966, http://tinshedgardencafe.com, 7am-9:30pm daily, $8-14) has a comfortable dining room that opens onto a large, pet-friendly outdoor patio with a fireplace and herb garden. Come here for breakfast, where creative egg scrambles—combinations of veggies and sausage, ham, or tofu served with a buttermilk biscuit and potato pancakes or cheese grits—are legendary.

Join Portland's late-rising hipsters for breakfast at **Tasty n Sons** (3808 N. Williams Ave., 503/621-1400, tastynsons.com, 9am-10pm Sun.-Thurs., 9am-11pm Fri.-Sat., $7-15) and you'll almost certainly plan to return for dinner. This popular spot is a great place for robustly flavored brunch, happy hour snacks, or dinner. Dishes are divided into small plates and bigger plates—all designed to be shared.

Sweedeedee (5202 N. Albina Ave., 503/946-8087, http://equinoxrestaurantpdx.com, 8am-4pm Mon.-Sat., 8am-2pm Sun., $7-11) is almost too cute…good thing the food is so delicious (egg sandwich plus bacon plus avocado) that you can put away the smart-phone camera and get to eating.

Barbecue
Podnah's Pit (1625 NE Killingsworth St., 503/281-3700, http://podnahspit.com, 11am-10pm Mon.-Fri., 9am-10pm Sat.-Sun., $11-20) serves up Texas-style barbecue, slow-cooked over oak in a pit. With one exception, Podnah's takes "don't mess with Texas" to heart—and that exception is a very tasty North Carolina-style pulled pork. Although smoked trout and sides of pinto beans and Texas caviar (black-eyed pea salad) are available, non-meat-eaters will feel a little lonely here.

Italian
Northeast Portland's top Italian restaurant is **DOC** (5519 NE 30th Ave., 503/946-8592, http://docpdx.com, 6pm-close Tues.-Sat., $19-29), which adds Pacific Northwest touches to the underlying Italian structure. Risotto may come with bay shrimp, snap peas, nasturtium, or chives; a steak is topped with maitake mushrooms and padron peppers. If you want to splurge, this is an excellent place to do it: Order the six-course tasting menu ($60 per person) with wine pairings ($45 per person). DOC is an intimate place, and you really get to see the chefs at work as you enter the restaurant—the kitchen is near the front door.

Mediterranean
A wine bar and small-plates restaurant with over 50 carefully selected wines by the glass, handcrafted Spanish, French, and Italian food (which you order off little paper menus as in a sushi joint), and a friendly low-key attitude make **Navarre** (10 NE 28th St., 503/232-3555, www.navarreportland.com, 4:30pm-10:30pm Mon.-Thurs., 4:30pm-11:30pm Fri., 9:30am-11:30pm Sat., 9:30am-10:30pm Sun., $4-20) one of Portland's top choices for flavorful artisanal cooking. Nearly everything is handmade with near-obsessive attention to authenticity, and the restaurant gets produce from a community supported agriculture farm just a few miles away in Southeast Portland.

Mexican
Like an unassuming beach taqueria in Baja, ★ **¿Por Qué No?** (3524 N. Mississippi Ave., 503/467-4149, and 4635 SE Hawthorne Blvd., 503/954-3138, www.porquenotacos.com, 11am-10pm Mon.-Sat., 11am-9:30pm Sun., $3-11) has a relaxed hole-in-the-wall vibe to go with its excellent tacos and other south-of-the-border street foods. You can't go wrong with any of the tacos; the guacamole is outstanding, as is the ceviche. Fresh-squeezed margaritas are utterly addictive. This place is tiny—line up to order your food, then find a

seat. Most people end up sitting at tables in the street, rain or shine.

The Mexican food at **Autentica** (5507 NE 30th Ave., 503/287-7555, www.autenticaportland.com, 5pm-10pm Tues.-Fri., 10am-2pm and 5pm-10pm Sat.-Sun., $18-23) is complex and sophisticated, but the restaurant doesn't take itself so seriously as to suck the fun out of the experience. The whole place is warm and colorful, and the patio out back is one of the best places to celebrate a warm evening in Portland. Although you can order enchiladas here, Autentica is a good place to stretch your idea of Mexican food, perhaps to include wild mushrooms with grilled poblano peppers simmered in a spicy tomatillo cream sauce.

Northeast Alberta Street is home to a couple of traditional taquerias. Favorites include **La Sirenita** (2817 NE Alberta St., 503/335-8283, 10am-10pm daily) and **La Bonita** (2839 NE Alberta St., 503/281-3662, 11am-9pm Tues.-Sat.).

Pacific Northwest

At **Beast** (5425 NE 30th Ave., 503/841-6968, www.beastpdx.com, seatings 6 and 8:45pm Wed.-Sun., 10am or noon Sun., reservations required) a prix fixe menu changes weekly. You have a choice of the tasting menu's six ($102) courses, but not much else. It's called Beast for a reason: chef Naomi Pomeroy has a deft hand with pork, and most meals feature a selection of house-made charcuterie and often feature braised pork shoulder or brined chops. An optional six-course wine pairing costs $48. Sunday brunch ($45) can also come with wine ($25).

Spanish

Toro Bravo (120 NE Russell St., 503/281-4464, www.torobravopdx.com, 5pm-10pm Sun.-Thurs., 5pm-11pm Fri.-Sat., $4-19) serves the kind of food that would be native to Portland had it been colonized by the Spanish: rich, seasonal, and full of vigorous flavor. The menu is extensive, covering many regions of Spain and offering everything from a bowl of olives to heaping platters of paella.

Argentinian

Fire is the raison-d'être of **Ox** (2225 NE M. L. King Jr. Blvd., 503/284-3366, http://oxpdx.com, 5pm-10pm Mon.-Thurs and Sun., 5pm-11pm Fri.-Sat., $24-47), where meats, seafood, and vegetables get licked by flames and are served in a style that recalls the hearty, smoky flavors of Argentina. Try the crispy beef, olive and raisin empanadas, or the clam chowder enriched with a beef marrow bone. Seared steaks are the stand-out main courses, but if you're not into beef, you can enjoy the house-made chorizo sausages, coal-roasted artichokes, or roasted sea scallops with sweet corn in bacon sherry cream.

Brewpubs

If your local pub has a children's play area, you know you must be in Portland. **Laurelwood Public House & Brewery** (5115 NE Sandy Blvd., 503/282-0622, www.laurelwoodbrewpub.com, 11am-10pm Mon.-Tues., 11am-11pm Wed.-Thurs., 11am-midnight Fri., 10am-midnight Sat., 10am-10pm Sun.) is a family-friendly brewpub with restaurant-quality food in Northeast Portland's Hollywood district. While the Space Stout (say that twice quickly) may look like a pint of pure opaque chocolate, it's not for the children. Instead, it's an award-winning stout, and Portland's version of Guinness.

You can't get much more casual than **Stormbreaker Brewing** (832 N. Beech St., 503/281-7708, www.stormbreakerbrewing.com, noon-10pm Sun.-Mon., noon-11pm Tues.-Thurs., noon-midnight Fri.-Sat.). Along busy North Mississippi Avenue, the brewery and the serving area are in a small converted metal shop, but you'll drink and dine outdoors at picnic tables underneath a huge tent. Dogs aren't just allowed, they are encouraged. In winter, some of the tables move indoors, and space heaters warm the beer garden.

At **Breakside Brewery** (820 NE Dekum St., 503/719-6475, www.breakside.com, 3pm-10pm Mon.-Thurs., noon-11pm Fri.-Sat., noon-8pm Sun), Portlanders prove they can drink something besides IPA; the pilsner here is excellent. Food is also good, but if you want something more, there's a good Italian restaurant across the street.

SOUTHEAST

Southeast Portland is filled with restaurant enclaves, where it's a good idea to just park the car and wander the streets before making a dining choice. Some neighborhoods, such as the six-block stretch of 28th Avenue near East Burnside Street or SE Division, especially from SE 27 to SE 38 Avenues, seem almost totally devoted to dining.

American

Bread and Ink (3610 SE Hawthorne Blvd., 503/239-4756, www.breadandinkcafe.com, 8am-8:30pm Sun.-Thurs., 8am-9:30pm Fri.-Sat., dinner $42-24) is a longtime gathering place in the Hawthorne neighborhood. For breakfast, an assortment of homemade breads and imaginative omelets will sustain you. Lunchtime diners line up for a massive burger topped with gruyère cheese and Bermuda onion as well as locally esteemed salmon sandwiches.

Step into tradition at Zell's (1300 SE Morrison St., 503/239-0196, www.zellscafe.com, 7am-2pm Mon.-Fri., 8am-2pm Sat., 8am-3pm Sun., $7-15), a longtime eastside favorite for hearty breakfasts and lunch. The setting is a historic pharmacy, complete with an antique soda fountain, and the food is outstanding: The complimentary scones with homemade jam served at breakfast are amazing.

A good place for a sandwich, especially if you want to experiment with high-end grilled cheese, is Cheese Bar (6031 SE Belmont St., 503/222-6014, http://cheese-bar.com, 11am-11pm Tues.-Sun., $8-14) on the west slope of Mount Tabor. It's a mix of a retail cheese shop with charcuterie, several great variations on grilled cheese sandwiches, and an extensive beer list (mostly consisting of limited releases).

Seafood

Two restaurant experiences in one: That's what is offered by Block + Tackle and ★ Roe (3113 SE Division St.). Block + Tackle (503/236-0205, http://blockandtacklepdx.com, 5pm-10pm Wed.-Sat., $6-22) is a casual but bustling seafood bar with a selection of raw oysters, seafood charcuterie, and fresh fish-based small plates that can be easily assembled into dinner. But in the back, behind the curtain, is Roe (503/232-1566, http://roe-pdx.com, 5:15pm-9:30pm Wed.-Sat., 4-course menu $75), a separate dining room with its own kitchen, where local seafood is transformed into a high-end, multicourse feast. The Roe dining room is small and reservations are required—but the always-changing, all-seafood menu is exquisite and stunningly fresh.

Chinese

Portland's contemporary Chinese community is centered in the SE 82nd Avenue and Division Street neighborhood, where Portland's best Chinese food can be found at Wong's King (8733 SE Division St., 503/788-8883, http://wongsking.com, 10am-10pm Mon.-Thurs., 10am-11pm Fri., 9:30am-11pm Sat., 9:30am-10pm Sun., $8-21). The chef has won prestigious cooking awards in China, and the huge dining room is always thronged with Chinese families, but the staff is very solicitous to non-Chinese diners who may be confounded by the extensive menu. The dim sum is terrific.

Indian

At ★ Bollywood Theater (3010 SE Division St., 503/477-6699, 2039 NE Alberta St., 971/200-4711, www.bollywoodtheater-pdx.com, 11am-10pm daily, $6-17) the focus is on Indian street food—the *Dahi Papri Chaat* (house-made crackers topped with chickpeas, potatoes, yogurt, cilantro, and tamarind chutney) is outrageously delicious, and other top dishes include pork vindaloo, egg masala, and fried okra with chile, lime, and raita. This is not a fancy, sit-down restaurant: You'll order at the counter and take a free table, inside or out, to eat your meal.

Expect long lines on weekends and food that's worth the wait.

Italian

Nostrana (1401 SE Morrison St., 503/234-2427, http://nostrana.com, 11:30am-2pm and 5pm-10pm Mon.-Thurs., 11:30am-2pm and 5pm-11pm Fri., 5pm-11pm Sat., 5pm-10pm Sun., $16-28, pizza $9-18) is part wood-fired pizza joint and part rustic Italian home-cooking restaurant. Order one of the excellent pizzas—perhaps prosciutto and arugula—and augment it with a selection of wonderful salads, soups, house-cured meats, and wood-oven-cooked meats. The menu changes nightly to ensure that everything here is absolutely fresh and seasonal.

★ **Ava Gene's** (3377 SE Division St., 971/229-0571, http://avagenes.com, 5pm-11pm daily, $19-38) focuses on Rome and its traditional cooking traditions, translated for the Pacific Northwest. Start with vegetable small plates, such as grilled pole beans, anchovies, and a poached duck egg; move onto a hearty plate of fusilli pasta and tripe; and if you're still hungry, perhaps a *secondi* of roast lamb, peperonata, and chickpeas. The tab does add up here. The handsome tiled dining room lends the perfect touch of formality.

Immediately next door and under the same ownership is **Roman Candle Bakery** (971/302-6605, 7am-4pm daily) with coffee, pastries, artisanal breads, and Roman-style white pizzas.

Japanese

Biwa (215 SE 9th Ave., 503/239-8830, www.biwarestaurant.com, 5pm-midnight daily, $4-13) is a Portland-style representation of an *izakaya,* a Japanese sake-and-beer bar where patrons gather to drink and dine on a multitude of highly flavored and shareable dishes. This semi-subterranean dining room is an exercise in industrial chic, with boisterous crowds and an open kitchen. In addition to *maguro poke,* raw yellowfin tuna showered with *shoyu* and feathered with seaweed, wonderful salads (the baby octopus and cucumber salad is marvelous), and house-made pickles, there are handmade ramen and udon noodles served both cold in salads and hot as steaming bowls of soup.

Bamboo Sushi (310 SE 28th Ave., 503/232-5255, bamboosushi.com, 4:30pm-10pm daily, rolls $8-17), with a stylish dining room and a vast selection of fish that has been harvested according to "green" and sustainable practices, has become Portland's

Ava Gene's is a wonderful spot for a special-occasion dinner.

top sushi restaurant. Indeed, with non-sushi dishes such as sesame-crusted tuna with caramelized eggplant, it's one of the city's best seafood restaurants. Find other outposts at 836 NW 23rd Ave. (971/229-1925), 1409 NW Alberta St. (503/889-0336), and downtown (not yet open at press time).

Mexican

Forget American-style Mexican food. **Xico** (3715 SE Division St., 503/548-6343, www.xicopdx.com, 5pm-10pm Sun.-Thurs., 5pm-11pm Fri.-Sat., $18-29) serves sophisticated Mexican cuisine, with tortillas handmade from corn ground in-house; the same masa is used to make tamales. A special take on posole is offered here; it's made with roasted trout and topped with tomatillo-avocado salsa.

Start with a wild boar taco or some chips and excellent guacamole at **Taqueria Nueve** (737 SE Washington St., 203/954-1987, www.taquerianueve.com, 5pm-10pm Tues.-Sat., 5pm-9pm Sun., $4-15). From there, keep going with tacos or order a plate of enchiladas or a grilled hanger steak with smoky chile sauce. Along with good food, enjoy a fun, high-energy atmosphere.

Pacific Northwest

No need to dust off your high school French when calling for reservations at ★ **Le Pigeon** (738 E. Burnside St., 503/546-8796, www.lepigeon.com, 5pm-10pm daily, $14-32)—rhymes with smidgen—a highly touted hot spot of meaty gastronomy. This lack of pretension is characteristic of chef-owner Gabriel Rucker's full-flavored cooking style and his slightly manic, pocket-size dining room. His cooking embraces a breadth of rarely encountered ingredients: lambs' tongues, beef cheeks, and pork belly along with less unusual meats, fish, and vegetables, all from local sources and prepared with a passion for robust flavors and inventive contrasts.

The sophisticated cuisine at **Castagna** (1752 SE Hawthorne Blvd., 503/231-7373, www.castagnarestaurant.com, 5:30pm-10pm Wed.-Sat., $95 tasting menu) is very refined:

Each dish is an epiphany of taste and texture. Expect a succession of small, exquisite tastes, such as hot-smoked halibut belly with roe and nasturtium cream and aged duck with black garlic and toasted alliums: This is some of Portland's most cutting edge dining. The dining room presents a minimalist decor that some find austere, others soothing. Immediately next door is **Café Castagna** (1758 SE Hawthorne Blvd., 503/231-9959, 5pm-10pm Tues.-Sat., 10am-2pm and 5pm-1pm Sun., $16-27), offering a less formal (and more affordable) dining experience.

Russian

Don't let preconceptions about Russian food keep you from visiting ★ **Kachka** (720 SE Grand Ave., 503/235-0059, kachkapdx.com, 4pm-10pm daily, $13-20); if nothing else, go there for a flight of vodkas, perhaps including horseradish-infused vodka. While at the bar, studying the Soviet-era posters on the walls, you may find yourself ordering a plate of pickled veggies. That might lead to a zakuski (appetizer) spread, including taranka (aptly described as "something like fish jerky") and on to pork-stuffed cabbage rolls. The food is shockingly good, and the atmosphere pure Portland.

Thai

One of the most exciting Thai restaurants in Portland is not the fanciest. In fact, ★ **Pok Pok Thai** (3226 SE Division St., 503/232-1387, www.pokpokpdx.com, 11:30am-10pm daily, $13-20) started out with just outdoor seating and a kitchen that was more a shed than a restaurant (there's now indoor seating). Nonetheless, the Thai food produced here—specializing in the cuisine of the Chiang Mai region—is incredible. The roast game hen with dipping sauces is delicious, and the *muu sateh* (charcoal-grilled pork loin skewers marinated in coconut milk and turmeric and served with cucumber relish) tastes exactly like freshly prepared Thai street food. When there's a wait for seating at Pok Pok, head across the street to the **Whiskey Soda**

Lounge for drinks and traditional Thai drinking food. In Northeast Portland? Head to sister restaurant **Pok Pok Noi** (1469 NE Prescott St., 503/287-4149, www.pokpoknoi. com, 5pm-midnight daily, $9-23), which offers many of the same dishes.

Vegetarian

Portobello (1125 SE Division St., 503/754-5993, 5:30pm-9pm Tues.-Thurs., 5:30-10pm Fri.-Sat., 9:30am-2pm and 5:30pm-9pm Sun, $7-18), a friendly "vegan trattoria," makes delicious pastas, pizzas, and burgers using fresh ingredients (no scary fake meat) and cashew-based "cheese." Dining here is in no way a compromise; try it even if you're not vegan.

Pizza

The staff at **Apizza Scholls** (4741 SE Hawthorne Blvd., 503/233-1286, apizzascholls.com, 5pm-9:30pm daily and 11:30am-12:30pm Sat.-Sun., pizzas $19-25) have earned the reputation as pizza snobs for their formidable resistance to allowing patrons to add more than three toppings. But they're right... the handmade crusts won't char properly if they're loaded up. The Diablo Blanco, with ricotta, tomato pesto, and pumpkin seeds, is a great house specialty. Reserve online or expect a wait.

You may also face long lines at another Portland favorite, **Ken's Artisan Pizza** (304 SE 28th Ave., 503/517-9951, kensartisan.com, 5pm-10pm Mon.-Sat., 4pm-9pm Sun.). Ken is first and foremost a bread baker, so it's no surprise that the wood-fired pizzas have nearly perfect chewy crusts; the toppings are also top-notch.

Vietnamese

A few blocks north of SE Division Street on 82nd Avenue is one of Portland's top purveyors of Vietnamese food. **Pho Van** (1919 SE 82nd Ave., 503/788-5244, www.phovanrestaurant.com, 10am-9pm Sun.-Thurs., 10am-9:30pm Fri.-Sat., $9-12) offers a broad selection of the namesake soup plus other rice and noodle dishes.

Brewpubs

Hopworks Urban Brewery (2944 SE Powell Blvd., 503/232-4647, http://hopworksbeer. com, 11am-11pm Sun.-Thurs., 11am-midnight Fri.-Sat.), or HUB, is about as Portland as you can get; it's an "ecopub" combining a bicycle theme with good beer and pizza. Along one of the city's busiest bike corridors, find

Experience authentic Russian food and pure Portland atmosphere at Kachka.

Hopworks' **Bike Bar** (3947 N. Williams Ave., 503/287-6258), where bike frames from local custom builders are displayed over the bar. The atmosphere is great, but the beer is even better.

Most beers made in Portland are strongly hopped, but there's starting to be a trend toward sour beers, such as the summer gose you'll find at **Cascade Brewing Barrel House** (939 SE Belmont St., 503/265-8603, http://cascadebrewingbarrelhouse.com, noon-11pm Sun.-Thurs., noon-midnight Fri.-Sat.).

Hair of the Dog Brewing Company (61 SE Yamhill St., 503/232-6585, www.hairofthedog.com, 11:30am-10pm Tues.-Sat., 11:30am-8pm Sun.), famous for its commitment to unusual and high-alcohol beers that are meant to be aged and drunk like fine wines, does serve up a wide range of beers with lower (and not-so-low) ABV values, from Little Dog Fred (3.5% ABV) to Adam from the Wood (12% ABV).

Although they don't brew at the **Loyal Legion** (710 SE 6th Ave., 503/235-8272, loyallegionpdx.com, 4pm-midnight Mon.-Wed., 4pm-2am Thurs.-Fri., noon-2am Sat., noon-10pm Sun., cash only) you can choose from 99 beers (well, a few ciders are thrown in) on tap, all from Oregon. The food menu is limited to sausages ($6), but they're good ones from Olympia Provisions.

A favorite of the Southeast Portland crowds is **Lucky Labrador Brewing Company,** whose original brewpub is at 915 SE Hawthorne Boulevard (503/236-3555, 11am-midnight Mon.-Sat., noon-10pm Sun.). This former sheet-metal warehouse is a comfortable and unpretentious place—slip on your flip-flops, bring your dog, and head down to the large shady patio for some brews.

Wine Bars

With its crisp lines and woodsy interior, **Bar Avignon** (2138 SE Division St., 503/517-0808, www.baravignon.com, 5pm-10 daily, small plates $5-15, entrees $24-27) is a cozy destination along a busy stretch of SE Division Street. The choice of wine is large, particularly the by-the-bottle selection, which naturally enough favors French vintages but with lots of local wines also included. The food choices are simple but nicely prepared, with mix-and-match cheese and cured meat platters, panini sandwiches, salads, and a few classic French main courses, such as a perfect roast chicken.

Information and Services

TOURIST INFORMATION

Portland's visitor information resources are far-reaching and extensive. Begin at Travel Portland's **Visitor Information Center** (701 SW 6th Ave., 503/275-8355 or 877/678-5263, www.travelportland.com, 8:30am-5:30pm Mon.-Fri., 10am-4pm Sat.), located in Pioneer Courthouse Square. Sharing the space with the visitor information center is the **TriMet Ticket Office** (www.trimet.org, 8:30am-5:30pm Mon.-Fri.), where you can buy bus tickets and pick up schedules.

NEWSPAPERS

The *Oregonian* (www.oregonlive.com), Portland's long-time newspaper, is joined by a host of alternative or community papers that circulate around the city. The paper's Arts and Entertainment section, the A&E, comes out each Friday.

Of all the free weeklies, most useful to travelers are the *Willamette Week* (http://wweek.com) and the *Portland Mercury* (www.portlandmercury.com). Both publications have live music and entertainment listings; their websites have archives of restaurant reviews.

Portland Monthly (www.portlandmonthlymag.com) is a glossy magazine dedicated to the good life in Portland. The magazine keeps an eye trained on the city's burgeoning dining scene and offers fairly comprehensive restaurant listings.

RADIO STATIONS

Portland is very much a public and community radio kind of city. **OBP** at 91.5 FM is the local NPR station. Of the top 50 public radio news stations in the nation, OPB has the largest share of listeners in its broadcast area. That doesn't exactly mean that Portland is the most public-radio-listening city in the United States (some cities have more than one NPR station), but almost.

For a taste of Portland's more alternative side, tune into **KBOO** at 90.7 FM for community radio, Oregon style. KBOO's mission statement just about says it all: "volunteer-powered, noncommercial, listener-sponsored, full-strength community radio for Portland, Oregon, Cascadia, and the world!"

Other noncommercial radio stations include **KMHD** at 89.1 FM for jazz and **KBPS** at 89.9 FM for classical music and the Metropolitan Opera radio broadcasts.

Transportation

GETTING THERE
Air

Portland International Airport (877/739-4636, www.flypdx.com), known by its airport code PDX, has been selected twice in recent years as the top airport in the country by readers of *Condé Nast Traveler* magazine, for its easy MAX connections to downtown, free WiFi, and great shopping and dinning. PDX is served by more than 17 major airlines, all of which can be accessed from the airport website's list of airlines.

PDX is 15 miles from downtown Portland, but if you're driving, allow at least half an hour to make the trip, more if you are traveling during rush hour. From downtown, take I-84 east toward The Dalles, then take I-205 north toward Seattle. Take Airport Way West (Exit 24) off I-205.

Airport MAX (www.trimet.org) makes it easy to avoid traffic with frequent light rail train service to and from PDX and downtown and other stops on the MAX system. The airport service is called the Red Line, and it runs every 15 minutes from Beaverton Transit Center through downtown Portland to PDX. Depending on the day, the earliest trains begin operation from the airport around 5am; the final trains of the day leave PDX by midnight. Travel downtown to or from the airport is $2.50. The trip to or from the airport and the city center takes approximately 40 minutes.

To find the MAX station at PDX, proceed to the lower level (follow signs for baggage pickup), then turn right (south) at the base of the escalators. Proceed to the end of the terminal; at the final set of doors you'll find automated ticketing machines for MAX, and right outside the doors is the train itself.

Several cab companies and shuttle services serve the airport; look for them at the center section of the airport terminal's lower roadway—go out the doors from the baggage claim level. Taxi fare to downtown is roughly $40 from the airport. Note that under current regulations, Uber and Lyft drivers aren't allowed to pick up riders at the airport (they can drop off, however).

To drive to Portland from PDX, exit the airport and follow signs to Portland. This takes you first to I-205 South; then, at Exit 21B, follow signs to Portland, which puts you onto I-84 West. In six miles, at the junction of I-5, take the exit for I-5 South but remain in the on-ramp lane, which exits onto the Morrison Bridge and downtown.

Train

Portland is served by three **Amtrak** (800/872-7245, www.amtrak.com) lines. The *Coast Starlight* travels between Los Angeles and Seattle, with a daily stop each way in Portland. Traveling much the same route is the *Cascades* line, which operates multiple trains daily between Eugene, Portland, Seattle, and Vancouver, British Columbia. The *Empire Builder* links Portland and Chicago with once-daily service in each direction.

Handsome **Union Station** (800 NW 6th Ave.) is a glorious 1890s vestige of the glory days of rail travel that's still in service as Portland's Amtrak station.

Bus

Greyhound (550 NW 6th Ave., 503/243-2361 or 800/231-2222, www.greyhound.com) provides intercity bus service from the Greyhound depot, one block south of Amtrak's Union Station.

A great addition to Pacific Northwest intercity bus transport is **Bolt Bus** (877/265-8287, www.boltbus.com), with direct service between Portland, Seattle, Bellingham, and Vancouver, British Columbia. Tickets between Portland and Seattle range $16-25 one way.

Car

Portland sits on or near the routes of interstates 5, 405, 205, and 84. I-5 runs from Seattle to San Diego, and I-84 goes east to Salt Lake City. I-405 circles downtown Portland to the west. I-205 bypasses the city to the east. U.S. 26 heads west to Cannon Beach on the coast and east to the Cascades.

GETTING AROUND

The city's layout is fairly straightforward, with most streets conforming to an easily understood grid. Most streets are named and run east-west; most avenues are numbered and run north-south. Generally speaking, the city is divided into quadrants by the Willamette River and Burnside Street. Therefore, streets and avenues with an SE (Southeast) prefix are south of Burnside and east of the river; streets and avenues prefixed by NW (Northwest) are north of Burnside Street and west of the Willamette, and so on. There is also a section of Portland with the single prefix N for North; it's best thought of as the part of Northeast Portland that is west of Williams Avenue. Also worth noting: Northwest Portland streets proceed in alphabetical order from Ankeny, moving north with streets keyed to the names of early settlers (hence Burnside, Couch, Davis, Everett, all the way to Yeon).

Bridges are a major part of getting around in a river city. The east and west sides of Portland are linked by a dozen bridges, 11 of them in the core of the city, including the new public transit, pedestrian, and bike bridge linking OMSI and the South Waterfront. Some of these are drawbridges and regularly lift to allow ship traffic to pass. This is particularly a feature of everyday life during the Rose Festival, when the naval fleet arrives at and departs from downtown moorages.

Public Transportation

Portland has an excellent public transport system called **TriMet** (503/238-7433, www.trimet.org), which includes buses, light rail (MAX), and commuter rail. There is also the Portland Streetcar and an aerial tram operated by the City of Portland. Nearly all Portland's primary tourist destinations are easily reached by this system, so unless you actually need a rental car for your visit, consider using public transport. In fact, riding MAX, the Portland Streetcar, and the tram can be part of the fun of visiting Portland.

The most widespread of TriMet's transport services are **buses,** with over 90 bus lines, most of which connect to MAX. For most lines, bus service begins 5am-5:30am; selected lines continue service until about 1:30am.

Like many large cities, Portland once had

an extensive streetcar system, but by the 1950s the antiquated lines were retired and replaced by buses. In 2001, Portland started streetcar service on the first modern streetcar system built in the United States in 50 years. Streetcar service currently links the Nob Hill district of NW 23rd Avenue, the Pearl District, and downtown (along 10th and 11th Aves.); Lloyd Center, the inner east side, and OMSI; and Portland State University, the South Waterfront development, and the Portland Aerial Tram. MAX is the Portland region's light rail system. It currently has four different lines, the longest being the 33-mile Blue Line that connects Gresham on the east through downtown and west to Beaverton and Hillsboro. The Red Line travels some of the same route from Beaverton in the west through downtown to the Gateway Transit Center, but then it turns north and travels to Portland International Airport. The Yellow Line runs between downtown and the Portland Expo Center via the Rose Quarter Transit Center and North Portland along Interstate Avenue. The MAX Green Line runs between Gateway Transit Center and Clackamas Town Center, and on 5th and 6th Avenues in downtown Portland

between Union Station and Portland State University. The new Orange Line links downtown Portland to the southern suburb of Milwaukie.

Throughout downtown, 5th and 6th Avenues are referred to as the "Portland Mall" or simply the "Bus Mall": Most buses run along these two one-way streets as they pass through downtown. Each part of the transit system uses the same tickets or fare structure, and bus transfers and streetcar or MAX tickets can be used throughout the system. Tickets are valid for a maximum of 2.5 hours of travel. Keep your ticket (or transfer, as it's also called) with you, as it is your proof of payment, and you can ride the system until the expiration time shown. Portland formerly offered free public transport in an area known as Fareless Square, but this free service has been discontinued. You'll need a ticket to ride on public transport, even in the city center.

As part of the discontinuation of Fareless Square, TriMet also did away with differential fares by transit zone. Now there is just a single ticket price for any journey on public transit, whether it's just one stop or a trip across the entire metro area. Basic ticket prices are $2.50 standard adult; $1 for "honored citizens"

one of Portland's light rail streetcars

(seniors, disabled, and people on Medicare); $1.65 children 7-17 and students; and $2.45 for lift or paratransit. Bus operators do not give change, so carry exact change (the ticketing machines accept both coins and bills). At the MAX stations, including transit centers, machines accept cash and credit or debit cards and will give change. In addition, an all-day ticket is available and is valid for unlimited rides on buses, MAX, and the Portland Streetcar until the end of the service day when the ticket was purchased; these cost $5 adult, $2 "honored" (senior) citizens, and $3.30 children, and are clearly a great deal if you're going to use public transport more than once a day.

Regular per-ride tickets can be purchased at TriMet's primary ticket and information center in Pioneer Courthouse Square (SW Yamhill St. and SW 6th Ave.), and as you board any bus or streetcar. In addition, there are ticket vending machines at all MAX stops. All-day tickets can be purchased from MAX ticket machines, from the TriMet office, and from bus operators; all-day passes are not available from streetcars. You'll need to insert and validate your all-day ticket in the validator machine if you're traveling on MAX or the streetcar.

The **Portland Aerial Tram** is a gondola that travels 3,300 linear feet between the South Waterfront District and the upper campus of the Oregon Health and Science University. Round-trip tickets are $4; the tram is not part of the TriMet system, so bus transfers and MAX or streetcar tickets are not valid on the tram. (However, TriMet monthly or annual passes are honored.) Tickets are available from ticket machines at the lower terminal and are checked only on boarding at the lower terminal. The tram is easily reached via public transport, as the lower tram station is adjacent to the Westside streetcar line SW Moody & Gibbs stop.

The tram operates 5:30am-9:30pm Monday-Friday, 9am-5pm Saturday, and, during June-September, 1pm-5pm Sunday.

Car

Apart from increasing gridlock on the freeways and major arterials, driving in Portland is mostly straightforward. Avoid taking the interstates at rush hour, if at all possible. Because Portland is a city of bridges, traffic tends to back up when approaching the rivers, particularly on the I-5 and I-205 bridges across the Columbia River.

the Portland Aerial Tram

Street **parking** downtown is metered, though parking meters have been replaced with parking-meter kiosks. Pay with change, a credit card, or a debit card and receive a ticket to place on the street-side window as proof of payment. Valid tickets (those with time left on them) can be used at more than one parking place. In addition, the city is filled with parking garages; the seven city-owned SmartPark parking garages are usually the cheapest options and also accept merchant validation stamps (on the garage receipt) for a limited period of free parking. Street parking is free 7pm-8am.

Taxi

In addition to **24-hour taxi service** (call Broadway Cab at 503/333-333 or Radio Cab at 503/227-1212), Portland has Uber and Lyft.

Tours

If you want to get the Portland Big Picture before setting out to explore on your own, consider Big Pink Sightseeing's **Hop-On Hop-Off Trolley Tour** (503/241-7373, www. graylineofportland.net, $32). A daylong ticket lets you jump off and on an open-air, covered bus anywhere along its 12-stop route, which includes many of Portland's top sights. This is an excellent introduction to Portland for first-time visitors.

Portland Walking Tours (503/774-4522, www.portlandwalkingtours.com) offers a variety of tours related to art, architecture, history, and food of the downtown area. Most depart from the visitors center at Pioneer Courthouse Square. The 2.5-hour Best of Portland tour visits public art, downtown parks, and the waterfront ($20 adults); for the same price, the Underground Portland tour captures the spirit of the city's historic Old Town and Chinatown, culminating in a visit to an underground business district and a Shanghai tunnel.

Join up with the folks at **Pedal Bike Tours** (133 SW 2nd Ave., 503/243-2453, www.pedalbiketours.com, tours from $49 includes bike) and you'll not only get some exercise, but you'll get a feel for Portland life. The downtown tour provides a good orientation to the city's layout and sights; other tours visit local coffee roasters, food shops, and cafés.

Get out on the Willamette aboard the *Portland Spirit* (503/224-3900 or 800/224-3901, www.portlandspirit.com), which offers a variety of sightseeing and dining

The *Portland Spirit* sails from the downtown waterfront.

cruises aboard a 150-foot yacht with three public decks. The usual tour route is between downtown and Lake Oswego, south (upstream) from Portland. Two-hour lunch cruises ($40 adults) and 2.5-hour dinner cruises ($68 adults) are available Monday-Saturday, and there are also two-hour brunch cruises ($46) Saturday-Sunday. Sightseeing passengers may also accompany any dining cruise ($28 adults for lunch and brunch sailings, $38 for dinner sailings) with drinks and snacks available on board. Most cruises depart from the dock at Salmon Street Springs Fountain (at the base of SW Salmon St. at Waterfront Park). Call or check the website for departure times and to learn about other cruise options.

Willamette Jetboat Excursions (503/231-1532 or 888/538-2628, www.willamettejet.com) offers jet-boat tours of the Willamette River. A two-hour cruise available daily May-September travels up to Willamette Falls at Oregon City ($41 adults, $27 children ages 4-11) while a one-hour Bridges and Harbor Tour (mid-June-early Sept., $29 adults, $20 children ages 4-11) explores the waterfront and all 11 of downtown Portland's bridges. Tours depart from the OMSI dock (1945 SE Water Ave.).

Ecotours of Oregon (3127 SE 23rd Ave., Portland 97202, 503/245-1428 or 888/868-7733, www.ecotours-of-oregon.com) runs tours blending ecological understanding with good times. Door-to-door van transport from anywhere in the Portland area, lunch, and commentary are included in itineraries such as Portland microbrewery tours ($50) and whale-watching ($109). Packages focusing on winery tours, Mount St. Helens, and the Columbia Gorge typify the focus of this small company. Trips are usually confined to vans of six, accompanied by a professional naturalist-historian guide.

If you're just interested in Portland beers, you have several brewpub tour options, including the minivan tours offered by **Brewvana** (503/729-6804, www.experiencebrewvana.com, $65-85, beers included). A more participatory option is **Brewcycle Portland** (1425 NW Flanders St., 971/400-5950, www.brewgrouppdx.com/brewcycle, $20-25) where you'll join up to 14 other beer lovers on a specially designed "brewcycle" that you'll help peddle from pub to pub (ticket prices don't include beers). These same folks also offer the BrewBarge, which gets you out on the Willamette on 1.5 hour cruises ($35), but you need to bring your own beer.

Columbia River Gorge and Mount Hood

Look for ★ to find recommended
sights, activities, dining, and lodging.

Highlights

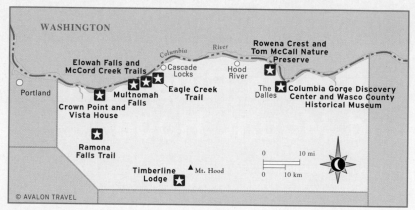

© AVALON TRAVEL

★ **Crown Point and Vista House:** This viewpoint provides the classic vista of the Columbia River and its mountain canyon (page 106).

★ **Multnomah Falls:** Plunging 620 feet, the second-highest drop in the nation, this is one waterfall you can't miss (page 109).

★ **Elowah Falls and McCord Creek Trails:** Leading to two fantastic overviews of the same beautiful waterfall, these trails comprise one of the Columbia Gorge's lesser-known hiking routes (page 111).

★ **Eagle Creek Trail:** The one trail you must hike in the Columbia Gorge leads to numerous waterfalls along a steep-sided valley (page 117).

★ **Rowena Crest and Tom McCall Nature Preserve:** One of the few drive-to vistas in the Columbia Gorge, this promontory is famed for its spring wildflower displays (page 132).

★ **Columbia Gorge Discovery Center and Wasco County Historical Museum:** The best museum in the Columbia Gorge relates the complex and fascinating history of the region (page 135).

★ **Timberline Lodge:** A fantastic log lodge built by hand in the 1930s, Timberline Lodge is an icon for the Pacific Northwest (page 138).

★ **Ramona Falls Trail:** An easy hike leads to a dramatic weeping-wall waterfall, one of the most beautiful near Mount Hood (page 140).

To Native Americans, the Columbia River Gorge was the great gathering place. To Lewis and Clark, it was the gateway to the Pacific. To visitors today, the Columbia River's enormous canyon carved through the Cascade Mountains is one of the Pacific Northwest's most dramatic and scenic destinations. The river, over a mile wide, winds through a 3,000-foot-deep gorge flanked by volcanic peaks and austere bands of basalt. Waterfalls tumble from the mountain's edge and fall hundreds of feet to the river. Clinging to the cliff walls are deep green forests filled with ferns and moss. It's the living rendition of a Pacific Northwest postcard.

While most visitors confine themselves to the cliffs and dense woodlands at the western end of the gorge, a surprise awaits the newcomer venturing farther east. Halfway through this cleft in the Cascades, the greenery parts to reveal tawny grasslands and sage-covered deserts under an endless sky. This 80-mile-long, 5-mile-wide chasm has as much variety in climate, topography, and vegetation as terra firma can muster.

Visitors can revel in a cornucopia of attractions: the world's largest concentration of high waterfalls, one of the planet's most diverse botanical communities, and a wide spectrum of recreational opportunities that includes skiing, fishing, hiking, rock climbing, windsurfing, and more—much of which can be enjoyed all in the same day.

Immediately south of the Columbia River Gorge rises 11,240-foot Mount Hood, Oregon's highest peak. Mount Hood is an all-season outdoor playground for all of northern Oregon. Besides boasting five popular ski areas, the mountain attracts hikers, mountain climbers, and those who come to marvel at the extravagant Works Progress Administration-era Timberline Lodge.

If there's one word to describe the forces that created the Columbia River Gorge, it's *cataclysmic*. During the last ice age, a 2,000-foot ice dam formed Lake Missoula, a vast inland sea in what is now northern Idaho and western Montana. The collapse of the ice dam some 15,000 years ago released a wall of water that steamrolled westward at 60 mph. These

Previous: hiking trail leading to Mount Hood; bridge at Latourell Falls in spring. **Above:** view from Crown Point.

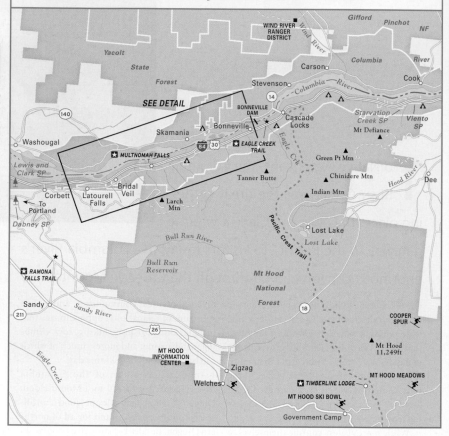

Columbia River Gorge and Mount Hood

torrents entered the eastern gorge at depths exceeding 1,000 feet. The floodwaters submerged what is now Portland and then surged 120 miles south, depositing rich alluvial sediments in the Willamette Valley. Scientists estimate there were at least 40 such inundations between 12,000 and 19,000 years ago.

THE COLUMBIA RIVER

The 1,243-mile Columbia River has its primary headwaters at Lake Columbia in British Columbia, and from there it flows north and west from Canada's Kootenay Range. Glacial runoff, snowmelt, and such impressive tributaries as the Kootenay and Snake Rivers

guarantee a fairly consistent flow year-round. At peak flows, the river pumps 250,000 cubic feet of water per second into the Pacific Ocean after draining 259,000 square miles, an area larger than France.

Flow peaks in spring and early summer, coinciding with the region's irrigation needs. Another leading use of the river is hydropower. The Columbia River Basin is the most hydroelectrically developed river system in the world, with more than 400 dams in place throughout the main stem and tributaries. As a result, the current incarnation of the Columbia is a stark contrast to the white water that filled its channel before the dams

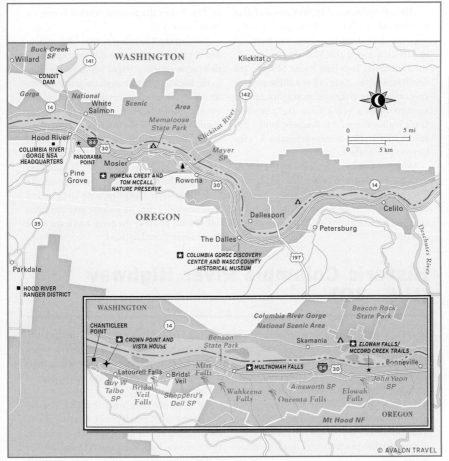

© AVALON TRAVEL

were built. Back in that era, spawning salmon had to jump over several sets of roiling cascades, and shipping was a hazardous enterprise. Floods were commonplace; the flood of 1894, for example, inundated Hood River and The Dalles. Although the Columbia no longer exerts so pervasive an influence on the topography, it is still more powerful than any river in North America except the Mississippi.

PLANNING YOUR TIME

The heart of the Columbia Gorge is just an hour from Portland, making this a major getaway for residents and travelers alike. Any trip to the gorge should include a drive along the

Historic Columbia River Highway, with hikes to waterfalls and a drive up the "Fruit Loop" (Rte. 35) from Hood River to Mount Hood. Even though the gorge is very popular, it's also vast, so it's easy to lose the crowds if you hike a lesser-known trail or get off the main routes.

While most people visit the gorge as a day trip from Portland, consider spending a night in Hood River or at Mount Hood to make this a more relaxing trip—and to get a feel for the youthful culture of windsurfers and cyclists that use this stunning landscape as their playground. In addition to excellent hotels and restaurants, you'll find wine-tasting rooms aplenty.

Also, if you're based in Portland and plan to drive out on I-84 to visit the gorge as a day trip, consider driving back to the Portland metro area along the Washington side of the Columbia. Two-lane Route 14 along the north side of the river offers a different perspective on the river and its mighty canyon and provides a break from the relentless truck traffic along I-84. Route 14 joins I-205 east of Portland for an easy detour back to the Oregon side of the Columbia.

Weather can be capricious in the gorge, making for dangerous driving conditions any time of the year. The Cascade summits can wring more than 200 inches of rain yearly from eastward-moving cloud masses, yet in The Dalles the annual rainfall is just six inches annually.

West of the Cascades, winter lows seldom dip below freezing. A notable exception to this happens when frigid winds originating in the Rockies blow through the gorge in winter, resulting in ice storms that can make for freezing rain and black ice, with the weather sometimes closing the interstate.

The **Columbia River Gorge National Scenic Area** (902 Wasco St., Hood River, OR 97031, 541/308-1700, www.fs.usda.gov/crgnsa) is the federal entity that oversees the Columbia River Gorge in both Oregon and Washington. From its website you can print out a handy guide to the gorge and learn more about recreational options.

Historic Columbia River Highway (U.S. 30)

In 1911, Samuel Hill, a wealthy and eccentric railroad lawyer, began promoting a dream for an automobile route through the Columbia River Gorge. Hill found supporters in the Portland business community who were swept up in the fervor stirred up by the national Good Roads campaign of the time. This movement supported the construction of paved highways with scenic qualities to foster tourism.

As the first Model T rolled off Henry Ford's assembly line in 1913, Hill's dream began to take form. Timber magnate and hotelier Simon Benson coordinated the project's fiscal management and promotion, and mill owner John Yeon volunteered as road master of the work crews. Samuel Lancaster, a visionary Tennessee engineer recruited by Hill, added the artistic inspiration for what came to be known as "a poem in stone." Together Hill and Lancaster journeyed to Italy, Switzerland, and Germany to view European mountain roads.

Hill and Lancaster were able to convince the Oregon government to finance the Columbia River Highway, the first road linking The Dalles to Portland through the gorge. To these idealists, the highway was not meant to be an intrusion on the wilderness; instead, the road was designed to be a part of the landscape.

This would not only be the Pacific Northwest's first paved public road but one of the defining events in the growth of modern U.S. tourism. Following the 1915 completion of this highway's first section, from Troutdale to Hood River, scores of middle-class Portland families in their Model Ts took to the cliffs above the Columbia on this architecturally aesthetic thoroughfare. After the stretch between Hood River and The Dalles was completed in 1922, it was dubbed "king of roads" by the *Illustrated London News*.

Service stations, roadside rest stops, motor courts (later called "motels"), and resort hotels that catered to the motorized carriage trade developed, contributing to the gorge's economic growth. Of the several dozen roadhouses that lined this highway 1915-1960, only a few structures remain today. A new interstate was constructed in the 1950s and 1960s that

Mount Hood Loop

By far the most popular day trip from Portland is the so-called Mount Hood Loop, which connects many of the sights in this area into a single day's driving adventure. Depending on side trips, the loop is about 160 miles in length—not too stressful if you get an early start and make frequent stops. Of course, the loop can be driven in either direction, but it's common to begin by heading out I-84 up the Columbia River Gorge and detouring onto U.S. 30, the Historic Columbia River Highway, which passes towering waterfalls and hiking trailheads—you should definitely make time for a short walk to an otherwise hidden waterfall to appreciate the gorge's striking natural history. After spending the morning in the mists of waterfalls, continue to Hood River for lunch. From here, head south on Highway 35 through orchards and farmland toward Mount Hood, which by this time will be filling the horizon. In summer and fall, this road is lined with farm stands selling fruit and vegetables. At Mount Hood, drive up to Timberline Lodge to go eye-to-eye with the mountain, Oregon's highest at 11,249 feet. Have a hot chocolate in the historic lodge and take a short hike around the base of the ski lifts (chances are you will be huffing due to the elevation). Then drop down the west face of Mount Hood on U.S. 26, following signs in Gresham, Portland's easternmost suburb, back to I-84 and Portland.

made gorge travel faster, but the charm of the earlier era was lost. Some sections of the old highway became part of the interstate; two sections remained open to car travel as U.S. 30.

Fortunately, the "king of roads" experienced a renaissance in the 1980s. Political activists, volunteers, government agencies, and federal legislation provided the spadework for the creation of the Historic Columbia River Highway, the first federally designated scenic highway in the United States. Thanks to its inclusion on the National Register of Historic Places (the only road on the list) as well as listings as an All-American Road, National Scenic Byway, National Heritage Road, and National Historic Landmark, the restoration has become a reality.

Currently, the old highway's sections from Troutdale to Ainsworth State Park and Mosier to The Dalles attract millions of motorists annually. Other segments of the old road are being rebuilt with attention to architectural nuance and potential recreational and interpretive uses. The reconstructed Mosier Twin Tunnels east of Hood River as well as restored sections between Cascade Locks and Eagle Creek and in the Bonneville-Tanner Creek corridor exemplify how parts of the highway have been rededicated as hiking and biking trails.

SIGHTS

Access to the Historic Columbia River Highway (U.S. 30)

There are several options for getting onto U.S. 30 from Portland. If you're in no particular hurry, head east on I-84 and take Exit 17, turning right at the outlet mall, left at the blinking light up the hill from the outlets, and onto the Historic Columbia River Highway (follow the signs to Corbett). This route snakes up the Sandy River and through the pleasant small towns of Troutdale and Corbett before reaching the Columbia Gorge's big attractions. The next 20 miles traverse historic bridges and stonework, lush orchard country, rainforested slot canyons, more than a half-dozen large waterfalls, and cliff-side views of the Columbia River Gorge. The attractions between Corbett and Horsetail Falls explain why both the American Automobile Association and Rand McNally rate the Historic Highway as one of the top 10 scenic roads in the country.

For quicker access to waterfalls and hikes from the west, take I-84 Exit 22 at Corbett, which joins U.S. 30 just before the first major viewpoints. To reach this section of U.S. 30 from the east, take Exit 35 at Ainsworth State Park.

Native People of the Gorge

Archaeological findings indicate that native people have lived in the Columbia River Gorge for some 10,000 years. When Lewis and Clark first came through in 1805, they found a gathering of Native Americans near present-day Wishram, Washington, whose numbers and variety surpassed any other native trading center on the continent.

The region hosted indigenous people from as far away as Alaska and the Great Lakes, who would come for barter fairs during salmon fishing season. Gambling, races, and potlatches (festivities in which individuals gave away possessions to gain status) supplemented trade and fishing.

Lewis and Clark encountered evidence of foreign contact on the Columbia from such disparate sources as a Chinook chieftain with red hair and gorge natives with swords, coins, and other European and Asian goods. Certain artifacts suggested trade with Native Americans from as far away as present-day Missouri and the southwestern United States. Lewis and Clark observed native currency of trade consisting of shells from Vancouver Island and blankets crafted by the British Hudson's Bay Company rather than indigenous articles.

When Lewis and Clark passed through, an estimated 13,500 native people lived in the Columbia River region. However, with the waves of European settlers and traders in the early 19th century came diseases to which the local people had no resistance. Measles and smallpox epidemics killed up to three-quarters of the region's native population, greatly reducing their ability to resist the influence of European and American colonists. While the arrival of settlers on the Oregon Trail brought about some isolated conflicts with gorge peoples, far more damaging to the long-term survival of Native Americans culture here was the destruction of their dietary staples, including the camas root and salmon. Native Americans were moved to reservations outside the gorge as a result of treaties enacted in 1855.

Portland Women's Forum State Scenic Viewpoint

The view east from Chanticleer Point, as this vista point is also called, is the first cliff-side panorama of the Columbia and its gorge that most travelers experience on U.S. 30. This classic tableau features Crown Point's domed Vista House jutting out on an escarpment about a mile to the east, giving human scale to the cleft in the Cascades 725 feet below.

Larch Mountain Turnoff

If you veer right on the road marked "Larch Mountain" at the Y intersection with the highway, you'll go 14 miles to an overlook featuring views of the snowcapped Cascades as well as the Columbia all the way west to Portland. There are also picnic tables and trailheads for hikes to the gorge below, and gorgeous beargrass blossoms in June. Later, August's huckleberries and mushrooms await foragers after the first rains.

To enjoy one of Oregon's classic sunsets, head to the northeast corner of the Larch Mountain parking lot around dusk and follow a gently rolling 0.25-mile paved path through forests of old-growth noble fir. The trail's last 100 yards are a steep climb up to an outcropping. This is **Sherrard Point,** and it has preeminent alpine views on a clear day.

★ Crown Point and Vista House

Driving the interstate, you might notice the distinctive outline of an octagonal structure on a high bluff in the western gorge. This is the **Vista House Visitors Center at Crown Point** (40700 E. Historic Columbia River Hwy., 503/695-2240, www.vistahouse.com, 9am-6pm daily Apr.-Oct.), 733 feet above the Columbia. Construction began in 1916 when the Columbia River Highway was formally dedicated. The occasion was marked when Woodrow Wilson pressed a button in the White House, which electrically unfurled Old Glory at the flat circular dirt area that was to become the visitors center.

Vista House was completed two years after

the highway's official dedication. The outside observation deck up the steps from the main rotunda showcases 30 miles of the Columbia River Gorge. A plaque outside pays homage to Samuel Lancaster for the "poetry and drama" the highway embodies. Photos of the various stages of the road's construction are displayed in the main rotunda, as are wildflower cuttings of the region's native plants. In the gallery of Vista House, volunteers run an information desk, while educational exhibits relate the history of the building and the highway.

Figure Eight Loops

The highway between Crown Point and Latourell Falls drops 600 feet in elevation in several miles. As you wend your way downhill from Vista House, it becomes apparent that Lancaster softened the grade of the road by means of switchbacks. With a grade never exceeding 5 percent and curve radii of not less than 100 feet, this section presents few problems for modern vehicles, but it challenged period cars and trucks during the highway's first decades. During construction, Scottish stonecutters and Italian masons sometimes hung suspended on ropes, singing while

they worked on the precipitous, circuitous roadbed.

Latourell Falls

Latourell Falls is the first of a half-dozen roadside waterfalls seen by motorists. When the highway was built, special care was taken to ensure the bridge crossing Latourell Creek provided a good view of the waterfall. Nonetheless, be sure to take the paved 150-yard trail from the parking lot to the base of this 249-foot cataract. The shade and cooling spray create a microclimate for fleabane, a delicate bluish member of the aster family, and other flowers normally common to alpine biomes. The misty tendrils of water against the columnar basalt formations on the cliffs make Latourell a favorite with photographers. Foragers appreciate maidenhair ferns and thimbleberries, but not enough to denude the slope.

Another trailhead begins in the middle of the parking lot and climbs around and above the waterfall, although bushes may obscure the overhang from which the water descends when you're looking down from the top. You'll probably be more inclined to stop after 50 yards and take in the distant perspective of Latourell from across the chasm. Latourell

Take in the view from Vista House, a postcard classic.

Creek flows from the waterfall underneath the highway bridge toward Guy Talbot State Park, where there are picnic tables shaded by an ancient forest.

Shepperd's Dell

A lush, forested canyon cut by a waterfall, Shepperd's Dell is one of the visual highlights of the gorge—despite the fact that little of this splendor is apparent from the road. It was named for a settler who retreated here for spiritual renewal because of the lack of good roads to a nearby church. An 80-yard sloping paved walkway descends from a bridge (and a parking lot east of it), the intricate architecture of which can be appreciated with a glance over your shoulder. Chances are, however, your gaze will be riveted by Shepperd's Dell Falls coursing down out of the forest to plummet sharply over a precipice.

Bishop's Cap

Bishop's Cap embodies the highway engineering genius of Samuel Lancaster. The base of a basalt outcropping was undercut as little as possible to accommodate traffic. Locals call this altered formation "mushroom rock" due to its similarity to a stem connecting to a mushroom cap. The same motif is repeated

around the bend. More highway architecture is visible in the form of dry masonry walls and stone guardrails.

Bridal Veil Falls State Park

Another legacy from the past can be experienced at the 1926-era Bridal Veil Lodge across from the state park. This establishment is one of the only lodgings from the heyday of the Columbia River Highway still operating.

Across from Bridal Veil Lodge is the waterfall for which the state park is named, reached by a trailhead at the east end of the parking lot. A short 0.7-mile round-trip hike takes you to the observation platform at the base of this voluminous gushing bi-level cascade.

Bridal Veil Falls State Park is also the western trailhead for the 33.5-mile **Gorge Trail 400.** Between here and Wyeth, this largely level trail takes in the gorge's highest waterfalls as well as newly opened sections of the old Columbia River Highway that are closed to vehicular traffic.

In addition to tree-shaded picnic tables and restrooms open all year, the park features the largest camas patch in the Columbia River Gorge. Blue-flowering camas and wapato were once the leading food staples for local Native Americans. The camas bulb looks like

Latourell Falls

Bridal Veil Falls State Park

footbridge abutting the road is a trailhead for the 0.6-mile hike to upper Wahkeena Falls. Follow this largely paved trail to a bench just beyond the waterfall and take in views of both the upper and lower falls. Higher up are panoramic vistas of the Columbia River and Gorge and the ridgeline pathway connecting Wahkeena to Multnomah. This trail is especially striking in October, when the cottonwoods and the bigleaf and vine maples sport colorful fall foliage. A picnic area is north of the Historic Highway, across from the waterfall.

★ Multnomah Falls

At 620 feet, Multnomah is the second-highest continuously running waterfall in the country. This huge cascade pours down from above with the authority worthy of the prominent Native American chief for whom it is named. The waterfall drops twice: once over 560 feet from a notch in an amphitheater of vertical rock, and then another 70 feet over a ledge of basalt. A short trail leads to an arch bridge directly over the second waterfall.

The 0.5-mile-long uphill trail to the bridge should be attempted by anyone capable of a small amount of exertion. You can bathe in the cool mists of the upper waterfall and appreciate the power of Multnomah's billowy flumes. The more intrepid can reach the top of the waterfall and beyond, but even the view from the base of the waterfall is astonishing. While some of the waterfalls in the surrounding area emanate from creeks fed by melting snows on Larch Mountain, Multnomah is primarily spring-fed, enabling it to run year-round. Roughly two million visitors per year make Multnomah Falls the most-visited natural attraction in the state.

The waterfall area has a snack bar as well as **Multnomah Falls Lodge** (503/695-2376, www.multnomahfallslodge.com, 8am-9pm daily). A magnificent structure, the lodge was built in 1925 as one of the original hostelries along the Columbia River Highway, and today is operated by a private concessionaire under license from the National Forest Service. The

an onion and tastes very sweet after it is slowly baked. Leave the camas alone, out of respect for a traditional food source as well as for your own safety—camas with white flowers are poisonous, a fact that is not always established when the bulb is being harvested.

If you're here in April, look for patches of camas along the short **Overlook Trail** to the Pillars of Hercules, a pair of giant basalt monoliths with I-84 and the Columbia River in the background. These formations are also called Spilyai's children, after the Native American coyote demigod. According to legend, Spilyai transformed his wife into Latourell Falls and his children into these volcanic formations to keep them from leaving him. Overlook Trail is about 20 yards west of the Bridal Veil Falls trailhead.

Wahkeena Falls

The name means "most beautiful," and this 242-foot series of cascades that descends in staircase fashion to the parking lot is certainly a contender. To the right of the small day lodge has an on-site restaurant, but no overnight accommodations. There's also a Forest Service visitors center.

Oneonta Gorge

Just east of Multnomah Falls, Oneonta Gorge is a narrow chasm cut into a thick basalt flow by Oneonta Creek. Walls more than 100 feet high arch over the stream, the cliff walls sometimes just 20 feet apart. This peculiar ecosystem, preserved as **Oneonta Gorge Botanical Area,** is home to a number of rare cliff-dwelling plants that thrive in the moist, shadowy chasm. There's no room along the sheer walls of Oneonta Gorge for a trail, but for those unperturbed by the thought of wet sneakers, the shallow stream can be waded for about 0.5 mile to Oneonta Falls, where Oneonta Creek drops 75 feet into the gorge.

Horsetail Falls

Only a few hundred feet east of Oneonta Gorge is Horsetail Falls, which drops out of a notch in the rock to fall 176 feet. While the waterfall is easily seen from the turnout along U.S. 30, hikers should strongly consider the three-mile **Horsetail-Oneonta Loop Trail.** Starting at Horsetail Falls, the trail quickly climbs up the side of the gorge wall and along the edge of a lava flow. The trail continues *behind* Ponytail Falls (also called Upper Horsetail Falls), which pours out of a tiny crack into a mossy cirque. The trail then drops down to Oneonta Creek, with great views over the narrow gorge and waterfalls. The trail returns to U.S. 30 about 0.5 mile west of the Horsetail Falls trailhead.

HIKING

There are many wonderful hikes along the Historic Highway. In addition to those described here, check out the National Forest Service's *Short Hiking Loops* map, available free at the Multnomah Falls Lodge.

Angel's Rest Trail

In early October 1991, massive fires engulfed portions of the Mount Hood National Forest off the Historic Highway. At the time, it was

Multnomah Falls is the second highest continual falls in the nation.

feared that massive erosion from the devastation of the trees and the understory would destroy the network of trails in and around the route of the waterfalls. But as you will see, this cloud had a silver lining.

For a good perspective on the fire as well as a great view of the gorge, Angel's Rest Trail 415 is recommended. To get there off I-84, take eastbound Exit 28 and follow the exit road 0.25 mile to its junction with the Historic Highway. At this point, hang a sharp right as if you were going to head up the hill toward Crown Point, but pull over into the parking area on the north side of the highway instead. The trailhead is on the south side of the road.

The steep 2.3-mile path to the top of this rocky outcropping gains 1,600 feet and takes you from an unburned forest through vigorous new brush growth beneath live evergreens with singed bark. Charred conifers dominate as you near the summit.

From the top you can enjoy a balcony-seat view overlooking the action. The stage in this case juts out over the Columbia River

Cruising the Columbia River

Thanks to a revival of interest in Lewis and Clark's journey, Columbia River cruises are more popular than ever. Most of these small cruise ships carry 80-180 people and offer weeklong trips, primarily out of Portland or Vancouver, Washington. These are rather pricey packages, but offer a highly scenic and relaxing alternative to a lengthy road trip. The well-appointed ships boast gourmet meals and ideal sightlines on the shipping locks and dam facilities. Add expert commentary by qualified interpreters and you have a trip to remember.

Un-Cruise Adventures (888-862-8881, www.un-cruise.com) offers a seven-night, eight-day cruises on the Columbia, Snake, and Willamette Rivers from April through November. Un-Cruise offers two different itineraries, one focusing on wine tasting and another featuring natural wonders and history; both itineraries depart from Portland. Per-person prices start at $3,195 based on double occupancy and include all meals and lodging.

Linblad Expeditions (800/762-0003, www.expeditions.com) packages trips on state-of-the-art craft with groups small enough to guarantee individualized attention from an attentive crew. In addition to luxury, these cruises offer an in-depth experience into the human and natural history of the region thanks to visiting authors, historians, and professors (the cruises are held in conjunction with National Geographic). There are frequent trips ashore, plus Zodiac explorations to remote side canyons. The ship is equipped with kayaks, which allow guests the freedom to explore on their own. The seven-day itinerary travels between Portland and ends at Clarkston, Washington, on the Snake River; cruises run in September and October, with prices starting at $4,590 per person based on double occupancy.

The **American Queen Steamboat Company** (888/749-5280, www.americanqueen-steamboatcompany.com) offers sternwheeler tours aboard the American Empress, the largest overnight riverboat west of the Mississippi, with over 100 staterooms and suites. Eight- to nine-day cruises travel up and down the Columbia between Astoria to Clarkston, Washington, from the ship's home port in Vancouver, Washington (across the Columbia from Portland). The price for a nine-day trip is $3,795 per person based on double occupancy.

with sweeping views toward Portland; to the northeast the snowcapped carapace of the Washington Cascades plays peekaboo behind a series of smaller ridges.

Wahkeena-Multnomah Loop

This is a hike of about five miles with panoramic river views, perspectives of four waterfalls, and ancient forests.

To get to Wahkeena Falls, drive I-84 to Exit 28, Bridal Veil Falls. Several miles later you'll come to the waterfall parking area and trailhead. If you take the trail to the right of the bridge, in about one mile you'll come to Fairy Falls, so named for its ethereal quality. Just past Fairy Falls, leave Trail 420 for Vista Point Trail 419 to see panoramas from 1,600 feet above the river. Old-growth Douglas firs usher you through higher elevations on this trail.

Rejoin Trail 420 one mile east of where Trail 419 began. Once you get past the first 1.5 miles of this trail's initial steep ascent, the rest of the route is of moderate difficulty. As you begin your descent, you might become confused by a lack of signs at the junction of Trail 420 and the Larch Mountain Trail. Hang a sharp left on Trail 441 to head west and down along Multnomah Creek. At the rear of this gorge is pretty Ecola Falls. There are several other cascades along the route.

When you hit the blacktopped section of Trail 441, hang a left to enjoy views from the top of Multnomah Falls; then descend, crossing the bridge and heading down into the parking area.

★ Elowah Falls and Upper McCord Creek Trails

To avoid the crowds while taking in

spectacularly varied gorge landscapes, try the Elowah Falls and Upper McCord Creek Trails.

From Portland, take I-84 past Multnomah Falls east to Exit 35, Ainsworth State Park. As you come off the access road, you'll have a choice of left turns. Take Frontage Road, with signs for Dodson. This road may also be accessed from the Historic Highway after driving five miles east of Multnomah Falls. Drive about two miles to the small parking lot of John Yeon State Park, named for one of the major advocates of the Columbia River Highway. In the western corner of the lot is the trailhead. Follow it 0.5 mile up the hill. When you reach a junction of two trails, turn right for Upper McCord Creek and left for Elowah Falls.

The Upper McCord Creek Trail leads to a mossy glade framing a creek at the top of a waterfall just under a mile from the junction. En route, the trail narrows to a ledge carved out of a cliff. From behind a railing, gaze hundreds of feet down at the Columbia River in the foreground of 12,306-foot Mount Adams. Across the chasm, layered basalt strata indicate successive lava flows. This is a good place to look for ospreys riding the thermals before they dive down to the Columbia for a fish. The trail continues to a view of dual cascades descending the rock face.

Retrace your steps to where the trail forks and descend 0.5 mile from the junction to Elowah Falls. This 289-foot feathery cascade is set in a steep rock amphitheater amid hues of green that conjure the verdant lushness of Hawaii.

SWIMMING

Swim in the Columbia River at historic and scenic **Rooster Rock State Park** ($5 per vehicle), Exit 25 off I-84 near Troutdale. West of the parking area is the monolith for which the park is named. According to some sources, Lewis and Clark labeled the cucumber-shaped promontory on November 2, 1805. Playing fields and a gazebo front a sandy beach on the banks of the Columbia. The water in the roped-off swimming area is shallow but refreshing. A mile or so east is one of only two nude beaches officially sanctioned by the state (the other is Collins Beach on Sauvie Island).

ACCOMMODATIONS AND FOOD

Columbia River Gorge sights are no more than 30 miles from Portland or Hood River, so most travelers will visit the waterfalls of the Columbia Gorge from the comfort of these cities. For a special escape, however, there are several wonderful accommodations in this area that deserve special consideration.

Imagine a 38-acre estate featuring a restaurant, a hotel, a brewery, a spa, a winery and tasting room, a movie theater, and a "pub golf" course amid lavish gardens and artwork at every turn. That's the McMenamins' ★ **Edgefield** (2126 SW Halsey St., Troutdale, 503/669-8610 or 800/669-8610, www.mcmenamins.com, $140-160). Oregon's preeminent brewpub-meisters have transformed what had been the Multnomah County Poor Farm and later a convalescent home into a base from which to explore the Columbia Gorge or Portland. This is truly the best of the country near the best of the city. Guests may choose from rooms with private bathrooms or with conveniently located common bathrooms down the hall. None of the rooms have TVs or phones. Remember, you're here to relax. Also, no A/C, but window fans are available. The **Black Rabbit Restaurant and Bar** (7am-10pm daily, $14-24) in the hotel offers McMenamins' version of fine dining, with main courses such as seared pankocrusted halibut with red-wine reduction or smoked rib eye steak with chipotle butter and cherry-syrah demi-glace. The **Power Station Pub** (11am-1am daily, $8-11) is in a separate building that once housed an electric power plant. Now it's where you go to enjoy a pint and dine on burgers, sandwiches, and pizza. In summer, a large open-air dining area sits just east of the pub.

Also unique is **Bridal Veil Lodge Bed & Breakfast** (46650 E. Historic Columbia River Hwy., Bridal Veil, 503/695-2333, www.

bridalveillodge.com, $195). The lodge, across the road from Bridal Veil Falls State Park, is one of the last surviving accommodations from the 1920s "roadhouse" era on this part of the Historic Columbia River Highway. Knotty pine walls, antique quilts, and historic photos set the mood. **Tad's Chicken 'n' Dumplins** (1325 E. Historic Columbia River Hwy., Troutdale, 503/666-5337, 5pm-10pm Mon.-Thurs., 4pm-10pm Fri.-Sat., 2pm-10pm Sun., $11-22) is a Portland-area original. Right on the Sandy River, its classic weather-beaten roadhouse facade has graced this highway since the 1930s. If you decide to forgo the restaurant's namesake dish, try the fried oysters, fried chicken, steak, or salmon. It's good ol' American food that'll taste even better with drinks on the deck overlooking the Sandy.

Service in the dining room at **Multnomah**

Falls Lodge (503/695-2376, www.mult-nomahfallslodge.com, 8am-9pm daily, $16-22) can be uneven, but the food is surprisingly good when the kitchen isn't overwhelmed. A cheery solarium adjacent to the wood-and-stone dining room makes a great setting to begin or end a day of hiking. On warm days the outside patio is delightful, and if you crane your neck, you can see the waterfall.

INFORMATION

The **Multnomah Falls Information Center** (at Multnomah Falls Lodge, 503/695-2372, 9am-5pm daily) has a ranger and volunteers on duty year-round to recommend campgrounds and hikes. Ask about nearby hikes to Horsetail Falls, Triple Falls, and Oneonta Gorge. Be sure to request the *Short Hiking Loops Near Multnomah Falls* map for a visual depiction of the network of trails.

Cascade Locks

The sleepy appearance of modern-day Cascade Locks belies its historical significance. The town is perched on a small bluff between the river and I-84, and its services and creature comforts are mostly confined to its main drag, Wa-Na-Pa Street. Below the town were rapids—called the Cascades—that blocked steamboat traffic between Portland and The Dalles and caused hardship for raft-bound Oregon Trail pioneers. Before the shipping locks that inspired the burg's utilitarian name were constructed in 1896 to help steamboats navigate around hazardous rapids, most boats had to be portaged overland.

The Bridge of the Gods, a steel cantilever bridge spanning the Columbia River at Cascade Locks, was built in 1926, the modern realization of a legendary bridge that, according to Native American myth, spanned this same channel.

The construction of the Bonneville Dam in the late 1930s inaugurated boom times

The Bridge of the Gods spans the Columbia River at Cascade Locks.

in the area. The dam created 48-mile Lake Bonneville, which submerged the shipping locks.

Reasonably priced food and lodging, a historical museum, the Bonneville Dam, and sternwheeler tours along with superlative hiking trails nearby make Cascade Locks a nice stopover.

SIGHTS
Bonneville Dam

The **Bonneville Dam** (541/374-8820, www.nwp.usace.army.mil) can be reached via Exit 40 off I-84. The signs lead you under the interstate through a tunnel to the site of the complex on Bradford Island. En route to the visitors center you drive over a retractable bridge above the modern shipping locks. On the other side are the powerhouse and turbine room. Downriver on the Washington side is the second-largest exposed monolith in the world (Gibraltar is first). This 848-foot lava promontory abutting the shoreline is known as **Beacon Rock,** a moniker bestowed by Lewis and Clark.

See the big ones that got away at the Bonneville Fish Hatchery.

Beyond the generating facilities is a bridge, underneath which is the fish-diversion canal. These fishways cause back eddies and guide the salmon, shad, steelhead, and other species past turbine blades. You'll want to stop for a brief look at the spillways of the 500-foot-wide Bonneville Dam, especially if they're open.

While it isn't anywhere near the largest or the most powerful dam on the river, Bonneville Dam was one of the largest and most ambitious of the Depression-era New Deal projects. Completed in 1937, it was the first major dam on the Columbia River. The building of the dam brought Oregon thousands of jobs on construction crews, and the cheap electricity that it produced promised future industrial employment. President Franklin D. Roosevelt officiated at the dam's opening in 1938, attended by a cheering throng of thousands. The two hydroelectric powerhouses together produce over one million kilowatts of power, and they back up the Columbia River for 15 miles.

Tours of Powerhouse 1 (541/374-4538, free) are offered at 11am, 1pm and 3pm daily June 15-Labor Day, and the same hours but Sat.-Sun. the rest of the year. Be aware that the dam may be closed to visits without warning due to security alerts.

The five-level **visitors center** (503/374-8820, 9am-5pm daily year-round) has exhibits on dam operations, pioneer and navigation history on the Columbia, and fish migration. A long elevator ride takes you down to the fish-viewing windows, where the sight of lamprey eels—which accompany the mid-May and mid-September salmon runs—is particularly fascinating. Outside the facility there's access to an overlook above the fish ladders. A walkway back to the parking lot is decorated with gorgeous roses spring through fall. Ask the Army Corps of Engineers personnel at the reception desk about public campgrounds, boat ramps, swimming, and picnic areas.

Retrace your route back to the mainland from Bradford Island and turn right, following the signs to the **fish hatchery**

Dams and Salmon

Beginning with Bonneville in 1938, the construction of the great dams on the Columbia changed the course of one of the world's mightiest rivers and the way of life in the gorge forever. Bonneville and Grand Coulee Dams supplied power for the World War II shipyards in Portland and Vancouver, Washington, and Boeing in Seattle. Besides billions of dollars' worth of pollution-free renewable energy at the lowest cost in the western United States, other Bonneville by-products include 370 miles of lucrative inland shipping, irrigation water for agriculture, and perfect windsurfing conditions.

Today, Pacific Northwest businesses and residents still benefit from hydropower, but at the possible cost of the greatest salmon runs ever known. Salmon are anadromous fish, meaning they live most of their lives in the ocean, but they breed in freshwater. They are hatched in rivers and then swim to the ocean where they mature. They then swim back up the same rivers they were born in, spawning in exactly the same spot where they were hatched, after which effort the fish die. The great salmon migrations up the Columbia were once so vast and strong that in the 1850s it was considered dangerous to row across the Columbia near Portland—the size and number of salmon were so great that they could inadvertently capsize small boats as they struggled upriver.

However, this massive population of salmon in the Columbia basin was not immune to the actions of humans. During the 1880s, 55 canneries operated on the Columbia, employing such then-new technologies as the salmon wheel, a Ferris wheel-like scooping device that extracted salmon from the river in such large numbers that the wheels were banned in the first decades of the 20th century. Starting with Bonneville Dam, the hydroelectric dams on the Columbia served as enormous barricades to the natural migrations of these fish, resulting in drastically smaller salmon populations.

(7:30am-5pm daily, free). Visit during spawning season (May and Sept.) to see the salmon make their way upriver. During spawning season, head to the west end of the hatchery, where steps lead down to a series of canals and holding pens. So great is the zeal of these fish to spawn that they occasionally leap more than three feet out of the water. This shady spot is a lovely spot for a picnic.

Inside the building, you can see the beginnings of a process that produces the largest number of salmon fry in the state. Fish culturists sort the fish and extract the bright-red salmon roe from the females. These eggs are taken to the windowed incubation building, where you can view trays holding millions of eggs that will eventually hatch into salmon. Once these fry grow into fingerlings, they are moved to outdoor pools where they live until being released into the Columbia River by way of the Tanner Creek canal. The whole process is annotated by placards above the windows inside the incubation building.

The salmon and trout ponds and the floral displays are worth your attention at certain times of the year, but the sturgeon pools to the rear of the visitors center are always something to see. Bonneville is the nation's only hatchery for white sturgeon, and the government has made this facility user-friendly. Biologists say the white sturgeon species of the Columbia River, with bony plates instead of scales, has remained unchanged for 200 million years.

Cascade Locks Marine Park

Down near the river is the **Cascade Locks Marine Park** (Exit 44 off I-84 East). Look for it on your left going east on Wa-Na-Pa Street; just follow the signs. Here the sternwheeler *Columbia Gorge* (reservations 503/224-3900 or 800/224-3901, www.portlandspirit.com) makes it possible to ride up the river in the style of a century ago. This 145-foot, 330-ton replica carries 599 passengers on three decks. There are several packages of varying themes and duration. The two-hour sightseeing cruise ($28 adults and seniors, $18 children plus a $4 pp landing fee) departure times vary; check the website for schedules. Lunch, dinner, and weekend brunch cruises are also available; cruises run May-October.

Port of Cascade Locks (541/374-8619, http://portofcascadelocks.org) houses the ticket office as well as an information center and gift shop, which sells an excellent map of local hiking trails.

About 0.25 mile west of the visitors center, **Cascade Locks Historical Museum** (503/374-8535, 10am-5pm daily May-Sept., free) is housed in an old lockkeeper's residence and exhibits Native American artifacts and pioneer memorabilia. Information about the fish wheel, a paddlewheel-like contraption that conveyor-belted salmon out of the river and into a pen, is especially fascinating. This diabolical device was perfected in Oregon in the early 20th century and was so successful at denuding the Columbia of fish that it was outlawed. Outside the museum is the diminutive Oregon Pony, the first steam locomotive on the Pacific coast. Its maiden voyage dates back to 1862, when it replaced the 4.5-mile portage with a rail route around the Cascades.

Take a walk over to the old locks. Construction began in 1878 to circumnavigate the steep gradient of the river; they were completed in 1896. By the time the Cascade shipping locks were completed, however, river traffic had decreased because cargo was being sent by train, so the impact of altering the river flow was negligible.

HIKING

The following hikes require a $5-per-vehicle day pass or a $30 annual Northwest Forest Pass.

Wahclella Falls and Old Columbia River Highway Hiker-Biker Trail

The best short hike in the Columbia Gorge that doesn't involve significant elevation gain is the walk along Tanner Creek to Wahclella Falls. After a mile of walking, you reach the terminus of the canyon framing the creek. En route, the gently hilly pathway shows off this pretty steep-walled arroyo to great advantage, but the destination is better than the journey.

In a scene evocative of a Japanese

Tour the Gorge on the sternwheeler *Columbia Gorge*.

along the Eagle Creek Trail

The highlight of the route is a reproduction of the Toothrock Viaduct, annotated by plaques and heritage markers. After exiting this section of the highway via a stairway into the parking lot of the Eagle Creek Fish Hatchery, head east a short distance to the second leg of this hiker-biker trail. The Eagle Creek-Cascade Locks section is highlighted by a pretty waterfall at the beginning and a well-rendered tunnel near the end. The distance between Bonneville and Moffet Creek is about seven miles.

★ Eagle Creek Trail

Hikes up a spectacular side canyon of the Columbia Gorge are the highlight of this popular recreational area. The Eagle Creek Trail 440, constructed in 1915, was an engineering feat. Volunteers blasted ledges for trails along vertical cliffs, spanned a deep chasm with a suspension bridge, and burrowed a 120-foot tunnel behind a waterfall. If you have time for only one day hike in the gorge, this should be it.

The classic Eagle Creek day hike leads up along the face of a cliff to a viewpoint over Metlano Falls. Part of the trail then drops back streamside near Punchbowl Falls, a good spot to break for lunch and splash in pools of cool water. Casual day hikers can return at this point, making for an easy 4.5-mile round-trip stroll.

More ambitious hikers can continue along to High Bridge, a suspension bridge spanning a deep crevice, and Tunnel Falls, so named because of the tunnel blasted into the rock behind the waterfall. Work your way through the tunnel for great views up and down Eagle Creek's canyon. The round-trip hike from the trailhead to High Bridge is 6.5 miles; to Tunnel Falls and back it is a strenuous 12 miles.

Be warned that the Eagle Creek Trail is very popular. Try to avoid summer weekends, when the trail is thronged with hikers. Some sections of the trail inch along vertical cliffs with cable handrails drilled into the cliff side for safety. Other steep sections lack handrails

brushstroke painting, a waterfall pours down dramatically at the canyon's end, best seen from a bridge over the creek. While the trail on the other side of the stream is worthwhile, it doesn't loop all the way back to the parking lot, so you'll have to retrace your steps. From I-84 eastbound, reach the trailhead by taking the Bonneville Dam exit (Exit 40) and making a right at the bottom of the exit ramp into a small parking lot (instead of a left under the highway to Bonneville Dam).

From this same parking lot you can access a resuscitated portion of the Columbia River Highway by heading east. However, with lanes barely wide enough to accommodate a golf cart, you'll have to leave the car behind. The state decided to repave this section of the old road for hikers and bikers, re-creating the arched guardrails, bridges, viaducts, and tunnels between here and Moffet Creek to join the surviving ones. In addition to the ornate stonework, the curving, undulating roadbed—which was blasted out of the mountainside prior to 1920—offers unsurpassed views.

altogether. This isn't a good trail for unsupervised children or unleashed pets.

ACCOMMODATIONS AND FOOD

If the best view of the Columbia from a hotel room is important to you, then make reservations at Cascade Locks's **Best Western Columbia River Inn** (735 Wa-Na-Pa St., 541/374-8777 or 800/595-7108, www.bestwestern.com/columbiariverinn, $143-184). Some rooms have hot tubs, and all rooms have microwaves and refrigerators. Many rooms also have balconies. In addition to views, there's a fitness room with a whirlpool, a pool, and exercise facilities. With the Cascade Locks Marine Park down the street, this property is in an excellent location.

Forget health food and haute cuisine until you get to Hood River. In Cascade Locks, you get down-home country cookin' at a decent price. The **Cascade Locks Ale House** (500 Wa-Na-Pa St., Cascade Locks, 541/374-9310, 11am-9pm daily, $6-16) is a small, dark brewpub whose smoked salmon chowder, pizza, and sandwiches fill you up on the cheap. Along the old locks in the historic Marine Park, **Thunder Island Brewing** (515 NW Portage Rd., 971/231-4599, http://thunderislandbrewing.com, 11am-9pm Mon.-Wed., 11am-10pm Thurs.-Sun., $7-10) has an off-the-beaten-path location and excellent beers. The menu is simple (salads, meat and cheese plates, and excellent meat pies) but the parklike location and the friendly welcome make this idyllic spot worth seeking out.

East Wind Ice Cream (395 Wa-Na-Pa St., Cascade Locks, 541/374-8380) is a traditional stop for families on a Columbia River Gorge Sunday drive.

Camping

There's no shortage of options for campers in this area. Keep in mind that the western gorge is Portland's backyard and can be very crowded, so avoid peak times when possible. In addition to first-come, first-served **Ainsworth State Park** (503/695-2301 or 800/551-6949, www.oregonstateparks.org, $17-24), several other sites are worth considering. These have been chosen for their location (near attractions or a prime trailhead) or for special amenities.

While the **Eagle Creek Campground** (541/386-2333, mid-May-Oct., $15) can be noisy and crowded, it's an ideal base camp for hiking as it's close to several trailheads. Established in 1915, this is the first campground ever created by the National Forest Service. Reservations are not accepted—it's first-come, first-served only—so try to get here early in the day. There are sites for tents and RVs up to 22 feet long, and have picnic tables, grills, and flush toilets. Sanitary services are available. Eagle Creek is located between Bonneville Dam and Cascade Locks off I-84. At the seven-mile point on the Eagle Creek Trail, there's a free primitive campground, but it fills up on summer weekends.

Herman Horse Camp (541/386-2333, mid-May-Oct., $10, no reservations) is 0.5 mile east of Cascade Locks, near the Pacific Crest Trail and 0.5 mile from Herman Creek. A full array of services, including a laundry, a store, a café, and showers are within two miles, supplementing the seven tent and RV sites. Piped water, grills, picnic tables, and stock-handling facilities are also welcome additions. There are trails for hiking and horse-packing, and other attractions include the historic Forest Work Center, a complex of stone and wood buildings (including an early ranger station and warehouse), which show the intricate handiwork of the 1930s Civilian Conservation Corps.

At I-84 Exit 51 is the **Wyeth Campground** ($10, no reservations, no phone), a beautiful and secluded Forest Service site that was used as a Civilian Conservation Corps camp in the 1930s. Today's it's popular as a windsurfing spot and has piped water and flush toilets.

Cascade Locks Marine Park (355 Wa-Na-Pa St., Cascade Locks, 509/637-6911, www.portofcascadelocks.org, year-round, $18-28) has campsites close to the center of town. The museum and the sternwheeler are housed in the complex. The amenities that are not available on-site are within walking distance.

Finally, two miles east of town near the banks of the Columbia is the **Cascade Locks KOA Kampground** (841 NW Forest Ln., Cascade Locks, information 541/374-8668, reservations 800/562-8698, Feb.-Nov. 30, $28 tents, $38-47 RVs, $3 each extra person). This private campground features the basics plus a spa (hot tub and sauna), hot showers, and a heated swimming pool. One-room (a queen bed and a set of bunk beds, $64) or two-room (a queen bed and two sets of bunks, $77) Kamping Kabins with shared bathroom facilities are available, as are two-bed cottages with private bathroom for $100-120; bring your own linens, pillows, towels, sleeping bags, etc. Kabins fill up quickly, especially on weekends, so reserve well in advance. To get there, take U.S. 30 east from town and turn left onto Forest Lane. Proceed 1.2 miles down, and you'll see the KOA on the left.

Hood River

In the past, Hood River was known as an especially scenic place to grow fruit. Since the early 1980s, however, well-heeled adherents of windsurfing have transformed this town into an outdoor recreation mecca. Instead of just the traditional dependence on cherry, apple, peach, and pear production, Hood River now rakes in tens of millions of dollars annually from the presence of "board-heads."

Bounded by picturesque orchard country and the Columbia River, with snowcapped volcanoes serving as a distant backdrop, this town of 6,500 enjoys a magnificent setting. The main thoroughfare, Oak Street, which becomes Cascade Street as you head west, is set

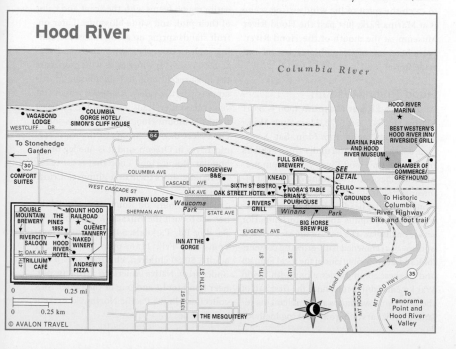

Hood River

© AVALON TRAVEL

on a plateau between the riverfront Marina Park to the north and streets running up the Cascade foothills to the south. Boutique shops and hip restaurants dress up old storefronts, and casual attire and sandals predominate.

Pick up a map to the **Fruit Loop** (www. hoodriverfruitloop.com), a 45-mile stretch of meandering highway and back roads, which directs area visitors to some of the richest farmland and most breathtaking scenery in the state—along the Hood River with Mount Hood as the backdrop to it all. Vineyards, orchards, farm stands, and country stores dot the route that crisscrosses the river, beckoning visitors to picnic, tour, or taste-test the fresh produce.

SIGHTS

Downtown Hood River is a lively place, with many shops and restaurants along Oak Street. A sense of fun and youthfulness pervades the town, the result of the many tanned, buff visitors who come here for the world-famous windsurfing and kiteboarding. A good spot to catch the spirit of the windsurfing scene is at Marina Park, just past the Hood River Museum, at the mouth of the Hood River. From here, lots of river athletes set sail and trade stories.

Hood River Museum

At the **Hood River Museum** (300 E. Port Marina Dr., 541/386-6772, 11am-4pm Mon.-Sat. Apr.-Aug., noon-4pm Mon.-Sat. Sept.-Oct., $5, children 10 and under free), exhibits trace life in the Hood River Valley from prehistoric times to the founding of the first pioneer settlement in 1854. Native American stone artifacts, beadwork, and basketry as well as pioneer quilts and a Victorian parlor set are on display. The story of the area's development as a renowned fruit-growing center is told, and the contributions of the local Finnish and Japanese communities, along with World War I memorabilia, introduce the first half of the 20th century. Photos and implements related to fruit harvesting and packing methods

round out the historical collections on the first floor.

Panorama Point

If you don't have time to drive up the Hood River Valley to enjoy the fantastic vistas of Mount Hood above the orchards, here's a close-to-town alternative. Drive to the east end of town and turn south on Route 35. Head south until you see the sign for **Panorama Point.** After a left turn, head south about a mile on East Side Road, then make a left on a road that'll take you to the top of a knoll; the views south and west do justice to the name. Panoramic vistas here afford a distant perspective on the orchards below Mount Hood that have for decades served as a visual archetype of the Pacific Northwest.

The Hood River Valley

South of the town of Hood River, the river of the same name drains a wide valley filled with orchards. During the spring, nearly the entire region brims with the scent and color of their pink and white blossoms. Later on, fruit stands spring up along roadsides, selling apples, pears, cherries, berries, and vegetables. Watch for wineries, as wine grapes are the most recent crop to find a home in this famously fertile valley. Route 35, which traverses the valley, leads up the south and east flanks of Mount Hood, only 25 miles south. On a clear day, this is one of the most scenic drives in Oregon, and it is one leg of the popular Mount Hood Loop that is for many Portland visitors their first glimpse of rural Oregon.

Driving south on Route 35 to Parkdale, be sure to visit the **Hutson Museum** (4967 Baseline Rd., Parkdale, 541/352-6808, 11am-4pm Wed.-Fri., 11am-6pm Sat.-Sun., $1 adults, $0.50 children, children ages 6 and under free). Native American artifacts, pioneer hand tools, and one of the better rock collections in the Pacific Northwest make it worthwhile.

Mount Hood Railroad

Train buffs will be delighted to ride the **Mount Hood Railroad** (541/386-3556 or 800/872-4661, www.mthoodrr.com, regular excursion $30-55 adults and seniors, $25-55 children under age 12, depending on style of railcar), which runs from the old Hood River railroad depot just off I-84 Exit 63 up the scenic Hood River Valley to its terminus in Parkdale—seemingly at the very base of Mount Hood due to the volcano's immensity and proximity. Riders sit in lovingly restored enclosed Pullman coaches or in more exclusive domed coaches. Also featured are an antique concession car and, of course, the obligatory red caboose. The standard ride takes about four hours round-trip, including a stop in Parkdale. The railroad also features dinner and brunch trains and many special-event rides, such as the Christmas Tree Trains, bedecked with carolers and other holiday trimmings. The main season is June-October.

Wine-Tasting

The moderate climate in the Hood River Valley favors production of cool-weather grapes such as pinot noir and pinot gris, while just across the Columbia River near Bingen and Lyle in Washington, the microclimate makes possible heavier reds such as syrah and whites such as viognier. There are now some 30 wineries in the Gorge, all open daily for tasting May-October (call to confirm opening times during the winter), and all easily found by using the readily available **Columbia Gorge Wine map** (www.columbiagorgewine.com).

Here are some of our favorite stops. **Naked Winery** (102 2nd St., 800/666-9303, www.nakedwinery.com, noon-7pm daily) has a tasting room right in downtown Hood River. The wines are moderately priced and marketed with a slightly naughty edge: Penetration Cabernet, anyone? **Cathedral Ridge Winery** (4200 Post Canyon Rd., 541/386-2882, www.cathedralridgewinery.com, 11am-6pm daily) is just west of town near the golf course. The valley's oldest winery, dating to 1981, is **Hood River Vineyards** (4693 Westwood Dr., 541/386-7772, http://hoodrivervineyardsandwinery.com, 11am-5pm daily). The microclimate at this winery is similar to that which produces Germany's Rhine wines. In addition to the Rieslings, chardonnays, Gewürztraminers, and other white wine varietals produced here, the area is famous for award-winning pinot noir and fruit wines such as Anjou pear, marionberry,

Mount Hood rises over the Hood River Valley.

Hood River's Japanese Settlers

The first orchards were planted in the Hood River Valley in the 1850s, and soon it became apparent that the valley's rich volcanic soil, glacier-fed rivers and streams, and mild climate were perfect for cultivation of apples, pears, stone fruit, berries, and vegetables. Strawberry farming was so successful at the turn of the 20th century that the Hood River Railroad was established in 1906 largely to hasten the delivery of the delicate berries to mainline trains at Hood River, from where they were shipped to markets across the country.

Many of the workers who built the Hood River Railroad were immigrants from Japan, and, after laying the track, many stayed on in the Hood River area and established farms and businesses. By 1920, over 350 Japanese people lived in Hood River, and of these, 70 were land-owning farmers. The Japanese were very successful and hardworking, and by 1940 there were 88 Japanese-owned farms in the valley.

Then in 1942, during World War II, came Executive Order 9066, issued by President Franklin D. Roosevelt, declaring that all people of Japanese ancestry were excluded from the entire Pacific coast. In a period of just two weeks, all people in the Hood River of Japanese ancestry, including U.S. citizens, were forced onto trains and sent to internment camps in California.

After the war, about 40 percent of Hood River's Japanese attempted to return to the valley and their businesses, but most found their property vandalized, possessions stolen, and farms untended. Many moved on, but some persevered; several large farms and orchards are still owned by Japanese American families.

and zinfandel, which are frequently delicious. Italian varietals are featured at **Marchesi Vineyards and Winery** (3955 Belmont Dr., 542/386-1800, www.marchesivineyards.com, 11am-6pm daily May 15-Oct., 11am-6pm Fri.-Sun. Nov.-mid-May).

Probably the oldest vineyard in Oregon—a plot of century-old zinfandel planted by an Italian stonemason near The Dalles—forms the foundation for the best wines at **The Pines 1852** (202 Cascade Ave., 541/993-8301, www.thepinesvineyard.com, noon-5pm Mon.-Wed., noon-7pm Thurs., noon-10pm Fri., noon-7 Sat.-Sun.). Rhone-style wines and an ice wine are other sure bets. On Friday evenings, live bands accompany winetasting from 6pm-9pm. Although the historic vineyards are near The Dalles, the tasting room is in Hood River.

Lost Lake

The postcard photo of Mount Hood from Lost Lake, with the white mountain peak rising above a deep-blue reflecting pool amid a thick green forest, is probably the most famous image of Oregon's most famous volcano.

The lake, about 25 miles southwest of Hood River, is a popular getaway when Hood River temperatures spike.

The 25-mile drive to Lost Lake from Hood River begins on 13th Street, which changes names (Hwy. 281, Tucker Rd., and Dee Hwy.) on its way up the flanks of Mount Hood. About 12 miles from downtown, take a right at the Dee Lumber Mill, where a green Lost Lake sign points the way. From here, bear left and follow the signs.

Lost Lake Resort (P.O. Box 90, Hood River, 541/386-6366, http://lostlakeresort. org, $8 day use, lodge rooms $125-200, cabins with pit toilets $65-170, yurts $60, campsites $26-32, some sites reservable through www. reserveamerican.com) offers rowboat rentals (no power boats allowed on the lake) and a small store along with campsites and cabins. In addition, there are standard guest rooms in the second story of the lodge (bedding is provided, but bring your own towels). Come prepared; the closest gas station is 20 miles away in Parkdale. The resort is usually open early May-late October.

Late August huckleberry season is a

highlight at Lost Lake, but September's weather and diminished crowds make it a preferable time to visit. The rangers have campfire programs on Saturday nights July-August. The Lakeshore Trail features a 0.5-mile boardwalk through an old-growth cedar grove; the boardwalk is two miles into the trail, where you pass eight-foot-thick cedars. Pick up a map with natural history captions that correspond to numbered posts along the route.

SPORTS AND RECREATION

The Hood River Marina offers an excellent family swim area and boat marina, and it also has personal watercraft rentals. The Hook offers a nice area (when the winds and windsurfers are absent) for some gentle canoeing or kayaking. Koberg Beach State Park, one mile east of town off I-84 but accessible from the westbound lanes only, offers a sandy swimming beach in a pretty setting. Be warned, however, that the drop-off is steep and not safe for little kids or weak swimmers.

Windsurfing

Hood River is recognized around the world as a major center for windsurfing and related sports for its gusty sailing sites, related businesses, and the sport's unique subculture. Blessed by a propitious mix of geography, climate, and river currents, the Columbia Gorge has strong and very reliable summer westerlies (winds blowing west to east) countered by the strong westbound Columbia River current.

Three of the top-rated sites for advanced windsurfers are accessed from the Washington side of the river. Doug's Beach, the Hatchery, and Swell City are just across the Hood River Bridge.

Three distinct windsurfing beaches are within the Hood River city limits. The Hood River Marina Sailpark is the largest and most developed of the three, including bathrooms with showers, food concessions, a picnic area, a grassy lawn for rigging, an exercise course, and a great family swimming beach

area with sheltered shallow water for tykes. As the name implies, you'll find the largest marina and boat launches. Beware of shallow sandbars off the shore as well as the boats entering and exiting the marina. Due to its amenities, including ample close-by parking, this can be one of the most crowded sites around.

The Event Site, a newer and somewhat smaller site, is to the west of the Hood River's confluence with the Columbia. Major events, including well-known windsurfing competitions, happen here. It has a lawn for rigging and lots of lawn space for spectators. These amenities, plus a location convenient to downtown, make this an ideal spot for casual onlookers. It provides quicker access to deeper water than the marina, but it can also be quite crowded at times. Toilets, water, and food carts are available on-site. The Event Site is off I-84 Exit 63, or at the north end of 2nd Street.

Several windsurfing schools in The Hook provide instruction in the gentle basin, an ideal location for beginners; once you're out in the main channel, winds can be strong. Conditions are quite variable, particularly as some places are in a wind shadow caused by nearby Wells Island, a sensitive wildlife area vulnerable to human impact. The views to the west (and hence, the sunsets) are just grand.

Access to The Hook is at the west end of Portway Avenue, the paved road that first takes you to the Event Site. All three in-town sites charge a day-use fee ($7 per vehicle). Call the Port of Hood River (541/386-1645) for more information.

About eight miles west of town, Viento State Park offers good river access for sailing in a beautiful natural setting. The park has a campground, a picnic area, restrooms, and water. Spectators won't have a lot of room, but the wind and wave action can get spicy. Viento is at Exit 56 off I-84.

In the opposite direction, six miles east of Hood River, you'll find the Rock Creek launch site in Mosier. Amenities are sparse but include chemical toilets. The river here is wide, and the chop can get high. You can reach Rock Creek off I-84 Exit 69. At the top

The Other Side of the Gorge

Although this guide focuses on the sights of Oregon, it's clear that the Columbia River has two shores, and only one is in Oregon. Cross a bridge and you're on the Washington side of the gorge, which offers a number of excellent destinations.

Across the Columbia from Hood River, the **White Salmon River** cuts a narrow canyon down through the gorge walls as it rushes to meet the Columbia. A number of white-water rafting guides offer half-day trips on the White Salmon, which bounces down through near-constant Class IV rapids. It's a short but exhilarating rafting trip and easily added to a gorge itinerary. Guided trips are roughly $60-65 per person and are available from **River Drifters** (800/972-0430, www.riverdrifters.net) and **All Star Rafting and Kayaking** (800/909-7238, www.asrk.com).

The area around Lyle is transforming into a wine-producing mecca. The hot summer weather is perfect for growing syrah, Grenache, Roussanne, viognier, and other wine grapes from France's Rhone Valley. Two notable wineries here are **Syncline Wine Cellars** (111 Balch Rd., Lyle, 509/493-4705, http://synclinewine.com, tasting 11am-6pm Thurs.-Sun. Feb.-mid-Dec.) and **Domaine Pouillon** (170 Lyle Snowden Rd., 509/365-2795, http://domainepouillon.com, 11am-6pm Thurs.-Sun.). For both, call to confirm winter hours.

Down the road a bit, there's **Maryhill Winery** (9774 Hwy. 14, 877/627-9445, 10am-6pm daily), in a very impressive clifftop tasting room 25 miles east of Lyle and directly across the Columbia from Biggs, Oregon; this winery offers a summer series of outdoor concerts in a natural amphitheater. The **Maryhill Museum** (509/773-3733, www.maryhillmuseum.org, 10am-5pm daily Mar. 15-Nov. 15, $9 adults, $8 seniors, $3 children ages 6-16) is an idiosyncratic collection of art and artifacts in a grand country estate. You'd be right to think that a 20,000-square-foot manor house is rather unusual in the Columbia Gorge. Maryhill was built by Sam Hill for his wife Mary. Hill was an early-20th-century mogul whose family controlled the Great Northern Railway and who was instrumental in the building of the Columbia River Highway in the 1910s. Atop an 800-foot cliff above the Columbia, Maryhill was designed to resemble a French château and to serve both as home for Hill and his wife and as the center of a utopian Quaker community. Although construction began on Maryhill in 1913, it wasn't completed until 1926, as Hill lost interest in the project after it became clear that his wife was unwilling to live in this godforsaken country and the imported Belgian Quakers found the arid cliffs unsuitable for agriculture. Maryhill opened as a museum in 1940 and has a very good collection of Native American artifacts, an impressive set of 19th-century landscape and portrait paintings, sculpture and drawings by Auguste Rodin, and French fashion mannequins from the early 20th century. The museum also offers classes, lectures, and concerts.

Just east of Maryhill is another of Hill's eccentric constructions. Dedicated to the area's fallen soldiers from World War I, a full-scale replica of **Stonehenge** looms above the gorge.

of the ramp, hang a right, then the first left on Rock Creek Road. The site is on the right just past the dry creek bed.

In business since 1986, **Big Winds** (207 Front St., 541/386-6086, www.bigwinds.com) offers board and full rig rentals starting at $69 per day and $389 per week, depending on the equipment. Big Winds also offers two levels of beginner lessons ($79 per lesson), or choose the "Discover Windsurfing" package ($149) that includes all three lessons. The price includes use of a wetsuit, booties, and all the necessary windsurfing equipment. There are many other windsurfing lessons and rental operations in Hood River with similar price ranges and options.

In addition to windsurfing, all the water sports outfitters also have rental gear for other sports, such as kiteboarding and stand-up paddling.

Adepts will tell you that windsurfing is best in the fall. It's less crowded, the water's warm, and the winds are lighter at school sites. It's easier to find parking and rigging space at launching areas, and there's a quality of light on the water, with enough clear days to add aesthetic appeal. Best of all for beginners is the availability of individualized instruction during fall. While conditions are generally good at most locations along the river during the season, the best places are in the east end of the gorge, notably around Three Mile Canyon and other launch sites in the Arlington, Oregon, and Roosevelt, Washington, areas.

Fishing

The area offers two different types of fishing. You can go for trout in several beautiful small mountain lakes, most of which are west and south of the Hood River Valley. Notable among the latter are Wahtum, Rainy, and North Lakes, all about 45 minutes west of downtown Hood River on good gravel roads. Then there is Lost Lake, the popularity of which might detract from the quality of the fishing during some seasons. Pick up licenses in any Hood River sports shop.

The other option is fishing the Hood River itself, or the Columbia River. The Hood has good trout fishing, and both have good seasonal steelhead and salmon fishing. The Hood River can be accessed from several county parks. Contact the **Gorge Fly Shop** (201 Oak St., 541/386-6977, www.gorgeflyshop.com, 9:30am-6pm Mon.-Sat., 10am-4pm Sun.) for information; this operation can also arrange fly-fishing lessons.

Golf

Offering great views of Mount Hood is the popular 18-hole, 6,150-yard **Indian Creek Golf Course** (3605 Brookside Dr., 541/386-3009, www.indiancreekgolf.com, $35-50). A little farther from town is **Hood River Golf Course** (1850 Country Club Rd., 541/386-3009, www.hoodrivergolf.net, $30). It has 18 holes that are a bit hillier than at Indian Creek, as well as beautiful views of Mount Hood, Mount Adams, elk, and geese. Come in fall if only to see the spectacular foliage.

Hiking

While the most famous gorge hikes tend to cluster around the west end waterfall area, the environs of Hood River have their fair share of great trails. Three of these trails are right on the gorge, eight miles west of town on the south side of the highway, accessible via the Viento Park exit (Exit 56) off I-84.

The **Starvation Creek to Viento Trail** hike is the shortest and by far the easiest of the three. Actually a restored segment of the Historic Columbia River Highway, this mostly paved path runs a little over one mile each way. It offers some decent gorge views but will be of more interest to history buffs who want to retrace extant remnants of the old highway. This trail also provides access to the other two trails in the area.

Both the **Mount Defiance Trail** (Trail 413) and **Starvation Ridge Trail** (Trail 414) used to be accessible through the Starvation Creek rest stop exit off I-84, which is now closed. So walk the Starvation Creek to Viento Trail, then look for signs for either of the other trails once you get to the west side of the rest stop. Both trails eventually head for the same place, converging high above the gorge just below the top of Mount Defiance. Being the highest point on the gorge proper at 4,960 feet, Mount Defiance presents a strenuous workout for anyone up for the challenge.

Either route rewards you with spectacular views of the gorge, as well as old-growth woods and pristine Warren Lake. The Starvation Ridge Trail is somewhat steeper than the Mount Defiance Trail. This long loop is about 12 miles round-trip. A short two-mile loop is also possible by following Trail 413 for one mile, then heading east (left) onto Trail 414. This eventually takes you back to the highway where you started. These trails are really best only for experienced hikers due to their steepness and narrowness.

The **Wygant Trail** is reached from the eastbound-only Exit 58 off I-84 at Mitchell Point. Go right (west) at the top of the ramp, then follow the road heading west. This eventually becomes the trail, and it follows the old route of the Historic Highway for a stretch. The trail eventually winds its way for almost four miles to the top of 2,214-foot Wygant Peak. Along the way you'll pass through some native Oregon white oak groves, mixed conifer forests, and some openings with lovely views.

There are many beautiful trails south of Hood River off Route 35 in Mount Hood National Forest. The **East Fork Trail** offers an easy but very scenic amble along the swift glacial-fed East Fork of the Hood River. Accessed from either the Robin Hood or Sherwood Campgrounds (24 miles south of Hood River) along Route 35, this trail is great on foot or mountain bike. It is about four miles between the two campgrounds, and the trail continues beyond the Sherwood Campground north into the Mount Hood Wilderness.

Tamanawas Falls Trail leads off from the East Fork Trail about 0.5 mile north of the Sherwood Campground. A short but steeper hike, this trail is uphill all the way to the reward—beautiful 150-foot-high Tamanawas Falls.

Perhaps the best place to experience the transition from western alpine conifer forest to interior high desert is **Lookout Mountain** in the Badger Creek Wilderness. This aptly named 6,525-foot peak is the second-highest in the Mount Hood National Forest. To get there, drive 25 miles south of Hood River on Route 35 to Forest Road 44 (the Dufur cutoff). Follow it east for five miles up a steep hill to Forest Service Road 4410, marked for High Prairie. This route takes you six miles to a parking area opposite the trailhead to High Prairie Trail (Trail 493).

The 20-minute walk to the top of Lookout Mountain on Trail 493 takes you through wildflower meadows to the former site of a fire spotter's cabin. Directly west looms Mount Hood. Turn 180 degrees and you face the sagebrush and wheat fields of eastern Oregon. To the south are the Three Sisters and Broken Top. West and north of those peaks rises Mount Jefferson's tricorn hat. The body of water to the southwest is Badger Lake. To the north, views of Mounts Adams, St. Helens, and Rainier (on a clear day) will have you reeling with visual intoxication.

Mountain Biking

Just west of town is a network of old gravel and dirt roads that local mountain bikers love. **Post Canyon Road** starts out as a typical paved rural road, with houses scattered along each side. Shortly past its start at Country Club Road, the pavement ends and the fat-tire fun begins. Several side roads branch off from Post Canyon Road into the Cascade foothills. You can ride for a long time without seeing any buildings, but you will undoubtedly encounter some clear-cuts and other logged areas, so don't expect pristine forests. Also, be warned: The road is used by groups of motorbikers at times, so stay alert.

To get there, take Exit 62 off I-84, turn right at the top of the ramp, then make an immediate right onto Country Club Road. Follow this road about a mile as it bends to the south, then turn right into the well-signed Post Canyon.

Surveyor's Ridge Trail (Trail 688) traverses the ridgeline on the east side of the upper Hood River Valley for 17 miles. It offers some great Mount Hood and valley views and is especially fun for mountain bikers. The trailhead is off Forest Service Road 17, which intersects Route 35 about 11 miles south of Hood River just past the big lumber mill to the left of the highway.

Stop by **Discover Bicycles** (116 Oak St., 541/386-4820, www.discoverbicycles.com, 10am-6pm Mon.-Sat., 10am-5pm Sun.) for advice on mountain bike trails and bike rentals (from $30 per day).

ENTERTAINMENT AND EVENTS

The second weekend in April brings the **Hood River Hard-Pressed Cider Fest** (3315 Stadelman Drive, 541/386-2000, $5 general admission, ages 14 and under free, $5 for cider glass and 4 drink tokens) which gives seasoned and novice cider drinkers alike the chance to sample cider from Hood River

County's very own cider makers, as well those from a variety of additional Northwest cideries. More than 20 cider makers usually participate, with more than 40 ciders on tap. The daylong event also features local food vendors, produce and arts vendors, a kid's area and a line-up of local music. Depending on the year, this is also prime apple and pear blossom season, so a drive up through Hood River orchards should also be part of the celebration—but before imbibing the cider.

For fans of the exciting Columbia Gorge beer and ale scene (and they are legion) the **Hood River Hops Fest** (541/386-2000 or 800/366-3530, http://hoodriver.org, $5 entry only for 21 and older, $15 beer garden ticket with tasting mug and five drink tickets) celebrates the hop harvest season with one of the largest fresh hop beer selections in the nation. The festival, usually held the last Saturday in September) offers more than 60 fresh-hop beers for sampling from over three-dozen breweries. The event is open to the public from noon to 9pm, and takes over about four blocks of downtown (the Columbia Parking Lot between 5th and 7th streets at Cascade Ave. is nominally the center of action). The one-day festival also features arts and crafts vendors from the region, a selection of Gorge wines, a children's play area, fun contests, and a day-long lineup of live music. Children and youths under 21 are welcome and have free admission throughout the afternoon until 5pm; in the evening, the venue is open to adults only until closing at 8pm.

ACCOMMODATIONS

Finding a room in Hood River in the summer isn't easy, and the rates reflect the area's popularity. In fact, don't set out to Hood River in summer or on weekends without room reservations; there are a limited number of rooms and a large influx of visitors. Some lower-end motels can be pretty battered—the young ski and windsurfing crowd can be hard on rooms. All prices listed reflect summer rates; remember to add the 9 percent room tax within the city of Hood River. Weekend rates can be substantially higher than those for weekdays.

$50-100
The ★ **Vagabond Lodge** (4070 Westcliff Dr., 541/386-2992, www.vagabondlodge.com, $80-140) is a couple of miles west of downtown near the Columbia Gorge Hotel. It has lovely landscaped grounds with a playground for kids and is set back from the highway. Three guest rooms have full kitchens, and a number have large stone fireplaces. The best are the view rooms (extra charge), which take in a spectacular vista of the gorge.

Riverview Lodge (1505 Oak St., 541/386-8719, www.riverviewforyou.com, $95-140) has basic rooms, a pool, and some units with kitchens. It's within easy walking distance of Cascade Commons, Hood River's shopping center, with several grocery stores and eating options.

$100-150
In the heart of downtown is the ★ **Hood River Hotel** (102 Oak St., 541/386-1900 or 800/386-1859, www.hoodriverhotel.com, $109-209), an impeccably restored turn-of-the-20th-century hotel with a good restaurant (Cornerstone Cuisine, 7am-9pm daily, $12-20). Special vacation packages are also featured. The oak-paneled, high-ceilinged lobby, with a cozy fireplace and an adjoining lounge and restaurant, is particularly inviting. Rooms that face the river also face the rail lines, so if you're a light sleeper, you may want to opt for a lower-priced town-view room. All in all, "the Hotel" (as locals call it) is a nexus of activity and the most charming in-town digs to be found.

Comfort Suites (2625 W. Cascade Ave., 541/308-1000, $139-179) is at the west end of Hood River, about a mile from downtown. It offers immaculate guest rooms and amenities, such as a pool and spa, as well as some suites with kitchens.

A large 1909 home right on the edge of downtown is home to the **Oak Street Hotel** (610 Oak St., 541/386-3845 or 866/386-3845, www.oakstreethotel.com, $149-199), a small boutique hotel with just nine rooms, all stylishly furnished. The hotel also represents a number of rental vacation homes in the area, if you are traveling with a group or require the extra comforts of a private home.

If being on the river is essential to you, **Best Western's Hood River Inn** (1108 E. Marina Way, 541/386-2200 or 800/828-7873, www.hoodriverinn.com, $140-200) is the only place in town to boast direct river frontage and even a small private beach. The rooms provide great opportunities to watch windsurfers, and there's a lounge and a decent restaurant (the Riverside Grill) on the premises. Best of all, however, are the heated outdoor pool and spa. The only downside is that the hotel is a bit of a trek to downtown. There's a complex formula for determining room rates, which can spike wildly from day to day, so it's worth visiting the website before calling to make reservations.

Two B&Bs are located in the leafy old neighborhood near the historic center of Hood River. **The Inn at the Gorge** (1113 Eugene St., 541/386-4429, www.innatthegorge. com, $119-159) is a nicely refurbished 1908 Victorian that offers the informality of a windsurfer hangout in the form of a classy B&B. Three of the five guest rooms are suites, and have very large rooms with full kitchens. All rooms have private baths.

Windsurfer-friendly, the **Gorgeview Bed and Breakfast** (1009 Columbia St., 541/386-5770, www.gorgeview.com, May-Oct.) is in a historic house with a great porch view and a hot tub. You'll have a choice of regular private rooms ($120-145) or hostel-style bunk rooms ($58 pp).

Up at Parkdale near Mount Hood, the **Old Parkdale Inn** (4932 Baseline Rd., Parkdale, 541/352-5551, www.hoodriverlodging.com, $135-170) has three rooms, two of which are spacious suites. All have private baths, TVs, VCRs, microwaves, coffeemakers, and refrigerators. The breakfast is gourmet quality, and the peaceful village will satisfy those looking for an escape from the rat race. The gardens,

full kitchens, mountain views, and rural setting will get you in relaxation mode.

$150-200

The ★ **Columbia Gorge Hotel** (4000 Westcliff Dr., 541/386-5566 or 800/345-1921, www.columbiagorgehotel.com, $175-289) was built in 1921 by lumber magnate Simon Benson. It has been called the "Waldorf of the West" for its neo-Moorish facade, glittering chandeliers, and 207-foot waterfall on the grounds. The hotel recently received a much-needed renovation and update. Large wing chairs around the fireplace and fresh-cut bouquets in the dining room bespeak the hotel's enduring refinement. In addition to a fine restaurant offering breakfast, lunch, and dinner, the hotel has lovely gardens. To get there, take Exit 62 off I-84, drive over the bridge to the north side of the highway, and follow Westcliff Drive west.

Immediately adjacent to the Columbia Gorge Hotel, **Columbia Cliff Villas** (3880 Westcliff Dr., 541/436-2660 or 866/912-8366, www.columbiacliffvillas.com, $179-299) shares its stellar views and offers hotel and condo lodgings with one- to three-bedroom units. The guest rooms can be put together into almost any layout, from basic hotel-style rooms to multibedroom suites with full kitchens.

Camping

Hood River County (www.co.hood-river. or.us) offers parks with campgrounds in the Hood River Valley.

Tucker Park (2440 Dee Hwy., 541/386-4477) is only four miles from town, in a lovely spot along the banks of the gurgling boulder-strewn Hood River. It's the most developed of the three parks, with a store, a restaurant, laundry, and an ice machine just four miles away in town. It has 14 RV sites with water and electricity ($29) and 80 tent sites ($19).

Tollbridge Park (Rte. 35, 541/387-6888) is also set along the Hood River in the upper valley. It's 17 miles south of Hood River and offers showers and two grocery stores a short distance away. Rates are $29 for full-hookup sites, and $19 for tent sites.

Oregon State Parks (www.oregonstateparks.org) offers two full-service campgrounds right on the Columbia River. **Viento State Park** (800/551-6949 or 800/452-5687, mid-Apr.-late Oct.) is eight miles west of Hood River on the river side of I-84. You'll pay $20 for one of the 57 sites with water and electric, or $17 to pitch your tent at the other 18 sites. Viento offers direct recreational access to the mighty Columbia.

Memaloose State Park (800/452-5687, $19-24) is 11 miles east of Hood River on I-84, accessible from the highway's westbound lanes only. On the Columbia, but with limited river access, the park offers 43 full-hookup sites ($28) and 67 tent spaces ($19), showers, and an RV dump station. It's only fair to mention that both of these campgrounds are not far from a main freight train line; in other words, expect to hear the trains go by, even at night.

There are several nice semiprimitive forest service campgrounds in the Mount Hood National Forest, which surrounds the valley on three sides. All are in pleasant settings. Call the **Hood River Ranger Station** (6780 Rte. 35, 541/352-6002) for information. Some of the Forest Service campgrounds south of town are Sherwood and Robin Hood, both on Route 35 and $14 per night, Laurence Lake (off Forest Rd. 2840, free), and Lost Lake ($25-30).

FOOD

Hood River's status as the premier windsurfing town in North America has brought sophisticated tastes to the gorge, with a resulting spike in restaurant quality. A cluster of casual deli, lunch, and coffee places are located along Oak Street in the downtown area; it's pleasant just to saunter the street and browse the menus. Few other small towns in the Columbia Gorge (or in the Pacific Northwest, for that matter) can boast such a roster of fine restaurants, not to mention gourmet coffee and options for vegetarians.

Coffee & Breakfast

Hood River has a number of excellent coffee shops with good pastries and other options for breakfast. Here are a few of our favorites. Just east of the major downtown intersection, **Ground** (12 Oak St., 541/386-4442, http://groundhoodriver.com, 6am-6pm Sun.-Thurs., 6am-7pm Fri.-Sat.) is the quirky kind of caffeinated outpost that you'd expect in Oregon. The coffee and ambience are great, and at lunch you'll find good panini sandwiches and fresh salads. Just to the west, **Dog River Coffee** (411 Oak St., 541/386-4502, 6am-6pm Mon.-Fri., 7am-6pm Sat.-Sun.) is where to find excellent Stumptown coffee and sustenance like breakfast burritos and muffins. For top-notch bread and baked goods, head to **Knead** (102 5th St., 541/436-2886, 8am-5:30pm Tues.-Sat.), where wonderful pastries and lunch-time sandwiches help provision picnics.

American

The **Sixth Street Bistro** (6th St. and Cascade Ave., 541/386-5737, http://sixthstreetbistro.com, 11:30am-9:30pm daily, $8-20) has a good selection of microbrews on tap and an eclectic menu featuring fresh, locally grown organic ingredients. Sample dishes ranging from red coconut curry to grilled rib eye with gorgonzola and port sauce. Good burgers, too, and the deck is a shady refuge on a hot summer day.

For great views of the gorge, climb the steps up to **3 Rivers Grill** (601 Oak St., 541/386-8883, www.threeriversgrill.com, 11am-10pm daily, $10-37) with expansive decks overlooking downtown and the Columbia. The selection of Pacific Northwest seafood and steaks is large and well prepared.

A classic old bar in the center of town has been refurbished into the **River City Saloon** (207 Cascade Ave., 541/387-2583, www.waucomaclub.com, noon-2:30am daily). This handsome spot is perfect for lunch or early evening dinner, with lots of sandwich and steak options. This is also Hood River's primary sports bar and late-night hangout, so the crowds can get intense late in the evening, which isn't a problem if that's what you're looking for.

East of downtown, in the Best Western Hood River Inn, is the **Riverside Grill** (1108 E. Marina Way, 541/386-2200, 6am-9pm daily, $1-29), with the best riverfront views in town. The menu features fresh seafood and steaks.

On "The Heights" (the plateau forming the start of the lower Hood River Valley, a few hundred feet above downtown) you'll find **The Mesquitery** (1219 12th St., 541/386-2002, www.thebestinhoodriver. com, 4:30pm-9pm nightly, $8-19), where wood-smoke and barbecue flavors issue a wake-up call to your taste buds. You'll find the best ribs in town, not to mention steaks, fish, and many other dishes.

In Parkdale (16 miles up the valley toward Mt. Hood), is another outpost of barbecue. The **Apple Valley BBQ** (4956 Baseline Dr., 541/352-3554, www.applevalleybbq.com, 11am-8pm Wed.-Sun., call to confirm winter hours, $8-24) is a hopping spot with St. Louis-Style ribs and local beers and wines.

Italian

Andrew's Pizza and Bakery (104 Oak St., 541/386-1448, 9am-9pm Mon.-Thurs., 9am-10pm Fri.-Sat., 10am-9pm Sun., large pizzas $14 and up) easily wins our vote for best pizza in the gorge. Lots of extravagant toppings are available, as well as microbrews and great coffee. Andrew also now offers his excellent pizza and brews at the **Skylight Theater** (541/386-4888, www.skylighttheater.com), an expansion into two movie theaters immediately next door to the pizzeria.

Romul's West (315 Oak St., 541/436-4444, www.romuls.com, 4pm-9pm Sun.-Thurs., 4pm-10pm Fri.-Sat., $13-25) offers high-quality pasta and traditional Italian main courses (osso bucco and veal piccata) in a stylized Roman dining room.

Pacific Northwest

Although the name makes it sound like a brewpub, ★ **Brian's Pourhouse** (606 Oak St., 541/387-4344, www.brianspourhouse. com, 5pm-10pm Sun.-Thurs., 5pm-11pm Fri.-Sat., $12-27) is in fact a restaurant notable for locally sourced seasonal cuisine. Few places in town can match the Pourhouse for sheer culinary creativity, and Brian's has become a local hangout for the under-40, outdoor sports-oriented crowd. The chef offers inventive dishes that combine the best of traditional Asian, European, and nouvelle elements, always with a flair for freshness. Chile-crusted calamari is served with lemon aioli, and Columbia River king salmon comes with Calabrian chilies and succotash.

A stalwart of the Hood River fine dining scene is ★ **Celilo Restaurant and Bar** (16 Oak St., 541/386-5710, www.celilorestaurant.com, 11:30am-3pm and 5pm-9pm daily, $14-24), with a daily changing menu and an updated lodge look that features hefty wood beams and splashes of soothing color. The food is very well executed, with up-to-the-minute preparations such as pickled asparagus and house-made prosciutto and seared albacore tuna with baby turnips and fava bean sauce.

Simon's Cliff House at the Columbia Gorge Hotel (4000 Westcliff Dr., 541/386-5566 or 800/345-1921, www.columbiagorgehotel.com, 7am-2pm and 5pm-10pm Mon.-Sat., 9am-2pm and 5pm-10pm Sun., $18-36) looks east at the Columbia River rolling toward the hotel from out of the mountains, and west toward sunset alpenglow. The menu includes pasta, steaks, Columbia River steelhead and trout, and specialties such as chicken chardonnay and smoked duck breast with sour cherry glaze.

Brewpubs

Hood River and environs have spawned a mini-microbrew scene, with several establishments brewing and selling their own suds. The most famous is the **Full Sail Brewery** (506 Columbia St., 541/386-2247, www.fullsailbrewing.com, 11am-9:30pm daily, $7-15), offering beautiful river views to accompany its renowned ales and soups, salads, and sandwiches. The **Big Horse Brew Pub** (115 State St., 541/386-4411, www.bighorsebrewpub.com, noon-9pm Mon. and Wed.-Thurs., noon-9:30pm Fri.-Sat., noon-8pm Sun., $9-16), in addition to selling its delicious ales (the India Pale Ale is recommended) also serves up a full menu of lunch and dinner items at pub prices; grab a seat by the window for good views.

★ **Double Mountain Brewery** (8 4th St., 541/387-0042, 11am-10pm daily, www.doublemountainbrewery.com, $16-22 for 16-inch pizza) offers excellent beers and a bustling hipster scene in a taproom with thrift store-chic decor. Food choices are simple—mostly grilled sausages and very tasty wood-fired pizza. Lines can get long on weekends—have a plan B if you're in a hurry.

One of Hood River's most recent brewpub additions is **Pfriem Family Brewers** (707 Portway Ave., 541/321-0490, www.pfriembeer.com, 11am-9pm Sun.-Thurs., 11am-10pm Fri.-Sat., $10-18), with Belgian-style brews and a small menu of soups, salads, and sandwiches. Up in tiny Parkdale is **Solera Brewery** (4945 Baseline Dr., 541/352-5500, www.solerabrewery.com, 4pm-10pm Mon.-Tues. and Thurs., noon-10pm Fri.-Sun., $6-10), offering sandwiches, good beers, and a postcard view of Mt. Hood from the back patio.

INFORMATION

The **Hood River County Chamber of Commerce** (at the Hood River Expo Center, 405 Portway Ave., 541/386-2000 or 800/366-3530, www.hoodriver.org) has an extensive array of maps, pamphlets, and other information about the area. They also have a huge 3-D model of the gorge's terrain that is an excellent way to get oriented to local geography. Take Exit 63 off I-84 and head north (toward the river), following the signs to the Expo Center. Another source of local visitor information, although limited to outdoor recreation, is the **National Forest Service Scenic Area Office** (902 Wasco Ave., 541/386-2333). To get there, head down 7th Street until it winds

around to the left, becoming Wasco Avenue, then follow the signs.

GETTING THERE AND AROUND

Greyhound (www.greyhound.com) serves Hood River with three buses daily in each direction, stopping at the former rail station (110 Railroad Ave.). There are no services here, so plan on buying your ticket online or from the bus driver. **Hood River Taxi and Transportation** (1107 Wilson St., 541/386-2255) provides taxi service in and around the city.

HISTORIC COLUMBIA RIVER HIGHWAY AND ROWENA CREST

East of Hood River, the highly scenic route up and over Rowena Crest is a segment of the Historic Columbia River Highway that remains open to motorists. Another section between Hood River and Mosier, the western gateway to Rowena Crest, was closed in the 1950s. However, in the 1990s public officials

Rowena Crest

reopened a five-mile stretch of the route, which contains a number of tunnels, to hikers and bikers, making it possible to view the amazing engineering and craftsmanship of the original 1920s highway.

Historic Columbia River Highway Trail

This five-mile-long segment of the Historic Columbia River Highway is worth a visit. It provides a great walking and biking experience (car traffic is verboten) with the spectacular engineering feat of the reopened **Mosier Twin Tunnels** in the middle. Carved out of solid basalt and adorned with artful masonry work, the highway has become famous for its tunnels. They are about a mile from the trail's east end and 600 feet above the river. To start on the east end, take Exit 69 off I-84, turn right off the ramp, then take the first left on Rock Creek Road. Go under the highway and continue for less than a mile. The parking area is on your left; the highway segment begins across the road.

Access the west-side parking area from downtown Hood River by going to the junction of State Street and Route 35, then head up the hill on Old Columbia River Drive. This road is actually the Historic Columbia River

Highway, officially numbered as U.S. 30. The west-side parking area has a small visitors center with restrooms.

Going west to east allows a hiker, in a mere five miles, to witness a rapid climate and vegetation transition rarely encountered in such a short distance. Starting on the Hood River side, the highway winds its way through lush towering Douglas fir groves. By the time you reach the east side of the tunnels by Mosier, you're in a dry oak savanna-grassland ecosystem.

About halfway down the trail, a short interpretive loop trail has been developed, rewarding hikers with stunning views of this varied and beautiful part of the gorge. Amateurs of geology will marvel at the dramatic precipice located across the river in Washington, visible from the east end. Locally called "Coyote Wall," it's technically part of a big syncline-anticline system in the area.

★ Rowena Crest and Tom McCall Nature Preserve

East of Mosier, a section of the Historic Columbia River Highway begins again for automobile traffic, climbing up over a spectacular volcanic promontory called **Rowena Crest.** For eastbound traffic, this route begins

Tom McCall Nature Preserve

at Mosier, at I-84 Exit 69, while westbound traffic can pick up the route at I-84 Exit 76.

The **Tom McCall Nature Preserve,** a 2,300-acre sanctuary on part of Rowena Crest created by the Nature Conservancy, is the site of a mid-May pilgrimage of wildflower lovers. Because the preserve lies in the transition zone between the wet west and the dry east, several hundred species flourish here, including four that occur nowhere else in the world. In the spring display you'll find yellow wild sunflowers, purple blooms of shooting stars, scarlet Indian paintbrush, and blue-flowered camas. While the flowers are enticing, beware of ticks and poison oak. Of course, as with any nature preserve or public park, enjoy the flowers, but leave them behind for the next person as well.

The Dalles

It hits you shortly after leaving Hood River. Verdant forests give way to scrub oak, which transition to sage and the grasslands of eastern Oregon. You've come to The Dalles, a place Lewis and Clark called the "Trading Mart of the Northwest" in 1805. Instead of seeing a Native American potlatch on the Columbia River, however, the modern visitor will see 10,000 souls living in the industrial hub of the Gorge. If you look carefully, you'll also glimpse Google's multimillion-dollar processor farms near the river.

These days, The Dalles (the name derives from the French word for flagstone) focuses on historical tourism as well as an emerging red-wine grape industry and already-thriving cherry-growing agriculture. The Google facilities provide about 175 jobs in the community.

For a traveler interested in Northwest history, gaining a complete perspective of Oregon's past is impossible without a day trip to The Dalles. Downtown is awash in bits of Oregon's heritage—the Oregon Trail Marker, the stunning 1897 Old St. Peters Landmark church, and the historic Baldwin Saloon. Explore the old Fort Dalles grounds and the Fort Dalles Museum, housed in the original surgeon's quarters from the days when the fort was active. Another early landmark, Pulpit Rock, still stands in the middle of 12th Street, just as it did in the 1800s when the Methodist ministers preached to the Native American population and settlers. Enjoy the work of local artists at The Dalles Art Center, located in the historic Carnegie Library.

The Dalles played a preeminent role in Oregon's early history. Five hundred years ago, nowhere in the Northwest boasted such a cosmopolitan mix of peoples as the area around The Dalles. During the great fall and spring migrations of salmon, the banks of the Columbia River—and particularly those near Celilo Falls, just upstream and now smothered by The Dalles Dam—were lined with many Native American groups trading, fishing, performing ceremonies, gambling, and socializing. Lewis and Clark first passed The Dalles in 1805, and in the 1840s the land route of the Oregon Trail terminated at The Dalles, as the Gorge's high cliffs and rapids precluded further wagon travel along the Columbia.

The first white settlement at this transport hub was a Methodist mission, established in 1838. In 1854, the town of The Dalles was platted, and a town charter was granted in 1857. Then as now, the Gorge was the principal corridor between eastern and western Oregon, and almost all freight bound in either direction passed through The Dalles. Steamboats docked at the riverfront; stagecoaches rattled off to far-flung desert communities. The streets were crowded with miners, ranchers, and traders.

The completion of the railroad and later barge lines through Columbia River reservoirs served to increase freight transport through The Dalles. The area is also the nation's largest

The Dalles

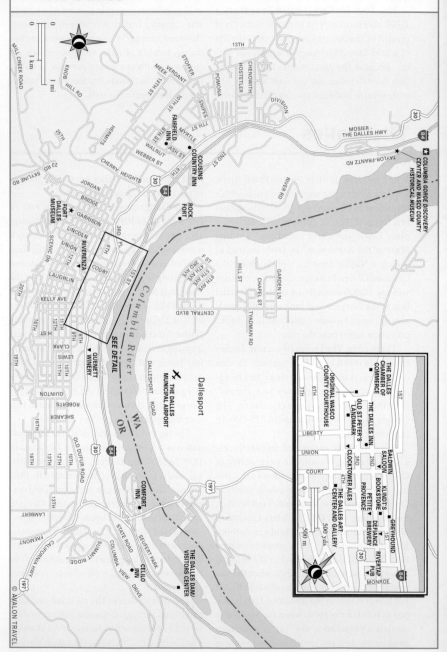

© AVALON TRAVEL

The Surgeon's Quarters at Fort Dalles Museum dates from 1856.

producer of sweet cherries, and orchard workers from Latin America impart the community with cultural influences from their countries of origin. Despite the recreational boom of the last 20 years, The Dalles remains largely hard-working and practical.

SIGHTS

Klindt's Booksellers (315 E. 2nd St., 541/296-3355, www.klindtsbooks.com, 8am-6pm Mon.-Sat., 11am-4pm Sun.) represents a bit of history in The Dalles. Established in 1870, it is the oldest bookstore in Oregon, complete with original wood floors, a high ceiling, and oak and plate-glass display cases.

Fort Dalles Museum

Established in 1850, **Fort Dalles** (15th St. and Garrison St., 541/296-4547, www.fortdalles-museum.org, 10am-4pm daily Apr.-Oct., $5 adult, $4 senior, $1 students 7-17) was meant to protect the incoming settlers along the Oregon Trail from the large Native American presence in the area. At the time it was built,

Fort Dalles was the only U.S. Army garrison between the Pacific Coast and Wyoming.

Of the original 10-square-mile encampment, only a grassy park with the Surgeon's Quarters, dating back to 1856, remains. The wooden structure serves as a museum for armaments, period furniture, and other pioneer items, as well as Native American artifacts. This is Oregon's oldest historic museum, dating back to 1905.

Just down the hill, **Pulpit Rock,** a curious thumb of rock near the corner of 12th and Court Streets, combines geology and theology. From this natural pulpit, early Methodist missionaries preached to the Native Americans. The rock still serves as a pulpit for local Easter services.

★ Columbia Gorge Discovery Center and Wasco County Historical Museum

The **Columbia Gorge Discovery Center and Wasco County Historical Museum** (5000 Discovery Dr. N., Crates Point, three miles west of The Dalles on U.S. 30, 541/296-8600, www.gorgediscovery.org, 9am-5pm daily, $9 adults, $7 seniors, $5 ages 6-16) brings together the rich historical, geological, biological, and cultural legacies of this region. The Discovery Center addresses the region as a whole, articulating a 40-million-year timeline with scale models and videos (as well as simulated "hands-on" experiences) that begins with the cataclysms that created the Gorge on through its Native American occupation to the coming of the pioneers and subsequent domination by European Americans. Along the way, native plants and animals are given attention, along with such diverse activities as road building, orchards, and windsurfing. A cafeteria is located on-site.

Wine-Tasting

The arid hills around The Dalles are home to a number of vineyards, and there's one standout winery right in town. **Quenett Winery** (901 E. 2nd St., 541/298-8900, noon-6pm daily) pours excellent wines in a tasting room that occupies a fantastic space: a renovated, century-old flour mill that has been brought back to life with all of its belts, pulleys, and chutes in place. It's worth a stop just to take in the magnificent infrastructure, but the wine is also a big draw, particularly the round and quenching viognier and velvety Grenache. On most Friday evenings, the winery remains open until 8pm with live music and light food service.

ACCOMMODATIONS

Conveniently located off I-84 Exit 87, the **Comfort Inn** (351 Lone Pine Dr., 541/298-2800, $119-139) has a pool, a fitness facility, and free continental breakfast. Rooms come equipped with microwaves and coffeemakers. **Cousins Country Inn** (2114 W. 6th St., 541/298-5161 or 800/848-9378, www.cousinscountryinn.com, $114-169) is a high-quality motel with an indoor hot tub and an outdoor pool. Guest rooms have microwaves, refrigerators, and coffeemakers; some have fireplaces. The on-site restaurant and lounge is one of The Dalles's most popular.

The new entry in The Dalles is the **Fairfield Inn and Suites** (2014 W. 7th St., 541/769-0753, $119-149), which has spacious and stylish rooms on the west side of town, and has an indoor pool, guest laundry, and free hot breakfast.

At the west end of the historic downtown is **The Dalles Inn** (112 2nd St., 541/296-9107 or 888/935-2378, www.thedallesinn.com, $99-129), a well-maintained motor court with a pool and guest rooms with microwaves, refrigerators, and coffeemakers. It's also within easy walking distance of downtown bars and restaurants. For clean, basic rooms at a good price, consider the **Budget Inn Motel** (118 West 4th St., 541/296-5464, www.motelthedalles.com, $75-99), convenient to historic downtown.

The area's top lodging choice, particularly if you're looking for Gorge views and a cool, sophisticated decor, is the ★ **Celilo Inn** (3550 East 2nd St., 541/769-0001, www.celiloinn.com, $109-139 and up). This unlikely boutique motel sits atop cliffs just east of The Dalles, and makes the most of its modest mid-20th-century heritage through a stylish transformation. Rooms are nicely furnished with a hip, retro-urban design—not something you expect in The Dalles. There's also a patio, an outdoor pool, and a fitness center. All rooms come with mini fridges and microwaves. The only problem is that the Celilo Inn is far from restaurants, but you can't beat the stylish atmosphere.

FOOD

In the heart of downtown, **Petite Provence** (408 E. 2nd St., 541/506-0037, 7:30am-3:30pm Sun.-Wed., 7:30am-5pm Thurs.-Sat., $5-12) is a French-style bakery and coffee shop that also offers sandwiches, soup, and light entrées at lunch.

Baldwin Saloon (1st St. and Court St., 541/296-5666, http://baldwinsaloon.com 11am-9pm Mon.-Thurs., 11am-10pm Fri.-Sat., $8-18) is in an 1876 building that has seen a bit of history—it was built as the dining hall for the local railroad crews. The redbrick interior houses a repository of early-20th-century oil paintings and an 18-foot mahogany bar. Fresh oysters are the house specialty, but the sandwiches, salads, steaks, and burgers are also good.

Downtown, The Dalles has its share of handsome historic structures, and one of the most notable is the 1881 Wasco County Courthouse, topped with a bell tower. After serving as a Masonic hall and funeral parlor, this landmark is now home to **Clock Tower Ales** (311 Union St., 541/705-3590, 11am-9 Tues. and Sun., 11am- 10pm Wed.-Sat., $7-14), a taproom serving over 30 regional brews and light meals such as sandwiches and salads.

The **RiverTap Pub** (703 E 2nd St., 541/296-7870, www.rivertap.com, 11am-10pm Sun.-Thurs., 11am-midnight Fri.-Sat., $8-17) is a convivial tap house with about 20 local brews on draft and a bar, dining room, and large outdoor seating area right on Main St. The menu includes a well-prepared selection of pub grub, with burgers, wraps, and salads.

Defiance Brewery became The Dalles's first brew pub in 2015.

Due to open in late 2015, **Defiance Brewery** (208 Laughlin St., 541/296-2337) is a new craft brewery and tap house right downtown in the historic Stadelman Ice House. Stop by and check it out!

Just up the hill from downtown is one of The Dalles's most captivating breakfast and lunch options, **Riverenza,** 401 E. 10th St., 541/980-5001, 7am-4pm Mon.-Sat., $5-8). In a century-old stone church, this small café offers excellent coffee, pastries, and lunchtime paninis and soups in a transformed religious space, with lovely shady patios off to the side. It's a great spot to recalculate and realize you're in one of the West's oldest settlements.

INFORMATION AND SERVICES

Shortly after you enter town via Exit 82 (City Center exit), stop off at **The Dalles Area** **Chamber of Commerce** (404 W. 2nd St. at Portland St., 541/296-2231 or 800/255-3385, www.thedalleschamber.com) and pick up its pamphlets *The Dalles: Historic Gateway to the Columbia Gorge* and *Walking Tours to Historic Homes and Buildings*. Take a gander at the restored Wasco County Courthouse next door, which was moved from its original location. This court presided over much of the country west of the Rockies in the mid-1800s. At the time, Wasco County comprised 130,000 square miles and included parts of Idaho and Wyoming.

GETTING THERE

Greyhound provides bus service from The Dalles west to Portland and east to Spokane and Boise. The terminal is at 201 Federal Street (541/296-2421).

Mount Hood

Oregon's highest peak, Mount Hood (or "Wy'east," as the region's Native Americans knew it), rises 11,249 feet above sea level less than an hour's drive from Portland and dominates the city's eastern horizon. Like Japan's Mount Fuji, California's Shasta, and Washington's Rainier, Adams, and St. Helens, Hood is a composite volcano (or stratovolcano), a steep-sided conical mountain built up of layers of lava and ash over millennia.

Mount Hood was formed about 500,000 years ago and has since erupted repeatedly, most recently during two periods over the last 1,500 years. Centuries before the first European explorers entered the region, native people of the Pacific Northwest witnessed the mountain's eruptions, and the retelling of the events became lore handed down over generations. According to one legend, Wy'east and Pahto were sons of the Great Spirit, Sahale, who both fell in love with a beautiful maiden named Loowit. She was unable to choose between the two, and the braves fought bitterly to win her affection, laying waste to forests and villages in the process. In his anger at the destruction, Sahale transformed the three into mighty mountains: Loowit became Mount St. Helens, Pahto became Mount Adams, and to the south, Wy'east became Mount Hood.

The first European to report seeing the mountain was British Navy Lt. William E. Broughton, who viewed it in 1792 from the Columbia River near the mouth of the Willamette River. Broughton named the peak after the British Navy's Admiral Samuel Hood, who would never see the mountain himself.

Hood's most recent volcanic episode ended in the 1790s, just prior to the arrival of Lewis and Clark in 1805. But since record-keeping began in the 1820s, no significant volcanic activity has been noted, though in 1859, 1865, and 1903 observers mentioned the venting of steam accompanied by red glows or "flames."

Although the mountain is quiet, volcanologists keep a careful watch on Mount Hood.

Today, the mountain is the breathtaking centerpiece of the Mount Hood National Forest, which embraces 1,067,043 acres of natural beauty and recreational opportunities right in Portland's backyard. Five downhill ski resorts and numerous cross-country trail systems, 1,200 miles of hiking trails, dozens of jewel-like alpine lakes, and more than 80 campgrounds are just the beginning.

SIGHTS
★ Timberline Lodge

Timberline Lodge (six miles north of Government Camp, 503/622-7979 or 800/547-1406, www.timberlinelodge.com) is one of the unquestioned masterpieces of rustic Craftsman design and an object of veneration for those who look back to the Depression-era building boom as a golden age of social and artistic idealism. Over two million people visit Timberline each year, making it one of the top tourist destinations in the state.

When it was built in 1936 and 1937, the four-story 43,700-square-foot log and stone lodge was the largest of the federal Works Progress Administration (WPA) projects in Oregon. It employed up to 500 workers and artists, for whom building Timberline was more than just a job; it was an expression of a cultural ideal. In a pamphlet from that time, one eager observer noted: "In Mt Hood's Timberline Lodge the mystic strength that lives in the hills has been captured in wood and stone, and in the hands of laborer and craftsman, has been presented as man's effort at approximating an ideal in which society, through concern for the individual, surpasses the standard it has unconsciously set for itself."

Nearly every part of the structure and its decor was handcrafted, from the selection of stones in the massive lobby fireplaces to the hand-loomed coverlets on the beds. Every effort was made to harmonize with the natural splendor of the location; stonecutters quarried local stone for the walls, and builders employed locally harvested timber for the floors, staircases, and monumental three-story lobby. The six-sided central tower was designed to echo the peak of Mount Hood; the steeply slanted rooflines are meant to resemble mountain ridges. Even the exterior paint color was specially created to match the hue of mountain frost.

The results of this astonishing attention to detail and handcraftsmanship is vividly on display in the lobby and central foyer. The massive fireplace built of local basalt rises 92 feet through three floors of open lobby; all the furniture in the hotel was made by hand in WPA carpentry halls, fanciful hand-carved animals adorn newel posts and stairways, and murals and paintings of stocky stylized workers grace the walls. It's hard to imagine a more powerful relic of the 1930s' glorification of the worker than this.

The lodge is open to nonguests, so be sure to stop by for a hot chocolate or a meal (there are three dining rooms and two bars). The **Rachael Griffin Historic Exhibition Center,** on the main floor, displays some of the history of the lodge in tools, drawings, weavings, and photographs. A free 30-minute video that illustrates the construction of the lodge is shown daily at 12:30pm in the Barlow Room, and Forest Service rangers offer free tours at 11am, 1pm, 2pm, and 3pm daily.

Cascade Streamwatch

Near the village of Welches, on the west side of Mount Hood, pull off U.S. 26 to visit the **Cascade Streamwatch** at the Wildwood Recreation site (between mileposts 39 and 40). This 0.75-mile, gently rolling and accessible wetlands trail goes through a beautiful second-growth mixed conifer forest along the Salmon River to several viewing windows built into the shoreline embankment, giving visitors a great opportunity to view fish in a natural river. Trailside fish carvings and sculptures along with information placards on forest ecology and salmon spawning enhance the experience, and you may see such species as the giant Pacific salamander, red-legged frog, and coho salmon. While spring and fall spawning seasons are optimal times to see the coho, it's possible to spot fish at other times of the year. The trail is located 39 miles east of Portland on the south side of the highway in the Bureau of Land Management's

Timberline Lodge

Wildwood Recreation corridor (503/375-5646), near the town of Zigzag. A nearby pull-out offers information about Barlow Road, the final leg of the Oregon Trail, which went through these woods.

HIKING

Hikes in the **Zigzag Ranger District** (70220 U.S. 26 E., Zigzag, 541/666-0704 or 503/622-3191 from Portland) are an excellent introduction to the wealth of recreation options in the Mount Hood National Forest off U.S. 26. Whether you're driving the whole **Mount Hood Loop** (U.S. 26-Rte. 35-I-84) or just looking for a nice day trip from the Portland area, the Zigzag District's relatively low elevation and spectacular views of the state's highest mountain can be enjoyed by neophyte hikers or trail-wise veterans.

If you're coming in from the west on Hwy 26, stop at the **Mount Hood Information Center** (65000 U.S. 26 E., Welches, 541/622-4822 or 888/622-4822, www.mthood.info) in the Mount Hood Village Resort on the south side of the highway. This facility will help you get your bearings with a wealth of pamphlets and an information desk. Pick up the free Forest Service flyer *Mount Hood Hikes*.

Salmon River Trail

The **Salmon River Trail** is pretty, easy, and low elevation, meaning that there's no excuse not to hike it. The 33-mile Salmon River is one of the very few waterways protected as a National Wild and Scenic River for its entire length—from its headwaters on Mount Hood to its confluence with the Sandy River near Brightwood. This trail, which runs 14 miles in the Salmon-Huckleberry Wilderness Area but is most often hiked in much smaller sections, runs right alongside the river; hikers can expect to see wildflowers, old-growth Douglas firs, and a number of campgrounds. In fall, enjoy red and gold maples; year-round, giant cedars and firs dominate. Access is easy, especially to the lower portion of the trail. From Sandy, follow U.S. 26 east for 17.9 miles and turn right (south) onto the Salmon

Ramona Falls cascades down a wall of columnar basalt.

River Road. Follow this road five miles to the trailhead.

★ Ramona Falls Trail

The **Ramona Falls Trail,** a 4.5-mile loop to a stunning waterfall, is one of the most popular on Mount Hood. From the trailhead, it initially parallels the Sandy River. In a little more than a mile you'll come to a seasonal bridge over the river with a pretty view of Mount Hood. On the other side of the river, Trail 797 will get you to Ramona Falls in about two miles. The grade of the slope is gentle throughout, and while much of the trail isn't especially scenic (except for the bridge over the Sandy River, June rhododendrons, and views of Mount Hood), Ramona Falls itself makes it all worthwhile.

Here a multitude of cascades course over a 100-foot-high, 50-foot-wide series of basalt outcroppings. This weeping wall is set in a grove of gargantuan Douglas firs. The spray beneath this canopy of trees can reduce the temperature by 20°F, making the place a popular retreat on hot summer days. This trail connects with the Pacific Crest Trail, and backpackers often use it as part of a longer trip.

To reach Ramona Falls, drive 18 miles east of Sandy on U.S. 26 to Lolo Pass Road, close by the ranger station. Turn left (north) and go five miles up Lolo Pass Road; stay right onto Forest Service Road 1825. From here, you'll take the road about four miles to its end.

McNeil Point Shelter

Although the **McNeil Point Shelter** hike is gorgeous and culminates at a cool, old stone shelter, it has some tricky trail nuances and requires a map and consultation, both available at the Mount Hood Information Center. The trailhead is not far from Ramona Falls, making this is a nice follow-up to that hike. (Between the two hikes, you can camp at the McNeil Campground.)

Start at the Top Spur Trailhead. A half-mile up the hiking trail, take a right on the Pacific Crest Trail and keep right, continuing up the trail to a four-way intersection. Views of Mount Hood—and in June, a spectacular wildflower display—will greet you.

The remaining three miles contain some twists and turns (essentially, you're skirting Bald Mountain) that need cartographic clarification from the Forest Service. Be sure to ask the information center as the trail can change from year to year, depending on conditions. Your reward will be breathtaking above-timberline views of the Mount Hood National Forest. This excursion is four miles each way and tame enough for weekend warriors. Just start early to give yourself sufficient daylight.

To reach the McNeil Point trailhead from U.S. 26, turn north onto Lolo Pass Road at Zigzag and follow it four miles. Veer right onto Forest Service Road 1828 and proceed 13 miles until you reach the Top Spur Trailhead 785.

Bigfoot

One of the secrets the Columbia Gorge might share if it could talk would be the whereabouts of Bigfoot, or Sasquatch.

Whether it exists outside the mind or not, the King Kong of the Pacific Northwest forests has attracted to the region everyone from hunters and academics to curiosity seekers and *National Enquirer* reporters. Although the notion of a half-man, half-ape eluding human capture seems implausible at first, a brief look at some of the evidence might convince you otherwise.

Native Americans of the region regarded this creature as a fact of life and celebrated its presence in art and ritual. As recently as the winter of 1991, reports from a remote area of eastern Oregon's Blue Mountains told of more than 60 miles of tracks left in the snow by a large five-toed creature. Scientists on the scene were of the opinion that the pattern of the prints and the gait could not have been faked. A similar conclusion was reached in 1982 about a plaster cast of footprints taken from the same mountain range. A Washington State University professor detected humanlike whorls on the toe portions of the prints, which he said showed that the tracks had to have been made by a large hominid.

Reports and evidence of actual encounters abound in Pacific Northwest annals, compelling the U.S. Army Corps of Engineers to list the animal as an indigenous species, accompanied by a detailed anatomical description. Skamania County, Washington, whose southern border is the Columbia River shoreline, declared the harming of these creatures a gross misdemeanor punishable by a year in jail and a $1,000 fine.

The unwavering belief in Bigfoot and the native insistence that it's a living entity have naturally met with skepticism. But considering that stories about black-and-white bears roaming the alpine hinterlands of China persisted for centuries until the 1936 discovery of pandas, there could be something new under the sun in the 21st century.

Mirror Lake Trail

It's easy to find the trailhead for the popular **Mirror Lake Trail**—it's right on U.S. 26, and it's usually marked by a fleet of parked cars. There's good reason for the crowd: The 1.5-mile trail gains 700 feet in elevation and passes wild rhododendrons and a passel of other wildflowers on the way up to the lake that, as its name suggests, forms a perfect reflecting mirror for Mount Hood. A trail circumnavigates the lake, and ambitious hikers can continue another two miles to the top of Tom, Dick, and Harry Mountain, named for its three distinct, but not very characteristic, summits.

Find the trailhead at the footbridge one mile west of Government Camp on U.S. 26. Because of its popularity, try to do this hike on a weekday.

Timberline Trail

More ambitious trekkers will take on the 40-mile **Timberline Trail,** a three- to five-day backpacking trip usually started at Timberline Lodge. If you undertake this loop, you'll finish up back at the lodge to cool off in the showers or swimming pool. While the alpine meadows on the Timberline Trail are beautiful, consult the rangers to see if water in the half-dozen creeks forded en route is too high during the June-July snowmelt season.

With almost two dozen trails branching off the Timberline, opportunities for shorter day-trip loop hikes abound. Most of the main trail follows the base of the mountain near the timberline at elevations of 5,000-7,000 feet. On the northwest side, however, it drops to 3,000 feet and merges with the Pacific Crest Trail. This means that there's snow on the trail most of the year. Make the trip in the early fall to avoid the crowds; in July and August, the mountain meadows are ablaze with wildflowers.

Backpackers must camp at least 200 feet from water and 100 feet from any trail, mountain meadow, or obvious viewpoint.

Buried Forest Overlook

An easy one-mile round-trip leads to the **Buried Forest Overlook,** which provides a dramatic view of the White River Canyon, where a thick forest was buried during one of the mountain's major eruptive periods 200-250 years ago. Superheated gases blew down giant trees like matchsticks, and in the next instant everything was buried underneath a mixture of water, ash, and mud. The forces of wind and water erosion have since exposed

Above Timberline Lodge the Timberline Trail and the Pacific Crest Trail are one and the same.

the remains of the Buried Forest. To get here, follow one of the trails behind Timberline Lodge up the mountain about 0.25 mile until you reach the Pacific Crest National Scenic Trail. Turn east (right) onto the Pacific Crest Trail and follow it another 0.25 mile or so to the overlook.

Cloud Cap

The best way to get up close and personal with Mount Hood is with a visit to **Cloud Cap**. A beautiful old lodge (now closed) and the entrance to the Mount Hood Wilderness are on the north side of the volcano. To get there, take Route 35 south of Hood River 24 miles to Cooper Spur Road. Drive past the ski area until you come to Cloud Cap at the end of a twisting, 10-mile gravel road. The road is passable only in summer months due to snow at that altitude. From here, hardy adventurers can rub elbows with glaciers, walking up Cooper Spur (a side ridge of Mount Hood) without climbing gear in late summer to almost 8,600 feet above sea level.

SKIING

Wherever you ski here, November-April, be sure to purchase and display a **Sno-Park permit** ($20 for the season, $10 for 3 days,

$7 one-day). Most ski shops near the slopes sell them.

From Portland you can hear road and ski condition reports on KINK 101.9 FM at 6:30 and 7:30am and 12:15pm Monday-Friday December-March. Log on to www.tripcheck.com or call 800/977-6368 for road conditions and traveler advisory information.

In addition to being the state's highest mountain, Mount Hood also boasts the most ski areas—five in all.

Mount Hood Meadows

The mountain's largest and most varied ski area is **Mount Hood Meadows** (503/287-5438, ext. 182, or 800/754-4663, www.ski-hood.com, $74 adults full-day, $59 adults afternoon, $39 children, with discounts if you purchase online), with 2,150 acres of groomed slopes, terrain parks, five high-speed quads, and half a dozen slower lifts. Even with all the lifts, this place is so popular at times you might have to wait. Night skiing is also popular.

Meadows is located 10 miles from Government Camp on Route 35. It's often sunny here on the east slope of the mountain when it's snowing and raining on the west side; call 503/227-7669 for a snow report and

cross-country skiing on Mount Hood

hours of operation. Check the ski area's website for current information about bus transportation from Portland.

Cooper Spur Ski Resort

A popular destination for families and beginners is **Cooper Spur Ski Resort** (541/352-7803, www.cooperspur.com, $32 adults, $28 seniors and youths 7-14). On the northeastern flank of the mountain, 24 miles south of Hood River on Route 35, the location occasionally offers protection from storms and prevailing westerlies, yet has more than enough snow for a good time and is more affordable than the other Mount Hood resorts. However, the trails are only served by a slow double chairlift and a rope tow. Nordic skiers appreciate the **Tilly Jane Trail.**

Mount Hood SkiBowl

Mount Hood SkiBowl (503/658-4385, www.skibowl.com, $50-53 adults, $34-35 night, $31-32 seniors and children) is only 53 miles from metropolitan Portland on U.S. 26 and features the most extensive night skiing in the country. The upper bowl has some of the most challenging skiing and snowboarding to be found on the mountain. In summer, the complex turns into a summer adventure park for bungee jumping, an alpine slide, mountain biking, and much more.

Timberline Ski Area

Timberline Ski Area (503/231-7979 information, 503/222-2211 snow report, www.timberlinelodge.com, $66-72 regular-peak adults age 18-64 full-day or $58-62 afternoon, children age 15-17 regular-peak $56-$59 full-day, $48 children afternoon) is known for its high-elevation Palmer lift and its nearly year-round season.

With the highest vertical drop of any ski area in Oregon (3,600 feet) as well as the highest elevation accessible by chairlift (8,600 feet), 60 percent of Timberline's ski runs are in the intermediate-level category. Timberline has the longest ski season in the nation.

Although you'll rarely find powder conditions at Timberline, the 31 runs are so well groomed that Timberline snow is easily navigable. The chairlifts (six in winter, two in summer) are mostly obscured by trees or topography, so you get a feeling of intimacy with the natural surroundings when you're schussing downhill. You can go up two lifts, enjoying a nearly two-mile-long run that drops 2,500 feet vertically.

The upper Palmer lift, highest on the mountain, is open late spring-fall, when conditions are safe for skiing on the Palmer glacier. The Magic Mile chair, directly below the Palmer, is open to the 7,000-foot level for sightseers as well as skiers ($15 per person).

Located 60 miles east of Portland on U.S. 26, the skiing starts where the trees end. To get here, go east of Government Camp on U.S. 26 and take Forest Service Road 50 for six miles. Check the resort's website for information about bus transportation.

Summit Ski Area

A mile south of the Timberline turnoff on U.S. 26 is **Summit Ski Area** (503/272-0256, www.summitskiarea.com, $35 adults, $25 seniors over 60 or children under age 12), the place for families, beginners, and people who just like to play in the snow. You can ski on beginners' slopes or rent an inner tube to barrel down the gently sloping surrounding hills. Several other good sliding hills are close by. To get to Summit, drive through the town of Government Camp off U.S. 26. Beyond the stores and concessions you'll see a large parking lot on the left side of the road with a structure housing a burger joint and equipment rentals.

Cross-Country Skiing

Across Route 35 from the Mount Hood Meadows turnoff, **Teacup Lake** offers a great network of cross-country skiing trails that are maintained by a club that requests a small donation. Another popular trail that's easy after you get past the first long downhill goes to

Trillium Lake. Find the Sno-Park for this trail about three miles east of Government Camp on U.S. 26.

Rent cross-country skis and get info about current conditions in the town of Sandy at **Otto's** (38716 Pioneer Blvd., 503/668-5947).

CLIMBING

Mount Hood (11,239 feet), the highest mountain in Oregon, has the additional distinction of being the second-most-climbed glacier-covered peak in the world. Nicknamed the Fujiyama of America, Mount Hood offers ascents that cater to everyone, from beginners to advanced climbers. Another similarity to its Japanese counterpart is that only a brief part of the year is safe for climbing, from May to mid- or late July.

Since the summer heat brings the threat of avalanche danger and falling rock hazards, the time of day that you depart is just as important as the time of year. Most expeditions set out in the wee hours of the morning when the snow is firm and rock danger is slighter. Although you won't get as much sleep, you will be able to enjoy beautiful sunrise scenery as you venture to the top.

Unless climbers are very experienced, it is best to go with a guide. All climbers should register at the kiosk by Timberline Lodge before climbing and check out after the climb. While the climb looks like just a few miles on the map, it takes 10-15 hours to make the trip from Timberline Lodge to the top and back. The four primary routes up Mount Hood—**Hogsback, Mazama, Wyeast,** and **Castle Crags**—are all technical climbs; there is no hiking trail to the summit. Having the right equipment means little if you don't know how to use it. That said, all climbers should rent a Mount Hood Locator Unit, or MLU, available at local climbing shops and at the Mount Hood Inn off of U.S. 26 in Government Camp.

Two-day guided climbs are offered by **Timberline Mountain Guides** (541/312-9242, www.timberlinemtguides.com, $590).

ACCOMMODATIONS

Remember that Mount Hood is just over an hour from Portland, so you can always return to the city if you don't want to spend the night on the mountain.

Timberline Lodge

Of all the lodgings on Mount Hood, one is nearly as archetypal as the mountain itself: ★ **Timberline Lodge** (27500 E. Timberline Rd., Government Camp, 503/622-7979 or 800/547-1406, www.timberlinelodge.com, $135-145 w/o bath, $160-340 w/bath). This massive log lodge, built during the Depression by craftspeople put to work by the Works Progress Administration, is one of the best examples of rustic Craftsman style in the world. Timberline gained even more fame when it was used as the setting for the 1983 film *The Shining* (walk by room 217 and recall "redrum, redrum," with a shiver of fright).

One of the many charms of Timberline is the individuality of each room, which range from bunk bed-equipped "chalet rooms," with a bath down the hall, to large fireplace suites. No matter how humble the room, it will have the lodge's signature hand-loomed curtains and handcrafted furniture. Guests also have access to a sauna and the year-round outdoor pool.

The lodge's lobby is a good place to visit even if you aren't a guest. The upstairs Ram's Head Bar is a classic spot for an après-ski or post-hike drink, and the **Cascade Dining Room** (7:30am-10am, 11:30am-2pm, 6pm-8pm Mon.-Fri., 7:30am-10:30am, 11:30am-3pm, 5:30pm-8pm Sun., $20-48) serves outstanding though pricey food.

Adventuresome groups of travelers should check out Timberline's **Silcox Hut** ($165-205pp, includes dinner and breakfast), a spacious but cozy onetime skiers' warming hut perched up the mountain, beyond the main lodge, at 7,000 feet. The hut does have electricity, running water, and toilets, but with its stone walls and big timbers, it definitely has rustic charm. The hut can sleep up to 24 people, and beds are bunk-style, in six rooms. Guests reach the hut either by snowcat or the ski area's Magic Mile chairlift and have the option of skiing back down to the base area in the morning. The hut's host prepares a family-style dinner (typically something like lasagna) as well as breakfast. A minimum of 12 people (16-18 on weekends and holidays) is required to rent the hut; it's also a popular spot for weddings.

Government Camp and Vicinity

Also operated by Timberline Lodge, the **Lodge at Government Camp** (along the Government Camp loop, www.thelodgeatgovernmentcamp.com, $190-245 weekdays, $305-375 weekends, for up to six people, two-night minimum stay) is a rather grand structure that offers eight condo units ranging 2-4 bedrooms. All units are fully furnished and have complete kitchens; guests have access to all facilities at Timberline Lodge.

More conventional lodgings are also available in Government Camp. The **Best Western Mount Hood Inn** (87450 E. Government Camp Loop, 503/272-3205 or 800/443-7777, www.mthoodinn.com, $129-149) is a good bet. If that's too expensive, the venerable **Huckleberry Inn** (88611 E. Government Camp Loop, 503/272-3325, www.huckleberry-inn.com, $90-140) has both standard guest rooms and a slightly funky bunkroom that you can rent for a group of up to 14 people ($185).

A new and outsized condo development, **Collins Lake Resort** (88544 E. Government Camp Loop, 800/234-6288, www.collinslakeresort.com, $189-369 chalet doubles) is in the heart of Government Camp and offers chalets and multibedroom condos. The resort offers a variety of pools and a sauna.

Speaking of housing large groups, cabins are a cost-effective way for groups of three or more to stay in beautiful surroundings near hiking trails, ski slopes, and other outdoor recreation. Some of the most popular and best-situated cabins on the mountain are

those at **Summit Meadow** (503/272-3494, www.summitmeadow.com, $190-265 weekday; $410-625 weekend, minimum two-night stay). The five cabins range from a cozy one-bedroom with a sleeping loft to a large two-bedroom cabin with a loft that'll sleep you and nine of your closest friends. These cabins are located 1.5 miles south of Government Camp in a secluded setting surrounded by national forest. The cabins are open year-round, but in the winter are accessible only by cross-country skiing or snowshoeing in, about 1.5 miles from the Sno-Park.

Mount Hood Village (65000 E. U.S. 26, Welches, 800/255-3069, cabins $68-189) is another good value. Although it is primarily an RV park, it also includes a cluster of wooden cabins and some yurts ($47-65) near the Salmon River. Close by the Forest Service information center and bookstore as well as the Ramona Falls trailhead, Cascade Streamwatch, and the Rendezvous Grill and Tap Room, the resort includes a fitness room and the Courtyard Cafe, which serves breakfast and lunch. Choose between basic "cabins in the woods" sleeping four and large "vacation cottages," with features like hot tubs and saunas.

Cascade Property Management (24403 E. Welches Rd., Suite 104, 503/622-5688 or 800/635-5417, www.mthoodrentals.com) posts dozens of enticing offerings on its website, most located down the mountain around the Sandy River. These cabins come with all the amenities you'd find in a hotel room and then some (firewood and kitchen implements included). Rates vary with the season and the size of the unit. A typical summer rate for a 1,500-square-foot unit with several bedrooms sleeping six might be $235 per night. Rates go as low as $160 for small units to over $500 for larger cabins sleeping more than a dozen people. Many of these cabins enjoy secluded locations, and the rental office provides discounted lift tickets to several Mount Hood ski areas. Look for the rental office just west of the Hoodland shopping center.

For more listings of cabins and property

management companies, see www.mthood.
info.

Camping

Most of the following campgrounds are in
Mount Hood National Forest (503/668-
1700, www.fs.fed.us). Those that accept reservations are so noted; to inquire about
reservations, contact 877/444-6777 or www.
recreation.gov.

Set along the banks of the Salmon River
is **Green Canyon** (Zigzag Ranger District,
65000 E. U.S. 26, Welches, 503/622-3191, May-
mid-Sept., $20-22). Here you'll find 15 camp-
sites for tents and RVs (22 feet maximum),
with picnic tables and grills, piped water, pit
toilets, and firewood available seasonally. The
Salmon River Trail is nearby, and a store and
a café are about five miles away. To get there,
go to Zigzag on U.S. 26 and take Salmon River
Road (Forest Rd. 2618) for four miles to the
campground.

Near the replica of the Barlow Road
Tollgate is **Tollgate Campground** (late May-
mid-Sept., $20-22). Set along the banks of the
Zigzag River, this campground has 15 sites for
tents and RVs up to 16 feet in length. Because
it's close to the Mount Hood Wilderness and
many hiking trails, it's so popular that finding
a campsite without a reservation on a summer
weekend is next to impossible. To get here,
take U.S. 26 one mile past Rhododendron.

Situated on the Clear Fork of the Sandy
River, **McNeil Campground** (May-late Sept.,
$15-17) has a good view of Mount Hood. The
campground has 34 sites for tents and RVs
up to 22 feet in length, with picnic tables and
grills, vault toilets, and firewood available. To
reach the campground, turn onto Lolo Pass
Road (County Rte. 18) at Zigzag and follow it
for four miles. Turn right onto Forest Service
Road 1825 and follow signs to the campground, about a mile farther.

A popular place for a night out in the
woods is **Camp Creek** (late May-late Sept.,
$18-20, reservations accepted). This camp-
ground has 25 sites for tents and RVs up to 22
feet, with piped water, picnic tables, and grills.

Vault toilets and firewood are also available.
Situated along Camp Creek not far from the
Zigzag River, the campground has double
campsites that two parties can share. To get
here, go three miles east of Rhododendron on
U.S. 26 and turn south to the campground.

About one mile down the road from
Timberline Lodge is **Alpine** (July-late Sept.,
$20-22). The high-elevation setting lives up to
the name, with snow remaining on the ground
until late in the summer in heavy snow years.
There are 16 campsites for tents, plus piped
water, picnic tables, and grills. In addition to
easy access to summer skiing up at Mount
Hood, the Pacific Crest Trail passes very close
to the camp.

Near the junction of U.S. 26 and Route 35
is **Still Creek** (mid-June-late Sept., $20-22,
reservations accepted). Here you'll find 27
sites for tents and RVs (16 feet maximum)
with picnic tables and grills. Piped water, pit
toilets, and firewood are also available. The
campground has many large trees and good
fishing, and it is close to a pioneer cemetery
and Trillium Lake. To reach this spot, drive
past Government Camp to Forest Service
Road 2650.

A good place for a base camp for those
who like to canoe is at **Trillium Lake** (late
May-late Sept., $20-22, reservations accepted).
Just 60 miles from Portland, the lake is a great
place for city kids. If they're ages 13 and under,
they don't need a fishing license and may keep
up to 10 fish per day. Crayfish also prowl the
lake bottom awaiting capture. Families appreciate the opportunity to cruise the lake in a
canoe or some other nonmotorized craft. At
night, a new amphitheater hosts campfire programs and nature talks. There are 57 sites for
tents and RVs (40 feet maximum), with picnic tables and grills. Piped water and flush
toilets were installed recently; boat docking
and launching facilities are nearby, but no
motorized craft are permitted on the lake.
To get here, take U.S. 26 two miles southeast
of Government Camp, then turn right onto
Forest Service Road 2656. Proceed one mile
to the campground.

A spot that offers good fishing, swimming, and windsurfing is **Clear Lake** (late May-early Sept., $21, reservations accepted). Here you'll find 28 tent and RV sites (32 feet maximum) with picnic tables and grills. Piped water, vault toilets, and firewood are also available. Boat docking and launching facilities are nearby, and motorized craft are allowed on the lake. To get here, go 11 miles southeast of Government Camp on U.S. 26, then a mile south on Forest Service Road 2630 to the campground.

A midsize county park called **Toll Bridge** (7360 Toll Bridge Rd., Parkdale, 541/352-6300, Apr.-Nov. and off-season weekends, weather permitting, $19-29) is 18 miles south of Hood River on Route 35. This campground has 18 tent and 20 RV (20 feet maximum) sites with electricity, piped water, sewer hookups, and picnic tables. Flush toilets, showers, firewood, a recreation hall, and a playground are also featured. Set along the banks of the Hood River, Toll Bridge includes bike trails, hiking trails, and tennis courts.

Nottingham (15 miles south of Parkdale) and **Sherwood** (11 miles south of Parkdale, Hood River Ranger District, 541/352-6002, www.mthood.info, Memorial Day-Labor Day, $14, no reservations) both include basic amenities. Both are located on the east fork of the Hood River and offer good hiking.

FOOD

Far and away, the top dining choice on Mount Hood is the ★ **Cascade Dining Room** (Timberline Lodge, 27500 E. Timberline Rd., Government Camp, 503/622-0700, 7:30am-10am, 11:30am-2pm, 6pm-8pm Mon.-Fri., 7:30am-10:30am, 11:30am-3pm, 5:30pm-8pm Sat.-Sun., $20-48, dinner reservations recommended). As at most of the top Oregon restaurants, the chefs here prepare meals to showcase regional foods—in this case, often wild mushrooms from Mount Hood's forested slopes and huckleberries from its meadows. Even if a full dinner doesn't fit into your plans or your budget, lunch in this huge timbered dining room is a hearty treat—take a break from skiing for some polenta served with roasted vegetables or a salmon BLT.

Down the hill at the west end of Government Camp, find the **Mount Hood Brewing Company** (87304 E. Government Camp Loop, Government Camp, 503/272-0102, www.mthoodbrewing.com, 11am-9pm daily, $8-14). Sandwiches, pasta, chili, and design-your-own pizza can be washed down with microbrews (try their own oatmeal stout), espresso drinks, and local wines. Also in town, the **Huckleberry Inn** (88611 E. Government Camp Loop, Government Camp, 503/272-3325, www.huckleberry-inn.com, $6-14) deserves mention if only for its 24-hour, 7-day-a-week restaurant—and, you guessed it, wild huckleberry pie.

INFORMATION

The **Mount Hood Information Center** (65000 E. U.S. 26, Welches, 503/622-4822 or 888/622-4822, www.mthood.info, 9am-5pm daily) is staffed by Forest Service rangers who can provide information about local places of interest. This is really an excellent stop, even for people who travel up to the mountain quite often.

The Willamette Valley

Highlights

★ **Carlton:** The area around Carlton in Yamhill County is a great place to tour some of the nation's top pinot noir and pinot gris wineries (page 155).

★ **McMinnville:** Wine country's largest town has charm to spare, excellent restaurants, and relatively inexpensive lodging (page 160).

★ **State Capitol:** The art alone in the Oregon capitol is worth the trip (page 166).

★ **Mount Angel Abbey:** This hilltop abbey is a good place for both quiet reflection and architectural tourism; the splendid library was designed by famed Finnish architect Alvar Aalto (page 176).

★ **Silver Falls State Park:** Aren't waterfalls what Oregon is all about? Here, a seven-mile trail passes 10 waterfalls (page 177).

★ **McKenzie River National Recreation Trail:** This 26-mile trail follows the McKenzie, with waterfalls cascading over lava rocks and lush green streamside vegetation (page 207).

★ **Oakridge Mountain Biking:** In the hills just outside this working-class mill town, you'll find some of the state's best mountain biking (page 212).

The Willamette Valley, the primary destination of the Oregon Trail pioneers, is one of the most productive agricultural areas in the world. This is meaningful not only to long-ago pioneers or present-day residents, but to nearly every visitor. Wineries abound, as do plant nurseries and U-pick berry fields. During the spring, the tulip and iris fields are beautiful, especially when (as is common) they're backed up by a rainbow.

The Willamette Valley is also the population nexus of Oregon, supporting 100 cities (including Portland) and 70 percent of the state's population. (Geographically speaking, Portland is part of the Willamette Valley, but is considered separate.) Nonetheless, once you get south of Portland's suburbs, you'll seldom have the feeling of being in a big metropolis. The broad Willamette Valley, 130 miles long and at some points nearly 60 miles wide, rolls out between the rugged Coast Range and the glaciered peaks of the Cascades. Along the way, the Willamette collects the waters of other large rivers, including the McKenzie, the Santiam, and the Yamhill. By the time it joins the Columbia, the Willamette is the 10th largest river in the United States.

PLANNING YOUR TIME

Although the Willamette Valley runs only about 100 miles from Portland to Eugene, it's worth exploring the back roads and smaller towns off I-5. Start with the valley's wine country. By spending the night along the way, you can relax and enjoy a dinner at one of the area's excellent restaurants. The greatest concentration of wineries is between Newberg and McMinnville in the North Willamette Valley Wine Country. If hiking is more your focus, head to Silver Falls State Park, home to 10 large waterfalls and within striking distance of the Oregon Garden (an 80-acre botanical paradise) and lovely Mount Angel Abbey (a working monastery).

Because of its youthful energy and high-quality facilities, Eugene—home to the University of Oregon—is a good place to spend a day or two, both to experience the town and to explore the river valleys and west slopes of the Cascades that lie to its east.

Previous: the Willamette Valley wine country; The Willamette Queen. **Above:** fishing the McKenzie River.

The Willamette Valley

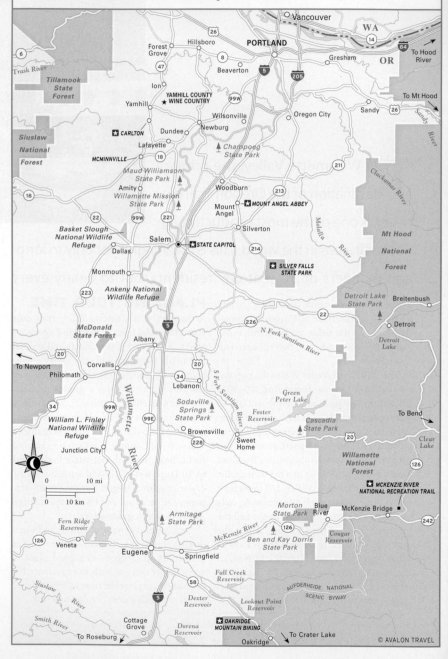

© AVALON TRAVEL

North Willamette Valley Wine Country

Although excellent wine is a product of southern Oregon and the Columbia Gorge, Oregon's most noted wine production area includes vineyards southwest of Portland in the hills of the northern Willamette Valley, particularly in Yamhill and southern Washington counties. This is where the rich soil and long, gentle growing season create conditions sustaining the greatest concentration of vineyards in the Pacific Northwest. In summer, Oregon's northern latitude makes for long sunny days without excessive heat, while slow-cooling fall days allow grapes to produce a complexity of flavor by inhibiting high sugar concentrations while maintaining the natural acidity of the grape.

While the Willamette Valley is known as one of the major pinot noir-producing regions in the world, local wineries also put out pinot gris, pinot blanc, chardonnay, gamay, Riesling, Gewürztraminer, sparkling wine, sauvignon blanc, cabernet, merlot, and other offerings.

Even locals find it difficult to keep up with the burgeoning northern Willamette Valley wine scene, with some 300 vineyards and wineries gracing the rolling hills. **Willamette Valley Wineries** (503/646-2985, www.willamettewines.com) maintains an excellent website. Look for their very handy map and guide distributed free at most wineries. **Travel Yamhill Valley** (503/883-7770, www.travelyamhillvalley.org) is another good source for winery, dining, and accommodations information.

Wine-Tasting

Tasting rooms in Oregon range from no-frills makeshift back rooms to relatively grand affairs. There's usually a tasting fee ($5-20), often waived with a minimum wine purchase. Wineries are generally open 11am to 4pm-5pm daily. If you have your heart set on visiting a particular winery, call in advance to confirm hours and details.

Some of the smaller and more exclusive wineries don't offer regular tastings, or offer them only by appointment. Since these wineries have no tasting staff on hand, don't be surprised if recreational visits are gently declined.

tasting pinot noir in the Willamette Valley

Almost all wineries are open on Memorial Day and Thanksgiving weekends, when thousands of people throng into the region to visit their favorite wineries.

Given the proximity of Portland, many folks visit the wine country as a day trip. Should you care to extend your stay, there are plenty of bed-and-breakfasts and a smattering of hotels, including a luxurious resort, to accommodate you.

Wine Tours

Hiring a tour company has become an increasingly appealing (and safer) alternative for many wine enthusiasts. Several wine tour companies offer door-to-door service from Portland hotels. One particularly well-established company is **Grape Escape Winery Tours** (503/283-3380, www.grapeescapetours.com), which offers a variety of private and semiprivate custom tours. Tours are also provided by **Eco Tours of Oregon** (503/245-1428, www.ecotours-of-oregon.com), which offers van tours with Portland-area pickup and returns.

If you're already in the Willamette wine country, contact **Insiders Wine Tour** (503/791-0005, www.insiderswinetour.com), based in McMinnville. Thanks to inside connections, you may get the chance to visit wineries not typically open to the public.

There are more exciting ways to tour wine country than in minivans. **Equestrian Wine Tours** (503/864-2336 or 866/864-5253, www.equestrianwinetours.com) provides horseback winery tours on Tennessee Walking horses. Hikers should consider the guided walking tours of Dundee-area wineries offered by **Oregon Dundee Hills Walking Wine Tours** (503/789-7629, markdartist@gmail.com). Portland-based **Pedal Bike Tours** (503/243-2453, http://pedalbiketours.com) offers bicycle tours of wine country. Want to see wine country from the air? Tour the wineries via helicopter with **Precision Aviation Tours** (503/537-0108, www.flyprecision.com) or ride a hot-air balloon with the folks at **Vista Balloons** (503/625-7385

or 800/622-2309, www.vistaballoon.com, Apr.-Oct.).

Getting Around

An unavoidable factor of Willamette Valley wine country: The traffic is often horrendous, particularly along Route 99W, the valley's main drag. (The route is also patrolled heavily by police.) The only way to avoid the traffic is to steer clear of it as much as possible.

The tour described below is an alternate route, following four-lane U.S. 26 west from Portland to Forest Grove and dropping south into the heart of the wine country through back roads. To return to Portland without driving in 99W traffic, there are a couple of choices. From Newberg, follow Hwy. 219 south across the Willamette River and turn left on McKay Rd., passing near Champoeg State Park and the verdant fields of French Prairie, before joining I-5 at Exit 278.

FOREST GROVE AND GASTON

The northernmost reach of Willamette Valley wine country is in Forest Grove, about 20 minutes west of Portland off U.S. 26. Forest Grove is home to Pacific University, the oldest chartered university in the western United States, established in 1849.

Wineries

David Hill Winery (46350 NW David Hill Rd., 503/992-8545, www.davidhillwinery.com) is a picturesque vineyard with a long history. The first wine grapes were planted here in the 19th century, and the vineyard produced award-winning wines until Prohibition. Part of the vineyards were replanted in the 1960s, making these some of the oldest pinot noir vines in the state.

Montinore Estate (3663 Dilley Rd., 503/359-5012, www.montinore.com) is just south and west of downtown Forest Grove. As is the practice at many Willamette Valley vineyards, the grapes are grown sustainably using biodynamic practices.

Don't leave Forest Grove without stopping

in at **Sake One** (820 Elm St., 503/357-7056, www.sakeone.com) to taste the local sake and tour the sakery. The sakes, made from California rice, range from the delicate Noma sake, a fresh, unpasteurized wine that's available only at the tasting room, to the milky coconut-scented Pearl and the clean-tasting, very slightly fruity Asian pear sake.

Seven miles south of Forest Grove on Route 47, the tiny town of Gaston is home to **Elk Cove Vineyard** (27751 NW Olson Rd., 503/985-7760, www.elkcove.com), one of the oldest and most respected operations in the area. Elk Cove's tasting room is especially lovely, and year-in and year-out their pinot gris is one of the region's best.

Accommodations and Food

One of the McMenamin brothers' largest projects is the **Grand Lodge** (3505 Pacific Ave., Forest Grove, 503/992-3442, www.mcmenamins.com), a hotel, brewpub, and entertainment center on 13 acres of lawns and gardens that was converted from a vast Masonic and Eastern Star retirement complex built in 1922. The Grand Lodge includes four bars and restaurants, a movie theater, a 10-hole disc golf course, and 77 hotel rooms. Guest rooms are a mix of European style ($65-120 w/o bath) or king rooms with private baths ($210). The entire establishment is rich with the McMenamins' signature funkiness; it's a fun place to stay if you appreciate old-fashioned atmosphere in an updated, but not utterly transformed, hotel.

YAMHILL

In the Chahalem Mountains east of Yamhill is the small **Ribbon Ridge American Viticulture Area**, one of Oregon's most heralded wine regions and home to some of the state's top-rated wines.

Wineries

From Yamhill, head east on Route 240 to find the hillside vineyards of **Willakenzie Estate** (19143 NE Laughlin Rd., 503/662-3280, www.willakenzie.com). In a beautiful rural setting,

the winery's three-level gravity-fed design (a tradition in Burgundy) ensures gentle handling of the wine. Along with several different estate-grown pinot noirs, the tasting room pours lush pinot gris, pinot blanc, and gamay noir. Top-flight pinot noir is the specialty at highly recommended **Penner-Ash Wine Cellars** (15771 NE Ribbon Ridge Rd., 503/554-5545, www.pennerash.com). Atypical for the region, wines made from viognier and syrah grapes are also featured. One of Oregon's pioneer wineries, **Adelsheim Vineyard** (16800 NE Calkins Ln., 503/538-3652, www.adelsheim.com) was established in 1971 and produces a range of single-vineyard pinot noir wines as well as excellent Chardonnay, pinot gris, and rarely encountered auxerrois wines.

★ CARLTON

South on Route 47, Carlton is a quiet, picturesque farm village with 18 wine-tasting rooms within a stroll of each other, plus good restaurants.

Wineries

Just north of Carlton, the cooperative **Carlton Winemakers Studio** (801 N. Scott St., 503/852-6100, www.winemakersstudio.com) houses 14 boutique wineries, including Andrew Rich, Hamacher, and Bachelder. The studio helps up-and-coming winemakers by providing space and support. Sharing the same access road, **Cana's Feast** (750 W. Lincoln St., 503/852-0002, www.canasfeastwinery.com) focuses on Mediterranean grape varietals, including sangiovese, barbera, nebbiolo, and primitivo. Occasional weekend meals are served on the winery's grape-shaded veranda during summer and early fall; call to inquire.

In Carlton's old rail station is **Ken Wright Cellars** (120 N. Pine St., 503/852-7010, www.kenwrightcellars.com), with six vineyard-specific pinot noir bottlings. Wright also makes a delicious Bordeaux-style Claret from eastern Washington fruit under the Tyrus Evan label. In a handsome old brick storefront,

Scott Paul Wines (128 S Pine St., 503/852-7300, http://scottpaul.com) specializes in elegant, French-style pinot noir. From Carlton, leave Hwy. 47 and travel the back roads. Follow Main Street east from downtown; it eventually turns into Hendricks Road and passes through lovely rolling hills lush with vineyards on the way to Newberg. Stop at **Lemelson Vineyards** (12020 NE Stag Hollow Rd., 503/852-6619, www.lemelsonvineyards.com, 11am-4pm Thurs.-Mon.) to taste outstanding organic pinot noir and pinot gris wines.

Accommodations

Within easy walking distance to tasting rooms and restaurants in downtown Carlton, the **Carlton Inn** (648 W. Main St., 503/852-7506, www.thecarltoninn.com, $170-200) is a charming B&B in a 1915 farmhouse-style home. Each of the four guest rooms has a private bath.

In the hills east of Carlton, the **Lobenhaus B&B** (6975 NE Abbey Rd., 503/864-9173, www.lobenhaus.com, $150-225) is a tri-level lodge on 27 acres with comfortable accommodations and a peaceful atmosphere. Each guest room has a private bath and a deck overlooking a spring-fed pond. Guests can take advantage of two common living rooms, each with a TV and a fireplace.

Nearby, the ★ **Abbey Road Farm B&B** (10501 NE Abbey Rd., 503/852-6278, www.abbeyroadfarm.com, $225) has elegant rooms located in—no joke—converted grain silos. This upscale B&B (think fine art and 600-thread-count sheets) is very nicely appointed; the 82-acre Abbey Road Farm has cherry orchards, goats, llamas, donkeys, and gardens; guests can ask about assisting with farm chores. In the interest of your own relaxation, there are no phones or TVs. In addition to the B&B rooms, the farm also rents a three-bedroom, two-bath home with full kitchen ($450, or $375 with two-night minimum).

Food

A great place for country-style French food

is **Cuvée** (214 W. Main St., 503/852-6555, www.cuveedining.net, 5:30pm-9pm Wed.-Sat., 5pm-8pm Sun., $21-27). French standards include *coquilles* St. Jacques; make sure to check out the sautéed oysters with horseradish sauce as an appetizer. Three-course fixed-price dinners ($30, reservations recommended) are offered Wednesday, Thursday, and Sunday nights.

For a lighter meal, head to **The Horse Radish** (211 W. Main St., 503/852-6656, www.thehorseradish.com, noon-3pm, Sun.-Thurs., noon-10pm Fri.-Sat., $6-12), a deli with good soups and sandwiches, plus a large selection of cheese—perfect for a picnic. A phalanx of local wines is available by the glass or bottle, and there's live music on weekend evenings.

NEWBERG

Busy Route 99W runs through the heart of Newberg, and the suburbs to the east are an unattractive sprawl. But Newberg is central to many wineries and home to the luxurious Allison Inn and Spa, one of the most impressive hotels in Oregon.

Wineries

The old redbrick downtown offers a number of tasting rooms, including the outstanding **Chehalem Vineyards** (106 S. Center St., 503/538-4700, www.chehalemwines.com). Chehalem produces estate pinot noir from three different American viticulture areas, giving you a chance to taste different *terroirs* side-by-side. Also good here are Rieslings and an unusual gamay-pinot noir blend.

Two miles east of Newberg is another wine country pioneer, **Rex Hill Vineyards** (30835 Rte. 99W, 503/538-0666 or 800/739-4455, www.rexhill.com), with excellent pinot noir and chardonnay. The tasting room is itself worth a visit; fashioned from an old prune- and nut-drying shed, it now features Persian rugs, antiques, an ornately carved front door, and a stone fireplace, all set in the midst of lovely gardens. Although generally not available for tasting, Rex Hill's popular and reasonably priced distribution line, **A to Z Wineworks,** is sold here.

Like most Willamette Valley wineries, **Bergström Wines** (18215 NE Calkins Ln., 503/544-0468, www.bergstromwines.com) is a family-run business, crafting pinot noir and chardonnay from the grapes grown in their five vineyards. Their tasting room is northwest of town, just south of Bald Peak.

Accommodations

If wine country B&Bs aren't your style, the **Best Western Newberg Inn** (2211 Portland Rd., 503/537-3000, www.bestwestern.com, $99-109) offers an indoor pool and hot tub in addition to well-appointed rooms.

The wine country's most opulent place to stay is the ★ **Allison Inn** (2525 Allison Ln., 503/554-2525 or 877/294-2525, www.theallison.com, $390-625), one of the finest hotels in all of Oregon. Set amid five acres of pinot noir vineyards, the Allison is a monumental structure of stone and wood, with sweeping wine country views from its many terraces and balconies. Each spacious guest room has a gas fireplace, soaking tub, large flat-screen TV, bay window seats, private terrace or balcony, and beautiful furnishings and art, all from local artists. Facilities are

top-notch and include Jory Restaurant, a casually elegant dining room with a noted wine list. The lounge features live music on weekend evenings. Perhaps most impressive is the 15,000-square-foot spa and fitness center, with indoor pool, steam room, sauna, and a dozen treatment rooms. With its Gold LEED certification, the Allison is not only a temple of refinement, it's easy on the earth.

Food

Defining itself as a "neighborhood kitchen," **Recipe** (115 N. Washington St., 503/487-6853, www.recipenewbergor.com, 11:30am-9pm Tues.-Sat., $19-29) is a friendly restaurant that welcomes you whether you are looking for a lunchtime sandwich ($9 13), a glass of wine, or a five-course meal. The menu features local and seasonal ingredients prepared with rustic, handmade aplomb.

A quiet block off busy Main Street, the **Painted Lady** (201 S. College St., 503/538-3850, www.thepaintedladyrestaurant.com, 5pm-10pm Wed.-Sun., tasting menu $85) is a highly regarded bastion of multicourse fine dining with a menu featuring the best of local farms. Located in an elegant Victorian home, the restaurant's seasonally changing menu features such delicacies as roasted rabbit

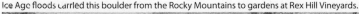

Ice Age floods carried this boulder from the Rocky Mountains to gardens at Rex Hill Vineyards.

GLACIAL ERRATIC BOULDER

THIS BOULDER WAS CARRIED HERE FROM THE ROCKY MOUNTAINS IN A PIECE OF AN ICEBERG DURING THE LAKE MISSOULA FLOODS AT THE END OF THE ICE AGE

roulade with morels or foie gras with apple butter and red-onion jam.

It's worth searching out **Subterra** (1505 Portland Rd., 503/538-6060, www.subterrarestaurant.com, 11:30am-close daily, $21-27), tucked behind Mike's Pharmacy and underneath the Dark Horse Wine Bar, for dinners ranging from "adult mac and cheese BLT" to seared scallops served on brussels sprout slaw. Of course, local wines are given the spotlight and can be enjoyed with small plates as well as entrées.

The beautifully furnished **Jory Restaurant** at the Allison Inn (2525 Allison Ln., 503/554-2525 or 877/294-2525, www.theallison.com, 6:30am-10:30am, 11:30am-2pm, 5:30pm-9pm Mon.-Sat., 9am-2pm, 5:30pm-9pm Sun., $32-45) offers sweeping views of wine country plus elegant preparations of hearty regional cuisine. Local and seasonal specialties include salmon, lamb, venison, and wild mushrooms. It's very entertaining to sit at the kitchen bar and watch the chefs in action. Or book the Chef's Table in the kitchen itself, where the chef will prepare a special dinner for up to 10 lucky diners. The wine list offers many rare and acclaimed bottles from both Oregon and France.

DUNDEE

At one time, Dundee was noted mostly for its filberts (known to most of the world as hazelnuts) and the roadside Dundee Nut House. Now the town is famous for the abundance of wineries in the hills above town. Some of Oregon's top-rated wines are grown in the Dundee Hills American viticulture area, but drive around—you'll still see filbert orchards.

No one would characterize Dundee as a charming town, mostly because busy Route 99W funnels an incredible amount of traffic right through its heart (a traffic bypass has been in the works for a long time but is yet to materialize). But with good restaurants and some excellent lodging options, Dundee offers many reasons to pull off the road and explore.

Wineries

Midway between Newberg and Dundee is **Duck Pond Cellars** (23145 Rte. 99W, 503/538-3199, www.duckpondcellars.com), which produces wines from both Oregon- and Washington-grown grapes. If you're a price-driven wine shopper, note that this is the place to pick up some less expensive (but still very drinkable) wine.

Downtown Dundee may not seem to be much more than an intersection, but look more carefully and you'll see a number of wineries and tasting rooms scattered along the road. A favorite stop is **Dobbs Family Estate** (240 SE 5th St., 503/538-1141, www.dobbsfamilyestate.com), where winemaker Joe Dobbs crafts high-end vintages on the Dobbs Family label and delicious entry-level wines on the Wine by Joe label.

Located in an old farmhouse, the **Argyle Winery** (691 Rte. 99W, 503/538-8520, www.argylewinery.com) tasting room is the place to sample sparkling wine good enough to have graced the Clintons' White House table (and a certain travel writer's wedding reception). It is the state's leading producer of sparkling wine in the tradition of French champagne. At the center of Dundee is the **Ponzi Wine Bar** (100 SW 7th St., 503/554-1500, ponziwinebar.com), where you can taste a selection of wines from Ponzi Vineyards, one of Oregon's oldest and most respected wineries (the actual vineyards are west of Portland). A number of other small wineries are also represented here, and you can order a sandwich or snack to accompany your wine. If you're growing weary of the subtle and nuanced wines of the Willamette Valley and long for hearty, heavier wines, stop at **Zerba Cellars** (810 Hwy. 99 W., 503/537-9463, www.zerbacellars.com). This tasting room in downtown Dundee is an outpost of the Zerba winery near Walla Walla, and offers tastings of their Rhone-style wines, as well as delicious sangiovese.

As Dundee's Ninth Street turns west, it turns into Worden Hill Road, a thoroughfare that climbs up through miles of vineyards.

This is, more or less, the glory road of Oregon wine.

Though the tasting room is new (and spectacular), the vineyards at **Winderlea Wine Co.** (8905 NE Worden Hill Rd., 503/554-5900, http://winderlea.com) date from the 1970s and produce some of the region's most compelling wines. Just up the road is one of Oregon's largest and oldest (dating from 1967) wineries, **Erath Winery** (9409 NE Worden Hill Rd., 503/538-3318, www.erath.com). Erath's wood-paneled tasting room sits high in the Red Hills of Dundee, where beautiful picnic sites command an imposing view of local vineyards and the Willamette Valley. Although Erath is no longer family-owned, its new owner, Washington's Ste. Michelle Wine Estates, is considered to have done a good job at maintaining Dick Erath's legacy.

Lange Estate Winery and Vineyards (18380 NE Buena Vista Dr., 503/538-6476, www.langewinery.com) is an excellent place to try handcrafted pinot noir, chardonnay, or pinot gris. If you want a behind-the-scenes experience, private tours and tastings are available for $40 per person.

Sokol Blosser Winery (5000 Sokol Blosser Ln., 503/864-2282, www.sokolblosser.com), two miles south of Dundee (follow signs), is another of Oregon's pioneer wineries. Its strikingly beautiful tasting room is perched on top of a hillside planted with grapes. In addition to acclaimed pinot noir, the chardonnay is especially recommended. Also good is the rosé of pinot noir.

On the southern flanks of the Dundee Hills is another clutch of notable vineyards. **Domaine Drouhin** (6750 Breyman Orchards Rd., 503/864-2700, www.domainedrouhin.com/en, 11am-4pm daily) is the Oregon outpost of France's famed Drouhin family, making excellent pinot noirs in the Burgundy style. Multi-award-winning **Domaine Serene** (6555 NE Hilltop Ln., 503/864-4600, www.domaineserene.com, 11am-4pm daily) is one of Oregon's top producers of ultra-premium wines. This is a must-sip for any serious wine lover.

Accommodations

Although it's right in the busy center of Dundee, the 20-room **Inn at Red Hills** (1410 N. Rte. 99W, 503/538-7666, www.innatredhills.com, $179-249) is a gracious and relaxing place to stay. There is a good restaurant on the main floor and other excellent dining choices within walking distance.

Just up the road from Sokol Blosser, at the crest of the Dundee Hills, **Wine Country Farm Cellars** (6855 Breyman Orchards Rd., 503/864-3446 or 800/261-3446, www.winecountryfarm.com, $150-225) combines wine-growing with homey bed-and-breakfast accommodations. Views stretch from Salem to Mount Jefferson over miles of vineyards. Watch the pinot noir grow, take a hike, get a massage, or ride horseback to neighboring wineries. Guest rooms all have private baths and wireless Internet. While not the last word in upscale luxury, Wine Country Farm is noted for its friendly welcome and relaxed farm-like atmosphere.

The area's top lodging choice is the nine-room ★ **Black Walnut Inn** (9600 NE Worden Hill Rd., 503/429-4114 or 866/429-4114, www.blackwalnut-inn.com, $279-529), a villa-like complex that looks like it's been transported from Tuscany (but with all the modern luxuries). The rooms are large and very comfortable, most with wondrous views across the vineyards to Willamette Valley. Rates include a multicourse breakfast and an afternoon of appetizers and wine tasting.

Food

One of the wine country's top restaurants, ★ **Tina's** (760 Rte. 99W, 503/538-8880, www.tinasdundee.com, 11am-2pm, 5pm-close Tues.-Sat., 5pm-close Sun.-Mon., $24-40) is right on the main drag in Dundee; look for a small red structure across from the Dundee fire station. Tina's uses the freshest Oregon ingredients to create simple yet elegant fare. This intimate institution is a gem, as one bite of the pan-fried oysters will tell you. (Come for the oysters, stay for the beef short ribs braised in chocolate-red wine sauce.) In what can only be interpreted as a good sign, it is common to see local winemakers hanging out at the tiny bar, sampling vintages from the wide-ranging wine list.

Affiliated with Ponzi Vineyards, **Dundee Bistro** (100-A SW 7th St., 503/554-1650, dundeebistro.com, 11:30am-close daily, $14-30) is a reliable spot for top-notch but not overly expensive food. The emphasis is on fresh and regional cooking, including delicious pizza, house-made pasta, and main courses such as roast pork loin with applewood-smoked bacon. The wine list is both tempting and reasonably priced.

Red Hills Provincial Dining (276 Hwy. 99W, Dundee, 503/538-8224, www.redhillsdining.com, 5pm-9pm Tues.-Sat., 5pm-8pm Sun., $24-32) is a cozy, charm-filled restaurant that uses fresh local ingredients to create award-winning French- and Italian-inspired food.

At the false-fronted **Red Hills Market** (155 SW 7th St., 971/832-8414, www.redhillmarket.com, 7am-8pm daily, $5-14), you can load up a picnic basket with tasty sandwiches, buy local wine and artisanal cheese, or settle in for a delicious, casual meal. Wood-fired pizzas are a menu stronghold, but there's also the veggie-laden breakfast bowl, with bacon, eggs, cheese, and spinach. Upstairs, find a wine tasting room and a cooking school.

In tiny Dayton, six miles south of Dundee off Highway 18, the ★ **Joel Palmer House** (600 Ferry St., 503/864-2995, www.joelpalmerhouse.com, 4:30pm-9:30pm Tues.-Sat., $20-37, reservations recommended) is considered one of Oregon's finest restaurants and historic homes—it's on the Oregon and the National Historic Registers *and* is top-rated by such publications as *Wine Spectator*. Many dishes include wild mushrooms; this is a touchstone restaurant for lovers of fungi. Indulge your passion for mushrooms with the $85 five-course mushroom madness dinner (must be ordered by everyone at your table).

LAFAYETTE

While cruising the wine country, antiques collectors can pull off Route 99 into the town

The Red Hills Market makes a good lunch stop in Dundee.

of Lafayette to visit **Lafayette Schoolhouse Antiques** (748 Rte. 99W, 503/864-2720, 10am-5pm daily), where Oregon's largest antiques market can be found in the old schoolhouse, mill, and auditorium. Imagine 10,000 square feet of antiques spread over three floors in a 1910 building, with an antique furniture showcase next door.

Just north of Lafayette, wine tasters can enjoy the beautiful tasting room and one of the most panoramic views in the valley at **Anne Amie Vineyards** (6580 NE Mineral Springs Rd., 503/864-2991, http://anneamie.com), where you'll also find top-notch pinot noir, pinot blanc, and pinot gris.

★ McMINNVILLE

By far the largest town in the wine country, with a population of some 33,000, McMinnville is also one of the most appealing. Though surrounded by grim big-box development, the charming turn-of-the-20th-century downtown is lined with excellent restaurants, wine bars, boutique shopping, and a superlative organic grocery and health food store. McMinnville makes a great spot to spend the night; there are a wide range of lodging choices and enough fine restaurants to tempt diners into lingering on another night just to sample another good meal.

Another very compelling reason to visit McMinnville is the **Evergreen Aviation and Space Museum** (500 NE Captain Michael King Smith Way, 503/434-4180, www.evergreenmuseum.org, 9am-5pm daily, $25 adults, $24 seniors, $23 children ages 5-16), just off Route 18 south of McMinnville. This massive complex features two separate museums. The Aviation Museum houses the *Spruce Goose*, the giant wooden seaplane built for billionaire Howard Hughes in the 1940s. (The plane, which Hughes called a "flying boat," flew only once for approximately one minute.) In addition to the *Goose*, the museum houses many other aircraft, including funky, hand-built planes, bombers, and large cargo planes. Next to this vast hangar is yet another complex home to the Space Museum, which celebrates the history of space exploration and travel. In addition, you'll find an **IMAX theater** (tickets $11 adults, $10 seniors, $9 children ages 5-16), a number of dining options, and a wine-tasting room.

As if this weren't enough, the enormous 70,000-square-foot **Wings and Waves Water Park** (10am-6pm Mon.-Fri., 10am-7pm Sat.-Sun., summer, weekends only winter, museum only: $12; museum and water park: $27 under 42 inches, $32 over 42 inches) features a children's museum focusing on hydrology and the power of water plus 10 waterslides. You can't miss it; it's the building with a Boeing 747 on its roof.

Wineries

McMinnville offers several wine-tasting rooms (and a brewpub) right in town, in addition to those found in the surrounding hills.

Third Street is the main street downtown, lined with trees and lots of wine-tasting action. A good place to start is the **Willamette Valley Wine Center** (300 NE 3rd St.,

503/883-9012, http://wvv.com/mcminnville, 11am-6pm Mon.-Wed., 11am-8pm Thurs.-Sat., noon-6pm Sun.), operated by Willamette Valley Vineyards, which offers wine-tasting and sales; there are always a few bottles from guest wineries around the valley available to sample along with Willamette Valley Vineyards wines.

More than almost any other winemaker, David Lett of **Eyrie Vineyards** (935 NE 10th St., 503/472-6315, www.eyrievineyards.com, noon-5pm daily) was responsible for shepherding Oregon's fledgling wine industry. Eyrie started up in 1966 and produced the Willamette Valley's first pinot noir and chardonnay as well as the first pinot gris in the United States. The winery, set in an industrial area, is a bit hard to find, but well worth the effort to taste some of the most refined of all Oregon wines.

Yamhill Valley Vineyards (16250 Oldsville Rd., southwest of McMinnville off Rte. 18, 503/843-3100, yamhill.com, 11am-5pm daily) is set amid an oak grove on a 200-acre estate and features a balcony overlooking the vineyard. This winery's first release, an '83 pinot noir, first distinguished itself at a 1985 tasting of French and Oregon vintages held in New York City. Since then, the winery has been a leader in producing high-quality pinot noir as well as Riesling and pinot gris.

Festivals and Events

McMinnville's biggest annual event is the mid-May **UFO Festival,** a McMenamins-sponsored event that began as a way to honor a 1950 UFO sighting by two McMinnville residents. Along with guest speakers, expect to see lots of quite elaborate costumes, a parade, and music.

Oregon's top wine festival is the annual **International Pinot Noir Celebration** (503/472-8964 or 800/775-4762, www.ipnc.org). More than 70 U.S. and international pinot noir producers are on hand for symposia, tastings, and winery tours. More than 50 chefs prepare wine-focused meals, many held at invitation-only winery events.

The three-day festival takes place at the end of July on the Linfield College campus in McMinnville. While the cost of registration ($1,095) is prohibitive for all but the most serious oenophiles, tickets to the final tasting can be purchased separately for $125. Register well in advance; this event always sells out.

Accommodations

McMinnville has the largest selection of lodging choices in wine country. If the high price of plush inns and B&Bs has you looking for a standard motel, this is the place to go.

For inexpensive lodgings, reserve a room at McMinnville's **Motel 6** (2065 SW Hwy. 99 W., 503/472-9493, $78) with an outdoor pool. Step up to the **GuestHouse Vineyard Inn** (2035 S. Rte. 99W, 503/472-4900, www.guesthouseintl.com/hotels/McMinnville, $110-129), a pet-friendly place with free breakfast and an indoor pool and hot tub. Another standard hotel that's a good bet if you're traveling with a dog is the **Comfort Inn** (2520 SE Stratus Ave., 503/472-1700, www.comfortinn.com, $115-155). **Red Lion Inn and Suites** (2535 NE Cumulus Ave., 503/472-1500, www.redlion.com, $80-135) has spacious, well-furnished rooms with an indoor pool.

If you're in McMinnville to enjoy the restaurants and nightlife on Third Street, you should stay downtown. McMenamins' **Hotel Oregon** (310 NE Evans St., 503/472-8427 or 800/472-8427, www.mcmenamins.com, $83-150) has the same spirit of fun, funky art, and good food and drink as other outposts of the Brothers McMenamin empire. Built in 1905, Hotel Oregon has updated and comfy guest rooms (some with private bath, most with shared bath, no TVs), and an outdoor rooftop bar, making this a winner for travelers looking for a relaxed good time. If traveling with a group of friends, inquire about the five rooms that share a private interior patio. Pets are permitted in a few of the rooms.

The top lodging in downtown McMinnville is the ★ **3rd Street Flats** (219 NE Cowls St., 503/857-6248, www.thirdstreetflats.com, $190-265, discounts for week-plus stays),

with 11 flats in two locations at the center of town (four are above a historic 1885 bank building, the rest in a converted Odd Fellow Lodge). Each flat is designed by a different local decorator and filled with regional art; all have full kitchens and living rooms, and the larger units have separate dining rooms. The showcase is the corner Retreat flat, with a fireplace and 750 square feet of living space. These highly original units (some sleep up to six) are perfect for cooks, as well as friends traveling together.

A short drive from McMinnville is the **Youngberg Hill Vineyards and Inn** (10660 SW Youngberg Hill Rd., 503/472-2727, www.youngberghill.com, $249-349), set atop a range of hills carpeted with vineyards. Excellent views take in the Coast Range, Mount Jefferson, Mount Hood, and the Willamette Valley, as seen from the rooms or from the covered decks that surround the inn. The eight rooms are large and nicely furnished; guests are treated to a wine-tasting of estate-grown wines plus a multicourse breakfast.

Food

For variety and quality, McMinnville has the best and liveliest dining scene in the Willamette Valley wine country, much of it centered on the pleasant, leafy downtown area on Third Street. Be aware that many of the top restaurants are closed on Monday.

If you're looking to provision a picnic or pick up some healthy snacks, **Harvest Fresh Grocery** (251 NE 3rd St., 503/472-5740, 8am-8pm Mon.-Fri., 8am-7pm Sat., 10am-7pm Sun.) is a well-stocked natural foods store with a deli and salad bar.

A major eating and entertainment anchor on Third Street is the **Hotel Oregon** (310 NE Evans St., 503/472-8427 or 800/472-8427, www.mcmenamins.com, 7am-11pm Sun.-Wed., 7am-midnight Thurs., 7am-1am Fri.-Sat., $8-17), McMinnville's outpost of the local McMenamins microbrew chain. In addition to the bar and dining room (characteristically decorated with over-the-top

You'll find good food in McMinnville.

they also serve good sandwiches and breakfast pastries.

A good spot for breakfast or lunch is **Community Plate** (315 NE 3rd St., 503/687-1902, www.communityplate.com, 7:30am-3:30pm daily, $5-9), which combines old-school diner cooking with an intense commitment to local and sustainable ingredients. Celebrate the local with a filbert butter and jam sandwich.

The commitment to local farmers and producers is sharply in focus at chef-owner Eric Bechard's much-lauded restaurant ★ **Thistle** (228 NE Evans St., 503/472-9623, www.thistlerestaurant.com, 5:30pm-close Tues.-Sat., $24-27), where the daily-changing menu features the bounty of farms, pastures, and waters within a 45-mile radius of the restaurant. The chalkboard menu doesn't distinguish between large and small plates, so it's easy to sample a number of dishes. An evening's choice may include gnocchi with fava beans, morels, tomato, and watercress; salmon with sweet peppers, fennel, and green olives; or elk with winter squash, kale, and huckleberry sauce. The wine list is divided between local and French wines.

For decades, ★ **Nick's Italian Cafe** (521 3rd St., 503/434-4471, nicksitaliancafe.com, 11am-3pm and 5pm-9pm Tues.-Sat., noon-8pm Sun., 5pm-9pm Mon., $15-28), had the well-deserved, outsize reputation as the best restaurant in wine country, with a wine list that was both extensive and distinctive. Now under second-generation ownership and with a new, fresher approach to Italian food, Nick's is better than ever, with house-made pasta such as lasagna with Dungeness crab, wild mushrooms, and pine nuts, and main courses such as calamari, clams, and sea scallops in leek and potato broth.

A top choice for a casual meal is ★ **La Rambla** (238 NE 3rd St., 503/435-2126, www.laramblaonthird.com, 11:30am-2:30pm and 5pm-close daily, tapas $4-11), an excellent Spanish restaurant that invites you to graze through a series of tapas and small plates. Feast on paella ($19 small, $32 large) or an

panache), there are many other quirky spaces in which to eat and drink. Stop in at the famous rooftop bar or the cellar bar (usually only open on weekends) when the hotel features live music—sometimes several bands at once in different venues. The pub grub here isn't exactly sophisticated (burgers, pizza, sandwiches), but when accompanied by a pint of McMenamins' ale, it's hard not to enjoy yourself.

Another brewpub is on the east end of downtown, in a former rail warehouse. **Golden Valley Brewery** (980 NE 4th St., 503/472-2739, www.goldenvalleybrewery.com, 11am-10pm Mon.-Thurs. 11am-11pm Fri.-Sat., 11am-9pm Sun., $9-17) offers beef from the owner's own Angus herd, vegetables from the kitchen garden, and most everything else is made in-house. The menu features soup, salads, and sandwiches, and the quality of the food is high; craft brews are also excellent.

Get your coconut macaroon fix at **Red Fox Bakery** (328 NE Evans St., 503/434-5098, redfoxbakery.com, 7am-4pm Mon.-Sat.);

assortment of traditional Spanish tapas. The wood-paneled, candle-lit dining room is flanked by a long copper bar, a perfect spot for a romantic dinner.

Traditional French provincial cooking is available at **Bistro Maison** (729 NE 3rd St., 503/474-1888, www.bistromaison.com, 11:30am-2pm and 5:30pm-9pm Wed.-Thurs., 11:30am-2 and 5pm-9pm Fri., 5pm-9pm Sat., noon-7pm Sun., $18-27), a charming farmhouse-like restaurant that serves delicious standards such as coq au vin, confit de canard, and steak tartare.

AMITY

At the southern edge of Yamhill County is the tiny community of Amity. In the steep hills east of town are a number of wineries. About five miles southwest of Amity is the **Priory of Our Lady of Consolation** (23300 Walker Ln., 503/835-8080, www.brigittine.org), a monastery for Brigittine monks. The monks fund the monastery in part through the sale of handmade fudge and other candies, available for sale at the **monastery store** (9am-5pm Mon.-Sat., 1pm-5pm Sun.). Visitors are welcome to attend mass (8am Mon.-Sat., noon Sun.).

Wineries

A classic Yamhill County winery is **Amity Vineyards** (18150 Amity Vineyards Rd. SE, 503/835-2362noon-5pm Wed.-Sun.). The tasting room is in a huge old barn on a 500-foot hill looking out over vineyards to the Coast Range. Amity, which was founded in 1974, is one of Oregon's oldest wineries and still has a homespun feel that belies its excellent wines.

The nearby **Kristin Hill Winery** (3330 SE Amity Dayton Hwy., 503/835-0850, www.kristinhillwinery.com) specializes in a traditional "Methode Champenoise" sparkling wine and a sweet port. Picnickers are welcome.

Northeastern Willamette Valley

Much of Oregon's early history played out on the fertile banks of the Willamette River between present-day Portland and Salem. Settlers made a break from the British Hudson's Bay Company and established an American-style provisional government. Over 160 years later, these Willamette Valley towns are still mostly small and the surrounding countryside is lush, inviting a ramble through history, particularly on a bicycle.

CHAMPOEG STATE HERITAGE AREA

Along the banks of the Willamette River, just southeast of Newberg on Route 219, is **Champoeg** (pronounced sham-POO-ee or sham-POO-eck; 503/678-1251, www.oregonstateparks.org, visitors center 9am-5pm daily, $5 day-use fee), often touted as the birthplace of Oregon. Far more than just a historic site, Champoeg is a beautiful park with broad meadows dominated by massive oak trees—it's a wonderful place for a walk or bike ride. The name Champoeg means "field of roots" in Chinook, referring to the camas coveted by Native Americans, who boiled it to accompany the traditional salmon feast.

This park commemorates the site of the 1843 vote to break free from British and Hudson's Bay Company rule and establish a pro-American provisional government in the Oregon country. At the time, Champoeg was the center of settlement in the Willamette Valley, and the smattering of settlers here were almost exactly evenly split between newly arrived Americans and British and French Canadian former employees of the Hudson's Bay Company.

In addition to a visitors center, the grounds contain several historic buildings, including the Old Butteville Jail (1850) and a one-room schoolhouse. The **Newell House Museum**

Champoeg State Park has trails along the Willamette River.

To reach Champoeg State Park, take I-5 Exit 278 and follow a rural route five miles to the park visitors center. The 568-acre park is equidistant from Portland and Salem along the Willamette River.

If you enjoy Champoeg and its mix of history and pastoral scenery, consider touring the **French Prairie Loop,** a 40-mile byway that passes through idyllic farmland and takes in a number of towns founded by the French Canadian traders, such as St. Paul, Donald, and Butteville. St. Paul is known for the Fourth of July **St. Paul Rodeo** (www.stpaulrodeo.com), which includes a fireworks display, barbecue, and art auction. French Canadian trappers from the Hudson's Bay Company started settling here in the 1820s and 1830s, establishing the first farms and villages in the Willamette Valley. This is an especially popular route for **bicyclists,** as the route is largely flat and traffic is light. Pick up a map and brochure at the Champoeg State Park visitors center.

(503/678-5537, newellhouse.com, 11am-3pm Fri.-Sun. Mar.-Oct., $4 adults, $3 seniors, $2 children), a replica of a 1852 house, showcases Native American artifacts and a collection of inaugural gowns worn by the wives of Oregon governors. The **Pioneer Mothers Cabin** replicates the dwellings in the Willamette Valley circa 1850. In addition to the historical exhibits, Champoeg features a botanical garden of native plants as well as four miles of hiking and biking trails beginning in the Riverside day-use area and heading to the historic Butteville Store, now an ice cream parlor.

Camping

Champoeg State Park (503/678-1251 or 800/452-5687, www.oregonstateparks.org, $19 tents, $26-28 RVs, $40-50 yurt or cabin) has year-round camping and is one of the few campgrounds within easy driving distance (25 miles) of Portland. Add beautiful Willamette River frontage and prime bike-riding on the nearby country roads, and you might consider this the consummate budget alternative to a night in the city or a pricey wine country B&B.

Salem

The used-car lots and fast-food outlets encountered on the way into Salem off I-5 contrast with the inspiring murals and displays in the capitol, where it is comforting to be reminded of Oregon's pioneer tradition and proud legacy of progressive legislation. Downtown Salem has had a bit of a renaissance in recent years; after visiting the capitol, walk a few blocks west past lovely old buildings, shops, and restaurants toward the Willamette River.

SIGHTS
★ State Capitol

If visiting the **state capitol** (900 NE Court St., 503/986-1388, www.oregonlegislature.gov, 7:30am-5pm Mon.-Fri., free) strikes you as the kind of saccharine excursion best reserved for a first-grade class trip, you're in for a pleasant surprise. The art deco-style capitol building is filled with attractive murals, paintings, and sculptures of seminal events in the state's history. The capitol is located on Court Street between West Summer and East Summer Streets, just north of Willamette University.

Atop the capitol dome is a gold-leafed bronze statue of a bearded, ax-wielding pioneer. Massive marble sculptures flank the main entrance—*Covered Wagons* on the west side, *Lewis and Clark Led by Sacagawea* on the east. Maps of the Oregon Trail and the route of Lewis and Clark are visible on the backs of the statues. The symbolism is sustained after you enter the double glass doors to the rotunda. Your eyes will immediately be drawn to a bronze state seal, eight feet in diameter and set into the floor, which juxtaposes an eagle in flight, a sailing ship, a covered wagon, and forests. The 33 marble steps beyond the cordoned-off emblem lead up to the House and Senate chambers and symbolize Oregon's place as the 33rd state to enter the Union. Four large murals adorning the rose travertine walls of the rotunda illustrate the settlement and growth of Oregon: Robert Gray sailing into the Columbia estuary in 1792; Lewis and Clark at Celilo Falls in 1805; the first European women to cross the continent being welcomed by Dr. John McLoughlin in 1836; and the first wagon train

The Capitol Mall is particularly lovely when the cherry trees bloom.

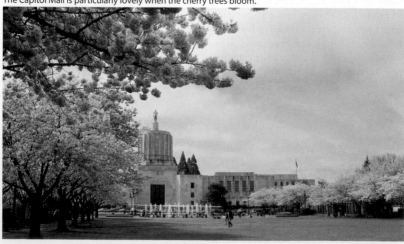

Salem

To
Interstate 5

D ST NE

99E

99E

221

SILVERTON RD

OREGON
STATE
FAIRGROUNDS

22

MAP AREA

CENTER ST

MUSEUM OF
MENTAL HEALTH

99E

22

BEST WESTERN
MILL CREEK INN

COMMERCIAL ST

5

CHURCH ST

COTTAGE ST

SUMMER ST

UNION ST

★ GILBERT HOUSE
CHILDREN'S MUSEUM

To Route 22W

MARION ST

GREYHOUND

CENTER ST

Riverfront
Park

FRONT ST

CHEMEKETA ST

BIBIM BAP
HOUSE

WINTER ST

★ WILLAMETTE
QUEEN

VENTI'S
CAFE

GOVERNOR'S
CUP

ELSINORE
THEATRE

★ STATE CAPITOL

COURT ST

Willson
Park

★ State Capitol

Capitol
Park

COURT ST

CASCADE BAKING
COMPANY

AMADEUS

THE KITCHEN

ARCHIVE
COFFE & BAR

SUPREME COURT
BUILDING

STATE ST

12TH ST

13TH ST NE

14TH ST

STATE ST

★ SALEM
CAROUSEL

WILD
PEAR

STATE ST

LA CAPITALE

HALLIE FORD
MUSEUM OF ART

SUPREME COURT
BUILDING

FERRY ST

22

99E

WINTER ST

WILLAMETTE

Word of
Mouth

To

GRAND HOTEL

22

TRADE ST

99E

UNIVERSITY

★ WILLAMETTE
HERITAGE
CENTER

FERRY ST

Willamette River

COMMERCIAL ST

LIBERTY ST

HIGH ST

CHURCH ST

PRINGLE PARKWAY

MILL ST

BELLEVUE ST

AMTRAK

13TH ST

OAK ST

OAK ST

SALEM HOSPITAL

CAPITOL ST

UNIVERSITY ST

99E

To Hwy 5
and Route
22E

22

LESLIE ST

MISSION ST

KEARNEY ST

BUSH HOUSE
AND PARK

★ DEEPWOOD
ESTATE

HINES ST

SAGINAW ST

COMMERCIAL ST

LIBERTY ST

HIGH ST

BUSH ST

OWENS ST

0   200 yds

0   200 m

© AVALON TRAVEL

on the Oregon Trail in 1843. The best part of the capitol is the legislative chambers, up the sweeping marble staircases.

Near the ceiling in the Senate and House chambers are friezes depicting an honor roll of people who influenced the growth and settlement of Oregon. Included are Thomas Jefferson, who sanctioned the Lewis and Clark expedition, and Thomas Condon, native son and naturalist extraordinaire. In both legislative chambers look for forestry, agricultural, and fishing symbols woven into the carpets; murals about the coming of statehood are behind the speakers' rostrums.

If you don't want to roam independently, free half-hour-long building **tours** are given on the half-hour 10:30am-2:30pm on weekdays, January-November.

A tower at the top of the capitol building gives a superlative view of the valley and surrounding Cascade peaks, worth the 121-step climb from the fourth floor. Tower tours depart hourly 10am-2pm on weekdays June-September (closed when the temperature reaches 90°F). Also worth a look is the ongoing exhibit of outstanding Oregon artists in the governor's ceremonial office upstairs. Downstairs is a café where visitors can eavesdrop on legislators and lobbyists. On the west side of the building (Court St. entrance) is an indoor visitors information kiosk.

To get to the Oregon State Capitol from I-5, take Exit 253 to Route 22 West. Take the Willamette University/State Offices exit and follow the signs for 12th Street/State Offices. Turn left onto Court Street.

Willamette University

Willamette University (900 State St., 503/370-6300, www,willamette.edu), just south of the Capitol Mall, is the oldest institution of higher learning west of the Mississippi. It began as the Oregon Institute in 1842, a school that Methodist missionary Jason Lee founded to instill Christian values among the settlers. Over the years, Willamette University has turned out its share of Oregon politicos, including longtime senators Mark Hatfield

and Bob Packwood. It also has to be one of the prettier campuses in the nation and has an exceptionally good art museum.

The **Hallie Ford Museum of Art** (700 State St., 503/370-6855, www.willamette. edu, 10am-5pm Tues.-Sat., 1pm-5pm Sun., $6 adults, $4 seniors, $3 educators or college students, free to all on Tues.) features Native American baskets and a third-century Buddhist bas-relief from Pakistan. Asian pieces are also prominent. Contemporary work—much of it very high caliber—is exhibited on a rotating basis.

Willamette Heritage Center

Just east of Willamette University, a complex of historic buildings along an old millstream make up the **Willamette Heritage Center** (1313 Mill St. SE, 503/585-7012, www.willametteheritage.org, 10am-5pm Mon.-Sat., $7 adults, $6 seniors, $4 students with ID, $3 children ages 6-17, free to all on Tues.). Its centerpiece is the reconstructed Thomas Kay Woolen Mill. The oldest frame house in the Pacific Northwest and water turbines converting fleece into wool fabric are interesting, and the local fiber arts guild uses the building for classes. Several historic homes, including the 1841 Jason Lee House and a Methodist Parsonage, which were part of a mission to the Native Americans, have been moved to this site.

To get to the museum from I-5, exit at Route 22, go west on Mission Street for two miles to the 13th Street overpass, turn north onto 12th Street, and go west on Mill Street. If you arrive by Amtrak, Mission Mill is within walking distance.

Deepwood Estate

The historic **Deepwood Estate** (1116 Mission St. SE, 503/363-1825, historicdeepwoodestate.org, gardens dawn-dusk daily, house tours on the hour 9am-noon Wed.-Mon. May-Sept., noon-3pm Wed.-Sat. Oct.-Apr., $6 adults, $5 seniors, $4 students, $3 youth 6-15) features tours of an elegant 1894 Queen Anne-style home with hand-carved woodwork, gorgeous stained-glass windows, and a well-marked nature trail. English formal gardens here were designed in the 1930s by the Pacific Northwest's first women-owned landscape architecture firm; the Pringle Creek Trail's native flora and the public greenhouse's tropical plants are also worth visiting. Parking is at 12th and Lee Streets near the greenhouse.

Bush House and Park

Bush House Museum (600 Mission St. SE, 503/363-4714, http://salemart.org, hourly tours 1pm-4pm Wed.-Sun. Mar.-Dec., $6 adults, $5 seniors, $4 students, $3 children ages 6-15) is located in 80-acre **Bush Pasture Park** off Mission, High, and Bush Streets. This 1877 Victorian with many original furnishings is the former home of pioneer banker and newspaper publisher Asahel Bush, who once wrote about his competitor, "There's not a brothel in the land that would not have been disgraced by the presence of the *Oregonian*." Even if you're not big on house tours, the Italian marble fireplaces and elegant walnut-and-mahogany staircase are worth a look. Besides being a sylvan retreat for picnickers and sports enthusiasts, the Bush Pasture Park is home to the **Bush Barn Art Center** (541/581-2228, 10am-5pm Tues.-Fri., noon 5pm Sat.-Sun., free). Next to the Bush House, this center features two galleries with monthly exhibits and a classy gift shop. To get there from I-5, take Exit 253 and drive two miles west on Route 22 (Mission St.). Turn south on High Street and enter the park on Bush Street, one block south of Madison.

Oregon State Hospital Museum of Mental Health

If you've seen the movie made from Ken Kesey's *One Flew Over the Cuckoo's Nest,* you have have an idea of what the **Oregon State Hospital Museum of Mental Health** (2600 Center St. NE, 971/599-1674, http://oshmuseum.org, noon-4pm Tues., Fri., Sat., $4 adults, $3 seniors and students, $2 youth 6-18) is like—the movie was filmed in this imposing brick building, which started accepting patients in 1883. Patients were confined to the hospital both voluntarily and by commitment, and their ailments ranged from alcoholism to dementia to "mania." Upon entering the museum, visitors are issued an ID badge with the name of a patient, staff member, or visitor; information about these individuals is revealed in museum exhibits. Exhibits look at conditions that patients were treated for, treatments offered (including straitjackets, lobotomies, ice baths, and sterilization, as well as those considered to be more progressive and humane), life on the ward, and the Cuckoo's Nest movie.

Riverfront Park

Downtown Salem is bordered to the west by the Willamette River, and **Riverfront Park** is a good place for a stroll, a riverboat excursion, or a ride on the **Salem Carousel** (101 Front St. NE, 503/540-0374, www.salemcarousel.org, 10am-7pm Mon.-Sat., 11am-6pm Sun. June-Sept., 10am-6pm Mon.-Thurs., 10am-7pm Fri.-Sat., 11am-5pm Sun. Oct.-May, $1.50). It's no antique—it was built in the late 1990s—and the carousel horses were hand-carved by volunteers.

Along the river near the carousel is the *Willamette Queen* (200 Water St. NE, 503/371-1103, www.willamettequeen.com), a stern-wheeler that cruises the Willamette year-round. Lunch cruises are offered noon-1pm Wednesday-Sunday ($25 adults, $16 children ages 4-10); one-hour afternoon cruises without food are less expensive (2pm, $12 adults, $6 children) and allow you to eat at a good restaurant a short walk away in downtown. Dinner and Sunday brunch cruises are also offered. This is a good way to get a decent look at the river and, if you're lucky, some of its wildlife.

The **Gilbert House Children's Museum** (116 Marion St. NE, 503/371-3631, www.acgilbert.org, 10am-5pm Sun.-Fri., 10am-7pm Sat., $8 visitors ages 3-59, $6 seniors, $4 children ages 1-2) inspired by A. C. Gilbert, a Salem native whose many inventions included the Gilbert Chemistry Set and the Erector Set, is a cheerful cluster of restored Victorians with hands-on activities incorporating art, music, drama, science, nature, and outdoor play. If you don't have participatory inclinations, you can still enjoy fascinating exhibits like the one dedicated to A. C. Gilbert, whose Olympian athletic exploits and proficiency as a world-class magician were overshadowed by his inventions.

Enchanted Forest

Seven miles south of Salem off I-5 on Exit 248 is the **Enchanted Forest** (8462 Enchanted Way, Turner, 503/371-4242, www.enchanted-forest.com), one man's answer to Walt Disney. In the 1960s, an enterprising Oregonian single-handedly built a false-front Western town, a haunted house, and many more attractions here. You can visit the old woman who lived in the shoe, the seven dwarves' cottage, or Alice in Wonderland's rabbit hole. It's a little dated, but still popular with kids.

The park has a few schedule quirks; it's best to check the website if you are going to be visiting 5pm-6pm. Basically, it is open 10am-5pm or 6pm daily March 15-March 31; weekends only in April; daily May-Labor Day; weekends only in September; closed October-March 15th. Admission is $10.95 for adults, $9.95 for seniors and children ages 3-12, $1-4 extra for many rides.

Gardens

Schreiner's Iris Gardens (3625 NE Quinaby Rd., 503/393-3232, www.schreinersgardens.com, 8am-dusk) is one of the world's largest iris growers; visit mid-May through the first week of June to take in the peak blossom seasons. Schreiner's is seven miles north of Salem next to I-5.

Wine and Beer

Some of Oregon's best wine is produced within a few miles of the State Capitol. **St. Innocent Winery** (5657 Zena Rd. NW, 503/378-1526, www.stinnocentwine.com, 11am-5pm daily) is just a few miles from downtown and is known for its good wines and sustainable farming. In the same neighborhood, **Witness Tree Vineyard** (7111 Spring Valley Rd. NW, 503/585-7874, www.witnesstreevineyard.com, 11am-5pm Tues.-Sun. May-Oct.), named for an ancient oak that towers over this lovely vineyard, is a small producer of top-notch pinot noir and chardonnay.

Due west of Salem, you'll find **Firesteed Cellars** (2200 N. Rte. 99W, Rickreall,

Head to Riverfront Park for a carousel ride.

The Willamette Valley is one of the world's best hop-growing regions.

the hops grow, taste beer, and grab a meal made from farm crops. Seven varieties of hops grow here by the Willamette River. Farm tours are offered at 1pm and 3pm on Saturday and Sunday.

SPORTS AND RECREATION
Bicycling

Although Salem is not the cycling paradise that you'll find in the nearby Willamette Valley cities of Portland, Eugene, and Corvallis, it is possible to have some fun on two wheels. The best news is the trail through Riverfront Park and the **Union Street Railroad Bicycle and Pedestrian Bridge** over the Willamette River (otherwise hard to cross without a car). The bridge links Riverfront Park with Wallace Marine Park on the west side of the river. Another good place to cycle, skate, or walk is **Minto-Brown Island Park** (2200 Minto Island Rd. SE), a large natural park with 20 miles of trails and an off-leash dog park. Find it along the east bank of the Willamette River south of the capitol area; a footbridge connects it to the south end of Riverfront Park.

ENTERTAINMENT AND EVENTS

Salem's recreational mix belies its reputation for being a town dedicated to legislation and little else. The **Elsinore Theatre** (170 High St. SE, 503/375-3574, www.elsinoretheatre. com) is a nicely restored vintage theater and downtown cultural venue that features music and dance performances and classic films as well as live theater. Other local venues include the L. B. Day Amphitheater at the fairgrounds, which hosts big-name acts; brewpubs featuring live music; and Salem Riverfront Park, which hosts summertime concerts.

Five miles west of downtown, the **Pentacle Theatre** (324 52nd Ave. NW, 503/364-7121, www.pentacletheatre.org) hosts an award-winning eight-play season.

The **Salem Art Association** (600 Mission

503/623-8683, www.firesteed.com, 11am-5pm daily), with some of the region's most affordable (but still delicious) wines, and **Eola Hills Wine Cellars** (501 S. Rte. 99W, Rickreall, 503/623-2405, www.eolahillswinery.com, 10am-5pm daily), one of the area's pioneering wineries, which has many vineyard holdings and reasonably priced wine.

A few miles south of town, just off I-5, **Willamette Valley Vineyards** (8800 Enchanted Way SE, Turner, 503/588-9463 or 800/344-9463, www.wvv.com, 10am-6pm Sat.-Thurs., 11am-8pm Fri.) is one of the state's largest wineries, with great views and a classy tasting room. Free tours are offered every day at 2pm; private tours ($20) are available by appointment and include a private tasting and cheese tray.

South of Salem, about seven miles southeast of the town of Independence, thoughts turn to beer. Stop by **Rogue Farms Hopyard** (3590 Wigrich Rd., Independence, 503/838-9813, www.rogue.com, 11am-9pm Sun.-Thurs., 11am-10pm Fri.-Sat.) to watch

St., 503/581-2228, http://salemart.org) puts on the mid-July **Salem Art Fair and Festival**, with 200 artists, performing arts, food, children's activities, a five-kilometer run, an Oregon authors' table, wine and cheese tasting, and art technique demonstrations.

The **Oregon State Fair** (2330 NE 17th St., 503/947-3247 or 800/833-0011, www.oregonstatefair.org) is an annual celebration held in Salem during the 12 days prior to Labor Day. Here you can admire prize-winning cattle, sheep, bunnies, quilts, and marijuana plants; ride carnival rides; watch dogs jump from a dock; get your tongue pierced; or attend a concert. The best way to get there off I-5 is via Exits 253 or 258. Signs point the way. Admission is $8 for visitors ages 12 and up, $6 for seniors and children 6-12, and free for children under 5; save a few bucks by buying tickets online in advance of the fair's start. Parking is $5. Carnival ride tickets add up quickly; concerts are usually free for general admission, but $20 and up for reserved seats.

Hello from the Oregon State Fair!

ACCOMMODATIONS

Salem's lodgings are largely mid-priced chain hotels clustered near I-5. The choice spot to stay is the downtown ★ **Grand Hotel** (201 Liberty St. SE, 503/540-7800 or 877/540-7800, grandhotelsalem.com, $159), an elegant hotel and conference center with large, nicely furnished guest rooms and a good restaurant.

A good bet that's close to the freeway on the south side of town is the **Best Western Mill Creek Inn** (3125 Ryan Dr. SE, 503/585-3332, www.bestwestern.com/millcreekinn, $145-187), with large rooms and a pool and hot tub, plus a free shuttle service to the Salem Airport and Amtrak as well as an included breakfast at a nearby Denny's. Take the Mission Street exit (Exit 253) from I-5.

If you don't mind staying a little north of town, the **Hopewell House B&B** (22350 Hopewell Rd. NW, 503/868-7848, www.hopewellbb.com, $169-189 with breakfast, $139-159 without) is a good place to relax in a newer B&B; cottages include kitchens and hot tubs in a rural setting.

FOOD

Downtown Salem is looking good these days, and its restaurants are better than ever.

Coffee Shops/Bars

The downtown **Governor's Cup** (471 Court St. NE, 503/581-9675, 6am-9pm Mon.-Thurs., 6am-midnight Fri., 7am-9pm Sat., 7am-7pm Sun.) is a friendly coffee shop that attracts everybody from high school kids to retirees; it turns into a bar in the evening. Friday nights bring live music.

Salem's hipsters hang out at the **Archive Coffee and Bar** (102 Liberty St. NE, www.archivecoffeeandbar.com, 7am-midnight daily). During the day, order coffee or "coffee cocktails" (such as espresso with orgeat and black walnut bitters). In the evening, a limited food service ($3-12) and boozy cocktail offerings ramp up.

American

★ **Word of Mouth** (140 17th St. NE, 503/930-4285, www.wordofsalem.com,

11am-11pm Wed.-Thurs., 11am-midnight Fri.-Sat., 11am-8pm Sun., $9-16) is a little bit Asian and a little bit Mediterranean, with falafels, rice bowls, wraps, Tibetan pork barbecue, and lots of vegetarian options. Venti's also has a great selection of craft beers and a few varieties of cider. Downstairs, find a club and a full bar.

Mediterranean

Amadeus (135 Liberty St. NE, 503/362-8830, www.amadeussalem.com, 11am-9pm Tues.-Thurs., 11am-11pm Fri.-Sat., $12-26) is a bit more formal than other downtown restaurants, and a good place to go for a special dinner. Along with a good selection of seafood dishes, Amadeus has choices for vegetarians and paleo diners.

Asian

Bibim Bap House (635 Chemeketa St. NE, 503/585-1530, www.happybibimbaphouse.com, 11am-9pm Mon.-Sat., $9-15) serves traditional Korean rice bowls topped with veggies, spicy gochujang chili pepper paste, and a fried egg and meat. The menu included Chinese-style dishes and sushi, but go for the Korean dishes.

Mexican

Among Salem's many Mexican restaurants, a local favorite is **Hacienda Real** (3690 Commercial St. SE, 503/5405537, www.lahaciendarealoregon.com, 11am-10pm Mon.-Thurs., 11am-11pm Fri.-Sat., $8-22), known for homemade tortillas and Jalisco-style food. This location is south of downtown; there are a couple of other locations around town.

INFORMATION

The **Travel Salem visitor information center** (181 High St. NE, 503/581-4325 or 800/874-7012, www.travelsalem.com, 9am-5pm Mon.-Fri., 10am-4pm Sat.) is downtown.

The Salem *Statesman Journal* (www.statesmanjournal.com) is sold throughout the Willamette Valley, central coast, and central Oregon. The newspaper's "Weekend"

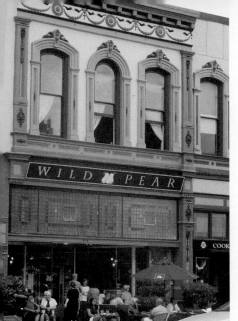

Wild Pear is one of Salem's most popular lunchtime restaurants.

7am-3pm Wed.-Mon., $8-14), located in an old house east of the capitol and Willamette University, is known for its delicious breakfasts, where corned beef hash is the signature dish and the crème brûlée french toast a local favorite.

A good, and extremely popular, downtown spot is **Wild Pear** (372 State St., 503/378-7515, www.wildpearcatering.com, 10:30am-6:30pm Mon.-Sat., $9-15), a lunchtime restaurant with a good selection of sandwiches and salads. Lunches are large, but you might still consider adding an order of white-truffle sweet potato fries with mustard aioli.

The **Kitchen on Court Street** (466 Court St. NE, 971/701-6902, 7am-9pm Mon.-Thurs., 7am-10pm Fri., 8am-10pm Sat., 8am-8pm Sun., $7-15) is a stylish spot, detailed out with brick, wood, and subway tiles. Lunches (and light dinners) are high-class comfort food; try the fish tacos, served either Mexican- or Korean-style.

Venti's Cafe (325 Court St. NE, 503/399-8733, ventiscafe.com, 11am-10pm Mon.-Tues., section features entertainment listings and reviews every Friday covering the week to come. Although these listings focus on Salem, considerable attention is also given to events throughout the Willamette Valley, central Oregon, and the coast.

GETTING THERE AND AROUND

Salem's State and Center Streets run east-west; Commercial and Liberty Streets run north-south. East and West Nob Hill Streets run southeast. With a profusion of one-way streets and thoroughfares that end abruptly, it's important to keep your bearings. One helpful frame of reference is supplied by remembering that Commercial Street runs north-south along the Willamette River on the western edge of town.

Salem provides a lot of ways to get in and out of town. **Greyhound** (450 NE Church St., 503/362-2428) runs about five buses a day through Salem. The **Amtrak** station (500 13th St. SE, 503/588-1551) sits across from Willamette University and is close to Mission Mill Museum. The **Salem airport** (503/588-6314) is a few miles east of downtown. A Salem-to-Portland airport shuttle is run by **Hut Limousine Service** (503/364-4444, www.portlandairportshuttle.com, $35 one way).

Mass-transit bus service in town is run by **Salem Area Mass Transit (Cherriots)** (216 High St., 503/588-2877, www.cherriots.org, $1.60). Terminals are in front of the courthouse.

Vicinity of Salem

SILVERTON

Silverton, located in the foothills of the Cascades about 10 miles east of Salem, is a thriving small town with a major attraction—the Oregon Garden—right out its back door. Don't rush past downtown Silverton; it's worth spending at least a few minutes wandering past or through the antiques and decor shops and checking out the murals on downtown buildings.

The big annual "do" in Silverton is **Homer Davenport Days** (503/873-5615, homerdavenport.com), usually held the first weekend in August, when locals enjoy crafts, food, music, and the spectacle of neighbors racing furniture down Main Street. Davenport was a nationally famous cartoonist in the 1930s and a Silverton favorite son. Most of the action takes place at **Coolidge-McClain Park** (300 Coolidge St.).

Oregon Garden

The **Oregon Garden** (879 W. Main St., 503/874-8100 or 877/674-2733, www.oregongarden.org, 9am-6pm daily May-Sept., 10am-4pm daily Oct.-Apr., $11 adults, $9 seniors, $8 students 12-17, $5 children 5-11) offers 20 different specialty gardens on 80 verdant acres. The gardens were designed by a dream team of landscape architects with the backing of the state's dynamic nursery industry—nursery plants are among Oregon's most important agricultural products. A lovely hotel and spa make an overnight visit an attractive option.

There are some innovative parts of the gardens. Especially intriguing is the wetlands section, which uses treated wastewater from Silverton to create the environment. The water travels through a series of terraced ponds and wetland plants to a holding tank; from there it is used to irrigate the entire garden. A garden of medicinal plants and a garden with a train running through it are also fun to visit.

An attraction that makes the trip to the gardens worthwhile for architecture buffs is **Gordon House** (869 W. Main St., Silverton, 503/874-6006, www.thegordonhouse.org,

Willamette Bird Sanctuaries

The federal government established several bird sanctuaries between Salem and Eugene in the mid-1960s because of the encroachment of urbanization and agriculture on the winter habitat of the dusky Canada goose, which now comes to **Baskett Slough National Wildlife Refuge** (NWR) west of Salem, **Ankeny NWR** southwest of Salem, and **Finley NWR** south of Corvallis each October after summering in Alaska's Copper River Delta. Forest, cropland, and riparian environments attract hummingbirds, swans, geese, sandhill cranes, ducks, egrets, herons, plovers, sandpipers, hawks and other raptors, wrens, woodpeckers, and dozens of other avian species. Migrating waterfowl begin showing up in the Willamette Valley in mid-October. By mid-March, large numbers of Canada geese, tundra swans, and a variety of ducks descend on the refuge.

The pamphlet "Birds of Willamette Valley Refuges" (available from Refuge Manager, Western Oregon Refuges, 26208 Finley Refuge Rd., Corvallis 97337, 541/757-7236, www.fws.gov) details the best months to spot birds, the frequency of sightings, and the locations of hundreds of kinds of birds.

Some refuge trails are closed in winter. A hike that can be enjoyed any time of year is Finley NWR's one-mile **Woodpecker Loop.** Forests of oak and Douglas fir as well as a mixed deciduous grove combine with marshes to provide a wide range of habitats. Look for the pileated woodpeckers in the deciduous forest. Take Route 99W from Corvallis to Refuge Road. Look for the footpath on the right after driving three miles. A dropbox has a pamphlet with pictures and information on the birds, wildlife, and plant communities.

Ankeny NWR is located 12 miles south of Salem off I-5 at Exit 243, and Baskett Slough NWR lies northwest of Rickreall on Route 22. Visit fall through spring for the best chance to see ducks, geese, swans, and raptors.

tours noon, 1pm, 2pm daily, $15 adults, children with adults free, reservations strongly recommended), a Frank Lloyd Wright-designed home located within the Oregon Garden complex. The house was moved to its current spot when the original property was sold and the new owners planned to demolish the house and rebuild to suit their own tastes. The modestly sized house is an example of Wright's populist Usonian style and has beautiful western red cedar trim, many built-in drawers and cabinets, and lots of natural light. Terraces bring the outdoors in, and low ceilings in the bedrooms create a sense of retreat. Docents lead tours on the hour; this is the only way to see the inside of the house.

Accommodations and Food

The ★ **Oregon Garden Resort** (895 W. Main St., 503/874-2500 or 800/966-6490, www.oregongardenresort.com, $179) is a great base for exploring this part of the Willamette Valley. The resort includes a restaurant, lounge, and spa; guest rooms are in a series of small six-unit buildings tucked behind the main lodge. All the guest rooms, which are decorated in a way that's pretty and upscale but not too designer-slick, have private patios or balconies and gas fireplaces; some are pet-friendly (as is part of the Oregon Garden itself). Many packages are offered, and special deals abound. Especially during the off-season, this can be a surprisingly affordable getaway.

In town, the **Silverton Inn and Suites** (310 N. Water St., 503/873-1000, www.silvertoninnandsuites.com, $99-149), a once-lackluster motel, has been transformed into a stylish suite hotel with kitchenettes in many guest rooms. Another good option right in the heart of Silverton is the **Birdwood Inn B&B** (511 S. Water St., 503/873-3247, www.birdwoodbandb.com, $100-125), a small inn with two bedrooms (private baths) and a separate cottage. The gardens at the Birdwood are a special delight.

A perfect spot for breakfast or lunch is **The Gathering Spot** (106 N. 1st St.,

503/874-4888, gatheringspotcafe.com, 8am-3pm daily, $9-12), a friendly up-to-date diner with fantastic omelets, cinnamon roll pancakes, and a breakfast sandwich worth getting up early for.

Downtown Silverton's ★ **Silver Grille** (206 E. Main St., 503/873-8000, www.silvergrille.com, 5pm-9:30pm Wed.-Sun., $18-27) has a big reputation among locals in the greater Salem area as *the* restaurant for casual fine dining, where local produce and wines create a seasonal Willamette Valley cuisine that's both innovative and classic.

MOUNT ANGEL

Mount Angel's location an hour south of Portland makes it an excellent day trip. Just take Exit 272 for Woodburn off I-5 and follow the blue Silver Falls tour route signs. If you're approaching the Mount Angel Abbey from Salem off I-5, take the Chemawa exit and follow the signs.

★ Mount Angel Abbey

Four miles northwest of Silverton off Route 214 and high above the rest of the Willamette Valley is **Mount Angel Abbey** (1 Abbey Dr., Benedict, 503/845-3345, www.mountangelabbey.org). The abbey itself is perched

above the faux-Bavarian town of Mount Angel; as you drive there you'll pass the neo-Gothic St. Mary's church, which is staffed by abbey monks.

The Benedictine abbey sits on a 300-foot hill overlooking cropland and Cascade vistas. From the bluff, look northward to Mount Hood, Mount St. Helens, Mount Adams, and, according to locals (that is, monks), on exceptionally clear days you can see Mount Rainier. The abbey **library,** designed by the famous Finnish architect Alvar Aalto, is an architectural highlight, with beautiful light and modern lines. The texts are also pretty amazing, especially those housed in the Rare Book Room. Also worth checking out are the display cases in the lobby; the exhibits are invariably interesting.

While at Mount Angel Abbey, visit its eccentric **museum** (9am-5pm Tues.-Sun., free), which is tucked in a basement to the side of the main church (get a map from the librarian and ask to have the museum pointed out). Displays include religious artifacts such as a crown of thorns, a world-class hairball, and a huge collection of taxidermy, including an eight-legged calf.

The abbey's late-July **Bach Festival** features professional musicians in an idyllic

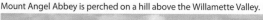
Mount Angel Abbey is perched on a hill above the Willamette Valley.

setting; call for tickets months in advance (503/845-3064).

Meditative retreats can be arranged at the abbey's **retreat house** (503/845-3025, www. mountangelabbey.org, $81 single occupancy includes all meals). Arrival days are Monday-Thursday. Although the accommodations are ascetic, the peace of the surroundings and the beauty of the monks' rituals will deepen your personal reflections no matter your spiritual orientation.

Wooden Shoe Bulb Company

Plant nurseries abound in the area. A visit to the **Wooden Shoe Tulip Farm** (33814 S. Meridian Rd., Woodburn, 541/634-2243, www.woodenshoe.com, $5 per person or $20 per car weekends during the tulip festival) in late March through May will colorfully illustrate Oregon's rites of spring. Take Exit 271 off I-5 and follow Route 214 east. It will become Route 211 to Molalla; turn right at the flashing yellow light onto Meridian Road and go two miles to the tulip fields. Afterward, you can head south through the town of Monitor and reach Mount Angel via a delightful rural route.

Recreation and Events

The town of Mount Angel's holds a big

Oktoberfest (541/845-9440) in mid-September, when folks flock here to enjoy the *Weingarten,* the beer garden, the oompah-pah of traditional German music, art displays, yodeling, and street dancing amid beautiful surroundings. The biggest attraction of all, however, is the food: stuffed cabbage leaves, strudels, and an array of sausages.

Bicyclists relish the foothills and farmland around Mount Angel. Lowland hop fields and filbert orchards give way to Christmas tree farms in the hills. This region is known as well for its crop of red fescue, a type of grass seed grown almost nowhere outside the northern Willamette Valley.

★ SILVER FALLS STATE PARK

With 10 major waterfalls, nearly 30 miles of trails, and over 9,000 acres of woodlands (much of it temperate rainforest), **Silver Falls State Park** (22024 Silver Falls Hwy., Sublimity, 26 miles east of Salem, 503/873-8681, ext. 31, www.oregonstateparks.org, $5 day use) was, in the 1920s, under consideration for national park status (it was rejected because parts of the land had just been clear-cut). Much of the park's infrastructure was created by the Civilian Conservation Corps

springtime at the Wooden Shoe Bulb Company

(CCC) during the 1930s using rustic stone and log construction typical of national parks. Be sure to visit the South Falls Lodge, which now houses interpretive displays and a café; nearby, find a viewpoint and the trailhead to South Falls.

Hiking

The **Trail of Ten Falls** is a seven-mile loop linking the falls; the "canyon" half of the loop is more interesting (that's where the falls are) and has a few steep sections. The highlights are 177-foot **South Falls** and 136-foot **North Falls;** in both cases, trails run behind the falls. The "rim" half of the trail is easy but not so scenic; leashed dogs are allowed on this section, but not on the canyon section. Bikers and horseback riders have their own specially designated trails.

If you don't want to hike the whole loop, a shorter loop starts at the North Falls parking area. North Falls itself is just a short (but steep) hike from the parking area; South Falls is easily reached from the large parking area at South Falls Lodge, a couple of miles south of the North Falls parking lot.

Camping

Silver Falls State Park's campground (22024 Silver Falls Hwy., Sublimity, 503/873-8681, www.oregonstateparks.org, www.reserveamerica.com, $19-26 campsites, $40-50 cabins) is in a wooded setting with relatively private sites separated into tent and RV loops. Large groups (up to 75 people) can rent dormitory-style bunkhouses, called "ranches," for $200 per night (extra fees when exceeding 25 guests). Tent sites are open May-October; RV campground and one of the "ranches" are open year-round. In addition to hiking, swimming, and biking, there are stables near the park's entrance and a horse camp.

OPAL CREEK

The old-growth forests and emerald pools of Opal Creek, which includes a grove of 1,000-year-old 250-foot red cedar, has been

North Falls is one of the most impressive of the 10 waterfalls at Silver Falls State Park.

called the most intact old-growth ecosystem on the West Coast.

To reach Opal Creek from I-5, take Route 22 for 22 miles east to Mehama. At a flashing yellow light, turn left off Route 22 onto North Fork Road and continue 20 miles (it will become the gravel Forest Service Road 2209) and be sure to veer left, uphill, at the Y intersection. About six miles past the Willamette National Forest sign, a locked gate will bar your car from proceeding farther down Road 2209. Park and follow the trail to a large wooden map displaying various hiking options. Dogs must be on leashes.

While old-growth trees abound not far from the parking lot, be sure to cross over to the south side of the North Fork of the Little Santiam River (indicated by trailside signs). Here you can take in the placid Opal Pool, a small aquamarine catch-basin at the base of a cascade that cuts through limestone. Located several miles from the parking lot over gently rolling terrain, Opal Pool is the perfect day-hike destination.

The **Opal Creek Ancient Forest Center** (503/892-2782, www.opalcreek.org) is an environmental education center three miles east of the trailhead with a few cabins for rent ($225-375; bring your own sleeping bag and towel; no dogs; access is on foot only). A Bureau of Land Management campground, **Elkhorn Valley** (503/897-2406, www.blm.gov/or, $14 mid-May-Labor Day) is a good place to camp and stage a day trip to Opal Creek. To reach the campground, drive 24 miles east from Salem on Highway 22 and turn north on the North Fork Road. Continue 8.5 miles to the campground.

DETROIT LAKE

It's a Salem tradition to take to the hills via Route 22 along the North Santiam River to enjoy the fishing and camping at Detroit Lake. This large and busy 400-foot-deep reservoir is known for its boating, waterskiing, swimming, and fishing for rainbow trout, landlocked chinook, and kokanee. Boat rentals are available at the marina. Because the reservoir was built for water storage, during drought years it can be drawn down enough to make recreation unappealing.

Camping

Although most Detroit Lake campers stay at the amenity-rich but very busy **Detroit Lake State Recreation Area** (503/854-3346, www.oregonstateparks.org, www.reserveamerica.com, $19-28) on the lake's north shore, the remoter south-shore Forest Service campground at **Cove Creek** (Blowout Rd., 503/854-3366, www.recreation.gov for reservations, $22, flush toilets, showers) is more peaceful, though still not exactly a wilderness experience.

BREITENBUSH HOT SPRINGS

Breitenbush Hot Springs Retreat and Conference Center (503/854-3320, www.breitenbush.com) offers natural hot springs, trails forested with old growth, and a wide variety of programs aimed at healing body,

mind, and spirit. Music, storytelling, yoga, and vegetarian meals are also part of the Breitenbush experience. Sweat lodge ceremonies are offered once a month. Although many visitors come to Breitenbush to take part in an organized workshop, it's also possible to come on your own for a personal retreat. Know before you go that most hot springs bathers forgo the option of clothing.

Cabins are Spartan but have electricity and heat, and some have indoor plumbing ($108 per person, using bathhouse; $127 pp with a bath in cabin; bring your own bedding or pay $17 extra); rates include three vegetarian meals daily and use of the facilities and waters. Single visitors may sometimes be assigned a cabin-mate unless they specify otherwise (and pay extra). Large tents on platforms ($90, June-Oct.) are also available, or you can camp in your own tent ($67 pp). Day-use fees for hot springs and other facilities are $16-30; it's essential to call and reserve in advance. Individual all-you-can-eat lunches or dinners for daytime visitors cost $13. Be sure to bring your own caffeine if that's something you require. Do not bring alcoholic beverages or marijuana.

On-site you'll find the Spotted Owl Trail near the entrance of the Breitenbush parking lot. Near Breitenbush are such remarkable natural areas as Breitenbush Gorge, Opal Creek, Bull of the Woods, and Jefferson Park; for more information, contact the Detroit Ranger Station at 503/854-3366.

To get to Breitenbush from Salem, take Route 22 to the town of Detroit. Turn at the gas station—the only one in town—onto Forest Service Road 46. Drive 10 miles and take a right over the bridge across Breitenbush River. Follow the signs, taking every left turn after the bridge, to the Breitenbush parking lot.

On the way up Forest Service Road 46 from Detroit to Breitenbush Hot Springs, you will pass a number of Forest Service campgrounds. **Breitenbush Campground** (10 miles northeast of Detroit, 503/854-3366, www.fs.usda.gov or www.recreation.gov, May-Sept.,

$16) is less than two miles from Breitenbush Resort and is a good spot for campers who want to visit the hot springs without staying at the resort itself. Nearby, the Breitenbush River has good fishing.

OLALLIE LAKE

To the east of Breitenbush, Olallie Lake is one of the nicest camping and hiking getaways in the area, with superb views of Mount Jefferson from the lake. The lake has a small **resort** (www.olallielakeresort.com) that offers cabins and yurts of varying sizes ($65-100 per night, usually July-Sept.) with woodstoves and outhouses and rents rowboats and canoes. Camp at the adjacent **Paul Dennis campground** ($15 per site). Olallie Lake is along the Pacific Crest Trail, and there are hiking trails galore, many leading to other small lakes. In the early summer, wildflowers are an attraction; late in summer, this is a great place to pick wild huckleberries. The season up here is pretty short—snows usually keep the resort closed until July.

From the Detroit area, head north and east on Forest Service Road 46, then turn right on Forest Service Road 4220 (a rough gravel road) and follow it 13 miles to the lake.

MOUNT JEFFERSON

Mount Jefferson, Oregon's second-highest peak at 10,495 feet, dominates the Oregon Cascades horizon between Mount Hood to the north and the Three Sisters to the south—though, unlike Mount Hood, Mount Jefferson is rarely visible from the west.

Mount Jefferson is 12 miles east of Detroit. Take Route 22 and turn left, following Forest Service Road 2243 (Whitewater Creek Rd.) 7.5 miles to the Whitewater Creek trailhead. From there, it's an easy 4.5-mile hike to **Jefferson Park.** This northern base of the mountain features an abundance of lakes and, in early summer, wildflowers. The alpine meadows are full of purple and yellow lupine and red Indian paintbrush in July.

Above Jefferson Park, the ascent of the dormant volcano's cone is a precarious endeavor and should only be attempted by truly experienced climbers. You'll reach the bottom of Whitewater Glacier at 7,000 feet. Thereafter, climbing routes steepen to 45 degrees, and snow and rock ridges crumble when touched. Near the top, the rocks aren't solid enough to allow the use of ropes or other forms of climbing protection; going down is even more dangerous than going up. Even if you head up the more sedate south face, you can expect difficulties due to the instability of the final 400 feet of rock on the pinnacle.

Sometimes the mosquitoes in Jefferson Park are bloodthirsty enough to pierce thick clothing, so bring insect repellent in summer. On occasion the area is so crowded with day-use visitors and folks trekking the nearby Pacific Crest Trail that Jefferson Park seems more like a city park than a mountain wilderness. No matter; the sight of Mount Jefferson in alpenglow at sunset or shrouded in moonlight will make you forget the intrusions of humans and insects alike.

Corvallis

The name "Corvallis" refers to the city's pastoral setting in the "Heart of the Valley." But just as much as its physical setting, it's the culture of Oregon State University that defines Corvallis.

Although Corvallis isn't a huge tourist destination, its beauty, tranquility, and central location in the heart of the valley make it a good base from which to explore the bird sanctuaries, the Coast Range, and nearby wineries farmland. It's an especially appealing base for easygoing (or vigorous) bike rides. Streets have wide bike lanes, and scenic routes for cyclists parallel the Willamette and Mary's Rivers.

SIGHTS

The beautiful parklike campus of **Oregon State University (OSU)** (follow the signs to Jefferson Ave. or Monroe Ave., 541/737-1000, www.oregonstate.edu), an 1868 land grant institution, is a major hub of activity in town and a good place to take a walk or attend a university-sponsored lecture or musical event. But even more intriguing is the

thriving downtown, filled with locally owned shops and edged by a splendid path along the Willamette River. A number of restaurants face onto the riverfront.

A good place to start a downtown walk is around 2nd Street and Jackson Avenue. On Saturdays during July and August, the **Historic Homes Trolley Tour** (541/757-1544, 1pm Sat., $5 donation suggested, call for reservation) leaves from this corner. This corner is also the hub of Wednesday and Saturday morning farmers markets.

WINERIES

Located less than 10 miles southwest of Corvallis off Highway 99W is **Tyee Wine Cellars** (26335 Greenberry Rd., Corvallis, 541/753-8754, www.tyeewine.com, noon-5pm Fri.-Sun. Apr.-Dec.). Pinot gris, pinot noir, chardonnay, and Gewürztraminer are featured. After wine-tasting, you can enjoy a picnic on the grounds of this historic farm site or walk a 1.5-mile loop to beaver ponds. Several other wineries are also located in the area and are easy to visit by bike from Corvallis; see

Corvallis, located in a rich agricultural area, has a good farmers market.

http://heartofwillamette.com for information on exploring these area wineries.

SPORTS AND RECREATION
Hiking

Marys Peak (541/750-7000, www. fs.usda. gov/recarea/Siuslaw, $5 parking) sits 16 miles southwest of Corvallis. Follow Route 34 west to the road's Coast Range Summit (1,230 feet); turn north onto Forest Road 30 and drive 10 miles to a parking area. A 0.7-mile hike across the meadow leads to the 4,097-foot summit, offering perspectives on Mounts Hood and Jefferson, the Three Sisters to the east, and the Pacific Ocean to the west.

A biome unique to the Coast Range exists up here, with such flora as alpine phlox, bear-grass, Pacific iris, tiger lily, Indian paintbrush, purple lupine, and the blue-green noble fir. Exceptionally large species of this fragrant tree grow on the Meadowedge Trail. This trail connects to a primitive campground (16 sites, May-Oct., $10 per night, no water) two miles below the summit (also accessible from the road). It's part of a nine-mile network of trails around the upper slopes of the mountain.

Snow, an infrequent visitor to most Coast Range slopes, can often be found here in winter, even at lower elevations. In fact, the road is sometimes impassable without tire chains from late fall until early spring. A Sno-Park permit is required for day use November 15-April 15.

Closer to town, the **McDonald Experimental Forest,** which includes **Peavy Arboretum** (541/737-6702, 8692 NW Peavy Arboretum Rd., http://cf.forestry.oregonstate.edu/peavy-arboretum), eight miles north of Corvallis on Route 99W, serves primarily as a research forest for the university's Forestry Department. The arboretum's Woodland Trail is a good place to start; bikes and horses are also permitted on logging roads and trails in the areas of the McDonald Forest outside the arboretum boundaries. This is a good place to come when your dog needs a run.

The McDonald Experimental Forest and Peavy Arboretum have miles of hiking and biking trails.

Find good info about local trails at http://therighttrail.org or pick up a trail map ($6.95) at local stores.

Biking

Corvallis has an excellent network of bike paths and on-street bike lanes. It's easy to bike anywhere in town in a few minutes, and the wide path along the downtown riverfront is a good place for kids or nervous cyclists to start out. More confident cyclists can begin in downtown Corvallis and ride eight miles on back roads to Philomath.

Low-traffic back roads also lead to Alsea Falls, 30 miles southwest of town, where several mountain bike trails exist, and more are being developed.

Mountain bikers can pedal to the west edge of town to Bald Hill Park. where six miles of trails offer a few routes to the summit. The McDonald Forest, a few miles north and west of town, offers many miles of old logging roads and trails open to bikes; Lewisburg Saddle is a popular destination here.

The Majestic Theatre is a good place to catch music or a play in downtown Corvallis.

Rent a bike or stop in for ride recommendations and a bike map at Peak Sports (135 NW 2nd St., 541/754-6444, www.peaksportscorvallis.com).

Spectator Sports

The **OSU Beavers** (www.osubeavers.com for schedules and tickets) dominate the sports scene in Corvallis. In fact, unless you're a fan, you might want to avoid town if the Beavs are playing the University of Oregon Ducks; these teams share a rowdy sibling rivalry.

ENTERTAINMENT AND EVENTS

The **Majestic Theatre** (115 SW 2nd St., 541/766-6976, www.majestic.org), a restored 1913 vaudeville house, is a lovely place to watch a play or catch a concert. Close by is the excellent **Grassroots Books and Music** (227 SW 2nd St., 541/754-7558, www.grassrootsbookstore.com).

This university town has no shortage of drinking establishments, including a couple

of typical college taverns on 2nd Street downtown. A step up (well, all the way to the rooftop) is **Sky High Brewing** (160 NW Jackson Ave., 541/207-3277, skyhighbrewing.com, 11am-10pm Sun.-Tues., 11am-11pm Wed., 11am-midnight Thurs.-Sat., rooftop open after 4pm daily), a family-friendly pub with good food and great views of town and the river.

The **Corvallis Fall Festival** (541/752-9655, www.corvallisfallfestival.org), a vibrant gathering of artists and craftspeople and a block of food concessions, including an Oregon wine garden, takes over Central Park the fourth weekend in September.

ACCOMMODATIONS

Hotel rates can vary dramatically in Corvallis, depending on what's going on at the university.

Of the older and less expensive lodging options in the city center, the **Rodeway Inn Willamette River** (345 NW 2nd St., 541/752-9601, www.rodewayinn.com, $50-150) is decidedly basic but has a good location downtown and near the river. Pets are permitted.

A prime place to stay downtown along the river is the ★ **Holiday Inn Express** (781 NE 2nd St., 541/752-0800 or 800/315-2621, www.hiexpress.com, $153-200). From here, it's an easy and pleasant walk to downtown riverfront restaurants; get a river-view guest room and perhaps you'll see an eagle flying upriver early in the morning.

The **Hilton Garden Inn** (2500 SW Western Blvd., 541/752-5000 or 800/445-8667, www.hiltongardeninn.com, $149-159) is practically part of the OSU campus; it's located near Reser Stadium (the football stadium), Gill Coliseum (the basketball arena), and the OSU Conference Center. It's a very comfortable hotel with good amenities for business travelers.

If you want to get out into the countryside, consider a farm stay at the **Leaping Lamb** (20368 Honey Grove Rd., Alsea, 541/487-4966 or 877/820-6132, leapinglambfarm.com, $250,

Willamette Water Trail

Ready for a new view of the Willamette Valley? How about seeing it from the river? An outing on the **Willamette Water Trail** (willamettewatertrail.org) can be as simple as an afternoon paddle from Peoria (Oregon) to Corvallis or as involved as a weeklong camping expedition.

Be prepared to pull out the binoculars and the camera repeatedly along the way, and to settle into a quiet profound enough to make you forget that I-5 is probably less than five miles away.

In addition to the very helpful Willamette Water Trail website, you'll find essential information on access points, campsites, and river hazards in a series of waterproof maps (available to order from the website).

Canoes and sea kayaks are the vessels of choice for Willamette River paddle trips. They're available for rent at the following locations:

- **Alder Creek** (200 NE Tomahawk Dr., Portland, 503/285-0464, www.aldercreek.com)

- **Portland Kayak Company** (6600 SW Macadam Ave., Portland, 503/459-4050, www.portlandkayak.com)

- **Next Adventure** (704 SE Washington St., Portland, 503/233-0706, https://nextadventure.net)

- **eNRG Kayaking** (1701 Clackamette Dr., Oregon City, 503/772-1122)

- **Chehalem Paddle Launch** (3100 SE 8th St., Dundee, 503/687-1706, www.cprdnewberg.org)

- **Peak Sports** (207 NW 2nd St., Corvallis, 541/754-6444, www.peaksportscorvallis.com)

- **Oregon Paddle Sports** (520 Commercial Ave., Eugene, 541/505-9020, www.oregonpaddlesports.com)

two-night minimum stay), where a private two-bedroom cabin with cooking facilities (basic breakfast items supplied) is perfect for families. It's well situated for hikes into the nearby forest or for just communing with farm animals. The farm is on the way to the coast, 17 miles southwest of Philomath, near Alsea, on Hwy. 34.

Camping

Camping in this part of the Willamette Valley can be delightful, especially in late spring and early autumn. **Marys Peak Campground** (541/750-7000, www. fs.usda.gov, $10) is open mid-May-October; the final stretch of road to this spot is unsuitable for trailers. It's about 19 miles from town, off Hwy. 34.

RV campers can stay at **Benton Oaks** (110 SW 53rd St., 541/766-6259, $21 tent, $31-37 RV year-round; tenting summer only), immediately adjacent to the county fairgrounds.

Special rates and reservations are required on OSU football weekends.

FOOD

The riverfront stretch of downtown is home to several good restaurants. The hottest restaurant in Corvallis for a fine dining experience is ★ **del Alma** (136 SW Washington Ave., 541/753-2222, delalmarestaurant.com, 5pm-9:30pm Mon.-Thurs., 5pm-10pm Fri.-Sat., $19-36), serving "New Latin cuisine" inspired by food from Latin America, the Caribbean, and Spain. From barbecued pork tacos to tapas such as albondigas and rockfish ceviche, the menu has something that'll please everyone.

Big River Restaurant and Bar (101 N. Jackson St., 541/757-0694, www.bigriver-rest.com, 11am-9:30pm Mon.-Thurs., 11am-10:30pm Fri., 10am-2pm and 4pm-10:30pm Sat., 10am-2pm and 4pm-9pm Sun., $12-22) is

- **REI** (locations in Portland, Tualatin, Salem, and Eugene, www.rei.com)

Put in at one of the many parks along the way. Although many paddlers set up their own vehicle shuttles, if you're renting a canoe or kayak, ask at the rental shop about shuttle services. **River Trail Shuttle** (541/228-4084, www.rivertrailshuttle.com) runs shuttles in the Eugene area and beyond ($30-130).

If you decide you want to paddle 107 miles of the Willamette along with some company, sign up for the mid-August **Paddle Oregon** event (www.paddleoregon. org, $749). Meals, side trips, yoga, and nightly entertainment round out the trip, which is run by Willamette Riverkeeper, a nonprofit organization dedicated to protecting, preserving, and restoring the river.

Although the Willamette is generally regarded as an "easy" river to paddle, certain precautions are necessary. Paddlers must be able to "read" the river for hazards, maneuver in a current, self-rescue if capsized, and dress appropriately so as to avoid hypothermia. Hone your skills by taking a class from Alder Creek, eNRG Kayaking, Next Adventure, Oregon Paddle Sports, or Portland Kayak Company.

access point for Willamette Water Trail at Champoeg State Park

Children 12 and under must wear a personal floatation device. Paddlers should be aware that DUI laws do apply on the river.

a lively, hip restaurant with Pacific Northwest cuisine and a farm-to-table sensibility. Big River also incorporates an on-site bakery and the more casual adjacent **101 Eat & Drink** (www.101atbigriver.com, 4:30pm-10pm Mon.-Thurs., 4:30pm-midnight Fri.-Sat.), with a cocktail bar atmosphere.

On the edge of downtown is **Luc** (134 SW 4th St., 541/753-4171, www.i-love-luc.com, 4:30pm-9pm Wed.-Sun., $16-30), an intimate chef-owned restaurant with French-influenced food prepared from fresh, local ingredients. The weekly changing menu features such delights as duck breast with pan-fried spaetzle and seared salmon with sweet corn quinoa and basil vinaigrette.

Near the university, **Bombs Away Cafe** (2527 Monroe St., 541/757-7221, www.bombsawaycafe.com, 11am-midnight Mon.-Fri., 5pm-midnight Sat., $7-13) is a busy restaurant with colorful murals on the walls, frequent

live music, and lines of lunchtime hopefuls anxious to sample Mexican-style food made with the freshest ingredients and organic produce. A gluten-free menu is available.

Block 15 (300 SW Jefferson Ave., 541/758-2077, http://block15.com, 11am-11pm Sun.-Thurs., 11am-1am Fri.-Sat.), a brewpub with a strong emphasis on doing business sustainably, is a pleasant low-key place to hang out and draw on the chalkboard tables. Their sister pub, **Les Caves** (308 SW 3rd St., 541/286-4471, www.biercaves.com, 4pm-midnight Tues.-Thurs., 4pm-1am Fri., 9:30am-1am Sat.-Sun.) has a wide range of beers from all over the world and pretty good food (though they seem to be best known for their bier bread pretzels).

It doesn't get much fresher or more local than lunch at **Gathering Together Farm** (25159 Grange Hall Rd., Philomath, 541/929-4270, www.gatheringtogetherfarm.

com, 11am-2pm Tues.-Wed., 11am-2pm and 5:30pm-9pm Thurs.-Fri., 9am-2pm Sat., lunch about $10, dinner $15-20), an organic farm five miles west of Corvallis. Lunches are the mainstay of this farm kitchen; during the winter, when produce is harder to come by, it might include a house-made sausage with sauerkraut, potatoes, and carrots.

Nearby Albany has an unexpected outpost of fine dining. ★ **Sybaris Bistro** (442 1st Ave. W., 541/928-8157, sybarisbistro.com, 5pm-8pm Tues.-Thurs., 5pm-9pm Fri., 10am-1pm and 5pm-9pm Sat., $18-30) is one of the top restaurants in the state, specializing in creative American cooking featuring the fresh bounty of local farms and waters. An appetizer of sticky rice "dumplings" is served with fresh veggies and Thai green curry; salmon is cooked with seeds, berries, and greens.

Corvallis also has a **farmers market** that takes place 9am-1pm Wednesday and Saturday mid-April-mid-November along the river (1st St. and Jackson Ave.).

INFORMATION

The **Corvallis Visitor's Information Center** (420 NW 2nd St., 541/757-1544 or 800/334-8118, visitcorvallis.com) maintains a good website.

To catch up on local events, read the *Corvallis Gazette Times* (www.gtconnect. com). **KOAC** (550 AM) is the public radio station.

GETTING THERE AND AROUND

Greyhound and **Valley Retriever** (153 NW 4th St., 541/757-1797) operate every day, with routes north and south as well as west to the coastal town of Newport. **Amtrak** (110 W. 10th St., 541/928-0885) makes a stop in nearby Albany.

Corvallis Transit (transit center at 5th St. and Monroe Ave., 541/757-6988, Mon.-Sat., free within Corvallis) operates city buses.

Eugene

Oregon's second-largest city and home to the University of Oregon, Eugene belongs on the itinerary of anyone who wants to experience a laid-back Pacific Northwest version of urban sophistication and active pursuits in a beautiful natural setting. The Willamette River curves around the northwest quarter of the community (pop. about 157,000), and from an elevated perch you can see the Coast and Cascade Ranges beckoning you to beach and mountain playgrounds little more than an hour away.

In town, the world-renowned Bach Festival and other big-time cultural events are showcased in the acoustically excellent Hult Center. The University of Oregon campus provides another forum for the best in art and academe, while its Hayward Field track has been the site of the U.S. Olympic Trials several times.

Outdoor gatherings such as the Saturday Market and Oregon Country Fair bring the community together in a potlatch of homegrown edibles, arts, and crafts. But it doesn't take an organized festival to draw the townsfolk outside. Even during persistent winter rains, locals can be seen jogging, bicycling, and gardening.

Eugene's labor, environmental, and human services organizations have labored with quiet effectiveness for several decades, giving the town a distinct lefty touch with worker-owned collectives, a wheelchair-friendly cityscape, preserved ancient forests, and wetland protection against industrial pollution.

SIGHTS

Two major areas of interest to visitors are immediately south of the Willamette River. The campus, in Eugene's southeast quadrant, and the downtown (bounded by 5th and 10th Avenues and Charnelton and High Streets) are only a five-minute drive from each other. Serious walkers and casual cyclists can manage the two-mile distance without trouble. Another excellent place to stroll, run, or bike with the locals, Alton Baker Park, is just across the river from downtown and the university.

Skinner Butte

A good place to get oriented in Eugene, visually as well as historically, is **Skinner Butte.** If you look north from almost anywhere downtown, you'll see this landmark. A park fronting the Willamette River is located at the butte's northern base. This riverfront site served as a dock for pioneer sternwheelers and was where founding father Eugene Skinner ran a ferry service for farmers living north of the river. The town tried to become a major shipping port, but the upper Willamette was uncharted as well as too shallow and meandering.

From downtown, head north on High Street, which becomes Cheshire Avenue as it curves to the left. Take a left onto Skinner Butte Loop and follow it to the top. You can also get here by traveling north on Lincoln

Street to Skinner Butte Loop or by walking up from the south side, which takes about 15 minutes. Kalapuyas, a local tribe, used this promontory for ceremonial dances. On a clear day you can still see the Cascade and Coast Ranges as well as pockets of greenery throughout the city. You can also spot another good reference point in your orientation, **Spencer Butte,** looming above the southern hills five miles away.

The 1888 Queen Anne-style **Shelton McMurphey-Johnson House** (303 Willamette St., 541/484-0808, www.smjhouse. org, 10am-1pm Tues.-Fri., 1pm-4pm Sat.-Sun., $6 adults, $3 children ages 12 and under), on the lower south slope of Skinner Butte, is a museum of Victorian-era life and the most eye-catching of some 2,000 designated historic properties in the city.

Owen Rose Garden

Near the base of Skinner Butte and along the banks of the Willamette, the 400 varieties of roses at the **Owen Rose Garden** (300 N. Jefferson St., 541/682-4824, open daily) peak in June and bloom until fall. Along with 4,500 roses and magnolia blossoms in spring, tremendous old cherry and oak trees also command attention. To get here from I-5, take

The Owen Rose Garden is a good place for a quiet stroll.

Eugene

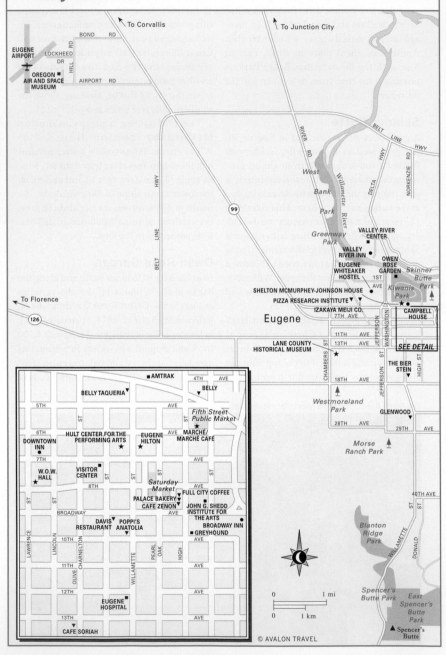

To Corvallis

To Junction City

EUGENE
AIRPORT

LOCKHEED
DR

OREGON
AIR AND SPACE
MUSEUM

BOND   RD

HILL   RD

AIRPORT RD

RIVER   RD

BELT   LINE   HWY

DELTA   HWY

NORKENZIE   RD

West
Bank
Park

Willamette   River

99

BELT   LINE   HWY

To Florence

126

Greenway
Park

VALLEY RIVER
CENTER

VALLEY
RIVER INN

EUGENE
WHITEAKER
HOSTEL

OWEN
ROSE
GARDEN

Skinner
Butte
Park

Kiwanis
Park

1ST
AVE

SHELTON MCMURPHEY-JOHNSON HOUSE

PIZZA RESEARCH INSTITUTE

IZAKAYA MEIJI CO.

Eugene

CAMPBELL
HOUSE

7TH   AVE

11TH   AVE

13TH   AVE

SEE DETAIL

CHAMBERS   ST

JEFFERSON   ST

WASHINGTON   ST

HIGH   ST

LANE COUNTY
HISTORICAL MUSEUM

18TH   AVE

THE BIER
STEIN

Westmoreland
Park

28TH   AVE

GLENWOOD

29TH   AVE

JEFFERSON   ST

Morse
Ranch
Park

40TH AVE

WILLAMETTE   ST

DONALD   ST

Blanton
Ridge
Park

AMTRAK

4TH   AVE

BELLY

BELLY TAQUERIA

5TH
AVE

ST

ST

Fifth Street
Public Market

6TH
AVE

DOWNTOWN
INN

HULT CENTER FOR THE
PERFORMING ARTS

EUGENE
HILTON

MARCHÉ/
MARCHÉ CAFÉ

AVE

7TH
AVE

W.O.W.
HALL

VISITOR
CENTER

ST

ST

Saturday
Market

AVE

FULL CITY COFFEE

8TH

ST

PALACE BAKERY
CAFE ZENON

JOHN G. SHEDD
INSTITUTE FOR
THE ARTS

BROADWAY

DAVIS
RESTAURANT

POPPI'S
ANATOLIA

BROADWAY INN

GREYHOUND

AVE

10TH

LAWRENCE   ST

LINCOLN   ST

CHARNELTON   ST

OLIVE   ST

WILLAMETTE   ST

PEARL   ST

OAK   ST

HIGH   ST

11TH

AVE

12TH

EUGENE
HOSPITAL

AVE

13TH

CAFE SORIAH

0   1 mi

0   1 km

Spencer's
Butte Park

East
Spencer's
Butte
Park

Spencer's
Butte

© AVALON TRAVEL

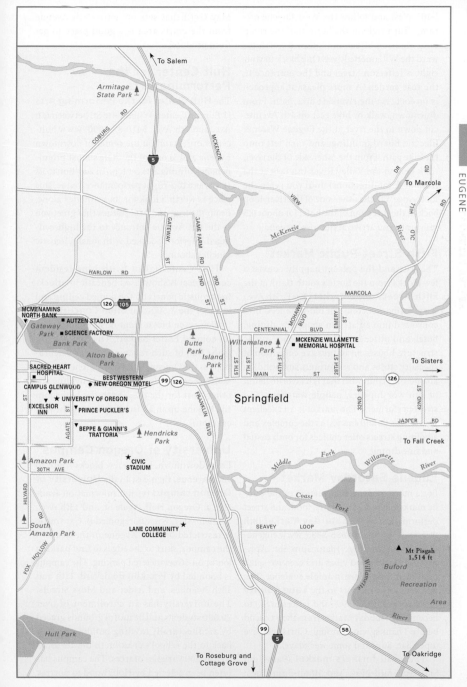

To Salem

Armitage
State Park

COBURG RD

MCKENZIE

5

To Marcola

VIEW

OLD HILL RD

DR RD

71ST

River

McKenzie

GATEWAY ST

JAME FARM RD

2ND ST

3RD ST

HARLOW RD

MARCOLA

126 105

MCMENAMINS
NORTH BANK

AUTZEN STADIUM

Gateway
Park

SCIENCE FACTORY

Bank Park

Butte
Park

Island
Park

Willamalane
Park

CENTENNIAL BLVD

MOHAWK BLVD

EMERY ST

MCKENZIE WILLAMETTE
MEMORIAL HOSPITAL

To Sisters

Alton Baker
Park

SACRED HEART
HOSPITAL

5TH ST

7TH ST

14TH ST

MAIN

28TH ST

ST

126

CAMPUS GLENWOOD

BEST WESTERN
NEW OREGON MOTEL

99 126

Springfield

32ND ST

42ND ST

ST

EXCELSIOR
INN

UNIVERSITY OF OREGON

PRINCE PUCKLER'S

JASPER RD

AGATE ST

BEPPE & GIANNI'S
TRATTORIA

Hendricks
Park

FRANKLIN BLVD

To Fall Creek

Amazon Park

30TH AVE

CIVIC
STADIUM

Middle Fork

Willamette River

Coast Fork

HILYARD RD

South
Amazon Park

LANE COMMUNITY
COLLEGE

SEAVEY LOOP

Mt Pisgah
1,514 ft

FOX HOLLOW

Buford

Recreation

Area

Willamette River

Hull Park

99

5

58

To Roseburg and
Cottage Grove

To Oakridge

I-105 West and follow the West Eugene off-ramp. Turn right at the bottom of the ramp onto Madison Street and follow it north toward the Willamette River. One block to your right is Jefferson Street and the entrance to the rose garden. A more pleasant approach is on foot, via the riverside bike path. From downtown, walk or bike east on 4th Avenue, cut down to the river at the Eugene Water & Electric Board building, and turn left onto the bike path. From the other side of the river, walk behind the Valley River Inn (ask at the front desk for directions) until you get to the footbridge. On the other side of the river, loop back in the direction of the hotel for about 0.5 mile until you arrive at the rose garden.

Fifth Street Public Market

The past and the present happily coexist a few blocks from the butte's south flank at the **Fifth Street Public Market** (296 E. 5th Ave., www.5stmarket.com), an old-time feed mill converted into an atrium shopping, dining, hotel, and office complex. This once-rustic structure houses an impressive collection of specialty stores and restaurants surrounding an open-air courtyard that is a favorite haunt of sun worshippers, people watchers, and street performers. The market is an excellent spot for meals and snacks, as the complex and adjoining streets offer choices for both casual and fine dining.

Eugene Saturday Market

For a more freewheeling version of the public market, explore the crafts, food, and street performances at the **Saturday Market** (8th Ave. and Oak St., 541/686-8885, www.eugene-saturdaymarket.org, 10am-5pm Sat. Apr.-mid-Nov.); the good vibes and creative spirit of the community are in ample evidence. The market moves indoors to the **Lane County Fairgrounds** (13th Ave. and Jefferson St.) to become the Holiday Market from the weekend before Thanksgiving through Christmas Eve (open Sat.-Sun. and some weekdays).

The small **farmers market** (9am-3pm Sat. Apr.-mid-Nov. and 10am-3pm Tues.

May-Oct.) that sets up across 8th Avenue from the crafts area is a good place to get fresh produce.

Hult Center for the Performing Arts

The **Hult Center for the Performing Arts** (1 Eugene Center, Willamette St. between 6th Ave. and 7th Ave., 541/687-5000, www.hult-center.org) stands at the center of downtown Eugene and is one of the state's most prominent performing arts centers. In addition to its status as a top-flight performance venue, this place is worth a look for its aesthetics alone. From the frog and troll statues that greet you at the 6th Avenue entrance to the high-ceilinged interior bedecked with masks, artistic touches abound.

Hult Center talent (with nine resident companies) is showcased beneath interlocking acoustic panels on the domed ceiling and walls of the 2,500-seat **Silva Concert Hall** (which resembles a giant upside-down pastel-colored Easter basket). The Hult Center is the hub of such renowned music celebrations as the Oregon Bach Festival. The **Jacobs Gallery** exhibits local artwork, providing another feast for the eyes. Even the bathroom tile is done up in a visually pleasing theatrical motif.

University of Oregon Campus

From downtown, head a few blocks south to 13th Avenue, then east to the **University of Oregon campus** (visitor information available at Oregon Hall, Agate St. and 13th Ave., 541/346-3111, www.uoregon.edu). Car traffic is restricted on 13th Avenue in the heart of the campus; skirt to the edges to find parking lots or on-street metered parking. The campus is bounded by Franklin Boulevard, 11th and 18th Avenues, and Alder and Moss Streets. The university has an enrollment of over 20,000 students and beautiful grounds graced by architecturally inviting buildings dating back to the school's creation in the 1870s, as well as 500 varieties of trees. The campus has often been selected by Hollywood to portray the ivy-covered halls of academe, most notably in the comedy *Animal House*.

Deady Hall, the oldest building on campus, was built in 1876. Also noteworthy are two museums: the **Jordan Schnitzer Museum of Art** and the **Natural History Museum.** A free **campus tour** leaves from Oregon Hall weekdays at 8:30, 9:30, and 11am and 12:30 and 2pm and Saturday at 10:30am. Unless you're a prospective student, you're better off just picking up the map or downloading the campus app and setting your own pace.

Across from the Schnitzer Museum is the **Knight Library.** (You'll notice that many buildings in campus are named for the Knight family, thanks to Nike cofounder Phil Knight's generosity toward his alma mater.)

Toward the eastern edge of the campus, Agate Street is dominated by **Hayward Field,** which regularly hosts championship meets and Olympic trials. Built in 1919 for the college football team, it's been used by the track program since a cinder track was installed in 1921. The Bowerman Building, on the northwest edge of the track, houses locker rooms, memorabilia, and the university's International Institute for Sport and Human Performance.

Museums

A must on any campus tour is the **Jordan Schnitzer Museum of Art** (next to the Knight Library, 1430 Johnson Ln., 541/346-3027, http://jsma.uoregon.edu, 11am-5pm Tues. and Thurs.-Sun., 11am-8pm Wed. year-round, $5 adults, $3 seniors, UO students and ages 18 and under free). This museum is a real gem, with a surprisingly good collection of contemporary art, including works by Chuck Close, Mark Tobey, Morris Graves, and many Pacific Northwest artists. Another major highlight is a nationally renowned Asian collection (don't miss the jade carvings); the revolving paintings and photography exhibits on the first floor are also usually worthwhile.

The university's other notable museum is entirely different: The **Natural History Museum** (1680 E. 15th Ave., 541/346-3024, http://natural-history.uoregon.edu, 11am-5pm Wed.-Sun., $3, $2 students and seniors) showcases Oregon's prehistory and includes artifacts from digs in eastern Oregon as well as bird and mammal fossils from around the state, including many collected by Thomas Condon, the discoverer of the John Day Fossil Beds. There's also a set of sagebrush sandals dated at 9,350 years old (from the collection of Dr. Luther Cressman), 15-million-year-old

Eugene's Hult Center is an acoustic marvel.

shell fossils, a whale vertebra, mammoth tusks, and an excellent collection of Arctic material. The museum is tucked behind the Knight Law School; to get there from Hayward Field on Agate Street, go east on 15th Avenue and look for a fish sculpture on your right, in front of an attractive wooden building.

Maude Kerns Art Center (1910 E. 15th Ave., 541/345-1571, www.mkartcenter.org, 10am-5:30pm Mon.-Fri., noon-4pm Sat., free) is just east of the University of Oregon campus. Set in an old church, this gallery and visual arts community center is dedicated to contemporary art of nationally known as well as regionally prominent artists. This gallery and others downtown are the focal points of a **gallery walk** (Lane Arts Council, 541/485-2278, www.lanearts.org, 5:30pm-8:30pm first Fri. of the month).

Just across the river in Alton Baker Park, the **Science Factory** (2300 Leo Harris Pkwy., 541/682-7888, www.sciencefactory.org, 10am-4pm daily summer, 10am-4pm Wed.-Sun. during the school year, closed on university home football game days, $7 exhibits and planetarium, $4 exhibits or planetarium alone) is designed to stimulate scientific understanding and curiosity in everyday life. The permanent exhibits are similar to those at Portland's Museum of Science and Industry and are complemented by a new set of traveling exhibits every three months.

The museum's planetarium, the **Exploration Dome** (shows usually on the hour 11am-2pm Sat.-Sun., check website, $4) is highly recommended. Reach the Science Factory-Exploration Dome complex from I-5 by taking I-105 West to the Coburg Road exit and following the signs to Autzen Stadium (look for Centennial Boulevard and the Leo Harris Parkway).

The **Lane County Historical Museum** (740 W. 13th Ave., 541/682-4242, www.lanecountyhistoricalsociety.org, 10am-4pm Tues.-Sat., $5 adults, $3 seniors, $1 children) is next to the fairgrounds. Just look for the steam donkey on the front lawn. There are other 19th-century logging vehicles and period rooms on display. The Oregon Trail exhibits are among the most interesting.

Close to the Eugene Airport, the **Oregon Air and Space Museum** (90377 Boeing Dr., 541/461-1101, www.oasm.info, noon-4pm Wed.-Sun. Apr.-Oct., noon-4pm Wed.-Sat. Nov.-Mar., $7 adults, $6 seniors, $3 children) has vintage aircraft, artifacts, and displays.

Wineries

Head to the Whiteaker neighborhood to find the **Territorial Vineyards & Wine Company** winery (907 W. 3rd Ave., 541/684-9463, www.territorialvineyards.com, 5pm-9pm Wed.-Sat.), where you can sample pinot noir, pinot gris, and Riesling. Although the grapes are grown out toward the Coast Range, the wine is made here in a former coffee warehouse.

Silvan Ridge Winery (27012 Briggs Hill Rd., 541/345-1945, www.silvanridge.com, noon-5pm daily), 15 miles southwest of downtown near Crow, is a perfect place to spend a summer afternoon. Drive west on 11th Avenue, turn left on Bertelson Road, then right on Spencer Creek Road. A left down Briggs Hill Road takes you to the tasting room on a hillside overlooking a valley. The ride out is a favorite of local bicyclists, some of whom continue on into the Coast Range via Vaughan Road. While at the vineyard, ask to sample Hinman's award-winning Gewürztraminer; the pinot gris is also delightful.

The lavish, state-of-the-art **King Estate Winery** (80854 Territorial Hwy., 541/942-9874, www.kingestate.com, 11am-8pm daily), the state's largest winery, is set on 820 acres and resembles a European château. Production focuses on organically grown pinot gris and pinot noir. In addition to wine, you can also sit down to a meal at the well-regarded restaurant (541/685-5189, 11am-8pm Mon.-Wed., 11am-9pm Thurs.-Sun., dinner $26-34, reservations recommended). To reach the winery from Eugene, take I-5 South to Exit 182 (Creswell), turn west on Oregon Avenue (which becomes Camas Swale Rd. and then Ham Rd.) to Territorial Highway. Turn left

the restaurant at King Estate Winery

onto Territorial Highway and follow it about 2.5 miles to King Estate.

SPORTS AND RECREATION

Eugene's identity is rooted in its reputation as "Tracktown, USA," and also in its superlative Parks and Recreation Department, miles of bike paths and on-street bike lanes, and backcountry cycling minutes from downtown.

The **Ruth Bascom Riverbank Trail System** comprises more than 20 miles of paths accessible to bikes and pedestrians along both banks of the Willamette River. Pedal, walk, or jog to the Owen Rose Garden, the bird-rich wetlands at Delta Ponds, the Valley River Inn, and Alton Baker Park (including the Science Factory and Autzen Stadium); the University of Oregon and downtown are just off the path. Five bike-pedestrian bridges cross the river and trailside signs abound, so it's easy to tailor a loop to your own ambitions. Access the trail from downtown by heading east on 8th Avenue to the river.

Connect with Eugene's track heritage by running **Pre's Trail,** on the north side of the Willamette River east of Alton Baker Park. A good route from the university is to head north on Agate Street, cross Franklin Boulevard, and cross the Willamette on a footbridge that takes bikers, hikers, and joggers to Pre's Trail, the Willamette River Bike Trail, Autzen Stadium, and other facilities found along the Willamette River Greenway.

Some of the best urban **rock climbing** to be found anywhere is at the Columns, a basalt cliff located on public land against the west side of Skinner Butte in downtown Eugene. Limited parking is available at the Columns, but it's more enjoyable to ride a bike here by following the road rimming the butte. Climbing is free.

Parks

If you're looking for what makes Eugene *Eugene,* try visiting the city's parks. Go for a swim in the indoor pools at **Echo Hollow Park** (1560 Echo Hollow Rd., 541/682-5525) or **Sheldon Park** (2445 Willakenzie Rd., 541/682-5314); drop-in visitors pay a few bucks.

★ ALTON BAKER PARK

Just across the Willamette River from downtown, the 400-acre **Alton Baker Park** is home to a world-class running trail, the Science Factory and its adjoining planetarium, gardens, ponds, picnic areas, a canoe

Hiking Kentucky Falls

Picturesque **Kentucky Falls** (www.fs.usda.gov/siuslaw) is set in an old-growth forest on the upper slopes of the Coast Range. From downtown Eugene, drive 33 miles west on Route 126 to the Whittaker Creek Recreation Area on the south side of the road, approximately six miles west of the Walton Store and post office. The route to Kentucky Falls winds through the clear-cut lower slopes of 3,700-foot-high **Roman Nose Mountain.**

From Whittaker Creek Recreation Area, drive 1.6 miles south and make a right turn. After 1.5 miles, bear left on Dunn Ridge Road. After about seven miles the pavement ends, and you'll turn left on Knowles Creek Road; go 2.7 miles. Make a right onto Forest Service Road 23 (gravel) and proceed 1.6 miles until you make a right onto Forest Service Road 919. Continue for 2.6 miles to the Kentucky Falls trailhead, marked by a sign on the left side of the road. An old-growth Douglas fir forest on gently rolling hills for the first 0.5 mile gives way to a steep descent into a lush canyon. The upper waterfall is visible a little less than a mile down the trail. Continue another 1.4 miles from the upper falls to an observation deck overlooking Lower Kentucky Falls, a 100-foot-high twin falls. On your drive back to Route 126, retrace your route carefully to avoid veering off on a hair-raising spur route to Mapleton.

canal, and part of a very cool scale model of the solar system (the sun and inner planets are here; Pluto, whether or not it's an actual planet, is 3.66 miles to the northwest, along the bike path). The western part of the park is more developed; to the east, it includes the 237-acre Whilamut Natural Area.

The four-mile **Pre's Trail** runs along the Willamette River east of Alton Baker Park. Named after runner Steve Prefontaine, whose world-record times and finishing kicks used to rock the Hayward Field grandstands before his untimely death in a car accident in 1975, this soft path meanders along the river and connects to the network of trails along the Willamette.

Reach Alton Baker Park from downtown by taking the Ferry Street Bridge and turning right just after crossing the river; if you're on foot or bike, the Peter DeFazio bike bridge is near the Ferry Street Bridge and is an easy walk from the Fifth Street Market area. From the U. of O. area, walk or bike across the Autzen Bike Bridge to the park.

HENDRICKS PARK

About two miles southeast of the campus on a forested ridgeline is **Hendricks Park** (Summit Ave. and Skyline Blvd., 541/682-4800), home to 850 naturally occurring

rhododendrons and azaleas and about 10,000 hybrids. There are several ways to get to the park, the easiest being to turn from Fairmount Boulevard onto Summit Drive. Two parking lots accommodate cars—one near the picnic area of stoves and tables, the other at the upper entrance on Sunset Boulevard. The rhododendron gardens are in their glory during May, and even though the display declines by late June, it's always a great place to stroll. Gorgeous views of the city can be enjoyed from the west end of the garden.

RIDGELINE TRAIL

The South Hills **Ridgeline Trail** is only minutes south of downtown Eugene and offers wildlife-watching opportunities and more species of fern than perhaps any other single spot in Oregon. In addition, old-growth Douglas fir and the lovely and increasingly hard-to-find calypso orchid grow here. The trail is seldom steep and has some spectacular views of the city through clearings. A steep and often muddy spur trail leads up to Spencer Butte. The Ridgeline Trail can be reached from several points, including Dillard Road; near the corner of Fox Hollow and Christenson Roads; near Willamette and 52nd; off Blanton Road near 40th; and the Spencer Butte parking area.

SPENCER BUTTE

The view is great from the highest point in Eugene, 2,052-foot **Spencer Butte**. On a clear day you can see all the way up to Mount Hood, and you look down on Eugene-Springfield, with Fern Ridge Reservoir in the northwest. Beyond the reservoir you can sometimes see Marys Peak. Other Cascade Mountains sometimes visible from the butte include Mount Jefferson, Mount Washington, the Three Sisters, and Mount Bachelor.

Allow an hour to hike to the summit; be sure to take water. The main parking lot for Spencer Butte is on Willamette Street. Just drive south on Willamette Street until you see the signs on the left side of the road. There's also parking on Fox Hollow Road.

MOUNT PISGAH ARBORETUM

The **Mount Pisgah Arboretum** (Buford Park, 34901 Frank Parrish Rd., 541/747-3817, www.mountpisgaharboretum.com, $4 parking fee) features seven miles of trails that pass through a number of different habitats. The arboretum at the end of Seavey Loop Road sponsors such events as a fall fair dedicated to area mushrooms and a spring wildflower show and plant sale (dates vary; check website). Reach Mount Pisgah by following

East 30th Avenue from Eugene past Lane Community College to the I-5 interchange. Cross the bridge over the interstate, turn left, and take the next right onto Seavey Loop Road. You'll cross the Coast Fork of the Willamette River and then turn left onto a gravel road (look for the Mount Pisgah signs) that leads to the trailhead; the arboretum is just beyond the parking lot.

Other trails skirt the arboretum and climb (steeply) to the top of the 1,514-foot peak. A summit monument honors author Ken Kesey's son and other members of the University of Oregon wrestling team who perished in a van accident (the celebrated author lived two miles to the east in Pleasant Hill). This memorial consists of a sculpture with a relief map depicting the mountains, rivers, towns, and other landmarks in the Eugene area. Supporting the map are three five-sided bronze columns upon which the geologic history of Oregon over the past 200 million years is portrayed, using images of more than 300 fossil specimens.

FERN RIDGE LAKE

Reservoirs beyond downtown Eugene provide a wide range of recreation. The one closest to town is **Fern Ridge Lake** (25950 Richardson

It's worth climbing Mount Pisgah to see the memorial at the top.

Park Rd., Junction City, 541/688-8147). This lake was formed when the Long Tom River was dammed in 1941, and its southeast shore was designated a wildlife refuge in 1979. Visitors can camp, picnic, swim, water-ski, sail, fish, or watch wildlife.

To reach the lake, drive 10 miles west of downtown Eugene on West 11th Avenue (Rte. 126) toward Veneta, or take Clear Lake Road off Route 99W. The lake is drained in winter to allow for flood control, but the resulting marsh and wildlife refuge provide wildlife habitat. The wildlife area is closed to the public January-March 15 for the protection of wintering birds.

Biking

Eugene and Springfield together boast 120 miles of on-street bike lanes, limited-access streets, and off-street bikeways. The two cities collaborate to publish a free bicycle map; find it online by going to the **Eugene city website** (www.eugene-or.gov) and searching for "bicycle map." Especially appealing and easy to get to is the **Ruth Bascom Willamette River Bike Trail.**

Rent a bike from **Paul's Bicycle Way of Life** (556 Charnelton St., 541/344-4105, bicycleway.com, 9am-7pm Mon.-Fri., 10am-5pm Sat.-Sun.). Another local bike business is **Bike Friday** (3364 W. 11th Ave., 541/687-0487 or 800/777-0258, www.bikefriday.com, 9am-5:30pm Mon.-Fri., noon-4pm Sat.), known for elegant custom-made folding bicycles.

Golf

Of the many courses in Lane County, **Tokatee** (54947 Rte. 126, Blue River, 541/822-3220 or 800/452-6376, www.tokatee.com, Feb.-mid-Nov., $47 for 18 holes) is the best. To get there, drive 47 miles east of Eugene on the McKenzie Highway (Rte. 126). The 18 holes are set in a mountainous landscape patrolled by elk and other forest creatures in the shadow of the Three Sisters.

Spectator Sports

Each spring, the University of Oregon track team, a perennial contender for the status of best team in the nation, holds meets at **Hayward Field** (Agate St. and 15th Ave.). This site has also hosted such world-class events as the National Collegiate Athletic Association Finals and the U.S. Olympic Trials.

Fall means Duck football at **Autzen Stadium** (Martin Luther King Blvd. on Day Island). To get there, head north on Ferry Street; just after crossing the Willamette River, take a hard right on Martin Luther King Boulevard. Expect traffic.

In summer, the **Eugene Emeralds** (541/342-5367), a farm team for the Chicago Cubs, play ball at the PK Park right behind Autzen Stadium.

Water Sports

Alton Baker Park, along the Willamette River, and the Millrace Canal, which parallels the river for three or four miles, provide escapes from Eugene's main downtown thoroughfares. The canal is easily accessed from the University of Oregon campus by crossing Franklin Boulevard. During the summer, canoes, kayaks, and stand-up paddleboards are available for rent in Alton Baker Park.

ENTERTAINMENT AND EVENTS

Keeping up with Eugene's multifaceted entertainment offerings involves previewing the listings put out by two local newspapers, *Eugene Weekly* (http://eugeneweekly.com) and the daily *Eugene Register Guard* (www.registerguard.com); both have good online events listings, with the *Weekly* being a little more alternative. Check with the **University of Oregon ticket office** (541/346-4461, http://tickets.uoregon.edu) for athletic event and concert information.

Cutting-edge theater can be enjoyed at **Oregon Contemporary Theatre** (194 W. Broadway, 541/465-1506, www.octheatre.org).

Live Music

The best spot in town for frenetic dancing is

the **W.O.W. Hall** (291 W. 8th Ave., 541/687-2746, www.wowhall.org). This old Woodmen of the World meeting hall has remained a monument to Oregon's activist past in labor history (well, sort of, anyway: Its unofficial motto is now "Fighting to save rock & roll since 1975"). The W.O.W.'s floating hardwood dance floor and good acoustics allow it to rise above its junior high school gym ambience, and it hosts some surprisingly famous rock and blues performers. In any case, this all-ages venue is probably the most crowded and features an interesting cross section of Eugenians. Beer and wine are served downstairs.

Local bands and national acts, including comedians, play at the **McDonald Theatre** (1010 Willamette St., 541/345-4442, www.mcdonaldtheatre.com), which was built in 1925 and is now owned by the Kesey family, who work to maintain the old-fashioned ambience.

The **John G. Shedd Institute for the Arts** (868 High St., 541/687-6526, www.theshedd.org) brings in some really fun music (think Buckwheat Zydeco, Dar Williams, Steve Martin playing his banjo) and offers a wide variety of programs, including a performing arts company, a cultural arts center, and a community music school.

Big concerts occasionally take place within the cavernous enclaves of **Autzen Stadium** (2727 Leo Harris Pkwy., 541/346-4461, www.goducks.com), the home field to the Oregon Ducks football team. Near the Science Factory in Alton Baker Park, the **Cuthbert Amphitheater** (541/762-8099, www.thecuthbert.com) is a slightly more intimate (5,000-seat) outdoor theater; this is where you might go to see the Shins or David Byrne.

For more sedate listening, the **Hult Center** (E. 6th Ave. and Willamette St., 541/682-5000, www.hultcenter.org) is next door to the Hilton. The Eugene Symphony and other estimable local groups such as the Eugene Concert Choir perform here, along with a wide-ranging array of headliners from the world of music and comedy. This is also where most of the Bach Festival concerts occur.

Several clubs are clustered within a two-block area around West Broadway and Olive Street: the "Barmuda Triangle." The venerable **Horsehead** (99 W. Broadway, 541/683-3154, www.horseheadbareugene.com) has just about everything except live music—pool tables, darts, a pinball machine, and barbecue. **Cowfish** (62 W. Broadway, 541/683-6319) is a dance club, with an easygoing atmosphere and a large roster of DJs. **Jameson's** (115 W. Broadway, 541/485-9913, jamesonsbareugene.com) is classy but not overly fussy, with a retro-lounge feel.

Out in the Whiteaker neighborhood, **Sam Bond's Garage** (407 Blair Blvd., 541/421-6603, www.sambonds.com) serves live music (including weekly bluegrass jams), microbrews, and a menu of vegetarian pub grub until dawn; it's open every day.

Festivals and Events

There is a lot happening in this south Willamette Valley hub of culture and athletics. Several events—particularly the Eugene Marathon, the Oregon Bach Festival, and the Oregon Country Fair—best impart the cultural flavor of the area.

A **gallery walk** the first Friday of every month lets culture vultures enjoy open house exhibitions all over town. Consult the preceding Sunday's *Register Guard* for a complete listing of participating venues.

Late April brings runners to town for the **Eugene Marathon** (877/345-2230, www.eugenemarathon.com), which has a relatively flat course, starting and finishing at Hayward Field.

Appealing to lowbrow and highbrow alike is **Art and the Vineyard** (www.artandthevineyard.org, admission $7-9 adult, $1 children ages 6-11), which generally takes place over the Fourth of July weekend in Alton Baker Park. This event brings together art, music, and wine with over 100 artists' booths and the offerings of a dozen vineyards, accompanied by live music (jazz, country, blues,

Oregon Country Fair

Don't go to the Oregon Country Fair expecting to see livestock displays and prize-winning jellies. This is a place where body paint, feathers, man kilts, tie-dye, and good-natured frivolity rule. At one level, it's like a giant street fair, with artisans, food, and music, albeit in a beautiful wooded setting along the Long Tom River about 13 miles west of Eugene. But for the hundreds of crafts-people, musicians, jugglers, and volunteers who keep the fair running, and for many devoted fairgoers, it's way more than that…it's a celebration of life outside the edges of corporate America, and a way of maintaining an identity as a part of an alternative reality.

And that other world is pretty wide-ranging, including old hippies, circus performers, mystics, masseuses, musicians, the early-man-tool guy, fairies, community activists, and people dressed as trees. It's also very accepting and is especially welcoming to kids, elders, and the "alter-abled."

The crafts are high quality, and there's no better place to shop for a tie-dyed t-shirt. But the performances, both on the 18 stages and along the wooded paths, are the best part of the Oregon Country Fair. Stages range from **Shady Grove,** a quiet venue for acoustic music, to the **Daredevil Stage,** hosting contemporary New Vaudeville stars and other rollicking performers, to the **Main Stage,** which hosts the big acts. Don't miss the Fighting Instruments of Karma Marching Chamber Band/Orchestra parading through the fair or playing up on **Stage Left;** various permutations of the band have been rocking the joint with everything from Sousa marches to Bollywood dance tunes for over 40 years.

The **Oregon Country Fair** (541/343-4298, www.oregoncountryfair.org, 11am-7pm Fri.-Sun. the weekend after July 4 holiday, $23-29, $59 for three days, $5 senior discount). is near Veneta on Route 126. Tickets must be purchased in advance at a Safeway store or through **Tickets West** (800/992-8499, http://ticketswest.rdln.com).

Due to the popularity of this event, which attracts more than 50,000 attendees, the best way to get there is to take the free shuttle from Eugene's Valley River Mall or the downtown Eugene bus station. Bus service usually begins at about 10:30am, with the last departure from the fair site at 7pm. Car access to the fair is open 10am-6pm, but on-site parking is limited; expect a long walk from your car to the gate. Parking costs $10 at the gate, a couple of bucks less when reserved in advance.

and folk) and food concessions. Contact the **Maude Kerns Art Center** (541/345-1571, www.mkartcenter.org) for details and tickets.

Join the free **Festival of Eugene** (Skinner Butte Park, 541/681-4108, www.festivalofeugene.com). This three-day fete in late August includes such events as a pet parade, food and craft vendors, a poetry stage, a kid zone, and three performance stages.

Note: When Eugene hosts the U.S. Olympic team's track-and-field trials, the town books up months in advance. If you are planning to visit in June 2016, when the trials will be held here again, book your room as soon as possible.

OREGON BACH FESTIVAL
The **Oregon Bach Festival** (541/346-5666 and 800/457-1486, www.oregonbachfestival.

com) takes place over two weeks late June-early July and features a sparkling array of internationally renowned opera and symphonic virtuosos. Festival-goers can choose from more than two dozen concerts (some are also performed in Portland, Ashland, and Bend), with musical styles ranging from the Baroque era to the 20th century. The centerpieces of the festival, however, are Bach works such as the *St. Matthew Passion,* numerous cantatas, and the Brandenburg Concertos.

Performances take place in the Hult Center and the Beall Concert Hall at the University of Oregon Music School. Free events, including "Let's Talk with the Conductor," mini-concerts, and lectures also take place at these venues during the festival.

ACCOMMODATIONS

Although there are abundant chain hotels at the I-5 exits, these lodgings are miles from the fun and bustle of downtown Eugene. Luckily, the campus and downtown neighborhoods offer lots of choices for motels within walking distance of the Eugene scene. Expect prices to bump up during football and back-to-school weekends.

Under $50

The **Eugene Whiteaker International Hostels** (970 W. 3rd Ave., 541/343-3335, http://eugenehostels.com, $20-38) offer inexpensive lodging in two older homes converted into well-run hostels in the funky, convenient Whiteaker neighborhood just west of downtown.

$50-100

A few older but well-kept motor court hotels have convenient locations in downtown Eugene. **Downtown Inn** (361 W. 7th Ave., 800/648-4366, downtowninn.com, $83) is an accessible bargain. If you don't expect luxury, you'll enjoy the 1950s ambience of this classic motel. Nearby, the **Courtesy Inn** (345 W. 6th Ave., 888/259-8481, www.courtesyinneugene.com, $90-105) is another good bet; it's a couple of blocks from the Hult Center and within easy walking distance of restaurants.

The **Timbers Motel** (1015 Pearl St., 800/643-4167, www.timbersmotel.net, $79-109) is one of our longtime downtown Eugene favorites; we like to bunk in the tiny timbered-topped budget room.

On the edge of downtown, the **Broadway Inn** (476 E. Broadway Ave., 541/344-5233 or 800/876-7829, www.eugenebroadwayinn.com, $83-93) offers clean, simple rooms and a very convenient location.

Over $100

The **Best Western New Oregon Motel** (1655 Franklin Blvd., 541/683-3669, www.bestwestern.com, $103-132) is a good choice for visiting parents of U. of O. students or for folks in town to attend a sporting or cultural event. It's right across the street from the Registration Office and dormitories. Although the motel is on a busy street, it backs up to the riverside millrace, and riverside paths lead to a footbridge to Alton Baker Park.

The **Campbell House** (252 Pearl St., 541/343-1119, www.campbellhouse.com, $129-319, breakfast included) is a 19-room Victorian mansion in the historic east Skinner Butte neighborhood. Proximity to the Fifth Street Market and the river, as well as the sophistication of a European-style B&B complete with a dinner restaurant, makes this antique-filled 1892 gem a good lodging choice. Note that the least expensive rooms are quite small.

At the center of downtown, the **Eugene Hilton** (66 E. 6th Ave., 541/342-2000, www3.hilton.com, $134-244, parking $15) has a great location right across the street from the Hult Center and within easy walking distance of the city's best restaurants. We mention it here because of its location and because it sometimes has very good weekend rates.

The upstairs of a popular eatery just a block from campus, the **Excelsior Inn** (754 E. 13th Ave., 541/485-1206, www.excelsiorinn.com, $135-300, breakfast included) offers 14 elegant bed-and-breakfast guest rooms featuring antiques, cherry furniture, marble tile, and fresh-cut flowers. An elevator makes the rooms wheelchair accessible. An excellent standard motel is the **Valley River Inn** (1000 Valley River Way, Valley River Center, 541/687-0123, www.valleyriverinn.com, $129-233, web specials often available). Don't be deterred by its location away from downtown behind a giant shopping mall; the Willamette River is in back of the inn, which provides easy access to the riverside trail network. In fact, it's easier to get downtown along the bike path than it is to drive. It's also a good place to stay if you're traveling with a dog; the inn is pet-friendly, and the riverside path makes for delightful dog walks. A decent restaurant, a crackling fire in the lobby, and pool and spa facilities add to the allure. If it's in your budget, pony up an extra $20 for a riverside room—the view is worth it.

Over $200

Eugene proves that it can be a little bit glamorous at its newest hotel, ★ **Inn at the 5th** (205 E. 6th Ave., 541/743-4099, www.innat5th. com, $204-460). This boutique hotel is the place to stay for a romantic weekend or when you want to feel pampered. Of course, this being Oregon, the luxury is all quite sustainable: The giant wood-slab table in the lobby was taken from an 80-year-old bigleaf maple that was sacrificed to build the hotel; pieces of the tree are featured in rooms throughout the hotel. With room service by next-door Marché restaurant and a spa on the ground floor, it's easy to hole up at the inn, but bikes are available in case you want to cruise the riverside trails.

Camping

Richardson County Park (25950 Richardson Park Rd., Junction City, 541/935-2005, www.lanecounty.org, Apr.-mid-Oct., $25, $10 reservation fee and small surcharge for some "premier" sites) has sites with hookups on the shores of Fern Ridge Reservoir six miles northwest of Eugene; take Clear Lake Road off Route 99 to its intersection with Territorial Road.

During Oregon Country Fair, many campgrounds spring up on private and public land near the fair site in Veneta; find a list at www. oregoncountryfair.org. **Zumwalt Park** (29652 Jeans Rd., Veneta, 541/935-2335, $35) is a privately owned RV campground and marina 12 miles west of Eugene convenient to the Oregon Country Fair. Although many spots are occupied by long-term residents, it's a well-kept place with a nice lakeside location.

FOOD

Eating out in Eugene has long been a delight, thanks to the staggering array of locally made gourmet products and organic foods available from local farms, ranches, and the nearby Pacific.

Fifth Street Public Market Area

The northern edge of downtown Eugene is dominated by the **Fifth Street Public Market,** a renovated market building that houses a number of restaurants, including a large food court with five food purveyors to choose from. The three-story, internal courtyard is overflowing with art and greenery, making a very pleasant spot for a casual meal.

Since it opened in 1997, ★ **Marché** (296 E. 5th Ave., 541/342-3612, www.marcheres-taurant.com, 7am-11pm Sun.-Wed., 7am-midnight Thurs.-Sat., dinner entrées $18-35) has set the standard for fine dining in Eugene. The restaurant, in the ground-floor southwest corner of the Fifth Street Public Market, is as close to a French bistro as you're going to find in this town, and the food is French-inflected, with an emphasis on fresh local produce and meat. The atmosphere is crisp but not fussy, and if you sit in the bar, you can while away an enjoyable but not particularly expensive evening with drinks and casual fare such as steak frites ($18).

For a more casual take on Marché's food, head upstairs in the Fifth Street Market to **Marché Provisions** (296 E. 5th Ave., 541/743-0660, 8am-8pm Mon.-Sat., 8am-7pm Sun., www.marcheprovisions.com, $7-17 for a light meal), where the food spans the hours from late breakfast to early dinner with quiche, tasty open-faced sandwiches, pizza, soups, salads, deli items, and dessert.

A few blocks west, near the train station, **Belly Taqueria** (454 Willamette Ave., 541/687-8226, www.eatbelly.com, 5pm-9:30pm Mon.-Thurs., 5pm-10:30pm Fri.-Sat., tacos $3-6) is high-end for a taqueria, with good cocktails and seasonal specials such as tacos filled with braised octopus and pork belly.

Central Downtown Area

Full City Coffee (842 Pearl St., 541/344-0475, www.full-city.com, 5:30am-6pm Mon.-Fri., 6:30am-6pm Sat., 7am-5pm Sun.) is locally noted for its daily grind; pick up a muffin or a sandwich to accompany your coffee at the adjacent **Palace Bakery** (844 Pearl St., 541/484-2435, 7am-5:30pm Mon.-Sat., 8am-2pm Sun.).

★ **Belly** (30 E. Broadway, 541/683-5896, www.eatbelly.com, 5pm-9:30pm Tues.-Thurs., 5pm-10:30pm Fri.-Sat., $11-19), in a noisy, consciously hip downtown location, offers country French cooking with a few Southwestern U.S. touches and specializes in house-made charcuterie, sausages, confit, and other meaty dishes.

Wander down Oak Alley to find **Falling Sky Brewing** (1334 Oak Alley, 541/505-7096, www.fallingskybrewing.com, 11am-midnight Sun.-Wed., 11am-1am Thurs.-Sat., $9-15) and snack on warm pretzel sticks or dig into a Cuban-style pork sandwich. Even when the weather's marginal, the covered and heated outdoor patio is a good place to sip one of the brews (which include a root beer).

In the heart of downtown, **Poppi's Anatolia** (992 Willamette St., 541/343-9661, http://poppisanatolia.com, 11:30am-9pm Mon.-Thurs., 11:30am-10pm Fri., 11:30am-3pm and 5pm-10pm Sat., 5pm-9pm Sun., $10-17) is a Eugene mainstay for Greek and Indian food. Spicy curries and vindaloo chicken are complemented by saganaki (fried cheese), spanakopita (spinach cheese pie), and gyro sandwiches. The best baklava in town with a shot of ouzo or retsina can finish off a richly flavored and moderately priced repast.

At the southwestern edge of downtown, **Cafe Soriah** (384 W. 13th Ave., 541/342-4410, cafesoriah.com, 5pm-10pm daily, $16-32) is a popular choice for a romantic dinner. Both its patio for summer outdoor dining and its bar offer great ambience, but the Mediterranean-Middle Eastern cuisine is the real attraction. Moussaka and various dishes featuring chicken and lamb with vegetables sautéed in olive oil stand out.

Classy and inviting, **The Davis Restaurant & Bar** (94 W. Broadway, 541/485-1124, 11am-11pm Mon.-Thurs., 11am-2am Fri., 4pm-2am Sat., $9-24) has a broad selection of tempting starters, such as BLT gougère sliders. Most salads and main courses are available as small plates or regular dinner portions, making it fun to graze through a variety of dishes. Braised pork shoulder is served with ramps and wild mushroom demi-glace, and grilled quail comes with fig agrodolce sauce. At night, a young and stylish crowd gathers for drinks and to listen to live music.

Between downtown and the university, find a couple of good places to drink beer. **16 Tons Taphouse** (265 E. 13th Ave., 541/345-2003, http://sixteentons.biz, noon-10pm Sun.-Wed., noon-midnight Thurs.-Sat.) is an easygoing beer shop and pub with nearly 20 taps dispensing a rotating selection of some of the state's best beers. The **Bier Stein** (1591 Willamette St., 541/485-2437, 11am-midnight Mon.-Sat., noon-10pm Sun.) has a warehouse-sized refrigerator case filled with beers and ciders from around the world and over 20 taps.

University Campus Area

The eateries on the campus periphery are a cut above those found in most college towns, and even the on-campus offerings are pretty good. One such campus food court, **Fresh Marketcafé** (Global Scholars Hall, 541/346-4277, 10am-10pm daily, $5-12), is behind the Natural History Museum and offers pastas, sushi and bento, rice bowls, salads, smoothies, and coffee.

Start the day at **Campus Glenwood** (1340 Alder St., 541/687-0355, www.glenwood-restaurants.com, 7am-9pm daily, $5-15) or at the south-side **Glenwood** (2588 Willamette St., 541/687-8201, 6:30am-9pm Mon.-Fri., 7am-9pm Sat.-Sun., $5-15). Although both restaurants are open for three meals a day, breakfast is what keeps people coming back. Come prepared for a wait on weekend mornings.

In the shadow of the campus, the **Excelsior Inn Ristorante** (754 E. 13th Ave., 541/485-1206, www.excelsiorinn.com, 7am-10am and 11:30am-9pm Mon.-Thurs., 7am-10am and 11:30am-10pm Fri., 8am-10am and 4pm-10pm Sat., 8am-2pm and 4pm-9pm Sun., $27-36) is an elegant restaurant in a charming old home. The Italian menu might include ravioli filled with Dungeness crab and buttered leeks or grilled prawns with red pepper risotto. Many ingredients are grown at the restaurant's farm south of town. Although the Excelsior is very close to campus, it draws an older crowd; when you see students here, they're often with their parents, who may be staying in the inn upstairs. Behind Hayward Field, find top-notch ice cream at **Prince Puckler's** (1605 E. 19th Ave., 541/344-4418, noon-11pm daily, $2-6), a Eugene institution since 1975. Although President Obama went for the mint chocolate chip when he visited, our favorite is the Velvet Hammer shake ($2.60), with Mexican chocolate and espresso.

South of Downtown

After a weekend morning run at Amazon Park, head to **Hideaway Bakery** (3377 E. Amazon Dr., 541/868-1982, 7am-6pm Mon.-Sat., 7am-4pm Sun., $4-8) for pastries, a breakfast sandwich, or a slice of wood-oven pizza. This popular bakery, tucked behind the venerable Mazzi's Italian restaurant) has a great patio and delicious sweet and savory treats.

Dinner on the outside deck at **Beppe & Gianni's Trattoria** (1646 E. 19th Ave.,

541/683-6661, http://beppeandgiannis.net, 5pm-9pm Sun.-Thurs., 5pm-10pm Sat.-Sun., $16-25) is one of Eugene's coveted summertime dining experiences. The menu features homemade pastas with light northern Italian cream- or olive oil-based sauces graced by fresh vegetables, meats, or fish. Try the *cappelli di vescovo* (bishop hats)—pasta stuffed with Swiss chard, prosciutto, and cheese in a brown-butter sage sauce.

Whiteaker Neighborhood

Just west of center city is Blair Boulevard and the Whiteaker neighborhood. A restaurant row has developed in this agreeably funky neighborhood. These places, for the most part, are easy on the pocketbook while offering an interesting variety of cuisines.

Wandering Goat (268 Madison St., 541/344-5161, www.wanderinggoat.com, 6am-11pm Mon.-Wed., 6am-midnight Thurs.-Sat., 6am-10pm Sun.) is Eugene's top coffee shop, with discerning hipster baristas serving coffee from beans roasted in the back room, music many evenings, good baked goods (many vegan), and beer.

Just across the street from Wandering Goat, find excellent beer at the **Oakshire**

Wandering Goat serves some of Eugene's best coffee.

Brewing Public House (207 Madison St., 541/688-4555, http://oakbrew.com, 11am-10pm daily). The brewers started out with an amber, added an IPA and some seasonal brews, and now offer a changing menu of single-batch brews such as a Belgian-style strong wit or a double IPA (with 100-plus IBUs for you hopheads). Although Oakshire's food offerings are minimal, customers are welcome to bring their own food to the pub.

By now, **Ninkasi Brewing Company** (272 Van Buren St., 541/344-2739, http://ninkasi-brewing.com, noon-9pm Sun.-Wed., noon-10pm Thurs.-Sat.), which has made some of Oregon's best beer in the Whiteaker area since 2007, is a neighborhood institution. The ancient Sumerian goddess of fermentation surely casts a fond eye on Total Domination IPA, as do the locals and visitors who gather at the tasting room. The focus is on beer, not food, but there's usually a food cart posted outside the tasting room.

One of the neighborhood highlights is the ★ **Pizza Research Institute** (530 Blair Blvd., 541/343-1307, www.pizzaresearchinstitute.com, 4pm-9:30pm daily, $16 for small pizza), which has the most innovative pizza in town. In this case, innovation equals excellence—try the chef's choice, which is invariably tasty and has ingredients arranged to form a mandala. PRI, which serves only veggie pies, has a friendly, spunky feel that's thoroughly Eugenian.

Chill out at **Izakaya Meiji Company** (345 Van Buren St., 541/545-8804, http://izakaya-meiji.com, 5pm-1am daily, $3-11) with very good Japanese-inspired small plates and a cocktail. Later in the evening, it's more of a bar scene.

If you need a treat to start the day, make it through the afternoon, or cap off a restaurant dinner, visit **Sweet Life Patisserie** (755 Monroe St., 541/683-5676, sweetlifedesserts.com, 7am-11pm Mon.-Fri., 8am-11pm Sat.-Sun.), where a hazelnut fig tartlet might just do the trick. Gluten-free and vegan options abound.

INFORMATION AND SERVICES

Find info about Eugene, the Cascades, and the coast at one of **Travel Lane County's** (www.eugenecascadescoast.org) two locations: downtown at 754 Olive Street (800/547-5445) or just off I-5 in Springfield (3312 Gateway St., 541/484-5307 or 800/547-5445). The Springfield location is better if you're looking for info on outdoor activities.

The **Smith Family Bookstore** (768 E. 13th Ave., 541/345-1651, and 525 Willamette St., 541/343-4717, www.smithfamilybookstore.com) purveys an excellent collection of used books. **Tsunami Books** (2585 Willamette St., 541/345-8986) is a local favorite for books and in-store events.

The main local public radio station, **KLCC** (89.7 FM), is an NPR affiliate with lots of news and music programming ranging from new wave jazz to blues. The University of Oregon station **KWAX** (91.1 FM) provides continuous classical music.

Eugene Weekly (1251 Lincoln St., 541/484-0519, www.eugeneweekly.com) has the best entertainment listings in Eugene. At the beginning of each season, the magazine's *Chow* edition will point you in the direction of Eugene's hot restaurants. This publication is available free at commercial establishments all over town.

GETTING THERE AND AROUND

If you're in your own car or on a bike, remember the campus is in the southeastern part of town; 1st Avenue parallels the Willamette River; and Willamette Street divides the city east and west. Navigation is complicated by many one-way roads and dead ends. Look for alleyways that allow through traffic to avoid getting stuck.

Amtrak (4th and Willamette, 541/344-6265, www.amtrak.com) offers three different transport options. The long-distance *Coast Starlight* links Eugene to major West Coast hubs from Los Angeles to Seattle. Two additional daily Amtrak Cascades trains (www.

Covered Bridges Scenic Bikeway

The town of Cottage Grove, some 20 miles south of Eugene, is known for its **covered bridges** (there are six in the area; details at www.cgchamber.com) and as being the gateway to the Bohemia mining district, the site of old abandoned mines. The 14.1-mile **Row River Trail** is a rails-to-trails route that follows the paved-over tracks of an old mining train from Cottage Grove to Culp Creek—perfect for mountain biking, birding, and mushroom hunting (especially after the first fall rains). A longer bike route that includes the Row River Trail, the **Covered Bridges Scenic Bikeway** (rideoregonride.com), starts in Cottage Grove and runs 38 relatively flat miles past six covered bridges and around Dorena Lake.

If you're looking for campsites in the covered bridge country near Cottage Grove, try the lakeside **Baker Bay County Park** (35635 Shoreview Dr., Dorena, 541/682-2000, www.lanecounty. org, mid-Apr.-mid-Oct., $20, $10 reservation fee). Take I-5 south to Mosby Creek Road (take the Cottage Grove exit), turn left, then left again on Row River Road, and then take the right fork. It's about 18 miles from Eugene.

amtrakcascades.com) link Eugene to Portland and Seattle, with connections to Vancouver, British Columbia. In addition, Amtrak runs through-way bus service each day to Portland and on to the northern Oregon coast.

Greyhound (9th Ave. and Pearl St., 800/231-2222) is the other major mode of long-distance public transport, heading south to San Francisco or north to Portland several times daily from Eugene.

Around town, **Lane Transit District** (541/687-5555, www.ltd.org, $1.75) has canopied pavilions displaying the bus timetables downtown. All buses are equipped with bike racks.

The **Eugene Airport** (541/682-5430, www.eugene-or.gov/airport) is a 20-minute drive northwest from downtown—just get on the Delta Highway off Washington Street and follow the signs. United Express, Horizon, American, Allegiant Air, SkyWest, and Delta Connection all operate flights in and out of Eugene. There is no city bus service to the airport. **OmniShuttle** (541/461-7959, www. omnishuttle.com, $25.50 from downtown) provides door-to-door shuttle service to and from Eugene Airport to various points in Lane County. **Budget Taxi** (541/683-8294) can also take you where you need to go (airport runs start at $15). **Rental car companies** Avis, Budget, Hertz, and Enterprise also have kiosks at the airport.

The McKenzie River Highway

From I-5 near Eugene, reach the scenic McKenzie River Highway by taking Highway 126 east. Just past Springfield, where the four lanes merge into two, the McKenzie River Recreation Area begins. For the next 60 miles, you'll see beautiful views of the blue-green McKenzie River with heavily forested mountains, frothy waterfalls, jet-black lava beds, and snowcapped peaks as a backdrop.

The first 15 miles of the McKenzie River Highway pass through many fruit and nut orchards (primarily apples, cherries, and filberts), Christmas tree farms, and berry patches.

The Leaburg Dam signals your entry into the middle section of the McKenzie; six dams on the McKenzie provide power, irrigation, and what the Army Corps of Engineers calls "fish enhancement." A favorite haunt of fishing enthusiasts, the mellow waters of the middle McKenzie teem with trout, steelhead, and salmon. Mild white-water rafting and drift boat fishing are popular here, and local guides and outfitters are ready to help you float your expeditions.

The McKenzie River National Recreation Trail and many less vaunted yet still lovely trails feature waterfalls, mountain lakes, or lava formations a short trek from the road. In addition to the myriad recreational opportunities, hot springs, abundant accommodations, and a relative dearth of crowds give you the western slopes of the Cascades at their finest.

SIGHTS
Aufderheide National Scenic Byway

The 58-mile **Aufderheide Drive** links Route 126 to Route 58 near Oakridge. You'll find the Aufderheide turnoff (Forest Service Rd. 19) at mile marker 45.9 about five miles east of Blue River. The road winds along the south fork of the McKenzie River, crests the pass, and then follows the north fork of the middle fork of the Willamette River down to Oakridge and Route 58. Sights along the way include the Delta Old-Growth Grove Nature Trail, Terwilliger (a.k.a. Cougar) Hot Springs, the

Willamette River Gorge, and the Westfir covered bridge. The Aufderheide makes a spectacular, though tough, ride on a road bike; it's also a popular motorcycle route.

Terwilliger (Cougar) Hot Springs

If you'd like to try soaking in hot springs in a natural setting, head for **Terwilliger Hot Springs** (also called **Cougar Hot Springs**) in a forested canyon at the end of a 0.25-mile trail. Hot water bubbles up out of the earth at 116°F and flows down through a series of log and stone pools, each a few degrees cooler than the previous one. The local custom is to forgo clothing.

To get there, take the Aufderheide Drive from Route 126 south toward Cougar Reservoir. The trailhead for the hot springs on the west (right) side of the road is marked by a sign just past mile marker 7. You can park in a large lot on the east side of the road about 500 feet past the trailhead (alongside the reservoir). Parking alongside the road is prohibited (and enforced) from sunset to sunrise a mile from the trailhead. A $6-per-person day-use fee is required, and it has enabled this place to be well maintained. The hot springs are open from sunrise to sunset daily.

The South Fork of the McKenzie River is backed up by a dam to form Cougar Reservoir.

Most bathers shed their clothes at Terwilliger Hot Springs (aka Cougar Hot Springs).

The several pools in this tranquil forest setting can be overcrowded on weekends. Although this hot spring offers an exceptionally nice soaking experience and is generally an easygoing, tranquil place to hang out, it can occasionally attract an unsavory crowd. Women traveling alone may want to scrutinize the scene before taking the plunge.

If it's too warm for hot springs, consider swimming in the lagoon that's below the hot springs trail. From the pay station, it's a short hike in, and a steep descent along a path to the swimming hole.

Proxy Falls

To get to **Proxy Falls,** follow the old McKenzie Pass road (Rte. 242, closed in winter, 35-foot vehicle limit) from the new McKenzie Pass highway (Rte. 126) for 10 miles. The 1.5-mile loop trail, on the south side of the road, leads to a spectacular pair of waterfalls, Upper and Lower Proxy Falls.

From the large bulletin board at the trailhead, a small arrow points to the right. However, that will be the longer route, and it also requires hiking over sharp stones for part of the way. Going to the left at that bulletin board leads you to the trail, which is a shorter and easier route.

Take a left at the trailhead for an easy 0.5-mile walk to Upper Proxy. Take a left at the first fork in the trail (marked by a sign) to Upper Proxy Falls.

Now that you've seen Upper Proxy Falls from the bottom up, check out Lower Proxy Falls from the top down. Go back to the fork in the trail and take a left. In less than 0.5 mile, you will suddenly be on a ridge looking across a valley at Lower Proxy Falls. The hike back to the trailhead passes over a lava field, so wear shoes that can withstand the sharp rocks.

Dee Wright Observatory

The **Dee Wright Observatory** (57600 McKenzie River Hwy. on Rte. 242, 541/822-3381, closed in winter at the first sign of snow), built in the early 1930s as a Civilian Conservation Corps project, is at McKenzie Pass about halfway between Route 126 and Sisters. The tower windows line up with views of Mount Jefferson, Mount Washington, and two of the Three Sisters, as well as the eight-mile-long, half-mile-wide lava flow that bubbled out of nearby Yapoah a little less than 3,000 years ago. On a clear day, you can even see the tip of Mount Hood.

The 0.5-mile Lava River Trail next to the observatory offers a fine foray into the surrounding hills of rolling black rock. Note that on Route 242, vehicle length is restricted to a maximum of 35 feet.

Koosah Falls

Koosah Falls is about 20 miles from McKenzie Bridge on Route 126. The visitor facilities here provide wheelchair access and excellent views of this impressive 70-foot-high waterfall on the McKenzie. If you look carefully, you can see many small springs flowing from crevices in the basalt at the base of the waterfall. The blue water may have inspired the name Koosah, which comes from the Chinook word for "sky."

Sahalie Falls

Sahalie Falls is only 0.5 mile east from McKenzie Bridge on Route 126 from Koosah Falls. From McKenzie Bridge, travel east on Route 126 to Road 2672. Follow Road 2672 to Forest Service Road 655. Follow Forest Service Road 655 to the Sahalie Falls Day Use Area. The result of a lava dam from the Cascade Range's not-so-distant volcanic past, the river tumbles 100 feet into a green canyon. This is the highest waterfall on the McKenzie River—sahalie means "high" in the Chinook language.

Clear Lake

Just north of Sahalie and Koosah Falls and east of Route 126 is Clear Lake, which forms the headwaters of the McKenzie River. The best way to appreciate this lake, which is indeed remarkably clear, is in a canoe, so that you can paddle out to the northern end of the lake and look down to see the 3,000-year-old underwater forest that was submerged when lava flows dammed the water and created it. A campground and a resort are at the lake; the resort rents out canoes.

SPORTS AND RECREATION

Hiking

DELTA OLD-GROWTH GROVE NATURE TRAIL

Find the 0.5-mile loop Delta Old-Growth Grove Natural Trail through an old-growth ecosystem on the west side of the Aufderheide Byway not far from Route 126. In addition to 650-year-old conifers, you'll see other layers of life from shrubs and ground cover plants to fish, mammals, birds, and amphibians. Many plant species are clearly marked along the trail.

★ MCKENZIE RIVER NATIONAL RECREATION TRAIL

The McKenzie River National Recreation Trail (Trail 3507) runs for 26.5 miles and is extremely popular with mountain bikers as well as hikers. It starts just east of the small town of McKenzie Bridge and goes to the Old Santiam Wagon Road, about three miles south of the junction of Route 126 and U.S. 20. But don't let the long distance scare you. There are enough access points to let you design treks of three, five, eight, or more miles along this beautiful trail. It is hard to say which section of the footpath is the best, as each portion has its own charms; the following highlights give you a sample of what to expect.

Start at the top of the McKenzie River Trail at the Old Santiam Wagon Road. Completed in the early 1860s, this was the first link of the route from the mid-Willamette Valley to central and eastern Oregon. Way stations were established a day's journey apart to assist the pioneers along their weary way. Although most of these primitive establishments are no more, some of the historic buildings have survived. There isn't much left of the Old Santiam Wagon Road either, as much of it was destroyed with the construction of Route 126. However, a seven-mile stretch remains from Route 126 through the rugged lava country to the Pacific Crest Trail. A short walk on this former road to the promised land helps you to appreciate both the hardiness of the pioneers and the comforts of modern travel.

From the Old Santiam Wagon Road, the McKenzie River Trail surveys many remarkable volcanic formations. Lava flows over the last few thousand years have built dams, created waterfalls, and even buried the river altogether. Koosah and Sahalie Falls were also created by lava dams, and the view of these white-water cascades from the McKenzie River Trail is much different than the version accessible from the highway. Another interesting sight is the Tamolitch Valley, where the McKenzie gradually sinks beneath the porous lava, disappearing altogether until it reemerges three miles later at cobalt-colored Tamolitch Pool (often called the Blue Pool). This area is accessible only on the National Recreation Trail.

If possible, arrange your McKenzie outing with friends and run a two-car shuttle; **McKenzie River Mountain Resort** (541/822-6272, www.rivermountainresort. com) runs a shuttle service. Also keep in mind that hikes starting at the upper end of the trail take advantage of the descending elevation. Mountain bikes are allowed on all sections of the McKenzie River Trail; McKenzie River Mountain Resort also runs a bike shuttle service.

ROBINSON LAKE TRAIL

The 0.25-mile **Robinson Lake Trail** takes you to a heart-shaped lake with some fishing and swimming. To get there, take Route 126 about 16 miles east of McKenzie Bridge and turn right onto Robinson Lake Road. Be on the lookout for logging trucks and rocks on the gravel road. Follow the signs marked Forest Service Road 2664. At the junction, drive straight onto the red pumice road (Forest Service Rd. 2664) and continue until you reach the parking lot. It takes about 10 minutes to drive the four miles in. The easy hiking trail is in good condition; the left fork takes you to the center shore of Robinson Lake. The shallow lake warms up considerably during the summer, making a swim all the more inviting.

Fishing

Sure it's crowded, but scenic beauty and the chance to bag a five-trout limit lines 'em up on one of the state's best trout streams. Unless you can get a drift boat, access is limited. On weekends, drift boats and rafters vie for space. You can cast worms or spinners, though you're better off using flies when you're fishing off a boat for rainbow trout April-October. Anglers might want to book a trip with **Helfrich Outfitters** (541/741-1905 or 800/507-9889, www.helfrichoutfitter.com, full-day trip $400 for two anglers). Consult the **Oregon Outfitters and Guides Directory** for other local guides (www.ogpa.org). The best pools tend to be west of Blue River, but it's harder to get to them because of private landholdings. Be sure to check for rules and regulations before you go fishing; the **Department of Fish and Wildlife** (503/947-6000, www.dfw.state. or.us) can give you the information you need.

Golf

If you like to play golf, you should plan your vacation around a visit to **Tokatee Golf Club** (54947 Rte. 126, Blue River, 541/822-3220 or 800/452-6376, www.tokatee.com, Feb.-mid-Nov., $47 for 18 holes), one of the Pacific Northwest's most beautiful courses. Good for all levels of experience; every hole has its own challenge. No houses are on the fairways to obstruct the knockout views of the forested mountains and the Three Sisters Wilderness.

Mountain Biking

In the upper sections of the McKenzie, most of the usable trails gain elevation rapidly due to the steep terrain and make for very challenging biking. The most popular route is the **McKenzie River Trail.** Contact the **McKenzie River Ranger District** (503/822-3381) for detailed information. **McKenzie River Mountain Resort** (541/822-6272, www.rivermountainresort.com) has bikes for rent and runs a shuttle service for trail users.

Rafting

The McKenzie River becomes navigable at the

Olallie campground, about 11 miles east of McKenzie Bridge. Between the Olallie campground and the town of Blue River, there are seven public boat launches, including at Paradise and McKenzie Bridge campgrounds. Expect to encounter Class II and III rapids along the Upper McKenzie. Many local outfitters can guide you down the river.

McKenzie River Adventures (541/822-3806 or 800/832-5858, www.mckenzieriveradventures.com) has half-, full-, and two-day white-water rafting trips May-September. The half-day (three-hour) trip is $60 adults; the full-day (six-hour) trip is $100, lunch included. The cruises range 7-18 miles and take in some Class II and III rapids. Reservations are recommended. **Oregon Whitewater Adventures** (39620 Deerhorn Rd., Springfield, 541/746-5422 or 800/820-7238, www.oregonwhitewater.com) has similar trips and a two-day overnighter for $325. All necessary gear and transportation back to your car are included.

ACCOMMODATIONS

A great place for families (including pets) and those who want to get away from the noise of the McKenzie Highway is the **Wayfarer Resort** (46725 Goodpasture Rd., Vida, 541/896-3613, www.wayfarerresort.com, $115-335), featuring over a dozen cabins on the McKenzie and glacier-fed Marten Creek east of Vida. Accommodating 1-6 people, the cabins have porches with barbecues overlooking the water, full kitchens, and lots of wood paneling. Two larger units can sleep eight and are equipped with all the amenities. Children can enjoy fishing privileges in the resort's private trout pond, while the folks play on the resort's tennis court. In the summer, advance reservations are a must for this popular retreat.

The riverside **Eagle Rock Lodge** (49198 McKenzie Hwy., Vida, 541/822-3630, www.eaglerocklodge.com, $130-225) is one of the more elegant places to stay along the McKenzie. The large 1947 house has five extra-comfortable rooms in the main house and three suites in the carriage house; beautiful gardens and places to lounge outside surround the buildings. Guests have the option of ordering dinner from the lodge's personal chef ($40), which is particularly nice since there aren't many restaurants in the area.

Heaven's Gate Cottages (50055 McKenzie Hwy., Vida, 541/896-3855, www.heavensgaterivercottages.com, $125-150) offers housekeeping cabins right on the McKenzie (and the highway); the cabins are sandwiched between the highway and the river. One cabin is right over a good fishing hole, and night lights illuminate the rapids for your contemplation. These cabins may be old, small, and semirustic, but their riverside location helps overcome a multitude of issues. Note: although the official address for Heaven's Gate is in Vida, the cabins are much closer to Blue River.

The former Blue River ranger station, which sits above the highway away from the river, has been repurposed as the lodge for the **McKenzie River Mountain Resort** (51668 Blue River Dr., Blue River, 541/822-6272, www.rivermountainresort.com, $80-190); vacation cabins used to house the rangers. This is a popular base for mountain bikers riding the McKenzie River Trail; the resort offers a shuttle service. It's common for groups to rent the entire lodge.

Although **Harbick's Country Inn** (54791 Rte. 126, Blue River, 541/822-3805, www.harbicks-country-inn.com, $75-115) may not be as charming as some of the other lodgings along the McKenzie (it's basically a motel), it's a friendly place and within walking distance of one of the finest public golf courses in the country, Tokatee. It also has a good restaurant next door. Because of this, it's quite popular—reserve in advance.

The ★ **Cedarwood Lodge** (56535 McKenzie Hwy./Rte. 126, McKenzie Bridge, 541/822-3351, www.cedarwoodlodge.com, Apr.-Oct., $125-185) is tucked away in a grove of old cedars just outside the town of McKenzie Bridge. The lodge has nine vacation housekeeping cottages with fully equipped kitchens, bathrooms (with showers), fireplaces (wood provided), and portable barbecues. This is a sweet place to spend a couple of nights, particularly in those units with decks on the river.

The spacious and attractive cabins at ★ **Inn at the Bridge** (56393 McKenzie Hwy., McKenzie Bridge, 541/822-6006, www.mckenzie-river-cabins.com, $199) are open year-round. Though these beautiful cabins look like they are part of the landscape, they were built in 2006 and are fully modern, with two bedrooms, full kitchen, river-rock fireplaces, two bathrooms, and a back porch overlooking the river.

Belknap Lodge and Hot Springs (59296 Belknap Springs Rd., McKenzie Bridge, 541/822-3512, www.belknaphotsprings.com, $25-425) offers lodge rooms, cabins, camping, and access to two hot springs swimming pools. The lodge rooms range $100-185 per couple; bathtubs are plumbed with hot springs water. The five simple cabins range $130-425; the least expensive are pet-friendly. Campsites are $25-35. The main attraction on the property is Belknap Springs. The water is filtered piping hot into a swimming pool on the south bank of the McKenzie. For $7, drop-in visitors can use the pool for an hour; a day pass is $12.The pool closes at 9pm. If you forget your towel, you can rent one.

Camping

The following campgrounds are under the jurisdiction of the Willamette National Forest's **McKenzie Ranger District** (info: 541/822-3381, www.fs.usda.gov/willamette; reservations: 877/444-6777, www.recreation.gov). Many are along the beautiful McKenzie River National Recreation Trail. Its prime location halfway between Eugene and Bend also helps make the area a popular vacation spot during the summer, so reservations should be made at least five days in advance. Sites at these campgrounds run $12-18 per night; except as noted, all of the listed campgrounds have drinking water, vault toilets, and picnic tables.

Several choice campgrounds are south of the McKenzie Highway, off the Aufderheide Highway; these places are convenient to Cougar Reservoir and Terwilliger Hot Springs. **Delta** campground is closest to the McKenzie Highway; it's alongside the river amid old-growth trees less than a mile south of the highway and about a mile north of the Aufderheide. **Slide Creek** campground is on the east bank of Cougar Reservoir; it's a busy place with a boat ramp and swimming area. A few miles south of the reservoir, find **French Pete** and **Frissell Crossing** campgrounds, both are quiet spots along the South Fork of the McKenzie.

A half-mile west of McKenzie Bridge on Route 126 is the 20-site riverside **McKenzie Bridge Campground,** with a boat launch onto the river. East of McKenzie Bridge about three miles on Route 126 is **Paradise Campground.** Although there are 64 tent/RV (up to 40 feet) campsites, only half of the sites are in premium riverside locations. The summer trout fishing here can be very good.

Olallie Campground is 11 miles east of McKenzie Bridge on Route 126 on the banks of the McKenzie River; boating, fishing, and hiking are some of the nearby attractions. A couple of miles past Olallie on Route 126 is **Trail Bridge Campground** on the north shore of Trail Bridge Reservoir. Boat docks are close by, and the reservoir is noted for its good trout fishing. This campground is first-come, first-served and not on the reservation system; it is open June-October.

Another ideal campground for boating enthusiasts is **Lake's End** on nearby Smith Reservoir. One of the few boat-in campgrounds in Oregon, this park can only be reached via a two-mile sail across the lake. To get there, take Route 126 for 12 miles northeast of McKenzie Bridge, turn left, and follow Forest Service Road 730 two miles to the south end of the reservoir. Boat across to the north shore for camping. Be sure to take along plenty of water, because the campground does not provide any. Lake's End is open May-September and has no fees or reservations.

On the south shore of Clear Lake, 19 miles northeast of McKenzie Bridge on Route 126, is

Coldwater Cove Campground, open mid-May-mid-October. A county-run cabin resort, Clear Lake Resort (541/967-3917, www.linnparks.com) is adjacent to the campground and has a store, a summer-only café, and rustic cabins ($64-117, bring cooking utensils and bedding), as well as boat docks, launches, and rowboat rentals. No powerboats are permitted on the lake. The road to the resort closes at the end of September; guests can hike in to rustic cabins during the winter.

A handful of small campgrounds dot Route 242, the old McKenzie Pass road, but none have piped water.

FOOD

Restaurants aren't exactly a big deal out here—most overnight visitors are camping or renting cabins with cooking facilities.

There are a couple of good dining options just west of McKenzie Bridge. Stop at Takoda's (91806 Mill Creek Rd., 541/822-1153, www.takodasrainbow.com, 8am-9pm daily, $8-12), next to Harbick's Country Store, for pizza, a burger, or a visit to the salad bar. During the summer, there's outside seating in a garden area. Right across the highway, the Rustic Skillet (54771 McKenzie River Hwy., 541/822-3400, www.rusticskillet.com,

7:30am-2pm Sun.-Fri., 7:30am-7:30pm Sat., $6-14) can be likened to a fancy truck stop—just good ol' American food. Lest this sound like damning with faint praise, we should add that the menu is diverse for its genre, including asparagus omelets and homemade cinnamon rolls.

INFORMATION

Read the local news online (www.mckenzieriverreflectionsnewspaper.com). Wilderness permits, camping, hiking, and mountain biking information are available from the McKenzie River Ranger District (57600 McKenzie Hwy., McKenzie Bridge, 541/822-3381, www.fs.usda.gov).

GETTING THERE

Amazingly, travelers without cars can get to the McKenzie National Recreation Trail from Eugene via Lane Transit District (541/687-5555, www.ltd.org, $1.75). Their route 91 bus starts at Thurston station in Springfield (with frequent bus connections to downtown Eugene) and heads up the McKenzie River Highway. The bus is equipped to carry a couple of bikes. The terminus point is the McKenzie River Ranger Station at McKenzie Bridge.

Oakridge and the Upper Willamette River

Halfway between Eugene and the Cascades' summit on Route 58 lies the town of Oakridge. Historically a timber town, mountain biking now helps to support this small community (pop. 3,200) tucked away in a foothill valley of the Cascades. Over 100 lakes and streams nearby wait for just about any nimrod to pull out his or her quota of trout from the cool waters. A short drive southeast of town, near Willamette Pass, are two central Oregon gems: Waldo Lake and Odell Lake (see Bend and Central Oregon chapter).

SIGHTS
Westfir Covered Bridge

A short distance out of Oakridge on the paved Aufderheide National Scenic Byway is the Westfir Covered Bridge, which has the distinction of being the longest covered bridge in Oregon (180 feet) as well as the tallest covered bridge west of the Mississippi. You can get a good photograph of the bridge from the road as you approach the nearby town of Westfir.

Salt Creek Falls

About 20 miles southeast of Oakridge, just

THE WILLAMETTE VALLEY

OAKRIDGE AND THE UPPER WILLAMETTE RIVER

west of Willamette Pass on the way to Odell Lake on Route 58, is Oregon's second-highest waterfall, **Salt Creek Falls,** which forms the headwaters of the Willamette River. Shortly after the turnoff from the south side of the highway, take the right fork in the road and head down to the parking area (NW Forest Pass required). The short walk to the viewing area of the 286-foot-high cascade provides a great photo opportunity. Trails access both the top and the bottom of the waterfall.

McCredie Hot Springs

McCredie Hot Springs is 10 miles southeast of Oakridge on Route 58 near mile marker 45. A short walk down to Salt Creek brings you to a small hot spring adjacent to the river. This location allows you to enjoy the rush of simultaneously hot and cold water. Depending on how you position yourself, you can take a bath at any temperature you choose—be careful, there are some extremely hot spots. Because it's so close to the road this place is often busy; many visitors bathe nude here.

The 180-foot-long Westfir Covered Bridge is Oregon's longest covered bridge.

SPORTS AND RECREATION
Hiking
FALL CREEK NATIONAL RECREATION TRAIL

The 14-mile-long **Fall Creek National Recreation Trail,** about 30 miles southeast of Eugene, is ideal for short day hikes or longer expeditions; several national forest entry/exit points crop up along the way. Another plus is the low elevation of the trail, which makes it accessible year-round. Strolling through the wilderness, you will pass many deep pools, white-water rapids, and over a dozen small streams.

To get there, take Route 58 about 15 miles to Lowell, then go north for two miles to the covered bridge at Unity Junction. Take a right onto Forest Service Road 18 (Fall Creek Rd.), and stay to the left of the reservoir. Follow the road for 11 miles to Dolly Varden Campground, where the trail starts. There are five campgrounds en route and three other spur trails that merge into the Fall Creek Trail. Bedrock Campground is a particularly popular spot for swimming.

LARISON CREEK TRAIL

The **Larison Creek Trail** (Trail 3646), shared by hikers and mountain bikers, is less than 10 minutes south of Oakridge. Multicolored mosses cover the valley floor, and its walls simulate a brushstroked backdrop to stands of old-growth fir. Further contrast is supplied by waterfalls and swimming holes. The mild grade and low elevation of this trail make it accessible year-round. To get there, take Route 58 to Oakridge. Turn onto Kitson Springs County Road and proceed for 0.5 mile. Turn right on Forest Service Road 21 and follow it three miles to the trailhead, which you'll find on the right side of the road. Note that this trail is shared with mountain bikers.

★ Mountain Biking

Mountain biking has become incredibly popular in the Oakridge area, which is not

Salt Creek Falls is Oregon's second-highest waterfall.

surprising given that there are an estimated 350 miles of single-track within an hour's drive of town. Find information and detailed trail descriptions at www.mtbikeoakridge.com.

Novice bikers and families can start with the **Salmon Creek Trail**, which originates in town and heads along generally flat terrain to Salmon Creek Falls.

Also just outside town, starting at Greenwaters Park near the fish hatchery, **Larison Rock** is a thrilling, technical five-mile downhill ride. Then, unless you've arranged a car shuttle, it's a bit of a slog back to the start. (An easier though longer route back follows Forest Road 2102.)

The nearly 30-mile-long **Middle Fork River Trail** is a good bet for more experienced mountain bikers who want to test their stamina. It starts at the Sand Prairie campground south of town and heads south and east along the Middle Fork of the Willamette River.

Oakridge hosts a couple of **mountain bike events,** one in mid-July and the other

in August (503/968-8870, www.mtbikeoakridge.com, $409) with guided rides of the area's trails, meals, beer, and camping.

Road cyclists needn't avoid Oakridge; the **Aufderheide National Scenic Byway** is an excellent low-traffic paved road along the North Fork of the Willamette River.

ACCOMMODATIONS

There are some reasonable lodging options in the area. the bike-friendly **Oakridge Lodge and Guest House** (48175 E. 1st St., 541/782-4000, www.oakridge-lodge.com, $50 pp bunks, $115-125 private room) is a large house with a shared bunkroom, four private rooms, and a good B&B-style breakfast, even for bunk dwellers. The lodge also serves dinner (not included in price) 4pm-9pm Thursday-Sunday. This is the site of the early August **Oakridge Ukelele Festival.**

The **Bluewolf Motel** (47465 Hwy. 58, 541/782-5884, www.bluewolfmotel.com, $48-67) is a small, simple motel with microwaves and refrigerators. It's pet-friendly and has nice, spacious grounds, including the "Wolf Den" (an outdoor kitchen with a gas grill, piped water, and seating).

In the former office building of Hines Lumber Company in Westfir, across the street from the covered bridge, is the **Westfir Lodge** (47365 1st St., Westfir, 541/782-3103, www.westfirlodge.com, $80-130). The building has been tastefully converted into seven guest rooms with private baths across the hall.

FOOD

If there are mountain bikers, there must be beer nearby. Find both at the **Brewers Union Local 180** (48329 E. 1st St., 541/782-2024, www.brewersunion.com, noon-9pm Sun.-Wed., noon-10pm Thurs., noon-11pm Fri.-Sat. summer, noon-8pm Sun.-Tues. and Thurs., noon-10pm Fri.-Sat. winter, $12-16), a family-friendly British-style public house where it's as easy to settle in with a cup of tea as with a pint of real ale, and you can either read a book or play pool.

Fuel up for the day's activities with a

muffin from **Lion Mountain Bakery** (48273 E. 1st St., 541/782-5797, 8am-noon Tues., 8am-4pm Wed.-Fri., 8am-3pm Sun.); if you're passing through at lunchtime, the soup here is homemade.

Lee's Gourmet Garden (47670 Hwy. 58, 541/782-2155, 11am-9pm Tues.-Sun., $7-12) is better than your average small-town Chinese restaurant. The owner used to be Jackie Chan's personal chef and brings a nice touch and a few special dishes to a pretty standard Chinese American menu.

INFORMATION

The **Oakridge/Westfir Chamber of Commerce** (48248 Hwy. 58, Oakridge, 541/782-4146, www.oakridgechamber.com) has a small visitors center in the rest area on the east side of town.

Additional information on biking, hiking, camping, and the Aufderheide National Scenic Byway can be obtained from the **Middle Fork Ranger Station** (46375 Hwy. 58, Westfir, 541/782-2283, www.fs.usda.gov/willamette).

North Coast

Look for ★ to find recommended
sights, activities, dining, and lodging.

Highlights

★ **Columbia River Maritime Museum:**
One of Oregon's top museums tells the story of
seafaring on the Columbia River (page 222).

★ **Fort Clatsop National Memorial:** This
replica of Lewis and Clark's 1805-1806 winter
camp offers a fascinating glimpse into frontier
life (page 226).

★ **Haystack Rock:** This soaring sea stack on
Cannon Beach is home to thousands of seabirds
(page 250).

★ **Saddle Mountain State Natural
Area:** This knobby mountain rises high above
the northern coast, with a hiking trail leading
through unusual plant life on the way to an eye-
popping vista (page 252).

★ **Cape Lookout Hikes:** Go for the great
views of rocks and surf, the chance of seeing a
whale, or to totally immerse yourself in the foggy
coastal atmosphere (page 276).

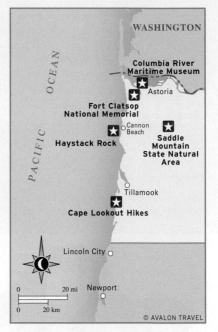

The enchanting north coast—from the mouth of the Columbia River south to Lincoln City—is little more than an hour's drive from the Portland metro area. It's the most popular part of Oregon's Pacific shoreline. Still, apart from the weekend crush at Cannon Beach and Seaside, there's more than enough elbow room for everyone.

Overlooking the Columbia River as it flows into the Pacific, the former shipping and fishing center of Astoria is fast rediscovering its own potential, with a lively arts scene, adventurous cuisine, and fine hotels and B&Bs hosting overnighters. Its long-idle waterfront is busy again with tourist attractions—most notably the Columbia River Maritime Museum, one of the best museums in Oregon.

West of Astoria, at Oregon's far northwestern tip, where the mighty Columbia River meets the Pacific, visitors to Fort Stevens State Park can inspect the skeleton of a century-old shipwreck and a military fort active from the Civil War to World War II, as well as revel in miles of sandy beaches. Fort Clatsop National Memorial, part of Lewis and Clark National Historical Park, includes a recreation of the Corps of Discovery's winter 1805-1806 quarters—a must-stop for Lewis and Clark buffs.

Cannon Beach and Seaside are two extremely popular resort towns that are polar opposites of one another. Cannon Beach, an enclave of tastefully weathered cedar-shingled architecture, is chockablock with art galleries, boutiques, and upscale lodgings and restaurants. A few miles north, Seaside is Oregon's quintessential family-friendly beach resort, with a long boardwalk, candy and gift shops, and noisy game arcades.

Just south of Cannon Beach, Oswald West State Park is a gem protecting old-growth forest and handsome little pocket beaches—as well as, some believe, a Spanish pirate treasure buried on Neahkahnie Mountain. Beyond Neahkahnie's cliff-top viewpoints along U.S. 101, the Nehalem Bay area attracts anglers, crabbers, and kayakers, as well as discriminating diners who come from far and wide to enjoy surprisingly sophisticated cuisine.

Previous: Haystack Rock at Cannon Beach; cows grazing in the Tillamook region. **Above:** Cape Falcon.

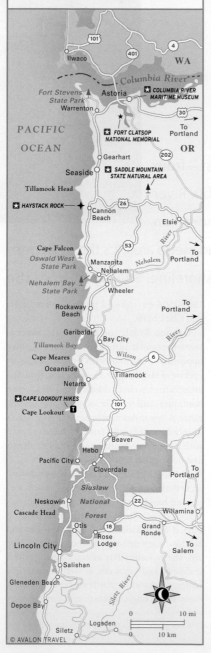

North Coast

Ilwaco
101
401
4
WA
Columbia River
Fort Stevens
State Park
Astoria
⊕ COLUMBIA RIVER
MARITIME MUSEUM
Warrenton
30
PACIFIC
OCEAN
⊕ FORT CLATSOP
NATIONAL MEMORIAL
To
Portland
OR
Gearhart
202
Seaside
⊕ SADDLE MOUNTAIN
STATE NATURAL AREA
Tillamook Head
⊕ HAYSTACK ROCK
Cannon
Beach
26
Elsie
River
Cape Falcon
Oswald West
State Park
Manzanita
Nehalem
53
Nehalem
To
Portland
Nehalem Bay
State Park
Wheeler
Rockaway
Beach
To
Portland
Garibaldi
Bay City
Tillamook Bay
River
Cape Meares
Oceanside
Wilson
6
Netarts
Tillamook
⊕ CAPE LOOKOUT HIKES
Cape Lookout
101
Beaver
Hebo
Pacific City
Cloverdale
To
Portland
Siuslaw
Neskowin
National
22
Cascade Head
Forest
Willamina
Otis
18
Grand
Ronde
Rose
Lodge
To
Salem
Lincoln City
Salishan
Gleneden Beach
Depoe Bay
Siletz River
0   10 mi
0   10 km
Logsden
Siletz
© AVALON TRAVEL

Tillamook County, home to more cows than people, is synonymous with delicious dairy products—cheese and ice cream in particular. It's no surprise that Tillamook's biggest visitor attraction is cheese-related. More than a million people a year come to the Tillamook Cheese Factory to view the cheese-making operations and sample the excellent results. The Tillamook Air Museum is another popular diversion, housing an outstanding collection of vintage and modern aircraft in gargantuan Hangar B, the largest wooden structure in the world. Tillamook Bay, fed by five rivers, yields oysters and crabs, while the active Garibaldi charter fleet targets salmon, halibut, and tuna in the offshore waters.

South of Tillamook, the Coast Highway wends inland through lush pastureland to Neskowin. It's a pleasant-enough stretch, but the Three Capes Scenic Loop, a 35-mile scenic coastal detour, is a more attractive, if time-consuming, option. The spectacular views and bird-watching from Capes Meares and Lookout are the highlights of this beautiful drive. At Pacific City, at the southern end of the Three Capes Loop, commercial anglers launch their dories right off the sandy beach and through the surf in the lee of Cape Kiwanda and mammoth Haystack Rock—a sight not seen anywhere else on the West Coast. Just north of Lincoln City, Cascade Head beckons hikers to explore its rare prairie headlands ecosystem.

PLANNING YOUR TIME

Although most Oregonians have a favorite beach town that they'll visit for weekends and summer vacations, if this is your grand tour of the Oregon coast, plan to spend a few days exploring the northern coast's beaches and towns. If you're interested in history, architecture, or ship-watching, be sure to spend a night in **Astoria**—it's one of our favorite coastal cities, even though it's several miles from the Pacific Ocean; if you can't wait to walk on Pacific beaches, head to **Cannon**

Beach (for a more upscale stay) or **Seaside** (which the kids will love) and begin your trip there. By driving from north to south, you'll be able to pull off the highway more easily into beach access areas. Campers might want to reserve a space at Nehalem Bay State Park, near the small laid-back town of **Manzanita,** a few miles south of Cannon Beach; Manzanita is also a good place to rent a beach house for a weekend. Aside from the

near-mandatory stop at the Tillamook Cheese Factory, you'll probably want to skip the town of Tillamook and head to the **Three Capes Loop,** where a night in Pacific City offers easy access to Cape Kiwanda as well as comfy lodgings and a good brewpub. On your way south to the central coast, or to the Highway 18 route back through the Willamette Valley wine country to Portland, do stop for a hike at **Cascade Head.**

Astoria and Vicinity

The mouth of the mighty Columbia River, with its abundance of natural resources, was long a home for Native Americans; artifacts found in the area suggest that people have been living along the river for at least 8,000 years. Early European explorers and settlers also found the river and its bays to be propitious as a trading and fishing center. Astoria's dramatic location and deep history continue to attract new settlers and travelers drawn to the area's potent allure.

Astoria (pop. about 10,000) is the oldest permanent U.S. settlement west of the Rockies, and its glory days are preserved by museums, historical exhibits, and pastel-colored Victorian homes weathered by the sea air. Hollywood has chosen Astoria's picturesque neighborhoods to simulate an idealized all-American town, most notably in the cult classic *The Goonies.*

What sets Astoria apart from other destinations on the northern Oregon coast is that it's a real city, not a waterfront town made over into a resort. While the decline in the logging and fishing industries dealt the city many economic blows in the late 20th century, there's plenty of pluck left in this old dowager, and her best years may be yet to come as a thriving haven for artists and free spirits.

Astoria has many charms: Colorful Victorian mansions and historic buildings downtown are undergoing restoration, cruise ships are calling, fine restaurants are

multiplying, a lively arts scene is booming, and there's new life along the waterfront, anchored by the excellent Columbia River Maritime Museum.

History

The Clatsop Indians, a Chinook-speaking group, lived in this area for thousands of years before Astoria's written history began. When Lewis and Clark arrived in 1805, the Clatsops numbered about 400 people, living in three villages on the south side of the Columbia River, but began a steady decline soon after contact with whites.

The region was first chronicled by Don Bruno de Heceta, a Spanish explorer who sailed near the Columbia's mouth in August 1775. He named it the Bay of the Assumption of Our Lady, but the strong current prevented his ship from entering. American presence on the Columbia began with Captain Robert Gray's discovery of the river in May 1792, which he christened after his fur-trading ship, *Columbia Rediviva.*

Thereafter, Lewis and Clark's famous expedition of 1803-1806, with its winter encampment at Fort Clatsop, south of present-day Astoria, helped incorporate the Pacific Northwest as part of a new nation. In 1811, John Jacob Astor's agents built Fort Astoria on a hillside in what would eventually grow into Astoria—the first American settlement west of the Rockies. The trading post was

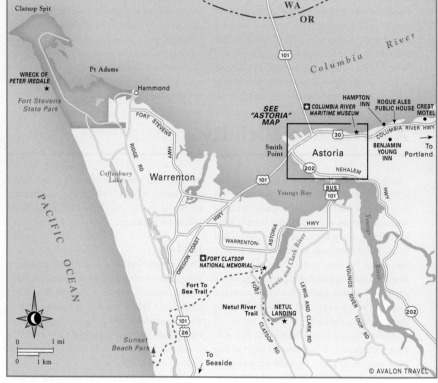

Astoria and Vicinity

Clatsop Spit

WA
OR

WRECK OF
PETER IREDALE
★

Pt Adams

Hammond

Fort Stevens
State Park

101

Columbia River

SEE
"ASTORIA"
MAP

HAMPTON
INN

✚ COLUMBIA RIVER
MARITIME MUSEUM

ROGUE ALES
PUBLIC HOUSE

CREST
MOTEL

COLUMBIA RIVER HWY

30

Smith
Point

Astoria

BENJAMIN
YOUNG
INN

To
Portland

202

NEHALEM

101

Youngs Bay

BUS
101

HWY

FORT STEVENS HWY

RIDGE RD

Coffenbury
Lake

Warrenton

PACIFIC OCEAN

HWY

WARRENTON-

ASTORIA

OREGON COAST

✚ FORT CLATSOP
NATIONAL MEMORIAL

Fort To
Sea Trail

Netul River
Trail

NETUL
LANDING
★

FORT

CLATSOP RD

Lewis and Clark River

LEWIS AND CLARK RD

YOUNGS RIVER LOOP RD

Youngs River

202

0   1 mi
0   1 km

Sunset
Beach Park ▲

To
Seaside

© AVALON TRAVEL

occupied by the British between 1813 and 1818, and the settlement was renamed Fort George. Real development began in the 1840s as settlers begin pouring in from the Oregon Trail. During the Civil War, Fort Stevens was built at the mouth of the Columbia to guard against a Confederate naval incursion.

Commerce grew with the export of lumber and foodstuffs to gold rush-era San Francisco and Asia. Salmon canneries became the mainstay of Astoria's economy during the 1870s, helping it grow into Oregon's second-largest city—and a notorious shanghaiing port, where young men, often drunk, were kidnapped from bars to serve as unwilling sailors on commercial and military ships. From that time through the early 1900s, the dominant immigrants to the Astoria area were

Scandinavian, and with the addition of these seafaring folk, logging, fishing, and shipbuilding coaxed the population up to 20,000 by World War II.

Some believe that the port city at the mouth of the Columbia might have grown to rival San Francisco or Seattle had it not been for the setback of a devastating fire in 1922. In the early morning hours of December 8, a pool hall on Commercial Street caught fire; the flames spread rapidly among the wooden buildings, many supported on wooden pilings, in Astoria's business district. By daybreak, more than 200 businesses in a 32-block area had been reduced to ashes. The downtown was rebuilt in the ensuing years, largely in brick and stone, but the devastation changed the fate of Astoria.

Near the end of World War II, a Japanese submarine's shelling of Fort Stevens made it the only fortification on U.S. soil to have sustained an attack in a world war. After the war, the region's fortunes ebbed and flowed with its resource-based economy. In an attempt to supplement that economy with tourism, the State Highway Division began constructing the Astoria-Megler Bridge in 1962 to connect Oregon and Washington.

Orientation

The waters surrounding Astoria define the town as much as the steep hills it's built on. Along its northern side, the mighty Columbia, four miles wide, is a mega aquatic highway carrying a steady flow of traffic, from small pleasure boats to massive cargo ships a quarter-mile long. Soaring high over the river is an engineering marvel that's impossible to miss from most locations in town. At just over four miles long, the Astoria-Megler Bridge is the longest bridge in Oregon and the longest bridge of its type (cantilever through-truss) in the world. When it opened in 1966, the bridge provided the final link in the 1,625-mile-long U.S. 101 along the Pacific Coast.

On Astoria's south side, Young's River, flowing down from the Coast Range, broadens into Young's Bay, separating Astoria from its neighbor Warrenton to the southwest.

A few miles to the west, the Columbia River finally meets the Pacific, 1,243 miles from its headwaters in British Columbia. Where the tremendous outflow (averaging 118 million gallons per minute) of the River of the West encounters the ocean tides, conditions can be treacherous, and the sometimes-monstrous waves around the bar have claimed more than 2,000 vessels over the years. This rivermouth could well be the biggest widow-maker on the high seas, earning it the title "Graveyard of the Pacific." Lewis and Clark referred to it as "that seven-shouldered horror" in a journal entry from the winter of 1805-1806.

Any visitor to Astoria should consider crossing the Astoria-Megler Bridge to visit the extreme southwest corner of Washington

State. Here the sands and soil carried by the Columbia create a 20-mile-long sand spit called the Long Beach Peninsula. Some of the West Coast's most succulent oysters grow in Willapa Bay, the body of water created by this finger of sand. Historic beach communities plus numerous Lewis and Clark sites also reward visitors to this charming enclave.

SIGHTS

After getting a bird's-eye view from the Astoria Column, you might want to take a closer look at Astoria on foot. The town is home to dozens of beautifully restored 19th-century and early-20th-century houses.

Here's a suggested route: From the Flavel House Museum at 8th Street and Duane Street, start walking south on 8th Street and turn left on Franklin Avenue. Continue east to 11th Street, then detour south one block on 11th Street to Grand Avenue; head east on Grand, north on 12th Street, and back to Franklin, continuing your eastward trek. Walk to 17th Street, then south again to Grand, double back on Grand two blocks to 15th Street, then walk north on 15th to Exchange Street and east on Exchange to 17th, where you'll be just two blocks from the Columbia River Maritime Museum. The route takes you past 74 historical buildings and sites.

Astoria Column

The best introduction to Astoria and environs is undoubtedly the 360-degree panorama from atop the 125-foot-tall **Astoria Column** (2199 Coxcomb Dr., 503/325-2963, www.astoriacolumn.org, dawn-dusk daily, $1 requested for parking) on Coxcomb Hill, the highest point in town. Patterned after the Trajan Column in Rome, the reinforced-concrete tower was built in 1926 as a joint project of the Great Northern Railway and the descendants of John Jacob Astor to commemorate the westward sweep of discovery and migration. The graffito frieze spiraling up the exterior illustrates Robert Gray's 1792 discovery of the Columbia River, the establishment of

American claims to the Northwest Territory, the arrival of the Great Northern Railway, and other scenes of the history of the Pacific Northwest. The vista from the surrounding hilltop park is impressive enough, but for the ultimate experience, the climb up 164 steps to the tower's top is worth the effort.

If you have kids in tow, be sure to stop by the tiny gift shop to buy a balsa wood glider. Lofting a wooden airplane from the top of the tower is an Astoria tradition.

Get to the Astoria Column from downtown by following 16th Street south (uphill) to Jerome Avenue. Turn west (right) one block and continue up 15th Street to the park entrance on Coxcomb Drive.

The Waterfront

While most of Astoria's waterfront is lined with warehouses and docks, the **River Walk** will get you front-row views of the river. The River Walk provides paved riverside passage for pedestrians and cyclists along a five-mile stretch between the Port of Astoria and the community of Alderbrook, at the eastern fringe of Astoria.

An excellent way to cover some of the same ground, accompanied by commentary on sights and local history, is by taking

a 50-minute ride on Old 300, the **Astoria Riverfront Trolley** (503/325-6311, www. old300.org, noon-6pm daily Memorial Day–Labor Day weather permitting, noon-6pm Fri., Sat.-Sun. fall and spring, $1 per ride or $2 all day), which runs on Astoria's original train tracks alongside the River Walk as far east as the East Mooring Basin. Trolley shelters are at nine stops along the route; you can also flag it down anywhere along the route by waving a dollar bill. The lovingly restored 1913 trolley originally served San Antonio and later ran between Portland and Lake Oswego in the 1980s.

Toward the eastern end of the River Walk, at Pier 39, the **Hanthorn Cannery** (100 39th St., 9am-6pm daily, free) is a rather informal but fascinating museum housed in an old Bumble Bee tuna cannery. Exhibits include some lovely old wooden boats, eye-catching photos, and canning equipment. There's also a coffee shop and a brewpub at this location, so it's a good place to take a break.

★ Columbia River Maritime Museum

On the waterfront a few blocks east of downtown Astoria, the **Columbia River Maritime Museum** (1792 Marine Dr., 503/325-2323,

the Astoria waterfront

© AVALON TRAVEL

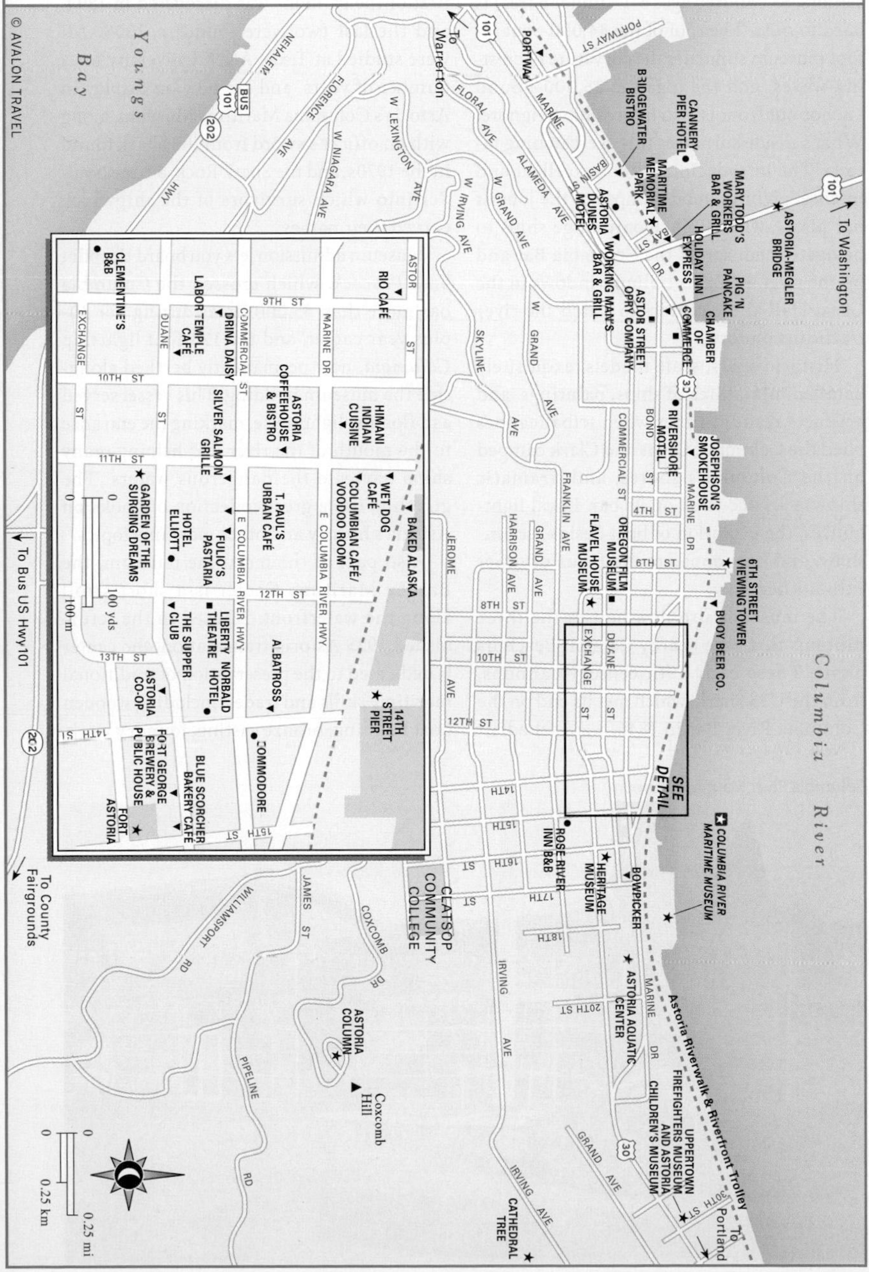

Youngs Bay

Columbia River

To Warrenton

To Washington

To Bus US Hwy 101

To County Fairgrounds

To Portland

Astoria Riverwalk & Riverfront Trolley

SEE DETAIL

Points of interest (map labels):

CANNERY PIER HOTEL
BRIDGEWATER BISTRO
MARITIME MEMORIAL PARK
MARY TODD'S WORKERS BAR & GRILL
ASTORIA-MEGLER BRIDGE
PIG 'N PANCAKE
HOLIDAY INN EXPRESS
ASTORIA DUNES MOTEL
CHAMBER OF COMMERCE
ASTOR STREET OPRY COMPANY
JOSEPHSON'S SMOKEHOUSE
RIVERSHORE MOTEL
OREGON FILM MUSEUM
FLAVEL HOUSE MUSEUM
6TH STREET VIEWING TOWER
BUOY BEER CO.
ROSE RIVER INN B&B
HERITAGE MUSEUM
BOWPICKER
COLUMBIA RIVER MARITIME MUSEUM
ASTORIA AQUATIC CENTER
UPPERTOWN FIREFIGHTERS MUSEUM AND ASTORIA CHILDREN'S MUSEUM
CLATSOP COMMUNITY COLLEGE
ASTORIA COLUMN
Coxcomb Hill
CATHEDRAL TREE

CLEMENTINE'S B&B
RIO CAFÉ
LABOR TEMPLE CAFÉ
DRINA DAISY
ASTORIA COFFEEHOUSE & BISTRO
HIMANI INDIAN CUISINE
SILVER SALMON GRILLE
WET DOG CAFÉ
COLUMBIAN CAFÉ/ VOODOO ROOM
T PAUL'S URBAN CAFÉ
BAKED ALASKA
FULIO'S PASTARIA
HOTEL ELLIOT
GARDEN OF THE SURGING DREAMS
THE SUPPER CLUB
LIBERTY THEATRE
A. BATROSS
NORBLAD HOTEL
ASTORIA CO-OP
14TH STREET PIER
COMMODORE
FORT GEORGE BREWERY & PUBLIC HOUSE
BLUE SCORCHER BAKERY CAFÉ
FORT ASTORIA

0 0.25 mi
0 0.25 km

0 100 yds
0 100 m

www.crmm.org, 9:30am-5pm daily, closed Thanksgiving and Christmas, $12 adults, $10 seniors, $5 children ages 6-17, under 6 free) is hard to miss. The roof of the 44,000-square-foot museum simulates the curvature of cresting waves, and the gigantic 25,000-pound anchor out front is also impossible to ignore. What's inside surpasses this eye-catching facade. The introductory film is excellent and intense, giving a good glimpse of the jobs of bar pilots, who climb aboard huge ships to navigate them across the Columbia Bar and up the river. Floor-to-ceiling windows in the Great Hall allow visitors to watch the river traffic in comfort.

Historic boats, scale models, exquisitely detailed miniatures of ships, paintings, and artifacts recount times when tribal canoes plied the Columbia; Lewis and Clark camped on the Columbia's shores; and dramatic shipwrecks occurred on its bar. Local lighthouses, the evolution of boat design, scrimshaw, and harpoons are the focus of other exhibits here.

The museum also now houses the three cannons that gave nearby Cannon Beach its name. These early 19th-century cannons, from the USS Shark, which met its end on the Columbia River Bar in 1846, were set adrift

and washed up some 30 miles south of the Columbia's mouth near Cannon Beach. The first of the cannons was discovered in 1894, and the last two were found in 2008. All were studied at Texas A&M University for a number of years, and are now on display in Astoria's Columbia Maritime Museum, along with an officer's sword from the Shark found in the 1970s, and the Shark Rock, a large boulder into which survivors of the shipwreck carved their names.

Museum admission lets you board the pilot boat *Peacock,* which crossed the Columbia bar more than 35,000 times during her 30-plus year career, and the 128-foot lightship *Columbia,* now permanently berthed alongside the museum building. This vessel served as a floating lighthouse, marking the entrance to the mouth of the river and helping many ships navigate the dangerous waters. The gift shop has a great collection of books on Astoria's history and other maritime topics.

Also part of the maritime museum, the Barbey Maritime Center is a short stroll along the waterfront. Housed in the refurbished 1925 Astoria train station, the center is dedicated to the preservation of traditional maritime skills and trades, including wooden boat building, bronze casting, foundry work,

Columbia River Maritime Museum

Astoria Goes to the Movies

In recent decades, the Victorian homes and ocean view in Astoria's hillside neighborhoods and the surrounding maritime settings have provided the backdrop for such fanciful modern sagas as *Free Willy I* and *II, Kindergarten Cop, Teenage Mutant Ninja Turtles III, Short Circuit, Come See the Paradise,* and *The Goonies.* The last movie, a cult favorite shot in 1985, concerns a gang of local kids hunting for pirate's treasure; happy memories of the movie continue to attract a steady stream of visitors looking for the locations used in the film. More recently, films shot in Astoria have gravitated toward horror, including *The Ring Two* and *Cthulhu,* a film based on the horror novels of H. P. Lovecraft. A guide to movie locations is available at the Oregon Welcome Center in Astoria, the Heritage Museum, Flavel House Museum, and the Warrenton Visitors Center. Stop by the **Oregon Film Museum** (732 Duane St., 503/325-2203, www.oregonfilmmuseum.org, 10am-5pm daily May-Sept., 11am-4pm daily Oct.,-April, $6 adults, $2 children ages 6-17), which ostensibly celebrates the various films shot in Oregon, but is mostly a paean to all things Goonie. The museum is housed in the old Clatsop County Jail (from 1914), which famously starred in *The Goonies* jailbreak scene.

wood carving, and tool making. The museum website lists current classes.

Heritage Museum and Research Library

The Clatsop County Historical Society operates three very worthwhile historic destinations in Astoria, and if you're planning on visiting the Heritage Museum, the Oregon Film Museum, and the Flavel House museum, you should consider the three-in-one tickets available at any of the locations for $12 adult, $10 seniors, $5 children 6-17.

The **Heritage Museum** (1618 Exchange St., 503/325-2203, www.cumtux.org, 10am-5pm daily May-Sept., 11am-4pm Tues.-Sat. Oct.-Apr., $6 adults, $5 seniors, $2 children ages 6-12), is housed in a handsome neoclassical building that was originally Astoria's city hall. It has several galleries filled with antiquities, tools, vintage photographs, and archives chronicling various aspects of life in Clatsop County. The museum's centerpiece exhibit concentrates on the culture of the local Clatsop and Chinook people, from before European contact up to the present day. Other exhibits highlight natural history, geology, early immigrants and settlers in the region, and the development of commerce in such fields as fishing, fish packing, logging,

and lumber. The **research library** is open to the public.

The historical society also operates the **Uppertown Firefighters Museum** (30th St. and Marine Dr., 503/325-2203, noon-3pm Sat. or by appointment, free), which displays an extensive collection of firefighting equipment dating from 1873 to 1963. Featured are hand-pulled, horse-drawn, and motorized fire engines, including a 1912 American LaFrance fire truck, a Stutz fire engine, and a 1946 Mack fire truck. The photos and information about the devastating fires of 1893 and 1922 are fascinating.

Flavel House Museum

Captain George Flavel, Astoria's first millionaire, amassed a fortune in the mid-19th century through his Columbia Bar piloting monopoly, and later expanded his empire through shipping, banking, and real estate. Between 1884 and 1886 he had a home built in the center of Astoria overlooking the Columbia River, now the **Flavel House Museum** (441 8th St., 503/325-2203, 10am-5pm daily May-Sept., 11am-4pm Tues.-Sat. Oct.-Apr., $6 adults, $5 seniors and students, $2 children ages 6-17, 5 and younger free), where he retired with his wife and two daughters. From its fourth-story cupola, Flavel could watch the comings and goings of his sailing fleet.

When the Clatsop County Historical Society assumed stewardship in 1951, the mansion was slated for demolition, to be paved over as a parking lot for the adjacent courthouse. Fortunately, thanks to the efforts of the historical society and many volunteers, the house still stands today at the corner of 8th and Duane Streets. The splendidly extravagant Queen Anne mansion reflects the rich style and elegance of the late Victorian era and the lives of Astoria's most prominent family.

The property encompasses a full city block. With its intricate woodwork inside and out, period furnishings, and art, along with its extravagantly rendered gables, cornices, and porches, the Flavel House ranks with the Carson Mansion in Eureka, California, as a Victorian showplace. The Carriage House, on the southwest corner of the property, serves as an orientation center for visitors with exhibits, an interpretive video, and a museum store.

The Flavel House is perhaps the grandest of Astoria's many Victorian mansions.

Garden of the Surging Dreams

This small garden and outdoor art display (11th and Duane Sts.) commemorates Astoria's Chinese heritage. At the center is a pavilion with nine stone columns ornately carved with dragons. The garden's east facade is a finely worked metal screen with quotations from Chinese pioneers. This park is the first feature in the repurposing of an underutilized downtown parking lot into the Astoria Heritage Square, which in time will also have an amphitheater and an open-air market.

Fort Astoria

In a tiny park at the corner of 15th and Exchange Streets, a reproduction of a rough-hewn log blockhouse and a mural commemorate the spot where Astoria began, when John Jacob Astor's fur traders originally constructed a small fort in 1811. It's worth a quick stop for buffs of early Pacific Northwest history.

Lewis and Clark National Wildlife Refuge

Six miles east of Astoria in the Burnside area is the **Twilight Creek Eagle Sanctuary.** To get there, drive seven miles east of town on U.S. 30 and turn left at Burnside. A viewing platform on the left 0.5 mile later overlooks the 35,000 acres of mudflats, tidal marshes, and islands (which Lewis and Clark called "Seal Islands") of the **Lewis and Clark National Wildlife Refuge.** Bald eagles live here year-round, and the area provides wintering and resting habitat for waterfowl, shorebirds, and songbirds. Beavers, raccoons, weasels, mink, muskrats, and river otters live on the islands; harbor seals and California sea lions feed in the rich estuary waters and use the sandbars and mudflats as haul-out sites at low tide.

★ Fort Clatsop National Memorial

In November 1805, after a journey of nearly 19 months and 4,000 miles, the Lewis and Clark expedition reached the mouth of the

Columbia River, where they decided to winter. They chose a thickly forested rise alongside the Netul River (now the Lewis and Clark River), a few miles south of present-day Astoria, for their campsite. There, the Corps of Discovery quickly set about felling trees and building two parallel rows of cabins, joined by a gated palisade. The finished compound measured about 50 feet on each side. The party of 33 people, including one African American and a Native American woman and her baby, moved into the seven small rooms on Christmas Eve and named their stockade Fort Clatsop for the nearby Indian people.

The winter of 1805-1806 was cold, wet, rainy, and generally miserable. Of the 106 days spent at the site, it rained on all but 12. The January 18, 1806, journal entry of expedition member Private Joseph Whitehouse was typical of the comments recorded during the stay: "It rained hard all last night, & still continued the same this morning. It continued Raining during the whole of this day."

While at Fort Clatsop, the men stored up meat and other supplies, sewed moccasins and new garments, and traded with local tribes, all the while coping with the constant damp conditions, illness and injuries, and merciless plagues of fleas. As soon as the weather permitted, on March 23, 1806, they finally departed on their homeward journey to St. Louis.

Within a few years the elements had erased all traces of Fort Clatsop, and its exact location was lost. In 1955, local history buffs took their best guess and built a replica of the fort based on the notes and sketches of Captain Clark. In 1999, an anthropologist discovered a 148-year-old map identifying the location of Lewis and Clark's winter encampment, and as it turns out the reproduction is sited very close to the original. In 2005, this replica of Fort Clatsop burned, and a new replica, built mostly by volunteers using period tools, was reopened in 2006. Compared to the previous one, this new Fort Clatsop is a more authentic replica of the actual fort that housed the intrepid Corps of Discovery.

Today, in addition to the log replica of the fort, a well-equipped visitors center, museum, and other attractions make **Fort Clatsop National Memorial** (92343 Fort Clatsop Rd., 503/861-2471, www.nps.gov/lewi, 9am-6pm daily mid-June-Labor Day, 9am-5pm daily Labor Day-mid-June, $3 adults, children under 16 free) a must-stop for anyone interested in this pivotal chapter of American history. The expedition's story is nicely narrated here with displays, artifacts, slides, and films, but the summertime "living history" reenactments are the main reason to come. Paths lead through the grove of old-growth Sitka spruce, with interpretive placards identifying native plants. A short walk from the fort leads to the riverside, where dugout canoes are modeled on those used by the corps while in this area. In addition, the 6.5-mile **Fort to Sea Trail** follows the general route blazed by Captain Clark from the fort through dunes and forests to the Pacific at Sunset Beach.

The winter of 1805-1806 put a premium on wilderness survival skills, some of which are exhibited here by rangers in costume. You may see the tanning of hides, making of buckskin clothing and moccasins, and the molding of tallow candles and lead bullets. In addition, visitors may occasionally participate in the construction of a dugout canoe or try their luck at starting a fire by striking flint on steel. Rangers also lead guided hikes and canoe trips.

This 1,500-acre park sits six miles southwest of Astoria and three miles east of U.S. 101 on the Lewis and Clark River. To get there from Astoria, take Marine Drive and head west across Young's Bay to Warrenton. On the south side of the bay look for signs for the Fort Clatsop turnoff; turn left off the Coast Highway about a mile after the bridge and follow the signs to Fort Clatsop.

Fort Stevens State Park

Ten miles west of Astoria, in the far northwest corner of the state, the Civil War-era outpost of **Fort Stevens** (100 Peter Iredale Rd., Hammond, 503/861-1671 or 800/551-6949,

The Long Beach Peninsula

If you've come as far as Astoria, at the edge of the continent and at the mouth of the Columbia River, you should consider crossing the soaring Astoria-Megler Bridge to explore sights on the Columbia's northern shore. There are both scenic and historical reasons to visit this remote corner of Washington State. The Lewis and Clark National and State Historical Parks aggregation includes a number of sites just across from Astoria in Washington, notably **Cape Disappointment State Park,** with a newly expanded Lewis and Clark Interpretive Center.

The **Long Beach Peninsula,** the thin sand spit just north of the mouth of the Columbia River, claims to have the world's longest beach. And with 28 unbroken miles of it, the boast has to be taken seriously. Like Seaside in Oregon, beach resorts at Seaview and Long Beach have a long pedigree, dating from the 1880s, when Portland families journeyed down the Columbia River by steamboat to summer at the coast. The bay side of the Long Beach sand spit creates **Willapa Bay,** known to oyster-lovers around the country for the excellent bivalves that grow in this shallow inlet, which is fed by six rivers. Most of Willapa Bay is protected as a national wildlife refuge, and it's an excellent bird-watching site. **Oysterville,** a tiny village along the bay, stands largely unchanged since the 1880s, and the entire town has been placed on the National Register of Historic Places. The very tip of the peninsula is preserved as 807-acre **Leadbetter Point State Park,** with informal hiking trails along both sandy beaches and the reedy bay.

www.oregonstateparks.org, $5 day use for historic military area and Coffenbury Lake, $21 tent camping, $29 RV camping, $45 yurt, $99 cabin) was one of three military installations (the others were Forts Canby and Columbia in Washington) built to safeguard the mouth of the Columbia River. Established shortly before the Confederates surrendered on April 9, 1865, Fort Stevens served for 84 years, until just after the end of World War II. Today, the remaining fortifications and other buildings are preserved, along with 3,700 acres of woodland, lakes, wetlands, miles of sand beaches, and three miles of Columbia River frontage.

Although Fort Stevens did not see action in the Civil War, it sustained an attack in a later conflict. On June 21, 1942, a Japanese submarine fired 17 shells on the gun emplacements

the remains of the 1906 wreck *Peter Iredale,* Fort Stevens State Park

The *Peter Iredale*

One of the best known of the hundreds of ships wrecked on the Oregon coast over the centuries is the British schooner *Peter Iredale*. This 278-foot four-master, fashioned of steel plates on an iron frame, was built in Liverpool in 1890 and came to its untimely end on the beach south of Clatsop Spit on October 25, 1906. En route from Mexico to pick up a load of wheat on the Columbia River, the vessel ran aground during high seas and a northwesterly squall. All hands were rescued, and with little damage to the hull, hopes initially ran high that the ship could be towed back to sea and salvaged. That effort proved fruitless, and eventually the ship was written off as a total loss. Today, nearly a century later, the remains of her rusting skeleton protrude from the sands of Fort Stevens State Park as a familiar sight to most who have traveled the north coast. Signs within Fort Stevens State Park lead the way to a parking area close to the wreck.

at Battery Russell, making it the only U.S. fortification in the 48 states to be bombed by a foreign power since the War of 1812. No damage was incurred, and the Army didn't return fire. Shortly after World War II, the fort was deactivated and the armaments removed.

Today, the site features a **Military Museum** (503/861-1470 or 503/861-2000, 10am-6pm daily June-Sept., 10am-4pm daily Oct.-May) with old photos, weapons exhibits, and maps, as well as seven different batteries (fortifications) and other structures left over from almost a century of service. Climbing to the commander's station for a scenic view of the Columbia River and South Jetty are popular visitor activities. The massive gun batteries, built of weathered gray concrete and rusting iron, eerily silent amid the thick woodlands, also invite exploration; small children should be closely supervised, as there are steep stairways, high ledges, and other hazards.

During the summer months, guided tours of the underground **Battery Mishler** (12:30 and 2:30pm daily, $4) and a narrated tour of the fort's 37 acres on a two-ton U.S. Army truck (12:30 and 2:30pm Mon.-Thurs., 11am, 12:30, 2:30, and 4pm Fri.-Sat., May 1-Sept. 30, $4) are also available. Summer programs include Civil War reenactments and archaeological digs.

Nine miles of bike trails and five miles of hiking trails link the historic area to the rest of the park and provide access to Battery Russell

and the 1906 wreck of the British schooner *Peter Iredale.* You can also bike to the campground one mile south of the Military Museum.

Parking is available at four lots about a mile from one another at the foot of the dunes. The beach runs north to the Columbia River, where excellent surf fishing, bird-watching, and a view of the mouth of the river await. South of the campground (east of the *Peter Iredale*) is a self-guided nature trail around part of the two-mile shoreline of **Coffenbury Lake.** The lake also has two swimming beaches with bathhouses and fishing for trout and perch.

To get to Fort Stevens State Park from U.S. 101, drive west on Harbor Street through Warrenton on Highway 104 (Ft. Stevens Hwy.) to the suburb of Hammond and follow the signs to Fort Stevens Historic Area and Military Museum.

SPORTS AND RECREATION
Bicycling

You don't need a fancy bike to pedal the River Walk; rent a hefty cruiser from **Bikes and Beyond** (1089 Marine Dr., 503/325-2961, www.bikesandbeyond.com, 10am-6pm Mon.-Sat., 11am-4pm Sun.). This friendly little shop also caters to bicycle tourists.

Diving and Kayaking

Astoria Scuba (on Pier 39, 503/325-2502,

www.astoriascuba.com, 8am-6pm daily) offers diving lessons and kayak rentals for $25 for half a day.

Fishing Charters

More than any other industry, commercial fishing has dominated Astoria throughout its history. Salmon canneries lined the waterfront at the turn of the 20th century. In the modern era, commercial fishing has turned to tuna, sole, lingcod, rockfish, flounder, and other bottom fish. If it's not enough to watch these commercial operations from the dock, try joining a charter.

Tiki Charters (350 Industry St., 503/325-7818, www.tikicharter.com, $120 pp per day) will take you out for salmon, halibut, bottom fish, and sturgeon, depending on the season. Trips depart from the dock just off Industry Drive near the West Mooring Basin. Given the retail price of fresh salmon, you could theoretically pay for a charter trip by landing a single fish. **Gale Force Guides** (trips depart from Warrenton, 503/861-1494, www.galeforceguides.com, $120 pp per day) takes sport anglers fishing for salmon in either salt- or freshwater, depending on the season. Sturgeon and crabbing trips are also offered.

On your own, go after trout, bass, catfish, steelhead, and sturgeon in freshwater lakes, streams, and rivers. Lingcod, rockfish, surfperch, and other bottom fish can be pursued at sea, off jetties, or along ocean beaches.

Hiking

An in-town hike that's not too strenuous begins at 28th and Irving Streets, meandering up the hill to the Astoria Column. If you drive to the trailhead, park along 28th Street. It's about a one-mile walk to the top. En route is the **Cathedral Tree,** an old-growth fir with a sort of Gothic arch formed at its roots.

The **Oregon Coast Trail** starts (or ends) at Clatsop Spit, at the north end of **Fort Stevens State Park** (100 Peter Iredale Rd., Hammond, 503/861-1671 or 800/551-6949, www.oregonstateparks.org, $5 day use). The most northerly stretch extends south along the beach for 14 miles to Gearhart. It's a flat, easy walk, and your journey could well be highlighted by a sighting of the endangered silverspot butterfly, a small orange butterfly with silvery spots on the undersides of its wings.

You might also encounter cars on the beach. This section of shoreline, inexplicably, is the longest stretch of coastline open to motor vehicles in Oregon. Call the **State Parks and Recreation Division** (800/551-6949) for an up-to-date report on trail conditions before starting out.

Fort Stevens State Park has nine miles of hiking trails through woods, wetlands, and dunes. One popular hike here is the two-mile loop around **Coffenbury Lake.**

In 2005, as part of the expansion of Lewis and Clark National Historical Park, the **Fort to Sea Trail** was created to link Fort Clatsop to the Pacific. The 6.5-mile trail follows the route through forest, fields, and dunes that the corps traveled as they explored and traded along the Pacific coast.

The Fort to Sea Trail starts from the visitors center at Fort Clatsop. The first 1.5 miles involve a gentle climb past many trees blown down in a big 2007 storm to the Clatsop Ridge, where on a clear day you can see through the trees to the Pacific Ocean. The ridge makes a fine destination for a short hike, but the really beautiful part of the trail is the hikers-only (no dogs) stretch from the overlook to the beach, where you'll pass through deep woods and forested pastures dotted with small lakes. The trail passes a tunnel underneath U.S. 101 and continues through dunes to the Sunset Beach-Fort to Sea Trail parking lot. From there, a one-mile path leads to the beach.

Unless you plan to return along the trail—which makes for a long day's hike—you'll need to arrange a pickup.

Water Parks

The **Astoria Aquatic Center** (20th St. and Marine Dr., 503/325-7027, www.astoria-aparks.com, 5am-8pm Mon.-Fri., 9am-5pm Sat., 11am-5pm Sun., $6.50 adult, $4.50 children ages 2-17, $15 family) houses four pools,

Lewis and Clark National Historical Park

On November 2, 2004, President George W. Bush signed a bill into law to create the 59th national park in the United States. The Lewis and Clark National and State Historical Parks honor explorers Meriwether Lewis and William Clark, whose journey in 1804-1806 paved the way for the U.S. settlement of the West. The park focuses on the sites at the mouth of the Columbia River, where the Corps of Discovery spent the famously wet winter of 1805.

The park is somewhat unusual in that it is essentially a rebranding of current National Park facilities and a federalization of current state parks. The new park includes a dozen sites linked to Lewis and Clark exploration, campsites, and lore. One of these, **Fort Clatsop National Memorial,** south of Astoria and where the Corps actually spent the winter, was already operated by the National Park Service, while **Cape Disappointment State Park** (formerly Fort Canby State Park), on the Washington side of the Columbia, remains a Washington state park but is managed by the national park entity.

Besides these two existing facilities, units of the new national park include the **Fort to Sea Trail,** a path linking Fort Clatsop to the Pacific; **Clarks Dismal Nitch,** a notoriously wet campsite near the Washington base of the Astoria-Megler Bridge; **Station Camp,** another improvident campsite for the Corps; the **Salt Works** in Seaside, where the Corps boiled seawater to make salt; **Netul Landing,** the canoe launch area used by Lewis and Clark near Fort Clatsop; and a **memorial to Thomas Jefferson** yet to be constructed on the grounds of Cape Disappointment State Park.

The new national park also encompasses the existing **Fort Columbia State Park** in Washington, which preserves a turn-of-the-20th-century military encampment, and **Fort Stevens, Sunset Beach,** and **Ecola State Parks** in Oregon.

The national park designation changes little for these once-disparate sites, at least for the moment. Fort Clatsop has been expanded to 1,500 acres, and the **Lewis and Clark Interpretive Center** at Fort Disappointment State Park was revamped. Visitors will mostly notice new and consistent signage throughout the park units. Ranger-guided hikes and living history reenactors promise to bring to life the famous, often very wet, events that took place here over 200 years ago.

including a 100-foot waterslide with a 20-foot drop and a lazy-river current; a six-lane, 25-yard lap pool; an adult hydro spa pool; a kiddies' wading pool; locker rooms; and a variety of fitness equipment.

ENTERTAINMENT AND EVENTS

For the lowdown on all the happenings in and around Astoria, get your hands on a copy of *Hipfish,* Astoria's spirited monthly tabloid, distributed free all over town.

Nightlife

Befitting of a vintage fishing port, Astoria has lots of old bars and watering holes. As a tribute to Astoria's scrappy spirit, explore some of the city's classic bars. The **Portway** (422 W. Marine Dr., 503/325-2651) is the oldest bar in the oldest American settlement west of the Rockies. Though the present building dates from 1923, it's loaded with character and characters. Directly under the bridge, **Mary Todd's Workers Bar and Grill** (281 W. Marine Dr., 503/338-7291) is a classic old bar with a notable drink special: the Yucca. Also try the marvelously crispy onion rings. **Phyllis & Bob's Labor Temple Café & Bar** (939 Duane St., 503/325-0801) is the oldest communal union hall in the Pacific Northwest and is not to be missed. The clientele is a mix of longtime union activists, twenty-something artists, and rowdy young sailors, making for some interesting dynamics. The **Voodoo Room** (1114 Marine Dr., 503/325-2233, www.columbianvoodoo.com) is a dark and cluttered bar with hipsters, cocktails, and occasional live music.

All of Astoria's brewpubs are friendly places to start a conversation or settle in with a pint and decent pub grub to quietly muse on the world. **Fort George Brewery and Public House** (1483 Duane St., 503/325-7468, www.fortgeorgebrewery.com) has free live music on Sunday evenings.

The Arts

The handsome **Liberty Theatre** (1203 Commercial St., 503/325-5922, www.liberty-theater.org), whose colonnaded facades along Commercial and 12th Streets converge at the corner box office, is a vibrant symbol of Astoria's ongoing rejuvenation. The ornate Mediterranean-style building in the heart of downtown began its life in 1925 as a venue for silent films, vaudeville acts, and lectures. The theater continued as a first-run movie house, but after decades of neglect this grande dame was badly showing her age, and it looked as though the Liberty would eventually meet the sad wrecking ball fate of so many fine old movie palaces. Fortunately, though, a nonprofit organization undertook efforts to restore the theater to its original elegance and equip it to be a state-of-the-art performing arts center, and the Liberty currently hosts concerts, recitals, theater, and other events.

Astoria's long-running *Shanghaied in Astoria* (122 W. Bond St., 503/325-6104, www.shanghaiedinastoria.com, evenings Thurs.-Sat. mid-July-mid-Sept., $17-21), based on the town's dubious distinction as a notorious shanghai port during the late 1800s, is a good old-fashioned melodrama. Chase scenes, bar fights, and a liberal sprinkling of Scandinavian jokes will have you laughing in between applauding the hero and booing the villain. Performed with gusto by the Astor Street Opry Company, the show has been running since 1985, and has spawned a number of related shows: a "junior" *Shanghaied in Astoria* for kids, a once-yearly drag version, and the holiday season *Scrooged in Astoria.* Check the website for children's theater productions in March and April and other off-season productions that this lively troupe of thespians dreams up.

Cinema

The **Columbian Theater** (1102 Marine Dr., 503/325-3516, www.columbianvoodoo.com, usually 7pm, $4, $2 children ages 12 and under) sits adjacent to the Columbian Cafe and screens the big movies you may have missed a month earlier in their first run. Enjoy beer, wine, cocktails, pizza, and other munchies while you watch.

Astoria Gateway Cinema (1875 Marine

The Liberty Theatre, a former movie palace, is a great place to catch musical performances.

Dr., 503/338-6575) is a modern movie multiplex, showing the usual stuff, where you can pass an afternoon trying to forget the often dismal weather.

Festivals and Events
FISHER POETS GATHERING
Modeled after Elko, Nevada's popular Cowboy Poets Gathering, the **Fisher Poets Gathering** (www.fisherpoets.org) provides a forum in which men and women involved in the fishing and other maritime industries share their poems, stories, songs, and artwork in a convivial seaport setting. The annual late February event, which dates back to 1998, draws writers and artists from up and down the Pacific coast and farther afield for readings, art shows, concerts, book signings, workshops, films, a silent auction, and other activities at pubs, galleries, theaters, and other venues around town. Participation isn't limited to fisherfolk but extends to anyone with a connection to maritime activity, and themes range from the rigors (and humor) of life on the water to environmental issues. Admission is by donation ($5) at the ticket booth of the **Columbian Theater** (1102 Marine Dr.). For more details and a full schedule, check the website.

ASTORIA-WARRENTON CRAB AND SEAFOOD FESTIVAL
The **Astoria-Warrenton Crab and Seafood Festival** (Clatsop County Fairgrounds, 503/325-6311 or 800/875-6807, 4pm-9pm Fri., 10am-8pm Sat., 11am-4pm Sun., $5-10 adults, children ages 5-12 half price), held the last weekend in April, is a hugely popular event that brings in crowds from miles around. Scores of booths feature a cornucopia of seafood and other eats, regional beers and Oregon wines, and arts and crafts. Activities include continuous entertainment, crab races, a petting zoo, and kids' activities. A traditional crab dinner caps off the evening. To get to the fairgrounds from Astoria, take Highway 202 for 4.5 miles to Walluski Loop Road and watch for signs. Parking is limited at the fairgrounds. Frequent shuttle service takes folks between the fairgrounds, park-and-ride lots, downtown, the Port of Astoria, and local hotels and campgrounds.

SCANDINAVIAN MIDSUMMER FESTIVAL
The legacy of the thousands of Scandinavians who arrived to work in area mills and canneries in the late 19th and early 20th centuries is still strong in Astoria. For many locals, the summer's biggest event is the **Scandinavian Midsummer Festival** (503/325-6311, www.astoriascanfest.com, $8 adults, $3 children ages 6-12), which usually takes place the third weekend of June, Friday through Sunday. Local Danes, Finns, Icelanders, Norwegians, and Swedes come together to celebrate their heritage; visitors and musicians from the Old Country keep the festivities authentic. Costumed dancers weave around a flowered midsummer pole (a fertility rite), burn a bonfire to destroy evil spirits, and have tugs-of-war pitting Scandinavian nationalities against each other. Food, dancing, crafts, musical concerts, and a parade bring the whole town out to the Clatsop County Fairgrounds on Walluski Loop Road just off Highway 202.

ASTORIA REGATTA WEEK
A tradition since 1894, **Astoria Regatta Week** is considered the Pacific Northwest's longest-running festival. Held on the waterfront in mid-August, the five-day event kicks off with the regatta queen's coronation and reception. Attractions include live entertainment, a grand street parade, historic home tours, ship tours and boat rides, sailboat and dragon boat races, a classic car show, a salmon barbecue, arts and crafts, food booths, a beer garden, and a twilight boat parade. For details and a schedule, contact the **Astoria Regatta Association** (503/325-6311 or 800/875-6807, www.astoriaregatta.org).

SHOPPING
On Sundays between Mother's Day weekend to early October, follow local tradition and

take a leisurely stroll up and down 12th Street between Marine Drive and Exchange Street for the **Astoria Sunday Market** (10am-3pm), where vendors offer farm-fresh produce, plants, crafts, and specialty foods.

A local store worth noting is **Finnware** (1116 Commercial St., 503/325-5720, www.finnware.com, 10am-5pm Mon.-Sat., 11am-4pm Sun.), which stocks Scandinavian crystal and glassware, jewelry, books, and kitchen tools. This is a store that takes its Finnish roots seriously.

Art Galleries

Astoria has a well-deserved reputation as an art center, with many downtown storefronts now serving as art galleries. Not to miss is **RiverSea Gallery** (1160 Commercial St., 503/325-1270, http://riverseagallery.squarespace.com, 11am-5:30pm Mon.-Sat., 11am-4pm Sun.), with a large and varied selection of work by local painters, glass artists, jewelry makers, and fine craftspeople. For a more quixotic art scene, go to **Imogen Gallery** (240 11th St., 503/325-1566, http://imogengallery.com, 11am-5pm Mon.-Tues. and Thurs.-Sat., 11am-4pm Sun.), dedicated to contemporary and conceptual art by local artists. **Lightbox Photographic Gallery** (1045 Marine Dr., 503/468-0238, http://lightbox-photographic.com, 11am-5 Tues.-Sat.) is the region's gallery for fine art photography.

The second Saturday of each month is the **Astoria Art Walk** (5pm-9pm), when most galleries and shops in downtown stay open late.

Bookstores

Several bookstores in town invite serious browsing, buying, and intellectual stimulation. **Lucy's Books** (348 12th St., 503/325-4210, 10am-5:30pm Tues.-Sat., 11am-3pm Sun.) is a small but bighearted locally owned bookshop with an emphasis on Pacific Northwest regional subjects. On the next block, **Godfather's Books and Espresso** (1108 Commercial St., 503/325-8143, 8am-8pm Mon.-Sat., 9am-6pm Sun.) sells a mix of new and used books and has a case of excellent antique maps and prints depicting the Columbia River and north coast.

Local Food

Josephson's Smokehouse (106 Marine Dr., 503/325-2190, www.josephsons.com, 9am-6pm Mon.-Sat.) was established in 1920 in a false-front clapboard building near the waterfront. Josephson's is Oregon's most esteemed purveyor of gourmet smoked fish, producing Scandinavian cold-smoked salmon without dyes or preservatives. The smokehouse caters to mail-order clientele and fine restaurants. You can buy direct here at cheaper (but not cheap) prices than the mail-order rates. Pickled salmon, salmon jerky, sturgeon caviar, crab, oysters, and a variety of alder-smoked and canned fish are also sold here. On typically foggy days here in midwinter, there's nothing finer than a cup of Josephson's very thick clam chowder.

To shop the daily catch, which can include Dungeness crab, wild salmon, halibut, albacore tuna, sardines, sole, and rockfish, go to **Warrenton Deep Sea Fish Market** (45 NE Harbor Pl., Warrenton, 503/861-3911, 9am-5:30pm Mon.-Sat, 10am-4pm Sun.). They carry the largest selection of locally caught fish in the area, and you'll find a variety of smoked fish and seafood here as well.

ACCOMMODATIONS

The prices noted are for high season (summer) double-occupancy rooms. Rates fall by as much as half off-season. Also note that Astoria has many festival weekends, and rooms can be limited and prices high on those occasions. In summer, plan your trip to avoid weekends if you're trying to save on lodging costs.

$50-100

Astoria's ★ **Commodore** (258 14th St., 503/325-4747, http://commodoreastoria.com, $89-199) has simple but stylishly decorated rooms in a renovated downtown hotel. The least expensive rooms ("cabins") are just sleeping chambers with a sink, a flat-screen

TV and DVD player, and an iPod docking station, with shared toilets and handsome tiled showers at the end of the hallway. Suite rooms are larger and include a private bathroom. The Commodore is very popular with hip young travelers, especially its coffee shop on the ground floor. Be aware that the Commodore is on a busy downtown corner, so if traffic noise will be a problem, bring earplugs.

Another vintage Astoria hotel made over into hip lodgings is the **Norblad Hotel and Hostel** (443 14th St., 503/325-6989, http://norbladhotel.com, $29 hostel beds, $59-$99 rooms and suites). Owned by the same local team that runs the Commodore, the Norblad has the same youthful, stylish vibe, with crisply-designed "Euro-style" rooms, nearly all with bathrooms down the hall. For the price, you can't beat the quality and the downtown location, though budget travelers looking for a real hostel experience might be disappointed with the perfunctory shared kitchen and lounge areas.

Astoria has several motels that offer basic but clean rooms. Except on summer weekends, the following should have rooms available without reservations. On the eastern edge of Astoria, the **Crest Motel** (5366 Leif Erickson Dr./U.S. 30, 503/325-3141 or 800/421-3141, http://astoriacrestmotel.com, $89-119 depending on views) offers cliff-side river views, a coin-operated laundry, a whirlpool set in a gazebo overlooking the river, and pet-friendly rooms (with no extra fees). Two blocks from the West Mooring Basin and its charter docks, the **Astoria Dunes Motel** (288 W. Marine Dr., 503/325-7111 or 800/441-3319, http://astoriadunes-motel.com, $90-125) has an indoor heated pool and whirlpool tub. About 0.5 mile east of the Astoria-Megler Bridge, the **Rivershore Motel** (59 W. Marine Dr., 503/325-2921, www.astoriarivershoremotel.com, $75-100) has 43 rooms with coffeemakers, microwaves, refrigerators, and Internet access. Some rooms include kitchens.

$100-150

Clementine's Bed and Breakfast (847 Exchange St., 800/521-6801, www.clementines-bb.com, $118-169, two-night min.), a handsome two-story home built in the Italianate style in 1888, stands in good company across the street from the Flavel House and is itself on Astoria's Historic Homes Walking Tour. From the gardens around the house come the fresh flowers that accent the guest rooms and common areas, as do the herbs that spice the delicious gourmet breakfasts. There are five rooms in the main house, all with feather beds and private bathrooms; upper-story rooms have private balconies with river views.

In addition to these guest rooms, two spacious sunny suites are available in the **Moose Temple Lodge** ($128-169), adjacent to the main house. Built in 1850, this is one of the oldest extant buildings in Astoria; it was the Moose Temple from 1900 to 1940 and later served as a Mormon church. Renovated with skylights, wood floors, fireplaces, small kitchens, and several beds, these are ideal for families or groups. Pets are welcome.

A couple of blocks away from busy downtown streets, the **Rose River Inn B&B** (1510 Franklin Ave., 503/325-7175, www.roseriverinn.com, $100-160) offers two river-view suites and three guest rooms in a large, cheerfully painted Victorian, decorated with European antiques and art and surrounded by a neatly tended garden. Each room includes a claw-foot tub, and the River Suite also has a Finnish sauna.

The **Benjamin Young Inn** (3652 Duane St., 503/325-6172, www.benjaminyounginn.com, $109-179) is an elegant 1888 Queen Anne-style mansion with four large guest rooms, all with private baths and great river views. The inn is in the eastern part of Astoria, away from the hubbub of downtown.

$150-200

Stay right downtown in the beautifully renovated ★ **Hotel Elliott** (357 12th St., 877/378-1924, www.hotelelliott.com, $149-259), a small boutique hotel that's an easy walk from good restaurants and the river. The Elliott first opened in 1924, and its current incarnation has preserved much of the original charm of its Craftsman-era details, including the mahogany-clad lobby, handcrafted cabinetry, and wood and marble fireplaces. An original banner painted across the hotel's north side proudly proclaims Hotel Elliott—Wonderful Beds. The new Elliott has made a point of living up to this claim, with goose-down pillows, luxurious 440-thread-count Egyptian cotton sheets, feather beds, and top-of-the-line mattresses to ensure a memorable slumber. In addition to standard rooms, the Elliott has a variety of suites, including the five-room Presidential Suite with access to a rooftop garden. The rooftop is open to all and is a fine place to enjoy a glass of wine and the sunset.

You can't top the views at the **Holiday Inn Express Hotel & Suites** (204 W. Marine Dr., 503/325-6222 or 888/898-6222, www.astoriahie.com, $180-243), directly under the Astoria-Megler Bridge. Guest rooms have a refrigerator, a microwave, a coffeemaker, a high-speed Internet connection, a TV, and a DVD player. Facilities include an indoor pool, breakfast bar, business center, and exercise room. Pets are welcome.

Over $200

★ **Cannery Pier Hotel** (10 Basin St., 503/325-4996 or 888/325-4996, www.cannerypierhotel.com, $289-375) is a modern luxury hotel on the former site of a historic cannery, jutting 600 feet out into the Columbia below the Astoria-Megler Bridge. The opulently furnished rooms have dramatic views, even from the shower; all rooms have balconies, fireplaces, and beautiful hardwood floors. Complimentary continental breakfast is included in the rates, as are hors d'oeuvres and wine in the afternoon. There's also a day spa in the hotel, plus a Finnish sauna, a fitness room, and a hot tub.

Hampton Inn & Suites Astoria (201 39th St., 503/325-8888, $219-249) is Astoria's newest hotel and located east of downtown near Pier 39, so not really within walking distance of the city center. However, the Astoria

Waterfront Trolley passes directly in front of the hotel, and you can ride it downtown and back during its operating season. The rooms are spacious and nicely furnished, and face directly onto the river. Amenities include a pool and business center, plus free breakfast.

Camping

Families flock to **Fort Stevens State Park** (100 Peter Iredale Rd., Hammond, reservations 800/452-5687, www.oregonstateparks.org, year-round, $21 tent camping, $29 RV camping, $45 yurt, $99 cabin). With over 500 sites, the campground is the largest in the state park system, and it's incredibly popular. The park's many amenities and attractions make it the perfect base camp from which to take advantage of the region. Just be sure to avoid spring break (mid to late March) if you want to be spared the rites of spring enacted here by Oregon teenagers.

Across the road from the state park, **Astoria Warrenton Seaside KOA** (1100 NW Ridge Rd., Hammond, 503/861-2606 or 800/562-8506, www.astoriakoa.com, $25 tents, $44 RVs w/electric, $53 RVs full hookup, cabins $67 and up, $10 resort fee) is another sprawling campground. Amenities include an indoor pool and hot tub, pancake breakfast, a game room, miniature golf, and bike rentals.

FOOD

In addition to the restaurants and cafés listed here, you'll find do-it-yourself options at **Astoria's Sunday Market** on 12th Street between Marine Drive and Exchange Street and **Josephson's Smokehouse** (106 Marine Dr., 503/325-2190, www.josephsons.com, 9am-6pm Mon.-Sat.). A good stop for fresh produce, health food, and deli items is the **Astoria Co-op** (355 Exchange Street, 503/325-0027, 8am-8pm daily).

Astoria also features a number of food carts—there are several on both the east and west entrances to downtown. Most notable is **Bowfingers,** with really good fish-and-chips served out of a converted boat near the corner of Duane and 17th Streets.

Bakeries and Cafés

Stop by the ★ **Astoria Coffeehouse and Bistro** (245 11th St., 503/325-1787, http://astoriacoffeehouse.com, 7am-10pm Sun.-Thurs., 7am-11pm Fri.-Sat., $13-22) for fresh breakfast pastries and coffee, salads and sandwiches, and home-cooked regional fare. It's an airy, friendly place to sit and read the paper, or to enjoy cocktails and local seafood specialties late in the evening. This the kind of place that makes everything from scratch, from slow-roasted turkey, corned beef, and cakes to even ketchup, apple butter, and ice cream. All this, and it's a fun and lively place for a cocktail at night, too.

At the collectively run ★ **Blue Scorcher Bakery Cafe** (1493 Duane St., 503/338-7473, 8am-5pm daily, $6-12), the motto is "joyful work, delicious food, and strong community," and it's all true. Settle in with a tasty veggie sandwich (if the tempeh Reuben is on the menu, don't turn up your nose at it) and watch the Astorians—any one of whom would make an excellent new friend—come and go. A personal favorite are cardamom almond rolls, an old-fashioned Swedish treat that's perfect with a cup of coffee on a brisk morning. A wide variety of freshly prepared seasonal dishes also appear, from nettle soup in spring to pumpkin-black bean chili in the fall. A range of gluten-free pastries are offered on Friday. If it's all too healthy and wholesome for you, there's a brewpub next door.

American

A good, if rather standard, choice for families with kids, the Astoria outlet of **Pig 'N Pancake** (146 W. Bond St., 503/325-3144, 6am-9pm Sun.-Thurs., 6am-10pm Fri.-Sat., breakfast and lunch $7-10, dinner $10-18), a small north-coast chain (others are in Seaside and Cannon Beach), excels at big, filling breakfasts at reasonable prices. The specialty is homemade pancakes and waffles, available in a dozen variations, including potato pancakes, Swedish pancakes (thin and crispy with lingonberries), pecan-filled pancakes, and, of course, pigs in a blanket.

Eastern European

There aren't a lot of Bosnian restaurants around, and the **Drina Daisy** (915 Commercial St., 503/338-2912, www.drinadaisy.com, 11am-8pm Wed.-Sun., $11-23) is worth a stop to sample foods from an unfamiliar part of the world. The cuisine is a cross between Greek and Central European cooking. You can't go wrong with the appetizers or salads, many of which come with smoked sausages and filo-wrapped goodies.

Italian

For Astoria's top Italian food, go to **Fulio's Pastaria** (1149 Commercial St., 503/325-9001, 11am-close daily, $11-30) with excellent pasta, Tuscan-style steaks, and a good wine list in a lively and convivial dining room.

Mexican

There are a number of serviceable Mexican restaurants in Astoria (including, at last count, four food carts), but the locals' favorite is the hole-in-the-wall **Rio Café** (125 9th St., 503/325-2409, http://theriocafe.net, 11am-3pm Mon., 11am-8pm Tues.-Thurs., 11am-9pm Fri.-Sat., $10-18). Everything is fresh and made from scratch; the home-style cooking here packs more flavor than you'll find at many upscale Mexican restaurants.

Pacific Northwest

As widely appreciated as it is small, the ★ **Columbian Cafe** (1114 Marine Dr., 503/325-2233, http://columbianvoodoo.com, 8am-2pm Mon.-Wed., 8am-2pm and 5pm-9pm Thurs., 8am-2pm and 6pm-10pm Fri., 9am-2pm and 5pm-10pm Sat., 9am-2pm Sun., breakfast and lunch $7-10, dinner entrées $11-25) is an Astoria institution. The menu changes according to season and the chef's whim (be daring and order the "chef's mercy") but generally includes a good selection of pastas, chilies, crepes, and fresh catch of the day, and always a selection of homemade garlic, jalapeño, and red-pepper jellies. Breakfast is a highlight here. If this is your first visit to the Columbian Cafe, don't let the tiny, slightly seedy-looking venue put you off. Just barge in and take a seat—the servers will make you feel comfortable, and the rest is all culinary pleasure. Expect to be here for a while; the Columbian is not a quick in-and-out dining experience.

Another good restaurant with an inspiring motto ("Eat well, laugh often, and love much") is the easygoing **T. Paul's Urban Cafe** (1119 Commercial St., 503/338-5133, http://tpaulsurbancafe.com, 11am-9pm Mon.-Thurs., 11am-10pm Fri.-Sat., $9-24). The menu of hip diner food with fresh Pacific Northwest twists includes towering turkey sandwiches, bay shrimp ceviche, Caribbean jerk quesadillas, prawn pasta, and clam chowder. Quesadillas are the specialty, with about a dozen innovative varieties served. T. Paul's has a second downtown location, ★ **The Supper Club** (360 12th St., 503/325-2545, http://tpaulssupperclub.com, 11am-9pm Mon.-Thurs., 11am-10pm Fri.-Sat., $12-28) with a wide-ranging menu, a rather swank dining room, and some of the most reliably delicious food in Astoria. Top choices are pasta dishes, burgers, salads, and fresh seafood. The tiny bar is the perfect spot for a cocktail.

A cross between a cocktail lounge and a restaurant, the **Albatross** (225 14th St., 503-741-3091, $8-20) has excellent craft cocktails and small menu of sandwiches and small plates, along with a few nightly dinner specials, all based on locally sourced food. The oysters on the half shell are excellent (from Netarts Bay), and if you find slow braised duck leg with morel mushrooms, asparagus, and brown butter grits as a special, be sure to order it.

Seafood

One of Astoria's more notable restaurants is **Silver Salmon Grille** (1105 Commercial St., 503/338-6640, www.silversalmongrille.com, 11am-9pm daily, $13-28), for fine dining in an atmosphere that's somewhat formal but not starchy. Attractive murals of the eponymous fish adorn the walls inside and out, and salmon takes pride of place on the

The Columbian Cafe is a quirky diner with great locally sourced food.

dinner menu as well in a variety of preparations that are fresh and cooked to perfection. Pasta dishes, seasonal seafood (if razor clams are offered, be sure to order them, as they are excellent here), and several meat choices fill out the extensive menu. The wine list includes reasonably priced house wines made especially for the restaurant by Maryhill Winery in the Columbia Gorge. The bar here is one of the nicest in downtown Astoria, and it's a favorite of locals out on the town.

Settle in for some excellent seafood at ★ **Bridgewater Bistro** (20 Basin St., 503/235-6777, http://bridgewaterbistro.com, 11:30am-close Mon.-Sat., 11am-close Sun., $12-26), where you can graze on tapas (small plates menu 3pm-5pm) or order regular-size or smaller entrées. The soaring ceiling and riverside setting of the historic building next to the Cannery Pier Hotel are almost as compelling as the food. At the end of 12th Street, directly overlooking the Columbia, **Baked Alaska** (1 12th St., 503/325-7414, 11am-9pm Sun.-Thurs., 11am-10am Fri.-Sat., $18-32) features a selection of small and large plates with modern, international inflections. Seared sea scallops are served with grilled peaches, shiso leaves, cider aioli, and shaved hazelnuts, while prawn and Dungeness crab spaghettini comes with figs, capered brown butter, and fresh lovage. But about that name—yes, you can get baked Alaska here: The restaurant's twist on this classic dessert is basically a flaming ice cream sundae served on chocolate-chip cookies. The views rival the food, particularly in summer, when there's deck seating. Baked Alaska now also operates a wood-fired pizzeria, and its pizzas are available in the dining room, bar, and to go.

Indian

★ **Himani Indian Cuisine** (1044 Marine Dr., 503/325-8171, www.himaniic.com, 11am-3pm and 5pm-9pm Mon.-Fri., 5pm-9pm Sat.-Sun, $9-20) serves a very wide selection of Indian cuisine, with a specialty in southern Indian dishes such as tandoori dishes (including tandoori salmon) and masala dosa. The naan breads are equally delicious. A buffet ($9) is available Monday-Friday for lunch, and also all day Sunday. Himani also serves food from its original stall at the Astoria Sunday Market.

Brewpubs

Astoria's oldest brewpub, the **Wet Dog Cafe** (144 11th St., 503/325-6975, 11am-9pm Sun.-Thurs., 11am-10pm Fri.-Sat., $9-20) is home to the Astoria Brewing Company, maker of excellent handcrafted microbrews. There's also a full bar and live music or entertainment Thursday-Saturday nights. The café is housed in a cavernous remodeled former waterfront warehouse, with good views of the river. The food is good basic pub grub: fish-and-chips, burgers (including seafood burgers), sandwiches, and salads.

The **Rogue Ales Public House** (100 39th St., 503/325-5964, 11am-9pm Sun.-Thurs., 11am-10 Fri.-Sat., $9-22) is east of downtown in the Hanthorn Pier development. The pub is set inside a wood-plank structure atop a former cannery pier and offers excellent ales, plus burgers, pizza, and sandwiches. It's hard to get more Astorian than this. For beer snobs, the place to go is **Fort George Brewery and Public House** (1483 Duane St., 503/325-7468, www.fortgeorgebrewery.com, 11am-11pm Mon.-Thurs., 11am-midnight Fri.-Sat., noon-11pm Sun., $7-12), whose powerful ales have won it a reputation as one of Oregon's top breweries. The regular pub grub is a bit basic, but the pizzas served on the pub's second floor are excellent. There's free live music every Sunday evening. In an old fish-processing warehouse right on the edge of the river is **Buoy Beer Company** (1 8th St., 503/325-4540, www.buoybeer.com, 11am-10pm Sun.-Thurs., 11am-11pm Fri.-Sat., $10-26), with good beer and an ambitious menu that ranges from chicken romesco sandwiches and Petrale sole with herbed caper sauce to rib-eye steaks with gnocchi.

INFORMATION AND SERVICES

The **Astoria Chamber of Commerce** (111 W. Marine Dr., 503/325-6311 or 800/875-6807, www.oldoregon.com, 8am-6pm daily May-Sept., 9am-5pm Mon.-Fri. Oct.-Apr.) operates the Oregon Welcome Center at its offices, providing a plethora of brochures and maps for visitors to Astoria and other destinations on the north Oregon coast and southwest Washington. The website has downloadable audio tours.

With 10,000 people, Astoria is the largest city and the media hub of the north coast. The local newspaper, the *Daily Astorian* (www.dailyastorian.com) is sold around town and worth a look. The free monthly *Hipfish* is a publication in the great tradition of the alternative press of the 1960s. Whether you agree with its take on regional politics or not, the thoughtful and lively articles and complete entertainment listings will enhance your visit to the north coast.

Throughout the north coast, **KMUN** (91.9 FM in Astoria and Seaside, 89.5 FM in Cannon Beach) is a public radio station with excellent community-based programming. Folk, classical, jazz, and rock music, public affairs, radio drama, literature readings, children's bedtime stories, and National Public Radio news will keep your dial set on this frequency. A sister station, KCPB, broadcasts classical music in addition to NPR news.

The **Astoria Post Office** is located in the Federal Building at 750 Commercial Street. Useful numbers to know include the **county sheriff** (503/225-2061), the **Coast Guard** (2285 Airport Rd., Warrenton, 503/861-6220), and **Columbia Memorial Hospital** (2111 Exchange St., Astoria, 503/325-4321).

GETTING THERE AND AROUND
Amtrak Thruway Motorcoach Service (800/USA-RAIL or 800/872-7245, www.

amtrak.com) runs two buses daily between the north coast and Portland Union Station. Board the coach in Astoria at the downtown transit center (9th St. and Astor St.). The bus also stops at Cannon Beach, Seaside, and Warrenton.

Car rentals are available from **Enterprise** (644 W. Marine Dr., 503/325-6500). For visitors willing to let go of their cars for a while, the Sunset Empire Transportation District, better known as **The Bus** (503/861-RIDE, 503/861-7433, or 800/776-6406, www.ridethe-bus.org), provides reasonably frequent transportation around Astoria and along the coast to Warrenton, including to Gearhart, Seaside, and Cannon Beach.

Seaside and Gearhart

Seaside is Oregon's quintessential, and oldest, family beach resort. The beach is long and flat, sheltered by a scenic headland, with lifeguards on duty during the summer months, beachside playground equipment, and a boardwalk winding through the dunes. Ice cream parlors, game arcades, eateries, and gift shops crowd shoulder to shoulder along the main drag, Broadway. The aromas of cotton candy and french fries lend a heady incense to the salt air, and the clatter of bumper cars and other amusements can induce sensory overload. Atlantic City it's not—thank goodness—but on a crowded summer day the town evokes the feeling of a carnival midway by the sea. During spring break, when Pacific Northwest high school and college students arrive, the town's population of 6,200 can quadruple almost overnight.

Neighboring Gearhart, a mainly residential community (pop. 1,100) just to the north, has a few lodgings away from the bustle of Seaside as well as a venerable 18-hole golf course.

Located along the Necanicum River, in the

shadow of majestic Tillamook Head, Seaside has attracted tourists since the early 1870s, when transportation magnate Ben Holladay sensed the potential for a resort hotel near the water. But better transportation was needed to get customers to the place. At that time, the way to get to Seaside was first by boat from Portland down the Columbia River to Skipanon (now Warrenton), and from there by carriage south to Seaside. To speed the connection, Holladay later constructed a railroad line from Skipanon to Seaside.

To escape Portland's summer heat, families in the late 19th century would make the boat and railroad journey to spend their summer in Seaside. Most men would go back to Portland to work during the week, returning to the coast on Friday to visit the family. Every weekend the families would gather at the railroad station to greet the men, then see them off again for the trip back to Portland. It wasn't long before the train became known as the "Daddy Train." As roads between Portland and the coast were constructed, the car took

Seaside and Gearhart

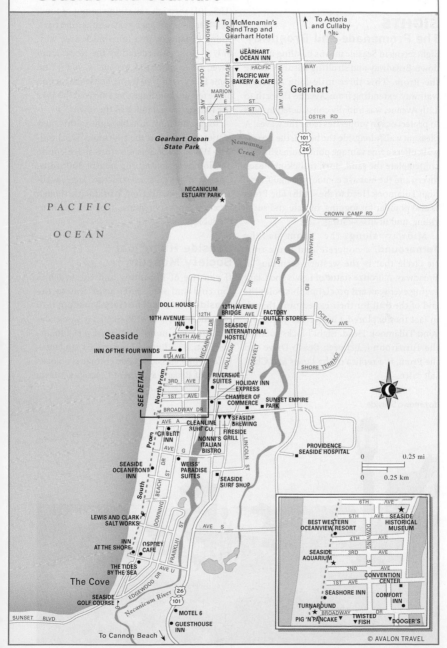

To McMenamin's
Sand Trap and
Gearhart Hotel

To Astoria
and Cullaby
Lake

GEARHART
OCEAN INN

PACIFIC
PACIFIC WAY
BAKERY & CAFE

Gearhart

MARION
AVE

E ST

F ST

G ST

OSTER RD

Gearhart Ocean
State Park

Neawanna
Creek

101
26

NECANICUM
ESTUARY PARK

CROWN CAMP RD

PACIFIC

OCEAN

WAHANNA RD

DR

DR

OCEAN AVE

DOLL HOUSE

10TH AVENUE
INN

12TH

12TH AVENUE
BRIDGE

10TH AVE

FACTORY
OUTLET STORES

SEASIDE
INTERNATIONAL
HOSTEL

HOLLADAY

ROOSEVELT

SHORE TERRACE

Seaside

INN OF THE FOUR WINDS

6TH AVE

NECANICUM DR

3RD AVE

1ST AVE

BROADWAY DR

RIVERSIDE
SUITES

HOLIDAY INN
EXPRESS

CHAMBER OF
COMMERCE

SUNSET EMPIRE
PARK

SEE DETAIL

North Prom

AVE A

CLEANLINE
SURF CO.

SEASIDE
BREWING

FIRESIDE

NONNI'S
ITALIAN
BISTRO

GILBERT
INN

AVE F

AVE G

LINCOLN ST

PROVIDENCE
SEASIDE HOSPITAL

Prom

SEASIDE
OCEANFRONT
INN

WEISS'
PARADISE
SUITES

SEASIDE
SURF SHOP

BEACH ST

DR

DOWNING ST

South Prom

0   0.25 mi

0   0.25 km

LEWIS AND CLARK
SALT WORKS

AVE S

INN
AT THE SHORE

OSPREY
CAFE

FRANKLIN ST

THE TIDES
BY THE SEA

AVE U

The Cove

SEASIDE
GOLF COURSE

EDGEWOOD DR

Necanicum River

26
101

MOTEL 6

GUESTHOUSE
INN

SUNSET BLVD

To Cannon Beach

6TH AVE

BEST WESTERN
OCEANVIEW RESORT

5TH AVE

4TH AVE

SEASIDE
HISTORICAL
MUSEUM

DOWNING ST

SEASIDE
AQUARIUM

3RD AVE

2ND AVE

1ST AVE

CONVENTION
CENTER

SEASHORE INN

COMFORT
INN

TURNAROUND

BROADWAY

PIG 'N PANCAKE

TWISTED
FISH

DOOGER'S

© AVALON TRAVEL

over, and the railroad carried its last dad in 1939.

SIGHTS
The Promenade and Broadway

Sightseeing in Seaside means bustling up and down Broadway and strolling leisurely along the Prom. This three-mile-long concrete walkway, extending from Avenue U north to 12th Avenue, was initially constructed in 1908 to protect ocean properties from the waves. A pleasant walk alongside the beach, the boardwalk offers a fine vantage point from which to contemplate the sand, surf, frolicking beach lovers, and the massive contours of 1,200-foot-high Tillamook Head to the south. The Prom is also popular for jogging, bicycle and surry riding, and in-line skating.

Midway along the Prom is the **Turnaround,** a concrete-and-brick traffic circle that is the western terminus of Broadway. A bronze statue of Lewis and Clark gazing ever seaward proclaims this point the end of the trail for their expedition, though in fact they explored a bit farther south, beyond Tillamook Head. Eight blocks south of the Turnaround, between Beach Drive and the Prom, is a replica of the Lewis and Clark salt cairn.

Heading east from the Turnaround, Broadway runs 0.5 mile to Roosevelt Avenue (U.S. 101) through a dizzying gamut of tourist attractions, arcades, restaurants, and bars. Along Broadway, in a four-block area west of U.S. 101 and bordered by the Necanicum River, 1st Avenue, and Avenue A, you'll find some fancy Victorian frame houses, a portion of the few old buildings that survived the 1912 fire that destroyed much of the town.

Today, the most notable sight in this busy section of Seaside is the enormous $73.3 million WorldMark Seaside time-share condo development containing nearly 300 units. Condos in this outsized structure aren't available for rent directly from Worldmark, though vacation property rental companies can handle sublets.

Seaside Historical Society Museum

If you tire of Broadway and the beach is too cold and wet, make your way to the **Seaside Historical Society Museum** (570 Necanicum Dr., 503/738-7065, www.seaside-museum.org, noon-3pm Mon.-Fri., 10am-3pm Sat., $3 adults, $2 seniors, $1 students), housed in a classic seaside cottage six blocks north of Broadway, where Clatsop artifacts

downtown Seaside

Lewis and Clark's men used ovens like these to make salt while in Seaside.

and exhibits on early tourism in Seaside impart more of a sense of history than anything else in town.

Seaside Aquarium

Right on the Prom north of the Turnaround is the **Seaside Aquarium** (200 N. Prom, 503/738-6211, www.seasideaquarium.com, 9am-7pm daily Mar.-Oct., 9am-5pm Wed.-Sun. Nov.-Feb., $8 adults, $6.75 seniors, $4 children ages 6-13). It's not quite the Oregon Coast Aquarium (find that in Newport), but if you're not going to make it that far south, it's an okay introduction to sealife for young children. Back in the era of the Daddy Train, this place served as a natatorium, but was converted to its current use in 1937. Today the pool is filled with raucously barking seals. In addition, a hundred species of marine life here include 20-ray sea stars, crabs, ferocious-looking wolf eels and moray eels, and octopuses.

Lewis and Clark Salt Works

Near the south end of the Prom at Lewis and Clark Way are the reconstructed salt works of Lewis and Clark. While camped at Fort Clatsop during the winter of 1805-1806, the captains sent a detachment south to find a place suitable for rendering salt from seawater. Their supply was nearly exhausted, and the precious commodity was a necessity for preserving and seasoning their food on the expedition's return journey. At the south end of present-day Seaside, five men built a cairn-like stone oven near a settlement of the Clatsop and Killamox people and set about boiling seawater nonstop for seven weeks to produce 3.5 bushels (about 314 pounds) of salt for the trip back east.

SPORTS AND RECREATION

Bicycling

Seaside has a bumper crop of places that rent bicycles, skates, and surreys, all for similar rates, about $10 per hour for a bike. The **Prom Bike Shop** (622 12th Ave., 503/738-8251, http://prombikeshop.com, 10:30am-5:30pm daily) is a full-service bike shop; rent cruisers or novelty bikes at **Wheel Fun Rentals Spoke 1** (21 N. Columbia St., 503/717-4337, 9am-sunset daily) or **Wheel Fun Rentals Spoke 2** (151 Ave. A, 503/738-7212, 9am-sunset daily).

Boating and Fishing

Just because you're smack-dab in the middle of a family resort town doesn't mean you can't enjoy some of nature's bounty; anglers can reel in trout, salmon, and steelhead from the Necanicum River right in the center of downtown. The **12th Avenue Bridge** is a popular spot for fishing and crabbing.

Cullaby Lake, on the east side of U.S. 101 about four miles north of Gearhart, offers fishing for crappies, bluegills, perch, catfish, and largemouth bass. At 88 acres, Cullaby is the largest of the many lakes on the Clatsop Plains. Two parks on the lake, **Carnahan Park** and **Cullaby Lake County Park,** have boat ramps, picnic areas, and other facilities. Cullaby is the only practical place to waterski in the area.

A half mile west of Highway 101, **Sunset Beach Park** on Neacoxie Lake (also known as Sunset Lake) has a boat ramp, picnic tables, and a playground. Anglers come for warmwater fish species, plus the rainbow trout stocked in the spring. From Astoria, drive south 10 miles on Highway 101 and turn west on Sunset Beach Road.

At **Quatat Park** (503/440-1548), beside the Necanicum River in downtown Seaside, rent kayaks, canoes, and pedal boats for exploring the waterway.

Golf

Golfers can escape to public courses south of Seaside and north in the small town of Gearhart. At **Seaside Golf Club** (451 Aye. U, 503/738-5261), greens fees are $15-17 for nine holes. The **Highlands at Gearhart** (1 Highland Rd., Gearhart, 503/738-5248, www. highlandsgolfgearhart.com, $17 for nine holes) is another public nine-hole course, with ocean views from most holes. The British-links-style course at **Gearhart Golf Links** (1157 N. Marion St., Gearhart, 503/738-3538, www.gearhartgolflinks.com, $70-80 for 18 holes in summer) was established in 1882, making it one of the oldest on the West Coast and Oregon's oldest.

Hiking

From the south end of Seaside, walk in the footsteps of Lewis and Clark on an exhilarating hike over Tillamook Head. In January 1806, neighboring Native Americans told of a beached whale lying several miles south of their encampment. William Clark and a few companions, including Sacajawea, set off in an attempt to find it and trade for blubber and whale oil, which fueled the expedition's lanterns. Climbing Tillamook Head from the north, the party crested the promontory. Clark was moved enough by the view to later write about it in his journal:

> I beheld the grandest and most pleasing prospect which my eyes ever surveyed. Immediately in front of us is the

ocean breaking in fury. To this boisterous scene the Columbia with its tributaries and studded on both sides with the Chinook and Clatsop villages forms a charming contrast, while beneath our feet are stretched the rich prairies.

Today, you can experience the view that so impressed Clark on the **Tillamook Head National Recreation Trail,** which runs seven miles through Ecola State Park. Prior to setting out, you could arrange to have a friend drive south to Indian Beach to pick you up at the end of this three- to five-hour trek (or you can be picked up another mile south at the Ecola Point parking lot just north of Cannon Beach). As you head up the forested trail on the north side of Tillamook Head, look back over the Seaside town site. In about 20 minutes, you'll be gazing down at the ocean from cliffs 1,000 feet above. A few hours later, you'll hike down onto Indian Beach.

To get to the trailhead from Seaside, drive south, following Avenue U past the golf course to Edgewood Street, and turn left; continue until you reach the parking lot at the end of the road.

Surfing

The best surfing spot in the Seaside area is the beach just south of town simply referred to as **The Cove,** directly north of Tillamook Head and reached from parking areas along Sunset Boulevard. While prevailing winds favor winter surfing rather than summer, this is in fact a popular destination year-round. Local surfers can be impatient with beginners, so this probably isn't a good spot for novices.

Seaside Surf Shop (1116 S. Roosevelt Dr., 503/717-1110, www.seasidesurfshop. com, 10am-6pm Mon.-Fri., 9am-6pm Sat., 9am-5pm Sun.) and **Cleanline Surf Co.** (60 N. Roosevelt Dr., 503/738-2061, www.cleanlinesurf.com, 9am-6pm daily) rent and sell surfboards as well as wetsuits, boots, and flippers; Cleanline Surf also offers instruction. **Northwest Women's Surf Camps** (503/440-5782, www.nwwomenssurfcamps.

com) will give you a bit of land training (the camp includes yoga to get you limbered up and in the right frame of mind) and then accompany you into the waves.

Swimming

Despite the lifeguard on duty in summer, swimming at Seaside's beach isn't the most comfortable, unless you're used to the North Sea. Gearhart boasts a quieter beach than Seaside's, although the water is every bit as cool. Warm-blooded swimmers can head to the facilities at **Sunset Empire Park** (1140 E. Broadway, Seaside, 503/738-3311, open daily), which includes three pools, waterslides, a 15-person hot tub, and fitness equipment.

Wildlife-Watching

Bird-watchers gather at **Necanicum Estuary Park**, at the 1900 block of North Holladay Drive across the street from Seaside High School. Local students have built a viewing platform, stairs to the beach, a boardwalk, and interpretive signs. Great blue and green herons and numerous migratory bird species flock to the grassy marshes and slow tidal waters near the mouth of the Necanicum River. During the fall and winter, buffleheads and mergansers shelter in the estuary, while in summer the waters are often thronged with pelicans. Occasionally, Roosevelt elk, black-tailed deer, river otters, beavers, mink, and muskrats can also be sighted.

ENTERTAINMENT AND EVENTS

Seaside predates any other town on the Oregon coast as a place built with good times in mind. A zoo and racetrack were among Seaside's first structures, and arcades are still thriving near the foot of Broadway. **Cannes Cinema** (U.S. 101 at 12th Ave.) is a five-screen multiplex showing first-run films.

The annual **Oregon Dixieland Jubilee** (800/738-6894, www.jazzseaside.com) takes place at the end of February. This event has been gaining momentum for more than 25 years and appeals to fans of Dixieland

and traditional jazz. The town celebrates the **Fourth of July** with a parade, a picnic and social at the Seaside Historical Society Museum (570 Necanicum Dr.), and a big fireworks show on the beach.

In early September, **Wheels and Waves** (503/717-1914) brings over 500 classic hot rods and custom cars (1962 and earlier, please) to downtown and the **Civic and Convention Center** (1st Ave. at Necanicum Dr.).

SHOPPING

Seaside is a shopping hub not only for its own population but also for Cannon Beach, which oddly doesn't even have a real grocery store, let alone a shopping mall. A number of shopping centers line U.S. 101 as it passes through Seaside; the **Seaside Factory Outlet Center** (1111 N. Roosevelt Dr., 503/717-1603) has 25 discount stores, including outlets for Eddie Bauer and Nike.

ACCOMMODATIONS

Whatever your price range, you'll have to reserve ahead for a room in Seaside during the summer and on weekends and holidays (especially spring break). If you do, chances are you'll be able to find the specs you're looking for, given the area's array of lodgings and over 1,800 hotel rooms. The **Seaside Visitors Bureau's** helpful website (www.seasideor. com) provides comprehensive listings and a handy booking engine for last minute rooms.

Generally speaking, there are three lodging areas in Seaside. First, there are several modern motels along busy U.S. 101, about eight blocks from the beach. If you're just passing through or waited too long to call for reservations, these offer inexpensive rooms, but little in the way of beachside charm. A second grouping of hotels is in the center of Seaside, along the Necanicum River. These have a quieter riverside setting but still aren't beachfront (though you won't have to cross U.S. 101 to get to the beach). Finally, there are numerous hotels that face directly onto the beach or are just a short stumble to the strand. Even here, there's quite a difference in price between rooms that face the beach and those that face the parking lot.

Under $50

The cheapest place in town is the quite nice **Seaside International Hostel** (930 N. Holladay Dr., 503/738-7911 or 888/994-0001, www.seasidehostel.net, dorm-style bunk $29 pp, private rooms $69-79), with special touches such as morning meditation and exercise classes. Unlike many hostels, it doesn't close down during the day and there's no curfew at night. There's an espresso bar on-site, and the Necanicum River runs through the backyard. Close by is the Necanicum Estuary Park.

$50-100

Out along U.S. 101 are two motels that provide good value and new rooms, but most people wouldn't consider them walking distance to the beach. **Motel 6** (2369 S. Roosevelt Dr., 503/738-6269 or 800/466-8356, $70-90), on U.S. 101 about 0.5 mile south of Broadway, isn't near the sand but does offer reasonably priced rooms. Just south is **Guesthouse Inns & Suites** (2455 S. Roosevelt Dr., 503/482-7666 or 866/482-7666, www.guesthouseseaside. com, $98-129), with free breakfast waffles, free high-speed Internet, and guest laundry. These two motels on the southern entry to Seaside are closest to Cannon Beach.

Well south of the bustling Broadway scene, the **Inn at the Shore** (2275 S. Prom, 503/738-3113 or 800/713-9914, www.innattheshore. com, $89-169) has nicely appointed rooms, each with a gas fireplace, a balcony, a wet bar, a microwave, a coffeemaker, a refrigerator, a flat-screen TV, and a DVD/VCR. The less expensive rooms don't have ocean views, but the beach is just steps away.

$100-150

There's a clutch of motels south of the Broadway-Prom axis that offer easy beach access at fair prices—and a much quieter beachfront experience than in the town center. The

Tides by the Sea (2316 Beach Dr., 503/738-6317 or 800/548-2846, www.thetidesbythesea. com, $107-252) is an older motel that has converted its large guest rooms and cottages into condos. About a quarter of the units face onto the Prom, but those that don't are just seconds away from the beach. If you can live without an ocean view, you'll save a bundle here. Each of the units is different, but most have kitchens and fireplaces. In high season, there is a two-night minimum stay policy.

The rooms at **Seashore Inn** (60 N. Prom, 503/738-6368 or 888/738-6368, www.seashoreinnor.com, $143-219) are right in the thick of it along the Promenade. Half the guest rooms face the beach, but half don't. These rooms are just steps from the beach but are a fraction of the cost of rooms on the other side of the building. All guest rooms have microwaves and mini-refrigerators, and some have full kitchens and balconies. There's also an indoor pool in case the weather turns foul.

While motels dominate the lodging scene in Seaside, a few B&Bs and small inns offer an alternative. The **Gilbert Inn** (341 Beach Dr., 503/738-9770 or 800/410-9770, www.gilbertinn.com, $149-159) is a well-preserved 1892 Queen Anne just a block south of Broadway and a block from the beach. Period furnishings adorn the 10 guest rooms, which all have private bathrooms, down comforters, and other nice touches (though this seems like a classic B&B, no breakfast is served). The third-floor "Garret" sleeps up to four in a queen and two twin beds, with ocean views from the dormer window.

North of Broadway, the **10th Avenue Inn** (125 10th Ave., 503/738-0643 or 800/745-2378, www.10aveinn.com, $125-150) is a comfortable 1908 home built just a few steps from the beach. In the parlor, a baby grand piano, a guitar, and other instruments are available for musically inclined guests. The three guest rooms have king-size beds, attached bathrooms, TVs, and small refrigerators. Next door and operated by the same folks is the **Doll House,** a sweet two-bedroom cottage ideal for four adults plus two or three children, with a full kitchen and a deck with a barbecue grill. It goes for $890 per week in summer (minimum 1-week rental), and $160 per night off-season (2-night minimum).

$150-200

Just north of the Necanicum River's mouth, Gearhart offers a respite from the bustle of Seaside. The ★ **Gearhart Ocean Inn** (67 N. Cottage St., 503/738-7373, www.gearhartoceaninn.com, $165-185) offers a choice of 12 New England-style wooden cottages with comforters, wicker chairs, and throw rugs, and the beaches are a short walk away. The two-story deluxe units have kitchens and hardwood floors. Pets are allowed in some units. Especially during the off-season, this spruced-up old motor court is one of the best values on the north coast.

A charmingly refurbished lodging just three short blocks from the beach, ★ **Weiss' Paradise Suites** (741 S. Downing St., 503/738-6691 or 800/738-6691, www.seasidesuites.com, $159-169) is south of the Broadway action but offers homey, recently upgraded units with lots of extras, including full kitchens, decks, two TVs, free DVDs, and robes.

The four-story, shingle-sided **Seaside Oceanfront Inn** (581 S. Prom, 503/319-3300 or 800/772-7766, https://theseasideinn.com, $159-319) stands right on the beach, with its north gable skewered by a clock tower. Each of the 14 guest rooms is decorated in a unique theme—the clock tower room has a huge round bed in the center of the room, but other than that, they're pretty tasteful. Most have a spectacular ocean view, and pets are permitted in certain rooms. The on-site restaurant is very good.

Seaside's most stylish rooms are at the ★ **Inn of the Four Winds** (820 N. Prom, 503/738-9524 or 800/818-9524, www.innofthefourwinds.com, $179-329). This 14-room boutique hotel has very comfortable rooms furnished with taste and panache. Each

guest room has a microwave, coffeemaker, refrigerator, MP3 player, gas fireplace, and deck or balcony with an ocean view. Best of all, the inn faces directly onto the beach eight blocks north of the frenetic Broadway strip.

In the center of Seaside, with balconies over the Necanicum River, the **Holiday Inn Express Hotel Suites Seaside Convention Center** (34 Holladay Dr., 503/717-8000, $188-208) has an indoor pool and spa and rooms with fridges, microwaves, coffeemakers, and CD and DVD players. Rates include a complimentary breakfast bar.

Just four miles north of Seaside at the sleepy town of Gearhart is the ★ **Gearhart Hotel** (1157 N. Marion Ave., 503/717-8159 or 855/846-7583, $175-190), a boutique hotel developed out of the historic Gearhart Golf Links club house by the McMenamin's local chain of hotels and breweries. It has all the trademark comfortable funkiness of other McMenamin properties, with the added benefits of sitting on the oldest golf course in the Pacific Northwest and Pacific beaches just across the street. Rooms have en suite bathrooms, and there's a lively pub on the main floor.

$200-250

Best Western Oceanview Resort (414 N. Prom, 503/738-3264 or 800/234-8439, www.oceanviewresort.com, $209-289) is a large hotel right on the beach near the center of town. Amenities include an on-site restaurant and lounge, a heated pool, and a spa; the majority of rooms face the ocean.

In the center of Seaside, right on the Necanicum River, the **Rivertides Suites** (102 N. Holladay Dr., 877/871-8433, www.rivertidesuites.com, $200-299) offers some of the most upscale accommodations in Seaside. All rooms have balconies, full kitchens, fine linens, and jetted tubs, plus complimentary breakfast, indoor pool and hot tub, exercise room, and great views from the rooftop viewing deck. In addition to the entry-level studio suites, there are also one- and two-bedroom suites.

Vacation Rentals

A good option for many travelers is one of the several dozen vacation rentals; options range from tiny cottages at less than $100 per night (minimum stays are often required, especially in summer) to large homes that can host groups of 10-12. Check with the **Seaside Visitors Bureau** (7 N. Roosevelt St., 503/738-3097 or 888/306-2326, www.seasideor.com, 8am-5pm daily), or contact one of the rental agencies: **Beachhouse Vacation Rentals** (503/738-9068, www.beachhouse1.com), **Oceanside Vacation Rental** (503/738-7767 or 800/840-7764, www.oceanside1.com), or **Northwind Vacation Rentals** (503/738-5532 or 866/738-5532, www.northwindrentals.com).

Camping

One mile south of Seaside in a lush green meadow is **Circle Creek RV Park and Campground** (85658 U.S. 101, 503/738-6070, www.circlecreekrv.com, mid-Mar.-Oct., RVs $40). The campground offers showers, a small store, picnic tables, and fire rings. No tent camping.

FOOD

While a stroll down Broadway might have you thinking that cotton candy, corn dogs, and saltwater taffy are the staples of Seaside cuisine, several eateries here can satisfy more refined palates as well. But there's no disputing the fact that Seaside, despite being one of Oregon's most popular Pacific-front towns, is not a mecca of fine dining.

American

If you're traveling with kids, you'll almost inevitably end up eating at **Pig 'N Pancake** (323 Broadway, 503/738-7243, 6am-9pm Sun.-Thurs., 6am-10pm Fri.-Sat., breakfast and lunch $7-10, dinner $10-18), where the Swedish pancakes and crab-and-cheese omelets are tops at breakfast, and the Frisbee-size cinnamon rolls will launch your blood sugar to new heights.

A top choice for home style American fare is **Firehouse Grill** (841 Broadway, 503/717-5502, www.firehousegrillseaside.net, 8am-3pm Thurs., 8am-3pm and 5-8pm Fri.-Sat., 8am-3pm Sun. and Mon., $8-14), where classic breakfasts feature biscuits and gravy and chicken fried steak, and lunch focuses on burgers.

An excellent destination for breakfast and brunch is the **Osprey Café** (2281 Beach Dr, 503/739-7054, 7:30am-3pm, $9-13) with breakfast all day (classic American egg dishes plus Mexican fare and Indonesian nasi goreng as well), and sandwiches for lunch. The Osprey is south of downtown, near the end of the Boardwalk, near some of Seaside's more affordable hotels.

Should the frenetic ambience of Seaside on a holiday weekend begin to wear thin, try the ★ **Pacific Way Bakery and Cafe** in Gearhart (601 Pacific Way, 503/738-0245, bakery 7am-1pm Thurs.-Mon., restaurant 11am-3:30pm, 5pm-9pm Thurs.-Mon., dinner $10-30, dinner reservations recommended). Pasta, crusty pizzas, and seafood dishes (including thick seafood cioppino) as well as Dungeness crab sandwiches with aioli pop up at lunch and dinner. Rib-eye steak and local razor clams are other frequent dinnertime highlights in the surprisingly urbane little café hidden behind a rustic old storefront. In the morning, the bakery side of the operation is *the* place to be for coffee and pastries.

Seafood

Dooger's (505 Broadway, 503/738-3773, 11am-9pm daily, $11-20), which also has an outlet in Cannon Beach, is a popular Broadway mainstay known for its clam chowder. Although it's kind of a frumpy-looking place, it serves good seafood. Local clams and oysters, fresh Dungeness crab legs, sautéed shrimp, and marionberry cobbler are also the basis of Dooger's reputation.

Right in the heart of busy Broadway, **Twisted Fish** (311 Broadway, 503/738-3467,

the Seaside Brewing Company

between. This small and popular restaurant fills up fast, so call ahead for reservations.

Brewpubs and Wine Bars

The **Seaside Brewing Company** (851 Broadway, 503/717-5451, http://seasidebrewery.com, 11:30am-9pm Sun.-Thurs., 11:30-10pm Fri.-Sat., $10-13) brews great ales and has a handsome location in Seaside's old 1914 city hall and jail. Expect burgers, sandwiches, and pizza. At the Gearhart Golf Links, the old clubhouse now houses **McMenamins Sand Trap** (1157 N. Marion Ave., 503/717-8150, 11am-10pm Mon.-Tues., 11am-11pm Wed.-Thurs., 11am-midnight Fri., 8am-midnight Sat., 8am-10pm Sun., $7-27); it has been decorated with the McMenamins' trademark whimsical artwork and serves the local chain's decent (not great, but always edible) upscale pub food.

INFORMATION AND SERVICES

The **Seaside Visitors Bureau** (7 N. Roosevelt St., 503/738-3097 or 888/306-2326, www.seasideor.com) is open 8am-5pm daily. **Providence Seaside Hospital** (725 S. Wahanna Rd., 503/717-7000) has 24-hour service and an emergency room.

GETTING THERE

Sunset Empire Transportation District operates **The Bus** (503/861-RIDE, 503/861-7433, or 800/776-6406, www.ridethebus.org), serving Cannon Beach, Seaside, Astoria-Warrenton, and points in between. **Amtrak** (800/872-7245, www.amtrak.com) buses pass through twice daily on their run between Portland and Astoria.

11am-10pm daily, $10-30) is a Pacific Northwest-style steakhouse, with hand-cut steaks, fresh fish and seafood, pasta and Mediterranean-inflected dishes such as chicken and prawn picatta. All bread and desserts are made in-house; live music is offered on weekend evenings.

Italian

The menu at **Nonni's Italian Bistro** (831 Broadway, 503/738-4264, 11:30am-9pm Thurs.-Mon., $11-29) extends from meatball sandwiches to crab- and salmon-rich cioppino, with a selection of pasta dishes in

Cannon Beach and Vicinity

In 1846, the USS *Shark* met its end on the Columbia River Bar. The ship broke apart, and a section of deck bearing cannons and an iron capstan drifted south, finally in 1894 washing ashore south of the current city limits at Arch Cape. And so this town got its name, which it adopted in 1922. In the winter of 2008, during an especially low tide, two additional cannons were revealed. After a thorough study by historians and archivists at Texas A&M University, the cannons are now on display at Astoria's Columbia Maritime Museum.

In 1873, stagecoach and railroad tycoon Ben Holladay helped create Oregon's first coastal tourist mecca, Seaside, while ignoring its attractive neighbor in the shadow of Haystack Rock. In the 20th century, Cannon Beach evolved into a bohemian alternative to the hustle and bustle of the family-oriented resort scene to the north. Before the recent era of development, this place was a quaint backwater attracting laid-back artists, summer-home residents, and the overflow from Seaside.

Today, the low-key charm and atmosphere conducive to artistic expression have in some part been quashed by development and the attendant massive visitor influx and price increases. While such vital signs as a first-rate theater, a good bookstore, cheek-by-jowl art galleries, and fine restaurants are still in ample evidence, your view of them from the other side of the street might be blocked by a convoy of Winnebagos.

Nonetheless, the broad three-mile stretch of beach dominated by the impressive monolith of Haystack Rock still provides a contemplative experience. And if you're patient and resourceful enough to find a space for your wheels (try the free municipal lot one block east of the main street), the finest gallery-hopping, crafts, and shopping on the coast await. Wood shingles and understated earth tones dominate the architecture of tastefully rendered galleries, bookstores, and bistros. The city is small enough for strolling, and its location removed from U.S. 101 spares it the kind of traffic blight seen on the main drags of other coastal tourist towns.

SIGHTS
★ Haystack Rock
Haystack Rock looms large above the long, broad beach. This is the third-highest sea

Haystack Rock at Cannon Beach

Cannon Beach

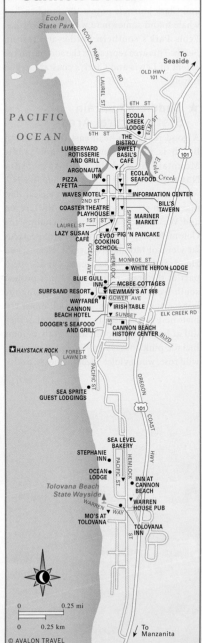

Ecola State Park

PACIFIC OCEAN

ECOLA PARK RD

OLD HWY 101

To Seaside

LAUREL ST

6TH ST

ECOLA CREEK LODGE

ELM ST

5TH ST

THE BISTRO/ SWEET BASIL'S CAFE

LUMBERYARD ROTISSERIE AND GRILL

Ecola Creek

101

ARGONAUTA INN

PIZZA A'FETTA

ECOLA SEAFOOD

WAVES MOTEL

2ND ST

INFORMATION CENTER

COASTER THEATRE PLAYHOUSE

SPRUCE ST

BILL'S TAVERN

1ST ST

MARINER MARKET

LAUREL ST

LAZY SUSAN CAFE

EVOO PIG 'N PANCAKE COOKING SCHOOL

OCEAN AVE

HEMLOCK

MONROE ST

WHITE HERON LODGE

BLUE GULL INN

MCBEE COTTAGES

SURFSAND RESORT

NEWMAN'S AT 988

WAYFARER

GOWER AVE

IRISH TABLE

CANNON BEACH HOTEL

SUNSET

ELK CREEK RD

DOOGER'S SEAFOOD AND GRILL

ST

CANNON BEACH HISTORY CENTER

BLVD

HAYSTACK ROCK

FOREST LAWN DR

PACIFIC ST

OREGON COAST

SEA SPRITE GUEST LODGINGS

101

SEA LEVEL BAKERY

STEPHANIE INN

HEMLOCK HWY

PACIFIC ST

OCEAN LODGE

Tolovana Beach State Wayside

INN AT CANNON BEACH

WARREN HOUSE PUB

WARREN WAY

MO'S AT TOLOVANA

TOLOVANA INN

HEMLOCK ST

0   0.25 mi

0   0.25 km

To Manzanita

© AVALON TRAVEL

stack in the state, measuring 235 feet high. As part of the Oregon Islands National Wildlife Refuge, it has wilderness status and is off-limits to climbing. Puffins and other seabirds nest on its steep faces, and intertidal organisms thrive in the tidepools around the base. The surrounding tidepools, within a radius of 300 yards from the base of the monolith, are designated a "marine garden"; they are open to exploration, but with strict no-collecting (of anything) and no-harassment (of any living organisms) protections in effect. Flanking the monolith are two rock formations known as the Needles. These spires had two other counterparts at the turn of the 20th century that have gradually been leveled by weathering and erosion. Old-timers will tell you that the government dynamited a trail to the top of Haystack in 1968 to keep people off this bird rookery. It also reduced the number of intrepid hikers trapped on the rock at high tide.

Volunteers from the **Haystack Rock Awareness Program** (503/436-1581) are often on the beach with displays, spotting scopes, and answers to many of your questions. Spend some time chatting with these folks, but don't forget to listen to the beach's own distinctive voices. You can't miss the cacophony of seabirds at sunset and, if you listen closely, the winter phenomenon of "singing sands" created by wind blowing over the beach.

Beach access is available at the west end of any public east-west street. From downtown, Harrison Street works well; south of downtown, Tolovana Beach Wayside has a large parking area and easy beach access.

Cannon Beach History Center

Permanent exhibits at the small **Cannon Beach History Center** (1387 S. Spruce St., 503/436-9301, www.cbhistory.org, 11am-5pm Wed.-Mon., free) chronicle the town's timeline, from prehistory to the modern expansion of tourism and recreation. The original eponymous cannon (the one found in 1894) from the ill-fated *Shark* is also on display here.

Ecola State Park

Ecola State Park (off U.S. 101, 800/551-6949, www.oregonstateparks.org, $5 day-use fee) is two miles north of Cannon Beach. Thick conifer forests line the access road to Ecola Point. This forested cliff has many trails leading down to the water. The view south takes in Haystack Rock and the overlapping peaks of the Coast Range extending to Neahkahnie Mountain. This is one of the most photographed views on the coast. Out to sea, the sight of sea lions basking on surf-drenched rocks (mid-Apr.-July) or migrating gray whales (Dec. and Mar.) and orcas (May) are seasonal highlights.

From Ecola Point, trails lead north to horseshoe-shaped **Indian Beach,** a favorite with surfers. Some prefer to drive the steep narrow road down to Indian Beach as a prelude to hiking up Tillamook Head, considered by Lewis and Clark the region's most beautiful viewpoint. The 2.5-mile Clatsop Loop Trail begins and ends at Indian Beach and climbs through Sitka spruce to a viewpoint. Ambitious hikers can do the first half of the loop, then continue another four miles north to Seaside.

The name Ecola means "whale" in Chinook and was first used as a place-name by William Clark, referring to a creek in the area. Lewis and Clark journals note a 105-foot beached whale found somewhere within present-day Ecola Park's southern border at Crescent Beach. This area represents the southernmost extent of Lewis and Clark's coastal Oregon travels.

★ Saddle Mountain State Natural Area

A good reason to head east from Cannon Beach is the hike up 3,283-foot Saddle Mountain at **Saddle Mountain State Natural Area** (off U.S. 26, 800/551-6949, www.oregonstateparks.org). On a clear day, hikers can see some 50 miles of the Oregon and Washington coastlines, including the Columbia River. Also possible are spectacular views of Mounts Rainier, St. Helens, and Hood, and miles of clear-cuts. On the upper part of the trail, plant species that pushed south from Alaska and Canada during the last ice age still thrive. The cool, moist climate here keeps them from dying out as they did at lower elevations. Some early blooms include pink coast fawn lily, monkeyflower, wild rose, wood violet, bleeding heart, oxalis,

Ecola State Park

Indian paintbrush, and trillium. Cable handrails provide safety on the narrow final 0.25-mile trail to the summit.

To get to the trailhead, take U.S. 26 from its junction with U.S. 101 for 10 miles and turn left on the prominently signed Saddle Mountain Road. (Although it's paved, this road is not suitable for RVs or wide-bodied vehicles.) After seven twisting miles, you'll come to the trailhead of the highest peak in this part of the Coast Range. The trail itself is steep, gaining more than 1,600 feet in 2.5 miles. Wet conditions can make the going difficult (allow four hours round-trip) and the scenery en route is not always exceptional unless you look down for the lovely May-August wildflower display; the view from the top is worth the climb.

The campground ($7-11) at Saddle Mountain is tiny and rustic and offers a secluded option for campers not attracted to the busy family scene at nearby Fort Stevens State Park.

Beaches

Stunning beaches don't end with Cannon Beach. Sandy expanses stretch seven miles south to the Arch Cape tunnel on U.S. 101, indicating the entrance to Oswald West State Park. Several of these beaches are reached via state park waysides. As you head south, views of **Hug Point State Recreation Site** (off U.S. 101, 800/551-6949, www.oregonstate-parks.org) and pristine beaches will have you ready to pull over. In summer, this can be a good escape from the crowds at Cannon Beach. Time your visit to coincide with low tide, when all manner of marine life will be exposed in tidal pools. Also at low tide, you may see remains of an 800-foot-long Model T-sized road blasted into the base of Hug Point, an early precursor to U.S. 101. The cliffs are gouged with caves and crevasses that also invite exploring, but be mindful of the tides so that you don't find yourself stranded. Hug Point got its name in the days when stagecoaches used the beach as highways; they had to dash between the waves, hugging the jutting headland to get around.

SPORTS AND RECREATION

Bicycling

Family Fun Cycles (1160 S. Hemlock, Cannon Beach, 503/436-2247, 10am-6pm Thurs.-Tues., $10-17 per 90 minutes) rents all manner of bikes, including mountain

Saddle Mountain

bikes, road bikes, beach cruisers, and three-wheeled recumbent "fun cycles," which zip up and down the hard-packed sand when the tide is out.

Horseback Riding

Sea Ranch Stables (415 Old U.S. 101, 503/436-2815, 9am-4:30pm daily mid-June-Labor Day, 9am-4:30pm weekends mid-May-mid-June, $80-140), at the north entrance to Cannon Beach off U.S. 101, offers a number of one- to two-hour guided rides, including night rides. Rides to Haystack Rock start at 9am, before the beach gets crowded.

Surfing

The area around Cannon Beach has several good surfing beaches. The most popular, and the best bet for beginners, is **Short Sands Beach,** at the end of the trail to the beach at Oswald West State Park, south of Arch Cape. It's a bit of a hike down to the beach, but the sheltered cove is a great place to spend the day, even if you're just bobbing around in the waves.

Another good spot for somewhat more advanced surfers (and surf kayakers) is **Indian Beach,** at **Ecola State Park** (off U.S. 101, 800/551-6949, www.oregonstateparks.org, $5 day-use fee). Rent a board and wetsuit at **Cleanline Surf** (171 Sunset Blvd., 503/436-9726, 10am-6pm Sun.-Fri., 9am-6pm Sat.).

ENTERTAINMENT AND EVENTS

Going strong since 1972, the **Coaster Theatre Playhouse** (108 N. Hemlock St., 503/436-1242, www.coastertheatre.com, $15-23) stages a varied bill of musicals, dramas, mysteries, comedies, concerts, and other entertainment. It's open year-round, in a building that started in the 1920s as a skating rink-turned-silent-movie house.

The half-dozen or so other sand-sculpting contests that take place on the Oregon coast pale in comparison to Cannon Beach's annual **Sandcastle Day** (503/436-2623, call to confirm dates). In 1964, a tsunami washed out a bridge, and the isolated residents of Cannon Beach organized the first contest as a way to amuse their children. Now in its fifth decade, this is the state's oldest and most prestigious competition of its kind. Tens of thousands of spectators show up to watch 1,000-plus competitors fashion their sculptures with the aid of buckets, shovels, squirt guns, and any natural material found on the beach. The resulting sculptures are often amazingly complex and inventive. This event is free to spectators, but entrants pay a fee. Recent winners included Egyptian pyramids and a gigantic sea turtle. This collapsible art show usually coincides with the lowest-tide Saturday in June and takes place north of Haystack Rock. Building begins in the early morning; winners are announced at noon. The American Legion serves a big breakfast buffet ($7 adult, $5 children ages 6-12) at 1216 South Hemlock Street, open to all.

Writers, singers, composers, painters, and sculptors take over the town for the **Stormy Weather Arts Festival** (503/436-2623), usually held the first weekend of November. Events include music in the streets, plays, a Saturday afternoon Art Walk, and the Quick Draw, in which artists have one hour to paint, complete, and frame a piece while the audience watches. The art is then sold by auction.

Beginning in July, the city park at Spruce and 2nd Streets hosts **Concerts in the Park** (5pm-7pm Sun.), a series of jazz, rhythm and blues, and popular music at the bandstand.

SHOPPING

Besides the beach, much of the attraction of Cannon Beach is window shopping up and down Hemlock Street, which, in addition to galleries, is lined with clothing stores, gift shops, and other boutiques. Cannon Beach supports a fine kite store: **Once Upon a Breeze** (240 N. Spruce St., 503/436-1112) and one of the better bookstores on the coast, the **Cannon Beach Book Company** (130 N. Hemlock St., 503/436-1301, http://cannonbeachbooks.com, 10:30am-6pm Sun.-Thurs., 10:30am-7:30pm Fri.-Sat.); it's the place to pick up regional titles or a good novel (lots of mysteries) for that rainy weekend.

Art Galleries

Cannon Beach has long attracted artists and artisans, and here art lovers and purchasers will find nearly two dozen galleries and shops with high-quality works. Most of the Cannon Beach galleries and boutiques are concentrated along Hemlock Street, where you can hardly swing a Winsor & Newton No. 12 hogbristle brush without hitting one. Not surprisingly, the seashore itself is the subject and inspiration of many works you'll see here, with Haystack Rock frequently depicted in various media. The **Cannon Beach Information Center** (201 E. 2nd St., 503/436-2623, www.cannonbeach.org, 11am-5pm Mon.-Sat., 10am-4pm Sun.) has a guide to all the galleries in town, or you can just stroll and discover them for yourself.

At the north end of town, **Northwest by Northwest Gallery** (232 N. Spruce St., 503/436-0741, www.nwbynwgallery.com, 11am-6pm daily) showcases photography, painting, sculpture, and ceramics and glass by noted regional artists. **White Bird Gallery** (251 N. Hemlock St., 503/436-2681, www. whitebirdgallery.com, 11am-5pm daily, call for winter hours), founded in 1971 and one of Cannon Beach's oldest galleries, casts a wide net with paintings, sculpture, prints, photography, glass, ceramics, and jewelry. Nearby, the **Bronze Coast Gallery** (224 N. Hemlock St., 503/436-1055, www.bronzecoastgallery. com, 10am-6pm Mon.-Sat., 11am-6pm Sun.) shows both traditional Western bronzes and innovative bronze works and paintings that may appeal to those who aren't crazy about traditional Western art. In midtown, **Icefire Glassworks** (116 Gower St., 503/436-2359, 10am-5pm Thurs.-Mon.) is a working glass studio where you can watch glassblowers and artists shape their work and then shop for unique pieces in the gallery.

DragonFire Gallery (123 S. Hemlock St., 503/436-1533, www.dragonfirestudio. com, 10am-6pm Mon.-Sat., 10am-5pm Sun.) shows the work of a wide variety of artists; on Saturday afternoons throughout the summer, everyone is invited to come and meet gallery artists.

ACCOMMODATIONS

Cannon Beach in summer is a very popular place, and even though there are a few moderately priced rooms—as well as many very pricey options—you need to make your

a busy shopping district along Hemlock Street

reservations as early as possible in the spring to even get a room at the inn. By Memorial Day weekend, many of the most popular spots will be completely booked. Plan well ahead if you have your heart set on staying here in summer. On the other hand, prices drop as much as one-half for mid-week, off-season stays.

$50-100

There aren't many inexpensive lodging options in Cannon Beach, but "mountain-view" rooms at the enormous **Tolovana Inn** (3400 S. Hemlock St., 503/436-2211 or 800/333-8890, www.tolovanainn.com, $79-105 mountain view, $169-269 ocean view, minimum stay in summer) hotel complex at the southern end of the Cannon Beach sprawl offer a good location at a fairly reasonable price. To make up for the rather cookie-cutter design and furnishings, you'll get a swimming pool, a spa, and a sauna, a number of restaurants sharing the same parking lots, and the beach right out the front door.

$100-150

About a one-minute walk to the beach, with friendly management and a great vibe, the **Blue Gull Inn** (632 S. Hemlock St., 503/436-2714 or 800/507-2714, www.bluegullinn.net, $139-209, two-night min. in summer) offers a choice between a beach house or less expensive motel units that come with housekeeping facilities. The modern cottages have in-room whirlpool tubs, fireplaces, and full kitchens. Cottages for larger groups are also available. Blue Gull Inn is one of several reliably comfortable and relatively inexpensive properties managed by **Haystack Lodgings,** which can be reached through the Blue Gull Inn website.

The **McBee Cottages** (888 S. Hemlock St., 503/436-0247 or 800/238-4107, www.mcbeecottages.com, $119-179) is a 1940s-era motel with semidetached units that have been nicely renovated. The rooms are simple, but the McBee is nonetheless a favorite of many visitors looking for cozy accommodations, and it's just a minute from the beach and within walking distance of downtown. McBee accepts pets in several of its homey cottages.

For more homey atmosphere, try the **Argonauta Inn** or **The Waves Motel,** which share an office (188 W. 2nd St., 503/436-2205 or 800/822-2468, www.thewavescannonbeach.com). The Argonauta ($144-299) is made up of four houses in the middle of downtown and has five furnished units just 150 feet from the beach. A cluster of six beachfront buildings makes up The Waves ($139-289), with units to fit the needs of families, couples, or larger groups. These are not cookie-cutter units, but the kind of individual lodgings you'd expect in Oregon.

The **Cannon Beach Hotel** (1116 Hemlock St., 503/436-1392 or 800/238-4107, www.cannonbeachhotel.com, $139-259) is a converted 1910 loggers' boardinghouse with 30 rooms and a small café and restaurant on the premises. The most expensive rooms have fireplaces, whirlpools, and partial ocean views. Meals are available in the restaurant adjacent to the lobby.

Just a few minutes' walk from downtown, **Ecola Creek Lodge** (208 E. 5th St., 503/436-2776 or 800/873-2749, www.ecolacreeklodge.com, $134-199) is a Cape Cod-style inn with 22 unique units set within four buildings. Accommodations range from simple queen-bed studios to two-bedroom suites. Special features include stained glass, lawns, fountains, flower gardens, and a lily pond. Les Shirley Park and Ecola Creek separate the lodge from the beach.

Over $200

The ★ **Surfsand Resort** (148 W. Gower St., 503/436-2274 or 800/547-6100, www.surfsand.com, $299-379) offers a great combination of location and amenities, with Haystack Rock right out the door and spacious, nicely furnished suites. The resort has an indoor pool and spa and on-site massage services; pets are permitted in some rooms. The popular Wayfarer Restaurant is adjacent.

The handsome **Inn at Cannon Beach** (3215 S. Hemlock St., 503/436-9085 or

800/321-6304, www.atcannonbeach.com, $259-289, minimum stay requirements in summer) has large and stylish cottage-like rooms in a beautifully landscaped garden setting with a courtyard pond, just a block from the beach. All guest rooms include a gas fireplace, fridge, microwave, coffeemaker, and TV/VCR/DVD combo; some rooms can accommodate pets.

The small, all-suites **Lighthouse Inn** (963 S. Hemlock, 866/265-1686 or 503/463-2929, www.cblighthouseinn.com, $239-269) offers eight attractive king and queen suites, some with full kitchens. The suites are quite spacious and nicely furnished, and all have balconies or patios, separate bedroom, dining area, fridge, fireplace, and other extras. The beach is just a block away.

The fabulously expensive (for Oregon) ★ **Stephanie Inn** (2740 S. Pacific St., 503/436-2221 or 800/633-3466, www.stephanie-inn.com, $561-664) offers attentive B&B-style service (breakfast buffet and evening wine gathering included), attention to detail, and luxury-level rooms with a low-key, not-too-fussy Oregonian touch. All guest rooms have balconies, fireplaces, wet bars, Jacuzzi tubs, fine linens, and all the extras you'd expect in an upscale resort hotel, including a fine dining restaurant. The Stephanie is a romantic, adult-focused inn; children under 12 are not permitted.

The **Ocean Lodge** (2864 S. Pacific Dr., 503/436-2241 or 888/777-4047, www.theoceanlodge.com, $239-389) feels like a long-established beach getaway, though in fact it was built recently. The high-end furnishings also give a clue that despite its venerable design, this rambling lodge isn't soaked in tradition. Rooms all have balconies, fireplaces, microwaves, and refrigerators.

For a more private experience just steps from the ocean, the **White Heron Lodge** (356 N. Spruce St., 503/436-2205 or 800/822-2468, www.thewavescannonbeach.com, $329, three-night minimum stays in summer) comprises two fully furnished oceanfront Victorian-style homes, both of which sleep up to four. Each

of the suites looks directly out on the Pacific. Wide sandy beaches and spacious front lawns make it a great location for families, especially those with small children. Located on a residential dead-end street, the lodge is only one block from downtown Cannon Beach.

Three miles south of Cannon Beach in quiet Arch Cape, the **Arch Cape Inn** (31970 E. Ocean Ln., 503/436-2800 or 800/436-2848, www.archcapeinn.com, $244-369) is a bit over-the-top in its turreted castle-like design, but it's supremely luxurious. Although it's not on the beach, it's an easy walk, and several rooms have good ocean views. Friday or Saturday lodging requires one night's dinner reservations at the on-site restaurant (Thurs.-Mon. May-Oct., Fri.-Sat. year-round).

Vacation Rentals

Several local property management companies offer a large selection of furnished rentals, ranging from grand oceanfront homes to quaint secluded cottages. **Cannon Beach Property Management** (3188 S. Hemlock St., 503/436-2021 or 877/386-3402, www.cbpm.com) and **Cannon Beach Vacation Rentals** (P.O. Box 723, Cannon Beach 97110, 866/436-0940, www.visitcb.com) both have good websites. During the summer, many beach houses are only available for weekly rentals.

Camping

Camping offers easier access to Cannon Beach's natural wonders at a bargain price. Although camping is not permitted on the beach or in Cannon Beach city parks, there are plenty of options for RV, tent, and outdoor enthusiasts.

Unlike most private campgrounds, the small, family-run **Wright's for Camping** (334 Reservoir Rd., 503/436-2347, www.wrightsforcamping.com, $32-36) is geared toward tent campers. It's just east of U.S. 101 and has 20 sites with picnic tables and fire rings as well as restrooms and a laundry. Wright's is wheelchair accessible; leashed pets are allowed.

For a more pampered RV-only experience, check out the **RV Resort at Cannon Beach** (345 Elk Creek Rd., 503/436-2231 or 800/847-2231, www.cbrvresort.com, $52). Open year-round, the RV Resort has 100 full hookups, an indoor pool and spa, free cable TV, an on-site convenience store, a laundry facility, restrooms, and a meeting room.

Roughly 20 miles east of Cannon Beach off U.S. 26 is **Saddle Mountain State Natural Area** (800/551-6949, www.oregonstateparks. org, Mar.-Oct., $7-11 tents, first-come, first-served), which offers 10 tent camping sites at the base of 3,283-foot Saddle Mountain, one of the highest peaks in Oregon's Coast Range. This more primitive and remote campground (although there are flush toilets and piped water, in addition to picnic tables and fire pits) might just be the tonic if you're weary of the crowds along the beach.

FOOD

If you're on a budget, keep dining prices down at the **Mariner Market** (139 N. Hemlock St., 503/436-2442, 8am-9pm daily), a dimly lit old grocery that's fully stocked with fresh meat, fruit, vegetables, and deli items.

American

The local **Pig 'N Pancake** (223 S. Hemlock St., 503/436-2851, 7am-3pm daily, $6-12) has large picture windows overlooking a leafy ravine. Choose from 35 breakfast dishes served anytime, including homemade pancakes (which are very good and extremely popular—expect to wait). For lunch, try the soups, chowder, or halibut and chips.

Try the wood-paneled sky-lit **Lazy Susan Cafe** (126 N. Hemlock St., 503/436-2816, www.lazy-susan-cafe.com, 8am-3pm Sun.-Mon. and Wed.-Thurs., $7-13) for a great breakfast (waffles are a specialty) or satisfying lunch (salads are very good).

If all you need is excellent coffee and delicious fresh baked goods, go to **Sea Level Bakery** (3116 S Hemlock, 53/436-4254, 7am-5pm daily, $4-12), where you'll find great bread for picnics, plus pastries and lunches

that include a charcuterie plate, soups, quiche, and sandwiches.

The **Lumberyard Rotisserie and Grill** (264 3rd St., 503/436-0285, www.thelumberyardgrill.com, noon-9pm daily, $8-35) is a block away from busy downtown Cannon Beach, but this spacious restaurant offers high-quality food at good prices. The specialty is rotisserie prime rib, but the pizza here is also good, as are burgers, local rockfish (the Steverino is baked with white wine and served with lemon-dill aioli), and a daily pot pie special. The Lumberyard is owned by the same company as the Stephanie Inn and the Surfsand Resort, and it has a similarly polished appearance.

Somewhat oddly, few of Cannon Beach's top restaurants have a view of the beach, so if excellent vistas of Haystack Rock and breaking waves are important to you, call to reserve a table at **The Wayfarer** (1190 Pacific Dr., 503/436-1108, www.wayfarer-restaurant. com, 8am-9pm daily, dinner $21-42), tucked above a beach entrance at Gower Street. The food, which is quite good but not as memorable as the views, features classic steak and seafood main courses. The lounge here is a good spot for a drink.

Italian

The pizza at **Pizza a'Fetta** (231 N. Hemlock St., 503/436-0333, 11am-8pm Sun.-Thurs., 11am-9pm Fri.-Sat., slices $3-4, whole pies $20-33) is Cannon Beach's best, with a selection of to-go slices available at a takeout window. Or crowd into the always-busy dining room for your choice of pies, salads, minestrone soup, and Oregon microbrew beer and Italian wines.

Mediterranean

Cozy and refined, **The Bistro** (263 N. Hemlock St., 503/436-2661, 4pm-9pm Wed.-Mon., $20-25) is tucked back in a maze of shops and gardens in downtown Cannon Beach. The atmosphere is a bit stark, particularly after a rebuild from a recent fire, but the menu brings a taste of Provençe to traditional fish and seafood dishes—the seafood stew is a wonderful blend of Pacific Northwest fish and shellfish prepared with Mediterranean zest. The dining room is truly tiny and the food superlative, so reservations are mandatory.

★ **Newman's at 988** (988 S. Hemlock St., 503/436-1151, www.newmansat988.com, 5:30pm-9pm Tues.-Sat. Oct. 16-June 30; 5:30pm-9pm daily July-Oct. 15, $19-26) is a good special-occasion restaurant in a tiny house, with an elegant atmosphere and excellent food. The chef-owner takes great pride in using fresh local ingredients to prepare seasonal menus with French and Italian influences, featuring such dishes as seared duck breast with foie gras and truffle oil or lobster ravioli with marsala cream.

While it's not a traditional restaurant, the **EVOO Cannon Beach Cooking School** (188 S. Hemlock, 503/436-8555, http://evoo.biz, cooking classes 6pm-9pm, $109-129 pp) is one of Cannon Beach's favorite "dinner theaters," where a small group of guests watch their meals cooked before their eyes. Dinners focus on seasonal ingredients and include starter plus a three-course dinner, dessert, and one glass of wine. You don't need to help prepare the food, though special "hands on" dinners are offered occasionally.

Irish

The **Irish Table** (1235 S. Hemlock St., 503/436-0708, 5:30pm-9pm Fri.-Tues., $11-22) makes the most of the Pacific Northwest bounty and hearty Irish cooking traditions, including meat pastries, grilled salmon, braised mussels, and variations on local lamb, including Irish lamb stew. The bar offers a wide selection of Scotch and Irish whiskies, plus Irish ales.

Pacific Northwest

Whether or not you're staying at the **Stephanie Inn** (2740 S. Pacific St., 503/436-2221 or 800/633-3466, www.stephanie-inn.com, 5pm-9pm nightly, $34-54, 4-course dinner $79), you are welcome to join guests in the dining room for creative Pacific Northwest cuisine (reservations required for non-guests). The atmosphere boasts mountain views, open wood beams, and a river-rock fireplace. Since guests get first shot at tables, those staying elsewhere should reserve well ahead of time.

For a much more casual dining experience, go to **Sweet Basil's Cafe** (271 N. Hemlock St., 503/436-1539, www.cafesweetbasils.com, 11am-10pm Wed.-Sun., $12-21), a tiny restaurant whose commitment is "natural, organic, wild." At lunch, enjoy mostly vegetarian sandwiches and salads. In the evening, linger in the wine bar, where tapas-style dishes are eclectic and creative, such as Dungeness crab-stuffed Portobello mushrooms and pork shank osso bucco with creamy Parmesan-cheese polenta.

Seafood

Hankering for some authentic West Coast chowder? Head to ★ **Dooger's Seafood and Grill** (1371 S. Hemlock St., 503/436-2225, 8am-9pm daily, dinners $12-45) for seafood that's always fresh and delicious. Don't overlook Dooger's for breakfast—during crab season (mostly winter and spring), the crab Benedict is a real treat. **Mo's at Tolovana** (195 Warren Way, Tolovana Park, 503/436-1111, www.moschowder.com, 11am-8pm Mon.-Thurs., 11am-9pm Fri., 8am-9pm Sat., 8am-8pm Sun., $3-16) has great views; although its clam chowder is locally famous (perhaps because of fondness for Mo and her family), the mostly fried food is not the big draw if you're looking for cutting-edge preparations.

In the fishing business for more than 25 years, **Ecola Seafoods** (208 N. Spruce St., 503/436-9130, 10am-9pm daily summer, 10am-7pm daily winter) features fresh-catch Dungeness crab and bay shrimp cocktails, as well as a decent clam chowder ($5). Or sample the smoked salmon and enjoy a big selection of fish-and-chips ($10-26). You'll find it across from the public parking lots and information center.

Brewpubs

Bill's Tavern (188 N. Hemlock St.,

503/436-2202, 11:30am-10pm Thurs.-Tues., 4:30pm-10pm Wed., bar open later, $7-13), once a legendary watering hole, is now a more traditional brewpub. Sweet thick onion rings, good fries, one-third-pound burgers, sautéed prawns, and grilled oysters are on the bill of fare.

Farther south near Tolovana, the **Warren House Pub** (3301 S. Hemlock St., 503/436-1130, 10:30am-1am daily, $7-14) serves local beers from Bill's Tavern, but in an English pub setting. The menu includes good smoked ribs, burgers, and seafood; in summer the backyard beer garden is a lovely spot to relax. Kids are allowed on the restaurant side of the pub.

INFORMATION AND SERVICES

The chamber of commerce operates the **Cannon Beach Information Center** (201 E. 2nd St., 503/436-2623, www.cannonbeach. org, 11am-5pm Mon.-Sat., 10am-4pm Sun.). This facility is close to the public restrooms (2nd St. and Spruce St.) and basketball and tennis courts.

Providence North Coast Clinic (171 N. Larch St., 503/717-7000) offers medical care and minor emergency services. It's located in Sandpiper Square behind the stores on the main drag.

GETTING THERE AND AROUND

From U.S. 101, there's a choice of four entrances to the beach loop (also known as U.S. 101 Alternate, a section of the old Oregon Coast Highway) to take you into town. As you wade into the town's shops, galleries, and restaurants, the beach loop becomes Hemlock Street, the main drag of Cannon Beach. Sunset Empire Transportation District operates **The Bus** (503/861-RIDE, 503/861-7433, or 800/776-6406, www.ridethebus.org), which serves Cannon Beach, Seaside, Astoria-Warrenton, and points in between. **Parking** can be hard to come by, especially on weekends, but you'll find public lots south of town at Tolovana Park and in town at Hemlock at 1st Street and on 2nd Street.

The **Cannon Beach Shuttle** runs every half-hour on a 6.5-mile loop, from Les Shirley Park on the north end of town to Tolovana Park; it operates 10am-6pm daily, with extended summer hours. The fare is $1.

Amtrak Thruway Motorcoach Service (800/USA-RAIL or 800/872-7245, www.amtrak.com) runs two buses daily between Portland Union Station and Cannon Beach (continuing on to Seaside and Astoria). The bus stops at 1088 South Hemlock Street, across the street from the Cannon Beach Mercantile store.

Nehalem Bay Area

MANZANITA AND VICINITY

Just south of Arch Cape, Neahkahnie Mountain towers nearly 1,700 feet up from the edge of the sea. U.S. 101 climbs up and over its shoulder to an elevation of 700 feet, and the vistas from a half-dozen pullouts (the highest along the Oregon coast) are spectacular—but do try to keep your eyes on the snaking road until you've parked your car.

This stretch of the highway, built by the Works Progress Administration in the 1930s,

was constructed by blasting a roadbed from the rock face and buttressing it with stonework walls on the precarious cliffs. The fainthearted or acrophobic certainly couldn't have lasted long on this job. The handiwork of these road builders and masons can be admired at several pullouts, along with the breathtaking vistas of Manzanita Beach and Nehalem Spit, stretching some 20 miles south to Cape Meares. Much of Neahkahnie Mountain and its rugged coastline are preserved in Oswald West State Park, one of the state's finest.

Immediately to the south, huddled along an expansive curve of beach at the foot of Neahkahnie Mountain, quiet Manzanita (pop. 700) makes a pleasant stop for lunch or for the weekend. When adjacent coastal areas are fogbound, the seven-mile-long Manzanita Beach often enjoys sunshine because of the shelter of Neahkahnie Mountain. As one of the few towns along the north Oregon coast that's not located directly on U.S. 101, Manzanita feels more peaceful and secluded than most others; like Cannon Beach, it's also a relatively wealthy and stylish town.

Just two miles south of Manzanita on Hwy. 101, tiny Nehalem occupies just a few blocks along U.S. 101 on the north bank of the Nehalem River. It's a lovely location with a few Old West-style storefronts. Sizable runs of spring and fall chinook salmon and winter steelhead make this a popular destination for anglers.

Oswald West State Park

Most of Neahkahnie Mountain and the prominent headlands of Cape Falcon are encompassed within the 2,500-acre gem of **Oswald West State Park** (off U.S. 101, 800/551-6949, www.oregonstateparks.org). Whether or not you believe in the stories of lost pirate wealth buried somewhere on the mountain, there is real treasure today for all who venture here in search of the intangible currency of extraordinary natural beauty. The state park bears the name of Governor Oswald West, whose farsighted 1913 beach bill was instrumental in protecting Oregon's virgin shoreline.

Several hiking trails weave through the park, including the 13 miles of the **Oregon Coast Trail** linking Arch Cape to the north with Manzanita. From the main parking lot on the east side of U.S. 101, a 0.5-mile trail follows Short Sands Creek to **Short Sands Beach,** a relatively sheltered beach that's popular with surfers year-round. Rainforests of hemlock, cedar, and gigantic Sitka spruce crowd the secluded boulder-strewn shoreline. From Short Sands Beach, hike north on the three-mile old-growth-lined **Cape Falcon Trail** to spectacular views.

From the trail to the beach, it's also possible to turn south and hike to **Neahkahnie Mountain** (4 miles one-way) with some stiff climbing. Shave about 1.3 miles off the hike by starting a mile south of the main Oswald West parking lot, where there's an access road to the Neahkahnie Mountain Summit Trail on the east side of the highway. It's not well marked; look for a subdivision on the golf

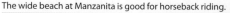

The wide beach at Manzanita is good for horseback riding.

NORTH COAST
NEHALEM BAY AREA

course to the west. Drive up the gravel road 0.25 mile to the trailhead parking lot and begin a moderately difficult 1.5-mile ascent. Allow about 45 minutes to get to the top. The summit view south to Cape Meares and east to the Nehalem Valley ranks as one of the finest on the coast.

Visitors who remember camping among the old-growth trees at Oswald West should treasure the memory. Due to the instability of the ancient trees, the campground remains closed.

Accommodations

Manzanita is a small town without an abundance of lodgings. Advance reservations are a must, especially in summer, and many accommodations require two- to three-night stays during the high season and on some holidays. A good alternative to motels for families here are the rentals available from the several property management agencies in town. Among these is **Manzanita Beach Getaway** (503/368-2929 or 855/368-2929, www.manzanitabeachgetaway.com), with fully furnished homes to rent, running $110-259 per night (most require weekly rentals in July and August).

If you're looking for a quiet retreat, the cedar-clad **Inn at Manzanita** (67 Laneda Ave., 503/368-6754, www.innatmanzanita.com, $179-225), set in a Japanese-accented garden just a short walk from the beach, promises guests the three R's: recreation, relaxation, and romance. Each of its 13 wood-paneled guest rooms features a gas fireplace and a two-person tub; most rooms have a balcony, offering glimpses through the evergreens of the nearby beach. Fresh flowers daily, robes, and other amenities help you feel pampered. Despite being in the middle of town near restaurants and the beach, a feeling of luxurious seclusion prevails.

The remodeled **Ocean Inn** (32 Laneda Ave., 866/3687701 or 503/368-7701, www.oceaninnatmanzanita.com, $139-229) has large and comfortable condo-like rooms (most with full kitchens); several have wood stoves,

Oswald West State Park offers wonderful hiking.

and two have patios. Most rooms have ocean views, and the beach is just moments away.

Six blocks from the beach, the six spacious, stylish, and airy cabins of ★ **Coast Cabins** (635 Laneda Ave., 503/368-7113, www.coastcabins.com, $215-440, two-night minimum stays in summer and weekends) comfortably sleep two (although two-story Cabin 5 is designed for up to four people) and offer kitchenettes or full kitchens, satellite TV, and goose-down pillows and comforters. The Coast Cabins folks also rent out a few sophisticated one- and two-bedroom condos in downtown Manzanita.

For a more standard motel experience, the **Sunset Surf** (248 Ocean Rd., 503/368-5224 or 800/243-8035, www.sunsetsurfocean.com, $130-165) offers guest rooms (many with kitchens) in three oceanfront units that share an outdoor pool. Although rooms are basic, the setting is great.

Another reasonably priced older motel, the **Spindrift Inn** (114 Laneda Ave., 503/368-1001 or 877/368-1001, www.spindrift-inn.com,

Grab a quick lunch at Manzanita Grocery & Deli.

$109-154) has rooms that are nicer than the rather plain exterior. It's a very short walk to the beach.

Camping

Just south of Manzanita and occupying the entire sandy appendage of Nehalem Spit is scenic, sprawling **Nehalem Bay State Park** (800/452-5687, www.oregonstateparks.org, year-round, $29 tents or RVs, $44 yurts, $5 day use for non-campers), a favorite with bikers, beachcombers, anglers, horse owners, and pilots (yes, there's a little airstrip and a fly-in campsite). Sandwiched between the bay and a beautiful four-mile beach stretching from Manzanita to the mouth of the Nehalem River is a vast campground with hot showers. Sites are a little bit close together, with few trees to screen the neighbors; dunes separate campers from the ocean. As big as this park is, it does fill up in summer, so reservations are recommended (particularly July-Aug., www.reserveamerica.com). To get there, turn south at Bayshore

Junction just before U.S. 101 heads east into the town of Nehalem.

Food

House renters, budget diners, and picnickers can take advantage of the excellent produce and impressive (for a coastal market) grocery section at **Manzanita Grocery & Deli** (193 Laneda Ave., 503/368-5362, 8am-8pm daily). One block away, **Mother Nature's Natural Foods Store** (298 Laneda Ave., 503/368-5316, 10am-7pm Mon.-Sat.) stocks natural groceries, coffees and teas, bulk foods, wine, and beer.

Stop at **Manzanita News & Espresso** (500 Laneda Ave., 503/368-7450, 7:30am-2pm daily, $2-5) for a coffee, pastry, and magazine (there are lots to choose from, and the selection is anything but generic).

The local bakery, **Bread and Ocean** (154 Laneda Ave., 503/368-5823, 7:30am-2pm Wed.-Sat., 8am-2pm Sun., $4-9), makes sandwiches as well as cinnamon rolls. The locals' favorite for hefty traditional breakfasts is **Big Wave Cafe** (822 Laneda Ave., 503/368-9283, 7am-9pm Fri.-Wed., 8am-9pm Thurs., $7-18), where you'll find Makin' Waves Eggs Benedict, dressed with spinach and chipotle-pepper hollandaise sauce.

Left Coast Siesta (288 Laneda Ave., 503/368-7997, 11:30am-8pm Mon.-Sat., noon-7pm Sun., closed Mon.-Tues. winter, $6-11) specializes in design-your-own burritos, the perfect takeout for a beach lunch or dinner. Options include spicy beef, spicy chicken, tequila-lime chicken, or black beans to fill a selection of flavored tortillas. It also serves tacos and enchiladas. And if you like it *caliente,* this is the place for you: Left Coast Siesta stocks a hot sauce bar with 200-plus different types of the hot stuff, many available to purchase by the jar.

Just a couple of blocks from the beach, **Marzano's** (60 Laneda Ave., 503/368-3663, 4pm-8:30pm Sun.-Mon. and Thurs., 4pm-9pm Fri., noon-9pm Sat., large pies mostly $20-25) serves the area's best slices of gourmet pizza. The roasted vegetable pizza is recommended, and the smoked prosciutto with aged monte-grappa cheese is another winner.

For relaxed fine dining, the best option is **Neah-Kah-Nie Bistro** (519 Laneda Ave., 503/368-2722, 3pm-8pm Tues.-Thurs and Sun., 3pm-9pm Fri.-Sat., $16-27), a small dining room serving local seafood and meats with up-to-date continental preparations. Halibut cheeks are sautéed in lemon butter, champagne, and capers, while grilled pork chops come with house-made pear chutney.

Blackbird (503 Laneda Ave., 503/368-7708, http://blackbirdmanzanita.com, 5pm-9pm Thurs. and Sun.-Mon., 5pm-10pm Fri.-Sat., $18-29) is a classy fine dining restaurant with inventive ways of preparing local produce, fish, and meats. The lamb burger is excellent, Brussels sprouts with bacon and cheese are deliciously decadent, and you can't go wrong with flank steak and truffled fries.

WHEELER

Wheeler (pop. 393) is a little town flanking the Nehalem River where most accommodations are low-cost efficiencies for visiting fisherfolk, but the 10 guest rooms of the **Wheeler on the Bay Lodge and Marina** (580 Marine Dr., 503/368-5858 or 800/469-3204, www.wheeleronthebay.com, $99-225), on U.S. 101 on the shore of Nehalem Bay, have more appeal. Most guest rooms have at least partial bay views, and several have jetted tubs. There's also a video store, kayak rentals, and on-site massage services, and they can help arrange fishing charters.

Guest rooms at **The Old Wheeler Hotel** (495 U.S. 101, 503/368-6000 or 877/653-4683, www.oldwheelerhotel.com, $99-169), a 1920s landmark across the road from the bay, may remind you of your great-aunt's guest room. They're old-fashioned in a very down-to-earth way. Although all guest rooms have private bathrooms, some bathrooms are down the hall from their rooms.

In a tiny cottage just off the main drag, the ★ **Rising Star Cafe** (92 Rorvik St., 503/368-3990, noon-3pm and 5pm-8pm Wed.-Thurs. and Sat., 5pm-8pm Fri., 10am-3pm Sun., $13-26) is a sweet spot for excellent pasta, sandwiches, and chowder—some of the best on the coast. There are only seven tables in this popular restaurant, so call ahead for reservations. The food can be very good here (the North Coast cioppino and pumpkin risotto are recommended) , and the atmosphere is comfortable and friendly.

Wheeler offers a number of antique and specialty stores.

ROCKAWAY BEACH

This town of 1,380 was established as a summer resort in the 1920s by Portlanders who wanted a coastal getaway. And so it remains today—a quiet spot without much going on besides walks on the seven miles of sandy beach, a **Kite Festival** in mid-May, and an **Arts and Crafts Fair** in mid-August. Shallow **Lake Lytle,** on the east side of the highway, offers spring and early summer fishing for trout, bass, and crappie. While the town of Rockaway is singularly unattractive from U.S. 101—a lengthy stretch of tacky shops, modest motels, and big new condos—the beach is quite nice, anchored at the south by the impressive Twin Rocks formation. The **Visitor Information Center** (503/355-8108, www.rockawaybeach.net), lodged in a bright red caboose in the center of town, can fill you in on other goings-on.

Accommodations

Rockaway's motels are basic and family-oriented; if you are planning in advance, take a moment to check out the beach houses available for rent on the **chamber of commerce website** (www.rockawaybeach.net).

The following motels are on the ocean side of busy U.S. 101, which dominates this long string bean of a town. **Surfside Resort Motel** (101 NW 11th St., 503/355-2312 or 800/243-7786, www.surfsideocean.com, $94-154 with no ocean view, $134-174 ocean view) is a large beachfront complex with an indoor pool. Some guest rooms with kitchens are available. **Silver Sands Oceanfront Resort** (215 S. Pacific Ave., 503/355-2206 or 800/457-8972, www.oregonsilversands.com, $116-166) is also right on the beach, with fairly basic rooms (some kitchenettes), an indoor pool and hot tub, and a sauna.

About a mile south of town, **Twin Rocks Motel** (7925 Minehaha St., 503/355-2391 or 877/355-2391, www.twinrocksmotel.net, $199-214) is a small cluster of dog-friendly two-bedroom oceanfront cottages. If you're looking for a simple, quiet getaway with family or a couple of friends, this might be your place.

Food

Cow Belle Cafe (194 U.S. 101 S., 503/355-2441, 8am-2pm Thurs.-Sun., $8-14) is a locals' favorite for breakfast. The biscuits and gravy here are renowned, as is the bovine-rich decor. The **Beach Bite** (162 U.S. 101 S., 503/355-2073, 11am-9pm Mon.-Thurs., 11am-11pm Fri., 8am-11pm Sat., 8am-9pm Sun., $6-20) is one of the classier dining places in town (don't worry, flip-flops and a sweatshirt will get you by), featuring burgers and pasta.

Tillamook Bay

GARIBALDI

Tillamook Bay's commercial fishing fleet is concentrated in this little port town (pop. 970) near the north end of the bay. Garibaldi, named in 1879 by the local postmaster for the Italian patriot, is a fish-processing center: Crabs, shrimp, fresh salmon, lingcod, and bottom fish (halibut, cabezon, rockfish, and sea perch) are the specialties. At the marina, **Garibaldi Cannery** (606 Commercial Dr., 503/322-3344, 7am-6pm Mon.-Sat.) gets crab, fish, and other seafood right off the boats, so the selection is both low-priced and fresh. If you want it fresher, you'll have to catch it yourself.

In addition to dock fishing, guide and charter services offer salmon and halibut fishing, bird-watching, and whale-watching excursions. North of Garibaldi on U.S. 101, the bay entrance is a good place to see brown pelicans, harlequin ducks, oystercatchers, and guillemots. The Miami River marsh, south of town, is a bird-watching paradise at low tide, when ducks and shorebirds hunt for food.

Bayocean Spit

At the western entrance to Tillamook Bay, a long narrow spit of land reaches north from Cape Meares nearly all the way to Garibaldi. Although today it's a good place for a long and sandy flat hike, it was once developed as the town of Bayocean, promoted as "the Atlantic City of the West."

In the early 1900s, two real estate developers, enchanted by the great views of the ocean, built a grand resort hotel on the spit and began selling lots. A giant natatorium—a heated, saltwater surf pool—was built in 1914. Initially, the only access was by boat or ferry; in 1928, a road was built from Tillamook.

The town that grew on the four-mile-long spit was thriving when the inevitable erosion began to chip away at the peninsula. Houses slipped into the sea, and by the late 1930s, most folks had packed up and left. By 1939 the natatorium had been swallowed up.

Since the early 1990s, the spit has been managed for protection and preservation of its ecosystem, which is dominated by beach grass and Scotch broom.

To reach Bayocean Spit from Tillamook, head west on the Three Capes Scenic Loop (3rd St. from downtown Tillamook) and travel three miles to the Bayocean Spit sign. Turn right and follow a gravel road 1.5 miles to the parking area.

Garibaldi Maritime Museum

The small but interesting **Garibaldi Maritime Museum** (112 Garibaldi Ave., 503/322-8411, http://garibaldimuseum.org, 10am-4pm Thurs.-Mon. April-Nov., $4 adults, $3 seniors, $4 children ages 11-18) retells the history of this longtime fishing village. It also focuses on the late-18th-century sailing world and the British sea captain Robert Gray and his historical vessels, the *Lady Washington* and the *Columbia Rediviva,* which explored the Pacific Northwest in 1787 and 1792. Among the museum displays are models of these ships, an eight-foot-tall reproduction of the *Columbia* figurehead, a half model of the *Columbia* showing how the ship was provisioned for long voyages, as well as reproductions of period musical instruments and typical sailors' clothing.

Oregon Coast Explorer Trains

The **Oregon Coast Scenic Railroad** (503/842-8206, www.ocsr.net, basic tours $18 adults, $17 seniors, $10 children ages 3-10) operates a number of rail excursions on a train pulled by a 1910 Heisler Locomotive Works steam engine between Garibaldi and Rockaway Beach. The basic tour is 1.5 hours round-trip; trains depart Garibaldi at 10am, noon, and 2pm, with opportunities to board

in Rockaway Beach at 11am and1pm. The train operates weekends only mid-May-mid-June and Labor Day-September, and daily mid-June-Labor Day as well as assorted holidays throughout the year. Dinner trains are also offered.

Fishing

The town's fishing and crabbing piers attract visitors looking to catch their own. Rent fishing boats, crab traps, and other gear at the **Garibaldi Marina** (302 Mooring Basin Rd., 503/322-3312, www.garibaldimarina.com).

The **Miami River** and **Kilchis River,** which empty into Tillamook Bay south of Garibaldi, get the state's only two significant runs of chum salmon, a species much more common from Washington northward. There's a catch-and-release season for them mid-September-mid-November. Both rivers also get runs of spring chinook and are open for steelhead most of the year.

Several charter companies have offices at the marina. **Garibaldi Charters** (607 Garibaldi Ave., 503/322-0007, www.garibaldi-charters.com) offers fishing excursions. A full day of light tackle bottom fishing or crabbing runs about $105, with salmon ($120-150) and tuna ($275) also offered, and wildlife-viewing or whale-watching trips ($40 per person).

Accommodations and Camping

If you want to wake up on the docks, spend the night at **Harbor View Inn** (302 S. 7th St., 503/322-3251, www.harborviewfun.com, $79-105), a motel popular with fishers and sports enthusiasts. A more standard motel is the **Garibaldi House Inn** (502 Garibaldi Ave., 503/322-3338 or 877/322-6489, www.garib-aldihouse.com, $139-189), which offers very pleasant rooms as well as an indoor pool, hot tub, sauna, fitness room, and complimentary hot breakfast.

Both tent and RV campers are welcome at **Barview Jetty County Park** (503/322-3522, $15-32, reservations accepted), a large campground in the tiny community of Barview (2.5 miles north of Garibaldi) with easy access to the beach forming the north side of Tillamook Bay. Most of the sites are for tents, with a section reserved for hikers and bikers; hot showers are a welcome amenity.

Food

One of the joys of eating on the Oregon coast is getting really good fish-and-chips from rough-edged dives on the docks. In Garibaldi, the **Fisherman's Korner Restaurant** (306 Mooring Basin, 503/322-2033, 7:30am-3pm Thurs.-Mon., $6-12) is right on the wharf and offers absolutely fresh fish-and-chips and excellent clam chowder. Breakfasts here are massive—meant for hungry sailors.

If you're looking for pub grub, a good choice is **Ghost Hole Public House** (409 Garibaldi Ave., 503/322-2723, 11am-2:30am daily, $6-15), with good burgers and sandwiches and a friendly vibe.

Just north of Garibaldi, **Pirate's Cove Restaurant** (14170 U.S. 101 N., 503/322-2092, http://piratesonline.biz, noon-9pm Mon.-Tues., 8am-9pm Wed.-Sat., 8am-8pm Sun., dinner $10-30) is one of the better restaurants between Manzanita and Lincoln City, with a dramatic vista of the mouth of Tillamook Bay. Try the local oysters and razor clams. Lunches are a better deal than the rather expensive dinners.

Four miles south at the little enclave of Bay City is another temple to seafood. **Pacific Oyster** (5150 Oyster Bay Dr., 503/377-2323, 10am-7pm Sun.-Thurs., 10am-8pm Fri.-Sat., $5-16) is mostly an oyster-processing center, but it's also an excellent spot for a few oyster shooters or a quick meal. Although there are a variety of seafood choices, the main draw is the oysters, which are both eating and entertainment here. As you eat, you can watch the oyster shuckers in action next door, as the dining area overlooks the oyster-processing area.

TILLAMOOK

Without much sun or surf, what could possibly draw enough visitors to the town of Tillamook (pop. 4,500) to make it one of Oregon's top three tourism attractions? Superficially speaking, cheese factories and a World War II blimp hangar, in a town flanked by mudflats and rain-soaked dairy country, shouldn't pull in more than a million tourists per year. But they do. And after a drive down U.S. 101 or along the scenic Three Capes Loop, you too will be mysteriously drawn to the huge white, blue, and gold building proffering bite-size samples of cheddar, not to mention ice cream.

Tillamook County is home to more than 26,000 cows, which easily outnumber the county's human population. They're the foundation of the Tillamook County Creamery Association's famous cheddar cheese and other dairy products, which generate about $85 million in annual sales—dwarfing the region's other important contributors to the local economy, fishing and oyster farming.

In 1940-1942, partially in response to a Japanese submarine firing on Fort Stevens in Astoria, the U.S. Navy built two blimp hangars south of town, the two largest wooden structures ever built, according to *The Guinness Book of World Records*. One of five naval air stations on the Pacific coast, the Tillamook blimp guard patrolled the waters from northern California to the San Juan Islands and escorted ships into Puget Sound. While all kinds of blimp stories abound in Tillamook bars, only one wartime encounter has been documented. Declassified records confirm that blimps were involved in the sinking of what was believed to be two Japanese submarines off Cape Meares. In late May 1943, two of the high-flying craft, assisted by U.S. Navy subchasers and destroyers, dropped several depth charges on the submarines, which are still lying on the ocean floor.

Until 1946, when the station was decommissioned, the naval presence here created a boomtown. Bars and businesses flourished, and civilian jobs were easy to come by. After the war years, Tillamook County returned to the economic trinity of "trees, cheese, and ocean breeze" that has sustained the region to the present day.

Tillamook Cheese Factory

With over a million visitors a year, the **Tillamook Cheese Factory** (4175 U.S. 101 N., 503/842-4481, www.tillamook.com/cheese-factory, 8am-6pm daily Labor Day-mid-June, 8am-8pm daily summer, free) is far and away the county's biggest drawing card. The plant welcomes visitors with a reproduction of the *Morningstar,* the schooner that transported locally made butter and cheese in the late 1800s and now adorns the label of every Tillamook product. The quaint vessel symbolizing Tillamook cheese-making's humble beginnings stands in contrast to the technology and sophistication that go into making this world-famous lunchbox staple today.

Inside the plant, a self-guided tour follows the movement of curds and whey to the "cheddaring table." Whey is drained from the curds, which are then cut and folded. These processes are coordinated by white-uniformed workers in a stadium-size factory. As you look down on the antiseptic scene from the glassed-in observation area, it's hard to imagine this as the birthplace of many a grilled cheese sandwich. Tastes of a few samples, however, prove it's true.

User-friendly informational placards and historical displays recount Tillamook Valley's dairy history from 1851, when settlers began importing cows. The problem then was how to ship the milk to San Francisco and Portland. Even though salting butter to preserve it allowed exportation, ships still faced the difficulty of negotiating the treacherous Tillamook bar. In 1894, Peter McIntosh introduced techniques here to make cheddar cheese, whose long shelf life enabled it to be transported overland.

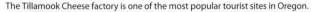

The Tillamook Cheese factory is one of the most popular tourist sites in Oregon.

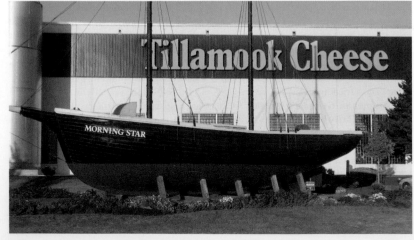

In the early 1900s, the Tillamook County Creamery Association absorbed smaller operations; the modern plant opened in 1949. Today, Tillamook produces tens of millions of pounds of cheese annually, including monterey jack, swiss, and multiple variations of the award-winning cheddar. Pepperoni, butter, cheese soup, milk, and other products are also available. There's a gift shop (more Holstein-themed tchotchkes than you've probably dreamed of) and a full-service restaurant, but the big attraction is the ice cream counter. Have a double-scoop chocolate peanut butter cone—worth every penny.

Blue Heron French Cheese Company

A quarter-million people per year visit Tillamook County's *second*-most-popular attraction, **Blue Heron French Cheese Company** (2001 Blue Heron Dr., 503/842-8282, www.blueheronoregon.com, 9am-6pm daily Labor Day-mid-June; 8am-8pm daily mid-June-Labor Day, free), a mile south of the Tillamook Cheese Factory. Housed in a large white barn, Blue Heron is famous for its brie-style cheese (though it's not produced on-site). In addition to cheeses and other gourmet foods, the shop sells gift baskets; over

120 varieties of Oregon wines are available in the wine-tasting room. A deli serves lunches of homemade soups and salads. For kids, there's a petting farm with the usual barnyard suspects.

Tillamook Air Museum

South of town off U.S. 101, you can't possibly miss the enormous Quonset hut-like building east of the highway. The world-class aircraft collection of the **Tillamook Air Museum** (6030 Hangar Rd., 503/842-1130, www.tillamookair.com, 10am-5pm daily, $9 adults, $8 seniors, $25 family) is housed in and around Hangar B of the decommissioned Tillamook Naval Air Station. At 1,072 feet long, 206 feet wide, and 192 feet high, it's the largest wooden structure in the world, and it's worth the price of admission just to experience the enormity of it. During World War II, this and another gargantuan hangar on the site (which burned down in 1992) sheltered eight K-class blimps, each 242 feet long.

Inside the seven-acre structure, you can learn about the role the big blimps played during wartime, as well as how they are used today. In addition, there's a collection of World War II fighter planes (many one-of-a-kind models) and photos and artifacts from

the Tillamook Air Museum

The Lost Treasure of Neahkahnie Mountain

Is there pirate gold on Neahkahnie Mountain? Local native legends tell of Spanish pirates burying a treasure here. One story relates that the crew of a shipwrecked Manila galleon salvaged its cargo of gold and beeswax (a valuable commodity in trade with Asia) by burying it in the side of the mountain. To deter natives from going to the site, the pirates killed a black man and buried him on top of the cargo. While this account taken from native histories has never been substantiated, a piece of crudely inscribed beeswax retrieved from the Neahkahnie region carbon-dated AD 1500-1700 (on display at the **Tillamook County Pioneer Museum**) keeps speculation alive. Further intrigue was added by the 1993 discovery of an ancient wooden rigging block. Found in the mud at the mouth of the Nehalem River, it was determined by a Spanish maritime expert to have been from a Manila galleon during that same time period. Lewis and Clark's 1805 reports of a Chinook with red hair, and similar accounts from the Vancouver Expedition's 1792 encounter with a redheaded native who claimed his late father had been a shipwrecked Spanish sailor, would tend to corroborate the shipwreck and treasure stories passed down in oral histories.

the naval air station days. Be sure to check out the cyclo-crane, a combination blimp, plane, and helicopter. This was devised in the 1980s to aid in remote logging operations; it ended up an $8 million bust. Note that a number of historic aircraft formerly housed in the Tillamook Air Museum have been moved to the Erickson Aircraft Collection in Madras, in central Oregon.

To get there from downtown, take U.S. 101 south two miles, make a left at the flashing yellow light, and follow the signs.

Tillamook County Pioneer Museum

East of the highway in the heart of downtown, **Tillamook County Pioneer Museum** (2106 2nd St., 503/842-4553, www.tcpm.org, 10am-4pm Tues.-Sun., $4 adults, $3 seniors, $1 children ages 7-10) is famous for its taxidermy exhibits as well as memorabilia from pioneer households. Particularly intriguing are hunks of ancient beeswax with odd inscriptions recovered from near Neahkahnie Mountain, which are thought to be remnants from 18th-century shipwrecks. The old courtroom on the second floor has one of the best displays of natural history in the state. There are many beautiful dioramas, plus shells, insects, and nests. The Beals Memorial Room houses a large rock, mineral, and fossil collection.

Latimer Quilt and Textile Center

The collection at the **Latimer Quilt and Textile Center** (2105 Wilson River Loop Rd., www.latimerquiltandtextile.com, 503/842-8622, 10am-5pm daily. Apr.-Oct., 10am-4pm Mon.-Sat. Nov.-Mar., $4 adult and children 13 and over, $3 senior, children 12 and under free) includes quilts from the 1850s to the present as well as looms, spinning wheels, and a variety of woven items. On Friday, you can see weavers at work; lessons can be arranged by calling ahead. The center, housed in a restored school, is just south and east of the cheese factory.

Munson Creek Falls

The highest waterfall in the Oregon Coast Range is lovely **Munson Creek Falls,** which drops 266 feet over mossy cliffs surrounded by an old-growth forest. A steep 0.25-mile trail leads to the base of the falls, while another, slightly longer trail leads to a higher viewpoint; wooden walkways clinging to the cliff lead to a small viewing platform. This is a spectacle in all seasons, but come in winter when the falls pour down with greater fury.

To reach the falls, drive seven miles south of Tillamook turn east from U.S. 101 on Munson Creek Road and then drive 1.5 miles on well-signed but very narrow, bumpy, dirt access road that leads to the parking lot. Note that motor homes and trailers cannot get into the park; the lot is too small.

Tillamook State Forest

A series of intense forest fires in the 1930s and 1940s burned vast amounts of land in the northern Coast Range. Most of this land was owned by private timber companies, who walked away from the seemingly worthless "Tillamook Burn," leaving property rights to revert to the counties, who then handed the land over to the state. A massive replanting effort ensued, and in 1973 the Tillamook Burn became the **Tillamook State Forest.** In 2006, the Tillamook Forest Center opened in a soaring timbered building in the middle of the once-burned, now-lush forest. Be sure to stop in to see the short movie about the area's history; the vivid fire scenes are a bit frightening—a sensation that's enhanced when the smell of smoke is released into the auditorium. Don't leave without walking out through the center's back door, crossing the footbridge, and taking at least a short hike, where you'll see an assortment of native wildflowers, shrubs, and trees. If you head west from the bridge, Wilson Falls is about two miles away.

If a short hike outside the Forest Center leaves you hankering for more, head east along Highway 6 to the Kings Mountain trailhead. On a clear day (ha!), there are good views from the top. Several more trails start at the summit of the Coast Range. The campgrounds along Highway 6, including Jones Creek, which is right next to the **Tillamook Forest Center** (45500 Wilson River Hwy., 503/815-6800 or 866/930-4646, www.tillamookforestcenter. org, 10am-5pm daily Memorial Day-Labor Day, reduced hours spring and fall, closed in winter, free), are popular with off-road vehicle drivers, who have their own trail network back in the hills.

Hiking

The Tillamook State Forest offers plenty of recreational opportunities. From a distance,

the forest seems like a tree plantation, but hidden waterfalls, old railroad trestles from the days of logging trains, and moss-covered oaks in the Salmonberry River Canyon will convince you otherwise. Bird-watchers and mushroom pickers can easily penetrate this thicket, thanks to 1,000 miles of maintained roads and old railroad grades.

Two challenging trails off Highway 6, **Kings Mountain** (25 miles east of Tillamook) and **Elk Mountain** (28 miles east of Tillamook) climb through lands affected by the Tillamook Burn, but with scenic views throughout. Thanks to salvage logging in the wake of the disaster and subsequent replanting, myriad trails crisscross forests of Douglas and noble fir, hemlock, and red alder. Stop at the visitor center for maps and trail descriptions.

Fishing

Among Oregon anglers, Tillamook County is known for its steelhead and salmon. Motorists along U.S. 101 can tell the fall chinook run has arrived when fishing boats cluster outside the Tillamook Bay entrance at Garibaldi. As the season wears on, the fish—affectionately called "hogs" because they sometimes weigh in at more than 50 pounds—make their way inland up the five coastal rivers—the Trask, Wilson, Tillamook, Kilchis, and Miami—that flow into Tillamook Bay. At their peak, the runs create such competition for favorite holes that the process of sparring for them is jocularly referred to as "combat fishing," as fishing boats anchor up gunwale to gunwale to form a fish-stopping palisade called a "hogline." Smokehouses and gas stations dot the outer reaches of the bay to cater to this fall influx.

Golf

Golfers choose between two public courses in Tillamook. Near the cheese factory and east of U.S. 101, find nine-hole **Bay Breeze Golf Course** (2325 Latimer Rd., Tillamook, 503/842-1166, 8am-6pm Mon.-Fri., 8am-7pm Sat.-Sun., $10-15 for 9 holes). Another two miles north, **Alderbrook Golf Course** (7300 Alderbrook Rd., Tillamook, 503/842-6413, www.alderbrookgolfcourse.com, 9am-dusk, $30-45 for 18 holes) has 18 holes.

Wildlife-Viewing

Bird-watchers flock to Tillamook Bay June-November to view pelicans, sandpipers, tufted puffins, blue herons, and a variety of shorebirds. Prime time is before high tide, but step lively, because this waterway was originally called "quicksand bay."

Accommodations

Most travelers seem to pass through Tillamook on their way to someplace else, and there are plenty of chain motels available all along the busy U.S. 101 strip north of town. A good local choice along this strip is **Ashley Inn** (1722 N. Makinster Rd., 503/842-7599 or 800/299-4817, www.ashleyinntillamook.com, $120-140), close to the cheese factory. Rooms have a refrigerator, microwave, iron and ironing board, coffeemaker, and cable TV. Amenities include an indoor pool, sauna, and hot tub, plus a complimentary continental breakfast.

There's not a lot going on in downtown Tillamook, but if you'd like to stay in the center of things, as opposed to the lengthy and busy commercial strip north of town, then book a room at the **Mar-Clair Inn** (11 Main Ave., 503/842-7571 or 800/331-6857, www.marclair.com, $79-99), a pleasant motor court tucked just off 101 with an outdoor pool and a restaurant.

Food

To sample the county's freshest produce, visit the **Tillamook Farmers Market** in downtown Tillamook. It runs every Saturday, mid-June-late September, at the corner of 2nd Street and Laurel Avenue.

The **Farmhouse Cafe** (8am-6pm daily Labor Day-mid-June, 8am-6pm Mon.-Fri., $4-10) at the Tillamook Cheese Factory serves breakfast and lunch. The deli at the **Blue Heron French Cheese Company** (2001 Blue Heron Dr., 503/842-8282, www.blueheronoregon.com, 11am-6pm daily) fixes sandwiches, soups, and salads daily; in polls conducted by the local paper, this is one of locals' favorite lunch spots. **La Mexicana** (2203 3rd St., 503/842-2101, 11am-9pm daily, $8-16) is the town's best Mexican restaurant. This restaurant, housed in a vintage home on the edge of downtown, goes way beyond tacos and burritos, preparing local fish and seafood with south-of-the-border zest and finesse.

In downtown Tillamook, attempts to open fine dining restaurants have faltered in recent years, but one promising spot is ★ **Pacific Restaurant** (2102 1st St., 503/354-2350, 11:30am-9pm Thurs.-Tues., $12-29), with an eclectic menu featuring local seafood and seasonal produce. The exterior of the restaurant (right downtown) is very unassuming, but the food—including pasta, salads, salmon, and chowders—is very well prepared. Also downtown is **Fat Dog Pizza** (116 Main St., 503/354-2283, 11:30am-9pm Sun.-Thurs., 11:30am-10pm Fri.-Sat., $15). Pizzas feature house-made dough (the Fat Dog Special is for meat lovers), and the submarine sandwiches, called Zeppelins in honor of Tillamook's dirigible history, are tasty. On the west side of U.S. 101, between the two cheese meccas, lunchtime do-it-yourselfers might check the locally raised and cured meat and smoked salmon at **Debbie D's Sausage Factory** (503/842-2622).

Take your time to savor a cup of tea at **La Tea Da Tea Room** (904 Main Ave., 503/842-5447, 11am-4pm Mon.-Sat. summer, 11am-4pm Tues.-Sat. winter, high tea $21). Go for the full high tea or settle for scones, soup, or little tea sandwiches.

Information

The **Tillamook Chamber of Commerce** (3705 U.S. 101 N., 503/842-7525, www.tillamookchamber.org, 9am-5pm Mon.-Fri.) is located across the parking lot from the cheese factory.

Three Capes Scenic Loop

The Three Capes Scenic Loop, a 35-mile byway off U.S. 101 between Tillamook and Pacific City, stays close to the ocean, which U.S. 101 does not. And although the beauty of Capes Meares, Lookout, and Kiwanda certainly justifies leaving the main highway, it would be an overstatement to portray this drive as a thrill-a-minute detour on the order of the south coast's Boardman State Park or the central coast's Otter Crest Loop. Instead of fronting the ocean, the road connecting the capes winds mostly through dairy country, small beach towns, and second-growth forest. What's special here are the three capes themselves, and unless you get out of the car and walk on the trails, you'll miss the aesthetic appeal and distinctiveness of each headland's ecosystem. The wave-battered bluffs of Cape Kiwanda, the precipitous overlooks along the Cape Lookout Highway, and

Cape Meares

the curious Octopus Tree at Cape Meares are the perfect antidotes to the inland towns along this stretch of U.S. 101. The majority of the Three Capes lodging and dining options are clustered in Netarts and Oceanside and at the other end in Pacific City. In between, it's mostly sand dunes, isolated beaches, rainforest, and pasture. To reach the Three Capes Scenic Loop from the north, turn west at Tillamook and follow signs to Cape Meares. From the south, follow signs north of Neskowin to Pacific City.

CAPE MEARES STATE SCENIC VIEWPOINT

With stunning views, picnic tables, a newly restored lighthouse, and a uniquely contorted tree a short walk from the parking lot, **Cape Meares State Scenic Viewpoint** is the most effortless site to visit on the Three Capes Loop. It was named for English navigator John Meares, who mapped many points along this coast in a 1788 voyage. The famed **Octopus Tree** is less than 0.25 mile up a forested hill. The tentacle-like extensions of this Sitka spruce have also been compared to candelabra arms.

The 45-foot diameter of its base supports five-foot-thick trunks, each of which by itself is large enough to be a single tree. Scientists have propounded several theories for the cause of its unusual shape, including everything from wind and weather to insects damaging the spruce when it was young. A Native American legend about the spruce contends that it was shaped this way so that the branches could hold the canoes of a chief's dead family. Supposedly, the bodies were buried near the tree. This was a traditional practice among the tribes of the area, who referred to species formed thusly as "council trees."

Beyond the tree you can look south at Oceanside and Three Arch Rocks Wildlife Refuge. The sweep of Pacific shore and

Three Capes Loop

© AVALON TRAVEL

offshore monoliths makes a fitting beginning (or finale, if you're driving from the south) to your sojourn along the Three Capes Scenic Loop, but be sure also to stroll the short paved trail down to the lighthouse, which begins at the parking lot and provides dramatic views of an offshore wildlife refuge, **Cape Meares Rocks.** Bring binoculars to see tufted puffins, pelagic cormorants, seals, and sea lions. The landward portion of the refuge protects rare old-growth evergreens.

The restored interior of **Cape Meares Lighthouse** (503/842-2244, 11am-4pm daily Apr.-Oct., free) was built in 1890. This beacon was replaced as a functioning light in 1963 by the automated facility behind it, and it now houses a gift shop. A free tour is occasionally offered by volunteers, who might tell you about how the lighthouse was built here by mistake and perhaps offer a peek into the prismatic Fresnel lenses.

OCEANSIDE

The road between Cape Meares and Netarts heads into the beach house community of Oceanside (pop. about 340). Many of the homes are built into the cliff overlooking the ocean, Sausalito style. This maze of very steep, very narrow streets reaches its apex atop Maxwell Point. You can peer several hundred feet down at **Three Arch Rocks Wildlife Refuge** (www.fws.gov), part-time home to one of the continent's largest and most varied collections of shorebirds. A herd of sea lions also populates this trio of sea stacks from time to time.

Accommodations and Food

There aren't many lodging options in Oceanside. While low prices and a window on the water can be found at **Ocean Front Cabins** (1610 Pacific Ave., 503/842-6081 or 888/845-8470, www.oceanfrontcabins.com, $70-140), the older, smallish guest rooms here might give upscale travelers pause. Nonetheless, for as little as $70 for a sleeping unit without a kitchenette—or $125 for

Cape Meares Lighthouse

a two-bed room with a full kitchen—you'll find yourself literally a stone's throw from Oceanside's beachcombing and dining highlights. Pets are accepted in some cabins.

For a more stylish lodging, consider

Thyme and Tide B&B (5015 Grand Ave., 503/842-5527, www.thyme-and-tide.com, $150-160), with two handsome rooms with ocean views and a location between Netarts and Oceanside.

Another good lodging option is **Bender Vacation Rental Properties** (503/233-4363, www.benderproperties.com/vacation-rentals), boasting six units with cliff-side ocean views, large private decks, and full kitchens (except for one unit). Other amenities include fireplaces, TVs, VCRs, and microwaves. Pets are welcome at most locations. For $80-110 per night with a two-night minimum, this is a great deal.

A popular draw for hungry Three Capes travelers, ★ **Roseanna's Oceanside Cafe** (1490 Pacific Ave. NW, 503/842-7351, www.roseannascafe.com, 9am-8pm Sun.-Thurs., 9am-9pm Fri.-Sat., call to confirm winter hours, $11-19) garners high marks from just about everyone. At first, the weather-beaten cedar-shake exterior might lead you to expect an old general store, as indeed it was decades ago. Once you're inside, however, the ornate decor leaves little doubt that this place takes its new identity seriously. From an elevated perch above the breakers, you'll be treated to expertly prepared local oysters, fresh salmon,

Three Arch Rocks Wildlife Refuge at Oceanside

a bevy of chicken dishes, and interesting pastas, such as gorgonzola and pear with penne noodles. Be sure to save room for blackberry cobbler; order it warm so the Tillamook Vanilla Bean ice cream on top melts down the sides, and watch the waves over a long cup of coffee.

Blue Agate Cafe (1610 Pacific Ave., 503/815-2596, 8am-5pm Mon. and Thurs., 8am-3pm Mon.-Thurs., 8am-9pm Fri.-Sat., 8am-8pm Sun., $7-15), is a happening little eatery in the center of Oceanside with fun breakfasts (try the Dungeness crab scramble), sandwiches, pasta, and excellent fish tacos.

NETARTS

Netarts (pop. about 750) has an enviable location overlooking Netarts Bay and the Pacific beyond. Along with nearby Oceanside, it's the closest coastal settlement to Tillamook and makes for a fine quiet getaway. Netarts Bay and seven-mile-long Netarts Spit are popular with clam diggers and crabbers, who can launch boats from Netarts Landing at the northeast corner of the bay. **Netarts Bay RV Park and Marina** (2260 Bilyeu St., 503/842-7774) and **Big Spruce RV Park** (4850 Netarts Hwy. W., 503/842-7443) rent motorboats and crabbing supplies.

Accommodations and Food

The **Terimore** (5105 Crab Ave., 503/842-4623 or 800/635-1821, www.terimoremotel.com, motel rooms $89-116, cabins $65-125) is situated a short walk from the water at the north end of Netarts Bay. Other than some units with fireplaces and kitchens, there are few frills, but for fair rates you'll find yourself close to the water, within easy driving distance of the Cape Lookout Trail, and a beach walk away from Roseanna's, the best restaurant on the Three Capes Scenic Loop.

For more up-to-date comforts, **Edgewater Motel and Vacation Rentals** (1st St. and Crab Ave., 503/842-1300 or 888/425-1050, www.oregoncoastmotels.com, $279) offers four luxury two-bedroom rentals directly above Netarts Bay. Each unit has two massive stone fireplaces (one in the master bedroom, one in the "great room"), a 650-gallon Jacuzzi tub, two balconies, and a well-equipped kitchen. Each unit sleeps up to eight people (with two queen-size foldout couches). The views can't be beat. If you don't require this level of sophistication, there are also vintage cabins and cottages on the same property, each with kitchens and TVs with a DVD player, and some have fireplaces ($129-250).

The view of Cape Lookout is tops at **The Schooner** (2065 Netarts Bay Rd., 503/842-4988, 11am-8pm Mon.-Thurs., 7am-9pm Fri.-Sat., 7am-8pm Sun. $10-25), and the food is a nice surprise also. Stop by for some steamer clams, fresh oysters, or tasty wood-fired pizza.

CAPE LOOKOUT STATE PARK

One of the scenic highlights of the Three Capes route, **Cape Lookout State Park** (off U.S. 101, www.oregonstateparks.org, $5 day use) juts out nearly a mile from the mainland, like a finger pointing out to sea. The cliffs along the south side of the cape rise 800 feet from the Pacific's pounding waves. The best way to take in the vista and the thrill of the location is on foot.

★ Hiking

Hiking to the end of mile-wide Cape Lookout is one of the top coastal hikes in Oregon. The trail begins either at the campground, where it climbs 2.5 miles up to a ridgetop trailhead with a parking lot, or from the Three Capes road at a well-signed trailhead. An orientation map at the trailhead details the options. The main 2.5-mile trail out to the end, along the narrowing finger of land, can give hikers the impression that they're on the prow of a giant ship suspended 500 feet above the ocean on all sides. Here, more than anywhere else on the Oregon coast, you get the sense of being on the edge of the continent. Giant spruce, western red cedars, and hemlocks surround the gently hilly trail to the tip of the cape. In March, Cape Lookout is a popular vantage point for whale-watching. June through August, a bevy of wildflowers and birds further enhance the rolling terrain en route to the tip of this headland, and in late summer red huckleberries line the path.

Halfway to the overlook, there are views north to Cape Meares over the Netarts sand spit. Even if you settle for a mere 15-minute stroll down the trail, you can look southward beyond Haystack Rock to Cascade Head. Right about where the trees open up, look for a bronze plaque commemorating the crash of a World War II plane and nearly a dozen casualties, which is embedded in the rock wall bordering the right-hand (north) side of the trail at eye level. If you're unable to take this hike, two unmarked turnouts along the Three Capes road between the sand dunes and Cape Lookout parking lot let you survey the terrain south to Cape Kiwanda. Don't be surprised if you see hang gliders and paragliders.

Another popular trail in the state park heads north from the campground through a variety of estuarine habitats along the sand spit separating Netarts Bay from the Pacific. It's a popular site for agate hunters, clammers, and crabbers.

Camping

At the southern end of Netarts Spit is the state park's **campground and beach extension** (13000 Whiskey Creek Rd. W., 503/842-4981 for information, 800/452-5687 or www.reserveamerica.com for reservations, $5-76), which also encompasses the entire cape and the seven-mile-long Netarts Spit within its boundaries. The campground has 173 tent sites ($21) and 38 full-hookup sites ($31), as well as 13 yurts ($44), three cabins (with bathrooms, a kitchen, and a TV/VCR, $88-98) and a hiker-biker camp ($6); discounts apply October-April. Some yurts accept pets ($10 fee). Amenities include showers, flush toilets, and evening programs. Reservations and a deposit are almost always needed at this popular campground.

South of Cape Lookout, the terrain suddenly changes. Extensive sand dunes surrounding the Sand Lake Estuary suddenly appear, drowning the forest in sand. The dunes and beach attract squadrons of dune buggy enthusiasts. Camping is available year-round at **Sand Beach Campground** (5 miles south of Cape Lookout on Galloway Rd., 503/392-3161 or 877/444-6777, $16, reservations at www.recreation.gov), a part of the Siuslaw National Forest, which has basic sites for tenters and RVs. This dramatic area is also popular with hikers.

PACIFIC CITY AND CAPE KIWANDA

As you approach the shore in Pacific City, the sight of **Haystack Rock** will immediately grab your attention. At 327 feet, this sea stack is nearly 100 feet taller than the similarly named rock in Cannon Beach. Standing a mile offshore, this monolith has a brooding, enigmatic quality that constantly draws the eye to it. Look closely, and you'll understand why some folks call it Teacup Rock.

The tawny sandstone escarpment of Cape Kiwanda juts half a mile out to sea from Pacific City and frames the north end of the beach. In storm-tossed waters, this cape is the undisputed king of rock-and-roll, if you go by coffee table books and calendar photos. While other sandstone promontories on the north coast have been ground into sandy beaches by the pounding surf, it's been theorized that Kiwanda has endured thanks to the buffer of Haystack Rock. In any case, hang gliding aficionados are glad the cape is here. They scale its shoulders and set themselves aloft off the north face to glide above the beach and dunes.

The small town of Pacific City, with about 1,000 residents, is at the base of Cape Kiwanda. It attracts growing numbers of vacationers and retirees, but remains true to its 19th-century origins as a working fishing village. In addition to the knockout seascapes and recreation, if you come here at the right time of day, you may be treated to a unique spectacle—the launch or return of the **dory fleet.**

It's a tradition dating back to the 1920s, when gillnetting was banned on the Nestucca

River to protect the dwindling salmon runs. To retain their livelihood, commercial fishers began to haul flat-bottomed double-ended dories down to the beach on horse-drawn wagons, then row out through the surf to fish. These days, trucks and trailers get the boats to and from the beach, and outboard motors have replaced oar power, enabling the dories to get 50 miles out to sea. If you come around 6am, you can watch them taking off. The fleet's late-afternoon return attracts a crowd that arrives to see the dory operators skidding their craft as far as possible up the beach to the waiting boat trailers. Others meet the dories to buy salmon and tuna.

In mid-July, **Dory Days** celebrate the area's fleet. The three-day fete includes craft and food booths, a pancake breakfast, a fishing derby, and other activities. For more information, call the **chamber of commerce** (503/965-6161). If you want to join the anglers for a summertime ocean fishing trip on a dory, contact **Haystack Fishing** (888/965-7555), across from the beach near the Inn at Cape Kiwanda.

In addition, the Pacific City area is besieged by surfers, who enjoy some of the longest waves on the Oregon coast. **Robert Straub State Park,** just south of town, offers access to Nestucca Bay and to the dunes and a long uninterrupted stretch of beach. Pacific City surfers should use *extreme* caution when the dories are returning to the beach.

Accommodations

The nicest motel on the Three Capes Scenic Loop is the large ★ **Inn at Cape Kiwanda** (33105 Cape Kiwanda Dr., 503/965-6366 or 888/965-7001, www.yourlittlebeachtown.com/inn, $229-279). All rooms face a beautiful beach and Cape Kiwanda's giant sand dune. If it's too rainy to go outside, fireplaces and spacious well-appointed rooms make for great storm-watching. Whirlpool tub rooms are available, and pets are permitted in some rooms.

For a more historic experience, head to the ★ **Craftsman B&B** (35255 4th St., 503/965-4574, www.craftsmanbb.com, $160-200), an exquisitely refurbished Craftsman-style home

At Pacific City, fishing boats launch directly into the surf.

with very stylish guest rooms. Built in 1921 (and perhaps Pacific City's oldest home), this B&B is a monument to sensitive historic preservation and also a very friendly, comfortable place to stay. All four guest rooms have private baths and are decorated according to the styles of Arts and Crafts luminaries such as Gustav Stickley, Charles Rennie Macintosh, and William Morris.

Camping

About 4.5 miles north of Pacific City on the Three Capes Loop Road, the **Clay Meyers Natural Area at Whalen Island** (4.5 miles north of Pacific City on Sandlake Rd., 503/965-6085, www.co.tillamook.or.us, $10-15) has a small campground run by Tillamook County. It's an open, sandy spot with a boat launch and flush toilets; nearby hiking trails traverse wetlands and provide a great look at the coastal Sand Lake Estuary.

Food

A popular and well-known Pacific City hangout is the ★ **Pelican Pub and Brewery**

(33180 Cape Kiwanda Dr., 503/965-7007, 8am-close daily, $6-23). Set in a most enviable spot right on the beach opposite Cape Kiwanda and Haystack Rock, this place boasts the best coastal view of any brewpub in Oregon. Buttermilk-beer pancakes, dory-caught fish-and-chips, pizzas, "shark bites," tasty chili, and IPA-poached salmon are some of the standouts. The pub's brews, including Tsunami Stout, Doryman's Dark Ale, India Pelican Ale, and MacPelican's Scottish Style Ale, have garnered stacks of awards.

Delicate Palate Bistro (35280 Brooten Rd., 503/965-6464, www.delicatepalate.com, 5pm-close Wed.-Sun., $17-25) is a classy little place where the chef brings a deft touch to classics—think pan-seared wild salmon with artichoke ragout or bouillabaisse made with a coconut curry broth and served with soba noodles—and the meals are backed up by an excellent wine list (or a long martini menu, if you prefer). The deck, which overlooks the local airstrip, is open for dining when weather allows.

Also on Brooten Road toward the north end

Pelican Pub and Brewery

of town, find the ★ **Grateful Bread Bakery** (34085 Brooten Rd., 503/965-7337 8am-4pm Thurs.-Mon., $5-9), where the challah bread, carrot cake, marionberry strudel, and other homemade baked goods deserve special mention. The full breakfast menu offers a range of tasty omelets served with oven-roasted spuds at great prices. Lunch sandwiches include a wide range of vegetarian options.

Neskowin and Cascade Head

NESKOWIN

The tiny vacation village of Neskowin (rhymes with "let's go in," pop. 170) has a quiet appeal based on a beautiful beach and a golf course in the shadow of 1,500-foot-high Cascade Head. It's the polar opposite of busy Lincoln City, 15 miles south. There's not much to do here but relax on the uncrowded beach and enjoy the views of Cascade Head and the dark beauty of **Proposal Rock,** a stony, forested hillock that stands right at the edge of the surf, with Neskowin Creek curving around it. The feature was named by Neskowin's first postmistress, whose daughter received a marriage proposal nearby. Neskowin has a reputation as a beach town for old-money, in-the-know Portland families.

The sleepy town has only one art gallery, and it's a good one. **Hawk Creek Gallery** (48460 U.S. 101 S., 503/392-3879, www.hawkcreekgallery.com, 11am-5pm daily summer, 11am-5pm Sat.-Sun. spring and fall) is the studio and showroom for the works of painter Michael Schlicting, who exhibits his work internationally but has made the Hawk Creek Gallery his home base since 1978.

Neskowin Marsh Golf Course (48405 Hawk St., 503/392-3377, $18 for nine holes) has streams and water hazards adding a challenge to most of the nine greens.

Accommodations

Proposal Rock Inn (48988 U.S. 101 S., 503/392-3115, www.proposalrockneskowin. com, rooms $67-137, suites $135-260) backs up on Hawk Creek and commands a fine view of the beach and the eponymous rock. Two-room oceanview suites with a full kitchen

Hawk Creek leads to the secluded beach at Neskowin.

fetch higher prices than the standard non-oceanview guest rooms, but all are right on the beach.

The nine two-bedroom condo units at **The Chelan** (48750 Breakers Blvd., 503/392-3270, www.rentoregoncoast.com, $125-285) are comfier than the boxy stucco exterior suggests, with fireplaces, kitchens, views, and direct access to the beach.

To rent a home in the Neskowin or Pacific City area, contact the property management firm **Neskowin Vacation Rentals** (503/392-4850, http://neskowinvacationrentals.com).

Food

Waits can be long at the tiny **Hawk Creek Cafe** (4505 Salem Ave., 503/392-3838, 8am-9pm Thurs.-Sun., 11am-9pm Mon.-Wed., $12-23), particularly at breakfast, but the food is worth it. Count on filling omelets for breakfast; sandwiches (about $10), burgers, and wood-fired pizza ($16-18) for lunch; and grilled fish and steaks for dinner. Hidden behind the general store is **Beach Club Bistro** (48880 Hwy 101 S., 503/392-3035, http://beachclubbistro.com, noon-8pm Wed.-Thurs., noon-9pm Fri.-Sun. $17-30), a friendly spot with a selection of small plates for grazing and such main courses as crab and Parmesan ravioli with seared scallops and prawns if you're looking for serious dining.

CASCADE HEAD
Cascade Head Scenic Research Area

About 10 miles north of Lincoln City, the 11,890-acre Cascade Head Experimental Forest was set aside in 1934 for scientific study of typical coastal Sitka spruce and western hemlock forests found along the Oregon coast. In 1974, Congress established the 9,670-acre **Cascade Head Scenic Research Area** (www.fsl.orst.edu/chef), which includes the western half of the forest, several prairie headlands, and the Salmon River estuary. In 1980, the entire area was designated a biosphere reserve as part of the United Nations Biosphere Reserve system.

The headlands, reaching as high as 1,800 feet, are unusual for their extensive prairies still dominated by native grasses: red fescue, wild rye, and Pacific reedgrass. The Nechesney Indians, who inhabited the area as long as 12,000 years ago, purposely burned forest tracts around Cascade Head, probably to provide browse for deer and to reduce the possibility of larger uncontrollable blazes. These human-made alterations are complemented by the inherent dryness of south-facing slopes, which receive increased exposure to the sun. In contrast to these grasslands, the northern part of the headland is the domain of giant spruces and firs because it catches the brunt of the heavy rainfalls and lingering fogs. Endemic wildflowers include coastal paintbrush, goldenrod, streambank lupine, rare hairy checkermallow, and blue violet, a plant critical to the survival of the Oregon silverspot butterfly, a threatened species found in only six locations. Deer, elk, coyotes, snowshoe hare, and the Pacific giant salamander find refuge here, while bald eagles, great horned owls, and peregrine falcons may be seen hunting above the grassy slopes. Today, in addition to its biological importance, the area is a mecca for some 6,000 hikers annually, and for anglers who target the salmon and steelhead runs on the Salmon River.

On the north side of the Salmon River, turn west from U.S. 101 onto **Three Rocks Road** for a scenic driving detour on the south side of Cascade Head. The paved road curves about 2.5 miles above the wetlands and widening channel of the Salmon River estuary, passes Savage Road, and ends at a parking area and boat launch at Knight County Park. From the park, the road turns to gravel and narrows (not suitable for RVs or trailers), and continues about another 0.5 mile to its end at a spectacular overlook across the estuary.

HIKING

Cascade Head offers some outstanding scenic hikes, with rainforest pathways and wildflower meadows giving way to dramatic ocean views.

A short but brisk hike to the top of the headland on a **Nature Conservancy trail** begins near Knight County Park. Leave your car at the park and walk 0.5 mile up Savage Road to the trailhead. It's 1.7 miles one-way, with a 1,100-foot elevation gain. No dogs or bicycles are allowed on the trail, which is open year-round.

Two trails are accessible from Cascade Head Road (Forest Rd. 1861), a gravel road open seasonally (July 16-Dec. 31) that heads west off U.S. 101 about three miles north of Three Rocks Road, near the highway summit of Cascade Head. Travel this road four miles west of U.S. 101 to the **Hart's Cove Trailhead.** The first part of the trail runs through arching red alder treetops and 250-year-old Sitka spruces with five-foot diameters. The understory of mosses and ferns is nourished by 100-inch rainfalls. Next, the trail emerges into open grasslands. The five-mile round-trip hike loses 900 feet in elevation on its way to an oceanfront meadow overlooking Hart's Cove, where the barking of sea lions might greet you. This trail can have plenty of mud, so boots are recommended as you tromp through the rainforest.

An easier trail accessible from Cascade Head Road heads to a viewpoint on the Nature Conservancy's preserve. (Again, no dogs or bikes are allowed on Nature Conservancy land.) The one-mile trail starts about 3.5 miles west of U.S. 101 and heads to a big meadow and an ocean overlook. It's possible to continue from the overlook, heading downhill to join up with the lower Nature Conservancy trail described above.

The **Cascade Head Trail** runs six miles roughly parallel to the highway, with a south trailhead near the intersection of Three Rocks Road and U.S. 101 and a north trailhead at Falls Creek, on U.S. 101 about one mile south of Neskowin. It passes through old-growth forest and is entirely inland, without the spectacular ocean views of other trails in the area.

Sitka Center for Art and Ecology

The region in the shadow of Cascade Head can be explored in even greater depth thanks to the **Sitka Center for Art and Ecology** (56605 Sitka Dr., Otis, 541/994-5485, www.sitkacenter.org, 8:30am-4:30pm Mon.-Fri.), located off Savage Road on the south side of the headland. Classes are offered June-August focusing on art and nature, with an emphasis on the strong relationship between the two. Experts in everything from local plant communities to Siletz Indian baskets conduct outdoor workshops on the grounds of Cascade Head Ranch. Classes can last from a couple of days to a week, and fees vary accordingly.

Central Coast

Look for ★ to find recommended
sights, activities, dining, and lodging.

Highlights

★ **Oregon Coast Aquarium:** Explore the life of Oregon's shores and oceans at this excellent aquarium (page 302).

★ **Yaquina Head Outstanding Natural Area:** A soaring lighthouse stands above a tide-pool-studded inlet at this small park, the quintessence of the Oregon coast (page 306).

★ **Whale-Watching:** *Thar she blows!* Newport is a great departure point for gray whale-watching tours (page 309).

★ **Cape Perpetua:** One of the most dramatic natural areas along the Oregon coast, Cape Perpetua is a top spot for hiking and exploring tidepools (page 318).

★ **Heceta Head Lighthouse and Devil's Elbow:** Climb to the top of this whitewashed lighthouse for wonderful views—or stay in the lighthouse keeper's house, now a B&B (page 324).

★ **Sea Lion Caves:** Take an elevator ride down to the caves at cliff's bottom to get a close look at the Steller sea lion rookery (page 325).

★ **John Dellenback Trail:** Explore 400-foot dunes in the Oregon Dunes National Recreation Area. It's like trekking the Sahara (page 337).

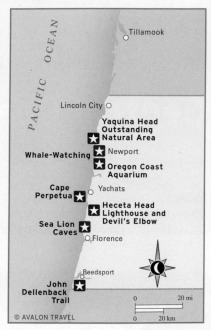

O regon's central coast, from Lincoln City to Reedsport and Winchester Bay, embraces such contrasts that it's difficult to generalize about the region.

In the north, Lincoln City's dense mix of lodgings and shopping, combined with its Native American casinos, generates the coast's worst traffic jams, especially on holidays and weekends. The sprawling town isn't everyone's first choice for a quiet getaway, but it's a long-time favorite with families. Depoe Bay—built around the world's smallest navigable natural harbor—is headquarters for the coast's busiest whale-watching fleet, and one of its largest and most sprawling condo developments.

A necklace of small state parks adorns the shore every couple of miles all the way from southern Lincoln City southward; inland, the Siuslaw National Forest safeguards several wilderness areas and groves of rare old-growth coastal forest, beckoning hikers to explore the primeval landscapes. Just north of Newport, Yaquina Head Outstanding Natural Area offers excellent vantage points for up-close whale-watching and bird-watching, plus tidepools accessible to wheelchair users.

The bustling harbor at Newport is home to the state's largest commercial fishing fleet and

second-largest recreational fleet, which runs charters year-round for rockfish and seasonally for salmon, tuna, and halibut. Newport also boasts the state-of-the-art Oregon Coast Aquarium, former residence of Keiko the beloved orca, and the bohemian resort community of Nye Beach, which has been attracting tourists since the 19th century.

Just south of Yachats, the panoramic view from Cape Perpetua can, on a clear day, extend 75 miles in each direction. Down at sea level, the tidepools here are some of the most fascinating on the coast. At Sea Lion Caves, a touristy but unique experience between Yachats and Florence, the world's largest sea cave is the only mainland rookery of Steller sea lions in the lower 48 states. Close by, photographers spend more time trying to capture the perfect image of Heceta Head Lighthouse than any other sight along the entire coast.

PLANNING YOUR TIME

It's easy to spend a few days exploring the central coast. Although **Lincoln City** has

---

Previous: Yaquina Bay Bridge; Oregon Dunes National Recreation Park. **Above:** Winchester Bay.

Central Coast

PACIFIC OCEAN

Pacific City
Cloverdale
22
Neskowin
Siuslaw National Forest
18
Otis
Lincoln City
Rose Lodge
Gleneden Beach
Salishan
Depoe Bay
Siletz River
Cape Foulweather
101
229
⭐ YAQUINA HEAD OUTSTANDING NATURAL AREA
Siletz
Logsden
Yaquina Head ★
Agate Beach
Newport
⭐ WHALE-WATCHING
Eddyville
20
Toledo
⭐ OREGON COAST AQUARIUM
To Corvallis
Waldport
Tidewater
34
Alsea River
⭐ CAPE PERPETUA
Yachats
⭐ HECETA HEAD LIGHTHOUSE AND DEVIL'S ELBOW
Siuslaw National Forest
Minerva
36
Swisshome
SEA LION CAVES ⭐
126
Siuslaw River
Florence
To Eugene
Oregon Dunes National Recreation Area
Siltcoos Lake
101
Sulphur Springs
Smith River
Tahkenitch Lake
Gardiner
Reedsport
Winchester Bay
38
⭐ JOHN DELLENBACK TRAIL
Scottsburg
Umpqua River
Lakeside
N. Tenmile Lake
Ash
Tenmile Lake
© AVALON TRAVEL

0   10 mi
0   10 km

abundant hotel rooms and is a good fallback during busy times of the year, tiny **Depoe Bay** is a great place to spend a night, perhaps with an early rise to take a fishing or whale-watching trip. And though **Newport** is a big city by Oregon coast standards, it's definitely worth spending a couple of nights here. In fact, if you're looking for a base for central coast explorations, Newport is well situated to visit sites from Lincoln City down to Florence. While in Newport, you may simply want to poke around the Nye Beach and Bayfront neighborhoods, beachcomb on Agate Beach, and check out the tidepools and lighthouse at the Yaquina Head Outstanding Natural Area; or you might decide to devote a day to the Oregon Coast Aquarium and the nearby Oregon State University Hatfield Marine Science Center.

Personally, when we have the opportunity to plunk down at the coast for a long week-end, we almost always head to **Yachats** to enjoy the low-key atmosphere, the incredible natural beauty, and the good restaurants of this tiny town. If you are touring the coast, we think it (and the incredible Cape Perpetua coastline just south) is worth a full day and night of your time.

Florence is a short hop from Yachats and is a good alternative if you'd rather stay in a slightly larger town with a lively Old Town and easy access to the north end of the Oregon Dunes National Recreation Area, a fantastic landscape of dazzling white sand mountains and jewel lakes stretched along nearly 50 miles of shoreline.

Although anglers may want to stay at **Winchester Bay,** for most coast travelers this little town is a good stop for fish-and-chips, but not an overnight destination. Nearby, **Reedsport** is in the heart of the dune country and a good place to camp while exploring the dunes, but it does not have a huge wealth of fancy hotels and restaurants.

Lincoln City

Back in 1964, five burgs that straddled seven miles of beachfront between Siletz Bay and the Salmon River came together and incorporated as Lincoln City. In commemoration, a 14-foot bronze statue of Abraham Lincoln was donated to the city by an Illinois sculptor. *The Lank Lawyer Reading in His Saddle While His Horse Grazes* originally occupied a city park; today the statue stands in a nondescript lot at NE 22nd Street and Quay Avenue. Look for the sign on U.S. 101 near the Dairy Queen.

In the following decades, what were discrete towns have grown and melded into an uninterrupted conurbation with a population of about 8,000 (which can balloon to 30,000 on a busy weekend). While the resulting sprawl and heavy traffic on U.S. 101 can be maddening at times, once you get off the highway, Lincoln City has some charming neighborhoods (check out the Taft area at the south end of town); wide sandy beaches; superlative wildlife-viewing around Siletz Bay; the large, freshwater Devils Lake; and two Native American casinos. Add prime kite-flying, some of the coast's better restaurants, and bibliophilic and antiquing haunts, and it's clear that there's more to the area than the pull of saltwater taffy and outlet malls.

SIGHTS AND RECREATION

Lincoln City Beach

Lincoln City boasts seven uninterrupted miles of sandy beach. From Siletz Bay north to Road's End State Recreation Area, there are more than a dozen access points. You can head west from U.S. 101 on just about any side street to get there, though high coastal bluffs lining the north-central portion of town may mean a climb down (and back up) long flights of stairs cut into the cliff. For something approaching solitude on a crowded day, follow Logan Road west from the highway near the north end of town to **Road's End State Recreation Area;** tidepools and a secluded cove add to the allure. This stretch is also popular with windsurfers.

Tidepool explorers should also check out the **rock formations** at SW 11th Street (Canyon Drive Park), NW 15th Street, and SW 32nd Street.

The **D River Wayside,** a small park on the beach in more or less the middle of town, is a state park property where you can watch what locals claim is the "world's shortest river" empty into the ocean. Flowing just 120 feet from its source, Devils Lake, to its mouth at the Pacific, it's short, all right; despite its unspectacular appearance, it was a cause

The Legacy of Ken Kesey

Two miles south of Lincoln City, you'll come to the turnoff for Highway 229 along the Siletz River. If you drive down the north side of the river about 1.25 miles, on the opposite shore you'll notice a showy Victorian-ish house. It was constructed for the movie version of *Sometimes a Great Notion.* The 1971 film, a so-so adaptation of Ken Kesey's memorable novel, starred Paul Newman, Lee Remick, Henry Fonda, and Michael Sarrazin. The plot concerns the never-say-die spirit of an antiunion timber baron, his not-always-supportive family, and life in the mythical Coast Range logging community of Wakonda. A huge porch once fronted the riverbank, heavily reinforced against the elements. It was taken down in the decade after the movie was made, but it lives on in the pages of the book. Much of the movie was shot in this area, with café scenes taking place at Mo's on Newport's bay front. Other scenes were shot near Florence.

Lincoln City

CHINOOK WINDS CASINO · LOGAN RD

LIGHTHOUSE SQUARE ★

VETERAN'S MEMORIAL ★ · 44TH ST

To Tillamook

40TH PL

SURFTIDES INN · 39TH ST · LINCOLN CITY PLAZA ★

PACIFIC

BREY HOUSE B&B ● · 36TH · DR · 101

KEEL · AVE

OCEAN · Beach

CONNIE HANSEN GARDEN ★

INLET AVE · 33RD · ST · HOLMES · RD

NORTH LINCOLN HOSPITAL ★

Wecoma · 30TH · ST · WEST DEVILS LAKE RD

28TH ST

JETTY

BLACKFISH CAFE ★

STARFISH MANOR HOTEL ●

22ND · ST

SEA HORSE OCEANFRONT LODGING ● · 21ST ST

HARBOR AVE

COHO OCEANFRONT LODGE ● · 17TH · ST · DAR · AVE

15TH ST

JASMINE THAI RESTAURANT ● · 13TH ST

12TH ST

11TH ST

INLET AVE · 6TH · DR

Devil's Lake State Recreation Area ⚓

Devil's Lake

'D' River ·

State Wayside · KYLLO'S ●

3RD · ST

STATE PARK

East Devil's Lake SP

EAST

EBB AVE · JETTY AVE · KEEL

DEVILS LAKE · RD

7TH ST · 8TH ST

VISITOR AND CONVENTION BUREAU ■ · GALLEY AVE

FACTORY OUTLET STORES ■

FLEET AVE · 14TH · ST

17TH ST

COAST AVE

BARD · RD

DORY COVE RESTAURANT ▼ · 101

ANCHOR AVE

NELSCOTT CAFE ▼

0 · 0.5 mi

0 · 0.5 km

ESTER LEE ●

INN AT SPANISH HEAD ● · HIGH · SCHOOL

Schooner · Creek

BEACH AVE · ROADHOUSE 101 ●

COAST AVE · GALLEY AVE

JENNIFER SEA'S ART STUDIO

50TH ST · NORTH LINCOLN COUNTY HISTORICAL MUSEUM ★

SILETZ BAY LODGE ● · 51ST ST · MO'S ▼

LOOKING GLASS INN ● · To Depoe Bay

© AVALON TRAVEL

---

célèbre when *The Guinness Book of World Records* withdrew the D's claim to fame in favor of a Montana waterway, the Roe. Local schoolkids rallied to the D's defense with an amended measurement, but the Roe, at a mere 53 feet long, carries the *Guinness* imprimatur as the shortest river. In addition to seeing the D River flow from "D" Lake into "D" ocean, you can fly a kite on the beach. It's one of the easier beach access points between stretches of high motel-topped bluffs, so it can get a little crowded.

Another convenient beach access is off SW 51st Street at the south end of town, just before **Siletz Bay.** A large parking area here in what's known as the Taft District stands beside the driftwood-strewn shore of the bay, where you can often see a group of harbor seals chasing their dinner or coming in for a closer look at you. It's a short walk to the ocean.

Time was when it was common for storms and currents to wash up that ultimate beach-comber's prize—**glass fishing floats**—on the Oregon coast. Lincoln City improves the beachcomber's odds by distributing over 2,000 glass floats along its beaches mid-October-Memorial Day. Handcrafted by Pacific Northwest glass artists, each of the colorful floats is signed and numbered and placed by volunteers on the beaches above the high-tide line. If you find one, it's yours to keep; you can call or stop in at the visitor center for a certificate and information about the artist who created it.

Devils Lake

Devils Lake, just east of the highway, is the recreation center of Lincoln City. In addition to windsurfing and hydroplaning, you can fish here—the lake is stocked with hatchery trout, and there's also a population of wild coho salmon (catch-and-release only) as well as lampreys. There's good bird-watching on and around this shallow 678-acre lake, which attracts flocks of migratory geese, ducks, and other waterfowl. Species to look for include

Drift Creek Falls

and Jet Skis can be rented at **Blue Heron Landing** (4006 W. Devils Lake Rd., 541/994-4708, www.blueheronlanding.net, 9am-7pm daily).

Drift Creek Falls

Although it requires a drive inland, it's worth heading about 10 miles east to hike **Drift Creek Falls** (503/392-3161, $5 NW Forest Pass to park). The relatively easy but steadily downhill 1.5-mile trail passes through a forest with mostly second growth, a little old growth, lots of big stumps, and an understory of lovely native plants, and it leads to a dramatic 240-foot-high suspension bridge overlooking the 75-foot falls. The bridge, built in 1998, is as much an attraction as the falls—it sways a little bit as you walk out to view the falls. From the bridge, the trail continues another 0.25 mile to the base of the falls.

From Oregon State Road 18, turn south at Rose Lodge onto Bear Creek Road (which becomes Forest Road 17) and follow it for about nine miles. At the fork with Schooner Creek Road, be sure to go left (uphill); a rustic sign notes that it's the way to "Drift Creek Camp."

From U.S. 101, turn east onto Drift Creek Road (at the south end of Lincoln City), then south onto South Drift Creek Road and east onto Forest Road 17. Follow Forest Road 17 for about 10 miles.

Siletz River

The **Siletz Bay National Wildlife Refuge** preserves coastal estuaries and wetlands on either side of U.S. 101 at the south end of Lincoln City. The skeleton trees here are reminders of times when the salt marsh was diked to provide pasture for dairy cows. Now these snags are used by red-tailed hawks, bald eagles, and other birds of prey. The wetlands provide habitat for great blue herons, egrets, and other waterbirds.

During the summer, refuge rangers lead a small number of **paddle trips** along the Siletz estuaries. Trips are free, but participants must register well beforehand (541/270-0610) and provide their own canoe or kayak. **Siletz**

canvasbacks, Canada geese, widgeons, gadwalls, grebes, and mallards. Bald eagles and ospreys nest in the trees bordering the lake.

The lake takes its name from a local Native American legend. The story goes that when Siletz warriors paddled a canoe across the lake one moonlit night, a tentacled beast erupted from the still water and pulled the men under. It's said that boaters today who cross the moon's reflection in the middle of the lake tempt the same fate, but the lake's devil has remained silent for years.

Of the five access points, East Devils Lake Road off U.S. 101 northeast of town offers a scenic route around the lake's east side before rejoining U.S. 101 near the day-use portion of the state park at the south end of the lake. To reach the camping area of **Devils Lake State Recreation Area,** take NE 6th Drive east from U.S. 101, about 0.25 mile north of the D River. The day-use area has a boat ramp, and there's a moorage dock across the lake adjacent to the campground.

Mountain bikes, canoes, fishing boats,

Moorage (82 Siletz Hwy., 541/996-3671) rents kayaks ($25 for 4 hours) from its location on the north bank of the river just east of the highway.

Casinos

One of the biggest draws in town is the **Chinook Winds Casino** (1777 NW 44th St., 541/996-5825 or 888/244-6665, www.chinookwindscasino.com, open 24 hours daily), operated by the Confederated Tribes of Siletz Indians, near the north end of town. In addition to slots, blackjack, poker, Keno, bingo, craps, and roulette, the casino has two on-site restaurants and a busy schedule of big-name (or formerly big-name) entertainment.

About 25 miles east of Lincoln City is the state's number-one visitor attraction, **Spirit Mountain Casino** (21700 SW Salmon River Hwy., Grand Ronde, 800/760-7977, http://spiritmountain.com, open 24 hours daily), operated by the Confederated Tribes of Grand Ronde. Games of chance include slots, craps, blackjack, poker, Keno, and bingo. No matter what you think of the casino, it should be noted that the Grand Ronde people have done a great job at getting their tribal status officially reinstated after the U.S. government officially terminated the tribe in 1954, leaving it with not much more than the tribal cemetery and a shed. They have amassed land and established a community fund that is a substantial supporter of nonprofit organizations in Oregon; 6 percent of the casino's proceeds go into this charitable fund.

North Lincoln County Historical Museum

The modest **North Lincoln County Historical Museum** (4907 SW U.S. 101, 541/996-6614, www.northlincolncountyhistoricalmuseum.org, 11am-5pm Wed.-Sun. June-Sept. and noon-5pm Wed.-Sat. Oct.-Dec. 14 and Feb. 1-May 31, free) tells the story of this area through exhibits of old-time logging machinery, homesteading tools, fishing, military life, and Native American history. A highlight is the great collection of Japanese glass fishing floats.

Connie Hansen Garden

Tucked into the neighborhood between busy U.S. 101 and the beach, the **Connie Hansen Garden** (1931 NW 33rd St., 541/994-6338, www.conniehansengarden.com, dawn-dusk daily, free) is a great example of a coastal rainforest garden. The late Connie Hansen bought the land because its dampness seemed well suited to growing irises, her favorite plants, but she soon expanded her vision, working with the site's ecology and her own artistic talents to create a horticultural showcase. Guided tours are available for a small fee with advance notice, and a gift shop is open 10am-2pm Tuesday, Saturday, and Sunday.

Glass Art

Spend a rainy day learning to blow a glass float or paperweight at the **Jennifer Sears Art Studio** (4821 SW U.S. 101, 541/996-2569, www.jennifersearsglassart.com, 10am-6pm daily, classes $65-135, reservations required). Kids ages 8-10 may participate with parental supervision. Be sure to wear closed-toe shoes, and no fleece!

About four miles south of town, near Salishan, you can watch the glass blowers at **Alder House** (611 Immonen Rd., 541/994-6485, www.alderhouse.com, 10am-5pm daily May-Oct.) and buy floats, paperweights, or other glass creations at very reasonable prices. Call ahead to confirm opening hours.

Golf

The area's most prestigious golf resort is seven miles south of Lincoln City at Gleneden Beach. **Salishan Spa and Golf Resort** (7760 N. U.S. 101, Gleneden Beach, 541/764-3632 or 800/890-8037, www.salishan.com, $79-119 for 18 holes) is an award-winning 18-hole course set in the foothills of the Coast Range and bordered by Siletz Bay and the sea. This challenging, 6,470-yard, par-71, championship layout course was redesigned by Oregon golf superstar Peter Jacobsen and includes stunning ocean views. Keep in mind that this is a Scottish links course, where the roughs are really rough.

The 18-hole **Chinook Winds Golf Resort** (3245 NE 50th St., 541/994-8442, http://chinookwindscasino.com, $35-40 for 18 holes) is set in hilly (and frequently windy) terrain amidst towering coastal mountains on the edge of Lincoln City. This course is another venture of the Chinook Winds Casino, operated by the Confederated Tribes of Siletz Indians. The golf course spans just 5,000 yards, with men's par 65 and women's 72.

ENTERTAINMENT AND EVENTS

Housed within the renovated Gleneden Brick and Tile Factory, five miles south of Lincoln City in Gleneden Beach, **Eden Hall** (6645 Gleneden Beach Loop Rd., 541/764-3826 performance info, 541/764-3825 restaurant, www.edenhall.com) stages live theater and hosts an impressively eclectic roster of regional and touring musicians. This spacious airy warehouse has an excellent sound system and is a wonderful place to take in a concert, with an emphasis on jazz, folk, and blues. Enjoy lunch or dinner at the adjacent Side Door Café.

The Arts

Lincoln City's homegrown theater company, **Theatre West** (3536 SE U.S. 101, 541/994-5663, www.theatrewest.com), stages half a dozen productions each year, with an emphasis on comedies, musicals, and drama. Visit the website for a list of current plays and their synopses.

Cinema

Catch first-run flicks at the **Bijou Theatre** (1624 NE U.S. 101, 541/994-8255), an old-time movie house dating back to the 1930s—making it a rare old survivor around here. The six-screen **Regal Cinemas** (3755 SE High School Dr., 541/994-7649), just east of U.S. 101 in the south end of town, is its modern competitor.

Festivals and Events

Lincoln City calls itself the kite capital of the world, pointing to its position midway between the pole and the equator, which gives the area predictable wind patterns. The town holds not one but two kite fiestas at the D River Wayside each year. The summer **Kite Festival** (541/994-3070 or 800/452-2151) takes place the last weekend in June; the fall festival is held the second weekend in October. The event is famous for giant spin socks, some as long as 150 feet.

SHOPPING

To sample the work of area artists, check out the **Ryan Gallery** (4270 N. U.S. 101, 541/994-5391, www.ryanartgallery.com, 10am-5pm daily). South of town at Salishan, the **Lawrence Gallery** (7755 U.S. 101 N., 541/764-2318, www.lawrencegallery.net, 10am-5pm daily) is a high-end gallery that's lots of fun to visit.

With some 65 shops, the **Tanger Outlet Center** (1500 SE East Devils Lake Rd., 541/996-5000), near the south end of town, is the largest outlet mall on the Oregon coast and has become something of a regional destination. Shops here include the ones you'd expect—Coach, Chico's, Eddie Bauer—plus the Oregon-based **Pendleton Woolen Mills** (541/994-2496, www.pendleton-usa.com).

Northwest Winds (130 SE U.S. 101, 541/994-1004) sells and repairs kites just across the highway from the D River Wayside, Lincoln City's kite-flying hub.

ACCOMMODATIONS

Lincoln City has more hotel rooms than any other coastal Oregon city. There are plenty to choose from, and many are very similar—basic hotel rooms within walking distance of the beach. However, there are some distinctions. Unless severely constrained by budget, one would not purposefully choose to stay on the east side of U.S. 101, necessitating an unpleasant fording of that great vehicular river just to walk to the beach, so, with one exception (Salishan), all the following hotels are on the beach side of the highway. Also, just because a hotel is new doesn't mean that it's preferred over older models. Many vintage hotels and motels have the best locations, and their slightly worn-in atmosphere is perfect for a summer holiday.

$100-150

The **Ester Lee** (3803 SW U.S. 101, 541/996-3606 or 888/996-3606, www.esterlee.com, $104-119) is a decades-old family motel complex, with some cottages and motel units on a bluff above miles of beachfront. All rooms have ocean views and fireplaces; some have kitchens and hot tubs. Pets are allowed in some of the cottage units, most of which have kitchens and fireplaces. It's not a fancy place, but it's clean and pleasant, with a great location and a good value.

The **Siletz Bay Lodge** (1012 SW 51st St., 541/996-6111 or 888/430-2100, www.siletz-baylodge.com, $128-148), on the north end of Siletz Bay on a driftwood-strewn beach, is a family-friendly and wheelchair-accessible (with elevators) lodging in a location ideal for bird-watching and viewing seals. About half of the standard rooms of this older hotel have balconies, with delightful views of the bay and the sunset over Salishan Spit. In-room amenities include microwaves, refrigerators, and coffeemakers, and a continental breakfast is offered.

A small oceanfront luxury hotel near the popular D River Wayside, the **Shearwater Inn** (120 NW Inlet Ct., 541/994-4121 or 800/869-8069, www.theshearwaterinn.com, $149-279) offers 30 units with balconies and gas fireplaces. Guests meet in the lobby every afternoon to sample Oregon wine. The hotel provides concierge and massage services and a continental breakfast, and accepts pets. The building is also wheelchair accessible.

A landmark that has had a recent makeover is the **Surftides Inn** (2945 NW Jetty Ave., 541/994-2191 or 800/452-2159, www.surftidesinn.com, $149-249 for updated oceanview rooms), a large complex hugging the beach at the northern edge of Lincoln City.

All of the oceanfront guest rooms have balconies, and most have fireplaces. All rooms include a small refrigerator, microwave oven, and coffeemaker, as well as cable TV with a DVD player. The inn has an indoor pool, a decent restaurant, a lounge, and meeting rooms. Prices vary by view; ask about partial or no-view rooms for up to 30 percent in savings. Pets are accepted in some rooms.

On the bluff above the beach, with fine views and easy access to the sand, **Sea Horse Oceanfront Lodging** (2039 NW Harbor Dr., 541/994-2101 or 800/662-2101, www.seahorse-motel.com, $129-249) has a dizzying selection of lodging options, from simple motel rooms to cottages, houses, and two- and three-bedroom units, all in an extensive and quiet oceanfront compound. While it's a bit hard to generalize, most rooms have kitchens, some have fireplaces, and all guests are welcome at the breakfast bar, indoor pool, and outdoor hot tub, which overlooks the beach. There are a handful of discounted partial or no-view rooms available. This friendly and venerable operation is one of the reasons Lincoln City is so popular with families.

Another good spot on the north end of Siletz Bay in Lincoln City's historic Taft area is the **Looking Glass Inn** (861 SW 51 St., 541/996-3996 or 800/843-4940, www.lookingglass-inn.com, $114-159), an attractive place that would be quiet and tucked away if it weren't for the busy Mo's restaurant just across the road. Most rooms have kitchenettes, and most are dog-friendly.

Close to the beach at the north end of town, **Brey House B&B** (3725 NW Keel Ave., 541/994-7123, www.breyhouse.com, $109-159) is one of the oldest bed-and-breakfast inns on the Oregon coast, a three-story Cape Cod-style home built in 1940 with four bedrooms, all with private baths and entrances. The excellent breakfast is served in a light-filled room overlooking the ocean. Rooms are for adults only.

$150-200

More a small boutique hotel than the typical

sprawling motel complex that typifies Lincoln City, ★ **Starfish Manor Hotel** (2735 NW Inlet Ave., 541/996-9300 or 800/972-6155, www.onthebeachfront.com, $179-399) has just 17 oceanfront guest rooms and suites perched above the beach. All units have large ocean-view whirlpool tubs, fireplaces, oceanfront decks, kitchenettes, tasteful furnishings, and fine linens. Some units have two bedrooms. The Starfish is in a quiet part of town, perfect for a romantic getaway. The folks who own the Starfish have two other small boutique hotels with even more upscale suites; see the Starfish website for links.

A longtime Lincoln City motel, the **Coho Oceanfront Lodge** (1635 NW Harbor Ave., 541/994-3684 or 800/848-7006, www.thecoholodge.com, $175-220), has undergone a multimillion-dollar renovation; guest rooms have a sleek and sophisticated modern look. A DVD library, indoor pool, hot tub, and sauna are available for guests to use; pets are allowed in some rooms.

Over $200

If you've been fantasizing about rolling out of bed, slipping on your robe and walking out—coffee in hand—onto a semiprivate stretch of beach, then the **Inn at Spanish Head** (4009 SW U.S. 101, 541/996-2161 or 800/452-8127, www.spanishhead.com, $225-349) may be your best bet. Oregon's only resort hotel right on the beach, the inn takes its place—large and looming—against the backdrop of rugged cliffs. Whether a suite, studio, or bedroom unit, every room has an ocean view. On-site amenities include Fathoms, the 10th-floor restaurant-bar, a fireplace lounge, meeting rooms, a heated outdoor pool, saunas, a spa, and an exercise room.

When asked to choose *the* place to stay on the Oregon coast, many Oregonians would select the ★ **Salishan Spa and Golf Resort** (7760 N. U.S. 101, Gleneden Beach, 541/764-3600 or 800/452-2300, www.salishan.com, $219-292), a few miles south of Lincoln City.

While there are distant Siletz Bay views, Salishan isn't a beachfront resort, but most folks quickly learn to appreciate the peace of the forest and the golf course. This paradigm shift is facilitated by art and landscape architecture that convey the vision of John Gray, who built Salishan and such other Pacific Northwest properties as Skamania Lodge (on the Washington side of the Columbia Gorge) and Sunriver (south of Bend) from native materials with respect for the surrounding environment.

Even if you don't stay here, the grounds and facilities are worth a look. The art gallery is free and features works by top Oregon artists; also check out master woodcarver Leroy Setziol's bas-relief panels in the dining room. In addition to the recreational and aesthetic appeal of the resort, the dining room contributes to Salishan's lofty reputation. The forested trails behind the golf course showcase the rainforested foothills of the Coast Range and the waterfowl near Siletz Bay. Across the street, the Salishan Marketplace features first-rate galleries and a good bookstore, Allegory Books.

In high season, Salishan attracts well-heeled nature lovers, corporate expense-account clientele, folks enjoying a special occasion, and serious golfers. You'll also find everyday folks and seminar attendees on winter weekend specials at half the summertime rates. Ask about multiday packages for big savings on your room rate.

Vacation Rentals

To rent vacation homes throughout Lincoln County, contact the **Lincoln City Visitor and Convention Bureau** (800/452-2151, www.oregoncoast.org), or try **Pacific Retreats** (541/994-4833 or 800/473-4833, www.pacificretreats.com), which features a selection of vacation home rentals.

Camping

Devils Lake State Recreation Area (1452 NE 6th St., 541/994-2002 information, 800/452-5687 reservations, www.reserveamerica.com, $21 tents, $29-31 RVs, $54 yurts, $6 hiker-biker) is the main public campground in Lincoln City, with 54 tent sites, 28 RV sites with full hookups, 10 yurts, and a hiker/biker camp. This campground is right in town, just off U.S. 101 at the northeast end of town, so it's hardly a quiet wilderness retreat, but it does provide easy access to swimming or boating on Devils Lake.

The **Salmon River RV Park** (6029 Salmon River Hwy., 541/994-3116, www.salmonriver-rvp.com, $20 tents, $20-30 RVs) is a good spot for anglers; it's on the Salmon River near the town of Otis. The **Lincoln City KOA** (5298 NE Park Ln., 541/994-2961 or 800/562-3316, www.koa.com, $27 tents, $37-41 RVs, $65 cabins) is also just a little ways inland, near the northeast corner of Devils Lake. At the south end of town, **Coyote Rock** (1676 Siletz Hwy., 541/996-6824, www.coyote-rock.com, $21 tents, $27-38 RVs, $46 "tree house" cabins) has a nice setting where the Siletz River meets its bay. All of these campgrounds, including the state park, have showers.

FOOD

Lincoln City offers many dining options, most of them very busy and family-dining focused. There are several fine dining and ethnic options, however, and the general quality of food is high.

American

If you're en route to the wine country or the Willamette Valley or just want a respite from resort traffic, a place that appeals to everybody is ★ **Otis Cafe** (1259 Salmon River Hwy., 541/994-2813, www.otiscafe.com, 7am-3pm Mon.-Wed., 7am-8pm Thurs.-Sun., $5-18), at the Otis Junction on Highway 18 five miles northeast of Lincoln City. Innovative variations on American road food have earned the Otis a devoted following (stop by to read the enthusiastic review by a satisfied *New York Times* reporter). Long waits on the porch are the rule on weekend mornings, though it's worth it for thick-crusted molasses bread, buttermilk waffles, and hash browns under a crust of melted Rogue Valley white

cheddar. Even if it's not mealtime, stop in for a slice of outstanding pie.

Two Native American gaming casinos are located within 25 miles of one another and offer dining alternatives to the coast-bound traveler. Both **Chinook Winds** (1777 NW 44th St., 541/966-5825 or 888/244-6665), and **Spirit Mountain** (21700 SW Salmon River Hwy., Grand Ronde, 800/760-7977), about 25 miles east of Lincoln City on Highway 22 in Grand Ronde, have many dining options. Each offers generous full buffets for breakfast, lunch, and dinner, and both have full-service fine dining restaurants offering moderate to expensive ($18-35) prices. Both casinos have nightly buffets in the $15-20 range. Chinook Winds' ocean views are also worth noting. Both casinos have outlets for 24-hour dining.

If you're looking for the perfect, homey spot for a traditional breakfast, the **Nelscott Café** (3237 SW Highway 101, 541/994-6100, 7am-3pm Thurs.-Mon., $6-12) might be what you're looking for. The breakfast standards such as omelets and French toast are very well prepared, and there are good burgers and sandwiches for lunch. This is a small place, and can get busy on weekends.

Asian

Jasmine Thai Restaurant (1437 NW U.S. 101, 541/994-2022, 11am-3pm and 4pm-9pm Mon.-Thurs, 11am-3pm and 4pm-10pm Fri., noon-10 Sat., noon-9pm Sun., $9-14) serves well-prepared traditional Thai cuisine. An extensive menu includes a number of seafood specialties, as well as daily specials that take advantage of seasonal vegetables and other local produce.

In the outlet mall, **Momiji** (1500 SE Devils Lake Rd., 541/996-8886, 10am-9pm daily, sushi rolls $4-14) offers both Chinese and Japanese cooking, but the reason this restaurant is so popular is the excellent sushi rolls and sashimi. You're welcome to watch at the bar as the sushi is made, eat family-style in the restaurant, or get your order to go.

Pacific Northwest

Some of coastal Oregon's top dining experiences are found just south of Lincoln City. The reasonable prices at the Salishan Lodge's **Sun Room Restaurant** (7760 N. U.S. 101, Gleneden Beach, www.salishan.com, 6:30am-10pm daily, $11-23) are a welcome surprise. This casual restaurant might be less elaborate and half the price of Salishan's signature **Dining Room** (5pm-9:30pm daily, $28-59), but its cuisine comes from the same kitchen. While prime steaks and other meats are the specialty in the Dining Room, fresh local seafood, such as halibut, crab, scallops, and salmon, are also featured. The wine list here is one of the largest in the state.

The ★ **Blackfish Cafe** (2733 NW U.S. 101, 541/996-1007, www.blackfishcafe.com, 11:30am-close Wed.-Mon., $12-28) is a great find. Presided over by former Salishan Resort executive chef Rob Pounding, who has longstanding relationships with local farmers, anglers, and mushroom foragers, the Blackfish Cafe is dedicated to fairly priced and delicious regional cooking. The emphasis is on what's fresh, homegrown, and creative, such as grilled Willamette Valley pork brisket rubbed with coriander and cumin and troll-caught chinook salmon with fennel-lime butter. There is no shortage of humbler fare, either, such as the self-proclaimed best clam chowder on the coast, Pacific City dory-caught fish-and-chips, and amazing fish tacos.

The **Bay House** (5911 SW U.S. 101, 541/996-3222, www.thebayhouse.org, 5:30pm-close Wed.-Sun., $27-40) combines oceanfront views with exquisite Pacific Northwest cuisine. Moscovy duck breast is served with French lentils and carrot-cardamom puree. A $68 five-course tasting menu is available, but must be ordered by everyone at the table. For a more casual and less expensive light dinner, eat from the small plates menu in the lounge. In either dining area, oenophiles will want to look at the wine list, praised by *Wine Spectator*.

A half-mile south of Salishan (five miles equidistant from Depoe Bay and Lincoln City) is a Gleneden Beach eatery with considerable appeal. The **Side Door Café** (6675 Gleneden Beach Loop, 541/764-3825, http://edenhall.com, 11:30am-9pm Wed.-Mon., $20-31) combines a gourmet restaurant with a musical venue. The airy yet cozy-feeling dining room features a menu where honey mustard and herb-rubbed salmon with marionberry glaze exemplifies the offerings.

Seafood

If coastal restaurants are eating a hole in your wallet, there's always tried-and-true **Mo's** (860 SW 51st St., 541/996-2535, www.moschowder.com, 10:30am-9pm Sun.-Thurs., 10:30am-10pm Fri., 8am-9pm Sat., $4-15). As at all Mo's locations, the view is great, and the seafood more than serviceable.

The chowder is a little tastier at the **Dory Cove Restaurant** (2981 SW U.S. 101, 541/557-4000, www.dorycove.com, 8am-8pm Sun.-Thurs., 8am-9pm Fri.-Sat., $5-23), but the views from this simple restaurant are out onto the highway. Rest assured that the focus is on the food—good old-fashioned deep-fried and sautéed seafood main courses (halibut fish-and-chips are recommended) and homemade pies.

Kyllo's (1110 NW 1st Court, 541/994-3179, www.kyllosrestaurant.com, 11:30am-9pm daily, $9-25) specializes in broiled, sautéed, and baked seafood, plus excellent pasta, sandwiches, and homemade desserts served with Oregon microbrews and wines. The restaurant is visible from U.S. 101 as you drive by the D River Wayside. With views of the water on all sides, this restaurant is a good place to linger, though waits can be long in the evening since no reservations are taken.

Brewpubs

The **Lighthouse Brew Pub** (4157 U.S. 101 N., 541/994-7238, 11am-10pm Sun.-Thurs., 11am-midnight Fri.-Sat., $9-20) is a welcome rehash of the successful McMenamin's formula. Just look for a lighthouse replica in a parking lot on the northwest side of U.S. 101 across from McDonald's. Pizza, burgers, sandwiches, and salads can be washed down with McMenamins' own ales as well as hard cider and wine.

The venerable **Roadhouse 101** (4649 SW U.S. 101, 541/994-7729, www.roadhouse101. com, 11:30am-9pm Sun.-Thurs., 11:30am-1:30am Fri.-Sat., $8-20) has added Rusty Truck Brewing to its already rockin' establishment, with a selection of house-made ales and a "south of the border" lager. The Roadhouse features hearty American-style food, frequent live music, and a lively crowd ready to party.

INFORMATION

The **Lincoln City Visitor Center** (540 NE U.S. 101, 541/994-3302 or 800/452-2151, www.oregoncoast.org, 10am-4pm Mon.-Sat.) has a website that's full of helpful information.

The **Central Oregon Coast Association** (541/265-2064 or 800/767-2064, www.coast-visitor.com) also maintains a useful website with details on Lincoln City and the rest of coastal Lincoln County.

GETTING THERE AND AROUND

Lincoln County Transit (541/265-4900, www.co.lincoln.or.us/transit) buses stop in town for service Monday-Saturday. The line goes as far south as Yachats and does not run on major holidays.

Peak traffic times in Lincoln City can result in 25,000 cars a day crawling through town. As an alternative to rush hour on U.S. 101, you could try detouring on NE West Devils Lake Road or NE East Devils Lake Road, which bypass the worst congestion.

Depoe Bay

In his classic travel tale *Blue Highways,* William Least Heat-Moon characterized Depoe Bay thusly:

> Depoe Bay used to be a picturesque fishing village; now it was just picturesque. The fish houses, but for one seasonal company, were gone, the fleet gone, and in their stead had come sport fishing boats and souvenir ashtray and T-shirt shops.

To be fair, tourists have come here since the establishment of the town. In fact, for all intents and purposes, the town didn't really exist until the completion of the Roosevelt Highway (U.S. 101) in 1927, which opened the area up to car travelers. Prior to that time, the area had been occupied mainly by a few members of the Siletz people. One worked at the U.S. Army depot and called himself Charlie Depot. The town was named after him, eventually taking on the current spelling.

Regardless of what you think of the busy commercial strip and the enormous time-share resort along the highway, the scenic appeal of Depoe's location is impossible to ignore. The rocky outer bay, flanked by headlands to the north and south, is pierced by a narrow channel through the basalt cliffs leading to the inner harbor. It's home to an active sportfishing fleet as well as the whale-watching charters that have earned Depoe Bay its distinction as the whale-watching capital of the state.

SIGHTS AND RECREATION
The Bayfront and Harbor

Depoe Bay is situated along a truly beautiful coastline that cannot be fully appreciated from the highway. A quarter-mile-long seawall and promenade invite a stroll. For a panorama of the harbor, continue along the sidewalks across the gracefully arching concrete bridge, designed by Conde McCullough and built in 1927. Other nice perspectives are offered from residential streets west of U.S. 101; try Ellingson Street, south of the bridge, and Sunset Street, at the north end of the bay. Two "spouting horns," natural blowholes in the rocks north of the harbor entrance, can send plumes of spray 60 feet into the air when the tide and waves are right.

East of the bridge is Depoe Bay's claim to international fame, the world's smallest navigable natural harbor. This boat basin is also exceptional because it's a harbor within a harbor. This topography is the result of wave action cutting into the basalt over eons until a 50-foot passageway leading to a six-acre inland lagoon was created. In addition to whale-watching, folks congregate on the bridge between the ocean and the harbor to watch boats maneuver into the enclosure. Depoe Bay's harbor was scenic enough to be selected as the site from which Jack Nicholson commandeered a yacht for his mental patient crew in the film *One Flew Over the Cuckoo's Nest*.

Whale Watching Center

Stop in at the **Whale Watching Center** (119 SW U.S. 101, 541/765-3304, www.oregonstate-parks.org, 9am-5pm daily summer, 10am-4pm Wed.-Sun. winter, free) where volunteers can help you spot whales and answer your

questions about them. The center, right on the seawall, is an ideal viewing spot. Peak viewing times are mid-December-January, when whales are migrating south; late March-early June, when they're traveling north (mothers and babies generally come later in the season); and mid-July-early November, when resident whales feed off the coast. The least likely times to see whales from the central Oregon coast are mid-November-mid-December and mid-January-mid-March.

Whale, Sea Life & Shark Museum

The private **Whale, Sea Life & Shark Museum** (234 S. U.S. 101, 541/912-6734, www.oregonwhales.com, 9am-5pm daily summer, 10am-4pm Wed.-Sun. winter, $5 adults, $3 children ages 4-10) on the harbor side of the highway, 100 feet south of the bridge, is run in conjunction with whale-watching tours in Zodiac craft. Carrie Newell, a marine biologist, runs both the museum and the tours ($30 for one hour, $50 for two hours). The museum, which is free with a whale-watching trip, features models of marine mammals, a large collection of shark jaws, and lots of photos of whales.

This fellow awaits outside the Whale Watching Center.

Boiler Bay State Scenic Viewpoint

Boiler Bay, half a mile north of Depoe Bay, is so named because of the boiler left from the 1910 wreck of the *J. Marhoffer.* The ship caught fire three miles offshore and drifted into the bay. The remains of the boiler are visible at low tide. This rock-rimmed bay is a favorite spot for rock fishing, birding, and whale-watching. A trail leads down to some excellent tidepools.

Whale Cove

This picturesque bay half a mile south of Depoe Bay has been scooped out of the sandstone bluffs. The tranquility of this calendar photo come to life is deceptive. There's considerable evidence to suggest that this tiny embayment—and not California's Marin County—was the site of Francis Drake's 1579 landing, but the jury is still out. During Prohibition, bootleggers used the protected cove as a clandestine port.

Rocky Creek State Scenic Viewpoint (800/551-6949, www.oregonstateparks.org) overlooks Whale Cove. There are picnic tables, and it's a good spot for whale-watching, but there's no beach access.

Drake's Lost Harbor?

In 1996 the media exploded with stories raising the possibility that the tiny hamlet of Whale Cove, two miles south of Depoe Bay, could supplant Plymouth Rock as the birthplace of a nation. Rotting timbers from what is theorized to have been a stockade built by Sir Francis Drake in 1579 were unearthed in an area where stories have long circulated that the English privateer made landfall.

Over the years, these notions have been fueled by several tantalizing pieces of evidence: an unsigned ship's log from Drake's voyage in a museum in England that identified 44 degrees north latitude—the same as Whale Cove—as a landing site; an English shilling dating from 1560 found on the central Oregon coast in 1982; a photo from the 1930s showing a local resident with a distinctly English sword he unearthed; and a ship's cutlass found in Newport in the early 19th century bearing the markings of a 16th-century English arsenal. Moreover, excavations of a nearby Indian village thought to have been buried in 1600 turned up brass items, blades, and Venetian beads.

An amateur British historian, Bob Ward, makes a compelling case for Whale Cove as the place where Drake spent five weeks in the summer of 1579. In his flagship *Golden Hynde,* the only one of his five-ship fleet to survive the stormy straits around Cape Horn, Drake harassed Spanish settlements throughout Latin America and plundered Spanish ships wherever he met them. Sailing west from Mexico on its return to England via the Cape of Good Hope, the treasure-laden *Golden Hynde* was beset by storms, and Drake had to retreat to land to make repairs. Conventional history has held that he made landfall around San Francisco, most likely on the Marin County coast.

Ward, however, believes that Drake continued his voyage farther north and sailed into the Strait of Juan de Fuca, thinking he had found the fabled Northwest Passage. Turning around before he realized his mistake, Drake then headed south down the Washington and Oregon coasts, where he found a sandy cove in which to drop anchor and make repairs before the long journey home.

On Drake's return to England after four years at sea, news of his exploits were suppressed. Queen Elizabeth confiscated the logs and charts, and it would be 10 years before an official account of the voyage would be published. Then, Drake's New Albion was described as being around 38 degrees north latitude (in northern California), in an attempt, Ward believes, to fool the Spanish into thinking the Northwest Passage was much farther south.

After Elizabeth's death in 1603, however, new charts began to appear that placed the landing site much farther north, and early 17th-century charts show a small shallow bay labeled Novus Albionis (New Albion) that is an uncannily accurate depiction of Whale Cove.

Since the initial blizzard of publicity, there has been no final word from the archaeologists and historians involved in corroborating these claims. Because most history books have placed New Albion, Drake's fabled lost settlement, near San Francisco, researchers will not be too quick to claim otherwise without definitive research.

Otter Crest Loop

The rocky bluffs of this coastal stretch take on an even more dramatic aspect as you leave the highway at the **Otter Crest Loop,** a winding three-mile section of the old Coast Highway, two miles south of Depoe Bay. The northernmost part of the loop, down as far as Cape Foulweather, is one-way southbound, with a generous bike lane.

From atop **Cape Foulweather,** the visibility can extend 40 miles on a clear day. The view south to Yaquina Head and its lighthouse is a photographer's fantasy of headlands, coves, and offshore monoliths. Bronze plaques in the parking lot tell of Captain Cook naming the 500-foot-high headland during a bout with storm-tossed seas on March 7, 1778.

The Lookout (milepost 131.5 U.S. 101, 541/765-2270, www.lookoutgiftshop.com, 9am-5pm daily), a gift shop on the north side of the promontory, is a good place to buy Japanese fishing floats for a few bucks. The million-dollar view from inside the shop is easily one of the most spectacular windows on the ocean to be found anywhere.

Another mile south, in the hamlet of **Otter Rock,** you'll find another of the Oregon coast's several diabolically named natural features, the **Devil's Punchbowl.** The urn-like sandstone formation, filled with swirling water, has been sculpted by centuries of waves flooding into what had been a cave until its roof collapsed. The inexorable process continues today, thanks to the ebb and flow of the Pacific through two openings in the cauldron wall. A state park viewpoint gives you a ringside seat for this frothy confrontation between rock and tide. When the water recedes, you can see purple sea urchins and starfish in the tidepools of the **Marine Gardens** 100 feet to the north.

To the south of the Punchbowl vantage point are picnic tables and a wooden walkway down to the beach. Close by in tiny Otter Rock, you'll find a small **Mo's** restaurant (122 1st St., 541/765-2442, 11am-8pm Mon.-Sat., 11am-6pm Sun., $4-16). Next door, the **Flying Dutchman Winery** (915 1st St., 541/765-2553, 11am-7pm daily) makes limited batches of handcrafted wines from grapes grown in southern Oregon and the Willamette Valley (grapes won't ripen on the coast).

Back on U.S. 101, a mile's drive south brings you to Beverly Beach State Park.

Fishing and Whale-Watching Charters

With the ocean minutes from Depoe Bay's port, catching a salmon or seeing a whale is possible as soon as you leave the harbor. Most charter operators here offer both fishing and whale-watching excursions. Bottom-fishing trips average $75 for a five-hour run; salmon fishing (available only when salmon season is open) are about $130 for a seven- or eight-hour day; and whale-watching excursions run $15-30 per person per hour.

Dockside Charters (541/765-2545 or 800/733-8915, docksidedepoebay.com) offers 1.5-hour whale-watching trips aboard its 50-foot excursion boat for $18 per adult and one-hour trips on Zodiacs for $25 per adult. **Tradewinds Charters** (541/765-2345 or 800/445-8730, www.tradewindscharters.com) hosts one- and two-hour trips December-May. Rates run $20-35 per adult.

Surfing

If you're itching to actually get into the water and catch a few waves, the beach at **Otter Rock,** a few miles south of Depoe Bay, is a good place to surf. Park in the lot at Devil's Punchbowl and walk down the long flight of steps to the beach, which is relatively protected and has a large area where beginners tend to hang out. (There's also a section that gets bigger waves and better surfers.)

ENTERTAINMENT AND EVENTS

The **Depoe Bay Classic Wooden Boat Show, Crab Feed, and Ducky Derby** is held the third weekend in April. Several dozen wooden craft, both restored and newly constructed vessels, including kayaks, skiffs, dinghies, and larger fishing boats, are displayed in the harbor and the adjacent Depoe Bay City Park. Rowing races, boatbuilding workshops, crab races, and other activities are scheduled. The big Crab Feed, held 10am-5pm both Saturday and Sunday, sees some 1,500 pounds of crab plus side dishes devoured at the Community Hall; it costs $12-18 for a crab dinner. The Ducky Derby is a raffle in which you purchase "tickets" in the form of rubber duckies that race down the harbor's feeder stream vying for prizes. For more information, contact the **Depoe Bay Chamber of Commerce** (223 SW U.S. 101, 541/765-2889 or 877/485-8348, www.depoe-baychamber.org).

The **Fleet of Flowers** happens each Memorial Day in the harbor to honor those lost at sea and in military service. Thousands come to witness a blanket of blossoms cast upon the waters.

The **Depoe Bay Salmon Bake** takes place on the third Saturday of September (10am-5pm) at Depoe Bay City Park, flanking the rear of the boat basin. Some 3,000 pounds of fresh ocean fish are caught, cooked Native American-style on alder stakes over an open fire and served with all the trimmings, to be savored to the accompaniment of live entertainment. The cost is $20 adults, $10 children. It always seems to rain on the day of this event, but that's life on the Oregon coast.

ACCOMMODATIONS

Lodgings in popular Depoe Bay require advance reservations on most weekends and holidays.

The **Inn at Arch Rock** (70 NW Sunset St., 541/765-2560 or 800/767-1835, www.innatarchrock.com, $89-309) is a cluster of white clapboard buildings that overlook Depoe Bay from a cliff-top perch at the north end of town. Most rooms have ocean views and are in the $140-200 range; a non-oceanview room goes for much less. Pets are permitted in several rooms.

Harbor Lights Inn (235 SE Bay View Ave., 541/765-2322 or 800/228-0448, www.

theharborlightsinn.com, $105-189), a small inn overlooking the harbor, has the distinct advantage of being distant from U.S. 101. Perched above the marina and the Coast Guard station, this homey inn with recently updated rooms affords views of sea otters, ducks, and geese while the whale-watching and fishing boats come and go. All rooms have a harbor view; rates include a hot breakfast. Small pets are allowed with prior approval.

The ★ **Channel House** (35 Ellingson St., 541/765-2140 or 800/447-2140, www.channel-house.com, rooms $140-330) features both standard B&B rooms and spacious suites boasting expansive views of the ocean, private decks with outdoor whirlpool tubs (in the majority of rooms), fireplaces, plush robes, and other amenities. This bluff-top B&B (there isn't a beach below, just miles of ocean and surrounding cliffs) may not look prepossessing from the outside, but inside, the place is all windows and angles—imagine *Architectural Digest* in a nautical theme. This is one of the best places on the Oregon coast to commune with whales, passing boats, winter storms, and the setting sun. A continental breakfast with tasty baked goods in an ocean-side dining area is included in the rates.

About a mile south of town, perched above scenic Whale Cove, find the boxy new **Whale Cove Inn** (2345 S. U.S. 101, 541/765-4300 or 800/628-3409, www.whalecoveinn.com, $425-825), a small boutique hotel that's a sister hotel to the Channel House. Here you can lounge in the hot tub on your private deck or on the Tempur-Pedic mattress in your bedroom alcove (all accommodations are in spacious suites; the top-end suites sleep six). Fine dining is available in the hotel restaurant, Restaurant Beck. This is as high-end as the Oregon coast gets; kids 16 and older are welcome, but pets are not.

About three miles south of Depoe Bay, at one of the most scenic spots on the central coast, is the **Inn at Otter Crest** (301 Otter Crest Loop, Otter Rock, 541/765-2111 or 800/452-2101, www.innatottercrest.com, $120-329), a large condo resort perched near the sandstone bluffs at the ocean's edge. Hotel rooms have a king or two queen-size beds, a refrigerator, coffeemaker, and private deck with picture windows. Studios have a queen-size Murphy bed (or a regular bed), full kitchen, fireplace, and dining area; larger one- and two-bedroom suites are also available. The least expensive rooms have a forest view.

The **Surfrider Resort** (3115 NW U.S. 101, 541/764-2311 or 800/662-2378, www.surfriderresort.com, $129-145) is a few miles north of Depoe Bay on picturesque Fogarty Creek's rockbound coast. Oceanfront suites and rooms have decks; some feature whirlpool tubs, kitchens, and fireplaces. A good restaurant, an indoor pool, and midweek specials are also noteworthy.

FOOD

Of Depoe Bay's several restaurants, **Tidal Raves** (279 NW U.S. 101, 541/765-2995, www.tidalraves.com, 11am-9pm daily, $12-25) has the best combination of flavor, views, and casual ambience. A number of seafood dishes take on an Asian twist, such as Thai barbecued shrimp or udon noodles with sesame-crusted scallops. A pasta dish features crab, shrimp, lingcod, snapper, and more on a bed of linguine with pesto. The Dungeness crab casserole is also noteworthy.

★ **Restaurant Beck** (2345 S. U.S. 101, 541/765-3220, restaurantbeck.com, 5pm-9pm daily, $27-30), in the Whale Cove Inn south of town, is Depoe Bay's only really elegant restaurant. It has a great view and excellent food, much of which originates on nearby farms. Be prepared to experiment: Pork belly confit and pickled sea beans are paired with miso ice cream; king salmon is served with popcorn, corn puree, and beet tops. Seasonal ingredients figure prominently; in June, Rainier cherries pair with ancho chilies atop a lamb loin.

INFORMATION

On the east side of the highway, opposite the seawall, the **Depoe Bay Chamber of Commerce** (223 SW U.S. 101, 541/765-2889 or 877/485-8348, www.depoebaychamber.org) offers literature about the town and the central coast in general.

GETTING THERE

On weekdays and Saturday, **Lincoln County Transit** (541/265-4900, www.co.lincoln.or.us/transit) runs buses four times daily, north to Lincoln City and south to Yachats.

the Inn at Otter Crest from Cape Foulweather

Newport

In January 1852, a storm grounded the schooner *Juliet* near Yaquina (pronounced yah-KWIN-nah) Bay, where her captain and crew were stranded for two months. When they finally made their way inland to the Willamette Valley, they reported their discovery of an abundance of tiny sweet-tasting oysters in the bay. Within a decade, commercial oyster farms were established—the first major impetus to growth and settlement in Newport. The tasty morsels, a Pacific Northwest species called Olympias, that delighted diners in San Francisco and at New York City's Waldorf-Astoria Hotel were almost harvested to extinction, but the oyster industry continued by introducing Japanese species. Dedicated oyster farmers have recently reestablished Olympias in Oregon waters. They can now be found in select restaurants around the state. They are often called Olys and have a snappy, briny flavor.

In 2011, Newport (pop. 10,000) became the National Oceanic and Atmospheric Administration's Pacific Marine Operations Center, managing a fleet of research ships. During the summer, these ships are usually out at sea conducting oceanographic research, but when they're in port, the large white vessels are easy to spot in the harbor.

The port also bustles with the activity of Oregon's largest commercial fishing fleet and second-largest recreational fleet. Factories to process *surimi* (a fish paste popular in Japan) and whiting have provided jobs, and a state-of-the-art aquarium that once housed Keiko the whale (from *Free Willy*) brings in the tourists. Wildlife observation facilities and access to tidal pools north of town at Yaquina Head make this park a highlight of the coast. The shops, galleries, and restaurants along Newport's historic bay front, together with the Performing Arts Center and quieter charm of Nye Beach, keep up a tourism tradition that goes back to when this town was the "honeymoon capital of Oregon."

SIGHTS
★ Oregon Coast Aquarium

There are 6,000 miles of water between the Oregon coast and Japan—the largest stretch of open ocean on earth. You can hear *our* side of the story at the **Oregon Coast Aquarium** (2820 SE Ferry Slip Rd., 541/867-3474, www.aquarium.org, 9am-6pm daily Memorial Day weekend-Labor Day weekend, 10am-5pm daily Labor Day-Memorial Day, closed Christmas Day, $19.95 adults, $17.95 seniors and youth 13-17, $12.95 children ages 3-12), one of the state's most popular attractions.

One of the gems of the aquarium is Passages of the Deep, a 200-foot-long acrylic tunnel offering 360-degree underwater views in three diverse habitats, from Orford Reef to Halibut Flats to Open Sea, where you're surrounded by free-swimming sharks. The jellyfish exhibit is a surprising highlight; it showcases several dozen kinds of jellyfish in an almost psychedelic display. If jellyfish aren't weird enough for you, check out the Oddwater exhibit, which looks at bizarre adaptations made by sea creatures.

At the large Jetty exhibit, visitors look through a window into a 35,000-gallon tank to watch white sturgeon and coho and chinook salmon swimming among large basalt boulders that simulate a coastal jetty, such as these anadromous fish might pass through in the wild on their upriver journey to their spawning grounds.

Of the several hundred species of Pacific Northwest fish, birds, and mammals on display in the rest of the facility, don't miss the sea otters, wolf eel, leopard sharks, lion's mane jellyfish, and tufted puffins. Kids will enjoy the sea cave with simulated wave action and resident octopus. Simulations of indigenous

Newport

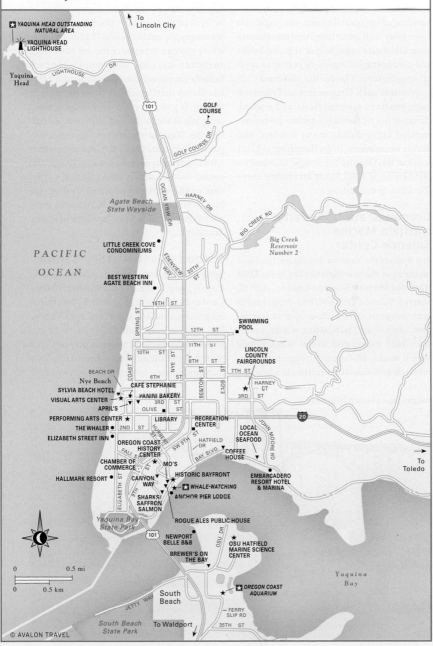

To Lincoln City

YAQUINA HEAD OUTSTANDING NATURAL AREA
YAQUINA HEAD LIGHTHOUSE

Yaquina Head

LIGHTHOUSE DR

101

GOLF COURSE

GOLF COURSE DR

OCEAN VIEW DR

HARNEY DR

BIG CREEK RD

Agate Beach State Wayside

Big Creek Reservoir Number 2

PACIFIC OCEAN

LITTLE CREEK COVE CONDOMINIUMS

EDENVIEW WAY

20TH ST

BEST WESTERN AGATE BEACH INN

SPRING ST

15TH ST

SWIMMING POOL

12TH ST

11TH ST

8TH ST

LINCOLN COUNTY FAIRGROUNDS

10TH ST

COAST ST

NYE ST

7TH ST

HARNEY CT

BEACH DR
Nye Beach
SYLVIA BEACH HOTEL
VISUAL ARTS CENTER
APRIL'S

6TH ST

CAFÉ STEPHANIE
PANINI BAKERY
3RD ST
OLIVE ST

BENTON ST

EADS ST

3RD ST

20

PERFORMING ARTS CENTER
THE WHALER
ELIZABETH STREET INN

2ND ST

HURBERT ST

LIBRARY

RECREATION CENTER

LOCAL OCEAN SEAFOOD

JOHN MOORE RD

To Toledo

OREGON COAST HISTORY CENTER

SW 9TH ST

HATFIELD DR

BAY BLVD

COFFEE HOUSE

CHAMBER OF COMMERCE

FALL ST

MO'S

HISTORIC BAYFRONT

EMBARCADERO RESORT HOTEL & MARINA

HALLMARK RESORT

ELIZABETH ST

CANYON WAY

9TH ST

SHARKS/
SAFFRON SALMON

WHALE-WATCHING
ANCHOR PIER LODGE

ROGUE ALES PUBLIC HOUSE

Yaquina Bay State Park

101

NEWPORT BELLE B&B

OSU DR

BREWER'S ON THE BAY

OSU HATFIELD MARINE SCIENCE CENTER

Yaquina Bay

0   0.5 mi
0   0.5 km

South Beach

JETTY WAY

FERRY SLIP RD

35TH ST

OREGON COAST AQUARIUM

South Beach State Park

To Waldport

© AVALON TRAVEL

ecosystems help visitors immerse themselves in the region's biology.

In addition to gaining a heightened understanding of the coastal biome, you might also come away with something from the museum shop's first-rate collection of regional books and oceanographic tomes, or perhaps a crystal or gemstone. The on-site Mermaid Cafe emphasizes such Oregon fare as Tillamook dairy products, seasonal fruits, and seafood. Advance tickets (available online) are recommended on weekends, major holidays, and during the summer. To get there from U.S. 101 south of the Yaquina Bay Bridge, turn east on OSU Drive or 32nd Street and follow Ferry Slip Road to the parking lot.

Oregon State University Hatfield Marine Science Center

Just south of the Yaquina Bay Bridge, head east on the road that parallels the bay to the **OSU Hatfield Marine Science Center** (2030 SE Marine Science Dr., 541/867-0100, http://hmsc.oregonstate.edu, 10am-5pm daily summer, 10am-4pm Thurs.-Mon. winter, 10am-4pm daily spring and winter break Whale Watch weeks, $5 donation suggested). This research and education facility is a low-key but interesting complement to the very popular Oregon Coast Aquarium, located half a mile south. At the door to greet you is an octopus in an open tank pointing the way to oceanography exhibits and a "hands-on" area, where you can experience the feel of starfish, anemones, and other sea creatures. The back hallway has educational dioramas, and a theater shows marine science films throughout the day. If you proceed left from the octopus tank, you'll see tanks with different sea ecosystems. Beyond the walls of the museum, guided field trips (daily at 11am in summer; a fee is charged) explore estuary, beach, and coastal forest habitats (check with the front desk or the website for details). Perhaps the biggest thrill is watching the octopus eat— it's fed at 1pm each Monday, Thursday, and Saturday.

Oregon Coast History Center

For a glimpse into the rich past of Lincoln County, stop at the **Oregon Coast History Center** (545 SW 9th St., 541/265-7509, http://oregoncoasthistory.org, 11am-4pm Thurs.-Sun. $5 adults and youths, children 12 and under free), which incorporates the Log Cabin Museum and the adjacent Queen Anne-style Burrows House, a former boardinghouse built

Newport has a busy fishing harbor.

in 1895. It's a half-block east of the chamber of commerce on U.S. 101. The logging, farming, pioneer life, and maritime exhibits (particularly Newport shipwrecks) are interesting, but the Siletz baskets and other Native American artifacts steal the show.

Here you can learn the heartbreaking story of the hardships—forced displacement, inadequate housing, insufficient food, and poor medical facilities—that plagued the diverse Native American groups that made up the Confederated Siletz Reservation.

The historical society also runs the **Pacific Maritime & Heritage Center** (333 SE Bay Blvd., 11am-4pm Thurs.-Sun. $5 donation suggested), which occupies a huge old mansion overlooking the Bayfront. Local residents have donated everything from ships' wheels to vintage surfboards to this museum, which is worth visiting for the setting and the building alone.

Bayfront District

Newport's Old Town Bayfront District can be easy to miss if you're not alert. At the north end of the Yaquina Bay Bridge, look for the signs pointing off U.S. 101 that lead you down the hill to Bay Boulevard, the Bayfront's main drag. Alternatively, turn southeast off the highway a few blocks north onto Hurbert Street; this runs into Canyon Way, which ends at Bay Boulevard. On summer weekends, forget about parking anywhere near here unless you arrive early. Spots close by the boulevard can often be found, however, along Canyon Way, the hillside access route to downtown.

Until 1936, ferries shuttled people and vehicles to and from Newport's waterfront. With the completion of the Yaquina Bay Bridge that year, however, traffic bypassed the Old Town area. Commerce and development moved to the highway corridor, and the Bayfront faded in importance. Within the last couple of decades, the pendulum has swung back, and the Bayfront District is now one of Newport's prime attractions, with some of its best restaurants and watering holes, shopping, and tourist facilities.

One of the first things that'll strike you about the Bayfront today is that it's still a working neighborhood, not a sanitized recreation of a real seaport. Chowder houses, galleries, and shops stand shoulder to shoulder with fish-processing plants and canneries, and the air is filled with the cries of fishmongers and the harmonious discord of sea lions and harbor seals. On the waterfront, sport anglers step off charter boats with their catches,

The Bayfront District bustles with restaurants, bars, and fish processing plants.

and vessels laden with everything from wood products to whale-watching tourists ply the bay. Unfortunately, the severe catch limits and cost of equipment make this less of a working port every year. In deference to the Oregon commercial fishers and other endangered species, wall murals on the Bayfront memorialize fishing boats and whales.

Yaquina Bay State Recreation Site

In 1871 a lighthouse was built here on a bluff overlooking the mouth of Yaquina Bay, and the lighthouse keeper, his wife, and seven children moved into the two-story wood-frame structure. It soon became apparent, however, that the location was not ideal, as the light could not be seen by ships approaching the harbor from the north. The station was abandoned after just three years once the nearby light at Yaquina Head was completed. The building was slated for demolition in 1934, when local residents formed the Lincoln County Historical Society to preserve it. In 1997 the government decided to turn Yaquina Bay's beacon back on.

Today, the handsome restored structure and surrounding grounds make up **Yaquina Bay State Recreation Site** (541/574-3129 or 800/551-6949, www.oregonstateparks.org, lighthouse hours noon-4pm daily, free), in a beautiful location at the north end of the Yaquina Bay Bridge. The last wooden lighthouse on the Oregon coast is also the oldest building in Newport. The living quarters, replete with period furnishings, are open to the public. Be sure to ask the volunteers about the resident ghost.

From the parking area, you have an excellent photo op of the bay and the bridge. The park is a good place to have a picnic, or you can descend the trails to the beach and dig for razor clams or hunt for agates and petrified wood.

Nye Beach

The 1890s-era tourism boom that came to Newport's Bayfront spilled over into Nye Beach. In 1891, the city built a wooden sidewalk connecting the two neighborhoods, and soon "summer people" were filling the cedar cottages. In the next century, thanks to an improved river-and-land route from Corvallis, health faddists (who came for hot seawater baths in the sanatorium) and honeymooners soon joined the mix.

A mile north from the Bayfront, to the west of U.S. 101 (look for signs on the highway), this onetime favorite retreat for wealthy Portlanders has undergone a revival in recent years. Rough times and rougher weather had reduced luxurious beach houses here to a cluster of weather-beaten shacks until a performing arts center went up in 1988. On the heels of the development of this first-rate cultural facility, the conversion of a 1910 hotel into a kind of literary hostel encouraged other restorations and plenty of new construction. Culture vultures, beach lovers, and people watchers now flock to Nye Beach, which feels a world away from the Coast Highway commercial strip just a few blocks to the east.

★ Yaquina Head Outstanding Natural Area

Five miles north of Newport, rocky Yaquina Head juts out to sea. Tools dating back 5,000 years have been unearthed at Yaquina Head. Many were made from elk and deer antlers and bone, as well as stone. Clam and mussel shells from middens in the area evidence a diet rich in shellfish for the area's ancient inhabitants.

Today, much of the headland is encompassed in the **Yaquina Head Outstanding Natural Area** (750 NW Lighthouse Dr., 541/574-3100, www.blm.gov, $7 per vehicle), managed by the federal Bureau of Land Management. "Outstanding" is indeed the word for this place; where the pounding ocean meets the land in a series of cliffs and tide pools; a visitor could easily spend several hours exploring all the site has to offer.

At its outer tip stands **Yaquina Head Lighthouse** (guided tours 10am-4pm Thurs.-Tues., weather permitting), the coast's tallest beacon. In the early 1870s, materials intended for construction of a lighthouse several miles north at Otter Crest were mistakenly delivered here. The 93-foot tower began operation in 1873, replacing the poorly located lighthouse south of here at the mouth of Newport's harbor. Walk up the 114 cast-iron steps for a spectacular panorama of the headland and surrounding coast.

Below, an observation deck provides views of seals, sea lions, gray whales, and seabirds. Of the half-dozen varieties of pelagic birds that cluster on Colony Rock—a large monolith in the shallows 200 yards offshore—the tufted puffin is the most colorful. It's sometimes called a sea parrot because of its large yellow-orange bill. Puffins arrive here in April and are most visible early in the day on the rock's grassy patches. The most ubiquitous species are common murres, pigeon guillemots, and cormorants. The murre's white breasts and bellies contrast with their darker bills and elongated backs. The guillemots resemble pigeons with white wing patches and bright red webbed feet, while the cormorants look like prehistoric pelicans.

Down a flight of steps from the observation area is Cobble Beach, covered with surprisingly round stones. At low tides, the tidepools at Cobble Beach are teeming with sea stars, purple urchins, anemones, and hermit crabs.

East of the lighthouse, the large **Interpretive Center** (541/574-3116, 9:30am-5pm daily summer, 10am-5pm fall and spring, 10am-4pm winter) features exhibits on local ecosystems, Native American culture, and historical artifacts such as a 19th-century lighthouse keeper's journal. Other highlights include a life-size replica of the Fresnel lens that shines from the top of the nearby lighthouse, a sea cave simulation with a life-size mural of a California gray whale (accompanied by an exhibit detailing its migratory pattern), statues of birds and harbor seals, and information on tidepool inhabitants.

Although the tidepools in an abandoned basalt quarry on the south side of the headland have now largely filled with sand, the short but steep paved path down to Quarry Cove has some great views of the headland, and frequently good close-up views of sea lions.

Beaches

The beach at **Yaquina Bay State Recreation Site** (541/574-3129 or 800/551-6949, www.oregonstateparks.org) is accessible via a trail from the bluff-top parking area.

Hip Nye Beach is packed with galleries and restaurants.

Agate Hunting

Hunting for agates after winter storms is a passion at several Oregon beaches, particularly around Newport. Deep in the earth, metals, oxides, and silicates fused together to create this type of quartz. Red, amber, blue, and other tones sometimes form stripes or spots in the translucent rocks. One of the best places to find these treasures is on the beach near the Best Western Agate Beach Hotel, not surprisingly called Agate Beach. Nearby Moolack Beach and the beach at Seal Rock, north of Waldport, as well as area estuaries and streambeds, are more spots worth a look October-May.

This is a popular spot for clam digging and agate hunting. There's also easy beach access from the Nye Beach neighborhood, with a large parking lot at the end of NW Beach St. Two miles south of the Yaquina Bay Bridge, **South Beach State Park** (541/867-4715 or 800/551-6949, www.oregonstateparks.org) draws beachcombers, anglers, campers, and picnickers to its miles of broad sandy beach.

North of town along U.S. 101, **Agate Beach** is a broad swath of coastline famed for its agate-hunting opportunities and its views of nearby Yaquina Head. In addition to the semiprecious stones, the contemplative appeal of Agate Beach inspired no less a figure than Ernest Bloch, the noted Swiss composer, who lived here from 1940 until his death in 1959. Famed violinist Yehudi Menuhin spoke

of Bloch and the locale thusly: "Agate Beach is a wild forlorn stretch of coastline looking down upon waves coming in all the way from Asia to break on the shore, a place which suited the grandeur and intensity of Bloch's character."

Moolack Beach, two miles north of Yaquina Head, is a favorite with kite flyers and agate hunters. **Beverly Beach,** 1.5 miles farther north, is a place where 20-million-year-old fossils have been found in the sandstone cliffs above the shore. Beverly Beach also attracts waders, unique for Oregon's chilly waters. Offshore sandbars temper the waves and the weather, so it's not as rough or as cold as many coastal locales. This long stretch of sand (panoramic photos are best taken from Yaquina Head Lighthouse looking north) is

Agate Beach, with a view of Yaquina Head

connected via an under-highway passage to a large state park campground.

SPORTS AND RECREATION
Fishing
Newport is one of the top spots on the coast for charter fishing, and opportunities abound at the home port of Oregon's second-largest recreational fleet. Bottom fishing (year-round), tuna fishing (Aug.-Oct.), crabbing (year-round), and salmon and halibut fishing (seasonal) are all possible. Typical rates here are $75 for a half-day of bottom fishing, $100 for a full day; $130 for an eight-hour chinook salmon outing; $225 for 12 hours of tuna fishing; and $180 for an all-day halibut charter.

In addition to a full menu of fishing excursions, most Newport operators also offer whale-watching charters. **Newport Marina Store and Charters** (2212 OSU Dr., South Beach, 541/867-4470, www.nmscharters.com) offers two-hour whale-watching trips for $30 per person. Two other local operators with similar trips and prices are **Newport Tradewinds** (653 SW Bay Blvd., 541/265-2101 or 800/676-7819, www.newporttradewinds.com) and **Captain's Reel Charters** (343 SW Bay Blvd., 541/265-7441 or 800/865-7441, www.captainsreel.com).

For those who prefer to take matters into their own hands, the clamming and Dungeness crabbing are superlative in Yaquina Bay. If you haven't done this before, local tackle shops, such as the Newport Marina Store in South Beach, rent crab pots or rings and offer instruction. The best time to dig clams is at an extremely low tide. At that time, look for clammers grabbing up cockles in the shallows of the bay. Tide tables are available from the chamber of commerce and many local businesses; they're also easy to find online.

Golf
The public course closest to Newport is nine-hole **Agate Beach Golf Course** (4100 North Coast Hwy., 541/265-7331, www.agatebeachgolf.net, year-round, $36 for 18 holes), just north of town. The views of Yaquina Head alone are worth a visit.

Kayaking
Join a ranger-led kayak tour at **Beaver Creek Welcome Center** (one mile east of Ona Beach off Hwy. 101, 541/563-6413, Thurs.-Mon. July-Labor Day, $20, reservations recommended). Kayaks, paddles, and life vests are supplied for the two-hour tours. Paddlers have a chance to see lots of wildlife, including great blue herons, immature bald eagles, turkey vultures, and signs of beavers, such as their lodges. Kayakers on evening tours have a pretty good chance of actually seeing beavers. This is pretty gentle paddling, but not suitable for children under age six; kids under 18 must be accompanied by an adult.

★ Whale-Watching
The best company on the coast in terms of state-of-the-art equipment and natural history interpretation is **Marine Discovery Tours** (345 SW Bay Blvd., 541/265-6200 or 800/903-2628, www.marinediscovery.com, $38 adults, $36 20seniors, $18 children ages 4-13). The two-hour SeaLife tour is narrated by naturalist guides and includes, depending on the time of year, whale-, seal-, and bird-watching, an oyster bed tour, estuary and ocean exploration, and a harbor tour. The 65-foot *Discovery* features video cameras that magnify the fascinating interplay between smaller life-forms, but the real attractions can be appreciated by the naked eye. Landlubbers will especially relish the full crab pots pulled up from the deep and the resident pod of whales often visible north of Yaquina Bay off Yaquina Head.

During the prime whale-watching weeks of late December and late March, volunteers from Whale Watching Spoken Here staff the **Don A. Davis City Kiosk** in Nye Beach to answer questions and help you spot whales.

ENTERTAINMENT AND EVENTS

Overlooking the sea in Nye Beach, the **Newport Performing Arts Center** (777 W. Olive St., 541/265-2787, www.coastarts.org), the Oregon coast's largest performance venue, hosts local and national entertainment in the 400-seat Alice Silverman Theatre and the smaller Studio Theatre. At the same address is the **Oregon Coast Council for the Arts,** which puts out a free monthly newsletter and has ticket information on the center venues. It also has updates on the **Newport Visual Arts Center** (777 NW Beach Dr., 541/265-6540), right above the beach two blocks north at the Nye Beach turnaround. Two floors and two galleries—**Runyan Gallery** (11am-5pm Tues.-Sun.) and the **Upstairs Gallery** (noon-4pm Tues.-Sat.)—offer art education programs and exhibition space for paintings, sculpture, and other works, often with a maritime theme. All exhibits are free.

In addition to its impressive schedule of music, dance, drama, and other arts, the Performing Arts Center screens a series of imported and art films—the ones you probably won't find at the multiplex **Newport Cinema** (5836 N. Coast Hwy., 541/265-2111).

In the Bayfront District, **Mariner Square** (250 SW Bay Blvd., 541/265-2206, 9am-8pm July-Aug., 10am-6pm June and Sept., usually 10am-5pm Oct.-May, $12 per attraction adults, $7 children 5-12, or $25 adult, $15 children for three-in-one tickets) is a complex of three attractions that mostly appeal to kids: **Ripley's Believe It or Not!, The Waxworks,** and the **Undersea Gardens.**

Festivals and Events

The biggest bash (and one of the largest events of its kind in the country) is late February's **Newport Seafood and Wine Festival** (541/265-8801 or 800/262-7844, www.seafoodandwine.com, $8-19), which features dozens of food booths and scores of Oregon wineries serving up palate pleasers, along with music and crafts, at the **South Beach Marina** (across Yaquina Bay from the Bayfront). A huge tent joins the exhibition hall, wherein festivalgoers wash down delights from the deep with Oregon vintages. The event is open only to the 21-and-over crowd.

The second event of note is **Loyalty Days and Sea Fair** (541/961-1466, www.loyalty-days.com, free) in early May. What began during the Depression as the Crab Festival, intended to stimulate the market for Dungeness crab, was recast during the depths of the Red Scare of the 1950s as a public expression of patriotism. Although that aspect still undergirds the events, it's really just a big community party stretching over four days, with carnival rides, veterans' events, bike races, and a parade.

ACCOMMODATIONS
$100-150

For location, you can't beat **The Whaler** (155 SW Elizabeth St., 541/265-9261 or 800/433-9444, www.whalernewport.com, $139-189). Each of the 73 rooms has a view, and some have fireplaces, wet bars, and private balconies. Guests can use the pool and exercise facilities; continental breakfast is served. Dogs are permitted in some guest rooms.

Stay on the Bayfront at **Anchor Pier Lodge** (345 SW Bay Blvd., 541/265-7829, www.marinediscovery.com, $125-199), up a long flight of stairs from street level, where you'll truly be living "above the store" (there's a gift shop down below). The rooms are simple, with wood-plank floors, but tastefully and individually decorated. Although the Bayfront can be a little noisy with carousing people and sea lions, the inn provides earplugs. Rooms that overlook the bay have balconies; they're the ones to go for.

North of town and above a great stretch of beach, the **Moolack Shores Motel** (8835 N. U.S. 101, 541/265-2326, http://moolackshores.com, $105-159) is a quiet spot, even though its parking area is just off the highway. The rooms are individually decorated and more than a little bit quirky, but most have good ocean views, and the beach is just down a long flight of wooden stairs from the motel.

The ★ **Sylvia Beach Hotel** (267 NW Cliff St., 541/265-5428, www.sylviabeach-hotel.com, $120-230), a favorite of many Oregonians, combines the camaraderie of a hostel with the intimate charm of a bed-and-breakfast. Built in the era when the Corvallis-to-Yaquina Bay train and seven-seater Studebaker touring cars from Portland ferried the summer folks to Nye Beach, the hotel and its National Historic Landmark designation and literary theme have attracted an enthusiastic following. The 21 guest rooms, named after different authors, are furnished with decor evocative of each respective literary legacy. The Edgar Allan Poe Room, for instance, has a pendulum guillotine blade and stuffed ravens, while the Agatha Christie Room drops such clues as shoes underneath the curtains and capsules marked "Poison" in the medicine cabinet.

Most of the rooms ("best-sellers") run $165, with several oceanfront suites ("classics") featuring a fireplace and a deck going for $230. "Novels" go for $120 (no ocean view, but still quite charming). All rates include a full breakfast and reflect double occupancy. At breakfast, you have a choice of entrées and share a table with eight other guests, so misanthropes beware! No smoking, pets, or radios are allowed on the premises, and small children are discouraged.

To get there, turn off U.S. 101 onto NW 3rd Street and follow it down to the beach, where NW 3rd and Cliff Streets meet. Look for a large, four-story dark green vintage wooden structure with a red roof on a bluff above the surf.

$150-200

Elizabeth Street Inn (232 SW Elizabeth St., 541/265-9400 or 877/265-9400, www.elizabethstreetinn.com, $169-209), in the Nye Beach neighborhood, sits on a bluff overlooking the ocean. All of the spacious rooms in this newer property face the ocean and have private balconies. They come fully equipped with fireplaces, refrigerators, microwaves, and coffeemakers. Guests also get a complimentary continental breakfast and have use of the indoor pool, spa, and fitness room. Pets are permitted in some rooms.

The **Hallmark Resort** (744 SW Elizabeth St., 541/265-2600 or 888/448-4449, www.hallmarkinns.com, $181-239) is a large hotel complex sitting atop the Newport bluffs, looking westward over the Pacific and miles of sandy beach. Of the many modern hotels that share this vista, the Hallmark is one of

The Elizabeth Street Inn is one of the top accommodations in the trendy Nye Beach district.

the nicest, with large, well-maintained guest rooms. Facilities include an indoor pool, a spa, and a restaurant. Many guest rooms are pet-friendly.

You may not find any riverboat gamblers aboard the **Newport Belle Bed & Breakfast** (2126 SE OSU Dr., 541/867-6290, www.newportbelle.com, closed Nov.-Jan., $160-175), a recently constructed sternwheeler designed as a floating inn, but this 97-foot-long B&B moored on the H Dock of the Newport Marina evokes the ambience of the sternwheeler heyday. Choose from five generous staterooms, each with its own personality and private bath. Most have fabulous vistas of the bustling marina and bridge area. In the evening, guests can retire to their staterooms, enjoy the open afterdeck, or socialize in the main salon, where a gourmet breakfast is served every morning. No children or smoking; pets are allowed in one room. Soft-soled shoes are required.

The extremely popular **Embarcadero Resort** (1000 SE Bay Blvd., 541/265-8521 or 800/547-4779, www.embarcadero-resort.com, $180-250) is bay-front but not beachfront; it overlooks Yaquina Bay and the soaring bay bridge, arguably one of the best views in Oregon. The Embarcadero has an assortment of suites and townhouses (including many timeshare units) with full kitchens and fireplaces. Facilities include an indoor pool, a sauna, two outdoor hot tubs, a restaurant and bar, a private dock, and boat rentals.

The **Best Western Plus Agate Beach Inn** (3019 N. Coast Hwy., 541/265-9411 or 800/547-3310, www.newportbestwestern.com, $165-185) is a tall oceanfront hotel with a fine view overlooking Yaquina Head Lighthouse and Agate Beach. The rooms are comfortable standard-issue hotel rooms, and although it's a little bit of a hike down to the beach, it is one of Newport's best beaches. A sports bar and a restaurant are on-site. Pets are permitted in some guest rooms.

If you want to get away from it all, **Little Creek Cove Condominiums** (3641 NW Oceanview Dr., 541/265-8587 or 800/294-8025, www.littlecreekcove.com, $159-259) is a small condo resort that might be what you're looking for. Little Creek Cove resort is two miles north of Newport, perched just above an isolated stretch of beach. You have a choice of studio, one-, and two-bedroom units, each with a private deck, full kitchen, and fireplace.

Camping

The campgrounds at Beverly Beach State Park and South Beach State Park are among the most popular on the Oregon coast. Their proximity to Newport, the absence of other camping in the area, and the special features of each explain their appeal.

Beverly Beach State Park (541/265-9278 or 800/452-5687 information, 800/452-5687 or www.reserveamerica.com reservations, $21 tents, $29-31 RVs, $44-54 yurts, $6 hiker/biker) is huge, multiloop campground set seven miles north of Newport on the east side of the highway in a mossy glade. A pedestrian tunnel passes under the highway and leads to a long, wide beach that is unfortunately directly bordered by the road. Devil's Punchbowl and Otter Crest are one and two miles up the highway, respectively.

It's just a hop over the sand dunes to the beach at **South Beach State Park** (541/867-4715 or 800/551-6949 information, 800/452-5687 or www.reserveamerica.com reservations, $21 tents, $29 RVs, $44-54 yurts, $6 hiker/biker), just south of the Yaquina Bay Bridge. The long beach has opportunities for fishing, agate hunting, windsurfing (for experts), horseback riding, and hiking; sign up in advance (541/867-6500) for kayak tours of nearby Beaver Creek.

FOOD

This is a town for serious diners—folks who know good food and don't mind paying a tad more for it. It's also the kind of place where wharf-side vendors supply fresh fish on the cheap. Mid-May through October, you can pick up the freshest garden produce the area has to offer, plus baked goods, honey, and other delectable, at the Lincoln County Small Farmers' Association's **Saturday Farmers Market,** held in the parking area of the **Newport City Hall** (U.S. 101 and Angle St., 9am-1pm, May-Oct.).

About seven miles east of the Bayfront, the **Oregon Oyster Farms** (6878 Yaquina Bay Rd., 541/265-5078, 9am-5pm daily) is the only remaining commercial outlet for Yaquina Bay oysters. Visitors are welcome to observe the farming and processing of these succulent shellfish. Try oysters on the half-shell, or sample smoked oysters on a stick. To get there, follow Bay Boulevard east six miles from the Embarcadero Resort.

Bakeries and Cafés

Down along the Bayfront is a wonderful breakfast haunt, the **Coffee House** (156 SW Bay Blvd., 541/265-6263, www.thecoffeehousenewport.com, 7am-2pm daily, $6-16). Scones, muffins, and such creative brunch fare as a wild mushroom omelet, crab cakes Florentine, various crepes, meat pasties, and oysters lightly breaded with Japanese panko breadcrumbs are complemented by well-made espresso drinks. In fair weather, the outside deck is a relaxing spot for soaking up some rays while you gaze out on the harbor.

In the Nye Beach neighborhood, a charming spot for breakfast (including a good breakfast burrito) and lunch sandwiches is **Café Stephanie** (411 Coast St., 541/265-8082, 7:30am-3pm daily, $6-11), a bustling cubbyhole with friendly service. Here both breakfast and lunch are served during open hours; consider starting your day with a bowl of smoked salmon chowder.

Nearby, the tiny ★ **Panini Bakery** (232 NW Coast St., 541/265-5033, 7am-7pm Thurs.-Mon., $5-12 sandwiches) is a great spot for a chocolate panini, a ginger scone, a slice of pizza, and the local vibe. It's the best bakery in town and has a few tables.

Italian

★ **April's at Nye Beach** (749 NW 3rd St., 541/265-6855, http://aprilsatnyebeach.com,

5pm-9pm Wed.-Sun., $16-28) is a small, stylish café just across the street from the Sylvia Beach Hotel. Roast duck with port sauce is a standout in a creative Mediterranean-influenced menu. House-made bruschetta and steamed clams with spicy sausage are excellent appetizers. In the summer, many vegetables come from the owners' farm. For dessert, have an éclair dipped in chocolate ganache and topped with slivered almonds. Affordable wines by the glass add to one of Newport's best dining experiences.

Pacific Northwest

You don't have to be a guest to have a meal at the **Tables of Content** (267 NW Cliff St., 541/265-5428, www.sylviabeachhotel.com, seatings at 7pm daily summer, 6pm Sun.-Thurs. and 7pm Fri.-Sat. winter, four-course prix fixe $28), the excellent restaurant at the Sylvia Beach Hotel. There's a nice view of the breakers and good company, and it's a good value for creatively prepared Pacific Northwest cuisine. Each night features several entrée selections with an appetizer, salad, bread, beverages (alcohol not included), and dessert. Diners share tables and are encouraged to break the ice with a game called Two Truths and a Lie, in which they regale each other with several stories, the object being to distinguish which one is untrue. Reservations are mandatory.

Seafood

If you're hankering for a broad selection of fresh local seafood but don't need a fancy dining room to enjoy it in, ★ **Local Ocean Seafoods** (213 SE Bay Blvd., 541/574-7959, http://localocean.net, 11am-9pm Sun.-Thurs., 11am-9:30pm Fri.-Sat., $6-28) is the place for you. Part fish market, part seafood grill, this bright and bustling restaurant spotlights sustainably caught, impeccably fresh fish and offers a lively atmosphere. Each item in the fish case is identified by name, where it was caught, how it was harvested, and who caught it. The menu items change depending on what's fresh, and though you can count on great fish-and-chips here, you may want to try the house-specialty fish tacos or albacore tuna kebabs.

Right on the bay front, with windows overlooking the active fishing port, ★ **Saffron Salmon** (859 SW Bay Blvd., 541/265-8921, http://saffronsalmon.com, 11:30am-2:15pm and 5pm-8:30pm Thurs.-Tues., $12-26) is one of Newport's finest choices for expertly prepared, sophisticated seafood. As you'd expect, the specialty is fresh wild salmon, grilled and served with citrus-saffron butter, while calamari are sautéed with olive oil and red cabbage. There's also a good selection of organic steaks and rack of lamb.

Also in the old-town harbor area, **Sharks Seafood Bar & Steamer Co.** (852 SW Bay Blvd., 541/574-0590, http://sharksseafoodbar.com, 4pm-9pm Sun.-Wed., 4pm-9:30pm Fri.-Sat., $10-25) specializes in steamed seafood. But don't worry—this isn't tasteless health food. The Catalina bouillabaisse packs a wallop, with 1.5 pounds of seafood in every spice-filled bowl. You'll also find a savory seafood gumbo, oyster stew, and a mix of stewed and sautéed fish called a pan roast. Fresh fish gets the steam treatment—in season, try halibut, salmon, and rockfish steamed and served with the chef's special sauces. Sharks is a fun, quirky place; the proprietors provide not just dinner, but a show. Be sure to sidle up to the bar in front of the cooking area to watch the chef in action.

The Newport Bayfront is where Mohava Niemi first opened the original **Mo's** (622 SW Bay Blvd., 541/265-2979, 11am-9pm daily, $4-16) several decades ago. When word got out about the good food and low prices, Mo's small, homey place soon had more business than it could handle. In response to the overflow, **Mo's Annex** (657 SW Bay Blvd., 541/265-7512, 11am-9pm daily, $4-16) was created across the street. While both establishments feature old-fashioned favorites, such as oyster stew, fried fish, and peanut butter cream pie, the Annex bay windows have the best view.

There are ample opportunities to buy fresh fish or crab along the bay front in Newport. About a half-mile south of the bridge, the **South Beach Fish Market** (3640 S. U.S. 101, 541/867-6800, 8am-8pm daily, $8-12) sells fresh fish, cooked and uncooked; 90 percent of what they sell comes from the Newport fishing fleet. It's a good place for the family to stop for fish-and-chips after a visit to the aquarium.

Asian

Although most Asian restaurants on the coast are merely serviceable, a good spot for anything from kimchee to ramen to pho is **Noodle Cafe** (837 SW Bay Blvd., 541/574-6688, www.noodlecafenewport.com, 11am-10pm Sun.-Thurs., 11am-midnight Fri.-Sat., $7-20). The noodles are homemade, and the restaurant makes good use of seafood.

Brewpubs

Rogue Ales Public House (748 SW Bay Blvd., 541/265-3188, 11am-midnight Mon.-Wed., Sat., 11am-1am Thurs.-Fri., $7-15) is along the bay in Old Town, serving seafood salads, shrimp-melt sandwiches, pizza, fish-and-chips, and seasonal fish dishes. In addition to the renowned Rogue ales, there's Rogue's draft root beer—a creamy concoction laced with honey and vanilla. Another Rogue Ales brewery, called **Brewers on the Bay** (2320 OSU Dr., 541/867-3660, 11am-9pm Sun.-Thurs., 11am-10pm Fri.-Sat., $7-15), is across Yaquina Bay near the Oregon Coast Aquarium. This is where the actual brewing is now done; tours are available weekdays at 3pm.

Rogue's third local outlet is the **Rogue House of Spirits** (2122 Marine Science Dr., 541/867-3670, 4pm-8pm Fri., noon-8pm Sat., noon-6pm Sun.), a distillery pub that produces rum, gin, vodka, and whiskey. The menu here is less extensive than at Rogue's brewpubs and features excellent cheese from Central Point, Oregon's Rogue Creamery. Tours are offered at 4pm daily.

INFORMATION

The **Greater Newport Chamber of Commerce** (555 SW U.S. 101, 541/265-8801 or 800/262-7844, www.newportchamber.org,

8:30am-5pm Mon.-Fri.) has lots of literature, but the most helpful website for a visitor is the chamber's visitor website: http://discovernewport.com. The **Central Oregon Coast Association** (541/265-2064 or 800/767-2064, www.coastvisitor.com) maintains a useful website with details on Newport and the rest of Lincoln County.

A public radio station, **KLCO,** a local repeater station for Eugene's KLCC, is heard on your dial at 90.5 FM. The **Newport Public Library** (541/265-2153, 10am-9pm Mon.-Wed., 10am-6pm Thurs.-Sat., and noon-5pm Sun.) is at 35 NW Nye Street. The **post office** (310 SW 2nd St., 541/265-5542) is one block west of the highway.

Samaritan Pacific Communities Hospital (930 SW Abbey St., 541/265-2244) is the central coast's only major hospital.

GETTING THERE AND AROUND

Newport is one of the few places on the Oregon coast that can be reached by public transportation. **Valley Retriever** (541/265-2253) buses connect Newport with Corvallis, Portland, and Bend Sunday-Friday. **Lincoln County Transit** (541/265-4900, www.co.lincoln.or.us/transit) runs buses several times daily Monday-Saturday, north to Lincoln City and south to Yachats, with numerous stops en route through Newport.

A **shuttle bus** (http://discovernewport.com, 8am-5:30pm daily) travels up and down the length of Newport on streets just east and west of U.S. 101, going as far south as the Newport Business Plaza in South Beach and north to NE 73rd Street. The wheelchair-accessible bus is equipped with a bike rack. It's free for those with a pass from their Newport hotel and $1 for others. The route is not straightforward; it helps to have a map and schedule (www.newport-chamber.org).

Newport's car rental agency of choice is **Enterprise Rent-A-Car** (533 E. Olive St., 541/574-1999).

Waldport and Vicinity

Originally a stronghold of the Alsea Native Americans, Waldport also has had incarnations as a gold rush town, salmon-canning center, and lumber port. This town of about 2,000, whose name means "forest port" in German, is pretty quiet today, with a nondescript main drag that gives no hint of the surrounding beaches and prime fishing and crabbing spots. Waldport provides a low-cost alternative to the big-name destinations; you won't have to fight for a parking spot or make reservations months in advance.

SIGHTS AND RECREATION
Alsea Bay Bridge Historical Interpretive Center
The small museum and visitors center known as the **Alsea Bay Bridge Historical Interpretive Center** (620 NW Spring St., 541/563-2002, www.oregonstateparks.org, 9am-5pm daily summer, 9am-4pm Tues.-Sat. fall-spring, free), operated by the Oregon Parks and Recreation Department and Waldport Chamber of Commerce, stands along the highway on the south side of the river. Exhibits here tell the story of how the sleek 1991 bridge replaced the aging Conde McCullough span across the bay, which has since been demolished. Displays about transportation methods along the central coast since the 1800s, information on the Alsea Native American people, and a telescope trained on the seals and waterfowl on the bay are worth a quick stop. On summer weekends, Oregon Parks and Recreation gives clamming and crabbing demonstrations (locations and times vary according to the tides; see website for calendar).

Seal Rock State Recreation Site

Four miles north of Waldport, **Seal Rock** (800/551-6949, day use only) attracts beachcombers and agate hunters, as well as folks who come to explore the tidepools and observe the seals on offshore rocks. The park's name derives from a seal-shaped rock in the cluster of interesting formations in the tidewater. The picnic area is set in a shady area behind the sandy beach. During Christmas and spring breaks, the volunteers of Whale Watching Spoken Here are on hand to help visitors spot passing grays 10am-1pm.

Ona Beach State Park

Ona Beach State Park (800/551-6949, day use only), a couple of miles north of Seal Rock, is a beguiling park on the west side of the highway. Attractions include a forested picnic area with a 0.25-mile trail and a footbridge over Beaver Creek leading to a fine stretch of beach.

Brian Booth State Park

Beaver Creek State Natural Area runs through **Brian Booth State Park** (541/563-6413, visitor center 10am-4pm June-Aug., noon-4pm Sept.-May); a visitor center is two miles east of Ona Beach, up Beaver Creek Road. This coastal wetland area has good paddling (ranger-led kayak tours, 8:30am Fri.-Mon., 6:30pm Thurs. July-Aug., $20, reservations required) and wildlife-watching, both from the creek and from a viewing blind that's just a short walk from the road. If you're not prepared to paddle, a seven-mile network of hiking trails starts near the visitor center.

Drift Creek Wilderness

Seven miles east of Waldport are the nearly 5,800 acres of the **Drift Creek Wilderness,** which protects the Coast Range's largest remaining stands of old-growth rainforest. Here you can see giant Sitka spruce and western hemlock hundreds of years old, nourished by up to 120 inches of rain per year. These trees are the "climax forest" in the Douglas fir ecosystem. They seldom reach old-growth status because the timber industry tends to replant fir seedlings after logging operations. The forest provides habitat for spotted owls along with bald eagles, Roosevelt elk, and black bears. Drift Creek sustains wild runs of chinook, steelhead, and coho salmon, which come up the Alsea River.

Steep ridges and their drainages, as well as small meadows, make up the topography, which is accessed via a couple of hiking trails. The trailhead closest to Waldport is the 3.5-mile **Harris Ranch Trail,** which descends 1,200 feet to a meadow near Drift Creek. The local access to Harris Ranch Trail and the conjoining Horse Creek Trail is via Highway 34; turn north off 34 at the Alsea River crossing, seven miles east of Waldport. Here, pick up Risely Creek Road (Forest Service Rd. 3446) and Forest Service Road 346 to the trailhead.

Fishing

Waldport's recreational raison d'être is fishing. World-class clamming and Dungeness crabbing in Alsea Bay and the Alsea River's salmon, steelhead, and cutthroat trout runs account for a high percentage of visits to the area. Before commercial fishing on the river was shut down in 1957, as much as 137,000 pounds of chinook were netted in a season. The wild fall chinook run remains healthy and starts up in late August. Catch-and-release for sea-run cutthroats starts in mid-August, while steelhead are in the river December-March. Crabbers without boats can take advantage of the Port of Waldport docks. **Dock of the Bay Marina** (1245 NE Mill St., 541/563-2003) rents and sells crabbing and fishing supplies and can guide you to the best spots.

ACCOMMODATIONS

Midway between Waldport and Yachats, the **Terry-a-While Motel** (7160 SW U.S. 101, 541/563-3377, www.terry-a-while.com, $60-200) has simple guest rooms that range in style from modern to vintage and in size from basic budget motel size to two-bedroom units with kitchens. Although the guest rooms are not extravagantly furnished, they all have decks with nice views.

The vintage **Cape Cod Cottages** (4150 SW U.S. 101, 541/563-2106, www.capecod-cottagesonline.com, $99-325) offer one- and two-bedroom oceanfront units with complete kitchens, cozy fireplaces, spectacular views, and private decks. The least expensive units are very basic motel rooms with no decks. A three-night minimum stay is required in summer.

The historic **Cliff House** (1450 Adahi Rd., 541/563-2506, www.cliffhouseoregon.com, $125-225) may appear rustic, but in fact this is a lovingly restored historic home, and the location can't be beat. Four guest rooms, some with whirlpools, are decorated with antiques; even the woodstoves are period. No pets are allowed, and children are best left home with the grandparents or a sitter.

Camping

Two excellent campgrounds sit about four miles south of Waldport on U.S. 101 along the beach. **Beachside State Park** (541/563-3220 for information, 800/452-5687 or www.reserveamerica.com for reservations, $21 tent, $29 RV, $44 yurt) is near a half-mile of beach not far from Alsea Bay and Alsea River. This is a paradise for rock fishers, surfcasters, clammers, and crabbers. Beachside fills up fast, so reserve early for space Memorial Day-Labor Day.

A half-mile south of Beachside, the Siuslaw National Forest's **Tillicum Beach** (877/444-6777 or www.recreation.gov, $24, reservations strongly recommended in summer) is set right along the ocean. Forest Service roads from here access Coast Range fishing streams. You'll also appreciate the strip of vegetation blocking the cool evening winds that whip up off the ocean.

Should Beachside and Tillicum be filled to

overflowing, you might want to set up a base camp in the Coast Range along Highway 34—especially if you have fishing or hiking in the Drift Creek Wilderness in mind. Just go east of Waldport 17 miles on Highway 34 to the Siuslaw National Forest's **Blackberry Campground** (877/444-6777 or www.recreation.gov reservations, $22). The 33 sites are open year-round; most are right on the river. A boat ramp, flush toilets, and piped water are on-site.

FOOD

Dining options in Waldport are limited. We recommend heading about 10 miles south to Yachats for dinner. If you just need a loaf of artisan bread or a pastry and time it right, **Pacific Sourdough** (740 NE Mill St., 541/563-3044, 10am-3pm Thurs. and Sat.) is the place to go. The bakers sell their bread to several restaurants in Yachats.

INFORMATION

The Waldport Chamber of Commerce operates a **visitors center** (620 NW Spring St., 541/563-2133, www.waldport-chamber.com, 9am-5pm daily summer, 9am-4pm Tues.-Sat. fall-spring) in the Alsea Bay Bridge Historical Interpretive Center, just south of the river. The **Siuslaw National Forest-Waldport Ranger Station** (1130 Forestry Ln., 541/563-8400) can provide information on area camping and hiking, including the trails in the Drift Creek Wilderness.

GETTING THERE

Highway 34 runs east from Waldport, following the Alsea River for several miles before veering northeast to Corvallis, about 65 miles away. This is one of the prettiest (and slowest) routes between the coast and the Willamette Valley.

The **Lincoln County Transit** (541/265-4900, www.co.lincoln.or.us/transit) buses run four times a day Monday-Saturday between Yachats and Newport.

Yachats and Cape Perpetua

Yachats (pronounced YAH-hots) is derived from an Alsea word meaning "dark waters at the foot of the mountain." The phrase aptly describes the location of this picturesque resort village of 700 people, clustered on the hillsides and coastal shelf beside the Yachats River mouth in the shadow of Cape Perpetua. Word of mouth has helped to spread the popularity of Yachats as a place for a quiet getaway and a base for enjoying the 2,700-acre Cape Perpetua Scenic Area and nearby beaches.

SIGHTS AND RECREATION
★ Cape Perpetua

The most notable sight near Yachats, indeed on the whole central coast, is the view from 803-foot-high Cape Perpetua. The name derives from Captain Cook's sighting of the promontory on March 7, 1778, St. Perpetua's Day. The road to the top of the cape affords 150 miles of north-to-south visibility from the top of the headland. On a clear day, you can also see nearly 40 miles out to sea.

Prior to hiking the 23 miles of foot trails or driving to the top of the cape, stop off at the **Cape Perpetua Visitor Center** (541/547-3289, 10am-5pm mid-June-Aug., 10am-4pm daily Sept.-mid-June, $5 per car or Northwest Forest Pass), three miles south of Yachats on the east side of the highway. A picture window framing a bird's-eye view of rockbound coast, along with exhibits on forestry, marine life, and monster storms provides an introduction to the region. Stick around to watch the excellent 15-minute film about Oregon's intertidal biome. From June through Labor Day, rangers give talks on Saturdays and Sundays at 11am, 1pm, and 3pm.

HIKING

Personnel at the visitor center have maps and pamphlets about such trails as Cook's Ridge, Riggin' Slinger, and Giant Spruce, as well as directions for the auto tour to the summit, from which you can take the 0.25-mile **Whispering Spruce Trail** through the grounds of a former World War II Coast Guard lookout built by the Civilian

birders at Yachats

Conservation Corps (CCC) in 1933. The southern views from the crest take in the highway and headlands as far south as Coos Bay. Halfway along the path, you'll come to a Works Progress Administration-built rock hut called the West Shelter, which makes a lofty perch for whale-watching. Beyond this ridgetop aerie, the curtain of trees parts to reveal fantastic views of the shoreline between Yachats and Cape Foulweather.

To begin your auto ascent, from the visitor center drive 100 yards north on U.S. 101 and look for the steep winding spur road (Forest Service Rd. 55) on the right. As you climb, you'll notice large Sitka spruce trees abutting the road. Halfway up the two-mile route, you'll come to a Y in the road. Take a hard left and follow the road another mile to the top of Cape Perpetua. If you miss the left turn and go straight ahead, you'll soon find yourself on a 22-mile loop through the Coast Range to Yachats. Along the way, placards annotate forest ecology.

If you'd rather hike to the top of the cape, the awe-inspiring 1.5-mile **Saint Perpetua Trail** from the Cape Perpetua visitors center to the summit is of moderate difficulty, gaining 600 feet in elevation. En route, placards explain the role of wind, erosion, and fire in forest succession in this mixed-conifer ecosystem.

The actual cape is only half the attraction at Cape Perpetua. At least as fascinating are the rocky coast and its tidepools, churns, and spouting horns of water. Just north of the turnoff for the top of Cape Perpetua (Forest Service Rd. 55) and U.S. 101 is the turnout for **Devil's Churn,** on the west side of the highway. Here the tides have cut a deep fissure in a basalt embankment on the shore. You can observe the action from a vertigo-inducing overlook high above or take the easy switchbacking trail down to the water's edge. While watching the white-water torrents in this foaming cistern, beware of "sneaker waves," particularly if you venture beyond the boundaries of the **Trail of the Restless Waters.** The highlights here are the spouting horns and acres of tidepools. All along this stretch of the coast, many trees appear to be leaning away from the ocean, as if bent by storms. This illusion is caused by salt-laden westerlies drying out and killing the buds on the exposed side of the tree, leaving growth only on the leeward branches.

Another hike from the Cape Perpetua visitors center goes down to a geological blowhole (called a spouting horn), where seawater

Drive to the top of Cape Perpetua to find this view.

Trails at Cape Perpetua lead to a giant spruce tree.

is funneled between rocks and explodes into spray. This is the **Captain Cook Trail,** which runs six miles through a dense wind-carved forest and the remains of an old CCC camp under U.S. 101 to an ancient lava deposit on the shore. Given enough wave action, water bubbles up through fissures in the basalt. There are also Native American shell middens built up 300-2,000 years ago in the area.

State Parks and Coastal Waysides

In this part of the coast, state parks and viewpoints abound with attractions. There's so much to see here that keeping your eyes on the road in this heavily traveled section is a challenge.

A mile north of Yachats, **Smelt Sands State Recreation Site** gives access to tidepools and the 0.75-mile 804 Trail, which

Devil's Churn

follows the rocky shore to a broad sandy beach to the north. In Yachats, turn west onto 2nd Street to loop around wave-battered **Yachats State Recreation Area,** overlooking Yachats Bay. The road heads north along the ocean, where it becomes Marine Drive. After going through a residential community, it eventually takes an easterly turn to reconnect with U.S. 101.

On the south bank of the Yachats River is a short but beautiful beach loop off U.S. 101 (going south, look for the "Beach Access" sign). The road runs between the landscaped grounds of beach houses and resorts on one side and the foamy sea on the other. A wide beach, tidepools, and blowholes on the bank by the river's mouth are a special treat.

A mile south of Cape Perpetua, **Neptune State Park** has a beautiful beach and is near the 9,300-acre **Cummins Creek Wilderness** east of U.S. 101. Just north of Neptune Park, Forest Service Road 1050 leads east to the Cummins Creek Trailhead. A half-mile south, gravelly Forest Service Road 1051 can take you to a point where a moderately difficult 2.5-mile hike leads to Cummins Ridge Trailhead. This pathway has some of the last remaining coastal old-growth Sitka spruce stands. Get maps and detailed directions for these and other area trails at the Cape Perpetua visitor center.

Close by, there's a chance to explore tidepools and sometimes observe harbor seals at **Strawberry Hill.** Scenic shorelines can also be found in the next few miles farther south at **Stonesfield Beach State Recreation Site** and **Muriel O. Ponsler State Scenic Viewpoint.**

ENTERTAINMENT AND EVENTS

This little village seems to be busy with some festival or other event just about every weekend. For a full schedule, see the local chamber of commerce website (www.yachats.org). What follows are some highlights.

In late March, the chamber-sponsored **Original Yachats Arts and Crafts Fair** (Yachats Commons, U.S. 101 and W. 4th St., 541/547-3530 or 800/929-0477, free) exhibits the work of some 75 Pacific Northwest artists and artisans.

Yachats pulls out all the stops for the **Fourth of July.** Events include the short and silly La De Da Parade at noon, a pie and ice cream social, lots of live music, and a fireworks show on the bay when darkness falls.

The weekend after July 4, the **Yachats**

Stop to explore the beach at Strawberry Hill, south of Yachats.

Music Festival takes place at the Presbyterian Church (360 W. 7th St., 510/845-4444). The lineup features classical virtuosi and vocalists from the San Francisco Bay Area for evening concerts as well as a Sunday matinee performance.

Fall is mushroom season on the coast, and the Yachats Village Mushroom Fest (541/547-3530 or 800/929-0477), held the third weekend in October, showcases the native mushrooms that abound in these temperate rainforests. Activities over the weekend include the fungi feasts, mushroom-cooking and -growing lessons, talks on forest ecology, and guided mushroom walks.

SHOPPING

Yachats has long been a center for artists and bohemians, and for proof of this you need go no further than Earthworks Gallery (2222 U.S. 101 N., 541/547-4300, http://earthworks-galleries.net, 10am-5pm daily). This excellent gallery displays the work of local painters, glass artists, and jewelers, as well as high-quality crafts. Touchstone Gallery (2118 U.S. 101 N., 541/547-4121, 10am-5pm daily) is another gallery with unique Pacific Northwest arts and crafts.

ACCOMMODATIONS
$50-100

Facing onto the beach loop south of town, the Yachats Inn (331 U.S. 101, 541/547-3456 or 888/270-3456, www.yachatsinn.com, $89-140) offers basic summer shelter with unfussy rooms that have little decks and TVs but no phones, though some have kitchens and fireplaces. There's great access to the beach. Suites with full kitchens and fireplaces are newer, but set back from the beach and don't permit dogs. An indoor pool overlooks the beach.

For those looking for budget prices close to the center of town, try Rock Park Cottages (431 W. 2nd St., 800/519-0437, www.sweethomerentals.com, $75-175), adjacent to Yachats State Recreation Area. Consisting of five rustic cottages arranged around a courtyard, Rock Park has to be one of the better

bargains on the coast. The kitchens are well equipped, and the vintage cottages couldn't be better located.

Another good old-fashioned budget choice, Deane's Oceanfront Lodge (7365 U.S. 101, 541/547-3321, www.deaneslodge.com, $89-139) is about halfway between Yachats and Waldport. The rooms are well-kept but not fancy; the least expensive don't share the great ocean views afforded by the top-end rooms. Pets are permitted in some rooms.

Set back from Highway 101, the Dublin House Motel (251 W. 7th St., 541/547-3703 or 866/922-4287, www.dublinhousemotel.com, $74-114) offers standard motel rooms and ocean views, each room having a microwave, a refrigerator, a coffeemaker, and cable TV; some kitchen units are also available. The indoor heated pool is especially nice in the winter months.

$100-150

A little north of the town center, the imposing Adobe Resort (155 U.S. 101 N., 541/547-3141, www.adoberesort.com, $160 for ocean view, $130 for hillside view) overlooks Smelt Sands Beach. Although the Adobe isn't what you'd call luxurious, it is one of the few full-service resorts in the area, with an on-site restaurant. All units have refrigerators, microwaves, satellite TV, DVD players, and a phone with voice mail. Pets are accepted in some guest rooms. Two-bedroom hot tub suites are 1,400 square feet and have all the comforts of a small home.

The Fireside Motel (1881 U.S. 101, 541/547-3636 or 800/336-3573, www.firesidemotel.com, $99-185) is known for its pet-friendly policies. The more expensive rooms have fireplaces, balconies and views of tide pools; the cheaper rooms are pretty basic, but you're still located right next to a beachside trail.

Over $150

A mile north of Yachats, above a thrust of wave-pounded tidepools, ★ Overleaf Lodge (2055 U.S. 101, 541/547-4880, www.overleaflodge.com, $210-315) offers the newest and nicest rooms in the Yachats area. Most guest rooms have balconies, hot tubs, and fireplaces, and all have fantastic views. Rates include a breakfast buffet plus access to a fitness area. A 3,000-square-foot spa has treatment rooms, steam rooms, and saunas, plus oceanview hot tubs. Adjacent to the lodge are six cottages ($295-345) tucked into the forest. With 2-4 bedrooms, these charming units with Craftsman-style decor have full kitchens and everything a family or small group will need for a great beach vacation.

The secluded **Sea Quest Inn** (95354 U.S. 101 S., 541/547-3782, www.seaquestinn. com, $190-355) is an antique-filled but contemporary inn of cedar and glass, with private entrances, seven miles south of Yachats. The innkeeper puts out a good breakfast, the wraparound deck affords superlative views of the beach, and telescopes and binoculars are always on hand for spotting whales and other marine life. Sea Quest is not appropriate for pets or children under 12 years of age; it is also not handicapped accessible.

Vacation Rentals

If you'd rather settle into a house, check out **Yachats Village Rentals** (541/547-3501 or 888/288-5077, www.97498.com), which offers a varied stable of vacation homes ($140-350) for long- or short-term rental.

Camping

Set along Cape Creek in the Cape Perpetua Scenic Area, the Forest Service's **Cape Perpetua Campground** (877/444-6777 or www.recreation.gov reservations, May-Sept., $24), with 38 sites for tents, trailers, or motor homes up to 22 feet long, is a great home base for exploring the wonderful Cape Perpetua area. Trails run from the campground to the top of the cape and to the beach. Flush toilets and piped water are available.

FOOD

For a town its size, Yachats has particularly good restaurant choices.

Start the day at **Green Salmon Bakery and Cafe** (220 U.S. 101, 541/547-3077, www. thegreensalmon.com, 7:30am-2:30pm Tues.-Sun., $2-10) for fresh breads and very good pastries plus soup and sandwiches for lunch. This lively café doubles as a hangout for the local alternative community. Lines can be long and slow-moving at the counter, so come equipped with patience.

Yachats Brewing (348 Hwy. 101 N., 541/547-3884, yachatsbrewing.com, 11am-6pm Mon.-Wed., 11am-7pm Thurs. and Sun, 11am-9pm Fri.-Sat., $5-6) is part of the Yachats FarmStore, a temple of fermentation. Sit at the bar and drink the local brew or one of the guest beers (or kombucha) and snack on pickled vegetables or a bowl of homemade soup. The menu is quite limited, but it's a fun stop for a look-see or a pint.

The carefully restored but easy-going ★ **Drift Inn Pub** (124 U.S. 101 N., 541/547-4477, https://the-drift-inn.com, 8am-10pm daily summer, 8am-9pm daily winter, $15-25) offers seafood dishes, crunchy salads, fish-and-chips, and other well-prepared pub grub in a relaxed atmosphere. There's often really good live music here, making this a lively spot whether you're here to eat or to quaff a pint or two. Families are welcome.

If you are looking for the quintessential fresh seafood experience, go to tiny **Luna Sea Fish House** (153 NW U.S. 101, 541/547-4794, www.lunaseafishhouse.com, 8am-9pm daily summer, 8am-8pm daily winter, $8-16) a fish restaurant owned by a local fisherman. Don't let the simple decor put you off; the food here is *good*. Using local ingredients, and particularly locally caught (never farmed) fish, Luna Sea offers superlative fish-and-chips and fish tacos. Breakfast omelets are also top-notch.

Heidi's (84 Beach St., 541/547-4409, 5pm-8pm Wed.-Sun., $15-25) is a quintessential Yachats business. This tiny Italian café serves brick-oven-baked pizza and homey Italian comfort food, including cioppino and butternut squash lasagna, in a modest little space that fronts the bay. Everything is homemade and served with charm and care. Takeout and dinner delivery are also available.

The simply decorated bay-view **Ona Restaurant** (131 U.S. 101 N., 541/547-6627, www.onarestaurant.com, 4-8:30pm Mon.-Fri., 11am-8:30pm Sat.-Sun., $15-26) serves grilled seafood, meatloaf, steak, and fresh pasta. For appetizers, you can choose between oysters, shrimp, clams, and crab cakes. Ona has a good happy hour (4pm-6pm Sun.-Thurs.), which is a good time to check out their offerings without emptying your wallet.

On a bluff overlooking Smelt Sands Beach is the glass-enclosed **Adobe Resort** (1555 U.S. 101 N., 541/547-3141, 8am-2:30pm and 5pm-9pm Mon.-Sat., 9am-1pm and 5pm-9pm Sun., $16-27). Two side-by-side semicircular dining rooms, with windows on the crashing surf, are a great place to start the day for breakfast or end it with a romantic evening meal, with such favorites as grilled oysters and steaks. Ask about the loft, where elevated coastal views provide photo ops; this is the perfect place to nurse a drink. A Sunday champagne brunch ($18) is served.

INFORMATION

The **Yachats Area Chamber of Commerce** (241 U.S. 101, 541/547-3530 or 800/929-0477, www.yachats.org, 10am-5:30pm daily mid-Mar.-Sept., Fri.-Sun. Oct.-mid-Mar.) has a central location on the highway (next to Clark's Market) and an enthusiastic staff. Ask them about fishing, rockhounding, bird-watching, and beachcombing in the area.

GETTING THERE

The bus stop is also in the parking lot of the **bead shop** (U.S. 101 and W. 3rd St.). Here you can catch **Lincoln County Transit** buses (541/265-4900, www.co.lincoln.or.us/transit), which run four times a day Monday-Saturday between Yachats and Newport, with a link to Lincoln City.

Florence and Vicinity

If you study the map of the central Oregon coast, you'll see that Florence is oriented along the Siuslaw River; a spit of dunes reaches up from the south, barring quick access from downtown to the ocean. But don't dismiss this riverfront town for its lack of oceanfront real estate; the views onto the river are plenty scenic, and Old Town is charming and easy to navigate on foot.

SIGHTS

If first and last impressions are enduring, Florence is truly blessed. A short way to the north of town, U.S. 101 passes over Heceta Head, with great views onto the lighthouse there. As you leave the city to the south, a graceful bridge over the Siuslaw ushers you away.

The Siuslaw River Bridge is an impressive example of Conde McCullough's Works Progress Administration-built spans. The Egyptian obelisks and art deco styling of McCullough's designs are complemented by the views to the west of the coruscating sand dunes. To the east, the riverside panorama of Florence's Old Town beckons for further investigation.

Old Town itself is a tasteful restoration, with all manner of shops and restaurants and an inviting boardwalk along the river. The quickest access to the beach and dunes is south of the bridge via South Jetty Road.

★ Heceta Head Lighthouse and Devil's Elbow

Twelve miles north of Florence, **Heceta Head Lighthouse** (541/547-3416, www.oregonstateparks.org, tours 11am-3pm daily, $5 day-use fee) is dramatically situated above a lovely cove at the mouth of Cape Creek and wedged into the flanks of 1,000-foot-high Heceta Head. The whitewashed lighthouse was completed in 1894 and beautifully restored in 2013; it's still in use, beaming the strongest light on the Oregon coast from its perch 205 feet above the pounding surf. A little below the lighthouse is Heceta House, where the lighthouse keepers used to live. Today, it serves both as an **interpretive center** (11am-4pm Thurs.-Mon. Memorial Day-Labor Day) and the **Heceta Head Lighthouse B&B** (92072 U.S. 101, 541/547-3696 or 866/547-3696, www.hecetalighthouse. com, $209-315). An easy half-mile trail leads up from the lighthouse's picnic and parking area to the tower. Other than the day-use fee, admission and tours are free.

Just south of the lighthouse, the graceful arc of Conde McCullough's Cape Creek Bridge spans a chasm more than 200 feet deep. From the lighthouse parking lot, a trail leads down to where Cape Creek meets the beach at **Devil's Elbow State Park.** Be conscious of tides here if you climb along the rocks adjoining the beach.

Heceta Head is said to be the most photographed lighthouse in the country; that may be difficult to verify, but it's impossible to quibble with the magnificent sight of the gleaming white tower and outbuildings on the headland, particularly when viewed from a set of highway pullouts just south of the bridge. The vistas from the lighthouse

and network of trails on the headland are no less dramatic: See murres, tufted puffins, and other seabirds as well as sea lions on the rock islands below; bald eagles soaring overhead; and in spring, northbound female gray whales and their calves as they pass close to shore. A trail leading to the north side of Heceta Head offers views to Cape Perpetua, 10 miles to the north.

★ Sea Lion Caves

Eleven miles north of Florence, you can descend into the world's largest sea cave to observe the only U.S. mainland rookery of Steller sea lions (*Eumetopias jubatus*). **Sea Lion Caves** (91560 U.S. 101, 541/547-3111, www. sealioncaves.com, 9am-5pm daily, closed Thanksgiving and Christmas, $14 adults, $13 seniors, $8 children ages 5-12, children 4 and under free) is home to a herd that averages 200 individuals, although the numbers change from season to season. These animals occupy the cave during the fall and winter, which are thus the prime visitation times. The Steller sea lions you'll see at those times are cows, yearlings, and immature bulls. In spring and summer, they breed and raise their young on the rock ledges just outside the cave. In addition, California sea lions (*Zalophus californianus*),

The Oregon Dunes spill into the Siuslaw River across from downtown Florence.

Florence's elegant McCullough Bridge spans the Siuslaw River.

common all along the Pacific Coast, are found at Sea Lion Caves from late fall to early spring.

Enter Sea Lion Caves through the gift shop on U.S. 101. A steep downhill walk reveals stunning perspectives of the coastal cliffs as well as several kinds of gulls and cormorants that nest here. The final leg of the descent is by an elevator that drops an additional 208 feet. After stepping off the lift into the cave, your eyes adjust to the gloomy subterranean light, and you'll see sea lions on the rock shelves amid the surging water inside the enormous cave. Flash photography is forbidden, so study your camera's settings if you want to take pictures inside. You have a better chance of seeing these animals inside during fall and winter. A set of stairs leads up to a view of Heceta Head Lighthouse through an opening in the cave.

Steller sea lions were referred to as *lobos marinos* (sea wolves) in early Spanish mariners' accounts of their 16th-century West Coast voyages, and their doglike yelps might explain why. You'll notice several shades of color in the herd, which has to do with the progressive lightening of their coats with age. Males sometimes weigh more than a ton, and dominate the scene with macho posturings

to scare off rivals for harems of as many as two dozen cows. Their protection as an endangered species enrages many commercial anglers, who claim that the sea lions take a significant bite out of fishing revenues by preying on salmon. In any case, the close-up view of these huge sea mammals in the cavernous enclaves of their natural habitat should not be missed—despite an odor not unlike sweat-soaked sneakers.

If you can't observe the animals to your satisfaction in the cave, or if you want a free look from a distance, go 0.25 mile north of the concession entrance to the "rockwork" turnout, where the herd sometimes populates the rocky ledges several hundred feet below. It's also a good place to snap a shot of the picturesque Heceta Head Lighthouse across the cove to the north from the turnout.

Darlingtonia Botanical Gardens

Three miles north up the Coast Highway from Florence, in an area noted for dune access and freshwater lakes, are the **Darlingtonia Botanical Gardens** (five miles north of Florence on the east side of U.S. 101, 800/551-6949, www.oregonstateparks.org, free). In a

Stop by the Darlingtonia Botanical Gardens to see these carniverous plants.

sylvan grove of spruce and alder are a series of wooden platforms that guide you through a bog where carnivorous *Darlingtonia californica* plants thrive. Shaped like a serpent's head, the darlingtonia is variously referred to as the cobra orchid, cobra lily, or pitcher plant.

The plant produces a sweet smell that invites insects to crawl through an opening into a hollow chamber beneath the plant's hood. Inside, thin transparent "windows" allow light to shine inside the chamber, confusing the bug as to where the exit is. As the insect crawls around in search of an escape, downward-pointing hairs within the enclosure inhibit its movement to freedom. Eventually, the tired-out bug falls to the bottom of the stem, where it is digested. The plant needs the nutrients from the trapped insects to compensate for the lack of sustenance supplied by its small root system. If you still have an appetite after witnessing this carnage, you might want to enjoy lunch at one of the shaded picnic tables.

Siuslaw Pioneer Museum

To fill yourself in on the early history of Florence and the Siuslaw River Valley and to get some notion of Native American and pioneer life, spend an hour or so at the **Siuslaw Pioneer Museum** (278 Maple St., 541/997-7884, www.siuslawpioneermuseum. com, noon-4pm daily May-Sept., noon-4pm Tues.-Sun. Feb.-Apr. and Oct.-Dec., $3 adults, children ages 16 and under free). You'll find it in Old Town in a renovated school building dating from 1905. Along with exhibits on early logging and farming, read an account of how the U.S. government double-crossed the Siuslaw people, who sold their land to the feds and never received the promised recompense. The museum can also set you loose on a walking tour of historic Old Town buildings.

Jessie M. Honeyman Memorial State Park

Jessie M. Honeyman Memorial State Park (84505 U.S. 101 S., 541/997-3641 information, 800/452-5687 reservations, $5 day-use fee or Oregon Coast Passport), three miles south of Florence, has a spectacular dune-scape and then some. Come here in May when the rhododendrons bloom along the short, sinuous road heading to the parking lot. A short walk west of the lot brings you to a 150-foot-high dune overlooking Cleawox Lake. From the top of this dune, look westward across the expanse of sand, marsh, and remnants of forest at the blue Pacific some two miles away. This is also a popular place to camp.

South Jetty

The northern boundary of the Oregon Dunes National Recreation Area is at the **South Jetty** ($5 per car or Northwest Forest Pass), where the Siuslaw River flows into the Pacific Ocean. May-September and on all weekends and holidays, the beach at the South Jetty is closed to motor vehicles, and even though there are no marked trails, it's a great place to explore the dunes in near solitude. The road into the jetty has several staging areas for off-highway vehicles; during the summer months, the area south of the road is open to motor vehicles. South Jetty Road is 0.5 mile south of the Siuslaw River Bridge.

SPORTS AND RECREATION

Huckleberry picking is an attraction just outside Florence. Some prime pickings are found about five miles north of Florence along the Sutton Creek Trail, which begins in the Sutton campground just off U.S. 101. During late summer or fall, these berries flourish below the dense canopy of shore pines.

Hiking

You'll find incredibly scenic hiking in the area around **Carl G. Washburne State Park,** 14 miles north of Florence on U.S. 101. At the southern end of the park is the **Hobbit Trail,** which winds 0.4 mile through dense forest thickets of pine, fir, and rhododendrons to the three-mile-long beach. From the same trailhead, another path takes off uphill to the **Heceta Head Lighthouse**. In its 1.75-mile run, the trail gains quite a bit of elevation and passes some outstanding viewpoints. Also starting at the same U.S. 101 parking area, the **China Creek Trail** (a.k.a. the Valley Trail) runs 1.7 miles on the east side of the highway through a series of elk meadows to the Washburne campground. The parking area for all these hikes is on the east side of U.S. 101. It's also possible to park in the day-use lot across the highway from the campground, catch the Valley Trail near the campground entrance, and hike to the Hobbit and Heceta Head Trails.

Up the North Fork of the Siuslaw River is the **Pawn Old-Growth Trail,** a half-mile pathway through 9-foot-thick, 275-foot-tall Douglas fir and hemlock trees that are several hundred years old. The trailhead, at the confluence of the North Fork of the Siuslaw and Taylor's Creek, is a good place to see salmon spawning in the fall and observe water ouzels (also called dippers). The trail follows the creek and offers interpretive placards along

the way. At one point in the trail, visitors walk through fallen Douglas fir logs 21 feet in diameter. Placards explain the science of tree rings. From Florence, take Highway 126 east for one mile, then turn north onto Forest Road 5070 and take it 12 miles to Forest Road 5084; stay right and go another five miles to the trailhead.

An excellent and not terribly difficult introduction to dune hiking can be found about 10 miles south of Florence at the **Oregon Dunes Day-Use Area** ($5 day-use fee). The **Overlook Beach Trail** runs for about a mile from a viewing platform to the beach. Follow the blue-topped wooden posts that mark the trail through the sand. To turn this into a more strenuous 3.5-mile loop, continue one mile south along the beach and head back inland (again following the posts) along the more rugged **Tahkenitch Creek Loop.** Find the turnoff from U.S. 101 near milepost 201.

Another good place to explore the dunes is along **Carter Dunes Trail** and **Taylor Dunes Trail.** Carter Dunes Trail starts near Carter Lake and heads west 1.5 miles to the beach. The first half of the mile-long Taylor Dunes Trail is wheelchair accessible; the trail passes some of the oldest (and gnarliest) conifers in the area. Both of these trails are good places to view wildlife, especially in the winter and spring, when the dunes take on wetland characteristics. The two trails link up, forming a Y rather than a loop. The turnoff for both trails is 7.5 miles south of Florence. Carter Lake also has a campground.

Hike the **Waxmyrtle Trail** along the Siltcoos River; the 1.5-mile trail travels along the estuary and ends up at the beach. The trail is closed March 15-September 15 to protect nesting snowy plover. This is a good spot for bird-watching. Find the trailhead near the Waxmyrtle campground about eight miles south of Florence at the Siltcoos Recreation Area.

Dune Rides

Ride into the dunes with the folks from **Sand**

Dune Country: Florence to Coos Bay

The Dunes Overlook, south of Florence, is a jumping-off point for trails in the Oregon Dunes.

Even though the 47-mile stretch of U.S. 101 between Coos Bay and Florence does not overlook the ocean, your eyes will be drawn constantly westward to the largest and most extensive oceanfront dunes in the world.

How did they come to exist in a coastal topography otherwise dominated by rocky bluffs? A combination of factors created this landscape over the past 12,000 years, but the principal agents are the Coos, Siuslaw, and Umpqua Rivers. The sand and sediment transported to the sea by these waterways are deposited by waves on the flat, shallow beaches. Prevailing westerlies move the particulate matter exposed by the tide eastward up to several yards per year. Over the millennia, the dunes have grown huge, with some topping 500 feet.

Constantly on the move, the shifting sands have engulfed ancient forests, a fact occasionally corroborated by hikers as they stumble on the top of an exposed snag. The cross-section of sand-swept woodlands seen from U.S. 101 demonstrates that this inundation is still occurring. Nonetheless, the motorist gets the impression that the trees are winning the battle, because the dunes are only intermittently visible from the road.

Dunes Frontier (83960 U.S. 101, 541/997-3544, http://sanddunesfrontier.com, 9am-6pm daily summer, 10am-4pm Tues.-Sat. Dec. 15-Mar. 15). Half-hour-long, 20-person dune buggy rides cost $14 for adults and $11 for children ages 4-11 years old. Protective goggles are provided, along with a driver. At the same location, **Torex ATV Rentals** (541/997-5363, $50-200 per hour) rents vehicles for travel in specially designated areas within the Oregon Dunes National Recreation Area. Go in the morning when the sand tends to blow around less.

Fishing

Oregon's largest coastal lake, 3,100-acre **Siltcoos Lake,** six miles south of Florence, offers excellent fishing and other recreation. The lake is stocked with rainbow trout in the spring, and steelhead, salmon (the lake is closed to coho fishing), and sea-run cutthroat trout move from the ocean into the lake via the short Siltcoos River in late summer and fall. But the real excitement here is the fishing for warm-water species, which are some of the best in the Pacific Northwest. Bluegill, crappie, yellow perch, and brown bullhead action is good through the summer, while fishing for large-mouth bass can be good year-round. Access points include several public and private boat ramps on the lake, as well as a wheelchair-accessible fishing pier at Westlake Resort.

Golf

Ocean Dunes Golf Links (3345 Munsel Lake Rd., 541/997-3232, $48 for 18 holes), part of the Three Rivers Casino complex, lets you tee off with sand dunes (some more than 60 feet tall) as a backdrop. The manicured 18-hole course has a driving range, a full pro shop, and equipment rentals on-site. For the ultimate in golfing by the dunes, however, try **Sandpines Golf Course** (1201 35th St., 541/997-1940, www.sandpines.com, $79 for 18 holes, $69 for Oregon and Washington residents). To get there, go west off U.S. 101 on 35th Street. In May and June rhododendrons line this drive, which heads into dune country as you move toward the sea. Follow the signs until you see a water tower not far from the pro shop. A par-72, 7,190-yard course, Sandpines's layout features fairways lined with lakes, Douglas firs, and beach grass on gently undulating terrain; the inward nine holes are traditional links style. Coastal winds that kick up in the afternoon can figure prominently in your shot selection.

Horseback Riding

Riding across the dunes into the sunset on a trusty steed sounds like a fantasy, but you can do it thanks to **C&M Stables** (90241 U.S. 101, 541/997-7540, www.oregonhorsebackriding.com, 10am-5pm daily). Rates range $60-125 per person for trips of 1-2 hours (with discounts for larger parties). The stables are open year-round and are located near 14 miles of horse trails that wind through the forest on a bluff above the beach. With beach rides, dune trail excursions, and sunset trips, there's something for everybody.

Sandboarding

Dude, it's a natural! Wax up a board, strap it onto your bare feet, and carve your way down the dunes. On the outskirts of Florence, you can rent a board and try out the rails and jumps at **Sand Master Park** (5351 U.S. 101, 541/997-6006, www.sandmasterpark.com, 9am-7pm daily mid-June-mid-Sept., 10am-5pm Mon.-Tues. and Thurs.-Sat., noon-5pm Sun. Mar.-May and mid-Sept.-mid-Jan., board rentals $10-25 includes admission). If you're more of a do-it-yourselfer, a number of roadside shops rent sandboards, and the dunes are certainly plentiful.

Water Sports

Although only the hardiest swimmers go into the ocean without wetsuits, **Cleawox** and **Woahink Lakes** warm up sufficiently to make summertime swimming enjoyable. Cleawox, the smaller of the two, is especially well suited for swimming. A lodge (10am-5pm Memorial Day-Labor Day) by the swimming beach rents pedal boats, canoes, and kayaks. Both lakes are within Honeyman State Park, three miles south of Florence ($5 per vehicle day-use fee).

Surfers head to the beaches at South Jetty, where the waves are best when small—they can often become overwhelming and unsuitable for novices. Look for more protection from the wind at the mouth of the river.

South of Florence, in the Oregon Dunes National Recreation Area, the **Siltcoos River** invites kayakers and canoeists to explore the two-mile stretch between Siltcoos Lake and the sea. Meandering two miles through dunes, forest, and estuary, the Siltcoos is a gentle Class I paddle with no white water or rapids, although a small dam midway must be portaged. Wildlife that you may encounter along the way include mink, raccoons, otters, beavers, and even bears. In the estuary, sea lions and harbor seals are common. Rent a canoe or kayak from **Siltcoos Lake Resort** (82855 Fir St., Westlake, 541/999-6941, www.siltcooslakeresort.com, $45 per day).

ENTERTAINMENT AND EVENTS

For current information on Florence area events, contact the **Florence Chamber of Commerce** (541/997-3128, www.florence-chamber.com).

During the third weekend of May, Florence celebrates the **Rhododendron Festival** co-inciding with the blooming of these flowers, which proliferate in the area. It's a tradition that goes back to 1908, when the festival was started as a way to draw attention and commerce to the town. A parade, carnival, flower show, 5K "Rhody Run," and the crowning of Queen Rhododendra are highlights of the festivities. This is a very popular event, attracting more than 15,000 visitors each year.

Fourth of July celebrations include live outdoor music and a barbecue in Old Town, along with a fireworks display over the river.

Authors, publishers, and readers gather at the **Florence Festival of Books** (541/997-1994) at the Florence Events Center the last weekend of September.

For general entertainment, the tribes run **Three Rivers Casino** (5647 Hwy. 126, 541/997-7529). Along with the slots and game tables, there's a hotel and golf course.

ACCOMMODATIONS

Like just about everywhere else, there are budget motels on the main drag. We've selected a few with some character, but urge you to consider one of the local B&Bs.

Unless otherwise noted, prices listed are for high-season doubles.

$50-100

One of the best bargains in town is the **Lighthouse Inn** (155 U.S. 101, 541/997-3221 or 866/997-3221, $86-145), a Cape Cod-style two-story motel on the highway close to the bridge and convenient to Old Town. With neatly kept rooms decorated with bric-a-brac and other homey touches, it may give you the feeling that you're spending the night at your grandmother's house. A pet-friendly suite includes a kitchenette, most rooms have

microwaves and refrigerators. Most guest rooms also have a queen- or king-size bed and sleep two; some are considered suites, with two rooms and a connecting bath, sleeping up to five guests. A few rooms are designated as pet-friendly.

If it's not important for you to be an easy walk from Old Town, consider staying three miles south of town at the charming and pet-friendly ★ **Park Motel** (85034 U.S. 101, 541/997-2634 or 800/392-0441, www.park-motelflorence.com, $89-145), a classic mom-and-pop place set well back from the highway in a stand of Douglas firs. The guest rooms are paneled in knotty pine and come in a variety of sizes and configurations, including a few cabins, making it a good place for families or groups of friends.

$100-150

For a river experience, try the ★ **River House Motel** (1202 Bay St., 541/997-3933 or 888/824-2454, www.riverhouseflorence.com, $119-189). It's worth paying extra for a river-front balcony ($159). This newer and attractive motel, which also has good views of the Siuslaw River Bridge, is just two blocks away from the heart of Old Town.

Just around the corner from Old Town and across the highway from the Lighthouse Inn, the pet-friendly **Old Town Inn** (170 U.S. 101 N., 541/997-7131 or 800/301-6494, www.old-town-inn.com, $115) provides guests with spacious rooms a short walk away from the river and Old Town. Although this motel is on U.S. 101, the guest rooms are fairly quiet.

$150-200

★ **The Edwin K B&B** (1155 Bay St., 541/997-8360 or 800/833-9465, www.edwink.com, $165-200) has six guest rooms, all with private bathrooms, and is just two blocks from Old Town, across the street from the Siuslaw River. River views, period antiques, and multicourse breakfasts with locally famous soufflés and home-baked breads served on fine china have established this gracious 1914 home as Florence's preeminent B&B. Add a private courtyard and waterfall in back, tea and sherry in the afternoon, and a restful atmosphere, and you'll understand the need to reserve well in advance.

At Heceta Beach, on the northern edge of Florence, **Driftwood Shores Resort** (88416 1st Ave., 541/997-8263 or 800/422-5091, www.driftwoodshores.com, $122-264) is unique among Florence lodgings in that it is oceanside. It is also a huge complex and in a pretty isolated area, far from Old Town and restaurants (except the resort restaurant). All rooms face the ocean and have decks or patios, as well as microwaves and refrigerators (some suites have full kitchens).

Over $200

Twelve miles north of Florence and just a short walk from Heceta Head Lighthouse is **Heceta Head Lighthouse B&B** (92072 U.S. 101, 541/547-3696 or 866/547-3696, www.hecetalighthouse.com, $209-315), built in 1893. It used to be the lighthouse keeper's home; today, it's a B&B with antique furnishings and vintage photos, which help recreate the lives of the keepers of the flame. Among the six bedrooms, the two Mariners' rooms command the finest views. The current caretakers maintain a garden on the grounds, as did the actual lighthouse keepers of yesteryear, and they use some of the produce to turn out amazing seven-course breakfasts, glorious 90-minute affairs replete with such dishes as d'Anjou pear with chevre and Oregon honey and vol-au-vent stuffed with eggs, chives, and asparagus. The innkeepers are more likely to tell you about resident ghosts during breakfast than right before bedtime.

On the south bank of the river, just across the bridge from Old Town, the **Best Western Pier Point Inn** (85625 U.S. 101, 541/997-7191 or 800/435-6736, www.bwpierpointinn.com, $215-220) offers spacious rooms, great bay views, sand-dune hiking across the street, and a complimentary hot breakfast. Rates at this large and classy motel drop by about half in the off-season.

Vacation Rentals

Elson Shields Property Management (3298 U.S. 101, 541/997-6235, www.florence-rentals.com) offers vacation home rentals in the Florence and Oregon Dunes area.

Camping

There are excellent campgrounds around Florence, several with recreational opportunities comparable to those at the nearby Oregon Dunes National Recreation Area but with more varied scenery.

Carl G. Washburne State Park (93111 U.S. 101 N., 541/547-3416 information, 800/452-5687 yurt reservations, www.oregonstateparks.org, year-round, $21 tents, $28-31 RVs, $44 yurts, $5 hiker-biker) is popular with Oregonians because of its proximity to beaches, tidepools, Sea Lion Caves, and hiking trails. The seven walk-in tent sites are secluded, and the remaining 57 have electricity and water (some also have sewer hookups); like almost all state park campgrounds, there are showers. Reservations are not accepted for regular sites, but the park's two yurts can be reserved. It's 14 miles north of Florence on U.S. 101 (three miles past Sea Lion Caves), then one mile west on a park road. This state park offers a number of good hiking trails and three miles of relatively isolated beach.

Three miles south of Florence's McCullough Bridge and on both sides of U.S. 101 is **Honeyman State Park** (84505 U.S. 101 S., 541/997-3641 information, 800/452-5687 reservations, www.oregonstateparks.org, $21 tents, $28-31 RVs, $54 pet-friendly yurts, $5 hiker-biker). This large and exceedingly popular campground gets very crowded in the summer—reservations are a must—but it empties out enough during spring and autumn to make a stay here worthwhile. The park is popular with ATV users, who camp in the H loop, where there's a two-mile ATV trail to the beach. (Hiking from the campground to the beach is discouraged.) In spring, pink rhododendrons line the highway and park roads.

If you're looking for something smaller and low-key, then two Siuslaw National Forest

Service campgrounds just north of Florence might be the ticket. **Sutton Campground** (877/444-6777 or www.recreation.gov, $22 regular site, $26 with electricity) is four miles north of Florence, and in addition to 80 campsites amid the dunes, it features a darlingtonia bog and a hiking trail network (flush toilets, but no showers). In high summer season, about a quarter of the sites can be reserved; the rest are available on a first-come, first-served basis.

Just another mile north is **Alder Dune Campground** (877/444-6777 or www.recreation.gov, $22) with two lakes with swimming beaches and trout fishing. Hiking trails lead out into the dunes and reach the Pacific beaches. During summer high season, all of the campground's 39 sites can be reserved. For more information on these campgrounds, contact the **Suislaw National Forest** (541/271-6000, www.fs.fed.us).

FOOD

The majority of Florence restaurants are along the Old Town waterfront. Walk along Bay Street and discover dozens of dining options, from casual to upscale.

Coffee and Tea

Under the bridge in Old Town, **Siuslaw River Coffee Roasters** (1240 Bay St., 541/997-3443, www.coffeeoregon.com, 7am-5pm daily, $2-6) serves good coffee and pastries. There's a little deck out back overlooking the river, and lots of books and hobnobbing inside.

If you're visiting on a rainy afternoon, a good place to while away the time is **Lovejoy's Tea Room** (129 Nopal St., 541/997-0502, lovejoysrestaurant.com, 11am-6pm daily, $8-16), owned by the founder of a famed San Francisco tearoom. Dine on a Cornish pasty or sausage roll or go for high tea service.

Mexican

It doesn't look like much from the front, but the best reason to seek out the **Traveler's Cove** (1362 Bay St., 541/997-6845, 9am-9pm daily, $9-20) is the lovely back patio, with tables directly over the river. The food is eclectic, with homemade clam chowder, tempting salads and sandwiches, and a number of Mexican dishes. Fresh Dungeness crab makes an appearance here with crab quiche, crab enchiladas, and "crabby" Caesar salad.

Italian

A good place to take a break from chowder (though not necessarily seafood) is **Pomodori Ristorante** (1415 7th St., 541/902-2525, www.lapomodori.com, 11:30am-2pm and 5pm-8pm Tues.-Fri., 5pm-8pm Sat., $14-24), an intimate northern Italian restaurant in a converted house. Specialties include fresh shrimp and halibut and pasta, as well as a pork chop stuffed with shrimp, pancetta, scallions, and tomatoes.

Down in Old Town, **1285 Restobar** (1285 Bay St., 541/902-8338, www.1285restobar.com, 11am-10pm daily, $8-17) is a lively trattoria with a focus on very good seafood entrées; pizza is also a popular choice. During happy hour, have a seat at a sidewalk table and watch the action on Bay Street; the patio out back is more secluded.

Pacific Northwest

The Oregon coast isn't really known for adventurous fine dining, but a handful of hip eateries are spicing up the scene. At the edge of Old Town, the ★ **Homegrown Public House** (294 Laurel St., 541/997-4886, www.homegrownpub.com, 11am-9pm Tues.-Sat., $8-23) is an easygoing place for a beer and a snack or a full meal. As the name implies, much of the food is locally grown or gathered (try the summer chanterelles if they're available) and seasonal.

Seafood

No one will ever accuse the ★ **Waterfront Depot** (1252 Bay St., 541/902-9100, www.thewaterfrontdepot.com, 4pm-10pm nightly, $14-18) of lacking in personality; it's a friendly, bustling place with good views out onto the river and lovely filtered evening light. This historic structure was formerly the rail station

Shoot a few baskets before dinner at the Homegrown Public House.

at nearby Mapleton before it was barged down the Siuslaw River to its current riverfront location. Ask for a table or sit at the bar, where you're likely to be next to a local regular in for the restaurant's signature dish, saucy crab-encrusted halibut fillet. For lighter appetites, try ordering from the tapas menu, which, like all the offerings, is written on a chalkboard up on the wall.

In Old Town, the local **Mo's** (1436 Bay St., 541/997-2185, www.moschowder.com, 11am-8pm Sun.-Thurs., 11am-9pm Fri.-Sat., $6-18) is the largest outlet of this famed Oregon chowder house, and its fresh fish, fast service, fair prices, and Siuslaw River frontage make it a good bet for a family meal.

Dessert

After dinner, have dessert at one of the two locations of **BJ's Ice Cream Parlor** (2930 U.S. 101 or 1441 Bay St., 541/997-7286, 10am-11pm daily summer, 11am-10pm daily winter, $2-6). BJ's churns out hundreds of flavors, with 48 on display at any given time. Full fountain service, ice cream cakes, cheesecakes, gourmet frozen yogurt, and pies complement the cones and cups.

INFORMATION AND SERVICES

The **Florence Area Chamber of Commerce** (290 U.S. 101, 541/997-3128, www.florencechamber.com, 9am-5pm Mon.-Fri.) is three blocks north of the Siuslaw River Bridge.

Peace Harbor Hospital (400 9th St., Florence, 541/997-8412) is open 24 hours, with a handful of specialists and an emergency room. The **post office** (770 Maple St., 541/997-2533), near the junction of Highway 126 and U.S. 101, is close to the library.

GETTING THERE

Porter Stage Lines (541/269-7183, www.pslporterstageline.com) offers Sun.-Fri. bus service between Coos Bay in the south and Eugene to the east. Eugene offers both Greyhound and Amtrak service, as well as air links to the rest of the country from Mahlon Sweet Field Airport (EUG).

Reedsport and Winchester Bay

If you're going fishing or coming back from a dunes hike, you'll appreciate a clean low-priced motel room in Reedsport. Otherwise, this town of 5,000 people might seem like a strange mirage of cut-rate motels, taverns, and burger joints in the midst of the Oregon Dunes National Recreation Area. Reedsport is not a tourist town, to put it politely. But there's lots of fascinating recreation available in the Oregon Dunes NRA that encircles the town, and the Umpqua River is itself a destination for anglers.

Three miles southwest of Reedsport, Salmon Harbor Marina in **Winchester Bay** (pop. 1,000), a busy port for commercial sportfishing at the mouth of the Umpqua, has given the whole area new life in recent years, following hard times precipitated by the decline in timber revenues. In many ways, Winchester Bay is the more interesting destination of the two side-by-side towns, with its busy harbor and collage of waterfront bars and restaurants.

SIGHTS
Oregon Dunes

A great place to start your explorations is the **Oregon Dunes NRA Visitor Information Center** (885 U.S. 101, Reedsport, 541/271-6100, www.fs.usda.gov/siuslaw), at the junction of the Coast Highway and Highway 38. In addition to the printed information on hiking, camping, and recreation, the Siuslaw Forest Service personnel are very helpful.

Note that a $5 day-use fee is charged per vehicle at most facilities and access points within the NRA. You can purchase an annual pass at the Dunes Visitor Center for $30.

Because the dunes are difficult to see from the highway in many places, the most commonly asked question in the visitors center is "Where are the dunes?" To answer that question for everybody, the National Forest Service opened **Oregon Dunes Overlook** just south of Carter Lake, midway between Florence and

Reedsport, at the point where the dunes come closest to U.S. 101. In addition to four levels of railing-enclosed platforms connected by wooden walkways, there are trails down to the sand. It's only about 0.25 mile to the dunes and then a mile through sand and wetlands to the beach.

You can hike a loop beginning where the sand gives way to willows. Bear right en route to the beach. Once there, walk south 1.5 miles. A wooden post marks where the trail resumes. It then traverses a footbridge going through trees onto sand, completing the loop. If you go in February, this loop has great bird-watching potential. A day-use fee is charged for cars.

Umpqua Discovery Center

In Reedsport's Old Town on the south bank of the river, the **Umpqua Discovery Center** (409 Riverfront Way, 541/271-4816, www.

The Umpqua Discovery Center is on the Reedsport waterfront.

umpquadiscoverycenter.com, 10-5pm Mon.-Sat., noon-4pm Sun. June-Sept., 10am-4pm Mon.-Sat., noon-4pm Sun. Oct.-May, $8 adults, $4 children ages 6-15) interprets the regional human and natural history through multimedia programs, dioramas, scale models, and helpful staff. The gift store is stuffed with local goodies. The boardwalk and observation tower give a good view of the broad lower reaches of the Umpqua.

Dean Creek Elk Viewing Area

Three miles east of Reedsport and stretching three miles along the south side of Highway 38, the **Dean Creek Elk Viewing Area** (48819 Hwy. 38, Reedsport, www.blm.gov, 541/756-0100) provides parking areas and viewing platforms for observing the herd of some 120 wild Roosevelt elk that roam this 1,100-acre preserve. The elk move out of the forest to graze the preserve's marshy pastures, sometimes coming quite close to the highway. Elk can reach 1,100 pounds at maturity, and the majestic rack on a fully grown bull can spread three feet across. Early mornings and just before dusk are the most promising times to look for them; during hot weather and storms, the elk tend to stay within the cover of the woods.

Umpqua Lighthouse State Park

Less than one mile south of Winchester Bay is **Umpqua Lighthouse State Park** (460 Lighthouse Rd., Winchester Bay, 541/271-4118, www.oregonstateparks.org, 10am-4pm daily May-Oct., $3). Tour the red-capped 1894 **lighthouse** (1020 Lighthouse Rd., 541/271-4631, 10am-4pm daily May-Oct., $5 lighthouse tours) or admire it from the roadside. Next door, in a former Coast Guard building, the park's **visitors center and museum** has marine and timber exhibits; this is also where tours begin. Directly opposite the lighthouse, overlooking the mouth of the Umpqua and oceanfront dunes, is a whale-watching platform with a plaque explaining where, when, and what to look for.

The squat Umpqua Lighthouse sits across the road from the beach.

Lake Marie, just south near the camping area, has a swimming beach and is stocked with rainbow trout. A one-mile forest trail around the lake makes for an easy hike. A trail from the campground leads to the highest dunes in the United States (elev. 545 feet), west of Clear Lake.

SPORTS AND RECREATION
Fishing

Winchester Bay and the tidewater reaches of the lower Umpqua River comprise Oregon's top coastal sturgeon fishery and one of the best areas for striped bass, particularly near the mouth of the Smith River, which enters the Umpqua just east of Reedsport. The best action for the Umpqua's spring chinook tends to be inland, below Scottsburg. Fall chinook enter the bay July-September. Other notable fisheries here are the huge runs of shad, which peak May-June, and smallmouth bass offer action upstream from Reedsport. Crabbing and clamming are also popular and productive pastimes in Winchester Bay and the lower reaches of the river. Every year August 1-mid-September, tagged crabs are released into the water in and around Winchester Bay—one of them worth a cash prize of $5,000 to whomever catches it.

Fishing charter services operating in the area include **Living Waters** (541/584-2295, www.fishinglivingwaters.com) and **Winchester Bay Charters** (541/361-0180, www.winchesterbaycharters.com).

Hiking

There are three excellent state parks and a dozen Siuslaw National Forest Campgrounds within the **Oregon Dunes NRA**. Although joyriding in noisy dune buggies and other off-road vehicles doesn't lack devotees, the best way to appreciate the interface of ecosystems is on foot. Dunes exceeding 500 feet in height, wetland breeding grounds for waterfowl and other animals, evergreen forests, and deserted beaches can be encountered in a march to the sea. Numerous designated hiking trails, ranging from easy half-mile loops to six-mile round-trips, give visitors a chance to star in their own version of *Lawrence of Arabia*. The soundtrack is provided by the 247 species of birds—along with your

heartbeat—as you scale these elephantine anthills. Deserted beaches and secret swimming holes are among the many rewards of the journey.

Before setting out, pick up the *Hiking Trails Recreation Opportunity Guide* from the Oregon Dunes NRA Visitor Center. Carry plenty of water and dress in layers—there are hot spots in dune valleys and ocean breezes at higher elevations.

★ JOHN DELLENBACK TRAIL

This spectacular dunes landscape can be found 10.5 miles south of Reedsport and 0.25 mile south of the Eel Creek Campground near Lakeside. After you emerge from a 0.5-mile hike through coastal evergreen forest, you'll be greeted by dunes 300-400 feet high. It's said that dunes near here can approach 500 feet high and one mile long after a windblown buildup. The trail, marked by blue-banded wooden posts, continues another 2.5 miles to the beach. Note that dune hiking can be a bit disorienting. If you lose the trail, climb to the top of the tallest dune and scan for the trail markers.

A shorter and easier one-mile loop trail leads through woodlands to the dunes for a quick introduction to this landscape.

Winchester Bay is a fishing hub.

Skate Park

Near the south end of Reedsport in Lions Park is a world-class **skate park** (U.S. 101 and S. 22nd St.). Here you'll find a funnel-shaped full pipe and a 360-degree full loop, as well as many more approachable features.

Water Sports

Ten miles south of Reedsport, the sleepy resort town of **Lakeside** hosted visits from Bob Hope, Bing Crosby, and the Ink Spots, among other luminaries, back in its 1930s and 1940s heyday. Today, it's still a popular destination, primarily for its proximity to the sprawling, many-armed Tenmile and North Tenmile Lakes. These large shallow lakes offer waterskiing and excellent fishing for stocked rainbow trout and warm-water species, including crappie, yellow perch, bluegill, and lunker largemouth bass, which can grow up to 10 pounds. A 0.25-mile channel connects the two lakes, and a county park on Tenmile Lake has a paved boat ramp, fishing docks, a sandy swimming beach, and a picnic area.

ENTERTAINMENT AND EVENTS

Every June over Father's Day weekend, chainsaw sculptors compete for $10,000 in prizes as they transform pieces of raw western red cedar into grizzly bears, giant salmon, and other rustic works of art during the **Chainsaw Sculpture Championships** (www.odcsc.com) at the Rainbow Plaza in Old Town Reedsport, near North 2nd Street and Greenwood Avenue.

Dunefest (541/271-3495, dunefest.com) brings ATV riders to town for races, freestyle shows, a treasure hunt, and more at the end of July.

ACCOMMODATIONS

Just off Highway 101 on the road to Winchester Bay, **Salmon Harbor Landing** (265 8th St., Winchester Bay, 541/271-3742, www.salmonharborlanding.com, $65-75) is a simple but clean and friendly motel. This is a good place to stay if you don't need fancy

amenities yet enjoy a personal touch. Each room is individually decorated, with many of the owner's antiques featured.

Anglers, or anyone who'd rather be in a location off the main drag, should consider the **Winchester Bay Inn** (390 Broadway, Winchester Bay, 541/271-4871 or 800/246-1462, www.winbayinn.com, $79-130), just across from the docks. Guest rooms are basic but clean. Even though this is a large sprawling complex, be sure to reserve ahead of time in fishing season. Pets are permitted in some guest rooms.

Another clean and convenient place for anglers, crabbers, and storm-watchers is the **Harbor View Motel** (540 Beach Blvd., Winchester Bay, 541/271-3352, $50-70), a small budget motel with easy access to charter boats.

The **Best Western Plus Salbasgeon Inn** (1400 U.S. 101, 541/271-4831 or 800/780-7234, $135-145) is Reedsport's largest and most full-service hotel, on U.S. 101 just south of the Umpqua River bridge. Amenities include an indoor pool, a fitness center, guest laundry, a hot tub, and complimentary breakfast.

Camping

Choices abound in this recreation-rich area. Just south of Winchester Bay is **Umpqua Lighthouse State Park** (460 Lighthouse Rd., Winchester Bay, 541/271-4118 information, 800/452-5687 reservations, www.oregonstateparks.org, $19-80). The campground alongside Lake Marie has firewood, flush toilets, showers, picnic tables, electricity, and piped water. The 20 RV sites go for $26; the 24 tent sites are $19; two basic yurts are $40; six deluxe yurts (with shower, small kitchen, refrigerator, microwave, and TV/VCR) are $80; and two rustic cabins are $39. The lake offers fishing, boating, and swimming. Trails from the campground lead to the highest dunes in the United States (elev. 545 feet), west of Clear Lake.

William A. Tugman State Park (541/759-3604 information, 800/452-5687 reservations, www.oregonstateparks.org, $24 tent or RV,

$43 yurt, $53 pet-friendly yurt) is eight miles south of Reedsport, in the heart of dune country. This larger campground with 115 sites sits on the west shore of Eel Lake, east of U.S. 101 across from the widest point of the dunes and two miles from the sea.

Windy Cove Campground (541/271-4138) is a county park with 24 full-hookup sites ($24) and four other sites with electric service only ($15). Located on the south side of Salmon Harbor Drive across from the Winchester Bay marina, it has restrooms, picnic tables, grass, and paved site pads. No reservations are accepted. It is legal to drive your off-highway vehicle (OHV) from this campground directly to the dunes, but that requires a couple of miles' drive on the pavement.

About nine miles south of Reedsport, set along Eel Creek near Eel and Tenmile Lakes, is **Eel Creek Campground** (877/444-6777 reservations, www.recreation.gov, mid-May-Sept., $20), a Siuslaw National Forest facility with 51 basic tent and RV sites; reservations are advised. The Umpqua Dunes Trail offers access to the dunes and the beach.

Eight miles north of Reedsport, the **Tahkenitch Campground** (877/444-6777 reservations, www.recreation.gov, mid-May-Sept., $20) is another Forest Service facility set among ancient Douglas firs and conveniently located near Tahkenitch and other lakes, dunes, and ocean beaches. A network of trails branch out through the dunes, along Tahkenitch Lake, and to the beach.

If you're coming to the dunes to ride ATVs and don't mind noise, consider spending the night at the all-in-one **Discovery Point Resort** (242 Discovery Point Ln., 541/271-3443, www.discoverypointresort.com, $18 tents, $34-37 RVs) near Winchester Bay. The resort offers OHV enthusiasts dune access and all-terrain vehicle (ATV) rentals, and provides condos, one- to three-bedroom cabins (which sleep up to six, $285), 60 RV spaces, and tent sites. To get there from Reedsport, head two miles south on U.S. 101 to Winchester Bay, then turn right at Pelican Market onto Salmon Harbor Drive. Go one mile, and you'll see Discovery Point Resort on the left. Reservations are strongly recommended.

FOOD

Seek not cuisine in Reedsport. Standard American fare is the norm in this hardscrabble town. The best bets for seafood are the wharf-side restaurants in Winchester Bay.

Reedsport

A popular diner on U.S. 101 is **Don's Main Street Restaurant** (2115 Winchester Ave., 541/271-2032, 8am-8pm daily, $7-10), with burgers, fried chicken, and a parlor serving local Umpqua ice cream. This is the locals' favorite place for pies.

The **Schooner Inn Café** (423 Riverfront Way, 541/271-3945, 10am-3pm daily, lunch $9-12), on the boardwalk next door to the Discovery Center, has a pleasant riverside patio and a good selection of delicious salads and sandwiches. It's a quiet spot for an al fresco lunch overlooking the Umpqua.

Winchester Bay

For the best fresh seafood in the dune country, head down to the Salmon Harbor Marina at Winchester Bay, where there are a number of

Winchester Bay has the best fresh seafood in the dune country.

casual seafood restaurants within easy strolling distance.

The friendly staff at the **Sportsmen's Cannery and Smokehouse** (182 Bay Front Loop, 541/271-3293, shop 9am-5pm daily) hosts a summer weekend seafood barbecue (4pm-7pm Fri., 11am-7pm Sat.-Sun., $12-18) that features salmon, halibut, and crab (and whatever else is fresh) and all the trimmings. Don't expect indoor seating for this meal—you'll eat at picnic tables set up in the parking lot. Peek inside and you may see cannery employees cutting up the day's catch. Visit the adjoining shop to purchase fresh, smoked, or canned fish; they'll even smoke your catch for you.

Another good bet for fresh seafood in an authentic dockside setting is **Fishpatrick's Crabby Cafe** (196 Bay Front Loop, 541/271-3474, 11am-3pm Sun. and Wed., 11am-8pm Thurs.-Sat., $8-25), which offers excellent fish-and-chips, crab, and fish sandwiches in a woodsy dining room.

INFORMATION

The **Oregon Dunes National Recreation Area Visitor Information Center** (885 U.S. 101, Reedsport, 541/271-6100, www.fs.usda.gov/siuslaw) and **Reedsport Chamber of Commerce** (541/271-3495 or 800/247-2155, www.reedsportcc.org) share a building at the junction of U.S. 101 and Highway 38. It's open 8am-4:30pm weekdays year-round and 8am-4:30pm daily mid-July-early September.

South Coast

Look for ★ to find recommended sights, activities, dining, and lodging.

Highlights

★ **Shore Acres State Park:** The regal manor house is gone, but the formal gardens from a onetime private estate still thrive above an especially rugged stretch of beach (page 348).

★ **Bandon Dunes Golf Resort:** This links-style course on the coastal headlands is evocative of Scotland. There are four golf courses, each expertly designed in a gorgeous setting (page 362).

★ **Cape Blanco State Park and Hughes House:** This is the only lighthouse in Oregon that allows visitors into the lantern room, with its massive Fresnel lens (page 369).

★ **Humbug Mountain:** The three-mile trail to the top of Humbug Mountain passes a spectacular array of native plants. Even if the promised mountaintop view is shrouded in fog, it's a great hike (page 370).

★ **Cape Sebastian:** Hike up Cape Sebastian for a front-row seat for springtime whale-watching (page 375).

★ **Rogue River Jet-Boat Ride:** Even die-hard paddlers won't regret succumbing to a jet-boat tour up the Rogue River. Boaters often get to see ospreys and eagles fishing along this stretch of river (page 376).

★ **Samuel H. Boardman State Scenic Corridor:** North of Brookings, the road winds hundreds of feet above the surf, allowing you to peer down at one of the most dramatic meetings of rock and tide in the world (page 384).

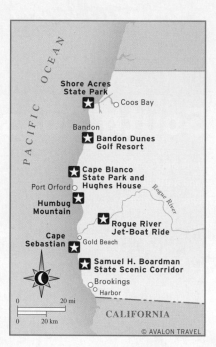

S tretching from the Coos Bay area to the California border, the southern Oregon coast is far from the population centers of Oregon's interior valleys, but amply rewards visitors who make the effort to get here. The foothills of the Klamath

Mountains tumble down the narrow coastal plain and fall off in precipitous headlands at the ocean's edge. Close to shore, the waters are a rocky garden of sea stacks and islets that are home to uncounted flocks of pelagic birds. With half a dozen wild rivers slicing through the mountains to the sea, the south coast is famed for its outstanding salmon fishing, especially on charters from the harbors of Charleston, Gold Beach, Bandon, and Brookings.

In addition, the southern region is blessed with the fairest weather on the Oregon coast and generally gets the most sunshine, the least rain, and the warmest temperatures—attributes as appealing to visitors as to the area's many retirees and other transplants.

Scenic highlights of the south coast include the weather-beaten bluffs and formal gardens at Cape Arago and Shore Acres State Parks, the gorgeous scenery of Boardman and Harris Beach State Parks, and just about every inch of the drive between Brookings and Port Orford.

Outstanding courses draws golfers to Bandon; some of the coast's top windsurfing and kiting are found near Cape Sebastian; and popular jet-boat tours run up the Rogue River from Gold Beach.

PLANNING YOUR TIME

Plan to spend at least a day or two exploring the **Coos Bay-Bandon** region. Coos Bay is the only real city along the southern coast, and like Tillamook to the north, it's a gateway to some spectacular areas, but pretty workaday itself. Be sure to head west and south from town to explore the wonderful shoreline parks at Sunset Bay and Cape Arago.

Don't overlook the coastal wetlands, especially the coastal estuary at **South Slough National Estuarine Research Reserve,** south of Coos Bay. **Bandon Marsh National Wildlife Refuge** protects the largest remaining tract of salt marsh within the Coquille River estuary. Major habitats

---

Previous: horses near Pistol River; Samuel H. Boardman State Scenic Corridor. **Above:** Gold Beach Bridge.

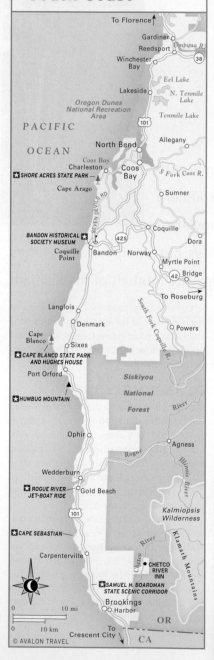

South Coast

To Florence
Gardiner
Reedsport
Umpqua R.
38
Winchester Bay
Eel Lake
Lakeside
N. Tenmile Lake
Oregon Dunes National Recreation Area
Tenmile Lake
PACIFIC
101
OCEAN
North Bend
Allegany
Coos Bay
Charleston
Coos Bay
S Fork Coos R.
★ SHORE ACRES STATE PARK
Cape Arago
Sumner
SEVEN DEVILS RD.
Coquille
BANDON HISTORICAL SOCIETY MUSEUM
425
Dora
Coquille Point
Bandon
Norway
Myrtle Point
42
Bridge
To Roseburg
Langlois
South Fork Coquille R.
Denmark
Powers
Cape Blanco
Sixes
★ CAPE BLANCO STATE PARK AND HUGHES HOUSE
Port Orford
Siskiyou
★ HUMBUG MOUNTAIN
National
Forest
River
Ophir
Rogue
Agness
Wedderburn
Illinois River
★ ROGUE RIVER JET-BOAT RIDE
Gold Beach
101
Kalmiopsis Wilderness
★ CAPE SEBASTIAN
River
Klamath Mountains
Carpenterville
Chetco River
● CHETCO RIVER INN
★ SAMUEL H. BOARDMAN STATE SCENIC CORRIDOR
Brookings
Harbor
OR
0   10 mi
0   10 km
To Crescent City
CA
© AVALON TRAVEL

include undisturbed salt marsh, mudflat, Sitka spruce, and alder riparian communities, which provide resting and feeding areas for migratory waterfowl, shore and wading birds, and raptors.

Although **Bandon** is known for its world-class Bandon Dunes Golf Resort, the old downtown area still hums to counterculture vibes. Bandon's beachfront, along with the Coos Bay sand spit, the beaches on the western side of Humbug Mountain, and the isolated shorelines of Boardman State Park are choice beachcombing spots.

Port Orford is often overlooked, but it's one of our favorite spots, with great ocean vistas from town and lots of hiking at nearby Humbug Mountain. It also doesn't hurt that there's good eating here. It's worth at least an afternoon stop.

Jet-boat tours start in **Gold Beach** and head up the Rogue River, offering those with just a morning to spare the chance to explore stunning river vistas—and perhaps help deliver the mail. Between Gold Beach and Brookings, save some serious time to explore beaches sequestered between steep cliffs and pounding surf at the 11-mile-long **Boardman State Scenic Corridor.**

Humbug Mountain

Charleston, Coos Bay, and North Bend

The towns around the harbor of Coos Bay—Charleston, Coos Bay, and North Bend—refer to themselves collectively as the Bay Area. In contrast to its namesake in California, the Oregon version is not exactly the Athens of the coast. Nonetheless, visitors will be impressed by the area's beautiful beaches and three wonderfully scenic and historic state parks. Because much of this natural beauty is away from the industrialized core of the area and U.S. 101, it's easy to miss. All that many motorists see upon entering Coos Bay and North Bend on the Coast Highway are the dockside lumber mills and foreign vessels anchored at the onetime site of the world's largest lumber port.

The little town of Charleston to the southwest makes few pretenses of being anything other than what it really is—a bustling commercial fishing port. Processing plants here can or cold-pack tuna, salmon, crab, oysters, shrimp, and other kinds of seafood. The town might occasionally smell of fish, but the few restaurants and lodgings are good values, and the area is the gateway to a trio of extraordinary state parks: Sunset Bay, Shore Acres, and Cape Arago.

To reach Charleston from points south, or to head south from town, take the slow but interesting **Seven Devils Road,** which has its southern terminus about three miles north of Bandon. This route runs 13 miles past forests, a few clear-cuts, and an estuarine preserve.

SIGHTS
Coos Bay Harbor
A good place to take in the bustling bay front is the **Coos Bay Boardwalk** (U.S. 101 and Anderson Ave.), where you can check out the oceangoing freighters, visit a restored tugboat, and learn of the harbor's history courtesy of interpretive placards. A 400-gallon saltwater aquarium holds fish and other marine life of Coos Bay. This is the largest coastal harbor between San Francisco and Puget Sound.

The Coos Bay Boardwalk is like an open-air museum.

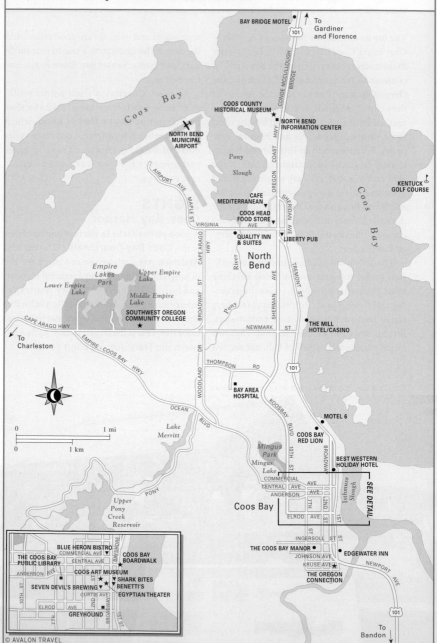

Coos Bay and North Bend

BAY BRIDGE MOTEL

To Gardiner and Florence

CONDE MCCULLOUGH BRIDGE

101

Coos Bay

COOS COUNTY HISTORICAL MUSEUM

NORTH BEND INFORMATION CENTER

NORTH BEND MUNICIPAL AIRPORT

Pony Slough

OREGON COAST HWY

SHERIDAN AVE

Coos Bay

KENTUCK GOLF COURSE

CAFE MEDITERRANEAN

COOS HEAD FOOD STORE

VIRGINIA AVE

QUALITY INN & SUITES

LIBERTY PUB

North Bend

CAPE ARAGO HWY

Pony River

TREMONT ST

Empire Lakes Park

Upper Empire Lake

Lower Empire Lake

Middle Empire Lake

BROADWAY ST

Pony

SHERMAN AVE

SOUTHWEST OREGON COMMUNITY COLLEGE

CAPE ARAGO HWY

NEWMARK ST

THE MILL HOTEL/CASINO

To Charleston

EMPIRE - COOS BAY HWY

WOODLAND DR

THOMPSON RD

101

OCEAN BLVD

Lake Merritt

BAY AREA HOSPITAL

KOOSBAY BLVD

0   1 mi

0   1 km

PONY

Mingus Park

Mingus Lake

MOTEL 6

COOS BAY RED LION

10TH ST

BROADWAY

BEST WESTERN HOLIDAY HOTEL

Upper Pony Creek Reservoir

COMMERCIAL AVE

CENTRAL   AVE

AVE

ANDERSON

Coos Bay

ELROD   AVE

7TH ST

2ND ST

1ST ST

Isthmus Slough

SEE DETAIL

INGERSOLL ST

THE COOS BAY MANOR

JOHNSON AVE

KRUSE AVE

THE OREGON CONNECTION

EDGEWATER INN

NEWPORT AVE

To Bandon

101

BLUE HERON BISTRO

COMMERCIAL AVE

CENTRAL AVE

COOS BAY BOARDWALK

THE COOS BAY PUBLIC LIBRARY

ANDERSON   AVE

10TH ST

7TH ST

COOS ART MUSEUM

SHARK BITES

BENETTI'S

SEVEN DEVIL'S BREWING

CURTIS AVE

EGYPTIAN THEATER

ELROD   AVE

2ND ST

BROADWAY

1ST ST

BAYSHORE

GREYHOUND

© AVALON TRAVEL

Coos Art Museum

The **Coos Art Museum** (235 Anderson Ave., Coos Bay, 541/267-3901, www.coosart. org, 10am-4pm Tues.-Fri., 1pm-4pm Sat., $5 adults, $2 seniors and students), in downtown Coos Bay, is the Oregon coast's only art museum and features primarily 20th-century and contemporary works by American artists, including pieces by Robert Rauschenberg and Larry Rivers. Etchings, woodcuts, serigraphs, and other prints make up a large part of the permanent collection, which includes several of Janet Turner's richly detailed depictions of birds in natural settings. Don't miss the Prefontaine Room on the second floor of the museum. Photos, trophies, medals, and other memorabilia of native-son world-class runner Steve Prefontaine illustrate his credo: "I want to make something beautiful when I run."

In addition to the permanent collection, recurring events worth detouring for are the May-July juried show of artists from the Western states, and the Maritime Art Exhibit, August-September.

Coos County Historical and Maritime Museum

The **Coos County Historical and Maritime Museum** (1220 Sherman Ave., North Bend, 541/756-6320, www.cooshistory.org, 10am-6pm Tues.-Sat., $5 adults, $4 ages 5-17) is near the south end of the Conde McCullough Bridge, one of several distinctive Depression-era spans by Oregon's master bridge-builder. The museum houses more than the usual bric-a-brac from earlier eras, thanks largely to the region's heritage as a shipping center. An early-1900s Regina music box, a piano shipped around Cape Horn, miniature boat models, and a jade Chinese plaque as well as Coos Indian beadwork and other artifacts make this collection especially memorable. Outside, old-time logging equipment and a 1920s steam train are also worth a look.

Sunset Bay State Park

The Cape Arago Highway west of Charleston leads to some of the most dramatic beaches and interesting state parks on the coast. Among the several beaches on the road to Cape Arago, the strand at **Sunset Bay State Park** (13030 Cape Arago Hwy., 541/888-4902 information, 800/452-5687 reservations, www.oregonstateparks.org, camping $19-28, yurt $50) is the big attraction because its sheltered shallow cove, encircled by sandstone

---

Coos Bay Shipwrecks

The *Captain Lincoln,* whose grounding on the treacherous North Spit of Coos Bay led to settlement of the area, would not be the last ship to meet its end on these dangerous shores. In 1910, the *Czarina* foundered in heavy seas on the bar; 24 people were killed in one of the worst shipwrecks on Oregon's south coast. The *Claremont* and the *Santa Clara* both wrecked on the bar in 1915, and the *Sujameco* grounded on Horsfall Beach in 1929. Although most of the ship was removed during salvage operations, iron projections can sometimes still be seen in the sand at low tide.

The most recent and infamous shipwreck here, though, was the February 4, 1999, grounding of the 640-foot wood-chip carrier *New Carissa,* on the North Spit. After the Coast Guard firebombed the freighter in an attempt to burn off the 150,000 gallons of fuel oil on board, the vessel broke into two parts. After weeks of failed attempts, the bow section was finally towed out to sea and sunk in 10,000 feet of water by a Navy torpedo. Most of the stern was finally removed, but a section of it remained mired in the sand on the North Spit, just beyond the surf, until 2008. During the shipwreck and months of salvage efforts, the hulk leaked some 70,000 gallons of oil, which killed an estimated 2,400 seabirds and destroyed oyster beds. The media circus that sprang up around the site generated a temporary economic boomlet for the region, but the long-term ecological damage is still to be determined.

bluffs, is warm and calm enough for swimming, a rarity in Oregon. (Local legend tells that pirates hid out in this well-protected cove.) In addition to swimmers, divers, surfers, kayakers, and boaters, many people come here to watch the sunset; the campground, just inland from the beach, is a good base for exploring the local parks.

A spectacular four-mile cliff-side segment of the **Oregon Coast Trail** runs from Sunset Beach south to Cape Arago. Good views of **Cape Arago Lighthouse** across the water can be seen along this route. Listen for its unique foghorn. For a short hike, follow the signs from the mouth of Big Creek to the viewpoint overlooking Sunset Bay.

The Cape Arago Lighthouse is on Chief Island and was once linked to the mainland by a steel-truss bridge. For the local Coos Indians, Chief Island and the adjacent shoreline were a traditional burial ground, though after the building of the first lighthouse in 1866, the Coast Guard no longer allowed native burials. However, the island continued to have a sacred significance for the Coos. After the lighthouse was decommissioned in 2006, the ownership of island, the lighthouse, and adjacent shoreline was transferred to the Confederated Tribes of the Coos, Lower Umpqua, and Siuslaw Indians. The bridge to Chief Island has been removed, and the lighthouse and Chief Island are currently not open to the public.

★ Shore Acres State Park

Less than one mile south of Sunset Bay at **Shore Acres State Park** (541/888-3732, 8am-sunset year-round, $5 per vehicle or Oregon Coast Passport, free with camping receipt from Sunset Bay State Park, no pets outside vehicles), the grandeur of nature is complemented by human endeavor. The park is set on the grounds of lumber magnate and entrepreneur Louis J. Simpson's early-1900s mansion, which began as a summer home in 1906 and grew into a three-story mansion complete with an indoor heated swimming pool and large ballroom. Originally a

Trails at Shore Acres State Park lead down to a secluded beach.

Christmas present to his wife, Shore Acres became the showplace of the Oregon coast, with formal and Japanese gardens eventually added to the 743-acre estate. After a 1921 fire, a second, larger (two stories high and 224 feet long) incarnation of Simpson's "shack by the beach" was built. Over the following years the building fell into disrepair; the house and grounds were ceded to the state in 1942. Because of the high cost of upkeep, the mansion had to be razed, but the gardens have been lovingly maintained.

The gardens are compelling attractions, but the headland's rim is more dramatic. Perched near the edge of the bluff, on the site formerly occupied by the mansion, a glass-enclosed observation shelter makes a perfect vantage point from which to watch for whales or marvel at the crashing waves. When there's a storm, the waves really slam into the sandstone reefs and cliffs, hurling up tremendous fountains of spray. It's not uncommon to feel the spray atop the 75-foot promontory. The history of the Simpson family is really the history of the Bay Area, and their story is captioned beneath period photos in the observation gazebo and in the garden in a small enclosure at the west end of the floral displays.

In the seven acres of neatly tended gardens, set back from the sea, the international botanical bounty culled by Simpson clipper ships and schooners is still in its glory, complemented by award-winning roses, rhododendrons, tulips, and azaleas. A restored gardener's cottage with antique furnishings stands at the back of the formal gardens. It's open for special occasions and during the winter holidays. Also in the gardens, note the copper egret sculptures at the pond and the greenhouse for rare plants from warmer climes.

From Thanksgiving until New Year's, during the annual **Holiday Lights and Open House** (4pm-10pm daily), the gardens are decorated with 250,000 colored lights and other holiday touches. The gardener's cottage opens and serves free refreshments during this time.

If you bear right and follow the pond's contours toward the ocean, you'll come to the **Simpson Beach Trail.** Follow it north for cliff-side views of the rock-studded shallows

below. Southward, the trail goes downhill to a scene of exceptional beauty. From the vantage point of a small beach, you can watch waves crash into rocks with such force that the white spray appears to hang suspended in the air. Pursuits for the active traveler include exploring tidepools and caves as well as springtime swimming in a cove, formed by winter storms, on the south side of the beach.

Cape Arago State Park

A little more than one mile south of Shore Acres is **Cape Arago State Park** (800/551-6949, day-use only, free), at the end of the Cape Arago Highway. Locals have made much of the fact that this was a possible landing site of the English explorer Sir Francis Drake in 1579, and put a plaque here commemorating him.

Beachcombers can make their own discoveries in the numerous tidepools, some of the best on the coast. The south cove trail (find it past the picnic shelter) runs down to a sandy beach and the better tidepools. The north cove trail leads to more tidepools, good spots for fishing, and views of the colonies of seals and sea lions at Shell Island, including the most northerly breeding colony of

Cape Arago State Park

enormous elephant seals. Their huge pups when just a month old may already weigh 300-400 pounds. Note that the north trail closes March 1-June 30 to protect seal pups. The picnic tables on the headlands command beautiful ocean panoramas and are superbly placed for whale-watching.

South Slough National Estuarine Research Reserve

Estuaries, where freshwater and saltwater interface, form some of the richest ecosystems on earth—capable of producing five times more plant material than a cornfield of comparable size while supporting great numbers of fish, birds, and other wildlife. The South Slough of Coos Bay is the largest such web of life on the Oregon coast. The **South Slough National Estuarine Reserve Interpretive Center** (61907 Seven Devils Rd., 541/888-5558, www.southsloughestuary.org, 10am-4:30pm Tues.-Sat., free), four miles south of Charleston, will help you coordinate a canoe trip through the estuary and offers guided hikes as well.

The center looks out over several estuarine arms of Coos Bay. These vital wetlands nurture a variety of life-forms, detailed by the placards captioning the center's exhibits. Eight miles of trails and boardwalks form a loop with many shorter options. The coastal ecosystem is introduced by the "10-minute trail" behind the interpretive center. The various conifers and the understory are clearly labeled along the gently sloping half-mile loop. Branch trails lead down toward the water for an up-close view of the estuary. Down by the slough, you may see elk grazing in marshy meadows and bald eagles circling above, while *Homo sapiens* harvest oysters and shrimp in these waters.

Whiskey Run Beach

Midway between Charleston and Bandon is the quiet beach at **Whiskey Run,** whose ore-bearing sands spread gold fever down the south coast in the early 1850s. As many as 2,000 miners worked here until a storm

washed away the deposit. Other forms of beachcombing at Whiskey Run and on the beaches to the north are still thriving, however. Agate-hunting after a season of winter storms and clamming at low tide make these solitary shorelines ideal places to forget worldly concerns. To get there, turn west from the lightly traveled Seven Devils Road onto Whiskey Run Road and drive 1.5 miles to this county park. Just to the north, you'll find Seven Devils State Wayside. Vehicles are permitted on the beach at Whiskey Run; Seven Devils is reserved for foot traffic.

Horsfall Beach and the North Spit

On the spit north of North Bend, the Oregon Dunes taper down to wide, sandy beaches and wetlands. **Horsfall Beach** is extremely popular with ATV riders, but it's also a good place to enjoy nature. It's worth exploring on foot, especially in the winter, when storms can expose old shipwrecks.

Myrtlewood

To see Oregon coast folk art in the making, visit the **Oregon Connection** (1125 S. 1st St., Coos Bay, 541/267-7804, www.oregon-connection.com, 9am-5pm Mon.-Sat., 11am-4pm Sun.), just off U.S. 101 at the south end of Coos Bay. The myrtlewood factory tour shows you how a myrtlewood log gets fashioned into bowls, clocks, tables, and other utensils. No admission is charged for this 25-minute guided run through a working factory. After you're done, the store is a delight, with Oregon gourmet foods and crafts supplementing the quality woodwork.

Five miles north of North Bend, **The Real Oregon Gift** (3955 U.S. 101, 541/756-2220, www.realoregongift.com, 9am-5pm Mon.-Sat., 9:30am-4:30pm Sun.) is another large myrtlewood factory and showroom.

SPORTS AND RECREATION

Wavecrest Discoveries (541/267-4027) offers a cornucopia of guided outdoor activities

The Myrtlewood Tree

When exploring the southern Oregon coast, you'll soon discover that myrtlewood is very popular hereabouts—nearly every town has a myrtlewood factory or showroom that peddles bowls, sculpture, furniture, and other products fashioned from this rare and unusual wood.

Myrtlewood is a member of the Lauraceae family of small trees and is a relative of the camphor, bay, and sassafras trees. Like these trees, the leaves and wood of the tree have a pungent odor. The myrtlewood tree grows only in a small area of southern Oregon and northern California, and it is large enough to harvest only after 100-150 years of growth. The wood is highly patterned, with the grain forming erratic bands of differing color in a single block of wood.

Myrtlewood is particularly popular for turning into bowls—salad and serving bowls make a lovely gift or keepsake of a trip to coastal Oregon. However, the tree and its wood have been used for myriad other functional and decorative purposes for many years.

Hudson's Bay Company trappers used myrtlewood leaves to brew tea as a remedy for chills. In 1869 the golden spike marking the completion of the nation's first transcontinental railroad (near Promontory, Utah) was driven into a highly polished myrtlewood tie. Novelist Jack London was so taken by the beauty of the wood's swirling grain that he ordered an entire suite of furniture.

During the Depression, the city of North Bend issued myrtlewood coins after the only bank in town failed. The coins ranged $0.50-10 in value and are still redeemable, although they are worth far more as collectors' items.

around the Bay Area and beyond, including clamming and tidepooling excursions, sea kayaking, dune and estuary tours, and more.

Fishing

Spring chinook salmon, which sometimes exceed 30 pounds and are renowned as an unrivaled dining treat, offer prime fishing in Coos Bay. However, their population levels and fishing rules vary from year to year.

Mid-August-November, Isthmus Slough sees a good return of fin-clipped hatchery cohos. In saltwater, chinook and coho are usually found in good numbers within a one- to two-mile radius of the mouth of Coos Bay June-August, although the legal season varies; carefully check the regulations.

Coos Bay is also one of the premier areas for crabbing and clamming. The Charleston Fishing Pier is a productive spot for crabs,

Charleston marina

while the best clamming spots are found along the bay side of the North Spit.

Fishing charters, bay cruises, whale-watching, and the like can be arranged through a number of charter outfits based at the Charleston Boat Basin. **Betty Kay Charters** (541/888-9021 or 800/752-6303, www.bettykaycharters.com) charges typical per-person prices: $75 for five hours of rock fishing; $140 for seven hours of salmon fishing; $200 for 12 hours of tuna or halibut fishing; and $40 for a two-hour bay cruise, whale-watching, or ecotour.

Golf

Tee up in a lovely setting at **Sunset Bay Golf Course** (11001 Cape Arago Hwy., Charleston, 541/888-9301, www.sunsetbaygolf.com, $20 weekends, $18 weekdays), a nine-holer close to Sunset Bay State Park.

Hiking

Although most hikers head to the coast, especially the four-mile stretch of the **Oregon Coast Trail** between Sunset Bay and Cape Arago, for a nice trail with spectacular views, it's also worth looking inland. Twenty-five miles northeast of Coos Bay in the Coast Range is **Golden and Silver Falls State Park** (800/551-6949, www.oregonstateparks. org). Two spectacular waterfalls are showcased in this little-known gem of a park. To find your way from Coos Bay, look for the Allegany/Eastside exit off U.S. 101. Beyond the community of Allegany, continue up the East Fork of the Millicoma River to its junction with Glenn Creek, which ultimately leads to the park. The narrow winding gravel roads make this half-hour trip unsuitable for a wide-body vehicle.

You can reach each waterfall by way of two 0.5-mile trails. The 100-foot cataracts lie about one mile apart, and although both are about the same height, each has a distinct character. For most of the year, Silver Falls is more visually arresting because it flows in a near semicircle around a knob near its top. During or just after the winter rains, however,

the thunderous sound of Golden Falls makes it the more awe-inspiring of the two. Along the trails, look for the beautifully delicate maidenhair fern.

Kayaking

From a canoe or sea kayak, as you pass tide flats, salt marshes, forested areas, and open water, you can really begin to grasp the richness of the estuarine habitat at the **South Slough National Estuarine Research Reserve** (541/888-5558, www.southsloughestuary.org). The estuary here has two main branches, offering plenty of territory for a day of exploration.

Although the waters are placid, they are strongly influenced by the tides—be sure to consult tide tables when you plan an outing. Wind can also affect your trip: Know that in the spring and summer, the prevailing winds are from the northwest; in the winter they're from the southwest. At all times of year, the wind blows hardest in the afternoon.

Surfing and Swimming

The best spot on the Oregon coast for swimming is **Sunset Bay State Park** (13030 Cape Arago Hwy., Coos Bay, 541/888-4902). The water is warm enough for most adults and gentle enough for most kids.

Surfing is best just northeast of Sunset Bay, at **Bastendorff Beach County Park** (63379 Bastendorff Beach Rd., Charleston, 541/888-5353). Rent a board in downtown Coos Bay at Waxer's Surf & Skate (240 S. Broadway, 541/266-9020, www.surfwaxers.com, 11am-6pm Mon.-Sat.).

ENTERTAINMENT AND EVENTS

The first event of note in summer is the **Oregon Coast Music Festival** (541/267-0938, www.oregoncoastmusic.com), which runs for two weeks in mid-July and has been bringing music to the coast since 1978. Coos Bay is the central venue for these classical, jazz, pop, and world music concerts, but

Bandon, North Bend, Charleston, and other neighboring burgs host some performances as well. Tickets to some events are free, with tickets to the majority of events under $25.

In late August, the ubiquitous Oregon blackberry is celebrated with the **Blackberry Arts Festival** (541/266-9706, blackberryartsfestival.com). Food and wine-tasting booths, a juried arts-and-crafts show, and entertainers fill the **Coos Bay Mall** (Central Ave. in downtown Coos Bay).

Polish up the spotting scope and head to the Oregon Institute of Marine Biology in Charleston during the last weekend of August to see migratory shorebirds with the **Oregon Shorebird Festival** (541/867-4550 or 541/756-5688, http://www.fws.gov/oregoncoast/shorebirdfestival.htm). Guided trips on land and water are offered; a boat trip out to see albatrosses and other seldom seen species that frequent the open ocean is a highlight. Other excursions visit the Bandon Marsh National Wildlife Refuge and Coos Bay to see plovers, loons, and a variety of other shorebirds.

In mid-September, perhaps the best-known Bay Area sports celebrity, Steve Prefontaine, is honored with a 10K race and two-mile walk in the annual **Prefontaine Memorial Run** (541/269-1103, www.prefontainerun.com). Prefontaine was a world-class runner whose gutsy style of running and record performances made him a major sports personality until his premature death at age 24 in 1974. Many top-flight runners pay homage by taking part in the race. Events begin and end at the runner's alma mater, **Marshfield High School** (4th St. and Anderson Ave., Coos Bay).

Occupying the former bay-side site of the Weyerhaeuser mill alongside U.S. 101 in North Bend, the **Mill Casino** (3201 Tremont Ave., North Bend, 541/756-8800 or 800/953-4800, www.themillcasino.com) is operated by the Coquille Indian Tribe. Open 24 hours a day, the casino offers blackjack, lots o' slots, poker, and bingo. A large hotel, lounge, and several restaurants are on-site.

ACCOMMODATIONS AND CAMPING

Most of the lodgings in Coos Bay and North Bend stretch along busy U.S. 101, and most are of the mid-century motor-court variety, but the majority are well-maintained and represent good value. Another option is staying in Charleston, particularly if your destination includes local state parks, ocean beaches, or South Slough. Charleston lodgings are pretty basic, but you'll stay near the fishing marina, not the highway.

Coos Bay

If you're just looking for a basic, clean room right on the highway, the local **Motel 6** (1445 Bayshore Dr., 541/267-7171, www.motel6.com, $70-100) is well maintained and offers a few rooms with microwaves and fridges. Close to downtown, the **Best Western Holiday Hotel** (411 N. Bayshore Dr., 541/269-5111, www.bestwestern.com, $155-175) is within walking distance of city center restaurants and offers a pool, hot tub, and hot breakfast buffet. Pets are welcome at both of these places.

The Coos Bay Manor (955 5th St., 800/269-1224, www.coosbaymanor.com, $145-235, full breakfast included) is a grand, high-ceilinged colonial-style home with cye-popping river views from the open-air second-floor breakfast balcony. The B&B's five spacious rooms have distinctive decor; two of the rooms can be combined to make a suite for families.

The waterfront **Edgewater Inn** (275 E. Johnson Ave., 541/267-0423 or 800/233-0423, www.theedgewaterinn.com, $120) is located off the highway facing the working waterfront. Many rooms have views, and the hotel also offers fitness equipment, an indoor pool, a spa and sauna, and a light complimentary breakfast.

Northwest of the Bay Area—2.5 miles north of the McCullough Bridge—is the Trans-Pacific Parkway, a causeway west across the water leading to Coos Bay's North Spit and the south end of the Oregon Dunes National

Recreation Area, with four **Forest Service campgrounds** (541/271-6000 or 877/444-6777, www.recreation.gov, year-round, $20) and expansive dunes that draw ATV enthusiasts. The main **Horsfall Campground** is popular with crowds of noisy ATVs and RVs. It's the only campground on the spit with showers. For more quiet and privacy, continue another mile on Horsfall Beach Road to **Bluebill Lake.** There isn't ATV dune access from this campground, and it tends to attract trekkers who use their feet to explore. Ask the campground hosts about area trails and the nearby oyster farm for the ultimate in campfire fare. Close by, **Horsfall Beach Campground** is in the dunes next to the beach. ATV access and beachcombing are popular activities. A half-mile away, **Wild Mare Horse Camp** has beach and dune access and a dozen primitive campsites, each with a single or double horse corral.

North Bend

One of the best values in the area is **Bay Bridge Motel** (33 Coast Hwy., 541/765-3151, www.baybridgemotel.com, $60-95), a small older motel just north of the McCullough Bridge, with good views of the bay from the higher-priced rooms.

Another option is the **Quality Inn & Suites Coos Bay** (1503 Virginia Ave., 541/756-3191, www.coosbayinn.com, $119-159), five blocks from U.S. 101. With 96 units and the standard chain-hotel amenities, this hotel provides a quiet escape.

★ **The Mill Hotel** (3201 Tremont Ave., 541/756-8800 or 800/953-4800, www.themillcasino.com, $153-170) is just south of the Mill Casino along the waterfront in a new seven-story tower and a building that once housed a plywood mill. Owned and operated by the Coquille (pronounced ko-KWELL in the local dialect) Indian Tribe, the hotel seeks to express its owners' patrimony: The exterior of this three-story hotel is the same cedar that the Coquille people used to build their plank houses, and the fireplace in the lobby is made of Coquille River rocks. The canoe displayed behind the front desk was carved by tribal members and is part of an interpretive display that tells the story of the Coquilles. Guest rooms are very nicely furnished, and waterfront views from the tower are especially dramatic. And, of course, all the pleasures of a modern casino are just a few feet away. In addition to gaming, the casino has a good restaurant, shops, and a performance center.

The Coos Bay Manor

Charleston

There are a few basic motels in Charleston, but even better are the nearby campgrounds. The **Plainview Motel** (91904 Cape Arago Hwy., 541/888-5166 or 800/962-2815, www.plainviewmotel.com, $81-120) is easy to spot—it's covered with colorful murals of sea life. If you'd like to catch your own dinner, the Plainview is a good base for clamming expeditions or fishing trips. This small older motel has rooms with kitchenettes, plus a cabin and a two-bedroom home.

If you want proximity to the area's parks, consider camping. Even though the crowds at **Sunset Bay State Park** (13030 Cape Arago Hwy., 541/888-4902 or 800/452-5687, www.reserveamerica.com for reservations, $5-50) can make it seem like a trailer park in midsummer, the proximity of Oregon's only major swimming beach on the ocean keeps occupants of the 66 tent sites ($19) and 65 trailer sites ($26-28) happy. Yurts go for $40 each ($50 for a pet-friendly yurt), and primitive hiker-biker sites are $5 each. Facilities include the standard state park showers, and there is a boat launch at the north end of the beach. This site, three miles southwest of Charleston, is popular with anglers, who can cast into the rocky intertidal area for cabezon and sea bass. It's also a good base camp for hikers.

Bastendorff Beach County Park (63379 Bastendorff Beach Rd., Charleston, 541/888-5353, www.co.coos.or.us, $16-24 campsites, $35 camping cabin) is a conveniently and beautifully located park two miles west of Charleston just off the Cape Arago Highway. It's open for camping year-round, with RV and tent sites as well as cabins and some hiker-biker sites. The campground has drinking water, flush toilets, and hot showers (for an extra $2). Fishing, hiking, and a nice stretch of beach are the recreational attractions, plus there's a good playground for toddlers.

FOOD

Oregon's Bay Area has many eateries where your nutritional needs can be met, if not in fine style then at least at the right price. With a couple of notable exceptions, in both Coos Bay and North Bend, you won't find it easy to dine on seafood—in these hardworking towns, eating well seems to require heartier fare. For fresh seafood, you're advised to head to the docks in Charleston.

Coos Bay

Nearly all the following are located along a two-block section of busy Broadway, which is the name given to southbound U.S. 101 as it passes through downtown Coos Bay. So just park the car and check out which of the following looks good.

The **Blue Heron Bistro** (110 W. Commercial Ave., 541/267-3933, 11am-9pm Mon.-Fri., noon-9pm Sat., noon-8pm Sun., $18-23) is in the heart of downtown Coos Bay—with its Bavarian-style half-timbered exterior, you can't miss it. The specialty is traditional German cooking, such as sauerbraten, schnitzel, and sausages, although fresh salmon and seafood are also featured.

For delicious old-school Italian food, try the family-run **Benetti's** (290 S. Broadway, 541/267-6066, benettis.com, 4pm-9pm daily, $9-25). Choose between pasta dishes such as spaghetti with house-made meatballs, chicken parmigiana, or a grilled steak.

One good spot for seafood in Coos Bay is ★ **SharkBites** (240 S Broadway, 541/266-7582, www.sharkbitescafe.com, 11am-9pm Mon.-Thurs., 11am-9:30pm Fri.-Sat., $8-22), a hip little eatery with a droll sense of humor and good, freshly prepared food, with several local seafood options. A variety of wraps and sandwiches—including a very tasty halibut burger—as well as pasta and fish tacos are favorites. Best of all, prices are fair and quality is high.

Spend an evening on the patio at **Seven Devils Brewing** (247 S. 2nd St., 541/808-3738, www.7devilsbrewery.com, 11am-10pm Sun.-Mon. and Wed.-Thurs. 11am-11pm Fri.-Sat., noon-8pm Tues., shorter hours in winter, $8-12), where the fire pit is a good place to get the local vibe and wash down an order of poutine fries with a hoppy Northwest-style ale.

If you're visiting the waterfront boardwalk and feel the hankering for seafood, stop by **Fishermen's Seafood Market** (200 S. Bayshore Dr., 541/267-2722, fishermensseafoodmarket.com, 10:30am-7pm Mon.-Sat., $5-13), a boat anchored off the boardwalk that serves as a seafood store for a local fishing family, plus a casual spot for (mostly) carry-out seafood sandwiches, fish-and-chips, and chowder.

North Bend

If you've had enough of the standard coastal fare, try ★ **Cafe Mediterranean** (1860 Union St., 541/756-2299, www.cafemediterranean.net, 11am-9pm Mon.-Sat., $8-19) for Middle Eastern-style Mediterranean food, including a locally famed lentil soup, in a friendly relaxed setting. This is a good spot for sharing a mezze platter, a Greek salad, and some kebabs.

Stop by the **Liberty Pub** (2047 Sherman Ave., 541/756-2550, 4pm-10pm Sun., Wed.-Thurs., 4pm-11pm Fri.-Sat., $8-13), with a good selection on Northwest beers on tap, tasty pizza, and music whenever possible. Half of the restaurant is family-friendly.

The **Mill Casino** (3201 Tremont Ave., 541/756-8800 or 800/953-4800, www.themillcasino.com) has a total of five dining options, including the **Timbers Café** (6am-3am Mon.-Thurs., 24 hours Fri.-Sat., $8-22), with burgers, sandwiches, and other light dining options. The more upscale **Plank House** (7am-2pm Mon.-Sat., 8am-2pm Sun., 5pm-9pm Wed., Thurs., Sun., 5pm-10pm Fri.-Sat., $12-28) offers three meals daily in a waterfront dining room. At the **Saw Blade** (4pm-8pm Mon.-Tues., $15), a buffet is offered on nights when the Plank House is closed.

Coos Head Food Co-Op (1960 Sherman Ave., 541/756-7264, 9am-7pm Mon.-Fri., 10am-6pm Sat., noon-5pm Sun.) has the largest selection of certified organic produce and food on the south coast.

Charleston

You can't go too far wrong looking for a fresh seafood meal down at the docks—a number of casual restaurants and seafood vendors (some more like shacks) cluster here, including one spot where the crab cooker is always on. If you're an oyster lover, you'll certainly want to visit **Qualman's** (4898 Crown Point Rd., 541/888-3145, 10am-5:30pm Wed.-Sat.), which sells incredibly fresh oysters from its nearby beds. Just look for the signs on the north side of the Charleston Bridge on the east side of the highway.

Part sports bar, part seafood restaurant, ★ **Miller's at the Cove** (63346 Boat Basin Rd., 541/808-2904, 11am-midnight Wed.-Mon., $7-14) has seafood every bit as fresh as it should be. Don't expect anything fancy, but it's a good place for fish tacos. Kids are allowed until 9pm.

Close by, the classier **Portside** (63383 Kingfisher Rd., Charleston Boat Basin, 541/888-5544, www.portsidebythebay.com, 11:30am-11pm daily, $15-55) has a view of the water and a wide menu of rather old-fashioned seafood specialties.

The casual **High Tide Cafe** (91124 Cape Arago Hwy., 541/888-3664, 11am-9pm Wed.-Sun., $17-23) is a good place for seafood dinners such as cioppino, albacore tuna fish-and-chips, or a plate of pasta (including seafood pasta). If the weather's nice, sit outside, where there's a view of South Slough near its entrance to the bay.

INFORMATION AND SERVICES

The **Coos Bay Visitor Center** (50 E. Central Ave., Coos Bay, 541/269-0215 or 800/824-8486, www.oregonsadventurecoast.com, 9am-5pm Mon.-Fri., 10am-2pm Sat.-Sun.) is right downtown across from the Boardwalk.

The Coos Bay World (www.theworldlink.com) is the largest daily paper on the south coast.

For health care and emergencies, the **Bay Area Hospital** (1775 Thompson Rd., Coos Bay, 541/269-8111), 0.5 mile west of U.S. 101 via Newmark Street, is the south coast's largest medical facility.

GETTING THERE AND AROUND

Improvements to OR 42 make it possible to get to and from Roseburg, 87 miles from Coos Bay, in less than two hours.

The **Point bus** (541/269-7183, http://high-desert-point.com) operates daily bus service between Coos Bay and Eugene via Reedsport and Florence. Eugene has Amtrak and regular Greyhound service, as well as an airport served by national carriers. **Coastal Express** buses (800/921-2871, www.currypublictransit. org), operated by Curry County Transport, run on weekdays between North Bend and Brookings to the south.

The **Southwest Oregon Regional Airport** (www.flyoth.com), at the north end of North Bend, offers flights to Portland and San Francisco.

Public transportation in the Bay Area is limited; one bus line, **Coos County Area Transit** (541/267-7111, www.coostransit.org), makes a loop in Coos Bay and North Bend.

Bandon and Vicinity

Between Coos Bay and Bandon, U.S. 101 veers inland through forests and bucolic farmland. The highway reencounters the Pacific at Bandon, near the mouth of the Coquille River. Bandon (pop. 3,000) is characterized by the style and grace of an earlier era, especially in Old Town, a picturesque collection of shops, galleries, and restaurants fronting onto a bustling waterfront.

Although logging, fishing, dairy products, and the harvest of cranberries have been the traditional mainstays of the local economy, in the early part of the 20th century Bandon also enjoyed its first tourism boom. In addition to being a summer retreat from the heat of the Willamette Valley, it was a port of call for thousands of San Francisco-Seattle steamship passengers. This era inspired such tourist venues as the Silver Spray dance hall and a natatorium with a saltwater pool. The golden age that began with the advent of large-scale steamship traffic in 1900, however, came to an abrupt end following a fire in 1936 that destroyed most of the town. The blaze was started by the easily ignitable gorse weed, imported from Ireland (as was the town's name) in the mid-1800s.

The facelift given Old Town decades later, and the subsequent tourist influx, conjured for many the image of the mythical phoenix rising from its ashes to fly again. Today, Bandon is a curious mixture of provincial backwater, destination golf resort, and artists' colony.

SIGHTS

One of the appealing things about Bandon is that most of its attractions are within walking distance of each other. In addition, on the periphery of town is a varied array of things to see and do, including a beautiful stretch of beach just south of downtown.

Old Town

Bandon's **Old Town** is a half-dozen blocks of shops, cafés, and galleries squeezed in between the harbor and a steep bluff. The renovated waterfront invites relaxed strolling, and crabbers and anglers pull in catches right off the city docks. The small commercial fleet based here pursues salmon and tuna offshore.

Preservation buffs should check out **Masonic Hall** (2nd St. and Alabama St.), one of the few buildings to have survived Bandon's 1914 and 1936 blazes. A photo in the local historical museum shows the same building and surrounding structures on Alabama Street (then called Atwater) circa 1914. The photo depicts boardwalks leading to a woolen mill, old storefronts, a theater, and the Bandon Popular Hotel and Restaurant, outside which

Bandon

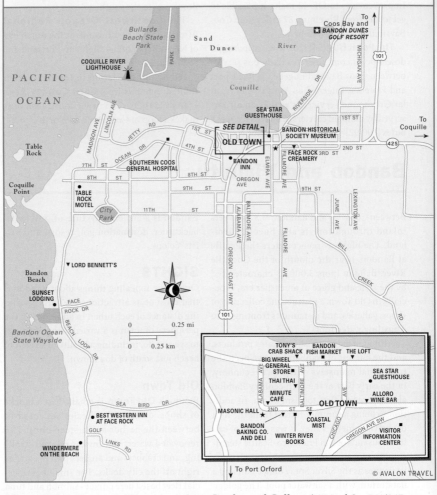

To
Coos Bay and
BANDON DUNES
GOLF RESORT

To
Coquille

PACIFIC

OCEAN

Bullards
Beach State
Park

Sand
Dunes

River

Coquille

COQUILLE RIVER
LIGHTHOUSE

SEA STAR
GUESTHOUSE

SEE DETAIL
OLD TOWN

BANDON HISTORICAL
SOCIETY MUSEUM

FACE ROCK
CREAMERY

Table
Rock

SOUTHERN COOS
GENERAL HOSPITAL

BANDON
INN

Coquille
Point

TABLE
ROCK
MOTEL

City
Park

Bandon
Beach

LORD BENNETT'S

SUNSET
LODGING

FACE

Bandon Ocean
State Wayside

0   0.25 mi

0   0.25 km

TONY'S
CRAB SHACK

BANDON
FISH MARKET

THE LOFT

BIG WHEEL
GENERAL
STORE

THAI THAI

SEA STAR
GUESTHOUSE

ALLORO
WINE BAR

MINUTE
CAFÉ

OLD TOWN

MASONIC HALL

COASTAL
MIST

BANDON
BAKING CO.
AND DELI

WINTER RIVER
BOOKS

VISITOR
INFORMATION
CENTER

BEST WESTERN INN
AT FACE ROCK

WINDERMERE
ON THE BEACH

To Port Orford

© AVALON TRAVEL

a horse and buggy await. The scene today has changed dramatically, but nonetheless an early-1900s charm still pervades the neighborhood.

Throughout Old Town are artists and artisans pursuing their crafts and selling their wares. The **2nd Street Gallery** (210 2nd St., 541/347-4133, http://secondstreetgallery.net, 11am-5:30pm daily) has a little of everything, from functional and art pottery to blown glass to paintings and sculptures. **WinterRiver** **Books and Gallery** (170 2nd St., 541/347-4111, www.winterriverbooks.com, 10am-6pm daily) has a wide-ranging assortment of travel titles, photo essays, and fiction that makes this the best bookstore on the south coast. Close by, the **Bandon Driftwood Museum** (130 Baltimore Ave., 541/347-3719, 9am-5:30pm Mon.-Sat., 10am-5pm Sun., free) shows off an interesting collection of natural sculptures, from gnarly root balls to whole tree trunks. It's housed at the **Big Wheel General Store,**

Bogged Down With Cranberries

From the vantage point of U.S. 101 between Port Orford and 10 miles north of Bandon, you'll notice what appears to be reddish-tinged ground in flood-irrigated fields. If you get closer, you'll see cranberries—small evergreen bushes that creep along the ground and send out runners that take root. Along the runners, upright branches 6-8 inches long hold pink flowers and, later, deep red fruit.

These berries are cultivated in bogs to satisfy their tremendous need for water and to protect them against insects and winter cold. Bandon leads Oregon in this crop, with an output ranking third in the nation. Oregon berries are often used in cranberry juice production because of their deep red pigment and high vitamin C content.

Fill up on cranberry confections at **Cranberry Sweets** (280 1st St. SE Bandon, 541/347-9475 or 800/527-5748, 9:30am-6pm Mon.-Sat., 9:30am-5pm Sun.). For sale are confections ranging from cranberry fudge to cranberry truffles. Other shops in town, including the local grocery store, stock **Vincent Family** (www.vincentcranberries.com) dried cranberries or cranberry juice. Three generations of Vincents have been tending cranberry bogs; they're committed to making the business sustainable and are working toward organic certification for their berries.

where you'll also find the Fudge Factory and 24 flavors of homemade ice cream and butter fudge.

As you enter Old Town, you may spot a giant fish sculpture. Take a closer look; it's made of plastic beach debris. The **Washed Ashore Project** (washedashore.org) draws attention to the problem of plastic pollution; the **Harbortown Events Center** (325 2nd St. S.E., 541/329-0317, 1pm-6pm Tues.-Sat.) hosts an exhibit of more beach litter art.

Bandon Historical Society Museum

The captivating **Bandon Historical Society Museum** (270 Fillmore St., 541/347-2164, http://bandonhistoricalmuseum.org, 10am-4pm daily, $3 adults, kids free), at the corner of U.S. 101 and Fillmore Street in Bandon's former city hall, traces the history of the Coquille people and their forebears. The chronology continues with the steamers and railroads that brought in white settlers. One room is

Bandon Beach

devoted to Bandon's unofficial standing as the cranberry capital of Oregon. Black-and-white photos showing women stooping over in the bogs to harvest the ripe berries are captioned with such quips as this classic from an overseer: "I had 25 women picking for me, and I knew every one by her fanny." Color photos spanning five decades of Cranberry Festival princesses also adorn the walls.

Another room depicts Bandon's Resort Years, 1900-1931, when the town was called the "Playground of the Pacific." The most compelling exhibits in the museum deal with shipwrecks and the fires of 1914 and 1936.

Scenic Beach Loop

U.S. 101 follows an inland path for more than 50 miles between Coos Bay and Port Orford, but you can leave the highway in Bandon and take the four-mile Beach Loop for a lovely seaside detour south of town. Several access roads lead west from the highway to Beach Loop Drive (County Rd. 29), each about 0.25 mile from the others. Most people begin the drive by heading west from Old Town on 1st Street along the Coquille. Another popular approach is from 11th Street, which leads to Coquille Point. The south end of the drive runs through the northern portion of **Bandon State Natural Area,** providing parking, beach access, and picnic tables.

The once-bucolic drive along the Beach Loop has changed a bit—trophy homes form pretty much the only view you have for the first mile or two. Still, there are state park parking areas that let you put the McMansions to your back and allow a look at the gorgeous ocean views or a trek down the bluff to a gorgeous beach.

Along this fine stretch of beach are rock formations with such evocative names as Table Rock, Elephant Rock, Garden of the Gods, and Cat and Kittens Rocks. The whole grouping of sea stacks (rocks eroded away from their original cliffs by the sea), included within the Oregon Islands National Wildlife Refuge, looks like a surrealist chess set cast upon the waters. The most eye-catching of

all is **Face Rock,** a basalt monolith that resembles the face of a woman gazing skyward. An Indian legend says that she was a princess frozen by an evil sea spirit. Look for the Face Rock turnout 0.25 mile south of Coquille Point on the Beach Loop.

Despite their scenic and recreational attractions, the beaches south of town can be surprisingly deserted, perhaps because of the long, steep trails up from the water along some parts. In any case, this dearth of people can make for great beachcombing. Agates, driftwood, and tidepools full of starfish and anemones are commonly encountered, along with bird-watching opportunities galore. Elephant Rock has a reputation as the Parthenon of puffins, while murres, oystercatchers, and other species proliferate on the other offshore formations.

Bullards Beach State Park

Two miles north of Bandon, bordering the Coquille River estuary and more than four miles of beachfront, **Bullards Beach State Park** (541/347-2209 or 800/551-6949 information, www.oregonstateparks.org, most campsites $26-28) is a great place to fish, crab, bike, fly a kite, windsurf, picnic, or overnight in the large sheltered campground. The beach and lighthouse are reached via a scenic three-mile drive paralleling the Coquille River. Look for jasper and agates amid the heaps of driftwood on the shore. Equestrian trails and horse-camping facilities make this a popular destination for riders. The boat ramp gives anglers, kayakers, and canoeists access to the lower Coquille River and Bandon Marsh National Wildlife Refuge.

The riverside road going out to the Coquille's north jetty takes you through the dunes to the picturesque **Coquille River Lighthouse** (tours 11am-5pm daily early May-mid-Oct., free), a squat tower with adjacent octagonal quarters. The last lighthouse built on the Oregon coast, it was completed in 1896, then abandoned in 1939 when the Coast Guard installed an automated light across the river. After years of neglect, the structure was restored in the late 1970s; its light is now solar-powered. Etchings of ships that made it across Bandon's treacherous bar—and some that didn't—greet you inside.

West Coast Game Park

Seven miles south of Bandon is the **West Coast Game Park Safari** (46914 U.S. 101 S., 541/347-3106, www.gameparksafari.com, 9:30am-5pm daily mid-June-Labor Day, call for spring, fall, and winter hours, $17.50 adults, $16.50 seniors, $10 children ages 7-12, $7 ages 2-6), the self-proclaimed largest wild animal petting park in the country. There are 450 animals representing 75 different species, including tiger cubs, camels, zebras, monkeys, and snow leopards. Visitors may be surprised to see a lion and tiger caged together, or a fox and a raccoon sharing the same nursery. The park trics raising different species together and often finds that animals can live harmoniously with their natural enemies. Free-roaming animals include deer, peacocks, pygmy goats, and llamas. An elk refuge is another popular area of the park. Even if you're not with a child, the opportunity to pet a pup,

a cub, or a kit can bring out the kid in you. The park is open year-round, but call during winter because of restricted hours of operation.

New River

In 1890, storm-blown sand blocked the outlet of Floras Lake (located south of Bandon), and flood water flowed into a low channel just east of a dune paralleling the beach, forming New River. The river runs north from the lake for nine miles, through a pretty remote area with only a couple of roads leading to it and a trail along its length. Hikers and paddlers have the chance to see birds, animals, and plants that are otherwise rarely spotted. Some areas are set aside for nesting snowy plovers from March 15 to September 15; check the information boards so you'll be sure to avoid these areas. A **nature center** (Croft Lake Ln., 541/756-0100, http://www.blm.gov/or/resources/recreation, sunrise-sunset daily, free) located at Storm Ranch, two miles west of the highway and about 8.5 miles south of Bandon, is a good place to learn more about the area and access trails. The trail is also easy to reach at Floras Lake, west of the town of Langlois.

The Coquille River Lighthouse is just north of Bandon.

SPORTS AND RECREATION

Bandon Beach Riding Stables (2640 Beach Loop Rd., 541/347-3423) is four miles south of Face Rock on the Beach Loop. Several beach rides are offered daily, plus sunset rides in the summer. Riders of all abilities are welcome, including those with disabilities. Prices range $40-60 for a 1- to 2-hour ride. Reservations are advised. Open year-round.

Golf

South of town, **Bandon Crossing Golf Course** (87530 Dew Valley Ln., 541/347-3232, www.bandoncrossings.com, $45-75 for 18 holes) is a forested, challenging, but fun course that's good for families, novices, and anyone looking for a less intense experience than at the Bandon Dunes Golf Resort.

★ BANDON DUNES GOLF RESORT

Bandon Dunes Golf Resort (57744 Round Lake Dr., 541/347-4380 or 800/742-0172, www.bandondunesgolf.com, May-Oct. greens fees $265 for hotel guests, $310 for nonguests, off-season $75-245 for guests, $100-290 for nonguests) has drawn accolades from the golf press and is far and away the most spectacular place to golf in Oregon. The original Bandon Dunes course has 7 holes along the Pacific and unobstructed ocean views from all 18. Three other 18-hole courses, Pacific Dunes, Bandon Trails, and Old Macdonald (inspired by golf course architect C. B. Macdonald), give golfers a chance to stay for a few days and keep encountering new territory.

In addition to the main courses, the 13-hole, par-3 Bandon Preserve course ($100 peak season, $50-75 non-peak) starts at the top of a sand dune and works its way down to the beach. Proceeds from this course go to the Wild Rivers Coast Alliance, an organization that supports conservation, community, and the economy along the southern Oregon coast.

To preserve the natural surroundings along the ocean bluffs, this Scottish links course doesn't allow carts (the only amenity missing), so you'll have to hire a caddie or schlep your own bag (a practice that is frowned upon here). A luxurious resort with Pacific views, attentive staff, and a fine restaurant are also available for those who come to worship in the south coast's Sistine Chapel of golf.

Golfers who have never played on the Oregon coast should come prepared for wind, especially in the afternoon. Oregon golfers may know about the wind, but we have a special piece of advice for you—dress up. This is a rather formal place, and you'll feel out of place in your baggy cargo shorts and faded polo shirt.

The resort is one mile north of the Coquille River. November through April, Oregonians are admitted at the guest rate. Caddies expect at least $100 per bag.

Fishing

The Coquille River runs 30 miles from its Siskiyou headwaters before meandering leisurely through Bandon. The north and south jetties are popular spots for perch and rockfish, while the city docks right in Old Town yield catches of perch and crab April-October and smelt July-September. The spring chinook run pales in comparison to those in the Rogue and Chetco Rivers to the south, but the fall runs of chinook (beginning Sept.-Oct.) and coho (Oct.-Nov.) are strong and productive. Steelhead usually arrive in November, and the run gathers steam January-February. A boat is necessary for the best steelhead and salmon water, but bank anglers can fish the mouth of Ferry Creek, just off Riverside Drive in Bandon. Fishing guides and gear can be arranged through **Bandon Bait & Tackle** (110 1st St., 541/347-3905, 6am-5pm daily), across from the boat basin. The shop also rents crab rings and other gear and can point you to productive spots for catching Dungeness crab. It's also not a bad place to grab a place of fish-and-chips.

Just off the south end of Beach Loop Drive, 30-acre **Bradley Lake,** protected from ocean winds by high dunes, offers good trout fishing and a boat ramp. Each spring the lake is stocked with trophy rainbows, averaging five pounds, reared at the Bandon Fish Hatchery east of town.

Wildlife-Viewing

Bird-watchers flock to the tidal salt marsh and the elevated observation deck of the **Bandon Marsh National Wildlife Refuge** (541/347-1470, http://www.fws.gov/refuge/bandon_marsh, daily sunrise-sunset), especially in the fall, to take in what may be the prime birding site on the coast. The extensive mudflats attract flocks of shorebirds, including red phalaropes, black-bellied plovers, long-billed curlews, and dunlins, as well as such strays from Asia as Mongolian plovers.

Reach Bandon Marsh by a short paddle across the river from the Bullards Beach State Park, or via Riverside Drive, which runs from Bandon to U.S. 101 on the south side of the Coquille River bridge. The refuge protects more than 700 precious acres of the Coquille estuary's remaining salt-marsh habitat along the southeastern side of the river. Migrating waterfowl, bald eagles, California brown pelicans, and other birds feast on the rich food sources. From U.S. 101 just north of Bandon, turn west onto Riverside Drive and continue for about one mile, where you'll reach the refuge.

ENTERTAINMENT AND EVENTS

A parade, cardboard boat races, and ice cream and apple pie are highlights of Bandon's **Fourth of July** celebration; at dusk, fireworks are launched across the Coquille to burst above the river.

The biggest weekend of the year for Bandonians comes the second weekend in September, when the **Cranberry Festival** (541/347-9616, http://www.bandon.com/cranberry-festival) brings everyone together in Old Town for a parade, a crafts fair, tours of a cranberry farm, and the Bandon High Cranberry Bowl—in which the local footballers take on traditional rival Coquille High.

ACCOMMODATIONS

For the best ocean views, often with nearby trails to the beach, look to the lodgings along the Beach Loop. If you want to be able to walk to dinner in Old Town, stay at one of the in-town locations. For the best of both worlds, bring a bike and cycle into town from a Beach Loop room. Bandon bills itself as America's storm-watching capital, and special packages are often available October-March.

$50-100

Right in the heart of Old Town, the ★ **Sea Star Guesthouse** (370 1st St., 541/347-9632, www.seastarbandon.com, $80-125) has just six rooms. Four rooms are spacious, charming, and uniquely decorated, with skylights, wood-beam ceilings, a verdant courtyard, and views onto the harbor. The other two rooms are less expensive and a bit less spacious, but are some of the best deals in town.

On a bluff at the top of Beach Loop Road, find an assortment of motel rooms and small cottages at **Table Rock Motel** (840 Beach Loop Dr., 541/347-2700 or 800/457-9141, www.tablerockmotel.com, $70-134). The least expensive rooms are small with no ocean views, but all are a short, steep walk away from one of the coast's prettiest beaches.

Farther down the Beach Loop is **Sunset Lodging** (1865 Beach Loop Rd., 541/347-2453 or 800/842-2407, www.sunsetmotel.com, $79-180), a motel complex with a variety of lodging types. With some units built right into the cliff above a scenic beach, the view here is hard to beat. Nonetheless, the steep steps down the 80-foot-high bluff to the beach, the busy atmosphere, and the rusticity of the least expensive guest rooms might not be to everyone's liking.

$100-150

Set on a bluff overlooking Old Town, the ★ **Bandon Inn** (355 U.S. 101, 541/347-4417 or 800/526-0209, www.bandoninn.com, $144-185) has spectacular views, comfortable rooms—all with balconies—and a path down to town. Pets are permitted in some rooms.

This is a great spot to stay if you want the wining and dining of Old Town within walking distance.

A favorite place to stay on the Beach Loop is the older but refurbished **Windermere on the Beach** (3250 Beach Loop Rd., 541/347-3710, http://www.windermereonthebeach.com, $135-198), where baby-boomers can relive their childhood beach getaways in old-fashioned cottages or motel rooms (some with kitchens), situated on a bluff above a wind-swept beach. Housekeeping facilities and proximity to restaurants (Lord Bennett's) and the West Coast Game Park also make this an ideal family vacation spot.

$150-200

Another popular place is the **Best Western Inn at Face Rock** (3225 Beach Loop Rd., 541/347-9441 or 800/638-3092, www.innatfacerock.com, $174-279). Part of its popularity has to do with the motel's location—set back from the road near the end of the Beach Loop, across the street from Bandon's coastline. Many of the modern well-appointed guest rooms have magnificent ocean views. An indoor pool, fitness room, whirlpool, and restaurant also make this an especially good choice for travelers looking for amenities. Some suites have fireplaces, kitchenettes, and private patios. There is a short path to the beach.

Over $200

For avid golfers or those seeking upscale accommodations, amenities, and service, the **Bandon Dunes Golf Resort** (57744 Round Lake Dr., 541/347-4380 or 888/345-6008, www.bandondunesgolf.com, most rooms $260-430) is the place to stay. Lodging is in several different locations around the resort and includes single lodge or inn rooms in various sizes, two- or four-bedroom suites, and multibedroom cottages (rates up to $1,900). View options vary from golf course and ocean views to dune and surrounding woods. Bandon Dunes is five minutes from Bandon, a mile north of the Coquille River,

and 27 miles (30 minutes' drive) from the North Bend Airport, which is served by daily flights from Portland.

Vacation Rentals

Bandon is an easy place to spend a weekend, and there are several property management companies that can help you find a house to rent.

Many of the places offered by **Exclusive Property Management** (541/347-3790 or 800/527-5445, www.visitbandon.com) are large and quite upscale, with great locations and lovely interior design. It also rents a few more modest homes, so don't be afraid to call or check the website. **Bandon Beach Vacation Rentals** (54515 Beach Loop Rd., 541/347-4801 or 888/441-8030, www.bandonbeachrentals.com) has several reasonably priced units available, including one that'll sleep 10 people.

Camping

Bullards Beach State Park (541/347-2209 or 800/551-6949 information, 800/452-5687 reservations, www.oregonstateparks.org, $26-28, horse camp $19, yurt $40-50, hiker/biker $5) is a very large and busy state park, with over 200 tightly packed campsites in a great location between the Coquille River and four miles of beach. To get there, drive north of town on U.S. 101 for about one mile; just past the bridge on the west side of the highway is the park entrance. The beach is reached via a scenic two-mile drive paralleling the Coquille River. Electricity, picnic tables, and grills are provided.

FOOD

If you want an edible souvenir or gift, stop by **Misty Meadows Jams** roadside stand (48053 U.S. 101 S., 541/347-2575, www.oregonjam.com, 9am-5pm daily) for a wide variety of jams and jellies, including products incorporating Bandon cranberries. In addition to preserves, the shop sells olives and fruit-based barbecue sauce, syrup, honey, and salsa. Look here and in other shops in town for Vincent Family dried cranberries or cranberry juice, produced by three generations of Vincents.

Face Rock Creamery

For over a century, Bandon was Oregon's "other" cheese-making center, and cheeses from the Bandon Cheddar Cheese Factory rivaled those of Tillamook until the operation closed in 2002. Cheese making returned to Bandon in 2013 with the opening of the **Face Rock Creamery** (680 2nd Street SE, just north of downtown Bandon on Hwy. 101, 541/347-3233, www.facerockcreamery.com, 9am-7pm daily). The factory and visitors center is small compared with Tillamook, but it's worth a stop to watch cheese production and to taste the many samples of cheese made from local milk (the Coquille River valley east of Bandon is lined with dairies). The creamery also sells a large selection of cheeses and gourmet food items from around the world—this is a good place to stock up for picnics—and offers freshly made ice cream, deli sandwiches, and a wine bar as well.

American

If you're after a full breakfast, head to the bustling **Minute Café** (145 2nd St., 541/347-2707, 5:30am-8pm Thurs.-Mon., 5:30am-3pm Tues.-Wed., $5-14), where locals and tourists settle in with the morning paper, omelets, and pancakes. Later in the day, the menu features burgers, sandwiches, and chowder. For coffee and a tasty cinnamon roll, head across the street to the **Bandon Baking Co. and Deli** (160 2nd St., 541/347-9440, www.bandonbakingco.com, 8am-5pm Mon.-Sat. June-Aug., 8am-4pm Tues.-Sat. Feb.-May and Sept.-Dec., closed Jan.).

Italian

Although it's called a wine bar, ★ **Alloro Wine Bar** (375 2nd St., 541/347-1850, www.allorowinebar.com, 4pm-9pm daily, closed Jan.-Feb., dinner $12-28) is the top choice in town for an Italian dinner. But don't come looking for spaghetti—the food is much more upscale than that. Instead, expect smoked steelhead Alfredo or duck breast served with cranberry cherry salsa and polenta. The food here is excellent, and the pace is relaxed. The pasta is house-made, and most of the produce is local. If you don't want a full dinner, there's a small bar where you can taste a flight of wines and nibble on olives or Italian cheeses.

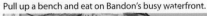

Pull up a bench and eat on Bandon's busy waterfront.

Pacific Northwest

From its second-floor perch above the harbor, ★ **The Loft** (315 1st St. SE, 541/329-0535, www.theloftofbandon.com, 5pm-9pm Wed.-Sun., $18-38) serves some of the best dinners in town—definitely with the best views. Abundant use is made of local produce, and there's always lots of good seafood on the menu. The dining room is fairly small, so reservations are a good idea.

If you don't want to leave the Beach Loop for dinner, **Lord Bennett's** (1695 Beach Loop Dr., 541/347-3663, lordbennett.com, 5pm-9pm daily, 10am-2pm Sun. $15-31) offers a dramatic ocean view. The food does justice to these surroundings with elegantly rendered pasta, steak, chicken, and seafood dishes. Jazz on selected evenings in the lounge adds a nice touch.

The **Bandon Dunes Golf Resort** (57744 Round Lake Dr., 541/347-4380 or 888/345-6008, www.bandondunesgolf.com) offers a number of dining options. In the main lodge is the **Gallery** (6am-10pm daily, $24-44), a good place to eat an excellent steak, and the many seasonal fish and seafood preparations are always noteworthy. If you're not staying at the resort, lunch is an interesting time to get a feel for the place and to enjoy the views out onto the Bandon Dunes course. If you're looking for a less formal atmosphere, check out the adjacent Tufted Puffin Lounge or the Bunker Bar downstairs, which has a gentlemen's club vibe; both serve snacks and light meals. Dinner has an Asian touch at the **Trails End Clubhouse** (6am-10pm daily, $24-36), in the Bandon Trails Clubhouse. In the evening, a good spot for an informal meal is **McKee's Pub** (2pm-midnight, $9-30), which has a Scottish country pub atmosphere, plus a wide-ranging menu that includes individual pizzas, burgers, steaks, and hearty favorites like meatloaf and fish-and-chips. In addition to a good selection of regional microbrews, in good weather McKee's also offers a marvelous outdoor patio fronting onto the course.

In the Pacific Dunes Clubhouse is the **Pacific Grill** (6am-1pm daily, $24-39) for a dining-in-the-round experience. The menu ranges from burgers and sandwiches for lunch to shrimp and grits or pork for dinner.

Seafood

If you're looking for inexpensive street food, check along 1st Street near the Old Town Marina, where **Tony's Crab Shack** (155 1st St., 541/347-2875, tonyscrabshack.com, 10am-7pm daily, $5-16) sells crab sandwiches, fish tacos, grilled salmon, steamer clams, and lots more. As the name implies, it's not really a sit-down place, though there are a few picnic tables on the dock.

Line up for your fish-and-chips to go at the **Bandon Fish Market** (249 1st St. SE, 541/347-4282, www.bandonfishmarket. com, 11am-6pm Mon.-Sat., 11am-3pm Sun., $10-15). Though it's takeout only, a picnic table outside near the harbor is the place to enjoy it all, with a trip across the street to **Cranberry Sweets** (280 1st St. SE, 541/347-9475 or 800/527-5748, 9:30am-6pm Mon.-Sat., 9:30am-5pm Sun.) for dessert.

Chocolates and Dessert

You'll want to know about **Coastal Mist** (210 2nd Street SE, 541/347-3300, coastalmist.com, 11am-6pm Mon.-Thurs., 10am-7pm Fri.-Sun., lunch $6-7), a chocolate boutique with house-made candies and desserts, plus lunchtime sandwiches and salads.

INFORMATION AND SERVICES

The **Bandon Chamber of Commerce** (300 W. 2nd St., Bandon, 541/347-9616, www. bandon.com) in Old Town distributes a comprehensive guide and a large annotated pictographic map of the town.

Southern Coos General Hospital (900 11th St. SE, 541/347-2426) features an ocean view that is in itself therapeutic, as well as a 24-hour emergency room.

GETTING THERE AND AROUND

North- and southbound **Coastal Express** buses (800/921-2871, www.currypublictransit.org) run on weekdays between North Bend and Brookings.

Between Bandon and Coos Bay, you can escape the tedium of U.S. 101's inland route by taking **Seven Devils Road** about three miles north of Bandon. This route runs 13 miles to **Charleston,** a fishing village that sits closer to the ocean than its larger neighbors to the northeast, Coos Bay and North Bend. En route, beaches, state parks, and an estuarine preserve make the drive interesting, although the miles of heavily logged mountainsides may take you aback.

Port Orford and Vicinity

Port Orford marks the northernmost end of one of the most spectacular stretches of coastline in the United States. From Bandon, the highway runs inland; when it hits Port Orford, the road nearly runs into the Pacific. And what a splendid place to encounter the ocean: The beach is perfect for long treasure-hunting walks, and the bluffs just to the north are also fun to explore. A few miles north, blustery Cape Blanco is the westernmost point of the continental United States; a short distance south, Humbug Mountain rises almost directly from the ocean. All of these places are great for a quick ogle and a snapshot, but even better for hiking and exploring. Port Orford is a good base for all of that, with a wide range of accommodations and a few good places to eat.

SIGHTS AND RECREATION

Port Orford has an ocean view from downtown that is arguably the most scenic of any town on the coast. A waterfront stroll lets you appreciate the cliffs and offshore sea stacks, as well as the unique sight of commercial fishing boats being hoisted by large cranes into and out of the harbor. With only a short jetty on its north side, Port Orford's harbor, the only open-water port in Oregon, is unprotected from southerly swells, so boats can't be safely moored on the water. When not in use, the fleet rests on wheeled trailer-like dollies near the foot of the pier.

A stroll or bike ride through town is a perfect way to visit Port Orford's impressive

Port Orford Indian Wars

In 1850, the U.S. Congress passed the Oregon Donation Land Act, allowing white settlers to file claims on Native American land in western Oregon. This was news, of course, to the Native American nations of the region, who had not been consulted on the decision. William Tichenor, captain of the steamship *Gull,* hoping to exploit the new act, had ambitions to establish an outpost on the coast at what's now Port Orford. When Tichenor observed the hostility of the Quatomah band of the Tututni in the tidewater, he put nine men ashore on an immense rock promontory fronting the beach because of its suitability as a defensive position. The Native Americans besieged the rock for two weeks before the white men escaped under cover of night. Tichenor returned with a well-armed party of 70 men and succeeded in founding his settlement.

From this inauspicious beginning, Port Orford established itself as the first town site on the south coast. Shortly thereafter, the town became the site of the first fort established on the coast during the Rogue Indian Wars. This conflict started when gold miners and settlers came into Native American lands. As a result of the clashes, hundreds of local natives were rounded up and sent to the Siletz Reservation near Lincoln City in 1856.

selection of galleries. These are, by and large, much different and far more interesting than the typical seaside-town collections of landscape paintings and sunset photos. Expect to find high-quality crafts, glass art, sculpture, and computer-generated art.

Battle Rock Park

As you come into town on U.S. 101, it's hard to ignore enormous Battle Rock on the shoreline, the site of the 1851 conflict between local Native Americans and the first landing party of white settlers. If you can make your way through the driftwood and blackberry bushes surrounding its base, you can climb the short trail to the top for a heightened perspective on the rockbound coast that parallels the town. You'll also notice the east-west orientation of the harbor. Once you get to the top of the rock, don't think the battle is necessarily over. Bracing winds often chill you, and high tides can sometimes render this coastal finger of land an island. The rock is also the site of a fireworks display at the **Fourth of July Jubilee Celebration.**

Even if you're not up for a scramble on Battle Rock, do take the short path down to the beach, which is relatively sheltered from the wind and a good place for a walk. It's also a good spot for beachcombing, with agates and fishing floats being the prize finds.

If you'd rather do your scavenging inland, try searching the nearby foothills for the lost Port Orford meteorite. The meteorite was found in the 1860s by a government geologist, who estimated its weight at 22,000 tons. Unfortunately, he was unable to locate the meteorite when he returned for another look.

Port Orford Heads State Park

Another shoreline scene, featuring a striking panorama from north to south, is up West 9th Street at **Port Orford Heads State Park** (541/332-6774, www.oregonstateparks.org, free). If you go down the cement trail to the tip of the blustery headland, you look south to the mouth of Port Orford's harbor. To the north, many small rocks fill the water, along with boats trolling for salmon or checking crab pots. On clear days, visibility extends from Cape Blanco to Humbug Mountain.

Also here is the historic **Port Orford Lifeboat Station** (10am-3:30pm Wed.-Mon., free), built by the Coast Guard in 1934 to provide rescue service to the southern Oregon coast. After it was decommissioned in 1970, the officers' quarters, the pleasingly proportioned crew barracks, and other outbuildings

Battle Rock Park

were converted into a museum depicting the work of the station. A trail leads down to Nellie's Cove, site of the former boathouse and launch ramp.

★ Cape Blanco State Park and Hughes House

Four miles north of Port Orford, west of U.S. 101, is **Cape Blanco,** whose remoteness gives you the feeling of being at the edge of the continent—as indeed you are here, at the westernmost point in Oregon. From the vantage of Cape Blanco, dark mountains rise behind you and the eaves of the forest overhang the tidewater. Below, driftwood and 100-foot-long bull kelp on slivers of black-sand beach fan out from both sides of this earthy red bluff. Somehow, the Spaniards who sailed past it in 1603 viewed the cape as having a *blanco* (white) color. It has been theorized that perhaps they were referring to fossilized shells on the front of the cliff.

With its exposed location, Cape Blanco really takes it on the chin from Pacific storms. The vegetation along the five-mile state park road down to the beach attests to the severity of winter storms in the area. Gales of 100-mph winds (record winds have been clocked at 184 mph) and horizontal sheets of rain have given

some of the usually massive Sitka spruces the appearance of bonsai trees. An understory of salmonberry and bracken fern help evoke the look of a southeast Alaskan forest.

Atop the weathered headland is Oregon's oldest, most westerly, and highest lighthouse in continuous use. Built in 1870, the beacon stands 256 feet above sea level and can be seen some 23 nautical miles out at sea. **Cape Blanco Lighthouse** (541/332-6774, 10am-3:30pm Tues.-Sun. Apr.-Oct., $2 adults, $1 children under 12) also holds the distinction of having had Oregon's first female lighthouse keeper, Mabel E. Bretherton, who assumed her duties in 1903. Tours of the facility include the chance to climb the 64 spiraling steps to the top. This is the only operational lighthouse in the state that allows visitors into the lantern room to view the working Fresnel lens.

Near Cape Blanco on a side road along the Sixes River is the **Hughes House** (541/332-0248, 10am-3:30pm Wed.-Mon. Apr.-Oct., free), a restored Victorian home built in 1898 for rancher and county commissioner Patrick Hughes. Owned and operated today by the state of Oregon, the house offers an intriguing glimpse of rural life on the coast over a century ago.

Cape Blanco Lighthouse

★ **Humbug Mountain**

Some people will tell you that 1,756-foot-high Humbug Mountain, six miles south of Port Orford on U.S. 101, is the highest mountain rising directly off the Oregon shoreline. Because the criteria for such a distinction vary as much as the tides, let's just say it's a special place. There's more than one version of how the peak, formerly called Sugarloaf Mountain, got its name. According to one, gold miners drawn here in the 1850s by tales of gold in the black sands nearby soon discovered that the rumored riches proved to be "humbug."

Once the site of Native American vision quests, Humbug Mountain now casts its shadow upon a state park campground surrounded by myrtles, alders, and maples. Just north is a breezy black-sand beach. A three-mile trail to the top of Humbug rewards hardy hikers with impressive vistas to the south of Nesika Beach and a chance to see wild rhododendrons 20-25 feet high. Rising above the rhodies and giant ferns are bigleaf maples, Port Orford cedars, and Douglas and grand firs. Access the trail from the campground or from a trailhead parking area off the highway near the south end of the park. In addition, the **Oregon Coast Trail,** which follows the beach south from Battle Rock, traverses the mountain and leads down its south side to the beach at Rocky Point.

Prehistoric Gardens

What can we say about this unique roadside attraction, featuring a 25-foot-tall Formica-green *Tyrannosaurus rex* standing beside the parking lot? Is it kitsch, or is it educational? You decide. In any case, if you've got children in the car, unless they're sleeping or blindfolded, you're probably going to have to pull over. **Prehistoric Gardens** (36848 U.S. 101, 541/332-4463, www.prehistoricgardens.com, 9am-dusk daily spring-fall, call for winter hours, $12 adults, $10 seniors 60 and over, $8 children ages 3-12), about 10 miles south of Port Orford, is the creation of E. V. Nelson, a sculptor and self-taught paleontologist who began fabricating life-size dinosaurs here back in 1953 and placing them amid the lush rainforest on the back of Humbug Mountain. Paths lead through the ferns, trees, and undergrowth to a towering brontosaurus, triceratops, and 20 other ferroconcrete replicas, painted in a dazzling palette of Fiestaware colors.

Grassy Knob Wilderness

The **Grassy Knob Wilderness** (Siskiyou National Forest, Powers Ranger District,

Find a black sand beach (and lots of birds) at the foot of Humbug Mountain.

Prehistoric Gardens is a classic roadside attraction.

541/439-6200, http://www.fs.usda.gov/recarea/ rogue-siskiyou) encompasses 17,200 acres of steep rugged terrain and protects rare stands of Port Orford cedar. The wood of this majestic fragrant tree is light, strong, and durable. Its use in planes during World War II and in Japanese construction has made it highly valued, but a fatal root fungus spread by logging trucks accounts for its rarity and astronomically high price. (As you travel around the area, you may notice the dead or dying cedars.) During World War II, Japanese submarines used Cape Blanco Lighthouse as an orientation mark to aim planes loaded with incendiary bombs at the Coast Range. The Japanese hoped to ignite forest fires that would destroy the region's Port Orford cedar trees, which were used to construct airplanes. Because of the perennial dampness, the results were negligible. A short (0.8-mile) but moderately difficult trail leads to the summit of Grassy Knob. To get here, follow U.S. 101 north of Port Orford about four miles, then go east on County Road 196 to Forest Service Road 5105, which ends at the trailhead.

Fishing

The **Elk River,** which empties on the south side of Cape Blanco, and the **Sixes River,** which meets the sea north of the cape, are two popular streams for salmon and steelhead fishing. Chinook and steelhead begin to enter both rivers after the first good rains of fall arrive, usually in November. Private lands limit bank access, with the exception of a good stretch of the Sixes that runs through Cape Blanco State Park. The salmon season runs to the end of the year, and steelhead through the following March. **Lamm's Guide Service** (541/784-5145, www.umpquafishingguide. com) leads trips on both rivers.

Boating and Waterskiing

In the northwest of town, drive west of the highway on 14th or 18th Streets to 90-acre **Garrison Lake** for boating, waterskiing, and fishing for stocked rainbow and cutthroat trout. **Buffington Memorial City Park,** at the end of 14th Street, has a dock for fishing or swimming, plus playing fields, tennis courts, picnic areas, hiking trails, and a horse arena. Half a mile north of the lake, look for agates on **Paradise Point Beach.**

Surfing

The south-facing beach at **Battle Rock Beach,** in downtown Port Orford, can be okay for surfing during the winter, when northwesterly winds blow in. Otherwise, surfers tend to go about a mile south of town to the beach at **Hubbard Creek** (best in the spring). What these spots may lack in intensity, they make up for in scenery.

Windsurfing and Kiteboarding

Between Port Orford and Bandon (just southwest of Langlois) is **Floras Lake,** one of the southern Oregon coast's two great windsurfing and kiteboarding spots (the other is south of Gold Beach at **Pistol River**). The lake, just barely inland from the beach, catches incredible breezes. **Floras Lake Windsurfing & Kiteboarding** (541/348-9912, www.floraslake.com) offers lessons and rentals; the proprietors also have a very nice B&B just above the lake. It's 11 miles north of Port Orford, about four miles west of the highway on Floras Lake Loop Road. On the lake is **Boice Cope County Park,** which has basic tent and RV sites and a boat ramp. When the wind's not blowing (fat chance, though), explore the hiking trails from the campground to the beach. From Floras Lake north to Bandon is the most isolated beachfront on the Oregon coast—ideal for beachcombing. Follow the New River north from Floras Lake. Grasses, dunes, and shore pines usher you the 25 miles back to Bandon, and chances are good you won't see a soul.

Bicycling

The **Wild Rivers Coast Scenic Bikeway** (rideoregonride.com) starts and ends in Port Orford, and over the course of 61 miles visits the Elk River, Cape Blanco State Park, Paradise Point, and Port Orford Heads State Park. It's easy to break this long ride down into shorter trips.

ACCOMMODATIONS

With one notable exception, Port Orford is the kind of place where a room with a view will not break your budget.

$50-100

The **Shoreline Motel** (206 6th St., 541/332-2903, $70-75) is right downtown, across the highway from Battle Rock. While not fancy, it's convenient and perfectly adequate for a basic night's stay.

Just south of town, the **Seacrest Motel** (44 U.S. 101 S., 541/332-3040, www.seacrest-oregon.com, $60-91) features views of coastal cliffs and a garden from a quiet hillside on the east side of the highway. Pets are welcome at this older motel.

★ **Castaway-by-the-Sea** (545 W. 5th St., 541/332-4502, www.castawaybythesea. com, $85-165) features ocean and harbor views from high on a bluff, fireplaces, and housekeeping units, and it allows pets. In addition to the motel rooms, the Castaway has

Winds rip at Pistol River, south of Gold Beach, attracting windsurfers and kiteboarders.

a two-bedroom lodge that'll sleep up to seven (from $185). The rates on the upper-end lodgings go down significantly in the off-season. It's said that Jack London once stayed in an earlier incarnation of this place.

$150-200

North of Port Orford, the **Floras Lake House B&B** (92870 Boice Cope Rd., Langlois, 541/348-2573, www.floraslake.com, $165-185, includes breakfast) is perfectly suited for windsurfers or others who want to explore the beaches in this unpopulated area. The spacious light-filled house looks out onto Floras Lake and the ocean, and the proprietors also offer windsurfing and kiteboarding lessons.

Over $200

Port Orford's serene luxury resort is ★ **Wildspring Guest Habitat** (92978 Cemetery Loop, www.wildspring.com, $298-328, including continental breakfast). The small (five-cabin) resort is in a forested setting on a bluff above the highway (but totally secluded from it), with views of the ocean from the main lodge and hot tub. The cabins are beautifully and meticulously designed and furnished (including a refrigerator, a massage table, and Wi-Fi access in each cabin, but no telephones or TVs) and are as comfortable as they are perfect-looking. The main guest hall has a kitchen that's available to guests as long as it's not being used to prepare breakfast. The well-tended grounds include a labyrinth and several meditation nooks, but perhaps the best place to hang out is the slate-lined hot tub, which looks out over treetops to the ocean. It's a good idea to take binoculars, as Wildspring is a stop along the Oregon Coast Birding Trail. This is a good place for a romantic retreat or a solo contemplative getaway.

Camping

Humbug Mountain State Park (541/332-6774, www.oregonstateparks.org, reservations 800/452-5687 or www.reserveamerica.com), six miles south of Port Orford on U.S. 101, features 62 tent sites ($17) and 32 electrical sites for RVs ($22), along with wind-protected sites reserved for hikers and bikers ($5). Flush toilets, showers, picnic tables, water, and firewood are available. A short trail leads under

the highway to the beach; a longer one goes up Humbug Mountain.

Reach **Cape Blanco State Park** (39745 U.S. 101 S., 541/332-6774 information, 800/452-5687 cabin reservations, $22 tent or RV, $17 horse camp, $5 hiker/biker, $40 rustic cabin) by driving four miles north of Port Orford on U.S. 101, then heading northwest on the park road that continues five miles beyond to the campground. Picnic tables, water, and showers are available. For horseback riders, there's a seven-mile trail and a huge open riding area; horses are also allowed on the beach. Only cabins can be reserved; regular sites are first-come, first-served.

Boice Cope County Park (92850 Boice Cope Rd., Langlois, 541/247-3386 general information, 541/373-1555 reservations, http://www.co.curry.or.us/Departments/Parks, $15-22), on the shore of Floras Lake, is a good base for windsurfers and kiteboarders. The area is known for its wind.

FOOD

Port Orford doesn't have a lot of restaurants, but there are a few good places to eat, including two of the best fish-and-chips joints on the coast.

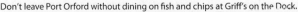
Don't leave Port Orford without dining on fish and chips at Griff's on the Dock.

Make sure to visit Port Orford's docks, where **Griff's on the Dock** (303 Dock Rd., 541/332-8985, 10:30am-8pm Mon.-Sat., 10:30am-7:30pm Sun., $7-20), a weathered shack amid the boats and tackle shops, serves up excellent fish-and-chips. The fish here is as fresh as it gets, and the atmosphere, with crusty old anglers eating hot dogs and talking crabbing, is not your cookie-cutter idea of a fish-and-chips place.

There are more really good fish-and-chips up on the highway, where **The Crazy Norwegians** (259 6th St., 541/332-8601, 11:30am-8pm Wed.-Sun., $10-20) also serves tasty tuna melts, burgers, and chowder. It's a busy place, so expect to wait on a summer weekend.

The best views and most upscale dinners are at **Redfish** (517 Jefferson St., 541/366-2200, www.redfishportorford.com, 9am-3pm and 5pm-9pm Mon.-Tues., 11am-10pm Wed.-Sat., 9am-9pm Sat.-Sun. $18-25). There's always a "fresh catch" fish dish, perhaps served over gnocchi and broccoli rabe. The food is a little hit or miss, but the setting is almost worth the price. Adjoining the restaurant is an upscale gallery.

INFORMATION AND SERVICES

Begin your travels at **Battle Rock Information Center** (Battle Rock Wayside, 541/332-4106, www.discoverportorford.com, 10am-3pm daily), on the west side of U.S. 101. The people here are especially friendly and helpful.

GETTING THERE

Curry County's **Coastal Express** buses (800/921-2871, www.currypublictransit. org) run up and down the south coast weekdays only between North Bend and the California border, including local service in Port Orford.

Gold Beach and Vicinity

This town is one part of the coast where the action is definitely away from the ocean. To lure people from Oregon's superlative ocean shores, the Rogue estuary has been bestowed with many blessings. First, the gold-laden black sands were mined in the 1850s and 1860s. While this short-lived boom era gave Gold Beach its name, the arrival of Robert Hume, later known as the Salmon King of the Rogue, had greater historical significance. By the turn of the 20th century, Hume's canneries were shipping out some 16,000 cases of salmon per year and established the river's image as a leading salmon and steelhead stream. This reputation was later enhanced by outdoorsman and novelist Zane Grey in his *Rogue River Feud* and other writings. Over the years, Herbert Hoover, Winston Churchill, Ginger Rogers (who had a home on the Rogue), Clark Gable, Jack London, George H. W. Bush, and Jimmy Carter, among other notables, have come here to try their luck. During the last several decades, boat tours focusing on the abundant wildlife, scenic beauty, and fascinating lore of the region have hooked other sectors of the traveling public.

At the north end of town, just before the road gives way to Conde McCullough's elegant Patterson Bridge, the harbor comes into view on the left, full of salmon trawlers, jet boats, pelicans, and seals bobbing up and down. Across the bridge is **Wedderburn,** a baby sister to Gold Beach and named for the Scottish birthplace of Robert Hume.

SIGHTS
Beaches

The driftwood-strewn strand of **South Beach,** just south of Gold Beach's harbor, is convenient but only so-so. You'll find more exciting stretches both north and south of town. Two miles south, there's easy access to a nice beach and some tidepooling at tiny **Buena Vista State Park,** at the mouth of Hunter Creek. Seven miles south of Gold Beach, there's more tidepooling amid the camera-friendly basalt sea stacks at beautiful **Myers Creek Beach,** part of Pistol River State Park south of Cape Sebastian. The south side of Cape Sebastian and **Pistol River State Park,** a couple of miles farther south, are the best places on the Oregon coast for windsurfers to sail in the ocean. The beaches around Pistol River are also great places to find razor clams.

Bailey Beach, north of town between the Rogue River jetty and Otter Point, is another popular spot for razor clamming, and **Nesika Beach,** seven miles north of Gold Beach, is another good tidepooling destination.

★ Cape Sebastian

Seven miles south of Gold Beach is **Cape Sebastian.** This spectacular windswept headland was named by Sebastián Vizcaíno, who plied offshore waters here for Spain in 1602 along with Manuel d'Alguilar. At 720 feet above the sea, Cape Sebastian is the highest south coast overlook reachable by a paved public road. On a clear day, visibility extends 43 miles north to Humbug Mountain and 50 miles south to California. This is one of the best perches along the south coast for whale-watching. A trail zigzags through beautiful springtime wildflowers down the south side of the cape for about two miles until it reaches the sea. In April and May, Pacific paintbrushes, Douglas irises, orchids, and snow queens usher you along. In addition, Cape Sebastian supports a population of large-headed goldfields, a summer-blooming yellow daisy-like flower found only in coastal Curry County.

In 1942, a caretaker heard Japanese voices drifting across the water through the fog. When the mist lifted, he looked down from Cape Sebastian trail to see a surfaced submarine. This sighting, together with the Japanese

bombing at Brookings and the incendiary balloon spotted over Cape Blanco, sent shock waves up the south coast. But the potential threat remained just that, and local anxiety eventually subsided.

Museums

At the **Curry County Historical Museum** (29419 S. Ellensburg Ave., 541/247-9396, www.curryhistory.com, 10am-4pm Tues.-Sat., closed Jan., $2), the local historical society has assembled a small collection of exhibits. Particularly interesting are a realistic reconstruction of a miner's cabin, vintage photos, and Indian petroglyphs.

In the harbor area on the west side of U.S. 101, **Jerry's Rogue Jets** (29980 Harbor Way, 541/247-9737, Mon.-Sat., 10am-5pm Sun., free) has assembled the best regional museum on the south coast in their gift shop. Centuries of natural and human history are depicted. Museum photos of early river runs—hauling freight, passengers, and mail—can impart a sense of history to your trip upriver or up the road.

Scenic Drives

From U.S. 101, two miles south of town, you can pick up **Hunter's Creek Road,** which loops north through the forest, finally following the course of the Rogue back into Gold Beach along Jerry's Flat Road. The three-hour drive follows Hunter's Creek inland for several miles, passing several picnic areas and campgrounds.

Other roads less traveled include the old **Coast Highway,** which you can pick up near Pistol River and Brookings; the **Shasta Costa Road** paralleling the Rogue from Gold Beach to Galice; and an unpaved summer-only road into the **Rogue Wilderness** from Agness (a town upriver on the Rogue) to Powers. Despite most of these routes being paved (except the last one), they are all narrow, winding, and not suitable for trailers or motor homes. Be sure to travel with a good map; don't just rely on your GPS.

SPORTS AND RECREATION

★ Rogue River Jet-Boat Ride

The most popular way to take in the mighty Rogue is on a jet-boat ride from Gold Beach. It's an exciting and interesting look at the varied flora and fauna along the estuary as well as the changing moods of the river. Three different lengths of river tours are available. Most of the estimated 50,000 people per year who "do" the Rogue in this way take the 64-mile round-trip cruise. An 80-mile trip goes farther up the Rogue, and the most adventurous trip is the 104-mile excursion that enters the Rogue River canyon. Meals are not included in the cost of the cruise, and you can either bring your own food or have a meal at one of the secluded fishing lodges upriver, where the tours stop for meal breaks. The pilot-commentators are often folks who have grown up on the river, and their evocations of the diverse ecosystems and Native American and gold-mining history can greatly enhance your enjoyment. Bears, otters, seals, and beavers may be sighted en route, and anglers may hold up a big keeper to show off. Ospreys, snowy egrets, eagles, mergansers, and kingfishers are also seen with regularity in this stopover for migratory waterfowl.

In the first part of the journey, idyllic riverside retreats dot the hillsides, breaking up stands of fir and hemlock. Myrtle, madrona, and impressive springtime wildflower groupings also vary the landscape. All of the jet-boat trips out of Gold Beach focus on the section of the Rogue protected by the government as a Wild and Scenic River. Only the longer trips take you into the pristine Rogue Wilderness, an area that motor launches from Grants Pass do not reach. The 13 miles of this wilderness you see from the boat have canyon walls rising 1,500 feet above you. Geologists say this part of the Klamath Mountains is composed of ancient islands and seafloor that collided with North America. To deal with the rapids upstream, smaller and faster boats are used to skim over the boulders with just six inches of water between hull and the rock surface.

The season runs May-October 15. Remember that chill and fog near the mouth of the estuary usually give way to much warmer conditions upstream. These tour outfits have wool blankets available on cold days as well as complimentary hot beverages. Also keep in mind that the upriver lodges can be booked for overnight stays, and your trip may be resumed the following day.

Just south of the Rogue River Bridge, west of U.S. 101 on Harbor Way, is **Jerry's Rogue Jets** (29985 Harbor Way, 541/247-4571 or 800/451-3645, www.roguejets.com). Jerry's offers 64-mile ($50 adult, $25 children 4-11), 80-mile ($70 adult, $35 children), and 104-mile ($95 adults, $45 children) trips. There are usually two departures for each trip daily: one in the morning, one near midday. This heavily patronized company is noted for personable, well-informed guides.

Fishing

Fishing is a mighty big deal in Gold Beach, which has one of the highest concentrations of professional guides in the state. There's something to fish for just about year-round, but salmon and steelhead are the top quarry. When the spring chinook pour in (Apr.-June), anglers will need to book guided trips well in advance to get a shot at them. Catches peak in May. Summer steelhead and fall-run chinook usually arrive July-September, then it's hatchery coho September-November (sometimes as early as August). In December, the first of the winter steelhead make their appearance and continue into March.

The **Rogue Outdoor Store** (29865 Ellensburg Ave., 541/247-7142, 8am-6pm daily) is well stocked with fishing, camping, and other gear, and its staff can advise on where, when, and what to fish.

Typical rates for guided salmon trips are $250-400 per person depending on the size of your group. Contact the **Gold Beach Visitor Center** (541/247-7526 or 800/525-2334, www.goldbeach.org) for a list of over two dozen licensed guides.

Fish Oregon (541/347-6338, www.fish-oregon.com) is a well-established guide service; Shaun Carpenter at **End of the Rogue** (541/247-2049, www.endoftherogue.com) and Ron Smith at **Sportfishing Oregon** (541/425-1318, www.sportfishingoregon.com) also guide salmon and steelhead fishing trips on a number of southern Oregon rivers.

Golf

The nine-hole **Cedar Bend Golf Course** (34391 Cedar Valley Rd., 541/247-6911, www.cedarbendgolf.com, $20 for 9 holes, $28 for 18) is in nearby Ophir. Eleven miles north of Gold Beach, pick up Ophir Road off U.S. 101. Follow it to Squaw Valley Road, turn right at the Old Ophir Store, and continue until you see the links. Woods line the fairways, and a winding creek offers a challenge on nine holes.

Hiking

The 40-mile **Rogue River Trail** (www.blm.gov/or) offers lodge-to-lodge hiking, which means you need little more in your pack than the essentials. The lodges here are comfortably rustic, serve home-style food in copious portions, and run $130-310 for a double room. They are also comfortably spaced, so extended hiking is seldom a necessity.

Before you go, check with the **Gold Beach Ranger Station** (29279 Ellensburg Ave., 541/247-3600, http://www.fs.usda.gov/rogue-siskiyou, 8am-5pm Mon.-Fri.) on trail conditions and specific directions to the trailhead. Pick up the western end of the trail 35 miles east of Gold Beach, about 0.5 mile from Foster Bar, a popular boat landing. Park there and walk east and north on the paved road until you see signs on the left marking the Rogue River Trail. Go in spring before the hot weather and enjoy yellow Siskiyou irises and fragrant wild azaleas. The trail ends at Grave Creek, 27 miles northwest of Grants Pass. Be careful of rattlesnakes, and note that summers are extremely hot on the trail.

Windsurfing

Although beginners may want to hone their skills up north at Floras Lake, experienced windsurfers head out into the ocean near the debouchment of the **Pistol River.**

ENTERTAINMENT AND EVENTS

The **Wild Rivers Coast Seafood, Art, and Wine Festival** is a two-day event that celebrates wine, fine dining, and arts and crafts of the southern Oregon coast in mid-May at the **Event Center on the Beach** (29392 Ellensburg Ave., 541/247-4541, admission fees vary).

The **Pistol River Wave Bash National Windsurfing Competition** (americanwindsurfingtour.com) brings four days of competitive riding to Pistol River State Park each June.

The **Curry County Fair** takes place at the **Event Center on the Beach** (29392 Ellensburg Ave., 541/247-4541, admission fees vary) in mid-August.

Since 1982, the **Pistol River Concert Association** (541/247-2848, www.pistolriver.com, $15 adults) has produced a top-notch **concert series,** encompassing bluegrass, folk, jazz, classical, and blues at the Pistol River Friendship Hall. Concerts are held roughly once a month throughout the year, and it's well worth fussing with your schedule in order to catch one. Past and present performers are a *Who's Who* of acoustic music, including Greg Brown, Mike Seeger, Peggy Seeger, Kevin Burke, Norman and Nancy Blake, Peter Rowan, and Tony Rice, to name a few. To get there from Gold Beach, take U.S. 101 for 10 miles south to the second Pistol River exit (Pistol River/Carpenterville), then take the first right. The Pistol River Friendship Hall is 0.5 mile ahead on the right.

ACCOMMODATIONS

As in most coastal towns, there is no shortage of places to stay along the main drag, Ellensburg Avenue (a.k.a. U.S. 101). In fact, Gold Beach offers the largest number and widest range of accommodations on the south coast, with intimate lodges overlooking the Rogue as popular as the oceanfront motels. A discount of 20 percent or more on rooms is usually available during winter, when 80-90 inches of rain can fall.

$50-100

The best bet for a clean, inexpensive room is the **Wild Chinook Inn** (94200 Harlow St., 541/247-6675, http://chinookinn.com, $85-105), where you get no-frills accommodations in a motor court motel across from the fairgrounds. Rooms have Wi-Fi, a fridge, and a microwave; some full-kitchen units are available.

Don't turn up your nose at this **Motel 6** (94433 Jerry's Flat Rd., 541/247-4533 or 956/668-7829, $85-130); the location—perched above the Rogue River—is great, and the rooms are modern and comfy. Pets are permitted.

If you're looking for a simple place to spend a night or two and don't care about frills, the **Azalea Lodge** (29481 Ellensburg Ave., 541/247-6635 or 866/381-6635, www.azalealodge.biz, $95-175) is a good bet, with friendly owners and clean rooms. No pets are allowed; all guest rooms are nonsmoking and have refrigerators.

$100-150

Though it's true that ★ **Ireland's Rustic Lodges** (29330 Ellensburg Ave., office 29346 Ellensburg Ave., 541/247-7718, www.irelands-rusticlodges.com, cabins $125-149, lodge rooms $104-159) include charming vintage cabins, it also offers more modern lodge rooms, condos, and beach houses. Many of the guest rooms have fireplaces, knotty-pine interiors, and distinctive decor. Best of all, the parklike grounds are lovingly landscaped with pine trees, flowers, and ocean views. A sandy beach is a short stroll to the west. There are 33 lodge units (some with kitchens), seven vintage but well-kept log cabins (recommended) that sleep up to five, and houses that sleep as many as 11. Immediately next door, and with the same owners, is the **Gold Beach**

Inn (29346 Ellensburg Ave., 541/247-7091 or 888/663-0608, www.goldbeachinn.com, non-oceanview rooms $90, oceanview rooms $129-159), a more modern (but far from new) hotel with oceanfront guest rooms, many with balconies. These two establishments share many facilities, including private beach paths and a series of outdoor hot tubs in the midst of an 11-acre property.

$150-200

For a more traditional oceanfront hotel, the **Gold Beach Resort** (29232 Ellensburg Ave., 541/247-7066 or 800/541-0947, www.gbresort.com, $150-170) offers nicely furnished ocean-view rooms, all with balconies. Also part of this large complex, with easy beach access, are one- and two-bedroom condos, all with fireplaces. Facilities include an indoor pool and a fitness center; a complimentary continental breakfast is available.

Over $200

★ **Tu Tu Tun Resort** (96550 N. Bank Rogue River Rd., 541/247-6664 or 800/864-6357, tututun.com, rooms $255-385, suites $435-505, house $530-915) is the most luxurious place to stay on the southern Oregon coast, where lucky guests take in river views through the floor-to-ceiling windows, enjoy a good book from the lodge's library in front of the massive river-rock fireplace, and savor delicious Pacific Northwest cuisine. As you sit on your patio overlooking the water along with the resident bald eagles, only the sounds of an occasional passing boat may intrude upon your Rogue River reverie. Rooms are graciously furnished, but not overly fussy—why interfere with the stunning views? The lodge is seven miles up the Rogue River from Gold Beach.

This acclaimed retreat also offers a heated pool and other recreational facilities. Meals are available on an inclusive Modified American Plan ($68 per person), which includes hors d'oeuvres, a gourmet four-course dinner, and a bountiful breakfast buffet. Nonguests are welcome to dinner ($60) with reservations. The dining room is only open

May-October. In the off-season, guests are served a continental breakfast only. Tu Tu Tun is not a secret, so reservations are required well in advance of your stay.

Upriver Lodges

Several lodges on the Rogue, some accessible only by boat or via hiking trails, lure visitors deep into the Rogue interior. Jet-boat trips can drop you off for an overnight or longer stay. Advance reservations are essential.

Also accessible by road and boat, the authentically rustic **Lucas Lodge** (3904 Cougar Ln., Agness, 541/247-7443, www.lucaslodgeoregon.com, $45-95) is 32 miles east of Gold Beach. Some cabins here come equipped with kitchen options. Lunch and dinner are served daily in the lodge—chicken, biscuits, and garden vegetables are standard fare. Reservations are required.

Accessible only by helicopter, boat, or on foot, the **Paradise Lodge** (541/842-2822 or 888/667-6483, www.paradise-lodge.com, $155-165 per person, $85 children, includes meals) attracts guests who want to immerse themselves in nature but still eat and sleep well. Electricity only operates during certain hours. A huge on-site garden provides ingredients for home-cooked meals.

Another backcountry lodge, the **Clay Hill Lodge** (541/859-3772, www.clayhilllodge.com, $165 per person, $100 per child, includes meals), is accessible via raft (from upstream), jet boat, or foot. By foot, it's about three hours (six miles) up from the trailhead near Foster Bar, east of Gold Beach.

Camping

There are no public campgrounds along the coast between Humbug Mountain, just south of Port Orford, and Harris Beach, at the northern entrance to Brookings. But campsites east of town up the Rogue River provide wonderful spots to bed down for the night. Those taking the road along the Rogue should be alert for oncoming log trucks, raft transport vehicles, and other wide-body vehicles. In addition to the public campgrounds listed,

there are *many* private RV resorts up the north bank of the Rogue.

Foster Bar Campground (Siskiyou National Forest, 541/247-6651, www.fs.usda. gov, open year-round, flush toilets available May-Oct., $10) is 30 miles east of Gold Beach on the south bank of the Rogue. Take Jerry's Flat Road east for 30 miles to the turnoff for Agness. Turn right on Illahe Agness Road and drive three miles to camp. Campsites here come equipped with drinking water, toilets, ADA-compliant facilities, picnic tables, fire rings, and a boat ramp. Sites are available on a first-come, first-served basis only. This is a popular spot from which to embark on an eight-mile inner-tube ride to Agness. It's also where rafters pull out, so the parking lot may be jam-packed. The rapids are dangerous—wear a life jacket. You are also within walking distance of the trailhead of the Rogue River Trail.

Lobster Creek Campground (541/247-3600, www.fs.usda.gov, $10) is nine miles east of Gold Beach via Forest Service Road 33. This campground is open year-round and has three tent sites, three trailer sites, one group site, picnic tables, fishing, and flush toilets—but no drinking water. The Schrader old-growth trail is two miles from the campground via Forest Road 090. It is a gentle one-mile walk through a rare and majestic ecosystem. Also nearby is the world's largest myrtle tree.

Honeybear Campground and RV Resort (34161 Ophir Rd., Ophir, 541/247-2765 or 800/822-4444, www.honeybearrv.com, open year-round, $20-39) is not up the Rogue; it's nine miles north of Gold Beach on U.S. 101, then two miles north on Ophir Road—but it could just as well be in the Black Forest. The owners have built a large rathskeller with a dance floor. Six nights a week during the summer, there are dances here with traditional German music. Check out their version of Oktoberfest, a traditional fall festival held two weekends in late September. Locals praise the Honeybear's on-site delicatessen for its homemade German sausage.

FOOD
American

Drive a mile up the south bank of the Rogue to eat breakfast in a relaxed riverfront setting at **Indian Creek Café** (94682 Jerry's Flat Rd., 541/247-0680, 5:30am-2pm daily, $8-12). In good weather, there's seating on a deck overlooking the Indian Creek, which flows into the Rogue here. Omelets, pancakes, and other traditional breakfast items are well prepared; lunch is mostly burgers and sandwiches.

Locals recommend the **Port Hole Café** (29975 Harbor Way, 541/247-7411, http://portholecafe.com, 11am-9pm daily, $8-20), with bay and river views in the Cannery building at the port, for hearty portions of fish-and-chips, chowder, and homemade pies at decent prices. If you don't want to stop for a meal, pick up some fresh seafood or the best canned tuna you'll ever taste next door at **Fishermen Direct Seafoods** (29975 Harbor Way, 541/247-9494, 9am-5:30pm Mon.-Sat., 9am-2pm Sun.).

Barnacle Bistro (29805 Ellensburg Ave., 541/247-7799, http://www.barnaclebistro.com, 11am-8pm Tues.-Sun., $8-15) is a lively spot for light meals, offering sandwiches, burgers, and fish tacos. The salad greens are local and organically grown, and all the sauces and dressings are made in-house.

Italian

Mangia Buff Café (29692 Ellensburg Ave., 541/247-4606, 11am-7pm Mon.-Fri., 4pm-7pm Sat., $11-25) is a small, art-filled dining room with excellent Italian cooking—not a cuisine you find often on the Oregon coast. At lunch, expect salads, meatball sandwiches and sausages, while in the evening the menu features fresh pasta (clam sauce ravioli) and meat dishes such as chicken Marsala and grilled Tuscan rib eye steak. This is a chef-owned operation, and the attention to detail shows on every plate. (Park in the lot out back; the restaurant is upstairs and down the hall in the Gold Rush building.)

Steak and Seafood

A very good dinner house is **Spinner's Seafood, Steak and Chophouse** (29430 Ellensburg Ave., 541/247-5160, http://www.spinnersrestaurant.com, 4:30pm-9pm nightly, $15-39). The menu is wide-ranging, and the dining room extremely pleasant. Look for fresh, well-prepared seafood, pasta, and prime rib, along with choice beef and chops. A children's menu is available.

Wine Bar

★ **Anna's By the Sea** (29672 Stewart St., 541/247-2100, http://www.annasbythesea.com, 5pm-8pm Wed.-Sat., $19-33, reservations recommended), tucked into a residential neighborhood a couple of blocks east of busy Ellensburg Avenue, is a wonderfully quirky wine bar/restaurant serving "nouvelle Canadian Prairie cuisine"—think Angus beef drizzled with black truffle oil or locally caught cod in a vegetable-based broth over dumplings. The chef-owner hates to make desserts; instead, enjoy an after-dinner drink and some excellent house-made cheeses. Anna's is a tiny place—just 15 seats—so come early if you don't want to wait (in summer, there's more seating on the deck).

INFORMATION AND SERVICES

The **Gold Beach Visitor Center** (94080 Shirley Ln., 541/247-7526 or 800/525-2334, www.goldbeach.org, 9am-5pm Mon.-Sat.) has an excellent and informative website. The **Gold Beach Ranger Station** (29279 Ellensburg Ave., Gold Beach, 541/247-3600, http://www.fs.usda.gov/rogue-siskiyou, 8am-5pm Mon.-Fri.) can provide information on camping and recreation in the district.

The **post office** (541/247-7610) is at the port on Harbor Way. A modern building houses the **public library** (94341 3rd St., 541/247-7246, 10am-7pm Mon.-Thurs., 10am-5pm Fri.-Sat.), one block east of the highway in the north end of town. **Curry General Hospital** (94220 4th St., Gold Beach, 541/247-6621) is the only hospital in the county.

GETTING THERE
Curry County's **Coastal Express** buses
(800/921-2871, www.currypublictransit.org)
run up and down the south coast weekdays
only between North Bend and the California
border, including local service in Gold Beach.

Brookings-Harbor and Vicinity

Brookings and Harbor sit on a coastal plain overlooking the Pacific six miles north of the California border, split by U.S. 101 (Chetco Ave.) and the Chetco River. Flowing out of the Klamath Mountains east of town, the Chetco drains part of the nearby Siskiyou National Forest and the Kalmiopsis Wilderness, extensive tracts encompassing some of the wildest country in the Lower 48 and renowned for their rare flowers and trees. The Kalmiopsis Wilderness is named for a unique shrub, the *Kalmiopsis leachiana,* one of the oldest members of the heath family (Ericaceae) that grows nowhere else on earth.

Don't form your opinion of Brookings by simply driving down U.S. 101. Just make your way past the somewhat drab main drag to Samuel Boardman State Park north of town, where 11 of the most scenic miles of the Oregon coast await you. Or head down

to the harbor to embark on a boating expedition, with some of the safest offshore navigation conditions in the region. Or drive up the Chetco River, where the fog that frequently drenches the coastline during the summer months burns away a couple of miles inland and hikers can find trails.

During winter, Brookings and its neighbor, Harbor, enjoy mild temperatures. Enough 60-70°F days occur during January and February in this south coast "banana belt" town that more than 50 species of flowering plants thrive—along with retirees, outdoor-sports lovers, and beachcombers. With two gorgeous state parks virtually inside the city and world-class salmon and steelhead fishing nearby, only the lavish winter rainfall, averaging over 73 inches a year, can cool the ardor of local outdoor enthusiasts. In the springtime, the area south of town is lush with lilies—it's the Easter lily capital of the world.

Brookings-Harbor

Brookings-Harbor

© AVALON TRAVEL

SOUTH COAST INN B&B

OXENFIRE PUBLIC HOUSE

WILD RIVERS MOTORLODGE

CAFE KITANISHI

ART ALLEY GRILLE

PACIFIC AVE

PINE ST

SPRUCE ST

REDWOOD ST

OAK ST

HEMLOCK ST

CHETCO AVE

RAILROAD ST

ALDER ST

PACIFIC OCEAN

Goat Island

Harris Beach State Park

To SAMUEL H. BOARDMAN STATE SCENIC CORRIDOR, Gold Beach, and Port Orford

OREGON COAST HWY

BY THE SEA B&B

BEACH AVE

101

Zwagg

Chetco Point

SPINDRIFT MOTOR INN

ARNOLD LN

FIFIELD ST

BROOKINGS HARBOR MEDICAL CENTER

1ST ST

2ND ST

3RD ST

4TH ST

5TH ST

6TH ST

FERN AVE

EASY ST

RANSOM AVE

3RD ST

5TH ST

BROOK LN

HASSETT ST

Brookings

CENTER ST

RAILROAD ST

PACIFIC AVE

WHARF ST

TANBARK RD

SEE DETAIL

HEMLOCK ST

CHETCO AVE

REDWOOD ST

OAK ST

ALDER ST

PINE ST

MAPLE ST

PACIFIC AVE

FIR ST

AZALEA ST

PIONEER RD

OLD COUNTY RD

MEMORY LN

DEL NORTE LN

SPORTHAVEN MARINA/ HUNGRY CLAM

VISITOR INFORMATION CENTER

CHETCO SEAFOOD

PARK AVE

AZALEA Park

Azalea Park

BEST WESTERN BEACHFRONT INN

BOAT BASIN RD

Port of Brookings

LOWER HARBOR RD

SHOPPING CENTER AVE

Crescent City, CA

OCEAN SUITES

Harbor

OCEANVIEW DR

101

To Crescent City, CA

Chetco River

NORTH BANK CHETCO RIVER RD

SOUTH BANK CHETCO RIVER RD

Bombsite Trail

To Alfred A. Loeb State Park

To Alfred A. Loeb State Park

0 0.25 mi

0 0.25 km

Brookings: From Box Factory to Retirement Haven

What is now the shopping hub of rural Curry County started out as a factory town for the Brookings Box Company in 1913. Owner J. L. Brookings hired the architect Bernard Maybeck (famous for designing the Palace of Fine Arts in San Francisco) to lay out the streets and design housing and community buildings for his mill workers. Maybeck drew up extensive plans for a model company town, but most of them were never realized; his central vision was eventually gutted when the state highway was laid through, rather than around, the town. Examples of Maybeck's craftsmanship can still be seen around Brookings, notably in the 1917 Craftsman-style residence (now the South Coast Inn B&B) he designed for lumber baron William Ward.

In the years that followed, the lumber industry was augmented with fishing, horticulture, and tourism. Omitting for the moment the possibility that the offshore waters here were visited by Juan Cabrillo (in 1542) and the English explorer Sir Francis Drake (in 1579), the local event with the greatest historical significance was a Japanese aerial bombing on September 9, 1942, when a Japanese incendiary bomb scorched the treetops of Mount Emily, southeast of town, in one of only two documented wartime air bombing missions against the U.S. mainland (the other occurred three weeks later near Port Orford). The resulting fires were quickly doused by the damp conditions, and no significant harm was done.

Since the late 1980s, Brookings's greatest growth industry has been as a haven for retirees, and that population has been booming in recent years.

SIGHTS

In Brookings, camellias bloom at Christmas, and flowering plums add color the next month. Daffodils, grown commercially on the coastal plain south of Brookings, bloom in late January and into February. Magnolia shrubs, some early azaleas, and rhododendrons bloom in late winter. The area also produces 90 percent of the world's Easter lily crop.

Azalea Park (640 Old Country Rd.) is a quiet place just off the main drag to picnic and enjoy the flowers. This Works Progress Administration-built enclave features 20-foot-high azaleas (which are several hundred years old), hand-hewn myrtlewood picnic tables, an excellent playground, and a band shell that hosts summer concerts. Wild cherry and crab apple blooms, wild strawberry blossoms, and purple and red violets round out the bouquet. Butterflies, bees, and birds all seem to concur with locals that this array smells sweetest around graduation time in mid-June.

Harris Beach State Park

At the northern limits of Brookings, **Harris Beach State Park** makes up for all the strip-mall architecture you'll find on Chetco Avenue. Besides its stunning views, this state park offers many incoming travelers from California their first chance to actually walk on the beach in Oregon. You can begin directly west of the park's campground, where a sandy beach strewn with boulders often becomes flooded with intertidal life and driftwood. The early morning hours, as the waves crash through a small tunnel in a massive rock onto the shoreline, are the best time to look for sponges, umbrella crabs, solitary corals, and sea stars.

Offshore, **Bird Island** (also called Goat Island) is the largest island along the Oregon coast and the state's largest seabird rookery. This outpost of Oregon Islands National Wildlife Refuge dispatches squadrons of cormorants, pelicans, tufted puffins, and other waterfowl, which dive-bomb the incoming waves for food.

In addition to beachcombing, you can picnic at tables above the parking lot, loll about in the shallow waters of nearby Harris Creek, or cast in the surf for perch.

Mill Beach is the southernmost part of the

Harris Beach area. Locals prefer the beach access from downtown, which is easy to miss. To get there, drive toward the ocean on Center Street in downtown Brookings, make a right at the plywood mill, and stop next to a small ballpark. An unimproved road leads to a hillock, from which trails take you down to a beach full of driftwood. Residents say that Japanese fishing floats occasionally roll up onto the beach after a storm.

Chetco Valley Historical Society Museum

The **Chetco Valley Historical Society Museum** (5461 Museum Rd., 541/469-6651, www.chetcomuseum.com, 1pm-4pm Fri.-Sun. Memorial Day-Labor Day, $3 donation suggested), in the red-and-white Blake House, sits on a hill overlooking U.S. 101 two miles south of the Chetco River. The structure dates to 1857 and was used as a stagecoach way station and trading post before Abraham Lincoln was president.

Oregon's largest Monterey cypress tree is located on the hill near the museum. The 130-foot-tall tree has a trunk diameter of more than 18 feet.

★ Samuel H. Boardman State Scenic Corridor

The stretch of highway from Brookings to Port Orford is known as the "fabulous 50 miles." Some consider the section of coastline just north of Brookings to be the most scenic in Oregon—and one of the most dramatic meetings of rock and tide in the world. The offshore rock formations and winding roadbed hundreds of feet above the surf invite comparison to Europe's Amalfi Drive. The "fabulous 50" sobriquet is perhaps most apt in the dozen miles directly north of Brookings, encompassed by **Samuel H. Boardman State Scenic Corridor.** You'll want to have a camera close at hand and a loose schedule when you make this drive, because you'll find it hard not to pull over again and again, as each photo opportunity seems to outdazzle the last. Of the 11 named viewpoints that have been cut into the highway's shoulder, the following are especially recommended (all viewpoints are marked by signs on the west side of U.S. 101 and are listed here from north to south).

Near the north end of Boardman State Park, a short walk down the hillside trail leads you to the **Arch Rocks** viewpoint, where an

Samuel H. Boardman State Scenic Corridor offers miles of dramatic coastline.

immense boomerang-shaped basalt archway juts out of the water about a quarter-mile offshore. This site has picnic tables within view of the monolith.

A few miles south, the sign for **Natural Bridges Cove** seems to front just a forested parking lot. However, the paved walkway at the south end of the lot leads to a spectacular overlook. Below, several rock archways frame an azure cove. This feature was created by the collapse of the entrance and exit of a sea cave. A steep trail through giant ferns and towering Sitka spruce and Douglas fir takes you down for a closer look. Thimbleberry (a sweet but seedy raspberry) is plentiful in late spring. As in similar forests on the south coast, it's important to stay on the trail. The rainforest-like biome is exceptionally fragile, and the soil erodes easily when the delicate vegetation is damaged.

Thomas Creek Bridge, the highest bridge in Oregon (345 feet above the water) as well as the highest north of San Francisco, has been used as a silent star in many TV commercials. A parking lot at the south end of the bridge offers the best views.

House Rock was the site of a World War II air-raid sentry tower that sits hundreds of feet above whitecaps pounding the rock-strewn beaches. To the north, you'll see one of the highest cliffs on the coast, Cape Sebastian. A steep circuitous trail lined with salal goes down to the water. The path begins behind the Samuel Boardman monument on the west end of the parking lot. The sign to the highest viewpoint in Boardman State Park is easy to miss, but look for the turnout that precedes House Rock, called Cape Ferrelo (for Juan Cabrillo's navigator, who sailed up much of the West Coast in 1543).

Carpenterville Road

The current roadbed of U.S. 101 was laid in southern Oregon in 1961. The previous coastal route still exists along **Carpenterville Road,** which can be picked up near Harris Beach. It comes out near the Pistol River, where it descends in a series of switchbacks. Its highest point is 1,700 feet above sea level at Burnt Hill. Views of the Siskiyous to the east and the Pacific panoramas to the west make the sometimes-rough road worth the effort. In very clear weather, it's possible to look back toward the southeast at Mount Shasta between the ridgelines. This route is best appreciated going south, and it makes a great 20-mile bike ride, with a long climb to 1,700 feet above sea level.

Alfred A. Loeb State Park

Eight miles northeast of Brookings, on North Bank Chetco River Road (which follows the Chetco River), the **Alfred A. Loeb State Park** preserves 320 acres of old-growth myrtlewood, the state's largest grove. Many of these aromatic trees are much older than 200 years.

The 0.25-mile Riverview Trail passes numerous big trees to connect Loeb Park with the **Redwood Nature Trail.** This trail winds 1.2 miles through the northernmost stands of naturally occurring *Sequoia sempervirens.* This is Oregon's largest redwood grove and contains the state's largest specimens. Within the grove are several trees more than 500 years old, measuring 5-8 feet in diameter and towering more than 300 feet above the forest floor. One tree has a 33-foot girth and is estimated to exceed 800 years in age. When the south coast is foggy and cold on summer mornings, it's often warm and dry in upriver locations such as this one, inviting the possibility of swimming in the Chetco.

Kalmiopsis Wilderness

The lure of untrammeled wilderness attracts intrepid hikers to the **Kalmiopsis Wilderness,** despite the summer's blazing heat and winter's torrential rains. In addition to enjoying the isolation of the wilderness, they come to take in the pink rhododendron-like blooms of *Kalmiopsis leachiana* (in June) and other rare flowers. The area is also home to such economically valued species as Port Orford cedar and, in the past, illegal marijuana grows. (Cannabis is a leading cash crop in this part of the state.) During the fall there's a lucrative mushroom harvest; take care not to encroach on pickers, who may be quite territorial.

In any case, the Forest Service prohibits plant collection *of any kind* to preserve the region's special botanical populations. These include the insect-eating darlingtonia plant and the Brewer's weeping spruce. The forest canopy is composed largely of the more common Douglas fir, canyon live oak, madrona, and chinquapin. Stark peaks top this red-rock forest, whose understory is choked with blueberry, manzanita, and dense chaparral.

Many of this wilderness's rare species survived the glacial epoch because the glaciers from that era left the area untouched. This, combined with the fact that the area was once an offshore island, has enabled the region's singular ecosystem to maintain its integrity through the millennia. You'd think that federal protection, remoteness, and climatic extremes would ensure a sanguine outlook for this ice-age forest, but an active debate still rages over the validity of some logging claims.

In summer 2002, the **Biscuit Fire** raged out of control for weeks, ravaging nearly half a million acres of southwestern Oregon, engulfing most of the Siskiyou National Forest and virtually all of the Kalmiopsis Wilderness. This inferno, the nation's largest wildfire of 2002 and the biggest in Oregon for more than a century, destroyed extensive habitat of the endangered northern spotted owl. The good news, however, is that flora of the region is well adapted to periodic fires; many of the old-growth trees survived the blaze, and within a few months green sprouts and new growth of many species were reappearing amid the ashes.

In the years since the fire, a new forest has taken hold. Certain tree species, including rare Brewer spruce and knob cone pine, have grown back abundantly, as their seed cones require fire for germination. With the once-thick overstory vegetation mostly dead, lower-growing plants such as ferns, huckleberries, and bear grass are thriving in the sun. Soils are moister, too, since massive adult trees

aren't sucking up the groundwater. Forest scientists estimate that it will take a century for trees of the mature forest, including stands of Douglas fir and sugar pine, to return and erase the evidence of the 2002 fire. Meanwhile, the charred snags of the former primary forest stand above the lush growth of quickly rejuvenating woodlands.

Even if you don't have the slightest intention of hiking the Kalmiopsis, the scenic drive through the **Chetco Valley** is worth it. From Brookings, turn off U.S. 101 at the north end of the Chetco River Bridge. Follow this paved road upriver past Loeb State Park and continue along the river on County Roads 784 and 1376 until a narrow bridge crosses the Chetco. From here, turn right for 18 miles along national forest roads 1909, 160, and 1917 to reach the Upper Chetco Trailhead (just past the Quail Prairie Lookout). The driving distance from Brookings is 31 miles. If you're not hiking into the wilderness, you can continue west on national forest road 1917 (portions are not paved), which will return you to the above-mentioned narrow bridge over the Chetco.

Crissey Field State Recreation Area

Crissey Field State Recreation Area lies south of Brookings, almost to the California border, and is set along the Winchuck River. The park, which was added to the state park system in 2008, is great place to watch birds, harbor seals, California sea lions, and other wildlife. A trail leads through a huge pile of driftwood logs to dunes that shelter native plants, tiny wetlands, and old-growth Sitka spruce trees. Crissey Field is also the site of a spacious **visitor center.** Incidentally, the park's name has nothing to do with the San Francisco park (that's Crissy); it's in the heart of the lily-growing area and is named for a lily bulb grower.

HIKING
Bombsite Trail

Brookings takes a peculiar pride in having

been bombed by the Japanese during World War II. In 1942, two incendiary bombs were dropped about 16 miles east of town on the slopes of Mount Emily. Although they were intended to start a fire, conditions were wet, and the small fire that resulted was easily controlled. A sort of mutual respect eventually developed between the Japanese pilot who dropped the bomb and the town of Brookings. The pilot was a guest of honor at one Azalea Festival, and his family later presented the town with his samurai sword, which he wore during the bombing and throughout the war. The sword is now on exhibit at the local library (420 Alder St.).

The Mount Emily **Bombsite Trail**, 19 miles by road from town, commemorates the bombing. It's a two-mile stretch with redwoods near the beginning and fire-dependent species such as knobcone pine and manzanita along the way. To reach the trail, head eight miles east up South Bank Road and turn right onto Mount Emily Road. At the fork, turn onto Wheeler Creek Road and follow the signs.

Oregon Redwoods Trail

In addition to the trail through redwood trees in Loeb Park, hikers can explore some not-huge but still old-growth redwoods along the 1.7-mile **Oregon Redwoods Trail** southeast of town. The first half-mile of the trail is wheelchair-accessible; a longer stretch leads downhill to a scattered collection of redwoods. Although redwoods here at the northern edge of their range aren't the monster trees that you see in California, this is a pretty trail.

From U.S. Highway 101, take the Winchuck River Road; turn right onto Forest Road 1101 and continue four miles up this narrow dirt road to the trailhead, which is 11 miles from town.

Vulcan Lake Trail

A good introduction to the Kalmiopsis Wilderness is along the one-mile trail to **Vulcan Lake** at the foot of Vulcan Peak, which is the major jumping-off point for

trails into the wilderness. The trail begins at Forest Road 1909 and takes off up the mountains past Pollywog Butte and Red Mountain Prairie. The open patches in the Douglas firs reveal a kaleidoscope of Pacific Ocean views and panoramas of the Chetco Valley and the Big Craggies. For the botanist in search of rare plants, however, the real show is on the trail; it's located in the area burned by the 2002 Biscuit Fire and shows the recovery since then. Despite steep spots, the walk from County Road 1909 to Vulcan Lake is not difficult. Before going, check with the Forest Service in Brookings to see if the road to the Vulcan Lake trailhead is open and passable, because weather-related closures occasionally occur and the road can be in really rough condition.

To reach the trailhead from Brookings, turn east off U.S. 101 at the north end of the Chetco River Bridge, follow North Bank Road (County Rd. 784) and Forest Road 1376 along the Chetco River for six miles, and then turn right and follow Forest Road 1909 to its bumpy end. Driving distance from Brookings is 31 miles. Hikers should watch out for the three shiny leaves of poison oak, as well as for rattlesnakes, which are numerous. Black bears also populate the area, but their lack of contact with humans makes them more shy than their Cascade counterparts.

SPORTS AND RECREATION

For some mellow fun in the sun, cruise down Easy Street, east off U.S. 101, to **Bud Cross City Park** for some tennis, a dip in the outdoor pool, or a visit to the skate park.

Fishing

Fishing on the Chetco was once one of southern Oregon's best-kept secrets, but word has gotten out about the river's October run of huge chinook and its superlative influx of winter steelhead. The late-summer ocean salmon season out of Brookings may be the best in the Pacific Northwest. Boatless anglers can try their luck at the public fishing pier at the harbor and on the south jetty at the mouth of the Chetco. Chinook season generally runs mid-May-mid-September, but that's subject to change, so check the regulations.

Guided fishing trips for salmon, steelhead, and ocean bottom fish can be arranged through **Wild Rivers Fishing** (541/813-1082, www.wildriversfishing.com). In addition to fishing charters, **Tidewind Sportfishing** (16368 Lower Harbor Rd., 541/469-0337, www.tidewindsportfishing.com) offers whale-watching excursions in season.

Golf

All the press about Bandon Dunes has obscured the development of another great course, **Salmon Run Golf Course** (99040 South Bank Chetco River Rd., 541/469-4888, salmonrun.net, $55 for 18 holes). This beautiful 18-hole public links—not far from the Kalmiopsis Wilderness—was designed with environmentally sensitive imperatives, so numerous wildlife sightings may be enjoyed here long into the future. Whether it's the chance to see salmon (usually after the first rains in November) and steelhead spawning (January), black bears, elk, and wild turkeys, or just the opportunity to play a first-rate course, golfers shouldn't overlook this one. Beginner and intermediate players may find the executive nine-hole ($29) course ideal. This par-34 course within a course is located on the back nine holes and measures 1,310 yards. Your Oregon coastal golf pilgrimage can begin here, then hit Bandon Dunes, Sandpines (Florence), and Salishan (near Lincoln City).

Surfing, Boogie Boarding, and Kayaking

The best surfing is usually found at **Sporthaven Beach,** at the north end of the jetty in Harbor. Reach it by driving to the end of Boat Basin Road to the RV park. There's plenty of parking at the very end of the road. Even if the surf is not spectacular (it's usually best in the winter), it's a pretty mellow place for beginners, and as a fringe benefit, it can be a good spot to see whales during their spring-time or December migrations.

Boogie boarders tend to favor **Harris Beach State Park.** From fall to spring, the waves are big and dangerous, and the water is cold. If you know what you're doing, come on in.

Rent a surfboard, stand-up paddleboard, boogie board, kayak, or wetsuit from the **Southern Oregon Surf Co.** (519 Chetco Ave., 831/235-6505, 10am-7pm Wed.-Sun.).

South Coast Tours (541/373-0487, www.southcoasttours.net) leads kayak tours in the ocean off Samuel Boardman State Park ($130). This 9.5-mile trip isn't suitable for beginners, but more experienced paddlers have the chance to paddle through arches, examine the Thomas Creek Bridge from below, and view sea birds, marine mammals, and kelp forests. They also lead stand-up paddling tours ($100, experience required) into coves and around the natural arches.

ENTERTAINMENT AND EVENTS

Brookings's big event is the **Azalea Festival** (541/469-3181 or 800/535-9469, Memorial Day weekend), which celebrates the local flower with carnival rides, street food, a fun run, and a parade. Most of the action is down at the harbor, which is thronged with vendors, food stands, music, and giant inflatables.

Like several other Oregon coast towns, Brookings puts its windy weather to good use with its annual **Southern Oregon Kite Festival** (www.southernoregonkitefestival.com), held over two days in mid-July. Individuals and teams display their aerial skills at the port of Brookings-Harbor.

Azalea Park is home to **Nature's Coastal Holiday Light Show** in December, with more than 75,000 lights.

ACCOMMODATIONS

Rooms in Brookings are generally rather expensive; there are more budget accommodations 29 miles north in Gold Beach. It's also harder to find pet-friendly lodgings here than in most other coast towns.

$50-100

Just north of the Chetco River Bridge, **Wild Rivers Motorlodge** (437 Chetco Ave., 541/469-5361, www.wildriversmotorlodge.com, $90-110) is the most attractive roadside budget motel in town. Rooms come with refrigerators and microwaves; some are pet-friendly.

The **Spindrift Motor Inn** (1215 Chetco Ave., 541/469-5345, $90) is a well-managed property and a decent value. However, its ambience is strictly roadside-budget, and it is a bit of a walk to the beach.

At the southern edge of the Brookings-Harbor stretch of U.S. 101, the **Harbor Inn Motel** (15991 U.S. 101 S., 541/469-3194 or 800/469-8444, www.harborinnmotel.com, $70-90) is not a bad place to land. It's nothing fancy, but it's pretty quiet and permits pets; all rooms have a fridge, a microwave, and Wi-Fi. If you head west from the stoplight at the motel, it's about a mile to the port of Harbor.

$100-150

The nicest places to stay in the Brookings area are bed-and-breakfast inns, and they aren't that much more expensive than the local run-of-the-mill motel rooms.

A coastal gem one block north of the highway, the ★ **South Coast Inn B&B** (516 Redwood St., Brookings, 541/469-5557 or 800/525-9273, www.southcoastinn.com, $119-159) is a 1917 Craftsman building and was once the home of lumber baron William Ward. Designed by famed architect Bernard Maybeck and situated in the heart of old Brookings just blocks away from the beach and shopping, this 4,000-square-foot B&B offers four guest rooms, a guest cottage, and an apartment. All rooms have TVs with VCR (and access to the inn's video library), private bathrooms, and other amenities. An indoor spa with a sauna and a hot tub and an included breakfast featuring a health-conscious menu are additional enticements to book space early. Ask the friendly innkeepers about other Maybeck structures in town.

For a B&B that's close to the ocean, **By the Sea B&B** (1545 Beach Ave., 541/469-4692 or 877/469-4692, www.brookingsbythesea.com, $175) offers a choice of two theme-decorated guest rooms and a cottage. Enjoy breakfast and breathtaking ocean views from the stained-glass-topped windows. On the upper veranda, a spa and a wood-burning fire pot are available for guest use.

Perhaps the best value in Brookings lodgings is **Ocean Suites Motel** (16045

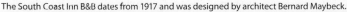

The South Coast Inn B&B dates from 1917 and was designed by architect Bernard Maybeck.

Lower Harbor Rd., 541/469-4004, www. oceansuitesmotel.com, $125), at the Harbor end of town. These really are suites—each has a full kitchen and a living room. No pets are allowed.

Another option is to rent a cottage at **Whaleshead Beach Resort** (19921 Whaleshead Rd., 541/469-7446 or 800/943-4325, www.whalesheadresort.com, $95-300) by the night or by the week. This sprawling development is on a bluff about eight miles north of Brookings, just across the highway from Whaleshead Beach, a beautiful spot in Boardman State Park. The little cabins are individually owned (and quite variable) but rentals are handled by the resort; all are fully furnished, and facilities include a restaurant and a 700-foot-long tunnel under the highway to the beach. There's also an RV park ($35) here.

$150-200

The best conventional hotels are south of the Chetco River in Harbor. The ★ **Best Western Beachfront Inn** (16008 Boat Basin Rd., Harbor, 541/469-7779, $184-250) sits on the beach at the mouth of the Chetco River, just past the port and marina. All units feature private decks, microwaves, and refrigerators. Kitchenettes as well as suites with ocean-view hot tubs and an indoor pool are available. Pets are permitted on a very limited basis; call the hotel directly to plead your case.

Camping

Harris Beach State Park (1655 U.S. 101, 541/469-2021, www.oregonstateparks.org or 800/452-5687, www.reserveamerica.com, $20 tent, $28-30 RV, $43-53 yurt, $5 hiker/biker), two miles north of town, is open all year, but even with over 150 sites, reservations are definitely necessary Memorial Day-Labor Day. Flush toilets, electricity, water, sewer hookups, sanitary service, showers, firewood, and a playground are available. Whale-watching is particularly good here in January and May, and the birding is good year-round. Note: At the time of our update, the campground here

was scheduled to be closed for renovations until May 25, 2016.

Alfred A. Loeb State Park (541/469-2021, www.oregonstateparks.org, campsites $22, cabins $40) is nine miles northeast of Brookings on North Bank Chetco River Road. There are 45 sites with electrical hookups for trailers/motor homes (50 feet maximum) and three cabins. Electricity, piped water, and picnic tables are provided; flush toilets, showers, and firewood are available. The campground is in a fragrant and secluded myrtlewood grove on the east bank of the Chetco River. From here, the Riverview Trail takes hikers to the Siskiyou National Forest's Redwood Nature Trail, where nature lovers will marvel at 800-year-old redwood beauties. Although cabins can be reserved (800/452-5687, www. reserveamerica.com), campsites are all first-come, first-served.

Beyond Loeb State Park is the more primitive **Little Redwood Campground** (contact Gold Beach Ranger District, 541/247-3600, www.fs.usda.gov, campground open mid-May-Sept., no water, free). To get there, go 0.5 mile south of Brookings on U.S. 101 to County Road 784, then go northeast for seven miles. At Forest Service Road 376, turn northeast and drive six miles to the campground. Little Redwood is on the main access route to the Kalmiopsis Wilderness, 20 miles away, and is a good spot for fishing during the winter steelhead run.

The Forest Service rents several cabins and fire lookouts ($40-50/night); advance booking is required. Contact the **Gold Beach Ranger District** (541/247-3600, www.fs.usda.gov, reservations 877/444-6777, www.recreation.gov) for information about renting Packer's Cabin, Ludlum House, or the Quail Prairie Lookout.

FOOD

Brookings has a profusion of family-friendly, though unexciting, restaurants that serve large portions at a good value—this is not a fine-dining capital. For slightly more distinctive fare than the usual fast food and family-dining joints, check out the following places.

A coastal town is certainly a safe place to eat sushi. In Brookings, find it at **Cafe Kitanishi** (632 Hemlock St., 541/469-7864, www.cafekitanishi.com, 11am-3pm Wed.-Fri., noon-3pm Sat. and 5pm-9pm Thurs.-Tues., $8-28), which also serves bento boxes to go and has an espresso bar with Internet access.

Down in the harbor area, you'll find a number of seafood shops. For fresh, traditional fish-and-chips, you can't miss at **Sporthaven Marina** (16374 Lower Harbor Rd., 541/469-3301, http://www.sporthavenmarina.com, 11am-6pm Sun.-Thurs., 11am-7pm Fri.-Sat., $6-15) with good clam chowder and fried seafood done up in traditional Oregon style. Yet more fresh fried seafood is ready for you at the adjacent **Hungry Clam** (16350 Lower Harbor Rd., 541/469-2526, www.hungryclam.com, 11am-7pm Sun.-Thurs., 9am-8pm Fri.-Sat., $8-15), with crab cake sliders, fresh tuna melts, crab cocktails, and a host of fried fish with slaw and chips.

A pleasant surprise in downtown Brookings is the ★ **Oxenfre Public House** (631 Chetco Ave., 541/813-1985, www.oxenpub.com, 4pm-9pm daily for dinner, open until 11pm or later for over age 21, $12-25), a self-proclaimed gastropub with a hip atmosphere and trendy meals such as Korean short-rib tacos with sesame cucumber relish and chili peanut slaw. There are also plenty of pub standards with tasty twists—have a late-night meal of parmesan truffle fries and a Kobe beef frankfurter on pretzel bread or hot pastrami on that same pretzel bread. Kids are welcome until 9pm.

Brookings's only real fine dining is at the intimate and charming **Art Alley Grille** (515 Chetco Ave., 541/469-0800, http://artalleygrill.com, 4:30pm-8:30pm Wed.-Sat., $20-28), a basement spot tucked downstairs from an art gallery. The menu is fairly wide ranging, with items such as pork with house-made harissa and seared tuna steak with ponzu sauce and wasabi.

INFORMATION

Pull off the highway and talk to the friendly folks at the **Crissey Field Welcome Center** (16633 Hwy. 101 S., 541/469-4117, 8am-5pm daily Apr.-Oct., 8:30am-4:30pm Mon.-Fri. Nov.-Mar.), where you can gather information and brochures about the coast and the rest of the state. For additional information pertinent to Brookings and environs, the **Brookings-Harbor Chamber of Commerce** (16330 Lower Harbor Rd., Brookings, 541/469-3181, www.brookingsharborchamber.com) is down at the harbor.

GETTING THERE

It takes determination to get to Brookings using public transportation. Curry County's **Coastal Express buses** (800/921-2871, www.currypublictransit.org) run up and down the south coast weekdays only between North Bend and the California border, including local service in Brookings. **The Point bus** (541/269-7183, http://highdesert-point.com) operates daily bus service between Coos Bay and Eugene via Reedsport and Florence. Eugene has Amtrak and regular Greyhound service, as well as an airport served by national carriers.

Ashland and Southern Oregon

When Oregonians talk about southern Oregon, they usually mean the southwestern corner of the state, including the upper valleys of the Umpqua and Rogue Rivers, the spine of the southern Cascade Mountains, and east to Klamath Falls. The outstanding features of this region include world-class culture-fests at Ashland and Jacksonville, the dramatically beautiful Rogue and Umpqua Rivers, and more summer sun and heat than you expect to find in Oregon.

It also includes Crater Lake National Park, Oregon's only national park, one of the most spectacular natural wonders in the United States. Driving up the desert slopes to the rim and then glimpsing the lake's startlingly blue water ringed by rock cliffs is a magnificent experience.

PLANNING YOUR TIME

Ashland and the **Oregon Shakespeare Festival** are undeniably the largest tourist draw in southern Oregon, although to make the most of this world-class theater festival you'll need to make plans and reserve seats and lodgings well in advance.

Increasingly, southern Oregon is becoming a major center for wine production, and it's easy to add a bit of wine-tasting to your theater itinerary. We've included some of our favorite wineries, and for a full listing of area wineries, go to the **Southern Oregon Wineries Association website** (www.southernoregonwines.org), where you can download a brochure and map.

Southern Oregon's other top destination is **Crater Lake National Park.** Even though a summer weekend visit to the park itself—which for most travelers involves driving the loop route around the rim of the caldera—can be hectic due to excessive traffic, the approaches to the park along the Rogue or Umpqua river valleys offer excellent opportunities for less-thronged outdoor recreation.

The larger cities of southern Oregon—Medford, Grants Pass, and Roseburg—are mostly utilitarian, with little to delay or seduce the traveler.

Previous: along the Upper Rogue River; Wizard Island rises out of Crater Lake. **Above:** along the Watson Falls trail.

Southern Oregon

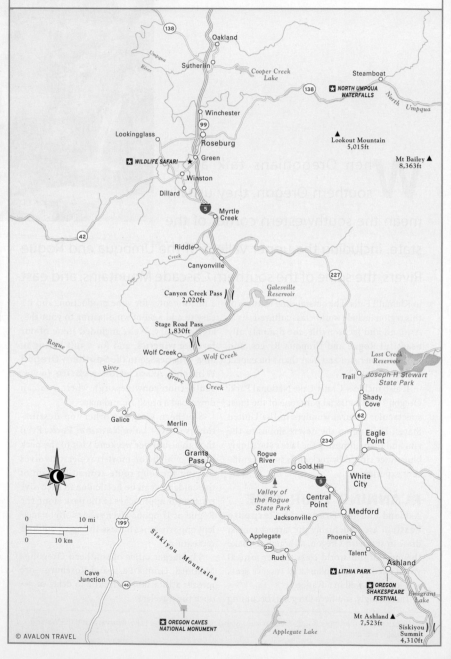

Umpqua River

138 Oakland

Sutherlin

Cooper Creek Lake

Steamboat

138 ★ NORTH UMPQUA WATERFALLS

North Umpqua

Winchester

99

Lookingglass

Roseburg

★ WILDLIFE SAFARI ★ Green

Winston

Dillard

5 Myrtle Creek

42

Riddle

Canyonville

Cow Creek

227

Canyon Creek Pass 2,020ft

Galesville Reservoir

Stage Road Pass 1,830ft

Wolf Creek

Wolf Creek

Rogue River

Grave Creek

Galice

Merlin

Grants Pass

Rogue River

5

Gold Hill

Valley of the Rogue State Park

Central Point

Lost Creek Reservoir

Trail ● Joseph H Stewart State Park

Shady Cove

62

Eagle Point

234

White City

Medford

Jacksonville

Phoenix

Talent

Lookout Mountain 5,015ft

Mt Bailey ▲ 8,363ft

Siskiyou Mountains

0   10 mi
0   10 km

199

Applegate

238 Ruch

★ LITHIA PARK

★ OREGON SHAKESPEARE FESTIVAL

Ashland

Emigrant Lake

Cave Junction

46

★ OREGON CAVES NATIONAL MONUMENT

Applegate Lake

Mt Ashland ▲ 7,523ft

Siskiyou Summit 4,310ft

© AVALON TRAVEL

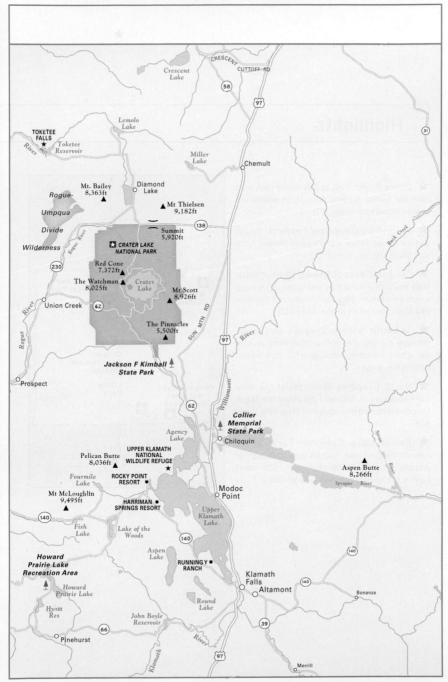

Highlights

★ **Lithia Park:** Trails at this lovely park lead from the formal gardens through an arboretum to wild woodlands (page 397).

★ **Oregon Shakespeare Festival:** Take in a show at one of the world's great theater festivals (page 401).

★ **Oregon Caves National Monument:** Here you'll find stalactites and stalagmites deep inside a mountain, plus the unexpected pleasure of a classic mountain lodge (page 422).

★ **Wildlife Safari:** Oregon's only drive-through zoo features 600 animals from around the world, including lions, giraffes, and hippopotamuses (page 424).

★ **North Umpqua Waterfalls:** The drive from Roseburg to Toketee Falls along the North Umpqua is dotted with stunning waterfalls (page 429).

★ **Crater Lake National Park:** At the nation's deepest lake, caused by a catastrophic volcanic eruption 6,600 years ago, you won't believe the color of the water (page 436).

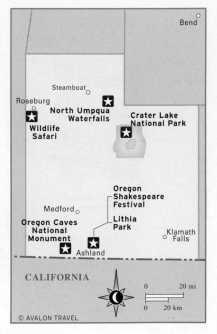

Ashland

Few towns are as closely identified with theater as Ashland (pop. 21,000). Tickets to the renowned Oregon Shakespeare Festival are the coin of the realm here, with contemporary classics and off-off-Broadway shows joining productions by the Bard. You can immediately sense that this is not just another timber town by the Tudor-style McDonald's, vintage Victorian houses, and high-end clothing stores on Main Street.

Ashland's tourist economy is also sustained by its auspicious location roughly equidistant to Portland and San Francisco. Closer to home, day trips to Crater Lake, Rogue River country, and the southern Oregon wineries have joined the tradition of "stay four days, see four plays" as a major part of Ashland's appeal.

SIGHTS
★ Lithia Park

Ashland's centerpiece is 100-acre **Lithia Park** (340 S. Pioneer St.). Recognized as a National Historic Site, the park was designed by John McLaren, landscape architect of San Francisco's Golden Gate Park. It is set along Ashland Creek, where the Takelma people camped and where Ashland, Ohio, immigrants built the region's first flour mill in 1854.

The park owes its existence to Jesse Winburne, who made a fortune from New York City subway advertising and in the 1920s tried to develop a spa around Ashland's Lithia Springs, which he said rivaled the venerated waters of Saratoga Springs, New York. Although the spa never caught on due to the Great Depression, Winburne was nevertheless instrumental in landscaping Lithia Park and was responsible for piping the famously sulfurous Lithia water to the plaza fountains so all might enjoy its beneficial minerals.

Pick up a guide to the park's trails at the plaza's visitors center kiosk. Paths line both banks of Ashland Creek. Park on the west side (to the right as you face the park) or drive up scenic Winburne Way. The park is nicely landscaped in a naturalistic way. A good destination on a hot day is the swimming reservoir, 1.4 miles up the east bank.

Spend a hot summer afternoon relaxing in Lithia Park.

Ashland

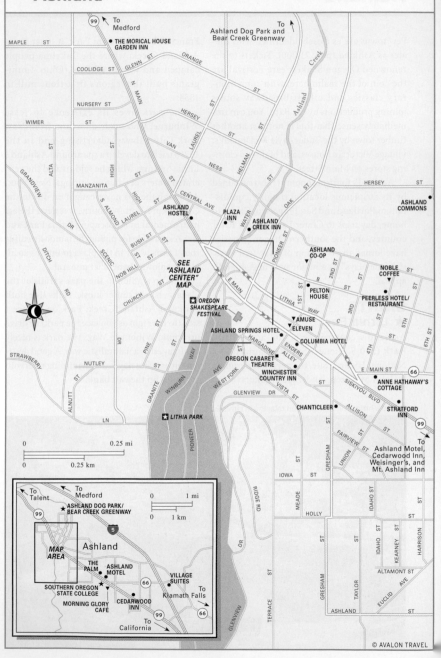

© AVALON TRAVEL

Ashland Center

CALDERA
TAP HOUSE

WATER ST
B ST
OAK ST

THAI
PEPPER
TAI
LITHIA WAY

CHURCH ST

MIX BAKESHOP
BLACK SHEEP PUB
GREENLEAF RESTAURANT

ADVENTURE
CENTER
STANDING STONE
BREWING CO.

EAST MAIN ST

HIGH ST
PINE ST

LITHIA SPRINGS FOUNTAIN

N PIONEER ST

WILL DODGE WAY

MARTOLI'S

BAUM ST

Bowmer

THE LUNCH
SHOW

GRANITE ST
WINBURN WAY

OREGON
SHAKESPEARE
FESTIVAL
Elizabethan

New
Theatre

LITHIA PARK

0   100 yds
0   100 m

© AVALON TRAVEL

ScienceWorks Hands-On Museum (1500 Main St. near Walker St., 541/482-6767, www. scienceworksmuseum.org, 10am-6pm daily Memorial Day-Labor Day, 10am-5pm Wed.-Sun. Labor Day-Memorial Day, $10 adults, $8 seniors and children ages 2-12, under age 2 free), a hands on museum that offers interactive exhibits, live performances, and activities.

Wine-Tasting

The climate of southern Oregon is ideal for many Bordeaux varietals such as cabernet sauvignon, sauvignon blanc, and merlot. Though the area's largest concentration of wineries is in the nearby Applegate Valley, a handful are close to Ashland.

Just south of town is **Weisinger's Vineyard** (3150 Siskiyou Blvd., 541/488-5989, www.weisingers.com, 11am-6pm daily May-Sept., 11am-5pm Wed.-Sun. Oct.-Apr.). The vineyard, which has received national and international awards, produces cabernet sauvignon, viognier, pinot noir, chardonnay, sauvignon blanc, and Italian varietals.

Just north of Ashland, **Paschal Winery** (1122 Suncrest Road, in Talent, Oregon, 541/535-7957, www.paschalwinery.com, noon-6pm daily) crafts refined viognier, Cabernet sauvignon, and a delicious red blend of tempranillo, sangiovese, dolcetto, and syrah called Civita Di Bagnoregio.

SPORTS AND RECREATION

Ashland Mountain Supply (31 N. Main St., 541/488-2749, 11am-6pm Mon.-Tues., 10am-6pm Wed.-Sat., 11am-5pm Sun.) sells and rents outdoor recreation equipment.

Golf

A few miles outside of Ashland on Route 66 is **Oak Knoll Golf Course** (3070 Hwy. 66, 541/482-4311, www.oakknollgolf.org, $16 for 9 holes), an affordable nine-hole municipal course.

Hiking

If you want more than a trek through Lithia

The hub of the park in the summer is the band shell, where concerts, ballets, and movies are shown. Children love to play at the playgrounds or feed the ducks in the ponds. **Dogs are not permitted** in the park.

Museums and Galleries

There are over 30 retail galleries in Ashland. Check out www.ashlandgalleries.com for an online guide and map. Two favorites are the **Hanson Howard Gallery** (89 Oak St., 541/488-2562, www.hansonhowardgallery. com, 10:30am-5:30pm Tues.-Sat.), which features monthly exhibits of contemporary artists in a bright airy shop next to the Standing Stone brewpub, and the **Gallerie Karon** (500 A St., 541/482-9008, 10:30am-5:30pm Tues.-Sat.), which features the works of 21 artists in an eclectic collection of sculpture, paintings, fiber arts, printmaking, photography, and jewelry. It is located in a thriving commercial strip by the railroad tracks.

Schneider Museum of Art (Southern Oregon University campus, 1250 Siskiyou Blvd., 541/552-6245, https://sma.sou.edu, 10am-4pm Mon.-Sat., $5 suggested donation) features contemporary art by national and international artists. Ashland is also home to the

Park, the walk to the top of **Mount Ashland** is an easy one, with good views of the Siskiyou Mountains and 14,162-foot Mount Shasta in California. It's prudent to bring along a sweater even in warm weather, as it can get fairly windy.

The **Pacific Crest Trail** crosses the Mount Ashland road about three miles past the ski area. By early July, the snow is mostly gone, and the wildflowers abundant.

Horseback Riding

Saddle up and head out for a trail ride with **City Slickers** (776 W. Valley View Rd., 541/951-4611, www.oregontrailrides.com, $50 and up). A variety of rides in and around Ashland are available, and horses and guides are experienced with beginning riders.

Biking

One of the more popular local bike rides, the **Lithia Loop Mountain Bike Route** (www.fs.usda.gov), is a strenuous 28-mile ride that starts and ends in Lithia Park, with a steep six-mile uphill stretch at the beginning and a screamingly steep seven-mile descent at the end. To avoid the steep ups and downs, you can drive up to the top and ride the fairly level 15-mile stretch. The Lithia Loop may be

closed during midsummer and fall when fire danger is high.

The **Siskiyou Crest Mountain Bike Route** (www.fs.usda.gov) begins at the Mount Ashland ski area parking lot. The 31-mile round-trip ranges from moderate to difficult and affords incredible views of Mount Shasta. The route ends at Dutchman Peak, where you'll find one of the few cupola-style fire lookouts left in the Pacific Northwest. This particular lookout was built in 1927. Note that bicycles are not allowed on the nearby Pacific Crest Trail.

The 26-mile paved **Bear Creek Bike and Nature Trail** crisscrosses town before going down the valley to Medford along Bear Creek.

The **Ashland Ranger District** (645 Washington St., 541/482-3333, www.fs.usda. gov) can provide directions and additional information about these and other mountain bike trails in the area.

Skiing

Perched high atop the Siskiyou range and straddling the California-Oregon border is 7,523-foot **Mount Ashland** (541/482-2897, www.mtashland.com, $39 weekdays, $46 weekends, $25 night for adults, $29 weekday, $36 weekend, $19 night ages 7-12). To get here,

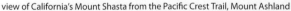

view of California's Mount Shasta from the Pacific Crest Trail, Mount Ashland

take the Mount Ashland exit off I-5 and follow the road eight miles uphill.

Skiers of all levels enjoy the 23 different runs, 100 miles of cross-country trails, and breathtaking vistas here, where the vertical drop is 1,150 feet. Although climate change has brought some low-snow winters to Mount Ashland, it's a great place to ski when the snow permits. Don't forget to purchase your Oregon Sno-Park permit.

Water Sports

Jackson WellSprings (2253 Hwy. 99 N., 541/482-3776, www.jacksonwellsprings.com, 8am-midnight Tues.-Sun. April 15-Oct. 14, noon-midnight Tues.-Sun. Oct. 15-April 14, $10 adult, $8 senior or student, $4 child, plus a once-yearly insurance charge of $5), a rather informal, decidedly hippie place, is two miles north of Ashland on the old highway and has a large naturally heated public swimming pool, hot soaking pool, and sauna and steam room, as well as private mineral baths. Clothing is optional in the evenings after 8pm. The pool is closed during the day on Monday but open after 6pm for "ladies night."

Meyer Memorial Pool (Hunter Park, Homes Ave. and Hunter Court, 541/488-0313, summer) includes a wading pool and a large swimming pool.

Six miles east of Ashland on Route 66 is **Emigrant Reservoir** (541/776-7001, http://jacksoncountyor.org/parks, $4 parking). In addition to waterskiing, sailing, fishing, and swimming, there is a 270-foot twin flume waterslide (noon-6pm daily Memorial Day-Labor Day, $6 weekdays, $7 weekends).

Outfitters

The **Adventure Center** (40 N. Main St., 541/488-2819 or 800/444-2819, www.rafting-tours.com) offers half-day, full-day, and multiday fishing, rafting, and cycling trips for any size party. The cost of the rafting trips includes gear (wetsuits, splash jackets, etc.), guides, and transport from Ashland. Half-day rafting trips on the Rogue River (9:30am-2pm or 1:30pm-5:45pm, $75) include a snack;

the longer white-water picnic trip (8am-4pm, $129) includes lunch. Rated one of the best floats in southern Oregon, the upper Klamath River trip ($135) generally runs 7:30am-5:30pm and includes all meals.

The Adventure Center also rents bikes and leads easygoing bike rides on quiet paved roads.

ENTERTAINMENT AND EVENTS

Shakespeare isn't the only act in town. Local companies include the **Oregon Cabaret Theatre** (1st St. and Hargadine St., 541/488-2902, www.oregoncabaret.com), with musical revues in a club setting and Southern Oregon State College productions.

Ashland's biggest summertime event, aside from the Shakespeare Festival, is the **Fourth of July parade,** which is more of an exuberant and slightly wacky celebration of the community than a patriotic event.

★ Oregon Shakespeare Festival

While Lithia Park is the heart of Ashland, Shakespeare is the soul of this community. The festival began when Angus Bowmer, an English professor at Ashland College, decided to celebrate Independence Day weekend in 1935 with a Shakespeare production. The city fathers were so unsure of the reception it would get that they asked him to allow boxing matches on the stage during the day prior to the performance. By the time he retired as artistic director of the festival in 1971, his Fourth of July dream had grown into an internationally acclaimed drama company with three theaters, one named in his honor.

Performances run from mid-February through late October or early November, though the famed outdoor **Elizabethan Theatre,** built on the site of Ashland's Chautauqua Dome and modeled after the Fortune Theatre of London circa 1600, is open in summer only. This is the largest of the festival's three theaters and primarily the domain of the Bard. While Shakespeare under the stars is incredibly romantic, it can also get very cold after sunset; bring warm clothing. Curtain times run 8pm-8:30pm, with most shows ending around 11pm. This outdoor theater opens in early June and closes by mid-October.

The 600-seat **Angus Bowmer** is an indoor complex with excellent acoustics, computerized sound and lighting, and nary a bad seat in the house, and the 150-seat **Thomas Theatre** is where modern works and experimental productions are the norm. This theater is small enough to stage plays that might be overwhelmed by a larger venue.

In addition to the plays themselves, two other events are popular with theatergoers. **Backstage Tours** (10am Tues.-Sun., high season $20, reservations required) explore the history, design, and technology of all of the festival's repertory theaters, including the fascinating Elizabethan Stage. The regular tour is a walking tour and has six flights of stairs; call ahead to schedule a tour without stairs.

Catch the free **Green Show** on the plaza outside the Elizabethan Theatre. It begins at 6:45pm and features live music, lectures, performance, storytelling, and other entertainment. It ends just before 8pm, when the outdoor performance starts in the Elizabethan Theatre.

TICKETS

Getting tickets to the **Oregon Shakespeare Festival** (15 S. Pioneer St., Ashland, OR 97520, 541/482-4331 or 800/219-8161, www. osfashland.org, box office 9:30am-performance time Tues.-Sun., 9:30am-5pm Mon., closed most holidays) is as much a part of the show as the performance. Seats often sell out months in advance. All seats are reserved; ticket prices range $30-100. Children under age six are not permitted. Once tickets are purchased, there are no refunds.

If you are unable to get advance tickets, your best bet is to show up at the Shakespeare Plaza an hour or two before the show with a sign stating what show you want to see. If you are lucky, you will score tickets from someone with extras. Avoid bidding wars with other would-be theatergoers, as ticket scalping is frowned upon. Otherwise, be at the ticket window at 6pm; any available seats will be released at that time. And remember, there is no late seating.

Catch the nightly Green Show before evening plays start; it's free!

ACCOMMODATIONS

Quoted rates are for June-September; expect prices to drop around one-third outside the summer high season. Look for chain motels at the freeway exits. If Ashland's prices seem too high, you can find less expensive rates in Medford, a 10-minute drive to the north.

The warmer traditions of Britain are represented in Ashland not only by the Oregon Shakespeare Festival but also by the town's numerous bed-and-breakfasts, the most of any locale in the state. Many B&Bs require a two-night minimum stay during summer. The **Ashland Bed and Breakfast Network** (800/944-0329, www.abbnet.com) can help you find quality B&B lodgings in town.

Under $50

Offering dorm beds and a handful of private rooms, the **Ashland Hostel** (150 N. Main St., 541/482-9217, www.theashlandhostel.com, $28 pp dorm bed, $55-64 d private room with shared bath, $79-129 suite with private bath) is a two-story 1902 house near the Pacific Crest Trail, only three blocks from the Elizabethan Theatre and Lithia Park and two blocks from the Greyhound station. Reservations are essential, especially March-October. The hostel has a coin-op laundry.

A newer hostel, **Ashland Commons** (437 Williamson Way, 541/482-6753, www.ashlandcommons.com, $28 pp dorm bed, $45-65 pp private room), is a little farther from the downtown hub in a quiet residential neighborhood.

$50-100

Moderately priced guest rooms are available from **Cedarwood Inn** (1801 Siskiyou Blvd., 541/488-2000 or 800/547-4141, www.ashlandcedarwoodinn.com, $75-115), with a pool and continental breakfast. Two-bedroom and kitchen units are also available.

$100-150

The **Ashland Motel** (1145 Siskiyou Blvd., 541/482-2561 or 800/460-8858, www.themmotel.com, $119) offers good value and clean,

cheery, and basic pet-friendly guest rooms. All rooms have fridges and microwaves; there are two 2-bedroom units, and a small outdoor pool.

A dollar-wise choice with some charm is the **Columbia Hotel** (262½ E. Main St., 541/482-3726 or 800/718-2530, www.columbiahotel.com, $105-149), in the center of town. This well-kept 1910 hotel with a grand piano in the lobby has 24 rooms. Most rooms share bathrooms.

The **Pelton House** B&B (228 B St., 541/488-7003 or 866/488-7003, www.peltonhouse.com, $135-185) is located in a historic Victorian just a few blocks from the Shakespeare Festival. Each of its seven rooms is themed, and two suites are available for families or groups.

$150-200

If you want to stay in the center of Ashland, **Best Western Bard's Inn Motel** (132 N. Main St., 541/482-0049 or 800/533-9627, www.bardsinn.com, $160-210) is a good choice. Just across the Main Street bridge from downtown, the Bard's Inn is no more than five minutes' walk from the theaters. There are a number of room types, all nicely furnished and well maintained. Facilities include a streamside restaurant and bar.

Clean and meticulously maintained, the privately owned and operated **Stratford Inn** (555 Siskiyou Blvd., 541/488-2151 or 800/547-4741, www.stratfordinnashland.com, $175-190) is just five blocks from the theaters. All guest rooms have a fridge and a couple of kitchen suites are available. A guest laundry, ski lockers during ski season, an elaborate continental breakfast, and an indoor pool and whirlpool tub all contribute to the inn's high occupancy rate.

Rooms at ★ **The Palm** (1065 Siskiyou Blvd., 877/482-2635, www.palmcottages.com, $169-179), are in a well-maintained cottage-style motel in the midst of lovely gardens. A saline pool, sundeck, and cabanas complete the oasis-like atmosphere. Pet-friendly rooms are sometimes available.

The 70-room **Ashland Springs Hotel** (212 E. Main St., 541/488-1700, www.ashlandspringshotel.com, $169-239), on the corner of 1st and Main Streets (a block from the Elizabethan Theatre), is a first-class historic hotel. A grand ballroom, a bar to enjoy parlor games and musical entertainment in, and English gardens add touches evocative of another era. Luxuriously appointed guest rooms aren't large but boast oversize windows highlighting nice views. Minimum stays may apply.

The historic ★ **Peerless Hotel** (243 4th St., 541/488-1082, www.peerlesshotel.com, $172-283) was established in 1900 to serve the needs of railroad travelers. The old hotel has been thoroughly modernized and converted into a boutique B&B-style hotel. One of the most distinctive places to stay in Ashland, the Peerless also offers a fine dining restaurant and a location in the art gallery-rich Railroad District.

The ★ **Morical House Garden Inn** (668 N. Main St., 541/482-2254, www.moricalhouse.com, $151-270) is a restored 1880s farmhouse with seven rooms and a guesthouse with three luxury suites, each with a picture-postcard view of Grizzly Mountain and the Siskiyou foothills. In season, the two acres of gardens provide organic produce for breakfast and habitat for birds and butterflies. Given this lovely setting, it's sometimes hard to remember that you are only a few blocks away from downtown theaters and shopping.

Plaza Inn and Suites (98 Central Ave., 541/488-8900 or 888/488-0358, www.plazainnashland.com, $179-289) is a large, modern hotel just below downtown and within easy walking distance of the theaters. Many of the rooms look onto a parklike courtyard that fronts onto Ashland Creek. Guest rooms are very nicely appointed; many have balconies, and some allow pets. A breakfast buffet is included in the rates.

The ★ **Chanticleer Inn** (120 Gresham St., www.ashland-bed-breakfast.com, 541/482-1919, $175-210), Ashland's oldest B&B and still leading the way, has five

The Ashland Springs Hotel is a block from the Elizabethan Theater.

romantic guest rooms and gourmet breakfasts. Dogs are permitted (with prior approval) in some of the rooms. Round-the-clock refrigerator rights, complimentary wines and sherry, and a full cookie jar on the kitchen counter help keep you wined and dined throughout your stay.

Anne Hathaway's Cottage (586 E. Main St., 541/488-1050, www.ashlandbandb.com, $175-235), four blocks from the theaters, was once a boardinghouse; the cottages across the street are part of this B&B complex. Kids and dogs are welcome here.

Bathe in naturally occurring hot springs at the **Lithia Springs Inn** (2165 W. Jackson Rd., 541/482-7128 or 800/482-7128, www.ashlandinn.com, $179-249). A couple of miles from downtown amid four acres of gardens, the inn is close enough to access Ashland culture, yet far enough away for some real peace and quiet. The rooms, suites, and bungalows are stylishly modern, with bathwater fed from the hot springs. Most rooms have soaking tubs, and an on-site spa can provide treatments.

Over $200

At the ★ **Ashland Creek Inn** (70 Water St., 541/482-3315, www.ashlandcreekinn. com, $245-425), you won't get any closer to Ashland Creek without getting wet. This small luxury-level inn is directly adjacent to the stream and has several guest rooms with cantilevered decks directly above the rushing water. Each of the 10 suites is uniquely decorated according to a theme—the Caribe, the Marrakech, the Edinburgh—and each offers complete kitchens, living rooms, private entrances, and decks. Best of all, this comfort and style are just moments from downtown shopping and the theaters.

Two blocks south of the theaters is the acclaimed **Winchester Country Inn** (35 S. 2nd St., 541/488-1113 or 800/972-4991, www.winchesterinn.com, $250-430), offering 19 guest rooms and suites with private baths and loads of personality. The individual attentiveness of the large staff recalls a traditional English country inn. Bay windows, private balconies, and exquisite English gardens add further distinction. Gourmet delicacies are featured at breakfast, and dinner and Sunday brunch are available in the inn's restaurant. Visit the website to check out their changing special lodging packages.

Camping

Emigrant Lake (5505 Hwy. 66, 541/774-8183, http://jacksoncountyor.org/parks, $20 tent, $30 RV), a few miles east of Ashland, has RV and tent camping at a Jackson County Parks Department campground. South of town, **Mount Ashland** has a primitive campground (free, no water) about a mile past the ski resort.

On the northern edge of town, **Jackson WellSprings** (2253 Hwy. 99 N., 541/482-3776, http://jacksonwellsprings.com, $25 one person in tent, $10 each additional adult) has tent sites on a grassy, tree-shaded lawn. It's highly informal (with a hippie vibe) and gets a bit of road noise, so it's not for the faint of heart. However, camping does gain you admission to the pool, sauna, and steam room, and it's only about a five-minute drive from downtown.

FOOD

Ashland's creative talents are not just confined to theatrical pursuits; some of Oregon's better restaurants can be found here. Even the humbler fare served in Ashland's unpretentious cafés and pubs can be memorable. The city has a 5 percent restaurant tax, a surcharge

Emigrant Lake, about five miles east of Ashland, is a good place to camp, boat, or swim.

seen nowhere else in the Beaver State except Lincoln City.

Stock up on groceries or pick up a deli sandwich at the **Ashland Food Co-op** (237 N. 1st St., 541/482-2237, www.ashlandfood. coop, 7am-9pm daily).

Bakeries and Cafés

Find Ashland's best coffee and a friendly place to hang out for a while at **Noble Coffee** (281 4th St., 541/488-3288, www.no-blecoffeeroasting.com, 7am-4pm daily), in the hip railroad district. A friendly spot for pastries and desserts is **Mix Bakeshop** (57 N. Main St., 541/488-9885, 7am-9pm daily), with Stumptown coffee and a bohemian atmosphere.

American

For Ashland's most popular breakfast café, head to **Morning Glory Restaurant** (1149 Siskiyou Blvd., 541/488-8636, www.greenlea-frestaurant.com, 8am-1:30pm daily, $10-12) for delicious omelets, pancakes, and breakfast sandwiches. Lines on weekend mornings can be long.

The **Greenleaf Restaurant** (49 N. Main St., 541/482-2808, 8am-8pm daily, $9-20) is known for its reasonably priced Mediterranean-influenced food and for its lovely patio overlooking Lithia Creek.

The **Lunch Show** (165 E. Main St., 541/488-7713, thelunchshowashland.com, 11am-3pm daily, $7-12) is a sweet little café with excellent sandwiches; be bold and try the yamwich, with roasted yams, feta cheese, and cilantro-lime chimichurri!

Asian

The **Thai Pepper** (84 Main St., 541/482-8058, thaipepperashland.com, 11:30am-2pm Fri.-Sat., 5pm-9pm daily, $15-19) has a lot to offer: Not only is the spicy, flavorful Southeast Asian cuisine well prepared and moderately priced, the dining room steps down into the steep gulch of Ashland Creek, offering a cool and quiet haven in the summer heat and one of the most pleasant patio dining areas in town.

For North Indian food, go to **Taj** (31 Water St., 541/488-5900, www.taj-indiancuisine. com, 11am-3pm and 5pm-9pm daily, $13-17), which has a number of vegetarian dishes, traditional curries, and tandoor oven specialties. At lunchtime, enjoy the $9 buffet.

Pizza

Stop by **Martolli's** (38 E. Main St., 541/482-1918, www.martollis.com, 11am-9pm daily, $8-11 for personal pie); it's the best pizza in town, and the cafe is a cheery place with a Deadhead theme.

Basque

Explore Basque cuisine at **Eleven** (11 N. 1st St., 541/905-1092, www.elevenon1st.com, 4:30pm-8:30pm Tues.-Sat., $9-15), where a few Pacific Northwest touches are added to traditional Basque dishes. Dishes are small plates, so it's good to order a few and share.

Pacific Northwest

The restaurant at the historic Winchester Inn, **Alchemy** (35 S. 2nd St., 541/488-1115, www. alchemyashland.com, 5pm-9pm daily, dinner $23-36), serves sit-up-and-take notice modern cuisine prepared with rarified techniques and ingredients. In the stately dining room, you can savor sous-vide filet mignon with wild mushrooms, parsnip puree, and scallop mouseline. The bar is a classy spot to enjoy a cocktail.

The ★ **Peerless Restaurant** (265 4th St., 541/488-6067, www.peerlesshotel.com, 5pm-9pm Tues.-Sat., $12-32) is part of a picturesque historic hotel; the garden is spectacular, so dine al fresco if possible. The impressive selection of small plates ($6-14) makes casual dining fun and exciting—start with lamb meatballs with blue cheese filling, and keep the plates coming. The menu also includes a couple of burgers, which can keep the price of dinner from skyrocketing.

★ **Amuse** (15 N. 1st St., 541/488-9000, amuserestaurant.com, 5:30pm-9pm Tues.-Sun., $26-38) is Ashland's top French-via-Pacific-Northwest restaurant, with a menu that changes weekly and features fresh local fruit, vegetables, and mushrooms as well as ranch beef and lamb and locally harvested fish. Expect such sophisticated dishes as crispy veal sweetbreads with roasted mission figs or black truffle-roasted game hen. Desserts ($10) are especially good. The small dining room is deceptive; the back patio is shady and expansive.

Just down the road from Ashland is the absolutely unique **New Sammy's Cowboy Diner** (2210 S. Pacific Hwy., 541/535-2779, noon-1:30pm and 5pm-9pm Wed.-Sat., $18-30, three-course prix fixe $54). The limited menu changes frequently, but expect delicious fish, rabbit, pork, and charcuterie—if the braised beef ribs are offered, by all means order them. The wine list has hundreds of choices. Ask to be seated in the old dining room with cow wallpaper and just six tables in what was once a gas station. Call for winter hours; reservations are strongly recommended.

Head down to Ashland Creek and search a bit to find the door to the ★ **Loft** (18 Calle Guanajuato, 541/482-1116, http://loftashland. com, 5pm-9pm Tues.-Sun., brunch 11am-2pm Sun., $24-32), an upstairs brasserie with a patio overlooking the creek. The French-Oregonian menu features locally sourced food, including seared steelhead trout served with tasty brussels sprouts and traditional rabbit paté.

Classy but casual, **Coquina** (542 A St., 541/488-0521, www.coquinarestaurant.com, 5pm-10pm Tues.-Sat., $18-32) serves refined Pacific Northwest cuisine based on local, seasonal ingredients. This Railroad District restaurant features such tempting creations as rabbit ravioli with porcini mushrooms and onion jam, and fresh scallops with pea tendril salad.

Brewpubs and Wine Bars
One story above Ashland Plaza, the **Black Sheep Pub and Restaurant** (51 N. Main St., 541/482-6414, www.theblacksheep.com, 11:30am-1am daily, $7-20) is a vast Olde English pub with better-than-average fare, plus a wide selection of British and Pacific Northwestern ales. This is the place to come for a late-night after-theater supper (burgers, steak pie, grilled salmon) with frothy pints of beer.

Bright, airy, and with a delightful back patio open in good weather, **Standing Stone Brewing Company** (101 Oak St., 541/482-2448, www.standingstonebrewing. com, 11am-midnight daily, $8-19) has one of the most pleasant dining rooms in Ashland. Not only are the beers tasty, the menu is also very broad, including soups, salads, burgers, wood-fired pizzas, and entrées verging on fine dining.

Tucked down near Ashland Creek, the **Caldera Tap House** (31 Water St., 541/482-4677, www.calderabrewing.com, 2pm-10pm Sun.-Tues., 2pm-11pm Wed.-Thurs., 2pm-midnight Fri.-Sat., $8-14) serves some of the best locally brewed beer (it's not brewed on-site, but at a brewery on Clover Lane) along with fairly typical pub food and live music.

If you're looking for a glass of wine or cocktail plus a delicious selection of snacks, try **Liquid Assets** (96 N. Main St., 541/482-9463, www.liquidassestswinebar.com, 3pm-midnight daily, small plates $8-20), a wine bar with a good choice of cheeses and cured meats, plus tempting house specialties such as Dungeness crab cakes, warm chèvre salad, and roast lamb loin with chimichurri.

INFORMATION
Ashland Visitor Information Center (110 E. Main St., 541/482-3486, www.ashland-chamber.com, 9am-5pm Mon.-Fri.) offers brochures, play schedules, and other up-to-date information on happenings.

The **Ashland-Siskiyou Visitor Center** (60 Lowe Rd., 541/488-1805, 9am-5pm daily May-Sept.) offers travel information on the whole state. The center is just off I-5 at Exit 19.

GETTING THERE AND AROUND

The local airport is in Medford. United Express and Horizon Air fly into **Medford/Jackson County Airport** (1000 Terminal Loop Pkwy., 541/772-8068 or 800/882-7488, www.co.jackson.or.us), 15 miles north of town.

Amtrak (800/872-7245) has a station 70 miles east at Klamath Falls and 75 miles south at Dunsmuir, California. The **Southwest Point bus** (585 Siskiyou Blvd., 541/482-4495) stops at the Ashland Safeway on its route between Brookings and Klamath Falls; it also stops in Medford.

Rogue Valley Transportation (541/779-2877, www.rvtd.org) is the local bus service; it has a line that runs up to Medford, with several stops in Ashland.

Medford

Along with a resource-based economy revolving around agriculture and timber products, Medford (population 77,600) is a popular retirement center. Some of the enticements are proximity to Ashland's culture, Rogue Valley recreation, Cascade getaways, and rainfall totals that are half those recorded in the Willamette Valley. All that summer heat is good for fruit production—the Rogue River Valley around Medford is a major center for peach and pear production, and wine grapes are displacing dairy cows and berries on area farms.

SIGHTS

Table Rocks

About 10 miles northeast of Medford are two eye-catching basaltic buttes, **Upper and Lower Table Rocks.** They are composed of sandstone with erosion-resistant lava caps deposited during a massive Cascade eruption about 4-5 million years ago. Over the years, wind and water have undercut the sandstone. Stripped of its underpinnings, the heavy basalt on top of the eroded sandstone is pulled down by gravity, creating the nearly vertical slabs that we see today.

Water doesn't readily percolate through the lava. Small ponds collect on top of the butte, nurturing the wildflowers that flourish in early spring. The wildflower display reaches its zenith in April. A dozen species of flowers cover the rock-strewn flats in bright yellow and vivid purple.

The **Lower Table Rock** protects an area of special biological, geological, historical, and scenic value. Pacific madrone, white oak, manzanita, and ponderosa pine grow on the flank of the mountain; the crown is covered with grasses and wildflowers, including dwarf meadow foam, which grows no place else on earth.

Hikers who take the 2.6-mile trail to the top of horseshoe-shaped Lower Table Rock should watch for batches of pale lavender fawn lilies peeking out from underneath the shelter of the scraggly scrub oaks on the way up the mountain. Walk over to the cliff's edge, past some of the "Mima mounds" or "patterned ground" that distinguishes the surface of the butte. How the mounds were formed is a matter of scientific debate. Some scientists believe they represent centuries of work by rodents; others think they are accumulated silt deposits; while still others maintain they were created by the action of the wind. However they got there, the mounds are the only soil banks on the mountain that support grasses, which are unable to grow on the lava. Lichens and mosses manage to grow on the lava, however, painting the dull black basalt with luxuriant green and fluorescent yellow during the wetter months.

The trail up **Upper Table Rock** is a little over one mile but can be muddy during the wet season. The trail affords wonderful vistas of the Rogue River and Sams Valley to the north. The ponds up here are smaller and

Medford

To Rogue Creamery

To Rogue Regency Inn

To Kaleidoscope Pizza and Pub

PROVIDENCE HOSPITAL

SOUTHERN PACIFIC CO

BIDDLE RD

99

5

Bear Creek

CRATER LAKE AVE

Jackson Park

TIKI LODGE

COLUMBUS AVE

JACKSON ST

Hawthorne Park/Pool

JACKSON BLVD

GREYHOUND

INN AT THE COMMONS

MEDFORD PHYSICIANS AND SURGEONS CLINIC

PORTER'S

5TH ST

BARTLETT ST

MAIN ST

4TH ST

PORTAL BREWING

ELEMENTS

SISKIYOU BLVD

To Jacksonville

238

W MAIN ST

MAIN ST

POST OFFICE

8TH ST

FIR ST

FRONT ST

RIVERSIDE AVE/ROGUE VALLEY HWY

CENTRAL AVE/ROGUE VALLEY HWY

SISKIYOU BLVD

HOLLY ST

GRAPE ST

5

Bear Creek Park

HIGHLAND DR

ALBA DR

BARNETT RD

STEWART AVE

HARRY AND DAVID

VISITOR INFORMATION

REAL DEAL CAFÉ

MILES FIELD

To Ashland

0   0.5 mi
0   0.5 km

99

BEAR CREEK GOLF COURSE

© AVALON TRAVEL

fewer than those on Lower Table Rock, but the Mima mounds are more clearly defined. It's easy to get disoriented out here, with hundreds of acres to explore. The point where the trail heads back down the mountain is marked by two large trees, a ponderosa pine and a Douglas fir, accompanied by a smaller cedar.

To get to the Table Rocks, take the Central Point exit (Exit 33) from I-5 east about a mile to Table Rock Road and turn north (left).

Continue 5.3 miles on Modoc Road, then turn north and go 1.5 miles to Upper Table Rock. For Lower Table Rock, go eight miles on Table Rock Road, turn left (west) onto Wheeler Road and continue 0.5 miles to the trailhead. The **Bureau of Land Management** (3040 Biddle Rd., 541/770-2200, www.blm.gov/or) has additional information on the Table Rocks. **Dogs are prohibited** on the Table Rocks trails.

Harry & David

Harry & David (1314 Center Dr., 541/776-2277, www.harryanddavid.com), the nation's leading purveyor of mail-order fruit, has a store just off I-5 Exit 27 in the south part of Medford. Here you'll find fresh fruit and vegetables, rejects from Harry & David's Fruit-of-the-Month Club that are nearly as good as the mail-order fruit but too small or blemished to meet their high quality standards, jams and fruit spreads, and a really large selection of Oregon wines. The local visitor center is right next door.

Wine and Cheese Tasting

RoxyAnn Winery (3285 Hillcrest Rd., 541/776-2315, www.roxyann.com, noon-7pm Mon.-Thurs., 11am-9pm Fri., 11am-7pm Sat.-Sun.) is one of the top wineries in southern Oregon, and conveniently the tasting room is immediately east of Medford in an old pear orchard. RoxyAnn makes particularly good, rich red wines—the claret and syrah are especially delicious. The tasting room is in an old barn, and it's the setting for music on Friday evenings.

Kriselle Cellars (12956 Modoc Rd., 541/830-8466, www.krisellecellars.com,

11am-5:30pm daily) is about 12 miles north of Medford, with a stunning tasting room overlooking the Rogue Valley. The wines here are notable, particularly the French-style viognier and award-winning cabernet sauvignon.

Central Point is home to the **Rogue Creamery** (311 N. Front St., Central Point, 541/665-1155, www.roguecreamery.com, 9am-5pm Mon.-Sat., 9am-6pm Sat., 11am-5pm Sun.), which makes some of the best cheese in the Pacific Northwest, with a focus on blue cheese; the Caveman Blue is exceptionally rich. In the same block, taste wine at **Ledger David Cellars** (245 N. Front St., 541/664-2218, ledgerdavid.com) and chocolate at **Lillie Belle Farms** (211 N. Front St., 541/664-2815, www.lilliebellefarms.com).

GOLF

Eagle Point Golf Course (100 Eagle Point Dr., Eagle Point, 541/826-8225, www.eagle-pointgolf.com, $47 weekdays, $55 weekends) is arguably the finest course in the Rogue River Valley. Designed by Robert Trent Jones Jr., the course boasts enough character to challenge beginners and experts alike. Impressive views of Mount McLoughlin and Table Rocks add to the experience.

Head just north of Medford to Central Point, where you can sample excellent blue cheese at the Rogue Creamery.

ENTERTAINMENT AND EVENTS

The **Jackson County Fair** (www.jcfairgrounds.com) is held at the county fairgrounds (1 Penninger St., Central Point) just north of town the third weekend in July, with livestock competitions, midway rides, and musical entertainment.

The **Pear Blossom Festival** (www.pearblossomparade.org) takes place the second weekend in April with arts and crafts exhibits, a parade, and a 10K run. The real attraction is the panorama of the pear orchards in bloom against the backdrop of snowcapped Mount McLoughlin. The parade and run take place downtown, and festivities continue at Commons blocks (N. Bartlett at 5th) with arts and crafts, food, music, and children's activities.

ACCOMMODATIONS

Medford has no shortage of motel rooms, with hotels and motels clustered near the interstate exits. Most are national chains, so there's no mystery as to what you're checking into. The cluster of hotels at I-5 Exit 27 is just 10 miles from Ashland, and offer a good alternative if you can't find affordable rooms there. Medford is the kind of place where it's good to check hotel websites to find deals, since the differences in the hotels aren't great and nearly all are at freeway exits.

You don't have to stay at a freeway exit, however. Just north of downtown on Highway 99 (here known as N. Riverside Ave.) are a number of inexpensive, older, but well-maintained motels, including the basic but perfectly acceptable **Tiki Lodge** (509 N. Riverside Ave., 541/773-4579, www.tikilodgemotel.com, $62-74). South of town, the quite nice **Pear Tree Motel** (300 Pear Tree Ln., 541/535-4445 or 800/645-7332, www.peartreemotel.com, $75-80) has a pool.

The closest hotel to downtown is the ★ **Inn at the Commons** (200 N. Riverside Ave., 541/779-5811 or 866/779-5811, innatthecommons.com, $90-129), a full-service establishment that offers a breakfast buffet, airport shuttle service, an outdoor pool, access to a local health club, and the excellent Larks restaurant.

A number of new upscale hotels have been built in recent years a bit out of town but convenient to I-5. One the nicest is **Rogue Regency Inn** (2300 Biddle Rd., 541/770-1234 or 800/535-5805, www.rogueregency.com, $113-350) which offers an indoor pool and spa, a fitness center, a business center, a complimentary shuttle to the airport, and a bar and restaurant.

FOOD

The local wine industry's recent boom has been the catalyst for a number of excellent new Medford restaurants.

The **Real Deal Café** (811 W. Stewart Ave., 541/770-5571, realdealcafe.com, 7am-2pm daily, breakfasts $6-11) serves old-fashioned breakfasts and casual lunches. Everything is made from scratch at this friendly diner, and in good weather there is seating on a shady patio. Medford's best pizza is at **Kaleidoscope Pizzeria and Pub** (3084 Crater Lake Hwy., www.kaleidoscopepizza.com, 541/779-7787, 11am-9pm Sun.-Thurs., 11am-10pm Fri.-Sat., small pizza $8-13), a bit north of town on Route 62. In addition to traditional toppings, Kaleidoscope also features unusual pizza choices like chipotle steak and spicy Thai chicken. There's also a good selection of local microbrews.

Jasper's Cafe (2739 N. Pacific Hwy., 541/776-5307, jasperscafe.com, 10:30am-7pm Mon.-Thurs., 10:30am-8pm Fri.-Sat., 11am-6pm Sun., $5-8) has been a Medford tradition since 1976, and it aims to do just a few things very well: Namely, serve the best hamburgers and hot dogs in the region. Add a hand-scooped milk shake, and you've got an authentic, delicious slice of Americana.

Larks (200 N. Riverside Ave., 541/774-4760, www.larksrestaurant.com, 11:30am-2pm Fri.-Mon. and 5pm-8pm Sun.-Thurs., 5pm-9pm Fri.-Sat., $19-35), the Medford outpost of an Ashland restaurant, has good farm-to-table dishes that take full advantage of the Rogue Valley's excellent produce.

For a traditional steak house atmosphere in Medford, go downtown to the old rail depot, where **Porters** (147 N. Front St., 541/857-1910, www.porterstrainstation.com, 5pm-9pm daily, $22-39) serves pasta, steaks, and plenty of local seafood options, including steelhead trout crusted with hazelnuts and drizzled with blackberry vinaigrette, or slow-cooked prime rib seasoned with rosemary and garlic.

One of the top places for a relaxed meal with excellent food is ★ **Elements** (101 E. Main St., 541/779-0135, elementsmedford. com, 4pm-midnight Sun.-Thurs., 4pm-1am Fri.-Sat., $7-15), a tapas and wine bar. The food is very sophisticated, but the atmosphere is friendly, which makes dishes like serrano-wrapped prawns, cinnamon-cherry seared duck breast, and chorizo-stuffed dates all the more enjoyable.

Downtown also has a couple brewpubs of note. **Bricktowne Brewing Company** (44 S. Central Ave., 541/973-2377, www.bricktownebeer.com, 11:30am-10pm Mon.-Thurs., 11:30am-late Fri.-Sat., noon-6pm Sun., $8-14) offers burgers, sandwiches, salads, and a friendly atmosphere. Housed in a historic fire station, **Portal Brewing Company** (100 E. 6th St., 541/499-0804, portalbrewingco.com, 4pm-10pm Mon.-Fri., noon-10pm Sat., $6-10) offers good brews plus simple food such as lamb schwarma, carrot soup, and pretzels. ★ **Bambu Asian Café and Wine Bar** (970 N. Phoenix Rd., 541/608-7545, www.

tigerroll.com, 11:30am-2pm Mon.-Fri. and 5pm-9pm Mon.-Thurs., 5pm-9:30pm Fri.-Sat., 5pm-8:30pm Sun., $14-24), located in a shopping center on the southeast edge of town, features updated and reinterpreted pan-Asian cooking with a mix of small and large plates that encourages sharing and exploring.

INFORMATION

The **Medford Visitors and Convention Bureau** (1314 Center Dr., 800/469-6307, www.visitmedford.org, 9am-6pm daily) has all kinds of useful maps, directories, and information for the asking. Find their visitors center near the Harry & David store.

GETTING THERE AND AROUND

A half-dozen buses dock daily at the **Greyhound** station (220 S. Front St., 541/779-2103), running along the I-5 corridor. **Rogue Valley Transportation** (200 S. Front St., 541/779-2877, www.rvtd.org) shares the same station and provides connections to Jacksonville, Phoenix, White City, Talent, and Ashland. Buses run Monday-Friday. **5 Star Taxi** (541/245-5555) has 24-hour service in the Medford area.

Medford/Jackson County Airport (1000 Terminal Loop Pkwy., 541/772-8068 or 800/882-7488, www.co.jackson.or.us), airport code MFR, is the air hub for southern Oregon and is served by SkyWest, United Express, Horizon, and Allegiant Air.

Jacksonville

Southern Oregon's pioneer past is vividly preserved in Jacksonville. Five miles west of Medford and cradled in the foothills of the Siskiyou Mountains, this small town of 2,800 residents retains an atmosphere of tranquil isolation. With more than 100 original wooden and brick buildings dating back to the 1850s, it has been designated a National Historic Landmark District.

Between 1873 and 1884, three major fires reduced most of the original wooden buildings to ash, prompting merchants to use brick in the construction of a second generation of buildings. To protect them from the elements and the damp season, the porous bricks were painted; cast-iron window shutters and door frames further reinforced the structures.

Today, Jacksonville paints a memorable picture of a Western town with its historic buildings, pretty surroundings, and beautiful pioneer cemetery. On summer Saturdays there's often a chance to catch an exhibit or reenactment in the historic Beekman House (452 E. California St., 541/899-8118, www.historicjacksonville.org; see website for schedule and details). In addition, a renowned music festival, colorful pageants, and rich local folklore all pay tribute to Jacksonville's golden age.

SIGHTS

Hop aboard the old-fashioned **Jacksonville Trolley** (541/899-8118, www.jacksonvilleoregon.org, $5 adults, $3 children ages 6-12) and learn a bit about local history from a period-dressed guide. Tours depart on the hour (11am-3pm summer) from the historic Beekman Bank at the corner of California and 3rd Streets.

On a hot afternoon, the hills of Jacksonville can seem pretty steep. Join up with **Segway of Jacksonville** (360 N. Oregon St., 541/899-5269, http://www.segwayofjacksonville.com, 10am and 2pm Tues.-Sat., $75) and spend a few minutes mastering your steed before heading out on a two-hour guided tour.

Peter Britt Gardens

Peter Britt came to Jacksonville not long after gold was discovered in Rich Gulch in 1851. After trying his hand at prospecting, he redirected his efforts toward painting and photography. The latter became his specialty, and for nearly 50 years, he photographed the people, places, and events of southern Oregon (Britt was the first person to photograph Crater Lake).

The Swiss-born Britt was also an accomplished horticulturalist and among the first vintners in southern Oregon. In addition to experimenting with several varieties of fruit and nut trees to see which grew best in the Rogue River Valley, he kept the first weather data records of the region. Another testimonial to his love of plants is the giant redwood tree on the western edge of the **Britt Gardens** (S. 1st St. and W. Pine St.), which he planted 130 years ago to commemorate the birth of his first child, Emil. A 0.5-mile hike begins 15 yards uphill from the Emil Britt redwood tree. This is a particularly nice walk in the spring when the wildflowers are in bloom and the mosses and ferns are green.

Wine-Tasting

Over 20 wineries are found near Jacksonville, many of them in the Applegate Valley west of town.

Four miles east of Jacksonville is **EdenVale Winery** (2310 Voorhies Rd., 541/512-2955, www.edenvalewines.com, 11am-6pm Mon.-Thurs., 11am-7pm Fri.-Sat., 11am-5pm Sun. summer, 11am-5pm Sun.-Thurs., 11am-6pm Fri.-Sat. winter), on the imposing Voorhies estate. EdenVale's most interesting wines are tempranillo, cabernet franc, chardonnay, and red blends. The tasting room also offers sales and samples of wines from other small Rogue Valley vintners.

About eight miles southwest of Jacksonville in the Applegate Valley is **Valley View Winery** (1000 Upper Applegate Rd., 541/899-8468 or 800/781-9463, www.valleyviewwinery.com, 11am-5pm daily). While focused on the grape varieties of southern France, Valley View also makes tempranillo, pinot gris, and port. The Bordeaux-style blends are especially good.

With a tasting room that resembles a French villa, **Troon Vineyard** (1475 Kubli Rd., 541/846-9900, www.troonvineyard.com, 11am-6pm daily summer, 11am-5pm daily winter) offers zinfandel, cabernet sauvignon, merlot, syrah, and chardonnay, all grown based on organic principles, plus a red and white blend called Druid Fluid.

If you want to taste wines without leaving town, stop by **Quady North** (255 California St., 541/702-2123, www.quadynorth.com, 11am-7pm Thurs.-Mon. summer, 11am-6pm Thurs.-Sun. winter). Their tasty rose is a pleasant sipper on a hot southern Oregon afternoon.

ENTERTAINMENT AND EVENTS

The **Peter Britt Music Festival** (Britt Pavilion, 1st St. and Fir St., 541/773-6077 or 800/882-7488, www.brittfest.org) began in 1962 on a grassy hillside amid majestic ponderosa pines near the site of the Britt home. Today, the scope of the small classical festival has broadened into a musical smorgasbord encompassing such diverse styles as jazz, folk, country, bluegrass, rock, and dance, in addition to the original classical repertoire. Michael Franti, Brandi Carlile, the Avett Brothers, the Decemberists, and Dwight Yoakam are just a few of the artists who have performed here in recent years.

The festival runs from the last week of June through the first week of September. Tickets typically range $25-90 for general admission, with most concerts running about $45. Reserved seats are available but are more expensive. Concertgoers often bring along blankets, small lawn chairs (allowed only in designated areas), wine, and a picnic supper to enjoy along with entertainment on balmy summer evenings. Be sure to order your tickets well in advance to avoid having to stand outside. Like the Oregon Shakespeare Festival,

The Applegate Valley is one of southern Oregon's top wine-tasting regions.

some shows sell out months in advance, especially for the well-known performers.

ACCOMMODATIONS

The **Wine Country Inn** (830 N. 5th St., 541/899-2050, www.countryhouseinnsjacksonville.com, $136-200) is the only place in town that deviates from the B&B model. Its exterior was designed to resemble historic stage stops along the stage route from Sacramento to Portland.

Also run by Country House Inns, the **McCully House Inn** (240 E. California St., 541/899-2050, www.countryhouseinnsjacksonville.com, $200-300) is a block from downtown, with a good restaurant on the premises. Built in 1861 in the classical revival style, this mansion has four beautifully appointed guest rooms with private baths.

The Craftsman-style **Touvelle House** (455 N. Oregon St., 541/899-3938 or 800/846-3992, www.touvellehouse.com, $139-199) offers five guest rooms and one suite, all with private baths. Out back, near the carriage house, is a heated swimming pool. Common areas include a library and large living room. A full breakfast is included; other goodies like fruit and cookies are available for snacking any time.

The **Jacksonville Inn** (175 E. California St., 541/899-1900 or 800/321-9344, www.jacksonvilleinn.com, $159-270, breakfast included) lies in the heart of the commercial historic district. In addition to eight air-conditioned guest rooms in the historic hotel itself, all furnished with restored antiques and private baths, the inn also offers four deluxe cottages complete with antiques, fireplaces, and canopied king beds. The inn has an excellent dining room.

FOOD

The **Jacksonville Inn** (175 E. California St., 541/899-1900 or 800/321-9344, www.jacksonvilleinn.com, 7am-10:30am and 5pm-10pm Mon.-Tues., 7am-10:30am, 11:30am-2pm, and 5pm-9pm Wed.-Sat., 7:30am-10am and 5pm-9pm Sun., $21-38, reservations recommended) offers steaks, seafood, and specialties of the inn like veal, duck, and prime rib in a Victorian atmosphere of red brick and velvet. Vegetarian dishes are also available. A cellar of over 2,000 wines further enhances your dining experience. There's also a bistro menu after 4pm for lighter appetites, and lovely patio seating during the summer.

The **Bella Union Restaurant and Saloon** (170 W. California St., 541/899-1770, www.bellau.com, 11:30am-10pm Mon.-Sat., 10am-2pm and 10am-9pm Sun., $13-30) is another popular spot. Soups, salads, sandwiches, chicken, steaks, pasta, and pizza are some of the items you'll find on the menu. Vegetarians have many choices to select from as well. The patio behind the restaurant is a pleasant place to eat lunch or enjoy a beer. Also available are picnic boxes, a good choice if you're going to a Britt festival concert. Be sure to call in your order by 2pm.

For the best Thai food in the valley, head for the **Thai House Restaurant** (215 W. California St., 541/899-3585, www.thaihouse-jville.com, 11:30am-2:30pm and 4pm-9pm Mon.-Fri., noon-9pm Sat., noon-8pm Sun., $13-16).

Ashland's outpost of contemporary fine dining is ★ **Gogi's Restaurant** (235 W. Main St., 541/899-8699, www.gogisrestaurant.com, 5pm-9pm Wed.-Sat., 10am-1pm and 5pm-9pm Sun., $21-36), where the dining room manages to be warm and modern at the same time and the food is absolutely of the here and now. A salmon filet is served with red onion jam and strawberry balsamic syrup; a cider-brined pork chop comes with polenta and bacon-apple compote.

INFORMATION

The **Jacksonville Chamber of Commerce** (185 N. Oregon St., 541/899-8118, www.jacksonvilleoregon.org, 10am-3pm daily May-Oct., 10am-3pm Mon.-Fri., 10am-1pm Sat. Nov.-Apr.) has the scoop on events and activities.

Grants Pass

The banner across the main thoroughfare in town proudly proclaims: "It's the Climate." But while the 30-inches-per-year precipitation average and 52°F yearly mean temperature might be desirable, the true allure of Grants Pass is the mighty Rogue River, which flows through the heart of this community. Outfitters in Grants Pass and the surrounding villages of Rogue River and Merlin specialize in fishing, float, and jet-boat trips. Riverside lodges, accessible by car, river, or footpath, yield remote relaxation in the shadow of the nearby mountains. Grants Pass also makes a good base for trips to Crater Lake and Oregon Caves.

The city itself has an active downtown area, with a large and dynamic **Farmers Market** (4th and F Sts., 9am-1pm Sat. mid-Mar.-Thanksgiving). On busy summer days, Grants Pass buzzes with high spirits and activity.

Don't miss the 18-foot-high statue near the north Grants Pass exit (Exit 58) off I-5; the **Caveman** welcomes travelers to Grants Pass.

SIGHTS
Palmerton Arboretum

Six miles down Route 99 in the town of Rogue River is the **Palmerton Arboretum** (West Evans Creek Rd., Rogue River, 541/776-7001, 8am-dusk, free). Originally a five-acre nursery, the arboretum features plant specimens from around the globe, including Japanese pines and Mediterranean cedars, in addition to redwoods and other trees native to the Pacific Northwest. While you're there, be sure to see **Skevington's Crossing,** a 200-foot-high swinging suspension bridge over Evans Creek that connects the arboretum to Anna Classick city park.

Wildlife Images Rehabilitation and Education Center

Originally a rehabilitation station for injured birds of prey, **Wildlife Images**

Rehabilitation and Education Center (11845 Lower River Rd., 541/476-0222, www.wildlifeimages.org, 9am-5pm daily, $12 adults, $7 children ages 4-17) has expanded into an outreach program to aid all kinds of injured or orphaned wildlife as well as to educate the public. Once the animals are well enough to survive in the wild, they are released. During the summer, tours are offered hourly on the half-hour; in winter, tours are every two hours. Tours last between an hour and an hour and a half; reservations are required for all tours. To get here from 6th Street downtown, head south, turn right onto G Street, continue to Upper River Road, and then turn onto Lower River Road.

Oregon Vortex

About 10 miles south of Grants Pass on I-5 is the **House of Mystery** at the **Oregon Vortex** (4303 Sardine Creek Rd., Gold Hill, 541/855-1543, www.oregonvortex.com, 9am-4pm daily Mar.-May and Sept.-Oct., 9am-5pm daily June-Aug., $12.50 adults, $11.50 seniors, $9 children ages 6-11). Called the "Forbidden Ground" by the Rogue Native American people because the place spooked their horses, it is actually in a repelling geomagnetic field where objects tend to move away from their center of alignment and lean in funny directions. For example, a ball at the end of a string does not hang straight up and down, and people seem taller when viewed from one side of the room as opposed to the other. It's truly a weird spot, and if nothing else, the drive through stands of madrone trees to the vortex is beautiful.

SPORTS AND RECREATION
Rafting

There are many ways to enjoy the Rogue River: oar rafts (which a guide rows for you), paddle rafts (which you paddle yourself), and one-person inflatable kayaks are all widely used.

The 40-mile section downstream from Grave Creek is open only to nonmotorized vessels, and river traffic is strictly regulated. For more information, stop at the **Smullin Visitor Center** (14335 Galice Rd., Merlin, 541/479-3735, 7am-3pm daily early May-mid-Oct.).

During the summer, limited float permits (apply during December at www.blm.gov/or/resources/recreation/rogue/permit.php) are needed for non-commercial rafters to float the Wild and Scenic portion of the Rogue, which begins seven miles west of Grants Pass and runs to 11 miles east of Gold Beach. These permits are prized by rafters around the world—this stretch of the Rogue not only has some of the best white water in the United States, but also guarantees a first-rate wilderness adventure. And yet it can be a civilized wilderness: Hot showers, comfortable beds, and sumptuous meals at several of the river lodges tucked away in remote quarters of this famous waterway welcome boaters after a day's voyage. Camping is also available. The BLM holds a lottery to award permits. Apply online at www.blm.gov/or between December 1 and January 31 for a spot the following summer. The best way to avoid this process is to sign on with an outfitter.

OUTFITTERS

Many outfitters can be found off I-5 Exit 61 toward Merlin and Galice just north of Grants Pass. Rafters hit Class III and IV rapids a little before Galice and, for 35 miles thereafter, the stiffest white water encountered on the Rogue. **Adventure Center** (541/488-2819 or 800/444-2819, www.raftingtours.com) has half-, full-, and multiday trips on oar or paddle rafts. Their adventures range from the mild to the wild. A half-day trip on the Rogue is $75.

Galice Resort and Store Raft Trips (11744 Galice Rd., Merlin, 541/476-3818, www.galice.com) offers raft or inflatable-kayak trips as well as river-craft rentals. A half-day float is $69 and a full day on the river is $99, which includes lunch at the resort.

Another river retreat with attractive packages is **Morrison's Rogue River Lodge** (8500 Galice Rd., Merlin, 541/476-3825 or 800/826-1963, www.rogueriverraft.com), about 16 miles from Grants Pass. Everything from half-day ($80) and one-day ($95) floats and excursions to two- to four-day trips is available. The longer excursions include either stays at river lodges or camping along the great green Rogue. Transportation back to Morrison's is included,

Laws of nature go a little awry at the Oregon Vortex.

or your car can be shuttled downriver to meet you at the end of the trip.

Orange Torpedo Trips (210 Merlin Rd., Merlin, 541/479-5061 or 800/635-2925, www.orangetorpedo.com) has half-day and one- to three-day adventures on rafts or inflatable kayaks. A six-hour day trip that covers nine miles of the Rogue is $95.

Ferron's Fun Trips (541/474-2201 800/404-2201, www.roguefuntrips.com) is a family-run business with guided raft tours and rentals ($35 a day and up). Half-day trips are offered both morning and afternoon ($75) and full-day trips ($95) include lunch. Ferron and his guides bring inflatable kayaks along on all the guided trips for anyone who gets the urge to paddle solo. Trips start at the Hog Creek Boat Landing, 8.5 miles west of the I-5 Merlin exit (Exit 61).

For more information on fishing and white-water rafting trips, contact the **Smullin Visitor Center** (14335 Galice Rd., Merlin, 541/479-3735) or the **Visitors Information Center** (1995 NW Vine St., Grants Pass, 800/547-5927, www.visitgrantspass.org).

Hiking

The Rogue River Trail was originally built for pack mules delivering supplies to miners. A three- or four-day hike here can include stays in riverside lodges or campgrounds. Summer is far too hot for pleasant hiking; arrange to go in the spring or fall, and even then, try to hike in the morning. Afternoons at swimming and fishing holes can add a special dimension to your hike.

Rogue Wilderness Adventures (325 Galice Rd., Merlin, 541/479-9554 or 800/336-1647, www.wildrogue.com, $1149 for four days) is one of several outfitters offering guided hikes. Hikes are lodge- and raft-supported, so hikers need carry only a day pack. Wilderness Adventures also offers raft and fishing trips as well as car shuttles.

Fishing

The upper Rogue River is renowned for one of the world's best late-winter steelhead fisheries. Numerous highways and back roads offer easy access to 155 miles of well-ramped river between Lost Creek Reservoir, east of Medford, and Galice, west of Grants Pass. With fall and spring chinook runs and other forms of river recreation, it's no accident that the Rogue Valley is home to the world's top aluminum and fiberglass drift boat manufacturers. Add rafters, kayakers, and plenty of bank anglers, and you can understand why peak salmon or steelhead season is sometimes described as "combat fishing." Contact southern Oregon visitors information outlets for rules, regulations, and leads on outfitters; many of the rafting outfitters listed above also offer guided fishing trips.

Jet-Boating

Hellgate Excursions (966 SW 6th St., 541/479-7204 or 800/648-4874, www.hellgate.com, May 1-late Sept.) is the premier jet-boat operator on this end of the river. Their trips begin at the dock of the **Riverside Inn** (971 SE 6th St.) and proceed downriver through the forested Siskiyou foothills. En route, black-tailed deer, ospreys, and great blue herons are commonly seen. If you're lucky, a bald eagle or a black bear might also be sighted. The scenic highlight is the deep-walled Hellgate Canyon, where you'll look upon what are believed to be the oldest rocks in the state. The least expensive way to experience this adventure is with a "scenic" cruise ticket ($41 Mon.-Fri., $43 Sat.-Sun.), but for a bit more money you can step up to a brunch, lunch, or dinner cruise. Another option is the white-water adventure trip that goes beyond Hellgate ($67 Mon.-Fri., $69 Sat.-Sun., adults). These excursions feature commentary by your pilot, who knows every eddy in the river. Be sure to call ahead for reservations, as space on all of their runs books up fast.

ACCOMMODATIONS

You'll find most motel accommodations clustered around the two Grants Pass exits on I-5, though there are a number of good choices right downtown. Near downtown, find the charming **Buona Sera Inn** (1001 NE 6th St., 541/476-4260 or 877/286-7756, http://buonaserainn.com, $64-109), with wall murals that

Rogue River Rooster Crow

The city of Rogue River, southeast of Grants Pass on I-5, has something to crow about. On the last weekend of June, the **Rogue River Rooster Crow** (http://rogueriverchamber.com) is held at the Rogue River Elementary School grounds. On Saturday, a parade and street fair take over downtown, but the big event occurs early in the afternoon: Farmers from all over Oregon and northern California bring their roosters to strut their stuff and crow to the enthusiastic crowds. Following a fowl tradition established in 1953, the rooster to crow the most times in his allotted time period wins the prize for his proud owner. Then it's the humans' turn, in which well-practiced revelers take their turn trying to mimic a rooster's crow. In the evening, there's live music and entertainment in the park, and Sunday brings the Rooster Crow Car Show's legions of antique cars.

travel from Grants Pass to Italy. The rooms at this courtyard-style motel are more "grandma's house" than Motel 6, with wood floors and nice linens.

Across the river from downtown is a charming option with riverfront access. **Motel Del Rogue** (2600 Rogue River Hwy., 541/479-2111 or 866/479-2111, www.moteldel-rogue.com, $95-155) is a classic 1930s motel that has been lovingly updated but not transformed. Most of the units overlook the river. The motel sits on two acres of parklike property and is very clean, comfortable, and quiet.

Just off I-5, about 20 miles north of Grants Pass, you'll find the **Wolf Creek Inn** (100 Front St., Wolf Creek, 541/866-2474, www.thewolfcreekinn.com). Originally a hotel for the California and Oregon Stagecoach Line, this historic property, built in 1883, is now owned by the state parks department and operated as a hotel and restaurant. Legend has it that President Rutherford B. Hayes visited the tavern in the late 1880s; you can also view the small room where author Jack London stayed and wrote part of his novel *The End of the Story*. The inn was closed for renovation as this book was being updated, but was expected to reopen in 2016.

The **Riverside Inn** (986 SW 6th St., 541/476-6873 or 800/334-4567, www.river-side-inn.com, $139-159) is both right downtown and right on the river. Rooms have decks overlooking the river, and the Hellgate jet-boat excursions depart from just below the hotel. Pets are permitted in some rooms.

Nearby, the ★ **Lodge at Riverside** (955 SE 7th St., 541/955-0600 or 877/955-0600, www.thelodgeatriverside.com, $145-209) offers very stylish rooms and suites, many with balconies facing the river. The lobby is in a huge log cabin with a stone fireplace, and in the middle of lush gardens beside the river is an outdoor pool. Just like at the chains, you'll get a free continental breakfast; there's also an evening wine reception.

Many guests use **Morrison's Rogue River Lodge** (8500 Galice Rd., 541/476-3825 or 800/826-1963, www.morrisonslodge.com, May-Oct., $116-284) as a base for raft trips. Morrison's was built in the 1940s as a fishing lodge and now has a small complex of cottages, suites, and lodge rooms, with an outdoor heated pool, basketball court, putting green, and bicycles.

One of the premium lodgings in the area, ★ **Weasku Inn** (5560 Rogue River Hwy., 541/471-8000 or 800/493-2758, www.weasku.com, $199-329) is a venerable river lodge that was the secret retreat of Clark Gable, Walt Disney, Carole Lombard, and other entertainment figures in the 1930s and 1940s. Only 17 guest rooms are available, ranging from lodge rooms and suites to an A-frame cabin. All look out on the Rogue River and have genuine rustic-chic decor. A deluxe continental breakfast is served, as is evening wine and cheese.

The longtime Redwood Motel has undergone a transformation to become **Redwood Hyperion Suites** (815 NE 6th St., 541/476-0878 or 888/535-8824, www.redwoodmotel.com,

$130-279). The venerable motel rooms have been updated and upgraded, and a new structure with luxury-level suites has been added. The park-like setting, complete with a grove of redwoods and a 350-year-old Palmer oak, is another plus. Add in a pool, hot tub, fitness center, and complimentary breakfast, and you've got one of the city's most unique lodging options.

Cabins

About 20 minutes outside of Grants Pass and well within the Wild and Scenic section of the Rogue River is the **Doubletree Ranch** (6000 Abegg Rd., Merlin, 541/476-0120, www.doubletree-ranch.com, Apr.-Oct., cabins $135-155). Originally homesteaded 100 years ago, this 160-acre fourth-generation working ranch offers cozy cabins, all set up for housekeeping with full kitchens. There's also a five-bedroom house available that is perfect for family groups.

No roads lead to the main lodge and sixteen cabins at **Black Bar Lodge** (541/479-6507, blackbarlodge.com, $130-230 per person includes two meals), but it's a good stop for rafters or hikers along the 40-mile Rogue River Trail. The Black Bar is 10 miles downriver from Grave Creek and is pretty much off the grid: Generators power lights and electricity, and are turned off at night.

Another off-the-grid lodge is **Marial Lodge** (541/471-3262 May-mid-Nov., 541/474-2057 winter, open May-mid-Nov., $115 per person includes three meals), located about 21 miles downriver from Grave Creek. Hikers should plan to stay a night at Black Bar and a second night at Marial Lodge or **Paradise Lodge** (541/842-2822 or 888/667-6483, www.paradise-lodge.com, $155-165 per person, $85 children, includes meals), 24 miles from Grave Creek. Book well in advance.

Camping

Many fine campgrounds are found along the banks of the Rogue River near Grants Pass, including **Valley of the Rogue State Park** (3792 N. River Rd., Gold Hill, 541/582-1118 or 800/452-5687, www.oregonstateparks.

org, www.reserveamerica.com, $19 tent, $26-28 RV, $40 yurt). About halfway between Medford and Grants Pass off I-5, the park is set along the banks of its namesake river. The Rogue supports year-round salmon and spring steelhead runs. Reservations are recommended during the warmer months.

Josephine County has several very nice full-service campgrounds (800/452-5687, www.co.josephine.or.us, www.reserveamerica.com, $20 tent, $25-30 RV, $30 yurt) near Grants Pass. **Indian Mary Park** (7100 Merlin-Galice Rd.), about eight miles west of Merlin, is located on the banks of the Rogue River. A boat ramp, hiking trails, a playground, and one of the best beaches on the Rogue make this one of the most popular county campgrounds on the river.

Griffin Park (500 Griffin Rd.) is a small campground west of Grants Pass. To get here, take the Redwood Highway (U.S. 199) to Riverbanks Road, then turn onto Griffin Road and follow it about five miles to where it meets the Rogue. **Schroeder Park** (605 Schroeder Ln.) is near town, off Redwood Avenue In addition to a picnic area and an excellent swimming hole, there's a dog park here.

At **Whitehorse Park** (7613 Lower River Rd.), eight miles west of Grants Pass via Upper River Road, the river channel shifted away from the park in the wake of the Christmas flood of 1964, but it's only about 0.5-mile walk to a fine beach on the Rogue.

FOOD

Grants Pass has a number of good dining choices, particularly along downtown's G Street. On a summer evening, take a stroll around the neighborhood on this bustling avenue and check out all the options. The neighborhood is also a good morning destination for fresh roasted organic coffee and friendly conversation at **Rogue Coffee Roasters** (237 SW G St., 541/476-6134, www.roguero-asters.com, 7am-pm Mon.-Fri., 8am-5pm Sat., 8am-4pm Sun.) and pastries from **DASSH Bakery** (102 SW 5th St., 541/474-1380, 7am-3pm Mon.-Sat.).

The **Laughing Clam** (121 SW G St., 541/479-1110, www.laughingclam.net, 11am-9pm Mon.-Thurs., 11am-10pm Fri.-Sat., $9-25) is an old bar and grill that has been transformed into a lively family-friendly tavern with good sandwiches, pasta, and steaks. The name might suggest that this is a seafood house, which it's not really, though a few fish dishes are offered.

Another old-time bar made young again, the ★ **Circle J** (241 SW G St., 541/479-8080, 11am-9pm Mon.-Sat., $10-13) is a redbrick cubbyhole with eclectic and funky decor and a hip and lively clientele. The specialties are pizza, burgers, and sandwiches (including some vegan ones) with sweet potato fries, all washed down with microbrews.

With marvelous views, **Taprock Northwest Grill** (971 SE 6th St., 541/955-5998, www.taprock.com, 8am-10pm Sun.-Thurs., 8am-11pm Fri.-Sat., $11-26) occupies a very handsome log-built dining room with spacious decks overlooking the river from between the downtown bridges. The menu is geared toward steaks and comfort food; a good selection of sandwiches and salads is also available.

A somewhat swanky G Street dining room is **Blondie's Bistro** (226 SW G St., 541/479-0420, www.blondiesbistro.com, 11am-9pm Mon.-Fri., noon-9pm Sat.-Sun., $16-22). The international menu includes Italian food such as chicken marsala and Thai curries.

A wine bar bordering on a full restaurant, ★ **The Twisted Cork** (210 SW 6th St., 541/295-3094, www.thetwistedcork-grantspass.com, 11am-8pm Tues.-Thurs., 11am-9pm Fri.-Sat., small plates $4-16, main courses $15-28, no minors allowed) makes the most of local wines and ingredients. In addition to some 30-odd small plates, flatbreads, salads and soups, the Twisted Cork also offers pasta and house specialty main courses such as pomegranate cinnamon flank steak.

INFORMATION

The **Grants Pass/Josephine County Visitor Information Center/Chamber of Commerce** (1995 NW Vine St., 541/476-7717, www.visitgrantspass.com) is open 8am-5pm Monday-Friday.

GETTING THERE

Greyhound (460 NE Agness Ave., 541/476-4513) offers access to the I-5 corridor.

CAVE JUNCTION

Cave Junction's hippie past is evident in some of the colorful local businesses, which include

The area around Cave Junction is colorful, with good wine and produce.

Bed-and-Breakfast in the Trees

Located in Takilma near Cave Junction, **Out 'n About Treehouse Institute and Treesort** (300 Page Creek Rd., Cave Junction, 541/598-2208, www.treehouses.com) is a unique lodging option that's worth driving a bit out of your way to discover. After all, how many bed-and-breakfasts do you find in tree houses?

This comfortable rural retreat blends the whimsy of the 1960s with 21st-century creature comforts. The well-appointed tree-house guest rooms are bolted to 100-year-old white oaks, some 18 feet above the ground. . Those desiring a more down-to-earth lodging option can stay in a peeled-fir cabin with a cozy woodstove. For the deluxe treatment, reserve a 300-square-foot structure built of redwood and Douglas fir that features a sink, tub, fridge, queen-size futon, loft, and 200-square-foot deck with mountain views.

Horseback trail rides, trips to the best Illinois River swimming holes, zip line adventures, and white-water rafting trips can be arranged through the management. Or swim in the river that runs through the property. Rates are $130-310 (some of the larger tree houses sleep four or more) and up with a two- or three-night minimum stay (Memorial Day-Labor Day) and include continental breakfast.

good farm stands, a couple of quirky galleries, and a (less hippie but still pretty groovy) sausage shop. Sample some of the local wines at **Foris Vineyards** (654 Kendall Rd., 541/592-3752 or 800/843-6747, www.foriswine.com) and **Bridgeview Vineyards and Winery** (4210 Holland Loop Rd., 541/592-4688 or 877/273-4843, www.bridgeviewwine.com). Both wineries offer tastings 11am-5pm daily year-round, although confirm their operating hours in winter.

★ OREGON CAVES NATIONAL MONUMENT

About 30 miles southwest of Grants Pass and 20 miles east of Cave Junction is the **Oregon Caves National Monument** (Rte. 46, 541/592-3400, www.nps.gov/orca, cave tours late March-October, 9am-6pm summer, shorter hours in spring and fall, $10 adults, $7 children 15 and under). The cave itself—as there is really only one, which opens onto successive caverns—was formed over the eons by the action of water. As rain and snowmelt seeped through cracks and fissures in the rock above the cave and percolated down into the underlying limestone, huge sections of the limestone became saturated and collapsed. When the water table eventually fell, these

pockets were drained and the process of cave decoration began.

First, the limestone was dissolved by the water and carried in solution into the cave. When the water evaporated, it left behind a microscopic layer of calcite. This process was repeated countless times, gradually creating the formations visible today. When the minerals are deposited on the ceiling, a stalactite begins to form. Limestone-laden water that evaporates on the floor might leave behind a stalagmite. When a stalactite and a stalagmite meet, they become a column. Other cave sculptures you'll see include helicites, hell-bent formations that twist and turn in crazy directions; draperies, looking just like their household namesakes but cast in stone instead of cloth; and soda straws, stalactites that are hollow in the center like a straw, carrying mineral-rich drops of moisture to their tips.

Tours

Tours are informative and entertaining, and you will leave the cave with a better understanding of its natural, geological, and human history. A recent discovery in an unexplored part of the caverns was a grizzly bear fossil believed to be over 40,000 years old. Children must be at least 42 inches tall and able to climb a set of test stairs to gain entry. The tour, limited to 16 people, takes 90 minutes and requires uphill walking, lots of stairs, and navigating some low passageways. Wear good walking shoes and warm clothing; the cave maintains a fairly consistent year-round temperature of 44°F. During summer you can wait in line up to an hour to go on a tour. Special tours include candlelight tours on Friday and Saturday evenings at 6:30 during the summer and off-trail tours (1pm-4pm Fri.-Sat. June-Aug., $45, reservations required at www.recreation.gov), which give novice spelunkers a chance to learn caving techniques and become rather intimately familiar with tight passageways through the cave.

Aboveground

Although the caves are clearly the big attraction, there are some good forest hikes at the monument. The three-mile **Big Tree Trail,** named for a huge Douglas fir estimated to be more than 1,000 years old, wends its way through virgin forest with tan oak, canyon live oak, Pacific madrone, chinquapin, and manzanita, as well as Douglas fir and ponderosa pine. The trail climbs over 1,200 feet,

so it's a bit strenuous, but the solitude and views of the surrounding mountains are as inspiring as the Big Tree. For a one-mile loop, try the **Cliff Nature Trail.** Placards will help you identify the plant life as you traverse the mossy cliffs, and there are also some good vistas of the Siskiyou Mountains. No pets are allowed on the trails in the monument.

Accommodations

The 23-room **Chateau at Oregon Caves** (541/592-3400, www.oregoncaveschateau.com, May-Oct., $109-199) offers food and accommodations at the caves. Built in 1934, this rustic structure blends in with the forest and moss-covered marble ledges. Indigenous wood and stone permeate the building so that you never lose a sense of where you are. The guest rooms feature views of Cave Creek canyon, waterfalls, or the Oregon Caves entrance. The old-fashioned bathroom fixtures, lack of in-room phones, cell service, TVs, and air conditioning (ceiling fans are usually all you need) add to the historical nuance.

The food at the château's main dining room is reasonably good, and having Cave

the 1934 Chateau at Oregon Caves

Creek running through the center of the room definitely adds to the unique atmosphere. Downstairs, the old-fashioned 1930s-style soda fountain dishes up classic American burgers, fries, and shakes, but is not open for dinner.

Camping

Camping is available at **Grayback** (Wild Rivers Ranger District, 541/592-4000, http://www.fs.usda.gov/recarea/rogue-siskiyou, $10, water available), a woodsy Forest Service campground 12 miles from Cave Junction on Route 46. There are 39 sites close to Sucker Creek, with one RV hookup and a one-mile

hiking trail. Closer to the caves is a smaller Forest Service campground, **Cave Creek** ($10, water); take Route 46 four miles south of the caves to Forest Service Road 4032.

Getting There

To get to Oregon Caves National Monument, take U.S. 199 to Cave Junction, then wind your way 20 miles up Route 46 (a beautiful old-growth Douglas fir forest lining the road might help distract the faint of heart from the nail-biting turns). The last 13 miles of this trip are especially exciting. Remember that there are few turnouts of sufficient size to enable a large vehicle to reverse direction.

Roseburg

Many people passing through the Roseburg area (pop. 22,000) might quickly dismiss it as a rural backwater. A closer look, however, reveals many layers beneath the mill town veneer, as evidenced by an award-winning museum, Oregon's only drive-through zoo, and wineries.

The true allure of Roseburg is not really in town, but in the surrounding countryside. The beautiful North Umpqua River to the east offers rafting, camping, hiking, and fishing. In addition to catching trout, salmon, and bass, anglers come from all over to enjoy one of the world's last rivers with a native run of summer steelhead. Numerous waterfalls along the river and the frothy white water make the Native American word Umpqua ("thundering water") an appropriate name.

SIGHTS
Douglas County Museum of History and Natural History
The **Douglas County Museum of History and Natural History** (123 Museum Dr., 541/957-7007, www.umpquavalleymuseums.org, 10am-5pm Tues.-Sat., $8 adults, $6 seniors and veterans, $2 students 5-17) is located at the Douglas County Fairgrounds

(Exit 123 off I-5). Its four wings feature exhibits that range from a one-million-year-old saber-toothed tiger to 19th-century steam-logging equipment. The museum houses the state's largest natural history collection and its second-largest collection of historic photos.

Winchester Fish Ladder
The **Winchester Fish Ladder** is just off I-5 at Exit 129 on the north bank of the North Umpqua River. Visitors can watch salmon and steelhead in their native environment as they swim by the viewing window at Winchester Dam. Spring chinook and summer steelhead migrate upriver May-August, and coho, fall chinook, and more summer steelhead swim past September-November. Winter steelhead is the primary species seen going through the fish ladders and on past the window December-May. The Umpqua River offers the largest variety of game fish in Oregon.

★ Wildlife Safari
Tucked away in a 600-acre wooded valley is **Wildlife Safari** (1790 Safari Rd., Winston, 541/679-6761, www.wildlifesafari.net, 9am-5pm daily, $18 adults, $15 seniors, and $12 children ages 4-12, no pets allowed), a

drive-through zoo that's a big hit with both kids and adults.

Once you are inside the park gates, the brightly colored birds and exotic game animals transport you to other lands, with an oddly appropriate Oregon backdrop. Be that as it may, at Wildlife Safari every possible step has been taken to re-create African and North American animal life zones, but with natural prey kept apart from natural predators. Similar precautions are taken with humans and their animal companions. People must remain inside their vehicles except in designated areas, and windows and sunroofs must be kept closed in the big cat and bear areas. Pets must be left in kennels at the entrance ($5 fee for padlock rental).

Throughout the day, many talks and opportunities to watch the animals being fed are scheduled (extra fees, mostly $12-15). If a short, free visit will suffice, the Safari Village has a selection of smaller, caged or fenced-in animals located right by the parking area and an area where you can take memorable ride on a camel ($10).

With 600 animals, including one of the most successful cheetah breeding programs in the country, Wildlife Safari is involved with various conservation and endangered species

programs. After your "safari," pull into the White Rhino restaurant, which serves food within view of lions, giraffes, and white rhinos.

To reach Wildlife Safari, take Exit 119 off I-5 and follow Route 42 for four miles. Turn right on Lookingglass Road and right again on Safari Road.

Wine-Tasting

Several wineries in the Roseburg vicinity offer tasting rooms and tours. The dry Mediterranean climate and rich variety of soils in the area are ideal for chardonnay, pinot noir, Gewürztraminer, Riesling, zinfandel, and cabernet sauvignon varietals. A wine tour pamphlet with a map showing the location of the wineries is available from the **Roseburg Visitors and Convention Bureau** (410 SE Spruce St., 541-672-9731 or 800/444-9584, www.visitroseburg.com), or go to the website www.umpquavalleywineries.org.

Abacela Vineyards and Winery (12500 Lookingglass Rd., 541-679-6642, www. abacela.com, 11am-6pm daily June-Oct., 11am-5pm daily Nov.-May) is notable for the large variety of wine grapes it grows, including tempranillo, malbec, and dolcetto. It's just a couple of miles north of Wildlife Safari.

Abacela Vineyards and Winery

Girardet Wine Cellars (895 Reston Rd., 541/679-7252, www.girardetwine.com, 11am-5pm daily) is one of the oldest in the area. Philippe Girardet, from a town at the headwaters of the Rhine River in Switzerland, brought European wine-blending techniques to Oregon in 1971. These processes produce unique chardonnay, pinot noir, cabernet sauvignon, and Riesling wines.

The **Henry Estate Winery** (687 Hubbard Creek Rd., Umpqua, 541/459-5120, www.henryestate.com, 11am-5pm daily) has produced a string of award-winning bottlings from chardonnay, Gewürztraminer, and pinot noir grapes. Picnic tables near the vineyard and the Umpqua River are a good place for lunch.

Oregon's oldest vineyard, dating to 1961, is **HillCrest** (240 Vineyard Ln., 541/673-3709, www.hillcrestvineyard.com, 9am-5pm daily Mar.-Dec.). A bewildering range of wine grapes are grown here, but some of the best to sample are the Riesling, syrah, and zinfandel.

SPORTS AND RECREATION
Fishing

The Umpqua River system comprises the North Umpqua, more or less due east of Roseburg; the South Umpqua, south and east of town; and the mainstem Umpqua River, which flows west from Roseburg to the ocean.

Spring chinook enter the North Umpqua River March-June, work their way upstream during July and August, and spawn September-October. Fall chinook are mainly found in the warmer South Umpqua River. Their migration starts in midsummer and peaks in September, when the rains increase water flow and lower the river's temperature. The best fishing for summer steelhead on the North Umpqua is June-October; the fish spawn January-March. This fish averages only 6-8 pounds, but it will make you think you are trying to reel in a chinook by the way it struggles.

Coho salmon, alias "silvers," are found throughout the Umpqua River system. The coho life cycle lasts about three years. Each spends its first year in freshwater, heads for the ocean to spend 1-2 years, and then returns to freshwater to spawn. The adults weigh an average of seven pounds each. This fishery has had some lean years recently.

You'll find rainbow trout in nearly all rivers and streams of the Umpqua River system, where the water is relatively cool and gravel bars are clean. This is the river's most common game fish, mainly because the rivers, lakes, and streams of the Umpqua are routinely seeded with over 100,000 legal-size (eight inches or longer) rainbows. The fishing season opens in April, with the best fishing in early summer when the fish are actively feeding. Visit the **Oregon Department of Fish and Wildlife website** (www.dfw.state.or.us) for additional information on the Umpqua.

ENTERTAINMENT AND EVENTS

Roseburg's big event is the **Douglas County Fair,** held annually at the fairgrounds (Exit 123 off I-5) the second week of August, with down-home events like 4-H livestock competitions, midway rides, food booths, and horse and stock car races. Contact the **Roseburg Visitors Center** (410 SE Spruce St., 541/672-9731 or 800/444-9584, www.visitroseburg.com) for specifics.

If you happen to be in Roseburg on a summer Tuesday evening, check out **Music on the Halfshell** (www.halfshell.org), a series of outdoor summer concerts held at the band shell in **Stewart Park** (NW Stewart Pkwy. and NW Harvey Ave.). The free concerts have featured big-name national and international stars such as Robert Cray, Taj Mahal, and Pink Martini. The park's bandstand is near the banks of the South Umpqua River.

ACCOMMODATIONS

There are over 1,500 motel rooms in Roseburg, and the competition keeps rates relatively low. A number of chain hotels are found at I-5 Exit 125.

Budget travelers can bunk down at the **Roseburg Travelodge** (315 W. Harvard

Ave., 541/672-4836, www.travelodge.com, $77-109). It's right on the Umpqua, though you'll pay a bit more to have a room and balcony overlooking the river. It's also convenient to downtown. Sharing the same river view and easy access to downtown, the **Holiday Inn Express Roseburg** (375 W. Harvard Ave., 541/673-7517, www.hiexpress.com, $171-205) offers a pool, whirlpool, business center, and some of the newest rooms in the area. Both these hotels are located just off I-5 Exit 124.

Get away from the freeway ramps at these comfortable lodgings just north of downtown. The flower-bedecked **Rose City Motel** (1142 NE Stephens St., 541/673-8209, www.rosecitymotel.com, $66) is an old-fashioned motor court motel that is very well-maintained, with full kitchens (extra $50) and a friendly welcome.

FOOD

Roseburg is not exactly the fine dining capital of Oregon, but you won't go hungry here. The **Umpqua Valley Farmers Market** (1771 W.

Harvard, 541/530-6200, 9am-1pm Sat. Apr.-Oct. Sept.) takes place in the parking lot of the Methodist church.

The McMenamins brewery empire has an appealing operation at **Roseburg Station** (700 SE Sheridan St., 541/672-1934, www.mcmenamins.com, 11am-11pm Mon.-Thurs., 11am-midnight Fri.-Sat., 11am-10pm Sun., $9-21). The 1912 Southern Pacific Station was purchased and restored while preserving original features like the 16-foot-high ceiling, tongue-and-groove Douglas fir wainscoting, and marble molding. Quality food and microbrews in a setting suitable for families enhance the appeal.

Some of Roseburg's best dining is Italian-style. ★ **Dino's Ristorante Italiano** (404 SE Jackson St., 541/673-0848, www.dinosristorante.com, 5pm-9pm Mon.-Thurs., 5pm-9:30pm Fri.-Sat., $15-20) is a cozy, family-run spot downtown with decor that's a sprawl of wine cases, travel guides, and cookbooks. The husband-and-wife cooking team spends part of each year in Italy, so the food is about as

Cow Creek Band of the Umpqua Tribe

As you pass Canyonville, along the remote stretch of I-5 between Roseburg and Grants Pass, you'll see the Seven Feathers Casino. It's operated by the Cow Creek Band of the Umpqua Tribe of Native Americans who, like many Oregon tribes, have rallied to regain land that they lost during the pioneer era.

The Cow Creek signed a treaty with the U.S. government in 1853, selling their land in southwestern Oregon for 2.3 cents an acre so that the government could sell it to pioneer settlers for $1.25 an acre. The treaty, which promised health, housing, and education, was ignored by the United States for almost exactly 100 years. The Cow Creek did not receive a reservation, but they stayed in their native area and continued to act as a tribe.

In 1954, the Western Oregon Indian Termination Act terminated federal relations with the Cow Creek and nearly every other tribe in western Oregon. Because the Cow Creek were not notified about their termination until after the act was passed, they sued in the U.S. Court of Claims and eventually won a $1.5 million settlement. The Cow Creek set up an endowment for their settlement money and draw on the interest to further economic development, education, and housing.

The tribe has also been buying back land. In the late 1990s they bought land along Jordan Creek and began clearing out old tires and other garbage that had accumulated there. A watershed assessment pointed to some habitat restoration opportunities, and the tribe set about trying to restore coho salmon and steelhead trout to a stretch of the creek that hadn't seen these fish since 1958, when I-5 was built. After installing weirs that allowed fish to swim through the culverts under I-5 and work on improving water quality and streambank habitat, coho are now spawning in Jordan Creek.

authentic as you'll find anywhere in southern Oregon.

Famous for its breakfasts, **Brix 527** (527 SE Jackson St., 541/440-4901, brix527.com, 7am-8pm or later Mon.-Sat., 7am-3pm Sun., breakfast $6-13, dinner $11-23) is also open for lunch and dinner. At breakfast, Brix 527 gets the basics, like delicious omelets and eggs Benedict, exactly right. At lunch expect soup, salad, and more inventive dishes like grilled bacon-wrapped salmon on saffron rice. At dinner, choose from burgers, steaks, fish, and pasta, or perhaps chipotle prawn tacos.

Head to **Salud Restaurant and Brewery** (537 SE Jackson St., 541/673-1574, www.saludroseburg.com, 2pm-10pm Mon.-Thurs., 2pm-11pm Fri.-Sat., $13-26) for Latin-inspired food and craft beer. "Street tacos" are filled with fresh fish or Coca Cola-marinated pork, chipotle slaw, and pineapple salsa. In addition to the beers brewed here, Salud serves good cocktails and has a bit of a late-night music scene on weekends.

INFORMATION
The **Roseburg Visitors Center** (410 SE Spruce St., 541/672-9731 or 800/444-9584, www.visitroseburg.com) has among its brochures a particularly useful drivers' guide to historic places.

GETTING THERE
Buses to and from the **Greyhound** bus depot (835 SE Stephens St., 541/673-5326) connect Roseburg with other cities along the I-5 corridor.

The North Umpqua River

One of the great escapes into the Cascade Mountains is via the Umpqua Highway, Route 138. This road runs along the part of the North Umpqua River fished by Zane Grey and Clark Gable as well as legions of less-ballyhooed nimrods during steelhead season. The North Umpqua is a premier fishing river full of trout and salmon, as well as a source of excitement for white-water rafters who shoot the rapids. Numerous waterfalls, including 272-foot Watson Falls, feed this great waterway and are found close to the road. Tall timbers line the road through the Umpqua National Forest, and many fine campgrounds are situated within its confines. Mountain lakes offer boating and other recreational opportunities. The Umpqua National Forest also boasts challenging yet accessible mountain trails up the flanks of Mount Bailey (8,363 feet) and Mount Thielsen (9,182 feet). And when snow carpets the landscape in winter, you can cross-country ski, snowmobile, and snowcat ski on Mount Bailey free from the crowds at other winter sports areas.

The recreational areas along the North Umpqua fall under the jurisdiction of the **Umpqua National Forest North Umpqua district** (541/496-3532, www.fs.fed.us, based in Glide) and **Diamond Lake district** (541/498-2531, www.fs.fed.us, based near Toketee Falls) and the **Bureau of Land Management** (777 NW Garden Valley Blvd., Roseburg, 541/440-4930, www.blm.gov/or).

SIGHTS
Colliding Rivers
Just off Route 138 on the west side of the town of Glide is the site of the **Colliding Rivers.** The Wild and Umpqua Rivers meet head-on in a bowl of green serpentine. The best times to view this spectacle are after winter storms and when spring runoff is high. If the water is low, check out the high-water mark from the Christmas flood of 1964. Water levels from that great inundation were lapping at the parking lot, a chilling reminder that *umpqua* means "thundering water" in Chinook.

★ North Umpqua Waterfalls
SUSAN CREEK FALLS

About 11 miles east of Glide is 50-foot-high **Susan Creek Falls,** whose trailhead sits off Route 138 near the Susan Creek picnic area. A well-graded one-mile trail through a rain-forest-like setting to the falls is accessible to strong wheelchair users. The cascade is bordered on three sides by green, mossy rock walls that never see the light of the sun and stay wet year round. Another 0.25 mile up the trail are the **Indian Mounds.** One of the rites of manhood for Umpqua boys was to fast and pile up stones in hopes of being granted a vision or spiritual powers. Also called the Vision Quest Site, the site still holds stacks of moss-covered stones in an area protected by a fence.

FALL CREEK FALLS

Four miles east of Susan Creek Falls is **Fall Creek Falls.** Look for the trailhead off Route 138 at Fall Creek. The one-mile trail goes around and through slabs of bedrock. Halfway up the trail is a lush area called **Job's Garden.** Stay on the Fall Creek Trail and in another 0.5 mile you'll come to the falls. It's a double waterfall, with each tier 35-50 feet in height. Back at Job's Garden, you may want

to explore the Job's Garden Trail, which leads to the base of columnar basalt outcroppings.

LITTLE FALLS AND STEAMBOAT FALLS

During early-summer steelhead season, it's fun to venture off Route 138 at Steamboat and go up Steamboat Creek Road 38 to see the fish battle two small waterfalls. The first, **Little Falls,** is one mile up the road. It's always exciting to see the fish miraculously wriggle their way up this 10-foot cascade. Travel four miles farther up Steamboat Creek Road and turn right on the road to Steamboat Falls campground to see **Steamboat Falls.** A viewpoint showcases this 30-foot waterfall, where some fish jump the falls and others swim the adjacent fish ladder.

TOKETEE FALLS

The word *toketee* means "graceful" in the Chinook language. After viewing **Toketee Falls** plunge over a sheer wall of basalt, you'll probably agree it's aptly named. Nineteen miles up Route 138 near the Toketee Ranger Station, this 0.5-mile trail ends at a double waterfall with a combined height of over 150 feet. To get to Toketee Falls, follow Forest Service Road 34 at the west entrance of the ranger

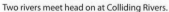
Two rivers meet head on at Colliding Rivers.

station, cross the first bridge, and turn left. There you'll find the trailhead and a parking area.

WATSON FALLS

On Route 138, take Forest Service Road 37 near the east entrance of the Toketee Ranger Station to reach the trailhead of **Watson Falls,** a 272-foot-high flume of water. A moderate 0.5-mile trail climbs through tall stands of Douglas fir and western hemlock and is complemented by an understory of green salal, Oregon grape, and ferns. A bridge spans the canyon just below the falls, providing outstanding views of this towering cascade. Clamber up the mossy rocks to near the base of the falls and get a face full of the cool billowing spray.

LEMOLO FALLS

Another waterfall worth a visit is **Lemolo Falls.** *Lemolo* is a Chinook word meaning "wild and untamed," and you'll see this is also the case with this thunderous 100-foot waterfall. To get here, take Lemolo Lake Road off Route 138, then follow Forest Service Roads 2610 and 2610-600 and look for the trailhead sign. The trail is a gentle one-mile path that drops down into the North Umpqua Canyon and passes several small waterfalls on the way to Lemolo Falls.

Umpqua Hot Springs

The **Umpqua Hot Springs** is mostly unknown and far enough from civilized haunts not to be overused, yet it's accessible enough for those who go in search of it to enjoy. The springs have been developed with wooden pools and a crude lean-to shelter. Weekends tend to attract more visitors, forcing you to wait your turn for a soak. Midweek is generally pretty quiet, though we've encountered some pretty dodgy folks up there at these times.

To get here, go north from the Toketee Ranger Station and turn right onto County Road 34, just past the Pacific Power and Light buildings. Proceed down Road 34 past

Toketee Falls

Toketee Lake about six miles. When you cross the bridge over Deer Creek, which is clearly signed, you will be a little less than 0.5 mile from the turnoff. The turnoff is Thorn Prairie Road, to the right, which goes 1 mile and ends at a small parking area. Note that in wet weather this road may be impassable, and it is not recommended for low-slung cars in any season. From the parking area, it's 0.5 mile down the blocked road to the hot springs trailhead and another 0.5 mile to the pool.

SPORTS AND RECREATION
Hiking

The 79-mile **North Umpqua Trail** is divided into 11 segments from over three miles to 13 miles in length. Beginning near the town of Glide, this thoroughfare parallels the North Umpqua River; the trail leads high into the Cascades and connects with the Pacific Crest Trail as well as many campgrounds. Route 138 affords many access points to the trail.

One segment of the North Umpqua Trail

Watson Falls drops 272 feet into a ferny glade.

is the five-mile **Panther Trail,** which begins near Steamboat at the historic Mott Bridge. Many wildflowers are seen late April-early June on the way up to the old fish hatchery. One flower to look for is the bright-red snow plant, *Sarcodes sanguinea,* which grows beneath Douglas firs and sugar pine trees. Also called the carmine snow flower or snow lily, the snow plant is classified as a saprophyte, a plant that contains no chlorophyll and derives nourishment from decayed materials. Growing 8-24 inches in height, the plant's red flowers are crowded at the crown of the stem.

A five-mile hike that ranges from easy to quite steep and rocky is found on the south slope of 8,363-foot **Mount Bailey.** (Bring plenty of water and good, sturdy hiking shoes.) To get to the trailhead, take Route 138 to the north entrance of Diamond Lake. Turn onto Forest Service Road 4795 and follow it five miles to the junction of Forest Service Road 4795-300. Proceed down 4795-300 for one mile until you see the trail marker. The easy two-mile **Diamond Lake Loop**

takes hikers through a mix of lodgepole pine and true fir to Lake Creek, Diamond Lake's only outlet. There are many views of Mount Bailey along the way, as well as some private coves ideal for a swim on hot days. But while the grade is easy, keep in mind that the elevation is nearly a mile high and pace yourself accordingly. To get to the loop, take Forest Service Road 4795 off Route 138 on the north entrance to Diamond Lake and look for the trailhead sign on the west side of the road.

The **Mount Thielsen Trail** offers experienced hikers and scramblers a million-dollar view from the top of the mountain. This challenging, scree-covered, five-mile trail winds to the top of Mount Thielsen's spire-pointed, 9,182-foot-high volcanic peak. You'll find the trailhead on the east side of Route 138 one mile north of the junction of Route 230. Extra care should be taken getting up and down the top 200 feet, which requires hand-over-hand climbing up a steep, crumbly pitch. If you make it to the top, be sure to enter your name in the climbing register found there. Then take a look at the view, which stretches from Mount Shasta to Mount Hood.

Fishing

The North Umpqua has several distinctions. First, it is known as one of the most difficult North American rivers to fish. No boats are permitted for 15 miles in either direction of Steamboat, and no bait or spinners are allowed either. This puts a premium on skillful fly-fishing. You can wade on in and poke around for the best fishing holes on the North Umpqua, one of the few rivers with a summer run of native steelhead—or better yet, hire a guide.

If you want to go with an experienced fishing guide, check out **Summer Run Guide Service** (541/496-3037, www.summerrun. net).

Rafting

The North Umpqua has gained popularity with white-water rafters and kayakers. But fishing and floating are not always compatible, so guidelines for boaters and rafters have been established by the Bureau of Land Management and the Umpqua National Forest.

The area around Steamboat has the most restrictions, mainly because of the heavy fishing in the area that boaters would disturb. Be sure to check with the **Forest Service** (541/496-3532) prior to setting out to make sure you are making a legal trip. A good way to get started rafting and avoid the hassle of rules, regulations, and gear is to go along with an experienced white-water guide. These leaders provide the safety equipment, the boats, and the expertise; all you have to do is paddle.

In addition to rafting, inflatable kayak trips are offered by outfitters. Inflatables are easier for the neophyte to handle than the hardshell type, though these craft expose you to more chills and spills. Whatever your mode of floating the river, expect more than a dozen Class III or IV rapids and plenty of Class IIs, as well as old-growth trees and osprey nests. Best of all, this world-class river is still relatively undiscovered. Spring and summer are the best times to enjoy the North Umpqua, although it's boatable year-round. Boaters are allowed on the river 10am-6pm only, leaving the morning and evening for fish.

North Umpqua Outfitters (541/496-3333 or 888/454-9696, umpquarivers.com) offers raft, kayak, and drift boat trips. Half-day raft trips start at $95 per person. Other outfitters with similarly price trips include the **Ouzel Outfitters** (800/788-7238, www. oregonrafting.com) and **Orange Torpedo Trips** (541/479-5061 or 800/635-2925, www. orangetorpedo.com).

Winter Sports
SKIING
Located 80 miles east of Roseburg off Route 138 in the central Cascades is Mount Bailey. The experienced skiers at **Cat Ski Mt. Bailey** (800/733-7593, www.catskimtbailey.com, $350 per day) know where the best runs are. Snowcats transport no more than 12 skiers up the mountain from Diamond Lake

Resort to the summit of this 8,363-foot peak. Experienced guides then lead small groups down routes that best suit the abilities of each group. The skiing is challenging and should be attempted only by advanced skiers. Open bowls, steep chutes, and tree-lined glaciers are some of the types of terrain encountered during the 3,000-foot drop in elevation back to the resort.

CROSS-COUNTRY SKIING
Over 56 miles of designated Nordic trails are found in the Diamond and Lemolo Lakes area along the upper reaches of Route 138. Some of the trails are groomed, and all are clearly marked by blue trail signs. Contact the **Umpqua National Forest** (Diamond Lake Ranger District, 541/498-2531, www.fs.usda. gov/umpqua) to request maps and information on these trails.

The **Diamond Lake Resort** (Diamond Lake, 541/793-3333, www.diamondlake.net, 8am-5pm daily) rents skis and snowshoes.

TUBING AND SNOWBOARDING
If you ski the bunny hill, you might enjoy inner-tubing or snowboarding near **Diamond Lake Resort** (Diamond Lake, 541/793-3333, www.diamondlake.net, $10 for 2 hours). A rope tow takes "tubers" to the top of the hill 9am-5pm weekends for nonstop thrills and spills on the way back down. The hill has a ticket system similar to other ski lifts, with full-day, half-day, and two-hour passes available. The tubing and snowboarding hill is located at the Hilltop Shop.

SNOWMOBILING
Approximately 133 miles of designated motorized snow trails are concentrated around the Lemolo and Diamond Lakes area. The trails are usually open in late November, as snow accumulation permits. Many of these trails are groomed on a regular basis, and all are clearly marked by orange trail signs and diamond-shaped trail blazes pegged up on trees above the snowline. Diamond Lake Resort is a hub of snowmobiling activity;

they rent snow machines and can advise you on trails.

One of the more exotic runs is into Crater Lake National Park. Snowmobiles and all-terrain vehicles must register at the north entrance of the park and stay on the trail. The trail climbs about 10 miles from the park gates to the north rim of the lake. Be aware that the mountain weather here can change suddenly, creating dangerous subzero temperatures and whiteout conditions. Also, watch for Nordic skiers and other people sometimes found on motorized vehicle trails.

ACCOMMODATIONS

The number of lodgings on the North Umpqua River is limited to a few properties that range from rustic quarters to full-service resorts.

The ★ **Steamboat Inn** (42705 N. Umpqua Hwy., Steamboat, 541/498-2230 or 800/840-8825, www.thesteamboatinn.com, Mar.-Dec., $195-325) is the premier dining and accommodation property on the North Umpqua, situated in the middle of a stretch of 31 miles of premium fly-fishing turf. The inn's rooms and cabins are extremely popular, so reservations are a must. It's an ideal getaway from civilization, near the hiking trails, waterfalls, and fishing holes for which the Umpqua is famous. Lodging is in handsomely furnished riverside cabins, cottages, and suites; a number of three-bedroom ranch-style houses are also available. The inn serves breakfast, lunch, and dinner to its guests; non-guests may also dine.

Near the summit of the Cascade Mountains about 75 miles east of Roseburg and 13 miles from Diamond Lake is **Lemolo Lake Resort** (2610 Birds Point Rd., Idleyld Park, 541/643-0750, www.lemololakeresort.com, cabins $160-260, hotel rooms $100), a more modest operation. Formed by a Pacific Power and Light dam, Lemolo Lake has good fishing for German brown trout as well as kokanee salmon, eastern brook trout, and rainbow trout. The lake is sheltered from wind by gently sloping ridges, and there are

many coves and sandy beaches along the 8.3 miles of shoreline. Waterskiing is permitted on the lake. Boats and canoes can be rented, and many miles of snowmobiling and cross-country skiing trails are nearby. The resort has both housekeeping and standard cabins as well as basic hotel rooms.

Diamond Lake Resort (Diamond Lake, 541/793-3333, www.diamondlake.net, cabins $110-230, motel rooms $100) is a rustic mountain resort with basic lodging, restaurants, groceries, a service station, a laundry, and showers. Diamond Lake is a good base camp for a Crater Lake excursion. Mountain bikes, paddleboats, kayaks, canoes, and fishing boats as well as an equestrian center keep you out of the very modest accommodations and busy enjoying the spectacular surroundings.

CAMPING
Little River Campgrounds

Camping is popular on the North Umpqua. Several alternatives are nearby, up the Little River south of Glide. **Cavitt Creek Falls** (541/440-4930, www.blm.gov/or, May-Sept., $8, water, vault toilets) is a small falls with a swimming hole at its bottom. To get to the campground here, head east of Roseburg on Route 138 to Glide, take Little Creek Road (County Road 17) for seven miles, then continue three miles down Cavitt Creek Road.

Oher small campgrounds suitable for tents and small RVs up Little River Road are managed by the Forest Service (North Umpqua Ranger District, 541/496-3532, http://www.fs.usda.gov/recarea/umpqua mid-May-late Oct., $10-15, water, vault toilets): **Wolf Creek** (five miles from Glide); **Coolwater** (15 miles from Glide) with good hiking trails nearby, including **Grotto Falls, Wolf Creek Nature Trail,** and **Wolf Creek Falls Trail; White Creek** (17 miles from Glide, then one mile down Red Butte Rd.), situated on the confluence of White Creek and Little River, with a good beach and shallow water; and **Lake in the Woods** (27 miles from Glide, last seven miles gravel), along the shore of a four-acre artificial lake at 3,200 feet elevation. Motorized craft are not permitted in this eight-foot-deep pond. Two good hikes nearby are to **Hemlock Falls** and **Yakso Falls.**

North Umpqua River Campgrounds

Set along the bank of the North Umpqua River 15 miles east of Roseburg a little ways north of Route 138 is **Whistler's Bend** (541/673-4863, www.co.douglas.or.us/parks, $15), a Douglas County park with reservable sites. Picnic tables and grills are provided at this county park, as are piped water, flush toilets, and showers.

About 30 miles east of Route 138 is **Susan Creek** (541/440-4930, www.blm.gov/or, reservations at www.recreation.gov, mid-Apr.-late Oct., $14, flush toilets, water, showers). This campground has 31 sites for tents and RVs (up to 20 feet). Situated in a grove of old-growth Douglas fir and sugar pine next to the North Umpqua River, the campground is enhanced by the presence of a fine beach and swimming hole as well as nearby trails.

Within easy access of great fishing (fly-angling only), rafting, and hiking, **Bogus Creek** (541/496-3532, www.fs.usda.gov/recarea/Umpqua, www.recreation.gov, May 1-Oct. 31, $15, flush toilets, water) offers you the real

thing. As the campground is a major launching point for white-water trips and within a few miles of Fall Creek Falls and Job's Garden Geological Area, it's good to reserve a site or get here early.

About 38 miles east of Roseburg on Route 138 near Steamboat and good fly-fishing is **Canton Creek** (541/496-3532, http://www.fs.usda.gov/recarea/Umpqua, May-mid-Oct., $10, flush toilet, water). Take Steamboat Creek Road off Route 138 and proceed 400 yards to the campground. **Horseshoe Bend** (541/496-3532, http://www.fs.usda.gov/recarea/Umpqua, mid-May-late Sept., $15, flush toilets, water) is 10 miles east of Steamboat. There are 34 sites for tents and RVs (up to 35 feet) with picnic tables and grills. Situated in the middle of a big bend of the North Umpqua covered with old-growth Douglas firs and sugar pines, this is a popular base camp for rafting and fishing enthusiasts.

Diamond Lake Campgrounds

Campgrounds surround beautiful, 5,200-foot-high Diamond Lake; boating, fishing, swimming, bicycling, and hiking are among the popular recreational options. The trout fishing is particularly good in the early summer,

Diamond Lake

and there are also excellent hikes into the Mount Thielsen Wilderness, Crater Lake National Park, and Mount Bailey areas. While no reservations are technically necessary, these campgrounds can fill up fast, so it's always a good idea to book a space ahead of time (877/444-6677 or www.recreation.gov). For general information, contact the **Diamond Lake Ranger District** (541/498-2531, www.fs.usda.gov/umpqua).

Diamond Lake campground (mid-May 15-Oct., $16, water, flush toilets), on the east shore of the lake with easy access to the north entrance of Crater Lake National Park, has over 200 sites. Numerous hiking trails lead from the campground, including the Pacific Crest National Scenic Trail. Boat docks, launching facilities, and rentals are nearby at **Diamond Lake Resort** (Diamond Lake, 541/793-3333, www.diamondlake.net).

Other large Diamond Lake campgrounds are **Broken Arrow** (mid-May-Labor Day, $15, flush toilets, water, showers), on the lake's south shore, and **Thielsen View** (mid-May-mid-Oct., $15, vault toilets, water), on the west side of the lake with picturesque views of Mount Thielsen.

FOOD

Make a reservation at the outstanding ★ **Steamboat Inn** (42705 N. Umpqua Hwy., 541/498-2230 or 800/840-8825, www.thesteamboatinn.com, 8am-9pm daily) to dine on main dishes of beef, fish, poultry, lamb, or pork served with fresh vegetables and homemade bread. Considered one of the top dining experiences in the state, the Steamboat also has a wide selection of Oregon wines. The prix fixe evening dinner ($50) is served nightly, and Winemaker's Dinners (Mar.-mid-June, $90) are scheduled frequently during the summer and on weekends the rest of the season. Reservations for dinner are required; feel free to drop in for lunch.

Crater Lake

High in the Cascades lies the crown jewel of Oregon: Crater Lake, the country's deepest at 1,943 feet. It glimmers like a polished sapphire in a setting created by a volcano that blew its top and collapsed thousands of years ago. Crater Lake's extraordinary hues are produced by the depth and clarity of the water and its ability to absorb all the colors of the spectrum except the shortest wavelengths, blue and violet, which are scattered skyward.

In addition to a 33-mile rim loop around the crater, the park, established in 1902, features two campgrounds, dozens of hiking trails, and boat tours on the lake itself. Admission to the park is $15 per vehicle or $10 per bicycle or motorcycle.

If you're seeing Crater Lake for the first time, drive into the park from the north for the most dramatic perspective. After crossing through a pumice desert, you climb up to higher elevations overlooking the lake. In contrast to this subdued approach, the blueness and size of the lake can hit you with a suddenness that stops all thought.

Geology

Geologically speaking, the name *Crater Lake* is a misnomer. Technically, Crater Lake lies in a caldera, which is produced when the center of a volcano caves in on itself; in this case, the cataclysm occurred 6,600 years ago with the destruction of formerly 12,000-foot-high Mount Mazama.

Klamath Native American legend, which tells of a fierce battle between the chiefs of the underworld and the world aboveground, resulting in explosions and ashfall, roughly parallels the scientific explanation for Crater Lake's formation.

The aftereffects of this great eruption can still be seen. Huge drifts of ash and pumice hundreds of feet deep were deposited over a wide area up to 80 miles away. The pumice deserts to the north of the lake and the deep ashen canyons to the south are the most dramatic examples. So thick and widespread is the pumice that water percolates through too rapidly for plants to survive, creating reddish pockets of bleakness in the otherwise green forest. The eerie gray hoodoos in the southern canyons were created by hot gases bubbling up through the ash, hardening it into rocklike towers. These formations have withstood centuries of erosion by water that has long since washed away the loosely packed ash, creating the steep canyons visible today.

Following the volcanic activity, over thousands of years the caldera filled with water. The lake is self-contained, fed only by snow and rain, with no outlets other than evaporation and seepage.

Wizard Island, a large cinder cone that rises 760 feet above the surface of the lake, offers evidence of volcanic activity since the caldera's formation. In fact, the crater (a true crater) at the top of the island is the source of the lake's name. The **Phantom Ship,** a smaller island formed from lava, is a much older feature.

Although Crater Lake often records the coldest temperatures in the Cascades, the lake itself has only frozen over once since records have been kept. The surface of the lake can warm up past the 60°F mark during the summer. The deeper water stays around 38°F, although scientists have discovered 66°F hot spots 1,400 feet below the lake's surface.

Rainbow trout, kokanee (a landlocked salmon), and crayfish were introduced to the lake many years ago by humans; crayfish are now threatening the lake's native newts. Some types of mosses and green algae grow more than 400 feet below the lake's surface, a world record for these freshwater species.

★ CRATER LAKE NATIONAL PARK
Visitors Center

The **Steel Visitor Center** (9am-5pm daily late Apr.-early Nov., 10am-4pm daily early Nov.-late Apr., closed Christmas day), is located below Rim Village near park headquarters and can provide information, maps, publications, and videos as well as backcountry permits and first aid. For information about weather and activities at Crater Lake, visit www.nps.gov/crla or call 541/594-3000.

The **Rim Visitor Center** (9:30am-5pm daily late May-late Sept.) is near the lodge. A rock stairway behind the small building leads

Crater Lake

Crater Lake National Park

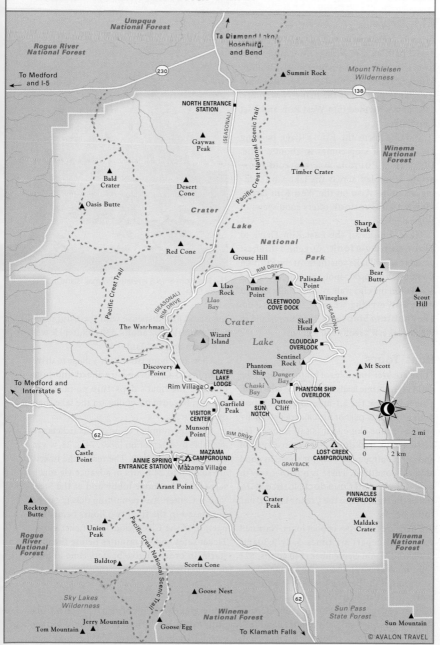

Umpqua
National Forest

Rogue River
National Forest

To Medford
and I-5

Mount Thielsen
Wilderness

▲ Summit Rock

230

138

NORTH ENTRANCE
STATION

To Diamond Lake,
Roseburg,
and Bend

Winema
National
Forest

▲ Gaywas
Peak

▲ Timber Crater

▲ Bald
Crater

▲ Desert
Cone

▲ Oasis Butte

Crater

Lake

National

Sharp ▲
Peak

Park

Bear
Butte

Scout
Hill

▲ Red Cone

▲ Grouse Hill

RIM DRIVE

Palisade
Point ▲

Pacific Crest National Scenic Trail

Pacific Crest Trail

(SEASONAL)

▲ Llao
Rock

Pumice ▪
Point

CLEETWOOD
COVE DOCK

Wineglass ▲

(SEASONAL)

Llao
Bay

(SEASONAL) RIM DRIVE

The Watchman ▲

Crater

Skell
Head ▲

▲ Wizard
Island

Lake

CLOUDCAP
OVERLOOK ▪

Discovery ▲
Point

Phantom
Ship

Sentinel
Rock ▲

▲ Mt Scott

CRATER
LAKE
LODGE

Chaski
Bay

Danger
Bay

Rim Village ○

PHANTOM SHIP
OVERLOOK

To Medford and
Interstate 5

VISITOR
CENTER

Garfield
Peak ▲

SUN
NOTCH

Dutton
Cliff

62

Munson
Point ▲

RIM DRIVE

Castle
Point ▲

MAZAMA
CAMPGROUND

ANNIE SPRING
ENTRANCE STATION

Mazama Village

GRAYBACK
DR

LOST CREEK
CAMPGROUND

0   2 mi

0   2 km

▲ Arant Point

Rocktop
Butte ▲

Rogue
River
National
Forest

▲ Union
Peak

Crater
Peak ▲

PINNACLES
OVERLOOK

Maldaks
Crater ▲

Pacific Crest National Scenic Trail

Winema
National
Forest

Baldtop ▲

▲ Scoria Cone

Sky Lakes
Wilderness

▲ Goose Nest

62

Winema
National Forest

Sun Pass
State Forest

Sun Mountain

Tom Mountain ▲   ▲ Jerry Mountain

Goose Egg ▲

To Klamath Falls

© AVALON TRAVEL

to Sinnott Memorial and one of the best views of the lake.

Rim Drive

Begin a driving tour with a walk along the paved path at Rim Village. Morning views from this path are especially lovely. It's best to drive clockwise around the lake; this makes it easier to pull off at the many viewpoints. The loop is divided into West Rim and East Rim Drives.

Starting from the Rim Village parking area, the first stop comes in about a mile; **Discovery Point** is where a gold prospector stumbled across the lake while riding his mule. Also on the West Rim Drive, **Watchman Overlook** offers good views of Wizard Island.

Head a mile off the East Rim Drive to **Cloudcap Overlook**; Oregon's highest paved road will take you there. At the **Pumice Castle Overlook**, spot the bright orange "castle" on the cliff wall. It's especially vibrant in the early evening, when the sun lights it up. The **Phantom Ship** looks like a tiny island in this big lake; it's really 170 feet tall.

Boat Tours

There are over 100 miles of hiking trails in the park, yet only one leads down to the lake itself. This is because the 1.1-mile-long Cleetwood Trail is the only part of the caldera's steep avalanche-prone slope that is safe enough for passage. The trail drops 700 feet in elevation and is recommended only for those in good physical condition. There is no other way to get to **Cleetwood Cove dock,** located at the end of the trail, where the **Crater Lake boat tours** begin.

There are two types of boat tours. Narrated excursions depart six times daily 9:30am-3:45pm July-mid-September ($40 adults, $27 children ages 3-12) and cruise counterclockwise around the perimeter of the lake. These tours do not stop at Wizard Island. Twice daily, at 9:30am and 12:45pm, a cruise departs with a three-hour stop at Wizard Island ($57 adults, $36 children). If you just want to get to

The Phantom Ship is a relatively small island in Crater Lake.

the island and dispense with the naturalist's talk, a shuttle ($32 adults, $30 children) leaves at 8:30am and 11:30am.

Allow one hour from Rim Village to drive 12 miles to Cleetwood trailhead and hike down to the boat's departure point. Dress warmly, because it's cooler on the lake than on terra firma.

A limited number of boat tour tickets are available by reservation (888/774-2728, www.craterlakelodges.com). The rest of the tickets are sold up to 24 hours in advance via touch screens in the lodge lobby and at the Steel Visitor Center. Any remaining tickets can be purchased in the final two hours before departure at the Cleetwood Trail ticket kiosk. Ticket sales end 45 minutes before the tour starts, in order to give boaters time to hike down to the dock.

Hiking

A short hike with lots of visual punch is from **Sun Notch**, on the East Rim Drive, 4.4 miles east of park headquarters. This 0.8-mile loop climbs 150 feet through a meadow to excellent views of the Phantom Ship and other lake features.

Park rangers often lead sunset hikes up **Watchman Peak**, 3.8 miles northwest of Rim Village. The 1.6-mile roundtrip climbs 420 feet to a fire lookout.

A suitable challenge of brawn and breath is the **Garfield Peak Trail.** The trailhead to this imposing ridge is just east of Crater Lake Lodge. It is a steep climb up the 1.7-mile trail, but the wildflower displays of phlox, Indian paintbrush, and lupine, as well as frequent sightings of eagles and hawks, give ample opportunity for you to stop and catch your breath. The highlight of the hike is atop Garfield Peak, which provides a spectacular view of Crater Lake 1,888 feet below.

Boat tour tickets aren't required for the steep hike down the **Cleetwood Cove Trail** (2.2 miles round trip, 700 feet elevation change) to the boat dock. There's no better way to know the lake than by swimming in it, and this is the place to do it!

A hike to **Wizard Island's summit** involves a boat ride, and a one-mile (770-foot elevation gain) climb. But once at the top you can see (or hike into) the crater and circumnavigate the rim on a blessedly flat 0.3-mile trail. Drop-offs are steep, but the views are spectacular.

Although it doesn't include views of the lake, the **Plaikni Falls Trail** leads to a pretty cascade that rolls down a glacier-carved cliff. The 1.1-mile trail is along a well-graded dirt path. Reach it from the Pinnacles Road, just off the East Rim Drive southeast of the Phantom Ship overlook.

One of the best places to view the mid-July flora is on the **Castle Crest Wildflower Trail.** The trailhead to this easy 0.5-mile loop trail is 0.5 mile from the park headquarters.

The 4.4-mile hike to the top of **Mount Scott** (8,926 feet), the highest peak in the area, gains 1,250 feet. Lake views and perspectives on a dozen Cascade peaks are potential rewards at the end of the trek.

Winter Sports

When snow buries the area in the wintertime, services and activities are cut to a minimum. However, many cross-country skiers, snowshoe enthusiasts, and winter campers enjoy this solitude. Park rangers lead **snowshoe hikes** (weather permitting) at 1pm on weekends, daily during Christmas week. Ski and snowshoe rentals are available at Rim Village.

Winter trekkers should be aware that there

A boat ride on Crater Lake will give you a different perspective, plus lots of information on geology and history from the ranger on board.

are no groomed cross-country trails, so it's imperative to inquire about trail, avalanche, road, and weather conditions at the visitor center. Circumnavigating the lake, which is visited by frequent snowstorms, takes 2-3 days, even in good weather. Only highly skilled winter hikers should attempt this 33-mile route that requires a compass and maps to traverse unmarked routes and avalanche paths.

Trolley Tours

Passengers can take two-hour round-trip tours on newly built but historically designed **trolley cars** (541/882-1896, www.craterlaketrolley.net, tours depart 10am-3pm on the hour mid-June-mid-Oct., fewer tours in June and Sept.-Oct., $27 adults, $24 seniors, $17 children ages 5-13) along Rim Drive, with several stops at scenic viewpoints. The natural gas-powered trolleys are ADA-compliant and feature commentary by a guide. Purchase tickets up to 24 hours in advance from a trolley parked by the Community House at Rim Village, near the Crater Lake Lodge.

Accommodations and Food

One of the nicest things about 183,180-acre Crater Lake National Park is that it's not very developed. Lodging and services are concentrated on the southern edge of the lake at **Rim Village;** the exact opening and closing dates for services changes from year to year, depending on the snowpack, which can exceed 50 feet. In general, restaurants and information services are open mid-May-mid-October, with the exception of the **Rim Village Cafe,** which is open year-round (9am-8pm in summer, shorter hours during rest of year). The café has grab-and-go sandwiches, salads, and rice bowls.

The 71-room ★ **Crater Lake Lodge** (541/830-8700, www.craterlakelodges.com, late May-mid-Oct., $180-309) is situated on the rim south of the Sinnott Overlook and is hewn of indigenous wood and stone. The massive lobby boasts a picture window on the lake and has decor echoing its 1915 origins.

The Castle Crest Wildflower Trail has a great mid-July display.

The stone fireplace is large enough to walk into and serves as a gathering spot on chilly evenings. Many of the rooms have expansive views of the lake below. Less expensive rooms face out toward upper Klamath Lake and Mount Shasta, 100 miles away in California.

Amid all the amenities of a national park hotel, it's nice to be reminded of the past by such touches as antique wallpaper and old-fashioned bathtubs (rooms 401 and 201 offer views of the lake from claw-foot tubs). This marriage of past and present in such a prime location has proven so popular that it's imperative to reserve many months in advance. The 72-seat **dining room** (541/594-2255, ext. 3217, 7am-10am, 11:30am-2:30pm, and 5pm-10pm daily, mid-May-mid-Oct., hours may vary early and late in season, $24-43, dinner reservations recommended) features Pacific Northwest cuisine in a classic setting. If you want to soak in the ambiance of the lodge but don't want to commit to a full dinner, consider ordering from a bar menu (orders taken in the lobby near the restaurant, $8-12) and relaxing with drinks and appetizers in the lobby or on the porch overlooking the lake.

Seven miles south of the rim is another cluster of services called Mazama Village. At the **Cabins at Mazama Village** (541/830-8700, www.craterlakelodges.com, late May-late Sept., $152), each room has one or two queen beds and a bath with shower (no TV, telephone, or air conditioning); two cabins are designed for wheelchair access. Be sure to reserve well in advance.

Also in Mazama Village, the **Annie Creek Restaurant** (7am-10:30am and 11am-9pm daily, early June-late Sept., dinner $9-20) serves American-style comfort foods, including burgers, pot roast, fried chicken, pizza, and vegetarian lasagna.

Camping

Mazama Village Campground (reservations at www.craterlakelodges.com, early June-late Sept., $23 tents, $32.50 RVs), seven miles south of the rim, has over 200 sites; in spite of its size, this is a pretty nice campground, with many spacious sites. **Lost Creek Campground** (early July-mid-Oct., $10 tents), about four miles down the Pinnacles Road from the East Rim Drive, has 16 sites, water, and vault toilets. Its more remote location is nice for many campers, but damage to the trees has left it feeling pretty hot and scrubby.

Campers should also consider **Diamond Lake** (877/444-6777, www.recreation.gov, mid-May-Oct., $16), just a few miles from the park's north entrance. The large lakeside campground here has many reservable sites.

Getting There

The only year-round access to Crater Lake is from the south via Route 62. To reach Crater Lake from Grants Pass, head for Gold Hill and take Route 234 until it meets Route 62. As you head up Route 62, you might spot roadside snow poles in anticipation of the onset of winter. This highway makes a horseshoe bend through the Cascades, starting at Medford and ending 20 miles north of Klamath Falls. The northern route via Route 138 (Roseburg to U.S. 97, south of Beaver Marsh) is usually closed by snow mid-October-July. The tremendous snowfall also closes 33-mile-long Rim Drive, although portions are opened when conditions permit. Rim Drive is generally opened to motorists around the same time as the northern entrance to the park.

Crater Lake Lodge has a spectacular setting.

CRATER LAKE HIGHWAY (HWY. 62)

Don't think that the vacation's over when you leave Crater Lake, at least for the first 40 miles or so. Highway 62 travels along the Upper Rogue River, where you'll find amazing river dynamics and lots of good camping and hiking.

Unfortunately, once you're west of Shady Cove, it's a long, slow suburban slog into Medford. If you intend to head north on I-5, definitely take the Sams Valley cutoff (Hwy. 234) toward Gold Hill.

Hiking and Walking

Many choice hikes are found along the 50-mile stretch of the Rogue River Trail from Lost Creek Lake to the river's source at Boundary Springs, just inside Crater Lake National Park. Those interested in more than just a short walk from the parking lot to the viewpoint can design hikes of 2-18 miles, with or without an overnight stay.

A two-mile hike down a cool and shady trail takes you to the source of the mighty Rogue River—**Boundary Springs.** Situated just inside Crater Lake National Park, it's a great place for a picnic. About one mile down the path from the trailhead, hang a left at the

fork to get to Boundary Springs. Once at the springs, you'll discover small cataracts rising out of the jumbled volcanic rock, which is densely covered with moss and other vegetation. Despite the temptation to get a closer look, the vegetation here is extremely fragile, so refrain from walking on the moss. To get here, take Route 230 north from Route 62 to the crater rim viewpoint, where parking can be found on the left-hand side of the road.

An easily accessible and particularly scenic stretch of the Rogue is near the hamlet of Union Creek. Several short trails are right near the highway and lead to deep gushing gorges and a natural bridge.

Just north of Union Creek is the spectacular **Rogue River Gorge.** At this narrowest point on the river, the action of the water has carved out a deep chasm in the rock. A short trail with several well-placed overlooks follows the rim of the gorge. Green mossy walls, logjams, and a frothy torrent of water are all clearly visible from the trail.

South of Union Creek, the **Natural Bridge** is about a mile off the highway. Here the Rogue River drops into a lava tube and disappears from sight, only to emerge a little way downstream. A paved path takes you to an artificial bridge that fords this unique section of

a dramatic stretch of the Upper Rogue River at the Natural Bridge area

the river. Keep going; the natural bridge is at the end of the paved path.

The 3.5-mile Rogue Gorge Trail connects these two viewpoints. Note the potholes in the dry riverbed above the gorge. They were formed by smaller rocks that were spun and drilled by river currents.

Many more hikes are accessible in this area if you're willing to drive a ways up Forest Service roads. Find more trails in the Rogue River-Siskiyou National Forest at http://www.fs.usda.gov/main/rogue-siskiyou/home or at the **Prospect Ranger Station** (47201 Hwy. 62, 541/560-3400).

Accommodations

The accommodations you'll find on Route 62 are rustic and simple. They're good bases for hiking in the area and for visiting Crater Lake. Both of the lodgings we've listed here have restaurants on site or a few steps away.

The **Union Creek Resort** (56484 Hwy. 62, Prospect, 866/560-3565, www.unioncreekoregon.com) was built in the early 1930s and little changed since then (it's listed on the National Register of Historic Places). Open year-round, it has rooms available in your choice of the original lodge, simple cabins with bathrooms, or housekeeping cabins with kitchens and

bathrooms. The lodge rooms ($79-84), paneled in knotty pine, have washbasins; guests share the bathrooms down the hall. The stone fireplace in the lobby was built of opalized wood from Lakeview, Oregon. The sleeping cabins with baths range $114-189. The vacation rental housekeeping cabins sleep up to 10 and range $249-309. If you like rustic cabins and lodges, the Union Creek is the real deal. The **Union Creek Country Store,** located at the resort, carries groceries and other essential items. Fishing licenses and Sno-Park permits can also be purchased here.

The **Prospect Hotel and Motel** (391 Mill Creek Rd., Prospect, 541/560-3664 or 800/944-6490, www.prospecthotel.com, historic hotel rooms $145-210 including breakfast, motel rooms $95-160) gives you a choice between something old and something new. The hotel, built in 1889 and listed on the National Register of Historic Places, has several small but comfortable guest rooms with baths. The rooms are named after local residents and famous people who have stayed at the hotel, including Zane Grey, Teddy Roosevelt, and Jack London. Because the hotel is small and old, no children, smoking, or pets are permitted. The adjacent motel features clean, spacious, and modern units, with

Prospect Hotel and Motel

some kitchenettes available. Pets are welcome in the motel.

Camping

Set along the woodsy bank of Union Creek where it merges with the upper Rogue River is **Union Creek campground** (541/560-3400, www.fs.usda.gov/recarea/rogue-siskiyou, late May-Oct., $16, vault toilets, drinking water). Other Forest Service campgrounds within a couple of miles of Union Creek are **Farewell Bend** ($20, flush toilets, drinking water) and **Natural Bridge** ($10, vault toilets, no drinking water).

Lost Creek Lake is the site of **Joseph Stewart State Park** (35251 Rte. 62, Trail, 541/560-3334, www.oregonstateparks.org, www.reserveamerica.com, Mar.-Oct., $17-22). The large campground here is set on a big grassy field above the reservoir and has all the usual state park amenities. Bike paths, a beach, and barbecue grills make this a family-friendly locale, if not exactly getting away from it all. Boat-launching facilities for Lost Creek Lake are located nearby, and eight miles of hiking trails and bike paths crisscross the park. Lost Creek Lake also has a marina, a beach, and boat rentals.

Klamath Falls

Klamath Falls, or "K Falls" as locals call it, is the population hub of south-central Oregon, with about 20,000 people within the city limits and an additional 40,000 in the surrounding area. This community is used to hard times after witnessing the decline of its previous economic engines, starting with the railroads and moving on to the timber industry. Farming and ranching are still an important part of the local economy, as are tourism and the influx of new settlers, particularly retirees. The climate is dry here, with more than 290 days of sunshine; winters are cool but not damp.

Downtown Klamath Falls has a clutch of handsome historic buildings, many revitalized with shops and dining spots, and museums that shed light on different aspects of local history and culture. But the real draw of Klamath Falls is out in the surrounding countryside, where the Klamath Basin national wildlife refuges, a complex of six lake and wetland units stretching into California, draw visitors—and lots of birds—to the area. The refuges host some 50 nesting pairs of bald eagles, as well as more than 400 other bird species.

SIGHTS
Favell Museum

A fine collection of Native American artifacts and Western art is found at the **Favell Museum** (125 W. Main St., 541/882-9996, www.favellmuseum.org, 10am-5pm Tues.-Sat., $10 adults, $5 children ages 6-16, children under 6 free, $25 family). Here you'll find beautiful displays of Native American stonework, bone and shell work, beadwork, quilts, basketry, pottery, and Pacific Northwest coast carvings. Another attraction is the collection of miniature working firearms, ranging from Gatling guns to inch-long Colt 45s, displayed in the museum's walk-in vault.

The museum also houses one of Oregon's best collections of Western art. The gift shop and art gallery specialize in limited edition prints and original Western art.

Two other museums are nearby: the **Baldwin Hotel Museum** (31 Main St., 541/883-4207, 10am-4pm Wed.-Sat. Memorial Day-Labor Day), adorned with original fixtures and furnishings, the legacy of photographer Maud Baldwin, and the **Klamath County Museum** (1451 Main St., 541/883-4208, http://museum.

Klamath Falls

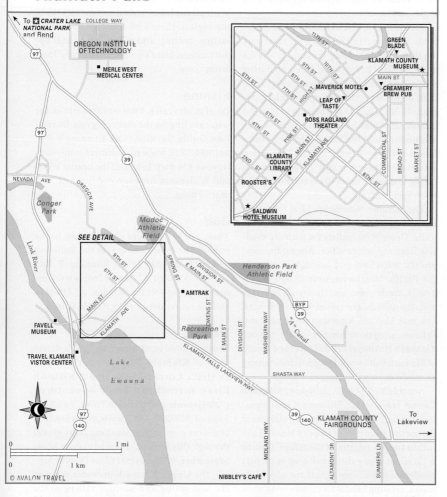

klamathcounty.org, 9am-5pm Tues.-Sat., $5 adults, $4 seniors and students, $5 children ages 5-12), with a good natural history section.

Wildlife Refuges

The lakes, marshes, and streams in the Klamath Basin are protected by six different wildlife refuges that stretch between southern Oregon and northern California and share

a **visitor center** at Tule Lake, in California (4009 Hill Rd, Tulelake, CA, 530/667-2231, www.fws.gov/refuge/Tule_Lake, 8am-4:30pm Mon.-Fri., 9am-4pm Sat.-Sun.). Overnight camping is not permitted in any of the refuges.

December-February the Klamath Basin is home to one of the largest wintering concentration of bald eagles in the Lower 48 states. The thousands of winter waterfowl that reside here provide a plentiful food source for these raptors. Ask at the Tule Lake Visitor Center about where the highest concentration of bald eagles can be seen.

March-May is when waterfowl and shorebirds stop over in the basin on their way north to their breeding grounds in Alaska and Canada. They rest and fatten up during the spring to build the necessary strength and body fat to carry them through their long migration. May-July is the nesting season for thousands of marsh birds and waterfowl. The **Klamath Marsh National Wildlife Refuge** (north of Klamath Falls off U.S. 97, www.fws.gov/refuge/klamath_marsh) is a good place in spring to observe sandhill cranes, shorebirds, waterfowl, and raptors.

The summer months are ideal for taking the self-guided auto tour routes and canoe trails. Descriptive leaflets for both are available from the refuge office. Among the most prolific waterfowl and marsh bird areas in the Pacific Northwest, over 25,000 ducks, 2,600 Canada geese, and thousands of marsh and shorebirds are raised here each year. You may also see American white pelicans, *Pelecanus erythrorhynchos,* at the **Upper Klamath National Wildlife Refuge** (north of Klamath Falls, www.fws.gov/refuge/upper_klamath) during the summer.

Another high point is the **Upper Klamath Canoe Trail,** which follows a 9.5-mile passage through lakes, marshes, and streams at the northwest corner of Upper Klamath Lake within the boundaries of the refuge. Birding is excellent along the canoe trail as mature ponderosa pines come right to the edge of the marsh, creating habitat for raptors, songbirds, and waterfowl. The trail departs from Rocky Point, about 25 miles northwest of Klamath Falls on Route 140. Canoe rentals ($60 per day) are available from **Rocky Point Resort** (28121 Rocky Point Rd., 541/356-2287, www.rockypointoregon.com).

The **Winter Wings Festival** (www.winterwingsfest.org) is held in February, with lots of workshops, field trips with celebrity birders, and photography workshops.

SPORTS AND RECREATION

With all the lakes, rivers, and mountains in the region, there's no shortage of fishing, rafting, golfing, and other recreational opportunities. Here's a short list of some local attractions.

Fishing

Local guides can get you outfitted and on the water angling for the elusive big one. **Darren Roe Guide Service** (5391 Running Y Rd., 541/884-3825, www.roeoutfitters.com) offers trips on Klamath Lake and the nearby Wood and Willamson Rivers, noted for their runs of wild trout.

Golf

There are several area courses open to the public. The most notable is at the **Running Y Ranch Resort** (5500 Running Y Rd., 541/850-5500 or 877/866-1266, www.runningy.com, $64-94 for 18 holes), a 7,138-yard 18-hole course designed by Arnold Palmer.

Rafting

Twenty miles (just under an hour's drive) west of Klamath Falls is what's known as Hell's Corner of the Upper Klamath River. **Arrowhead River Adventures** (720 Greenleaf Dr., Eagle Point, 541/830-3388 or 877/217-4387, www.arrowheadadventures.com) offers daylong trips ($149) through this remote, secluded canyon June-September. With several Class IV-plus rapids, the Upper Klamath provides some of the best spring and summer rafting in the state.

You can also arrange a raft trip in the Upper Klamath River canyons through Ashland's **Adventure Center** (40 N. Main St., Ashland, 541/488-2819 or 800/444-2819, www.raftingtours.com). In addition to a day trip ($135, includes transportation to and from Ashland), they offer a two-day trip down the river with a night of fully catered riverside camping ($339).

ENTERTAINMENT AND EVENTS

The region's cultural hub is the **Ross Ragland Theater** (218 N. 7th St., 541/884-5483, www.rrtheater.org). The Klamath Symphony, community theatre groups, country stars, and touring Broadway troupes grace the stage of this 800-seat auditorium.

ACCOMMODATIONS

Travelers on a budget will appreciate **Maverick Motel** (1220 Main St., 541/882-6688 or 800/404-6690, www.maverickmotel.com, $59). It serves continental breakfast and allows pets.

Midrange properties are mostly the domain of the chains. The non-chain **Olympic Inn** (2627 S. 6th St., 541/882-9665, www.olympicinn.com, $119-149) is the nicest standard hotel in the area; soup is served every afternoon at 4:30, cookies come out at 8pm, and breakfast is complimentary.

The **Running Y Ranch Resort** (5500 Running Y Rd., 541/850-5500 or 800/851-6013, www.runningy.com, $177-223 d hotel rooms) offers the total Klamath Basin package experience. This upscale golf resort has country club homes, and travelers can stay in the deluxe guest rooms at the ranch lodge. The 82 guest rooms are a mix of comfortable hotel-style rooms and well-appointed one-bedroom suites. Two- and three-bedroom houses are also available. Pets are welcome here, and the resort has plenty of trails for ambles with a dog.

Camping

Most of the campgrounds you'll find in the vicinity of Klamath Falls are privately owned RV campgrounds, often in prime locations. **Rocky Point Resort** (28121 Rocky Point Rd., 541/356-2287, www.rockypointoregon.com, Apr.-mid-Nov., tents $22, RVs $28-30, cabins $140) is close to the Upper Klamath National Wildlife Refuge, about a half-hour from Klamath Falls. This resort has a summer-camp vibe, with tent and RV sites with hookups as well as rustic cabins and a

restaurant. Ask about canoe rentals for trips on the Upper Klamath Canoe Trail.

Several other campgrounds are also found on Upper Klamath Lake. **Hagelstein Park** (17301 Hwy. 97 N., 541/883-5371, Apr.-late Nov., free), a small park just off the highway with boat ramp. It's the only campground on the east shore of the lake; to get there, head north of Klamath Falls for 10 miles and look for signs on the right side of the road.

Approximately seven miles farther north on U.S. 97 is **KOA Klamath Falls** (3435 Shasta Way, 541/884-4644, year-round, $28-38, cabins $56). Set along the shore of Upper Klamath Lake, the park has flush toilets, showers, a pool, a laundry, a recreation hall, and other amenities

The pretty campground at **Collier Memorial State Park** (547/783-2471, www.oregonstateparks.org or www.reserveamerica.com, $19-26) is set near the convergence of the Williamson River (locally famous for its trout) and Spring Creek. Across the road you'll find a logging museum. It's about 40 miles north of K Falls on Highway 97.

FOOD

The popular spot for breakfast and lunch is **Nibbley's Cafe** (2424 Washburn Way, 541/883-2314, www.nibbleys.com, 6am-4pm Mon., 6am-9pm Tues.-Fri., 7am-9pm Sat., 8am-2pm Sun., breakfast $5-11). The oatmeal pancakes are locally renowned, and the omelets are yummy.

We're suckers for a good artisan bakery, and were happy to find the **Green Blade** (1400 Esplanade St., 541/273-8999, greenblade.com, 7am-5:30pm Mon.-Fri., 8am-2pm Sat.) with excellent morning pastries and sourdough breads.

Right downtown, **A Leap of Taste** (907 Main St., 541/850-9414, www.aleapoftaste.com, 7:30am-6pm Mon.-Fri., 8am-4pm Sat., $4-11) is a great place for a sandwich or coffee, but it's a bit more than that. It also stocks a small selection of organic groceries, including locally raised meat, and serves as a place for young adults to learn job skills (in a way that's a bit more intentional than most coffee shops).

Rooster's Steak and Chop House (205 Main St., 541/850-8414, 4pm-10pm daily, $22-38) is the place for fine dining in K Falls, with excellent steaks and a classy atmosphere.

A good spot for casual dining is the **Creamery Brew Pub & Grill** (1320 Main St., 541/273-5222, kbbrewing.com, 11am-9:30pm daily, $10-24), with good beer and serviceable pub food. One of the great attractions of the Creamery is its outdoor seating on the building's old loading dock.

INFORMATION

Over 2.2 million acres of Klamath County is publicly owned. The **Klamath Falls Ranger District Office** (2819 Dahlia St., 541/885-3400) can provide outdoor recreational information on the Fremont-Winema National Forest.

You'll find the **Oregon Welcome Center** (11001 Hwy. 97 S., 541/882-7330, May-Oct.)

at a U.S. 97 rest area about halfway between Klamath Falls and the California-Oregon border. They have a broad collection of brochures and information about locales all over the state.

For information on Klamath Falls, contact **Discover Klamath** (205 Riverside Dr., 541/882-1501 or 800/445-6728, www.discoverklamath.com).

GETTING THERE

Amtrak (1600 Oak Ave., 541/884-2822) can connect you with northern and southern destinations via the *Coast Starlight* train. The **Klamath Shuttle** (445 S. Spring St., 541/883-2609) provides daily bus service between Klamath Falls and Medford, with connections to Amtrak in K Falls and Greyhound in Medford. The **Point** bus (also at 445 S. Spring St., 541/883-2609, www.oregon-point.com) provides connections to Ashland and Brookings.

Bend and Central Oregon

Look for ★ to find recommended
sights, activities, dining, and lodging.

Highlights

★ **High Desert Museum:** This indoor-outdoor museum has exhibits on contemporary Native American life, the development of the West, photography, and wildlife (page 454).

★ **Mount Bachelor:** When weather permits, you can ride the Summit Lift all the way to the top of the mountain (page 457).

★ **Deschutes River Trail:** This trail ushers runners, walkers, and bicyclists along the Deschutes. Cyclists can ride from downtown Bend all the way to Benham Falls (page 460).

★ **Metolius River:** At the headwaters of the Metolius, the water emerges from hillside springs and immediately becomes a full-sized river (page 484).

★ **Smith Rock State Park:** Famed for its rock climbing, Smith Rock has just as much to offer hikers, who can search for golden eagles on the cliffs (page 489).

★ **Museum at Warm Springs:** Not only does this museum display a wide variety of Native American artifacts, it also features audio and visual exhibits portraying the cultures of the Paiute, Warm Springs, and Wasco people (page 497).

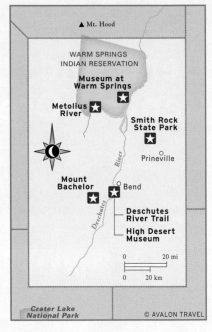

Central Oregon is one of the most magnificent natural playgrounds in this part of the world, with a scenic collage of green forest and black basalt outcroppings topped by extinct volcano cones covered with snow. Plenty of lakes,

rivers, and waterfalls provide a sparkling contrast to the earth tones. It's easy to find ways to explore these natural areas: hiking, biking, and cross-country ski trails abound, as do resorts both luxurious and rustic, waterways teeming with fish, and, increasingly, good restaurants and shopping.

The central Oregon Cascades, and especially Mount Bachelor, are a haven for winter sports that range from alpine and Nordic skiing to snowmobiling, snowboarding, and snowshoeing. Skiing here can be a special treat for westside Oregonians accustomed to Mount Hood's fierce weather and frequently dense, heavy snow. Of course, Bachelor *is* in Oregon, not Utah, so don't expect all powder all the time.

Central Oregon has gained recognition for world-class golfing. And no wonder: With over a dozen courses, this region of the state offers just about every kind of golf challenge. The warm sunny days, cool evenings, and

spectacular mountain scenery make every shot a memorable one.

With respect to everything except rain, the climate is a bit more extreme here than it is on the west side of the Cascades. Expect it to be fairly dry, though perhaps not as constantly sunny as advertised in many tourist publications—that snow on Mount Bachelor has to come from somewhere. It's cold in the winter, and hot in the summer, with cool to cold evenings year-round.

PLANNING YOUR TIME

Plan to spend a few days exploring this part of the state. A long weekend will do for a taste or if you're very focused on skiing or a particular hiking trip or fishing destination. **Bend** is a natural base in the area, but it's also worth considering **Sunriver,** especially if you're visiting with family or a group of friends. Both of these places allow easy access to the Deschutes

---

Previous: Smith Rock State Park; the Deschutes River near Benham. **Above:** the Deschutes River drops into a narrow fissure at Sherar's Falls.

Bend and Central Oregon

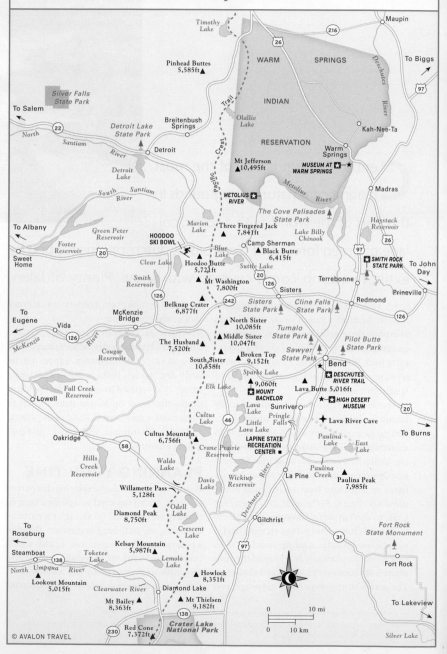

Maupin

To Biggs

Timberlake

216

26

97

WARM   SPRINGS

Pinhead Buttes
5,585ft ▲

Silver Falls
State Park

INDIAN

To Salem

Deschutes River

Kah-Nee-Ta

Breitenbush
Springs

Detroit Lake
State Park

22

Ollalie
Lake

RESERVATION

Warm
Springs

North   Santiam

River

Detroit

Crest

Pacific

Trail

Mt Jefferson
▲ 10,495ft

MUSEUM AT
WARM SPRINGS ✚ ★

Madras

Detroit
Lake

METOLIUS
RIVER ✚

Metolius   River

The Cove Palisades
State Park

Haystack
Reservoir

To Albany

South   Santiam

River

Marion
Lake

Three Fingered Jack
7,841ft ▲

Camp Sherman

Lake Billy
Chinook

26

97

Green Peter
Reservoir

Blue
Lake

▲ Black Butte
6,415ft

SMITH ROCK
STATE PARK ✚

Foster
Reservoir

20

HOODOO
SKI BOWL

Clear Lake

Hoodoo Butte
5,721ft ▲

Suttle Lake

20   126

Terrebonne

To John
Day

Sweet
Home

Smith
Reservoir

126

▲ Mt Washington
7,800ft

Sisters

Prineville

To
Eugene

Vida

126

McKenzie
Bridge

Belknap Crater
6,877ft ▲

242

Sisters
State Park

Cline Falls
State Park

Redmond

126

McKenzie   River

▲ North Sister
10,085ft

Tumalo
State Park

Pilot Butte
State Park

Cougar
Reservoir

The Husband
7,520ft ▲

▲ Middle Sister
10,047ft

Sawyer
State Park

Bend ★

Fall Creek
Reservoir

South Sister
10,358ft ▲

Broken Top
9,152ft ▲

DESCHUTES
RIVER TRAIL ✚

Lowell

Sparks Lake

▲ 9,060ft

Lava Butte 5,016ft ▲

20

Elk Lake

✚ MOUNT
BACHELOR

Lava
Lake

Sunriver

★ ✚ HIGH DESERT
MUSEUM

Oakridge

58

Cultus
Lake

46

Little
Lava Lake

Pringle
Falls

✦ Lava River Cave

To Burns

Cultus Mountain
6,756ft ▲

Paulina
Lake

East
Lake

Hills
Creek
Reservoir

Crane Prairie
Reservoir

LAPINE STATE
RECREATION
CENTER ■

Waldo
Lake

Davis
Lake

Wickiup
Reservoir

Paulina
Creek

Paulina Peak
7,985ft ▲

Willamette Pass
5,128ft

Odell
Lake

La Pine

Diamond Peak
8,750ft ▲

Deschutes   River

To
Roseburg

Crescent
Lake

Gilchrist

31

Fort Rock
State Monument

Kelsay Mountain
5,987ft ▲

Lemolo
Lake

97

Steamboat

138

Toketee
Lake

Fort Rock

North   Umpqua   River

Clearwater River

▲ Howlock
8,351ft

Lookout Mountain
5,015ft ▲

Diamond Lake

Mt Bailey ▲
8,363ft

▲ Mt Thielsen
9,182ft

0   10 mi

To Lakeview

138

0   10 km

© AVALON TRAVEL

230

Red Cone
7,372ft ▲

Crater Lake
National Park

Silver Lake

River, the High Desert Museum, and the Lava Lands sights.

If you plan to do a bit of hiking in the national forests, pick up a **Northwest Forest Pass** (www.fs.usda.gov/main/r6/passes-permits, $5 one-day, $30 one-year), which is required for parking at most trailheads and will get you into sites such as the Lava Lands Visitor Center. Passes are sold online and at trailheads, ranger stations, visitors centers, most local resorts, and many sporting goods and outdoors stores.

In the summer, camping is a good option. There are few campgrounds prettier than the ones along the Cascades Lakes Highway, and most have good places to fish and hike nearby.

However, if fishing is going to be your main activity, don't overlook **Prineville;** the Crooked River offers outstanding fly-fishing and a string of campgrounds below the Prineville Reservoir.

Resorts

There are several premier resorts in Deschutes County that have helped transform it from a primarily agricultural area to the Aspen of the Pacific Northwest. Golf, horseback riding, tennis, swimming, biking-jogging-hiking trails, saunas, and hot tubs grace these year-round playgrounds, along with first-rate lodgings and restaurants. Ski packages and other special offers are also available at each establishment. Among the best resorts are **Black Butte Ranch** near Sisters, **Brasada Ranch** outside Prineville, **Sunriver Lodge** in Sunriver, **Mount Bachelor Village** and **Tetherow** resorts on the outskirts of Bend, **Eagle Crest Resort** near Redmond, and **Kah-Nee-Ta** on the Warm Springs Reservation.

Tours

A great way to explore central Oregon in depth is through **Wanderlust Tours** (143 SW Cleveland Ave., Bend, 541/389-8359 or 800/962-2862, www.wanderlusttours.com), where the focus is on the area's geology, history, flora, fauna, and local issues. Wanderlust has been in this business for years and really does it right; it's generally thought to be the best tour company east of the Cascades. Day trips to Crater Lake, the Lava Lands, the Deschutes River, and the Cascades Lakes Highway are featured. Canoe lakes in the high Cascades ($65), or take a hike that's selected for your group's interests and abilities. Snowshoe tours ($65 half-day) are available in winter, and special moonlight trips can be arranged too. All-day trips include lunch; vegetarian meals are available on request. Wanderlust Tours also offers guided lava tube tours to a different lava tube than the forest service Lava River Cave near Highway 97. These naturalist-led tours include all necessary gear and equipment ($55 for half-day tour).

Bicyclists can sign on with **Cog Wild** (http://cogwild.com) for single- or multiday mountain bike tours.

Bend

There are two important things to know about Bend. First, it's different than it was last year. Growth went crazy in the early 2000s, with a good bit of the population of 81,000 housed in expensive new developments, earning Bend a ranking in 2006 as the nation's fifth-most-overvalued real estate market—then the crash came, leaving many partially built-out developments and some practically empty new subdivisions, from which there's been a substantial recovery.

And oh, yes, there is one other thing about Bend: no matter what the economy's doing, it's a fantastic place to visit. The hiking trails, fishing streams, golf courses, white-water runs, and ski slopes are top-notch; and the downtown is lively, with good restaurants and lovely places to stay.

The Old Mill District, a huge housing, office, and shopping area just south of downtown, opens up access to the Deschutes River in this formerly industrial part of town. The actual old mill smokestacks now soar above an REI store, and they serve as a fitting symbol of Bend's transformation from mill town into recreational hot spot.

Visitors will notice that a massive boom-time road-building effort has focused on the use of traffic circles rather than stoplights. Slow down and drive carefully, and you may be surprised how well this system works.

SIGHTS
Drake Park
The Deschutes River has a dam and diversion channel just above downtown Bend. It provides valuable irrigation water for the farmers and ranchers of the dry but fertile plateau to the north and creates a placid stretch of water called Mirror Pond that is home to Canada geese, ducks, and other wildlife. **Drake Park** (777 NW Riverside Blvd.) is on the east bank of this greenbelt and is a nice place to relax, have a quiet lunch, walk the dog, or toss a Frisbee around. (However, you had better be careful where you step, as the birds leave behind numerous land mines.) The neighborhoods surrounding the park have many older homes surrounded by lawns and trees and are also good places to walk.

★ High Desert Museum
Six miles south of Bend is the **High Desert Museum** (59800 U.S. 97 S., 541/382-4754, www.highdesertmuseum.org, 9am-5pm daily May-Oct., 10am-4pm daily Nov.-Apr., $15 adults, $12 seniors, $9 children ages 5-12, children ages 4 and under free, reduced off-season rates). Although the admission may seem steep, this is an excellent indoor-outdoor museum that will take half a day to explore in detail.

Along the many trails that wind through the 150-acre facility, visitors can observe river otters at play, porcupines sticking it to each other, and birds of prey dispassionately watching over the whole scene. Replicas of a sheepherder's cabin, a settler's cabin, forestry displays, and other historical interpretations are also along the museum walkways. Join a naturalist for a nature walk or a meet-up with the museum's raptors. Another highlight is the **Donald M. Kerr Bird of Prey Center,** with resident bald and golden eagles, a great horned owl, and more.

Inside the museum's main building, you'll find unique exhibits, slide and movie presentations, galleries, and pioneer history demonstrations. The "desertarium" is a special delight, populated by native plants and 37 small critters whose nocturnal lifestyles often keep them from view in the wild. Bats, lizards, mice, toads, snakes, and owls reveal that the desert is more alive than its superficially barren landscape might suggest.

The **Earle A. Chiles Center** exhibit on the spirit of the West features eight "you are there" life-size dioramas. This walk through time begins 8,000 years ago beside a still marsh and takes you to a fur brigade camp, into the depths of a gold mine, and down Main Street in a boisterous frontier town.

The **Spirit of the West Gallery** has representative arts and artifacts of the early American West, as well as tools, clothing, and other personal belongings from the 19th century. The Bounds collection of Native American artifacts and the Hall of Plateau Heritage balance out the museum's coverage of the peoples of the high desert, while the Changing Forest exhibit addresses old-growth life cycles and other issues of forest ecology. The **Henry J. Casey Hall of Plateau Heritage,** an 8,000-square-foot venue, showcases the Doris Swayze Bounds Native American artifact collection as well as other Native Americana.

The scope and interactive nature of this facility make it appealing for people who don't usually like museums. If you end up staying longer than you expected, stop for lunch or a snack at the museum café.

Bend

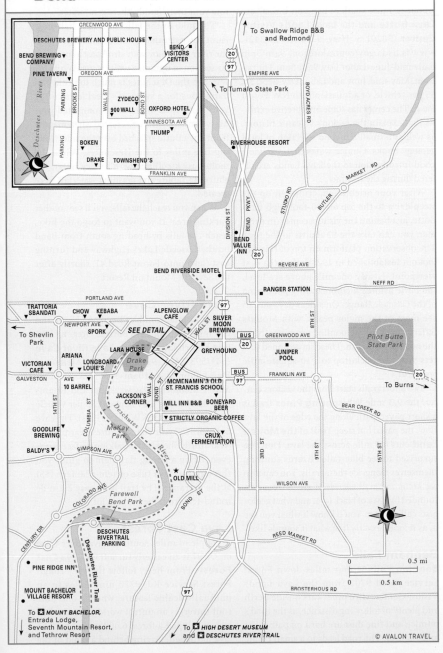

Text labels within the map:

GREENWOOD AVE
DESCHUTES BREWERY AND PUBLIC HOUSE ▼
BEND BREWING ▼ COMPANY
PINE TAVERN ▼
BEND VISITORS CENTER
Deschutes River
PARKING
BROOKS ST
WALL ST
OREGON AVE
ZYDECO
900 WALL
BOND ST
OXFORD HOTEL
MINNESOTA AVE
PARKING
THUMP ▼
BOKEN ▼
DRAKE ▼
TOWNSHEND'S ▼
FRANKLIN AVE

To Swallow Ridge B&B and Redmond
20
97
EMPIRE AVE
BOYD ACRES RD
To Tumalo State Park
RIVERHOUSE RESORT
STUDIO RD
BUTLER
MARKET RD
DIVISION ST
BEND PKWY
BEND VALUE INN
20
REVERE AVE
BEND RIVERSIDE MOTEL ●
NEFF RD
PORTLAND AVE
97
RANGER STATION ■
TRATTORIA ▼ SBANDATI
CHOW ▼ KEBABA ▼
ALPENGLOW CAFE ▼
SILVER MOON BREWING ▼
18TH ST
Pilot Butte State Park
NEWPORT AVE
SPORK ▼
WALL ST
SEE DETAIL
GREENWOOD AVE
BUS 20
To Shevlin Park
ARIANA ▼
LONGBOARD ▼ LOUIE'S
LARA HOUSE ●
Drake Park
GREYHOUND ●
JUNIPER POOL ●
VICTORIAN CAFÉ ▼
AVE
10 BARREL ▼
BUS 97
FRANKLIN AVE
20
GALVESTON
14TH ST
COLUMBIA ST
JACKSON'S CORNER ▼
WALL ST
BOND ST
McMENAMIN'S OLD ST. FRANCIS SCHOOL ●
To Burns
Deschutes River
MILL INN B&B ●
BONEYARD BEER ▼
BEAR CREEK RD
GOODLIFE BREWING ▼
McKay Park
▼ STRICTLY ORGANIC COFFEE
3RD ST
16TH ST
15TH ST
BALDY'S ▼
SIMPSON AVE
CRUX FERMENTATION ▼
Farewell Bend Park
★ OLD MILL
WILSON AVE
COLORADO AVE
BOND ST
CENTURY DR
DESCHUTES RIVER TRAIL PARKING
Deschutes River Trail
REED MARKET RD
0   0.5 mi
0   0.5 km
PINE RIDGE INN ●
97
MOUNT BACHELOR VILLAGE RESORT ●
BROSTERHOUS RD
To 🎿 MOUNT BACHELOR, Entrada Lodge, Seventh Mountain Resort, and Tethrow Resort
To 🎿 HIGH DESERT MUSEUM and 🎿 DESCHUTES RIVER TRAIL
© AVALON TRAVEL

Lava Lands Visitor Center and Lava Butte

About 11 miles south of Bend on U.S. 97 are **Lava Butte** and the **Lava Lands Visitor Center** (58201 S. Hwy. 97, 541/593-2421, www.fs.usda.gov/centraloregon, 9am-5pm daily mid-June-Labor Day, 9am-5pm Thurs.-Mon. May-mid-June and Labor Day-Sept. 30, $5 per vehicle, or admission with NW Forest Pass). The center has some interpretive exhibits that explain the region's volcanic history, as well as a small but good selection of local geology books. Guided walks that provide a good introduction to the Lava Lands are offered during the summer.

After your orientation, cruise on up the steep drive to the top of 500-foot-high Lava Butte, just behind the visitors center (in summer, you can take the $2 shuttle to the top). The observation platform on top of this fire lookout (established in 1928) offers the best viewpoint. Nearly one mile above sea level, the butte affords a commanding panorama of the Cascade Range. On a clear day you can see most of the major peaks, with Mounts Jefferson and Hood looming prominently on the northern horizon. These snowcapped turrets form the backdrop to a 10-square-mile lava field.

Two short trails start from the visitors center: the 0.3-mile **Whispering Pines** trail is a short paved path along the edge of the lava flow; the paved but steep **Trail of the Molten Land** cuts 0.5 mile across the lava. Don't be surprised to see blue-tailed lizards sunning themselves alongside these trails. You can also see *kipukas,* small islands of green trees surrounded by a sea of black lava, and what geologists call splatter. You'll know it when you see it, as it looks exactly like what it sounds like.

Benham Falls

Benham Falls is four miles down Forest Service Road 9702 from the Lava Lands Visitor Center. Give other cars a wide berth and plenty of following distance, as the road's pumice and fine dust are hard on paint jobs and engines. The road leads to a small picnic area in a grove of old-growth ponderosa pines on the bank of the Deschutes River. Be sure to tote your own liquids; there is no water.

The hike to the falls is an easy half-mile jaunt downstream. Take the footbridge across the river and enjoy your stroll past a spectacular section of untamed white water. While the water in the Deschutes is much too cold and dangerous for a swim, it's ideal for soaking your feet a little after you've completed your hike. Benham Falls was created when magma from Lava Butte splashed over the side, flowing five miles to the Deschutes. When the molten rock collided with the icy water, the churning rapids and crashing waterfall were created.

When you reach the falls, you'll see another parking area. If you want to forgo the hike, reach the falls by heading south from Bend on the Cascade Lakes Highway and turning east (left) onto Forest Road 41, shortly after the Seventh Mountain Resort.

Lava River Cave

About 12 miles south of Bend on U.S. 97 and one mile south of Lava Butte is Oregon's longest known lava tube, the **Lava River Cave** (541/593-2421, 9am-5pm daily Memorial Day-Labor Day, 10am-5pm Thurs.-Mon. May 1-Memorial Day weekend, and 10-am-5pm daily Labor Day-Sept. 30, $5 per vehicle or admission with NW Forest Pass). The cave is a cool 42°F year-round, so dress warmly and wear sturdy shoes—the walking surface is uneven. Bring a strong flashlight to guide you through this lava tube or rent a lantern ($5) at the entrance. The trail is an easy 2.4-mile round-trip from the parking lot.

Lava Cast Forest

A couple of miles south of Lava River Cave on US 97 is an easterly turnoff for **Lava Cast Forest.** From here, follow the very rough Forest Service Rd. 9720 nine miles to an unusual volcanic feature, where a one-mile trail traverses an unreal world created when lava enveloped a forest 6,000 years ago. The lava hardened, leaving behind a mold of the

Tumalo Falls

once-living trees, much like how the eruption of Mount Vesuvius in Italy left casts of Pompeii's residents.

Tumalo Falls

About 12 miles west of downtown, the 89-foot **Tumalo Falls** plummets down a sheer cliff. Although the falls are visible from the parking area, a short walk leads to better views, and a slightly longer walk takes you to the top of the falls. From here, follow the trail up Tumalo Creek, where there are a couple of smaller waterfalls. Several other hiking and mountain biking trails leave from the area; it's possible to make a loop, but part of the loop falls in an area where the watershed is protected and dogs and bikes are prohibited.

From downtown, head west on Franklin Street, skirt Drake Park, and continue west on Galveston. At the traffic circle, continue west; the street name changes to Skyliners Road. After about 10 miles, follow the signs for the falls and turn onto Tumalo Road. The last couple of miles are on a good gravel road.

Be sure to bring your Northwest Forest Pass or $5 to purchase a day pass at the trailhead.

Pilot Butte

On the east side of Bend is **Pilot Butte,** a 511-foot-high volcanic remnant. A road and a trail to the top offer a sweeping view of nine snowcapped Cascade peaks and their green forests. It is also pretty at night, with the twinkling lights of the city below and the stars above. Full moons are especially awesome, illuminating the ghostly forms of the mountains as icy light-blue silhouettes. The scent of juniper and sage adds to the visual splendor. Bring water if you're hiking.

SPORTS AND RECREATION
Winter Sports
★ MOUNT BACHELOR

The Pacific Northwest's largest and most complete ski area is **Mount Bachelor** (541/382-2607 information, 541/382-7888 hours and snow report, www.mtbachelor.com, $84 adult 19-64, $71 teen 13-18 or senior 65-69, $49 senior over age 70 or children 6-12; arrivals after noon pay about $15 less). Located 22 miles southwest of Bend on Century Drive, this venue's 12 ski lifts, including seven high-speed quads, and trails that range from beginner to expert make for some of the most popular skiing in the state. This is the winter training grounds for the U.S. Olympic Ski Team. If you're at the other end of the expertise spectrum, note that Bachelor's beginners' lift, the Carrousel, is free.

The Summit Express lift takes you right to the top of the mountain, yielding great sunny-day views of the neighboring Cascade peaks. You may also see puffs of steam coming off the slopes, which serve as reminders that Bachelor is a still-kicking volcanic peak. Although central Oregon is known for its clear skies, the truth is that storms do pass through quite regularly. This is a good thing for skiers and snowboarders, who count on the snow piling up deep enough on Bachelor for the ski season to extend into late spring, but it can mean skiing or boarding in high wind and flying snow pellets. Conditions are often best in late winter and early spring.

Expert skiers and boarders should ride the Northwest Express lift (a high-speed quad) to the mountain's Northwest Territory, where trees and bowls keep skills honed. The Summit lift is a must, both for the views and the trails, which include some blue runs. Another good area is the part of the mountain served by the Outback Express; runs here are mostly blue. Snowboarders and freestyle skiers head to the mile-long terrain park at Bachelors Park or the 400-foot-long super pipe.

With a top elevation over 9,000 feet and steady northwest airflow, skiing here can run into the early summer. However, avoid skiing after 1pm in May and June, when conditions become slushy. If you must ski then, choose the west-side snowfields, which hold up better in the late afternoon light. Finally, while there may not be enough snow to ski in summer, you can still ride the chairlift to the peak of this volcano for an unsurpassed view of the surrounding countryside.

Or, skip an afternoon of skiing and join **Trail of Dreams Sled Dog Rides** (Sunrise Lodge parking area, 541/382-1709 or 800/829-2442) for a one-hour sled dog ride ($85-99 for anyone over 80 pounds, $40 for anyone under 80 pounds) with Jerry Scdoris and his daughter Rachael, an Iditarod finisher. A daylong tour goes to Elk Lake and costs $550 for two people.

Even when ski season is over, **chairlift rides** (541/382-1709, 11am-4pm Mon.-Thurs. 11am-4pm and 5pm-8pm Fri.-Sun. July-Labor Day, $18 adults, $15 seniors, $12 children ages 6-12, less for evening rides) give visitors a chance to ride (roughly 15 minutes) from the West Village base area to the Pine Marten Lodge perched at 7,775 feet, with tremendous views of Cascade lakes and peaks. Sunset dinners at the Pine Marten Lodge restaurant are offered on Friday, Saturday, and Sunday (5pm-8pm). On summer days, a U.S. Forest Service ranger gives **interpretive talks** on the deck of the lodge (11:30am and 1:30 and 3:30pm daily, free with lift ticket).

Unlike most ski resorts of its size, Mount Bachelor has no slope-side lodging. The closest lodging is down the hill at the Seventh Mountain Resort. Sunriver is also about a 20-minute drive.

snow-capped Mount Bachelor

CROSS-COUNTRY SKIING

Just west of downtown Bend on the road to Mount Bachelor, **Virginia Meissner** and **Swampy Lakes** are excellent cross-country ski areas. The Sno-Park area at Virginia Meissner is about 13 miles west of town; Swampy Lakes is about two miles up the road from Meissner. The two trail systems join up and together access more than 25 miles of ski trails dotted with strategically placed warming huts. There are also snowshoe trails leading from each Sno-Park. Dogs and motorized vehicles are prohibited at both Virginia Meissner and Swampy Lakes. Sno-Park permits are required. In the summer, these trails are good for mountain biking.

Up the mountain at **Dutchman Flat Sno-Park,** what you gain in elevation and early-season snowpack you'll lose in peacefulness. This Sno-Park, almost directly across from the turnoff to Mount Bachelor's Sunrise Lodge, has trails for both skiers and snowmobilers and can be extremely busy on weekends and holidays. Snowmobilers can use this spot to access roughly 150 miles of trails; skiers find about 19 miles of trails, including some fairly challenging ones.

A trail system at **Edison Butte** is a good alternative for cross-country skiers with dogs.

It's south on Forest Road No. 45 from the Cascades Lakes Highway. Travel four miles to the trailhead; snowmobilers access trails from the same parking area, which can also be very busy on snowy weekends.

Hiking and Biking

The area in and around Bend boasts a rich network of hiking and mountain biking trails, ranging from short barrier-free interpretive walks in town to strenuous wilderness treks. The best hiking is on trails accessed by the Cascade Lakes Highway. Snow can lock up many of these high-elevation trails until as late as June or July, so you'll want to inquire locally before heading out fall-spring. The offices of the **Deschutes National Forest** (63095 Deschutes Market Rd., 541/383-5300, www.fs.usda.gov/centraloregon) can provide information. Note that parking at most trailheads in the national forests requires a **Northwest Forest Pass** (www.fs.fed.us/r6/passespermits, $5 one-day, $30 one-year), available at most outdoor stores and resorts as well as at trailheads.

For mountain bikers, the **Central Oregon Trail Alliance** (http://cotamtb.com) is a good resource. This volunteer group works with the Forest Service, the Bureau of Land

The Bend area has an excellent cross-country ski trail network.

Management, and other land managers to enhance mountain biking in and around Bend. Their website briefly describes area trails and shows current conditions.

★ DESCHUTES RIVER TRAIL

The best thing about Bend's boom years was the development of the **Deschutes River Trail** (download a map at www.bendparksandrec.org). The trail, which will ultimately run 19 miles from Tumalo State Park north of town to the Meadow Picnic Area near Widgi Creek Golf Course, offers excellent river access to walkers, runners, and cyclists (mountain bikes or cruisers are best). Pick up the trail downtown in Drake Park or in the Old Mill District, from Farewell Bend Park on the east side of the river (lots of parking on Reed Market Rd.), or from the Les Schwab Amphitheater on the west side. The trail is a patchwork of paved and unpaved surfaces.

If you want to keep going when you reach the trail's southern terminus, hop up onto Century Drive and head past the golf course and the Seventh Mountain Resort to the turnoff for Dillon Falls. This road will quickly reconnect you with riverside hiking and mountain biking trails that go all the way to Benham Falls. This section of the trail runs 9.1 miles through riverside pine forests and lava flows. It is actually a set of three parallel trails—one each dedicated to hikers, cyclists, and horseback riders—beginning about seven miles southwest of Bend. To get here via the road, follow Century Drive southwest, then turn south onto Forest Road 41 (Conklin Rd.), which has several access points to the trails at **Lava Island, Big Eddy, Aspen, Dillon, Slough, Benham West,** and **Benham Falls** day-use areas. The season is spring-fall, although most of the trails may remain open in winter during years with low snowfall. A Northwest Forest Pass is required for parking along Road 41, and dogs must be leashed. Four trail sections—at Big Eddy Rapids, Dillon Falls, Benham Falls West, and Benham Falls Picnic Area—are wheelchair accessible. They're

Trails run for miles along the Deschutes River; this stretch is below the Seventh Mountain Resort.

surfaced with crushed gravel and are of intermediate difficulty.

SHEVLIN PARK

About five miles west of town, **Shevlin Park** lures both hikers and mountain bikers with an easy five-mile loop through the pines along the Tumalo Creek gorge and along a ridge burned in the Awbrey Hall fire of August 1990. It's open year-round with no fees for parking or access. Several picnic areas offer quiet spots for lunch. To get there, follow Greenwood Avenue west from U.S. 97 in Bend; Greenwood becomes Newport Avenue after a few blocks, then changes again to Shevlin Road as it angles northwest.

PHIL'S TRAIL

A trail close to town that's very popular with mountain bikers is **Phil's Trail,** an eight-mile segment of a larger network of eponymous bike trails (Kent's, Paul's, Jimmy's, etc.—named for the riders who established or popularized them) among the canyon and butte country just west of Bend. Difficulty is generally easy to moderate, with some steep climbs to challenge your lower gears the farther west you ride. To get to the trailhead, head 2.5 miles west on Skyliners Road, then turn left on the first paved road to the south and travel 0.5 mile. A little farther west, Roads 4610 and 300 also intersect the network. A **Northwest Forest Pass** (www.fs.fed.us/r6/passespermits, $5 one-day, $30 one-year) is required for parking.

MOUNT BACHELOR SUMMIT TRAIL

Farther afield, Mount Bachelor beckons hikers in the summer and fall to walk the four-mile **Mount Bachelor Summit Trail** (2-3 hours one-way) to the mountain's top. This is one of the easiest and safest routes to the top of any Cascade peak, requiring no climbing skills or equipment. An even easier way to reach the top is via the chairlift at the ski area, which runs during the off-season.

To get to the trailhead, follow signs for the upper (east) parking lot at the ski area. The trail begins at the western end of the lot and climbs to a forested ridge on the mountain's northeastern side to the upper station of the first section of the ski lift. From there, the trail climbs steeply through the timberline area and continues up to a talus ridge leading to the mountain station of the second lift segment. It's a short hike from this lift station to the summit.

Plaques at viewpoints along the way identify lakes and mountains visible from this 9,000-foot vantage point, including Diamond Peak to the south and the Three Sisters, Broken Top, Mount Jefferson, and sometimes even Mount Hood, 100 miles away, to the north. The hike involves an elevation gain of 2,600 feet. Mountain bikes are not recommended on the trail.

BIKE RENTALS AND TOURS

Rent a mountain bike at **Pine Mountain Sports** (255 SW Century Dr., 541/385-8080, www.pinemountainsports.com, from $50 for 4 hours, $75 for 24 hours). Upstairs from Pine Mountain are the offices for **Cog Wild** (255 SW Century Dr., 541/385-7002, http://cog-wild.com), which leads mountain bike tours that include short family cruises ($75 adults, $60 children ages 12 and under), vigorous daylong tours (about $1100), and multiday trips (about $700-800).

If your bicycling style is a little more easygoing, rent a cruiser (or a tandem, kid's bike, trailer, or tag-along) or a multi-passenger surrey from **Wheel Fun Rentals** (603 SW Mill A Dr., 541/408-4568, 10am-sunset daily, $10-50 per hour) near the Deschutes River Trail in the Old Mill District.

Fishing

With over 100 mountain lakes and the Deschutes River within an hour's drive of Bend, your piscatorial pleasures will be satisfied in central Oregon. The high lakes offer rainbow, brown, and brook trout as well as landlocked Atlantic and coho salmon. The Deschutes River is famed for its red-sided rainbow trout and summer steelhead. Not surprisingly, the best fishing is outside of the Bend metropolitan area near Sunriver, Cascade Lakes, and Prineville. If you're stuck in town, head over to the Old Mill District, where you'll find the **Confluence Fly Shop** (375 SW Powerhouse Dr., 804/221-7748, www.confluenceflyshop.com) and a clever 18-station fly-fishing course on the edge of the Deschutes (think miniature golf with a fly rod). The fly shop teams up with **Deep Canyon Outfitters** (541/323-3007, www.deepcanyonoutfitters.com), a well-established guide service.

A full-service pro shop with everything for the fly fisher is **The Patient Angler** (822 SE 3rd St., 541/389-6208, www.patientangler.com), where you can stock up on information as well as gear; a guide service is also part of this business.

Deschutes River Outfitters (541/760-0956, www.deschutesoutfitters.com) features float trips, lake walk-in trips, and steelhead fishing trips that can be customized into single-day or multiday excursions. They have so many different packages and rates that it's best to refer to their outstanding website for specifics.

Floating and Paddling

You can either sit down or stand up to paddle through town on a relatively quiet stretch of the Deschutes. Put in at either **McKay Park** (166 SW Shevlin Hixon Dr., on the river's west bank) or **Farewell Bend Park** (on the east bank along Reed Market Dr.) and take out at Drake Park, where a **Ride the River shuttle bus** (www.cascadeseasttransit.com, 11:30am-6:30pm Fri.-Mon. July 5-Labor Day, $1.50 for one ride, $3 all day) will ferry you back to the starting point. Rent a kayak ($40 for 2 hours), canoe ($50 for 2 hours), float tube ($10 for 2 hours), or stand-up paddleboard ($40 for 2 hours) at **Tumalo Creek Kayak & Canoe** (805 SW Industrial Way, 541/317-9407, www.tumalocreek.com, 9am-7pm Mon.-Sat., 9am-6pm Sun.), where you can also sign up for paddling lessons.

Float the river on a specially designed river tube available for rent from **Sun Country Tours** (541/382-6277 or 800/883-8842, www.suncountrytours.com, $15 adults, $10 kids 12 and under, 10am-5:30pm daily). Find the rental location at **Riverbend Park** (799 SW Columbia St.).

Golf

Widgi Creek (18707 Century Dr., 541/382-4449, www.widgi.com, $29-79, reservations strongly recommended), just north of the Seventh Mountain Resort, was designed by Robert Muir Graves. The course's strategically placed trees, lakes, and sand traps have given this place the reputation as the "mean green" golf course of central Oregon. The 18 holes are mentioned in the same breath as Sunriver's North Course and Black Butte's Glaze Meadows—good company indeed.

Close to town along the Deschutes River, the hillside **River's Edge Golf Course** (3075 N. Business Rte. 97, 541/389-2828, www.riverhouse.com, $38-59) is a convenient and pretty alternative.

A couple of products of Bend's boom years are the lavish semiprivate golf courses at **Pronghorn** (65600 Pronghorn Club Dr., 866/372-1009, www.pronghornclub.com, $145-210), which has courses by Jack Nicklaus and Tom Fazio, where the eighth hole features a lava canyon; and **Tetherow** (61240 Skyline Ranch Rd., 541/388-2582, www.tetherow.com, $145-175), a links-style course designed

Rent a paddleboard and take it to the river in Bend's Old Mill District.

by Davis McLay Kidd, known for his work at Bandon Dunes.

sleigh rides are available, but must be reserved in advance.

Gyms

One of the finest aquatic and fitness centers east of the Cascades is found at **Juniper Aquatic and Fitness Center** (800 NE 6th St., 541/389-7665, www.bendparksandrec. org, single visits $6-7). Part of the Bend Metro Park and Recreation District, the center is located in 20-acre Juniper Park and features two indoor pools and a large 40-yard outdoor pool providing plenty of space for splashing around. Serious swimmers can enjoy frequent lap swims and adults-only swim times daily. An aerobics room, weight room, group exercise classes, jogging trail, and tennis court offer other exercise options. A sauna and a whirlpool tub provide you with yet another way to sweat it out.

Horseback Riding

Saddle up at the **Seventh Mountain Resort Stables** (18575 SW Century Dr., 541/693-9732, www.seventhmountain.com, Mar.-Oct.), where kids age 2-6 can take pony rides ($10) while older folks can head out on guided trail rides along the Deschutes River (starting at $35 for half an hour). During the winter,

Rafting

The Deschutes River offers some of the finest white water in central Oregon. The numerous lava flows have diverted the river to create tumultuous rapids that attract raft, kayak, and canoe enthusiasts. From short rafting trips to multiday adventures, you'll find many options available to enjoy the exciting Deschutes River. You will need swimwear, footwear, sunblock, and sunglasses for all rafting trips. It's also advisable to have a set of dry clothes handy at the end of the voyage.

The prime spot for daylong trips is actually the Lower Deschutes, out of the town of Maupin, but there are a couple of spots close to Bend that'll satisfy that urge to be in the river on a hot summer day.

A few miles upstream from town, the Big Eddy section of the river offers a few whitewater thrills. Several outfitters lead trips on this section of the Deschutes: The **Seventh Mountain River Company** (18575 SW Century Dr., 541/693-9124, http://seventhmountainriverco.com, $43) offers a 1.5-hour raft trip down a three-mile section of the Deschutes that takes in some Class I-IV

Tetherow has luxurious accommodations and a golf course.

rapids. With names like Pinball Alley and the Souse Hole, you can be assured of a good ride! Transfer between the inn and the river is included.

Sun Country Tours (531 SW 13th St., 541/382-6277 or 800/883-8842, www.suncountrytours.com, $53 adults, $46 children ages 6-12) runs a 1.25-hour three-mile Big Eddy Thriller that takes in Class I-III rapids on the Deschutes River.

ENTERTAINMENT AND EVENTS

Downtown Bend's striking art deco moderne **Tower Theatre** (835 NW Wall St., 541/317-0700, www.towertheatre.org) hosts music, films, and other performances. This is a good venue to see some relatively big-name acoustic musicians.

Bend's other main music venue, the **Les Schwab Amphitheater** (541/322-9383, www.bendconcerts.com), is on the edge of the Old Mill District, on Shevlin-Hixon Drive between Simpson Avenue and Columbia Street. This is the place to see performers such as Pink Martini, Bonnie Raitt, or Michael Franti. It's also the site of events such as the Bend Brewfest.

Festivals and Events

Quintessentially Bend, the mid-May **Pole Pedal Paddle** (541/388-0002, www.pppbend.com) is a relay or, for the exceptionally tough, a single-person event that starts at the top of Mount Bachelor and ends at the Les Schwab Amphitheater in Bend's Old Mill District. Between the two points, participants downhill ski, cross-country ski, bike, run, and canoe or kayak to the finish line. Although some participants take the event quite seriously, most enter in a spirit of fun.

The **Bend Summer Festival** brings out food booths, Oregon wine and microbrews, art exhibits, and live music all in one big downtown block party the second weekend in July. Contact the **Bend Visitors Information Bureau** (541/382-8048, www.c3events.com) for more details.

In mid-August, the Les Schwab Amphitheater (Shevlin-Hixon Dr.) is home to the **Bend Brewfest** (541/322-9383, www.bendbrewfest.com), with over 80 craft beers available for tasting.

ACCOMMODATIONS

Bend is the largest full-fledged resort town in the state. On holidays or ski weekends, it's hard to find a room if you don't have reservations, although during the shoulder seasons of spring and fall, rooms and deals often abound. For a comprehensive list of motels, see www.visitbend.org.

One longtime Bend favorite is in transition. In 2013, the **Seventh Mountain Resort** (18575 SW Century Dr., 541/382-8711 or 800/452-6810, www.seventhmountain.com) was sold to Wyndam, which planned to add it to its stable of WorldMark timeshare developments. Since many of the studios and condo units at Seventh Mountain had been privately owned, the conversion is not immediate and seamless. Wyndam is converting the resort to timeshares block by block, and at the time of updating, both timeshares and the original resort units are both available. If you want to stay in a great location (the closest place you'll find to Mount Bachelor with trails to the Deschutes), it's worth checking the website or looking at vrbo.com to see if any units are available for rent.

$50-100

Most of the least-expensive motels are along 3rd Street; except during busy weekends in the middle of the summer, you can just drive the street to check out these older, basic, but perfectly adequate lodgings. One reasonable bet is the **Bend Value Inn** (2346 NE Division St., 541/382-6222, www.bendvalueinn.com, $59-69), which has microwaves and fridges in the rooms.

Just south of downtown, on the edge of the Old Mill District, is the **Mill Inn B&B** (642 NW Colorado Ave., 541/389-9198 or 877/748-1200, www.millinn.com, $95-165). Originally an early 1900s hotel and boardinghouse, it has been remodeled into a 10-bedroom inn. Some rooms have a bath down the hall, but many have private baths, and some rooms adjoin to accommodate families. All rates include a full breakfast, and access to a washer and dryer, barbecue grill, hot tub, and "cocktail deck."

$100-150

The **Riverhouse Hotel** (3075 Business Rte. 97 N., 541/389-3111 or 866/453-4480, www.riverhouse.com, $128-309) is situated along the Deschutes River at the north end of town. Although this hotel features a conference center and other business amenities, it's also a good place for vacationers. The rooms are well kept and equipped with wireless Internet access, microwaves, and refrigerators. Pets are permitted, and guests have access to indoor and outdoor pools, an exercise room, and tennis courts. There's also a golf course on-site.

On 3rd Street not far from downtown, **Three Sisters Inn** (721 NE 3rd St., 541/382-4949, www.bendthreesistersinn.com, $134-219) is a tidy place with free breakfast buffet, a pool, and family suites.

Up the road toward Mount Bachelor, find the ★ **Entrada Lodge** (19221 Century Dr., 541/382-4080, www.entradalodge.com, $109-149), a rather standard motel in an exceptionally nice setting. It's nestled in among the ponderosa pines at a nexus of hiking and mountain bike trails that can take you toward town or down to the Deschutes River (about a 20-minute walk). A small pool, a large hot tub, a rather basic breakfast buffet, and in-room microwaves and refrigerators are the amenities. It's a good place to bring your dog . . . and a pleasant place to take dog walks. (Note: wireless Internet is difficult to connect to at the Entrada.)

$150-200

Pine Ridge Inn (1200 SW Century Dr., 800/600-4095, www.pineridgeinn.com, $179-429) is a small, romantic inn above the Deschutes River near the foot of Century Drive, not too far from downtown. Guest rooms are spacious (mini-suites and larger suites) and well decorated.

★ **McMenamins Old St. Francis School** (700 NW Bond St., 541/382-5174 or 877/661-4228, www.mcmenamins.com, $185-245) is right downtown but is in its own little world, surrounded by gardens with quiet sitting areas. Rooms in this historic 1936 Catholic school are nicely appointed with televisions, telephones, wireless Internet access, hair dryers, private bathrooms (showers only),

Stay in downtown Bend at McMenamin's Old Saint Francis School.

BEND AND CENTRAL OREGON

BEND

and comfy bathrobes to wear on the way over to the wonderful Turkish-style soaking pool. In addition to the standard rooms, several cottages ($185-395) are available. This is one of the few McMenamins hotels that allows pets. Guests also have free admission to movies at the school theater and easy access to the four bars on the premises; we recommend the fire pit outside O'Kane's pub, located behind the main hotel in a former garage.

★ **Mount Bachelor Village Resort** (19717 Mount Bachelor Dr., 541/452-9846 or 800/547-5204, www.mtbachelorvillage.com, $159-425) is a couple of miles from downtown, just off Century Drive. Some of the units, which include a wide variety of condos and hotel room suites, overlook the Deschutes River. The guest rooms are some of the nicest in Bend. It's easy for guests to get onto the Deschutes River Trail, and they can also use the adjacent Athletic Club of Bend, the most upscale gym in town.

Right downtown, the **DoubleTree by Hilton** (300 NW Franklin Ave., 541/317-9292, $199-239) is a good choice for business travelers or anyone who wants spacious guest rooms, although some of the "suites" don't exactly fit the usual definition of that term (they don't have separate rooms for sleeping).

Over $200

Downtown, the gorgeous ★ **Oxford Hotel** (10 NW Minnesota Ave., 541/382-8436 or 877/440-8436, www.oxfordhotelbend.com, $368-429) is a stylish and ecofriendly boutique hotel in a great location. From the subtle tree motif decor to the French press coffee (locally roasted and grounds composted), everything is designed to make you feel good about relaxing in luxury. The latex Natura beds are comfortable, hypoallergenic, and breathable; even the pull-out sofa beds have Tempur-Pedic mattresses. All rooms have a microwave and fridge and suites have a full kitchen, including dishwasher. At seven stories, the Oxford is Bend's tallest building, and the top-floor fitness center has some of the best views this side of the Bachelor summit

chairlift. It also has a steam room, a sauna, and a saline hot tub. Guests should inquire about gaining access to private golf courses in the area. Since the Oxford opened in 2010, this block of Minnesota Avenue has come alive with coffee shops, restaurants, and galleries, including a good restaurant in the hotel's basement. And, if you're willing to pay a fairly stiff ($55) fee, your pet will be enthusiastically welcomed.

Close to downtown, Drake Park, and Mirror Pond is **Lara House** (640 NW Congress St., 541/388-4064 or 800/766-4064, www.larahouse.com, $199-275). This large three-story house was built in 1910 and features six large bedrooms with private baths. All rooms are furnished with antiques and reflect individual grace and charm. A delicious homemade breakfast is served in the bright solarium overlooking the colorful gardens and Drake Park.

A ten-minute drive from downtown and bordering the Deschutes National Forest, the ★ **Tetherow Lodge** ($279-404) is a new and luxurious hotel set above the links-style course at Tetherow Golf Club. The rooms are large and beautifully furnished, most with a fireplace, spa-like bathroom, balcony or patio, and sumptuous bedding. Though the setting and exteriors feature a western lodge look, the rooms themselves are coolly modern and sophisticated—anything but woodsy. The lodge also features a restaurant and bar, while hotel guests get special pricing on greens fees.

Camping

With the Three Sisters Wilderness and the Deschutes National Forest flanking Bend, there are many wonderful spots to enjoy camping out under the stars. But for those who want to stay closer to civilization, **Tumalo State Park** (64120 O.B. Riley Rd., 541/382-3586, 800/551-6949, or 800/452-5687, www.oregonstateparks.org, year-round, $21 tents, $31 hookups, $44 yurts) is convenient and not overly urbanized. This park is located five miles northwest of Bend, off of U.S. 20 along the banks of the Deschutes River, and offers 54 tent sites, 23 sites for RVs up to 35 feet long, and showers.

A couple of decent RV parks can be found near Bend. **Crown Villa** (60801 Brosterhous Rd., 541/388-1131 or 866/500-5300, http://crownvillarvresort.com, $63-84), southeast of town, is exceptionally well maintained and has lots of amenities.

FOOD

The scenery around Bend feeds the soul, and restaurants here do the rest. While area restaurants run the gamut from fast-food franchises to elegant dinner houses, many travelers also want something between those extremes. Some alternatives for every budget are listed below.

Bakeries and Cafés

Downtown coffee lovers head to **Thump** (25 NW Minnesota Ave., 541/388-0226, www.thumpcoffee.com, 6am-5:30pm Mon.-Fri., 7am-5:30pm Sat., 7am-4:30pm Sun.) for Stumptown brew, good pastries, and friendly conversation. If you'd rather sip a cup of tea, try **Townshend's** (835 NW Bond St., 541/312-2001, www.townshendstea.com, 9am-10pm Mon.-Thurs., 9am-11pm Fri.-Sat., 9am-9pm Sun.), which serves high-quality teas in an atmosphere that's more hip than stuffy. South of downtown, near the Old Mill District, **Strictly Organic Coffee** (6 SW Bond St., 541/330-6061, www.strictlyorganic.com, 6am-7pm Mon.-Wed. and Fri.-Sat., 6am-8pm Thurs., 7am-6pm Sun.) is a great place for coffee or tea and a snack. They have a second location in the Old Mill shopping center.

Ask Siri to help you find the tiny ★ **Sparrow Bakery** (50 SE Scott St., 541/330-6321, www.thesparrowbakery.net, 541/330-6321, 7am-2pm Mon.-Sat., 8am-2pm Sun., sandwiches $7.50-8.50). Although it's just off the Bend Parkway near the Colorado Street exit, it can be tricky to locate this gem of a shop. The cardamom-scented "ocean rolls" make the search worthwhile, as do the fantastic sandwiches, which can take surprisingly long to make. If the weather's nice, that's no problem; a patio has tables and is surrounded by local artisans' studios and shops. And if you can't get here, find Sparrow's pastries downtown at both Thump and Townshend's.

American

★ **Chow** (1110 Newport Ave., 541/728-0256, www.chowbend.com, 7am-2pm daily, $7-14), in a charming little house across from the Newport Market, is a deservedly popular breakfast spot. Chow's aim is to keep their business sustainable and true to the food, and this care is evident: one of the top picks on the menu is always the locavore omelet, made with whatever is in season. Lunch sandwiches are inventive, and lunch isn't limited to sandwiches and salads; there's also a daily interpretation of mac and cheese. In nice weather the deck seating is great.

Just outside of downtown, diners linger at the **Victorian Café** (1404 NW Galveston Ave., 541/382-6411, www.victoriancafebend.com, 7am-2pm daily, $4-16), one of the few breakfast and lunch joints that has a full bar. Bloody Mary or no, breakfasts here are an extravaganza; for a real treat, order any of the eggs Benedict options.

Drop by ★ **Jackson's Corner** (845 NW Delaware Ave., 541/647-2198, www.jacksonscornerbend.com, 7am-9pm daily, $6-17) almost any time of day for a casual meal. The pizzas are excellent, as are the sandwiches and the salads. It's a casual neighborhood place where you order at the counter and may possibly share a big table with others. The side yard has a place for kids to play and adults to lounge at picnic tables.

Stop by **Longboard Louie's** (1254 NW Galveston Ave., 541/383-2449, www.longboardlouies.com, 7am-close Mon.-Fri., 8am-close Sat.-Sun., $3-10) for an easygoing lunch or casual dinner on the deck. The seafood tacos are excellent (get the halibut if it's in season).

Set on a corner in the heart of downtown, ★ **900 Wall** (900 NW Wall St., 541/323-6295, www.900wall.com, 3pm-close daily, $15-29) fairly pulses with energy, and the food is delicious and reasonably priced. Try a wood-fired pizza (the prosciutto and arugula pizza is drizzled with truffle oil and absolutely delicious) or some high-class comfort food, such as a pork chops or flatiron steak, prepared with just enough inventiveness to keep them interesting. The selection of wines by the glass is huge and well chosen. During summer, the restaurant is usually open until about 10pm weeknights, 11:30pm on weekends; in the winter it usually closes a bit earlier.

Drake (801 NW Wall St., 541/306-3366, http://drakebend.com, 11am-9:30pm Mon.-Thurs., 11am-10pm Fri.-Sat., 11am-9pm Sun., $14-30) offers upscale comfort food in a bright and airy dining room. While the menu seems to offer many classic American dishes, look again: the fish-and-chips features ale-battered Pacific cod with dried cherry coleslaw and the cheeseburger can be accessorized with roasted bone marrow or pear kimchi. More fine dining options are also offered: a grilled pork chop comes with coconut sweet potatoes, charred pineapple, and chimichurri.

International

Spork (937 NW Newport Ave., 541/390-0946, 11am-9pm Mon.-Thurs., 11am-10pm Fri.-Sat., $3-12) started out as a food cart, and now, as a brick-and-mortar restaurant, it retains a hip and casual atmosphere. There are no reservations, and you order at the counter without a table assignment—but it always seems like a table opens up before the food arrives. The food is a small-plates selection of delicious Asian and Latin American dishes, with excellent tacos, Chinese sweet and spicy pork noodles, and amazing spicy fried chicken with sambal sauce.

Barbecue

Find shockingly good barbecue on the road to Mount Bachelor at **Baldy's** (235 SW Century Dr., 541/385-7427, www.baldysbbq.com, 11am-9pm daily, $8-24). Be warned: If you're a rib-lover, once you eat here you'll be spoiled for any other restaurant in town. If ribs aren't your thing, the hickory-smoked chicken and the pulled pork are also delicious. A good selection of local beers is on tap. If you're headed out of town toward Burns, stop at the eastside Baldy's, near the Safeway (2670 NE Hwy. 20, 541/388-4227).

Italian

Head west of downtown to find ★ **Trattoria Sbandati** (1444 NW College Way, 541/306-6825, www.trattoriasbandati.com, 5pm-close Tues.-Sat., $14-30, reservations recommended), a family-run Italian restaurant that manages to be simultaneously romantic and homey. Go with the intention of making a night out of it; this is not a dine-and-dash spot. Start with a salad of gorgonzola and golden beets, move on to homemade pasta or gnocchi, perhaps try some polpette (meatballs), and make sure to take advantage of the excellent wine list. If you are in a hurry, stop by for deli items; the Sbandatis sell a good selection of cheeses and cured meats.

Mediterranean

Just out of the downtown core in a small bungalow, **Ariana** (1304 NW Galveston Ave., 541/330-5539, www.arianarestaurantbend.com, 5pm-9pm Tues.-Sat., $20-30, reservations recommended) is one of the most appealing and intimate dinner restaurants in town. The Mediterranean-influenced cuisine is prepared with care, elevating dishes as simple as beet salad to remarkable heights. To fully experience Ariana, go for the five-course tasting menu ($65). In the summer, seating expands to a deck.

Middle Eastern

For affordable and tasty Middle Eastern food, go to the colorful **Kebaba** (1004 Newport Ave., 541/318-6224, www.kebaba.com, 11am-9pm Mon.-Sat., 11:30am-9pm Sun., $5-15). There's a good mix of authenticity and innovation here; your lamb shawarma can come in a pita-bread wrap with za'atar fries or in a Middle Eastern rice bowl on top of pilaf. Kebaba is a good place to find excellent vegetarian food.

Southern

Zydeco (919 NW Bond St., 541/312-2899, www.zydecokitchen.com, 11:30am-2:30pm Mon.-Fri. and 5pm-close daily, $11-26) is one of the hottest spots in town. In the summer, its fun bright atmosphere spills out from the open kitchen to sidewalk tables. Inside, a good selection of wine is stored behind glass-fronted cabinets and strategically placed mirrors give views of the crowd—a mix of young partiers and older serious diners—and the open kitchen. The food, not surprisingly, has creole and Cajun influences, but also includes other good options, such as pan-roasted steelhead trout in a lemon-caper sauce.

Steak

★ **Jackalope Grill** (750 NW Lava Rd., 541/318-8435, www.jackalopegrill.com, 4pm-9pm daily, $26-32, reservations recommended), around the corner from the Oxford Hotel, is more upscale than its name. The restaurant, which used to be in a funky strip mall location, is a great addition to downtown Bend. Main courses range from steak or salmon to jaeger schnitzel or pork osso bucco, but don't skip the starters. Chef Tim Garling's soup du jour is invariably good, whether it's a rich butternut squash topped with chanterelles or a smooth concoction made from beets. During the summer, diners can sit in an intimate outdoor courtyard.

Also in the downtown core, **The Pine Tavern Restaurant** (967 NW Brooks St., 541/382-5581, www.pinetavern.com, 11:30am-3pm and 5pm-close daily, $16-32, reservations recommended) has been in business since 1936, and although it isn't a trendy place, it keeps current enough to continue drawing crowds. It's in a garden setting overlooking Mirror Pond, with an ancient ponderosa pine that's been growing up through the floor since it opened. Prime rib, meat loaf, and hot sourdough scones with honey butter are among the many specialties. Most dinners are in the $15-20 range and come with scones.

Brewpubs and Distilleries

Bend has seen an explosion of good local brewers in recent years. Many are alumni of central Oregon's first brewery and brewpub, **Deschutes Brewery and Public House** (1044 NW Bond St., 541/382-9242, www.deschutesbrewery.com, 11am-11pm Mon.-Thurs., 11am-midnight Fri.-Sat., 11am-10pm Sun., $9-16), which still serves fresh hand-crafted ales and food that is better than most pub food. Along with the burgers, veggie burgers, sandwiches, and pizza, you can get asparagus risotto or a grilled flatiron steak. The beer, including the always-satisfying Mirror Pond pale ale, is some of Oregon's best. The main brewery is in the Old Mill District at 901 SW Simpson Avenue, where tours and tastings are offered.

A visit to the tasting room at **Crux Fermentation** (50 SW Division St., 541/385-3333, http://cruxfermentation.com, 4pm-10pm Mon., 11:30am-10pm Tues.-Sun., 5pm-10pm Sun., $6-12) is a real treat, especially for beer nerds, who can appreciate the nontraditional brewing methods such as decoction mashing, open fermentation, and use of wild yeast strains and hops from all over the world. Here the beer flows directly from the finishing tanks to the taps (18 when we counted), and hops scent the building, a former auto transmission shop. Pub grub consists of good sandwiches, except on Monday evenings, when the kitchen is closed and food trucks pull up to make sure no one goes hungry.

Perhaps the hottest brewpub in town is **10 Barrel** (1135 NW Galveston Ave., 541/678-5228, www.10barrel.com, 11am-11pm Sun.-Thurs., 11am-midnight Fri.-Sat.). Wash down good pizza with an award-winning S1NIST0R black ale.

Although it (so far) has only a tasting room, not a full brewpub, **Boneyard Brewing** (37 NW Lake Place, 541/323-2325, www.boneyardbeer.com, 11am-6pm daily) is worth a visit. The brewery, just a short walk from downtown, got its name from scavenging old equipment from larger breweries. They also

Touring Bend's Brewpubs

Twenty years ago, the Deschutes Brewery was the only artisan brewery in town, but it turns out to have been an incubator for many local brewers. Bend's microbrewery scene is the fastest-growing in the state, and the local visitors center has developed the **Bend Ale Trail** to help you explore it.

Pick up a copy of the Discovery Map of Central Oregon (available at many hotels and at the Bend visitors center) and use its Bend Ale Trail Map and Passport to track down seven Bend breweries. (The Ale Trail is also available as an app for iPhones and Androids.) At each stop, get your passport stamped—and for extra credit, head over Sisters to visit an eighth pub. When you get all seven stamps, stop by the visitors center and to receive a commemorative silicone beer glass. All of the seven Bend breweries are within walking distance of each other.

Although it's easy to explore Bend's ever-expanding brewpub scene on your own, a couple of local companies are offering tours that give you a little extra insight into the breweries and remove any temptation to drive.

The **Bend Brew Bus** (541/389-8359, $65) is operated by Wanderlust Tours, whose guides know both the outdoors and their way around a tasting room. You'll get to go behind the scenes at the breweries and, of course, do some sampling. There's also a "Local Pour" tour that visits Bend distillers, cideries, wineries, and kombucha makers. The bus can pick you up at your hotel, eliminating the need to drive.

If you can get a group of about 14 folks together and want a slightly more active tour, board the **Cycle Pub** (541/678-5051, www.cyclepub.com) and start pedaling. And, um, drinking. The 16-person "bike," which looks more like a trolley, operates out of the Old Mill District and can be booked for pretty much any sort of tour you want to design. Two-hour tours ($350) are BYOB, but can include stops at brewpubs.

scavenged some excellent brewers, and their beers are first-rate. If you don't visit the tasting room, be sure to look for Boneyard brews on tap at local restaurants.

There's more good pub food at **Silver Moon Brewing** (24 NW Greenwood Ave., 541/388-8331, www.silvermoonbrewing. com, 11:30am-10pm Mon.-Thurs., 11:30am-2am Fri.-Sat., 11:30am-8pm Sun.), a normally low-key sports bar that kicks into gear several nights a week with live music.

The **Bend Brewing Company** (1019 NW Brooks St., 541/383-1559, www.bend-brewingco.com, 11:30am-close daily, $9-13), one of the few woman-owned breweries, is a local staple. Come for the good beer, the nice waitstaff, and the great patio (Brooks St. is a pedestrian-oriented street just to the river side of downtown). Food is good—grilled tacos, pizza, sandwiches, and excellent fish-and-chips. Happy hour is a good bet at this pub that's especially popular with the locals.

GoodLife Brewing (70 SW Century Dr.,

541/728-0749, www.goodlifebrewing.com, noon-10pm daily, $9-14) opened in 2011 in a warehouse with a 30-barrel brewing system and quickly established itself as a major player in the Bend beer scene, with Descender IPA winning raves. The brewpub (they prefer to call it a "bierhal") serves decent, somewhat healthy, pub fare; during the summer, you and your dog can enjoy it by the fire pit out back.

A few miles from downtown on the way to Sisters, find great handcrafted spirits at **Crater Lake Spirits** (19330 Pinehurst Rd., 541/318-0200, www.craterlakespirits.com, 11am-5pm Mon.-Sat., 11am-4pm Sun.). The distillery has tours and a tasting room; however, it's not a bar and doesn't serve food.

INFORMATION

Bend Visitor and Convention Bureau (750 NW Lava Rd., 541/382-8048 or 877/245-8484, www.visitbend.com) has an office downtown, around the corner from the Oxford Hotel. The **Central Oregon Visitors Association** (705

SW Bonnett Way, 541/389-8799 or 800/800-8334, http://visitcentraloregon.com) is in the Old Mill District.

The Bend and Fort Rock **Ranger Station** (63095 Deschutes Market Rd., 541/383-4000, www.fs.usda.gov/centraloregon) is the place to go for permits and information on the vast array of lands in central Oregon managed by the Forest Service. Passes are also available online; NW Forest Passes for hiking are sold at trailheads where they are required, and Sno-Park passes can be purchased at many local businesses, including ski shops and some grocery stores. The **public library** (507 NW Wall St., 541/388-6677) is a good place to get on the Internet; it is a wireless hotspot.

GETTING THERE
By Air

With flights to and from Portland, Seattle, San Francisco, Denver, Los Angeles, and Salt Lake City, access to central Oregon is quite good. The air hub of this section of the state is Redmond's **Roberts Field** (2522 SE Jesse Butler Cir., Redmond, 541/548-0646), 16 miles north of Bend and east of U.S. 97. Alamo, Avis, Budget, Hertz, National, and Enterprise have car rental offices in the terminal. Taxis, limos, and shuttle buses connect the traveler to Bend at nominal costs.

By Bus

The **Central Oregon Breeze Shuttle** (541/389-7469 or 800/847-0157, www.co-breeze.com, $52 one-way, $95 round-trip, fuel surcharge added when gas prices reach $4.39 a gallon) serves Bend to and from Portland International Airport and the Portland train station. **Redmond Airport Shuttle** (541/382-1687 or 888/664-8449, www.redmondairportshuttle.net) offers door-to-door service to and from the Redmond airport.

Cascades East Transit (541/385-8680, www.cascadeseasttransit.com) is a regional bus system with lines running to Mount Bachelor, Redmond, Prineville, Madras, Sisters, and La Pine. During the winter, Cascades East partners with Mount Bachelor to run a **ski shuttle** ($9 round-trip from a park-and-ride lot at the corner of Columbia and Simpson) to West Village on the mountain.

Get to and from the airport or the Chemult Amtrak station on **High Desert Point** (541/382-4193, www.highdesert-point.com), which also travels between Bend and Eugene. **Bend Cab** (541/389-8090) can always haul you around if you need a ride.

By Train

The closest you can get to Bend via **Amtrak** (800/872-7245, www.amtrak.com) is Chemult, 60 miles to the south on U.S. 97. Amtrak will assist you in scheduling your transfer to Bend.

By Car

U.S. 97 and U.S. 20 converge on Bend, much as the Native American trails and pioneer wagon roads did 150 years ago when this outpost on the Deschutes River was called Farewell Bend. Portland is three hours away via U.S. 97 and U.S. 26; Salem is two hours away via U.S. 20 and Route 22; and Eugene is two hours away via U.S. 20 and Route 126. Crater Lake National Park is about two hours south down U.S. 97. There are also many loops worth investigating, including the Cascade Lakes Highway, Newberry Crater, and the Lava Lands.

The Bend Parkway (U.S. 97) moves traffic fairly smoothly north and south through town. It parallels 3rd Street. On the road up to Bachelor and in some of the newer developments, including the area around the Old Mill District, traffic circles are used instead of stoplights. Your awareness of other vehicles should naturally heighten as you approach a traffic circle; traffic slows but doesn't necessarily stop at these junctions.

You can rent a car starting at around $40 per day from **Hertz** (2025 NE Hwy. 20, 541/388-1535, and Redmond Airport, 541/923-1411) or **Budget** (519 SE 3rd St., 800/527-0700).

Sunriver and Vicinity

The seeds of growth were planted in central Oregon in the mid-1960s, when a onetime military encampment a dozen miles south of Bend was transformed into the Sunriver Resort community. The resort, with its mix of private houses, rental units, and a lodge, has an increasing number of year-round residents, but it is still largely a hub for families looking to rent a house in central Oregon. And indeed, this is an ideal spot for a family get-together, with miles of bike paths, swimming pools, tennis courts, and the lovely Deschutes River. It's also an easy base for exploring the nearby volcanic landscape and sites along the Cascade Lakes Highway and, in the winter, for skiing Mount Bachelor.

SIGHTS
Newberry Volcano

Newberry Volcano, a vast shield volcano that reached to about 10,000 feet before it blew its top about 1,500 years ago, covers 500 square miles. Its caldera alone is five miles in diameter and contains two alpine lakes, Paulina and East Lakes. A 1981 U.S. Geological Survey probe drilled into the caldera floor and found temperatures of 510°F, the highest recorded in an inactive Cascade volcano.

The volcano itself is at the southeastern end of the area designated the **Newberry National Volcanic Monument,** which extends in a swath from Newberry Crater, south and east of Sunriver, all the way north to Lava Butte, on the highway between Bend and Sunriver. It preserves the obsidian fields, deep mountain lakes, and lava formations left in the wake of a massive series of eruptions. While lacking the visual impact (and great depth) of Crater Lake, this preserve is more accessible and less crowded than its southern Cascade counterpart.

The main focus of interest here are the two lakes in the caldera: **Paulina Lake** and **East Lake.** A 9,500-year-old circular structure called a wickiup was excavated at Paulina Lake in 1992, which dates back well before the latest eruptions of the volcano and indicates that native people used this area through

the lava flow at Newberry National Volcanic Monument

various stages of volcanic activity. Several campgrounds and two resorts are located along the shores of these lakes, which are noted for their excellent trout fishing, said to be best in the fall. In Paulina Lake, fisherfolk can troll for kokanee, a gourmet's delight, as well as brown and rainbow trout. Paulina's twin, East Lake, features a fall run of German brown trout that move out of the depths to spawn in shoreline shallows.

Be sure to take the four-mile drive (summer only) to the top of 7,985-foot-high **Paulina Peak,** the highest point along the jagged edge of Newberry Crater, on Forest Service Road 500. Towering 1,500 feet over the lakes in the crater, the peak also allows a perspective on the forest, obsidian fields, and basalt flows in the surrounding area. To the far west, a palisade of snow-clad Cascade peaks runs the length of the horizon.

The other must-see site on the volcano is the **Big Obsidian Flow,** which was formed 1,300 years ago and served as the source of raw material for Native American spear points, arrowheads, and hide scrapers. Prized by the original inhabitants of the area, the obsidian tools were also highly valued by other Native American nations and were exchanged for blankets, firearms, and other possessions as far away as Taos, New Mexico. These tools and other barter items helped to spread Newberry Volcano obsidian all across the West and into Canada and Mexico. Centuries later, NASA sent astronauts to walk on the volcano's pumice-dusted surface in preparation for landing on the moon. A 0.9-mile trail now crosses the obsidian flow. Find the trailhead on the road between the two lakes.

Newberry National Volcanic Monument is managed by the Deschutes National Forest; contact the **Lava Lands Visitor Center** (58201 S. U.S. 97, Bend, 541/593-2421, www. fs.usda.gov/centraloregon) for more information. During the summer, a Forest Service guard station is staffed at Paulina Lake. A Northwest Forest Pass or a three-day monument pass ($10, available at Lava Land Visitor Center or at the monument entrance) is required for day use.

To reach Newberry Crater, head south from Sunriver about 12 miles (or 27 miles from Bend) on U.S. 97 to the turnoff to Paulina and East Lakes. The 16-mile paved but ragged County Road 21 twists and turns its way up to the lakes in the caldera of Newberry Crater.

Sunriver Nature Center

Educational programs and interpretive exhibits, including a nature trail and a botanical garden, help orient visitors to the high desert ecology of the area around Sunriver. Programs at the **Sunriver Nature Center** (River Rd., Sunriver, 541/593-4394, www. sunrivernaturecenter.org, 9am-5pm daily late May-Labor Day) include nature walks, classes, and summertime day camps for kids.

SPORTS AND RECREATION
Bicycling

For many visitors, a visit to Sunriver is a chance to ride a bike. The gentle off-street bike paths provide the perfect way to get around the resort area. Sunriver's **Bike Barn** (541/593-3721), near the Great Hall, can set you up with a rented bike. **Village Bike and Ski** (541/593-2453), in the Sunriver Mall, is another good place to rent a bike. Be sure to pick up a map of the local bike trails. A popular ride from Sunriver is the easy eight-mile loop to Benham Falls on the Deschutes River.

If you like to bike but would rather have gravity do all of the work, consider the **Paulina Plunge** (541/389-0562 or 800/296-0562, www.paulinaplunge.com, May-Oct., $68-70), a six-mile downhill mountain bike ride. The outfitter provides high-quality mountain bikes, helmets, experienced guides, and the shuttle transfer from Sunriver and back. The action starts at Paulina Lake, where you begin your coast down forested trails alongside Paulina Creek. You'll pass by 50 waterfalls on your 2,500-foot descent, as well as abundant wildlife and varied vegetation. Three short nature hikes are necessary to experience the waterfalls and natural waterslides that make this trip famous. (Yes, you will want to plunge into the water!) You may bring your own bike, but this will not afford you a discount from the tour price. Bring your own lunch and water or pay $10 for a sack lunch, $2 for a water bottle.

Bird-Watching

About an hour south of Sunriver near Fort Rock is **Cabin Lake Campground** (Deschutes National Forest, 541/383-5300), an exceptional spot for viewing a wide variety of birds and wildlife. There is no lake at Cabin Lake, and the campground is pretty marginal, but the Forest Service has built two small ponds that blend in with the natural surroundings. Permanent wildlife-viewing blinds made of logs, built and donated by the Portland Audubon Society, are adjacent to the small 12-site campground and give close visual access to the ponds. In fact, the blinds are so close that binoculars aren't really needed.

Since there is little water in this 3,000-foot-high meeting of desert and mountain biomes, both mountain and desert birds are regularly attracted, usually in large quantities. The red crossbill, an increasingly rare member of the finch family, is a regular visitor to this avian oasis. The pinyon jay is another fairly uncommon bird that can be seen here with frequency. Woodpeckers, including Lewis's woodpecker, the common flicker, the white-headed woodpecker, and the hairy woodpecker, are also often sighted. Park checklists show the California quail, bluebirds, chickadees, flycatchers, sparrows, warblers, and the Western tanager making appearances too. Best viewing times are in the morning, but birds can usually be seen all day long.

Fishing

Although some people do fish the Upper Deschutes River from the bank in the area around Sunriver, most anglers use drift boats. If you don't have a boat, consider fishing the Fall River, off Route 43 (Century Dr.) southwest of Sunriver.

You can get equipment, licenses, advice, or a fishing guide at the **Sunriver Fly Shop** (56805 Venture Ln., Sunriver, 541/593-8814, www.sunriverflyshop.com), near the Chevron station in the business park and shopping area across the road from the entrance to Sunriver.

Families are catered to by **Garrison's Fishing Service** (541/593-8394, www.garrisonguide.com), which features pontoon boats with padded swivel chairs that cruise the lakes and rivers of central Oregon looking for the big ones.

Golf

Three 18-hole courses and a family-oriented nine-hole course are found at **Sunriver Resort** (541/593-4402 or 800/801-8765, www.sunriver-resort.com). The Meadows Course ($49-109) is many golfers' favorite. The Woodlands Course ($49-109) has water, abundant bunkers, and constricted approaches to the greens, making club selection and shot accuracy very important. The private Crosswater Course ($59-189) is touted by the management as the best course north of Pebble Beach. You must be a resort guest or member to play on it. The nine-hole Caldera Links ($39 adults, $10 children ages 12-17) is the newest course, designed to introduce new players to the sport; it's also limited to resort guests and local homeowners.

A nearby and economical golf course is **Quail Run** (16725 Northridge Dr., La Pine, 541/536-1303 or 800/895-4653, golfquailrun.com, $35), an 18-hole championship course in La Pine. Sand traps, ponds, and tree-lined fairways challenge golfers of all levels without seriously threatening their pocketbooks.

Horseback Riding

During the spring and summer, the **Sunriver Stables** (541/593-6995, www.sunriver-resort.com) offers rides ranging from short pony rides to eight-hour trail rides; riding lessons are also available. During the winter, horse-drawn sleigh rides ($100) travel along the Deschutes River and through the forest.

Paddling

The Sunriver marina (541/593-3492, 11am-3pm daily May, 9:30am-4:30pm daily June-early Oct.), on the Deschutes River west of Circle 3, rents canoes, kayaks, stand-up paddleboards, and rafts; offers kayak classes; and leads float trips on the Deschutes. Aspiring anglers can also rent a fishing rod here. Passes are available with many Sunriver rentals; ask about this when you're booking if it's important to you.

Swimming

The **Cove at Sunriver** (541-593-1000, 10am-10pm daily) is an expansion of the Lodge Village pool complex, with a new restaurant and bar, a vast zero entry pool, hot tub, water slide, private cabanas and nature trails. Sunriver Resort guests have exclusive and complimentary access to The Cove.

Sunriver homeowners and guests can also swim at **SHARC** (57250 Overlook Rd. off Circle 2, 541/585-5000, www.sunriversharc. com, $25 adults, $20 children ages 4-17, multiday passes available, rates less in winter), a huge 2-acre aquatic and recreation center with large indoor and outdoor pools, two waterslides, and an outdoor hot tub reserved for adults as well as playgrounds and basketball and bocce courts.

ENTERTAINMENT AND EVENTS

The mid-August **Sunriver Music and Arts Festival** (541/593-1084 or 541/593-9310, www.sunrivermusic.org), held in the magnificent log-and-stone structure called the Great Hall at Sunriver Resort and in Bend's Tower Theatre, has been pleasing capacity crowds since the festival's inception in 1977. The concert series features top performers from around the world. Highlights include the gala pops concert and the gourmet dinner as well as four traditional classical concerts and a family concert.

ACCOMMODATIONS

The Pacific Northwest's most complete resort, ★ **Sunriver Lodge** (800/801-8765, www. sunriver-resort.com) not only has proximity to Mount Bachelor skiing, Deschutes River canoeing and white-water rafting, and hiking and horse trails in the Deschutes National Forest, but also boasts golf courses, pools, tennis courts, 35 miles of paved bike routes, and a nature center with an astronomical observatory. There's pretty much something for everybody here.

Sunriver Lodge has rooms ranging from up-to-date lodge guest rooms ($225) to relatively large suites featuring a large fireplace, a fully equipped kitchen, a sleeping loft, and tall picture windows that open onto a patio ($289). Nearby "river lodges" are even more elegant and run about $309-325. About two miles south of the lodge, in the newer Caldera Springs development, swank three- to four-bedroom cabins start at about $440.

Note that it can be a much better deal to rent a condo or a house. Sunriver Resort's website allows you to set your criteria and browse available properties, which start at about $200.

Condo rentals are also available through **Mountain Resort Properties** (541/593-8685 or 800/346-6337, www.mtresort.com). All units have a fully equipped kitchen, linens, a washer and dryer, TV, and a barbecue, as well as access to Mavericks, a large fitness center. Since these are privately owned units, other amenities like hot tubs, saunas, and bicycles will vary. Most of these condos do not allow pets or smoking, but there are exceptions; inquire when making reservations. Other agencies brokering vacation house rentals include **Village Properties** (541/593-1653, www.village-properties.com) and **Discover Sunriver** (866/534-4668, www.discoversunriver.com). Many houses have hot tubs, and quite a few allow pets; rates are all over the map but can be as low as $150 a night for a two-bedroom condo.

Up on Newberry Crater, **Paulina Lake**

Resort (541/536-2240, www.paulinalake-lodge.com, $96-252) books up early with 14 rustic log cabins. Although all cabins have kitchenettes or full kitchens, hearty lunches and dinners (9am-4pm Sun.-Tues., 11am-7pm Wed.-Thurs., 9am-9pm Fri.-Sat., summer, 11am-8pm Wed.-Sat., 11am-4pm Sun. winter, dinner $13-25, dinner reservations required in winter) can be had in the resort's log-paneled dining room. Boat rentals and a general store are also on-site. During winter, although the road to the resort is snowed in, the resort itself is open December-March to cross-country skiers and snowmobilers, giving access to over 330,000 acres of designated snowmobile areas.

East Lake Resort (541/536-2230, www.eastlakeresort.com, mid-May-mid-Oct., $84-207) offers 16 cabins with at least rudimentary cooking facilities (most have full kitchens). A snack bar, a general store, and boat rentals are on-site, and the nearby RV park ($32) and tent sites ($25) have a laundry and pay showers. The lake itself is stocked with trout and Atlantic and kokanee salmon. The cold water and abundant freshwater shrimp make for excellent-tasting fish.

Camping

The nicest campgrounds near Sunriver are in the Newberry Volcano area. The creekside McKay Crossing (541/383-5300, www.fs.usda.gov/centraloregon, $10, no drinking water) is about three miles east of U.S. 97 on the road up to Newberry Volcano. Paulina Lake, Little Crater, Cinder Hill, and East Lake (reservations at 877/444-6777, www.recreation.gov, all $16, drinking water) are at the top of the Newberry Volcano; the season runs from late May to mid-October.

La Pine State Park (541/536-2071 or 800/452-5687, www.oregonstateparks.org, year-round, $24 tents, $23-26 RVs, $44 rustic cabin, $86 deluxe cabin) is a large campground south of Sunriver. Look for a sign on the west side of the highway marking the three-mile-long entrance road located eight miles north of La Pine off U.S. 97. This park also claims Oregon's tallest ponderosa pine tree (162 feet) and offers easy access to the Cascade Lakes Highway and an array of volcanic phenomena. The campground offers such amenities as flush toilets, firewood, and showers.

FOOD

There are a number of casual eateries in and around Sunriver's main shopping area as well as a well-stocked grocery store. Food isn't really one of the high points of a visit here, but it's fun to visit the Twisted River Tavern (541/593-3730, www.sunriver-resort.com/dining, 11:30am-midnight daily, $7-17), the lounge in Sunriver Resort's main lodge to enjoy a drink, pub food, and great views. Kids are allowed until about 8pm. Next door in the lodge, Carson's American Kitchen (www.sunriver-resort.com/dining, 541/593-3740, 7am-9pm daily, $17-35) offers steak, pasta, fried chicken, and burgers. For Sunriver's fine dining option, head to The Grille (www.sunriver-resort.com/dining, 541/593-3400, 11:30am-9pm, $14-47), where you can dine simply on tacos or crab macaroni and cheese, or go all out for rack of lamb with Bing cherry chutney or thyme-honey-glazed grilled salmon—though no matter what you eat, you'll need to meet the "country club casual" dress code.

Beyond the resort itself, there are more great views and decent Mexican-Peruvian food at Hola! (57235 River Rd., 541/593-8880, www.holabend, 11am-9pm Sun.-Thurs., 11am-10pm Fri.-Sat., $12-19), next to the Sunriver marina. The menu includes braised pork in Coca-Cola with yams, onions, tomatoes, or wild prawns with fried bananas, red onion, and spicy mole sauce. Hola! also has a couple of restaurants in Bend, including at the Old Mill.

Cascade Lakes Highway

The Cascade Lakes Highway (a.k.a. Century Dr. or Rte. 46) is an 89-mile drive leading to more than half a dozen lakes in the shadow of the snowcapped Cascades. These lakes feature boating, fishing, and other water sports, and just about every lake has at least one campground on its shore. Hiking, bird-watching, biking, and skiing also attract visitors. From downtown Bend, drive south on Franklin Avenue, which becomes Galveston Avenue, to the traffic circle at Galveston Avenue and Century Drive (at 14th St., about a mile from downtown). Go three-quarters of the way around the circle and you'll be headed south on Century Drive. The route is well marked, and the road climbs in elevation for a significant portion of the drive.

Although there are many places to stop and explore along the highway, the stretch between Mount Bachelor and Crane Prairie Reservoir is the most spectacular, so if you're just out for an eye-popping drive, you can take the shortened version described in the sidebar.

The area around the Cascade Lakes Highway is part of the **Deschutes National Forest** (541/383-5300, www.fs.usda.gov/

A Three-Hour Tour of the Cascade Lakes Highway

If you just want a gourmet taste of the Cascade Lakes Highway, a shortened version of the loop manages to take in some of the highlights. The following tour can be enjoyed in several hours, even allowing for several stops. In contrast, driving the entire loop takes a whole day with only limited time spent out of the car.

Begin by taking U.S. 97 south of Bend 13 miles and getting off at the exit for Sunriver. After about 1.5 miles, the turnoff to Sunriver Resort will be on your right; stay on the main road as it curves to the left. Follow this road (Rte. 40/Spring River Rd.) to Cascade Lakes Highway (Rte. 46) and turn right to reach Little Lava Lake. The Deschutes River begins its 252-mile course to the Columbia from here. Head just down the road to Lava Lake, where there's a small rustic resort, camping, and a store with a grand view of South Sister from the store's porch; in the summer your attention could be diverted by the hummingbirds that flock to a hanging feeder.

Follow the highway north to the shores of Elk Lake, a favorite of windsurfers and sailors. The year-round cabins at **Elk Lake Resort** (541/480-7378, www.elklakeresort.net) are popular, as is picture-taking from the lake's beach picnic grounds at the southernmost tip of shoreline. Here you have the full length of Elk Lake before you, with South Sister and Mount Bachelor in the background. During the snowbound months of winter, access to Elk Lake is by snowmobile, Sno-Cat van, or dogsled (really!) to a world of groomed cross-country ski and snowshoe trails amid spectacular alpine scenery.

Not far away, the red volcanic cinder highway contrasts with the black lava flows en route to aqua-tinted Devils Lake. From the northern end of this lake, on the other side of the highway, you'll find Devil's Pile, an agglomeration of lava flows and volcanic glass where *Apollo 11* astronauts reportedly culled a rock to deposit on the lunar surface. The road winds around to the Mount Bachelor Summit ski lifts. From the deck in front of the sport shop-cafeteria complex, you can see the Three Sisters and Broken Top.

You might want to hike the short trail to Todd Lake, canoe Sparks Lake in the shadow of Broken Top and South Sister, or visit the Ray Atkeson Memorial, dedicated to Oregon's "photographer laureate." All are between Devil's Pile and the ski lifts. From Mount Bachelor it's a 20-minute drive back to Sunriver.

main/deschutes). A **Northwest Forest Pass** ($5 one-day, $30 one-year) is required to park at most trailheads; passes are sold at the trailhead (bring exact change or a check).

SIGHTS
Todd Lake

Shortly after you pass Mount Bachelor, you'll find the turnoff to the exceptionally beautiful but equally rustic National Forest Service campground (NW Forest Pass, no extra camping fee, June-Oct., depending on snow) at **Todd Lake.** It's a short walk up the trail from a parking area to the campsites at this 6,200-foot-high alpine lake. Tables, grills, and a vault toilet are provided, but you will need to pack in your own water and supplies, as no vehicles are allowed—a good thing, because the drone of a Winnebago generator would definitely detract from the grandeur of this pristine spot. You'll find good swimming and wading on the sandy shoal on the south end of the lake, and you can't miss the captivating views of Broken Top to the north. Hardy explorers can portage a canoe up the trail for a paddle around Todd Lake. Because of the lake's high elevation, it is often socked in by snow until about the Fourth of July.

Sparks Lake

Clear and shallow **Sparks Lake,** about 25 miles west of Bend, is a favorite stop for photographers; most visitors can't resist trying to capture views of Mount Bachelor, South Sister, and Broken Top reflected in the lake. Broken volcanic rock forms the lakebed, and water slowly drains out during the course of the summer, leaving not much more than a marsh by late summer. This is a good place to let go of the idea of a formal trail and just explore the lakeshore on foot or in a canoe.

There is a campground, Soda Creek (June-Sept., $10); bring your own drinking water, or be prepared to filter lake water.

The lake is open to fly-fishing only for the local brook trout and cutthroat trout, and the use of barbless hooks is encouraged.

Green Lakes Trailhead

Begin a hike into the Three Sisters Wilderness Area from the **Green Lakes Trailhead,** 27 miles west of Bend. It's about 4.5 miles from the trailhead along waterfall-studded Fall Creek, past a big lava flow, to Green Lakes. From Green Lakes the trail continues to the pass between Broken Top and South Sister. This trail is extremely popular, so it's best to hike it on a weekday.

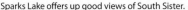

Sparks Lake offers up good views of South Sister.

Devils Lake

The eerily green **Devils Lake,** 29 miles west of Bend, is home to a very nice walk-in campground (Northwest Forest Pass required, no piped water) and an easy lakeside trail. Just across the highway from the lake is a popular trailhead used by South Sister climbers. The climb up 10,358-foot South Sister (Oregon's third-highest peak) is challenging but not technical. Many choose to do this 11-mile round-trip as an overnight backpacking trip. Many more hike the trail just as far as the pretty Moraine Lake area (about 3.5 miles), then return along the same route.

Elk Lake

A resort and a marina mean that this is not the quietest lake in the Cascades. **Elk Lake** is just about the only place along this road that you'll see sailboats, and it's also a good swimming lake by about August. The cabins at the **Elk Lake Resort** (541/480-7378, www.elklakeresort.net, $29-239) make a good base for exploring the local trails if you are not up for camping, and are open during the winter for cross-country skiers and snowmobilers. Accommodations range from small rustic cabins ($29) to larger, though still fairly rustic, cabins ($139-199) and modern homes ($239).

An on-site restaurant is surprisingly good. During the summer, the resort offers a marine and camp sites ($15-35); in addition, there's a Forest Service campground ($14).

Hosmer Lake

Just off the highway and 39 miles from Bend, **Hosmer Lake** is a favorite fishing and canoeing lake. It's stocked with Atlantic salmon, but don't count on eating them. Fishing is limited to catch-and-release fly-fishing with barbless hooks.

Even if you don't fish and don't have a canoe, it's worth visiting Hosmer Lake for its spectacular views of Mount Bachelor, South Sister, and Broken Top. Of the two campgrounds on the lake, **South** ($10, late May-late Sept., no drinking water) has the best views and the best lake access.

Lava Lake

Lava flows formed a dam that created **Lava Lake,** which is fed largely by underground springs. Rainbow trout, brook trout, whitefish, and illegally introduced tui chub live in the lake, which is 30 feet deep at its deepest point and open to bait fishing as well as fly-fishing. A lakeside **lodge** (541/382-9443) rents boats and operates an RV park; there is

Elk Lake

also a Forest Service campground (mid-May-mid-Oct., $14, drinking water) near the resort.

Little Lava Lake

Make a pilgrimage to **Little Lava Lake** and stand at the headwaters of the Deschutes River. Groundwater from the snowpack percolates down from the Mount Bachelor and Three Sisters area to fill the lake (it's thought that a large groundwater reservoir exists upstream from the lake); the Deschutes exits the lake as a meandering stream, flowing south about 8.4 miles to Crane Prairie Reservoir. Little Lava Lake shares a highway turnoff with Lava Lake.

Cultus Lake

Glacier-formed **Cultus Lake** is popular with campers, swimmers, boaters, water-skiers, Jet Skiers, and windsurfers. Anglers go for the big lake trout, also called mackinaw. An easy hiking trail follows the northern shore of the lake and then heads north along the Winopee Lake Trail to Teddy Lakes. From the trailhead to Teddy Lakes is about four miles.

The **Cultus Lake Resort** (541/408-1560 summer, 541/389-3230 winter, www.cultus-lakeresort.com, mid-May-mid-Sept.) rents rustic cabins ($85-140), motorboats, canoes, kayaks, and Jet Skis; it also operates a restaurant. During the peak of the summer season, cabins are only rented by the week.

Crane Prairie Reservoir

Crane Prairie Reservoir, an artificial lake, is a breeding ground for ospreys. These large birds, sometimes known as fish hawks, nest in the snags surrounding the lake and fish by plunging headfirst into the water from great heights. Cormorants, terns, bald eagles, and a variety of ducks are also commonly seen. Humans also like to fish—the most-prized fish is a "cranebow," a rainbow trout that grows almost freakishly large in this shallow, nutrient-rich reservoir.

A Forest Service campground (reservations at www.reserveamerica.com, $16, late Apr.-mid-Oct., drinking water) and the private **Crane Prairie Resort** RV park ($33), cabins ($55-80), marina, and fishing guide service (541/383-3939, www.crane-prairie-resort-guides.com) are located here.

Wickiup Reservoir

The area of the Deschutes River around present-day **Wickiup Reservoir** was a traditional Native American camping area during the fall. When the dam was completed in 1949, these campsites were flooded. Today, the reservoir (about 60 miles from Bend) is known for its relatively warm water and good fishing, especially for brown trout, which can weigh in at over 20 pounds. Kokanee and coho salmon as well as rainbow trout, brook trout, whitefish, and the nasty and invasive tui chub also live here. Campgrounds are **Gull Point Campground** (reservations at www.recreation.gov, $16, drinking water), at Wickiup Reservoir and across an access road at **North Twin Lake** ($12, no drinking water) and **South Twin Lake** ($16, drinking water), small natural lakes that flank the large reservoir.

From Wickiup Reservoir, Route 42 heads east and north along the Fall River toward Sunriver. The Cascade Lakes Highway, Route 46, continues south past Davis Lake.

Davis Lake

It takes a little doing to get to large and shallow **Davis Lake,** and many of those who make it come for fly-fishing. It's known for large rainbow trout as well as illegally introduced largemouth bass. Most anglers use boats or float tubes because the vegetation along the shoreline and the muddy lake bottom make it difficult to wade.

Davis Lake was formed about 6,000 years ago when a lava flow cut off Odell Creek. A fire in 2003 wiped out the West Davis campground; the **East Davis Campground** ($12, drinking water), though reduced in size by the fire, still exists and is looking a little less bare every year.

INFORMATION

For information about sites along the Cascade Lakes Highway, contact the **Deschutes** National Forest (63095 Deschutes Market Rd., Bend, 541/383-5300, www.fs.usda.gov/main/deschutes).

Willamette Pass and Vicinity

In the area around Willamette Pass, it's easy to see the shift from the greener, damper, Douglas fir-dominated west side of the Cascades to the dry east side, forested by lodgepole and ponderosa pines. Each of the lakes in the high country has its own partisans—families who have camped in the same spot for decades—and its own personality. Campgrounds are available at Crescent, Odell, and Waldo Lakes.

Pick one place to explore in depth, or hop between lakes—perhaps you'll carve out a new personal tradition.

SIGHTS
Crescent Lake

On the sun-drenched east side of Willamette Pass, **Crescent Lake** is home to a tremendously popular campground ($18 May-Nov., $12 Dec.-Apr.; yurts $30 May-Nov., $40 Dec.-Apr.) and the **Crescent Lake Resort** (541/433-2505, http://crescentlakeresort.com, open year-round, cabins $95-215, three-night minimum stay in summer), an easy place to while away a few days. Rent a fishing boat, kayak, or bike from the resort. Large lake trout (including one whopping 30-pounder) are regularly pulled from the lake. Crescent Lake is about three miles south of Route 58 via Deschutes National Forest Road 60 from Crescent Lake junction.

Odell Lake

Two resorts, several summer homes, and campgrounds surround 3,582-acre **Odell Lake,** 30 miles southeast of Oakridge on Route 58. Situated in a deep glacial trough, the lake probably filled with water about 11,000 years ago when a terminal moraine blocked the drainage of Odell Creek. Due to the depth of the lake and the nearly perpetual west-to-east winds that blow through Willamette Pass, the water averages a cold 39°F. Those breezes, however, help to keep pesky mosquitoes and other obnoxious insects away and make for some of the best sailing in the Cascades.

★ **Odell Lake Lodge** (541/433-2540 or 800/434-2540, www.odelllakeresort.com, year-round, lodge rooms $65-99, cabins $100-320, tent and RV sites $14-18) is a particularly charming, though rustic, typical old-time Oregon resort. It is popular with cross-country skiers during the winter. Skiers may want to take advantage of large cabin 12, which comfortably houses as many as 16 people for $320 per night. Since the lodge is extremely popular, reservations are strongly recommended as much as a year in advance for weekends.

Moorages at Odell Lake are available for rent through the lodge, as are canoes, powerboats, and sailboats. The lodge has a complete tackle shop to help outfit you to catch the kokanee and mackinaw that inhabit the icy waters, and rental equipment is also available if you didn't bring your own. The restaurant at the lodge is open for all meals. The lodge also maintains its own system of trails, which provide good biking in the summer and cross-country skiing in the winter. The owners of the resort have put together an area map to guide you to various waterfalls. Bikes and ski equipment can be rented from the lodge. In addition to these outdoor pursuits, basketball, volleyball, badminton, and horseshoes round out the fun. Tots and toddlers will enjoy the sandbox, the toy library, and the swings.

Across the lake from the lodge is **Shelter Cove Resort** (W. Odell Lake Rd., Cascade Summit, 541/433-2548 or 800/647-2729, www.

sheltercoveresort.com, lodge rooms $225-275, cabins $105-250, camping $20-36), which features nine cabins complete with kitchens, over 70 campsites, and a marina with moorages. The resort's general store handles everything from groceries, tackle, and boat rentals to Sno-Park permits and fishing or hunting licenses. The September-October spawning displays by Odell Lake's landlocked salmon are unforgettable.

Two Forest Service campgrounds, **Sunset Cove** ($16, late Apr.-mid-Oct., drinking water) and **Trapper Creek** ($16, late May-mid-Oct., drinking water, reservations at www.recreation.gov) are on the lake.

Willamette Pass Ski Area

Willamette Pass (541/345-7669, www.willamettepass.com, 9am-4pm Wed.-Sun., Dec.-Mar., $49 adults, $30 children 6-10 and seniors), 69 miles southeast of Eugene on Route 58, has some of the most challenging runs in the state as well as a multitude of beginner and intermediate trails. You'll find some of the steepest runs, unlike the open chutes or powder bowls at other ski areas. Since Willamette Pass plows its own parking lot, you will not need a Sno-Park permit. Night skiing runs Friday-Saturday nights December-March. In addition to regular lift

tickets, tickets are available for $13 an hour, with a two-hour minimum.

The ski area grooms trails for both regular cross-country and skate skiing (10am-4pm Sat.-Sun. and holidays, adult trail pass $12). In addition, there are several popular Sno-Park areas near Willamette Pass, including one right by the ski area with several fairly challenging trails; a couple follow the Pacific Crest Trail, which crosses Route 58 at Willamette Pass. For information on cross-country skiing from this and other local Sno-Park areas, contact the **Middle Fork Ranger District** of the Willamette National Forest (46375 Hwy. 58, Westfir, 541/782-2283, www.fs.usda.gov/willamette).

Waldo Lake

The Waldo Lake Wilderness is a 37,000-acre gem 70 miles southeast of Eugene via Route 58 (take Forest Service Rd. 5897 before the Willamette Pass turnoff to go 10 miles to the lake). The centerpiece of this alpine paradise is 10-square-mile **Waldo Lake,** the third largest in Oregon, whose waters were once rated the purest in the country in a nationwide study of 30 lakes. Peer down into the green translucent depths of this 420-foot-deep lake to see rocky reefs and fish 50-100 feet below.

Waldo Lake

No motorized craft are allowed on the lake, but canoeing, sailing, trout fishing, and windsurfing complement hiking and cross-country skiing to give you different ways to experience the lake and the surrounding region. Add wildlife-watching highlighted by the early September rutting season of Roosevelt elk, and you'll quickly understand why Waldo Lake is a favorite with Cascades connoisseurs. The 22-mile loop trail around the lake is popular with mountain bikers and backpackers, and day hikes on the south end edify less diehard recreationists.

To best savor it, visit the area late August-mid-October to avoid a plague of summer mosquitoes and early winter snowfall. Whenever you go, you can catch views of 8,744-foot Diamond Peak in the distance and find first-rate trails and campgrounds.

Waldo Lake has three very popular campgrounds: **Shadow Bay, North Waldo, and Islet** (541/822-3799, www.fs.usda.gov/willamette, reservations at www.recreation.gov, late June-mid-Oct., $20, drinking water). Shadow Bay usually has the most mosquitoes; North Waldo and Islet are windier. To get to the lake, take Route 58 for 24 miles southeast of Oakridge. Take a left on Forest Service Road 5897. It is five miles to Forest Service Road 5896, which takes you to Shadow Bay, and 10 miles down Forest Service Road 5897 to North Waldo. Boat docks and launching facilities are available, plus good sailing and fishing; gas motors are prohibited on the lake. Many trails lead to small backcountry lakes from here, so this is a good place to establish a base camp.

From the North Waldo boat launch, hike up to **Rigdon Lakes** via Trail 3555. It's about a half-mile to the first lake. If you want a longer loop hike, continue north to two more lakes and the intersection with Trail 3583, turn left, then hike generally southward back to the lake and take a left onto Trail 3590, which follows the lakeshore east to your starting point.

Sisters

Sisters, named after its backdrop to the south, the Three Sisters peaks, was established in 1888 when nearby Camp Polk, a short-lived military outpost, was dismantled.

The town's 19th-century flavor has been preserved with wooden boardwalks, 1880s-style storefronts, and good old-fashioned Western hospitality. Some people are quick to lambaste the thematic zoning ordinances of Sisters as a cheap gimmick to lure tourists, while others enjoy the lovingly re-created ambience and the abundance of charming, independently owned shops, including one of the world's best clock shops.

As well as being a food, fuel, and lodging stop, Sisters (pop. 2,000) is also a jumping-off point for a wealth of outdoor activities. Skiing at Hoodoo Ski Bowl, fly-fishing and rafting on the Metolius River, and backpacking into the great Three Sisters Wilderness are just a few of the popular local pursuits. Nearby luxury resorts such as Black Butte Ranch, an annual rodeo, and a nationally famous quilting event add to the appeal of this vintage village.

SIGHTS
Three Creek Lake and Tam McArthur Rim

Three Creek Lake, tucked under **Tam McArthur Rim,** is a good place for a summer swim, especially if you have an inflatable raft to prevent full-body immersion in the often quite cold water. A tiny lakeside store rents rowboats; from the center of the lake you'll get a good view of Tam McArthur Rim, named for the original author of the classic and fascinating reference book *Oregon Geographic Names*.

From the lake, trails head into the Three Sisters Wilderness Area. One leads up to the

7,700-foot rim, and from the top the views of the Three Sisters and Broken Top are quite astounding. Snows can be heavy (the lake itself is at 6,500 feet), so don't count on hiking this trail before July.

A small lakeside campground ($14, no drinking water) at Three Creek Lake is a pleasant place to spend a couple of days in midsummer, but be forewarned that most return campers bring insect repellent.

To get here from Sisters, turn south on Elm Street, which becomes Forest Road 16. Follow Road 16 south about 17 miles to the lake. Be prepared for a couple of miles of fairly rough dirt road. During the winter, Road 16 between the lake and Sisters has a couple of Sno-Park areas that mark cross-country ski trails.

Black Butte

Hike up to the **Black Butte** lookout towers for a bird's-eye view of the Sisters area. It's about two miles of uphill hiking, often in full sun, to the top of the cinder cone; bring plenty of water. To reach the trailhead, take U.S. 20 west from Sisters, turn north (right) onto Forest Road 11 (Green Ridge Rd.), and pass Indian Ford campground; turn left onto Road 1110 and follow it 5.1 miles to the trailhead.

★ Metolius River

About 10 miles from Sisters is the second-largest tributary of the Deschutes River, the **Metolius.** To get here, take the Camp Sherman Highway off U.S. 20 five miles west of Sisters. This road will take you around Black Butte. On the north face of this steep, evergreen-covered cinder cone lies the source of the Metolius. A 0.25-mile trail takes you to a railing where you can see the water bubbling out of the ground.

Known simply as "the Spring," the water wells up out of the earth at a constant 48°F. Native rainbow trout thrive in the cold spring-fed waters of the upper Metolius, but they are not necessarily easy to catch—the water is so clear that the fish are extremely selective about what they'll take, and flies must be both perfect looking and perfectly presented. A beautiful riverside trail follows the Metolius as it meanders through the ponderosa pine trees past many excellent fishing holes. Drift boats are used to tackle the harder-to-reach places along this 25-mile waterway. Bring a bike along to the Metolius; bike trails are being developed here all the time, and they are perfect for easygoing family rides.

Five miles downstream from Camp

the glaciered Three Sisters peaks

Sherman (seven miles from the head of the Metolius Trail) is the **Wizard Falls Fish Hatchery,** which is open to visitors daily. Over 2.5 million fish, including Atlantic salmon, brook and rainbow trout, and kokanee salmon, are raised here annually. The hatchery is the only place in the state that stocks Atlantic salmon, which are transferred to Hosmer Lake.

SPORTS AND RECREATION
Skiing
Twenty miles (a little more than 30 minutes' drive) west of Sisters on Route 126 is one of Oregon's most family-oriented skiing areas, **Hoodoo** (541/822-3799 or 541/822-3337 snow phone, www.hoodoo.com, 9am-4pm Sun.-Tues. and Thurs., 9am-9pm Fri.-Sat., closed Wed., $48-51 adults, $31-34 seniors and children). Hoodoo has five chairlifts and a rope tow. The maximum vertical drop is 1,035 feet, and the runs are fairly evenly divided among advanced, intermediate, and beginner levels of difficulty. Prices go up a few bucks during holidays.

Horseback Riding
Black Butte Stables (541/595-2061, www.blackbuttestables.com) at **Black Butte Ranch** (eight miles west of Sisters on U.S. 20) has several packages that take you down trails in the shadow of the Three Sisters. Rides range from the one-hour Big Loop trail ride for beginning riders ($50) to the all-day Black Butte Posse ride ($175-225). Kids' pony rides go for $20.

Golf
Two well-groomed courses, **Big Meadow** and **Glaze Meadow,** are found at **Black Butte Ranch** (eight miles west of Sisters on U.S. 20, 855/253-2562, www.blackbutteranch.com, $77 for 18 holes during peak time). Big Meadow is more open and forgiving, while Glaze Meadow, which was extensively renovated in 2011, demands precise shots. Both have tall trees and lush fairways from tee to green. Tee times can be reserved online.

Three miles outside of Sisters, the highly regarded **Aspen Lakes** (541/549-4653, www.aspenlakes.com, $75 for 18 holes at prime time) offers 27 holes in the shadow of the Three Sisters. Bent-grass fairways and distinct volcanic red-cinder bunkers add to the stunning mountain vistas.

The Metolius is one of Oregon's most enchanting rivers.

ENTERTAINMENT AND EVENTS

The annual **Sisters Rodeo** (541/549-0121 or 800/827-7522) happens the second weekend of June. In addition to the normal assortment of calf-roping and bucking broncos, country dances, a buckaroo breakfast, and a parade round out the fun. A huge **quilt show** takes place during the second week of July; the outdoor show blankets the town with color. Also noteworthy is the annual **Sisters Folk Festival,** held in early September, the weekend after Labor Day. This even attracts some of the biggest names in blues and folk. Contact the **Sisters Chamber of Commerce** (291 E. Main St., 541/549-0251 or 866/549-0252, www.sisterscountry.com) for the schedule of events.

ACCOMMODATIONS

The ★ **Sisters Motor Lodge** (511 W. Cascade St., 541/549-2551 or 877/549-5446, www.sistersmotorlodge.com, $129-179) was built in 1939, when the North Santiam Highway first opened to auto traffic. It's set back from the highway, within easy walking distance of the shops and boutiques of Sisters. Beds are decorated with quilts, and the kitchenettes have charmingly retro appliances and Formica tables; pets are allowed in some guest rooms.

The **Best Western Ponderosa Lodge** (505 U.S. 20, 541/549-1234 or 888/549-4321, www.bestwesternsisters.com, $149-249) is a large ranch-style resort motel set back from the road in the scattered pines. Rooms feature private balconies with views of the mountains and the adjacent Deschutes National Forest. Other amenities include a spa, a heated pool, and free continental breakfast.

Eight miles west of Sisters on U.S. 20, **Black Butte Ranch** (541/595-1252 or 866/901-2961, www.blackbutteranch.com, $150-650) sits in line with other Cascade peaks in a setting of ponderosa pines, lush meadows, and aspen-bordered streams. Over 16 miles of trails thread through the 1,800 acres of forested grounds. Accommodations include deluxe hotel-type bedrooms, one- to three-bedroom condominium suites, and resort homes. The resort includes golf courses, bike trails, tennis courts, several swimming pools, organized kids' activities and day camps, and a fitness center with yoga and other classes.

Right on the edge of town, ★ **FivePine Lodge** (1021 Desperado Tr., 541/549-5900 or 866/974-5900, www.fivepinelodge.com, $209-293) is a lovely newer resort with convention center facilities and an environmentally sensitive approach. Stay in a spacious suite in the large stone-and-timber lodge or in a classy Craftsman-style cabin with Amish-built wood furniture (pets are permitted in a couple of the cabins). All accommodations include breakfast, a wine reception, and access to the on-site Sisters Athletic Club, which has a 25-yard lap pool and a variety of fitness classes. During the summer, an outdoor pool is open, and use of cruiser bikes is complimentary. Also in the FivePine complex you will find a very posh spa, a brewpub, a movie theater, and a Mexican restaurant.

In a residential area close to downtown, find the **Blue Spruce Bed & Breakfast** (444 S. Spruce St., 541/549-9644 or 888/328-9644, www.blue-spruce.biz, $169). Designed and built from the ground up as a B&B, the four guest rooms have outdoorsy Western themes but plenty of comfort. All bathrooms have a shower and a two-person whirlpool tub. Bikes are available for guests' use, and rooms have minifridges and fireplaces.

Lake Creek Lodge (13375 SW Forest Service Rd. 1419, Camp Sherman, 541/595-6331 or 800/797-6331, www.lakecreeklodge.com, $170-320, about $50 less off-season, minimum stays may be required) is near Camp Sherman in the Metolius Recreation Area. This full-service resort has individual houses and cottages that vary in price depending on the unit and the number of people. Tennis, swimming, and fishing are some of the many activities available. Although the cabins have kitchenettes, many summertime guests like to eat at least one dinner at the lodge restaurant (8am-11am and at 7pm Tues.-Sat., 8am-noon and at 6pm Sun. July-early Sept., dinner $24-38 adults, $12 children under age 10); dinner is served family-style on the deck or in the pine-paneled main lodge and features a different selection of entrées each day, complemented by homemade breads, salads, and desserts. Lake Creek caters especially well to families; pets are allowed in selected cabins.

Another Metolius retreat is at **Cold Springs Resort** (25615 Cold Springs Resort Ln., Camp Sherman, 541/595-6271, www.coldspringsresort.com, $168-175). The cabins feature naturally pure artesian well water. A footbridge across the Metolius River connects the resort to Camp Sherman, where groceries, a church, and a café are within easy walking distance. Pets are allowed for $10 per night but must be kept on a leash at all times and never left unattended. The resort also operates an RV park with full hookups ($40).

The cabins at the ★ **Metolius River Lodges** (12390 SW Forest Service Rd. 1419-700, 541/595-6290 or 800/595-6290, www.metoliusriverlodges.com, $135-329) are tucked in by the Metolius River right near the Camp Sherman store. The most coveted pair have decks extending over the river, and the majority have fireplaces and kitchens.

Wedged between giant ponderosa pines and the banks of the Metolius are the 12 elegant cabins of the ★ **Metolius River Resort** (25551 SW Forest Service Rd. 1419, 541/595-6281 or 800/818-7688, www.metoliusriverresort.com, $265). These beautiful wooden structures are bright and airy with lots of windows. The cabins are two stories high with more than 900 square feet of living space, comfortably sleep 4-6 people, and feature a fully equipped modern kitchen, full bath, river-rock fireplace stocked with all the firewood you'll need, and a river-view deck. Reservations made well in advance are a must. You'll find the resort behind the Kokanee Cafe.

A few miles west of the Metolius River turnoff on U.S. 20 is the turnoff to Suttle Lake and the elegant **Lodge at Suttle Lake** (13300 U.S. 20, 541/595-2628, www.thelodgeatsuttlelake.com, camping cabins $100, lodge rooms, suites, and deluxe cabins $250-400), where a Native American theme predominates. The least expensive accommodations are in newly built and very clean but rustic cabins that share a central bathhouse; lodge rooms and waterfront cabins are much more posh. Unlike several of the other Metolius area lodgings, the Suttle Lake lodge is pet-friendly. The lodge restaurant serves three meals a day.

If you want a horse-centered stay in the area, consider the **Long Hollow Ranch** (541/923-1901, www.lhranch.com, $825 three days, $1,500 six days), a guest ranch offering trail rides, cattle drives, and horsemanship lessons. Rates are per person based on double occupancy, and include all meals and on-ranch activities.

Camping

Bend Sisters Garden RV Resort (67667 Hwy. 20, 541/549-3021, www.bendsistersgardenrv.com, $54-59 RV, $64-180 cabins) is a sprawling and amenity-laden (pool, fishing pond, miniature golf) RV park on the road to Bend. It's about four miles from downtown Sisters, with good views of the mountains.

Six miles northwest of Sisters on Route 126, find **Indian Ford Campground** (541/549-7700, www.fs.usda.gov/main/deschutes, $12, mid-May-mid-Oct., no water), the closest public campground to town. Farther west on Route 126, you'll hit the turnoff to the **Metolius River campgrounds** ($12-18, drinking water available at all but Candle Creek), a number of very pleasant Forest Service campgrounds strung along the river both upstream and downstream from the hub of Camp Sherman. The only Metolius campground with reservations available is called **Camp Sherman** (877/444-6777, www.recreation.gov).

Several campgrounds on Suttle Lake have boat ramps (reservations at 877/444-6777, www.recreation.gov, $16, drinking water, May-early Oct.); the lake is a popular place to fish, water-ski, windsurf, and swim. **Link Creek campground** has the longest season, and also has a few yurts ($40, no pets).

A handful of campgrounds open only in

summer can be found near Sisters on the old McKenzie Highway, Route 242. **Cold Springs Campground** ($14, drinking water) is just five miles west of town on Route 242. This campground, at 3,400 feet in elevation, has 23 sites for tents and small trailers (up to 22 feet). It's a pretty spot near the source of Trout Creek. Near the pass at 5,200 feet is the rustic 10-site **Lava Camp Lake Campground** (free, no water, mid-June-Oct. depending on snow), where the main allure is its close proximity to the Pacific Crest Trail and the Three Sisters Wilderness.

Information about these campgrounds is available from **Sisters Ranger Station** (Pine St. and U.S. 20, 541/549-7700, www.fs.usda.gov/main/deschutes).

FOOD

A number of pretty average but often busy restaurants line Sisters's main street, Cascade Avenue. The hottest spot among them and a fun place is **Bronco Billy's Ranch Grill & Saloon** (190 E. Cascade Ave., 541/549-7427, www.broncobillysranchgrill.com, 11:30am-10pm daily, $10-22). Built in 1912, the upstairs rooms of this historical hotel have been refurbished into intimate mini-dining rooms. Barbecued ribs are the specialty of the house, but you can also find fresh seafood, steaks, salads, sandwiches, and Mexican fare. In one corner of the building, on the other side of the Western-style saloon doors, is Bronco Billy's. This funky watering hole must look much the same as it did 80 years ago. A racy painting that used to grace the local brothel is proudly displayed behind the bar, and cowboy hats on most heads complete the picture of a town whose Old West ambience gets better with age. For the price of a beer, you can get one of the local guys to tell you the inside scoop on what to do in this neck of the woods.

A somewhat hip and healthy alternative lies a block off the main drag: **Angeline's Bakery & Cafe** (121 W. Main Ave., 541/549-9122, http://angelinesbakery.com, 6:30am-6pm daily June-Oct., 6:30am-4pm daily Nov.-May) serves homemade baked goods,

salads, wraps, and fresh juices, with lots of gluten-free and vegan options. Try the raw zucchini "noodles" with pumpkin-seed pesto; if you really want a nutritional boost, chase it with a green smoothie. During the summer, Angelina's stays open late some nights and hosts music.

The best breakfast and lunch food in town is at ★ **Cottonwood Cafe** (403 E. Hood Ave., 541/549-2699, www.intimatecottagecuisine.com, 7:30am-3pm Wed.-Sun., $9-13), an intimate cottage with casual but delicious fare. Breakfast is fantastic, with Dutch apple crepes, smoked salmon scramble, and huevos Motulenos (eggs over ham, black beans and tortillas), and lunch sandwiches include a ratatouille wrap and an open-faced ocean melt. In nearby Camp Sherman, a special treat awaits at the ★ **Kokanee Cafe** (25545 SW Forest Service Rd. 1419, 541/595-6420, www.kokaneecafe.com, 5pm-close daily summer, reservations recommended, $20-30), which is known for its fresh and innovative cuisine served in a small, simply furnished dining room. The local lamb chop is brined with fennel and coriander before roasting and served with wild mushroom bread pudding; the steelhead is served atop faro and black olives, accompanied by wasabi vinaigrette. Dinner reservations are crucial during the summer and fishing season, given the small size of the building. The Kokanee usually takes a break during the winter and has scaled-back hours in the spring; this varies year to year, so call ahead or check the website if you're traveling in the off-season.

INFORMATION

Detailed information about the geology, natural history, wildlife, wilderness areas, and numerous recreational opportunities in the Metolius Recreation Area can be obtained from the **Sisters Ranger Station** (Pine St. and U.S. 20, 541/549-7700, www.fs.usda.gov/centraloregon). More information is available from the **Sisters Chamber of Commerce** (291 E. Main St., 541/549-0251 or 866/549-0252, www.sisterscountry.com).

Redmond

Sixteen miles north of Bend is Redmond (population about 26,000), another rapidly growing central Oregon city. Redmond is a hub, centrally located among Madras, Prineville, Bend, and Sisters, so even with a new bypass, traffic can get congested.

The city got its start when the Deschutes Irrigation and Power Company established irrigation canals here in the early 1900s. The railroad soon came, and real estate traders shortly followed. Like most central Oregon towns, it was once home to several lumber mills, but now, thanks to its regional airport and nearby resorts, tourism plays a major role in the economy.

SIGHTS
Peter Skene Ogden Scenic Wayside

Nine miles north of Redmond on U.S. 97, stop to peer into the dramatic Crooked River Gorge, a 300-foot-deep canyon. The old railroad trestle spanning the gorge was built in 1911 and helped to establish Redmond as a transportation hub. The old highway bridge, now open only to foot traffic, was built in 1926; before it was constructed, travelers had to descend the canyon walls to ford the river. The current highway bridge was built in 2003.

★ Smith Rock State Park

The majestic spires towering above the Crooked River north of Redmond on U.S. 97 are part of 623-acre **Smith Rock State Park** (9241 NE Crooked River Dr., Terrebonne, 541/548-7501, www.oregonstateparks.org, $5 day use). Named for a soldier who fell to his death from the highest promontory (3,230 feet) in the configuration, the park is a popular retreat for hikers, rock climbers, and casual visitors. Picnic tables, drinking water, and restrooms can be found near the parking area. The more adventurous can camp out in the park's primitive (except for the showers) walk-in camping area ($5 per person, campfires prohibited), located near the park entrance.

Although Smith Rock is known for its rock climbing, many visitors come here to hike. Seven miles of well-marked trails follow the

The Crooked River runs through Smith Rock State Park.

Crooked River and wend up the canyon walls to emerge on the ridgetops. Because the area is delicate and extremely sensitive to erosion, it's important not to blaze any trails, because they may leave visible scars for years.

Some of the sport-climbing routes at Smith Rock are as difficult and challenging as any you'll find in the United States. Most of the mountain's 17-million-year-old volcanic rock is soft and crumbly, making descents extra challenging. Chocks, nuts, friends, and other clean-climbing equipment and techniques are encouraged to reduce damage to the rock. On certain routes where these methods would prove impractical, permanent anchors have been placed. Climbers should use these fixed bolts (after testing them first for safety, of course) to minimize impact on the rock face. Stop in at the park-side store to pick up a climbing guide to the routes at Smith Rock that do not require mounting additional fixed protection.

Climbers should never disturb birds of prey and their young in their lofty aeries. Golden eagles nest on the cliffs past the far end of the parking area; bald eagles have nested in a tree visible from the camping area. Stop in at the park visitors center (housed in a yurt by the parking area) for details on these birds and other park flora and fauna.

Finally, pack plenty of water. The Crooked River is contaminated with chemicals from nearby farmlands and isn't suitable for drinking, and even a short hike in this often-hot park will leave you thirsty.

SPORTS AND RECREATION
Golf
Eagle Crest Resort (1522 Cline Falls Rd., 541/923-4653, www.eagle-crest.com) has three 18-hole golf courses: Resort and Ridge ($74 for 18 holes, $55 resort guests) as well as Challenge (a short 18 holes designed for a three-hour playing time, $44).

Crooked River Ranch (5195 SW Clubhouse Rd., 541/923-6343 or 800/833-3197, www.crookedriverranch.com, $43-50

for 18 holes), an 18-hole par-71 course, is wide open with few trees, but that doesn't detract from the challenge or the scenic vistas.

A true desert course found in Redmond that requires shot accuracy is the **Juniper Golf Club** (1938 SW Elkhorn Ave., 541/548-3121, www.playjuniper.com, $60-66 for 18 holes). This is an 18-hole par-72 course that snakes through the juniper and lava of the high desert. The prevailing winds and abundance of rocks off the fairway challenge your shot-making abilities.

Rock Climbing
Redpoint Climbing Supply (8222 N. Hwy. 97, Terrebonne, 800/923-6207, www.redpointclimbing.com, 7am-8pm Mon.-Thurs., 7am-10pm Fri.-Sat.) at the corner of U.S. 97 and Smith Rock Way is a good information and supply stop for climbers. Climbing lessons, both private and group, are offered by **First Ascent** (541/318-7170 or 800/325-5462, www.goclimbing.com), which is known for its women's programs, and **Smith Rock Climbing Guides** (541/788-6225, www.smithrockclimbingguides.com).

ACCOMMODATIONS
The newly renovated **Lodge at Eagle Crest** (1522 Cline Falls Rd., 888/306-9643, www.eagle-crest.com, $144-171), five miles west of Redmond, is now operated by Holiday Inn and offers hotel rooms and one-bedroom suites. The terrain and vegetation are representative of the high desert, and the backdrop is views of eight Cascade peaks. Ask about ski and golf packages. This is a low-key family-oriented place. Vacation rental homes are also available through the resort.

In town, the **Best Western Plus Rama Inn** (2630 SW 17th Pl., 541/548-8080, www.bestwestern.com, $179-194) is a comfortable place to spend a night or two, with continental breakfast and an indoor pool.

Rock climbers tend to camp, but when that gets old, the **Hub Motel** (1128 NW 6th St., 541/548-2101 or 800/784-3482, http://

thehubmotel.com, $52-62) is inexpensive, close to Smith Rock, allows dogs, and has kitchenettes.

FOOD

Redmond makes its mark on the culinary world more by the quality of the local Juniper Grove goat cheese and its locally raised Kobe beef than by its restaurants, but increasingly there are good places to eat here.

The **Brickhouse** (412 SW 6th St., 541/526-1782, http://brickhousesteakhouse.com, 4:30pm-close Tues.-Sat., $18-39) is a popular and very good steak and seafood restaurant, serving high-quality meat and using many local ingredients. The interior, with its exposed brick walls and local art, is inviting and classy.

★ **Diego's Spirited Kitchen** (447 SW 6th St., 541/316-2002, 11am-10pm daily, $15-27) is an upscale Mexican restaurant, emphasizing Southwestern-Mexican cuisine with French and Italian influences. Pork osso bucco slow-roasted with mushrooms is served over mashed potatoes with truffle oil; pork carnitas ravioli and seafood pasta are cooked up alongside burritos and enchiladas.

The **Seventh Street Brew House** (855 SW 7th St., 541/923-1795, 11:30am-11pm Mon.-Thurs., 11:30am-midnight Fri.-Sat., noon-9pm Sun., $7-10) is just a block off busy 6th Street and serves Cascade Lakes beer as well as pizza and pub food.

Redmond has a couple of other noteworthy pubs: **Pig and Pound** (427 SW 8th St., 541/526-1697, 4pm-9pm Mon.-Thurs., 4pm-10pm Fri., noon-10pm Sat., noon-9pm Sun., $8-12) is an English-style pub, complete with bangers and mash and local and imported beers on tap; two women head up the brewing operations at **Smith Rock Brewing Company** (546 NW 7th St., 541/279-7005, http://smithrockbrewing.com, 11:30am-8pm Tues.-Thurs., 11:30am-9pm Fri., noon-9pm Sat., $6-12), where Smith Rock brews and a few other local beers share rotating taps—in nice weather, this pub has good outside seating. Burgers and sandwiches are the specialty here.

On the road to Smith Rock, the **Terrebonne Depot** (400 NW Smith Rock Way, Terrebonne, 541/548-5030, www.terrebonnedepot.com, 11:30am-8:30pm Sun. and Wed.-Thurs., 11:30am-9pm Fri.-Sat., $10-24) offers fresh food, including a good selection of vegetarian options and pizza, in the gorgeously renovated historic Terrebonne train depot. Climbers and hikers can also get picnic lunches to go.

Prineville

Prineville (pop. 9,200), near the geographic center of Oregon, is the oldest incorporated town in central Oregon and still feels a bit like the Old West, even as it becomes a bedroom community for Bend and home to Facebook and Apple data centers. Prineville gets a meager 10 inches of rain per year, a positive factor for retirees and recreationalists seeking sun.

Prineville is also known as the Gateway to the Ochocos, a heavily wooded mountain range that runs east-west for 50 miles. One of Oregon's least-known recreational areas, the Ochocos are ruggedly pristine. Beyond these mountains stretches the long valley of the John Day River.

SIGHTS

A. R. Bowman Museum

A good place to begin your travels in Ochoco country is at the **A. R. Bowman Museum** (246 N. Main St., 541/447-3715, www.bowmanmuseum.org, 10am-5pm Mon.-Fri., 11am-4pm Sat.-Sun. summer, 10am-5pm Tues.-Fri., 11pm-4pm Sat. winter, free). This museum's two floors of exhibits and displays are a notch above most small-town historical museums. Fans of the Old West will enjoy the

Willows, Wagon Trains, and Range Wars

The Ochoco country, named after a Paiute word for willows, was heavily populated by Native Americans who lived off a bounty of deer, elk, fish, and camas roots. The first significant passage of Europeans other than trappers through the area was the Lost Wagon Train of 1845. Led by Stephen Meek, brother of the Oregon Territory spokesperson Joe Meek, the pioneers were seeking a route to the Willamette Valley that would be easier than the arduous trek over the Blue Mountains.

Instead, they found hardship, starvation, thirst, and death on a tortuous journey through the deserts of Malheur and Harney Counties and along the rugged ridges of the Ochoco Mountains. Their hardships finally ended when they found the Crooked River and followed it north to The Dalles. Somewhere during the trek, members of the party scooped up gold nuggets and kept them in a blue bucket. Although the legend of the Blue Bucket Mine has since captivated Oregon history buffs, its actual site has never been found.

In 1860, Major Enoch Steen led an expedition through the region, which resulted in a number of geographic features being named after him, including Steens Mountain and Stein's Pillar. Eight years later, Barney Prine built a blacksmith shop, a store, and a saloon near the bank of Ochoco Creek; the outpost grew into the city of Prineville, the only town in 10,000 square miles. It was settled by the sons of the pioneers who had come west on wagon trains.

At the turn of the 20th century, cinnabar, the raw ore in which mercury is found, was discovered in the Ochocos, resulting in an influx of miners. About the same time, a range war broke out between the cattle ranchers and the sheepherders. Groups like the Ezee Sheep Shooters and the Crook County Sheep Shooters Association bragged that they had slaughtered 8,000-10,000 sheep in 1905 alone. Incensed by this lawlessness, the citizens of Oregon moved to stop the killing; still, troubles continued for cattle and sheep ranchers and farmers. Harsh winters took their toll on livestock, and the hope that the plains would be receptive to wheat farming was unrealized.

During World War I, many homesteaders gave up and moved to the cities to work for the war effort. In 1917, Prineville made a decision that wound up boosting the local economy. The town built a railroad to Redmond, linking its line with the Union Pacific. Used primarily to haul ponderosa pine logs, the railroad remains the only city-owned railroad still in operation in the United States. In the 1950s a new industry was added to the mainstays of logging, ranching, and farming: Gemstones of high quality were discovered in the Ochocos, prompting a rockhounding and tourism boom that continues to this day.

tack room with saddles, halters, and woolly chaps. Rock hounds will be delighted with the displays of Blue Mountain picture jasper, thunder eggs, and fossils. Other classic displays include a moonshine still, a country store, an upstairs parlor of the early 1900s, and a campfire setup with a graniteware coffeepot and a pound of Bull Durham tobacco.

SPORTS AND RECREATION
Hiking
Stein's Pillar is a distinctive rock outcropping in the Ochoco National Forest about 15 miles northeast of Prineville. A four-mile round-trip hike passes through meadows and old-growth forest with some lovely panoramic views and a final steep, challenging stretch of trail before reaching the rock. From town, head east on U.S. 26 for nine miles and turn north onto Mill Creek Road. Continue for 6.5 miles to the turnoff for the trailhead.

Farther up Mill Creek Road, find Wildcat Campground and a trailhead for the **Mill Creek-Twin Pillars** trail. From the campground, the trail follows Mill Creek into the Mill Creek Wilderness Area. This wet area supports lots of wildflowers and also a few cattle. If you go the full 8.3 miles to the Twin Pillars, a pair of 200-foot-tall volcanic plugs, it's necessary to ford the creek a number of times, which can be difficult early in the season.

Another worthwhile place to visit is

Lookout Mountain, the highest point in the Ochocos. It's a unique biosphere with 28 plant communities, one of the finest stands of ponderosa pines in the state, lots of elk and deer, a herd of wild mustang, and creeks full of rainbow and brook trout. A seven-mile trail starts near the **Ochoco Ranger Station** (541/416-6500) 22 miles east of Prineville on Forest Service Road 22 at the campground picnic area and ends at the summit of Lookout Mountain, from which 11 major peaks are visible. June is the time to visit to see one of the best wildflower displays in the state. To get there, drive 14 miles east from Prineville on U.S. 26, and bear right at the sign for the ranger station.

About halfway between Prineville and Madras on U.S. 26, **Rimrock Springs Wildlife Management Area** has a 1.35-mile trail (0.5 mile paved) through fragrant sagebrush and juniper to a wetland created by a small dam. Spring and early summer brings a good display of wildflowers, including bitterroot; lizards, snakes, and many species of birds are also easy to see on this short hike.

Fishing

The 310-acre **Prineville Reservoir,** 17 miles south of Prineville on Route 27, was built for irrigation and flood control. A popular year-round boating and fishing lake, it is famous for its huge bass and is also stocked with rainbow trout.

Just downstream from the reservoir dam is a winding stretch of the **Crooked River** that offers some of the best fly-fishing in the state, in an incredibly scenic atmosphere beneath basalt rimrock cliffs. This section of the river is also dotted with a series of campgrounds, all of which are good places to camp and fish. This is a fine place to learn to fly-fish; it's easy to wade into the water away from streamside brush. Non-anglers can climb the short trail up Chimney Rock (from the Chimney Rock campground) to the top of the rimrock. From there, it's possible to walk along the ridge all afternoon.

Ochoco Reservoir, six miles east of Prineville on U.S. 26, is a favorite recreational spot for locals, with year-round fishing, boating, and camping.

ACCOMMODATIONS

The **Rustlers Inn Motel** (960 NW 3rd St., 541/447-4185, www.rustlersinn.com, $82-93) was designed in the Old West style. Art by local artists and antique furniture grace the large rooms.

A budget motel that's popular with anglers is the **Executive Inn** (1050 NE 3rd St., 541/447-4152, $65-80), east of downtown. The large multiroom family unit is recommended as a base for a family weekend visit to the Painted Hills, as motel accommodations in Mitchell are limited.

More upscale accommodations are available at the **Best Western Prineville Inn** (1475 NE 3rd St., 541/447-8080, $122-151), near the east end of town.

The **Prineville Reservoir Resort** (19600 SE Juniper Canyon Rd., 541/447-7468, www.prinevillereservoirresort.com) is on the shoreline of Prineville Reservoir, 17 miles southeast of Prineville on the Paulina Highway (Rte. 27). This resort offers motel accommodations with kitchenettes ($75), camping units ($27-29), and rustic cabins (bring your own bedding, $35). The resort also rents fishing boats.

One of Central Oregon's newest resorts, ★ **Brasada Ranch** (16986 Brasada Ranch Rd., Powell Butte, 866/373-4882, www.brasada.com, $309-929) lies in the open hills of the ranch country between Prineville and Bend. *Brasada* is the Spanish cowboy term for "brush country," and that pretty much describes the landscape here, although it doesn't include the beautiful views of Cascade peaks you'll find here. This resort, which is very popular with golfers, is an easy place to hunker down for a few days—the rooms are luxurious, but comfortably so; there's a good fitness center and an outdoor pool that resembles those found in upscale Hawaiian resorts, an excellent restaurant, a golf course, and biking, hiking, and horse trails. It's also a convenient location for Crooked and Deschutes

Rivers anglers who want to stay in an upscale resort. Lodgings range from suites in the main "ranch house" lodge ($339) to one- to three-bedroom cabins ($545-929); they're all lovely, and the cabins have fully equipped kitchens.

Camping

For good campsites in the **Ochocos** (www.fs.usda.gov/main/deschutes, mid-Apr.-late Oct.), take Ochoco Creek Road approximately 10 miles east of Ochoco Lake. Camp beneath big ponderosa pines at **Wildwood** ($8, drinking water), **Ochoco Divide** ($13, no water), and **Walton Lake** ($15, water), where you can fish, boat, or hike the trail to Round Mountain. While on this loop, stop at the mining ghost town of Mayflower. Founded in 1873, the community was active until 1925; a stamp mill is still visible.

Camp alongside the Crooked River at any of the nine **Bureau of Land Management** campgrounds (541/416-6700, www.blm.gov/or/resources/recreation, $8) on Route 27; they are about 15-20 miles south of Prineville. Be sure to bring water, or be prepared to filter river water.

FOOD

For lunch, the **Sandwich Factory** (277 NE Court St., 541/447-4429, 7am-7pm Mon.-Fri., 8am-3pm Sat., $6-15), just west of the courthouse, has a huge menu of really good sandwiches. It's also an excellent place to people watch at lunch—most of downtown Prineville seems to eat here.

Behind a downright scary exterior lies an extremely popular (and not at all frightening) steak house: **Club Pioneer** (1851 NE 3rd St., 541/447-6177, www.clubpioneer.com, 11am-9pm Sun.-Thurs., 11am-10pm Fri., 4pm-10pm Sat., $14-26). The competition,

downtown's **Barney Prine's Steakhouse and Saloon** (389 NE Main St., 541/362-1272, http://barneyprines.com, 11am-2pm Wed.-Fri., 5pm-close Tues.-Sun., $10-24), is a bit more stylish, with beechwood floors salvaged from a Jim Beam distillery, a huge and beautiful bar, and a good wine list. The menu goes well beyond steaks to include pasta, chicken, and seafood.

Even Prineville now has a brewpub! **Solstice Brewing Company** (234 N. Main St., 541/233-0883, 11:30am-9pm daily., $7-15) is a family-friendly, very casual pub with decent sandwiches, fish tacos, and Double Dam IPA on tap.

It's about 20 miles (a 20-minute drive) from Prineville to the Brasada Ranch resort, where you'll find sophisticated farm-to-table cuisine in the area at the resort's **Range** (16986 Brasada Ranch Rd., Powell Butte, 866/373-4882, 5pm-9pm Tues.-Sat., $19-44). The restaurant has an upscale Western ambience and offers both indoor and outdoor seating and impressive views of the Cascades. The food, both here and at the resort's more casual restaurant, the **Ranch House** (7am-9pm daily, light dinner $11-19), is very good.

INFORMATION

The **Prineville-Crook County Chamber of Commerce** (785 NW 3rd St., 541/447-6304, http://visitprineville.org,) has a helpful staff and lots of information to dispense. The **Ochoco National Forest** (3160 NE 3rd St., 541/416-6500, www.fs.usda.gov/central-oregon) can offer details on hiking in the Ochocos; the website is an excellent resource for trail information. The **Bureau of Land Management** (3050 NE 3rd St., 541/416-6700, www.blm.gov) can guide you to rock collecting sites.

Warm Springs and Lower Deschutes River

North of the Bend-Redmond area, the juniper- and sage-lined roadsides and fields of mint and wheat stand in welcome contrast to the busy main drags of the Bend-Redmond-Sisters urban complex to the south.

MADRAS

Madras (pop. 6,000) is mostly known as a supply town for the surrounding agricultural area, which in places comes right up to downtown's doorstep. West of town, the Crooked, Metolius, and Deschutes Rivers join up and are impounded by Round Butte Dam to form Lake Billy Chinook. The main access to the lake is via Cove Palisades State Park. Downstream from the lake, the Deschutes River continues on its path to the Columbia. The most popular place for rafting the Deschutes is the area around Maupin, 47 miles north of Madras.

Madras is one of the region's most culturally diverse towns: Over 35 percent of its residents are Latino, and over 5 percent are Native American. Many more Native Americans live on the nearby Warm Springs Reservation.

Lake Billy Chinook

Heading north from Bend, travelers needn't put away their recreational gear. Just outside of Madras is a park that offers hiking, boating, fishing, waterskiing, and bird-watching. **Cove Palisades State Park** (541/546-3412 or 800/452-5687, www.oregonstateparks.org, $5 day use, $20 tent camping, $28-30 RV, $85 cabin) is 14 miles southwest of Madras off U.S. 97. Towering cliffs, Cascade vistas, gnarled junipers, and **Lake Billy Chinook** with its 72-mile shoreline create a stunning backdrop for outdoor activities. The lake was created when Round Butte Dam backed up the waters of the Deschutes, Metolius, and Crooked Rivers. For the best views of how these rivers come together, hike up the Tam-a-lau Trail (a quick 600-foot elevation gain) to the top of the Peninsula, a plateau of land between the backed-up Crooked and Deschutes Rivers. At the top, the trail makes a loop around the

BEND AND CENTRAL OREGON
WARM SPRINGS AND LOWER DESCHUTES RIVER

Three river canyons meet at Lake Billy Chinook.

Peninsula with good views onto the Cascades and the river canyons. In total it's six miles round-trip, best done in the springtime when it's not too hot and when the balsamroot and lupine are in bloom.

The lake is popular with boaters ($10 moorage fee); **Cove Palisades Resort & Marina** (5700 S.W. Marina Dr., 541/546-9999 or 877/546-7171, www.covepalisadesresort.com) rents everything from stand-up paddleboards to houseboats.

Richardson's Recreational Ranch

If you're a rock hound, you'll want to visit **Richardson's Recreational Ranch** (6683 NE Haycreek Rd., 541/475-2680 or 800/433-2680, www.richardsonrockranch.com, 7am-5pm daily March.-Oct., $1 per pound and up). This family-owned and operated enterprise has extensive rock beds loaded with thunder eggs, moss agates, jaspers, jasper-agate, Oregon sunset, and rainbow agates, and it is a huge hit with most kids. If you want to chip agates out of one of the many exposed ledges on the ranch, you will need to bring chisels, wedges, and other necessary hard-rock mining tools. Once you've completed your dig, you drop your rocks off at the office and pay for them by the pound. And if you don't care for dirt under your fingernails, you can always find rocks for sale from all over the world in the ranch's rock shop. To get there, take U.S. 97 north of Madras for 11 miles and turn right at the sign near mile marker 81. Follow the road for three miles to the ranch office. Rock diggers must start by 3pm, and the eight-mile road to the digging site is closed when wet.

Accommodations and Food

Most of the lodgings in Madras are on the spartan side. **Sonny's Motel** (1539 SW U.S. 97, 541/475-7217, www.sonnysmotelmadras. com, $85-99), a basic but thoroughly decent place on the south end of town, is a good deal and allows pets. The **Quality Inn Madras** (12 SW 4th St., 541/475-6141, www.choice-hotels.com/oregon , $90-140) is a step up; both

Sonny's and the Best Western have small outdoor pools, which are quite nice on a hot afternoon in Madras. The **Inn at Cross Keys Station** (66 NW Cedar St., 541/475-5800 or 877/475-5800, http://innatcrosskeysstation. com, $112-156) is by far the most luxurious and restful place to stay in town. It has an indoor pool and conference facilities.

Amid all the fast-food joints in Madras, there's a shining beacon of healthy eating: **Great Earth Natural Foods** (46 SW D St., 541/475-1500, www.greatearth.biz, 7am-6pm Mon.-Fri., 10am-3pm Sat., $6-9) is a small food store with an exceptionally good deli. Stop in for a roasted vegetable salad, a sandwich, or a smoothie. A longtime Madras favorite, **Pepe's** (221 SE 5th St., 541/475-1144, 10am-8pm Mon.-Sat., $7-11), is a friendly all-around Mexican restaurant.

Geno's Italian Grill (212 SW 4th St., 541/475-6048, www.genositaliangrill.net, 11am-9pm Tues.-Sun., $12-25) is the best bet for a relaxed and tasty Italian meal. Though the menu features pasta and pizza, you'll also find a wide selection of American fare such as burgers, steaks, and entree salads.

CAMPING

Two overnight campgrounds at **Cove Palisades State Park** (541/546-3412 or 800/452-5687, www.oregonstateparks.org, $5 day use, $20 tent camping, $28-30 RV, $85 cabin) offer all the amenities: Deschutes campground (May-mid-Sept.) has 82 full-hookup sites and 92 tent sites; the year-round Crooked River campground, perched right on the canyon rim, has 93 sites with electricity and water. Reserve in advance (800/452-5687, www.reserveamerica.com), as these are extremely popular campgrounds.

Rent a houseboat on Lake Billy Chinook from **Cove Palisades Resort & Marina** (5700 S.W. Marina Dr., 541/546-9999 or 877/546-7171, www.covepalisadesresort.com, $1,500-4,200 for three days, $2,275-6,750 for a week).

Culver, a little town southwest of Madras, is home to the **Redmond/Central Oregon**

KOA (2435 SW Jericho Ln., Culver, 541/546-7972 or 800/562-1992, www.madras-koa.com, $29 tent, $34-41 RV, $59-104 cabin). An outdoor pool plus some sites with shade are the big attractions at this well-run campground.

WARM SPRINGS INDIAN RESERVATION

Within the 600,000-acre **Warm Springs Indian Reservation** (www.warmsprings.com), which straddles U.S. 26 north of Madras, you can see the age-old practice of dip-net fishing on the Deschutes River, as well as the richest collection of Native American artifacts in the country at a 27,000-square-foot museum. But the reservation is hardly divorced from modern-day U.S. culture—tribal members operate a dam, a resort hotel, a casino (on Hwy. 26 across from the museum), and a lumber mill. It's interesting to note that these entrepreneurs are the descendants of the same Native Americans who greeted Lewis and Clark and Deschutes explorers Peter Skene Ogden (in 1826), John Frémont, and Kit Carson (both in 1843).

★ Museum at Warm Springs

You'll find an impressive display of Native American culture at the **Museum at Warm**

the Museum at Warm Springs

Springs (541/553-3331, www.museumatwarmsprings.org, 9am-5pm Tues.-Sat. $7 adults, $6 seniors, $4.50 teens, $3.50 children), just east of the town of Warm Springs below the viewpoint at the bottom of the Deschutes River Canyon. Audiovisual displays, old photos, and tapes of traditional chants of the Paiute, Warm Springs, and Wasco peoples (the three groups that live on the Warm Springs Reservation) are artfully presented. Each group's distinct culture, along with the thriving social and economic community they collectively formed, constitutes the major theme of this museum.

Replicas of a Paiute mat lodge, a Warm Springs tepee, and a Wasco plank house, along with recordings of each group's language, underscore the cultural richness and diversity of the area's original inhabitants. The exhibits, curated from a collection of more than 20,000 artifacts, range from primitive prehistoric hand tools to a push-button-activated Wasco wedding scene. Native American foodstuffs and art are on sale in the bookstore.

Kah-Nee-Ta

Kah-Nee-Ta Resort (541/553-1112 or 800/554-4786, www.kahneeta.com), a golf and hot springs resort at the bottom of a canyon

about a dozen miles off U.S. 26 from the town of Warm Springs, is a good place to find the sun when western Oregon seems unrelentingly gloomy. The 1,000-foot elevation and 12-inch annual rainfall enable golfers to play year-round; Kah-Nee-Ta is even snow-free in February. Spa Wanapine offers a variety of massage, aesthetic, and therapeutic treatments. Owned by the Confederated Tribes of Warm Springs, this arrow-shaped hotel is a focal point of the reservation, which includes a working ranch and wild horses.

Lodging possibilities include tepees ($79, bring your own sleeping bags and pads) and RV sites ($69) as well as hotel rooms, suites, and cottages ($139-640). The hot mineral baths and a spring-fed Olympic-sized swimming pool are among the highlights. There are also bike rentals, tennis, horseback riding, and hiking. Day visitors can take advantage of Kah-Nee-Ta's Big Village hot spring pool (92°F in the cool weather, and cooled in the summer) and hot tubs (included in overnight room rates) for $15; the 184-foot waterslide costs $4. A separate (generally quieter) pool in the lodge area is for lodge guests only.

Resort guests who aren't camping are pretty much forced to eat at one of the resort's two restaurants (it's a long drive anyplace else): the **Chinook Northwest Grille** (6:30am-11am and 5pm-8:30pm daily, $12-25) and the casual arcade-like **Warm Springs Grill** (11am-11pm Sun.-Thurs., 11am-1am Fri.-Sat., $9-22). The summertime Saturday-night **salmon bake** ($30, $15 children ages 12 and under, reservations recommended), featuring traditional dancing and salmon cooked outside on cedar sticks over an alder fire, is quite popular.

MAUPIN

The riverside town of Maupin is usually a pretty quiet place, catering mostly to anglers who come to fly-fish the native Deschutes River redside trout. On summer weekends, however, it becomes a bit of a zoo when river rafters descend.

Sherar's Falls

Downstream from the Sandy Beach raft takeout is **Sherar's Falls,** a cascade that demands a portage if you're rafting to the Columbia. A bridge crosses the Deschutes just downstream from the waterfall. At the bottom of the waterfall is a traditional Native American fishing area, still used by Warm Springs community members. You'll see the rather rickety-looking fishing platforms perched over the river, and you may also see people dipnetting from them. If you're in the mood for tooling around, cross the bridge to the west side of the Deschutes and follow Route 216 a few miles to **White River Falls State Park** (800/551-6949, www.oregonstateparks.org), a day-use park with another excellent waterfall and a short trail to the remains of an old hydroelectric power plant.

Rafting

Just about every tour company operating in central Oregon runs raft trips down the 13-mile "splash and giggle" stretch of the Deschutes, from Harpham Flat Campground to Sandy Beach, just above Sherar's Falls. Wapinita, Box Car, Oak Springs, White River, and Elevator Rapids are the highlights of this trip; look also for the resident ospreys as you pass the Maupin Bridge.

Sun Country Tours (531 SW 13th St., Bend, 541/382-6277 or 800/883-8842, www.suncountrytours.com) runs a full-day trip ($108 adults, $98 children) along the Harpham Flat-Sandy Beach stretch of the river. A hearty grilled chicken lunch is included. Transportation from Bend or Sunriver to Maupin is also part of the day-trip packages.

Rapid River Rafters (500 SW Bond St., Bend, 541/382-1514 or 800/962-3327, www.rapidriverrafters.com) offers a series of fullday and multiday packages on the Deschutes River. The one-day trip ($85 adults, $75 children) takes in 17 miles of the river from Harpham Flat to Lone Pine. A hearty lunch is included. The two-day trip ($275 adults,

$220 children) floats 44 miles of exciting white water from Trout Creek to Sandy Beach. The three-day trip ($400) runs 55 miles from Warm Springs to Sandy Beach. On all of the multiday trips, the camping and meal preparations at pleasant riverside locations are taken care of by guides. The season is late April-early October, and camping equipment is available for rent if you don't have your own. Among its many trips in Oregon, **Ouzel Outfitters** (1441 SW Chandler Ave., Bend, 541/385-5947 or 800/788-7238, www.oregon-rafting.com) offers a full-day trip ($105) on the Lower Deschutes out of Maupin.

Experienced rafters can rent a boat from **All Star Rafting and Kayaking** (405 Deschutes Ave., 541/395-2201 or 800/909-7238, www.asrk.com, raft from $80-190 per day, inflatable kayak from $35-45 per day) or **River Trails Deschutes** (301 Bakeoven Rd., 541/395-2545 or 888/324-8837, www.rivertrails.com, rafts from $90 per day, single kayas from $25 per day). Both of these Maupin outfitters also offer guided trips and shuttles. Currently no permits are needed to run the river, but there is a $2 per day/per person fee collected by the Oregon State Parks at the Harpham Flat put-in site. Call **Affordable Deschutes Shuttle** (541/395-2809, www.affordabledeschutesshuttle.com) if you need someone to take your car from put-in to take-out ($40 for Harpham Flat to Sandy Beach).

Fishing

Downstream from Maupin, anglers fish the Deschutes River year-round for trout; steelhead are in the river August-November. Part of the reason to fish here, especially in the spring and fall, is the beautiful canyon.

Deschutes Canyon Fly Shop (599 S. U.S. 197, 541/395-2565, www.flyfishingde-schutes.com, 8am-5pm Mon.-Sat., 8am-1pm Sun.) sells supplies and can advise you on the hatches and other conditions. They can also set you up with a guide (about $325-450 per day depending on the type of trip). John, the shop's owner, is very helpful, and really encourages women anglers. Maupin's other fly shop, the **Deschutes Angler Fly Shop** (504 Deschutes Ave., 541/395-0995, www.deschutesangler.com, 8am-6pm daily), is also worth a visit for both gear and information. The owners of this shop are experts on Spey casting, a two-handed technique, and they hold regular

the Dechutes River upstream from Maupin

fly-fishing the Deschutes near Maupin

casting clinics. The **Oasis Resort** (609 S. U.S. 197, 541/395-2611, www.deschutesriveroasis. com) also runs a guide service.

Accommodations and Food

If you don't want to camp, stay in a simple cabin at the **Oasis Resort** (609 S. U.S. 197, 541/395-2611, www.deschutesriveroasis.com, $50-95); it's a local classic. The **Deschutes Motel** (616 Mill St., 541/395-2626, www. deschutesmotel.com, $95-129) is above the river near Maupin's main downtown area. The fanciest place in Maupin is the **Imperial River Company** (304 Bakeoven Rd., 541/395-2404 or 800/395-3903, www.deschutesriver. com, $99-256), which has a riverside lodge. Some rooms have balconies overlooking the river, and all are nicely decorated and quite comfortable.

Right in town, the **Maupin City Park** (206 Bakeoven Rd., just downstream from the bridge, 541/395-2252, $24 tents, $32 RVs, reservations recommended for summer weekends) is on a grassy riverbank lot. Unlike almost all of the Bureau of Land Management (BLM) campgrounds along the Deschutes, Maupin City Park has water and showers.

Eat a hearty prefloat breakfast at the **Oasis**

(609 S. U.S. 197, 541/395-2611, www.deschutes-riveroasis.com, 7am-8pm Fri.-Sat., 8am-4pm Sun., $7-10)—it's also a good place for a burger and a beer. The **Imperial River Company** (301 Bakeoven Rd., 541/395-2404, 11am-10pm daily late Apr.-mid-Sept., 4pm-9pm Mon.-Fri., 11am-9pm Sat.-Sun. mid-Sept.-Oct., 4pm-9pm Fri., 11am-9pm Sat.-Sun. Nov.-late Apr., $8-22) is the most full-service restaurant in town, featuring steaks from the family cattle. The eatery that is most attractive to rafters coming off a hot day on the river, however, is the ice cream shop by the bridge.

CAMPING

Both upstream and downstream from Maupin are several riverside **BLM campgrounds** (541/416-6700, Memorial Day-Labor Day, $8-12). Bring water, or be prepared to filter it from the river. **Harpham Flat Campground** is the main launching spot for day trips on the Deschutes, and this place can be a little more hectic than the neighboring campgrounds. The nicest spots are actually a ways downstream at **Beavertail** and **Macks Canyon,** 21 and 29 miles north of Maupin, respectively. Reservations are not accepted.

Northeastern Oregon

Look for ★ to find recommended sights, activities, dining, and lodging.

Highlights

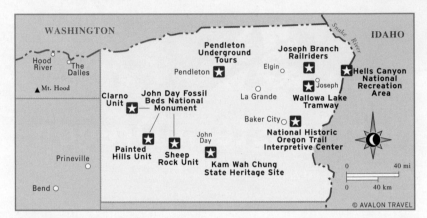

★ **John Day Fossil Beds National Monument:** At these three separate fossil bed units, you'll learn about saber-toothed tigers and wind through remote outposts of Miocene-era life (page 505).

★ **Kam Wah Chung State Heritage Site:** This is a fascinating remnant of the time when Chinese laborers outnumbered European settlers in gold camps of the West (page 511).

★ **Pendleton Underground Tours:** These tours explore everything from a Chinese jail to a brothel, the true underground of 1880s frontier life (page 514).

★ **Joseph Branch Railriders:** Hop aboard a railriding car (a cross between a recumbent bike and a rail car) and coast most of the way from Joseph to Enterprise on an abandoned rail line. It's an easy pedal back to Joseph (page 530).

★ **Wallowa Lake Tramway:** Hitch a ride on a gondola and whiz to the top of Mount Howard, with views over the Wallowa Mountains and nearby Hells Canyon (page 534).

★ **Hells Canyon National Recreation Area:** The world's deepest river gorge is trenched by the Snake River. The best way to see this otherwise almost inaccessible canyon is by raft or jet boat (page 538).

★ **National Historic Oregon Trail Interpretive Center:** This excellent museum tells the story of the Oregon Trail pioneers and their treacherous traversal of the West (page 541).

F or jaw-dropping scenic grandeur, outdoor recreation, and escapes from the urban world, Oregon's north-eastern corner is hard to top. The magnificent Wallowa Mountains easily invoke comparisons to the Swiss Alps. Hells

Canyon, carved by the Snake River, is one of the deepest river-carved gorges in the world, averaging 6,600 feet in depth. West of the Wallowas rise the Blue Mountains. The high country of the Blue Mountains is often dusted with snow by September, which was when Oregon Trail pioneers crossed these mountain passes. With its headwaters in the Blue Mountains, the John Day River cuts one of Oregon's most dramatic canyons, with fascinating fossil beds and an insightful interpretive center to help make sense of the region's long-buried natural history.

Just as the fossil beds provide a cross section of the earth's history, a trip through northeastern Oregon will give you a feel for the leather-tough people who settled here. In country towns and larger centers like Baker City, La Grande, and Pendleton, history is not very old; what may seem like the Old West is still a way of life. And while it remains primarily rural ranch country, the area is

becoming an increasingly popular haven for painters, sculptors, and writers.

PLANNING YOUR TIME

For many travelers on a road trip, northeast-ern Oregon will either be the first or the last part of Oregon they will encounter. If the Willamette Valley or the Oregon coast is the focus of your Oregon vacation, you might find it tempting to hurtle right through this corner of the state on I-84. However, plan to devote at least a day or two to explore the area's rich history and astoundingly dramatic scenery. Don't forget: The world's deepest river gorge is here, as are some of its richest fossil beds

In order to really explore this wild country, get off the interstate. From Ontario, consider crossing the state on U.S. 26, which travels through pine-clad mountains to the John Day River Valley, one of Oregon's most scenic. The river trenches through a layer cake of dramatic geologic formations to expose the **John Day**

Previous: Mount Howard; Painted Cove Trail. **Above:** riding the rails between Enterprise and Joseph.

Northeastern Oregon

© AVALON TRAVEL

To Portland

To Toppenish

To Spokane

To The Dalles

To Madras

To Bend

Prineville

Prineville Reservoir State Park

Ochoco Lake State Park

Stein's Pillar

Ochoco Summit 4,720ft

Painted Hills

John Day Fossil Beds National Monument Clarno Unit

Antelope

Mitchell

Crooked River

Paulina

Dayville

John Day Fossil Beds National Monument Painted Hills Unit

John Day Fossil Beds National Monument Sheep Rock Unit

Spray

John Day River

JOHN DAY FOSSIL BEDS NATIONAL MONUMENT

Fossil

Condon

Cottonwood Canyon State Park

Day River

John Day River

Biggs

Arlington

Columbia River

Umatilla

To Burns

Canyon City

John Day

STRAWBERRY MOUNTAIN WILDERNESS

Strawberry Mountain 9,038ft

KAM WAH CHUNG STATE HERITAGE SITE

Blue Mountain Hot Springs

Prairie City

Dixie Pass 5,280ft

Granite

Sumpter

Phillips Reservoir

ELKHORN DRIVE NATIONAL SCENIC BYWAY

Haines

North Powder

Lehman Hot Springs

McKay Creek Reservoir

Hermiston

Pendleton

COLD SPRINGS NATIONAL WILDLIFE REFUGE

PENDLETON UNDERGROUND TOURS

Emigrant Springs State Park

La Grande

HOT LAKE MINERAL HOT SPRINGS

Milton-Freewater

Walla Walla

WASHINGTON

OREGON

Elgin

Grande Ronde River

To Lewiston

To Burns

Baker City

Thief Valley Reservoir

Union

Cove

Wallowa Mountains

Matterhorn 10,004ft

Eagle Cap 9,685ft

Enterprise

Wallowa

Wallowa River

NATIONAL HISTORIC OREGON TRAIL INTERPRETIVE CENTER

Halfway

WALLOWA LAKE TRAMWAY

Mt Howard 8,200ft

Chief Joseph Mountain 9,617ft

Joseph

JOSEPH BRANCH RAILRIDERS

Imnaha

Imnaha River

HELLS CANYON NATIONAL RECREATION AREA

Vale

Ontario

Farewell Bend State Park

Snake River

To Boise

IDAHO

0   20 mi

0   20 km

Fossil Beds National Monument. Even if you stay closer to the interstate, consider branching off and making a loop around the Wallowa Mountains, a soaring piece of real estate that contains 17 individual peaks over 9,000 feet high. This side road also takes you to the brink of Hells Canyon, where the Snake River carves a gorge beneath 6,500-foot cliffs.

If you stick to I-84 and the fast track, at least realize that this route parallels the original Oregon Trail, the wagon route that brought in upward of 50,000 pioneers to the Pacific Northwest between 1843 and 1860. Stop at the National Historic Oregon Trail Interpretive Center near Baker City to learn more about this great human migration. (Baker City is also a good place to spend a night, with a lovely old downtown hotel, an excellent brewpub, and plenty of restaurants.) Then pull off the interstate at Pendleton to experience the city's colorful past on Pendleton Underground Tours, which explores a subterranean business district and a brothel from the turn of the 20th century.

John Day Fossil Beds and Vicinity

The canyon-cutting John Day River drains the western slopes of the Blue Mountains, trenching through north-central Oregon before spilling into the Columbia River. The John Day River Valley also offers some of Oregon's most tantalizing human history, plus fascinating glimpses into the region's prehistory. In the 1860s, self-taught geologist Thomas Condon discovered what is now known as the John Day Fossil Beds, which provide a paleontological record of 40-plus million years of ancient life.

★ JOHN DAY FOSSIL BEDS NATIONAL MONUMENT

The 14,000-acre John Day Fossil Beds National Monument is divided into three areas: the Sheep Rock Unit, about 40 miles west of John Day, with the monument's excellent interpretive center; the Painted Hills Unit, another 45 miles farther west; and the Clarno Unit, northwest of the other units, about 20 miles from the town of Fossil. For further information, contact John Day Fossil Beds National Monument (32651 Hwy. 19, Kimberly, 541/987-2333, www.nps.gov/joda). Admission is free to all units.

The days of 50-ton apatosaurs and 50-foot-long crocodiles, as well as delicate ferns and flowers, are captured in the rock formations of the three beds, easily visited in a day's road trip. This is the richest concentration of prehistoric early mammal and plant fossils in the world. More than 120 species have been identified, documenting a period dating from the extinction of the dinosaurs to the beginning of the last great ice age.

Accommodations are in short supply in this remote part of Oregon. The small towns near the monument's individual units have motels, and the town of John Day has the largest selection. A few campgrounds lie along the main fossil route; more are off the beaten path.

Painted Hills

The highly photogenic Painted Hills are a series of low-slung hills created around 30 million years ago by red, yellow, green, ocher, gray, and black-hued ash deposited into drifts hundreds of feet deep. Erosion has cut through the multicolored layers and sculpted the hills into soft mounds. While many casual visitors are satisfied snapping photos from the monument's designated overlook, easy hiking trails lead to more interesting vistas; the springtime wildflower display here is exceptional.

The half-mile Painted Hills Overlook Trail provides a view of mineral-bearing clays exposed by erosion. Nearby, the 1.5-mile Carroll Rim Trail has a spectacular all-encompassing view of the Painted Hills.

Oregon Paleo Lands Institute

Although geologists and other scientists have long traveled to eastern Oregon for their research, Pacific Northwesterners and visitors to the state are often only vaguely aware of the area's rich paleontology and geology. The **Oregon Paleo Lands Institute** (401 4th St., Fossil, 541/763-4480, www.paleolands.org, 9:30am-4:30pm Fri.-Sat summer, 1:30pm-5pm Thurs. winter) was established to bring these resources to a wider range of people and also to help boost the struggling rural economy.

In downtown Fossil, with exhibits on local geology and paleontology, the institute is a good resource for those who want to explore Oregon's John Day country. It also sponsors occasional trips guided by local geologists, photographers, and other experts.

This is a good place to come for information about floating the John Day River, biking through the John Day Basin, or hiking in the John Day Fossil Beds National Monument. You'll find books and maps (some with an intensely local focus and unavailable elsewhere), and friendly, informative staffers.

The most vivid colors of all are found at the **Painted Cove Trail,** a 0.25-mile loop where viewing the red mounds up close is a highlight. Close by, the 0.5-mile **Leaf Hill Trail** (another loop) leads to remnants of a 30-million-year-old hardwood forest. Take a look at the exhibit describing how our knowledge of Oregon's most ancient forests emanated from studies of this area. To reach the Painted Hills, drive three miles west of Mitchell on U.S. 26, turn left at the sign, and travel six miles along Bridge Creek to the site. Stop at the visitor center to get oriented and fill your water bottle. If possible, visit around dusk or after a rain shower, when the colors really pop.

ACCOMMODATIONS

Mitchell, which has a store, a couple of cafes, and a few places to stay, is the closest town to the Painted Hills. The historic **Oregon Hotel** (104 E. Main St., Mitchell, 541/462-3027, http://theoregonhotel.net, rooms with private baths $49-69, Mar.-Nov.) offers pleasantly vintage guest rooms right downtown. The less expensive guest rooms at the hotel ($49-59) share a bath; kitchenettes are

the Painted Hills

available for $105, and you can even get a hostel bunk for $20. Several hotels have existed on this site since the 1800s, with the current incarnation dating back to 1938. More up-to-date accommodations that sleep up to eight are available from **Painted Hills Vacation Rentals** (541/462-3921, paintedhillsvaction. com, $125-180), with three cheery rental cottages in the area.

Campers can pitch a tent ($5) or plug in an RV ($17) at the **Mitchell City Park** (541/462-3121), a grassy spot on the edge of the two-block-long downtown.

Clarno Unit

Right on the John Day River, the Clarno Formations are the monument's oldest and most remote. The 40-million-year-old **Clarno Unit** exposes mudflows that washed over an Eocene-era forest. The petrified mudslide here is one of the few places in the world where the stems of ancient plants, along with their leaves, seeds, and nuts, are preserved in the same location. Fossilized imprints of palm, gingko, and magnolia leaves point to a subtropical forest capable of supporting flowering trees. The formations eroded into distinctive chalky-white cliffs topped with spires and turrets of stone. The 0.25-mile **Clarno Arch**

Trail leads you into the formations where boulder-size fossils containing logs, seeds, and other remains of an ancient forest await. It links up with two other quarter-mile trails: **Trail of the Fossils,** where boulders are strewn with plant fossils, and the **Geologic Time Trail,** which lacks fossils but leads to a picnic area. Picnic facilities, drinking water, and restrooms are available at the monument.

The Clarno Formations are 18 miles west of the town of **Fossil** on Route 218. When you are traveling in the John Day country, Fossil makes an intriguing and perhaps necessary stop—in this remote area, chances are you'll need to gas up or get a bite to eat, and this Old West town has a full range of services for travelers. Fossil also offers fossils: When the townspeople began digging into a hillside to build a football field, they exposed an ancient lakebed rich with fossil leaf prints and petrified wood. The site (just behind the high school) is open to amateur fossil hunters for a $5 fee.

ACCOMMODATIONS AND FOOD

The closest facilities to the Clarno Unit are in Fossil. Escape city life at the **Wilson Ranches Retreat** (16555 Butte Creek Ln., 541/763-2227, www.wilsonranchesretreat.

Clarno Unit of the John Day Fossil Beds

Floating the John Day River

Oregon's longest free-running river, the John Day, spends most of its time far from roads, which makes it ideal to see from a boat. From May to early July, it's relatively easy to navigate the river in a canoe, raft, or inflatable kayak. The only rapid of note, a Level III-IV at Clarno, can be tough to run when the water level is low, and since there are no dams on the John Day, flow levels fluctuate widely in response to snowpack and rainfall. When water level is high, canoeists should have white-water experience.

The Bureau of Land Management (BLM) oversees boating on the John Day; their website (www.blm.gov/or) is a good source of up-to-date information, with links to water-flow forecasts. The BLM website is also the place to go for the permit that is required to boat on the John Day.

Most people float the John Day as a multiday trip. Service Creek is a common put-in for river trips; it's 48 miles (usually three days) to the bridge at Clarno. From Clarno to Cottonwood Canyon State Park, it's 70 miles, which usually takes five days to float. One-day floats are also possible from the town of Spray to mile marker 86 on Highway 19 or from mile 86 to Service Creek. Much of the time during any trip, the river is bounded by private land; it's important to carry a good map (available from the BLM by calling 541/416-6700) in order to know where to camp.

The **Service Creek Stage Stop** (38686 Hwy. 19, south of Fossil, 541/468-3331, www.servicecreek.com) rents rafts ($125 for a day rental with delivery and pickup), and shuttles are provided by the following people:

- **Donna's Shuttles** (541/763-4884)
- **Service Creek Stage Stop** (541/468-3331)
- **Bobbie Jo's Shuttles** (541/460-0858)
- **Ron and June Rollins** (541/763-0909 or 541/410-0933)

com, $105-145). Guests can ride horses ($45 for a one-hour ride), hike, help fix fences, and even ride along on a cattle drive.

Tent campers should head five miles south of town to the forested **Bear Hollow County Park** (45260 Hwy. 19, 541/763-2010, $10, drinking water, vault toilets).

RJ's Steaks, Spirits, and Sports (415 1st St., 541/763-3335, 11am-9pm daily, $7-20) is a good place to dine on anything from steak to ice cream with strawberry sauce accompanied by a friendly vibe.

Twenty miles south of Fossil, the **Service Creek Lodge** (38686 Hwy. 19, 541/468-3331, www.servicecreek.com, lodge rooms $85-125) is a handy all-purpose business, especially for folks who would like to paddle the easygoing, free-flowing (undammed) John Day River. It has food, lodging in nicely decorated rooms, raft rentals, and a shuttle service. The lodge also rents a five-bedroom vacation home in Fossil ($375).

Twenty miles north of Fossil is the town of **Condon,** where the renovated 1920s-era ★ **Hotel Condon** (202 S. Main St., Condon, 541/384-4624 or 800/201-6706, www.hotel-condon.com, $100-199) is the swankiest lodging choice in this part of Oregon. While in Condon, don't neglect to visit **Country Flowers** (201 S. Main St., 541/384-4120, 9am-6pm Mon.-Fri., 9:30am-5:30pm Sat., noon-5pm Sun.), an eclectic gift store with an outpost of Portland's Powell's Books and a classic old soda fountain. This is a good place for lunch.

North of Condon, where Highway 206 crosses the John Day River, find **Cottonwood Canyon State Park** (541/394-0002, www.oregonstateparks.org, $10 camping), one of the state's newest and largest parks. Many John Day rafters use this as a takeout spot, and the canyons and bottomlands are beautiful places to explore, with 4.5-mile-long trails on either bank of the river. During the summer, this area is quite warm, but it's a great spot to camp in spring and fall.

Sheep Rock Unit

The Sheep Rock Unit is the largest of the monument's three divisions and offers the most visitor facilities. The **Thomas Condon Paleontology Center** (eight miles northwest of Dayville, 541/987-2333, www.nps.gov/joda, 10am-5pm daily, free) serves as the monument's visitors center. It features a fossil museum with exceptional discoveries from local digs, a mazelike series of dioramas, and displays telling the geological and biological history of the fossil beds—plus short films that help explain the area's prehistory and current research. While here, pick up good printed information that's not available online, such as a mile-by-mile geology road log detailing the striking stretch of road from the visitor center to the Painted Hills. **The Cant Ranch House,** a handsome 1917 ranch house across the highway from the paleontology center, houses a museum on the human history of the ranch and its vicinity. A former bunkhouse and a small log cabin behind the ranch house contain additional exhibits on fossil history. The tree-shaded grounds surrounding the ranch house are perfect for picnicking,

and short trails lead to the fast-flowing John Day River.

North of the visitor center on Route 19 are two fossil-viewing areas. Two miles north is the parking area for **Blue Basin,** with several hiking trails leading into fossil-rich formations. The one-mile-long **Island in Time Trail** climbs into a badlands basin of highly eroded, uncannily green sediments. Along the trail are displays that reveal fossils protruding from the soil. The trail dead-ends at a natural box canyon; high around are barren, castellated walls rich in 25-million-year-old life-forms. The **Overlook Trail** offers a longer three-mile loop to the rim of Blue Basin, with views over the fossil beds and the layer-cake topography of the John Day Valley.

Two miles farther north at the day-use **Foree Picnic Area** are more hiking trails that explore green mudstone formations capped with basalt from ancient lava flows.

The drive between the junction of Route 19 and U.S. 26 and the small community of Spray is highly scenic; interesting geology and spectacular scenery don't always occur together, but they form an amazing team here. Along this route you'll see **Sheep Rock,** a steep-sided mesa rising hundreds of feet to a small rock cap, and **Cathedral Rock,** where

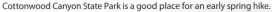

Cottonwood Canyon State Park is a good place for an early spring hike.

Sheep Rock rises above the Cant Ranch, which houses a museum devoted to the area's human history.

erosion has stripped away a hillside to reveal highly colored sediments beneath a thick overlay of basalt. Most astonishing of all is **Picture Gorge,** where the John Day River rips through an immense 1,500-foot-high lava flow and begins trenching its canyon to the Columbia River. The gorge, wide enough for only the river and the road, is named for the pictographs drawn there by early Native Americans; look for them near mile marker 125 on the west side of the road.

The Sheep Rock Unit of the John Day Fossil Beds is eight miles northwest of Dayville, and 40 miles from John Day.

ACCOMMODATIONS AND FOOD

The closest lodgings to the Sheep Rock Unit are in the tiny community of Dayville, where the **Fish House Inn** (110 Franklin St., Dayville, 541/987-2124, www.fishhouseinn. com, $55-130) offers accommodation in a cottage and a vintage Craftsman home. These pleasant digs are decorated with antique farm tools and fishing gear, hence the inn's name. Tent ($15) and RV sites ($30) are also available. The terrific **Dayville Cafe** (212 Franklin St., 541/967-2122, 7am-7pm Wed.-Sat., 8am-4pm

Sun., $8-17) serves burgers from local beef, tasty pie, and real milkshakes.

JOHN DAY AND VICINITY

The early history of John Day and nearby Canyon City centers on the discovery of gold in 1862. According to most estimates, $26 million in gold was taken out of the streams and mines in the Strawberry Mountains. At the peak of the gold rush, Whiskey Flat, later called Canyon City, was populated by 5,000 miners, which made it larger than Portland at the time. Thousands of Chinese came to the area to work the tailings, or leftovers, from the mines. Their fascinating history is vividly retold at the Kam Wah Chung and Company Museum in John Day.

One of the more colorful denizens of Canyon City was the celebrated poet Joaquin Miller, who served as the first elected judge in Grant County. Known as the "Byron of Oregon," this dashing figure dressed like Buffalo Bill and recited his florid sonnets to a baffled audience of miners.

Today John Day is principally a market town for local farmers and ranchers, with adequate facilities for travelers passing through to visit nearby fossil beds or hike in the lovely Strawberry Mountains.

★ Kam Wah Chung State Heritage Site

A must-stop in the town of John Day, the **Kam Wah Chung State Heritage Site** (250 NW Canton St., 541/575-2800, www.oregonstateparks.org, visitors center 9am-noon and 1pm-5pm daily May-Oct., tours on the hour except noon, free) was the center of Chinese life in the John Day area, serving as a general store and pharmacy with over 500 herbs. People came from hundreds of miles away for the herbal remedies of Doc Hay, who lived here. It also served in more limited capacities as an assay office, fortune-teller's studio, and Taoist shrine.

The building began as a trading post on The Dalles Military Road in 1866. With the influx of Chinese to the area during the gold rush, the outpost was purchased in 1887 by two Chinese apothecaries and evolved into a center for Asian medicine, trade, and spirituality. It remained a gathering place for the Chinese community in eastern Oregon until the early 1940s. While it admirably fulfilled this role, the opium-blackened walls, bootleg whiskey, and gambling paraphernalia are evidence of the less salutary aspects of the Kam Wah Chung lifestyle. At the time of the 1879 census, eastern Oregon had 960 East Coast emigrants and 2,468 Chinese, proof that the current museum is not an arcane exhibit but rather a significant window on the past. In fact, in 1983 scholars from China came to categorize the herbs and religious objects.

It's the little touches in the faithfully restored building that stay with you. First, your eye may be drawn to the metal shutters and outside wooden staircase on this rough stone edifice. Inside, there's a locked and barred herb cage where Ing Hay prepared medicine and where gold dust was weighed. A Taoist shrine graces the room where groceries and opium were dispensed. The meat cleaver by Doc Hay's bed bespeaks the fear and despair of Chinese life here near the turn of the 20th century.

Tours begin at the interpretive center, two blocks south on NW Canton Street.

Grant County Historical Museum

Another repository of local history, the **Grant County Historical Museum** (101 S. Canyon City Blvd., Canyon City, 541/575-0509, www.

Kam Wah Chung State Heritage Site

Who Was John Day?

John Day is such a common name in this part of Oregon (it is affixed to a two rivers, three towns, a dam, a series of fossil beds, a valley, and several parks) that you might assume the original John Day was an early pioneer settler. In fact, the eponymous John Day never visited most of the places that now carry his name. Day was hired to provide meat for a Pacific Fur Company expedition in 1812. Thirty miles east of The Dalles, near what was then known as the Mau Hau River, Day and another mountain man were ambushed by Native Americans, who robbed them and left them naked and injured. The two survived the ordeal and eventually made their way to Fort Astoria. The Mau Hau River soon became known as Day's River; mapmakers later changed it to the John Day River, and the name spread like wildfire. Even at Astoria, John Day's place-naming achievement continued: A *second* John Day River flows into the Columbia just east of Astoria.

gchistoricalmuseum.com, 9am-4:30pm Mon.-Sat. May-Sept., $4 adults, $3 seniors, $2 children ages 7-17, children 6 and under free) is in Canyon City, a couple of miles south of John Day on U.S. 395. Joaquin Miller's cabin and a jail building stand in the courtyard.

Accommodations

The **Best Western John Day Inn** (315 W. Main St., John Day, 541/575-1700 or 800/243-2628, $120-130) is a very nice conventional motel, with a fitness center, an indoor pool, and free Wi-Fi. A family restaurant is adjacent. The **Dreamers Lodge** (144 N. Canyon St., John Day, 541/575-0526 or 800/654-2849, www.dreamerslodge.com, $60-100), a classic, well-maintained pet-friendly motor court motel, is close to the town center but on a quiet side street.

The most amenity-laden campground in the area is **Clyde Holliday State Recreation Site** (seven miles west of John Day, 33 miles east of the Sheep Rock Unit, 541/932-4453, www.oregonstateparks.org, $24 tent or RV, $5 hiker/biker, $44 tepee). In addition to showers and shady sites with electrical and water hookups near the John Day River, the park offers a couple of large tepees. Although campsites are all first-come, first-served, tepees are best reserved in advance (541/932-4453, www.reserveamerica.com).

Food

For a Western meal, dine at the **Snaffle Bit**

Dinner House (830 S. Canyon Blvd., John Day, 541/575-2426, 4:30pm-9:30pm Tues.-Wed., noon-2:30pm and 4:30pm-9:30pm Thurs.-Sat., $8-32, dinner reservations recommended), known for its steaks and friendly staff. Locals say it's the best place for miles around.

Stop in for a beer and a flatbread or sandwich at the family-friendly **1188 Brewing Company** (141 E. Main St., John Day, 541/575-1188, http://1188brewing.com, 11am-9pm Mon.-Sat., $8-12). The brewery's Desert Monk IPA is particularly good, and guest taps flow with beers from around the West.

Information

For information on John Day and vicinity, contact the **Grant County Chamber of Commerce** (301 W. Main St., John Day, 541/757-0547 or 800/769-5664, www.gcoregonlive.com). The **Malheur National Forest** (www.fs.usda.gov/malheur) and the **Bureau of Land Management** share an office (431 Paterson Bridge Rd., John Day, 541/575-3000).

STRAWBERRY MOUNTAINS AND VICINITY

Thirteen miles east of John Day, the landscape becomes more mountainous and forests begin to encroach on the ranchland. **Prairie City** is an attractive small town in this lovely locale. The **DeWitt Museum** (Main St. and Bridge St., Prairie City, 541/820-3330, www.prairiecityoregon.com, 10am-5pm Wed.-Sun.

May 15-Oct. 15, $3) is housed in the Sumpter Valley Railroad's old depot, which operated between Baker City and Prairie City 1909-1947. The building was restored in 1979 and today has 10 rooms full of artifacts from Grant County's early days.

Just south of Prairie City are the Strawberry Mountains, a pocket mountain range that offers a good system of trails, seven lakes, volcanic rock formations, and, if you're lucky, glimpses of bighorn sheep. Trails head out from Strawberry Campground, 11 miles south of Prairie City, for the short hike to **Strawberry Lake,** with options to continue to Strawberry Falls or make a loop backpacking trip in the Strawberry Mountain Wilderness Area. Although there are some wild strawberry plants along the trails, late-summer hikers will be more apt to notice the abundant huckleberries.

For information on hiking the Strawberry Mountains' 120 miles of trails, contact the Prairie City Ranger District at the **Malheur National Forest office** (327 SW Front St., 541/820-3800, www.fs.usda.gov/malheur). Ask about the 11-mile loop circumnavigating 9,000-foot Strawberry Mountain.

Prairie City enthusiastically welcomes **bicyclists.** The 1976 cross-country Bikecentennial route went through town, and it's still a popular stop with long-distance cyclists. In addition, a number of road, gravel road, and mountain bike routes have been established: find details at www.prairiecityoregon.com or www.rideoregonride.com.

Accommodations and Food

The nine-room ★ **Historic Hotel Prairie** (112 Front St., Prairie City, 541/820-4800, http://hotelprairie.com, $84-144) is a renovated 1910 hotel. Even if you're not staying the night, drop by the lobby to examine the historical photos. The rooms aren't huge—they are authentic in that regard—but the beds and amenities are very comfortable. The top choice is a one-room suite; six regular bedrooms have private baths, while the two remaining rooms share a bath. The hotel is pet friendly, and a wine and beer bar gives guests a chance to mingle.

Strawberry Campground (541/820-3800, www.fs.usda.gov/malheur, June-mid-Oct., $8, no reservations) is a great bet for tent campers, but the final stretch of road to this sweet spot, at 5,700 feet in elevation, is too steep for trailers and RVs; tiny **Slide Creek** campground (nine miles south of Prairie City on Forest Rd. 6001, no water,

Strawberry Lake

free), another Forest Service campground a couple of miles closer to town, is a better bet for folks with larger rigs. **Depot Park** (Main St. and Bridge St., Prairie City, 541/820-3605, $18 RVs, $14 tents, $8 bikes, $1.75 showers) has an in-town campground surrounding the DeWitt Museum and offers both RV and tent camping; it's also a good place to stop for a shower after a few nights in the Strawberry Mountains. This campground is a great home base for cyclists exploring the many loop roads in the nearby mountains.

Chuck's Little Diner (142 W. Front St., Prairie City, 541/820-4353, 5am-2pm Wed.-Sun., $4-10) is a good place for a big breakfast on the outside patio or an afternoon slice of pie. The **Oxbow Restaurant and Saloon** (128 W. Front St., Prairie City, 541/820-4544, meals noon-9pm Tues.-Sun., $12-21) offers burgers, steaks, and other comfort foods with a good helping of Western atmosphere, including a lovely antique bar adorned by carved figureheads and taxidermy.

Pendleton

For a lot of people in the West, Pendleton is synonymous with rodeo and woolens, both pointing to the city's history as a frontier trade settlement. Pendleton still has Western spirit to spare, but proximity to the highly successful wineries in Washington's Walla Walla Valley is bringing change to this bastion of cowboy country.

With a population of 16,900, Pendleton is the largest city in eastern Oregon. It's an economic force thanks to vast wheat fields (Umatilla County is one of the top wheat-producing counties in the United States), rows of green peas, its famous woolen mills, and tourism from the Pendleton Round-Up, the September rodeo and weeklong party that brings in cowboys, cowgirls, and the crowds that love them. The Umatilla Reservation is just outside town, and the Pendleton area has a large Native American population; an Indian encampment is a traditional part of the Round-Up.

SIGHTS
★ Pendleton Underground Tours

One of the area's liveliest attractions is **Pendleton Underground Tours** (31 SW Emigrant Ave., 541/276-0730, www.pendletonundergroundtours.org, schedule varies, $15, reservations required). This visit to the wild and woolly days of the Old West takes you through the tunnels underneath the downtown historic district. At one time a series of 90 passageways, originally dug as freight tunnels by Chinese workers who weren't allowed to walk above ground, crisscrossed beneath the downtown area. During the Prohibition era, bootleggers, gamblers, opium dealers, and Chinese railroad laborers frequented the businesses that developed here.

The 90-minute tour starts at SW 1st Street and Emigrant Avenue and visits the old Shamrock Cardroom, filled with the bouncy sounds of honky-tonk music, where bartenders were once paid with gold dust; Hop Sing's laundry and bathhouse (a Prohibition speakeasy with secret escapes and a dank opium den); and the well-preserved Cozy Rooms Bordello. After this tour you'll understand how the old town of 3,000 once supported 32 saloons and 18 bordellos.

To get here from I-84, take Exit 209 and turn north into Pendleton. Continue up Emigrant Avenue to SW 1st Street.

Pendleton Woolen Mills

Next to the Round-Up, the town is best known for the **Pendleton Woolen Mills** (1307 SE Court Place, 541/276-6911, www.pendleton-usa.com, 8am-6pm Mon.-Fri., 9am-5pm Sun.), where they make those colorful wool

Pendleton

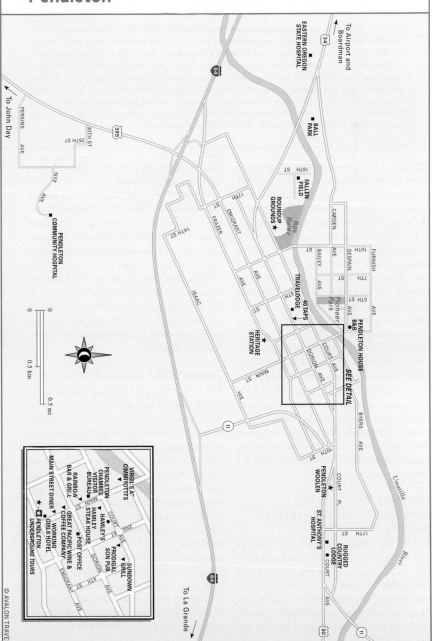

To Airport and Boardman

EASTERN OREGON STATE HOSPITAL

To John Day

PERKINS AVE

30TH ST

25TH ST

NYE AVE

BALL PARK

FALLEN FIELD

18TH ST

ROUNDUP GROUNDS

Roy Raley

CARDEN

17TH ST

FRAZER AVE

EMIGRANT AVE

15TH ST

16TH ST

ISAAC AVE

PENDLETON COMMUNITY HOSPITAL

BAILEY AVE

DESPAIN ST

10TH ST

FURNISH AVE

7TH ST

5TH ST

TRAVELODGE

11TH ST

40 TAPS

Pioneer Park

HERITAGE STATION

MAIN ST

COURT AVE

DORION AVE

PENDLETON HOUSE B&B

SEE DETAIL

BYERS AVE

10TH ST

PENDLETON WOOLEN

COURT Pl.

ST ANTHONY'S HOSPITAL

17TH ST

RUGGED COUNTRY LODGE

COURT AVE

Umatilla River

0   0.5 km
0   0.5 mi

N

To La Grande

84

11

30

11

Detail inset:

VIRGIL'S AT CIMMIYOTTI'S

PENDLETON CHAMBER VISITOR BUREAU

HAMLEY'S STEAK HOUSE

RAINBOW BAR & GRILL

GREAT PACIFIC WINE & COFFEE COMPANY

MAIN STREET DINER

PENDLETON UNDERGROUND TOURS

WORKING GIRLS HOTEL

POST OFFICE

PRODIGAL SON PUB

SUNDOWN GRILL

MAIN ST

COURT AVE

2ND ST

DORION AVE

EMIGRANT AVE

© AVALON TRAVEL

The SAGE Center

The long trip across eastern Oregon on I-84 may require more than a perfunctory rest stop. Pull off at Boardman (Exit 164) to learn about the region's sustainable agriculture and energy at the **Sustainable Agriculture and Energy Center,** or SAGE (101 Olson Rd., Boardman, 541/481-7243, www.visitsage.com, 10am-5pm Mon.-Thurs., 10am-6pm Fri.-Sat. Memorial Day-Labor Day, 10am-5pm daily Labor Day-Memorial Day, $5 adults, $3 students and seniors). Exhibits educate visitors about eastern Oregon's agricultural economy—expect to learn how irrigation works; the ins and outs of sources of power such as biofuels, hydropower, and wind energy; how food products such as corn and grains are processed and shipped around the world; and how these modern farming methods differ from those historically used.

blankets. After shearing, the wool goes to a scouring mill near Portland, where it's graded, sorted, and washed. Then the dried wool returns to the Pendleton mill for dyeing, carding, spinning, rewinding, and weaving.

Production began here in 1909 with Native American-style blankets, which are still going strong, along with men's and women's sportswear. Pendleton carved its lucrative niche by copying traditional designs for blankets used by Native Americans in Arizona and New Mexico. It introduced Western-style woolen shirts in the 1920s.

Twenty-minute-long tours run at 9am, 11am, 1:30pm, and 3pm Monday-Friday. Large groups are asked to make an appointment. To get to the mills, take I-84 Exit 207 and follow Dorion Street through Pendleton. Do not cross the viaduct, but turn left and proceed four blocks. Even if you can't go on a tour, stop by the company store, where you can pick up blankets and clothing, often at a good discount.

Heritage Station: The Umatilla County Historical Society Museum

In 1881 the Oregon-Washington Railway and Navigation Company, a subsidiary of the Union Pacific Railroad, constructed the northern branch of its transcontinental railroad through northeastern Oregon, and Pendleton served as an important stop on the route. By 1910, Pendleton had become the second-largest city in eastern Oregon, meriting a new railroad depot.

The attractive **Heritage Station depot** (108 SW Frazer Ave., 541/276-0012, www. heritagestationmuseum.org, 10am-4pm Tues.-Sat., $5 adults, $4 seniors, $2 students, $10 families), an adaptation of the California mission style, no longer serves railroad passengers, but instead houses the Umatilla County Historical Society's collection of Oregon Trail pioneer and Native American artifacts. Gold miners, sheep ranchers, and moonshiners are also given attention in well-designed displays.

Tamastslikt Cultural Institute

The Confederated Tribes of the Umatilla Indian Reservation—which include the Walla Walla, Umatilla, and Cayuse nations—had little reason to celebrate the 150th anniversary of the Oregon Trail, which was marked by celebrations in other parts of the West. For these eastern Oregon nations, the Oregon Trail led to war and to a huge loss of land and people. Native Americans felt that it was important for their view of the Oregon Trail story to be told, and they built the **Tamastslikt Cultural Institute** (72789 Hwy. 331, 541/966-9748, www.tamastslikt.org, 10am-5pm Mon.-Sat., $10 adults, $9 seniors, $6 students, $25 family of four). Exhibits depict Native American life prior to the pioneers' arrival; the impact of the horse (brought to North America by Europeans) on native people; and an Oregon

Pendleton is a classic Western town.

Held in mid-September, this high-spirited weeklong celebration includes a lot more than just a rodeo. On Friday, the **Westward Ho Historical Parade** brings together covered wagons, mule teams, buggies, and hundreds of Native Americans in full regalia. Wednesday-Saturday evenings at the Round-Up grounds (at Raley Park, west of downtown), the **Happy Canyon Pageant** depicts the opening of the West in a series of vignettes, complete with strutting cowboys and traditional Umatilla dancing. The pageant is an object of much love and some contention; its old-fashioned script is rife with stereotypes. During Round-Up week, Pendleton's Main Street is converted into a street fair and carnival. The **tepee encampment** on the Round-Up grounds and the **cowboy breakfast** served Wednesday-Saturday at 6am in Stillman Park exemplify the traditions that take the Old West beyond the rodeo ring.

Of course, the Round-Up is also a rodeo—one of the largest and richest in the United States. Cowboys and cowgirls come from across North America to compete for nearly $500,000 in prize money in such classic rodeo events as bulldogging, calf-roping, barrel racing, and wild-horse races. Rodeo events are held Wednesday-Saturday 1:15pm-5pm. Tickets for each day run $15-25, depending on day and seat location. Tickets are available by calling the Round-Up office and also through Ticketmaster (www.ticketmaster.com).

The **Round-Up Hall of Fame** (13th St. and SW Court Ave., 541/278-0815, 10am-4pm Sat., $5 adults, $4 seniors, $2 children ages 10 and under), located under the south grandstand area at the Round-Up Stadium, tells the history of the country's biggest rodeo in photos of past champions and displays of their saddles and clothing. The star of the show is a stuffed horse named War Paint.

Hotel rooms in Pendleton are totally booked up months in advance for the Round-Up, so call to make reservations as early as possible.

Trail retrospective from the point of view of the Cayuse, Umatilla, and Walla Walla nations.

The interpretive center adds a living encampment, interpretive trails, and an outdoor amphitheater. Sharing this 640-acre site at the base of the Blue Mountains is a casino, golf course, RV park, hotel, and restaurant.

The institute is six miles east of Pendleton on I-84 and one mile north of Exit 216. Museum admission is free on the first Friday of every month.

PENDLETON ROUND-UP

In 1910, Pendleton farmers and ranchers got together to celebrate the end of the wheat harvest. This was the first year of the **Pendleton Round-Up** (1205 SW Court Ave., 541/276-2553 or 800/457-6336, www.pendletonroundup.com). The annual event now draws 50,000 rodeo fans in the grand tradition started by legendary rodeo stars like Jackson Sundown and Yakima Canutt.

Pendleton Round-Up grounds

SPORTS AND RECREATION

Lots of sun is conducive to such outdoor activities as golf at **Pendleton Country Club** (seven miles south of town on U.S. 395, 541/443-8874), and boating and waterskiing on **McKay Reservoir** (541/922-3232), near the country club. Fishing enthusiasts can head north and arrive at the Columbia River in a little over an hour for salmon, steelhead, and bass, or try the area's reservoirs for bluegills, bass, and catfish.

The over three-mile-long **River Parkway,** a paved strip on a levee paralleling the Umatilla River through much of downtown Pendleton, is recommended for walkers and cyclists.

During the winter months, skiing is on tap up at **Spout Springs** (79327 Hwy. 204, Athena, 541/566-0320, www.spoutspringsski-area.com, $35 adults, $30 children ages 12-17, $25 children ages 5-11), 40 miles northeast of Pendleton in Athena. It's one of the oldest ski resorts in the Pacific Northwest. It's a small place, with two double chairlifts and relatively easy terrain. **Cross-country ski trails** are also maintained ($10 trail pass). To get here, drive north on Route 11 to Weston, turn east on Route 204, and travel a few miles past

Tollgate to the ski area. Spout Springs usually holds on to its dry powder longer than other ski areas in the state.

SHOPPING

If you're starting to like the look of pearl-snap shirts and cowboy boots, make your way to **Hamley's** (30 SE Court Ave., 541/278-1100, www.hamleyco.com, 9am-6pm Mon.-Thurs. 9am-8pm Fri.-Sat., 11am-5pm Sun.), a classic Western clothing and tack store complete with saddle makers in the back. Hamley's also has an impressive collection of Western art on the mezzanine level of the store. A walk through downtown will reveal several less vaunted and possibly less expensive places to buy Western clothing, boots, and saddles. It's a fun place to shop, and merchants are quite happy to help city folk with finer points of Western style.

ACCOMMODATIONS

Pendleton lodging is concentrated in two areas. A number of chain motels are found along the I-84 exits south of town. Older motor courts are close to downtown and within walking distance of Pendleton's famed nightlife. Rooms at these older downtown motels are usually cheaper than those in venues on the outskirts of town.

But first, a word about lodging at Round-Up time: If you show up at Pendleton in mid-September without a reservation or unprepared to pay double the usual room rate, you will almost certainly be out of luck. The town—and all those within easy driving distance—will be completely booked. If you find yourself in this situation, try booking a room in La Grande. If that doesn't work, consider staying in The Dalles and making a day trip out to Pendleton. The chamber of commerce has a list of private homes that rent for a little less than a motel room, but they are also normally booked well in advance. If you bring a tent, camping may be available in schoolyards and other special sites set up for Round-Up crowds.

Just west of downtown, the family-run **Rugged Country Lodge** (1807 SE Court Ave., 541/966-6800 or 877/778-4433, www.ruggedcountrylodge.com, $54-65) is a 1950s vintage motel that has been lovingly refurbished—rooms are small but charmingly decorated, and the grounds are nicely landscaped.

A bit closer to downtown, within walking distance of downtown shopping, dining, and entertainment, the **Travelodge** (411 SW Dorion Ave., 541/276-7531, www.travelodge.com, $75-95) is another good deal, with continental breakfast and pet-friendly rooms. The rooms are basic but clean and remodeled.

For something uniquely Pendleton, consider a night at the **Working Girls Hotel** (17 SW Emigrant Ave., 541/276-0730, www.pendletonundergroundtours.org, $75-95). An offshoot of the popular Pendleton Underground Tours, this five-guest room downtown hotel once served as a brothel in the Pendleton's rowdy heyday. The rooms have been modernized, but the hardwood floors, 18-foot ceilings, and exposed brick walls point to the hotel's 1890s birthright.

Equally historic but from the other end of the economic ladder, the ★ **Pendleton House Bed and Breakfast** (311 N. Main St., 541/276-8581, www.pendletonhousebnb.com, $135) is a fantastic 1917 mansion with five guest rooms and 6,000 square feet of

period luxury. Filled with antiques, oriental rugs, and original silk wall coverings, the Pendleton House even boasts a formal ballroom. A comfy porch, a backyard garden, and a fire blazing in the dining room while you enjoy creative breakfast fare evoke blissful thoughts of the good old days. The Byzantine shower in the shared bathroom evokes less gauzy thoughts.

Six miles east of Pendleton, the new tower hotel at the **Wildhorse Resort Hotel and Casino** (46510 Wildhorse Blvd., 541/278-2274 or 800/654-9453, www.wildhorseresort.com, $110-180, rates lower on weekdays) is an impressive place, worth checking out whether or not you're there to play the slots. Rooms in the tower have some of the best views in eastern Oregon; the older courtyard rooms ($110) aren't particularly remarkable, but some of these rooms are pet-friendly. Although the hotel lobby is immediately adjacent to the casino, where smoking is permitted, the hotel itself is nonsmoking, and good ventilation keeps the lobby air pretty clean. The adjacent RV park ($20-37) is also very well maintained. Facilities include a golf course, an indoor pool, a good restaurant, and, of course, 24-hour gaming.

FOOD

Dine in style at the **Hamley Steak House** (8 SE Court Ave., 541/278-1100, http://hamleysteakhouse.com, 5pm-9pm Sun.-Thurs., 5pm-9:30pm Fri.-Sat., bar open later nightly, $10-41), a gorgeous and opulent restaurant with good steaks, house-smoked ribs, and comfort food "ranch cookin'" such as biscuits and gravy and pot roast. Penny pinchers can eat a burger ($11) at the bar and soak up the atmosphere. Sharing a grassy plaza with the steak house is the casual but cowboy-chic **Hamley's Café and Coffee Company** (16 SE Court Ave., 541/278-1100, 8am-3pm daily, $5-10), with light breakfasts and lunchtime sandwiches and salads.

Also quite Western but considerably less tony than Hamley's is the **Rainbow Café** (209 S. Main St., 541/276-4120, rainbowcafependleton.com, 6am-2am Mon.-Sat., 6am-midnight Sun., dinner $8-24, no credit cards) a famous saloon and restaurant for rodeo fans and local buckaroos, in business since 1883. The Rainbow serves decent American diner food, which you shouldn't pass up, if only for the local color. It's a favorite for breakfast or late-night bar food.

Virgil's at Cimmiyotti's (137 S. Main St., 541/276-7711, 4pm-9pm Tues.-Thurs., 4pm-10pm Fri.-Sat., $14-33) is the newest incarnation of this dark, cozy, and very red spot that has been around for decades. Cimmiyotti's is an old-style Pendleton institution, with steaks and fare such as beef stroganoff and osso bucco, but the more up-to-date specials and the excellent service make it a local favorite. In addition, there is a good selection of Walla Walla wines.

Barbecue is the focus at the **Sundown Grill** (233 S.E. 4th St., 541/276-8500, 11am-1:30pm and 4:30pm-8pm Wed.-Sat., 10am-1:30pm Sun., $9-24), in a nicely decorated historic house with patio seating during the summer. Dinner specials such as smoked trout served with homemade baked beans are offered along with ribs, sausages, and burgers.

The **Great Pacific Wine and Coffee Co.** (403 S. Main St., 541/276-1350, www.greatpacific.biz, 10am-9pm Mon.-Sat. $7-14), in a classy old downtown building (the former Masonic Lodge), features imported cheeses, desserts, salads, pizza, sandwiches, microbrews, a good wine selection, an espresso bar, and occasional live music.

Out at the Wildhorse Casino, **Plateau** (46510 Wildhorse Blvd., 541/966-1610, www.wildhorseresort.com, 5pm-9pm nightly, $18-42) is a boon to those staying at the hotel and worth a visit even for folks staying in town. Traditional Pacific Northwest fare such as grilled salmon, halibut cheeks, elk, and steak is well prepared and presented with elegance that's a bit unexpected at an eastern Oregon casino hotel. It's possible to order half portions of some entrees ($11-14).

Pendleton's first microbrewery is ★ **Prodigal Son Brewery and Pub** (230 SE

The Rainbow Café has been in business for over 125 years.

Court Ave., 541/276-6090, http://prodigalsonbrewery.com, 11am-10pm Tues.-Sat., noon-9pm Sun., $9-12), a lively family-friendly pub on the edge of downtown. Come for the tasty Pacific Northwest-style brews and stay for the food, which includes burgers, sandwiches, and an excellent locally made bratwurst with sauerkraut.

Take a beer tour of the Pacific Northwest at **40 Taps** (337 S.W. Emigrant Ave., 541/612-8559, www.fortytaps.com, 2pm-10pm Sun.-Thurs., 2pm-1am Fri.-Sat., $4-7). Food is almost an afterthought here; it's provided by the taco truck parked outside.

INFORMATION

Travel Pendleton (501 S. Main St., 541/276-7411 or 800/547-8911, www.pendletonchamber.com) can steer you to local sights and special events. A self-guided walking-tour map of the historic downtown district is helpful. The tour starts at the corner of Main Street and Frazer Avenue and takes in many historic buildings.

GETTING THERE AND AROUND

SeaPort Airlines (seaportair.com) flies between the Portland and Pendleton airports. **Greyhound** (2101 SE Court Ave., 541/276-1551) offers two buses daily in each direction on the I-84 corridor between Portland and Boise. The stop is at the Pendleton Market.

Be aware that the mountainous stretch of I-84 east of Pendleton known as Cabbage Hill is treacherous to drive during icy winters. In addition to the slickness of the road surface, sudden blizzards and high winds can result in whiteout conditions. Be sure to pack snow chains for your car tires, and if you're looking to leave Pendleton and a snowstorm comes up, consider staying another day.

La Grande and Vicinity

La Grande is in the Grande Ronde Valley, which the indigenous peoples called Copi Copi ("Valley of Peace"). The broad valley is completely ringed by mountains and gives the impression of being circular, hence the valley's French name, which translates as "the big circle." The Nez Perce once gathered here for their summer encampments until the Oregon Trail cut through their territory. At La Grande, the Oregon Trail pioneers rested and prepared to traverse the Blue Mountains, a substantial challenge since the passes were often snow-filled by the time the wagon trains reached eastern Oregon.

More than a few of the pioneers were impressed with the agricultural possibilities of the Grande Ronde country, and they stayed to build a town that became the market center for a broad stretch of wheat and grass seed farms. Lumber from the Blue Mountains and livestock fattened on lush fields of tall grass also propelled the community's early growth. Now home to Eastern Oregon University, La Grande (pop. 13,000) has an economy based on beef ranching, wheat farming, and timber. In addition to serving as a gateway to Wallowa Lake and the northern flank of the Wallowa Range, La Grande is a pleasant destination in itself, with a historic downtown and several good restaurants.

The town of Union, 11 miles southeast of La Grande, has a very well-preserved town center of late Victorian homes and storefronts.

In fact, nearly the entire town is protected as a National Historic District.

SIGHTS

The Oregon Trail Interpretive Park at Blue Mountain Crossing

The **Oregon Trail Interpretive Park** (9am-7pm Tues.-Sun. Memorial Day-Labor Day, Northwest Forest Pass required) commemorates the crossing of the Blue Mountains by the Oregon Trail pioneers. Paved, easily accessible trails follow some of the best-preserved and most scenic traces of the Oregon Trail. Sign panels describe the pioneers' struggle through the thick forests and over the rugged mountain passes, and living history interpretive events are offered on summer weekends. To reach the park, take the I-84 Spring Creek exit 12 miles west of La Grande.

Mount Emily Recreation Area

When La Grande residents want to go on trail runs, bike rides, or cross-country ski or horseback outings, they don't have to travel far. The 3,669-acre **Mount Emily Recreation Area** is only two miles from downtown and has about 12 miles of trails. Climb the mountain for great views of the Grande Ronde Valley and the distant Eagle Cap Wilderness Area. Owsley Canyon Road leads from downtown (catch it just east of the fairgrounds) north to a Mount Emily trailhead. Stop by the local bike shop, **The Mountain Works** (1307 Adams

The Oregon Trail

The pioneer trek along the Oregon Trail, a tide of migration starting in 1841 and lasting over 20 years, is among the largest voluntary human migrations ever recorded. When it was all over, about 50,000 pioneers followed the trail to the end and settled in Oregon Country—present-day Oregon, Washington, and Idaho.

The wagon trains started in Independence, Missouri, as soon as the spring grass was green. Then the race was on to get across the far mountains before the winter snows. Although the first few hundred miles were easy traveling across the plains, the hardships were not long in coming. Contrary to the stereotype of hostile Native Americans being a major cause of casualties, cholera was by far the leading cause of death on the 2,000-mile journey.

The route—which usually required six months to complete—followed the North Platte River to South Pass in Wyoming, then crossed the Snake River Plain in Idaho, then across the Snake River and up and over the Blue Mountains in eastern Oregon to The Dalles. Here the pioneers faced a decision: Either they put themselves and all their belongings onto rafts to float the rapids of the otherwise impassable Columbia Gorge, or they struggled up the flanks of Mount Hood, descending into the Willamette Valley via the precipitous Barlow Trail.

At Fort Hall in eastern Idaho, there was a fork in the trail and a sign that read "To Oregon." It was here that the pioneers had to make a key decision. They could head south to California and the goldfields shining with the promise of instant wealth, or they could continue west to Oregon, where the fertile Willamette Valley offered its own allure for serious farmers and homesteaders. Some Oregonians like to tell a more pointed version of the story, which claims that the sign for the California road was marked by a pile of gold-painted rocks, in contrast to the "To Oregon" sign. The implication was that people who could read—or who were more interested in domestic pursuits than quick wealth—would head to Oregon. While this interpretation is not seriously accepted by historians, it remains a source of good-natured humor between the two states.

Ave., 541/963-3220, 10am-6pm Mon.-Sat.), for advice on where to mountain bike.

Hot Lake Mineral Hot Springs

Hot Lake Mineral Hot Springs was considered to be powerfully healing by the Western Native Americans who camped nearby. A steady flow of superheated water reaches the surface at nearly boiling point and pours into a large pond. During the 1800s, a hotel, bathhouse, and hospital were built, and the facility became known as the Mayo Clinic of the West. During that era, the healing waters were thought to give relief from arthritis and rheumatism, and the medical team was noted for its success treating tuberculosis. The sanatorium was also a fashionable place to have a spa vacation. After the hospital closed in the 1930s, the building was used variously as a resort, hotel, boardinghouse, restaurant, and nursing home. Subsequently, for many years, the resort sat vacant.

In 2004, David Manuel, an artist who owned a bronze foundry and gallery in the nearby town of Joseph, and his wife Lee took over the crumbling resort and embarked on an ambitious remodel and revival of the historic structure.

The resort (66172 Hwy. 203, 541/963-4685, www.hotlakesprings.com) now includes bed-and-breakfast guest rooms ($222, packages available), a hot mineral-water spa with a selection of treatments, a museum and history center, artist marketplace, restaurant and coffee shop, and gift shop. Tours of the property focus on the museum and history center (9am-4pm, Mon.-Sat., $10); call to check on exact times if you want to tour the bronze foundry.

Ladd Marsh

The 3,200-acre **Ladd Marsh** (I-84 Exit 268, five miles south of La Grande off Foothill Rd.) is one of northeastern Oregon's largest remaining wetlands. Both upland and wetland habitats are represented, and the habitat diversity contributes to the wide array of plant and animal species found on the marsh. It's an excellent place to go bird-watching, especially in the springtime when waterfowl are in the area; attentive birders can see up to 80 species in a morning.

SPORTS AND RECREATION
Golf

The **Buffalo Peak Golf Course** (1224 E. Fulton St., Union, 541/562-5527, www.buffalopeakgolf.com, $27 weekdays, $31 weekends) is an 18-hole, par-72, links-style course set in the Grande Ronde Valley. The course offers a variety of landscapes with native vegetation and natural terrain, such as patches of native prairie, streams, and lakes incorporated into the play.

Swimming

Hot Lake is not the only natural hot spring in the area. In the little community of Cove, 17 miles southeast of La Grande, the **Cove Warm Spring Pool** (907 Water St., Cove, 541/568-4890, coveoregon.org, noon-6pm Thurs.-Sun. Memorial Day-Labor Day, $8) is

a great outdoor swimming pool; the water is naturally heated to a constant 86°F.

ACCOMMODATIONS

Most of La Grande's hotels are not exactly grand. Out at I-84 Exit 261, **Best Western Rama Inn and Suites** (1711 21st St., 541/963-3100 or 800/780-7234, www.bestwestern.com, $140-185) has more amenities than other places in town, including an indoor pool. The adjacent **Best Value Sandman Inn** (2410 E. R Ave., 541/963-3707, www.bestvalueinnlagrande.com, $99-130) has an indoor pool and spa, wireless Internet, a continental breakfast included, and bright clean rooms. Downtown, the pet-friendly **La Grande Royal Motor Inn** (1510 Adams Ave., 541/963-4154 or 800/990-7575, www.royalmotorinn.net, $65-71) offers basic rooms within easy walking distance of good restaurants and bars.

Eleven miles southeast of La Grande on Route 203, the nine-unit **Union Hotel** (326 N. Main St., Union, 541/562-6135, www.theunionhotel.com, $74-119) will take you back to the 1920s, when this imposing hotel was built to satisfy the needs of sophisticated travelers between Portland and Boise. The hotel has been partially renovated (it's definitely a work in progress) and is one of the

Hot Lake Mineral Hot Springs.

most charming and unusual hotels in eastern Oregon, best suited now for those who don't mind very simple accommodations.

Hike, fly, or pack a horse into the remote **Minam River Lodge** (541/508-2719, www.theminamlodge.com), in the backcountry about 26 miles from La Grande. Although many guests arrive via private plane, it's possible to hike or ride a horse in via a steep 8.5-mile trail from the Moss Springs trailhead, east of the town of Cove. Once there, the lodgings are in a beautiful log cabin ($295-395), a wall tent ($149), a tepee ($95), your own tent ($40), or under your plane wing ($30). Along with the beautiful setting, the simple but carefully prepared, locally sourced family-style meals are a big attraction; breakfast is $20, lunch is $25, and dinner is $55. Even if you're camping, reserve your meals in advance. Package deals are available.

Camping

Between La Grande and Pendleton in the midst of the Blue Mountains, **Emigrant Springs State Heritage Area** (541/983-2277 or 800/551-6949, www.oregonstateparks.org, reservations www.reserveamerica.com, $17 tents, $22-24 RVs, $24-50 cabins, flush toilets, showers) is in a wooded area immediately off busy I-84.

The **Hilgard Junction State Park** campground (I-84 Exit 252, 541/983-2277 or 800/551-6949, www.oregonstateparks.org, no hookups, no reservations, $10) is eight miles west of La Grande on the Grande Ronde River, at the foot of the Blue Mountains. The campground, which is on the original route of the Oregon Trail, is convenient to the interstate, which also means that it's noisy and not particularly private. Consider driving eight miles up Route 244 (Starkey Rd.) to **Red Bridge State Wayside** for more appealing campsites ($10).

Another option off Route 244 is **Spool Cart Campground** (541/963-7186, www.fs.usda.gov, May-Nov., $5, no water) a small site on the banks of the Grande Ronde River. From I-84 Exit 252, drive 13 miles southwest

on Route 244 as it meanders along the river and its valley, where stands of ponderosa pine and aspen are broken by meadows and farmland; from there, drive six miles south on Forest Service Road 51.

Southeast of La Grande, near the town of Union, Catherine Creek State Park (Hwy. 203, 541/983-2277, www.oregonstateparks.org, $10, flush toilets, water) is a pretty spot on a trout stream.

FOOD

Stop for morning coffee and pastries is **Joe and Sugar's** (1119 Adams Ave., 541/975-5282, 7am-3pm Mon.-Fri., 9am-noon Sat., $2-8), a tiny bakery right downtown that also turns out excellent breakfast sandwiches and burritos. Some of the state's best fast food is available at the drive-through **Nells In 'n' Out** (1704 Adams Ave., 541/963-5733, 10:30am-11pm daily, $5-8). You'll find creative variations on shakes and floats, hand-curled french fries, and a full array of burgers.

Ten Depot Street (10 Depot St., 541/963-8766, http://tendepotstreet.com, 5pm-10pm Mon.-Sat., $10-32), in a classy old brick building, offers an up-to-date menu that might include grilled local lamb kabobs, grilled halibut, good salads and pasta, and perfectly prepared prime rib (the house specialty). The saloon is as popular as the restaurant—it's a great place to indulge in a burger.

INFORMATION

For information on La Grande and Union County, contact the **Union County Chamber of Commerce** (207 Depot St., 541/963-8588 or 800/848-9969, www.visitlagrande.com). The La Grande Ranger Station of the Wallowa-Whitman Forest Service is at 3502 U.S. 30 (541/963-7186).

GETTING THERE

Two **Greyhound** buses travel each day between Portland and Boise with stops in La Grande. The station is at 2204 E. Penn Avenue, 541/963-5165.

The Wallowas

Unlike any other of Oregon's peaks, the snow-capped Teton-like spires of the Wallowa Mountains soar 5,000 feet above Wallowa County farmlands and six-mile-long Wallowa Lake. Rather than the basalt that covers much of the state, these mountains are made of granitic rocks and limestone. Much of the range is in the **Eagle Cap Wilderness Area,** which contains 17 of the state's 29 mountains over 9,000 feet and 50 glacial lakes sprinkled throughout 300,000 acres. Campers and cross-country skiers are regularly treated to glimpses of bighorn sheep, mountain goats, elk, and mule deer, as well as snow-streaked peaks rising above meadows dotted with an artist's palette of wildflowers. Seashells in limestone and greenstone outcroppings attest to the age of the range, some 200 million years.

The Wallowa Valley is formed by the drainages of the Wallowa, Minam, and Grande Ronde Rivers, and its backdrop is the half-moon-shaped Wallowa Range, 80 miles long and 25 miles at its widest.

History

The Wallowa Valley, set apart by deep river canyons and mountain ranges, is the ancestral home of the Nez Perce, a nation known for its horse-training skills and fierce independence. These proud people, astride their spotted Appaloosas, first encountered Europeans when mountain men wandered onto their land. Lewis and Clark believed that the Native Americans' generosity with food saved their lives. Their willingness to feed and care for the Bonneville Party, which had struggled up out of the Snake River Canyon in 1834, reinforced their reputation for honor and largesse. Later, however, when a dry spell in the Grande Ronde Valley to the south prompted homesteaders to farm the Wallowas, native and settler cultures clashed.

One source of tension was the settlers permitting their hogs to trample the camas fields where the Native Americans came to gather food. The U.S. government attempted to resolve the situation by creating a 7-million-acre reservation in 1855, but reneged on the land treaty five years later when gold was discovered in the Wallowas. This breach initiated an era of bad feelings, during which various drafts of different treaties generated confusion and distrust.

The settlers later successfully lobbied the

Chief Joseph

Chief Joseph is known for his brave resistance to the government's attempts to force his people onto a reservation. A nation that spread from Idaho to northern Washington, the Nez Perce had peacefully coexisted with European Americans after the Lewis and Clark expedition; indeed, they had given the newcomers much-needed horses.

But with the incursion of miners and settlers, and because of misunderstandings surrounding the annexation of Native American land through a series of treaties never signed by Chief Joseph, tension increased to the breaking point. White disregard of native property spurred some rash young Nez Perce to retaliate. The ensuing 11-week conflict, during which the Nez Perce engaged 10 separate U.S. military commands in 13 battles (the majority of which the Nez Perce won), guaranteed Chief Joseph's fame as a brilliant military tactician. However, after many hardships, including starvation and many lost lives, Chief Joseph surrendered, only 50 miles from the sanctuary of the Canadian border.

Chief Joseph appealed repeatedly to the federal authorities to return the Nez Perce to the land of their ancestors, but to no avail. In 1885 he and many of his band were sent to a reservation in Washington, where, as the presiding doctor was heard to have said, he died of a broken heart.

government to evict the Native Americans, which led to the Nez Perce War of 1877. Chief Joseph and his people fought a running battle that covered 1,700 miles and ended with their surrender in the Bear's Paw Mountains, 50 miles from the Montana-Canada border. The Nez Perce Reservation is in central Idaho.

EAGLE CAP EXCURSION TRAIN

Trains didn't reach the remote canyon country of the Wallowas until 1908, and passenger service lasted only into the 1920s. In the 1990s, freight service stopped along this lonely rail line that passes through stunning mountain meadows and deep river gorges. Local citizens banded together to purchase the track, and today the system operates both freight and excursion services between Elgin and Joseph.

The **Eagle Cap Excursion Train** (800/323-7330, http://eaglecaptrainrides.com) offers occasional trips leaving from the small Wallowa Valley town of Elgin. The train passes through spectacular scenery and culminates by traveling along the Wild and Scenic stretch of the Wallowa River. In general, the excursion

train operates most Saturdays August-mid-October. Trips have different focuses, ranging from faux train robberies to wine and cheese tours; most depart at 10am and return around 2pm, with lunch included in the fare, which for most tours is $70 adults, $60 seniors, $35 kids 3-16. Call or check online for details.

ENTERPRISE

Enterprise is the larger of the two towns that dominate the Wallowa Valley, with a population of around 1,800, and, unlike Joseph, it has the feel of an authentic Western town. Much of the original downtown, built in the 1890s, still exists and functions as the mercantile center. The **Bookloft and Skylight Gallery** (107 E. Main St., 541/426-3351, http://bookloftoregon.net, 9:30am-5:30pm Mon.-Fri., 10am-4pm Sat.), just across the street from the county courthouse, is a gathering spot for artists and community activists.

ZUMWALT PRAIRIE

North of Highway 82, about halfway between Enterprise and Joseph, roads head north through rangeland to high plateaus. One good destination about 45 minutes

downtown Enterprise

Floating the Wallowa and Grande Ronde Rivers

The Wallowa and Grande Ronde Rivers offer an easygoing raft trip.

From the dot on the map that's Minam, rafters can float 46 miles north along the Wallowa and Grande Ronde Rivers through steep basalt canyons to Troy, a tiny town near the Washington border. Depending on flow and the amount of time you spend exploring on foot, the trip takes two or three days; there are options for shorter or longer trips.

Because the rivers are primarily free-flowing, water levels and river character change dramatically with the seasons. Higher, faster river flows typically occur in the spring and early summer.. By August, river flows are typically very low, with shallow water and exposed rocks. Early in the summer, this is a popular family trip, especially if parents are experienced rafters or the trip is a guided one; mid-summer, and again when the water cools, anglers dominate the scene.

Minam Raft Rentals (541/437-1111, www.minamraftrentals.com), operated out of the **Minam Motel** ($69-89), has rentals, shuttles, and guided trips. For full details on do-it-yourself trips, contact the **Bureau of Land Management River Station** (Minam, 541/437-5580, www.blm.gov/or).

from Enterprise is **Zumwalt Prairie,** the largest remaining native Pacific Northwest bunchgrass prairie. The prairie, which is managed by **The Nature Conservancy** (541/426-3458, www.nature.org), has several hiking trails (dogs, bikes, and horses are not permitted on the trails). To reach the prairie from Highway 82, head north on Cow Creek Road and, after five miles, turn right onto Zumwalt Road, which is paved for only the first few miles. Travel 14 miles on Zumwalt Road; at the junction, turn right (toward Imnaha) and follow The Nature Conservancy sign 1.4 miles to the

Duckett Barn, which has interpretive signs and a trailhead. Another trailhead, for the Horned Lark Trail, is on the main Zumwalt Road about three miles past the junction with the Imnaha road.

In addition to providing public access via the trails, The Nature Conservancy works to maintain the prairie with controlled burns, hunting, and carefully managed cattle grazing.

If you're up for more back road exploration, continue north on the Zumwalt Road to the Buckhorn Lookout; it's a slow 35 miles from the highway, and has amazing views.

Zumwalt Prairie

Entertainment and Events

Northwest of Enterprise in the town of Wallowa, the **Wallowa Band Nez Perce Trail Interpretive Center** (209 E. 2nd St., Wallowa, 541/886-3101, www.wallowanezperce.org) holds the late-July **Tamkaliks Celebration,** which celebrates the continuing Nez Perce presences in the Wallowa Valley. A Native American encampment, dancing, and feasting are highlights of the festival.

Hells Canyon Mule Days (www.hellscanyonmuledays.com), held the weekend after Labor Day at the **Wallowa County Fairgrounds** (668 NW 1st St., Enterprise), is where pack animal fanciers can get their kicks. The action includes mule races, a parade, a speed mule-shoeing contest, and endurance competitions.

Accommodations

Lodging in Enterprise can be less expensive than other Wallowa area options—and it's not booked up months in advance like the lodges at Wallowa Lake. The fairly large **Ponderosa Motel** (102 SE Greenwood St., 541/426-3186,

$82) is just south of downtown and has refrigerators and microwaves in the guest rooms. **Wilderness Inn** (301 W. North St., 541/426-4535, $76) has everything you need for a comfortable night in Enterprise.

The 1910 Historic Enterprise House B&B (508 1st South St., 541/426-4238 or 888/448-8825, www.enterprisehousebnb.com, $121-189) is a large rambling farmhouse from the turn of the 20th century and has a big front porch and great mountain views. Each of the five guest rooms has a private bath, and the massive third-floor suite ($189) can sleep up to six.

A different sort of B&B experience is offered at **A Barking Mad Farm Bed and Breakfast** (65156 Powers Rd., 541/886-0171, www.barkingmadfarm.com, $135-195), an elegant and exceedingly pet-friendly inn. The three suites are all beautiful, but it's hard to top the Treetop Suite, which you enter through a hatch and which has a deck snug up against an ancient yew tree.

Travel 30 miles north of town to the ★ **Rimrock Inn** (83471 Lewiston Hwy., 541/828-7769, www.rimrockinnor.com, open late May-Sept.), where you can choose between staying in a fully furnished, futon-equipped but nonelectrified tepee ($88-108, restrooms and bathhouse separate), a suite in the inn proper ($119), or your own tent ($25) or RV ($30). It's worth heading off the beaten path to stay at the Rimrock, and not only because of the views of beautiful Joseph Canyon; the inn's restaurant (open during peak summer season, reservations mandatory) is remarkably good. Breakfast is included for all but those camping in their own tents or RVs.

Food

About 10 miles northwest of Enterprise, the 1900 building housing the ★ **Lostine Tavern** (125 Hwy. 2, Lostine, 541/569-2246, http://lostine-tavern.com, 11am-10pm Wed.-Sun., $8-20) has long been a local gathering place; now it houses a wonderful pub-style restaurant where the emphasis on farm-to-table cooking supports local farmers and ranchers. In the evening, the sandwich-leaning menu adds a few homey dinner specials, such as barbecued chicken.

Red Rooster Cafe (309 W. Main St., 541/426-2233, www.red-rooster-cafe.com,

6am-2pm Wed.-Sun., $6-12) is an especially cheery place for breakfast or lunch in downtown Enterprise. The food here is homemade, using as many fresh, local ingredients as possible; baked oatmeal and a cup of the café's custom-roasted coffee are a great way to get ready for the day.

★ **Terminal Gravity Brewing** (803 SE School St., 541/426-0158, www.terminalgravitybrewing.com, 11am-10pm daily summer, 11am-10pm Wed.-Sat., $8-14) is a top-notch brewpub with excellent beer, decent pub food, and a perfectly laid-back atmosphere. Customers congregate on the porch and front lawn in an idyllic creek-side poplar grove.

Drive 30 miles north of Enterprise on Route 3 to the tiny town of Flora, where the **Rimrock Inn** (83471 Lewiston Hwy., 541/828-7769, www.rimrockinnor.com, 5pm-7pm seatings Tues.-Sat., $19-23, reservations required) awaits. Each night a different entrée is prepared—but be prepared to eat some meat, such as barbecued back ribs or Swiss steak, accompanied by organically grown vegetables. A staggering view of Joseph Canyon as it trenches its way toward Hells Canyon is as good as the (very good) food.

The Lostine Tavern serves food from local farms and ranches in a 100-year-old building.

Terminal Gravity Brewing

Information

The **Wallowa County Chamber of Commerce** (309 S. River St., 541/426-4622, www.wallowacountychamber.com, 8am-5pm Mon.-Fri.) stocks a full complement of brochures, maps, and other information on the area.

JOSEPH

At the base of the Wallowa Mountains is Joseph (elevation 4,150 feet), a lively community of about 1,000 that's named after the famous Nez Perce chief. Joseph is noted across the West as an arts town; however, the colorful main street is increasingly lined more with gift shops than galleries, and on a busy summer weekend, finding the artsy charm of this pretty town takes a little doing.

That said, there are still plenty of galleries and arts-related shops to visit, and **Valley Bronze** (18 Main St., 541/432-7445, www.valleybronze.com), Joseph's original bronze-casting operation—and the second-largest in the nation—displays works and offers tours of their **foundry** (307 W. Alder St., 541/432-7551, 11am Mon.-Thurs., 10am Fri. May-Sept., reservations required).

If a foundry tour doesn't fit into your schedule, at least take a walk down Main Street to look at many bronze sculptures; each was done by a different artist.

★ Joseph Branch Railriders

Ride the rails between Enterprise and Joseph using your own steam with the **Joseph Branch Railriders** (304 N. Main St., 541-910-0089 or 541-910-0981, http://jbrailriders.com, office hours 8am-4pm Fri.-Mon. mid-May-early Oct., reservations recommended). The vehicles are a cross between recumbent bicycles and railcars; the routes, which are no longer used by trains, pass through beautiful country that you won't see from the highway. A popular 12-mile round-trip route (9am, noon, 3pm, $20 adults, $10 children under 12) is a gentle downhill from Joseph to Enterprise and back. Another route goes from Minam to Wallowa, a relatively flat 26-mile round trip along the Wallowa River (9am Fri.-Mon., $45).

Josephy Center for Arts and Culture

The **Josephy Center** (403 N. Main St., 541/432-0505, www.josephy.org, noon-4pm Mon.-Sat.) aims to revitalize the area's "creative capital," with its attractive gallery space,

Wallowology!

Much as the Josephy Center celebrates the area's arts, **Wallowology!** (508 N. Main St., 541/263-1663, www.wallowology.org, 10am-6pm Tues.-Sun. June-Sept., free) gives visitors a chance to learn about the Wallowas' natural history. In addition to the exhibits, the center leads free three-hour hikes several times a week; longer outings and talks on geology, wildlife, fire, and other natural history topics are also offered (check the website for schedules).

Iwetemlaykin State Heritage Site

On the road from Joseph to Wallowa Lake, stop off and hike the trails at the **Iwetemlaykin State Heritage Site** to get a feeling for the Nez Perce homeland. It's easy to see why this grassland laced with streams and surrounded by mountains is sacred to the Nez Perce. Short trails offer a chance to get away from the hubbub of downtown Joseph without launching into a rigorous mountain hike. The site is adjacent to the Old Chief Joseph gravesite.

Wallowa County Museum

A must-stop for history buffs is the **Wallowa**

downtown Joseph

library, and workshops. The library, which honors Alvin Josephy (1915-2008), a Western historian who focused much of his work on the Nez Perce, is a treasure trove of books, journals, artifacts, and manuscripts from the Josephy family.

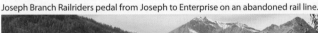
Joseph Branch Railriders pedal from Joseph to Enterprise on an abandoned rail line.

County Museum (110 Main St., 541/432-6095, www.co.wallow.or.us, 10am-4pm daily Memorial Day-late Sept., $4 adults, $3 seniors, $2 students). Built in 1888, the museum building has served as a newspaper office, a private hospital, a meeting hall, and a bank (one of the crooks who robbed the bank later became its president). The museum includes displays of pioneer life and the Nez Perce.

Fishing

The Wallowa Valley area is home to several fine fishing streams, including the Wallowa, Grande Ronde, Lostine, and Imnaha Rivers. The **Joseph Fly Shoppe** (203 N. Main St., 541/432-4343, www.josephflyshop.com, 9am-5pm Mon.-Sat., 9am-4pm Sun.) is a good source for information and gear; **Winding Waters** (877/426-7238, www.windingwatersrafting.com) is a local outfitter.

Entertainment and Events

The **Wallowa Valley Festival of the Arts** (www.wallowavalleyarts.org) is held at the Joseph Civic Center on the first weekend of June. Along with awards for Pacific Northwest artists, there are wine-tasting parties, a silent auction, and a quick-draw competition (using pencils, not sidearms).

Held the last week of July, **Chief Joseph Days** (541/432-1015, www.chiefjosephdays.com) is a weeklong festival in Joseph that features dances along with a carnival, Grand Parade, ranch-style breakfast, and three-day rodeo, one of the largest in the Pacific Northwest. **Bronze, Blues, and Brews** (www.bronzebluesbrews.com) takes place in early August, featuring music, gallery and foundry open houses, and locally brewed beer.

A couple of times a year, Joseph hosts a low-key but talent-laden literary gathering known as **Fishtrap** (541/426-3623, www.fishtrap.org). Authors writing in different genres attend; past participants have included William Kittredge, Ursula K. LeGuin, Ivan Doig, Sandra Scofield, and Terry Tempest Williams. Writers of all levels come to read their works and discuss social issues.

Accommodations

There are few lodging options in Joseph itself; many visitors stay a few miles away at Wallowa Lake, where there's a large campground, a couple of RV parks, and several cabin resorts. But in town, for clean, basic motel rooms, try the **Indian Lodge Motel** (201 S. Main St., 541/432-2651, www.indianlodgemotel.com, $100-110), known by old-timers as "Walter Brennan's place," after the motel's original owner, the TV and movie actor. **Mountain View Motel and RV Park** (83450 Joseph Hwy., 541/432-2982, www.mtviewmotel-rvpark.com, $75-105) is about a mile out of town toward Enterprise; in addition to pet-friendly motel rooms, they have a space for RVs ($40) and tent campers ($30).

Bronze Antler Bed & Breakfast (309 S. Main St., 541/432-0230, www.bronzeantler.com, $145-258) is a friendly B&B in a 1925 bungalow originally built by a local sawmill supervisor who filled the Craftsman-style home with custom millwork and beautiful wood floors. The three guest rooms and one suite have private baths and luxurious linens and towels—the room appointments rival those at upscale hotels.

Chandler's Inn (700 S. Main St., 541/432-9765, www.josephbedandbreakfast.com, $85-170) is a large house, long a B&B, on the edge of town. Options range from smaller rooms with a shared bath to large two-bedroom suites.

Food

Don't limit yourself to a latte at **Red Horse Coffee Traders** (306 N. Main St., www.redhorsecoffeetraders.com, 541/432-3784, 7am-5pm Mon.-Sat., 7am-4pm Sun., $7-10); this is a wonderful place for a scone, a breakfast burrito, or a sandwich on homemade bread.

The log-sided **Old Town Café** (8 S. Main St., 541/432-9898, 7am-2pm daily, $6-9) looks the part of a vintage frontier town eatery—it's a great spot for oniony hash brown potatoes topped with cheese, bacon, and homemade salsa. In nice weather, the outdoor seating is particularly appealing.

Red Horse Coffee Traders, in Joseph, is a good spot for breakfast.

Outlaw Restaurant & Saloon (108 N. Main St., 541/432-4321, www.theoutlawrestaurant.com, 11am-7:30pm Mon.-Thurs., 11am-8:30pm Fri.-Sat., $10-22) offers standard American fare, but in summer there's ample outdoor seating; this is a good bet for dinner for a family.

Embers Brewhouse (204 N. Main St., 541/432-2739, www.embersbrewhouse.com, 11am-close Mon.-Sat., noon-close Sun., $9-13) offers regional microbrews on tap plus pizza and deli sandwiches; try for a spot outside on the deck.

The front yard of ★ **Mutiny Brewing** (600 N. Main St., 541/432-5274, mutinybrewing.com, 3pm-8pm Wed.-Thurs., 11am-9pm Fri.-Sat., 11am-8pm Sun., $8-12) is a great spot for a pint of microbrew ale and a sandwich or delicious rice bowl.

Mutiny Brewing has good food and beer in downtown Joseph.

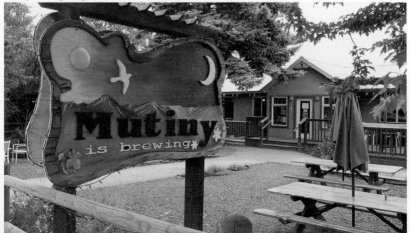

WALLOWA LAKE

The biggest attraction in the Wallowas is the 5,000-foot-elevation Wallowa Lake, which is bordered by the peaks of the Eagle Cap Wilderness. This moraine-held glacial lake begins a mile south of Joseph on Route 82 at the east end of the Wallowa Valley, though most development is at the south end of the lake, about six miles from Joseph. Although it is beautiful, the area around the lake takes on a carnival atmosphere during the summer, with arcades, bumper boats, miniature golf, go-karts, and—for adults—parasailing. In addition to these amusement park attractions, there are lodges, a large state park with a campground, packhorse corrals, boat launches, a marina, and perhaps the **Wallowa Lake Monster,** a creature with a gentle disposition and a length varying 30-100 feet, depending on the sighting. Reports of the critter go back several centuries to Native American tales.

Exercise caution before you dive in to join the monster. Invitingly clear, the lake waters are extremely cold and should not be experienced until August (and not much thereafter). The beach in the county park at the northern end of the lake is a good spot to test the waters.

Wallowa Lake State Park

One of the most popular in the Oregon state park system, **Wallowa Lake State Park** (541/432-4185, www.oregonstateparks.org) is set lakeside amid big old ponderosa pines. It's a beautiful spot, and the perfect place for an outdoorsy family vacation. Even if you're not camping here, the large lakeside day-use area is a fine post from which to enjoy the scenery. The **Wallowa Lake Marina** (541/432-9115, www.wallowalakemarina.com), located in the day-use area, sells fishing gear and rents watercraft ranging from stand-up paddleboards to motorboats. The park is moments from wilderness hiking trails and horseback riding as well as bumper boats and miniature golf. For high season, reserve a campsite at this busy park several months in advance.

★ Wallowa Lake Tramway

The gondola up Mount Howard, the **Wallowa Lake Tramway** (544/432-5331, www.wallowalaketramway.com, 9am-5:45pm daily June-late Sept., reduced hours early and late in season, $29 adults, $26 seniors, $25 students ages 12-17, $19 children ages 4-11, $4 age 3 and under), lifts passengers 3,700 feet from the edge of Wallowa Lake to the 8,200-foot summit.

Wallowa Lake

The 15-minute ride ends at the Summit Grill. But forget about the beer and burger; the best reason for taking the trip is the view. About 2.5 miles of mostly easy trails lead to various overlooks, where you have amazing views of the Wallowa Range, Snake River country, and Idaho's Seven Devils area.

The gondola operates fewer days per week and for fewer hours mid-May-mid-June and mid- to late September; check the website for the schedule during the shoulder season.

Hiking and Horseback Riding

Although many visitors hike the trail network at the top of the tram, there's a good trailhead at the end of Wallowa Lake Highway, less than one mile from the lake. From here you can hike the steep uphill trail six miles to Aneroid Lake, or turn around at the waterfall that's about four miles in. The last couple of miles, between the waterfall and the lake, are the prettiest. From the same trailhead you can catch the seven-mile trail to Chief Joseph Mountain, with good views along the way of Wallowa Lake. Expect to share the trail with horses.

If you'd rather ride a horse up one of these trails, the **Eagle Cap Wilderness Pack Station** (59761 Wallowa Lake Hwy.,

541/432-4145, www.eaglecapwildernesspackstation.com) is right near the trailhead; two-mile rides start on the hour (8am-11am and 1pm-4pm, $35). A variety of longer rides are also offered.

Accommodations and Camping

The following lodgings on Wallowa Lake reflect the special woodsy flavor of this outback locality. These accommodations are all at the south end of the lake, near the state park, which offers campsites.

The **Wallowa Lake Lodge** (60060 Wallowa Lake Hwy., 541/432-9821, www.wallowalakelodge.com, $115-255) is a renovated 1923 hunting lodge on the lakefront that fairly drips with vintage atmosphere. Some guest rooms are quite small; others have two bedrooms. All have private bathrooms and are decorated in a somewhat feminine style (no knotty pine). In addition, eight 1950s-era cabins feature knotty pine cabinets, stone fireplaces, and fully modern kitchens and bathrooms; most have lake views. It's hard to imagine a more enchanting setting.

The **Flying Arrow Resort** (59782 Wallowa Lake Hwy., 541/432-2951, www.flyingarrowresort.com, cabins $99-450), offers lodging

The Wallowa Lake Tramway lifts passengers 3700 feet up the side of Mount Howard.

ranging from one-room cabins to four-bedroom houses that can sleep 14. All but the $99 studio cabins have kitchens, fireplaces, and bathrooms; they're all unique, so visit the website to find out which cabin matches your needs. The resort also features a swimming pool, hot tub, chocolate shop, bookstore, and market. The Flying Arrow is kid- and pet-friendly.

Wallowa Lake Resort (84681 Ponderosa Ln., 541/432-2391, www.wallowalakeresort. com) rents over 30 different properties in the Lake Wallowa area, from small cabins perfect for a couple (starting at $95) to large homes that will sleep up to 10 ($260). No two are alike, so get on the website and make your selection.

On the quieter western side of the lake, **Trouthaven Resort** (61841 Lakeshore Dr., 541/432-2221, www.trouthavencabins.com, mid-May-mid-Sept., $110-120) is another venerable cabin resort. The cabins come in two sizes (the larger ones can sleep six) and have knotty pine paneling and a covered porch with an outdoor dining table. The Trouthaven also has a half-mile of Wallowa Lake frontage with a couple of docks; boats and fishing gear are available for rent. The cabins and this location are perfect ingredients for a family

Horseback rides head to mountain lakes.

vacation; during the busy months of July and August, a five-day minimum stay is usually required.

Although it's not what you'd call a secret hideaway, if you're looking for a campground

Wallowa Lake Lodge

surrounded on three sides by 9,000-foot-high snowcapped peaks and a large clear lake, the **Wallowa Lake State Park campground** (541/432-4185, www.oregonstateparks.org, reservations 800/452-5687 or reserveamerica. com, $20 tents, $30 RVs, $43 yurts) is for you.

Food

Most of the cabins along Lake Wallowa have kitchens, and Joseph's restaurants are just a short drive away, so even though this is a major tourist destination, there's not a vast selection of restaurants. Nonetheless, there are a couple notable places to eat. **Vali's Alpine Delicatessen** (59811 Wallowa Lake Hwy., 541/432-5691, www.valisrestaurant.com, seatings at 5 and 7pm Wed.-Sun. Memorial Day-Labor Day, 5 and 7pm Sat.-Sun. Apr.-Memorial Day, $13-22, no credit cards, reservations required) features a different fixed dinner menu each day with German and Hungarian specialties such as cabbage rolls or schnitzel (only one entrée is served each night). Stop by on Saturday and Sunday mornings (9am-11am), when freshly made doughnuts are on offer.

The dining room at the 1920s-era **Wallowa Lake Lodge** (60060 Wallowa Lake Hwy., 541/432-9821, www.wallowalake.com, 8am-11:30am daily and 5pm-6pm Fri.-Tues. summer, $11-26) is beautifully preserved, though the food—steaks, pasta, fresh seafood—is up to date. Early and late in the season, restaurant hours are reduced, so call to check.

THE WALLOWA MOUNTAINS HIGH COUNTRY

The Wallowa Mountains are some of Oregon's most rugged, beautiful, and least visited: 715 square miles of this craggy backcountry are preserved as the **Eagle Cap Wilderness Area.** Glacier-torn valleys, high mountain lakes, and marble peaks are some of the rewards that await backpackers. In addition, there's good fishing in streams and lakes, and in winter the heavy snowfalls attract both downhill and Nordic skiers. Forest Service

campgrounds serve as bases for Wallowa Mountains exploration. For more information on recreation and camping in the Wallowas, contact the **Wallowa-Whitman National Forest** (201 E. 2nd St., Joseph, 541/426-5546, www.fs.usda.gov/wallowa-whitman).

Hiking and Camping

Most Eagle Cap Wilderness Area trails are long and steep, and most alpine lakes are at least five miles from a trailhead, so opportunities for easy day hikes into the wilderness are limited. Camping is the best way to enjoy the area. Before heading out, pick up the Eagle Cap map from a Forest Service office or at local sporting goods stores. Higher elevations are usually free of snow by early July, but streams may be running high and fast until later in July.

The easily accessible **Minam State Recreation Area** (541/551-6949, www.oregonstateparks.org, $10, no reservations) off Route 82 about 15 miles east of Elgin puts you within relatively easy striking distance of trailheads.

The **Two Pan** trailhead is one of the most popular gateways into the Wallowas; **Williamson** and **Shady** campgrounds ($6, no water) are along the road to the trailhead. To get here, head south from Lostine on County Route 551 for seven miles and down Forest Service Road 5202 for 11 miles. This is a rough and rocky road, so take your time. Trails leave Two Pan for the Lostine River Valley and the glacial lakes at the base of Eagle Cap.

Farther east, **Hurricane Creek** ($6, no water) is three miles southwest of Joseph on Forest Service Road 8205. The Hurricane Creek trailhead leads to a hike along the east slope of the Hurricane Divide past Sacajawea Peak and the Matterhorn to the glacial lakes basin. An ambitious trek would start at Two Pan and end at Hurricane Creek. The lake basin area south of Joseph can get crowded, especially on weekends July-August.

If your budget allows, hire a guide to ease your way into the wilderness. The **Eagle Cap**

Wilderness Pack Station (59761 Wallowa Lake Hwy., Joseph, 541/432-4145, www.eagle-capwildernesspackstation.com) runs many day rides to lakes and streams in the Eagle Cap high country and outfitting expeditions into the backcountry. For $200 per person per day, the outfitters will furnish your complete camp, including riding horses, pack stock, a guide, wranglers, a cook, and food. These outfitters also offer "drop" trips, where horses and mules carry people and supplies to a lake, then leave and return at an appointed time to pack you and your gear out. This service costs $300 per person each way.

Wallowa Llamas (36678 Allstead Ln., Halfway, 541/742-2961, www.wallowallamas.com) offers a unique way to venture into the wilderness. One surefooted, even-tempered llama will carry 20 pounds of your gear; you carry the rest. The outfit offers three-to seven-day trips to Hells Canyon and the Wallowas. The expeditions are designed for those with some backpacking experience or anyone in reasonably good shape. The outfitters provide tents, eating utensils, and all meals—and of course the llamas. Four-day excursions begin at $695.

Skiing

The recreational delights of the Wallowas are not reserved for summer only; the skiing in this alpine wonderland can be excellent. **Ferguson Ridge Ski Area** (541/426-3493, www.skifergi.com, 10am-4pm weekends and holidays, $20 adults, $10 children) is a small and laid-back downhill facility with a rope tow and T-bar that climb from a 5,100-foot base to 5,800-foot-high Ferguson Ridge. The light eastern Oregon powder, when there's enough of it, makes for good skiing. Make sure to bring a full water bottle; no water is available at the ski area. To get there, drive east from Joseph about five miles on the Wallowa Loop Highway, then follow signs south on Tucker Down Road.

Cross-country skiers can head to the **Hurricane Creek.** Take Hurricane Creek Road west from Joseph to the trailhead. Another popular spot is **Salt Creek Summit,** about 20 miles southeast of Joseph on Wallowa Loop Highway. The facility has five miles of marked but ungroomed ski and snowmobile trails and a plowed snow park.

Backcountry ski mountaineering is the focus of **Wallowa Alpine Huts** (541/398-1980, www.wallowahuts.com), which offers four- or five-day trips to several backcountry huts, including one at 7,500-foot McCully Basin within the Eagle Cap Wilderness. Ski seven miles in to a yurt base camp and spend the days exploring the high country on backcountry snowboards, telemarking skis, or randonée skis, then return to cooked meals, warm yurts, and even a sauna. Four-day trips begin at $900 and include all backcountry meals, accommodations, bedding, and guides; forgo the guide and cook for yourself for $200 per person for a four-day stay at the yurts.

Hells Canyon

★ HELLS CANYON NATIONAL RECREATION AREA

The **Hells Canyon National Recreation Area** (Oxbow, OR 97828, 541/785-3395, www.fs.usda.gov) straddles a 71-mile portion of the Snake River and encompasses the 215,223-acre Hells Canyon Wilderness Area. Most of the canyon's terrain is made up of precipitous rock walls and steep, slot-like side valleys, which means that just about the only way to experience this epic landscape is on foot, horseback, or—most accessibly—by boat.

The remote Hells Canyon is the deepest river gorge in North America. For a distance of 106 miles no bridge crosses the river, and few paved roads come even near the canyon.

At its deepest point, the gorge walls rise nearly 8,000 feet.

Hells Canyon by Vehicle

There are several ways to get to Hells Canyon from Oregon. From Baker City, take Route 86 for 50 miles east to **Halfway.** Stop here to stock up on groceries and gas, continue on Route 86 another 16 miles to Oxbow Dam, and then downstream (north) 20 miles on the Idaho side of the Snake River to **Hells Canyon Dam.** A visitors center is adjacent to where rafts put in on the Snake River at the beginning of the river's Wild and Scenic stretch. This site affords a spectacular view of the canyon.

Another approach is via Route 82 through the Wallowa Valley to Enterprise, Joseph, and Imnaha. From Imnaha, one of the most isolated towns in the country, drive 24 miles to **Hat Point Lookout.** The first five miles of ascent is not for the faint of heart—the guardrail-free dirt road is vertigo-inducing. However, once on the ridgetop, the road edges to Hat Point and a view into Hells Canyon and the Snake River, a dizzying 7,000 feet below.

An simpler but less satisfying way to glimpse the canyon is from the **Wallowa Mountain Loop Road** (a.k.a. Forest Rd. 39), which runs between Joseph and Halfway. The **Hells Canyon Lookout,** the only paved viewpoint into Hells Canyon, is 31 miles north of Halfway. The vista looks into the canyon, but the river isn't visible from here.

Hiking

More than 900 miles of trails await hikers and backpackers in the Hells Canyon National Recreation Area, and hiking is just about the only way to get to some of the canyon's remoter areas. However, it's not a hiking destination for novices. Before lacing up your hiking boots, consider that summer temperatures soar above 100°F, rattlesnakes abound, and potable water can be hard to find. Ticks and poison oak can be problems here too. Black widow and brown recluse spiders can constitute the biggest danger, however. Major trails are maintained, but others are difficult to follow. It's a good idea to talk to rangers before setting out, as this is an extremely remote and challenging wilderness. You'll also want a detailed map.

Long-distance riverside trails run on both the Oregon and Idaho shores of the Snake River, but reaching them is a challenge. The rugged cliffs along the Hells Canyon Dam are too steep for hiking trails, although a mile-long trail from the jet-boat launch area does pick its way down the Oregon side before ending precipitously.

Reach the **Oregon Snake River Trail,** on the river's western edge, by driving 27 miles north of Imnaha to Dug Bar; this will put you on the river. The road is OK for passenger cars in good weather, but it can be very slippery when wet. Another option is the **Western Rim Trail.** There are comparatively few steep ups and downs, and daytime temperatures are much less oppressive than within the canyon. There is also plenty of shade among the rim's evergreen forests. On the other hand, the rim route has fewer water sources, so camping choices are limited. To reach the southern end of this 37-mile trail, from Joseph, follow Forest Road 39 to the Hells Canyon Viewpoint and head about 10 miles northeast on Forest Road 3965 to the PO Saddle Trailhead (www.fs.usda.gov/recarea/wallowa-whitman).

Boating

Outfitters arrange Snake River float trips on rafts, dories, or kayaks, providing high adventure as the river bounces though 34 named rapids rated Class II-IV in the most commonly floated part of the canyon, the two- to three-day passage between Hells Canyon Dam and Pittsburgh Landing in Idaho (longer trips are available). For travelers with less time, turbine-powered jet-boat tours are also available—a less idyllic but equally exciting way to see the canyon in as little as a day. These turbine-powered flat-bottomed boats are able to maneuver shallow water and rapids, though they are also very noisy. The recreation area website (www.fs.usda.gov/detail/

wallowa-whitman) provides a list of outfitters licensed to guide trips on the Snake River. Be sure to check the offerings available, as they are abundant. The brief selection below is just a taste of what's available and is intended to provide a guideline to prices and trips.

From the landing just below Hells Canyon Dam, **Hells Canyon Adventures** (541/785-3352 or 800/422-3568, www.hellscanyonadventures.com) offers a variety of jet-boat tours daily (Apr.-Sept.). The briefest and least expensive excursion is a two-hour afternoon jet-boat trip into the deepest part of the canyon that costs $85 adults, $60 children. A six-hour $177 tour ($88 children) leaves at 10am, runs all the principal rapids of the canyon, and includes lunch and a stop at the Kirkwood Ranch Museum, a frontier ranch at the base of the canyon. Hells Canyon Adventures offers other tours, including float trips and fishing charters. Reservations are required.

A local outfitter that specializes in whitewater raft trips is **Winding Waters** (877/426-7238, www.windingwatersrafting.com). Trips of 3-6 days are offered May-October and include guide services, tent accommodations, transport to and from Joseph, a night's lodging in Joseph, and food. A three-day trip starts at $995 adults, $796 children.

Fishing for trout, catfish, smallmouth bass, and, if you're lucky, 100-year-old sturgeon can add to the pleasure of a raft trip. **Canyon Outfitters** (541/742-4110, www.canyonoutfitters.com) offers summer white-water float trips (four days, $1,350) with ample time for fishing.

If you plan to shoot the Class III and IV rapids of the Snake River on your own, you'll need a permit from the **Hells Canyon National Recreation Area office** in Oxbow (541/785-3395).

Camping

Of the 12 campgrounds on the Oregon side of the national recreation area, we recommend the following three. **Lake Fork** **Campground** ($6, no water) is 18 miles northeast of Halfway on Forest Service Road 39, and the fishing is good at nearby Fish Lake. **Indian Crossing** ($6, water at nearby trailhead), 45 miles southeast of Joseph on Forest Service Road 3960, has a trailhead for backpacking into the Eagle Cap Wilderness. On the northern end of the recreational area, **Buckhorn** (free, no water) is 43 miles northeast of Enterprise and features a great view.

Accommodations and Food

The town of Halfway (pop. 286), 17 miles from the Oxbow Dam on the Snake River, is a popular way station for Hells Canyon-bound travelers. The ★ **Pine Valley Lodge** (163 N. Main St., Halfway, 541/742-2027, www.pvlodge.com, $80-150) is an unexpected pleasure in rugged Hells Canyon country. You can't get much more Old West-meets-Western chic than this! Nearly a dozen guest rooms have been created in vintage log and wood structures in downtown Halfway, and each is filled with cowboy decor that's part history, part whimsy.

Reasonably priced standard guest rooms can be had at the **Halfway Motel** (170 S. Main St., Halfway, 541/742-5722, www.halfwaymotel-rvpark.com, $60).

Twelve miles north of Halfway, at the southern edge of the Eagle Cap Wilderness Area, the **Cornucopia Lodge** (Queen Mine Rd., 541/742-4500 or 800/742-6115, www.cornucopialodge.com, $110-150) is a great place from which to launch or conclude a backpacking trip, or just relax. The cabins and lodge are in a spectacularly scenic setting, and guests can head out on horseback rides, hikes, or fishing trips. Breakfast is included in rates and dinner is available for $24; no cooking is allowed in the cabins.

Restaurants are few and far between in this country, and it would be prudent to pack a few picnic items. Halfway has a few cafés that will cover your basic feeding needs. There's also a restaurant down at Oxbow, near the Snake River on Route 86.

Baker City

Baker City, set in a valley between the Wallowas and the Blue Mountains, is the quintessential Western ranch town, with a handsome downtown area filled with classic stone and redbrick storefronts. Ranchers hereabouts still drive their herds down the highways, and folks wave howdy to passersby. Baker City (pop. 9,700) is a friendly place that has held on to its pioneer spirit. There's lots of history here—highlighted by the nation's foremost Oregon Trail interpretive center—and with its abundant and high-quality facilities, Baker City is a good jumping-off spot for Hells Canyon, the deepest gorge in North America. Baker City was the hub of the eastern Oregon gold rush; stop by the downtown U.S. Bank and check out the 80.4-ounce **Armstrong gold nugget,** found in 1913. It's a remnant from the days when this wealthy raucous frontier boomtown was the biggest and most important in the region.

West of town along Route 7 and its offshoots leading into the Elkhorn and Blue Mountains, ghost towns like Granite, McEwen, and Sumpter are remnants of the gold rush days of the 1860s. The route, which follows the twisty contours of the Powder River, is particularly pretty when the deciduous trees take on fall hues.

SIGHTS
★ National Historic Oregon Trail Interpretive Center

Six miles east of Baker City is the 23,000-square-foot **National Historic Oregon Trail Interpretive Center** (22267 Hwy. 86, 541/523-1843, www.blm.gov/or/oregontrail, 9am-6pm daily Apr.-Oct., 9am-4pm daily Nov.-Mar., $8 adults, $4.50 seniors, children ages 15 and under free, discounts in winter). The museum is perched atop Flagstaff Hill overlooking a picturesque section of the famous frontier thoroughfare. The exhibit halls are arranged to simulate the route and experiences of pioneers on the 547-mile section of the trail within Oregon's borders. The life-size dioramas of Oregon Trail scenes, accompanied by taped renditions of immigrant voices and wagon wheels, make you feel like part of the great migration.

Baker City's 19th-century downtown is worth exploring.

Outside the museum, your historical reverie is sustained by living-history exhibits and the chance to stand in the actual ruts left behind by pioneer wagons at **Virtue Flat,** a two-mile walk from the center. Surrounded by the 10,000-foot Elkhorn Mountains to the west, the Blues to the south, and the craggy Eagle Cap to the northeast, the "land at Eden's gate" becomes more than just another florid phrase from a pioneer diary.

Baker Heritage Museum

Housed in a showcase natatorium built in 1920, the **Baker Heritage Museum** (2490 Grove St., 541/523-9308, www.bakerheritage-museum.com, 9am-4pm daily mid-Mar.-Oct., $6 adults, $5 seniors and children ages 13-17) shows off an extensive collection from Baker City's frontier days as well as exhibits depicting the great Oregon Trail migration. The museum is across from Geiser Pollman Park, which has picnic tables and playgrounds.

Eastern Oregon Museum

Ten miles northwest of Baker City in the town of Haines is the **Eastern Oregon Museum** (610 3rd St., Haines, 541/856-3233, 9:30am-4:30pm Thurs.-Sun. mid-May-mid-Sept., $2). One of the largest historical museums in this part of the state, it boasts over 10,000 artifacts. It has an outstanding collection of vintage farming equipment, mining tools and paraphernalia, and pioneer relics.

SPORTS AND RECREATION
Skiing

Anthony Lakes Ski Area (541/856-3277, www.anthonylakes.com, Thurs.-Sun. and holidays, $35 adults, $29 students ages 13-18, $21 children ages 7-12, free for children ages 6 and under) is 18 miles west of Haines on the Elkhorn Scenic Byway. This ski resort offers a triple chairlift, Nordic trail system, day lodge, ski shop, and ski lessons. This is Oregon's first and highest (7,000 feet) ski area. Come to this remote spot for its pristine dry powder and a family-oriented environment. The 1,100 acres of slopes offer plenty of challenge—80 percent of the runs are intermediate or expert.

During the summer, the area around Anthony Lakes is a beautiful place to hike; several trailheads sprout from the road near the ski resort.

ACCOMMODATIONS

Baker City's preeminent lodging choice is the ★ **Geiser Grand Hotel** (1996 Main St.,

The 1889 Geiser Grand Hotel is still eastern Oregon's finest hotel.

Northeastern Oregon's Scenic Byways

Northeastern Oregon is road-trip country, and several routes in this region are federally designated as scenic byways.

The **Wallowa Mountain Loop Road** is a scenic 51-mile drive through Hells Canyon Country. The route begins with the Joseph-Imnaha Highway, which winds past farms and canyons. Turn south on Wallowa Mountain Loop Road to the Imnaha River, then ascend into alpine forests along Dry Creek Road to Halfway. You'll come out on the south flank of the Wallowas. Turn east for a shoreline view of the Snake River and Hells Canyon. Closed in winter.

Explore the high country behind Sumpter by driving the **Elkhorn Drive National Scenic Byway,** which takes you northwest from Sumpter through the gold-mining territory to Granite, across the north fork of the John Day, past Anthony Lake, and on to Baker City. Because much of this road is above 5,000 feet in elevation, the loop is open only a few months of the year. The portion south of Anthony Lakes and north of Granite is closed by snow from early November through June or early July. The Elkhorn Byway climbs higher than any other paved road in Oregon (7,392 feet) after passing North Fork John Day Campground and the junction with Blue Mountains Scenic Byway. The craggy granite peaks of the northern Elkhorns—several higher than 8,000 feet—are near this area.

The longest of eastern Oregon's scenic byways is the **Journey through Time Scenic Byway.** Departing from (or ending at) Biggs, on I-5 and the Columbia Gorge, this highly scenic route takes the back roads through the canyon-cut Columbia Plateau, extending to Baker City. The highlight of this tour is the John Day River canyon, where millennia of erosion have sculpted a dramatic gorge through layers of volcanic formations, in the process unveiling the fossil remains of ancient life, which can be seen at the various units of the John Day Fossil Beds National Monument. This route makes an excellent bike ride, especially during the spring and early fall; it's also popular with motorcyclists.

541/523-1899 or 888/434-7374, www.geisergrand.com, $99-209), a showplace of period grandeur and refinement. Built in 1889 as the finest hotel between Portland and Salt Lake City, the Geiser Grand was updated and refurbished in the 1990s and sparkles with old-fashioned charm and modern comforts. Amid Viennese chandeliers, mahogany columns, and a stained-glass skylight 40 feet above the dining room, you'll feel like you've traveled back in time. The standard guest rooms are large, and for a real treat you can step up to a suite—particularly one on a corner or including the cupola—and have 10-foot-high windows on two sides to drink in the Blue Mountain views.

Within walking distance of downtown is a good value motel, the **Oregon Trail Motel** (211 Bridge St., 541/523-5844 or 888/523-5882, http://oregontrailmotelandrestaurantbakercity.com, $45-55). Nothing fancy, but it's a clean and pleasant place to spend the night. The adjoining restaurant is a good spot for breakfast. Just across the street, rooms at the friendly but basic **Bridge Street Inn** (134 Bridge St., 541/523-6571, www.bridgestreetinn.net, $43-58) are about the same price.

The **Best Western Sunridge Inn** (1 Sunridge Ln., 541/523-6444, www.bestwesternoregon.com, $80-96) is a large motel complex with the feel of a small resort. Five motel blocks surround a nicely landscaped central garden, pool, and fitness area, which is also linked to the motel's two restaurants. The disadvantage of the Best Western is that it is near the interstate exchange No. 304, over a mile from downtown. Also out near the interstate is the **Always Welcome Inn** (175 Campbell St., 541/523-3431, www.alwayswelcomeinn.com, $70-78), a newer motel that offers clean comfortable rooms, an indoor pool, and—to set it apart from other interstate motels—a fossil bed out back.

Camping

The area's best camping is up in the Elkhorn Range near Anthony Lakes. **Anthony Lakes Campground** (541/523-6391, www.fs.usda.gov, $10, water, no reservations) is right at the base of the Anthony Lakes Ski Area, with campsites tucked among huge boulders a short walk from the lake. About a mile farther east along Forest Road 73, find **Grande Ronde Lake Campground** ($5, water, no reservations), a pretty spot at the headwaters of the Grande Ronde River.

FOOD

A great addition to Baker City's Main Street is **Zephyr Deli and Bakery** (1917 Main St., 541/523-4601, 9am-2pm Thurs.-Sun. and other hours as posted, $5-9), a hip and sociable spot for a breakfast sandwich or a salad (with as many organically grown veggies as possible), or hanging out with a cup of coffee and chatting with the locals. The orange rolls, baked fresh every morning, are worth seeking out.

Just across the street, the **Corner Brick Bar and Grill** (1840 Main St., 541/523-6099, 11am-9pm Mon.-Thurs., 11am-10pm Fri.-Sat., $10-15) is a friendly little spot with huge portions of pasta, pizza, salads, and sandwiches.

The **Lone Pine Café** (1825 Main St., 541/523-1805, 8am-3pm Fri.-Tues., $7-17) is another outpost of good food on Main Street. The menu isn't complicated—breakfast standbys, burgers, and excellent sandwiches (try the Reuben!)—but the quality is high. There's always a daily special that features local and seasonal ingredients, such as Blue-Mountain-harvested morel mushroom risotto.

Barley Brown's Brew Pub (2190 Main St., 541/523-4266, www.barleybrowns.com, 4pm-10pm Mon.-Sat. $8-19) serves some of Oregon's best brews (no small feat in this state). Most of its beer is only available at the pub and the Barley Brown's taproom across the street (2200 Main St.), so make a pilgrimage for a pint and enjoy well-prepared food as well. The menu goes far beyond pub grub, including steak, seafood, barbecued ribs, and pasta. If you're mostly just looking to sample the beer, head to the taphouse (2200 Main St.,541-523-2337, 2pm-10pm daily), just a block down the street, with 22 Barley Brown ales on tap.

Earth and Vine Gallery and Wine Bar (2001 Washington Ave., 541/523-1687, 11am-9pm Tues.-Thurs., 11am-10pm Fri., 8am-11pm Sat., 8am-8pm Sun., $8-15) is, as its name suggests, a combo gallery and light restaurant. It's a bright and airy place to enjoy a drink (beer is also available, including a couple of taps from Barley Brown's) and an appetizer or sandwich. Breakfasts are good, particularly if they have fresh strawberries and waffles (available seasonally). The **Palm Court** in the Geiser Grand Hotel (1996 Main St., 541/523-1899, www.geisergrand.com, 5pm-9pm daily, $9-27) is easily the classiest place to eat in Baker City, if not in all of eastern Oregon. The setting is splendid—a soaring stained-glass ceiling surmounts a wood-paneled dining room sparkling with linen, crystal, and candles. The food's pretty good too, though dinners are sometimes dwarfed by the atmosphere. Specialties include mesquite smoked prime rib, fresh Northwest salmon, and home-made desserts. A less formal option in the Geiser Grand is the **1889 Café** (7am-10pm, $5-15), in the old hotel bar, where you can start out with big eggy breakfasts in the morning, enjoy burgers and salads for lunch, and have light meals with cocktails and microbrews in the evening.

Ten miles north of Baker City is the beloved **Haines Steakhouse** (910 Front St., Haines, 541/856-3639, www.hainessteakhouse.com, 4:30pm-9pm Mon. and Wed.-Fri., 3:30pm-9pm Sat., 12:30pm-9pm Sun., $20-30), known for its tender prime rib and authentic Western atmosphere. Antiques and cowboy Americana decorate the restaurant, enhancing what may be described as first-rate chuckwagon fare.

INFORMATION

Contact the **Baker County Chamber and Visitor Center** (490 Campbell St.,

541/523-5855, www.visitbaker.com) for more information.

The *Baker City Herald* (www.bakercity-herald.com) publishes a good annual travel guide to the local area. It's available free at area museums and tourist facilities.

Sumpter and Vicinity

In the Elkhorn Mountains west of Baker City, Sumpter is a former gold-mining town, one of many small communities in this area that hovers between ghost town and tourist town status. The heyday of gold mining in the area was 1900-1905, when over 3,000 miners worked the hard-rock mines and dredged the Powder River. By 1905 most of the easily accessed gold was gone, but dredging continued until 1954. Today, Sumpter has about 150 year-round residents—a few of whom actually still run small gold mines—and the old storefronts are now antiques shops and art galleries. A few vintage watering holes still provide food and drink to locals and travelers alike. Sumpter is 30 miles west of Baker City and 57 miles east of John Day.

GETTING THERE

Greyhound buses serve Baker City on runs between Portland and Boise. There are two buses daily in each direction, and the terminal is at 515 Campbell Street (541/523-5011).

SIGHTS
Sumpter Valley Dredge State Heritage Area

A state park-managed site, the **Sumpter Valley Dredge State Heritage Area** (541/894-2486 or 800/551-6949) preserves one of three gold dredges that scooped up and sifted gold-rich Powder River gravels. With a hull 125 feet long and 52 feet wide, this is the longest and most accessible gold dredge in the country, in its day capable of chewing up 225 cubic feet (8.33 cubic yards) per minute, or an average of 100 acres of riverbed per year. Sticking out from the dredge's hull is a massive boom bearing 72 one-ton buckets. The buckets, moving like the chain of a chain saw, would bore into the riverbank and carry the loose rock back into the dredge interior. Once

The Sumpter dredge is a massive piece of equipment.

inside, the rock passed through a series of steel cylinders that separated the material by size, sending the smaller components deeper into the dredge. Using water and sluices, the gold was separated from the sediment, which passed through the back of the dredge along with the gravel and larger rocks and was deposited as mine tailings. In its lifetime, this dredge alone made $4.5 million when gold prices were a mere $35 per troy ounce. The dredge passed to Oregon state parks in 1995, which has restored it and in summer offers interpretive displays and tours. Access to the park is free, with trails leading out into wildlife viewing areas—the orderly piles of mine tailings along the Powder River have become an unlikely wetlands habitat.

Sumpter Valley Railroad

Another piece of local history is the **Sumpter Valley Railroad** (12259 Huckleberry Loop Rd., Baker City, 541/894-2268 or 866/894-2268, www.sumptervalleyrailroad.org, $12/17.50 adults one-way/round-trip, $10/15 seniors and military, $7/11 children ages 6-16, $30/50 family), a rebuilt narrow-gauge excursion train pulled by steam engines. The railway originally ran 1890-1961 between Baker City and Prairie City, transporting logs and ore in addition to passengers. Today, passengers ride the five miles between McEwen Station and Sumpter in two vintage observation cars; a restored 1890 caboose is also part of the train. Runs depart Sumpter station at noon and 3:15pm (Sat.-Sun. Memorial Day-last weekend in Sept.).

Granite

Back-road and ghost town connoisseurs will want to stop and take a gander at the remains of **Granite** (pop. 38). With its false-fronted buildings of unpainted and splintered boards, Granite is a true "ghost town." Hard as it is to believe, this place once had four saloons, a 50-room hotel, several smaller hotels, a boardinghouse, a church, and a wooden jail. Founded in 1862, its mining legacy sustained the town through the 1930s. The need for miners in World War II defense industries at that time compelled President Franklin D. Roosevelt to shut down the mines. Today, community ties are maintained by regular visits to the Granite store, where miners, retirees, and other residents meet up to keep the ghost alive.

EVENTS

On Memorial Day, Fourth of July, and Labor Day weekends, folks head to the fairgrounds

Nearly a ghost town, Granite is Oregon's smallest incorporated town.

for the **Sumpter Flea Market.** Collectibles, crafts, and food are arrayed in a beautiful mountain setting. This event is legendary among Oregon's bargain hunters.

ACCOMMODATIONS

The **Sumpter Stockade Motel** (129 E. Austin St., Sumpter, 541/894-2360, www. sumpterstockade.com, May-mid-Oct., $65-75) offers individually decorated rooms, including a suite with a full kitchen, in a newly built structure designed to resemble an Old West military fort complete with a pole stockade. Tent campers can set up on the lawn inside the stockade ($10 pp, $15 for 2), and there's a

tiny bunkroom ($20 pp) used mainly by bicycle tourists, a surprising number of whom pass through town on cross-country tours. This is an unusual but comfy place to stay in this little town.

For more traditional guest rooms, the **Depot Inn** (179 S. Mill St., 541/894-2522, www.thedepotinn.com, $75) is a handsome log-built motel; rooms have fridges, microwaves, and wireless Internet.

Sumpter's original 1900 hospital is back in business as **Sumpter Bed and Breakfast** (344 NE Columbia St., 541/894-0048, www. sumpterbb.net, $80), with six antique-filled guest rooms and a hearty breakfast.

Ontario

Midway between Portland and Salt Lake City in Oregon's far east, Ontario is where "Oregon's day begins." (Indeed, it begins an hour earlier here—Ontario is on Mountain Time.) It's the biggest city in Malheur County, with a population of 11,000. Ontario ships over 5 percent of the nation's onions and provides a good portion of the sweet russet potatoes used for french fries by national fast-food chains. Other local crops include sugar beets, peppermint, grains, and ornamental flowers. This abundance derives from the fertile plains at the confluence of the Snake, Owyhee, Payette, and Malheur Rivers.

In 1942, President Franklin D. Roosevelt ordered the removal of 120,000 Japanese Americans from the West Coast to 10 inland concentration camps located in isolated areas of seven states. About 5,000 Japanese Americans were moved to an internment camp near Ontario. Under the leadership of Ontario mayor Elmo Smith, the eastern Oregon farming community invited internees to help fill service and farm jobs. By the end of the war, 1,000 Japanese Americans had settled in the Ontario area, giving Malheur County the largest percentage of Japanese Americans in Oregon. As a result, Japanese

surnames grace many a ranch or farm in eastern Oregon. Some of the migrant workers in an influx from Latin America who came to work the crops in the 1950s and 1960s also stayed to start new lives, adding yet another ethnic flavor to a cultural stew that already contained Basques and the Paiute people.

SIGHTS

Four Rivers Cultural Center

Ontario's rich mix of cultures is celebrated at the **Four Rivers Cultural Center** (676 SW 5th Ave., 541/889-8191, www.4rcc.com, 9am-5pm Mon.-Fri., 10am-5pm Sat., $4 adults, $3 seniors and children) at Treasure Valley Community College. The four rivers—the Snake, Malheur, Owyhee, and Payette—represent the flow of people of different ethnicities into this part of Oregon: Native Americans, Basques, Hispanics, other Europeans, and Japanese. The complex includes a museum, theater, convention center, and formal Japanese garden.

Snake River Crossing

Remnants of the Oregon Trail still cross this remote corner of Oregon. Museums, historic markers, and wagon-rut memorials stud the area. South of Ontario, between Nyssa and Adrian along Route 201, a roadside monument commemorates the trail's **Snake River Crossing** into Oregon. Directly across the Snake from this point was Fort Boise, a Hudson's Bay Company fur-trading fort that doubled as a landmark and trade center for often-desperate pioneers. The fort was swept away by floods years ago; the site is now part of a wildlife refuge.

Follow the Oregon Trail from Nyssa to Vale to find several other historic sites. Take Enterprise Avenue just west of Nyssa and turn right on Lyttle Boulevard; from here the paved road closely follows the tracks of the Oregon Trail to Vale.

Keeney Pass Oregon Trail Historic Site

The **Keeney Pass Oregon Trail Historic Site,** four miles south of Vale, has a display of the deep ruts cut into the earth by ironclad wagon wheels. This exhibit marks the most-used route of the wagon trains as they passed through the Snake River Valley on their way to Baker Valley to the north. From the top of this pass you can see the route of a whole day's journey on the trail to Oregon over 160 years ago. Ponder the fact that one pioneer in 10 died on this arduous transcontinental trek. In June and July, Indian paintbrush and penstemon add a dash of color to the sagebrush and rabbitbrush that surround the ruts in the trail.

Farewell Bend

Twenty-two miles north of Ontario on I-84 is Farewell Bend, where travelers along the old Oregon Trail left the valley of the Snake River, which they had more or less followed from central Idaho, and climbed up into the desert uplands of eastern Oregon.

Before undertaking the strenuous journey through desert landscapes to the imposing Blue Mountains, Oregon Trail travelers usually rested at Farewell Bend, grazing livestock, gathering wood, and otherwise preparing themselves for the arduous trip ahead. Today,

Farewell Bend State Park (800/452-5687, www.oregonstateparks.org, $5 day use, $18-24 camping) commemorates this placid pioneer wayside with a picnic and play area, interpretive displays, a boat launch, and a large campground.

FESTIVALS AND EVENTS

The **Vale Rodeo** is a four-day fete that takes place over the July 1-4 holiday. It's highlighted by the Suicide Race, an event held at nearby Vale Butte in which cowboys race their horses off a steep slope into an arena.

The **Obon Festival,** celebrating Ontario's Japanese heritage, is held in late June at Ontario's **Buddhist temple** (286 SE 4th St., 541/889-8562). Japanese folk dancing is the highlight of the festival.

ACCOMMODATIONS AND FOOD

There is a cluster of motels at I-84 Exit 376. If you're hot and tired of driving, the deluxe sheets, indoor pool, and fitness center at the **Holiday Inn Express** (212 SE 10th St., 541/889-7100, $101-125) might sound pretty good. This is the high end of what you'll find in Ontario. The **Best Western Plus Inn** (251 Goodfellow St., 541/889-2600, $102-119) is also one of the nicer places to stay in town; it has an indoor pool, exercise room, and guest laundry, plus continental breakfast included. All rooms have microwaves and refrigerators. If you want a simple, friendly, '50s-style courtyard motel well off the interstate, check out the **Ontario Inn** (1144 SW 4th Ave., on the road to Vale, 541/823-2556, www.ontarioinnmotel.com, $64-74). It's pet-friendly, and even has a large fenced backyard where dogs can play.

There are plenty of fast-food and chain restaurants at the freeway exits, but for more authentic options, head to Ontario's old downtown area. Mexican restaurants abound in Ontario. Although **Tacos Mi Ranchito** (2520 S. Oregon St., 541/889-6130, 8am-8pm, $8) is just a simple order-at-the-counter taco joint, it's a very good one. Another good Mexican restaurant is **Casa Jaramillo** (157 SE 2nd St., 541/889-9258, 11:30am-10pm Tues.-Sat., 11:30am-10pm Sun., $6-15), an Ontario tradition since 1967. The chili verde has a local reputation, and don't forget to end your meal with deep-fried ice cream, topped with dulce de leche.

Ontario's Japanese heritage is represented at **Ogawa's Wicked Sushi, Burgers, and Bowls** (375 E. Idaho Ave., 541/889-2725, http://ogawasrestaurant.com, 11am-8pm Mon.-Thurs. and Sat.,, 11am-9pm Fri., Oct.-Mar., 11am-8pm Mon., 11am-9pm Tues.-Sat. Apr.-Sept., $5-27), which is one of the few places in this part of the state where you can get good sushi, in addition to well-prepared burgers and steaks. Downtown, **Romio's** (375 S. Oregon St., 541/889-4888, 11am-2pm Mon., 11am-8pm Tues.-Wed., 11am-9pm Thurs.-Sat., noon-8pm Sun., $8-18) serves pasta, pizza, calzones, and sandwiches, including gluten-free options. Even though it's a regional chain, it's a satisfying place for Italian American standards such as eggplant parmesan or fettuccine carbonara. If you're looking for your first steakhouse experience in Oregon, head to **Mackey's Steakhouse and Pub** (111 SW 1st St., 541/889-3678, 11am-9pm, Sun.-Mon., 11am-10pm Tues.-Sat., $8-25), a lively Irish-style establishment with steaks, burgers and curious "traditional Irish fare" such as salmon Alfredo. Oh, and corned beef and cabbage too!

Another downtown enterprise worth noting is **Jolts and Juice** (298 S. Oregon St., 541/889-4166, 6am-9pm Mon.-Sat., 7am-6pm Sun., $4-12). In addition to house-roasted coffee, smoothies, fresh squeezed juice, breakfast pastries, and muffins, you'll find panini sandwiches, soups, and salads. This lively coffee shop is also the home of **Tandem Brewing Company,** and you can sample the ales or pick up a growler to go. If you're staying out at the chain hotels at I-84 exit No. 376, you'll find a convenient Jolts and Juice outlet in the Ontario Marketplace Mall (215 East Lane, 541/881-8989, 6am-9:30pm Mon.-Sat., 7am-7pm Sun.), though this location doesn't serve their excellent ales.

INFORMATION

Contact the **Malheur County Chamber of Commerce** (876 SW 4th Ave., 541/889-8012, www.ontariochamber.com) for more information on the area.

GETTING THERE

Greyhound buses pass through Ontario on twice-daily trips in each direction between Portland and Boise. The terminal is at 842 SE 1st Street (541/823-2567).

Southeastern Oregon

Southeastern Oregon is a place where travelers shed their notions of what Oregon is supposed to be like. It's largely desertlike, but has huge wetland areas. It's backcountry, but also surprisingly sophisticated. It's out in the

middle of nowhere, but it has a couple of the state's most charming hotels. And it does deliver on what many travelers seek: wildlife galore. Malheur National Wildlife Refuge is one of the Pacific Northwest's top birding areas, especially during the spring and fall migrations, when it's easy to spot well over 50 species in a day. Hart Mountain has a refuge for pronghorn antelope, which can be seen across all of southeastern Oregon, and there are even wild mustangs living on Steens Mountain.

Although it's handy to come to southeastern Oregon prepared to camp, there are enough lodgings, mostly simple, to make your trip a little less rugged.

The Christmas Valley area has some of the most intriguing geological formations in the Pacific Northwest. Evidence of the cataclysmic forces that shaped the Columbia Plateau and the Great Basin are on display in this starkly beautiful part of the state. Fissures in the ground and wave patterns left by ancient lakes on the flanks of mountains are some of the fingerprints left by the hand of nature.

The sparsely populated sagebrush, rimrock, and grassy plains around Malheur National Wildlife Refuge and Steens Mountain are home to cattle ranches, a usually dry alkaline lake bed, and some hot springs. The tiny town of Crane has one of the few public boarding schools in the United States. Students reside in dorms on campus, because most come from ranches located many miles from town.

In the very southeast corner of the state, the area carved out by the Owyhee River is wild and beautiful, with only a handful of very small settlements.

If you're looking to get away from it all, you've found your piece of Oregon.

PLANNING YOUR TIME

If you're looking to explore the open spaces and wildlife of southeastern Oregon, be prepared to take your time. Once you settle into

Previous: Wildhorse Lake; Fort Rock. **Above:** the Alvord Desert.

Look for ★ to find recommended
sights, activities, dining, and lodging.

Highlights

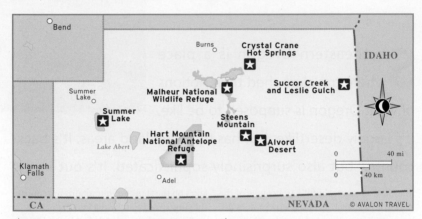

★ **Summer Lake:** Here, you're surrounded by geological curiosities such as Crack-in-the-Ground and Hole-in-the-Ground, birds, and minimally developed hot springs (page 555).

★ **Hart Mountain National Antelope Refuge:** This refuge is home to pronghorn, along with much more wildlife, rock art, and hot springs (page 561).

★ **Crystal Crane Hot Springs:** Here, you can actually swim in the big hot springs-fed pond (page 564).

★ **Malheur National Wildlife Refuge:** This wet spot in the desert supports a huge variety of bird life. Birders may get to witness the sage grouse courtship ritual (page 566).

★ **Steens Mountain:** This fault-block mountain drops straight off to the Alvord Desert. Take your time, hike the trails, and bring binoculars—you may catch a glimpse of the local wild mustangs (page 569).

★ **Alvord Desert:** It's hard to believe that this dry, blindingly white alkaline playa, or lake bed, is in the same state as the lush forests of western Oregon (page 572).

★ **Succor Creek and Leslie Gulch:** This epic geologic formation results from a tiny creek cutting a narrow chasm beneath towering spires and cliffs. It takes some planning to reach this backcountry gem, but it's worth it (page 573).

Southeastern Oregon

To Crater Lake

Sunriver

Bend

Lava River Cave

Pauina Lake

East Lake

Newberry National Volcanic Monument

97

Tule Lake

39

To Klamath Falls

140

Gerber Reservoir

Quartz Mountain

Ely

Quartz Mtn Pass 5,504ft

GEARHART MOUNTAIN WILDERNESS

Gearhart Mountain 8,634ft

Fremont

Dyeus Reservoir

Lakeview

Mountains

Fort Rock State Monument

31

Silver Lake

Summer Lake

Christmas Valley

Fort Rock

SUMMER LAKE

31

Lake Abert

Fossil Lake

Lost Forest

395

Clear Lake Reservoir

CA

Goose Lake

To Alturas

Goose Lake State Park

Adel

395

Cramp Lake

Hart Lake

Lower Campbell Lake

Flagstaff Lake

Swamp Lakes

Blue Joint Lake

HART MOUNTAIN NATIONAL ANTELOPE REFUGE

Blizzard Gap 6,131ft

Roaring Springs Ranch

Frenchglen

Jackass Mountains

205

Blitzen

Sagehen Summit 4,596ft

Silver Lake

Harney Lake

Malheur Lake

MALHEUR NATIONAL WILDLIFE REFUGE

Harney

Basin

Riley

Burns

20

Silvies River

395

Poison Creek Summit 5,340ft

Stinkingwater Pass 4,848ft

Buchanan

20

Charles Sheldon Antelope Range

Pueblo Mountains

Fields

Steens Rec Lands

Catlow Valley

Steens

Steens Mtn.

STEENS MOUNTAIN

STEENS MTN BYWAY

Mountain

Andrews

Alvord Desert

ALVORD DESERT

Alvord Lake

Mann Lake

Diamond

Baca Lake

Donner and Blitzen

New Princeton

Crane

CRYSTAL CRANE HOT SPRINGS

78

Malheur River

NEVADA

95

Blue Mtn 7,420ft

Blue Mtn Pass 5,293ft

Bowden Hills

Andrews

Burns Junction

Rome

95

Owyhee River

Antelope Reservoir

Jordan Valley

Mahogany Mtns

Lake Owyhee

Lake Owyhee State Park

Grassy Mountain

Mahogany Mtns

SUCCOR CREEK AND LESLIE GULCH

201

Vale

26

Nyssa

Ontario

84

FORT MCDERMITT INDIAN RES

© AVALON TRAVEL

ID

Snake River

0   20 km
0   20 mi

the rhythm of driving, poking around, and pausing to look at a kingfisher or some pronghorns, you may find that the rest of the world seems very far away. You'll get the most out of this tour if you combine motel or hotel lodgings with camping. Likewise, you're not going to find much fine dining out here, so bring provisions for picnicking—the landscapes and vistas make for better dining ambience than a small greasy spoon.

Distances are grand out here in Oregon's Outback, as the locals have taken to calling it, so it's a good idea to gas up frequently, especially if you're taking back roads.

This remote area of Oregon is famed for its wildlife—there are both a pronghorn and a waterfowl refuge—so be sure to bring binoculars and a wildlife guide. Southeast Oregon is also highly photogenic—landscapes are epic, geological wonders like **Fort Rock, Crack-in-the-Ground, Succor Creek,** and **Steens Mountain** are fantastic otherworldly photographic destinations, and it's worth it to plan your day to be there when the light is favorable for photography.

When you get out a map and start planning a trip across southeastern Oregon, you'll notice that there's a distinct absence of paved roads across the southern tier of the state, particularly from Plush to Frenchglen across the Hart Mountain National Antelope Refuge, just where it would be really handy to cut over to Steens Mountain. In fact, there is a gravel and hardpan dirt road through this desert landscape, and most vehicles will be able to make it across if driven slowly. If the weather is rainy or if a lot of snow has fallen, you may want to inquire locally before setting out, but the average driver in an average car has nothing to fear from this shortcut.

Note that the backcountry route linking Hwy. 95 from near Jordan Valley to Hwy 210 near Adrian, which passes through Succor Creek State Park, is shown on some maps as a paved road. It is not, however, and though average passenger vehicles can easily cross this graded dirt road in dry weather, it can be slow going.

Lake County

One of Oregon's three largest counties, Lake County is home to just 7,900 people, or about one person per square mile. This land of open spaces and geological marvels spawns a hardy breed that clings to Old West traditions. Cowboys herd cattle on horseback, itinerant prospectors dig for color in the Quartz Mountains, and farmers tend to their crops in the remote outback. The county is called the Gem of Oregon partly because the region is the best place to find Oregon's official gemstone, the sunstone or "Plush diamond," a semiprecious stone found in the area north of Plush. The nickname also pays homage to the gemlike beauty of the county's wide vistas beneath skies of pastel blue.

Visitors can climb the ancient citadel of Fort Rock, camp along a high mountain stream in Fremont National Forest, or enjoy wildlife-viewing at Hart Mountain National Antelope Refuge. Because of the varied vertical topography and wind drafts, hang gliding has drawn a fair number of visitors to the cliffs around Lakeview.

The semiarid climate here is generally cool, with 250 days of sunshine per year. Summer temperatures stay in the mid-80s; winter temperatures drop to the low 30s. Precipitation averages about 16 inches per year. At higher elevations in Lake County, there are as few as 20 frost-free days per year. This area can be a harsh land with little tolerance for the foolish, so take sensible precautions like toting extra water and gas. Despite a low density of creature comforts, you'll enjoy exploring this high desert country loaded to its sandy brim with wonders found nowhere else.

History

The history of human occupation here and in the Pacific Northwest has been authenticated to as far back as 13,200 years through carbon-dating of grass sandals found in Fort Rock Cave. Early desert dwellers who roamed the Great Basin in search of game and food witnessed the eruption of Mount Mazama 6,000-8,000 years ago. Their descendants, the Northern Paiutes, were also hunter-gatherers. This Lake County indigenous group was known as the Groundhog Eaters, and they left more petroglyphs and pictographs in Lake County than in all the rest of Oregon and Washington.

The first Europeans to venture into the area were French Canadian trappers working for the Hudson's Bay Company in the early 1800s, and they were eventually joined by U.S. mountain men. The journals kept during these expeditions noted broad valleys with grasses "belly-high to a horse." This information attracted a new cast of players: the cattle and sheep barons. The white influx resulted in frequent tensions with the original occupants, often culminating in bloodshed on both sides. After the Bannock-Paiute uprising in 1878, the local Native Americans were herded up and forced onto a reservation.

In the growth spurt that followed, the town of Lakeview was chartered in 1889; it burned to the ground in 1900 and was rebuilt with brick and corrugated-iron roofs. Other hopeful hamlets with names like Arrow, Buffalo, and Loma Vista sprang up around the county, thanks to a reactivated Federal Homestead Act in 1909 that sanctioned 320 free acres per settler. Many of these tiny burgs dried up and blew away after the 1918-1920 drought. However, larger communities like Lakeview, Paisley, and Summer Lake held on, and local farmers figured out how to irrigate and cultivate this ornery land, which is incredibly fertile if you just add water.

ALONG ROUTE 31: LA PINE TO LAKEVIEW

A vehicle with a bit of clearance is indispensable in this region if you value your oil pan (a Subaru wagon made it to all the places described, but did suffer one flat tire along the way). Stock up on provisions in Bend or La Pine.

La Pine State Park

Located in Deschutes County, this huge state park (www.oregonstateparks.org) lies just a few miles off U.S. 97. Visitors come to the 2,333-acre park to picnic, camp, mountain bike, and fish the Fall River; it is so vast that visitors rarely see one another. The 15 miles of single-track mountain biking trails are mostly flat and perfect for beginners. Bikes can be rented at Bend and Sunriver cycle shops. The park's **campground** has 137 campsites ($24) and 10 cabins ($44 rustic, $86 deluxe) that can be reserved (800/452-5687).

Hole-in-the-Ground

An interesting geological feature called Hole-in-the-Ground is found about 25 miles southeast of La Pine Junction off Route 31. Although this 300-foot-deep indentation looks like a meteor crater, scientists believe molten lava came into contact with water here, causing a massive explosion that quarried out a 7.5-mile-diameter crater, or maar. Astronauts came here in 1966 to experience the moonlike terrain.

To find this unusual and awe-inducing sight from U.S. 97, drive 22 miles southeast from La Pine Junction on Route 31; turn left at the Hole-in-the-Ground sign. Drive 3.1 miles to the next sign. Turn right and go 1.1 miles to the final sign. Turn left and go 0.2 mile to the rim of the hole. From the parking area, you can hike a moderately steep trail to the bottom of the crater.

★ Summer Lake

The region surrounding **Summer Lake** sits at the interface of desert and mixed conifer forest. Abundant wildlife, geological wonders, Native American sites, and historic structures beckon further investigation. The 20-mile-long and 10-mile-wide lake is surrounded by the mountains of the Fremont National Forest and Winter Ridge.

The tiny community of Summer Lake lies on Route 31 about halfway between La Pine and Lakeview and is a good place to stop for a night or two while you explore the area. Just north of Summer Lake on Route 31, pull into **Picture Rock Turnout.** Take the trail 80 feet to the southeast; behind the tallest rock is a pictograph. In the town of Summer Lake, the old **Harris School** is worth a photo. This classic one-room schoolhouse, complete with bell tower, is straight out of *Little House on the Prairie.*

The highway also passes through the **Summer Lake Wildlife Refuge** (541/943-3152, www.dfw.state.or.us, parking permit required), home to 170 species of migratory birds. Spring is the best time to see an amazing showing of waterfowl, including snow geese, avocets, black-necked stilts, and snowy plovers. An eight-mile wildlife-viewing trail around the lake is a recommended diversion at mile marker 70.

Anglers should head due west of Summer Lake to the **Thompson Valley Reservoir,** which has been known to yield large rainbow trout. It's most easily reached by driving south from Silver Lake on County Road 4-12.

ACCOMMODATIONS AND FOOD

Rustic and interesting is the concept here. ★ **Summer Lake Hot Springs** (41777 Hwy. 31, Paisley, 541/943-3931, www.summerlake-hotsprings.com), six miles north of Paisley on the southern tip of Summer Lake, is a private operation where you can enjoy a dip in the 30-foot-long **pool** (8am-8pm daily May-Sept, call for off season hours, $10 ages 6 and over, children under 6 free, overnight guests free), housed in a rustic shed originally built in 1927 as a bathhouse for local cowboys. This hot spring resort has campsites ($20 tents, $45 RVs) on a bluff above the lake, a couple of

small cabins ($95-110 double), and two-bedroom cottages ($145-210) for rent. This rustic resort is usually pretty laid-back, with an old-time Oregon hippie vibe; however, it's a popular stopover for people traveling to Burning Man, so during the week before Labor Day it can take on a bit of a party atmosphere.

The 1940s-era accommodations of the **Lodge at Summer Lake** (53460 Hwy. 31, 541/943-3993, www.lodgeatsummerlake.com) feature seven motel units ($66-78) and cabin and house rentals ($65-121), including one unit that can sleep up to six. There is an on-site restaurant and a private bass pond.

Wildlife Refuge Campground (53447 Hwy. 31, 541/943-3152, www.dfw.state.or.us, free) is on the Ana River just north of Summer Lake on Route 31. Bird-watchers like to camp here and walk the dikes of Summer Lake looking for waterfowl.

The one local eatery that has gained a statewide reputation is the ★ **Cowboy Dinner Tree Steakhouse** (50836 E. Bay Rd., 541/576-2426, www.cowboydinnertree.net, 4pm-8:30pm Thurs.-Sun. June-Oct. or Fri.-Sun. Nov.-May, $28 adults, $11 children 7-13, 6 and under free, cash only, reservations required), in a remote rustic shack 4.5 miles south of Silver Lake. You must specify when you make your reservations whether you'd like the nearly 30-ounce top sirloin steak or the chicken (and we do mean "the chicken"— an order is an entire chicken), and no split orders are allowed. Sides include soup, salad, fresh rolls, beans, a baked potato, dessert, and nonalcoholic beverages served in mason jars. This isn't just pretend rustic; as the sign says, "No Credit Cards—No Electricity—No Kidding." If you're too stuffed to drive after the meal, bunk down in a cabin ($124 for two people includes dinner).

Paisley

Thirty miles south of Summer Lake is the town of Paisley, with some 200 residents. The **Paisley Ranger Compound** features several structures built by the Civilian Conservation Corps during the 1930s. Check out the pine dugout canoe carved by CCC workers for Forest Service personnel. Trout fishing on the Chewaucan River west of town and deer hunting also draw visitors. Paisley is home to the **ZX Ranch,** the state's largest at over 1.3 million acres. The ranch property is 137 miles long and 64 miles wide.

Caves outside of Paisley have produced fossilized human excrement dating back about 14,400. These coprolites, as they're called, were found along with bones of horses and camels that went extinct in North America prior to 13,000 years ago.

The town's other main claim to fame is its annual **Mosquito Festival,** a fundraiser for mosquito control in this swampy neighborhood, held the last full weekend of July.

ACCOMMODATIONS AND FOOD

If you need to stay in Paisley, the **Sage Rooms** (441 Main St., 541/943-3145, $80-85) offer basic but comfortable accommodations, and a couple of restaurants, including the historic **Pioneer Saloon** (327 Main St., 541/943-3289, 11am-9pm daily, $8-15) offer a taste of the West. Campers should head west out of downtown, up the Chewaucan River; **Marster Spring** campground ($6, drinking water) is about six miles from town on Forest Road 33.

Plan ahead to rent the historic and quite scenic **Bald Butte Lookout** cabin (541/943-3114 information, 877/444-6667 reservations, www.recreation.gov, mid-June-mid-Oct., $40, no drinking water), in the Fremont National Forest near the Gearhart Mountain Wilderness.

Christmas Valley and Vicinity

Christmas Valley, considered a remote destination even in Oregon's outback, is a rather nondescript alfalfa-farming community in the midst of some spectacular geologic formations. The town got its picturesque name by accident. Southeast of here, the explorer and adventurer John C. Frémont spent Christmas at a lake during one of his mid-19th-century treks and called it Christmas Lake. A turn-of-the-20th-century mapmaker mistakenly affixed this name to a seasonal lake near the present-day town site, which also took on the cheery moniker. Although the expanse of sagebrush dotted with mobile homes is not immediately appealing (an attempt to turn the town into a retirement mecca in the 1980s largely failed), there are plenty of fascinating areas nearby.

Christmas Valley is home to the 5-megawatt Outback Solar Project, the first commercial-scale solar project in Bonneville Power Administration's territory. The 40-acre array is just east of Christmas Valley, and contains 20,000 solar modules that track the sun, tilting from east to west. At peak capacity, the array can soak up enough rays to serve 3,000 homes.

If you'd like to plunge even further into the Oregon outback, continue driving east on the Christmas Valley-Wagontire Rd. From Christmas Valley, you'll drive along a good paved road for 40 miles through scrub desert to Hwy. 395, with scarcely a sign of human habitation in sight. Once you get to the junction, you're still scores of miles from the nearest gas station, so if you decide to make this trek, be sure to refuel before leaving Christmas Valley.

ACCOMMODATIONS AND FOOD

Although accommodations are generally more appealing at Summer Lake, Christmas Valley is not without lodging options. The **Lakeside Terrace Motel** (1 Spruce Ln., 541/576-2309, www.lakesideterracecv.com, $50-65) offers basic motel rooms and rents full houses to larger groups; RV spaces are also available. The Lakeside Terrace is also the main place to eat in Christmas Valley (6am-2pm and 4:30pm-8pm Mon.-Sat., $8-15).

Fort Rock State Park

Rising like an enormous and eerie stone castle from the desert floor, Fort Rock towers 400 feet above the surrounding sagebrush. A series of underwater volcanic blasts created this very unusual formation when the entire area was a huge ice age lake stretching for hundreds of miles across central Oregon. Rising molten rock came into contact with mud and lake water, creating a series of massive explosions. As the ash and rock were thrown into the air, they came to rest in a perfect ring whose walls eventually reached hundreds of feet high. Fall and winter here offer wildlife-viewing par excellence; large herds of mule deer can be seen mid-November-mid-April, and pronghorn range over the alfalfa fields year-round. Many birds nest in the rocks, and golden eagles, hawks, kestrels, and peregrine falcons soar overhead.

The state park (800/551-6949, www.oregonstateparks.org, toilets and picnic facilities only, free), offers trails and amenities for rock climbers and sightseers. An easy trail rings the inside base of the crater walls, and the intrepid can follow more adventurous trails that explore the rims (some bouldering required). This is a great family destination: It's hard not to imagine this as the remains of a mythic fortress, and kids of all ages will love clambering up the rock walls exploring the trails. Fort Rock State Park is seven miles east of Route 31, or 30 miles northwest of Christmas Valley.

As the ice-age lake waters receded, ancient Native Americans also made their homes in caves and shelters in and around Fort Rock.

At **Fort Rock Cave** (a.k.a. Sandal Cave) in a nearby but separate formation, waves carved a 50-foot-deep cave in what was once a basalt island. In 1938, anthropologist Luther Cressman discovered over 70 ancient sandals woven from sagebrush in the cave. Dated at almost 10,000 years old, the sandals are some of the oldest human artifacts found in the Pacific Northwest; they're now on display at the University of Oregon Natural History Museum in Eugene.

Fort Rock Cave is a National Heritage site and is now open to a limited number of tours operated by Oregon State Parks. The tours are offered three days only during each June, July, and August; see the Fort Rock Cave page at www.oregonstateparks.org for exact dates, which change yearly. Tours are limited to 10 people only, and reservations (call 800/452-5687, $8) are required. Directions to the cave are given when you make your reservation.

The nearby town of Fort Rock has an old-time flavor that has been accentuated by the recent restoration of homestead cabins in a pioneer village at the **Fort Rock Valley Historical Homestead Museum** (541/576-2251, www.fortrockoregon.com, 10am-4pm Fri.-Sun. May-mid-Oct., $4 adult, $2 children 6-17).

Fort Rock is an enormous splatter cone.

Crack-in-the-Ground is exactly what you would expect.

precaution. The lower section of the cave does not have natural skylights and requires artificial lights or lamps.

Derrick Cave is part of a larger set of volcanic features called the Devils Garden, a 45-square-mile series of lava flows that include a set of splatter cones called The Blowouts and other volcanic oddities. These lava flows are likely between 50,000 to 10,000 years old.

To reach Derrick Cave, drive east from Fort Rock village on route 5-10 and follow signs north on Route 5-12. The final six miles are unpaved and quite bumpy.

Crack-in-the-Ground

Another really magical geologic feature in the Christmas Valley area, Crack-in-the-Ground is weirdly compelling and worth the journey to anyone with an interest in natural history. Crack-in-the-Ground is a volcanic fissure about two miles long, 10-15 feet wide, and up to 70 feet deep. On hot days, it's nice and cool within this chasm. In fact, the crack is so deep that cold winter air sometimes gets trapped within, preserving ice into summer. According to geologists, this dramatic fissure has been open for at least 1,000 years; the opening was once larger, but lava from nearby volcanoes filled it in to its present dimensions.

There are numerous sections to Crack-in-the-Ground. The first one you come to when walking in from the parking area (one-quarter mile) is also the easiest to explore. Go ahead and walk down into the crack: With a bit of rock clambering, you'll be able to negotiate the entire length of this section. Another couple fissure sections follow, but these don't have smooth floor passages and require some rock climbing skills to explore. However, the less intrepid can follow trails along the edge of these chasms, and if you have no vertigo, you can peer down into the rocky void and marvel.

To reach Crack-in-the-Ground, drive one mile east from Christmas Valley's main intersection (with the gas station) and turn north on Route 6109-D (watch for the BLM signs on the south side of the road).

There's not much to the town of Fort Rock, but there is the **Fort Rock Pub and Restaurant** (64591 Fort Rock Rd., 541/576-3988, 11am-8pm daily, $7-18), with burgers, sandwiches, and a friendly welcome.

Derrick Cave

Discover an exciting journey down into the bowels of the earth at Derrick Cave, 22 bumpy miles northeast of Fort Rock. This large lava tube is 1,200 feet long with rooms up to 80 feet wide and 46 feet high. During the Cuban missile crisis of 1962, the cave was turned into a fallout shelter. Metal doors were installed and provisions for 1,000 people were stockpiled. The supplies were later plundered by vandals, and the cave's civil defense status was eventually dropped.

Today, Derrick Cave is open to visitors year-round. Because the ceiling of the cave has collapsed in a number of places, these natural skylights allow visitors to explore the first section of the cave without flashlights, though a good strong flashlight is an excellent

Crack-in-the-Ground is seven miles north along a fairly bumpy dirt road.

Five miles northwest of Crack-in-the-Ground (along the same rough BLM road) is **Green Mountain Campground** and fire lookout, which sits high above the Devils Garden site. This primitive campground (large enough for three cars, but without water or toilets) sits atop a small cinder cone overlooking hundreds of square miles of high desert, lava beds, and forest from 5,190 feet above sea level.

Fossil Lake

During wetter times thousands of years ago, Fossil Lake was a watering hole for ancient camels, enormous beavers, flamingos, mammoths, and miniature horses. It was once part of a much larger body of water in the Fort Rock basin that was perhaps 40 miles wide and 200 feet deep. The water and animals disappeared when the climate changed, but their fossilized remains are still unearthed by paleontologists on sanctioned digs. Be aware that it is illegal to remove *any* fossils from the beds without proper authorization.

To reach Fossil Lake, drive two miles east from Christmas Valley and turn north on Route 5-14C (a.k.a. Fossil Lake Road). Follow signs toward Lost Forest and/or Sand Dunes, and in 16 miles, you'll pass beneath a high-tension powerline. Turn south on a dirt road and drive an additional 1.5 miles. You'll see an interpretive sign for Fossil Lake at a parking area. You'll need to hike in half a mile to reach the lake bed itself.

Lost Forest

Amid hundreds of miles of scrub desert and sand dunes, Lost Forest is a 9,000-acre stand of ancient ponderosa pines intermixed with the largest juniper trees in Oregon—all that's left of a grove that dates back thousands of years. Surprisingly, studies of tree rings show this area has received on average only nine inches of rain per year for the last 600 years, half the amount normally needed to sustain the growth of ponderosa pines. A layer of pumice-like soil beneath the surface traps and retains enough moisture to allow the trees to draw water up through shorter-than-usual root systems.

This island of green is 40 miles from the nearest forest, accentuating the isolation and solitude of these stately sentinels. Many of the junipers here are over 1,000 years old. On hot summer days this place is a welcome source of shade. The forest borders the largest inland sand dunes in the state.

To reach the Lost Forest, follow directions for Fossil Lake, but continue an additional eight miles east along Lost Forest Rd.

LAKEVIEW AND VICINITY

The "big city" in this part of the world is Lakeview (pop. 2,260), 142 miles south of La Pine on Route 31, east of Klamath Falls 96 miles on Route 140, and 139 miles from Burns on Route 395. Lakeview, the county hub, bills itself as the highest town in Oregon, at 4,800 feet in elevation.

Most of what's appealing about Lakeview lies outside the main downtown area. But if you're spending time in town, the **Schminck Memorial Museum** (128 S. E St., 541/947-3134, 11am-4pm Tues.-Sat., $3 adults, $2 seniors, children ages 12 and under free) has antiques and Native American artifacts assembled by the Oregon chapter of the Daughters of the American Revolution.

This town's fault blocks and winds have made Lakeview a center for hang gliding enthusiasts—look for hang gliders coming off 2,000-foot Black Cap Hill above the east side of Lakeview May-October.

You may hear stories about the local geyser, Old Perpetual, which used to erupt quite reliably in the front yard of **Hunter's Hot Springs Resort** (18088 Hwy. 395), on U.S. 395 north of town. In recent years, the geyser's been finicky, but it's worth checking to see if it's spouting.

Abert Rim

Fifteen miles north of Lakeview on U.S. 395 is

the **Abert Rim,** the highest fault escarpment in the United States. The rim rises 2,000 feet above Lake Abert. This unusual body of water has no outlet and is rich in brine shrimp, which attract countless waterfowl and shorebirds. As at Summer Lake, fall is prime birdwatching season; expect thousands of plovers and other shorebirds. Due to its high alkalinity, it is hazardous to swim in the lake.

Below Abert Rim along the east shore of Lake Abert, the slope is covered with boulders, some of which sport petroglyphs. Several are located right off the highway near the Abert Rim geological marker. Forest Service roads lead through the North Warner Mountains to Bureau of Land Management trails up the back side of Abert Rim; obtain routing information on these obscure byways from the **Lakeview Ranger Station** (18049 Hwy. 395 N., 541/947-6300). Although reaching the rim requires an arduous journey down bumpy back roads and a steep hike up the mountain, the view from the top is spectacular. Watch for rattlesnakes in the rocks.

★ Hart Mountain National Antelope Refuge

North and east of Lakeview, **Hart Mountain National Antelope Refuge** stretches across a high plateau rising above Warner Lakes. From U.S. 395 just north of Lakeview, head east on Route 140 for 15 miles to the Plush Cutoff Road, go northeast 19 miles to Plush, and take the road up the steep west face of Hart Mountain to the refuge headquarters. The **U.S. Fish and Wildlife Service office** (18 S. G St., 541/947-3315) in Lakeview has information on the refuge. There's also information and a small visitor center at refuge headquarters (541/947-2731, 9am-5pm Mon.-Fri.), about 10 miles east of the refuge's western entrance, along with rest rooms. Rangers are usually available, though don't be surprised if they are out on duty.

In summer, hundreds of the agile tan-and-white pronghorn gather at sunset along the dirt road south of the refuge. The refuge is also home to bighorn sheep, mule deer, 213 species of birds, and many small mammals.

The **campground** (free, no water), a few miles south of the refuge headquarters, features a hot spring surrounded by a cinder-block privacy wall; a dunk in the spring is highly recommended to loosen the stiffness from bouncing down the dirt roads to get here. Fill your water containers at the refuge headquarters.

The refuge is also a popular place for rock

pronghorn at Hart Mountain National Antelope Refuge

hounds searching for agates, fire opals, crystals, and sunstones. Check with the **chamber of commerce** (126 N. E St., Lakeview, 541/947-6040, www.lakecountychamber. org) or the ranger at Hart Mountain for more information.

Despite the name of the preserve, you won't find any antelope here; in fact, there are no wild antelope in North America, only pronghorn. Because these animals shed the outer sheaths of their horns each year, they differ from their Asian and African counterparts—true antelope—which have permanent horns. Male pronghorn have prongs, protrusions extending from their sheaths, to further distinguish them from antelope. The lingering misnomer was bestowed on these Oregon animals by Lewis and Clark. At any rate, many scientists believe that pronghorn could be the world's fastest land mammals over a long distance, barely edging out the cheetah on distances exceeding 1,000 yards. It's said they can cruise at more than 35 mph, maintain 60 mph for half a mile, and reach 70 mph in short bursts.

Besides pronghorn, the refuge also protects a number of areas rich in prehistoric rock art. The easiest to visit is **Petroglyph Lake** (follow signs from the refuge road), where early Native Americans etched symbols and animal likenesses on a rocky cliff above a small water hole. Follow the path to the cliff's end for the best display.

Most state maps show an unpaved road between Plush and Route 205 near Frenchglen, designated a Bureau of Land Management Scenic Byway. It's about 50 miles across a frequently rough and dusty road that's equal parts gravel and hardpan, but most vehicles will make it across without problems as long as you drive slowly and carefully. Inquire locally if there has been a lot of snow or rain, as the road is not regularly maintained.

Rockhounding

Rockhounding is a popular hobby in Lake County. Best known for its abundance of sunstones (also known as aventurine or Plush diamonds), the area has jasper, agates, petrified wood, fire opals, wonder stones, thunder eggs, and obsidian as well. To get to the sunstone-hunting grounds, go east on Route 140 to the Plush junction and turn north. Another spot for rockhounding can be reached by taking Hogback Road just north of the upper section of the Abert Rim; the Hogback junction is about 50 miles north of Lakeview on U.S. 395. For more information, visit the **Hi Desert**

Petroglyph Lake is ringed with rock art.

Craft Rock Shop (244 N. M St., 541/947-3237, 9:30am-5pm Mon.-Sat.).

Skiing
Warner Canyon Ski Area (541/947-5001, warnercanyon.org, $32), seven miles east of Lakeview on Route 140, is a small ski area with 23 runs, one chairlift (but no lines), and over 25 miles of marked but ungroomed cross-country trails. Thanks to a mile-high base elevation and the dry southeastern Oregon climate, excellent dry powder conditions are common. The area has a day lodge near the base of the hill with a snack bar that serves breakfast and lunch. The season may start as early as mid-December and run through the end of March.

Accommodations and Food
In Lakeview, the **Fremont Inn** (524 N. G St., 541/947-2060, www.fremontinnlakecounty. com, $99-149) is a converted old folks' home with spacious, comfortable rooms. The **Best Western Skyline Motor Lodge** (414 N. G St., 541/947-2194, $101-126) has a pool and a hot tub as well as large guest rooms. Just north of Lakeview, **Hunter's Hot Springs Resort** (18088 Hwy. 395, 541/947-4242 or 800/858-8266, www.huntersresort.com) has basic motel rooms ($69-74) as well as an RV park and restaurant. The rooms aren't exactly luxurious, and the hot springs pool has seen better days, but it's a place to really soak in the local atmosphere.

Lakeview isn't known for its cuisine. However, **Mario's Dinner House** (9 N. F St., 541/947-3102, 5pm-9pm Tues.-Sat., $11-26) serves good steaks, salmon, prime rib, home-made breads, and other standards in a historic downtown building. It's a really popular place on the weekends, when folks drive in from surrounding areas.

Camping
Goose Lake State Park (541/947-3111 or 800/551-6949, www.oregonstateparks.org, mid-Apr.-early Oct., $22 campsite) is a big spread 15 miles south of Lakeview on U.S. 395. The campground has tent sites, electrical hookups, and a boat launch on the shore of the huge lake. **Corral Creek Campground** (no water, free) is a good headquarters for an exploration of the Gearhart Mountain Wilderness, an area of high meadows, cliffs, and worn-down volcanoes. To get to the campsite, turn off Route 140 at Quartz Mountain, 24 miles west of Lakeview, and drive north on Forest Service Road 3600.

Junipers Reservoir RV Resort (541/947-2050, www.junipersrv.com, May 1-Oct. 15 depending on weather, $32-39) is 10 miles west of Lakeview on Route 140. This private reservoir with campgrounds (including some tent sites, $20) is situated on a working cattle ranch. Designated as one of six private wildlife-viewing areas in the state, this spread offers an excellent chance to view longhorn cattle, deer, eagles, ospreys, and coyotes.

Information
Stop by the **Lakeview Welcome Center** (126 N. E St., 541/947-6040) at the Lake County Chamber of Commerce for maps and brochures.

Steens Mountain Country

If you judge this part of southeastern Oregon by a drive-through on U.S. 20, you probably won't find it too memorable. But off the main thoroughfares are recreational retreats worthy of closer investigation. The Malheur National Wildlife Refuge is nationally recognized as one of the best bird-watching sites in the country, and Steens Mountain is famous for its stunning scenery.

BURNS

The town of Burns, named after the Scottish poet Robert Burns, was founded in 1884. By 1889 it had a population of 250, which has since grown about tenfold. A significant boost to the town's economy came in 1924 when a rail line reached Burns. Its sister city, **Hines,** was incorporated in 1930. Named after Chicago lumberman Edward Hines, this town of 1,400 residents is primarily a bedroom community for Burns.

Sagehen Hill Nature Trail

The **Sagehen Hill Nature Trail** is 16 miles west of Burns at the Sagehen rest stop on U.S. 20. This 0.5-mile nature trail has 11 stations on a route that takes you around Sagehen Hill through sagebrush, bitterbrush, and western juniper. Other plants found along the way include lupine, larkspur, owl clover, and yellowbell. The lucky early morning visitor in March and April might also catch the sage grouse courtship ritual. The male will display his plumage and make clucking noises to attract the attention of the females. The puffed-up necks and bobbing heads of these feathered philanderers are something to see. If these creatures are not visible, the views of Steens Mountain (elevation 9,733 feet) to the southeast will make the hike worthwhile.

Harney County Historical Museum

The **Harney County Historical Museum** (18 W. D St., 541/573-5618, 10am-4pm Tues.-Sat. Apr.-Sept., $5 adult, $8 couple, $3 seniors or children) started out as a brewery and then became a laundry and a wrecking yard. Descendants of local pioneer families have donated quilts, furniture, a complete kitchen, a wagon shed, and machinery to the museum. Of special interest are artifacts from pioneer Pete French's ranch.

★ Crystal Crane Hot Springs

Spend an idyllic couple of hours at **Crystal Crane Hot Springs** (59315 Hwy. 78, 541/493-2312, www.cranehotsprings.com, 9am-9pm daily, $4.25 pp day use), 25 miles southeast of Burns just west of the town of Crane. The local hot springs feed a large pond that's big enough to swim in if you have the energy. It's more likely that you'll lounge at the pond's edge and watch the coots and shoveler ducks paddling around in the adjacent cool pond. For visitors who prefer private soaking tubs ($7.50 pp per hour), several bathhouses have cattle troughs filled with hot spring water. A range of cabins ($45-69, shared bathhouse a bit of a walk away), two three-bedroom houses, and a camping area ($20 tents, $23-25 hookups) make it possible to spend the night and greet the morning with a dip in the pond.

Rockhounding

Southeastern Oregon is rockhounding country. Each year, thousands of enthusiasts flock to this far-flung corner of the state to collect fossils, agates, jasper, obsidian, and thunder eggs. The **Stinking Water Mountains,** 30 miles east of Burns, are a good source of gemstones and petrified wood.

Warm Springs Reservoir, just east of the Stinking Water Mountains, is popular with agate hunters. **Charlie Creek** and **Radar,** west and north of Burns, respectively, produce black, banded, and brown obsidians. Be sure to collect only your limit—be a rock hound, not a rock hog. Also keep in mind that it is illegal to take arrowheads and other artifacts from public lands.

Entertainment and Events

Held in Burns in early April, the **John Scharff Migratory Waterfowl Conference** (541/573-2636, www.migratorybirdfestival.com) celebrates the spring return of waterbirds to the region with lectures, movies, slides, a high-quality art show, and guided bird-watching tours, including early morning visits to the sage grouse leks, or strutting grounds. This is an excellent opportunity to learn more about birds, and it attracts some really knowledgeable and interesting people.

Accommodations

The pet-friendly **Silver Spur Motel** (789 N. Broadway, 541/573-2077 or 800/400-2077, www.silverspurmotel.net, $49-57) is a well-maintained family-owned motel on the north edge of downtown, with refrigerators and microwaves in the guest rooms.

The **Best Western Rory and Ryan Inn** (534 N. Hwy. 20, Hines, 541/573-5050 or 800/780-7234, $119-127) is newer and very comfortable, with an indoor pool, hot tub, hot breakfast, and all the extras you would expect with a hotel of this caliber.

By far the most distinctive place to stay in Burns is the ★ **Sage Country Inn** (351½ W. Monroe St., 541/573-7243, www.sagecountryinn.com, $105-115). This lovely, spacious house is set back just far enough from the main drag to make it quiet, but it's still easy to walk to restaurants in the downtown area. If frilly B&Bs turn you off, book a night in the Cattle Baron's room.

Camping

A couple of campgrounds to the north of Burns up in the Malheur National Forest are **Idlewild** and **Yellowjacket** (541/573-4300, www.fs.usda.gov, $10). Idlewild is right off U.S. 395 about 17 miles north of Burns in a pretty setting. The more remote Yellowjacket is on the shore of Yellowjacket Lake, 37 miles northwest of Burns on Forest Service Road 3745. From Burns, take County Road 127 out of town, then take Forest Road 47 to Road 37 and follow signs to the campground. Be sure to keep your food under wraps, especially meat, if you want to avoid being visited by the namesake hosts of the lake. Yellowjacket Lake is stocked with trout.

steam rising from the lake at Crystal Crane Hot Springs

Food

Although Burns isn't known as a culinary mecca, there are a few decent places to eat in town, especially if you're hankering for a steak dinner. The **Pine Room Restaurant and Lounge** (543 W. Monroe St., 541/573-2673, 5pm-9pm Tues.-Sat., $12-32) is a steakhouse with multicourse meals, including bread, shrimp cocktail starter, salad, soup, and main course. The barbecued pork ribs are especially good. Also, this is one of the few places to find beers from local Steens Mountain Brewing, the state's smallest craft brewery.

If the timing is right, treat yourself dinner at ★ **Rhojo's** (83 W. Washington St., 541/5737656, 11am-2pm Mon.-Fri., 11:30am-2pm Sun. and 6pm-9pm Fri.-Sat., $20-25). Lunchtime sandwiches and salads are good, but the weekend nights offering two entrees (changing weekly) such as seared halibut or marinated rib eye steak, plus full fixings, including delicious vegetables, are special events in downtown Burns.

Information

For general information on the region, stop by the **Harney County Chamber of Commerce** (484 N. Broadway, 541/573-2636, www.harneycounty.com, 10am-4pm Tues.-Sat.). For information on recreation, contact the **Bureau of Land Management** office (12533 U.S. 20 W., Hines, OR 97738, 541/573-5241, 9am-5pm Mon.-Fri.). The **Emigrant Creek Ranger District** (265 U.S. 20, Hines, OR 97738, 541/573-4300, 9am-5pm Mon.-Fri.) is also nearby.

★ MALHEUR NATIONAL WILDLIFE REFUGE

Malheur and Harney Lakes, fed by the mountain snow runoff filling the Blitzen and Silvies Rivers, have been major avian nesting and migration stopovers since prehistoric times. The contrast between the stark dry basin land, with its red sandstone monoliths and mesas, and the lush green marshes is startling. These vast marshes (the longest freshwater marsh in the western United States), meadows, and riparian areas surrounded by the eastern Oregon desert attract thousands of birds and hundreds of bird-watchers. The **Malheur National Wildlife Refuge** (36391 Sodhouse Ln., Princeton, 541/493-2612, www.fws.gov/refuge/malheur) is dominated by three fluctuating lakes—Malheur, Mud, and Harney. These are nourished by a scant eight inches of rain per year.

At this refuge, one of the West's most renowned birding areas, a total of 312 different species have been sighted over the last century. Prime bird-watching times are spring and fall, when migratory flocks pass through. Late spring is an especially good time to visit, before summer's scorching heat. In March, the first Malheur arrivals include Canada and snow geese, and in the vast Malheur Marsh, swans, mallards, and other ducks. Also look for sandhill cranes in the wet meadows. Great horned owls and golden eagles are two other early arrivals. Shorebirds are followed by warblers, sparrows, and other songbirds in spring. Red-tailed hawks can be seen swooping over the sage-covered prairies throughout spring, summer, and fall. In the late spring, ponds and canals at Malheur occasionally host the trumpeter swan, a majestic bird with a seven-foot wingspan. This is one of the few places where you can observe this endangered species nesting. Flocks of pelicans are a summertime spectacle worth catching. See them before they head south to Mexico in the fall.

August-October is another prime time when birders might see 100 species, and lucky visitors might see the magnificent snow goose. Another fall arrival is the wood thrush, graced with one of the most beautiful songs in the bird kingdom. A September-October highlight is the concentration of greater sandhill cranes, Canada geese, and mallard ducks foraging on Blitzen Valley grain fields. The first two weeks of September are particularly nice because hunting season has yet to begin and the aspens have turned golden.

Be sure to visit the refuge headquarters in a grove of cottonwoods looking out over the huge expanse of Malheur Lake. Here you can pick up maps for the self-guided auto tour of the refuge. A short distance downhill is a small museum where more than 250 bird specimens are beautifully arrayed. Also of interest is the charming park on the edge of the lake.

While the absolute numbers of birds at Malheur are not as great as they are at the Klamath Lakes or along the Oregon coast, the variety here is unsurpassed anywhere in the area. Among birders, however, it is the "accidental list" of 55 infrequently sighted species that makes this preserve special. Many of these "exotics" are sighted nowhere else in the region.

In the late 1800s, settlers enjoyed unrestricted hunting, and at the turn of the 20th century, hunters killed thousands of swans, egrets, herons, and grebes for feathers for the millinery trade. In 1908, President Theodore Roosevelt put a stop to the slaughter by protecting the area as a bird sanctuary. The Blitzen Valley and P Ranch were added to the refuge in 1935. Today, 185,000 acres are protected.

Not everybody comes to Malheur just to watch birds—some folks come to fish. Krumbo Reservoir is a good bet for trout or largemouth bass.

To get to the refuge, drive 25 miles south from Burns on Route 205 and then nine miles east on the county road toward Princeton. The Buena Vista Ponds are an excellent place to stop along the way.

Accommodations

A convenient though bare-bones place to stay on the refuge is the **Malheur Field Station** (34848 Sodhouse Ln., 541/493-2629, www.malheurfieldstation.org, $55-150), where you can bunk in dorm rooms (groups only, $22-30 pp), trailers, or a three-bedroom house. RV sites are also available ($19). Guests should bring bedding and towels; dorm dwellers should be prepared to share a restroom. Although most accommodations have kitchen facilities, during the peak season meals are available. Note that the trailers are the most coveted accommodations here; they're often full during spring and fall birding seasons. Reserve a room in advance to avoid driving 35 miles to Burns for bed and board.

FRENCHGLEN

Named for famous rancher Pete French and his wealthy father-in-law Dr. Hugh Glenn, the town of Frenchglen was originally known as P Station and was part of the nearby P Ranch.

The Frenchglen Hotel is over 100 years old and still welcomes guests.

Today, this historic community with its hotel, store, corral, and post office remains essentially the same as it was 70 years ago. The town is about 60 miles south of Burns on Route 205.

In Frenchglen, the ★ **Frenchglen Hotel** (60 miles south of Burns on Rte. 205, 541/493-2825, www.oregonstateparks.org, mid-Mar.-Oct., $75-135) is an excellent place to stay while visiting Steens Mountain or Malheur National Wildlife Refuge. Built in 1914 as a stage stopover, the main hotel has eight smallish rooms with a shared bath down the hall. Just behind the hotel building are several modern rooms with private baths in the Drover's Inn, a separate unit. Ranch cooks prepare delicious family-style dinners ($23-26, reservations required) served at 6:30pm sharp; breakfast and lunch are also available. Watching thunderstorms sweep across Steens Mountain from the hotel's screened-in porch while you chat with birders from all over the West can provide after-dinner entertainment.

DIAMOND AND VICINITY
Diamond Craters

Diamond Craters have been described by scientists as the most diverse basaltic volcanic features in the United States. To tour these unique formations, drive 55 miles south of Burns on Route 205 until you reach the Diamond junction. Turn left and begin a 40-mile route ending at New Princeton on Route 78. On the way you'll see why this area is called "Oregon's Geologic Gem." There are craters, domes, lava flows, and pits that give an outstanding visual lesson on volcanism. To aid your self-guided tour, pick up the "Diamond Craters" brochure at the **Bureau of Land Management office** (12533 U.S. 20 W., Hines, 541/573-5241) in Hines.

Round Barn

While in the Diamond Craters area, stop at the Round Barn, a historic structure built in the 1870s or 1880s by rancher Peter French as a place to spend the winter breaking his saddle horses. Located 20 miles north of Diamond, the barn is 100 feet in diameter, with a 60-foot circular lava rock corral inside. Twelve tall juniper poles support a roof covered with 50,000 shingles. Hundreds of cowpokes have carved their initials in the posts of this famous corral.

Just up the road from the barn, the privately owned **Round Barn Visitors Center** (541/493-2070, www.roundbarn.net, 9am-5pm daily, free), a combination gift shop, cold drink vendor, and historical museum, is worth a stop. Its architecture mirrors that of

Nineteenth-century rancher Peter French built Round Barn to break saddle horses.

the historic barn, and the genial proprietor, a third-generation Diamond Valley rancher, leads daylong tours of the area with stops in some rather remote areas, focusing on the area's colorful history.

Accommodations and Food

Tall Lombardy poplars mark the tiny hamlet of Diamond, which is a cluster of buildings tucked in at the bottom of a hill. The focal point of the town is the ★ **Hotel Diamond** (541/493-1898, www.central-oregon.com/hoteldiamond, Apr.-Oct., $74-97), a wonderfully and unpretentiously restored hotel dating from the late 1800s. Don't worry about where to eat when you book a stay: breakfast, lunch, and family-style dinners (about $20) at the hotel are quite good. Reserve a seat at the table at least a day in advance so there will be plenty of food to go around.

★ STEENS MOUNTAIN

Steens Mountain—named after Major Enoch Steen, a U.S. Army officer assigned the task of building a military road through Harney County—is one of the great scenic wonders of Oregon. A 30-mile fault block, the eastern flank of the mountain rises straight up from the Alvord Desert to a row of glacial peaks. On the western side, huge gorges carved out by glaciers one million years ago descend to a gentle slope drained by the Donner and Blitzen River, which flows into Malheur Lake.

Steens Mountain has five vegetation zones, ranging from tall sage to alpine tundra. The best way to see the transition is to drive the **Steens Mountain Byway** out of Frenchglen to the top of Steens Mountain. This is the highest road in Oregon, rising to 9,000 feet in elevation. The first 15 miles of the road are gravel, and the last nine miles are dirt. The latter section is not recommended for low-slung passenger cars. Expect to spend the entire day traveling this 59-mile byway.

Starting and ending at Frenchglen, the route up Steens Mountain, sans significant tree cover save for some beautiful aspens, evokes Alaskan alpine tundra. Multicolored low-to-the-ground wildflowers and a vast spaciousness give the feeling of being on top of the world. This impression is accentuated by standing in snow while you look 5,000 feet straight down into the sun-scorched Alvord Desert, which records just seven inches of rain annually.

The first four miles of the trek lead across the Malheur National Wildlife Refuge and

Steens Mountain drops 5,000 feet to a desert playa.

up to the foothills of Steens Mountain. **Page Springs,** the first campground on the route, is a popular spot offering campsites along the bank of the Donner and Blitzen River. Approximately 13 miles beyond Page Springs is **Lily Lake,** a good place for a picnic. This shallow lake has an abundance of water lilies, frogs, songbirds, and waterfowl.

After Lily Lake, you really start to climb up the mountain to **Fish Lake, Jackman Park** (both with campsites), and viewpoints of Kiger Gorge and the East Rim. **Kiger Gorge** is a spectacular example of a wide U-shaped path left by a glacier. Blanketed in meadow grasses, quaking aspen, cottonwood, and mountain mahogany at lower elevations, tiny tundra-like flowers proliferate on the 8,000-foot viewpoint.

The **East Rim** is a dramatic example of earth-shifting in prehistoric epochs. The lava layers that cap the mountain are thousands of feet thick and formed 15 million years ago when lava erupted from cracks in the ground. Several million years later, the Steens Mountain fault block began to lift along a fault below the East Rim. The fault block tilted to the west, forming the gentler slope that stretches to the Malheur Lake Basin. At the summit (9,670 feet) on a clear day, you can see the corners of four states—California, Nevada, Oregon, and Idaho.

From the summit, it's about one mile and 1,300 vertical feet down the slopes of Wildhorse Canyon to **Wildhorse Lake.** Expect the hike back up to the parking area to be tough—after all, you're climbing to 9,670 feet!

A good time to visit is August through mid-September—Indian summer. Nights are cold, but daytime temperatures are more pleasant than those of summertime scorchers. Later in the fall, red bushes and yellow aspens attract photographers. Some of the aspens are located at Whorehouse Meadow and are indirectly responsible for its name. Lonely shepherds would scratch love notes and erotica in the tree bark, pining for a visit from the horse-drawn bordellos that serviced these parts. Wildlife-viewing highlights include bighorn sheep, seen around the East Rim viewpoint in summer; hummingbirds, often observed at high elevations; and hawks, which can be spotted anywhere and anytime, especially from the ridge above Fish Lake.

The area has off-highway vehicle restrictions to protect the environment. Five gates controlling access to the Steens Mountain area are located at various elevations and are opened as road and weather conditions permit. Normally, the Steens Byway is not open until early July and is closed by snow in October or November. Gas is available only in Burns, Frenchglen, and Fields. Take reasonable precautions when driving the loop: sudden storms, lightning, flash floods, and extreme road conditions can be hazardous to travelers. The loop returns to Route 205 about 10 miles south of Frenchglen.

Visit Steens Mountain the first Saturday of August for the **Chris Miller Memorial Steens Mountain Rim Run** (541/573-2636, www.steensrimrun.com), a 10K run or walk along the East Rim of Steens Mountain that starts at an elevation of 7,835 feet and finishes at above 9,700 feet.

Blitzen

Four miles south of the southern terminus of the Steens Mountain Loop Road, turn west off Route 205 to take a side trip to the ghost town of Blitzen. This eight-mile jaunt will take you to the ruins of the little town of a half-dozen dilapidated buildings, founded in the late 1800s. Blitzen was named after the Donner and Blitzen River, which flows nearby. *Donner und Blitzen* is German for "thunder and lightning," the label given this stream by Captain George Curry, who tried to cross it during a fierce thunderstorm.

Camping

As for summertime Steens weather, the

100°F temperatures in the high desert give way to 50-80°F daytime temperatures atop the mountain. Nonetheless, be aware that the summit can see severe thunderstorms and lightning, and at night the mercury can drop below freezing, even on days with high noontime temperatures.

There are three high-elevation campgrounds along the Steens Mountain Loop Road. No reservations are accepted, and sites are $8 per vehicle per night. For more info, contact the **Bureau of Land Management** (541/573-4400). **Page Springs** (year-round) is four miles southeast of Frenchglen. Close to the Malheur National Wildlife Refuge, the campground is a good headquarters for bird-watching, fishing, hiking, and sightseeing. **Fish Lake** (July 1-Nov. 15) is 17 miles east of Frenchglen. The namesake lake is stocked with eastern brook, cutthroat, and rainbow trout. Aspens surround the campsites, which have toilets, well water, and fire pits; firewood is included in the campsite fee. Climb up on the ridge above the campground to watch hawks. **Jackman Park,** three miles east of Fish Lake, is particularly popular with backpackers, who use it as a

takeoff point. It has six sites with toilets and potable water.

Another alternative is the **Steens Mountain Resort** (N. Loop Rd., Frenchglen, 541/493-2415 or 800/542-3765, www.steens-mountainresort.com, $65-90 cabins and trailers, $15 tents, $30 RVs, reservations recommended), just before you get to the Page Springs campground. Views of the surrounding gorges are spectacular, and there are more amenities than at the Bureau of Land Management facilities, including showers, a small store, laundry, dumping facilities, and a public phone. Some of the cabins and trailers (all heated and air-conditioned) require guests to bring towels and bed linens.

ALVORD DESERT AND VICINITY
Fields

Fields, the largest community on the east side of Steens Mountain (pop. 120) and perhaps the friendliest place in the state, was established as a supply station in 1881, and a supply station it still is. Fields now has a gas station, a store, a café (open 9am-4:30 Mon.-Sat.), and a motel. All are part of the same business,

Fields Station is the only business in minute Fields.

Fields Station (541/495-2275 8am-6pm Mon.-Sat., 9am-5pm Sun.). The accommodations, though very simple, are perfectly sufficient and very reasonably priced; there are a couple of one-bedroom units and an old hotel that'll sleep up to 10 people ($65-90).

★ Alvord Desert

About 20 miles north of Fields, the vast hardpan playa of the **Alvord Desert** comes into view. This usually dry and stark white alkali lake bed, or "playa," gets about six inches of rain per year, which quickly evaporates. It's possible to drive down to, and even on, the playa (unless it's wet, in which case it's quite slick). But rather than driving, get out of the car and walk. One popular activity here is land-sailing, which is done in a "boat" that's sort of like a go-kart with a sail.

There is a small informal camping area nestled under the east face of Steens Mountain along Pike Creek. Look for a spur road leading off to the west about two miles north of Alvord Hot Springs. Some folks also camp on the edge of the playa.

Alvord Hot Springs

North of Fields, look for **Alvord Hot Springs,** a rustic spa recognizable by its corrugated-steel shack on the east side of the road. Two pools of hot mineral water piped in from spring runoff will warm your muscles and soak away your aches and pains at $5 admission for 24 hours.. The view from the hot springs up onto the east face of Steens Mountain is magnificent.

Mann Lake

North of the Alvord Desert, just west of the road, **Mann Lake** is a popular fishing destination. Early spring trout fishing is especially good, and the lake is the repository for the breeding stock of Lahontan cutthroat trout, a subspecies that's adapted to alkaline water. Although the lakeshore is pretty sagebrushy and unshaded, there is a campground.

The Alvord Desert is a hardpan playa.

OWYHEE RIVER COUNTRY

It's a long way from just about anywhere to the far southeastern corner of Oregon, but the canyons of the Owyhee are enchanting for those visitors who don't mind roughing it. If you aren't prepared to camp, you can stay in one of the two very basic motels in Jordan Valley, or come down from the north, where Ontario has more services.

Jordan Valley

This town, located almost on the Idaho border where U.S. 95 takes a sharp bend north, is mostly visited by long-haul truckers. For years, the Old Basque Inn, a former boarding house, was the place to eat and sleep in this remote territory. Now reopened as the **Flat Iron Steakhouse** (306 Wroten St., 541/586-2800, 7am-9:30pm, $8-24), you won't find many Basque options remaining on the menu, but the steaks and burgers are good. And there's

The Grave of Jean-Baptiste Charbonneau

One of the early West's most colorful characters is buried at the old Inskip Ranch, near the ranching community of Danner, just west of Jordan Valley. Jean-Baptiste Charbonneau was the son of Toussaint Charbonneau and Sacajawea, who accompanied Lewis and Clark's Corps of Discovery on their journey across the western U.S. between 1805 and 1806. In all those images of Sacajawea, young Pomp, as he was known to the corps, is the one in the papoose—but having served as the youngest member of the expedition was just the beginning of his incredible life. Captain Clark was so taken with the young half-French, half-Shoshone infant that he sent the child to private schools in St. Louis at his own expense. Later, at Fort Union in Montana, the adolescent Charbonneau met German nobleman-cum-scientist Prince Paul von Wertemberg, who was impressed by the well-educated boy. He took Charbonneau back to Germany with him, where Charbonneau spent the next six years as a courtier. During this time, he learned five languages fluently and traveled across Europe and to Africa with the prince. Charbonneau eventually returned to the western United States. He served as a guide through the Montana wilderness, trapped furs, served as alcalde at a California mission, and prospected for gold in the 1850s California Gold Rush. In 1866, he hankered to return to Montana, where gold fever had broken out. He got no further than Danner, then a stage stop, where he died of pneumonia at age 61. To visit the gravesite, follow signs north off Highway 95, 17 miles east of Jordan Valley or 28 miles east of Burns Junction. The grave site is about two miles north on a good gravel road.

even talk of opening the guest rooms upstairs B&B style. If you're headed to Jordan Valley, give a call to find out if the rooms are open. Otherwise, the **Basque Station Motel** (801 Main St., 541/586-2244, $50-65) has basic rooms that will look pretty inviting after a long day's drive.

Owyhee River Trips

The big treat for visitors to this area is a four- to six-day raft trip down the Owyhee River. The river can be run only for a few weeks in the spring, and during drought years it can't be run at all. Most trips start in the tiny town of Rome, east of Jordan Valley, and end at the southern edge of the Owyhee Reservoir, at the base of Leslie Gulch. Expect to pay $1,000-1,800, depending on the length of the trip, to float (with an occasional run through hair-raising rapids) through deep rugged canyons past tall rock pillars, petroglyphs, many species of birds, and a number of hot springs. The following outfitters offer Owyhee River trips: **Ouzel Outfitters** (541/385-5947 or 800/788-7238, www.oregonrafting.com), **Oregon**

Whitewater Adventures (541/746-5422 or 800/820-7238, www.oregonwhitewater. com), and **Momentum River Expeditions** (541/488-2525, www.momentumriverexpeditions.com).

★ Succor Creek and Leslie Gulch

From Jordan Valley, head north 18 miles on U.S. 95, then turn left onto unpaved Succor Creek Road (just shy of the Oregon-Idaho border) to discover one of Oregon's most remote and spectacularly scenic areas. Note that some maps show this route as paved. It is not. It's passable for most passenger vehicles, though high clearance is a plus.

Follow Succor Creek Road nine miles north to a signed junction with Leslie Gulch Road, which drops through a wildly eroded landscape on its way to Lake Owyhee. This steep, though usually passable gravel road careens down a narrow creek channel incised through vividly colored volcanic rock that's been eroded into amazing pinnacle and turreted formations. The 16-mile route ends at a lake-side campground (no potable water). Watch for bighorn sheep along the cliffs.

Back on Succor Creek Road, continue another 11 miles north to Succor Creek State Park, where small but mighty Succor Creek (and the twisting road) plunges between cliffs of volcanic tuff hundreds of feet high, a landscape reminiscent of Utah's Zion National Park. You'll find a number of stream-side campsites and picnic areas (bring water). Wander along the stream to explore the geology and wildflowers, but be sure to watch out for rattlesnakes and for thundereggs—spherical, baseball-size geodes filled with agate, and Oregon's state rock. This is one of the top spots in the state for discovering these unusual specimens.

Continue north 15 miles on Succor Creek Road to reach paved Route 201, which runs between Homedale, Idaho, and Nyssa, Oregon. If you are beginning your Succor Creek journey from the north, you'll find the well-signed Succor Creek Road eight miles south of the small Oregon town of Adrian.

A twisting road cuts through cliffs of volcanic tuff.

Background

The Landscape

GEOGRAPHY

If Oregon were part of a jigsaw puzzle of the United States, it would be a squarish piece with a divot carved out of the center top. To the west is the Pacific Ocean, with some 370 miles of beaches, dunes, and headlands; to the east are the Snake River and Idaho. Up north, much of the boundary between Oregon and Washington is defined by the mighty Columbia River, while southern Oregon lies atop the upper borders of California and Nevada.

Highs and Lows

Moving west to east, the major mountain systems start with the Klamath Mountains and the Coast Range. The Klamaths form the lower quarter of the state's western barrier to the Pacific; the eastern flank of this range is generally referred to as the Siskiyous. To the north, the Oregon Coast Range, a younger volcanic range, runs north-south in parallel to the coastline. The highest peaks in each of these cordilleras barely top 4,000 feet and stand between narrow coastal plateaus on the west side and the rich agricultural lands of the Willamette and Rogue Valleys on the other. Running up the west-central portion of the state is the Cascade Range, which extends from northern California up to Canada. Five of the dormant volcanoes in Oregon top 10,000 feet above sea level, with Mount Hood, the state's highest peak, at 11,239 feet.

Beyond the eastern slope of the Cascades, semiarid high-desert conditions begin. In the northeast, the 10,000-foot crests of the snow-capped Wallowas rise less than 50 miles away from the hot, arid floor of Hells Canyon, itself about 1,300 feet above sea level.

The Great Basin desert—characterized by rivers that evaporate, peter out, or disappear into underground aquifers—makes up the bottom corner of eastern Oregon. Here the seven-inch annual rainfall of the Alvord Desert seems as if it would be more at home in southeastern California and Nevada than in a state known for blustery rainstorms and lush greenery.

In addition to Hells Canyon, the country's biggest hole in the ground (7,900 feet maximum depth), Oregon also boasts the continent's deepest lake: Crater Lake, with a depth of 1,958 feet.

Last of the Red-Hot Lavas

Each part of the state contains well-known remnants of Oregon's cataclysmic past. Offshore waters here feature 1,477 islands and islets, the eroded remains of ancient volcanic flows. Lava fields dot the approaches to the High Cascades. East of the range, a volcanic plateau supports cinder cones, lava caves, and lava-cast forests in the most varied array of these phenomena outside of Hawaii.

The imposing volcanic cones of the Cascades and the inundated caldera that is Crater Lake, formed by the implosion of Mount Mazama some 6,600 years ago, are some of the most dramatic reminders of Oregon's volcanic origins. More fascinating evidence can be seen up close at Newberry National Volcanic Monument, an extensive area south of Bend that encompasses obsidian fields and lava formations left by massive eruptions. (Incidentally, geologists have cited Newberry on their list of volcanoes in the continental United States most likely to erupt again.) Not far from the Lava Lands Visitor Center in the national monument are the Lava River Cave and Lava Cast Forest—created when lava enveloped living trees 6,000 years ago.

the contours of what are now the Columbia River Gorge and the Willamette Valley.

Earthquakes and Tsunamis

Scientists exploring Tillamook County in 1990 unearthed discontinuities in both rock strata and tree rings indicating that the north Oregon coast has experienced major **earthquakes** every several hundred years. They estimate that the next one could come within the next 50 years and be of significant magnitude.

With virtually every part of the state possessing seismic potential that hasn't been released in many years, the pressure along the fault lines is increasing.

In coastal areas, one of the greatest dangers associated with earthquakes is the possibility of **tsunamis**. When the March 2011 9.0 earthquake hit Japan, Oregon's coastal residents fled to higher ground; although most of the state's coast was spared, 8-foot waves along the southern coast damaged the harbor in Brookings.

The Great Meltdown

However pervasive the effects of seismic activity and volcanism are, they must still share top billing with the last ice age in the grand epic of Oregon's topography.

At the height of the most recent major ice age glaciation, the world's oceans were 300-500 feet lower, North America and Asia were connected by a land bridge across the Bering Strait, and the Oregon coast was miles west of where it is today. The Columbia Gorge extended out past present-day Astoria. As the glaciers melted, the sea rose.

When that glacial epoch's final meltdown 12,000 years ago unleashed water dammed up by thousands of feet of ice, great rivers were spawned and existing channels enlarged. A particularly large inundation was the Missoula Floods, which began as ice dams broke up in what's now northern Idaho and western Montana, releasing epic floods of glacial meltwater. These floodwaters carved out

CLIMATE
The Rain Shadow

Oregon's location equidistant from the equator and the North Pole subjects it to weather from both tropical and polar airflows. This makes for a pattern of changeability in which calm often alternates with storm, and extreme heat and extreme cold seldom last long.

Oregon's weather is best understood as a series of valley climates separated from each other by mountain ranges that draw precipitation from the eastbound weather systems. Moving west to east, each of these valley zones receives progressively lower rainfall levels until one encounters a desert on the eastern side of the state.

The Coast

Wet but mild, average rainfall on the coast ranges from a low of 64 inches per year in the Coos Bay area to nearly 100 inches around Lincoln City. The Pacific Ocean moderates coastal weather year-round, softening the extremes. Spring, summer, and fall generally don't get very hot, with highs generally in the 60s and 70s and seldom topping 90°F. Winter temperatures only drop to the 40s and 50s, and freezes and snowfall are quite rare occurrences.

Western Oregon

If there is one constant in western Oregon, it is cloudiness. Portland and the Willamette Valley receive only about 45 percent of maximum potential sunshine; more than 200 days of the year are cloudy, and rain falls an average of 150 days. While this might sound bleak, consider that the cloud cover helps moderate the climate by trapping and reflecting the earth's heat. On average, fewer than 30 days of the year record temperatures below freezing. Except in mountainous areas, snow usually isn't a force to be reckoned with. Another surprise is that Portland's average annual rainfall of 40 inches is usually less than totals recorded in New York City, Miami, or Chicago.

In the southern valleys, Ashland and Medford typically record only half the yearly precipitation of their neighbors to the north, as well as higher winter and summer temperatures.

Central and Eastern Oregon

The landscape of central and eastern Oregon

by and large determines the weather, but you can almost always count on weather out here to be more extreme than in western Oregon. In summer, mountainous areas will be cooler, while the extensive desert basins of eastern Oregon can be scorching. Winter can bring snow and cold temperatures across the entire region.

Plants and Animals

PLANTS

With 4,400 known species and varieties, Oregon ranks fourth among U.S. states for plant diversity, including dozens of species found nowhere else.

Trees

The mixed-conifer ecosystem of western Oregon—dense far-reaching forests of Douglas fir, Sitka spruce, and western hemlock interspersed with bigleaf maple, vine maple, and alder—is among the most productive woodlands in the world.

In southern Oregon, you'll find redwood groves and rare myrtle trees (prized by woodworkers for their distinctive coloring and grain), while huge ponderosa pines are a hallmark of central and eastern Oregon. A particularly striking natural display along the McKenzie River mixes red vine maple and sumacs with golden oaks and alders against an evergreen backdrop.

Of the 19 million acres of old growth that once proliferated in Oregon and Washington, less than 10 percent survive. Naturalists describe an old-growth forest as a mixture of trees, some of which must be at least 200 years old, and a supply of snags or standing dead trees, nurse logs, and streams with downed logs. Of all the old-growth forests mentioned in this volume, **Opal Creek** in the Willamette Valley most spectacularly embodies all of these characteristics.

Coastal Plant Life

While giant conifers and a profuse understory of greenery predominate coastal forests, this ecosystem represents only the most visible part of the Oregon coast's bountiful botany. Many coastal travelers will notice **European beachgrass** (*Ammophila arenaria*) covering the sand wherever they go. Originally planted in the 1930s to inhibit dune growth, the thick, rapidly spreading grass worked too well, solidifying into a ridge behind the shoreline, blocking the windblown sand from replenishing the rest of the beach and suppressing native plants.

Freshwater wetlands and bogs, created where water is trapped by the sprawling sand dunes along the central coast, provide habitats for some unusual species. Best known among these is the **cobra lily** (*Darlingtonia californica*), which can be viewed up close just north of Florence. Also called pitcher plant, this carnivorous bog dweller survives on hapless insects lured into a specialized chamber, where they are trapped and digested.

Coastal salt marshes, occurring in the upper intertidal zones of coastal bays and estuaries, have been dramatically reduced due to land "reclamation" projects such as drainage, diking, and other human disturbances. The halophytes (salt-loving plants) that thrive in this specialized environment include pickleweed, saltgrass, fleshy jaumea, salt marsh dodder, arrowgrass, sand spurrey, and seaside plantain. Coastal forests include Sitka spruce and alder riparian communities, which provide resting and feeding areas for migratory waterfowl, shore and wading birds, and raptors.

Flowers and Fruits

While not as visually arresting as the evergreens of western Oregon, the state's several varieties of berries are no less pervasive. Found mostly from the coast to the mid-Cascades, invasive **Himalayan blackberries** favor clearings, burned-over areas, and people's gardens. They also take root in the woods alongside **wild strawberries, salmonberries, thimbleberries, currants,** and **salal.** Within this edible realm, wild-food connoisseurs especially seek out the thin-leafed **huckleberry** found in the Wallowa, Blue, Cascade, and Klamath Ranges. Prime snacking season for all these berries ranges from midsummer to mid-fall.

No less prized are the rare plant communities of the Columbia River Gorge and the Klamath-Siskiyou region. A quarter of Oregon's rare and endangered plants are found in the latter area, a portion of which is in the valley of the Illinois River, a designated Wild and Scenic tributary of the Rogue.

Kalmiopsis leachiana, a rare member of the heath family endemic to southwestern Oregon, even has a wilderness area named after it.

Motorists will treasure such springtime floral fantasias (both wild and domesticated) such as the **dahlias** and **irises** near Canby off I-5; **tulips** near Woodburn; irises off Route 213 outside Salem; the **Easter lilies** along U.S. 101 near Brookings; **blue lupines** alongside U.S. 97 in central Oregon; **apple blossoms** in the Hood River Valley near the Columbia Gorge; **pear blossoms** in the Bear Creek Valley near Medford; **beargrass, columbines,** and **Indian paintbrush** on Cascades thoroughfares; and **rhododendrons** and **fireweed** along the coast.

East of the Cascades, the undergrowth is often more varied than the ground cover in the damp forests on the west side of the mountains. This is because sunny openings in the forest permit room for more species and for plants of different heights. And, in contrast to the white flowers that predominate in the shady forests in western Oregon, "dry-side" wildflowers generally have brighter colors. These blossoms attract color-sensitive pollinators such as bees and butterflies. On the

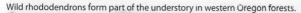
Wild rhododendrons form part of the understory in western Oregon forests.

opposite flank of the range, the commonly seen white **trillium** relies on beetles and ants for propagation, lessening the need for eye-catching pigments.

Mushrooms

Autumn is the season for those who covet wild chanterelle and matsutake mushrooms. September through November the Coast Range is the prime picking area for chanterelles—a fluted orange or yellow mushroom in the tall second-growth Douglas fir forests. In the spring, fungi lovers' hearts turn to morels. Of course, you should be absolutely certain of what you have before you eat wild mushrooms, or any other wild food. Farmers markets are usually good places to find an assortment of wild mushrooms.

ANIMALS

Oregon's creatures great and small are an excitingly diverse group. Oregon's low population density, abundance of wildlife refuges and nature preserves, and biomes running the gamut from rainforest to desert explain this variety. Throughout the state, numerous refuges, such as the **South Slough National Estuarine Research Reserve,** the **Malheur Bird/Wildlife Refuge,** the **Jewell Preserve for Roosevelt Elk,** and the **Finley Bird and Wildlife Preserve** provide safe havens for both feathered and furry friends.

Tidepools

For many visitors, the most fascinating coastal ecosystems in Oregon are the rocky tidepools. These Technicolor windows offer an up close look at one of the richest—and harshest—environments, the intertidal zone, where pummeling surf, unflinching sun, predators, and the cycle of tides demand tenacity and special adaptation of its inhabitants.

The natural zone where surf meets shore is divided into three main habitat layers, based on their position relative to tide levels. The **high intertidal zone,** inundated only during the highest tides, is home to creatures that can either move, such as **crabs,** or are well adapted to tolerate daily desiccation, such as **acorn barnacles** and **finger limpets, chitons, green algae,** and **limpets.** The turbulent **mid-intertidal zone** is covered and uncovered by the tides, usually twice each day. In the upper portion of this zone, **California mussels** and **goose barnacles** may thickly blanket the rocks, while ochre **sea stars** and green **sea anemones** are common lower down, along with **sea lettuce, sea palms, snails, sponges,** and **whelks.** Below that, the **low intertidal zone** is exposed only during the lowest tides. Because it is covered by water most of the time, this zone has the greatest diversity of organisms in the tidal area. Residents include many of the organisms found in the higher zones, as well as **sculpins, abalone,** and purple **sea urchins.**

Standout destinations for exploring tidepools include Cape Arago, Cape Perpetua, the Marine Gardens at Devil's Punchbowl, and beaches south and north of Gold Beach—among many other spots. Tidepool explorers should be mindful that, despite the fact that the plants and animals in the pools are well adapted to withstand the elements, they and their ecosystem are actually quite fragile, and they're very sensitive to human interference. Avoid stepping on mussels, anemones, and barnacles, and take nothing from the tidepools. In the Oregon Islands National Wildlife Refuge and other specially protected areas, removal or harassment of any living organism may be treated as a misdemeanor punishable by fines.

Gray Whales

Few sights along the Oregon coast elicit more excitement than that of a surfacing whale. The most common large whale seen from shore along the West Coast of North America is the gray whale (*Eschrichtius robustus*). These behemoths can reach 45 feet in length and 35 tons in weight. The sight of a mammal as big as a Greyhound bus erupting from the sea has a way of emptying the mind of mundane concerns. Wreathed in seaweed and sporting barnacles and other parasites on its back, a

With warming oceans, sea lions are more numerous than ever in Oregon.

leave Mexico and move more slowly, passing Oregon late April-June. During the spring migration, the whales may pass within just a few hundred yards of coastal headlands, making this a particularly exciting time for whale-watching from any number of vantage points along the coast.

Seals, Sea Lions, and Otters

Pacific harbor seals, California sea lions, and Steller sea lions are frequently sighted in Oregon waters. California sea lions are the animals you might have seen in circuses. These 1,000-pound mammals are characterized by their large size and small earflaps, which seals lack. Unlike seals, they can point their rear flippers forward to give them better mobility on land. Lacking the dense underfur that covers seals, sea lions tend to prefer warmer waters.

Steller sea lions can be seen at the Sea Lion Caves. They also breed on reefs off Gold Beach and Port Orford. In the largest sea lion species, males can weigh more than a ton. Their coats tend to be gray rather than the nearly black California sea lions. They also differ from their California counterparts in that they are comfortable in colder water.

Look for Pacific harbor seals in bays and estuaries up and down the coast, sometimes miles inland. They're nonmigratory, have no earflaps, and can be distinguished from sea lions because they're much smaller (150-300 pounds) and have mottled fur that ranges in color from pale cream to rusty brown.

Salmon and Steelhead

In recent decades, dwindling Pacific salmon and steelhead stocks have prompted restrictions on commercial and recreational fishing in order to restore threatened and endangered species throughout the Pacific Northwest. Runs are highly variable from year to year; for more information about fish populations and fishing restrictions, see the Oregon Department of Fish and Wildlife's website (www.dfw.state.or.us).

The salmon's life cycle begins and ends in

California gray whale might look more like the hull of an old ship were it not for its expressive eyes.

Some gray whales are found off the Oregon coast all year, including an estimated 200-400 during the summer, though they're most visible and numerous when migrating populations pass through Oregon waters on their way south December-February and northward early March-April. This annual journey from the rich feeding grounds of the Bering and Chukchi Seas of Alaska to the calving grounds of Mexico amounts to some 10,000 miles, the longest migration of any mammal. On the Oregon coast, their numbers peak usually during the first week of January, when as many as 30 per hour may pass a given point. By mid-February, most of the whales will have moved on toward their breeding and calving lagoons on the west coast of Baja California.

Early March-April, the juveniles, adult males, and females without calves begin returning northward past the Oregon coast. Mothers and their new calves are the last to

Species of Fish

Touted as the best-tasting salmon, king (also known as chinook) salmon are also the largest species, sometimes weighing in at over 80 pounds. Coho (or silver) salmon are known among anglers as fish that fight fiercely, despite a weight of just 10-20 pounds.

Chum salmon (known derogatorily as "dog salmon" because Canadian and Alaskan native people thought them worthy only of being fed to their dog teams) are found only in the Miami and Kilchis Rivers near Tillamook.

Steelhead are sea-run rainbow trout averaging 5-20 pounds whose life cycle generally resembles that of salmon—save for the fact that steelhead generally survive after spawning and may live to spawn multiple times. Runs of steelhead, often heavily supplemented by hatchery-raised fish, are found in rivers and streams up and down the coast. They provide great—if challenging—sport angling, but are not fished commercially (though you will find farm-raised steelhead in the grocery store).

a freshwater stream. After an upriver journey from the sea of sometimes hundreds of miles, the spawning female deposits 3,000-7,000 eggs in hollows (called redds) she has scooped out of the coarse sand or gravel, where the male fertilizes them. These adult salmon die soon after mating, and their bodies then deteriorate to become part of the food chain for young fish.

Within 3-4 months, the eggs hatch into alevin, tiny immature fish with their yolk sac still attached. As the alevin exhaust the nutrients in the sac, they enter the fry stage, and begin to resemble very small salmon. The length they remain as fry differs among various species. Chinook fry, for example, immediately start heading for saltwater, whereas coho or silver salmon will remain in their home stream for 1-3 years before moving downstream.

The salmon are in the smolt stage when they start to enter saltwater. The 5- to 7-inch smolts will spend some time in the estuary area of the river or stream while they feed and adjust to the saltwater.

When it finally enters the ocean, the salmon is considered an adult. Each species varies in the number of years it remains away from its natal stream, foraging sometimes thousands of miles throughout the Pacific. Chinook can spend as many as seven years away from their nesting (and ultimately their

resting) place; most other species remain in the salt for 2-4 years. Spring and fall mark the main upstream runs of the Pacific salmon. It is suspected that young salmon imprint the odor of their birth stream, enabling them to find their way home years later.

The salmon's traditional predators such as the sea lion, northern pikeminnow, harbor seal, black bear, Caspian tern, and herring gull pale in comparison to the threats posed by modern civilization. Everything from pesticides to sewage to nuclear waste has polluted Oregon waters, and until mitigation efforts were enacted, dams and hydroelectric turbines threatened to block Oregon's all-important Columbia River spawning route.

Land Animals

Oregon is home to cougars, also known as mountain lions. As human development encroaches on their territory, sightings of these large cats become more common. Although they tend to shy away from big people, they've been known to attack children and small adults. For this reason, if no other, keep your kids close to the adults when hiking. Oregon also supports several packs of grey wolves.

Wild "Kiger" mustangs, descendants of horses that the Spanish conquistadors brought to the Americas centuries ago, live on Steens Mountain and are identified by their hooked ears, thin dorsal stripes, two-toned manes, and faint zebra stripes on their legs. Narrow trunks and a short back are other distinguishing physical characteristics.

Bears

Black bears (*Ursus americanus*) proliferate in mountain and coastal forests of Oregon. Adults average 200-500 pounds and have dark coats. Black bears shy away from people except when provoked by the scent of food, when cornered or surprised, or when humans intrude into territory near their cubs. Female bears tend to have a very strong maternal instinct that may construe any alien presence as an attack upon their young. Authorities counsel hikers to act aggressively and defend themselves with whatever means possible if a bear is in attack mode or shows signs that it considers a hiker prey. Jump up and down, shout, and wave your arms. It may help to raise your jacket or pack to make yourself appear larger, but resist the urge to run. Bears can run much faster than humans, and their retractable claws enable black bears to scramble up trees. Furthermore, bears tend to give chase when they see something running.

If you see a bear at a distance, try to stay downwind of it and back away slowly. Bears have a strong sense of smell, and some studies suggest that our body scent is abhorrent to them. Our food, however, can be quite appealing. Campers should place all food in a sack tied to a rope and suspend it 20 feet or more from the ground and away from your tent.

Deer, Elk, and Pronghorn

Sportspeople and wildlife enthusiasts alike appreciate Oregon's big-game herds. Big-game habitats differ dramatically from one side of the Cascades to the other, with Roosevelt elk and black-tailed deer in the west, and Rocky Mountain elk and mule deer east of the Cascades. The Columbian white-tailed deer is a seldom-seen endangered species found in western Oregon. Pronghorn reside in the high desert country of southeastern Oregon. The continent's fastest mammal, it is able to sprint at over 60 mph in short bursts. The low brush of the open country east of the Cascades suits their excellent vision, which enables them to spot predators.

Small Mammals

Many of the most frequently sighted animals in Oregon are small scavengers. Even in the most urban parts of the state, it's possible to see raccoons, skunks, chipmunks, squirrels, and opossums.

West of the Cascades, the dark-colored Townsend's chipmunks are among the most commonly encountered mammals; east of the Cascades, lighter-colored pine chipmunks and golden-mantled ground squirrels proliferate in drier interior forests. The latter two look almost alike, but the stripes on the side of the chipmunk's head distinguish them from each other. Expect to see the dark-brown, cinnamon-bellied Douglas squirrel on both sides of the Cascades.

Beavers

Beavers (*Castor canadensis*), North America's largest rodents, are widespread throughout the Beaver State, though they're most commonly sighted in second-growth forests near marshes after sunset. Fall is a good time to spot beavers as they gather food for winter. The beaver has long been Oregon's mascot, and for good reason: It was the beaver that drew brigades of fur trappers and spurred the initial exploration and settlement of the state. The beaver also merits a special mention for being important to Oregon's forest ecosystem. Contrary to popular belief, the abilities of Mother Nature's carpenter extend far beyond the mere destruction of trees to dam a waterway. In fact, the activities associated with lodge construction actually serve to maintain the food chain and the health of the forest by slowing waters to create a habitat for a variety of freshwater and woodland creatures.

Banana Slugs

You won't go far in the Oregon coast woodlands or underbrush before you encounter the state's best-known invertebrates—and lots of them. There are few places on earth where these snails-out-of-shells grow as large (3-10 inches long) or as numerous. The reason is western Oregon's climate: moister than mist but drier than drizzle. This balance, combined with calcium-poor soil, enables the native banana slug and the more common European black slug (the bane of Oregon gardeners) to thrive.

Desert Critters

Because most desert animals are nocturnal, it's difficult to see many of them. Nonetheless, their variety and exotic presences should be noted. Horned lizards, kangaroo rats, red-and-black ground snakes, kit foxes, and four-inch-long greenish-yellow hairy scorpions are some of the more interesting denizens of the desert east of the Cascade Mountains.

Birds

The Pacific Flyway is an important migratory route that passes through Oregon, and the state's varied ecosystems provide habitats for a variety of species, ranging from shorebirds to raptors to songbirds. The U.S. Fish and Wildlife Service has established viewpoints for wildlife- and bird-watching at 12 Oregon national wildlife refuges.

In the winter the outskirts of Klamath Falls become inundated with bald eagles. Along the lower Columbia east of Astoria and on Sauvie Island, just outside Portland, are other bald eagle wintering spots. Visitors to Sauvie Island will be treated to an amazing variety of birds. More than 200 bird species come through here on the Pacific Flyway, feeding in grassy clearings. Look for eagles on the island's northwest side. Herons, ducks of all sorts, and geese also live on the island.

Other birds of prey, or raptors, abound all over the state. Northeast of Enterprise, near Zumwalt, is one of the best places to see hawks. Species commonly sighted include the ferruginous, red-tailed, and Swainson's hawks. Rafters in Hells Canyon might see golden eagles' and peregrine falcons' nests. Portlanders driving the Fremont Bridge over the Willamette River also might get to see peregrine falcons. Along I-5 in the Willamette Valley, look for red-tailed hawks on fence posts, and American kestrels, North America's smallest falcons, sitting on overhead wires.

Turkey vultures circle the dry areas during the warmer months. Vultures are commonly sighted above the Rogue River. In central Oregon, ospreys are frequently spotted off

great blue heron

the Cascades Lakes Highway south of Bend, nesting atop hollowed-out snags near water (especially Crane Prairie Reservoir).

In terms of sheer numbers and variety, the coast's mudflats at low tide and the tidal estuaries are among the best birding environments. Numerous locations along the coast—including Bandon Marsh, Three Arch Rocks near Cape Meares, and South Slough Estuarine Research Reserve near Coos Bay—offer outstanding opportunities for spotting such pelagic species as pelicans, cormorants, guillemots, and puffins, as well as waders such as curlews, sandpipers, and plovers, plus various ducks and geese. Rare species such as tufted puffins and the snowy plover enjoy special protection here, along with other types of migratory birds. The **Oregon Islands National Wildlife Refuge,** which comprises all the 1,400-plus offshore islands, reefs, and rocks from Tillamook Head to the California border, is a haven for the largest concentration of nesting seabirds along the West Coast,

thanks to the abundance of protected nesting habitat.

Malheur Wildlife Refuge, in the southeast portion of the state, is Oregon's premier bird and birder retreat and stopover point for large groups of sandhill cranes, Canada and snow geese, whistling swans, and pintail ducks.

In the mountains, look for Clark's nutcracker or the large Steller's jay, whose grating voice and dazzling blue plumage often commands the most attention. Mountain hikers are bound to share part of their picnic lunch with these birds. At high elevations, the quieter Clark's nutcracker will more likely be your guest.

Unfortunately, the western meadowlark, the state bird, has nearly vanished from western Oregon due to loss of habitat, but thanks to natural pasture east of the Cascades, you can still hear its distinctive song. The meadowlark is distinguished by a yellow underside with a black crescent pattern across the breast and white outer tail feathers.

History

NATIVE PEOPLES
Early Days

Long before Europeans came to this hemisphere, native peoples thrived for thousands of years in the region of present-day Oregon. The leading theory concerning their origins maintains that their ancestors came over from Asia on a land or ice bridge spanning what is now the Bering Strait.

Despite common ancestry, the people on the rain-soaked coast and in the Willamette Valley lived quite differently from those on the drier eastern flank of the Cascade Mountains. Those west of the Cascades enjoyed abundant salmon, shellfish, berries, and game. Broad rivers facilitated travel, and thick stands of the finest softwood timber in the world ensured that there was never a dearth of building materials. A mild climate with plentiful food and resources allowed the wet-siders the leisure

time to evolve a complex culture rich with artistic endeavors, theatrical pursuits, and such ceremonial gatherings as the traditional potlatch, where the divesting of one's material wealth was seen as a status symbol.

After contact with traders, Chinook, an amalgam of Native American tongues with some French and English thrown in, was the common argot among the diverse nations that gathered in the Columbia Gorge each year. It was at these gatherings that the coast and valley dwellers would come into contact with Native Americans from east of the Cascades. These dry-siders led a seminomadic existence, following game and avoiding the climatic extremes of winter and summer in their region. In the southeast desert of the Great Basin, seeds and roots added protein to their diet.

The introduction of horses in the mid-1700s made hunting much easier. In contrast

What's in a Name?

One rather peculiar theory of how Oregon got its name derives from a reputed encounter between Native Americans and the Spanish mariners who plied West Coast waters in the 17th and 18th centuries. Upon seeing the abalone shell earrings of the coastal Salish people, the European sailors are said to have exclaimed, *"¡Orejon!"* ("What big ears!")—later anglicized to Oregon. Others point out the similarity between the name of the state and the Spanish locales Aragon and Obregon (in Mexico). Additionally, the word *Oregon* belonged to a Wisconsin group of Native Americans who purportedly traded with Columbia River natives during salmon season.

A less fanciful explanation has it that the state's name was inspired by the English word "origin," conjuring the image of the forest primeval. The French word *ouragan* ("hurricane") has also been suggested as the source of the state's name, courtesy of French Canadian fur trappers who became the first permanent European settlers in the region during the early 19th century. In this vein, the reference to the Columbia River as the "Oregan" by some French Canadian voyageurs who came here with the "beaver brigades" of the Northwest and Hudson's Bay Companies is another possible etymological ancestor.

It was recently noted that *oregonon* and *orenogonia,* two Greek words pertaining to mountainous locales, were seen on old navigators' maps marking the area between northern California and British Columbia. Given that the famous Pacific Northwest explorer Juan de Fuca was actually Greek (born Valerianos) and that many navigators were schooled in Greece, perhaps Oregon's name originated in the Mediterranean.

to their counterparts west of the Cascades, who lived in 100- by 40-foot longhouses, extended families in the eastern groups inhabited pit houses when not hunting. The demands of chasing migratory game necessitated caves or simple rock shelters.

Twelve separate nations populated Oregon. Although these were further divided into 80 tribes, the primary allegiance was to the village. The "nation" status referred to language groupings such as Salish and Athabascan.

Conflicts with European Settlers

The coming of European settlers meant the usurpation of Native American homelands, exposure to European diseases such as smallpox and diphtheria, and the passing of ancient ways of life. Violent conflicts ensued on a large scale with the influx of settlers doing missionary work and seeking government land giveaways in the 1830s and 1840s. In the 1850s, mining activity in southern Oregon and on the coast incited the Rogue River Indian Wars, adding to the strife brought on by annexation to the United States.

These events compelled the U.S. federal government to send in troops and eventually to set up treaties with Oregon's first inhabitants. The attempts at arbitration in the 1850s added insult to injury. Tribes of different—indeed, often incompatible—backgrounds were rounded up and grouped together haphazardly on reservations, often far from their homelands. In the century that followed, the evils of modern civilization destroyed much of the ecosystem on which these cultures were based. An especially regrettable result of settlement was the decline of the Columbia River salmon runs due to overfishing, loss of habitat, and pollution. This not only weakened the food chain but treated this spiritual totem of the many Native American groups along the Columbia as an expendable resource.

For a while, there was an attempt to restore the balance. In 1924 the federal government accorded citizenship to Native Americans. Ten years later, the Indian Reorganization Act provided self-management of reservation lands. Another decade later, a court of treaty claims was established. In the 1960s, however, the government, acting on the premise that Native Americans needed to assimilate into mainstream society, terminated several reservations.

Recent government reparations have accorded many native peoples preferential hunting and fishing rights, monetary and land grants, and the restoration of status to certain disenfranchised bands. In Oregon, there are now nine federally recognized tribes and six reservations: Warm Springs, Umatilla, Burns Paiute, Siletz, Grand Ronde, and Coquille. Against all odds, their culture is still a vital part of Oregon; the 2010 census estimated that over 53,000 Oregonians are Native American. Native American gaming came to Oregon in the mid-1990s, and Native Oregonians now operate a number of lucrative casinos in the state; the Confederated Tribes of Grand Ronde, owners of the phenomenally popular Spirit Mountain Casino, are among the state's biggest philanthropists.

EXPLORATION, SETTLEMENT, AND GROWTH

In the 17th and 18th centuries, Spanish, British, and Russian vessels came to offshore waters here in search of a sea route connecting the Atlantic with the Pacific. Accounts differ, but the first sightings of the Oregon coast have been credited to either Juan Rodríguez Cabrillo (in 1543) or the English explorer Sir Francis Drake (in 1579). Other voyagers of note included Spain's Vizcaíno and de Aguilar (in 1603) and Bruno de Heceta (in 1775), and Britain's James Cook and John Meares during the late 1770s, as well as George Vancouver (in 1792).

Sea otter and beaver pelts added impetus to the search for a trade route connecting the Atlantic and Pacific Oceans. While the Northwest Passage turned out to be a myth, the fur trade became a basis of commerce and contention between European, Asian, and eventually American governments.

U.S. Expansion in Oregon

The United States took interest in the area when Robert Gray sailed up the Columbia River in 1792. The first U.S. overland excursion into Oregon was made by the Corps of Discovery in 1804-1806. Dispatched by Thomas Jefferson to explore the lands of the Louisiana Purchase and beyond, Captains Meriwether Lewis and William Clark and their party of 30 men—and one woman, Sacajawea—trekked across the continent to the mouth of the Columbia, camped south of present-day Astoria during the winter of 1805-1806, and then returned to St. Louis. Lewis and Clark's exploration and mapping of Oregon threw down the gauntlet for future settlement and eventual annexation of the Oregon Territory by the United States. The expedition also initially secured good relations with the Native Americans in the West, thus establishing the preconditions to trade and the missionary influx.

Following Lewis and Clark's journey, there were years of wrangling over the right of the United States to settle in the new territory (when Lewis and Clark made their journey, Oregon and Washington were British territory). Nonetheless, American John Jacob Astor's Pacific Fur Company established a trading fort at Astoria in 1811, though British war ships soon dispersed the settlement. It wasn't until 1818, as part of the settlement of the War of 1812, that the country west of the Rockies, south of Russian America, and north of Spanish America was open for use by U.S. citizens as well as British subjects.

During the 1820s, the British Hudson's Bay Company continued to hold sway over Oregon country by means of Fort Vancouver on the north shore of the Columbia. More than 500 people settled here under the charismatic leadership of John McLoughlin, who oversaw the planting of crops and the raising of livestock. Despite a growing number of farms and settlements along the Willamette River, as the trappers began to put down roots, several factors presaged the demise of British influence in Oregon. Most obvious was the decline of the fur trade as well as Britain's difficulty in maintaining her far-flung empire.

Less apparent but equally influential was the lack of European women in a land populated predominantly by European trappers and explorers. If the Americans could attract settlers of both genders, they'd be in a position to create an expanding population base that could dominate the region.

The first step in this process was the arrival of missionaries. In 1834, Methodist soul-seekers led by Jason Lee settled near Salem. Four years later, another mission was started in the eastern Columbia River Gorge. In 1843, Marcus and Narcissa Whitman's missions started up on the upper Columbia in present-day Walla Walla, Washington. The missionaries brought alien ways and diseases for which the Native Americans had no immunity. As if this weren't enough to provoke a violent reaction, the Native Americans would soon have their homelands inundated by thousands of settlers lured by government land giveaways.

The Oregon Trail

Despite Easterners' ignorance of western geography and the hardships it held, more than 53,000 people traversed the 2,000-mile Oregon Trail between 1840 and 1850 en route to the Eden of western Oregon. Though many of these settlers were driven by somewhat utopian ideals, there was also the attraction of free land: This march across the frontier was fueled by the offer of 640 free acres that each adult white male could claim in the mid-1840s.

In 1850, the Donation Land Act cut in half the allotted free acreage, reflecting the diminishing availability of real estate. But although a single pioneer man was now entitled to only 320 acres, and single women were excluded from land ownership, as part of a couple they could claim an additional 320 free acres. This promoted marriage and, in turn, families on the western frontier and helped to fulfill Secretary of State John C. Calhoun's prediction that American families could outbreed

the Hudson's Bay Company's bachelor trappers, thus winning the battle of the West.

The Applegate Trail

Another route west was the Applegate Trail, pioneered by brothers Lindsay and Jesse Applegate in the mid-1840s. Each had lost sons several years before to drowning on the Columbia River. The treacherous rapids here had initially been the last leg of a journey to the Willamette Valley.

On their return journey to the region, the brothers departed from the established trail when they reached Fort Hall, Idaho. Veering south from the Oregon Trail across northern Nevada's Black Rock Desert, they traversed the northeast top of California to enter Oregon near present-day Klamath Falls. A southern Oregon gold rush in the 1850s drew thousands along this route.

Early Government and Statehood

There was enough unity among American settlers to organize a provisional government in 1843. Then, in 1848, the federal government decided to accord Oregon territorial status.

The new Oregon Territory got off to a rousing start thanks to the California gold rush of 1849. The rush occasioned a housing boom in San Francisco and a need for lumber, and the dramatic population influx created instant markets for the agriculture of the Willamette Valley. The young city of Portland was in a perfect position to channel goods from the interior to coastal ports and prosper economically.

However, strategic importance and population growth alone do not explain Oregon becoming the 33rd state in the Union. In 1857, the Dred Scott decision had become law. This had the effect of opening Oregon to slavery, as a territory didn't have the legal status to forbid the institution. While slavery didn't lack for adherents in Oregon, the prevailing sentiment was that it was neither necessary nor desirable. If Oregon were a state instead of a territory, however, it could determine its own policy regarding slavery. A constitution (forbidding slavery as well as "free blacks") was drawn up and ratified in 1857, and sent to Washington DC for approval. However, the capital was engulfed in turmoil about the status of slavery in new American states, and only after a year and a half of petitioning did Oregon finally enter the Union on Valentine's Day 1859.

Economic Growing Pains

During the years of the Civil War and its aftermath, internal conflicts were the order of the day within the state. By 1861, good Willamette Valley land was becoming scarce, so many farmers moved east of the Cascades to farm wheat. They ran into violent confrontations with Native Americans over land. Miners encroaching on Native American territory around the southern coast eventually flared into the bloody Rogue River Wars, which would lead to the destruction of most of the native peoples of the coast.

In the 1870s, cattle ranchers came to eastern Oregon, followed by sheep ranchers, and the two groups fought for dominance of the range. However, overproduction of wheat, uncertain markets, and two severe winters spelled the end to the eastern Oregon boom. Many eastern Oregon towns grew up and flourished for a decade, only to fall back into desert, leaving no trace of their existence.

In the 1860s and 1870s, Jacksonville in the south became the commercial counterpart to Portland, owing to its proximity to the Rogue Valley and south coast goldfields as well as the California border. The first stagecoach, steamship, and rail lines moved south from the Columbia River into the Willamette Valley; by the 1880s, Portland was joined to San Francisco and the east by railroad and became the leading city of the Pacific Northwest.

Progressive Politics

In the modern era, Oregon blazed trails in the thicket of governmental legislation and reform. The so-called Oregon system of initiative, referendum, and recall was first conceived in the 1890s, coming to fruition in the first decade of the 1900s. The system has since become an integral part of the state's democratic process.

In like measure, Oregon's extension of suffrage to women in 1912, a 1921 compulsory education law, and the first large-scale union activity in the country during the 1920s were red-letter events in U.S. history.

The 1930s were exciting years in the Pacific Northwest. Despite widespread poverty, the foundations of future prosperity were laid during this decade. New Deal programs such as the Works Progress Administration and the Civilian Conservation Corps undertook many projects around the state. Building roads and hydroelectric dams created jobs and improved the quality of life in Oregon, in addition to bolstering the country's defenses during wartime. Hydroelectric power from the Bonneville Dam, completed in 1938, enabled Portland's shipyards and aluminum plants to thrive. Low utility rates encouraged more employment and settlement, while the Columbia's irrigation water enhanced agriculture.

World War II

Thanks to mass-production techniques, 10,000 workers were employed in the Portland shipyards. But in addition to laying the foundations for future growth, the war years in Oregon and their immediate aftermath were full of trials for state residents. Vanport—at one time a city of 45,000—grew up in the shadow of Kaiser aluminum plants and the shipyards north of Portland, but it was washed off the map in 1948 by a Columbia River flood. Tillamook County forests, which supplied Sitka spruce for airplanes, endured several massive fires that destroyed 500 square miles of trees.

The Modern Era

With the perfection of the chain saw in the 1940s, the timber industry could take advantage of the postwar housing boom. During that decade, the state's population increased by nearly 50 percent, growing to over 1.5 million. During the 1950s and 1960s, the U.S. Army Corps of Engineers carried out a massive program of new dam projects, resulting in construction of The Dalles, John Day, and McNary Dams on the main stem of the Columbia River as well as the Oxbow and Brownlee Dams on the Snake River. In addition, flooding on the Willamette River was tamed through a series of dams on its major tributary watersheds, the Santiam, the Middle Fork of the Willamette, and the McKenzie.

Politically, the late 1960s and 1970s brought environmentally groundbreaking measures spearheaded by Governor Tom McCall. The bottle bill, land use statutes, and the cleanup of the Willamette River were part of this legacy.

The 1990s saw the Oregon economy flourishing, fueled by the growth of computer hardware and software industries here as well as a real estate market favorable to an Oregon Trail-like stream of new settlers. The demographics of Oregon's new arrivals as well as its changing economic climate helped to sustain the state's image as a politically maverick state, with Oregon leading the way in physician-assisted suicide, extensive vote-by-mail procedures, legalized marijuana , and the Oregon Health Plan, a low-cost health insurance program for low-income Oregonians.

Today's Economy

Oregon's economy has traditionally followed a boom-bust cycle. Even though it has in recent decades diversified away from its earlier dependence on resource-based industries, the economic bust of 2008 left over 10 percent of Oregonians unemployed, second only to Michigan in unemployment rate.

The state's major industries today include a booming high-tech sector (Intel is the state's largest employer), primary and fabricated metals production, transportation equipment

Ranching and farming are important in northeastern Oregon.

fabrication, and food processing. Important nonmanufacturing sectors include wholesale and retail trade, education, health care, and tourism. Portland is home to a number of sports and recreational gear companies, including Nike, Adidas America, Columbia, and other sportswear companies with headquarters in the Rose City area.

In agriculture, organic produce, often sold in farmers markets, and other specialty products have helped many small farmers to survive. Other agricultural products include nursery crops (Monrovia is the nation's largest Christmas tree nursery, and Oregon is the number one Christmas tree state); wine grapes; berries, cherries, apples, and pears; and gourmet mushrooms, herbs, and cheese. Wheat, cattle, potatoes and onions are the stalwarts of the eastern Oregon economy. Oregon wineries, most of them small operations, turn out increasingly excellent wine to meet the demands of a thirsty global market. With the legalization of marijuana in 2015, the enormous black market in pot production has edged into the mainstream economy, with yet-to-be-determined consequences.

Essentials

Transportation

AIR

It is a simple enough matter getting to and around Oregon by air. The main point of entry is Portland International Airport (PDX), which is served by over a dozen airlines, but there are also airports in Eugene, Redmond, and Medford. If eastern Oregon is your destination, consider flying into and out of Boise, Idaho.

Horizon Air (800/547-9308, www.horizonair.com), the commuter-league farm club of Alaska Airlines, connects Portland to Redmond, Eugene-Springfield, and Medford, as well as numerous other cities around the western states. Horizon operates commuter prop planes with 10-40 seats. If you are sensitive to loud noises and pressure change, bring earplugs.

TRAIN

Thanks to **Amtrak** (800/872-7245, www.amtrak.com) and its high-speed Spanish-made Talgo trains, the stretch from Eugene to Vancouver, B.C., enjoys an efficient and scenic mass-transit link. Four *Cascades* trains make daily round-trips between Portland and Seattle; one continues on to Vancouver, B.C. Two trains go from Portland south to Eugene daily. The *Coast Starlight* runs between L.A. and Seattle with stops in Oregon at Klamath Falls, Chemult, Eugene, Salem, and Portland.

Note that getting a sleeper on the extremely popular *Coast Starlight* requires reservations 5-11 months in advance any time of the year.

The *Empire Builder,* which connects Portland with Chicago, shows off the Columbia River Gorge to good advantage. Trains run on the Washington side of the Columbia, giving a distant perspective on the waterfalls and mountains across the river. In summer this train stops in Glacier Park, Montana.

Amtrak also runs bus service in such corridors as Portland-Eugene, Portland-Astoria, and Chemult-Bend. The latter service makes Bend accessible to *Coast Starlight* passengers who disembark in Chemult.

BUS

Greyhound (800/229-9424, www.greyhound.com) has cut most of its service to rural Oregon and now travels only along the interstate corridors of I-5 and I-84, but many smaller companies have picked up the slack. Porter, Valley Retriever, Central Oregon Breeze, Southwest and Northwest Point, and other smaller companies operate on former Greyhound routes. Visit www.tripcheck.com to find details on bus service to Oregon's cities and towns.

CAR

For the vast majority of visitors (and residents), the automobile is the vehicle of choice for exploring the state. Speed limits top out at 65 mph on sections of I-5 and I-84; the rest of the roads in the state have a 55 mph maximum speed limit.

Many Oregon roads are strikingly beautiful. The magnificent scenery prompted the building of the first paved public road in the state with the Columbia River Highway, constructed 1913-1915, now known as the Historic Columbia River Highway. The Oregon Coast Scenic Highway, U.S. 101 along the entire Oregon coast, is another internationally renowned drive. Entirely different in character, but equally stunning, is the Cascade Lakes Highway out of Bend.

The **Oregon Department of Transportation** advises on **road conditions** by phone (503/588-2941 out of state, 800/977-6368 within Oregon) and via the TripCheck website (www.tripcheck.com).

Gas is readily available on the main routes, but finding it can be a little trickier in remote eastern Oregon, especially after 5pm. Fill up before you leave the city. Another thing to remember is that Oregon is one of the few states that does not have self-service gasoline outlets; pull up to the pump and wait for an attendant. In some eastern Oregon communities, self-service gas is available outside of regular opening hours.

Winter Driving

The first rule to follow when rain, snow, or hail make pavement slick, or when fog reduces visibility, is to slow down. From late fall to early spring, expect snow on the Cascade passes and I-5 through the Siskiyous; snow tires or chains are often required.

A **Sno-Park permit** is required to park at most ski areas and plowed parking lots leading to cross-country ski trails. Without the daily sticker or season pass in your left-hand windshield, a car left in a Sno-Park area can receive a ticket. This permit is essentially a fee levied by the state to pay for the upkeep of parking and rest areas and for snowplowing in the mountains. Pick these up at a Department of Motor Vehicles office, ski shops, sporting goods stores, and other commercial establishments. They apply to travel November 15-April 15 and cost $4 for 1 day, $25 for the season; stores selling the permits often levy an extra service fee.

If you are traveling into the mountains in the winter, make sure your car has tire chains in the trunk. During snowstorms, many mountain passes are closed to vehicles without chains, and the state patrol takes the task of enforcing this requirement very seriously.

"Go by bike" is a common mantra across Oregon.

BICYCLE

Oregon is user-friendly for bicyclists. In the 1970s the Oregon legislature allocated one percent of the state highways budget to develop bike lanes and encourage energy-saving bicycling. In addition to establishing routes throughout the state with these funds, many special paths were developed with bicycle and foot access specifically in mind. For example, Eugene's Willamette River Greenway bike path system winds through a string of parks. In Portland, many streets are marked as bike corridors, and signs direct cyclists to nearby destinations. A decent cyclist can easily beat a car across town during rush hour.

The **Oregon Department of Transportation** (503/986-3555, www.oregon.gov) produces some useful and free resources for cyclists, which can be ordered by phone or downloaded online—you can find maps of bike trails and routing suggestions for the entire state, the Columbia Gorge, the coast, and a number of cities.

Sports and Recreation

PARK FEES AND PASSES

Oregon has more state parks than almost any other state, as well as a natural environment suited to all manner of recreational activities. In recent years, numerous state and federal parks, national recreation areas, trails, picnic areas, and other facilities have begun charging day-use fees, which are separate from overnight camping fees (the exception to this is camping at rustic sites in national forests, covered by the Northwest Forest Pass). At sites that charge fees, the day-use fee is currently $5 per vehicle at state parks or federal sites. Visitors can pay for day use at individual sites or purchase one of the annual passes described here.

Oregon Pacific Coast Passport

The best deal if you plan to visit many parks along the Oregon coast, this pass covers entrance, day-use, and vehicle parking fees at all state and federal fee sites along the entire Oregon portion of U.S. 101. It does not cover the cost of camping at state parks, which is a separate fee.

Two basic passports are available, depending on your needs and preferences. An **annual passport,** valid for the calendar year, is $35. A **five-day passport** is $10. Passports may be purchased at welcome centers, ranger stations, national forest headquarters, national memorials, and state park offices. Call 800/551-6949 to purchase an annual pass by credit card or for directions to a convenient purchase location near you.

State Park Passes

Another option valid for day-use fees at Oregon state parks that levy fees is to buy a one-year ($30) or two-year ($50) **State Park Pass.** It's available from state park offices, at day-use fee booths, and by phone (800/551-6949). See the **Oregon State Parks website** (www.oregonstateparks.org) for more details and a complete list of vendors.

Northwest Forest Pass

In response to major reductions in timber harvests and cutbacks in federal money, a revenue shortfall has made it hard to keep up trails and campgrounds at a time when the region's population has put more demand on these facilities. The **Northwest Forest Pass** ($5 for 1 day, $30 for 1 year) is a vehicle-parking pass for the use of many improved trailheads, picnic areas, boat launches, and interpretive sites in the national forests of Oregon and Washington. Funds generated from pass sales go directly to maintaining and improving the trails, land, and facilities. You will see "Northwest Forest Pass Required" signs posted at participating sites. Fees are

Get out of the car and hike!

collected at trailhead kiosks. Passes are also available at many local vendors and online at www.fs.usda.gov. You can also check this website before you head out to find out if a pass is required.

These passes are good at most Forest Service sites all over the Pacific Northwest, but they are not valid for campground fees (with the exception of rustic free campsites), concessionaire-operated sites, or Sno-Parks.

Golden Passport Program

Most National Park Service sites, such as national parks and monuments, charge a fee for their use. You can pay an entrance fee at each site or park you visit, or you can purchase an annual **America the Beautiful Pass** ($80), which allows the owner to use all U.S. Forest Service, Park Service, Bureau of Land Management, and Fish and Wildlife sites, as well as developed day-use sites and recreation areas. The $10 **America the Beautiful Senior Pass** is a lifetime pass covering entrance fees for U.S. citizens over the age of 62 (proof of age required). Pass holders also get a 50 percent discount at some campgrounds, boat launches, and swimming areas. The third pass, the free **Access Pass,** is available only to those who are permanently disabled (check with the National Park Service for eligibility requirements). It offers the same benefits as the Senior Pass.

BICYCLING

While not for everybody, biking all or part of the Oregon coast is the surest way to get on intimate terms with this spectacular region. Before going, get a free copy of the **Oregon Coast Bike Route** map from the **Oregon Department of Transportation** (503/986-3555, www.oregon.gov) or from coastal information centers and chambers of commerce. This brochure features strip maps of the route, noting services from Astoria to the California border. With information on campsites, hostels, bike repair facilities, elevation changes, temperatures, and wind speed, this pamphlet does everything but map the ruts in the road.

Because the prevailing winds in summer are from the northwest, most people cycle south on U.S. 101 to take advantage of a steady tailwind. You'll also be riding on the ocean side of the road with better views and easier access to turnouts, and generally wider bike lanes and shoulders. The entire 370-mile trip (or 380 miles if you include the Three Capes Scenic Loop) involves nearly 16,000 feet of elevation change. Most cyclists cover the distance in 6-8 days, pedaling an average of 50-65 miles daily.

If you're looking for a medium to long recreational ride, check out www.rideoregonride.com, which has excellent route information for road and mountain bike rides all over the state.

A number of companies offer preplanned group bicycle trips, with everything from the bicycle to the meals and lodging included. For example, **Bicycle Adventures** (425/250-5540 or 800/443-6060, www.bicycleadventures.com) offers several coast packages, including a six-day fully supported tour from Astoria to Lincoln City for $2,895 (a budget tour with fewer fancy perks is about $500 less).

Cycle Oregon (503/287-0405 or 800/292-5367, www.cycleoregon.org) sponsors an annual weeklong supported tour of rural Oregon in September. Considered one of the best bike tours in the country, Cycle Oregon tours cover about 500 miles and attract up to 2,000 riders each year. Fees, which include all meals, showers, support, and entertainment, are around $975 per person. A mid-July weekend Cycle Oregon ride ($199 adult, $99 student) is a bit more family-oriented, with a variety of daily routes ranging from 25 to 75 miles.

CAMPING
State Parks

Oregon's state parks have great amenities (including showers at most campgrounds), and given that, fees are reasonable. Fees for RV sites run about $24, tent sites about $20, yurts and rustic cabins about $40. The fee for reserving a site is $8. During the winter, camping fees drop slightly.

Most state park campgrounds have at least a couple of yurts—canvas-walled, wood-floored shelters equipped with fold-up beds, heaters, and lamps; they sleep five. Although pets have traditionally been banned from state park yurts, many parks now have at least one pet-friendly yurt.

Many state park campgrounds accept campsite reservations, and reservations are accepted for all special facilities such as cabins, yurts, and tepees. The state park system has a central **information hotline** (800/551-6949) and a website (www.oregonstateparks. org) where you can get park maps, campground layouts, rates, and other information.

Reservations for state parks can be made by phone (503/731-3411 in Portland metro area, 800/452-5687 elsewhere, 8am-7pm Mon.-Fri.). Online reservations, with a Visa or MasterCard, are handled by a private vendor, **ReserveAmerica** (www.reserveamerica.com). Reservations may be made from two days up to nine months in advance. In addition to the campsite fee, a processing fee is charged.

If you need to **cancel your reservation** three days or more before your scheduled arrival, call one of the numbers above. Two or fewer days before your trip, call the park directly to cancel your reservation. Phone numbers for all parks are found on each individual park's web page (www.oregonstateparks.org). Cancellation service fees and requirements for special facilities, such as yurts and cabins, may vary. Your reservation fee is nonrefundable, and a small cancellation fee will be charged if you cancel in the last two days.

National Forests
The U.S. Forest Service maintains hundreds of campsites, trails, and day-use areas. National forest campsites are usually much less developed than those at state parks; electric hookups are not available, although most campgrounds have water and vault or flush toilets. Most overnight sites charge a user fee. Fees are generally $10-18 for campsites, $5-7 for an extra vehicle. Campsites can be reserved online with a Visa or MasterCard through www.recreation.gov.

HIKING
While every corner of Oregon features hiking trails, a couple of long-distance trails deserve special notice. For 362 miles, from the Columbia River to the California border, the **Oregon Coast Trail** hugs the beaches and

camping at the Alvord Desert

headlands, leading hikers into intimate contact with some of the most beautiful landscapes anywhere. Most of the trail runs through public lands, though some portions traverse easements on private parcels and the trail follows the highway and city streets in a number of places. The only coastal long-distance treks separated from U.S. 101 are the 30 miles between Seaside and Manzanita, and between Bandon and Port Orford. A free trail map and directory are available from the **Oregon State Parks information center** (800/551-6949, www.oregonstateparks.org). This pamphlet makes clear where this trail crosses open beaches, forested headlands, the shoulder of the Coast Highway, and even city streets in some towns. Be sure to bring water, particularly on northerly sections of the trail, as much of the trek is on beachfront away from a potable supply.

The other long-distance trail through the state is the Oregon portion of the **Pacific Crest Trail,** which runs from southern California to the Canadian border. The PCT through Oregon is exceptionally scenic and not too hard for sturdy, experienced backpackers; much of it runs along ridgelines, avoiding constant ups and downs.

FISHING AND HUNTING

Oregon takes a backseat to few other places when it comes to sportfishing and hunting opportunities, with varied shooting and angling possible all over the state. Rules and bag limits for both are subject to frequent change, so get a copy of the **Oregon Department of Fish and Wildlife** hunting and fishing regulations, available online (www.dfw.state. or.us) or at the agency office (4034 Fairview Industrial Dr. SE, Salem, 503/947-6000), as well as at sporting goods stores, some grocery stores (such as Fred Meyer), and other outlets.

Fishing

Fishing for trout, both wild native cutthroat and rainbows as well as planted hatchery fish, is popular all across the state. Standout areas include the Deschutes River, a blue-ribbon stream noted for its large "redband" rainbow trout, as well as excellent steelhead fishing. Other notable steelhead streams include the coastal Rogue and Umpqua Rivers, as well as the Sandy and Clackamas Rivers, right in Portland's backyard. Smallmouth bass provide excellent sport on the John Day and Umpqua Rivers, and largemouth bass draw anglers to warm-water lakes across the state.

Weighing into the hundreds of pounds, sturgeon is another extremely popular game fish in the larger rivers, particularly the Columbia and the Umpqua. Off the coast, bottom fishing for rockfish and other species is a year-round activity, depending on the weather. Warm ocean currents bring albacore tuna in August-September, and halibut are usually available in summer, though the season is variable and set yearly by the Pacific Fishery Management Council.

About 1,000 fishing guides are licensed in Oregon. Fishing opportunities on your own are almost limitless, but hiring a guide can be money well spent if you're exploring unfamiliar waters or you lack a boat. Major **charter-fishing** centers on the coast include Astoria, Hammond, Warrenton, Garibaldi, Depoe Bay, Newport, Winchester Bay, Charleston, Gold Beach, Bandon, and Brookings. Charter rates vary a bit, but typical prices up and down the coast are $80-100 for a half day (5-6 hours) of bottom fishing, about $125 for a full day; $125-175 for an 8-hour salmon outing; $200-300 for 12 hours of tuna fishing; $175-200 for a 12-hour halibut charter. Inland, expect to pay at least $175-300 per person per day for guided trips for salmon, steelhead, sturgeon, and other species. Chambers of commerce in each town can also provide extensive listings.

Fishing licenses cost $16.75 (for 1 day), $31.50 (2 days), $46.25 (3 days), $58 (4 days), $59.75 (7 days), or $106.25 (full year for nonresidents; $33 for Oregonians). Nonresident licenses include Combined Angling Tags (allowing the taking of salmon, sturgeon, steelhead, and halibut).

Hunting

Hunters enjoy a broad range of opportunities throughout Oregon. Shooting for upland game birds—chukar, Hungarian partridge, pheasant, grouse, and quail—can be good to excellent in eastern and central Oregon, the Cascades, and the coastal ranges. The eastern half of the state as well as the Willamette Valley, Columbia River basin, and coastal areas offer waterfowl hunting. Wild turkeys, introduced successfully on the eastern side of Mount Hood, have proliferated and are now hunted in almost every county of the state. Bigger game includes elk, black bears, cougars, black-tailed deer in western Oregon, and mule deer in the east. A limited number of special tags are also issued for pronghorn, bighorn sheep, and mountain goats.

The rules governing hunting in the state are more complex and variable than those for fishing. Check the regulations carefully for seasons, restrictions, and bag limits, and consult the **Department of Fish and Wildlife's website** (www.dfw.state.or.us) for the latest information.

WHITE-WATER RAFTING

With 90,000 river miles in the state and hundreds of outfitters to choose from, neophyte rafters have an embarrassment of riches. To help navigate the tricky currents of brochure jargon and select the experience that's right for you, here's a list of rivers to run and questions to ask before going.

Raft the famous **Rogue River** June-September to avoid the rainy season and be spared current fluctuations due to dams upstream. This run is characterized by gentle stretches broken up by abrupt and occasionally severe drop-offs as well as swift currents. In fact, Blossom Bar is often cited as one of the state's consummate tests of skill for rafters. The Rogue is ideal for half- and full-day rafting trips, with most outfitters putting in near the town of Merlin and continuing downstream as far as Foster Bar. Water turbulence on the Rogue is often intensified by constricted channels created by huge boulders. Depending on the season, rafters can expect Class II, III, and IV rapids interspersed by deep pools and cascading waterfalls. At day's end, superlative campsites offer repose and the chance to savor your adventures.

Despite the dryness and isolation of Oregon's southeast corner, the **Owyhee River** has become a prime springtime destination for white-water enthusiasts. The 53 miles from Rome to the Owyhee Reservoir have two

rafting the Deschutes River

sections of exceptionally heavy rapids, but the many pools of short intense white water alternating with easy drifts make for a well-paced trip. The best times to go are May-early June. Before going, check conditions with the **Vale Bureau of Land Management District office** (541/473-3144, www.or.blm.gov/vale), because the Owyhee can only be run in years with high snowmelt. Access to rafting takeout points in this part of the state is greatly facilitated by a four-wheel-drive vehicle.

The **John Day River** in northeastern Oregon offers an even-flowing current as it winds 175 miles through unpopulated rangeland and scenic rock formations. Below Clarno, the grade gets steep, creating the most treacherous part of the state's longest river (275 miles). The 157-mile section of the John Day that rafters, canoeists, and kayakers come to experience also has falls near the mouth that require a portage. The special charm of this Columbia tributary is the dearth of company you'll have even during the river-running seasons of late March-May and then again in November. Just watch out for rattlesnakes along the bank, and remember that the silt load in this undammed river reduces it to an unboatable trickle in summer months. Contact the **Prineville Bureau of Land Management office** (541/416-6700) for more information.

Unlike the John Day and the Owyhee Rivers, the **Deschutes River** rapids aren't totally dependent on snowmelt, and it is the busiest vacation waterway in the state. The 44 miles between Maupin and the Columbia River contain sage-covered grasslands and wild rocky canyons where you might see bald eagles, pronghorn, and other wildlife. If there's a good run of salmon or steelhead, you might also encounter plenty of fishing boats. This area averages 310 days of sunshine annually, so weather is seldom a problem except for excessively hot summer days.

Typical rafting outfitter services include meals, wetsuits or rain gear, and inflatable rafts and kayaks. Guided raft trips begin at about $50 for a half-day trip and increase to

$200 and up per day for longer trips. To ensure an intimate wilderness experience, ask about the number of people in a raft and how many rafts are on the river at one time. Are there any hidden costs such as camping gear rental or added transfer charges? What is the cancellation policy? Another consideration is the training and experience of the guide. Can he or she be expected to give commentary about history, geology, and local color? You might also want to check on the company's willingness to customize its trips to special interests such as photography, bird-watching, or hiking.

WINDSURFING AND KITEBOARDING

Windsurfing conditions near the town of Hood River have made the Columbia River Gorge world-famous. In recent years, kiteboarding has become almost as popular. Other than the San Francisco Bay Area, no other place in the continental United States boasts summertime airflows as consistently strong as those in the gorge. Championship events and top competitors have coalesced on the shores of the river here, 60 miles east of Portland. The Columbia River runs in the opposite direction of the westerly airflows, which can cause large waves to stack up and allow windsurfers to maintain their positions relative to the shore. In short, the area offers the perfect marriage of optimal conditions and scenic beauty.

Some coastal waters are also gaining popularity for windsurfers. Floras Lake, near Port Orford, and the area around Pistol River, just south of Gold Beach, are top destinations. The latter hosts the Pistol River Wave Bash National Windsurfing Competition each June.

WINTER SPORTS

One of the silver linings to Oregon's legendary precipitation is that so much of it falls in the form of snow in the mountains. Mount Hood, for example, has been buried by as much as 100 feet of snow in a single year. That makes a lot of people happy from late fall through spring and even into summer, as Oregon snowpacks support the longest ski season in the country (at Timberline on Mount Hood), as well as snowboarding, snowmobiling, and snowshoeing. For snow reports and other updated information throughout the season, a good source is OnTheSnow.com (www.onthesnow.com/OR).

Alpine resorts are concentrated in the northern and central Cascades and in the state's northeast corner. A little over an hour's drive away on **Mount Hood,** Portlanders have their choice of five developed ski resorts—Mount Hood SkiBowl, Cooper Spur, Mount Hood Meadows, Timberline, and tiny Summit, the Pacific Northwest's oldest ski resort, dating to 1927. In the central Cascades, there are family-friendly **Hoodoo Ski Bowl** southeast of Salem, **Willamette Pass** southeast of Eugene, and **Mount Bachelor,** the Pacific Northwest's largest and most developed ski area, southwest of Bend. At **Mount Bailey,** near Diamond Lake in the southern Cascades, downhillers can experience snowcat skiing, a more affordable alternative to being dropped off on inaccessible slopes by helicopter. The area also offers extensive cross-country, skating, sledding, and snowmobiling terrain. Near the California border in southern Oregon, **Mount Ashland** offers downhill action in addition to 100 miles of cross-country trails.

In the northeast, skiers have their choice of Anthony Lakes Ski Area, between Baker City and La Grande, and **Ferguson Ridge Ski Area,** east of Joseph.

Cross-country skiing can be as simple as heading to the nearest mountain pass and looking for a Sno-Park trail head (remember to buy the parking permit). You may need to share your trail with snowmobiles, however. Ski rental stores and forest service offices can offer suggestions. In addition, most of the larger downhill ski resorts also offer miles of groomed and backcountry ski trails.

Sno-Park Permits

Note that for winter sports in many areas November 15-April 30, you'll need to purchase a Sno-Park permit ($4 for 1 day, $25 for the season) to park your vehicle in posted winter recreation areas. Sporting goods stores, ski shops, and resorts near the slopes sell them.

Travel Tips

LIQUOR AND MICROBREWERIES

Liquor is sold by the bottle only in state-sanctioned liquor stores, open Monday-Saturday. Many stores also keep Sunday hours. Beer and wine are also sold in grocery stores and retail outlets. Liquor is sold by the drink in licensed establishments 7am-2:30am. The minimum drinking age is 21.

CANNABIS

Recreational marijuana (whatslegaloregon. com) is legal for adults 21 and older in Oregon. Buy it in a medical marijuana dispensary (which won't be hard to find, just look for the green—instead of red—cross) or, after retail stores are set up (probably sometime in 2016), at a pot store. Use it only on private property (not in campgrounds!) and don't drive under the influence or take your purchases out of the state.

ENTRY REQUIREMENTS

Entry requirements are subject to change. For current information, see the **U.S. Department of State's Bureau of Consular Affairs website** (www.travel.state. gov). All visitors from abroad must be in possession of a valid passport in order to enter the United States. Also required in most cases is a round-trip or return ticket, or proof of sufficient funds for a visit and a return ticket.

Visitors from many countries must also have a valid visa for entry. (See the State Department website, www.state.gov, for a current list of countries for which the visa requirement is waived.) Applicants for visitor visas should generally apply at the U.S. embassy or consulate with jurisdiction over their place of permanent residence. Although visa applicants may apply at any U.S. consular office abroad, it may be more difficult to qualify for the visa outside your country of permanent residence.

ACCESS FOR TRAVELERS WITH DISABILITIES

Oregon is generally proactive with regard to providing accessible facilities for people with disabilities, though there's always room for improvement. The great outdoors and some older buildings (lighthouses, for example), of course, can pose some insurmountable challenges, but many parks and recreation areas work to accommodate visitors with mobility

Oregon Festivals and Events

The majority of large crowd-drawing events take place June-September, but there are plenty of cool weather and ongoing activities to keep you entertained throughout the year. The free local weekly magazines are a great source for listings of events and entertainment and can be found in most of the larger burgs and college towns.

Oregon loves to celebrate its heritage, as well as its artistic and gastronomic bounty. The following seasonal sampler highlights some of the festivals and celebrations throughout the state.

In spring, two coastal gourmet affairs of note are the **Newport Seafood and Wine Festival** and the **Astoria Crab Feed and Seafood Festival.** Also around this time, Florence's **Rhododendron Festival** and Brookings's **Azalea Festival,** both on the coast, attract blossom connoisseurs.

If you have kids in tow, in June take advantage of the parades, carnival rides, air shows, and floral splendor of Portland's **Rose Festival** or the Cannon Beach **Sandcastle Festival.** You could fill up July and August with such varied musical talents as the new vaudeville acts of the **Oregon Country Fair** and the gold-record performers at Jacksonville's **Peter Britt Music Festival,** not to mention the blues icons who appear at the **Waterfront Blues Festival** in Portland, the West Coast's largest.

During the last full weekend of July, festivalgoers can toast their appreciation of Oregon at Portland's **Oregon Brewers Festival,** where more than 60 microbreweries are showcased, or at the **Annual International Pinot Noir Festival** in McMinnville, attracting master vintners from around the world. Summer festival-hoppers might also want to take in **Da Vinci Days** in Corvallis, uniting the community's scientific and artistic elements, and Portland's **Bite,** featuring the best in food.

In the fall and winter, the leading events west of the Cascades include Mount Angel's **Oktoberfest,** the **Eugene Celebration,** the **Corvallis Fall Festival,** and Thanksgiving open houses in the wine country. At Christmastime the leading events are Albany's **Victorian Parlor tours,** Portland's **Christmas Ships,** and light displays all over the state.

While most of Oregon's celebrations take place west of the Cascades, there are notable exceptions to the rule. Bird-watchers relish the Klamath Basin **Bald Eagle Conference** in February and the springtime **John Scharff Migratory Waterfowl Conference** in Burns. Highbrows can take in the summertime literary festival at **Fishtrap** in the Wallowas or rock out at the **Bend Summer Festival** in central Oregon. Rock hounds flock to summer mineral shows in the central Oregon hamlets of Madras and Prineville. Rodeo fans can whoop and holler at the venerable **Pendleton Round-Up** in September.

Such celebrations of ethnicity as Portland's **Cinco de Mayo** (one of the largest celebrations of this kind in the nation) and **Scandinavian festivals** in Astoria and Junction City express the state's diversity.

issues. Many campgrounds have accessible sites.

The **Access Pass,** which allows free entry to designated federal recreation areas such as national parks and monuments, Bureau of Land Management lands, and U.S. Fish and Wildlife sites, is available to those who are blind or permanently disabled. The pass is free to qualified applicants ($10 processing fee); get details from the **U.S. Geological Survey** (http://store.usgs.gov).

TRAVELING WITH CHILDREN

Oregon is a great place to travel with kids, with plenty of attractions and activities to keep them interested. One of the first things travelers by car will notice is the ample number of rest stops, with one every 30-60 miles or so on most major routes. In most towns and cities, public parks offer play structures and open spaces where kids can burn off some energy. Many Oregon state parks offer excellent recreational opportunities for families such as guided hikes, nature programs, and campfire presentations.

Many B&Bs discourage children. Where possible, we've indicated policies (for and against) in accommodations listings, but it's always a good idea when making a reservation to inquire as to whether the lodging is appropriate for children.

GAY AND LESBIAN TRAVELERS

In Portland, college towns such as Eugene and Corvallis, and most touristed areas, gay and lesbian visitors can expect to find progressive attitudes. In these places there are venues that specifically cater to same-sex couples; Portland's **Q Center** (4115 N. Mississippi Ave., 5037234-7837, www.pdxqcenter.org) is an LGBTQ community center. Outside of these places, one may find the attitude considerably less open and accepting; in more rural parts of the state, the attitude may be downright hostile. On the other hand, gays and lesbians live all over the state, and the relationships that these folks have built with their neighbors and coworkers often pave the way for acceptance of gay and lesbian travelers.

Health and Safety

EMERGENCY SERVICES

Throughout Oregon, dial 911 for medical, police, or fire emergencies. Most hospitals offer a 24-hour emergency room. Remember that medical costs are high here, as in the rest of the United States, and emergency rooms are the most expensive places for medical care; for nonemergency situations, look for urgent care clinics. In Portland and its suburbs, the ZoomCare clinics charge about $125 for a visit, and take most insurance.

HEALTH HAZARDS
Hypothermia
In this part of the country, anyone who participates in outdoor recreation should be alert for problems with hypothermia—when

your body loses more heat than can be recovered and shock ensues. The damp chill of the Pacific Northwest climate poses a greater hypothermia threat than colder climes with low humidity. In other words, it doesn't have to be freezing for death from hypothermia to occur; wind and wetness often turn out to be greater risk factors. Remember that a wet human body loses heat 23 times faster than a dry one.

One of the first signs of hypothermia is a diminished ability to think and act rationally. Speech can become slurred, and uncontrollable shivering usually takes place. Stumbling, memory lapses, and drowsiness also tend to characterize the afflicted. Unless the body temperature can be raised several degrees by a knowledgeable helper, cardiac arrhythmia or arrest may occur. Getting out of the wind and rain into a warm, dry environment is essential for survival. This might mean placing the victim into a sleeping bag with another person. Ideally, a ground cloth should be used to insulate the sleeping bag from cold surface temperatures. Internal heat can be generated by feeding the victim high-carbohydrate snacks and hot liquids. Placing wrapped heated objects against the victim's body is also a good way to restore body heat. Be careful not to raise body heat too quickly, as that could also cause cardiac problems.

Measures you can take to prevent hypothermia include eating a nutritious diet, avoiding overexertion followed by exposure to wet and cold, and dressing warmly in layers of wool and polypropylene. Wool insulates even when wet, and because polypropylene tends to wick moisture away from your skin, it makes a good first layer. Gore-Tex and other waterproof breathable fabrics make for more comfortable rain gear than nylon because they don't become cumbersome and hot in a steady rain. Finally, wear a hat to prevent heat loss through your head.

Frostbite

Frostbite is not generally a major problem until the combined air and wind-chill temperature falls below 20°F. Outer appendages such as fingers and toes are the most susceptible, with the ears and nose a close second. Frostbite occurs when blood is redirected out of the limbs to warm vital organs in cold weather, and the exposed parts of the face and peripherals cool very rapidly. Mild frostbite is characterized by extremely pale skin with random splotchiness; in more severe cases, the skin will take on a gray ashen look and feel numb. At the first signs of suspected frostbite, you should gently warm the afflicted area. In more aggravated cases, immerse hands and feet in warm water. Do not massage the skin, or you risk further skin damage. Warming frostbitten areas against the skin of another person is suitable for less serious frostbite. The warmth of a campfire cannot help once the skin is discolored. As with hypothermia, it's important to avoid exposing the hands and feet to wind and wetness by dressing properly.

Poison Oak

Neither the best intentions nor knowledge from a lifetime in the woods can spare the western Oregon hiker at least one brush with poison oak. Major infestations of the plant are seldom encountered in the Coast Range but are prevalent in the Columbia Gorge. In the fall, the leaves are tinged with red. Even when the plant is totally denuded in winter, the toxicity of its irritating sap still remains a threat.

When hiking in hardwood forests, it's a good idea to wear long pants, long-sleeved shirts, and other covering. When you know you've been exposed, try to get your clothes off before the resin permeates your garments. Follow up as soon as possible by washing with Tecnu, a type of soap that seems to help remove the poison oak oil from skin. It's available at REI and at many drugstores. If you get the rash, cortisone cream is effective at temporarily quelling the intense itching.

Giardia

Known medically as giardiasis but colloquially called "beaver fever," this syndrome afflicts those who drink water contaminated by *Giardia lamblia* parasites. Even water from cold clear streams can be infested by this microorganism, which is spread throughout the backcountry by beavers, muskrats, livestock, and other hikers. Boiling water for 20 minutes or applying five drops of chlorine, or preferably iodine, to every quart of water and letting it sit for half an hour are simple ways to kill the giardia spores. Backpackers should use water pumps that filter out giardia and other organisms.

Mosquitoes

Mosquitoes can be a problem especially in the Cascades, the Willamette Valley, and parts of the Columbia River Gorge. West Nile virus is not common in Oregon, though every year at least a few infected mosquitoes are detected, mostly in the eastern part of the state. When mosquitoes are present, it's a good idea to apply insect repellent and wear long pants and long-sleeved shirts to reduce the chance of getting bitten. Otherwise, you may want to stay indoors during prime mosquito time, around dusk.

Ticks

Of approximately 20 species of hard ticks found in Oregon, only four species are commonly found on humans. Of these, the western black-legged tick (also known as the Pacific tick and deer tick) is the only known carrier in the western United States of the bacterium that causes the debilitating Lyme disease.

A prescription for prevention is to layer insect repellent on thickly before venturing into potentially infested areas. Also, be sure to check your body and clothing frequently during and after possible exposure. Ticks often may be found attached in the underarms, the groin, behind the knees, and at the nape of the neck.

If you find an attached tick, remove it promptly by grasping it with tweezers, as close to the skin as possible, and pulling it straight out, steadily and firmly. Don't twist it, as this increases the chance of breaking off mouth parts and leaving them embedded in your skin. Afterward, wash up with soap and water and apply an antiseptic to the bite area. The same routine applies for the removal of ticks from pets.

Information and Services

COMMUNICATIONS AND MEDIA

The state's two largest-circulation newspapers, the *Oregonian* and the *Eugene Register Guard,* come out of the most populous cities, Portland and Eugene. The *Oregonian* is distributed statewide, while the *Register Guard* is carried in newspaper dispensers as far away as the southern coast of Oregon.

Alternatives to the big dailies are found in a number of excellent tabloids, including Portland's *Willamette Week,* the *Eugene Weekly,* Astoria's monthly *Hipfish,* and others.

Portland and Eugene also dominate the broadcast media, serving far-flung rural communities by means of electronic translators. **Oregon Public Broadcasting** (www.opb.org) is also a statewide presence both in TV and radio. Some standout TV programs of interest to visitors include the long-running *Oregon Field Guide,* which explores natural history, outdoor recreation, travel, and environmental issues; and *Oregon Art Beat,* which profiles local artists, craftspeople, and performers of all stripes.

Warm Springs Indian Reservation's KWSO (91.9 FM) is a progressive country radio station spiced with elders chanting in the morning and topical discussions on Native American issues by younger community members.

Even though regional monthlies such as *Northwest Travel* and *Sunset* do not have a strictly Oregon focus, there are usually several destination pieces about the state in each edition of these magazines. **Oregon Coast** magazine confines its coverage to subjects closer to home. All these periodicals can be obtained at newsstands throughout the state.

Telephones

Oregon has three area codes. **503** is the main area code in use for the greater Portland metropolitan area, including Mount Hood and the westerly portion of the Columbia River Gorge, Astoria to Lincoln City on the coast, and Portland to Salem in the Willamette Valley; it's supplemented by **971.** The area code **541** is for the rest of the state. Note that when using a landline in Oregon, you must dial the area code, even for local calls. **Cell**

phone service in some parts of Oregon—including mountainous regions, the southern coast, and the state's eastern areas—can be spotty to nonexistent.

MAPS AND TOURIST INFORMATION

Travel Oregon (775 Summer St. NE, Salem, 800/547-7842, www.traveloregon.com) is an outstanding resource for visitors and residents alike. The state-run organization maintains an informative website and produces a number of useful free maps and publications, with extensive listings of lodgings and activities, suggested itineraries, events, and more.

Nine welcome centers, located near the borders along major routes into the state, are a good first stop for newly arriving visitors. They stock literature and maps on the entire state, though their regional offerings tend to be best represented.

Other useful contacts are the **Oregon Parks and Recreation Department** (725 Summer St. NE, Salem, 503/986-0707 or 800/551-6949, www.oregonstateparks. org), the **Bureau of Land Management** (333 SW 1st Ave., Portland, 503/808-6002, www.or.blm.gov), and the **National Forest Service** (333 SW 1st Ave., Portland, 503/808-2971, www.fs.fed.us/r6). All offer free information and maps on the specific recreation areas and preserves under their respective auspices.

For members only, **AAA Oregon/Idaho** (600 SW Market St., Portland, 503/222-6734 or 800/452-1643, www.aaaorid.com) offers roadside assistance such as towing and retrieving keys locked in cars and provides tour guides and high-quality maps of the state and major towns.

Visitor information offices are all good sources for free state, regional, and town maps. Some of the best road and city maps available are those produced by AAA for their members. Particularly useful for outdoor recreation is *Oregon Road & Recreation Atlas,* a large-format book of beautiful shaded-relief maps of the entire state, published by **Benchmark Maps** (www.benchmarkmaps. com). The atlas is available in bookstores and sporting goods shops and directly from the publisher. In addition, several regional tourism authorities offer information and services for their corners of Oregon.

Trail Maps

Accurate trail and topographical maps are worth their weight in gold for hikers, mountain bikers, anglers, and other outdoors enthusiasts. A wide variety of maps, including those published by the U.S. Geological Survey, can be purchased at **Pittmon's Map store** (825 SE Hawthorne Blvd., Portland, 503/233-2207, http://www.pittmonmaps.com, 8am-5pm Mon.-Fri.) in Portland.

Another good series of paper maps is put out by **Green Trails.** Unlike USGS maps, these maps show trail mileage and campsites. Look for them at outdoors stores and ranger stations.

Resources

Suggested Reading

In addition to the titles cited in the text, Oregon-bound travelers may want to read some of these books. We advise readers to search for out-of-print books at www.powells.com.

ATLASES

Benchmark Maps. *Oregon Road and Recreation Atlas.* Medford, OR: Benchmark Maps, 2005. Use this atlas to help plan your trip or as a travel companion. You'll find that it has lots of detail and shaded relief.

Loy, William G. *Atlas of Oregon.* Eugene, OR: University of Oregon Press, 2001. Find graphic details on economics, climate, geology, and historic trails in this gorgeous detailed reference atlas.

MacArthur, Lewis. *Oregon Geographic Names.* Portland: Oregon Historical Society, 2003. This text might be physically weighty, but its alphabetic historical rundown of place-names makes for light and informative reading.

FICTION

Davis, H. L. *Honey in the Horn.* Moscow, ID: University of Idaho Press, 2004. This reprint edition of a 1935 Pulitzer Prize-winning novel about rowdy southern Oregon settlers makes the pioneer days seem quite real.

Doyle, Brian. *Mink River.* Corvallis, OR: Oregon State University Press, 2010. Part crime novel, part magical realism fantasy, this book beautifully evokes the personalities and rhythms of the Oregon coast.

Duncan, David James. *The River Why.* San Francisco: Sierra Club Books, 1983. A coming-of-age story and an epic of fly-fishing set along the Deschutes River.

Kesey, Ken. *Sometimes a Great Notion.* New York: Viking, 1964. One of the best novels ever about life in rural Oregon.

Leslie, Craig. Winterkill. New York: Picador Publishing, 1996. A touching father-son saga set on the reservations of central Oregon.

GUIDEBOOKS

Fanselow, Julie. *Traveling the Lewis and Clark Trail.* Helena, MT: Falcon Publishing, 2003. This guidebook for the modern-day explorer acquaints readers with what to see and do along Lewis and Clark's celebrated route from Illinois to Oregon.

Fanselow, Julie. *Traveling the Oregon Trail.* Guilford, CT: Globe Pequot Press, 2001. The adventures continue with Fanselow's scenic and informative guide to the present-day Oregon Trail.

Jewell, Judy. *Oregon.* New York: Fodor's Compass American Guides, 2005. Read this guide before traveling to the state to complement *Moon Oregon* as your on-the-road reference. Beautiful color photos and insightful travel tips liven up this literary rendition of Oregon's greatest hits.

Jones, Shawn, and Nell Nix. *Out and About: Portland with Kids.* Portland: Sasquatch Books, 2009. A must-have for those exploring Portland with children.

McRae, W. C., and Judy Jewell. *Moon Coastal Oregon.* Berkeley: Avalon Travel Publishing, 2012. Comprised of the coastal Oregon chapters in this book with new and specific Discover, Background, and Essentials chapters for the Oregon coast.

Vaughn, Greg. *Photographing Oregon.* Alta Loma, CA: PhotoTripUSA, 2009. Good tips on selecting subjects and setting up your shots.

HISTORY

Ambrose, Stephen. *Undaunted Courage.* New York: Touchstone Press, 1996. A classic book on the country's seminal voyage of discovery, the Lewis and Clark expedition. It gives a historical context to the explorers' journals in an entertaining, enlightening way. Read this before taking on *The Journals of Lewis and Clark* themselves. The latter work is available through many different publishers, but the antiquated grammar and archaic English make it difficult reading.

Federal Writers' Project (editor). *WPA Guide to Oregon.* Portland: Binford and Mort, 1940. The granddaddy of them all, this 1941 guide is the primary inspiration for *Moon Oregon.* The product of dozens of authors working in the Federal Writers' Project, this post-Depression guidebook still sets the standard for thorough coverage and vivid description. Although much of the information is dated, its rundown of pioneer history and glimpses of early 20th-century Oregon make it a valuable tool for any modern traveler. Available in many public libraries.

Jackman, E. R., and R. A. Long. *The Oregon Desert.* Caldwell, ID: Caxton Press, 2003; and Jackman, E. R., John Scharff, and Charles Conkling (photographer). *Steens Mountain in Oregon's High Desert Country.* Caldwell, ID: Caxton Press, 2003. These two works are the classics for eastern Oregon. Within the volumes, history and local color fill in the east side of the state's wide-open spaces.

O'Donnell, Terrence. *Portland: An Informal History and Guide.* Portland: Oregon Historical Society, 1964. This book is widely available used, and it makes for entertaining reading.

Robbins, William G. *Landscapes of Promise: The Oregon Story 1800-1940.* Seattle: University of Washington Press, 1999. In this fascinating environmental history of Oregon, Robbins examines ways that Oregonians have interacted with the land; he shows that Native Americans altered the landscape in a number of ways, and that the landscape encountered by early European settlers was, in some areas, highly managed.

Stark, Peter. *Astoria: John Jacob Astor and Thomas Jefferson's Lost Pacific Empire.* New York: Ecco Press, 2014. Though solidly founded in history, this is a ripping good yard about the founding of Astoria.

NATURAL HISTORY

Alt, David, and Donald W. Hyndman. *Roadside Geology of Oregon.* Missoula, MT: Mountain Press Publishing Company, 2003. This book's mile-by-mile approach makes it a good reference to have in the car to answer your questions about Oregon's geology.

Evanich, Joseph E., Jr. *Birders Guide to Oregon.* Portland: Audubon Society of Portland, 2003. A good all-around guide to the state's birdlife, with a useful breakdown of specific coastal locations and details on what species to watch for and when.

Jolley, Russ. *Wildflowers of the Columbia Gorge.* Portland: Oregon Historical Society Press, 1988. An exhaustive study of the gorge's plant species, with excellent color photos identifying 744 of the Columbia Gorge's more than 800 species of flowering shrubs and wildflowers.

Littlefield, Caroll D. *Birds of Malheur Refuge.* Corvallis, OR: Oregon State University Press, 1990. Recommended for serious birders.

Sept, J. Duane. *The Beachcomber's Guide to Seashore Life in the Pacific Northwest.* Vancouver, BC: Harbour Publishing, 1999. This ideal guide for the casual and curious observer aids in understanding the intertidal zone and in identifying more than 270 species encountered there, including crabs, clams, and other mollusks, seaweeds, sea stars, sea anemones, and more.

OUTDOOR RECREATION

Ostertag, Rhonda, and George Ostertag. *75 Hikes in Oregon's Coast Range.* Seattle: Mountaineers Books, 2001. A well-chosen selection of hikes along the length of the coastal ranges covers a broad variety of terrain and difficulty levels. Detailed trail descriptions and maps make this guide particularly useful.

Giordano, Pete. *The Soggy Sneakers Guide to Oregon Rivers.* Seattle: Mountaineers Books, 2004. An indispensable guide to Oregon's rivers, replete with maps, class ratings, gradient listings, river lengths, and best seasons to visit.

Hill, Sean Patrick. *Moon Oregon Hiking.* Berkeley: Avalon Travel Publishing, 2010. Details more than 490 hikes throughout Oregon, including hiking tips and top 10 lists of Oregon's best trails.

Ostertag, Rhonda, and George Ostertag. *75 Hikes in Oregon's Coast Range.* Seattle: Mountaineers Books, 2001. A well-chosen selection of hikes along the length of the coastal ranges covers a broad variety of terrain and difficulty levels. Detailed trail descriptions and maps make this guide particularly useful.

Stienstra, Tom. *Moon Oregon Camping.* Berkeley: Avalon Travel Publishing, 2010. Details nearly 700 campgrounds across the state, with an excellent selection on the coast. Rich with tips on gear, safety, and other topics.

Sullivan, William L. *100 Hikes in Northwest Oregon and Southwest Washington.* Eugene, OR: Navillus Press, 2006. Sullivan's excellent hiking guides also include *100 Hikes* books for the central Oregon Cascades, southern Oregon, eastern Oregon, and the Oregon coast and Coast Range.

Wozniak, Owen. *Biking Portland.* Seattle, WA: Mountaineers, 2013. Guided tours through Portland's neighborhoods, with history and interesting commentary along the way.

Internet Resources

ACCOMMODATIONS

Oregon Bed and Breakfast Guild
www.obbg.org
800/944-6196
Lists links to Oregon bed-and-breakfasts by region.

ENTERTAINMENT AND EVENTS

Oregon Craft Beer
www.oregoncraftbeer.org
Proffers merchandise and features a calendar of statewide beer-related events, along with an extremely useful map of Oregon's microbreweries.

Oregon Wine
www.oregonwine.org
Everything you ever wanted to know about Oregon wines, wineries, and events.

Wines Northwest
www.winesnw.com
A guide to the world of wine in the great Pacific Northwest (and a useful link to guides and driving services).

HISTORY

Haunted Places
www.ghostsandcritters.com
An eerie look into Oregon's underworld. Offers advice for novice ghost hunters and info about haunted places in the state.

Oregon Historical Society
www.ohs.org
A resource for Oregon history.

OUTDOOR RECREATION AND CAMPING

The Dyrt
www.thedyrt.com
Find and review campsites; the Yelp of camping.

ORbike
www.orbike.com
Statewide calendar of bike rides and cycling events.

Oregon Department of Fish and Wildlife
www.dfw.state.or.us
Information on fishing and wildlife in Oregon.

Oregon Hiking
www.oregonhiking.com
Information on outdoor adventures such as hiking, snowshoeing, rafting, and climbing.

Ride Oregon
http://rideoregonride.com/
Bike ride options throughout the state.

State Parks
www.oregonstateparks.org
Find a state park or campsite, make a reservation, or download brochures.

U.S. Forest Service
www.fs.usda.gov/r6
Links to national forests, camping information and reservations, ranger station contact info, maps and brochures, fees, passes, and permit info.

REGIONAL INFORMATION AND SERVICES

Central Oregon Visitors Association
http://visitcentraloregon.com
P.O. Box 4489
Bend, OR 97707
800/800-8334

Columbia River Gorge Visitors Association
www.crgva.org
800/98-GORGE (800/984-6743)

Eastern Oregon Visitors Association
www.visiteasternoregon.com
541/523-9200 or 800/332-1843

Eugene, Cascades & Coast
www.eugenecascadescoast.org
754 Olive St.
Eugene, OR 97401
541/484-5307 or 800/547-5445

Oregon Coast Visitors Association
http://visittheoregoncoast.com
137 NE 1st St.
Newport, OR 97365
541/574-2679 or 888/628-2101

Oregon's Mt. Hood Territory
www.MtHoodTerritory.com
150 Beavercreek Rd., Suite 305
Oregon City, OR 97045
503/655-8490 or 800/424-3002

Portland Oregon Visitors Association
www.travelportland.com
701 SW 6th Ave., Suite 1
Portland, OR 97204
503/275-8355 or 877/678-5263

Southern Oregon Visitors Association
www.southernoregon.org

Willamette Valley Visitors Association
www.oregonwinecountry.org
866/548-5018

STATEWIDE INFORMATION AND SERVICES

Travel Oregon
www.traveloregon.com
The official state tourism department offers a
fun website with information about lodging,
recreation opportunities, and a statewide calendar of events.

TRANSPORTATION

Amtrak
www.amtrak.com
Train schedules, fares, and booking
information.

Greyhound
www.greyhound.com
Schedules, fares, and booking information.

Oregon Department of Transportation
www.tripcheck.com
Great site with webcams, road conditions,
public transportation, and mileage calculator.

Portland International Airport
www.flypdx.com
Portland International Airport's website provides a list of carriers, ground transport, and
other useful information on the area.

Index

XYZ

List of Maps

Photo Credits

Title page photo: Paradise Loop trail sign © Rcphoto | Dreamstime.com; page 4 Willamette Valley vineyard © Jamiehooper | Dreamstime.com; page 5 Haystack Rock at Cannon Beach © Bill McRae; page 6 (top left) © Bill McRae, (top right) © Sarawinter | Dreamstime.com, (bottom) © Tondafoto | Dreamstime.com; page 7 (top) © Adeliepenguin | Dreamstime.com, (bottom left) © Judy Jewell, (bottom right) © Paul Levy; page 8 © Groovysoup | Dreamstime.com; page 9 (top) © Joshuaraineyphotography | Dreamstime.com, (bottom left) © Bill McRae, (bottom right) © Judy Jewell; page 11 © Chiyacat | Dreamstime.com; page 12 © jsquirephotography | Dreamstime.com; page 13 © Judy Jewell; page 14 © Rcphoto | Dreamstime.com; page 16 © Judy Jewell; page 17 © Bill McRae; page 21 © Toynutz | Dreamstime.com; page 22 © Paul Levy; page 23 © Ruth Gibian; page 25 (top) © Judy Jewell, (bottom) © Diro | Dreamstime.com; page 27 © Judy Jewell; page 36 © Bill McRae; page 37 © Bill McRae; page 40 © Bridgetjones | Dreamstime.com; page 41 © Judy Jewell; page 42 © Paulbradyphoto | Dreamstime.com; page 43 © Judy Jewell; page 46 © Judy Jewell; page 47 © Bill McRae; page 50 Judy Jewell; page 51 © Judy Jewell; page 52 © Judy Jewell; page 57 © Bill McRae; page 60 © Bill McRae; page 62 © Bill McRae; page 63 © Bill McRae; page 65 © Jit Pin Lim/123rf. com; page 67 © Bill McRae; page 69 © Judy Jewell; page 72 © Bill McRae; page 73 © Judy Jewell; page 79 © Judy Jewell; page 81 © Bill McRae; page 83 © Judy Jewell; page 89 © Judy Jewell; page 91 © Judy Jewell; page 95 © Andreykr | Dreamstime.com; page 96 © Wollertz | Dreamstime.com; page 97 © Judy Jewell; page 99 (top) © Rcphoto | Dreamstime.com, (bottom) © Qwntm | Dreamstime.com; page 101 © Jeanneprovost | Dreamstime.com; page 107 © Bill McRae; page 108 © Tusharkoley | Dreamstime.com; page 109 © Livingstonatlarge | Dreamstime.com; page 110 © Bill McRae; page 113 © Judy Jewell; page 114 © Bill McRae; page 116 © Bill McRae; page 117 © Judy Jewell; page 121 © Tusharkoley | Dreamstime. com; page 131 © Bill McRae; page 132 © Paul Levy; page 135 © Bill McRae; page 137 © Bill McRae; page 139 © Judy Jewell; page 140 © Judy Jewell; page 142 © Judy Jewell; page 143 © Judy Jewell; page 149 (top) © Judy Jewell; (bottom) © Judy Jewell; page 151 © Jamiehooper | Dreamstime.com; page 153 © Bill McRae; page 157 © Judy Jewell; page 160 © Judy Jewell; page 163 © Bill McRae; page 165 © Judy Jewell; page 166 © Paul Levy; page 170 © Judy Jewell; page 171 © Judy Jewell; page 172 © Judy Jewell; page 173 © Judy Jewell; page 176 © Judy Jewell; page 177 © Paul Levy; page 178 © Paul Levy; page 181 © Judy Jewell; page 182 © Judy Jewell; page 183 © Judy Jewell; page 185 © Judy Jewell; page 187 © Judy Jewell; page 191 © Bill McRae; page 193 © Bill McRae; page 195 © Judy Jewell; page 202 © Judy Jewell; page 205 © Judy Jewell; page 206 © Judy Jewell; page 212 © Judy Jewell; page 213 © Judy Jewell; page 215 (top) © Tusharkoley | Dreamstime.com, (bottom) © Tracy Fox/123rf.com; page 217 © Judy Jewell; page 222 © Bill McRae; page 224 © Bill McRae; page 226 © Judy Jewell; page 228 © Bill McRae; page 232 © Judy Jewell; page 238 © Bill McRae; page 242 © Judy Jewell; page 243 © Bill McRae; page 249 © Bill McRae; page 250 © Bill McRae; page 252 © Bill McRae; page 253 © Bill McRae; page 255 © Bill McRae; page 261 © Bill McRae; page 262 © Kathryn Osgood; page 263 © Judy Jewell; page 264 © Bill McRae; page 268 © Bill McRae; page 269 © Iwhitwo | Dreamstime.com; page 273 © Judy Jewell; page 275 (top) © Judy Jewell, (bottom) © Bill McRae; page 278 © Judy Jewell; page 279 © Bill McRae; page 280 © Bill McRae; page 283 (top) © Judy Jewell, (bottom) © Capricornis | Dreamstime.com; page 285 © Judy Jewell; page 289 © Judy Jewell; page 297 © Bill McRae; page 301 © Bill McRae; page 304 © Bill McRae; page 305 © Bill McRae; page 307 © Bill McRae; page 308 © Bill McRae; page 311 © Bill McRae; page 318 © Judy Jewell; page 319 © Bill McRae; page 320 (top) © Judy Jewell, (bottom) © Bill McRae; page 321 © Judy Jewell; page 325 © Bill McRae; page 326 © Paul Levy; page 327 © Bill McRae; page 329 © Judy Jewell; page 334 © Judy Jewell; page 335 © Bill McRae; page 336 © Paul Levy; page 337 © Judy Jewell; page 339 © Judy Jewell; page 341 (top) © Judy Jewell, (bottom) © Paul Levy; page 343 © Bill McRae; page 344 © Rruntsch | Dreamstime. com; page 345 © Bill McRae; page 348 © Judy Jewell; page 349 © Judy Jewell; page 351 © Judy Jewell; page 354 © Judy Jewell; page 359 © Judy Jewell; page 361 © Paul Levy; page 365 © Bill McRae; page 368 © Judy Jewell; page 369 © Judy Jewell; page 370 © Paul Levy; page 371 © Paul Levy; page 372 © Paul Levy; page 373 © Judy Jewell; page 381 © Bill McRae; page 384 © Paul Levy; page 389 © Judy Jewell;

Also Available

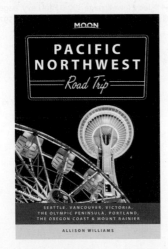

MAP SYMBOLS

⚏	Expressway	○	City/Town	✈	Airport	⚜	Golf Course
	Primary Road	◉	State Capital	✖	Airfield	🄿	Parking Area
	Secondary Road	⊛	National Capital	▲	Mountain	⬗	Archaeological Site
╌╌╌	Unpaved Road						
	Feature Trail	★	Point of Interest	✛	Unique Natural Feature	⛪	Church
╌ ╌ ╌	Other Trail	●	Accommodation				Gas Station
⋯⋯	Ferry	▼	Restaurant/Bar	⚑	Waterfall		Glacier
	Pedestrian Walkway	■	Other Location	▲	Park		Mangrove
▥▥▥	Stairs	Λ	Campground	☗	Trailhead		Reef
				⛷	Skiing Area		Swamp

CONVERSION TABLES

°C = (°F - 32) / 1.8
°F = (°C x 1.8) + 32
1 inch = 2.54 centimeters (cm)
1 foot = 0.304 meters (m)
1 yard = 0.914 meters
1 mile = 1.6093 kilometers (km)
1 km = 0.6214 miles
1 fathom = 1.8288 m
1 chain = 20.1168 m
1 furlong = 201.168 m
1 acre = 0.4047 hectares
1 sq km = 100 hectares
1 sq mile = 2.59 square km
1 ounce = 28.35 grams
1 pound = 0.4536 kilograms
1 short ton = 0.90718 metric ton
1 short ton = 2,000 pounds
1 long ton = 1.016 metric tons
1 long ton = 2,240 pounds
1 metric ton = 1,000 kilograms
1 quart = 0.94635 liters
1 US gallon = 3.7854 liters
1 Imperial gallon = 4.5459 liters
1 nautical mile = 1.852 km

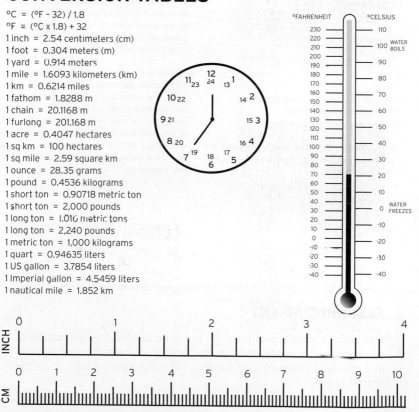

MOON OREGON

Avalon Travel
a member of the Perseus Books Group
1700 Fourth Street
Berkeley, CA 94710, USA
www.moon.com

Editor: Erin Raber
Series Manager: Kathryn Ettinger
Copy Editor: Kristie Reilly
Graphics Coordinator: Elizabeth Jang
Production Coordinator: Elizabeth Jang
Cover Design: Faceout Studios, Charles Brock
Moon Logo: Tim McGrath
Map Editor: Mike Morgenfeld
Cartographers: Sierra Willems, Brian Shotwell
Proofreader: Rachel Feldman
Indexer: Greg Jewett

ISBN-13: 978-1-63121-254-3
ISSN: 1080-3394

Printing History
1st Edition — 1991
11th Edition — June 2016
5 4 3 2 1

Text © 2016 by Judy Jewell and Bill McRae.
Maps © 2016 by Avalon Travel.
All rights reserved.

Some photos and illustrations are used by permission and are the property of the original copyright owners.

Front cover photo: orchard in the Hood River Valley © Dennis Frates / Alamy

Back cover photo: Fairy Falls © Light & Magic Photography | Dreamstime.com

Printed in China by RR Donnelley

All recommendations, including those for sights, activities, hotels, restaurants, and shops, are based on each author's individual judgment. We do not accept payment for inclusion in our travel guides, and our authors don't accept free goods or services in exchange for positive coverage.

Although every effort was made to ensure that the information was correct at the time of going to press, the author and publisher do not assume and hereby disclaim any liability to any party for any loss or damage caused by errors, omissions, or any potential travel disruption due to labor or financial difficulty, whether such errors or omissions result from negligence, accident, or any other cause.

KEEPING CURRENT

If you have a favorite gem you'd like to see included in the next edition, or see anything that needs updating, clarification, or correction, please drop us a line. Send your comments via email to feedback@moon.com, or use the address above.